上海交通大學
百年报刊集成

第一辑（1896—1949）

学 术 学 科

经管卷（第四册）

上海交通大学
档案文博管理中心　编

目 录

《管理》简介

该刊由交通大学管理学院所办的《交通管理学院院刊》改组而来，于1936年4月交大四十周年校庆纪念日时创刊发行，为双月刊。出版7期后，于1937年抗战爆发后停刊。1947年4月复刊1期，发行周期由双月刊变为季刊。刊名"管理"二字由北洋政府交通总长、交通大学校长叶恭绰亲笔题写。本书收录全部8期（1936年第1卷1—4期；1937年第1卷第5期；1937年第2卷第1—2期；1947年季刊第1期）。

该刊属于管理类学术刊物，创刊背景乃是1931年交通大学管理学院成立定名后，师生鉴于"欧美各国，对于管理学术之研究，已有相当之成绩，吾国自宜急起直追，庶可不落人后"①的使命意识，遂由管理学院学生于课余之暇，编行此刊，取名《管理》，以"唤起国人对于管理学术之注意与研究，并求实施于各种事业，藉以推进吾国之建设"②。该刊设有论著、译述、书评、古今领袖人物言行札记、转载、演讲、报告、通讯等栏目。

刊登的内容"包罗各种事业之管理；关于铁道管理，工商管理，公务管理及财务管理方面，尤为侧重"③。代表性论文如沈奏廷的《吾国铁路实行货物夜间装卸制度之审订》，林叠的《人事行政组织之研究》，许靖的《美国铁路管理到达货运事务之组织与方法》，王烈望的《现代企业组织问题之检讨》等等。这些管理类的学术研究文章，主要由管理学院的教员与学生投稿。

值得注意的是，该刊"为鼓励管理人才，注意人格修养起见"④，每期设置"古今领袖人物言行札记"一栏，成为该刊特色所在。旨在使"读者于学术研究之余，得着高尚观感的

① 钟伟成：《发刊例言》，《管理》1936年第1卷第1期。
② 钟伟成：《发刊例言》，《管理》1936年第1卷第1期。
③ 钟伟成：《发刊例言》，《管理》1936年第1卷第1期。
④ 钟伟成：《发刊例言》，《管理》1936年第1卷第1期。

指导，与修身治事的箴规”[①]。此外，该刊作为“管理学院的喉舌”[②]，除了研究管理学术外，还负有沟通校友消息的使命，遂设“毕业同学消息”一栏，专载毕业同学最近服务的状况。在1937年第2期的首篇，还载有院长钟伟成《送别本届毕业生》一文，劝勉毕业生需具备五德，即“诚实不欺”“工作正确”“办事勤恳”“学识充裕”“精神愉快”。“五德”标准至今仍是现代社会从事管理者为人行事之指南。

① 钟伟成：《发刊例言》，《管理》1936年第1卷第1期。

② 《编后语》，《管理》1936年第1卷第1期。

管理

二月刊

第一卷 第一期 二十五年四月

本期要目

交通大學管理學院出版

管理二月刊

第一卷第一期
民國二十五年四月

發刊例言

管理爲近代之新科學。其方法之應用，雖因事業而互有差異，然基本上固有共同之原則可循。歐美各國，對于管理學術之研究，已有相當之成績，吾國自宜急起直追，庶可不落人後。本院自民國二十年改組後，定名爲管理學院，分設鐵道管理，實業管理，公務管理，及財務管理四科，實負有此特殊之使命者也。玆於課餘之暇，編行此刊，顏曰「管理」；惟仝人等能力淺薄，實地資料，又非常缺乏，尙祈海內同志，進而教之。

關於本刊編例，聯誌數語於後：

一　本刊目的，在喚起國人對于管理學術之注意與研究，並求實施於各種事業，藉以推進吾國之建設。是一個提倡者，並不敢自居爲一個指導者。

二　本刊內容，包羅各種事業之管理；關于鐵道管理，工商管理，公務管理及財務管理方面，尤爲側重。

三　本刊論著譯述書評三欄，每編之首，均貫有編號，爲讀者事後分類之用，編號方法，詳載雜誌論文索引首頁。

四　本刊爲鼓勵管理人才，注意人格修養起見，每期選載「古今領袖人物言行札記」，使讀者於學術研究之餘，得着高尚觀感的指導，與修身治事的箴規。

五　本刊爲便利讀者研究管理學術起見，按照本刊規訂暫行分類編號方法，逐期編製雜誌論文索引。

鍾偉成

論著

闢誤解「管理」者（A 1.）

鍾偉成

自物質文明發達以來，工商業的組織，日趨於複雜，政府的機構亦大爲擴展，各種事務之處理，不復如昔日之簡單。於是管理科學乃應時代而產生。歐美各國利用其原理，實施於工商業，實施於一切社會企業，均大見成效。民國十九年孔祥熙氏長實業部時，有鑒及此，組織中國工商管理協會，負責領導科學管理運動。五年以來，該會同仁雖努力提倡，大聲疾呼，徒以我國「人治」心理，中根已深，一般人提到「管理」都不免有種種誤解之處，如果不加辯正，實足爲科學管理運動之障礙。故不辭簡陋，特在本文提出最重大之幾種誤解，加以辯正。

（一）管理不成其爲科學而僅是一種常識

這一點是最普通的誤解。其所持論調，大概如此：

管理科學根本沒有這麼一回事。所謂管理不過是一種常識和應變的方法。因其頭緒太繁，變態太多。「未知之數」，不一而足。要把這隨機應變的管理技術或實務，縮成一套確實的法則與一定的系統，是不可能之事。管理的實務，雖然僅是對付物料，金錢和人事，但是這三種東西，彼此作用起來，其相互間關係的複雜和紊繁，可以說是千變萬化，那裏能建立一般的公例和特殊的原則？

這種見解是完全錯誤的。我們正因爲現代管理機能的複雜，不是僅憑個人的手腕所能勝任，所以愈是有使管理成爲科學化的必要。要使管理成爲科學化，不用說，當然要從繁複的事實中，用歸納的方法，抽出一般的公例和特殊的原則，編成一個系統，使各種事業的管理者，有所憑籍。然而這是可能的嗎？我可以肯定的說，這是可能的。管理的實務，不外是對物和對人。物是呆板的，管理牠們的方法，可以說是一種機械式的管理。人是活動的。管理人事，不能完全用機械式的方法。管理的實務之所以複雜和變化，也就是因爲人事活動之難於控制，然而這並不是說，人事的活動，就沒有一般的原則，可爲管理人事的依據。現在的社會科學差不多就是以人事的活動爲對象，而其所定的原則，已獲得大家的公認。管理在對物方面因其可用機械式的方法，固然不成問題；在對人方面，也可以依據其他社會科學的先例，用歸納的方法，去抽繹原則，編成一個系統，使工商業的管理者，有所憑籍。所以說是管理因其對象的複雜和變化，不能成爲科學這句話是不成立的。

管理科學一如其他社會科學有種種原則與法則的根據。法則大半是對物而言，原則是對人而言。前者因爲可以應用自然科學的定律，有十分之八九是拿得穩的，所以可稱爲法則；後者因爲祇能仿照其他社會科學的先例，祇能說大體是不錯的，但不能保證沒有例外，所以祇能稱爲原則。

簡單地說，管理科學的法則，第一是關於管理物料設備和生產過程方面，大體是根據自然科學的定律與法則；第二關於管理個人行動及其相互的反應作用，應用心理學與生理學的法則；第三關於管理金錢應用會計學與理財學的法則。至於原則亦可分爲二種：一種是關於集團方面的，一種是關於個人方面的。前者指組織中所有一切人員間之關係，諸如分工原則就是說各部仍都要功能化，抵衝原則就是要獲得員工間之權責均衡，紀律原則，其目的不但在服從命令，而尤在取得調和，以及其他。後者是組織中所有一切人員之個別管理，第一要爲事擇人，第二要加以訓練，求其精進，第三要擴充專門化於最大限度，第四，一切行動過程均根據預訂計劃受一定的控制，第五，要用適當的獎勵方法，在不妨害健康的範圍以內，以刺激工作人員的努力。這集團的和個人的管理原則，可以總稱之爲組織原則。一個企業苟知充分引用這原則與法則，「增高效能」和「掃除浪費」二目的是必然可以達到，是絕對可以達到的。

上面所述，可以說是管理學大體的輪廓。至於說管理是一種常識不是一種科學，也是不難加以辯正的。第一常識與科學之間並沒有一定的界綫。「科學就是有組織有系統的常識」，這是黑胥黎教授(Prof. Huxley)所說的話。況且常識與科學間的界限又是因人而不同，因時代而不同，工程師之常識在會計師即可認爲科學。反之會計師認爲常識，工程師或須引爲科學。再則昔日之科學到現代可以變爲常識。反之今日之常識到明日也可變成科學。

從上文所述，可知管理不成爲科學一說，不攻自破。

(二)管理不能成爲一獨立職業

有人說管理不過是企業經營中的一種機能，牠本身尚不能像「工程」和「會計」等成爲一種獨立職業。這種說法是否正確我們可以從事實上來證明。

我們要問「管理」固然爲企業經營中的一種機能，「工程」和「會計」何獨不是？爲什麽「工程」和「會計」會變成一種獨立的職業呢？這是因爲這兩種機能跟着時代的進展而日趨於專門化，非訓練有素的人，是辦不來的。在產業革命以前，企業的規模狹小，生產技術幼稚，舉凡製造理財記帳管理都可以由一個人來辦，那時當然不會有工程師，更不會有會計師。自從機械倡明以後，生產技術突飛猛進，工程已經成爲一種極專門的智識和技能。因生產力的膨脹，企業規模也跟着擴大，營業的變動需要更精密的紀錄和分析，因此會計也就成了一種專門智識和技能，各種實業都非得請教工程師和會計師去做顧問不可。於是工程師和會計師，遂成了一種獨立的職業，到了現在，各種實業的顧問除了工程師和會計師以外，還得請教管理專家。不但工商界如是，即歐美各國政府都延聘行政專家，來設計預算制度物料管理制度人事管理制度等等。這都是應着時代的需要而產生的必然現象。單就工商業說，在手工業時代商業資本家約定手工業勞動者去製造商品，勞動者各自在家裏工作，那時當然沒有所謂工業管理。自工廠制度發生以後，勞動者集合在一起生產，分工合作。於是管理問題也就跟着發生。不過那時企業規模不大，一切情形還很簡單，担任管理的職務者還是資本主自己。他們自己出資經營，自己管理廠務，也不感什麽困難。自工業革命以後，生產技術猛進，市場亦大爲擴展。企業家覺得一人的能力智識有限，不能不用各種專門人才，採辦，推銷，會計，機械等職務，都以用專門人才來辦爲有利。因此企業的組織，逐漸龐大，而管理的事務，亦日形複雜。接着，有限公司組織的風行，資本的所有者與企業的經營者就截然劃成二體，而資本的集合尤形便利迅速。因之就產生下列三種顯著的進展。

(1)大規模的生產，龐大的設備，和職工與業務的分化，需要更大的管理能力。

(2)企業所有者的分散隱含了「所有」與「管理」的分離。以指揮和組織實業團體爲職業的人，成爲一新興的階級。

（3）各公司因競爭的劇烈，合併，協同，和互相諒解，成爲不可避免的結果。在另一方面加入集團的每一個公司，都需要有永久性的專家委員會來指揮監督，使全部政策可以得到調整。

在二十世紀的開端，「管理」所佔的地位，比較從前更爲顯著，以前「管理」受「資本」的驅策，現在資本一反而爲管理者所利用。管理者在生產要素中，已處於超然地位，他一方面利用資本，一方面統率勞工，策動生產。

「管理」地位的重要既如此。而其機能之複雜又如彼。自科學管理倡明以來，除了經驗以外，更加上了學理的研究。現代工業的管理如果不合於科學原則，是很難立足的。因此歐美各國工商界對於管理專家的重視，已不在會計師和工程師之下。管理專家在歐美已經成爲一種獨立的職業，間接方面，代理公司或工廠計劃一切管理問題，如組織設計，會計制度，人事管理，生產管理，設備佈置採辦及銷售制度等等，處于顧問之地位。直接方面，充任總經理或各部主任，司行政之職責。

（三）管理在中國與工程及自然科學相較爲不切要之學科

我們已經證明「管理」是可以獨立成爲一種科學的。但是又有人說這種科學在中國遠不及工程與自然科學之重要，因爲中國的產業尚未發展到和歐美一樣，所以先要從工程和自然科學的研究來開發中國的產業。產業發達到相當程度，再來研究管理科學亦不爲遲。

此如從前有人主張馬達救國及時人所提倡狹義的生產教育，同爲一孔之見。中國自輸入馬達以來，至少已有五六十年的歷史，歐戰時，應用馬達的輕工業(如紗廠絲廠麵粉廠等等)，更有風起雲湧之概，但是中國的經濟始終不能獨立起來，經此次大恐慌反有日暮途窮之感，許多新興的工業，虧本的虧本，倒閉的倒閉，拍賣的拍賣。差不多沒有一種企業，可以說站得住脚。這是什麽緣故呢？其外來的原因，固然可以說是帝國主義者的經濟侵略；其內在的原因，則管理的落伍不能不負一大部份的責任。現代的工業，非用現代的管理去經營不可。現在中國的新興工業實在談不上什麽科學管理。最壞的現象，就是把家庭制度搬到工廠中去。好像一個工廠專爲供養親戚朋友而開的一樣。生產的效能當然更談不到了。我可以打個比方，好的酒用不乾淨的瓶去裝，好酒也會變成壞的。如果祇知道去研究酒的質地，而不去研究裝酒的瓶，始終，是拿不出好酒來的。同樣，我們也可以說，祇知道去研究製造方法，而不去研究企業之管理和組織，也是不中用的。往往有好些工業成功在製造方面，而失敗則在於管理不善。在歐美產發展的過程中，也曾經有這種經驗。以前歐美的企業家，視機器爲萬能，人人偏重於物質的研究，對於人事方面，不甚注意，管理一事亦由技術家兼理，不知技術家善於物質的管理，未必善於人事的應付。在大規模的企業中，技術家就是能應付人事，也沒有餘力可以兼顧。管理科學乃是應着時代的需要而產生的。以前他們因爲不知道管理的重要，走了好些寃枉路，一直到二十世紀的開始，美人泰婁氏(Taylor)篤信管理是可以科學化的，經多年的研究，首創所謂「科學管理法」，始奠今日管理科學之基石，亦可謂管理科學的發軔時期。迨至歐戰爆發，更給管理科學一巨大的推動，因戰時物質需要至形緊張，歐美各國當局益覺管理有改進擴張之必要。同時大學校對于生產方法，工人心理，勞資關係，市場統制，社會心理，成本會計，統計應用，生理變化，預算統制，人事管理等問題，詳加研究，至是管理學之理論和系統乃得以確定。這一時期可以說管理科學進展時期。自從泰婁氏發現「科學管理法」以來，距今不足三十餘年，管理學之進步已有一日千里之勢。世界生產量都因着管理的實施，激急增加。這比單靠機器時代，又進一步，所以有人說管理科學的發現，是世界第二次工業革命。這一段短短的歷史，正可以做我們的借鑑。

發展中國的產業，無疑地是要利用外資借用外國的機械技術。如果僅限於此，那是很危險的。新式的企業，恐怕不免再重演舊式的官僚統治和親戚朋友的給養。所以我們利用外資和外國的機械技術，同時也得全盤接受他們的科學管理；否則在機械方面即使可以迎頭趕上，而在管理方面依然落後，這好比他們雙腿齊起，而我們蹺着一脚，試問怎麽還追得上呢？所以中國於利用機械之中，同時必須採用管理科學，雙管齊下，急起直追，然後方能達到迎頭趕上的目的。不然，我進一寸，人進一尺，經濟的落後，是沒有方法可以補救的。

或曰，如子所言，管理與機械雙管齊下，就有辦法，何以科學管理運動，近幾年來雖經社會人士竭力提倡，與工商管理協會努力推行，依然沒有效果？這一點，我認爲近年來中國科學管理運動之所以沒有成績，大都因爲祇是支支節節地在方法上兜圈子，沒有從科學管理的原則作打算，舍本耘末，當然得不到好結果的。

管理科學的幾個重要原則，在第一節中已略爲述及，我現在要多列舉幾點，以資詳盡。

(1)精密與合理的分工　分工是給各個或各組人員利用能力的最好方法。其目的在以同等的勞力，獲得更多和更好的效果，工人專做同一部份工作，經理常管同一種類的問題，自然可以得到技巧和正確，而增加他們的生產能力。

(2)權力與責任並重　權力與責任應永遠相等。有一分權力即應負一分責任。擁大權而不負責任謂之瀆職。反之如果祇有責任而不賦與相當的權力，那末他的責任，一定也是辦不了。同時處於最高地位的人也要把自己的權限劃定，如果細大必親，弄得其屬下之主管人員，無事可爲，而自己則不勝其繁劇。結果各部份的事，也終於辦不好。

(3)廠規公允與賞罰嚴明　要員工服從廠規，廠規必須公允。如果以偏面的廠規，不合時代的廠規叫員工去遵守，一定要引起他們的反感，結果一廠的紀律，便因之而破壞。同時有了公允的廠規，必須嚴格地執行，有功必賞，有過必罰，否則有廠規等於無廠規，還有什麽紀律可講？

（4）號令統一與事權集中　一個職工，關於一樁事情，只能接受一個上司的命令。這就叫做號令統一。如果有兩個人對於同一職工，或同一機關，行使權力，這就叫做兩重命令。(Dual Command)。兩重命令足以紛亂辦事的手續，使聽受命令的人有無所適從之感。這對於工作效能是一個極大的阻礙。所謂事權集中就是以一個經理和一個計劃，管理同一目的的業務。號令統一，在乎各員工有適當之工作，而事權集中在乎組織有正確之安排。

（5）「先公後私」精神的樹立　利己之心，人人同具。我們雖然不能使人人爲公忘私，但在無論何種團體中，不能不有先公後私的精神，沒有了團體就沒有了自己；但是失去了自己的利益，也就不肯竭力替團體謀利益。兩方面的利益都能顧到，自然是最好的管理方法，然而私利和公利往往有衝突的地方，怎樣調和二者的衝突？在管理上確是一個最困難的問題。第一還是要當局者以身作則，第二僱主與僱員之間要有公允的規約。第三要互相監察。

（6）報酬制度的合理　職工的報酬，應以公平爲原則，在訂定報酬率的時候，一面應顧到員工的才能，經驗與智識。一面應注意到生活程度，一般的經濟情形，人工的供求狀況以及本公司的經濟地位等。

（7）員司職位的穩固　一個僱員離去他的職位，無論對他自己或該服務機關，差不多總是一種損失，尤其對於高級的職員，他經過了許多的創造與閱歷，熟悉了機關內外的情形，認識一切有關係的人物，他有預定的計劃，他相信自己同時也得別人的信任。往往因爲他的離職，就不能實現他所預定的計劃，甚至還使該機關逐漸衰替，這是一種極不好的現象。所以在可能範圍內總須使職員的位置穩固。

（8）創造力的培養　能提出一種計劃而能保證牠的成功，這是智識份子所感到最有生氣的滿足，也是人類事業裏最有力量的鼓勵，這種玄想和實行的能力，就叫做創造力。創造力是由機警和特殊才能產生出來的。牠是促成該機關活力的來源，有時候下屬的創造力可補充或替代上司的。尤其在困難時，更有這創造力的必要，所以一個聰明的上司，應該犧牲他自己的尊嚴而盡量地鼓勵和發展下屬的創造力。

（9）團體精神的保持　統一就是力量(Unity is strength)，每一機關的首領應該認取這句成語。所以職工的合拍與統一，實是最大力量的發源，也是穩健鞏固的柱石，這就叫做團體精神。(Esprit de Corps) 通常損害團體精神的有兩種危險，因管理能力的欠缺，因問題未全部了解，更因自私自利的慾念，上司們往往會分割內部同事們的力量，有時不能利用他們各個的才能，有時使他們互相猜忌，這是第一種危險。還有在需要用當面商量的事而用書面接洽，往往不能表達其中曲折之處，以致發生誤會，發生隔膜等情，這是第二個危險。

或許有人要說，以子之所云：管理科學如此之重要，但觀上述管理之九條原則，固亦平談無奇。這種說法就是表示問者沒有了解管理科學之內容。九條原則固似老生常談。試問，要使一個企業能完全適合這幾種原則的神髓，其間的組織問題，人事問題，財政問題，技術問題，正是錯綜複雜，非有深切研究與適當訓練，能抓着問題的核心嗎？能獲得矯正的途徑嗎？中國過去推行科學管理之所以沒有成效，就是因爲人們沒有抓着問題的核心，祇是在泰婁「科學管理法」幾個方法上兜圈子，尋生路，毫無成效，這是必然的結果。

我請工商業領袖和政府官吏根據這幾個原則平心靜氣地反躬自省一下，再把自己所管理的事業透視一下，假使自省的反應覺得我的事業全合乎這九個條件，那嗎，你去推行各種新管理方法，——科學管理法——我可以保證行得通，并且包管收穫一百分的成功。但是假使你透視的膠片上，發現你事業的肺部是有了黑影，我奉勸趕快去治本病。如其仍然支支節節地去亂求丹方，亂投江湖郎中，結果必是死期更促。我敢大胆說，中國的一切企業，全都有肺病徵象，所不同者，程度深淺而已。我們既然覺察自已染了肺病，那麼，我們是不是應當知道一些治肺病的驗方，和一些預防的醫學常識？再進一步說，我們能不希望政府辦幾個醫學校，多培植幾個肺病專科醫生，來供應我們的需要？因此我確信：

第一、全國工商界行政界以及一切社會企業都需要研究管理科學，職位愈高需要愈切。全國大學各學院均應列管理科學爲必修科之一。

第二、政府應當多辦幾所訓練管理人才的學校，以供應將來建設新中國的需要。中國的新建設，就政治方面說，爲管理的改進，以求防奸杜弊，發揮效率。就工商方面說，一方面要改良技術，一方面是改良管理。就鐵路方面說，一方面要建築新路，一方面是整頓舊路。在這種形勢之下，管理人才的訓練，能說他是不急之務嗎？

管理原則是燈塔

偉成

吾輩司管理之責者，苟不熟知管理原則，有如暗中摸索，混亂紛爭將爲必然的結果。合理的原則，更益以經驗與果斷，可使吾人辦事無往不利。原則有如港外之燈塔，航行者賴之辨別方向，避免危險，不致走入歧途。然而苟操舟者并進港正路亦不識，則燈塔無補于事也。（譯法國工業管理家費堯語）

中華國有鐵路現行行車時刻表

隴海綫

混合列車		特別快車			車次 / 站名	特別快車		混合列車		
74	72	6	4	2	站名 ↑ / ↓	1	3	5	71	73
		18.25			連雲			1.00		
	20.30	↑			大浦			↑	8.20	
	20.04	16.48			新浦			11.46	9.01	
0.15	10.30	8.53		7.10	徐州	12.40		19.47	18.25	19.05
18.50				3.02	商邱	17.18				1.36
13.12			13.40	22.59	開封	21.36	14.[illegible]0			7.04
10.27			11.51	20.50	鄭州南站	23.47	16.17			9.44
4.11			7.36	16.30	洛陽東站	3.51	20.23			19.33
20.27				10.30	陝州	9.20				0.09
18.56				9.09	靈寶	10.06				1.10
15.33				6.36	潼關	12.53				5.21
11.47				3.15	渭南	15.37				8.59
8.10				0.30	西安	17.55				12.15

附註：表內時刻除到達站外均係開行時刻

本路一次及二次特快與滬平通車301.302次在徐州聯接

本路一次特快與平漢21次又本路2次特快與平漢22次在鄭州相聯接

本路73次與平漢62.72次又本路73.74次與平漢61次在鄭州接聯

THE IMPORTANCE OF THE STUDY OF PUBLIC ADMINISTRATION

By

Dr. Kalfred Dip Lum (林疊)

Meaning and Nature

The word "administration" may be defined in various ways. In its general sense, it denotes the work involved in the actual conduct of governmental affairs without referring to any particular branch of government. In its restricted sense, it denotes the operation of the administrative branch of government only. In its broadest sense from the standpoint of public affairs, it may be defined as the act of supervising or the act of executing a public function. Thus, public administration may be defined as the systematic execution of a public function, particularly the administrative branch of the government. The object of its study is to secure competent personnel, proper organization, efficient control of material, and sound management of finance. The fundamental principle underlying its study is the one of economy and efficiency.

At the present day, public affairs are becoming more numerous as society develops. The government of any political society, otherwise known as the state, is getting closer and closer to the individuals, and that governmental affairs are getting to be more predominant. Consequently, the business of government is expanding and that the management of public affairs has gradually become a profession. Thus, the task of management of any function has increased in difficulty, responsibility and complexity, and that the objective of public administration is the efficient conduct of business. It calls to its service, men and women equipped with tacts and ideals, with the highest scientific qualifications and with a strong organization and leadership capacity. So the purpose to study public administion is to improve or seek to improve executive methods from the confusion and costliness of inexperienced experimentation.

The Studying of the Subject

In the study of public administration, we should observe things as a unit, and not to conceive things separately as this is city, that is state, and the other is national. The problems in the study of each may be different, but the method of study is the same since the objective of the administration of any branch of government or any function is the efficient conduct of business and the efficient utilization of resources at the disposal of officials and employees. The utilization of resources includes not only the current appropriations and material equipments, but also the human resources bounk up in the hundreds of thousands of men and women who take part in the work. It must be remembered that good administration seeks to eliminate waste, conserve material and energy, and secure the most rapid and complete achievement of purpose and result. How to accomplish this is not an easy task.

The common problems which we will study in public administration are organization, personnel, material and finace, and that the study should start from the base of management in a scientific way. In the study of government, we usually divide the government activities into legislative, executive and judicial. But in the study of public administration, we study all three types of activities together since administration tends to reach more and more into the field of legislation and adjudication. Administration has now become the heart of study of modern governmental problems. Consequently, it is not only a necessity, but it should be a demand for colleges or universities to establish courses in public administration.

The Growth of the Subject

It was due to the industrial revolution in Europe and its political, economic and social implications that brought forth the new idea of public administration. It was about 1815 that the chair of public administration and politics that was established at the University of Tubingen, Germany. By the time of the twentieth century when industry began to be expanded, both on a national and international scale, modern transportation facilities began to be developed, and modern communication system such as the installation of the telegraph, telephone, wireless and radio was introduced, all of which had not only increased the scale and intensity of administrative activity, but also brought forth new types of problem. All of these newly created activities have caused the state to act as the great agency of administration and regulation. The state therefore becomes the important organ of administration in the interest of public welfare and for the preservation of its own existence. In every respect to-day, the function and task of the state is also being extended with additional administrative activity. Consequently, increasing attention has been given to the business side of government which should be managed with skill and by men and women who have received sufficient training in administration. Thus, by the twentieth century, a great deal of interest was shown in the study of public administration.

The interest shown in public administration is due to the outcome of several natural causes. Of these, the rapidly increase of cost of government is the most significant one. During the last two decades, the governmental expenditures of every modern government increased to about two hundred percent. How to balance the annual budget is the most difficult task of modern government. The increase of expenditure, the heavy burden of taxation, and the drastic effort to uphold economy have given rise to the demand of gaeater efficiency in administration. The competition in trade and industry, both national and international, also calls for the demand for more efficiency in administration.

At the present time, the greatest interest shown by any country in efficient administration is, perhaps, the United States of America. The chief phases of American public administration to attract national attention before the World War were the spoils system and the reform of municipal government. It was not until after the World War with the subsequent increase of public expenditure that there was a realization which called for more responsibility and for the efficient conduct of public affairs. Within the last twenty years, every city and state as well as the national government have introduced some type of budget system, some kind of centralized purchasing agency, and some system of fiscal supervision. In some cities, a new type of municipal executive, namely, the city manager, has been evolved; and on all phases the administrative power of the chief executive has been greatly increased. The whole trend of public administration in the United States to-day is toward centralization.

Its Relation to Science and Research

Efficient administration is nevertheless considered as scientific administratien. As such, it may be of interest to note its relations to science and research. It is of course not easy to describe as to what extent administration depends upon science. But the whole technical equipment of the present-day administration rests upon scientific achievement. A good administrator should be both a good scientific scholar and a good research scholar, or at least he should have the constant advice of some expert scientific persons, if he is not a scientific man himself. Few of the important tasks fo modern administration can be carried on without the constant support of the technician. The management of any administrative process requires the service of the specialists. Even the care of the poor and the feeble-minded and the custody of criminal and the insane requires to have the attention of an experienced custodian, if not a specialist. Likewise, one might go on to enumerate all the elaborate equipments of technology, investigation and scientific procedure.

The impact of science upon administration gave rise to several questions. Among the most outstanding of all is the effective organization of the scientific personnel. Sometimes it requires to introduce research, which means that a department of research and information should be established with the administration. It was only during the last thirty years rhat bureaus of research were established in the United States. To-day, the United States is unique in the scope, variety, and extent of research agencies with a large number of them established throughout the country.

The research bureau movement in the United States commenced in 1906 with the founding of the New York Bureau of Municipal Research and soon spread rapidly throughout the larger cities in the country, as it was followed by Philadelphia in 1908, Cincinnati in 1909, Chicago and Seattle in 1910, etc. The first state research bureau was established by Ohio in 1913, which was followed by Arizona in 1914, New York in 1915, etc. In 1915 the Governmental Research association was established for the exchange of experience and information among the various research agencies in the United States. This Association usually holds annual convention with the National Municipal League in New York City. In 1931, the National Institute of Public Administration was established and affiliated with Columbia University. Then there are also researches made by organizations of public officials as well as private institutions on crime statistics, social service, street cleaning and disposal of refuse, etc.

How Research Leads to the Study of Public Administration

In conjunction with the various subjects of research, American colleges and universities have also adopted programs of research and established ressearch bureaus in connection with the study of public administration. University interest in puplic administration in the United States was first shown at Columbia University in 1890 after an emphasis made dy Woodrow Wilson in 1887. By 1910 university interest in public administration had shifted to problems of municipal government with emphasis on issues of democracy rather than on administration. Also the general courses in political science emphasized constitutional issues instead of administration. In the University of Wisconsin under the leadership of Professor Van Hise, an intereet was shown from 1903 to 1918 toward the study of public administration. Other universities such as Johns Hopkins under Professor W. F. Willoughby, and the University of Illinois under Professor J. A. Fairlie, also emphasized the study of administration. But the World War temporarily diverted the interest to other fields, particularly international affairs and reletions. In 1920 the emphasis on the study of administration was finally ascertained when the University of Chicago specially created a chair in public administration, and in 1928 established the first university chair in police administration, which was followed by the University of California and other universities.

Further Interest Shown on the Subject

In 1924 the American Political Scienç e Association established a round table on public administration which has become a regular feature of all succeeding annual meetings of the Association. In 1928 the Social Science Research Council established a committee on the study of administration. In the last ten years, therefore, there has been a decided interest and concentration develped in the study of public administration due to the growing importance and interest on the subject, particularly in the present era of world-wide economic emergency.

The interest shown in the study of this subject evidently reveals the fact that the government of a nation is like a machine, which should not only make to work but make to work in snch a way that greatest efficiency and highest productivity are obtained. The way to increase administrative efficiency of a governmental machinery lies in the elimination of unnecessary waste and directing it to more usual enterprises. This can only be achieved by scientific management aims at obtaining the amount of productivity with the least amount of time, money and energy. In other words, it means simplicity of the organization ard working procedure of a government organ and effective exertion of all human and financial power. Thus, scientific management has pecome the watchword of the present industrial and commerial world, and that such management can only be achieved through the proper study of the principles and methods of public administration.

It is true, however, that we cannot expect all administrative officials to be well versed in high technical knowledge, but if the importance of the study of publc administration is realized, there will be plenty of opportunity for one to possess some of the fundamental knowledge of this study. If one is loyal-minded and energetic, he will be able to improve his ability which is instrumental to all advancement of his work.

Fundamental Characteristics

During the World war, national emergency or war government organs were established. The distinctive characterisitics were the unusual simplicity of organization, retrenchment in expenditures, and the effective centralization of human and financial power. The important procedure therefore is to organize or group services inot integrated departments or bureaus in accordance with their purposes or functions rather than on the character of activities engaged in. Each department should be made unifunctional, that is, it will embrace only those services whose special functions pertain to the general functions of the department. In other words, the integrated system should be adopted with the attempt to group all services whose operations fall in the same general field and which maintain intimate working force or relation with each other instead of being independent or uncorreated. For an example, army and navy have the same function for self-defene which should be grouped into one department with a proper title as the name of such a department. It may be called as the Department of Self-Defense. Likewise, railway and communication have practically the same general function for transportation and communication which can be grouped together under one department as the Department of Communication. There is no reason why functions shonld be divided when they are similar or identical in nature. The rule is to decrease rather than to increase the number of departments or bureaus for any plan of economic and efficient administration.

In the organization of operating services, however, it may be organized either of the departmental or bureau type, or of the board or commission plan. If responsibility is to be vested in a single individual, the departmental or bureau type of organization should be adopted. If responsibility is to be vested in a number of persons exercising joint authority, then the board or commission plan of organization may be employed. Both types of organization are being used at the present day. Whether the departmental or board or commission type of organization should be adopted depends upon the existing conditions. If the condition of the work to be done is essentially of an administrative character, that is, one calling for the direct performance of work, the departmental or bureau type of organization should be adopted. If the duties are to be performed by a service which are not primarily of an administrative character but call for the exercise of quasi-legislative, quasi-judicial or general policy determining functions, they should be vested in a board or commission. This is the basis for the distinction in organzing the two types of service. If the service calls for both types of duties or where the dutes to be performed fall in both fields, as those of public education, public health, police, correction and charities, it is necesaary to make provisions where two classes of service can be carried out in a harmonious way. The problem is usually met by making provision for the two authorities, a board or commission, and an executive officer known as a superintendent, such as the superintendent of the board of education or of the board of health, or the chief of police of the police commission. The relative jurisdiction of these two authorities and their relation to each other should be determined. One method is that of vesting all authority in the first instance in the board or commission and making its executive officer its executive secretary or administrative head to have charge of the general direction of the whole board or commission. Another method is to make the two offices independent but cordinate. Whichever these two methods is employed, it is necessary to see that powers and duties of the two be clearly distinguished, and that the board or commission be granted no administrative authority.

Boards and commissions may be composed of members serving full time and receiving emuneration on the same basis as other officers of the government, or of private persons receiving no salaries and giving only a small part of their time, or of members holding other offices under the government and by virtue of such offices being ex officio members, or of members representing a combination method of selection. But it is difficult to lay down any general rule as to which of these two types of board or commission should be chosen. It has to depend upon the circumstances of each case and the amount and character of the work to be done. It would be unwise to provide for a non-salaried honorary board or commission when there are enormous duties to be done. But when the work is to attend a few meetings and merely of approving a few important proposals, the non-salaried honorary board or commissien should be adopted.

The Importance of Studying the Subject in China

A striking phenomena in Chinese officialdom to-day is the lack of proper organization and administration. There are too many commissions or committees and that they are not properly organized. The greater part of the time of the officials is occupied in attending meetings and conferences with the result that administrtive work has been greatly neglected. Abolishing some of the commissions or committees, abrogating the unimportant meetings, and simplifying documentary procedure should at least be effected as a means toward heightening administrative efficiency. On the other hand, the ability of most staff members in the Chinese governmental organizations is exceptionally low. Measures should be devised to increase their knowledge and to arouse their interest in their work, and the measures lie in their training while they are in school or university. The only way to solve the problem is to realize the importance of the study of public administration.

Administration Courses at Chiaotung University

It is due to this realization that administration courses are established at Chiaotung University under a separate college, known as the College of Administration which is the first of its kind as well as the only one to be instituted in China up to the present time It was first instituted in 1924 under the administration of President Sun Fo, who is now the president of the Legislative Yuan in the National Government. About four years ago complete courses in the various fields of administration were introduced. President J. Usang Ly of the University is a keen and far-sighted administrator. He exerts great interest and influence in bringing this College of the University to its present standard. As at present constituted, the College is divided iuto four different departments, namely, the Department of Railway Administration, the Department of Industrial Administration, the Department of Finance Administration, and the Department of Public Administration, each of which fullfils a unique demand. The last mentioned Department was instituted with a due consideration of its importance and need with a full four-year program of studies as given in the University Catalogue, reference of which can be readily made by any one who is interested in such studies. With the introduction of snch courses of study, it is hope that the ability of the personnel will be raised gradually, and proper organization and efficient administration will ensue toward the rejuvenation of the Chinese nation.

THE CHAIR OF ADMINISTRATION AND POLITICS AT THE UNIVERSITY OF TUBINGEN AND FREDERICK LIST.

By

B. H. Li, (李炳華)

A college offering courses in Administration may be a new thing here in China and therefore may have caused different comments from various quarters, but it was nothing new in some universities of the most advanced countries in Europe. One of the earliest departments of instruction in Administration was to be found in the University of Tubingen, Germany, where in 1817 under the liberal minister, Wangenheim, a chair of Administration and Politics was bounded and Frederick List was appointed its first professor.

The lack of materials under our command makes it difficult to know just exactly what he covered in his courses. But judging from the conditions existing in Germany at the time, and the extra-ordinary interest he had shown in them as he remarked in the preface of a book that "the history of my book is the history of half of my life," and to that remark one writer added "He might have added that it was also the history of Germany from 1800 to 1840."; and the subsequent reform projects he had proposed, it would not be impossible to divine the mission he had set for the Chair and himself to accomolish. In an introduction to his lectures at Tubingen published in 1818 he exposed the evils of the practice of the levying of tolls and taxes on goods passing from one locality to another and between the different German States. He advocated the abolition of local burdens upon commerce and industry and the extablishment of a customs union. In 1841 he published the best known of his works entitled, The National System of political Economy, since translated into several languages.

List was working through the Chair of Administration and Politics in the University of Tubingen to create an economic system for Germany based upon the conception of nationality in that country where the dominant political note throughout the 19th century was the realization of national unity. Since some of the economic conditions existing in China to-day are in many respects similar to those existing in Germany then, which List tried to remedy and, since we are striving to attain our national unity let us see what lessons we can learn from List's message. But first of all let us examine briefly Germany's conditions.

Germany was unique among the nations of Europe in the 19th centruy. Her population was for the most part agricultural and the various states were politically and economically isolated. Her industry was fettered by the corporative regime and her agriculture was still in feudal thraldom. Freed from these encumbrances and having established first her economic and then her political unity, she took her place, during the last three decades of the century, among the foremost of industrial powers.

The Act of Union of 1800 had resulted in the economic unity of the Brisish Isles and Adam Smitn regarded it as "one of the chief causes of the prosperity of Great Britain. "France had accomplished the same end by the abolition of domestic tariffs in 1791. But Germany even in 1815 was still a congeries of provinces, varying in importance and separated from one another by tariff walls. "In short," says List in one of his petitions, "while other nations cultivate the sciences and the arts whereby commerce and industry are extended, German merchants and manufacturers must devote a great part of their time to the study of domestic tariffs and taxes." During the period when he was working hard for the establishment of the Zollverin, which was completed in 1841, List also carefully studied the causes of national progress and decay.

After sketching the economic development of Western Europe he gives his theorectical conclusions regarding the causes which underlie and explain such developments. He takes as his starting point Adam Smith's discussion of the nature and causes of the wealth of nations and comes to the conclusion that productive powers to create wealth are far more important than wealth itself. While criticizing Smith for not developing this he credits him with having clearly recognized it, A nation like a person may be poor and weak at one point of time but if possessed of productive powers it is, in the long run, far better off than one which merely possesses wealth but is lacking in productive powers. The contrast is best illustrated in the economic history of Spain and Germany.

"The powers of producing wealth," he says, "is therefore infinitely more important than wealth itself; it insured not only the possession and the increase of what has been gained, but also the replacement of what has been lost. This is still more the case with entire nations(who cannot live off mere rentals) than with private individuals"(1)

Next we were told of the rich sources of productive power which spring from the teachings of religion, from the adoptions and spread of socializing influences, like a free press, the postal system, sound systems of money, and wlights and measures, of police administration, the introduction of the principles of freehold and especially property, of the means of mass transport. The differences between the conditions of European states and of Oriental countries are to be explained principally in terms of the absence and differences in the above mentioned agencies. The influence of liberty of thought and conscience upon the productive forces of nations are likewise stressed and illustrated in accounting for the differences in the economic development of Great Britain and Spain.

Unlike the classical theory, human labor is not to be considered the cause of wealth according to List. Modern nations using mechanical power have employed less human labor than have Oriental countries; yet they are incomparably richer, more powerful, and prosperous. Later, as if commenting on the existing conditions in China, List wrote; "The prevailing school of economists (the classical) does not perceive that between a State devoted merely to agriculture and a State possessing both agriculture and manafacture, a much greater difference exists than between a pastoral state and an agricultural one. In a condition of merely agricultural industry, caprice and slavery, superstition and ignorance, want of means of culture, of trade and of transport, poverty and political weakness exist. In the merely agricultural State only the least portion of the mental and bodily powers existing in the nation is awakened and developed, and only the least part of the powers and resources placed by nature at its disposal can be made use of, while little or no capital can be accumulated.

...Manufactories and manufactures are the mothers and children of municipal liberty, of intelligence, of the arts and sciences, of internal and external commerce, of navigation and improvements in transport, of civilization and political power. They are the chief means of liberating agriculture from its chains, and of elevating it to a commercial character and to a degree of art and science, by which the rents, farming profits, and wages are increased, and greater value is given to landed property.......

If, however, trade in the manufactures of far distant lands exercises admittedly so beneficial an influence on our agricultural industry, how much more beneficial must the influence be of those manufacturers which are bound up with us locally, commercially, and politically, which not only take from us a small portion but the largest portion of their requirements of food and of raw materials, which are not made dearer to us by great costs of transport, our trade in which cannot be interrupted by the chance of foreign manufacturing nations learning to supply their own wants themselves, or by wars and prohibitory import duties?" 2

In a later chapter he draws the contrast between an agricultural country and one possessing a more rounded development in the following language; "A nation which only carries on agriculture is an individual who in his material production lacks one arm. Commerce is merely the medium of exchange between the agricultural and the manufacturing power, and between their separate branches. A nation which exchanges agricultural products for foreign manufactured goods is an individual with one arm which is supported by a foreign arm." 3

That China to-day is a country with preponderantly agricultural interests to the neglect of manufacturing industries is a well known fact. About eighty per cent of our people are directly dependent for their living upon the soil. Therefore, it is not only important that improvements in the methods of agriculture must be effected, but that new industries must be encouraged along lines used in the factory production of the West. That such industrial development has not sufficiently occurred in China has been due largely to a lack of desire on our part to make the most of the natural resources of the country, an idea inculcated through age-long teachings by sages and philosophers. In the past the thoughts and the desires of the leaders of the people have not been along industrial or commercial lines. More than that, they deprecated excessive attentions being paid to industry or commerce. They were anti-capitalistic and preached the doctrine of moderation in industrial as in other concerns. As a consequence of this unfavorable attitude toward industries on our part, we neglected the necessary training to cope with nature, altho by no means without natural aptitudes, as demonstrated by the number of significant inventions credited to us. Moreover, the experience of our people for centuries gave a fear for the uncertain future, and men learned that the way to have wealth was to hide it. Foreign invasions, inter-sectional wars and civil strife were hardly calculated to induce people to put their wealth into enduring forms.

In the large centers of trade this lack of confidence in the future has already passed away, altho it still lingers to a certain extent in other places. Many of the educated people realize, more and more, that factory production on a large scale must come to China. The lack of desire to develop the resources is gone but the lack of training for production on a large scale is still present.

It is here I feel that the college of Administration of Chiao-tung University can be of much service to our country by training men to carry out the various administrative duties especially in the field of banking and finance. Before the war, the prevailing thought of the economists appeared to be that banking and credit were more or less mechanical phenomena whose purpose was little more than that of facilitating the exchange of goods. The War had changed this line of thinking, the most important of which is the change of the point of view. The banking question of the present day is undoubtedly recognized by careful students as being fundamentally a question of social organization and control. Its immediate significance is to be found chiefly in its effect upon the distribution of wealth, while its ultimate significance is to be found in connection with the bearing it has upon production and in its power to direct production into new and different channels.

Hence, if we can agree with List that a country must encourage her industries to supplement agriculture in order to have a balanced and wholesome economic development, then we cannot afford to neglect the whole field of financial organization which is pre-requisite to any industrial development on a large scale. No country can do much to encourage her industries without having a unified monetary system and a sound, uniform banking law and practice. These can only be accomplished by training men with rasonable patriotism and intelligence to guide and direct the growth of such important economic institutions.

1. List, F., National System of Paliti eal Economy, P. 108
2. List, F., of cit., pp. 114, 115
3. List, F., of cit., p. 130

中國財務行政組織（E 1.）

衞挺生

財務行政可分廣狹二義，狹義言之可分爲積極的四種，曰收入行政，曰支出行政，曰公債行政，曰金庫行政。廣義言之，更包括預算決算會計，統計報告等事，此四者可稱爲積極之財政監督。查攷財務行政是否合法辦理，有事前審計，收支是否確行，有事後審計，事實是否實在，則有稽察以爲監視。審計爲書面上之稽察，稽察爲事實上之審計，可稱爲消極的財政監督。

依現在政府組織，合四種狹義行政加以貨幣金融行政等，爲財政部所主持事項。預決算統計之事務歸掌於主計處，合審計統稱爲計政。審計稽察事項則歸監察院審計部處理。

我國廣義財務行政制度與他國不同，財政在經濟科學中，發源至早，經濟史上，不絕所載，經濟學之研究亦由財政而漸入於私經濟。所可注意者，財政學發達雖早而進步甚遲，故各國財政制度相差彌遠，因參差之故，我國設任意摹仿他國，實不合度。蓋各有歷史經濟制度爲背景。以不同之背景，勉强傚學他人，自不能求其適合。故我國今日之財政制度非由於抄襲，亦非由自造，而爲依照本國經驗，他國成規，挹長補短，所得之結果。

全部財政之得當與否，全視預算，預算之妥當與否，又根據政治與事業之設計，此種設計，基於統計，故統計實爲財政制度之始。蘇俄有經濟計劃之成功，促世人與經濟計劃化之念。經濟生活，當有完善之計劃，國家之富强，更非經濟計劃不能完成之。言包工，工料之値，應有統計，應有計劃，以達僱方及被僱方經濟上之目的，是可見計劃及統計之要，根據精密之計劃及統計雙方始能得利。國家每種政事皆可以影響全國人，是政事之決定，豈可無精密之統計及計劃。經濟計劃完善，仍未能求整個國家之富强，更須進而求教育，政治社會之種種計劃以爲補助。今日預算之造成乃由於精密之施政及實業之計劃與統計。前者國人亦嘗注意統計，然法不精，意不誠，統計之成績，未能可靠，尤以地方統計爲甚。爲改良計，現在統計制度訂定之原則，注意於人員，方法，及資料。所有政府辦理統計人員歸國府統計局管理，其任免，遷調，攷績，升降，均由該局主管，如此，全國人員可有標準之訓練及監督，至如方法，資料，亦有集中機關以爲計劃，收效自宏，如是範圍劃定，以免重複或欠缺之弊。

統計整理後，次言施政及實業計劃。每年於預算決定前，各種機關應先定施政計劃，以爲預算決定之張本。現在對於辦理預算人員，設法使與行政機關相脫離，故由歲計局委派，而成超然之組織。辦理預算人員對行政機關之施政，有簽註獨立意見之權，故預算之估計分爲兩欄，一爲機關長官之估計，一爲預算人員簽註意見，所以爲牽制，而免浪費也。然而人情不能免除，主管長官及辦理預算人員仍有妥協折中之惡習，不能盡殺其弊，但至少已可得較爲合理之預算矣。

至於會計制度，國民革命成功後，財政部卽有會計獨立之倡。該部附屬機關會計主任有獨立地位，惟當時財務行政長官及會計主任均由財部派遣，會計主任之直隸於財部也，雖比較的有超然獨立之可能，然事實上成績仍未見顯著，通同作弊，隨地皆是，卽會計主任能清明無私，而各財政長官均有背境，不能實行牽制，更難達到會計獨立之目的。其後有進一步之改革，乃欲使各部各院會計之獨立，財部無力管馭，而以獨立之機關直接隸於國府。其時預算統計亦有超然之議，乃以預算，統計及會計三者，併合而成一超然機關，蓋三者有連帶之關係，以之歸同一機關辦理，經濟上又可節省，於理論於事實均有其利也。主計之名，非新創，民三袁世凱時代，總統府設政事堂，下設主計局，辦理財政預算事，今日之主計處，實與當時之主計局相仿。

再言審計制度，審計名稱，起於宋代，歐洲各國歸爲司法監督。我唐代歸刑部主管，稱比部郎中，歐洲稱會計法院（Court of Accounts）程序亦似司法。日本稱會計檢查院。英美則不然，英審計長（Comptrollor & Audit Gnrcl）對國會負責，不取司法形式，美審計有General Accounting office設審計長，及審計官，分掌事務，對國會負責，程序亦不採司法，故英美對審計實為立法監督。我國五權分立，審計歸監察院辦理，故不可稱為司法之監督。

審計之辦理在昔有送請審計猶今日之事後審計，事前審計亦曾採用，而稽察事務則並未創立。送請審計，弊端百出，謊報揑造，不一而足，徒耗審計之經費；為補救計，乃有就地審計制度及稽察之設。各省市設審計處，兼理中央及地方審計。

金庫制度，古代確有庫房之設，至今日貨幣信用經濟制度下，庫無設房之必要，而成抽象之名詞，僅代表公家所有資產之集體，而有法人之資格，故國庫(國庫司Public Treasury)之任務為收入及支出之彙總。至於金庫（Fiscal Agency）實際管理收支事務，可分為官廳金庫，各部金庫，二種制度均有操縱之弊，而各機關間無調節之效。更進，乃有集中之金庫，然於經濟上有不良之影響，再進有銀行代理金庫辦法，日亦採此制，又進為銀行存款法，政府以錢存銀行，金融市場，可資流通。我國現在採用銀行存款制，法規方在草擬，其辦法為以稅款由人民交銀行，銀行一方面報告政府一方面通知金庫。金庫基金劃分為三，曰普通總基金，經費基金及各特種基金。如需經費由總基金撥入經費基金，每當支出，機關開支票領取現金以便交付政府債權人，事實上在劃撥後，未入債權人前，各機關並無現金，歸公庫記帳。所謂特種基金有如營業基金(郵政，鉄道等)，公債基金等，此種基金另有管理程序。故公庫僅掌帳目，錢存銀行，以免行政人員之舞弊營私。

收入行政在已往爲最不名譽之政府事務，顯著有如厘卡。現在主計審計金庫制度已次第實行，內部有所牽制，或可少戢弊誤。

至於公債行政，問題複雜，昔日均爲祕密，弊端百出，皆因監督不嚴之故。現在則亦見改良，蓋亦內部牽制組織能力之發揮也。

總之新舊財政之不同，乃爲職務之絕對劃分，造成牽制組織，今稱爲聯綜組織。

中華國有鐵路現行行車時刻表

津浦綫

上行車

站名	公里	時刻	302次 滬平通車(餐臥頭二三等車)	72次 浦徐區間車 頭二三等車	22次 津浦快車(餐臥頭二三等車)	306次 平浦通車(餐臥頭二三等車)	74次 徐濟區間車(三等車)	76次 濟津區間車(三等車)	78次 濟津區間車(三等車)
上海北站		開	16.00						
浦口		開	1.40	7.10	9.45	16.20			
滁州	50	開	3.05	9.02	11.20	17.42			
蚌埠	176	開	6.38	13.55	15.18	21.15			
南宿州	266	開	8.47	16.42	17.49	23.24			
徐州府	341	開	11.05	19.00	20.18	1.39	6.40		
臨城	408	開	13.05		22.22	3.31	8.59		
兗州府	502	開	15.47		1.28	6.00	12.28		
曲阜	519	開	16.14		1.55	6.35	13.01		
泰安府	586	開	18.15		4.02	8.38	15.37		
濟商府	658	開	20.45		6.44	10.59	18.05	12.00	22.40
德州	776	開	0.25		10.15	14.04		15.34	3.20
滄州	889	開	3.29		13.30	16.46		19.21	7.39
天津總站	1010	開	6.55		17.19	20.03		23.15	12.00
天津東站	1 14	開	7.30		17.29	20.45			
北平東站	1154	到	10.21			23.45			

下行車

站名	公里	時刻	21次 津浦快車(餐臥頭二三等車)	75次 津濟區間車(三等車)	77次 津濟區間車(三等車)	301次 滬平通車(餐臥頭二三等車)	305次 平浦通車(餐臥頭二三等車)	73次 濟徐區間車(三等車)	71次 徐浦區間車(頭二三等車)
北平東站		開				15.05	19.30		
天津東站		開	8.50			18.20	23.00		
天津總站	5	開	9.30	7.00	16.30	18.40	23.30		
滄州	125	開	13.22	11.04	22.50	21.[illegible]9	3.18		
德州	239	開	16.58	15.21	2.18	0.20	6.49		
濟南府	357	開	20.37	18.40	6.05	3.33	10.31		
泰安府	428	開	23.07			5.43	12.51	7.20	
曲阜	496	開	1.01			7.14	14.42	10.29	
兗州府	513	開	1.41			7.50	15.31	12.[illegible]8	
臨城	607	開	4.25			10.10	18.04	13 44	
徐州府	673	開	6.44			12.11	20.21	16.58	
南宿州	749	開	8.53			14.00	23.16	19.05	7.50
蚌埠	839	開	11.23			16.19	1.43		10.26
滁州	963	開	15.14			19.36	5.32		13.37
浦口	1014	開	16.40			20.45	6.45		18.33
上海北站		到				7.45			20.15

注意　南下赴京旅客請購下關站客票　由京北上旅客請在下關站購票

車務處　浦口　電話41394　問訊處　浦口車站　電話41152轉

中國鐵路的管理問題

葉子剛

中國的鐵路，自始就不曾當作商業經營過。清季如此，民國成立後，仍是如此，路政都旁落在軍人政客手中。割截路段，濫用私人，和扣留路款等怪劇，是司空見慣。十幾年來，鐵路在這種混亂情形之下，路產的維持尙談不到，科學的管理與合理的經營更是無從說起了。

軍人政客之所以能干涉路政，因爲鐵路在人事上沒有一定政策。大凡一件事業，如果它的人事組織能長久維持他的系統，必能走上軌道，我國的銀行就是一個好例子。鐵路如能滲入銀行的經營精神，則今日組織的龐大與鬆懈，用人的漫無標準及經營的不合理化等現象，必可逐漸消滅。所以作者以爲目今整頓鐵路的前提，在樹立一定的人事組織，使鐵路行政與政治少發生關係；如果爲了應付環境，寗可協助款項，不可讓軍人政客等參與路政，這樣，最低也可保存路產的完整。至於鐵路在專家經營之下，如何才能走上軌道，如同火車在鐵軌上安穩地駛行，作者也有一些小意見，分別寫出來向行家請教。

組織與用人

鐵路既受政治的影響很大，則組織的龐大與鬆懈自在意中，因爲濫用私人既受容許，則因人設事的現象便不能免掉。例如總務處，就有文書，機要，編查，審核，公益，衛生，庶務等課，每課起碼有二十餘人，路線稍長的還不止此數。就鐵路經營的範圍說，這種組織不免稍大，各課很可併爲數課。組織縮小，用人自然減少；這樣，各人的工作緊張，效能自然大見，有用的人才便不致投閒置散，而事務因組織的縮小，也不會因手續之轉折錯誤而有所延誤了。

我國鐵路，素以總務費特高著名。據統計，二十二年全國國有各路的總務費共計一八、三九〇、一四〇、〇五元，佔該年用款總數百分之二六・七六，佔該年進款總數百分之一九・一四。這種百分率，如與外國的比較，(外國最多不過百分之三)，未免太高，雖然我國鐵路總務費所包括的項目較多。在其他各國，工務維持費和機務維持費都佔用款的大宗，而在我國，則在民國二十二年，工務維持費佔用款總數百分之二〇・七七，機務維持費佔用款總數百分之十八・七七，均不及總務費所佔的成數，可見我國鐵路用款用於直接經營的微小與經營的不合理，更證明總務處之組織之過於龐大。

各路員工總數，在民國二十二年，爲一二七、一五一人，較民國二十一年增加一、九二五人，每營業路線公里有員工一七・七人。依據歷年統計，員工數目只有增加，并無減少，這固然是因爲業務有相當進展，但是否完全因事置人，則頗値得考究。據實際的考察，人浮於事是我國各機關的普通現象，鐵路又何能免此，然則鐵路員工人數之增加，足供我們長思了。近年來，政府對於各機關的用人問題很注意，新進的須經考試或銓叙，在任的須經考績以定其去留晉降，但對於現有人員的過多，仍無妥當的處置辦法。作者以爲在用人方面，鐵路應按照現實的需要，規定各處的員司名額，在未有名額空出前，不准添一新人。如現有人數較定額爲多，則應施行嚴密公正的考績，依照員司的學識，經驗和資歷來核定員司的名次，凡是在名額之內的爲正式員司，在名額之外的爲記名員司，仍舊支薪供職，遇正式員司出缺時卽依照考績所定的記名員司的名次，依序晉補，留下來的記名員司缺卽行取消。這個辦法的好處在不斥退一人，而收緊縮用人的功效。近來各方面雖感覺有人浮於事的現象而仍不敢裁員者，大都因爲中國在另一方面失業問題很是嚴重，如果一裁人，就難免使社會不安，如採用上法，就可避免這種不安，而仍舊可達到裁員的目的。

關於選用新人，鐵路本已有很好的辦法。鐵道部特設交通大學，培養交通專門人才，幷每年派遣交大畢業生赴各路實習，使其得資歷練，而各路常常招考低級員司。但這種選用的新人，每年不過一兩百人，在每年新人總數中佔數很微，大多數人還是由推薦來的；其間不能說沒有人才，但根據經驗，在中國，推薦是難得適當人才的。爲了求得人得其位，事得其人，應當廢除推薦制度，採用考試方法。每年由鐵道部或委託考試院舉行公開考試，依照所需人數，招收各大學有志於鐵道事業的畢業生，分發各路實習，然後授與實職，對於交大學生則或仍用現行辦法，或亦加以考試而酌量免除應試科目。於下級員司則責成各路舉辦考試。能如此則倖進之路絕，復加以名額的有定與考績的施行，現在鐵路用人紊亂的情形，無須責成當局勿援用私人，便可解決了。

設備品的運用與提高運輸能力

鐵路的設備，應當好好維持，并應充分運用。近十餘年來，因了天災人禍，鐵路路產所受的破壞很大，同時因爲國內經濟情形不佳，鐵路收入不豐，也無力維持路產。如同平漢路的黃河鐵橋保險早已滿期，而仍在將就使用；又如湘鄂路的枕木壞爛甚多，車行其上，猶船走在江中，顚播不已，而且行走甚慢。在車輛方面，因各路無力多購，一方面車輛使用過度，致時需修理，而一方面因爲車輛不夠用，修理也就馬虎。據民國二十四年十月份統計，全國各路機車共有一、一二八輛，在廠修理和待修的，有三一五輛，佔全數百分之二十八；貨車共有一四、六五六輛，在修理和待修的有二、二五八輛，佔全數百分之十五·五。百分數之高，中外罕有，這是由於車輛太少和修理不善所致。在這裏，機廠修理工作的效率和修理的方法乃問題的焦點，是急待解決的。因爲這種情形，不僅減低鐵路的運輸能力，而且增加用款，甚不經濟。

車輛不僅應好好維持，幷應好好運用，因爲能多運用一點，就可多得一點收入，同時也就減少一點成本，這在鐵路本身和國民經濟兩方面，都是有益的。

運用車輛當注意減少空車里程，減少車輛在站內留滯之時間及增加列車裝載量等。據統計，民國二十二年全國各路空車延噸公里佔貨車延噸公里之百分之三十六，比率甚高。空車里程數之大，固由於鐵路沿線的經濟情形，但也繫於鐵路的營業政策和車輛支配的方法。平綏路曾利用東運減價政策，減少空車里程不少。又如能支配車輛得法，使空車勿在長途駛行，也是減少空車里程的一法。

據民國二十二年的統計，全國各路每貨車平均停站之公噸鐘點爲六七〇，爲數不小。貨車在站內停留的原因不外「調車及站務」，「起卸貨物」，「軍用延期」，「候車」等項，所以要減少這種留滯時間當從改善調車制度，改善裝卸貨物手續，增進站上辦事效率入手。如能減少車輛在站內停留的時間，則無形中增加可用之車輛，鐵路之運輸能力自必因之而提高。

列車裝載量在近九年有減低之勢。據統計，全國各路每貨運列車平均貨物噸數，民國十九年爲二九七，民二〇爲二五九，民二一爲二四六，民二二爲二三三。列車裝載噸數一方面與成本有關。一方面與進款有關，所以增加列車裝貨噸數也是一個急應研究的問題。

機車也應好好用，尤其是在路線長的路，運用機車的方法與提高運輸力很有關係。從前津浦路的機車是每段更換，這既多需機車，而且增加卸車掛車的手續，很不經濟。現在改用機車長途行駛法，據說，結果很好，這是可供有志鐵路的人研究的。

材料的購用

鐵路用款的最大項目是薪資和料價。材料的價值比薪資的數目還大，其中的弊端最難看出，歷來鐵路當局都把主管材料當作肥差。近來購料採用投標法，舞弊的事情大爲減少，但不經濟的地方還很多。作者以爲凡大宗的常用材料應該集中購辦，由鐵道部大批採購，分發各路使用，因爲大批購辦的價格較廉，手續較省。如果須向外國買，則宜乘外匯有利或物價跌落的時候，預先買就。日本就採用這種辦法，常屯集大批材料，以供數年之用。至於自己可製造的小件，則應自造。前時某路因需用撑軌架(Rail－Brace)，本擬由機廠自製，成本僅須一元左右一個，因照章制零件須由部代購，結果過時數月，每個費價三四元，這是很不經濟的。此外，購料應有預算，既不可濫買而致呆擱，又不可少買致有缺乏，這就有賴於用料處，購料處和存料處的通力合作。材料廠應時時有精確的存料統計，用料處應有精確的用料預算，購料處根據這統計和預算，籌劃購料。這種辦法可免去一方面廢料堆積一方面停工待料或高價購料的矛盾現象。

材料購來後，應妥當存儲，將材料分門別類，編號庋藏，使它不受風雨的剝蝕和蟲鼠的傷壞。從前有些鐵路對於材料的存放不甚注意，過了週年半載，新料變爲舊料，舊料變爲廢料，廢料復棄而不用，虛耗不少資金。以理論講，材料購買原依用料處的請求，不應發生廢置。如因中途改變建築計劃而致，猶有可原，但現在多半是因不預先籌劃亂購所致，所以當有了廢料，材料廠應與用料處商議，設法利用，如利用不可能，則應招商承買，決不可棄而不問。

各用料處向材料廠領料，應依照一定手續。領來後，應即使用，不可有領而不用的情事。料用後應即編造用料報告或統計，以供購料的參考。

關於材料，如能這樣整頓，每年必可替國家省一筆很大的金錢，拿這筆款子去擴充鐵路，成績必定很可觀的。

很早以前，鐵路當局就知道購買材料須先儘國貨，但實際上所購的仍以外貨爲多。這是一個技術問題，除了我國生產事業發達之外，別無辦法可想。自從杭江鐵路建築以來，便有借材料這一方法，近來南玉路便是借德國材料造成的，而剛剛開工的南萍路，也在採用這種借料方式。這比借錢的辦法好，因爲建築一條鐵路，大宗費用是薪資和料價，直接借料很可免除借款的被人挪用和款項的虛糜。在借用外資諸法中，這是一個值得注意的辦法。

在用料問題中，值得一注意的是機車用煤問題。民二二年全國各路機車用煤佔機車用款百分之五十八，佔運務費百分之四十三，佔營業用款總數百分之九，爲數甚是可觀。這種費用的大小和煤的質量，價格，及燒煤的技術與當心大有關係，是值得管理鐵路的人注意的。

營業和運價

近幾年，鐵路漸知自己招攬營業，各路大都設立營業所，創辦負責運輸，直接和商人接洽，幷改運輸的設備和手續，朝便利商人的方向走去，這是很可喜的現象。希望服務鐵路人員能更加努力，使鐵路成爲純粹商業機關，好像非營業發達便不能立足似地；這樣鐵路才算盡了它的義務，也必須這樣，鐵路才有發達的可能。

此外，鐵路更應減輕人民的負担。據統計，中國鐵路的票價和運費，如與外國的相比，稍嫌過高，所以第九次運輸會議曾議決凡票價在每公里一分五厘以上者，減按一分五厘計算。減低票價幷不一定減低收入，正如增加票價不一定增加收入一樣，如能減抑適當，反能增加收入，因爲這可刺激人們的旅行欲。

運價的高對於一國的經濟影響很大，這件事已爲國內研究鐵路的人所公認，用不着細說；但應如何調整運價，使國民經濟能夠發展，却是一件繁難的工作。現在各路只注重維持現有收入，很少顧及運價政策的運用，這是很危險的，因爲殺死了金鵝，金蛋就永遠不會再有的。例如平綏路改低運價後，收入即增加三四百萬元。這還不過就收入這一端說，在另一端，商業情形因此較形活潑，經濟情形也就會漸趨良好。但這裏有一個問題，就是鐵路運價應該取一般經濟政策呢？還是取營利政策呢？這兩說都有人主張，作者以爲在不蝕本的原則之下，鐵路應該以發展國民經濟爲目的。這就是說，鐵路應用極經濟的經營方法，節省糜費，減輕成本，然後利用運價政策，在不虧本的條件之下，發展國民經濟。例如發展經濟的最大條件是使全國各地同沾惠益。像現在，離市場遠的貨物便不能與離市場近的貨物競爭，致使產地有偏枯偏榮，這種情形應該利用運價去改正。

鐵路財務

我國鐵路，沒有一條不與借債有關。民二十一年底止，我國鐵路債款共有一、三〇六、三二五、七一九、四三元。這十萬萬元的鉅額債款是中國鐵路一個重大的負担，凡是想減輕鐵路負担的理財家都曾設法整理。歷來整理債務的意見，不外下列數種：

一、另發低利新債以抵償高利舊債；

二、將零星各債併而爲一，發行一新債以抵償之；

三、舊債仍舊存在，僅減低其利率；

四、延長舊債的償還期限。

整理債務原不外這幾種辦法，作者所要提出的是如何償還。有些人主張應將鐵路的盈餘完全償付債款本息，以維信用。這不是一個辦法。如果將盈餘完全用在還債，則鐵路用什麽去維持和發展自己呢？樹立信用并不在乎還債，而在有還債的能力和還債的願意。所以作者以爲應將鐵路的盈餘分爲兩部份，一部份用去還債，其他一部份用去擴充鐵路的設備，增大鐵路的運輸能力，使之能獲得更多的收入。這樣，不特舊債能還，而且還得更快，同時外人看見我們鐵路的經濟能力日見强大，不特不來逼債，而且會更願意借款給我們。這是一種攻補兼施的方劑，比卽專主攻的方子有用得多，因爲攻勢大峻，病人的身體太弱，受不住的。

論到建築新路，在民窮財盡的今日中國，自非借用外資不可。但今日環境，借用外資都有限制了，我們該怎樣呢？難道不建設嗎？最好的方法當然是用鐵路的盈餘造鐵路，但舊的鐵路雖有盈餘，却用在償還舊債，和改善設備方面，并無力量顧到新路。其次當然是向國內籌款，但在今日之中國，人民既無財力，銀行也沒有這麽大的手面，所以最後仍不得不向借外資一途走。要借外資，得先整理舊債，所以整理舊債很重要。從前各路整理債務都是各自爲政，這雖也有方便之處，但也有缺點。最好的辦法是由鐵道部來統籌，就全國各路的經濟情形通盤籌畫，并須以償還舊債爲借新債的張本，這才一舉兩得，既解决了舊債，又解决了新路理財問題。

借用外資，應只是技術的，不應是政治的，這是近來理財者一致的意見。作者以爲宜更進一步，借款只取借料的方式。這種辦法已有玉萍路在行，它的結果很好，是值得仿行的。

過去吾國鐵路之錯誤與今後新路建設之方針

沈奏廷

吾國之有鐵路也，遠在距今六十年以前，而迄今全國所有之鐵路里程，除東三省外，幹綫不過七千餘公里，若連枝綫，副軌及岔道等計算在內，亦僅一萬公里有奇，以視交通發達之美國，固屬瞠乎其後，卽與印度南非等國相較，亦覺望塵莫及，無怪農工商業俱無振興之望，地方經濟永無發展之期，良堪浩歎。嘗考建築鐵路固不如建築公路之易舉，然果下相當之決心，要亦非難能之事。最近如山西之興築同蒲鐵路，浙江江西之興築浙贛鐵路，與夫粵漢之完成，隴海之西展，均收良好之效果，具見事在人爲，非不能也。或有以爲年來我國公路勃興，交通日便，鐵路似可緩修者，不知公路運輸能力極小，取費甚昂，舉凡價廉或笨重之貨物均不能由公路運送，欲求實業之發展，仍非增修鐵路不可也。乃者鐵道最高當局似有鑒於斯，有積極籌集資本，展修新路之意，國人聞之，自當引爲快事。吾人除以十二分之熱忱，希望其一一見諸事實外，深覺過去吾國鐵路之興修與經營，尙有種種之錯誤與缺陷，均爲此後新修之路所應竭力避免或糾正者，甚願主其事者以高瞻遠矚之眼光而愼之於始，以免貽患於將來，此尤吾人之所期望於今後之新路者也。請申論之。

一 路軌

路軌問題之要點，一爲軌距，一爲軌重。吾國國有鐵路、除正太外，向均採用標準軌距(四呎八吋半)，而軌重大都爲八十五磅。惟近年來，國人鑒於國內資金之缺乏，建築鐵路工事之艱巨，并爲求完成迅速獲利較易起見，頗有傾向於輕窄軌之一途者。遠如杭江，近如同蒲，皆其著例。杭江，軌重爲三十五磅，惟仍用標準軌距；同蒲則軌重僅三十二磅、軌距僅一公尺，實爲一輕窄軌之鐵路。究竟吾國此後興修新路，應採用輕軌乎，採用輕窄軌乎、抑採用標準軌距與重軌乎？關於軌距之寬窄一點，管見以爲窄軌鐵路往往弊多於利，非有特殊之原因，不應貿然採用窄軌；蓋除在山嶺綿延，羊腸曲徑之地帶外，窄軌之建築費用，較諸寬軌所省極微。而考其弊害，則不一而足，舉其著者，則有下列數端：(一)窄軌鐵路之車輛不能與寬軌鐵路互通，平時固有礙於聯運，戰時尤不利於軍運。(二)窄軌鐵路改修標準軌時，全部機車車輛不能復用，最初所省者小，而後日所耗者大。(三)軌距既窄，車輛容積亦不得不小，對於運輸經濟，影響滋巨。(四)幹綫既修成窄軌，則其枝綫及聯絡綫亦非修成窄軌不可，他日積重難返，更張非易。有此數因，故窄軌非不得已時不應採用；山西同蒲路之修成窄軌，亦屬基於一種錯誤的觀念，殊非計之得者。

其次則爲軌重問題。查路軌之輕重，影響於行車之速度與列車車輛之載重者綦巨，因路軌愈輕，則列車之行駛速率愈小，列車與車輛之載重愈少也。故同一之運量，在輕軌之路，必須以較多之車輛與列車次數運送之。嘗考輕軌之利在建築費用之節省，而其弊則在行車費用與機車車輛修理折舊等費之增加。是以採用輕軌，非有下列三種條件，往往不能合算，即：(一)運量小，(二)運輸成本低，(三)資本利息重是也。據作者最近赴晉考察之所得，同蒲路採用輕軌之所以合算者，亦以適合上述條件之故；蓋在山西，利息按年約須一分，築路資金亦須負担同樣利率，而煤價及工資甚廉，鐵路營業用款遠較他處爲節省，且同蒲現有運量尙小（貨運年約五〇、〇〇〇、〇〇〇延噸公里，客運年約六〇、〇〇〇、〇〇〇延人公里），列車及車輛之載重能力尙能符合需要；有此特殊情形，故同蒲之採用輕軌，目前尙稱有利。惟就個人研究所及，該路之貨物運量每年若增至四〇〇、〇〇〇、〇〇〇延噸公里時，即除客運不計，輕軌已不合算。他路之運輸成本較高資本利息較輕者，更不待運量增至此數；而必已有改修重軌之必要矣。由上所述，可知今後興修新路，是否將得用輕軌，以節經費，當視其能符合上項條件與否而定，且須顧及將來運量之發展程度，而爲之蠡測規定焉。

二 車輛

過去吾國各路所購之車輛，形式不一，構造不同，情形異常複雜，若各路不相聯絡，不辦聯運，則彼此分歧，尙不覺其有害。今各路聯運暢通，車輛必須過軌，爲求車輛返還原有路計，乃用原車返還之法，限制其使用及返還之路徑，并核收車租及延期費，以爲督促其返還之助。考此制行於美國，耗費滋多，彼邦人士亦早思有以改進，徒以種種關係，尙難實現。因實行此制，則各路間勢必互送空車，空車里程因以增加，一面造成軌道及車場之擁擠，一面增多行車及調車之耗費；且因回程裝貨須有路徑之限制，有時貨物之路徑與車輛回程之路徑不符，遂致有車不能裝貨，有貨無車可裝，事之矛盾，莫逾於此。欲圖改良，惟有採用貨車公用制度，廢除原車返還之法。而後他路貨車可與本路貨車同樣使用，祇須按期結算過軌之差數，無須互送多數之空車，徒增種種之耗費。按此制行於英國及歐陸諸國，收效甚宏。惟欲實行此制，則公用之車輛必須有統一之構造，統一之容量，否則窒碍孔多，決難推行盡利。今後吾國建築新路，購置車輛，對此似應特別注意。卽除特種車輛外，所有通常各路共同需用之車輛，務須使之統一化，標準化，對於舊路添置新車時，亦應令其嚴守統一之標準，庶幾將來舊車漸去，新車漸增，貨車公用制度乃得通行於全國，車輛利用必見增加，行車耗費必見減少，其有裨於鐵路運輸之前途也審矣。

三　車站設備

曩時吾國建築鐵路，對於車站設備大都不加重視，事前既無詳盡之設計，事後亦少改進之計劃，以致布置不合理者有之，地位不敷用者有之。對外既多不便，對內尤多耗費。良以車站一物，爲鐵路客貨呑吐之咽喉，咽喉不健全，則臟胃亦隨之而病矣·故鐵路客貨車站設不善，則全路運輸之效能必減、耗費必增。先進諸國之鐵路，對於終點大站之設計，事前莫不有切實之規劃，且往往顧及數十年後客貨運量之發展，以爲擴充改良之地步，其用意至爲深長，其思慮極爲週到，故客貨運量雖多，而車站皆能井然有序，而無擁擠龐雜之患，運輸效率隨以增加，而耗費隨以減少，所謂工欲善其事，必先利其器也。吾人對於今後新修之鐵路，深盼其能力矯過去之錯誤，對於客貨大站之設備，事前能有眞正完善之設計，藉以增進運輸業務之效能。茲請就客貨兩種車站分別討論之。

旅客車站　吾國鐵路旅客車站秩序之紊亂，已爲共見共聞之事實，雖旅客習慣之不良，訓練之缺乏，常爲其原因之一，而車站設計之不善，尤爲原因中之重要者。嘗考美國鐵路對於旅客車站之設備，莫不注意下列各點，請列舉之：(一)各種主要設備，如售票房，行李房、男女待車室，問訊處，盥洗所，餐室、包件貯藏室・電話間、電報房(收音電者)、售品所等，應聚集於一處，(通常聚集於總待車室 Main Waiting Room 之兩旁及中間)勿使分散，致碍找尋，俾旅客一入站門，各種設備，均一一羅列眼前，無須往來尋覓。(二)行李房之地位須與售票房取得聯絡，俾旅客先購車票，後掛行李，行李掛就，即行上車，均係順路前進。無須後退，徒多往返。(三)行李之裝車卸車，應竭力避免與旅客混雜，致碍旅客之行動，而增站台之擁擠。其法或用地道及電梯，使月台與行李房聯絡，或用特設之行李裝卸月台，使行李無通過旅客月台之必要；或將大量之行李在特別指定之月台裝卸，使不必佔用其他月台之地位。而行李房之應鄰近軌道，使出入之行李不必經過站內旅客會集之所（如總待車室是），尤爲要圖。（四）笨大之行李應與輕便之行李劃分，前者應令直送行李房，勿使通過站內待車室等處，旅客可向行李房取得臨時收據，然後入站，購票，換取正式收據，庶幾笨重之物件不至與站內之旅客混雜，徒增紛亂。（五）到達之旅客，多數無須入站停留，應於大月台Concourse上另闢門戶，俾下車後卽可出站，無須行經站內總待車室等處，而與出發之旅客發生衝突混亂，致礙秩序。（六）各種設備之大小與多寡，應視客運數量而異，事前須有相當之考查與計算，使無不敷應用之患。例如待車室、盥洗所·餐室等之大小與夫售票窗戶之多寡，應視每日最繁忙時之旅客人數而定；行李房及包件，貯藏室之大小，應視每日行李及包件之件數而定。且須顧及今後客運增加之需要，以免將來捉襟見肘之患。以上各端，雖非全豹，然均爲吾國鐵路之應特別注意者，此後新建各路果能切實注意及此，則車站秩序之改進，工作效率之增加，當不難收相當之效果也。

貨物車站　鐵路承運之貨物，分整車與零担兩類，凡處理零担貨物之車站設備，與處理整車貨物者應有不同，不能視同一物。蓋零担車站之前部應爲月台，後部應爲軌道，其設計上應注意之點，就起運站觀之，約有下列數端：（一）月台前面須有多數之收貨門戶，使貨物備能隨到隨收，無守候與擁擠之患；(一)月台上須有多數之磅秤，俾貨物能隨收隨磅，無積壓之弊。(三)整個月台應爲一打通之空間，不得隔成數部，致碍貨物之搬移；(四)月台應與車底齊平，以增搬貨入車之便利；(五)每兩股軌道之間，應築一島式月台，以便貨物之搬送，而免車門之配對；(六)站內軌道不應用以調車，凡每一軌道停留待裝之空車，非俟全數裝畢，不得移動，以免擾亂裝車工作；(七)月台應力求平整，并減少柱脚等障碍物，以便搬貨車之行動。(八)軌道容積應足敷全日各車停站裝貨之用，使在裝之車輛竟日不必移動，迨傍晚貨已裝齊，乃調入車場編組列車，庶幾工作進行不至受何阻礙。凡此諸端，多爲吾國現有之貨站所未能實行者，無怪秩序凌亂，效率減少也。

整車貨物與零担貨物性質逈異，蓋前者以直接裝車裝畢過磅爲最經濟，而後者則非通過站台，先事過磅，而後分析裝車不可。故整車裝卸軌道應與零担貨站不同，前者無須月台之設置，而應以兩股道爲一組，兩組之間應爲車行道，以便貨商車輛之出入，軌道長度應較零貨裝車軌道爲短，以免調車之不便，因整車貨物不能各車同時裝竣，如軌道太長，則調動裝畢之車時，勢必擾及在裝之車輛也。整車裝卸軌道亦不應作調車之用，裝畢之車應拖入調車場內，從事編配。地磅之設置應在重車調動必經之地，使調車過磅能同時進行，一舉兩得，而免機力與時間之耗費。現在吾國鐵路對於整車貨物，規定須先請求貨位，入站堆裝，而後從事撥車，實爲一種極不經濟之辦法，（其弊詳見拙著改革吾國鐵路貨站支配貨車制度之商榷一文，載京滬杭甬鐵路日刊第一五〇九及一五一〇期）。此後建築整車貨站，應辨明整車貨物之性質，勿與零担貨站混淆，視同一物，而後工作效率乃能增加，耗費乃能減少也。

四　行車設備

西國鐵路雖皆竭力講求用款之經濟，耗費之減少，然對於必要之設備，則往往不惜工本，力求完善；行車設備關係行車安全與行車效率，至深且鉅，先進諸國講求尤不遺餘力。吾國鐵路於此，雖不能追蹤歐美，而與之並駕齊驅，然必要之保安設施終不可少，蓋寧省他種之靡費而移用於有益之途也。吾國各路之行車設備除北寧路較爲優勝外，大都均屬因陋就簡，異常陳舊，對於行車安全，殊多影響今後建築新路，似宜注意下列各點，以策安全而增效率：（一）分路轍尖宜有保險之鎖扣 Lock 辦法，使搬動之後不能跳易地位，無須分路夫用足踏住，免肇出軌等危險；（二）轍尖宜有 Detector Bar 或 Detector Locking 辦法，俾列車行經分道尚未離去時，轍尖絕對不能搬動；（三）轍尖與其號誌應一律有聯鎖之關係，務使分路尚未搬妥或軌道未清之前，號誌絕對不能表示平安，庶免搬錯分路發生撞車之危險，（四）在較大之站，號誌及轍尖應集中於一處管理，卽設一號誌樓，所有號誌，轍尖等物均由該號誌樓搬動，集中支配，無須一轍尖由分路夫一人管理，藉免分路搬錯與指揮不靈之患；（五）平交道所在之處，除列車次數甚少之路綫外，須一律裝置固定號誌，俾列車瞭望較易，不至撞壞柵門或竟肇撞車之禍；(六)固定號誌應一律改用上弦式 Upper Quadrant 以增進安全之程度；(七)沿途各站之蛇綫佈置，應一面爲直道，一面爲彎道，俾某一方向(上行或下行)之列車均可行徑直道，無須經過彎道，藉以增加行車之安全與效率，勿使兩旁僅有彎道，而直道反居中間，徒供停放閒車之用。以上各點，均係必要之保安設施，而非騖遠之論，建築新路，自始卽應注意及之。查已成國有諸路所有號誌及軌閘之建築費，除北甯較多外，餘均備極渺小，列表如次，以資例證：(民國二十年一之統計)

路別	營業公里(幹枝綫)	號誌及軌閘建設費		
		金額(千元)	每公里金額(元)	當路綫及設備品原價百分數
平漢	一、三二一·四	一、四五八	一、一〇三·〇〇	一·一%
北甯	四六四·九	三、二六九	七、〇三一·〇〇	二·六
津浦	一、一〇四·九	一、三四一	一、二一三·〇〇	一·〇
京滬	三二七·一	二七一	八二八·〇〇	〇·七
滬杭甬	二八六·五	二五二	八七九·〇〇	〇·九
平綏	八七六·五	八五三	九七三·〇〇	一·四
正太	二四二·二	四一七	一、七二一·〇〇	一·五
道清	一六五·四	一〇五	六三四·〇〇	一·二
汴路	一八四·〇	一六九	九一八·〇〇	一·〇
隴海	七一〇·一	三〇二	四二五·〇〇	〇·二

廣九	一四三·三	七九	五五一·〇〇	〇·五
湘鄂	五一三·〇	二一四	四一七·〇〇	〇·三
膠濟	四五三·三	三三五	七三九·〇〇	〇·七
南潯	一二八·四	三九	三〇三·〇〇	〇·三
國有鐵路合計	六、九二一·〇	九、一〇四	一、三一五·〇〇	一·一

觀上表可見各路用於號誌及軌閘之建築費，除北甯外，多則每公里不過一千元有奇，少則竟在五百元以下；其當路綫及設備品原價之總數，多則大都僅百分之一有奇，少則僅千分之三，而各路平均亦不過千分之十一，其爲數之渺小，卽足以表示各路行車設備之簡陋。今後築路，固應力事撙節，然對於此種行車保安必要之設備，似不應過於吝嗇，徒增將來之耗費。假定號誌及軌閘之建設費每公里能有五千元之數，則較諸平漢津浦等路，每修一千公里之路綫，亦不過多費三百餘萬元，爲數並不甚巨，而將來行車費用之節省，歲月累積，或且倍蓰，至於安全之保障，更不能以數字計矣。

× × × × ×

以上四端，均管見以爲今後建設新路時所應注意之要點，實施不難，所費有限，而其效甚宏，其利甚溥。想新路建設當局必亦已計劃及此，惟一得之愚，不敢緘默，芻蕘之見，或亦足供參考耳。

鐵路管理與理財

王炳南

一 引言

我國舉辦鐵路歷有多年，言路綫，現所存者僅約及一萬公里；言營業，則收入微薄，支出膨大，既不努力於招徠發展運輸，復視鐵路爲致富之源，營私舞弊，任意刁難，宜乎商賈視鐵路爲畏途，裹足不前也；言路產，非特不能年有添增擴充，即原置產業亦破壞不堪應用；如民國十三年各路共有機車一千一百四十六輛，客車一千七百六十六輛，貨車一萬六千八百三十一輛，總計共有一萬九千七百四十三輛。至十八年止，僅有機車七百三十六輛，客車一千二百九十一輛，貨車一萬零六百八十四輛，共有一萬二千七百十一輛，約少去七千輛之多，再加平漢路應換鋼軌約有十四萬條，而實際上至一九三一年底止，僅換四萬二千九百條枕木，應更換者，至少有六百四十萬根。而實際上更換之數僅約五百萬根，平綏枕木路軌等工事之待整理，更有甚於平漢；言財政，則債務與時俱增，民國十四年國有鐵路之負債額總計五萬萬餘元，至民國二十二年已激增至十二萬萬餘元，而各路資金資產原價約有八萬萬餘元，實際上之價值或僅達負債總額之半數。然則以千孔百瘡之鐵路，而負此鉅額之債務，能不積欠日深，而勢將頻於破產乎？當考其原因：由於我國鐵路環境之惡劣所致，政局不安，內戰頻仍，軍人佔據路產，扣留車輛，以路款爲餉源，予取予求，一也；組織不良，加以借款合同之束縛，難收統一管理之効，二也；鐵路事業不能脫離政治，居高位者，往往與政局同進退，不能久安其位，自難望其專心發展鐵路事業，至若事不得其人，人不盡其材，升降任免，毫無標準，工作效率降低，三也；凡此皆爲我國事業失敗結癥之所在。今者國事粗定，政局已漸入正軌，軍事已告段落，整理鐵路財政，挽回經濟危勢，實爲當務之急。整理之方，應從改善管理入手，開闢財源，節省費用；而後財政始有辦法。

二　鐵路管理與理財

鐵路管理之責任有公私之別，對公衆以服務爲前提，雖在財政困難之時，亦不能制定過高之運價，阻礙國內工商業之活躍，甚至因新創工業，技術幼稚，成本過高，定專價以扶助之，農村經濟，日趨衰落，農產品運銷不暢，則減費以救濟之，所定專價特價不必斤斤求其適合於運輸成本也；對私之責任，須求自給；蓋鐵路投資既鉅，所負債務年須還本付息，且設備品必須修理擴充改良，工事必須維持，此等大宗款項，應自鐵路營業進款中積餘之。故爲公須實行社會化；爲私須實行商業化；欲完成如此重大之使命，惟有求經濟及有効能之管理。

管理之効能，最易從鐵路財政狀態以測驗之，蓋管理之得失，與鐵路營業，及支出皆息息相關也。管理上一切問題，皆不出下列公式之範圍：

收入－用費＝淨益

茲分別論之。

三 鐵路管理與收入

鐵路營業之消漲，有外界原因，及本身原因之分。外界勢力之影響，非鐵路所能操縱，故不能作爲測驗之標準。如：

（一）商業循環——鐵路運輸之繁簡，往往被視爲商情之測驗。蓋遇商業欣欣向榮之時，製造工廠大都增加產量，原料運輸量必增，尤以基本工業所需之煤鉄爲尤甚。反之，則鐵路貨運必減，此種變動與鐵路管理之成績無關也。

（二）農村經濟——若鐵路沿線以農產品爲主體，則客貨往來之盛衰，全恃年歲豐歉爲進退。連年我國各地水旱相互爲災，農村瀕於破產。各路營業之不振，此亦爲重要原因。政府爲調劑糧食救濟農村計，迭令各路將各項糧食，以及其他農產運價，多改等減低收費，如米，小麥，豆，玉蜀黍，等農產品，運價由四等減至五六等，此外尚有特價，其等級在六等之下。平均較原來運價減百分之五十，至百分之八十，損失達數百萬元。

（三）社會安寧——至若國內戰爭，國際侵略，地方匪患，直接足以破壞路產減低運輸能力；間接則交通阻礙，市場衰敗，人民無力購買，客商交受其害，鐵路營業以至銳減。此爲國家政治及治安問題，非鐵路所能過問也。茲將我國各路營業所受此類之損失，列舉於左：

因國際事變所受直接損失者，有東北各路，北甯路，京滬滬杭甬等路。

東北各路九一八事變後營業損失表

自民國二十年十月一日起至二十一年三月底止

四洮	吉長	吉敦	洮昂	齊克	瀋海	呼海	吉海	洮索
3,375,666元	1,947,380元	897,792元	1,073,754元	600,000元	2,671,542元	2,370,789元	1,200,000元	600,000元

（鐵道年鑑1卷480頁）

京滬滬杭甬鐵路一二八事變營業損失表

	客貨運輸	租金及報照費	餐車	共計
京滬路	4,660,952元	6,324元	29,077.46元	4,686,353.97元
滬杭甬路	900,927.57元	550.80元	13,013.79元	914,492.16元

（鐵道年鑑1卷533頁）

北甯路營業進款，民國二十年爲四千二百七十五萬元，二十一年減爲三千五百二十七萬元，二十二年減爲三千三百十九萬元。

因內戰鐵路營業所受損失，尚無有系統統計可查，祇得略舉一二，以供參考。

平漢路歷年軍事損失表

年別	營業(單位元)
民國五年	8,867,163
九年	3,570,229
十一年	6,563,823
十三年	2,574,496
十四年	4,740,340
十五年	14,817,126
十六年	17,862,180
十七年	11,171,900
十八年	21,237,320
十九年	9,222,415
二十年	6,153

(平漢年鑑 641 卷頁)

二十一年份各路軍運記帳表

路別	軍運
津浦	1,021,192.58
濟膠	48,827.90
隴海	808,677.56
汴路	428,939.99
北寧	458,000.00
平漢	3,414,663.20
京滬	317,000.00
滬杭甬	180,000.00
正太	255,576.45
平綏	686,144.00
湘鄂	44,860.00
道清	95,248.37
廣九	83,494.79
廣韶	261,437.00
南潯	672,403.36
總計	8,231,605.20

(鐵道年鑑1卷290頁)

鐵路營業不振，其由本身管理之不良者，亦有數因：

(一)官廳化——我國鐵路在昔管理人材極感缺乏，且政潮不定，辦路政者，不得不移用精力於政治活動，對鐵路本身事業反置之不顧，下級員工，又因待遇菲薄，於是相率營私舞弊，貪贓枉法，賄賣車皮，百弊叢生。結果貨物或捨陸而就航運，或委託轉運公司代辦手續，鐵路客商間隔膜之深如此，安望其營業之蒸蒸日上！

(二)缺乏伸縮性之運價——鐵路供給運輸業務之代價爲運價。惟運價釐訂不得其宜，小者鐵路營業受其影響：大者全國農工商業受其害；我國運價制度過於重視運輸成本，採取里程原則，殊不知里程運價，在版圖狹小之國家，運輸距離甚短，尙無流弊。我國幅圓廣大，若用里程運價，貨品負担太重，不能暢銷各地，而洋貨反因運輸成本較低，爭奪國貨市場，有失國家築造鐵路之本旨。且鐵路爲招徠客貨，及調節運輸起見，有時可以特減運費，以免車輛空回。有時因氣候關係，對客貨之運費，而需異其率者，蓋運價之制定，本不可依算學公式演出。在能善於運用，以獲最大量之運輸，我國運價則悉以里程爲標準，殊鮮伸縮性，於業務之發展頗多阻礙。

(三)運輸能力薄弱——我國鐵路運輸能力薄弱，由於車輛缺乏。致沿線有時積貨如山，而貨運仍無法使之暢旺，造成私賣車皮等惡習。軍事破壞，固爲公認原因。而各路調度之不得法，管理不周，亦難辭其咎！據鐵道部業務司調查所得，每百輛貨車，各路實際上僅能當作若干輛，運用之情形如下：

膠濟	二〇・五	京滬杭	一九・六	北甯	一五・九	平綏	六・二
隴海	五・八	津浦	五・五	平漢	五・三	湘鄂	四・七

車輛運用效率之最高者爲膠濟，約可至百分之二十；湘鄂爲最低，祇百分之五；平均約在百分之十。如按科學方法管理，加以改革，平均可增至百分之六十以上。以全國貨車一萬二千輛計，若善於運用，以應付目下貨運，足有餘裕。

我國鐵路既受惡劣環境之支配，又因本身管理之不良，以致營業甚爲不振。茲將國有鐵路歷年營業進款用款與南滿鐵路收支總數，列表比較於下：

國有鐵路營業進款用款表

年份	營業進款	營業用款	營業淨益	附註（以下各路該年份未報告）
十四年	127,522,217.90	73,328,263.40	54,193,954.50	株萍，廣三，漳厦
十五年	99,341,879.30	69,291,201.14	30,050,078.16	株萍，廣三，漳厦
十六年	105,018,254.25	70,078,655.21	34,939,599.04	株萍，廣三，漳厦
十七年	87,520,465.68	54,229,024.99	53,291,390.69	平漢，汴洛，隴海，廣九，漳厦，
十八年	105,428,289.60	64,461,489.72	40,966,799.88	平漢，汴洛，隴海，廣三，平綏，廣九，南潯，
十九年	136,712,347.07	92,340,612.96	44,371,734.11	吉長，四洮，漳厦，
二十年	158,233,799.16	104,856,482.50	53,377,316.66	東北四省各路
二十一年	107,578,482.15	76,473,222.70	31,105,249.45	
二十二年	112,598,289.00	80,327,113.00	32,271,176.00	

（鐵路年鑑）

南滿鐵路收支狀況表（單位日元）

年度	客運收入	貨運收入	總收入	總支出	盈餘
1908	2,964,587	9,542,262	12,537,142	6,101,515	6,435,627
1915	4,842,338	17,260,655	23,532,118	—	—
1921	12,194,288	59,615,833	78,204,132	33,172,717	45,031,415
1927	16,102,953	94,040,819	113,244.180	45,235,835	68•008,345
1928	17,619,293	97,738,147	118,639,C90	44,358,065	74,281,025
1930	11,461,175	77,936,688	95,330,730	36,768,576	58,562,154

(Fellner: Communications in the Far East, P.104)

南滿鐵路全長不過一千一百三十五公里，每年平均收入爲一萬一千餘萬圓　每公里每年收入十萬餘圓。我國國有鐵路路線長度共有九千餘公里，每年平均收入爲一萬二千餘圓，每公里收入約一萬數千圓，不及南滿路收入六分之一，以盈餘而論，每年不過三四千萬圓，以全部償還路債本息尙不足遠甚，故子息相加，債務繼長增高，無法清理。

鐵路營業，亦有因管理努力改善，而有成績表現者。如：

（一）推行負責運輸——泰西各國，對於鐵路之貨物皆負全責，除因人力不能避免之災害外若有遺失損壞概由鐵路負責賠償，蓋非如此不足以發展運貨也。獨我國辦理鐵路，已具有五十年之歷史，而此項根本要政，尙付闕如，以致貨物滯積，實業不振，鐵路營業亦受不良之影響。近年鐵道部已令各路分別緩急施行，成効卓著，據津浦路報告，自完全實行負責運輸以來，二十一年十一月份之收入爲二百十六萬一千八百八十六圓，而二十年同月收入爲一百六十一萬九千二百九十九圓，計增加五十四萬二千五百八十七圓。以前各項貨物原由運河水道及青島海運者，近以負責聯運，多改由津浦南下運至京滬路沿線，平均每日約達一千餘噸。其次京滬滬杭甬路，亦收同等效果，該路二十一年十一月份獨貨運一項之收入，較上年同月增加六萬餘圓，二十一年十二月份，因榆關事變，貨運不免受打擊，然較二十年同月仍有增加，此者我國鐵路管理改進所收之功效也。

(二)推進聯運事業——鐵路辦理聯運事業，於發展業務至爲重要。我國鐵路聯運之舉辦，已有多年，中間曾因戰事一度停頓，民國廿一年鐵道部令飭各路實行負責貨物聯運，近又次第實行水陸聯運，與夫開行定期聯運直達貨車，聯運進款，遂破以前紀錄。

(三)鐵路商業化——鐵路事業之性質本爲商業機關而我國往昔鐵路管理，處處違反商業化之原則，客商託運皆由轉運公司代理，每於運費之外，尙有其他負担，在鐵路營業方面，亦損失不貲。自京滬滬杭甬路創辦營業所以來，各路已有倣尤，雖成績如何，尙難判斷，然爲客商謀利便，爲鐵路招徠運輸業務，間接增加收入，則至明顯也。

鐵路官僚化之結果，遂使客商與路局頗多隔膜，鐵路營業，往往居於被動，而非自動向各方發展，故欲糾正以往習慣，必須路商打成一片，互謀利益，商討合作之方。最近京滬滬杭甬路曾招待上海市重要各業代表，並擬就該路沿線各站物產運銷合作辦法綱要，及合作緣起，實行招待各商講習貨運手續，其辦法足爲各路倣照推行。

各路努力整頓之結果，營業進款均有顯著之進步，如平漢路民十八年收入爲二〇、一三八、六四八圓，二十年增至二三、七四四、八二〇圓，民二十三年超出三千萬圓。津浦路十九年收入爲一三、三七一、八二三圓，二十一年增至二〇、四三三、四三一圓，二十三年爲二千四百萬圓；因此各路財政狀況亦隨之轉佳，此可由我國債票價格在國外市場暴漲情形反映之。

中國鐵路公債在國外市價表

路債名稱 \ 年月	1132年1月	1932年7月	1933年1月	1933年7月	1934年1月	1934年7月	1935年1月
北寧關內外借款	65.1/2	75.1/2	86.3/8	92.1/4	94.5	100.1	——
平漢匯豐理借款	46.0	65.3/4	83.1/2	73.0	92.1/2	92.1/2	99.1/2
京滬借款	37.0	30.0	31.0	39.1/2	60.0	67.5/8	82.1/2
廣九借款	6.1/8	7.5/8	6.1/2	8.0	14.0	18.1/4	——
津浦原借款	6.3/8	17.3/4	25.0	27.5/8	40.0	35.1/2	36.0
津浦續借款	6.1/2	15.1/8	22.0	25.0	32.0	27.0	31.1/2
滬杭甬借款	63.1/4	57.7/8	88.0	84.0	27.0	99.1/2	101.0
道清借款	7.3/8	7.1/2	12.0	7.0	26.1/2	31.1/2	35.1/2
隴海借款	——	——	——	——	——	17.3/4	19.1/2

（中國銀行經濟研究室：中國外債彙編）

四 鐵路管理與支出

美善經濟管理之第二種測驗爲鐵路支出，鐵路之付息償債能力，來自收入與支出之差別，亦卽爲淨餘，故收入與支出，實爲相關之問題，未可偏重。經濟之管理，非指消極節省，裁員減薪因陋就簡，卽可達到目的；乃謂以最經濟之用費，而獲最高之效果也。

鐵路支出，款目繁多，若歸納之，亦可得下列公式：

薪工＋材料＋間接費用＝支出

由此以觀，鐵路支出問題可從人事管理，材料管理，及總務管理，分別研究之。

人事管理我國鐵路用人向不經濟，如辦鐵路者非鐵路人材，此其一；工作人員，不時更調，無一貫之精神，此其二；隨意添派人員，冗員大增，工作効率降低，路局支出激長，此其三。若以各國鐵路每百英里工作人數(職員在內)比較，我國居其首位：

國別	人數
中國	二五五四人
英國	二五〇四人
美國	一六六七人
法國	一一四三人
意大利	一六七一人

上列人數，僅就每百英里鐵路長度而言。若再進而比較其每百英里之運輸量，則工作之效率，更不可同日而語矣！

鐵路人事問題，非裁員減薪所可解決：裁員增加社會失業人數，且被裁者未必皆爲應裁之人；減薪增加員司生活艱難，更易促成舞弊風氣。爲挽救起見，惟有提高工作效率，其方法約有下列數端：

(一)規定用人標準——鐵道業務爲專門性質，非任何人所能濫竽充數，故編制專章中，對於職務皆應詳爲標明，並各項職位應具之資格一一申叙，然後可因缺擇人，有一定標準，夤緣之風以減，不平之事以泯。

(二)訓練——鐵路員司，有上中下三級。上中級職員，類皆受有專門訓練，惟中下級員司，學識不足，各路應設訓練所分別抽調，予以學識及技能上之訓練，並施以考試，成績優良者，予以升遷，工作性質不適宜者，予以改調，若此：則勤者有鼓勵，怠者知警惕。

(三)提高下級員司及工人待遇——鐵路下級員工，薪給微薄，年來生活程度日高，而待遇標準依舊，欲其安分守己，盡忠職務，事實上蓋不可能。故整理鐵路業務必先定工人最低待遇標準，然後積弊可除，而貪污以去矣。

(四)實行養老金制度——養老儲金，實爲安定員工生活使盡忠厥職之良法。歐美鐵路實行已久，我國各路，亦知逐漸舉辦，惟應再事推廣，以期普及。

(五)實行機廠科學管理——各國凡規模宏大事業，皆必竭力實施科學管理，所以減低用費，而增加產量也。惟鐵路採用者尚不多見，因其性質與普通工廠有根本上之不同：(一)鐵路路線延長數千里，員工分散各地，不易管理；(二)鐵路工會往往聲勢浩大，實施科學管理必遭反對。惟科學管理雖不能行之於全路各部，亦不妨先試行於機廠，因機廠工人集中一處監督較易。且工作種類性質亦不若其他各處之複雜，若繩之以標準，勉之以獎勵，則工作迅速，機車車輛之在機廠待修期限縮短，而車輛缺乏之情形可以避免。

材料管理——材料佔鐵路一切費用支出之大部：其管理方法是否合乎經濟原理，自難忽視，我國鐵路對於材料之處理，尙須加以深切之研究，以免糜費路款：

(一)統一材料名稱以杜流弊；

(二)統一材料規範書，

(三)設法利用各路舊存廢料；

(四)盡量採辦國產材料；

(五)節用行車材料費用——材料大量消耗，尤推日常行車必需之大宗煤斤油類棉紗等，倘能於購買，驗收，保管，使用諸項均力求經濟嚴密，所省費用必不在少數；如關於購料一層，最好各路每半年將所需用之行車材料消耗預算數量呈部，由部合成整批購買，其價必較廉，並須規定消耗標準，以免浪費。

總務管理——我國鐵路營業用款最不合理者，卽爲總務費之高出其他費用。總務費爲間接生產之費用，其數宜低，使鐵路之財力集中於直接生產，如設備品及工務之維持，產業之改良擴充，而收益能力始得增强。日本鐵路總務費僅佔全部營業用費百分之二·五五，美國鐵路之總務費佔營業用款百分之三·八八，反視我國各路，總務費平均佔營業用款百分之二四·八二，而平漢路高至三二·三二，此種現象，足以證明我國鐵路管理之失當。

五 鉄路管理與淨益

營業進款減去營業用款，爲營業淨益，此卽鐵路賴以付債務之利息及償還本金也。故淨益之多寡，足以表示一路之財力；例如淨益爲債務百分之五時，僅足支付五厘債券之利息，而無餘力還本，若淨益爲債務百分之十時，則財政狀況鞏固多矣。我國鐵路負債在二十二年底達十三萬萬元，營業淨益爲三千二百萬圓，僅及債務百分之二·四六卽以全部償付利息，尚有不足，財政之危急，不問可知！其原因由於金價高漲，債務不借自增，而管理不良，開支日增，實爲根本原因。故近年我國鐵路營業雖稍有起色，而用費增加更速，卒致淨益無多，此可於歷年營業百分率遞增情形見之。在民國十四年，營業百分率爲五七·五，十七年爲百分之六〇・二，二十年爲百分之六五・九，二十一年爲百分之七一・五，數年中逐步上升。用款之中亦有因修補殘缺，加固工事，而驟形增高者，爲將來營業樹立基礎計，其政策本未可厚非，然用款中之總務費始終過高，不能不爲我國鐵路管理之一大缺點也。

六　結論

我國鐵路今日財政之危機已極嚴重，以數千英里殘破之鐵路，而負十餘萬萬圓之債額，不可謂不鉅，所以希圖自救者，端在管理之進步，一方面發展營業，增加收入，一方減低費用，增加淨益，以清積欠，事業前途庶幾有望。

經濟之戰

經濟之戰，較武力之戰，尤爲重要。吾人試以都市等于營盤，關稅等于溝壘，國貨等于鎗砲，交通等于戰線，工廠商店等于武庫，銀行錢莊等于後路粮台，行政長官等于主帥，羣衆等于小卒，而經濟學說之宣揚，則爲最效之戰略。今觀吾國所謂營盤如何，溝壘如何，鎗砲戰線如何，主帥小卒又如何，思之眞不寒而慄，此實有關我國眞正存亡問題，而有待于舉國上下共同籌謀者也。

中華國有鐵路現行行車時刻表

膠濟綫

2次各等	74次二三等	22次各等	72次二三等	52次各等	上行(東)列車	站名	下行(西)列車	51次各等	21次各等	71次二三等	73次二三等	1次各等
22.00	14.40	11.40		7.00	開	濟南	到	18.00	22.12		13.35	7.30
22.06	14.47	11.47		7.09	開	北關	開	17.55	22.07		13.29	7.25
22.13	14.55	11.54		7.16	開	黃臺	開	17.47	21.55		13.20	7.17
不停	15.10	12.08		7.30	開	王舍人莊	開	17.34	21.41		13 05	7.01
不停	15.23	12.20		7.40	開	郭店	開	17.23	21.36		12.52	6.50
22.48	15.39	12.36		7.57	開	龍山	開	17.08	21.15		12.35	6.34
23.03	15.55	12.52		8.13	開	棗園莊	開	16.54	21.0[illegible]		12 18	6.19
不停	16.07	13.03		8.24	開	明水	開	16.44	20.49		12.05	6.09
23.28	16.3[illegible]	13.20		8.41	開	普集	開	16.39	20.34		11.48	5.53
不停	19.42	13.31		8.52	開	王村	開	16.19	20 24		11.36	不停
不停	16.54	不停		9.03	開	大臨池	開	16.07	不停		11.22	不停
0.01	17.13	13.56		9.20	到	周村	開	15.43	19.48		10.47	5.13
0.04	17.16	13 59		9.23	開		開	15.40	19.51		10.04	5.10
不停	17.35	不停		9.40	到	馬尚	開	15.21	不停		10.20	不停
0.26	17.43	14.21		9.48	開	張店	到	15.12	19.23		10.10	4.34
0.41	17.58	14.36		10.03	開		到		19.08		9.55	4.46
不停	18.11	14.49		10 15	開	湖田	開	14.48	18.59		9.44	不停
不停	18.2	14.58		10.24	開	金嶺鎮	開	14 35	18.5		9.33	不停
1.10	18.3,	15.12		10.38	開	辛店	開	14.21	18.36		9.17	4.05
不停	18.51	15.25		10 51	開	淄河店	開	14.08	18.19		9.02	不停
不停	19.03	不停		11.01	開	普通	開	13.58	不停		8.50	不停
1.39	19.16	15 44		11.13	到	青州	開	13.46	18.0[illegible]		8.36	3.36
1.42	19 19	15.47		11.16	開		到	13.43	17.56		8.33	3.34
不停	19.35	16.02		11.31	開	楊家莊	開	13.28	17.41		8.14	不停
不停	19.46	16.13		11.42	開	譚家坊	開	13.17	17.30		8.00	不停
不停	19.5[illegible]	16.25		11.54	開	堯溝	開	13.05	17.18		7.46	不停
2.22	20412	15.37		12.06	開	昌樂	開	12.53	17 06		7.33	2.53
2.39	20.26	16.51		12.19	開	朱劉店	開	12.40	16.52		7.17	2.40
不停	20.37	17.01		12.30	開	大圩河	開	12.29	不停		7.14	不停
2.58	20.50	27.13		12.42	到	濰縣	開	12.15	16.30		6.49	2.18
3.01	20.54	17.16	7.00	12.45	開		到	12.12	16.28	20.35	6.44	2.16
3.10	21.04	17.25	7.10	12,54	到	二十里堡	開	12.04	16.20	20 26	6.34	2.08
3.22	21.17	17.37	7.23	13.06	開	坊子	開	11.52	16.08	10.13	6.20	1.56
3.37		17.51	7.38	13.21	開		到	11.37	15.54	20.02		1.41
3.52		18.06	7.54	13.36	開	蝦蟆屯	開	11 24	15.41	19.48		1.28
不停		不停	8.09	13.50	開	南流	開	11.09	不停	19.31		不停
不停		18.24	8.17	13.57	開	黃旗堡	開	11.01	15.21	19.23		不停
4.18		18.35	8.29	14.0[illegible]	開	岞山	開	10.52	15.12	19.13		1.02
不停		18.54	8 48	14.2[illegible]	開	丈嶺	開	10.33	14.53	18.53		不停
不停		19.03	8.58	14.42	開	塔耳堡	開	10.23	14.43	18.39		不停
不停		19.12	9.08	14.51	開	蔡家莊	開	10.13	14.32	18.23		不停
不停		不停	9.20	15.02	開	康家莊	開	10.02	不停	18.16		不停
5.04		19.31	9.32	15.13	到	高密	開	9.50	14.12	18.03		0.12
5.12		19.42	9.48	15.24	開		到	9.39	14.01	17.52		0.01
不停		不停	9.56	15.36	開	姚哥莊	開	9.28	不停	17.41		不停
不停		20.00	10.05	15.45	開	芝蘭莊	開	9.19	13.44	17.32		不停
5.47		10.17	10.23	16.02	到	膠州	開	9.02	13.27	17.14		23.30
5.49		10 19	10.26	16.04	開		到	9.00	13 25	17.11		23.38
不停		不停	10.39	16.16	開	膠東	開	8.48	不停	16.58		不停
不停		不停	10.51	16.27	開	李哥莊	開	8.36	本停	16.45		不停
6.15		20.46	11.01	16 37	開	藍村	開	8.27	12.58	16.36		23.02
不停		20.59	11.15	16 50	開	南泉	開	8.18	12.43	16.18		不停
6.41		21.15	11.34	17.08	開	栻陰	開	7.57	12.27	16.01		2.342
不停		21.24	11.44	17.17	開	女姑口	開	7.48	12.18	15.51		不停
6.29		21.36	12.07	17.29	開	滄口	開	7.36	12.06	15.38		2.16
7.19		21.59	12.2.	17.45	開	四方	開	7.20	11.50	15.26		22.00
7.30		22.10	12.35	17.55	開	大港	開	7.11	11.41	15.11		21.51
7.35		22.15	12.40	18.00	到	青島	開	7.50	11.30	15.00		21.40

公路管理方法之檢討（C 1.）

熊大惠

公路事業，經緯萬端，欲期運輸業務之發駿，端在管理得法，苟管理精密，則營運自增，反是設或管理不善，在路方既感營業不克發展，在社會民生方面，亦僉以運輸不便爲苦，是以公路管理問題，洵爲當今公路建設之要圖，作者于役公路，深以今後我國公路管理方法，實有亟予改進之必要，茲擇其輕而易舉者數端，略貢芻蕘，願與公路建設當局，管理專家，共商榷焉：

（一）組織——繇交通事業管理之得失，繫于組織之完善與否，苟組織不健全，則管理不便，必難收指臂之効，是故事業範圍較大之機關，爲增進管理上之效率，尤非有縝善之組織不可。愚意我國公路管理組織，應予改進如左：

（甲）車機工務合併——嘗查現今我國各省公路管理機關之組織，車機工三務，大多分立，以致各自爲政，隔閡時生，苟能設法合併，則關聯縝密，管理統一，行政設施，自能益臻敏活。

（乙）分區管理組織——公路組織，規模闊遠，路綫加長，運輸頻繁，爲管理上之便利計，實應將所屬路綫，劃分若干區，分區管理，以收相機行事就地處置之功，浙省公路，實行此項管理制度，已見成効。

(二)業務——公路既經營運輸業務，是則顧名思義，應隨時隨地，以推廣其營業爲前提，非惟廣拓業務，增進收入，而便利民衆，俾運輸之功益彰，推廣業務之道不一，愚意應注意左列二點：

(甲)厲行商業化——公路運輸機關，應本服務國家社會之旨，隨事隨時，謀民衆之便利，所有服務員工，尤應與民衆相接近，刻刻懷「爲民衆服務」之心理待人接物，無論答覆問訊，解釋章則，徵收運費，指示各項手續等等，均應抱謙和誠摯之態度，以袪往昔路商間隔閡之遺詬，而臻業務商業化之成功。

(乙)減低運價——運價係出售汽車運輸業務之代價，但其價率之厘訂，應有一定之準則，苟不得其宜，過高客運則旅客負担增加，行旅因以減少，貨運則商貨成本重，以致銷路呆滯，影響農工商業，但運價過低，不能抵補本身之運輸成本，則路收減絀，業務不能發展，客貨仍蒙其害，故竊以爲今後公路厘行運價，除顧及自身之運輸成本外，應設法以低廉爲原則，俾應客貨之負担能力，而擴增公路運輸業務數量也。

(三)人事——近代各種事業組織，尤其大規模之經營，任用之員工既夥，人事之管理益難，夫公路事業，規模旣廣，欲圖其業務之發展，殆全恃良善之人事管理，蓋有縝察之組織，完美之設備，而人事問題，不先妥當解決，則一切設施計劃，悉將成爲空譚，是故業務效率之增加與否，全視人事效率之程度若何？愚意今後公路人事管理應予改進者，有如左述：

（甲）嚴格甄別——任用員工，應以該人之學識經驗爲標準，按其才能及旨趣，予以相當之工作，務以「因事設缺因缺擇人」爲原則，其不適宜者，則應隨時甄別，分別更調裁撤，或予以嚴格之訓練，如此人浮于事事浮于人之弊可免，而冗員裁汰，開支亦可減少，加以厘訂嚴密之獎懲，確實之保障，則懦者不敢懷京兆五日之心，黠者亦不敢爲泄沓貪污之謀，人人以公路之利害爲利害，休戚相關，憚忠竭智，爲公路服務，則工作效率之增加，不卜可期矣。

（乙）提高待遇——年來社會生活程度日高，反觀各公路機關對于所屬員工之待遇，頗形菲薄，有尅打折扣發放者，有薪餉積欠數月不發者，以此種待遇，丁此時艱，而欲其勤奮將事，斯誠難矣！故爲增進工作效率計，亟應提高員工之薪級，俾生活安定，無後顧之憂，則人事效率，自能與日俱晉也。

（四）材料——夫材料一項，自積極而論，係營運之要素，就消極言之，實爲路帑支出之大宗，省耗之間，公路之經濟繫焉，是故近今各種事業機關，對于材料管理一事，莫不精研詳究，舉凡材料之購買，收發，保管，稽核等，悉以經濟效率爲原則，此無他，蓋爲收實施科學化管理材料之功效也，關于公路材料管理尚應予以改善之點，玆臚陳如次：

(甲)材料管理組織——良以公路材料，如汽車，汽油，輪胎等，大多屬于機務運務方面，故其管理上之組織，最好由機務部份統制，俾事權劃一，管理效率增加。

(乙)汽油代替品——汽車燃料，當以汽油發動力爲最高，惜以我國煤油礦未開採，致汽油一項，多仰給于外邦，根據國際貿易局統計，去年汽油進口值，竟達進口貨第三位，總計達三千七百餘萬元之鉅，此項數額之龐大，實令人寒慄不止，但公路建設，在今日之中國，尚屆萌芽時期，前途之進展，正未可限量，汽油之消耗，將何可勝計，誠不應因噎而廢食，亟宜積極研究運用汽油代替品，如煤氣，酒精，柴油，植物油等之行車效率，藉挽漏巵，而利營運。

以上不過晐要簡述而已，祗以其有關管理之得失，業務之盛衰，用特不揣簡陋，草陳個人觀感之所及，拋磚引玉，尙幸高明指正之！

管理與統計(A 1.)

汪仲良

文明進步，人事日繁。其間關係聯絡，錯綜複雜，一有變化，千百隨之。然事固無有一定不變者。於是互相影響，互爲因果，大者如是，小者亦然。若無治紛理亂之方，察變求常之道，將何以窺其全豹，探其趨勢，究其既往，斷其未來，俾居處其間者得競爭以求生存乎。此則統計尚矣。然如何運用統計所得之結果，以常處變，以往備來，一一見諸實施，俾競而能勝，生而能存，則非管理不爲功。無統計則不能爲有效之管理，非管理亦難得確切之統計，二者實相互爲用者也。

吾國事事落後，地大物博人衆而逼處於弱小民族之地位者，一言以蔽之，無管理無統計耳。言政治則自上及下，由內達外，從未能收心臂之效；言社會則一切團體，一切集結，莫不漫無組織，存既鮮有貢獻，滅卽銷聲匿跡。凡稍留意國情者，必知吾國一切事業之運行，僅僅依賴習慣，憑恃個人。充其極，不過成規墨守，進展毫無。偶有成功，端賴英才之傑出。英才既歿，功業隨亡。試觀國家事業；則秦皇漢武唐太宗元世祖以迄清之康乾，當其在世，莫不盛極一時，及其既歿，曾未能略作持久之繼續。再觀私人事業；始也主持得人，蒸蒸日上，一旦易主，覆敗隨之。夫使事業隨人而消長，則才智之輩安可必其按時產生。一人之壽命幾何，其不能長久也甚明。何況移體養氣，賢者有時而不免。始有成就，中途變節以招致禍患者，比比皆是也。法之內閣，嘗數日一更迭，美之政府，歷四年必變遷。繼起者豈盡英豪，其所以長爲强盛之國家者，以有管理與統計耳。欲垂事業於永久，進展而不頹壞，無他道也。中材之人，世所恆有，欲其手造時勢，實乃奢望。有管理之方法，欲其保持而利用之，以與他人較長短，爭存亡，未必不可。今日吾國事業之急需適當之管理者，大別之：有公衆、理財、交通、實業、四端。請分別言之。

服公務而無效率，則將百事不舉，弊竇叢生，內則自受其殃，外則貽人口實。吾人習聞公務之窳敗，由於人員之不能奉公守法矣，然公何因而不奉，法何由而不守也，人類劣性與有生以俱來者，厥爲自私。若守法奉公不如毀法損公之有利而易爲，則不奉公守法勢耳。嚴刑峻法，或可收宏效於一時，然必非久長之道。如能對於公務人員之工作效能，報告獎懲等，有嚴密之統計以管理之，則公務員之一舉一動，將無所逃形，所作所爲，盡同透視，雖極端自私之人，亦必奉公守法矣。吾人又習聞吾國幅員遼闊，人民衆多，不易爲治之言，則土地散播之廣，人種集合之雜，無過英國，然未聞其不治也。若對於土地之肥瘠，人民之習俗，有翔實之統計，則全國各地之狀況，將有簡單之呈現，窵遠之地，如在目前，中央之與地方，聯絡而無隔核，上下聲氣，交通而不擁塞，爲政者乃能洞悉各方，通盤籌劃，又何至顧此失彼，視龐大複雜爲難乎。

理財之道，在於詳源悉流，發源以致充裕，節用以省糜費，然如何能詳悉財源，以謀開發，統制財用，以謀節省，則胥賴統計與管理。今之理財，莫不以舉債置捐、高利廣告爲開源，裁員減薪，折價倒閉爲節用。倘有完美之統計，認眞管理，則歲收月入，應有幾何、趨勢增減：成何比例，比較分析，作何象徵，鈎稽考察，何者事出偶然，何者勢所不免。何項啓疑，何項應究，作一事經常需用幾人，臨時幾人，均將纖毫畢現，而遺漏收入，將僅屬偶然，中飽營私，殆將絕跡，增益財用，恐不止倍蓰也。不觀吾國之田賦乎，早徵者有之，隱匿者亦有之，瘠地而納重賦者有之，良田而得逃賦者亦有之。於是滑吏豪紳，乃得利用紛亂複雜之情形，上下其手，廣事朦蔽。整頓之言 習聞之矣，終未見效也。倘能記其面積，分其腴瘠，析其賦稅，稽考舊徵，推行新制，所入豈止現額哉。夫以羅掘爲開源，以緊縮爲節用，將見羅掘緊縮之無已時。而財用之終於不給耳。

交通事業，不止利人民之行旅，便商賈之運輸已也，溝通風氣，使分者合，遠者近。國家有事之秋，則因應軍事，承平之世，則增補稅收。吾國交通事業，雖屬微尠，然近年來實有長足之進展。但若徒事道路之增長，船舶之建造，而不同時講求管理，則欲收利便聯絡之功，因應增補之效，而不爲人詬病恐不可得也。若統計綫路所經之人口分布情形，物品出產種類，與所需用材料之數量，及其維持業務之結果，各段乘客之異動，貨運之增減，以至於車行時刻之長短，視其性質，按期而計劃之，則避免失事，減少稽遲，非難事也。若僅以宣傳展覽爲招徠，增減運率爲維持，視擁擠爲當然，目遲悞爲不免，傎矣。

實業之成功，殆同建屋。精良之技術爲基，嚴密之管理爲幹，市場之周旋爲頂。企業家之難事，不在專門技術之覔取，而在如何能使工作有效而無耗損，各部相輔而不衝突，人事糾紛之解决，臻於圓滿，市場之應付，能獲利益。蓋技術可以養成於平時，急需且得借材於異地。而其他則非可自由統制者也。原料耗費之多寡，產品之良窳，產量之遲速，非集合比較無以明顯而求適當改進。各部之分工，有否完美之合作，非統計工作之詳情，不能爲有效之監督，而爲公平之懲獎。市場因素複雜，瞬息萬變。應付之機，稍縱卽逝，非有統計分析，不能察其盈虛消長，而作未雨之綢繆。然今之企業家，其創業也，因他人獲利而效顰。始或得僥倖遂欲於一時，終必竭蹶而爲國家社會之累。若先調查容量以決參加，根據統計以定政策，施行管理以爲競爭，則在平時必能獲得自然之發展，卽在非常時期亦必不至遂遭淘汰。今吾國實業之不振，人謀不臧，實居太半也。

由是觀之，管理之於事業，猶腦之於人。甯靜則運用思想，審既往，明現在，察未來。波動則發號施令，明責職，致聯絡，策應付。並非巧立名目，增用人員，苛章細則之謂也，事無不需管理。有效之管理，又無不賴統計。有用之統計，在於將所求得之適當資料，經過適當之編製，以具體表示某時期某地方某情形事物之如何遵循常態以生變化，俾吾人得樹立標準，以比較得失。測度變化，研求關係，而推衍終結。非僅廣集數字，製作圖表之謂也。若徒慕管理與統計之空名，而不務其實，吾恐反足以僨事，而令不知者悞解其爲有害無益之贅尤，則又大失管理與統計之本意矣。善用之者，當不河漢斯言。

行政之寶

政之所興，在順民心；政之所廢，在逆民心。民惡憂勞，我佚樂之。民惡貧賤，我富貴之。民惡危墜，我存安之。民惡滅絕，我生育之。能佚樂之，則民爲之憂勞。能富貴之，則民爲之貧賤。能存安之，則民爲之危墜。能生育之。則民爲之滅絕。……故從其四欲，則遠者自親；行其四惡，則近者叛之。故知予之爲取者，政之寶也。

管子牧民四順篇

委員制之利弊

(甲)委員制的長處：

(1)可以防止專制　委員制的國家，行使政治權，既是由多數人的合議，自不易爲一人所操縱。所以要防專制，最好行委員制；

(2)可以避免政潮　委員制可以適合下面兩種環境：

(一)民主勢力未曾養成，全國重心未曾樹立，不得不網羅各派的中心人物組織委員會，遇事可以共同商議，使政令易於推行。

(二)民主習慣已經養成，人民又能和衷共濟，可以免黨派的鬥爭，而得集思廣益的利益。如瑞士，黨派若有糾紛，其委員往往因職務的關係不只牽入漩渦，且能努力使其諒解。

(3)可以多網羅人才　委員制的名額較多，可以使多方面的人才以平等的資格，擔負首腦責任；較少「滄海遺珠」的憾事。

(乙)委員制的短處：

(1)責任不明　一切政策，既要經過會議，多數取決，個人意見卽使不贊成，也不能不服從且有不使向局外人宣示自己異議的態度；所以政策的失敗或成功，是什麼人的責任，不容易淸楚。

(2)欠缺敏活　當一個重要緊急的機會，應付方法理應當機立斷的，因爲要經過會議的手續，使不能不遲滯。

(3)易洩機密　關於軍事，外交的機要，要絕對秘密的，在個人運用，還需要若干烟幕彈，委員間各因立場不同，或偶不謹愼，易致洩漏。

(4)天才不易發展　人性是大智不常，而多是中才之士，那末雄才大略，遠瞻高矚的委員，很不容易得中才的委員的了解，不免受着相當的掣肘，使不能充分發展其天才。

(5)政策不易貫澈　委員間因黨派不同，而地位又是平等，若彼此不願合作，對於多數決定的政策，也不允犧牲成見切實贊助或更從事破壞，則該項政策的實施，將更感困難。

(6)難收合議的善果　委員制的委員名額，常是很多，在委員會內勢不能每人都有適當的位置，那些有適當位置的委員，便會形同「伴食」，會議時唯唯諾諾，無所可否，故雖有合議之名未必符合議之實。

——李樸生：改善現行委員制的必要，行政效率　三卷三期。

汪精衛先生語：「實行之機關應採獨任制，以專責任，諮詢機關可採委員制，以博採衆意」。

新路建設之經濟觀 (C·1.)

黃宗瑜

一　緒言

處今日杌隉不安之世界，値經濟恐怖之時期，倡言鐵道建設，戛乎其難矣，環睹四週，國內市場以貿易不振，銀根奇緊，而國外市場，亦以經濟衰落資金缺乏，加之匪禍連年，災疫四起，非但鉅額資金籌集爲難，卽購料施工，亦感棘手，是故倡言建設，實爲目前最困難之問題，但就國勢以觀，吾國今日實處最窮最危險之境地，欲以救亡圖存，非實現經濟政策中之生產建設不可，生產建設之道繁多，而最要者，乃鐵道建設。觀夫鐵道公報中載有曾次長養甫先生之有言曰：

「……近年雖以種種關係　本部（鐵道部）暫時管轄之路，里程較以前爲少，而新路建築，則較以前益形迫切，因　總理鐵道計畫，規定我國須築十萬英里，而今日已成者，不及十分之一……」

又謂「目前建築鐵路之根本目的有二，一爲救亡一爲救貧，欲救亡則非迅速不成，欲救貧又非省儉不可・須以最少之經費，迅速完成最急要之工作……」

由是可知，鐵道建設，其使命非僅爲復興經濟改良生產而已且實爲救亡圖存之關鍵，其

需要之急迫自不待言，惟是漫言建設，漫無標準，殊涉空泛，總理建設十萬英里鐵道之計劃中，曾有四大原則之規定，其要點：即

一、必選最有利之途，以吸外資。

二、必應國民之最大需要。

三、必期抵抗之最少。

四、必擇地位之適宜。

以上四者，乃鐵道建設之基本原則，無論國家財力如何，均應遵守，但當茲國難方殷，財源竭蹶之時代，所謂非常時期之經濟建設自非有非常之辦法，不足以資應付，夫非常辦法之原則爲何，卽前節所謂「迅速」與「省儉」是也，蓋建設新路，非迅速不足以應非常之需要，非省儉不足以籌興建之資本，而「迅速」與「省儉」者，卽美國鐵道一九二〇年運輸法中，所列之「經濟」與「效率」之謂也，惟建築之際，施工如何可使之迅速，費用如何可使之節省，是又不可不明乎鐵道建設，其經濟及工程上之要素，考鐵道建設，經濟上之要素凡四，卽資本土地勞力及材料是也，工程上之要素凡七，卽路線，軌道坡度，灣度，列車阻力，行車設備，及車站設備是也。

茲篇所述，首論管理新建設之經濟要素，繼論管理新路建設之工程標準，末殿以建築成

本之稽核方法，全文着重於建築之經濟及效能，雖管窺蠡測，未足以質高明。而一得之愚，或有補於萬一也。

甲、經濟要素　鐵道建設之經濟要素凡四，前已述及，茲詳爲分析如下。

一、資本

資本爲建設之基礎，路綫建築之初，必先集有充分之資本，否則工程進行，時斷時續，其費用殊不經濟，惟資本之籌集與運用，如何始合乎經濟原則，似應從下列三點，加以考察。

一、資本構成之方式　鐵路資本大別之分爲二類，第一類爲股票，企業者以其所有之資本，投入鐵路資產中換取股票，并組織董事會以管理鐵路行政，其所享之利益乃鐵路經營最後之餘利，又以財產爲最後之擔保，雖股票有優先普通之分，而其對於鐵路資產及盈利之享有權，則恆在債券之後，第二類爲債票，乃經營鐵路者以其信用，向持券人借貸之資金，發行債券，以爲憑證，持券人既爲債主，自無管理鐵路之權，惟對於鐵路財產及餘利則有儘先享有之利益，以故就投資之穩妥方面言之，債券實較股票爲優，但就鐵路財政構成之方式而言債券與股票則應兼採並用，方爲經濟。若專恃債券，以資建築，似非計之得者，美國公共事業經濟專家雷芒氏 (Dr. W. G. Raymonds) 曾用統計方法，加以研究，其結果以鐵路財政之構成，三分之二爲債券，三分之一爲股票，最爲經濟，此種假定經一般人之試驗，認爲合理，且美國鐵路資金，大都均合乎此種比例，平均百分之七五爲債券，百分之廿五爲股票，茲將雷芒氏之解說，詳爲介紹如左。

「設某鐵路公司，其資本總額約需一二〇、〇〇〇、〇〇〇元，而市上公債利息法定爲四釐，根據雷芒氏之解說，以債權人希望公司將來之收入，須二倍其所應付之利息，而後債券本息有穩妥保障，而鐵路企業家（或股東）亦希望其資本所得之報酬率，須爲債券利率之二倍，而後所得之報酬，始可認爲有利之投資，根據此項解說，將債券與股票其構成全部資本之各種比例及其所得結果，列表比較如下。

債券佔資本總額之比例	債券人希望之收入	股東希望之收入	應有收入之數	所得報酬率	股票佔資本總額數
1/4	2,400,000	7,200,000	8,400,000	7%	3/4
1/3	3,200,000	6,400,000	8,000,000	6 2/3%	2/3
1/2	4,800,000	4,800,000	7,200,000	6%	1/2
2/3	6,400,000	3,200,000	6,400,000	5 1/3%	1/3
3/4	7,200,000	2,400,000	7,200,000	6%	1/4

由上表觀，可知債券與股票最經濟之比例，卽債券資本總額三分之二，股票佔資本總額

三分之一，蓋在此種比例之下，全部收益爲六、四〇〇、〇〇〇元，債權人得所三、二〇〇、〇〇〇元爲債券總數八〇、〇〇〇、〇〇〇元之百分之四，且收入亦等之利息支出之二倍，而股東之紅利共計三、二〇〇、〇〇〇元，適合股票總額四〇、〇〇〇、〇〇〇元之百分之八，且報酬率亦等於債券利率之二倍，是債主與股東之利益均能滿足且收入限制亦爲最低。但若債券所佔之比例苟較全體資本三分之二稍大或較小，則鐵路應賺之收益數，均應較大，在新興之路綫，沿綫實業，未盡發達，營業數量不多，規定應有之收入，自以愈低爲愈宜，故債券與股票自以上述之數目爲適當之比例」。

由是可知，鐵路財政之組成，應有適當比率，若專恃借債築路，殊非所宜，我國鐵路，昔時均爲借債興築，條件苛嚴，莫可比擬，各路除還本付息之外，兼有其他負擔，而政府股本與債款數目之比例，亦無適宜之調節，以致每年營業盈餘，大部份流入債權人之手，而政府應得之報酬，反只有懸記之賬項，爲數亦極有限，就財政政策上言之。殊非得計，惟說者又謂現在經濟組織，大都均藉信用以換資金，且籌借資金，亦較招募股本爲易，蓋債券有穩妥之保障，固定之利息，且自信託業務發達之後，大部份資本，均集中于保險公司銀行及信託公司之手，此種理財組織對於委託代管之資金，大都均擇較爲穩妥之途，設法存放，以故爲購買債劵較投資股票者爲多是鐵路債票銷售較易，即就鐵路本身而論，借款數目愈大，而支出利息，愈爲固定，在業務發達時，股東(或政府)所得之盈利，亦愈多，是借債築路就財政政策上言之，亦不能認爲錯誤，此理誠屬至當，惟謹約之財政組織，債票與股本，似宜有適當之比例其多少視事業之性質而定，在收入固定之企業，借款本息可按期還付，債款較多，尚無問題，若收益增減無常則債款本息不能按期還付，因之而負擔日增，殊極危險，我國鐵路，今日財政限于窘迫之原因，未始不由昔時財政組織未加調節而起也。是故今後鐵路財政，似採債股兼募之政策，視將來營業情形而規定適當之比例，斯爲最善之道也。

二、資本募集之方式　建築鐵路募集資本，就我國目前情形以觀，有下列五種。

一、發行債券　我國鐵路，大都均爲募債興築，而當時之公債，又以外人投資者爲多，本國募集之公債殊尠，時以迫于情勢，故條件異常嚴刻，所有債務，除按期還本付息之外，尚有其他條件，舉其要者，約有數端。

一、回扣及發行佣金

二、分攤餘利

三、購料權及佣金

四、工程監理及建築權

五、支線展築權

六、業務經營權

七、進款存放權

八、還付本息手續費

是此項借款合同，債權人非但享財政上之利益，且有監督及管理之特權，以致鐵路其行政上財政上以及業務上一切措施，往往因條件縛束，無可發展，茲者當局鑒于以往之經驗，募借債款，力避干涉行政及業務上之權限，最近鐵道部頒行之鐵道建設公債條例，均以平等互惠爲原則，大都由本國銀行承銷，較諸以前，全憑外資者，相差遠甚，惟是國內資金，爲數有限，而建設費用，支出浩繁，欲于最短期內，興築數萬英里之鐵道，勢非利用外資不可，但外人之投資我國者，除希圖較高之利潤外，每兼含有侵略之性質，以故借款立約，自須先定原則，前交通部長葉玉甫先生，對於利用外資，曾有明切意見，其宗旨頗爲平允足爲師法，茲摘述如下。

一、贊成國際投資　其大意謂「……利用外資，與其借一國之資金，使其勢力範圍過於增長，何若准各國共同投資，其勢力範圍得以破除……」又謂「共同投資，所應注意之點有二郎（一）以不失管理主權爲前提。（二）不可使單獨的勢力範圍變爲統合的勢力範圍……」

二、反對共同管理　其大意謂「若干人以共同投資，卽爲共同管理，在外人之意，以爲非此不足以保障其利權，而謀鐵路之發展，在我國則宜分別研究，共同投資祇須條件平允，無損主權，自可酌量承認，若共同管理，則國家人民生死存亡有密切之關係，不能不極端反對……」

以上所錄二大原則，誠爲利用外資必要之條件，至國內公債之發行，部頒條件，極爲允當堪爲模範。

二、募集股款　我國鐵路，以國有國營爲政策，政府卽爲股東，政府資金，卽猶鐵路股本，昔時狃於成例，民股商股，一律排除，民有鐵路收歸國有時，其商股幷由政府收買或掉換公債，就最近情勢以觀，國家辦理之機關，如銀行實業，均有招集或擴充商股之議，而海外僑胞，擁有巨資，無法利用，因之進而爲投機或危險之事業，往往因而失敗，坐耗資金，殊深可惜，是以建設鐵道，其支線或完全以經濟爲目的之幹線似可兼設商股，採行官商合組之董事會制度，以共同管理其業務，旣可誘致國外僑胞之遊資，而建築時資金之運用，亦可期經濟，卽將來營業之商業化，亦較完全國營者爲易，惟商股不可過多，股東應以華人爲限，且股票亦須規定不得轉讓，否則外人將乘機攫取，而喪失國權矣。

三、盈利撥用　在國有各鐵路，苟特別會計制度，能確切維持，則每年盈利，自可隨意調撥，以充建築新路之用，惟各路債款負擔過重，每有盈餘，還付本息，尙虞不足，卽偶有一二路，稍有盈餘可資撥用，亦大都劃爲他路協款，拔還舊債，以故新路建設，欲藉已成線之盈餘，以資挹注，殊爲困難，況整理舊路債款，還本付息，卽所以維持鐵道信用，增高公債市價，對於募集新債，關係至切，似又不可顧此而失彼也。

四、增稅築路　增稅築路辦法，歐美各國政府，多有採行，惟因徵稅手續太緩，一時難籌鉅款，大都均用稅款以爲擔保或用爲還本付息之基金，而發行公債，此種辦法我國不乏先例，卽前鐵道部長孫哲生先生，亦有增加關鹽稅築路之計劃，但現時中央財政異常急迫，國庫支絀所有可征之稅，大都均已舉辦，其稅收亦已指定用途，如關稅鹽稅烟酒印花稅，均經劃定開支，卽新增之稅，亦歲入不旺，欲提高稅率，反足以傷稅源，減少收額，卽增稅亦無濟於事，由是可知，增稅築路，在今日情形之下，決無可行之理。

五、庚款輔助　庚子賠款，自經各國退回以後，我國建設及文化事業之基金，每以此爲唯一財源，彼借此撥，支配殆盡，且大部份經債權國指定爲辦理特種文化及實業之用，以故剩餘之數無多，孫前鐵道部長，曾有庚款築路計劃之擬訂，迄未見行，而目前其他建設事業，需款孔急此宗款項，似難移撥，欲由此而籌集較大之資金以興築鐵路，恐非易易也。

由上所述，建設新路，其資金之籌集，自以借債及募股爲較便易，惟股票公債，其銷售之市場，發行之條件，利率之高下，債票與股票之比例，均須就金融市場之情形過去之經驗以及將來營業上之負擔，詳細研究，務須以束縛少，募集易，負擔輕，爲基本原則，庶可免重蹈昔時濫借外債之弊也。

三、資金分配之比例　資本募集之後應如何支配其用途實爲大問題，我國鐵路昔時之建築計畫，就其資本支出之支配情形言之，大都偏重於路線之建築及車輛機車之購置，而管理費一項如總務費籌辦費，爲數尤鉅，且以建築時期過長，因之而建築時之利息及維持費亦隨之而增加，又因國外購料及雇用洋員以外幣支付薪俸，又須蒙匯兌上之損失，凡此種種。均爲無謂之消耗，並非不可避免之支出，至於行車號誌，車站設備，車場貨棧，料庫，機廠，則往往以經費限制，因陋就簡，其結果使行車無安全之保障，事變叢起，調車無適當之車場，週轉需時，其他如站棧狹小，岔道短少，非但營業運輸上時生阻礙，卽員司工作效率亦無形減低，其損失之鉅，莫可數計，然實際支出之款項，並不因此而稍減，考其原因，實資本分配，未得其當，設計工程，未盡相宜，以致資本消耗於無形資產之內，殊深可惜，此後建築新路，於資金運用自宜詳細規定，應以「節省」及「便用」爲原則，下列四點，似宜注意，茲分述。

一、建築鐵道先從工程運輸及營業方面，詳細計劃，然後根據此項計劃，籌集的款，在款項未籌集之先，寧可展緩開工。

二、工程上一切設計，以國有鐵路互通車輛爲原則，初期資本，務須設法減輕，但與列車行駛，運輸能力及營業方法有切實關係之設備，如車站車場號誌岔道機廠等項，應與路基及車機等，一律重視，應按其效用及需要情形設法採用新式設備，以圖一勞永逸之計。

三、總務費籌辦費應儘量緊縮建築時期，亦宜嚴格限定，藉以節省靡費。

四、所用材料以採用國貨爲原則，以免匯兌上之損耗。

根據此項原則，規定工程預算，嚴厲執行，則資本分配，當爲公允合理矣。

（未完待續）

關於吏治者

國有德義未明於朝者，則不可加於尊位。功力未見於國者，則不可授以重祿。臨事不信於民者，則不可使任大官。故德厚而位卑者，謂之過。德薄而位尊者，謂之失。寧過於君子，而毋失於小人。過於君子，其爲怨淺；失款小人，其爲禍深。是故國有德義未明於朝而處尊位者，則良臣不進。有功力未見於國，而有重祿者，則勞臣不勸。有臨事不信於民，而任大官者，則材臣不用

管子立政三本

中華國有鐵路現行行車時刻表

平漢綫

64 普通客	62 普通客	52 普通客	42 普通客	44 普通客	22 快車	2 特快（每星期一三五由漢口開）	北上列車	站名	南下列車	1 特快（每星期一三五由北平開）	21 快車	43 普通客	41 普通客	51 普通客	61 普通客	63 普通客	71 混合車
每日開行											每日開行						
7.15	9.35						開	漢口玉帶門	到						7.56	18.10	11.40
7.35	9.52				—	—	到	漢口大智門	開	—	—				7.39	17.50	10.53
8.00	10.20				23.50	9.30	開		到	22.20	18.50				7.19	17.32	10.13
8.10	10.30				24.00	9.40	到	漢口江岸	開	22.10	18 40				7.09	17.20	10.02
8.15	10.35				0.05	9.42	開		到	22.08	18 35				7.05	17.15	9.27
9.05	11.19				0.46	—	到	橫店	開	21.34	17.54				6.20	16.25	8.26
9.08	11.21				0.48	10.16	開		到	—	17.52				6.18	16.20	8.22
10.42	12.44				2.05	11.25	到	孝感縣	開	20.25	16.35				4.54	14.45	6.05
10.57	12.57				2.20	11.39	開		到	20.11	16.20				4.46	14.30	5.45
12.10	14.02				3.25	11.35	到	花園	開	19 15	15.18				3.40	13.15	4.02
—	14.07				3.35	12.37	開		到	19.13	15.13				3.32	—	2.42
	15.34				4.55	13.50	到	廣水	開	18.00	13.51				2.03		0.46
	15.49				5.15	14.10	開		到	17.45	13.35				1.51		24.00
	16.51				6.27	15.12	到	新店	開	16.53	12.40				0.52		22.16
	16.66				6.32	15.14	開		到	16.52	12.35				0.49		22.06
	18.16				7.56	16.20	到	信陽州	開	15.35	11.10				23.17		19.35
	18.36				8.21	16.35	開		到	15.20	10.55				23.02		18.35
	20.04				9.57	—	到	明港	開	14.05	9.24				21.31		16.27
	20.09				10.02	17.46	開		到	—	9.19				21.27		16.02
	22.12				12.00	19.23	到	駐馬店	開	12.28	7.27				19.25		12.50
	22.44				12.40	19.53	開		到	11.58	6.52				18.54		11.36
	1.00				14.55	21.45	到	郾城縣	開	10.05	4.46				16.39		7.55
	1.15				15.15	21.55	開		到	9.55	4.31				15.24		6.55
	2.58				16.56	23.18	到	許州	開	8.32	2.59				14.35		4.20
	3.18				17.11	23.33	開		到	8.17	2.44				14.20		3.17
	6.40	—			20.10	1.56	到	鄭州	開	5.55	24.00				11.15		22.20
	—	7.45			21 00	2.11	開		到	5.40	23.20			22.35	—		20.20
		10.50			23.32	4.2	到	新鄉	開	3.22	20.34			19.30			15.35
		11.05			23.47	4.44	開		到	3.07	20.14			19.15			14.05
		14.40			2.41	7.13	到	彰德府	開	0.37	16.55			15.39			8.20
		15.20			3.21	7.43	開		到	0.07	16.15			14.59			6.42
		17.30			5·17	9.16	到	邯鄲縣	開	22.33	14.10			12.51			2.48
		17.38			5.25	9.17	開		到	22.32	14.02			12.41			2.08
		19.17			6.50	10.30	到	順德府	開	21.18	12.32			10.59			23.43
		19.32			7.05	10.45	開		到	21.03	12.12			10.44			22.43
		21 49			8.59	—	到	高邑縣	開	19.19	10.10			8.32			19.30
		21.54			9.04	12.27	開		到	—	10.05			8.27			19.00
		23.35	—		19.25	13.38	到	石家莊	開	18.08	8.35		—	6.50			16.40
			8.05		11.00	13.58	開		到	17.48	8.02		17.10	—			14.25
			10.29		13.13	15.51	到	定州	開	15.55	5.54		14.32				10.30
			10.39		13.23	16.01	開		到	15.45	5.44		14.12				9.35
			12.24	—	14.58	17.25	到	保定府	開	14.20	4.15	—	12.25				6.45
			12.45	6.50	15.13	17.40	開		到	14.05	4.00	19.35	12.03				5.30
			14.43	8.45	16.47	19.05	到	高碑店	開	12.40	2.26	17.40	10.15				2.02
			14.58	8.55	16.57	19.15	開		到	12.30	2.16	17.30	10.05				1.32
			17.03	11.03	18.38	20.41	到	長辛店	開	11.04	0.37	15.03	8.03				21 20
			17.18	11.11	18.48	20.51	開		到	10.54	0.27	14.50	7.48				22.17
			18.05	2.058	19.30	21.25	到	北平前門	開	10.20	23.45	14.00	7.00				20.00

工廠材料檢查之效用與方法（B 4.）

張宗謙

檢查二字（Inspection）一般人往往僅以爲乃關於工廠之設備及工作狀況而言，殊不知其尙有不止於此者，工廠所用材料亦有檢查之必要，各種原料檢查之需要，當視其情形而定，如所購原料爲數甚微，或其品質之優劣對於製造部之工作，並無問題，卽可不必多此一舉，但普通實行科學管理之工廠，對於採購原料。必有一種固定之制度，大抵採取大批採購方法，以圖經濟，同時實行標準化，於是檢查工作益爲不可疏忽之事。

檢查原料之功用

A.節省成本　檢查原料與成本之減低，殊有密切之關係，在科學管理未實行以前，工廠均係小規模事業，故所購原料，爲數甚小，檢查員卽有不能盡職者，所蒙損失，亦甚有限，至現代之工廠，受激烈之競爭，唯一方法，乃以大規模製造，（Mass production），以求成本之減低，於是所購原料，亦因之而增多，但對於所購之材料，必須先經嚴密之檢查，以視其是否合用，原料進廠尙未送入製造部之際，此時最關重要，一有疏忽，非獨影響於製造部之工作非淺，且成本亦因而增高矣。

B.時間經濟　科學管理化之工廠，對於時間問題，頗爲重視，其製造部對於出產數目及時間，均有規定，採購部之工作，乃係供給製造部所需要之材料，故其所購之材料必須與對方約好，在規定之時間內交貨，以便按時送交製造部應用，但對方(卽賣方)在製造之時，往往發生誤會，致材料雖按時送到廠中，而其品質不合，結果雙方俱受影響，故美國有若干大工廠，以及陸軍部海軍部等購置材料，皆派有專員駐守對方廠中，隨時檢查及監督其工作，此種情形雖屬特殊，然檢查工作之重要於此可見一斑。

C.維持標準　一科學管理，對於出產品，旣有一定之標準，則其所需之原料，亦必須定一標準，並切實遵守檢查，如試驗所收之材料，與標準規定，是否符合，因該項原料，將來須進製造部，若稍有不愼將未合標準者，大意收入，以致出產品質，降爲次等之貨，大不合算也。

檢查科之位置

檢查科在工廠組織中所佔之位置普通可分三種。

(1)歸製造部管轄　支加哥大學敎授密巧所著生產管理(Production Management, by W. N. Mitohell) 一書中卽主張將檢查工作歸製造部管轄，其理由有三：

(1)製造工作之成敗，須根據於所用之原料是否合格，同時有多種原料須至製造之時始發現其缺點，故製造部應有檢查原料之主權。

(2)在配合工業中(Assembly industry)有多種材料可不必經過製造之手續而直接加入生產品者，如錶中之發條，及汽車中之電池等，檢查科普通既負責檢查出產品，亦應同時負責檢查此類材料。

(3)製造部檢查原料可以測驗採購部工作之效率。

上述理由雖表面觀察似尚充足但一般專家之意見均認爲不妥，如台維司(R.C. Davis)，金堡(D. S. Kimball)，及劉意史(H.L. Lewis)等根本反對檢查科應歸製造部管轄，蓋因製造部之工頭，爲求生產額加多起見，每任工人超越所定寬容額(tolerance)而至損及品質，檢查科負檢查出產品之責任者，若隸屬於製造部往往受其指使隱諱不報。故檢查科不可直接隸屬於製造部。

(二)歸採購部管轄　哈佛教授劉意史等主張採購部應管轄材料檢查科其理由有下列各點：

(1)製造部不能直接管轄出產品檢查科，恐有指使隱諱之弊，須組織一獨立機關以行之，但採購部之管轄材料檢查科，則可不成問題。蓋因材料之檢查，乃測驗對方之效率，與本廠之採購部本身效率初無多少影響也。

(2)材料檢查科與採購部合作之後，大可以使採購部明瞭各供給材料廠家之優劣，以便從事選擇。

(3)檢查科可貢獻採購部以參考關於材料之缺點及其代替品。

(4)檢查科可以隨時糾正採購部重價格輕品質之政策。

(5)檢查科可時常測驗對方送來之樣品將其測驗之結果報告採購部，作爲參考。

(6)檢查科可以時常派人檢查各材料供給廠家之效率，能力，及工作情形。

(7)檢查科可以指點供給廠家關於其製造方面不合格及缺點所在地有改善之必要者。

(三)直接歸工廠經理之管轄　若干工廠對於貨物之品質極關重要者，如科學儀器等物之製造，乃有設立一獨立之檢查部建有測驗室，專門測驗出產品者，此時卽可利用此種測驗室及其人員兼管檢查原料以期經濟上之節省及可靠之檢查。但此種情形不易多見耳。

歐海歐電力公司之檢查科

美國歐海歐電力公司(Ohio Light and Power Company)對於檢查原料一部份之工作，可稱盡善盡美，用將其大概情形略述於下：

(一)組織——檢查科之位置根據多數專家之意見隸屬於採購部，科長以下設檢查員八人，每人專門研究數種原料之品質及其檢查方法。

(二)職務——檢查科之職務分爲三點：

(1)檢查手續。

(a)採購部將進貨單之第七份每日送交檢查科。

(b)檢查員將應需檢查之進貨單檢出，然後預備檢查單四份。

(一)第一份留存檢查科，俟檢查工作完畢，塡寫明白後再轉送需要原料之部份。

(二)第二份由檢查員携帶於檢查時作爲參考。

(三)第三份送交需要原料之部份表示對於上列各種材料將實行檢查。

(四)第四份寄交收貨地點以便校對。

(c)如檢查之後發覺原料有不合格之處，應預備拒絕報告書(Rejection Report)三份。

(一)第一份送交採購部主任，購料員，及發票股閱後再收入採購部擋卷中。

(二)第二份送交需要材料部份，通知拒絕之理由及情形。

(三)第三份留存檢查科擋卷中作爲以後之參考。

(2)監督編訂原料品質確定單——原料品質之確定乃實行標準化所應有之步驟，檢查旣負責檢查購買之原料品質以符標準，則其與品質確定之工作，頗有密切之關係，故檢查科應負責保管所有確定單，同時應搜集下列各機關之原料品質確定書作爲參考

(a)美國國家政府(United States Government)

(b)國家電光協會(National Electric Light Association)

(c)美國標準化研究協會(American Standards Association)

(d)大衆汽車公司(General Motors Corporation)

(e)美國電話電報公司(Amrican Telephone and Telegraph Company)

(f)美國海軍部(United States Navy)

若干原料尚無相當之確定單可供採用者，則檢查科職員應將該項原料用後之效能爲標準，自行塡寫，但無論如何須先經各關係部份之主任及購料員通過後方能使用。

(3)檢查供給廠家之新出品，以謀品質之優越。

(4)調查與檢查各種原料之代替品，以圖經濟上之節省。

(5)隨時派人到供給廠家調查其下列各點。

(a)所用之機器。

(b)生產之能力。

(c)出品之種類。

(d)職員之才能。

鉄道管理學之系統與內容(C 1.)

周世正

自喬治斯帝芬生發明蒸汽機車，鐵道經一百年之發揚光大，已佔陸地交通之主要地位，總理稱『交通爲實業之母，鐵道又爲交通之母』，舉凡人物之懋遷，訊件之傳送，以至經濟之開發與繁榮，文化之溝通與進步，實利賴焉。但鐵道爲一極專門之事業，於建築工程及輪機方面，因非特殊研究不可；而鐵道之組織管理財政法規及業務上之進行與發展，又非專門學識不爲功；且鐵道爲公用事業，如何適應國民之需要，促進社會之繁榮，亦爲一專門之問題，於是鐵道管理學尚焉。故鉄道管理學者，『運用科學管理之方法於鐵道事業，以最經濟有効之手段，維持並發展鐵道事業，並使其最適應國家社會之需要』也。

鐵道管理學之定義既明，即可因以分析其系統，系統既定，應包括於各系統之學科，便可分別歸納。

根據定義，鐵道管理學應分爲三大部份：

(甲)關於管理方法之研究，包括達到科學化管理之各種學科。

(乙)關於鐵道事業之特殊性質及各種工作之研究，此種研究，係站在科學的立場，故應融合科學管理方法與特殊之鐵道事業包括一切應用科學管理方法於鐵道事業之學科。

(丙)如何使鐵道事業適應社會國家需要之研究、包括與鐵道有關之各種學科，及直接所發生關係之敘述與改善之學科。

茲將各系統所包括學科分敘於次，同時整個鐵道管理學之內容，卽可知之矣。

(甲)關於科學管理方法的研究之學科。

(A)一班的科學管理之主要條件，卽對於事業，有一極準確之調查與認識，舉凡組織上財務上業務上各種情況，俱宜以最準確之數字，加以記載，計算，彙集，編列與分析，然後整個事業之內容，可以明悉，進行方針，可以決定，以往之缺點，可以免除，於是最重要之二科尙焉，卽會計學與統計學也。會計學可將事業資產負債營業盈虧及財務上一切狀況，詳爲表示，於財政上及整個事業之存亡興衰，有極大之關係，成本會計將成本精確算出，事業之盈虧，原賴成本之高低，故尤具特殊之意義，統計學以數字圖表記載計算並表示各種事務，可應用於業務人事商情等，方面，使各方面俱可以切實表明，爲事業進行及發達之根據，在科學管理方法上，此二科誠最重要者。

(B)更進一步求事業之管理得法，組織之合理，職工工作之有効亦極關切要，此一方面之學科，不可不有者爲。

(一)人事管理。

(二)勞工問題。

(三)工商組織與管理。

(C)又在科學管理上，財務方面，除可用會計學作記載計算實際情形外，又宜講究開源節流之理財方法，以及資本之募集，各種證券之比較等，於是理財學公司理財公用事業經濟預算學等不可不讀，而於事業所需材料之購買存儲使用，如何趨於有利少費之途亦甚重要，故宜分列一科研究，而相隨以來之商業知識亦不可不先行探討也。

各學校各學者研究科學管理方法，將上述三方面之內容，或互相合併而研究，或更從而細分之，大概總不外如是也。

(乙)關於應用科學管理於鐵道事業之研究的學科。

此系統所包括，爲鐵道之特殊意義及工作之原理與實踐之研究，而處處與科學管理之原則與方法相融合，綜合卽特殊之鐵道事業的本身科學管理法也。

更將上述範圍分述於次：

(A)一班的研究——(一)鐵道運輸原理——給予總的概念。

(二)鐵道發達史——從事史的觀察。

(B)組織及財務方面——(一)鐵道組織與管理。

(二)鐵道理財學。

(三)鐵道會計學——此三者俱將科學管理法運用於鐵道。

(C)業務方面——(一)營業方面。

(子)客運——包括行李運輸包裹運輸，郵政及雜項運輸在內。

(丑)貨運——進行及發展方法之研究。

(寅)聯運——各鐵道間分爲國內國際二種。

(二)運輸方面。

(子)鐵道行車學。

(丑)終點及車場運務學。

關於業務方面必須分開營業及運輸二者研究，前者多關於商務部分，如運輸票據運送規則，承運及取貨手續與運送責任賠償及發展運輸方法等是。後者直接研究鐵道之車輛在站內外之行駛調度，如車輛之調佩，車站之設備，號誌路軌之設置與使用，及種種行車上之規則與實踐此二者性質與工作逈異，必須分別研究，於實用於鐵道時，亦貴分別處理，方能收科學管理上分工之利益，省費有而効也。

(D)材料方面——鐵路用料，爲極重要之部門，如在美國，每年鐵道耗于購料在十萬萬至二十萬萬元之間，全國所產煤量之三分之一，鋼鐵產物之百分四十，及木料之百分四十，俱爲鐵道購用，在中國購料費用，在支出亦佔第一位，故科學的材料管理，應用于大規模之鐵道事業，更歲特殊之學科，且爲極重要者，卽稱爲「鐵道材料管理學」也。

(E)尙有分等運價，與鐵路本身有絕大之存亡關係，由運價所得之總收入，必不能在總成本之下，但定之過高，又不符客商能力，如何得其中庸，誠屬治鐵道學者不可不注意者。

(丙)關於使鐵道事業適應公衆需要之研究的學科

鐵道事業，係公共性質，影響整個社會之經濟文化，攸關國家之安全福利，故除在第二系統中對事業本身之管理加以研究外，更應以公衆對鐵道之要求爲基礎，站在鐵道客觀的立場，廣吾人之研究立脚點，其應包括之學科于後：

(A)鐵道分等運價學——此學科與第二系統亦有關，蓋分等運價非特必須使鐵道補償其成本，且運價之規定，實爲鐵路與社會發生關係中最密切之一點。觀夫美國鐵路可因運價之差異，決定兩商或兩地之生死興衰，更觀各國保護本國製造業，以增高他國貨物進口稅與給予本國貨物以低廉運價並重，則運價與公衆之關係密切可知。故運價學實介在第二第三系統之中，爲最重要之一科，如何使鐵道與公衆之利害調和，實鐵道管理學一大問題。

(B)運輸調整——僅賴鐵道之聯運，猶不足適應完整之交通需要，因各種交通工具，俱有其特殊之優點與缺點，因而各有其經濟範圍，如公路適於短距離，飛機之迅速及其載重量之有限是。故須有整個之調整計畫，合併各工具之優點，而避其短，以發揮最大之運輸効能，當然各工具之性質定應首先承認，是以所包括之學科，應爲：

(子)公路運輸。

(丑)水道運輸。

(寅)航空運輸。

(卯)運輸調整。

(C)法律方面——鐵道非超越國家範圍之組織，故自發起成立以及事業之進行，處處須受法律之制限，是以法學知識，必須具備。切要之學科爲

(子)法學通論。

(丑)商法。

(寅)鐵道法規。

(D)政治經濟方面——政治學之對象爲全體國民及其活動；鐵道上爲國民之一種企業，自不能離政治之領域。至言經濟，則交通原爲經濟事業之一部門，其與商業金融的關係之密切更無待贅爲空言，茲將其各科列左：

(子)政治學原理。

(丑)中國行政組織。

(寅)經濟學原理。

(卯)貨幣銀行學。

(辰)國際貿易與國際匯兌——此在吾國常向國外購料，尤極重要。

(E)國家之鐵道政策——國家對鐵道事業所採政策，當然爲鐵道事業活動之楷模，此在美國等民營鐵道多者尤關重要，所包括者應爲：

(子)鐵道所有問題。

(丑)監督民路之制度及對於運價業務諸點之規定與限止。

(寅)對民路之稅率。

(卯)全國鐵道系統之籌計。

(F)軍事時期之鐵道運輸——鐵道平日服務於國家者固多，戰時爲軍事輸送之迅速，尤爲極重要之工具，但軍事時期之運輸與平日頗有不同，實有特加研究之必要。

綜上所述，鐵道管理學之系統與內容已見梗概，筆者在校選脩鐵道管理，本文乃根據學校規定之課程，加以分析歸納，似可作爲研究鐵道管理者之索隱，且可更明確地表示鐵道管理，實爲一獨立整個的學程，非加專門之研究不可。今日我國鐵道，正在方興未艾之秋，管理之學，其將日臻完善乎！

一個關於管理的小故事

盩屋縣西門，有個玉女洞，洞旁邊有一條飛泉。味道極好；且有益健康。蘇東坡狠愛吃這水，常常叫用人去取。但是路狠遠，恐怕用人偷懶，不眞的到那裏去取，隨便弄些水來哄他。於是他想了一個管理的方法。用些竹筒，一劈兩半，上面刻些符號，一半交給靠近玉女洞旁邊廟裏的和尚收着。當每次用人去取過一囘水，便帶一個囘來，作爲工作報告。東坡就把帶囘來的那一個，和自己的一個相對。這樣一來，那個用人再也不敢做假了。這個竹筒，當時人都稱爲「調水符」。

譯述

財務行政義

法國Goston Jeze著 方善桂譯

財務行政者，政府事務之一部，論及公款之征收、保管、與分配，公家收入與支出之調整，國家信用之管理，以及公家一切理財事務之統制者也。其詞復見財政學中，財政學者，研究政府財務管理之理論與實務者也。

財務行政之見重于今世，厥有數因：(一)政府權責，逐日擴大，收支日見浩繁；(二)民主政體，普遍建立，議會政治，統制國家之財庫；(三)行政之道，有趨于簡單化及合理化之勢。

欲求財務行政制度之良善，有數原則焉：組織必求嚴密，權責務須集中，一也；立法之原意，見於預算者，必須督責嚴峻，二也；工作之進行，求其簡單化迅捷化與秩序化，三也；財務之統制，宜乎簡繁適中效能顯著，四也。而制度之健全，猶待有技術與可靠之官員，則人員之銓叙，亦屬要務，與組織之本身，有同等之重要性焉。

財務行政組織，經過長時期之發展，始能臻于健全，並未一蹴卽就者，而發展之過程，尤與政治制度，有密切之關係。英法兩國之財務行政制度，完成最早，歷久無繼者。英國憲法中，關于財務行政組織之立法爲一八六六年六月廿八日之「財政及審計部條例」(Exchequer & Audit Department Act)。據一八六七年三月二日「財政備忘錄」(Treasury Minute)所載規則補充云：「此法乃集中財政與審計部之職責，以執物公家銀錢之收入，監管，與發行並稽查其帳目者」。法國財務制度，之法條，載于「主計章程」(Réglement Général Sur la Comptabilité Pupliqu e)初版載于一八三八年五月卅一日，末版載于一八六二年同日「皇家法權」(Royal Donnance)。其在他國，則多仿英法之制；法制行于大陸，較英制爲有系統，惟滿意之程度不若焉。各國有酌改其體而圖進者，若比利時，一八四六年五月十五日及一八六八年十二月十日之法律涉，及政府會計；意大利一八八四年二月十七日之法律及一八八五年五月四日之規例規定政府之財務管理及會計；德國一九二二年十二月卅一日之法律規定國家預算條例，一九三〇年四月十四日之法令及一九二七年八月六日之法令制定國庫之職權者是。

際乎諸國，以英之制度，最見縝密與統一。全部組織之中心爲財政部(Treasury)。自一六一二年起，財政部採委員制，設首席一人由首相担任名義，一席由財政部長担任，次席數人(常三人)。事實上，權皆集于財長。在其管督之下，有人員一批，訓練完備，與之合作，能保制度之持續，與錯誤之避免。部中要員，首推「常務祕書」其人，全部行政，統歸指揮，次則「理財秘書」掌管各部事務。此兩職以地位衝要，選任維愼。

政府歲出之概算，由財部集中之。財政部長係國王之財政顧問；請求下院撥補全國之歲出，以便統制各部。下院則將此概算，表決之。無提議歲出或要求增加法定支用之權。常視財政部長所提之數，照准之。

財政部對全國財政之監督，直接永久。下議院所予法定支用之權，係給予國王，而非授諸閣員者。全國財政，任憑國王、而財政部不過執行其意志耳。故每一支出之先，閣員須先得財政部之同意。法定支用如有不足，閣員可書面提出于財部，俟財部審核支出可否縮減延後，以及應否向下議院提請通過追加預算。財政部有督察政府機關行政效率之權，遇有應興應革，宜予指示。

稅款之征收及公債之管理事務，另設兩處分理之，均受財部監督。財部所監督者，尙有公款之保管與分配(保管委英蘭銀行辦理)。財部與英蘭銀行，備有往來帳册，各處收得款項，均入財部戶下，凡財政部之付款命令，由英蘭銀行轉帳。公款存儲集中于英蘭銀行後，使政府之款項，亦流通于外，不致因稅款之征收，而影響金融市場也。

英國財政中，尙有審計長 (Comptroller and Auditor General) 一職，極爲重要。該員之任命，權操國王，惟該員係對國會負責，非財部之職員。國會有權撤換之。其職務在監視財部向英蘭銀行支款，是否合乎議會之意志，每次支款，均須得其核准。謂之審計核准。

財政如有入不敷出情事，財部得借取短期債款，以資彌補。借款方法，或由英蘭銀行墊付，(Ways & Means Advauces) 或由其轉銷國庫券(Treasury Bill)。倘政府開辦建設生產事業，籌措基金，得由財部發行公債，期限較國庫券爲長，以事業收入逐次償還。

財政部對政府簿記，直接並不審計。每週出版財政週報一種，載述收支數字及財政法令。此外，每年編造財政總册，呈送國會，報告財政狀況。政府簿記之審計，由國會另組委員會担任之，稱主計委員會(Committee on Public Accountant)常由審計長及財部派員一人共同組織之。該會並檢查財政部之業務。該會調查所得，即爲財政備忘錄之根據，由財部編印，分送各部。自一八五七以來，此項文書，印成主計委員會報告書概要，一八五七——一九一〇，及財政備忘錄，(Epitome of the Reports from the Committees on Public Accountantand of Treasury Minute Thereon)不啻英國計政之縮影焉。

法國財政行政制度，由財政部長獨負全責，財政計政，並不分立。及一九二五年，由于政治上之原因，設立預算部，與財政部相並立。預算部之主要職權，爲編造預算送呈國會。兩部分立後，未收著效。預算部長之職位，較財政部長爲次，且亦非高于其他閣員。其他閣員雖須將支出計劃送達預算部，但預算部長無權管轄之。下議院及上議院設財政委員會，有斟酌全國財政之權，故財政部長及預算部長之權，爲之減弱。國會所討論之財政計劃，注重財政委員會所提者。下院議員，有提議增加新支出案及增加法定支用案之權。立法之密，不足防弊。依照憲法，上議士無提議增加歲入分配之權，但按諸實際，此輩以詐取勝，于討論預算時，虛予減低。迨預算案再送下院時，下院議士提議增加，即上議士欲增之數。故法國預算案，無人負責，猶之書之無作者，兒子之無父親也。

財政部于各部財務，無直接的永久的及有效的統制。各部閣員照其預算核准法定支用之數支用，不受財政部長之干涉。預算應增撥時，預算部長得有關之閣員請求，向議會請求之。由于預算部長權力之微弱，由于財政委員會勢力之膨脹，上下議院所提增減分配，遂成重要之一着。當一八九〇年，財政部長集權之時，財部分設已定支出監理員 (Controleur des Dépenses Engagées) 一職，專司綜核各部支出事務。凡支出之先，必須經該員審查法律，參酌議決之預算，得其副署方可。但不能改變其設計。監理員有批評行政效率之權。倘監理員拒絕副署，各部得遞抗辨書於財政部長，由部長取決之。官吏支出金額，故意不經監理員之副署，依一九二二年八月十日之法律，應負民事及刑事責任，但此法從未執行。監理員之職務，均屬必要，惜無充分權力，以求其工作之有效耳。

財政部長綜理歲入之征收與分配。公款之監守，則由法蘭西銀行 Bank of France 任之，故金融易于流通。銀行與財部間，成立往來戶，凡征得公款，胥入戶內。至于公款之支付，先由各關係閣員發出支付命令，由領款人（或稱國家之債權人）持向該行支取。財政部長則令該行存銀于出納主任，以備支付。此項支付命令，必須有監理員及財政部公款流通總所 (Direction du Mouvement Général des Fonds du Ministére des Finances) 之副署。前者之責任，在確定財政部長支款之權；後者則担保此項支付，已有的款備用。每月終，財政部長結算支付之數，咨照各部，並通知其下月尚可支領之數。倘支付款項，未完上述手續，付款之職員應個人負其全責，但負責之範圍，由財政部長最後處决之。

財政部長爲對國會及法律之惟一負責者。在法國制度中，並無如英國審計長之設，防止財政部長于法案之違背。財政部長得支用國款，不問合法與否，苟有命令，監理員及付款職員均須服從。並可任意解除付款職員之責任。一九二二年八月十日之法律，予政府以增加法定支用之權，以應公債利息之需，惟須事後卽得國會之追認，政府之弄權，遂使國會統制之權，失其效率。法律條件，置之不顧。例如一九二九年國庫有二千萬萬法郎之支付準備，而議會不知其情。一九三〇年，曾有新法之制，意圖稍以約制國庫，以其條件之空虛無力，終未稍奏膚功。

財政部長，並負國債行政之責。如遇國庫收支不得平衡，則發短期國庫券(Treasury Certificate) 此外則一九二八年以前，法蘭西銀行長期無息墊款。常在六萬萬法郎，戰後法郎價格平穩成功，始無形消滅。

財政部長指揮全政府各部分會計事務，並審查其報告書，遂後始送交「會計法庭」(Cour des Comptes)，作最後之審查。惟此項報告書送請審計，事實上常相隔至數年之遙，故審計之效，完全喪失，可謂無意義之至。此種查核工作，議會亦無意爲之也。

德國之財務制度，雖取法于法國，然以其傳統之習慣，集權于行政，而議會則軟弱無能。以此傳統故，財政部長遂成財務制度中之領袖，財政部長有編造預算之權，雖未見大于英國財政部，然强于法國財長多矣。編造預算，有一定格式，先由各部墊就，遂後送交財政部長，財政部長則憑各部之施政計劃，親自列定歲出歲入數字。並有批評之權，如遇爭議，則由閣議決定之；但財政部長得要求重開會議複決之。閣員要求之法定支用，倘與財政部長發生爭議，必須閣議多數贊同，並得首相之贊同方能照准。閣議核准之預算，再送呈各州代議士合組之上議院(Reichsrat)，組專門委員會討論之，而財政部長復爲該會之主席。財政部長得要求將修正之預算案再付閣議，經分別准駁，再送衆議院。衆議院得審議之，財政部長不得過問，故表面似損折財長之權，但事實上衆議院不如法國下院然，得增加法定支用案重造豫算也。衆議院之議士，人人皆有提議增加歲出之權，惟皆結成政黨操縱之，與政府個別交涉。一九三一年，衆議院之法律修改，凡衆議院議士提核減收入增加支出之案，必須提補救平衡之法。此種補救法猶須送請政府同意之。又如修正法定支用，增加之數，尙須送請上議院核准。設遇不准，德國總統應于三月內舉行國民投票，或發交衆議院再度核議，增加案須三分之二議士之贊同，方得存在。歷來以應用後法爲多。但雖有三分之二之贊同，總統仍得舉行全國總投票。依據一九一九年韋碼憲法過衆議院反對預算或應解散以徵民意時，德統得宣布財政法令。故當一九三〇年七月十八日衆議院反對預算解散時，總統曾發布此種法令。一九三〇年之預算，遂得依此確立。

德國財務行政之方法，未能得財政上滿意的平衡。自一九二四年以來，年年虧耗。依法上年度之虧耗。乃下年度之支出，因收得之稅款須補上年度之損失也。事實上虧耗皆由公債補足之，尤以短期借款爲多。截至一九三〇年八月，數已超一百三十萬萬馬克以上。

當預算執行後，財政部長無權管轄其同級官員，其職位不若英國財政部長，而頗似法國之財政部長。但尙有不及者，德國財長不能委任各部之會計官，各部部長得自行委人管理帳冊。預算之月份分配，則倣自法國者。財政部長取決應付款項之總數，但于支付超過限度，並不担保，遇支付超出總數時，付款職員僅能出之拒絕支付之一途。

政府收入之大宗，悉由財政部長掌之。財政部中，分設司科辦理稅款查定，及稽查其他收入事務。各地分金庫，將收入之款，彙解中央金庫，或存入國家銀行政府戶下，或由郵局匯寄。各分庫亦有與國家銀行成立往來戶者。德國國家銀行在財務行政制中之地位，較之英之英蘭銀行，法之法蘭西銀行爲遜。

財政部長得上議院授權，發行公債，並負責淸償之。國債行政，另設機關 (Reichsschuldenverwaltung) 辦理之。一九二四以前，國庫偶有不足，輒由國家銀行墊款，以國庫券作担保。惟是年以後國家銀行放出三個月短期信用，以一萬萬馬克爲限，須于會計年度終了後（三月底）三個月半內淸訖。國家銀行，得貼現國庫券，以三個月爲期，四萬萬馬克爲限，國庫券須有殷實人士簽名。國庫亦能向鐵路郵局借款，以其爲進款機關，經濟獨立故也。

在德國之財務機構中，並無對法律議案負責之機關，僅由各行政機關設預算處，由該管上司委令一人，在上司監督下執行工作。衆議院于預算執行之監督，並不嚴峻。倘有浮支情事，恆未經衆議院之同意，俟報告書編妥，始送請核銷，而衆議院亦竟樂予從同，不加駁斥焉。

自一九二九年五月起，財政部長印行按月收支報告書，及國庫報告另附一債務說明書。並聯合各部編成預算帳目，咨送衆議院。支出之帳目，則由付款職員逕送獨立組織之預算監理員（Rechnungshof），該員以監查預算之執行，法案之符合，支出之手續，支付之經濟，及編製年報貢納改進意見于政府爲職志。所編年報，經國會及衆議院通過後，政府之責任卽被解除。然事實上衆議院亦殊不斤斤于此也。

美國之財務制度，在一九二一年預算會計法未公布前，極爲腐敗。預算之編製，由參衆議院分設委員會掌理，對于預算之平衡，亦不注重。財部于各部支款請求之審查，並未受合法權力之賦予，法定支用之謬誤，支付之不當，均熟視無覩，不以爲奇。議院以爲政府用款，係出强迫，非由隨意，故政府須在賦予之範圍內，使用金錢。寖假狼狽爲奸，虛靡浪費，遂成美國財務制度特有之現象矣。

一九二一年，財務制度，全部改組，英國之制度，雖有採酌，但非抄襲成法。在美國政制下，財政部長（Secretary of Treasury）之地位，不能與英國財政部長相比，故以英國財長之職權賦之美國財政部長，實不可能。考一時無劇烈之改革，實緣于總統有優厚之力量，閣員處補弼之地位，議會財權之重大，及傳統習慣之强盛故耳。

美國預算之編製，研究，及公布，權均在總統之手。總統之下，依一九二一年之法律，設預算局（Bureau of Budget）以主理之。預算局之職權，與英財政部常務祕書之權相似，專任彙編各機關之概算，加以訂正及增加，此項職權，無異統制全國各機關。預算局下，有概算委員會，專事與聯邦中各機關取得聯絡。聯邦各分支機關中，均有專司預算之人員，由該管上司委任，担任概算之編製，及與預算局聯絡。全國各機關，凡遇預算局徵取各項資料時，務須盡量供給。預算局之職員，並可奉命查閱各部帳册。

各行政機關均有法定支用。其支用聽各主管人員之便，毋須預算局之批准。但爲另作他用，則必須通知預算局並請許可。在預算公布或六月卅日之前各行政機關須報告其預定之每月或每三個月之支用分配（Apportionment of Appropriations）于預算局，嗣後如有更改，亦須隨時報告並請核准。此外每隔三個月，各機關尙須報告支用實數。預算局並設調整員（Coordinator）專司研究支用經濟效能，及減少阻碍之方法。

由于總統及其屬下之預算局權力甚大，美國財政部長之職權，遂未能如英法財政部長之重要。財政部長僅能向總統建議稅餉公債及其他財源之增減，公款之征收及保管。當初美國中央銀行未成立時，公款之保管，頗生困難。起先分在于各銀行，但因選擇銀行憑職員之好惡，常遇信用破産情事，公款遂存于國庫。由于公款存儲國庫之故，當稅餉征收時，大批金錢，脫離金融市場，造成通貨緊縮，流弊甚大。內戰之後數年，復恢復銀行存款辦法。自聯邦準備制度成立後，聯邦準備銀行，代理公庫，惟財政部長仍有選擇銀行存儲之權。一九二○年，設立存款科，專司管理存款事宜。邊遠之區，無聯邦準備銀行者，則存于國家銀行，或爲支付當地薪給便利計，亦可如此辦理、一九二八年，財政部長復被授權指派州立銀行及信託公司，兼充公庫。

國庫得向外借款。凡短期借款，常由庫發行庫劵或鈔票借得，以補財政之不足。政府信用之運用，可使國用之支出，分配均勻，並可穩定國內之經濟焉。

全國會計事務，依據一九二一年法律之規定，設總會計署 (General Accounting Office) 歸全國金融總監及副總監(Comptroller and Assistant Comptroller)節制。總監由總統委任，參院批准，任期十五年。須憑兩院通過，方得撤換。總會計署係對議會負責，性質頗似英國之審計長。一九二一年起，擴大職權，專司會計格式之設計、會計制度之擬訂、會計審查之計劃事宜，對于美國官廳會計之統一改良，頗著功績。該署並可調集資料，及稽查各機關之帳册，並調查政府行政是否與議會立法相符。由各機關之咨詢，該署須解釋預算之原意，執者應付。執者應靳。惟解釋得由議會變更之。該署之職權雖廣，然不及法國支出監理員。該署雖可統制各機關長官之支付請求於款項未付之前，但並不普遍。該署呈報總統及上院之報告，建議財務行政經濟有效之道。兩院及所屬委員會，預算局等處，常委任其調查政情，苟查得國家支用或合同有違反法律情事，則另繕報告書，呈報議院。

總會計署分設各組辦事，（一）控訴組，依據行政法調查控訴事宜。行政長官之缺信，常有不能滿意之服務，總會計處如認控訴有理則轉報國會。(二)查帳部，審查各機關及郵政局之帳目。(三)顧問處，担任法律顧問，關于預算解釋事宜。(四)文書部，專司文書保管擋案事宜。(本文譯自 Encyclopedia of Social Sciences, 1931, "Financlal Administratian")

中華國有鐵路現行行車時刻表

北甯綫

41次 普通客車 中騎各等	71次 平津客貨 三等慢車	3次 特別快車 騎車各等	23次 快車 騎車各等	301次 平滬特快 騎臥各等	5次 平津特快 騎車各等	305次 平浦特快 騎臥各等	401次 平津客貨 平滬通貨	1次 平瀋特快 騎臥各等	上行列車 ↓	站別	上行列車 ↑	2次 瀋平特快 騎臥各等	302次 滬平特快 騎臥各等	6次 津平特快 騎車各等	72次 津平客車 三等慢開	42次 普通客車 中騎各等	4次 特別快車 騎車各等	24次 快車 騎車各等	402次 津平客貨 滬平通貨	306次 浦平特快 騎臥各等
5.45	7.10	9.30	13.00	15.35	17.10	20.00	20.10	21.15	開	北平前門	到	9.25	10.00	11.38	16.35	17.40	18.25	22.30	23.40	23.15
6.04	7.56		13.16				20.54		開	永定門	開				16.03	17.23		22.15	23.13	
6.20	9.01	10.00	13.30	16.00		20.26	22.10	21.40	開	豐台	開	9.02	9.36		15.15	17.05	18.03	22.02	22.17	22.50
6.44	10.24		13.48					21.58	開	黃村	開	5.43			13.53	16.37				
7.39	12.59		14.37			21.20	0.50	22.38	開	郎坊	開	8.05			11.42	15.41		20.54	19.15	21.51
8.03	13.48		14.53				1.29	22.55	開	落	開	7.43			10.28	15.20			18.31	
8.36	15.35		15.20				2.24	23.16	開	楊村	開	7.21			9.10	14.50		20.19	17.30	
9.14	17.28	11.44	15.47	17.51	19.10	22.24	3.43	23.42	開	天津總站	開	6.56	7.45	9.40	7.08	14.14	16.10	19.55	16.22	20.54
9.23	17.45	11.52	15.55	18.00	19.18	22.32	4.00	23.50	到	天津東站	開	6.45	7.35	9.30	6.20	14.00	16.00	19.45	15.20	20.45
9.35	停	12.05	16.05	18.20	停	23.00		24.00	開	天津東站	到	6.30	7.05			13.46	15.48	19.32		20.15
10.38		13.04	17.06	開往上海		開往浦口		1.01	開	塘沽	開	5.30	由上海開來			12.46	14.55	18.35		由浦口開來
11.46		14.00	18.13					2.07	開	蘆台	開	4.26				11.41	14.00	17.25		
12.34			19.00					2.58	開	胥各莊	開	3.30				10.45		16.34		
12.47		14.55	19.13					3.12	到	唐山	開	3.15				10.30	13.05	16.20		
12.52		15.00	19.18					3.15	開	唐山	到	3.10				10.23	13.01	16.17		
13.06		15.11	19.29					3.30	開	開平	開	2.55				10.10	12.51	16.07		
13.39		15.35	19.54					4.03	開	古冶	開	2.30				9.44	12.34	15.50		
14.29		16.07	20.28					4.53	開	灤縣	開	1.32				8.45	11.55	15.07		
15.32		16.49	21.18					5.59	開	昌黎	開	0.31				7.40	11.14	14.22		
15.56			21.37					6.24	開	留守營	開	0.01				7.12		13.59		
16.16		77.22	21.55					6.47	開	北戴河	開	23.42				6.54	10.43	13.45		
16.43		17.42	22.17					7.16	開	秦皇島	開	23.09				6.25	10.20	13.20		
17.05		18.00	22.35					7.40	到	山海關	開	22.40				6.25	10.00	13.00		
								8.20	開	山海關	到	22.00				6.00				
								16.40	開	遼甯總站	到	14.00								

書評

『良好公務人員』

任家誠

原　名——Better Government Personnel

著　者——Report of the Commission of Inquiry on Public Service Personnel

出版處——McGraw—Hill Book Company

版　期——一九三五年

定　價——美金二元

自從管理科學的進展，技術行政的提倡以來；世界各國的政治由祕密而入於公開，由朦混攏統而趨于條分縷析。行政四大部份的劃分，管理合理化的施行，行政效能的推進，一切設施皆以合乎經濟為目的。凡此種種都表明科學管理領域的擴張；從工商業的成就，而移植于政府機關。

人事行政（Civil Service）無論是英美或者德法的學者，誰都認為行政四大部分最要的一部。良以沒有合格的人才，管理整個行政的機紐，無論制度怎樣優良，政策怎樣完備，決不能運轉自如。所以公務員在行政上，正像工人在管理着機械的發動，正像人生的腦部，把握住人生的靈魂。看吧！英美現在的發展，何嘗不是公務員管理之得法，我國今日政治的窳敗，又何嘗不是官吏的腐化和引導的失當。

美國自從加非爾總統（President Garfield）之被刺，一八八三年本特爾登法案（Pendleton Act）之通過，分贓制（Spoil System

）之淘汰，成績制(Merit System)之推進，文官攷選委員會(Civil Service Commission)之成立，人事行政邁步走向科學化合理化的大道，數十年來劃分一個前後優劣判然的鴻溝。誰也不能夠否認美國一切的飛黃騰達，政治的上軌道，是由於公務員統制之得法。近年以來，還不以為一八八三年革新為滿意，官職分類之重行劃分，俸給厘訂之嚴加擬定，攷績制度之逐步推進，退職方法之次第改良，成為世界執政施政的楷模，世界學者研究探討之中心。其革新的發凡，雖然後于英倫，到底因為科學原理引用之得當，把握着世界行政科學的權威。

因為美國政府文官攷選委員會工作的努力，產生良好的制度和方法；而學術界方面猶以為未足，幫同作改進的研究。過去人事行政研究團體的經過茲不贅述，最新的結果，有光明燦爛的人事行政諮詢委員會(Commission of Inquiry on Public Service Personnel) 之成立。該會始于一九三三年十二月，由社會科學研究聯合會 (Social Science Research Council) 組成，攷察現行制度，指示將來工作，以為整個國家和人民的介紹。牠們的研究及諮詢有三方面：第一方面從各大城中探詢，如華盛頓，紐約，芝加哥等，更進而擴展至英京倫敦；第二方面委託專家編製英德法各國人事行政之歷史及其他有關資料；第三方面聘請研究人員蒐集及研究所有資料。當然，有這種完整的諮詢組織，良好資料的獲得是必然的。

『良好公務人員』一書，就是該會成立後一年中調查和研究的報告。雖然是限于美國一國，和我們的國情及制度有所不同，作為參證的資料是十分有價值的。不是嗎，幾年來提倡我國改革人事行政的學者，都十分推崇美國的文官制度。

因為這書是一報告，所以不述基本的原則，而着眼于現行制度的批評，將來致進的貢獻。是一本宜于對於人事行政已有相當

註：社會科學研究聯合會為一自動集會，由七大國家專門社會科學組織所組成，此七大團組織為：The American Anthropological Association, the American Historical Association, the American Economic Association, the American Political Science Association, the American Psychological Association, the American Sociological Society, 及 the American Statistical Association.

研究的人士作爲探討的參攷，所以與其說他是一本良好的教科書，不如說他是一本完整的參攷書。

全書開宗第一編便是具體的建議，可以說是調查結果的心得的流露。對於職位的分類；成績制度的推進；攷銓，升遷，退休的辦法；試用時期的規定；地方與中央人員的聯繫；都有詳盡的意見。

關于職位分類，誰都知道美國分職制的優點，而該會還認爲現行制度太過複雜，主張分爲下列五大級：

一、管理級（Administrative Service）

二、專門技術級（Professional & Technial Service）

三、辦事級（Clerical Service）

四、精工級（Skill & Trade Service）

五、工事級（Unskilled Service）

升擢方面，主張高級人員與下層的熟悉，工作訓練的提倡，公事攷績記載的翔實，揭發公務員工作的能力，而予以升擢的機會。

至於公務員的保障，主力避因小小錯誤而任意撤退人員，或以宗教，政治，種族的關係，而影響公務員服務的安全；除非因爲不合任用及試用原則，攷績的不良應予調整或降俸和已至給予養老金命其退休的時期。

至於合作，主張中央及地方間管理上之聯繫；這意見不特對於美國的制度有特別提出討論的必要，就是我國也何嘗不然，「令不出於都門」，中央對於地方政府有臂長莫及之痛苦，而地方政府認爲「天高皇帝遠」，任意調遷人員，絕無顧忌，破壞人事行政制度的集中和一致性。此書對於此點的補救辦法，或由中央管理，或由地方政府組織集團（League of local governments），互商對於中央的聯絡。我國現在各地分設攷銓委員會，正和其第一主張相吻合。

還有比較偏于美國特有的情形，茲不贅述。

至報告本身，內有五大章，第一章述政府與人員之關係，其中值得介紹的就是美人對於人事行政觀念上的錯誤，美人所犯的錯誤正和我國一樣，而此書竟能言人之所不能言，讀了一定令人拍案叫絕呢！牠說：

『第一點是分贓制度（Spoil System），黨魁獲勝，任用私人的缺點。一人得志，雞犬升天，來報酬運動的成功，黨同伐異，飽飫自己的黨羽……』這點誠概乎言之，然而美國的人事行政已有相當的成就，尚且不能免此錯誤，想到我國更不必談了。

『第二點是把政府的工作當作十分容易，正如傑克遜總統（President Jackson）所說的：簡單，平凡，任何智識階級都可勝任愉快……』

『第三點把俸給當作慈善事業看待，公務員的任用，不過因為他們需要職務，…領俸以外，又何嘗注意到工作的成績……』

『第四點錯誤見解「以恩意（Patronage）當做民主政治的代價」，黨派而求其存在，不能避免分贓的辦法……把黨看作找尋職務的機器也似……』

『第五點以為「最良好的公務員即為最劣的一個」。……能任澈底工作的公務員即為腐敗，此種人士將侵蝕我人之自由，成績愈佳工作愈久，為莫大之危機」，此說雖然是堂堂一九二八年美國總商會（U.S. Chamber of Commerce）會長所言，然而揆之事實，當然不對。……』

『第六點以為「工作期乃為分贓制度治療的方法」……』

『第七點以為廢除分贓制應自下級人員起，……實際上高級人員之影響為最大，假使高級人員的任用，出于分贓的結果，當然制度是永遠不會改良的』

『第八點以為「本地之職務應由本地人士担任」……此種劃分最為不良』。關于此點我國亦有人主張，其錯誤的出發點正與美人如出一轍。

『第九點以為「行政必不及私人事業為有效」……實際上私人事業亦有任用私人，獻媚持寵，不合道德之弊，公務人員未必弱于私人事業的雇員……』

『第十點以爲分贓制及腐敗的習尙，可以因爲特種舞弊的禁止，而制止之。然而事實上反而之法律不足爲糾正，而需乎正面及軍事之手段藉公衆之力量，力加矯正。

以上十點的陳述，可以見該會對現行制度觀察精細之程度，當然得了病源，對症下藥，其效必著。我國現在亦在改革行政了，但是頭痛醫頭，脚痛醫脚，今天想到處理案案，明天想到整頓人事，對於病症，沒有深刻的於驗，又何能講到開藥方，配藥料呢。

第二章講到良好人事制度的本身，對於人事行政和人事行政制度二者有良好的定義，牠說：

『人事行政(Career in Service Government)是一種公共服務，組織之，管理之，以勉勵公務人員。』

『人事行政制度是人事行政施行之法律，組織，規程及程序的薈集』

對於人事行政，牠主應有公開的認識，應有法律的規定；應有良好的組織，來督促行政推進；應有良好的任用制度；應有根据工作之成績，予公務員以升擢的機會；應有良好的俸給制度，以工作之優劣爲增減之準繩；應有良好的退休和養老金制度，以推進工作之效能，以鼓勵下級人員之努力；應有公平的懲戒辦法以相對於公務之獎勵；公務雖應依其興趣團結合作，互爲有益公務和社會的探討。

對於人事行政制度牠主張：舊有法規應時加修改，以合需要而作準繩；應組織人事行政機關辦理一切，人事行政機關應派遣專家辦理，以圖人事行政之推進，此種制度應永久維持，時加改進，以達于化境。

第三，四二章講到人事行政的種種問題，也可以說以前各章所指出要點之實在報告；關於美國現行制度有翔實之調查，明確之報告，如任用，如升遷，如訓練，如任期的規定，如養老金制度，以及其他較爲次要的問題如郵務人員的管理等。

最後一章是全書的歸結，從現行的制度說到今後改進的步驟。以爲良好之政府建築在良好的人事行政制度上專門人員的工作必較門外漢之主持爲可靠。牠又說到美國現行教育制度之不切國家需要，大中學的教導不能注意及中央或地府行政工作的實況與管理上的學科，又因分贓制度沒有完全淘汰，學識和任用，失掉聯覺，造成種種若卽若離的現象。關於教育問題二點的陳述，當然我們可以得到不少感觸和教訓，我國對於公務員的任用，又何嘗注意到人才主義呢！對於公務員的訓練，又何嘗有事前的準備呢！所以這本書的結論，正好似對我們而說的！

本書的特點也算介紹了一部份，特長的地方未免恭維了些，但是我以爲亦不能倖免于欠缺。其缺點最明顯的就是書名和內容之不能脗合；因爲這書名之爲『良好公務人員』，而其內容不過爲美國現行制度的報告。但是美國現行制度亦有牠的缺點，好比分贓制之未全廢除，中央和地方因國體的關係而不能合作，人事行政也蹈此覆轍；我們當然不能認爲美國的人事行政制度是十分善良而無瑕可擊的。所以與其名之爲『良好公務人員』，莫若名之爲『美國現行人事行政之報告及建議』。

其次就是內容的失之空洞，說牠切於實際，則沒有具體改進的方案，說牠近乎理論，則未曾涉及原理；可以作爲研究的，到還是前幾十頁。但是這也不能苛責，因爲是一份正式的報告，這種半官式或全官式的報告，往往有所顧忌易生空洞的弊病。

又次，該會能夠揭發現行政的缺點，而不能貢獻良善的辦法；正如一個醫生祇會看病，不會開方。像前面介紹的美人對於人事行政觀念上的錯誤。你看他陳述得多麼透澈，但是翻遍書也找不出個對於此種錯誤的糾正來。說句笑話，他們祇會看病；但是我們今日言行政改革者，則確巧相反，祇會發藥，不會看病；以藥試病危險孰甚。視彼美人又復不如。

最後，此書的附錄，對於美國現行制度下的詳況，有數字的表解；又各州及中央政府人事行政法規之分類彙集等，都可作爲我人參證的資料。

結言之，該書不失爲一完備的參攷書，藉此可以觀光美國的人事行政，有詳加閱讀的價值！

「實業管理指南」

胡健

書　名——Executive Guidance of Industrial Relations: An Analysis of the Experience of Twenty-Five Companies.

著　者——C. Canby Balderston

出版者——University of Pennsylvania Press, Philadelphia

（本書共四百三十五頁，美金三元七角五分，一九三五年出版）

本書是從二十五個公司的經驗分析而得的結晶。

牠們三分之二是列入美國二百個最大公司之中，差不多可以代表各式各樣的企業。牠們各個別的人事管理都寫在書里。

一九三一年，爲要使各公司產生一最完善最强勁的工人管理關係的計劃起見，福勃君（Mr.B.C. Forbes）設立一個有獎競賽，四個得獎的公司全在這二十五個公司之內。

這書的最大目的，正像作者所說，是觀察雇主與雇員間相互關係的最好焦點。爲的近來各公司都樂爲人事管理的先鋒，他大部份用了案件制（The Case Method）描寫和解釋人事管理的性質。他先討論關于「人事裁決」的要素，然後及于企業的特性：如年代，經濟力量，眞勢力的地位，和其他別的實際要素。他繼續說着——一種可以採擇的組合方針；衝突動機的鑑定；用案件研究的企業分析；以及參酌各種統計資料所定的人事標準。每一章每一節里，他說得清晰而有趣，尤其在「利害衝突」的一節。

總之，這書有人事的基本哲學在里面。凡注意近代管理方法的人事首領，在尋求別的公司如何管理而要改進自己公司的管理的時候，從這書裏面，可以無疑地獲得極大的帮助與益處。

「企業管理」

胡健

書名——Management of an Enterprise

著者——C. Canby Balderston, Victor S. Karabasz, Robert P. Brecht

出版者——Prentice-Hall, New York

（本書共四百七十頁，美金五元，一九三五年出版）

此書乃美國白而段斯頓教授和他的兩個助教根據了教室裏許多年的經驗總寫成的。開始寫着的是產品，是物質的便利，最後寫着的是組織，是人事的關連。

作者相信管理教授的重要點在乎實用的問題，而不在乎原理的解釋；他們設了許多問題和案件，務使原理脗合着實況。何謂管理？何謂出產計劃？何謂價格的劃定？房屋要否購置？要否建築？要否租賃？誰應做採辦的職務？怎樣獲得存料管理？怎樣明了標準成本？——這些問題，書裏面統統明白指示出來。

最後一章是討論着人事的管理。公司聯合會(Company Union)和管理合作聯社(Union Management Cooperation)的比較，對于雇員保障的强迫捐款和自由捐款的檢討，以及誰該負責經濟的安全——個人工作者呢，企業呢，抑或國家呢，都包括在這章裏的。

關於教育者

一年之計，莫如樹穀。十年之計，莫如樹木。終身之計，莫如樹人。一樹一穫者，穀也。一樹十穫者，木也。一樹百穫者，人也。

管子權修篇

古今領袖人物言行札記

凡百事業之成敗，均以人爲根本。而事之能成與否，尤視領袖者之管理合於機宜與否。如確立計劃，妥定組織，登用賢能，分工治事，調整各部，發施號令，考核事功等等，均爲領袖者職分內應盡之責任。欲求盡此責任而無所愧怍，第一，須有高尙人格，堅强意志。次則須有閎偉襟抱，遠大眼光。再加以優深之學理，沉着之經驗，自能措施悉當，攸往咸宜矣。本刊特設此欄，一則砥礪有爲之青年，於修養上須切用工夫。一則撮舉治事之標準，於中外領袖知有所效法。但最要之目的，則在於使治管理學者知成功之領袖，斷非無因而獲有良果。蓋其一言一行，莫不與今之管理學精神，暗相契合也。

偉成附誌

曾文正公函牘摘錄

菊臞

(一)京官之辦事通病有二：曰退縮，曰瑣屑。外官之辦事通病有二：曰敷衍，曰顢頇。退縮者，同官互推，不肯任怨，動輒請旨，不肯任咎是也。瑣屑者，利析錙銖，不顧大體，察及秋毫，不見輿薪是也。敷衍者，裝頭蓋面，但計目前，剜肉補瘡，不問明日是也。顢頇者，外面完全，而中已潰爛，事實粉飾，而語無歸宿是也。有此四者，習俗相沿，但求苟安無過，不求振作，將來一有艱鉅，國家必有乏才之患。

★ ★ ★

(二)唯天下滔滔，禍亂未已。吏治人心，毫無更改；軍政戰事，日崇虛僞。非得二三君子，倡之以樸誠，導之以廉恥，則江河日下，不知所屆。默察天意人事，大局殆無挽回之理。鄙人近歲在軍，不問戰事之利鈍，但課一己之勤惰。蓋戰雖數次得利，數十次得利，曾無小補，不若自習勤勞，猶可稍求一心之安。

★ ★ ★

(三)凡事之須逐日檢點者，一日姑待，後來補救則難矣。況進德修業之事乎！

★ ★ ★

(四)每日臨睡，須默數本日勞力者幾件，勞心者幾件。

★ ★ ★

(五)凡有血氣，必有爭心。人之好勝，誰不如我，施諸己而不願，亦勿施於人，此强恕之事也。一日强恕，日日强恕；一事强恕，事事强恕：久之則漸近自然。以之修身則順而安；以之涉世則諧而祥。孔子之告子貢仲弓，孟子之言求仁，皆無先於此者。若不能勉强而聽其自至，以頑鈍之質，而希生安之效。見人之氣類與己不合，則隔膜棄置，甚或加之以不能堪，不復能勉强自抑，舍己從人，傲惰彰於身，乖戾着於外，鮮不及矣。

★ ★ ★

(六)强毅之氣，決不可無，古語曰，自勝之謂强。曰强制，曰强恕，曰强爲善，皆自勝之義也。如不慣早起，而强之未明即起。不慣莊敬，日强之立尸坐齋。不慣勞苦，而强之與士卒同甘苦。强之勤勞不倦，是即强也。不慣有恆，而强之貞恆，是即毅也。

★ ★ ★

(七)余觀自古聖賢豪傑，多由彊作而臻絕詣，淮南子曰，功可彊成，名可彊立。中庸曰，或勉强而行之，及其成功一也。近世論人者，或曰，某也向之所爲不如是，今强作如是，是不可信。沮自新之途，而長偷惰之風，莫大乎此。吾之觀人亦嘗有因此而失賢才者，追書以志吾過。

★ ★ ★

(八)心者何？一曰實心。國家澂敘官方，吏治章程，纖悉具備。特患視爲具文故事，苟可以塞上司之責，免功令之罰，便爲了事，巧於趨避競尚浮華；則雖有良法美意，都成虛設，於地方毫無補益。苟能將士習民風獄訟賦役水利盜賊諸事，凡一切令申之所垂，憲檄之所飭，民生之所繫，國計之所關，一一實心整理。如飲食衣服之切己，饑必求飽，寒必求煖，不因上台督責而粉飾，不因同列異同而依違；一民未安，一事未究，寢食不敢甯也，焦勞不敢恤也，由是才高者尋理必細，操持必堅。更無難事足以沮我，何患政之不立。雖才識稍下，而心之所至，識自開明，才自展拓，於境內必日有起色矣。二曰虛心。夫心本靈明，不虛則蔽，有欲念則不虛。好利好名皆欲念也。有成見則不虛，務嚴務寬皆成見。心既不虛，於是是非之衡不能定，情僞之隱不能燭；動則輒誤，無所適從，要皆蔽之爲患也。惟徹其所蔽，使好名好利之念，無所介於其中。不計祿位之得失，不問俗情之毀譽，則事之是非，民之情僞，自無遁形。事至而應，就事論事，不以姑息市恩，不以執泥行法，成見一空，漸歸無我，有過即改，何舍妨己從人；有善不矜，常覺彼長我短，虛則能受，虛則生明，豈獨居官之切務，實亦治心之要訣矣。

莫索里尼的生活和治事

王樹德

聞莫索里尼名字的，誰不知他是二十世紀的怪傑、『法西斯蒂』的首領，他在世界政治舞臺上眞與俄國的列寧享同樣的盛名。身兼數職，獨掌大權，『法西斯蒂』的將來，我們雖不敢預料，但自『法西斯蒂』統治了意大利以來，意國的國際地位和國內政治社會經濟，都向着蓬勃的路上邁進，這也可以說是『法西斯蒂』的一些成功；尤其是莫索里尼個人的精神和能力，很値得我們佩服，所以我把他生活的片段和治事的方法，介紹給讀者，以窺偉人的特殊。

莫索里尼有幹鍊耐勞和專心致志的精神，在他的自述中，他說：「我生活上的主要原則，即盡量應用身心的能力。世人常不能利用他們的體力智力，達到可稱爲有効率的步地。時處現代，我們要竭盡我們的能力，使底於成而後已。我深信美國心理學家惠廉姆奇末司的話，他以爲人類倘能盡量利用他們的智力與體力，他們成功的境地，往往出於常人所不及料。我做事必盡量發展我能力之所及。對於着手辦理的事情，必用全力去做；大自政府大計，小至馳馬細事，都是這樣。我的心靈往往隨我的志願而工作。如一事未畢，萬不得已而須另辦他事時，必將前事完全擱諸腦後，用全副精神辦理新着手的事。……有此種能力，心靈方能不爲他事所擾，而妨害工作的功能。」他又說：「此種克服身心的能力，無論晝夜，都跟着我，所以我的睡眠，與孩童一樣，絕無煩擾之弊，神經系統極其安靜。我深信我能在極紛擾的環境裏面，安然入睡鄉。在戰爭時，雖砲聲隆隆，我也靜睡。但若我的將領需我日夜督戰，雖僅獲薄睡數分鐘，亦不覺困頓。」在前述幾句話中，又見得他有鎮靜的態度，與堅强的體魄。

莫索里尼的生活，和一部機器似的，要牠工作，馬上可以開動。他不使他的精神鬆弛和體力倦懶。他平日晚間，七小時安睡，清晨醒來，精神體力，完全恢復，先稍事欠伸，以蘇筋骨，然後即時離床，從未於欠伸以後，再入夢鄉。他以爲既醒以後，還臥床不起，足以使人疲倦，且足以頹唐精神，爲最不良的惡習慣。

領袖人物的時間，當然比普通人寶貴！他每晨浴罷，報已送到案上，他一面整裝，一面讀報，閱讀報紙。他自謂頗有經驗，瀏覽一過，其中要聞，絕無遺漏。他每日時間的分配是：運動一小時，安眠七小時，工作自十四小時至十六小時，就餐不過數分鐘而已。他以爲此種辦法，由於經驗得來，既可使他盡量工作，又可使他身體健康。

在他自述中，他又說：「我以爲人生此世，作事宜勇往直前，決不可事事顧慮，有所畏縮。我時以此種精神，灌輸於『法西斯蒂』的黨員心中。我既爲首領，勢必以身作則。我常對他們高聲疾呼：『生活於危險之中，無所用其逃避。』……做領袖的，須能當機立斷，富有犧牲的精神；若遇危難的時候，必須鼓十分勇氣以赴之。」所以他又是一個負責任的，有決斷的，和日求進步的人。

古今中外難有完人——倘若不是絕對沒有——往往各有所長，各有所短，其爲人物的大小，即在其長短的性質程度如何爲斷。這樣說來，他們有整個的模範給我們，固所欣幸；僅有局部的模範給我們，亦大可歡迎；全在我們能去短取長，作爲修養上淬勵奮發的借鏡。像莫索里尼者，至少可以給我們局部的模範罷？

華盛頓

章景瑜

稱爲美國國父之華盛頓，以軍事家而兼政治家理財家，其豐功偉績，幾爲人所共知。考華氏並無若何超人之才能，其成功亦係時勢所造就；惟華氏一身治事方法中，有三特點，確爲其事業成功之基礎。

第一　華氏對於無論何事，皆以數字爲出發點。彼幼年卽嗜數理，於治田時曾研究每磅荷蘭翹究含草子若干粒，於彼日記中曾將故鄉各家窗牖數目一一記入。及長，精於測量，嘗爲測量官，所繪之圖，纖悉無誤。故華氏以後行軍則注重地勢之測量，理財則注意價格之漲落。總之華氏對於任何事均有精密之統計。此種科學化治事方法，使其在軍事上政治上獲得極大成功。

第二　華氏爲一實行家，彼一身工作範圍，均限於實際生活——行軍、理財、治政，彼以爲理想不具何等力量，貴在能將此理想施諸實行。方華氏爲代議士時，發言極少，但能按時出席。及被舉爲元帥爲總統，則不避巨艱，毅然自任，結果卒底於成。

第三　華氏酷愛秩序。彼幼年修身原則中有若干條皆關於團體生活應如何遵守秩序，及爲軍事領袖，則嚴格整頓軍紀。爲總統時有時竟不惜用武力以維持國家秩序。迄於彌留，且將一切家庭細事與公私文件，囑左右預爲整理。要之華氏始終爲一有秩序之人，故辦事井井有條，能負巨任。

至於華盛頓之人格，則勇敢忠實，謙和大量，十足具有領袖人物之氣度者也。

拿破崙

蔡秋琴

拿破崙起自微細，乘法國革命，以戰功顯，數載而成帝業，其兵力所及，幾遍全歐，其氣概可謂雄矣。而其用意，則殊非甘於窮兵黷武，惟以武力爲前驅，而欲置世界於大同，其規模之宏遠，爲世人所共曉。是以其功業之傳於後世者，不專在乎武功，而尤在乎文治，其所手訂之民法，法國人民至今猶視爲至寶。其主義之益於歐洲諸邦者亦至今弗衰。故略述其生平事蹟中，有關於治事方法者，以供吾人之借鏡：

（一）賞罰分明　每當拿破崙出戰時，必嚴禁官兵任意擄掠，或爲其他有損軍隊及法國名譽之事。如有違背者，則必從嚴究辦，毫不徇私，如有勇往直前，爲國效勞者，則必從優獎勵，以酬其勞，是以軍隊有紀律，軍人有死戰之心，而得稱霸全歐也。

（二）迎合民心　拿氏固一軍人也，然於心理學，亦頗有心得，故當其克服城市時，必先向民衆宣言其治政之方，及接人待物之法，並力言必以民心爲依歸，故人民心服之。孟子曰：「以力服人者，非心服也，力不贍也，以德服人者，中心悅而誠服也。」拿氏可謂得其道矣。

（三）治事有條理　當拿氏批閱案卷公文，必逐一觀看，依次而進，一卷未畢，决不另閱他卷，是以秩序井然。

（四）計劃精密處事鎭靜　拿氏規劃戰略時，細心考慮，無微不至，凡有發生危險之可能性者，必設法免除之。戰戰兢兢，惟恐有失，惟於左右部下，則鎭靜如常，全無懼態。戰略一經決定，則傾全力以求目標之到達，是以軍民威服，成其帝業。

（五）善於用人　拿氏對於部下士卒，詳悉其個性，各安置於適宜之職務，以求優良之收獲。拿氏曰「科學家與之交談則可，選之爲大臣則不可，」即此謂也。是以拿氏之部下，均得盡其能，展其長，而爲拿氏效勞。

由此可見拿氏之治事方法，有條不紊，精明過人，其能享盛名於世，非偶然也。

納爾遜

袁玄同

當法皇拿破崙（Napoleon Bonaparte）逞雄歐陸之際，於脫佛加（Trafalgar）重創法西二國聯合艦隊之英海軍名將納爾遜，其事蹟久經膾炙人口，按其治事方法固亦極合管理學之精神。

納氏年十二入海軍習業，弱冠卽顯，其擢遷迅速之原因，於機警伶俐外，待人接物之仁慈和藹，與夫外表之整齊軒昂，致博得儕輩及長官有良好印像而加以青睞，亦居其一，故知言語謙和，儀容整潔，舉止安詳，極爲重要。

納氏之天資深合領袖之條件，如頭腦清楚，舉動敏捷，富於膽量，善於指揮，長於辭令，嫻於交際等，均得自其傳略中覓見，是以北極圈遇熊，獨無驚惶失措與其伴同逃奔，而卒手斃之，於法西聯軍大舉進攻時，能完成前往挨而巴（Elba）之艱難使命，……此僅信手拈得之例，已可見其不凡，因能態度鎮靜，當機立斷以應付事變，乃信脫佛加之捷非屬倖致。

吾人知凡集團生活於秩序外，尙須有感情連繫，感情之於人羣，蓋猶機油之於機械，所以減少其各部之磨擦阻力，與所需要之動力，人與人間若有感情，則動作便利，阻礙減小，納爾遜深知個中三昧，故以親愛處其屬，至稱以「弟兄們」(Band of Brothers) 凡有設施計劃，必與其弟兄們公開商討，以是部屬於其所發命令皆極了解悅服，從未有以不知該令之意志爲言者，以是得人信仰，且樂受其指揮。

納氏以善用人稱，能役各種性情不同者使爲之效命，脫佛加之役，其號召之名句初爲：「納爾遜深信各人能盡其職責」(Nelson Confides That Every Man Will Do His Duty)其後改爲：「英吉利望各人能盡其職責。」(England Expects That Every Man Will Do His Duty) 士氣果爲之旺盛，而敵船殲焉。

世無完人，納氏自亦有所短，卽才氣不斂是，喜炫耀自負，此或爲一般才人之通病，蓋有才氣之人始爲可造人才，然才氣之爲物，易露不易藏，而涉足社會則宜藏不宜露，才氣横溢。鋒芒易見，鋒芒見則挫折自多，是以納氏釋兵柄閒居者屢，如一七九九年地中海艦隊司令愷斯 (Lord Keith) 廬米諾架島 (Minorca) 爲西法二國所攻，檄氏率兵往爲之備，納氏不以其令爲然而不從，遂被責違命而辭職，此外納氏復極易興奮，亦爲治事者所當切忌。

最後，納氏治事頗富責任之心，脫佛加之役雖於艦首指揮時受創倒地垂危，猶念念不忘軍事，彌留之際得知捷報，乃言曰：「予已滿意，謝上蒼，予已盡予職責矣。」。始瞑目云。

帳目不清

當然，賬目不清，是認爲有營私舞弊侵吞公款的嫌疑，是一種重大的案件。其實賬目不是專限於金錢方面。物品也可以有賬目，人事也可以有賬目，所以賬目也就是一種記錄。人事記錄是辦理人事，研究人事所必需的。人事記錄，種類很多，但不妨按性質的重要，來先後次第保存，人事記錄若是不完整可靠，那亦等於金錢上的賬目不清，是與整個的組織有害的。

哲隱人事管理第二號

中華國有鐵路現行行車時刻表

京滬滬杭甬綫

上行車

車次	92	32	2	62	34	94	12	222
站名	嘉滬二三等混合區間車	閘滬快車 餐	閘京聯運特快通車 餐	閘三四等慢車	閘滬快車 餐	閘嘉二三等混合區間車	閘滬特別快車 餐	新龍上南區間車
閘口開		6.40	8.30	9.00	13.25	16.30	17.25	
杭州到 開		7.01 7.10	8.47 8.55	9.25 9.35	13.45 13.55	16.46 16.55	17.42 17.50	
長安到 開		8.09 8.14	9.40 9.45	10.45 10.55	14.54 14.59	17.58 18.03	18.43 18.48	
硤石到 開		8.46 8.48	10.11 10.13	11.53 11.56	15.31 15.33	18.41 18.43	19.14 19.16	
嘉興到 開	 6.50	9.23 9.30	10.42 10.47	12.35 12.46	16.08 16.14	19.20	19.45 19.50	
松江到 開	8.09 8.14	10.40 10.46	11.45 11.50	14.12 14.22	17.24 17.29		20.52 20.57	
上海南站到	9.45	11.50	—	15.50	18.38		21.55	7.55
上海北站到 開	9.55	12.00	13.45 12.20	16.05	18.45		22.00	

上行車

車次	46	74	42	4	22	2	302	24	72	6	44
站名	滬錫三四等區間車	錫京二三等混合區間車	滬京三四等車	滬京特別快車 餐	滬京快車 餐	閘京聯運特快通車 餐	滬平聯運特快通車 餐	滬常區間特別快車 餐	滬錫二三等混合區間車	滬京夜特快車 餐臥	滬鎮三四等區間車
上海北站到 開	 0.50		 5.15	 8.00	 9.50	12.45 13.20	 16.00	 16.50	 17.55	 23.00	 24.00
蘇州到 開	2.41 2.50		8.18 8.25	9.27 9.34	11.56 12.05	14.47 14.53	17.51 17.59	18.43 18.50	20.40 20.47	0.57 1.05	1.51 1.58
無錫到 開	3.45	 6.00	9.41 9.48	10.17 10.21	13.02 13.05	15.36 15.40	18.46 18.51	19.37 19.41	22.00	1.57 2.05	2.49 2.45
常州到 開		7.09 7.19	11.40 11.48	11.01 11.06	13.57 14.03	1?.21 16.2	19.39 19.47	20.35		2.53 3.04	4.15 4.25
丹陽到 開		8.36 8.41	13.03 13.11	11.51 11.44	15.02 15.06	17.11 17.13	20.38 20.40			4.13 4.17	5.46 5.50
鎮江西站到 開		9.38 9.45	14.12 14.21	12.30 12.35	15.47 15.52	17.45 17.50	21.18 21.26			5.00 5.10	6.50
南京到		12.00	16.30	13.50	17.30	19.15	22.50			7.00	

下行車

車次	93	31	11	61	1	91	33	221
站名	嘉閘二三等混合區間車	滬閘快車 餐	滬閘特別快車 餐	滬閘三四等慢車	京閘聯運特快通車 餐	滬嘉二三等混合區間車	滬閘快車 餐	上南新龍區間車
上海北站到 開		 7.00	 8.35	 9.05	14.15 15.00	 16.30	 18.10	
上海南站開		7.05	8.40	9.15	—	16.40	18.10	14.55
松江到 開		8.11 8 16	9.36 9.41	10.43 11.00	15.56 16.01	18.04 18.11	19.18 19.23	
嘉興到 開	 6.55	9.27 9.34	10.44 10.49	12.44 12.52	16.58 17.03	19.30	20.37 20.44	
硤石到 開	7.32 7.34	10.08 10.15	11.18 11.20	13.31 13.34	17.32 17.34		21.18 21.20	
長安到 開	8.12 8.22	10.47 10.52	11.46 11.51	14.16 14.26	18.00 18.05		21.50 21.55	
杭州到 開	9.32 9.40	11.51 12.00	12.36 12.45	15.42 15.52	18.50 19.00		22.47 22.55	
閘口到	9.53	12.20	13.05	16.15	19.15		23.10	

下行車

車次	71	23	1	45	43	41	21	3	73	5	301
站名	錫滬二三等混合區間車	常滬區間快車 餐	京閘聯運特快通車 餐	錫滬三四等區間車	鎮滬三四等區間車	京滬三四等車	京滬快車 餐	京滬特別快車 餐	京錫二三等混合區間車	京滬夜特快車 餐臥	滬平聯運夜特快通車 餐臥
南京開			8.20			9.00	12.35	17.05	17.45	23.00	24.00
鎮江西站到 開			9.36 9.41		 10.00	11.15 11.21	14.19 14.24	18.20 18.25	19.59 20.10	0.49 0.57	1.40 1.48
丹陽到 開			10.18 10.20		10.56 10.59	12.19 12.24	15.04 15.08	18.59 19.01	21.07 21.10	1.45 1.48	2.33 2.35
常州到 開		 8.00	11.03 11.08		12.16 12.24	13.49 14.05	16.12 16.23	19.44 19.49	22.13 22.20	2.50 2.58	3.32 3.40
無錫到 開	 5.55	8.55 9.02	11.49 11.53	 12.25	13.35 13.40	15.18 15.38	17.20 17.30	20.30 20.34	23.20	3.52 3.58	4.32 4.38
蘇州到 開	6.55 7.02	10.06 10.15	12.36 12.42	13.41 13.50	14.51 15.00	16.49 16.55	18.35 18.45	21.17 21.22		4.55 5.00	5.34 5.41
上海北站到 開	9.45	12.30	14.15 15.00	16.30	17.20	19.55	20.50	22.50		7.00	7.40

轉載

我們的財政往何處去（轉載自鐵道公報第一四一〇期）

江英志演講

兄弟今天奉命報告，因職守關係，只好三句不離本行，將財務司主管的財政情形，向各位長官及同事報告。但兄弟來部不久，對於事體還沒有深切的研究，所報告的財政情形也許有錯漏之處，萬望各位長官及同事指正。

今天的題目便是『我們的財政往何處去?』這不消說是我們本部的財政快到山窮水盡的意思。俗語說，眞的是山窮水盡時就有柳暗花明的境界，那末，我們自然也有柳暗花明的一天，尤其是在賢明的部長次長領導之下，更不成問題會有柳暗花明的一天。

要說到我們的財政往何處去，我們必須稍爲說說我們的鐵路歷史。這怪得很，好像我們的鐵路歷史，總是苦命兒一般，始終是苦命的，我們的鐵路和外國人的鐵路拿來相比，那簡直小巫見大巫。外國動不動是十幾萬公哩，而我國只有萬多公哩。就是這萬多公哩的鐵路還是無數的血肉換來的，

中國歷史告訴我們一八四〇年的鴉片戰爭以後，接連着就是太平天國的暴動，而我們有鐵路的觀念也就在這太平天國被平定以後之一八六三年。聽說那時候有二十七位英美商人向江蘇巡撫李鴻章請願建築上海至蘇州的鐵路，但是給李鴻章拒絕了。接着一八六四年七月，英國商人有在北京玄武門外表演其木頭火車軌者，無非希望中國人相信他的那種把戲而覺悟到非即刻建築鐵路不可。可是，這種把戲，又給當局所禁止，并不發生任何新的刺激。同年，又有位名叫做 Sir Macdonald Stephenson從印度來中國。鼓其如簧之舌，說其在印度之經歷，希望其所預定之大鐵路計劃，如(一)漢口東至上海；(二)鎭

江北至北平；(三)上海至甯波；(四)漢口至四川雲南及緬甸；(五)蘇州至內地等的鐵路計劃會被當時我們的政府採取的。可是不幸得很，這一番苦口婆心恰恰收得相反的結果。

外國人自從那兩個把戲失敗以後，他們從一八七二年開始，便以個人資格向中國私人在虹口到吳淞一帶收買地皮，等到地皮買到相當程度時，那是一八七六年，淞滬鐵路居然出現了，那時的火車頭只是一噸左右重的，鐵軌也只是二十六磅的，自然是個 Bady Train。這事一發生。上海道台呈報江蘇巡撫李鴻章將此事鬧到總理衙門裏，而且中外兩造還爭執得非常利害。最後是由英國大臣Sir Thomas Wade 和李鴻章作這樣的解決：中國提出二十八萬五千兩在一年內分三期攤還英國人，贖回這條鐵路，翌年即是一八七七年，當最後一期款付清，這第一條鐵路便被拆掉了。這便是中國鐵路第一次閃現和第一次的夭亡。

一八七八年李鴻章發起的開平煤礦公司成立了，以運煤的關係，公司工程師 R. R. Burnett 建築一鐵路由礦坑通至北塘，李鴻章並沒有反對，馬上接受工程司的建議，且馬上就鳩工起來。一八八〇年這一條鐵路由唐山展築至胥各莊，接着，又展築至蘆台，而至天津關外展築至瀋陽，成爲今日的北甯路。

各位長官，各位同事，這兒，也許會懷疑李鴻章何以一下會變成兩個不同的人呢？這點，我想所謂『需要便是發明之母，』這一句話可以說明了。他前此之所以反對，是因爲沒有看到『需要，』後此之所以贊成者，却是看到了『需要。』何況李鴻章在當時總算是民族意識相當濃厚的人，且已經看懂了外國人是利用鐵路做工具來侵掠中國！對鐵路覺醒了的李鴻章無形中得了個張之洞做同伴。張不像李只認定鐵路與國防有關係，他說漢口應築條鐵路通北京，蓋漢口是中國之中心，有許多貨物均可靠這條鐵路運輸到各方面去交換，而使內地農村經濟均活躍起來。於是平漢路便在一八八九年開始工作着，李鴻章與張之洞在這十九世紀八、九十年來的中國總算是鐵路方面的雙柱了。這一個時期可說是我們鐵路的啓明時期。這一個啓明時期到了一八九〇年的中日戰爭以後，特別是俄國仗義立言，强迫日本退還遼東半島以後，各種鐵路計劃，及各鐵路之興工等等才像雨後春筍，一齊出現來了。

膠濟、株萍、道清、廣韶、滇越、廣三、正太、隴海、潮汕、平綏、彰廈、新甯、廣九、南潯、浦津、京滬、滬杭甬等等都是這個時期逼出來的，可是這十幾條路綫不久又遭遇八國聯軍的事體而擱置着，幾乎都是一九〇四年拳匪亂後才繼續完成的。這許多鉄路共長有一萬多公哩。我們就大胆說這一萬多公哩的鉄路就是中國近代文明的撑持者罷！

一萬多公哩鉄路中，只有八百七十七公哩的平綏路算是完全中國資本，中國人力及中國設計出來的。其餘都是向外國借款築成的。中國自然想按照平綏路的過程來建築所有鉄路的，無奈這十九世紀末葉的中國特別是國難多端，中國無論怎樣想均難得如願。借款築路是開端于一八九六年，那是向法俄比三國借款築廣西龍州路，東三省中東路，及貫通河北河南與湖北的平漢路。歷史翻進到廿世紀的第一頁，中國更是傷心慘目了。義和團的幾聲符咒，竟把中國淪於次殖民地了。一萬多公哩的鐵路是外國人十萬萬以上的借款換來的。日本有兩萬萬五千幾萬，英國有兩萬萬三千多萬，比國有一萬萬八千餘萬，德國有一萬萬五千餘萬，荷蘭有一萬萬零六百多萬，美國有六百五十幾萬，法國有兩百八十幾萬。這十幾萬萬的外債眞是吸血鬼，把我們整個鉄道部，乃至於四萬萬同胞的血，吸得面黃肌痩，氣息奄奄。各位長官，各位同事，像這樣鐵路歷史還不是苦

命的歷史嗎？

假定十幾萬萬借款利息都是年利五厘吧，那一年的總利息便在五六千萬以上。再加上合同規定還本的話，那就將一年的收入整個交把外國人亦恐不夠了。現根據我們財務司所有的材料看來，各位長官及各位同事總會天大的驚奇起來。好罷，兄弟姑且勉爲其難地將過去一年中國有鉄路的收支情形說說：

國有各路過去一年中全部收入，除廣九路以報告未全未行計入外，綜計約爲國幣一萬六千六百二十餘萬元，軍運約佔百分之七，計一千一百九十萬餘元，實際現金收入計共一萬五千四百三十餘萬元。

營業用款連同歲計帳盈虧撥補帳所列用款全部合計約需一萬五千〇九十四萬餘元，比照現金收入僅餘三百三十餘萬元，而軍事協餉即需四百八十萬元，其他償還已整理之債款本息及指定某項收入償付借款本息共達二千五百萬元以上，均屬額外擔負。其情形之竭蹶，可想而知。所幸各路政府長期資金應付五厘利息不必支付現款，而各路應付債款本息亦多愆期未付，收支尙可勉相適合。但關於資本支出則毫無的款，補充、改良，均屬無從着手。這幾句話分明表示我們的鉄路是完全靠賴債

之一途而存在了。

我們爲明瞭實際情形起見，不厭瑣煩，再將各路段情形摘要說說：

平漢路　該路全年收入據報告共達三千三百七十萬元，軍運約佔六分之一，計六百二十餘萬元。現金收入凡三千另另五十萬元，除用款外，計可餘現金五百萬元，爲財政狀況較佳之路。但因以前積欠債款整理之後，每年約需付出本息約六百三十餘萬元，担負太重，潼西借款本息，及協助湘鄂整理款項一百二十萬元，軍事協餉一百二十萬元，故仍不敷。

津浦路　全年收入凡二千五百八十萬元。軍運約佔百分之六，計一百三十五萬元。現金收入計二千四百四十餘萬元。用款乃達二千四百一十餘萬元，故所餘僅約三十萬。軍事協餉須付八十四萬元，已整理之債款，應付本息約需三百八十萬元，亦是不敷。

北甯路　全年收入約共二千四百萬元，軍運記帳八十餘萬元。現金收入可達二千三百餘萬元，除用款二千萬元外，尚約餘二百七十餘萬元，比較情形亦尚良好，惟該路額外負担，如軍事協餉卽須一百八十萬元，如攤還滬楓借款，雙軌借款餘額，太潼潼西借款，開灤完成粵漢借款，此外尚須担負戰區經費，總計七百四十餘萬元，亦是不敷。

京滬滬杭甬路　兩路全年收入共計二千一百二十餘萬元。軍運約五十四萬餘元。用款約二千萬元。從表面觀察尚有盈餘約計六十萬元，惟按月各該路應提準備金，備付積欠債款本息約計二百六十萬元，又須支付兩路資本支出及劃分餘利。亦是不敷。

膠濟路　全年收入計一千五百三十萬餘元。軍運甚少僅五萬元。用款約需一千三百二十餘萬；可盈餘約二百萬元。但每年應提贖路準備金二百四十萬元，備付資本支出約一百萬元。亦是不敷。

隴海路　該路連汴洛潼西兩段全年收入共約一千四百二十餘萬元。軍運一百萬餘元。實際收入僅一千三百十餘萬元，而用款乃至二千餘萬元。亦是不敷。

平綏路　該路全年收入約爲一千一百餘萬元，軍運五十六萬元，用款需九百餘萬元，結餘僅約二百萬元，而該路復興計劃以外之資本支出，卽須四百餘萬元，應付已整理之債款約需一百九十餘萬元。軍事協餉六十萬元。亦是不敷。

正太路　全年收入約六百七十餘萬元，軍運約四十萬元，用款約三百五十餘萬元。約可剩餘二百七十餘萬元。比較成績最屬良好，惟該路代還太潼潼西借款本息及巴黎電機廠料款本息，年達二百六十餘萬元，故實際亦感困難。

其他如廣韶、湘鄂、道淸諸路，更毋庸詳細贅述，同仁均已知其狀況之匪佳。

這幾條路告訴我們一些什麼印像呢？是『也是不敷。』大有大的不敷，中有中的不敷，小有小的不敷。……不敷從什麼地方來彌補？便是賴債。像這樣的情形還能維持得久嗎？好比病入了膏肓的人，專門靠興奮劑，可以延年益壽麽？債是賴不了的。尤其是外國人的債，更是賴不了的。他們會用外交，外交用不了時，便會用强權。若長此賴債，兄弟相信他們必始則曰：中國人無信用，次則曰無組織，最後則必曰非他們來經營不可。這樣一來，豈不是加添了我們的恥辱？……

鉄路的財政情形，既然壞到這步田地，我們以後往何處去呢？自然開源節流是唯一有效的方法，我們要推廣營業，我們要發展鉄路沿線的產業，我們要以鐵路爲推進國民經濟的原動力，這一方面是鉄路自救之策，同時也是救國的工作，再其次我們便不能不談到用款的節約了，根據上面的報告，國有各路的營業率，實在太不像樣了，財政上的情形，關於運用靈活，固然是一個緊要的關鍵，但這是也靠各方面努力的，倘使管理事項，都往浪費的路上走，根本上便無所謂盈餘，也就談不到調度整理，每天的工作，不過救窮而已，救窮的結果，便是債務增加，愈陷愈深，推廣營業，是無濟於事的，這不是趨絕路嗎？所以節約運動，是一項極關重要的工作，我們必須採用經濟原則，用極少的資金，得最大的效果。先決問題解決了，我們擁有餘力，進行改良補充的工作，便可同時整理債務，免去賴債的恥辱。

各位同事……部次長常常告訴我們，過去種種，譬如昨日死，今後種種亟須迎頭趕上，那末，我們希望賴債的過去，會從此死去。接着，我們須從整債方面重生過來。要整債必須要一切工作均從……部次長所招示的康莊——那是營業化和社會化，邁步走去。必須社會化，人民才曉得鉄路是與他們有切身的關係，急起而効力於鉄路事業。必需營業化，往後的財政始能裕如，財政一裕如，我們便有把握來整理債款。部次長雖只給了我們一個理財方案，然而我們可在這種方案中找出我們的手段來。兄弟年紀還輕，若能說得上有認識的話，那我想想部次長所指示的方案之下可以產生如此的邏輯；本部之與各路局自應是銀行總行之與各分支行一樣。本部果能統制各路的財政，取得盈虛相劑，各路收入解部，各路支出由部照核定預算數撥發，各路的盈虧，就是本部的盈虧，各路爲增加業務擴充設備時，如財力不敷，本部得儘量補助，一方面我們還要嚴格管理各路的預決算。這樣一來，各路的財政，可以調撥靈活，在消極方面，各路的支出無形中可以減少。在積極方面，各路必要增進業務的設備，就不致因爲本路財力不足而躭置，收入自然也可以逐漸增加。另一方面，我們可以用各路全部的財力，統籌支配，來整理債務，兄弟相信，上述鉅額的債務也有辦法了，前途自是光明。所謂柳暗花明者不就是很容易實現出來了麼？完了。

雜誌論文索引暫行分類方法

管　　理

A. 管理總論

A1. 管理理論　A2. 管理教育　A3. 其他

B. 工商管理

B1. 工商組織　B2. 計劃與行政　B3. 生產管理

B4. 物料管理　B5. 推銷與市場　B6. 人事管理

B7. 其他

C. 鐵道管理(附公用事業管理)

C1. 概論　C2. 鐵道組織　C3. 工程與機械

C4. 鉄道材料管理　C5. 鐵路業務　C6. 行車管理

C7. 鐵路會計與統計　C8. 鐵路人事問題　C9. 其他

D. 公務管理

D1. 概論　D2. 中央及地方政府　D3. 人事管理

D4. 物料管理　D5. 法制　D6. 其他

E. 財務管理

E1. 概論　E2. 豫算　E3. 會計與統計

E4. 金融管理　E5. 其他

分 類 索 引

索引類別	題　　目	著　者	雜誌名稱	發行年月	號數
A類					
A 3：	人類天性與人事管理	張天福	人事管理	25—1	6
B類					
B 2：	確定最低勞工工資的商榷	逸	工商管理月刊	25—2	3：2
B 3：	工場設備生產能力之勘測	張心雄	會計雜誌	,,	7：2
B 5：	進貨問題	何昇餘	工商管理月刊	25—1	3：1
	市場研究	何昇餘	,,	25—2	3：2
B 6：	商店售貨員之人事管理	何清儒	,,	25—1	3：1
	工人之測驗	屠哲隱	,,	,,	,,
	合作行政主管人員之使命	姜炳麟	中國實業	,,	2：1
	一張關于人事管理之普通方法	乙 般	商專季刊	,,	9
	小賣商店之人事對策	井上員藏	,,	,,	,,
	面談與評量	屠哲隱	人事管理	25—1,2	5—6
	怎樣訓練學徒	朱通舟	,,	25—1	5
	防止『揩油』	曹昂千	,,	,,	,,
	歐美工廠的人事管理	顧炳元	,,	,,	,,
	人與事之適應	徐春霖	,,	,,	,,
	人事管理問題	何清儒	,,	,,	,,
	商店職員之聘用與訓練	劉仲廉	商業月報	25—2	16：2
B 7：	工場管理	曹亦民	工商管理月刊	25—1	5
	蘇俄管理國內貿易概說		國際貿易導報	25—2	8：2
	不景氣中職業界青年應有之覺悟	愼微之	商業月報	25—1	16：1
	談工業心理學	鄭丕留	人事管理	,,	5
C類					
C 1：	首都鐵路之回顧與前瞻	李鍾魯	鐵路雜誌	25—1	1：8

	玉南段通車後有關國計民生之效用		浙贛鐵路月刊	25—1	2:8
C 3:	二十五年來廣九鐵路機車運用上之經濟研究	羅廣垣	鐵路雜誌	,,	1:8
C 5:	經濟蕭條期之美國鐵路貨運與復興運動	朱翰譜	,,	,,	,,
	遞遠遞減制與裝卸費	李起濤	,,	,,	,,
	鐵路之副業—擴充鐵路苗圃間接增進農產品運量	勞 勉	,,	,,	,,
C 8:	購料委員會同人應有之修養	曾養甫	,,	,,	,,
C 9:	創設國有鐵路總印刷廠芻議	王學海	,,	,,	,,
	中國鐵路利用外資問題的研究		東方雜誌	,,	33:2
	我國鐵路與公路平行線問題	俞棪	交通雜誌	25—2	4:1,2
	船舶管理		航業月刊	25—1	3:9

D類

D1:	論法令如毛	陳之邁	獨立評論	25—1	186
	論政治貪污	,,	,,	,,	184
	菲希特之政治思想	浦薛鳳	社會科學	,,	1:2
D2:	北伐以來中央政治制度變遷略史		時事月報	25—2	14:2
	中國地方政府之特質與中央政府之控制權	沈乃正	社會科學	25—1	1:2
	中央政務宜全局整頓	大公報	國聞週報	,,	13:4
D3:	人力合理化	陶孟和	,,	,,	13:1
	公務員懲戒機關	陳之邁	獨立評論	,,	1:2
D6:	美國舊政與新政改革	希爾斯特	時事類編	25—2	4:4
	新恣態的行政院	參 也	獨立評論	25—1	184

E類

E3:	審計之趨勢	錢素君	會計雜誌	25—1	7:1
	查帳開始前後之注意事項	陸善熾	,,	,,	,,
	和解及破產會計概要	潘序倫	,,	25—1,2	,,
	統一公路會計制度之數大問題	夏鄭鳴	交通雜誌	25—2	4:1,2
	幣值變動與會計	顧 準	會計雜誌	,,	7:2

	合作膳堂之會計制度		會計雜誌	25—2	7:2
	會計上之法與人	余肇池	社會科學	25—1	1:2
	去年全國失業人數		銀行週報	,,	20:1
	杭州市金融統計		浙江商務	,,	1:1
	準備與基金	潘誌甲	會計雜誌	25—2	7:2
E 4:	管理的貨幣制度與計劃的銀行制度芻議	陳長蘅	時事月報	25—1	14:1
	財政部幣制改革後之經過及今後急待解決之問題	何廉	,,	,,	,,
	我國銀行制度中之幾個問題	蔡可達	社會科學	,,	1:2
	一年來全國經濟統制之情況及其効果	葉樂羣	復興月刊	25—1,2,3	4:5,6,7
	銀行人事管理與防弊問題	胡明理	工商管理月刊	25—2	3:2
	整理舊債與發行新債	受百	商業月報	,,	16:2
	穩定外匯問題	譚秉文	,,	,,	,,
	安定銀潮之我見	直夫	商職月刊	,,	1:6
	新貨幣制度的檢討	古天戈	淮海	,,	9

編後語

編者

經過短時期的籌備和同人等的努力，在交通大學開四十週紀念慶祝會的那天，我們的小孩——管理二月刊創刊號——終于哇的一聲產生出來了。他將來是强勁肥白的呢，抑是瘦削枯黃的呢，我們此刻還不敢逆料——當然，我們是希望前者的；我們以爲這不單是我們幾個編輯者的能力和責任，而同時最要緊的，却是靠着喜歡研討管理科學的讀者們會一天天地增加起來，會時時在可能範圍內給我們以共同的提攜與培養。這樣，唯其這樣，他纔能毫無阻礙而且很有價值地立足于現社會之中，不斷地發育着，滋長着。

就本期的質量方面上說，我們自信還沒有很好的成就；可是只要牠有一點兒可取之處，只要牠能夠引起一般的國人對于管理科學漸漸地有着深切的了解和注意，那我們就覺得很安慰，而且也很以爲牠的生命就有存在的必要了。

本刊的封面是承葉遐厂先生親筆賜題的，我們覺得很榮幸，並且很感激。

在這一期里，本校教員投稿的有鍾偉成，林疊，汪仲良，李炳華，沈奏廷，王炳南和張宗謙諸先生，學生投稿的有周世正，方善桂，任家誠，王樹德，章景瑜，蔡秋琴和裘玄同諸君，我們很感謝他們的熱忱；而尤其是對外界投稿的衞挺生，葉子剛，熊大惠三位先生，我們更應當表示特殊的感謝。

還有，蔣士麒先生的「管理與會計」，和許靖先生的「美國鐵路管理起運貨棧之報告及統計」，都因爲時間上趕排不及，只好留在下期披露了，這是應該向這二位先生抱歉的。

本刊旣是管理學院的喉舌，所以除了研究管理學術的目的而外，還負有媾通校友消息的使命。從下期起，我們打算添設「畢業同學消息」一欄，專載畢業同學最近服務的狀況。我們曉得畢業校友大都老遠地分播在全中國的，我們只有希冀他們每個人都能讀着這「管理」的刊物，迅速地報告他自己及他所熟悉的校友的一切。

當然，畢業校友能夠根據着獨到的服務經驗，趕早的投寄些稿件來，那是我們最歡迎的。

本院教員著作一覽表

行政學大綱	林　叠著
中國政府（英文）	林　叠著
法律大綱（英文）	林　叠著
研究科學之方法（英文）	林　叠著
鐵路經濟論文集	沈奏廷著
鐵路貨運業務	沈奏廷著
鐵路運價之理論與實際	沈奏廷著
鐵道經濟論叢	鍾偉成編
鐵道材料管理	鍾偉成著
公路運輸	王炳南 熊大惠合著
運輸學水道編	熊大惠著
東北鐵路問題之研究	王同文著

本刊投稿簡章

一、投稿以有關於管理者為限。

二、投稿不拘文言白話，須繕寫清楚，並加標點，如係外國文稿件，並請打印之，均不得於一紙兩面寫字。

三、論著稿中，如有譯名或引文，須分別註明原文及出處。

四、譯稿須將原文題目，原著者姓名，出版日期及地點，詳細載明，如能附寄原文尤佳。

五、稿末請簽名蓋章，並註明住址。

六、來稿文字，本院有酌量修改之權，如投稿人不願有何增刪，則應於投稿時聲明。

七、來稿登載與否，概不寄還，惟附寄郵票預先聲請寄還者，亦可照辦。

八、來稿一經登載，當酌贈以每千字一元至三元之薄酬。

九、來稿請寄上海徐家匯交通大學管理學院。

中華民國二十五年四月出版

第一卷第一期

每本大洋四角
全年五期大洋一元六角

主編者 鍾偉成

發行者 交通大學管理學院

印刷者 華豐印刷鑄字所 上海浙江路五三六號

本刊廣告價目表

等級	地位	全頁價目	半頁價目
甲	底封面外頁	伍拾元	
乙	底面裏頁及封面裏頁	三十五元	二十元
丙	封面裏頁底面裏頁之對面	二十五元	十五元
丁	普通	二十元	十二元

一、乙丙丁四分之一頁按照半頁價目六折計算
二、廣告概用白紙黑字如用彩印紙色價目另議
三、廣告如用銅鋅版由本刊代辦照收製版費
四、連登多期價目從廉請逕函本校出版處經理組接洽

二月刊

第一卷 第二期 二十五年七月

本期要目

交通大學管理學院出版

編者導言

本刊出版，甫及一期，猥荷各方重視，紛紛訂閱，尤以路界方面爲最。足徵社會上對於管理學術之需要。此本刊同人所引爲自慰，而更以自勉者也。

本刊規定，年出五期，分四月份，七月份，九月份，十一月份，與二月份。本期應爲七月份，茲因稿件已足，故提前於六月出版，以供本校本屆畢業典禮時來賓之流覽。

本期文稿，極爲擁擠。限於篇幅，祇得就時間之先後，留出若干篇，以待下期披露，計有俞希稷先生之「管理上的法律問題，」錢素君先生之「會計與企業管理」，曹麗順先生之「各種運輸事業之聯系，」黃宗瑜先生之「新路建設之經濟觀（續），」王烈望先生之「事權之分離及其聯整，」王同文先生之「平時之軍運組織適於戰時需要，」以及黃恭儀先生之「參觀電動統計機後」等。此外葉子剛先生之「鐵路統計分析與管理」一篇，來文極長，亦因篇幅關係，僅先載其一部。以上各節，編者應向作者與讀者抱歉者也。又書報索引，及畢業同學通訊兩欄，亦以同樣原因暫缺。

科學管理之實施於政治，各國試行，已著成績；學者專究，不乏其人。而在吾國，則「公務管理」一名詞，似猶未爲國人所注意。比者，蔣院長召集十省行政

管理二月刊

第一卷 第一期 民國二十五年四月

管理二月刊

第一卷 第二期 民國二十五年七月

書評

古今領袖人物言行札記

論 著

讀蔣院長在十省行政會議席上訓詞之感想（D 1.）

林 叠

此次行政院召集十省高級行政長官，舉行行政會議（時在本年五月十一日至十六日），濟濟一堂，堪稱盛舉，到會長官，各將地方行政情形，以及個人之閱歷經驗，儘量貢獻於大會，藉以檢討地方行政之實況，俾資興革利弊，促進效能，此不特十省政治，從之而益見改善，加速推進，且可助進整個政治之發展，誠政治上之一大轉機，細讀蔣院長之訓詞（發載上海申報之五月十七日及十八日兩期），而益足置信焉。

蔣院長在行政會議席上訓詞，所啓示諸端，寓有充份之行政學理，恰當於現在社會之需要，其對於任用人員，則主嚴格考驗，綜覈名實，對於行政措施，則主通力合作，密切連繫。對於財務行政，則主節約踏實，善用人力，對於教育事項，則主政教合一，相助爲理，於所謂教民，養民，衛民，三大綱領，擇要加以訓示之外，尤置重於管理與統制之施行。其所謂管理，係在於執行法紀，納民軌物，統制則爲管理最終之目的，而在於對人，對地，對事，對物，統籌監督，斟酌損益，爲調劑其關係，支配其功能，使得發揮其最高之效用，此乃就工作綱領上扼要言之。其次對於各地行政人員今後所應努力之途徑與方法，若經濟建設，組織民衆。厲行保甲，綏靖地方，整理土地，修路造林，興修水利，處理犯人，促進衛生，改良教育等等，言之尤爲詳盡，誠屬至理名言，切中時要。吾國有此偉大之政治領袖，指導在上，各地方行政長官，果能遵照所有訓示各點，身體力行，埋頭苦幹，則所謂「現代政治」，何難確立，「現代國家之建設」，亦何難完成之。

吾人細讀蔣院長之訓詞，於深佩其政治眼光之卓絕，立論之偉大外，尙覺猶有進者：

（1）行政制度。在政治進行上，甚關緊要，蓋有良善之政制，便有嚴密之組織，有嚴密之組織，則政事之措施，當有條理而易收效，吾國改元迄今，一切尙在艱難創造之中，在行政制度上，難免有未臻完善之處，外人竟因此而譏誚吾國爲無組織之國家，爲散漫頹廢之民族，欲免除此種譏誚，趕上現代政治，對於政制，應力求完善，以適合各地方之情形，俾得運用靈活，措施得當，關於行政制度與組織問題，中西各行政學理書籍，已有詳細敘述，各地行政人員，尙望參考及之。

（2）欲使所有行政，獲得最高之效率，視於管理與統制之運用如何。如果運用得當，則不難做到「人盡其才，地盡其利，物盡其用，貨暢其流」。輓近歐美各國，盛倡統制之說，各大學多有管理學科之設立，以製造此項專門人才，各地亦或有會社之組織，以資研究管理與統制之運用，返觀吾國之大學，其有設立管理一類之學科，供學生之研究探討者尚少，如上海交通大學設有管理學院，僅有四科，卽公務管理，財政管理，實業管理，及鐵道管理，此項設備，在吾國誠屬創舉，可謂應時代之要求，以訓練人才，備國家之用。管理學科，在行政效率上，既有上述之關係，吾人自應深切注意，力事提倡，俾得多所訓練造就，以收政教合壹，相助爲理之效。至於各都市地方，亦應有組成管理研究學會一類之社團，備公務人員於公餘之暇，前往研究探討，互相觀摩，增進其對於管理統制之實際知識，以利政事之推行。

(3)吾國行政機關，素來對於形式上，較爲重視，就公文一事，已可概見之。凡行一公文，必拘於上行平行下行之格式，設有一事件發生，由最上級遞呈至最下級，或由最上級輾轉令飭至最下級，經過數個機關之承接，則該公文中之「等因奉此」，「等情據此」，一類之承接套語，觸目多是，占去不少篇幅，此種套語，於事件之實體，未見有若何之關係，而參雜太多，殊碍閱讀繕寫，甚或使所言事件之眞情眞意，反不能顯著，此種公文格式，實屬過於呆板累贅。至於公文之收發處理，往往須經過數層之手續，遲滯延擱，在所不免，或因手續之繁多重叠。以致廢時失事者。亦爲常有之事。是以對於公文程式及公文收發處理手續，吾人認爲應設法改善，力求迅速簡單，以利公務，蓋呆板累贅，繁多重叠，均有影響於行政效率之增進也。

（4）物料管理，亦爲行政上之一要務，蓋管理不得其宜，不特虛糜公帑；暴殄天物，且足以啓貪汚侵佔之風，影響政事之進行，故歐美各國對於物料管理制度，均甚重視，此項制度，概言之則爲品物之購置，須有精密之計算，物品之領用，須有完善之手續，品物之保藏與修理，須有適當之處置，以期錢無虛費，物無虛用，杜絕舞弊，保存公款，盡經濟之效能，助政事之進展。吾國値茲財政拮据，百端待舉之秋，對於經費；固應力求樽節，尤要在對於用款，力求其最高效用，務使一文錢得收十文錢之用，從辛勤刻苦，節約踏實之中，圖謀各種建設之完成，政務之推進，是則對於物料管理方面，誠不可忽視也。

以前所陳四點，係吾人於讀蔣院長訓詞之後，有所感觸，濡筆寫此，以就正於各地行政長官，深望於此次會議之後，各遵奉蔣院長所訓示各點，以及大會所決議之重要方案，本快幹硬幹實幹之精神，以身作則，切實力行，務期從今以後，吏治臻於修明，庶政趨於畢舉，復興國家，以慰四萬萬人之喁望。

非常時期的管理經濟（E 1.）

馬寅初

一 何謂非常時期

非常時期亦即所謂緊急時期（Emergency）第一爲準備時期，第二爲戰爭時期，第三爲整理時期，非常時期包括此三個時期，總稱之爲非常時期。故非常時期較戰時經濟之範圍爲廣，現在雖未到戰爭時期，但已到準備時期，故現在已踏入非常時期之階段。

二 何謂非常時期之經濟

非常時期之經濟原則與平時不同。平時之經濟原則甚多，舉其大者有二：一曰自由競爭，二曰價格制度，平時之經濟活動，受此二種原則之支配。例如南京城內之電影院，營業興旺，獲利甚厚，新設者接踵而起，互相競爭，政府不能阻止之。一至非常時期，社會資金應集中於國防一點，以戰勝爲目的，不應再供建築戲院之用。政府應出而阻止。務使此項資金，用以購買國防公債。於是自由競爭之作用失矣。平時財貨之分配，以價格爲之主宰。能給價者得之，不能給價者不得也。例如米賣十元一石，能出十元者得米一石、不能出十元者不得也。但一至戰時，米價必漲，如漲至五十元一石，則必有一大部份人民不能得米，是致亂之道也。前方未敗而後方先亂，非自取滅亡而何？故政府必將出而統制糧食。定糧食之最高價甚至定量分配，富者不能多購，貧者亦可得食，例如歐戰時，德國麵包由政府分配，每人發給麵包券若干張，憑券取物，其他類是。於是價格制度之作用失矣。上述二者卽爲非常時期經濟與平時經濟根本不同之點。

三　中國不能採用歐美在歐戰時所用之統制方法

現在旣已踏入非常時期之第一階段——準備時期，平時之經濟原則，雖不能立卽廢止，然一旦戰事爆發。必代之以政府之管理經濟，然則如何管理？此爲今日亟待解決之問題，目前關於戰時經濟之書籍，坊間已出有多種。然皆爲介紹外國學說或歐戰時參戰諸國之經驗，以之作爲參考則可，採用其法則不可也。蓋當時歐美各國所用之統制方法，於我有適用者有不適用者，請言其故。

第一，歐美諸國工業已發達至最高階段，生產集中於幾百個託辣斯之手。此種大公司在平時製造普通用品，一至戰時，普通用品銷路驟減。非改造軍需品不可。例如牽引機廠之改造坦克車，橡膠廠之改造防毒面具，曹達廠之改造毒瓦斯，傢具公司之改造子彈箱等等。政府爲軍需品之大顧主，故各工廠情願受政府之統制。第二，戰事之期限不可預料，若戰事於短時期爲停止，則大量產生之軍需品將賣與何人？倘受政府統制，企業合理的利益，有政府爲之保障，虧損有政府爲之賠償，便可大胆進行。故各大工業一至戰時，無不願受政府統制。第三，戰時運輸機關已爲政府管理，工業上之運輸，受政府之支配，政府許其運則運，不許卽不能運。運輸爲工業之血脈，血脈已受政府支配，何如將整個企業請政府統制之爲愈也。請政府統制，企業利益有保障，否則血脈一斷，生命絕矣，第四，大工業國家，生產旣集中於幾百個託辣斯，政府祇須抓住此幾百個託辣斯，卽可以統制全國生產。第五，全國生產有統盤之籌劃，與管理，生產效率可以增加。因此諸種原因，大工業國家實行戰事統制，較爲易辦。中國爲農業國家、若謂歐美所用之統制方法，亦可移植於中國，實屬大謬。第一，在大工業國家。工廠改造軍用品，必須靠政府收買，否則卽無銷路。若在農業國家。米麥等農產，爲軍需品並爲普通品，非必須賣與政府，而今年賣不出，待至明年亦可，不必靠政府之收買。第二，在大工業國家，一至戰時，全國之運輸機關，受政府之支配，各種工業上之運輸，不能不聽從政府之命令。至若中國農產品之運輸，有一大部份仍靠人力獸力之挑馱，以及竹筏民船之載運，走鐵路者，不過爲一小部份，走汽車路者爲數更少。政府雖把持鐵路與汽車路，但不能禁止人民之挑馱與水運。第三，至戰時，工廠必須改造，軍需品才有銷路，農產品無論在戰時或平時均有銷路，不必依賴政府也。第四，在大工業國家生產集中於幾百個大公司之手，易於統制。農業經營單位甚小，中國爲小農經營，幾乎每一個農民，成一單位，單位愈多，統制愈難。第五，工業一經統制，可以加速生產，農業則不能，以其播種收穫。均有定時故也。是以農業國家之戰時經濟，甚難統制，歐美之方法。决不能適用也。

四 戰時經濟之重心爲接濟問題

中國既不能採用歐美之戰時統制方法，然則將如何？準備之聲，聽之熟矣。然則如何準備？戰時經濟，是否僅憑準備所能解决？所謂準備者，無非爲屯積糧食軍火，建築防禦工程等項，但屯積糧食軍火祇能供短時期之需，倘戰事延長，斷賴接濟，况今日之軍備，日新月異，在今年爲最新式之軍器，至明年或有更新者出，則今年之軍器卽不能與明年新出者敵，近聞西方發明以無線電駕御軍艦之法，此法果成，日本現在所有之海軍，已非其敵手矣。故與其現在以鉅資屯積武器，不如留鉅資以備將來購買或製造最新式之武器。如現在已將所有資本變成武器，則將來有更新者出，其將何以得之？故現在祇須有相當之準備，足供一年半載之用，當可暫時應付事變，往後則全在乎接濟。接濟之法，最好爲自己生產，其次當取給於外國。就目前中國之情形而論，大規模之準備，—自己生產；已爲時間所不許，故以後所需之武器，惟有取給於外國，但戰事一起，沿海各大口岸必被封鎖，如何能得外國之接濟？問題之中心，卽在於此，此爲軍事問題，諒軍事當局已注意及之也。

五 戰時財政與物價統制

以上所論爲應戰方面之問題、同時吾人對於戰時之社會經濟問題，亦須有應付之辦法，余在報上曾發表談話，極端反對貨膨脹，誠恐物價高漲，而人民之所得未增，生計堪虞，易啓亂端，一至戰時，即使未採通貨膨脹政策，物價亦將飛漲，政府爲保障人民生活，維持社會秩序，制止之不暇，安可再爲火上加油之計？以糧食爲例，一至戰時，其價必漲，因（一）糧食進口驟減，（二）運輸機關盡歸軍用，糧食之運輸受影響，（三）有米者私藏不出（四）政府大批購買，以充軍食，（五）市儈奸商，屯積居奇，（六）耕田淪爲戰場，（七）農人宰牛爲食，生產因以減少，（八）農產富庶之區或被敵人佔領，或受敵威脅，凡此種種原因，皆可以使米價騰貴，其他物品，亦復類是，第一。由於政府消費之大量增加，第二，物價既貴，邊際生產以下之土地與工廠，均將墾植開工。生產成本因以提高，物價祇能上漲，不能下降，第三，戰時危險甚大，保險費增加，銀行不敢放款，金融緊急，利息增加，鐵路輪船汽車，忙於軍用，運費亦將增加，於是生產成本愈重，物價豈能不漲？倘再膨脹通貨，眞不啻火上添油，物價高漲之結果爲資本家獲暴利；勞動者則工資未增而實物所得反減去大半，生活無法維持，其他貧民更不得了，倘亂民乘機煽動，變起肘下，豈非大患？戰時資本家之暴利，爲不可避免之事，在歐戰時，歐洲各國雖徵收暴利所得稅（Excessive profit tax），但發財者仍復不少，此點亦應早爲之計，以免貧富階級之尖銳化，否則將有不測之危險，故余極端反對通貨膨脹，一則恐物價騰貴，貧民無以爲生，不免挺而走險，二則物價飛漲，造成暴富，階級仇恨愈深，內部容易發生變亂，三則通貨一經膨脹，無法制止，卒至愈發愈多，一若德之馬克，俄之盧布，結果鈔票一錢不値，人民儲蓄，如數冲銷，戰後欲圖復興，活動資本已不可得，清初之揚州，太平天國時之南京，自經軍事破壞以後，亘數百年而不能恢復元氣，可爲殷鑑，如有資本，當可徐圖復興。紙幣濫發之結果，必使活動資本完全消滅，復興永無望矣。若向外國借款，則美國已上德國之當，（德國於戰後向美借款以圖復興，結果則爲賴債，）於我未必有特殊之信用也。環顧各方舉借外債，實未容我，是以顧到戰後復興之計，尤不能膨脹通貨。

六 戰時財政之出路

反對通貨膨脹，各方意見，殆已一致，惟戰時財政，餘膨脹通貨以外，如何籌劃？則各方意見大有出入，余則始終主張開徵所得稅，關於此層，余在各報已發表談話多次，頗引起各方熱烈之討論，彼等以爲中國經濟落後，產業幼稚，大多數人爲農民，所得甚微，卽使舉辦所得稅，亦屬杯水車薪，無濟於事，其說雖不無理由，但亦僅憑個人之視察，並無實在之根據，以前未辦統稅之時，亦必以爲中國產業落後，所收無幾，統稅係在民國十七年開徵，其時收入僅三四十萬元，至今已達一萬三千萬元，爲中央大宗稅收之一，豈初料之所及哉？

中國國民所得究有幾何，無統計可考，安知開徵以後，亦如統稅之一躍而爲中央大宗收入之一？豈能遽定其收入甚微，無濟於事？若謂徵收困難，則事屬技術問題。未始不能設法解決，事在人爲，何可因噎廢食？

余之所以主張徵收所得稅者，第一卽爲避免紙幣政策，其理由已如上述，第二，則因關鹽統三稅，皆爲貨物稅，戰事一起，海口被封，關稅斷絕。產鹽區域，多在沿海各省，萬一失守，不但鹽稅無着，卽食鹽亦成問題，中國工廠均在沿海口岸，倘被敵人佔領，則統稅亦去，此三稅者實爲中央政府之生命線，而今不絕如縷，安可不易籌新稅以謀抵補？第三，新稅之籌劃，固不僅限於所得稅一項，其他如遺產稅，地價稅、無不可辦，但余則以爲所得稅尤須先辦，使人民養成納稅之習慣，至戰時始可提高稅率，以資挹注，遺產稅亦爲余所主張，自宜相繼籌辦，以裕稅收，但遺產稅最好充教育經費，以之充戰時經費，不如所得稅之易於收效也。至於貨物稅如爲生活所必需之品，不宜加稅，以其易於轉嫁。使物價提高，結果仍落於窮人身上，故不宜採用，但如無關生計之品、如浙江之錫箔，儘可加重稅率以禁止之，俾其所用之錫，盡歸軍用。土地增值稅爲黨綱所規定，自當及時籌備，但地價在戰時跌落，此稅亦未必可靠。且中國地價最高之處，爲沿海各大都市，倘被敵人佔領，或一朝繁華，毀於炮火，則此稅終必有一大部份落空。有人主張以增加田賦爲戰時財政之出路者，余竊以爲未可，蓋中國田賦大部份爲農民負担，以今日田賦之重，農民已不勝其苦。若再增加，惟有相率逃村，戰時糧食，反因此而起恐慌矣。雖曰糧價提高，農民收入可以增加，負担能力亦因之而大，然大多數小農，仍須出錢購米，米價提高，生計反而困難，得其利者恐爲少數富農而已。且今日豪富之家，大都坐擁無形資産，如股票，公債，外匯，以及銀行存款之類，此外如銀行家，洋行買辦，名醫生，名律師，政府官僚，收入皆以萬計，不令彼等有所負担，而專從窮苦無告之農民身上着想，豈非大謬？如徵收所得税遺産税，則直接爲富人所負担，不能轉嫁，亦不影響於物價，所得税之基礎既立，則於戰時可以徵收暴利所得税，以服一般人之心，如此辦理，窮人出力，富人出錢，負担公平，策之上也。

七　結論

綜上所述，非常時期經濟與平時不同，平時經濟變自由競爭與價格制度之支配，一至非常時期，政府出而統制，此二種原則卽爲統制經濟所代替，歐美諸國之統制方法，不適用於中國，中國在準備時期，應從接濟方面設法，自己不能生產，應與外國取得聯絡，打通出口路綫，是爲最要。在社會經濟方面，凡生活上以及軍用上所必需之品，於戰時如有必要，應採定量分配方法，例如汽油爲吾國所最感缺乏之物，此時民間應極力節約，每戶每週所用，不得超過若干加侖。他如糧食煤鹽銅鐵等物，亦須加以統制。如此當可防止物價之飛漲，至在财政方面，萬萬不能採紙幣政策，應另籌新稅或增加舊稅稅率，以資挹注，但不能再加重農民之負担。所得稅與遺產稅爲富人負担之直接稅，最適合公平原則，應卽籌辦。此外如用募捐方法。雖可得極大之資助，例如一二八之役，十九路軍所得於民衆之輸將，不知其數、九一八以後，馬占山將軍遠在黑龍江抗日，南方各省民衆捐助匯往之數，亦頗可觀；但募捐决不能持久而勒捐又無客觀之標準，非計之得也。

戰時統制經濟之必要

爲求戰時軍需之合理的充足，由以下之理由。以藉統制經濟爲必要。

(一)由軍事上之見地。

所要求之多量且迅速之軍需品生產，若僅依各個人營利心之發動，則終不能達到如所希望之充足。國家須藉企業之國營，補助或强制，以獲得所必要之生產品。

(二)由經濟上之見地

藉統制防止重復設備及資源勞力之浪費，爲戰爭目的以圖一國生產諸力之完全利用，至爲必要。在戰時，已不能將緊要之諸產業，置於所謂無政府狀態。

(三)由財政上之見地

國家對其需要，苦提供高昂價格，至某程度，固然可以刺戟增進其生產，但於財政上受極大之損失，尤於使軍資金在不能不發揮其最大效果時爲然。價格常須合理的統制之。

(四)由思想上之見地

對於軍需生產者及其他企業給與高利之結果，各有「戰時暴富」迭生時，則挑發多數國民之反感，且害及戰時舉國一致之精神。德國哈巴(Fritz Haber)博士來日之時，曾敍述關於德國致敗之原因，然言及戰時暴富之情狀時，頗現聲淚俱下之慨。

——森武夫戰時統制經濟論第七三頁。(商務譯本)

美國鐵路整車貨場之組織及管理

許 靖

一 整車貨場之性質及作用

鉄路貨運，大別之，分整車與零担兩種：凡零担貨物之托運與裝車，概須經過貨棧，而其卸車與交付，亦必經過貨棧。所謂貨棧者，即 Freight Houses 是也。然在整車貨運則反是，其裝卸之工作，概由貨主自理（惟我國則由鉄路代理），其裝卸之場所，又非貨棧而在貨場，即英文所謂 Team Tracks 或 Team Yards 者是也。故貨棧與貨場雖同爲鉄路辦理貨運之必要車站建築設備，然其性質截然不同，各有特殊用途；用途既各不同，故二者之事務性質，與夫組織管理；均有分別研究之必要，試分論之。

鉄路建築一切物質設備，各有特殊作用存乎其間，設備未善，固當改良，而運用不當，影響更大，故一切設備之建築，一面當於設計諸端力求完善，期合實用，而在運用上更不容許發生顛倒錯亂之現象。依貨棧及貨場而言，前者之建設，乃爲適應零担貨運之需要，設備後者之目的，在謀辦理整車貨運之便利；故零担貨運之一切收裝卸交事宜，以在貨棧處理爲不易原則，而整車貨物之裝卸收授，無論係由鐵路代理，或由貨主自理，要以均在貨場直接裝車卸車，無須經過抑且不應經過貨棧爲原則。其理可得而言者如左：

(一)在零担貨運，照例係以多數貨主寄往不同站地之貨物同用一車裝運，而在裝車以前，又須經過鐵路人員按照運輸上種種經濟原則之分類手續。爲便於辦理種種裝車手續之經濟敏捷起見，鐵路不得不設備貨棧，以資利用；在整車貨物則不然，凡屬同一貨主者，大抵專用一車運至同一到達站，無分類手續之煩。貨物一到車站，卽可直接裝入車內，故整車貨場大都設於露天敞地，非若貨棧有採取形同一般房屋構造之必要也。此其一。

(二)零担貨物當由何車裝載運出，貨主不得而知，必待鐵路收到之後，始能決定裝入何車，故當收到與裝車之間，須有貨棧設備，以資暫時堆放貨物之用；而整車貨運。則係事前由鐵路撥定車輛，貨物一經送站，卽可逕由貨主自其送貨車輛直接裝入鐵路貨車，無卸出停放之必要，因而在整車貨場照例不爲商人預備堆放貨物之位置，英美各國，大抵相同。此其二。

(三)零担貨物之件數多而體積小，必藉貨棧之特殊構造，分由多數門道同時收進，及由多數門道同時卸車，而後方能提高承運及卸車之效能；整車貨物之數量旣大，體積亦重，以之出進貨棧，不惟極感不便，且笨重之件，往往因貨棧門道高低大小寬窄均有一定限制，竟有不能通過者，是又整車貨物不應通過貨棧理由之一。此其三。

(四)到達零担貨物，亦須經過繁重之分類手續，非若整車之一到卽可交貨，故爲便於辦理到達零担貨物之種種卸車手續，及爲暫時存放待領之便利，亦非利用貨棧不可；而整車貨物則於運到之後，照例，就原車存放不動，等待貨主到站直接由原車卸出提走，其間並不佔用鐵路地面，故在到達貨物方面，鐵路亦無在貨場特闢位置停放整車貨物之必要。此其四。

(五)依前述第(三)項同一理由，到達之零担貨物，亦有分由多數門道卸車及由多數門道交貨之必要，而整車貨則係以原車交付貨主直接卸貨，故以整車貨通過貨棧，殊屬徒增無謂麻煩，擾亂辦理零担貨運之秩序，故在實際上徒爲有害無益之舉。此其五。

總上觀之，無論起運或到達之整車貨物，均用直接裝車與直接交貨制度，零担貨則用間接裝車及間接交貨辦法；間接者必須經過貨棧，不可使用貨場。直接者必須使用貨場，不應通過貨棧。如以不應通過貨棧之整車貨物而通過之，不但徒費無謂手續，抑且糜費貨棧內部面積；反之，若以不能使用貨場之零担貨運而使用之，則又不僅感覺收貨，交貨，裝車，卸車，及無處儲存貨物之種種不便，抑又妨礙整車貨物之裝卸收授。良以貨棧者原爲用於零擔貨運之設備，貨場者本爲整車貨運而設置，二者功用各殊。界限極嚴，不容顚例爲用，此在歐美各國爲然。試繪圖如次，表示三種情狀之實況：

第一圖：爲零擔貨棧之經常正當運用情狀。

第二圖：爲整車貨物運用貨場直接裝車卸車之正當情狀。

第三圖：爲整車貨物由零擔貨棧裝卸之乖謬情形。

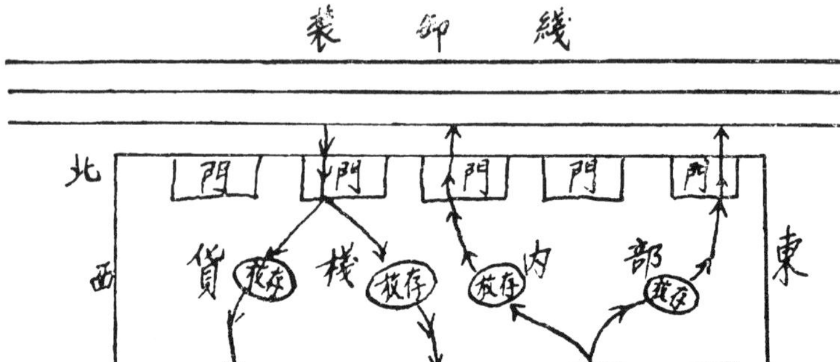

說明：（1）北方各門，爲裝車卸車時必經之道。

（2）南方各門，爲收貨交貨時必經之道。

（3）貨棧內部，爲堆存貨物之用。

（4）箭頭向南之線，表示貨物卸車時由各門入棧存放，然後再由各門交貨之狀。

（5）箭頭向北之線，表示貨物由各門收進存放，然後再由各門裝車之狀。

第一圖　零擔貨物經由貨棧裝卸之狀。

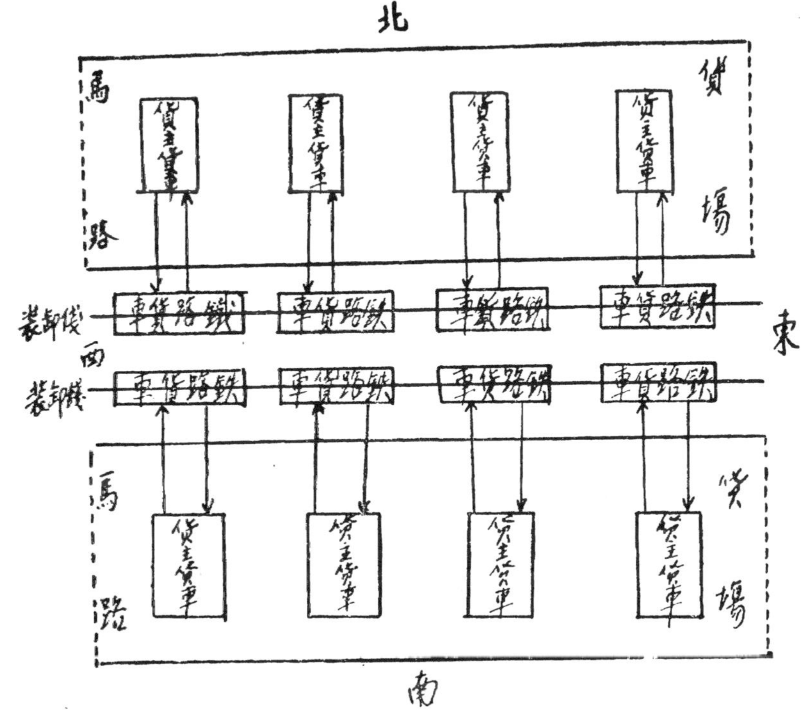

說明：（1）貨場馬路，爲停放貨主送貨或提貨車輛之用。

（2）箭頭向鐵路貨車之線，顯示貨物直接由貨主運貨車直接裝入鐵路貨車之狀。

（3）箭頭向貨主貨車之線，乃爲貨主由鐵路貨車直接卸車提貨之狀。

第二圖　整車貨物經由貨場直接裝車卸車之狀。

北

鐵路貨車

门　门　门

零担貨棧內部

西　A　B　東

门　门　门

貨主貨車

南

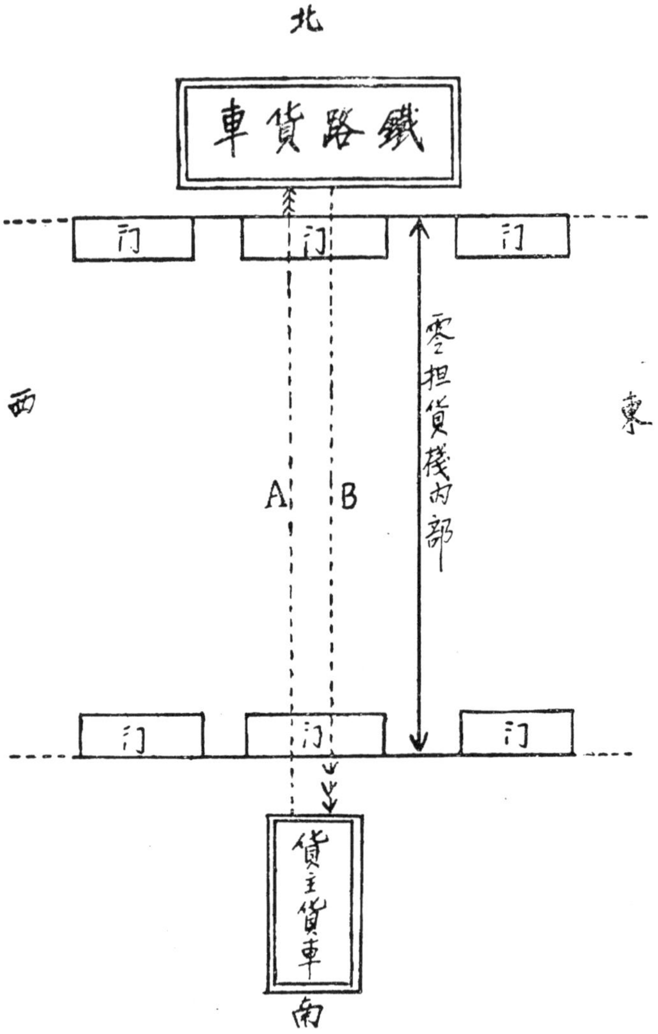

說明：（1）箭頭向北之虛線，表示整車貨物經過零擔貨棧裝車之象。

（2）箭頭向南之虛線，表示整車貨物經過零担貨棧卸車之象。

（3）A，B，兩虛線，代表整車貨物通過零担貨棧所走之無謂距離。

第三圖　整車貨物因通過貨棧變成間接裝卸之謬誤現象。

我國現時辦理整車貨運，多由貨棧裝卸，即犯上面第三圖所示之病，是由對于貨場與貨棧之本來作用未加深察之所致耳。卽曰吾國整車貨物，例由鐵路工人裝卸，與歐美由貨主自理之習慣不同，爲求車輛運用經濟，在鐵路代客卸車制度之下，貨物一經運到，卽可由鐵路脚行卸車，不致因等候貨主自卸，增加車輛在站停留時間。然究不應舍貨場而用貨棧，何況在現行辦法之下，貨物卸車雖快，然而貨主幷非卽能將貨提走，仍須佔用棧內位置爲之保管，以用於暫時存放零貨之貨棧，同時用於收存整車貨物，無怪本不充分之貨棧設備，益覺不敷應用之感，是誠得不償失之舉也。蓋以不問貨物所佔用者，究爲車輛，抑爲站內設備，結果同爲不利於鐵路，是故與其由鐵路代裝代卸整車貨物，直接加重鐵路必須擴充保管貨物設備之負擔，間接又足影響零擔貨車之裝卸，似不如仿照歐美辦法，改用貨主自理裝卸制度，既省無謂手續，復又免去無謂煩瑣，較爲上策。如曰脚力勢力，根深蒂固，實行貨主自理裝卸制度，則失業工人勢必羣起反對，是又過慮之杞憂也。蓋以裝卸方法雖有改變，而原有鐵路工人仍可照舊利用，其道爲何？請分述之：（一）現時所行之先看貨後派車之辦法，極不妥當，應卽首先改正，採用歐美事前撥定車輛辦法，貨主托運整車貨物必須先向鐵路請求派車，俟車輛派撥後，然後將貨送站，鐵路原有工人卽可於貨物到站時代替貨主直接裝車。如是則先行收存之手續卽可省去。此其一。（二）到達之整車貨物，亦俟貨主接到通知來站提貨時，仍由脚行代其卸車，直接提走，勿令中間在站停留，此其二。倘能按此改良現時制度，不但鐵路工人仍可照舊不動，代客裝卸制度亦可不變，而又省去擴充存放整車貨物設備之無謂費用。其法簡而易行，而又一舉數得。卽在美國鐵路，亦有臨時雇用包工代客卸貨之先例，我又何不可酌量變通而改進之耶？

且也，整車貨物不應在站存放，尙有一極大之理由在焉，卽整車貨運之數量極大，在貨運發達車站，一日之內，出進車數，往往以數百輛計，如若一一先收後運，或先卸後交，姑無論鐵路難得如是廣大空地，建築存儲設備，卽令能之，終有不敷容納應付之勢。所以任何鐵路先進國家，對於整車貨運，均採用直接裝車及直接卸交原則，其中原有深意存焉，一則可免無謂之手續，二則車站不致發生無謂擁塞之患，三則可以免除無謂之建築及耗費。惟獨我國對于整車貨運，於其起運之前，必先將貨收下，待車運出；於其到達之後，亦先卸車，然後交付。因此任何整車貨物，均須與零擔貨物經過同樣在站停放之手續，此種辦法，不僅極不合理，抑亦未免庸人自擾，殊有改正之必要也。

二 建築整車貨場之重要設計問題及原則

鐵路着手建築貨場之先，關於重要設計問題，應有縝密妥善之研究及規劃，應於建築完成之後，便於運用管理，得收運輸調度經濟與靈敏之效用，請撮要分陳於次：

甲、**關於位置者** 決定貨場建築位置之原則有三：

（一）**接近工商中心區域**——經過工商繁盛城市之鐵路，往往不止一路，而各路，所經各地之出產品，又恆有在同一市場而銷售者，客商托運貨物，不僅常取里程較短之路，以圖節省運費，卽於鐵路托運貨物場所與其商號或工廠相距遠近關係，亦甚重視。蓋因利之所在，錙銖必較，遠則於托運提貨均不便利，耗時旣久，人工亦費；近則便於托運，亦利於提貨。商人對於一切運輸成本，卽分釐絲毫，亦在計算之列，以日積月累，爲數則可觀也。是故欲求避免此種無形競爭損失，不宜因地價高昂，忽視交通便利，當於可能範圍內擇其適中地點，以爲建築貨場之用，愈能接近一市之工商實業中心

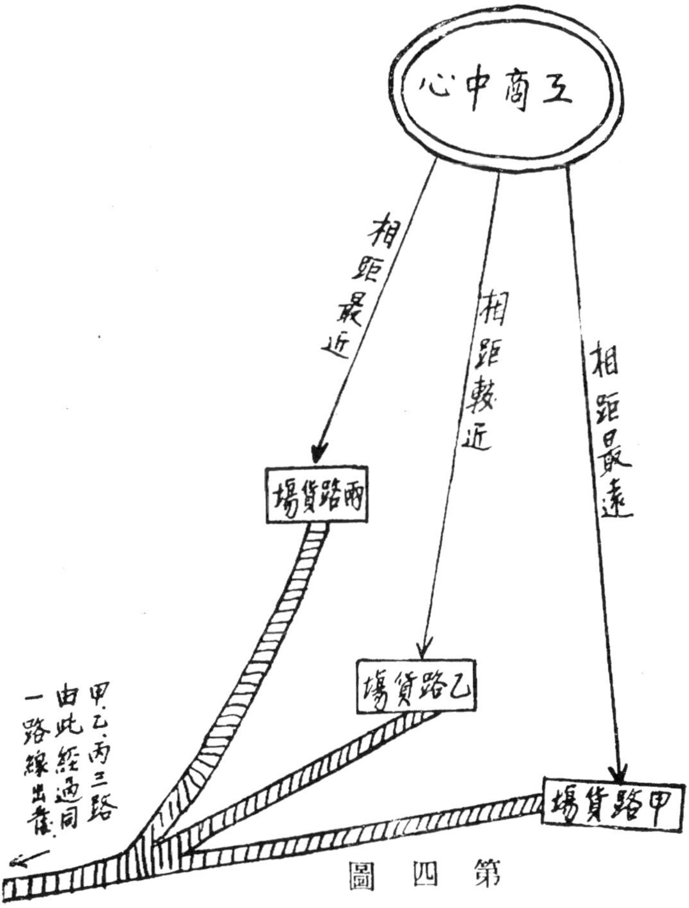

工商中心
相距最近
相距較近
相距最遠
丙路貨場
乙路貨場
甲路貨場
甲.乙.丙三路由此經過同一路線出發

第四圖

區域，則在貨運競爭上愈爲有利，附圖所示(圖四)，是卽甲、乙、丙、三路同一城市之貨場與工商實業中心相距遠近關係之簡例：

(二)接近站內其他貨運設備——通常用於貨運之主要建築設備，莫過於編組列車及調動車輛之調車場，裝卸零担貨物之各種貨棧，及用於整車貨運之貨場三種；故除貨場而外，所謂其他貨運設備者，卽指調車場及貨棧而言。三者均極重要，在位置上應以彼此互能接近發生密切聯絡爲原則，蓋愈能互相接近，則愈能省時與省力，並能增進直接間接種種經濟及便利。約言之，則有如下數端：(1)貨棧之重車一經卸空，如無待裝之零貨，而貨場需要車輛甚急，則可立刻撥至貨場備用。反之，在貨場方面不用之空車，亦可隨時調至貨棧，裝運零担貨物。所謂酌盈劑虛，增進車輛運用效能，此其一也。(如第五圖)(2)因貨棧與貨場相距甚近，故撥調車輛時，極爲靈便，旣省時而又省事，此調車方面之經濟也。(3)再就商人方面觀察，貨主一面先以零担貨物送至貨棧托運，同時可以利用原車回到貨場，順道提取運到之整車貨物，如第六圖上部虛線所示之狀；反之，如先送整車貨物至貨場托運，則裝車之後，亦可利用原來送貨之車，於回程中順便經過貨棧，提取運到之零担貨物，如第六圖下部實線所示之狀；歸納

整車貨場
空車撥至貨場
空車撥至貨棧
零担貨棧

第五圖

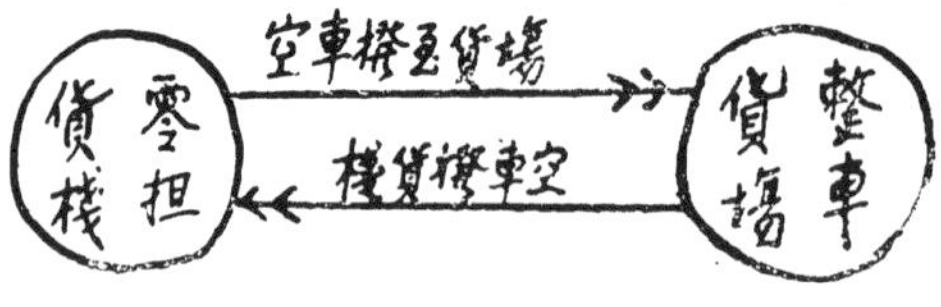

言之，是在同一時間以同一車輛兼辦送貨提貨兩種事務，所謂省人省時省事，三者兼而有之。其於貨主之便利如此，而間接上亦卽增進鐵路之效能，此其三也。倘若當初建築之始，於此種種不加考慮，東建一貨棧，西築一貨場，或方面相同，而相距甚遠；甚或場棧之間，隔有行車正線或其他建築物，均非正當辦法。我國北寧天津東站貨運設備之情況，卽犯此病，零担貨棧設在車站之東，整車貨場（卽所謂之西貨場）則在車站之西，不僅相距太遠，且無避開正線之聯絡調車線，往返甩掛撥調車輛，必須通過站內旅客月台，經過行車正線，影響所及，非獨商人無從得到前述第六圖之便利，卽鐵路本身撥用車輛，亦極感不便，是爲我國鐵路建築上設計錯誤之一例也。

第六圖

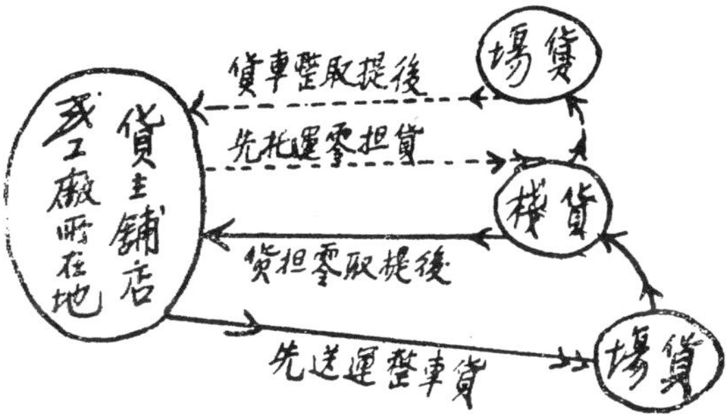

（三）地面宜寬大——其次，在設計建築貨場時。應先審察現時之需要，幷顧及將來之發展，預定一發展之計劃，先從目前之需要着手，俟日後貨運發展時再爲擴充之。故其所選定之地面，不宜過於狹隘，有礙將來隨時擴充範圍及添設軌道之便利。

乙、關於軌道者

（一）軌道數目與長度——貨場之軌道，數目宜多而長度宜短，蓋多而短，則可隨時將貨物裝卸經由之一部分空重車輛拖出或拖入，不致因欲拖出或拖入少數空重車輛，必須同時將整個貨物裝卸線上之多數車輛牽動，幷影響各貨主之裝卸工作。反是則調動不靈。影響甚大。通常一道之長度，以能容車十輛至十五輛爲適中，假定某站一日之內能有三百輛整車貨運，則與其建築平均長度能容三十輛之長道十股，致滋種種弊害，毋寧改建平均長度僅容十輛之短軌三十道，較爲合宜，是其例也。

（二）軌道排列與軌距——貨場之軌道及馬路，原爲便於裝卸整車貨物而設，故其建築之方式，宜採分組平列制（如第七圖）。其法卽以每兩股道爲一組，每兩組間築一行車馬路，以便貨主出入貨場停車裝卸之用，而各組軌道與裝卸貨物馬路，均須成平行形勢建築，如是既省地面。又便管理，而調撥車輛及裝卸貨物均極靈便。且爲節省地面之同樣理由、每兩股軌道之相隔距離，亦不宜留之太大，通常以約有十二呎之間隔（自甲道中心點至乙道中心點）爲適中。其每兩組軌道間之馬路，蓋爲商人往來通行及停車裝卸貨物之必要道常，不宜太窄，其闊度當視各站通常多用何種車輛搬運貨物而定。如用馬車，則其所佔地面常較新式載重汽車爲多，按新式運貨汽車之長度計算，約須四十呎寬之馬路，卽能容納兩車同時對立停放裝卸貨物，中間尙有隙地通過行駛汽車一輛而有餘。若在使用馬車送貨之鐵路，則其闊度又當略爲加大矣。

(三)軌道編號——貨場所有之設備，惟軌道與馬路。軌道數目太多，而又散布各處，爲便於考察場內各車所在地點，指導裝車卸車事務，及管理全場運用經濟種種起見，須用數字規定各道之號數，此後方可按號劃分管理區域，分配員工工作，例如第一道，第二道，第三道等等是其例也。

(四)調車線與馬路——除上述各項外，貨場軌道兩端之橫面，不宜均有調車線之設置，當在一端用梯形軌道使各軌連成一片，以與調車場相通連，而在他端則與貨主之往來通行大道相連接，如是則商人送貨提貨，可以不斷由此一端出入貨場，而他端之梯形軌道又可不斷用於抽調或撥動空重車輛，彼此各不妨礙。而又安全便利。其次，各組軌道間之裝卸貨物馬路，均當用士敏士鋪修，使其整平堅固，雖遇雨天，亦可卸車，切不可聽其自然，不加修理，一遇天雨，卽變成渠，滿泥偏地，妨礙卸車之便利。此又關於設計貨場建築時應行注意之兩大要項也。茲以整車貨場各項設備形勢關係圖示如下，以便研究：

丙、我國整車貨場現狀及其改良方法——貨場之設備，在吾國鐵路中本已有之，惟因一般路員對於此專門建築之性質作用未能深切瞭解者多，因之在名稱上發現不少錯誤。有將貨棧與貨場視爲同物者，有以貨棧而稱貨場者，亦有視貨場爲岔道者。假令學者對於英文名稱

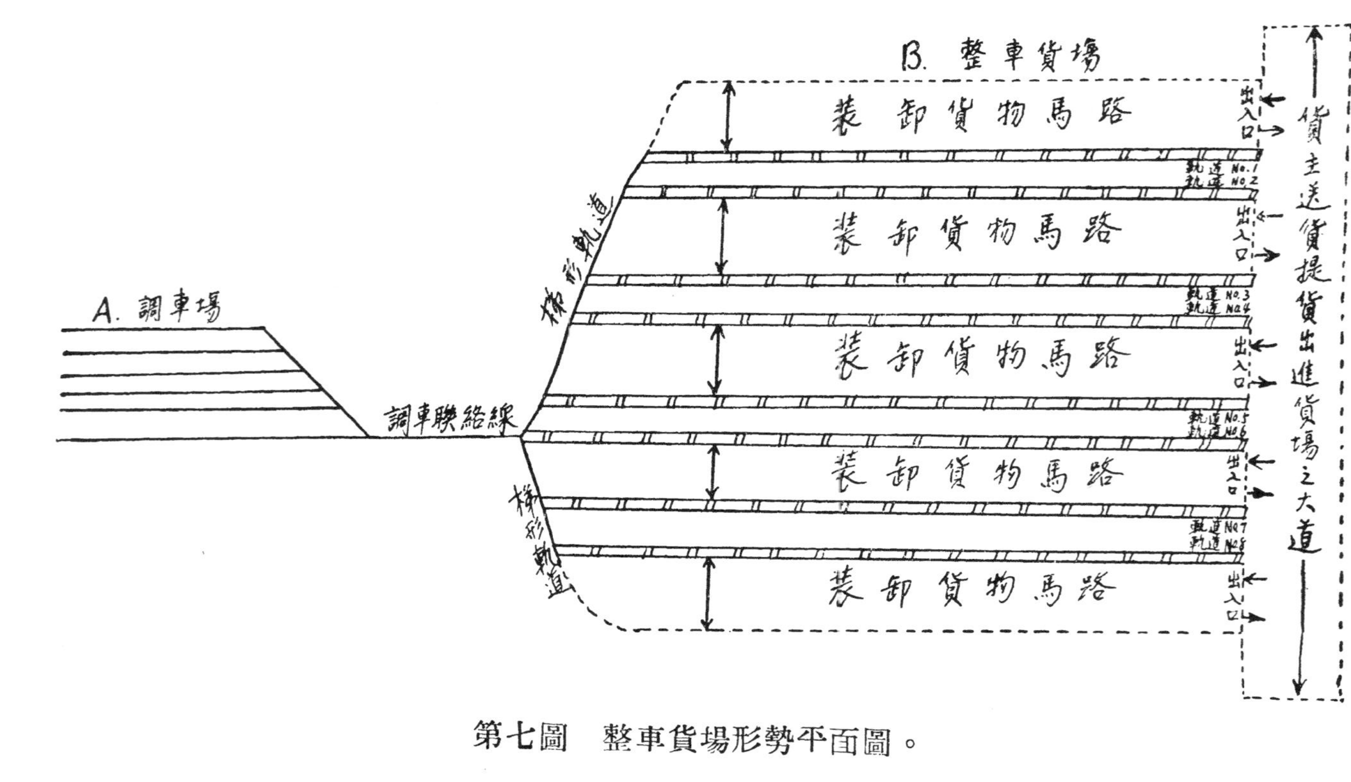

第七圖 整車貨場形勢平面圖。

及所代表之設備本身性質如何，先無透澈之了解，徒就中文譯名研究，直如墮入五里霧中，不知所指究爲何事，此貨場之名稱與意義在我國鐵路上尚待切實規定及統一者也。名稱而外，關於設計及管理方法，尚有可議之處甚多：(1)論位置，多與零担貨棧不生聯絡關係，及北寧天津東站之貨棧與西貨場各在車站之一邊，是爲最顯著之例。(2)論軌道之排列，則分岔之處太窄，(如第八圖甲甲線)，而兩道之盡頭處又復分散太遠(如第八圖乙乙線)，加以各道方向不一，長短不齊，紛然雜陳，毫無秩序，直與前述分組平行排列原則背道而馳，不獨糜費地面太甚，抑且不便裝卸貨物。蓋以接近分岔處之各軌道相距太近，如甲甲線所代表者，不便排車，運貨汽車不能進入，故甲甲線所代表之一段軌道及馬路，在實際上等於虛費；而乙乙線所代表之距離又復相隔太寬，除容納兩輛汽車對停裝車卸車以外，所餘空地太多，亦屬糜費貨場有用之地面，

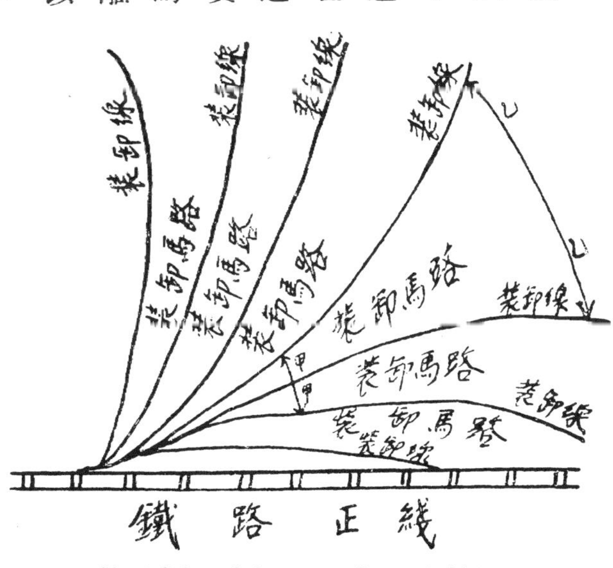

第八圖　中國整車貨場形勢圖。

均非經濟之道。年來已有識者感覺吾國貨場軌道排列之不合理。因有「撇蘭式之岔道」之譏諷稱謂，蓋以各軌道之散布情況，一若蘭草散開之形狀。余則以爲不如逕稱爲「蘭草式」之貨場，更較名符其實也。(3)論各軌道間之裝卸貨物馬路，則毫未修理，高低不平，一遇天雨，泥土滃亂不堪，全場頓成澤國。(4)其尤甚者，場內隙地及各軌道間之馬路。往往有租與商人，聽其自由堆存貨物及建築房屋者，於是原爲一般商人運輸整車貨物便利之貨場，一變而爲少數商家之居住地及存貨地，殊屬令人大感不解其故。其他種種違反鐵路管理貨場原則之處，不勝枚舉。總之吾國貨場之功用，多數不甚了解，因而發生意想不到之離奇現象，改良之道，首當確定名稱意義，亟早取銷一切租地契約，收回一切地面。然後當依前述(甲)(乙)各項原則，對全部貨場軌道馬路佈置加以重新澈底改造，庶有談及改良管理方法之可能也。

三　美國鉄路管理整車貨場事務之辦法

由貨場處理之整車貨物，雖其裝車卸車，例由貨主自理，(亦有少數笨重零担貨物由貨場起運及交付者)，從表面觀之，事務似極簡單，然在裝車前後及卸車前後，鐵路究應如何撥給車輛，如何登記空車，如何處置空車，如何通知取貨，如何準備交車手續，以及如何監督裝卸等等，非有分工合作之簡捷完密方法，決不能收辦事靈活，內外各部事務同時並舉之效。請依下列各項分別撮要陳之。

甲、關於託運貨物者

(一)承運及簽收托運單手續——凡貨商欲托運整車貨物者，在美國亦如托運零貨然，照例先由貨主塡妥托運單三聯。其格式亦與用於托運零担貨物者完全相同。塡妥之後，連同貨物一併送站，逕至貨場地磅 (Wagon Scale) 處，一面就原車過磅，一面卽以托運單交於場內副監工。副監工立卽察對貨物名稱種類是否與托運單所列者相符。一面簽收，一面決定裝運車輛，幷以車號隨手記入托運單。其簽收之情形，如「起運貨棧」收貨員之簽收零担貨運，惟須在托運單上加蓋一種「貨主自裝自點」(Shipper's load and Count) 之戳記。以示整車貨物係由貨主自行點數裝車之意，祇要運抵到達站時。車門車鎖並無異狀，縱然發現不符情事，鐵路不負賠償短少之責。凡此過磅，點驗，簽收托運單，決定裝車車號，等項手續，均在同一短促時間一律辦完，總共所費不過一二分鐘之譜，其敏捷之程度可想見矣。此貨場承運整車貨物時第一步手續及其簡捷辦法也。

(二)裝車，塡寫貨票，計算運費，及塡發車牌手續——貨物一經過磅簽收，貨主卽就原車開進場內指定車輛地點裝車，此時鐵路有人在場領導照料，但不負檢查貨物件數多寡之責一任貨主自裝自理。而托運單一共三聯，除在簽收過磅之際，已以第一三兩聯當卽交還貨主收執，作爲鐵路收到貨物憑證并可用作裝車外，其餘一聯名曰 Shipping Order ，則由貨場辦公室立卽轉送站內「貨票處」(Billing Department) 計算運費及改塡貨票 (Waybill)，與零担貨物之由托運單改換貨票，同一辦法。其詳已於拙著美國鐵路起運貨棧之組織及管理一文論及之矣，茲不復贅。(見北去改進專刊第九期)而貨場辦公室則亦同時塡具車牌(Card)兩方，以備車一裝完，卽可用作根據調車。

車牌之內容，等於托運單之摘要，載明每一車輛之：(1)裝車站名 (Loading Station)，(2)車號及路號，(3)貨物種類，(4)總噸數，(5)塡發車牌日期 (Date Carded)，(6)聯軌站 (Junction)，(7)到達站，及(7)摘車地點 (Spot Station) 等項，均用硬塊方紙預先印製就緒，用時逐項照塡而已。車牌之名稱顏色不一。用於鮮貨者，名曰鮮貨車牌 (Perishable Card)，用於急運貨物者，名曰急貨車牌 (Dispatch or Manifest Card)，二者均用白底紅字紅線，表示緊要重視之意；用於普通貨物者、則稱噸量車牌 (Tonnage Card)，均爲白底黑字黑線，以示不如以前二者貨物之重要，此外尚有客車車牌及外路車牌等等。故車牌之種類性質極不一致，當視貨物之性質分別塡用也；語其功用，隱而不顯，試申述數點如次：(1)車牌之內容，既如前述係由托運單摘要而來，故在正由托運單改換貨票之內部事務尚未完畢以前，貨物裝車就緒以後，調車場卽可依照釘於各車兩旁之車牌，利用時間，先將裝好車輛拖出，從事編組列車。迨列車組成，而內部填換貨票手續亦已竣事，較之必待貨票填妥之後，始能調車組車，則時間上之損失將有不可言喻者矣。(2)因有車牌制度(Carding System)，內部填票與外部調車得以同時並行不悖，兩不妨礙，故貨票一經辦妥，逕由貨票處送至調車場，不必經過貨場，徒費周折。列車長由調車場取得貨票之時，卽可點票對車。開始行車。因而任何貨物，自托運時以至正式運出，其間毫無無謂之躭誤，直接減少貨物在起站之停留時間，間接卽爲提高鐵路之運輸能力。(3)行車員工沿途甩摘車輛，可憑車牌直接行事，無待檢查貨票，荒廢時間，是又對於行車及甩車事務之便利也。至車牌之形式如何，作者曾於調車場之組織及管理文中揭舉一二。故於此間略而不及。(見北甯改進專刊第十一期)

總之，裝車乃貨主在貨場外部之事務、預備車牌乃貨場內部之事務，計算運費及改換貨票，又爲貨票處之內部事務。而編組列車又爲調車場之外部事務，欲收內外各處同時辦理各項手續及同時完畢之功，勢非同時採用兩種制度不可！卽托運單與貨票分開制度及車牌制度是也。蓋以不有以托運單完全對外及貨票完全對內之辦法，則商人必須在站等候鐵路計算運費，發給貨票之後，方有簽收憑證，始能進行裝車，裝車之後再能辦理車牌。反之。如先以托運單用於裝車。則計算運費及改換貨票諸事又必受其延誤。蓋一切事務，均賴托運單以進行，而由鐵路留存之托運單又止一聯，用於裝車，卽不能同時用於計算運費與填寫貨票；用於填寫貨票，則又不能同時用於裝車，或用於預備車牌。無論如何，二者不能兼顧。必待一事辦完之後，方能進行第二步之事務。彼此互相牽制，時間損失極大。所以美國鐵路規定托運單爲三聯，經過鐵路簽收之後，貨主當即取回一二兩聯，故得立即據以裝車。第二聯由鐵路用作填寫貨票，故裝車與填寫貨票得以同時進行，而貨票純爲鐵路內部用作行車統計，會計，之工具，與托運人不生關係。鐵路既不藉貨票以爲收貨憑證，托運人亦無等候鐵路填換貨票之必要，是爲美國鐵路承運貨物制度上之最大優點。然以僅有托運單與貨票分開之辦法，則又不能兼顧編車方面之時間經濟，蓋調動車輛亦須有所根據，托運單既用於填寫貨票，其手續往往不能與裝車同時辦完。換言之，即填票不如裝車之快，若必待貨票齊備而後編車，是又不免時間上之損失，故爲節省此項等候貨票之時間計，不得不同時實行車牌制度，以爲預先編組列車之便利，及至車已編妥，而貨票亦已辦齊，時間毫不虛糜，內外事務同時並舉。如此簡便經濟辦法，吾人殊有亟於採用之必要。茲以整個事務聯繫情狀及內外同時辦理程序圖示於后，以求顯豁：

乙、**關於到達貨物者**

(一)**檢查到達車輛方法及作用**——按美國鐵路辦理貨運之制度，無分整車零担，亦不問其爲寄出者，或爲運到者，舉凡裝車卸車調車，均不依賴貨票。換言之，即無貨票亦可裝貨

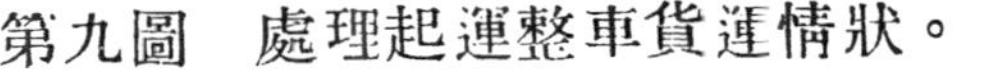
第九圖　處理起運整車貨運情狀。

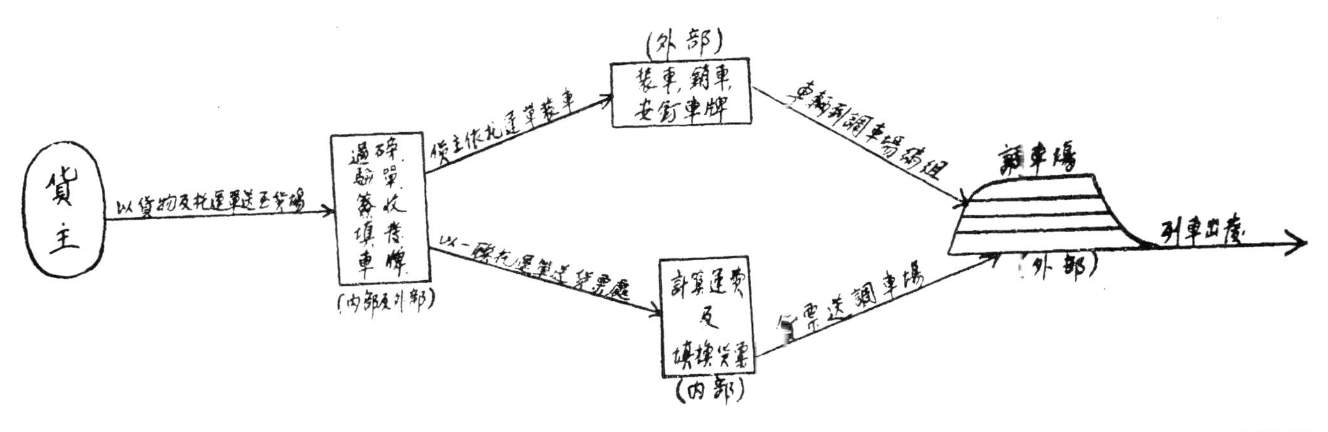

卸貨及調動車輛也。除關於起運整車貨物者業於前面述及外，茲就到達者一略言之。其辦法則爲凡屬一列貨車運到之後。其列車先進調車場停放，列車長卽以關係貨票交於場內辦公室。由其轉送站內「到達貨物處」(In-freight Department)，以憑審核票內運費計算有無錯誤，及用以改換收費，卸車，交貨，到達通知種種單據。此時貨票雖已離開車輛，另有作用。然各車兩旁均有代表貨票內容之車牌在焉。故何車應行甩入零担貨棧，或應甩入整車貨場，調車員工一望車牌，卽可分別按照甩送，并不因貨票脫離列車而受其影響，斯又車牌制度在到達站無形中輔助內外事務同時進行之偉大功用也。

貨場之檢查運到車輛，亦係利用車上之車牌。其法則係按照規定表格，由各交貨員(Deliverymen) 於每日上班之時，分途點查所轄軌道以內之車輛，蓋貨車甩入貨場，多在夜間行之，因是每日檢查時所發現之新車，即爲最近運到之車輛，而各車何時由調車場甩入貨場之日期，亦由調車場於車牌內詳爲塡明。故貨場雖然不見貨票，仍可根據車牌所示種種要目，同時單獨辦理車輛狀況檢查，預爲準備一切交車卸貨手續。檢查時携帶如附式0203號之空白「各道車輛狀況單」(Track Report)，一面點查，一面依照車牌所指各項轉抄於空白報單，無論新舊重車空車，一律塡入，每日如是。

各道車輛狀況單(Track Report) 附式0203

車號 Car No.	路別 Initial	收貨人姓名 Consignee	貨物種類 Contents	車抵調車場日期 Date Car Arrival at Nearest Yard	車輛甩到貨場日期 Date Car Placed on Tracks	軌道號數 Track No.

此項「各道車輛狀況報單」之作用有四，故填造時當用複寫紙一次填造四份，以省手續而免轉抄費時，及妨礙各方同時運用之便利。以一聯交收費員，以爲計算貨車延期費（Demurrage）與軌道佔用費（Track Storage Charges）之根據；一聯用作轉錄新到鮮貨車於「鮮貨車通知簿」（Perishable Notice Book），以便用電話特別從速通知貨主；一聯交加冰員（Icing Clerk）用作轉填關於冷藏貨車之「加冰報單」（Icing Report）；第四聯則用作編造如附式0206號之「全場逐日待卸車輛單」（Daily List of Cars on Team Tracks），凡新舊未卸重車，一律列入，每日更換一次格式至爲簡單，僅記各車之車號及軌道號數，而車號最

全場逐日待卸車輛單　　附式0206

車號 Car No.	軌道號數 Track No.	車號 Car No.	軌道號數 Track No.	車號 Car No.	軌道號數 Track No.	車號 Car No.	軌道號數 Track No.	車號 Car No.	軌道號數 Track No.
30118									
25238									
4019									

末一字相同者，則併列一處，如末數爲8者爲一類。9號者另爲一類，餘類推。於填妥後張貼辦公室內，如是全場雖有千百待卸之車輛散佈各處，隨時一目瞭然。如貨主電向貨場查詢

任何車輛及其所在地點，可於頃刻之間予以圓滿答復。其法簡而明，殊有採用之價值也。

(二)鮮貨車通知法——整車貨物書面到達通知，概由「到達貨物處」依據到達貨票填發，而貨場方面因有直接檢查車輛方法，並於鮮貨各車別提出另行單獨登記，註明(1)車號，(2)路別，(3)貨物種類及(4)收貨人姓名四項，故能依之直接用電話先行通知貨主，俾得預爲提貨卸車之準備。并以電達日期時刻及接話人姓名一併在鮮貨通知簿內切實註明，作爲電話通知記錄。此蓋重視鮮貨及易壞貨物之意，無論整車零担均用之，故到達貨棧對於零担鮮貨亦有於書面通知外另行電話通知之辦法也。

(三)交車卸貨之方法與手續——美國鐵路交付整車貨物，亦無憑藉貨票之必要。貨主接到通知來場提貨，各交貨員即依前述「各道車輛狀況單」以車號及停放地點告知提貨人前往開車卸貨。且爲受授手續淸楚責任分明起見，一面如是交車卸貨，一面依照「各道車輛狀況單」另外加塡一種交貨單，每車一張。但有兩車或三車同係交於一個貨主時，則不必分塡，即可共用一單。此項整車交貨車。與到達貨棧所用之零担貨物交貨收據名實均不相同，其格式如附式168號之Delivery Sheet。此單不僅作爲收授整車貨物之唯一憑證，且爲遇有損壞賠償要求時之主要參考，故記載當力求翔實。除照格式上各項塡寫外，尙須在單內註明(1)軌道號數，(2何時開始卸車(Time Started Unloading)，(3)何時卸完 (Time Finished

Unloading），（4）貨主提貨車號（5）提貨人簽收，（6）交貨員簽字等項。如貨物發現異狀或

整車交貨單(Delivery Sheet)　　附各168

We, the under signed, hereby acknowledge receipt of Freight, from cars named below, in good order, Except otherwise noted.　站名______日期______

路別 Initial	車號 Car No.	收貨人姓名 Consignee	貨物種類 Contents	卸車日期 Date	提貨人簽字 Signature	編號備考 File

損壞，亦應說明原因，例如裝車失當，或因包裝不當，或因到站傾覆，分列填入。然後彙繳辦公室，經過編號之後，連同六聯收費單據內之交貨收據 (Delivery Receipt) 轉送站內賠償處 (Local Claim Department) 存查。特在轉送以前，尚須先行用以登記各車車號，路別，及卸空時刻於空車簿(Empty Car Book)之內，是又足以附帶表明所以在交貨車內註明卸空時刻之用意也。

(四)**登記卸空車輛與填發空車車牌**——車輛爲鐵路主要生產工具，凡有重車卸貨之場所

，不問其爲本路車，抑爲外路車，當於各車卸空時刻，有一隨時明瞭方法。庶幾卸空之後，不致投閑置散，影響車輛運用之經濟。所以美國鐵路責令交貨員在交貨單內填明各車卸空時刻，其意卽在便於事後登記空車。然僅有登記，而無處置之辦法，則調車員工亦因無所依據，無從拖出空車，更不知當作如何發落。所以於登記之外，又有空車車牌之運用。所謂空車車牌者。復分兩大類別：一爲本路空車牌（System Empty Car Card），用以指示撥給他站本路空車，一爲外路空車牌（Home Car Card），係爲送還外路空車之用；填發時當依總局發交各站之貨車支配規則妥爲辦理，不得草率將事，致背車輛支配經濟原則。

空車牌由辦公室依照空車簿隨時填具，隨時發交主管交貨員安置于空車兩邊，當其安置新車牌時，必須注意先將原有車牌一律撤下，以免新舊混淆，致滋錯誤。關於車牌上所填之事項，應同時在0203號「各道車輛狀況單」內關係車旁一併註明，蓋該單對於各車所在軌道記之極詳，於分送車牌及清查車輛，均有莫大之便利。此又貨場處理空車最爲簡捷周密之方法，足資吾人借鑑者也。

總上以觀，是美國鐵路處理關於到達貨物之一切事務。亦以內外同時並舉分途並進爲原則，而其所以能致此者，其最要之關鍵，則爲於到達貨票外另行填用一共六聯之收費單據（Expense Bills），及同時運用車輛制度。他如貨場直接檢查車輛，直接預備交車卸貨手續，清理空車，以及塡發車牌程序等等辦法，亦皆與有力焉。我國貨運繁複情狀，不及美國百分之一，而站內辦理一切手續之遲鈍，則又數倍於美國原因雖非一端，而以一切均賴貨票方能進行，實爲最大之病根。蓋貨票之張數有限，用於甩送車輛，卽不能卸車；用於卸車，卽不能計算運費；用於計算運費，卽無從甩送車輛；因在同一時間不能辦理兩項以上之事務，無形中所受之直接間接損失，實極異常重大。改良之道，當於貨票之外，添設一共六聯之單據，使六聯名稱各殊而實質相同，可用複寫紙由貨票一次塡就，分作六方面同時運用，卽卸車，通知，交貨，收費，收費憑證，及稽核到達貨物運費是也。此外同時推行空重車牌制度，使車輛不賴貨票亦可單獨調動，藉以改進調車事務之效率。試更以美國鐵路處理到達整車貨運之程序圖示如左：

四 整車貨場之組織及人事

(一)人事及職稱——貨場之職務，既在處理一站之出進整車貨運，復以裝車卸車，例由貨主自理，故貨場之範圍雖大，而事務之性質殊甚單純，人事亦不若零担貨棧之多而且繁。惟二者在支配人事及規定職稱上頗有相異之處。爰就大體標準情況略其梗概。并於各職稱附註英文原名，以我國貨場組織及員司職稱均尙缺乏統一規定，或有足供他日改進參考之處耳。

1.監工(Foreman)一人——監督及計劃全場內外事宜。

第十圖　處理到達整車貨運情狀。

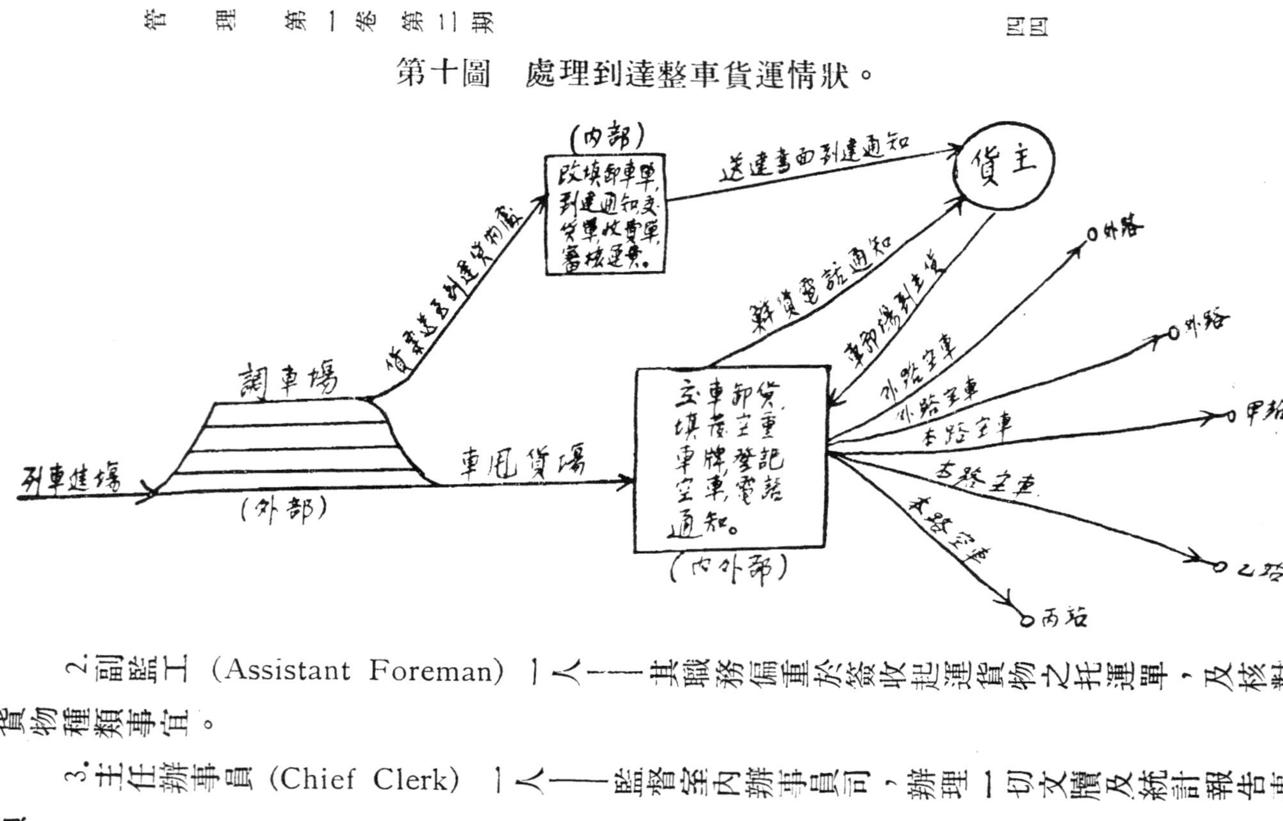

2.副監工（Assistant Foreman）一人——其職務偏重於簽收起運貨物之托運單，及核對貨物種類事宜。

3.主任辦事員（Chief Clerk）一人——監督室內辦事員司，辦理一切文牘及統計報告事項。

4. 辦事員（Office Clerks）三四人——分掌檢查車輛，登記出進空重車輛，填發車牌，答復商人電話問訊，及填造各種報單等項事務。

5. 審核員（Revisor）一人——審核起運貨物之托運單。及到達貨物之交貨單，幷辦理關於短少損壞事件之調查考核事宜。

6. 通知員（Notice Clerk）一人——經理到達通知事宜。

7. 收費員（Cashier）一人——收受運費幷辦理一切關係事務。

8. 司磅員（Weighmaster）一人——經理貨物過磅及其關係事項。

9. 交貨員（Deliverymen）數人——辦理交車卸貨手續。填具各項關係單據，清理及調換新舊車牌。其名額當視裝卸軌道多寡及裝卸事務繁簡隨時增減之。

10. 車鎖員（CarSealers）一二人——分管全場出進裝卸車輛之車鎖及封車事務。

11. 其他員工——如包裝匠（Coopers），巡羅夫（Watchmen），及其他工人等。

我國鐵路員司，在總局者多稱課員，在外站者多稱司事，外站員司之待遇，亦遠不如總局員司之優厚，是乃我國鐵路遇事重內輕外之一種表現：揆之歐美鐵路用人定職。一以事務重要與否爲準標，絕無因內外地域不同關係，遂在名義上及待遇上劃分階級，顯出種種不公允之事實，是又中外鐵路在人事上極爲懸殊之點。因此吾輩研究管理學者，在人事問題方面，往往感覺缺乏適當名稱之困難。爲合於中國習慣起見，則在貨場服務之一般員司，如交貨員，審核員，收費員等等，似宜改稱交貨司事，審核司事，或收費司事，然如此而又與外國情狀不符，亦欠妥當，其他類此之處甚多。究應遷就我國特殊習慣，譯稱司事，抑應仍照一般國外辦法，不稱司事，是乃關係整個鐵路組織人事問題，性質至爲複雜，何去何從，尚有待於商榷者也。

（二）**組織系統**——辦理整車貨運之貨場，與辦理零擔貨運之起運貨棧或到達貨棧，在組織上處於平行地位。三者鼎足而立，各有監工一人，主管其事。惟以三者同爲貨運車站實地辦理貨物收授裝卸之機構，彼此在事務上殊有通力合作維持密切聯絡之必要，故於三者之上，往往設置總監工（General Foreman）一人，藉以集中管理，統一事權。不獨三處車輛可以互相撥用，即員工亦當隨時互相調用。是故總監工者，實爲一站內各貨棧各貨場之最高管理者，直接對貨運站長負責，而各監工則爲各處之主管，均對總監工直接負責，茲就貨場組織系統及上下內外關係表列於左，以便參考：

五　管理整車貨場工作效率之統計方法

歐美各國管理鐵路任何部分之事務，均有簡明統計，以資日常考察工作成績或效能之用，尤以美國最爲詳盡。起運貨棧有其特殊統計，到達貨棧亦有其專門統計，二者均於其他文

整車貨場組織系統表

- 貨站站長
  - 總監工（主管貨棧及貨場）
    - 貨場監工
      - 外部
        - 副監工
          - 交貨員(Deliverymen)
          - 司磅員(Weighmaster)
          - 車鎖員(Car Sealers)
          - 包裝員(Coopers)
          - 巡羅夫(Watchmen)
          - 其他工人
      - 內部
        - 主任辦事員
          - 辦事員(Office Clerks)
          - 審核員(Revisor)
          - 收費員(Cashier or Teller)
          - 通知員(Notice Clerk)

中論及之矣。茲就用於貨場者詳爲述之。以便比較其異同。其日常用於管理貨場者，計凡三種：一曰全場員工人數及正班鐘點薪資統計，二曰全場員工人數及加班鐘點薪資統計。三曰全場逐日工作狀況比較統計(Daily Report of Team Track Operation)。前二者之格式，與用於起運貨棧及到達貨棧者完全相同，故略而不贅。而最後第三種，則係根據前二者之內容及參合其他材料編製而成，是爲貨場中最重要最有用之管理統計、故於其格式，項目，各項用意詳爲分析陳列如次：

(一)員工人數 (No. Men) ——包括全場上自監工下至員工之共計人數。惟收貨員係由收費處(Cashier Department) 列支，不在其內。設立本項之用意，乃在隨時考核人數是否合於事務之需要，以防人浮於事。如出進裝卸車數減少，而員工人數反形增多，卽宜裁員，以資撙節人工薪資。故此項統計卽係統計學中一種代表費用「或」「成」本之單位，所謂 Units of Cost 是也。

(二)裝運車數—— (Total No. Cars Loaded) ——卽在一日內所有裝貨運出之車數。此數愈大愈佳，以車數之增減，卽爲營業消長之反映也。

(三)卸完車數 (Total No. Cars Unloaded)——卽在一日內已經交出卸貨之車數，其性質適與第(二)項相反，然其同爲表現運輸狀況則一。不特數目愈大。愈足顯示運輸之發達，而貨主卸車之快慢亦可藉以考察。貨主卸車之數愈大，則貨場之軌道設備運用效能愈能增高，而貨車在站待卸停留時間亦必大爲減少也。

(四)裝卸車數共計 (Total Loaded and Unloaded)——是卽第(二)項「裝運車數」與第(三)項「卸完車數」之共計。換言之，卽在一日內全場運出及交卸之總共車數，其增減卽爲鐵路運輸數量暢旺或衰落之象徵。

(五)費用或成本共計 (Total Cost)——指全場逐日全體員工薪資之總計而言，惟收費員之開支在外也。此項數目當隨第(四)項「裝卸車數共計」之變化而增減。蓋裝卸車數愈少，卽爲運輸衰落之反映，運輸既衰落，場內事務亦必較少。爲貫澈用人經濟之原則，則當隨時比照運輸狀況，裁減工作人員，而使本項人工費用減低。亦爲統計學中表示費用之單位也。

(六)**每車平均費用或成本**(Total Cost Per Car)——以第(四)項「裝卸車數共計」除第(五)項「費用或成本共計」，卽得每裝一車或每卸一車所費之平均員工薪資。此爲統計學上表現工作成績之一種平均數，所謂 Units of Result 是也。此項平均數目，以愈低爲愈經濟，亦卽成績愈優之表現，蓋其所表現者，乃爲辦理整車貨運所費之人工開支，愈少則爲於鐵路愈爲有利也。

以上六項，代表美國各路日常考核貨場成績之統計方法，在編製上復分「本日」「累計」兩類數字，意在便於多方比較，期收運用完密之效。吾國類似此等管理統計，迄今一無所有，誠有亟宜舉辦之必要，用附整個格式於后，以供研究而便參考。

美國鐵路管理貨場工作狀況比較統計(Daily Report of Team Track Operation)

A.本日數——Today:

年 份	日 期	員工人數 (No. Men)	裝運車數 (Total No. Cars Loaded)	卸完車數 (Total No. Cars Unloaded)	裝卸車數共計 (Total Loaded and Unloaded)	費用共計 (Total Cost)	每車平均費用 (Cost Per Car)
本 年							
上 年							
本年上月							

B.累計數——Total Todate:

本 年	日 期						
上 年							
本年上月							

鐵路統計分析與管理

葉子剛

經營鐵路事業，固賴善法良策，然策雖良，法雖善，非皆準放於一切而皆宜，亦非經營鐵路需用此策此法，蓋各路之內部情形及外界環境不盡相同，處理之辦法亦自應有異，否則未有不枘鑿者。故管理鐵路事業者，於其定大計之先，必先觀察事業既往及現在之經營情形并分析其致此之原因，然後相情度勢，設計一切。凡此觀察，攸賴統計。統計以確實之數字，表現經營之情勢與各部負責者之成績與效率，善用者排比而觀，以得事業過往成績或病態，以爲改進之參考。

論統計有二法，一爲研究統計之編製，一爲研究統計之利用。於前一論題，頗有筆之而成書者；著者以爲苟不知利用統計之法，則難盡統計之用，故敢略誌所得，以就教於世之同志焉。

營業進款之衡量

一 客運進款

衡量營業進款之增減，應就各類進款分別行之，因各類進款增減之原因各異也。據我國鐵路營業進款分類則例，鐵路營業進款分爲運輸進款及其他進款二類。前者復分爲客運進款貨運進款及渡船進款三類，後者亦分爲雜項進款附屬營業進款及互用車輛三類。

客運進款詳分下列各類：

進—一 客運業務—旅客

進—一—一 尋常

進—一—二 政府

進—一—二—一 屬於行政者

進—一—二—二 屬於軍事者

進—一—三 優待票

進—一—四 遊覽票

進—一—五 補價票

進—一—六 睡車票

進—一—七 特別費

進—一—八 定期票

進—二 客運業務—其他

進—二—一 行李

進—二—一—一 公衆

進—二—一—二 政府

進—二—二 包裹

進—二—二—一 公衆

進—二—二—二 政府

進—二—二—三 本路

進—二—三 車輛及動物

進—二—三—一 公衆

進—二—三—二 政府

進—二—四 專車

進—二—四—一 公衆

進—二—四—二 政府

進—二—五 郵運業務

進—二—六 裝卸力

進—二—七 貨幣

上海交通大学百年报刊集成·第一辑（1896—1949）·学术学科

進—二—七—一　公衆

進—二—七—二　政府

進—二—八　其他　手

客運業務—旅客（進—一），及客運業務—其他（進—二），之性質不同，故應分別比較，客運業務—旅客（進—一）中尋常（進—一—一），與政府（進—一—二），優待票（進—一—三），遊覽票（進—一—四）；補價票（進—一—五），睡車票（進—一—六），特別費（進—一—七），及定期票（進—一—八），亦須分別比較。因尋常（進—一—一），之增減原因與其他各類之增減原因均不相同。政府（進—一—二）與優待票（進—一—三），係減價票—其最高數年有一定。遊覽票（進—一—四），與定期票（進—一—八），亦爲減價票，其數額之大小與運價減低之程度，鐵路之營業方針，及社會之狀況有關。補價票（進—一—五），與鐵路之管理方法有關。睡車票（進—一—六）與特別費（進—一—七），雖與尋常（進—一—一）有關，但以分別研究爲當。至客運業務—其他（進—二）亦宜依此分別各加以分析，其關係於政府項下之數，更應注意。

分析營業進款之第一步手續爲本期與上期營業進款之比較，視其爲增或減，再推究本期進款增減之原因。

客運進款增減之原因可求之於(一)票價之變動，(二)客運性質之變動，(三)鐵路經營之得失，(四)外界之影響。票價本高，如有減低，則營業有增加之望，惟進款總數是否因而增加，則須視減低之程度如何而定。票價本低，如提高之，則營業有減少之可能，惟進款總數是否因而減少，須視提高之程度如何而定。蓋票價之高低，一方固與進款總數有關，一方尤與運輸者間之競爭及旅客之心理有關，其增加程度苟有過分，則既足以減抑旅客之乘車慾。幷足以啓劇烈之競爭；減低程度如過分，則以客觀環境之限制，營業亦不能陡增也。

旅客之等級，行程之長短及旅行之性質與進款總數頗有關係，因等級高，行程長，均爲增加進款之因數，而尋常客運之收入又較政府運輸及遊覽票等之收入爲大也。等級高低與鐵路沿線之社會經濟情形有關。行程遠近與路線之長短有關。大凡一鐵路沿線之經濟發達或其路經過政治都會者，高級乘客較多，如昔之北寧平津段及今日京滬路，頭二等旅客均較其他各路爲多。路線長者，其旅客之行程亦多較路線短者爲遠，此蓋由於路線長，乘客有機會旅行長途；我國各路之情形與此甚合。惟亦有不盡然者，即若鐵路兩端幷非大都會，而大都會反在沿線，則短程乘客較長程者多，每旅客之平均行程卽不甚遠。

鐵路本身之經營方法亦與進款之增減有關，蓋鐵路之設備，對旅客之服務及招攬旅客之方法，如能運用得當，甚能增加營業。近時我國各路頗注意及此，於車行之舒適，旅客之便利等。均有改進，各路營業近年漸見好象者，此一原因也。

此外，社會情况，政事變遷，經濟消長，均能間接或直接影響鐵路之進款。在昔軍閥時代，各處內戰。行旅褁足，鐵路收入大爲減少。不特此也，自南京定都以來，京滬路上旅客如雲，鐵路收入，較前倍增，皆此之證。又如經濟興旺。則人民富力加增，不僅旅行興趣增加，且有求舒適之欲，凡此皆足以增加鐵路之進款也。

客運進款增減之原因已如上述。惟每期進款之增減，非必所有原因之結果，亦非必某一原因之結果，研究者須仔細分析，度定其因。而分析客運進款增減之工具則有三；一爲每延人公里之平均進款，二爲每旅客列車公車之平均進款，三爲每旅客之平均進款。

每延人公里之平均進款係由延人公里除客運進款之數而得，亦稱之曰「客運平均價」。以此數與基本運價相比較，可得知客運進款之增減係由於運價之有提抑，抑由於旅客人數或其行程之有增減；由此并可測知此項變動係由於何級客運增減所致。當運用此工具時，最好能分別等級，分別全價票與減價票，以求得較繁原因。

每旅客列車公里之平均進款，係由旅客列車公里除客運進款之數而得，由此單位可測知營業進款與經營之關係。如此平均數之增係由於列車里程之減少，乃屬管理得當之果，如此平均數之減係由於列車里程之增多，則爲經營不善所致。如此平均數與列車里程具同一趨勢，則當追究列車里程是否應當增加，此則屬於經營效率之研究。容待後文論之。

每旅客之平均進款，係以旅客人數除客運進款之數而得，係補助每延人公里之平均進款一單位者，當運用時應按照旅客乘車之等級，分計人數而求得各個平均數，藉以知悉各等旅客之收入及各等間相互之比例。如票價未改，則每旅客之平均行程一單位卽已足用。

今試以某路爲例，逐步分析其二十二年份客運進款增減之原因。

一 觀察進款總數之變動，係由於何項之增減，其法卽爲比較二十二年份與二十一年份各項客運進款之數。

進款類別	二十二年	二十一年	增減實數	增減百分數
客運進款總數（元）	三、七九五、四三四・二四	三、八四八、一二一・六四	減 五二、六八八・四〇	減 一〇〇
旅客（進—一）（元）	三、四四九、二一五・六九	三、五八八、三〇五・八〇	減一〇七、〇九〇・一一	減 二〇七
其他（進—二）（元）	三四六、二一八・五五	六八九、八一六・八四	增 五六、四〇一・七四	增 一〇七

二 觀上表，二十二年份客運進款之減少殆純係旅客業務（進—一）減少之所致，故第二步當觀察旅客業務各項之變動情形。

款類	二十二年	二十一年	增減實數	增減百分數
旅客（進—一）（元）	三、四九九、二一五・六九	三、五五八、三〇五・八〇	減一〇九、〇九〇・一一	減一〇〇・〇〇

尋常(進—一—一)(元)	三、二四九、六九六・二七	三、三七九、五九一・七三	減一二九、八九五・四六	減一一九・○○
政府(進　一—二)(元)	一四、四三七・六○	二三、八五六・三五	減　九、四一八・七五	減　八・六○
優待票(進—一—三)(元)	一二、七五七・二二	九、七二六・四○	增　三、○三○・八二	增　二・八○
遊覽票(進—一—四)(元)	五二、九九六・五八	三四、四三六・○四	增　一八、五六○・五四	增　一七・○○
補票(進—一—五)(元)	一、六○四・六五	一、四二六・二五	增　一七八・四○	(數過小不列)
睡車票(進—一—六)(元)	一五、一三一・五○	一○、二八一・○○	增　四、八五○・五○	增　四・四○
特別費(進—一—七)(元)	一○三、五四三・八七	九八、九八八・○三	增　三、五五五・八四	增　三・三○
定期票(進—一—八)(元)	四八・○○	…………	增　四八・○○	(數過小不列)

三　觀上表，可知旅客進款十萬餘元之減少，純係尋常旅客與政府旅客二項業務之減少所致，而以前者爲最，故第三步當研究尋常旅客業務減少之原因。

項目	二十二年	二十一年	增減實數	增減百分數
1.尋常旅客(進—一—一)(元)	三、二四九、六九六・二七	三、三七九、五九一・七三	減一二九、八九五・四六	減　三・八四
2.尋常旅客延人公里	二四五、一一三、七三一	三三七、九四九、一七三	減九二、八三五、四四二	減　二・七四
3.旅客列車公里	一、一九九、一五三	一、二七○、六○四	減　七一、四五一	減　五・六二
4.旅客列車車里(註)	一○、二四八、三七三	一○、一五七、七四八	減　九○、六二五	減　○・八九

5.每旅客公里之平均延人公里(2÷3)	二〇四	二〇〇	增	四	增 二·〇〇
6.尋常旅客人數	二、七七〇、三八五	三、〇三〇、七七七	減	二六四、三九二	減 八·七一
7.每延人公里之平均進款(1÷2)(元)	一·三二	一·三三	減	〇·〇一	減 〇·七五
8.每旅客列車公里之平均進款(2÷3)(元)	二·七一	二·六六	增	〇·〇五	增 一·八九
9.每旅客列車車里之平均進款(1÷4)(元)	〇·三一七	〇·三三三	減	〇·一六	減四八·〇〇
10.每旅客之平均進款(1÷6)(元)	一·一七	一·一一	增	〇·〇六	增 五·五六
11.每旅客列車之平均車輛數(4÷3)	八·五四	七·九九	增	〇·五五	增 六·九〇
12.每輛車之平均旅客數(2÷4)	二三·九二	三三·二七	減	九·三五	減 六·一〇
13.每旅客之平均行程(2÷6)	八八	八四	增	四	增 四·七〇

（註）我國僅有客坐里程統計，如欲求客車車里，則以七五除客坐里程卽得。

分析上表，每旅客之平均行程及每旅客之平均進款均有增加，旅客列車公里及旅客列車車里均有減少，而旅客列車公里之平均進款反有增加，由此可見二十二年客運進款之減少，既非由於旅客行程之減少，亦非由於列車與車輛運轉之失計，更非由於票價之變更（此觀於上表每延人公里之平均進款無甚變動及是年該路并未減低票價可知，）實由於旅客之減少二十六萬餘人，尤多短程者；故延人公里數，每旅客列車車里之平均進款數及每輛車之平均旅

上海交通大学百年报刊集成・第一辑（1896—1949）・学术学科

客數均見減少。又由每延人公里之平均進款之減少。可知高級旅客業務亦稍有減少，而此數與三等票價率相近，可知業務大都爲三等。至每旅客列車之平均車輛數稍有增加者，則因旅客列車所掛車輛數本有一定，而在該年其他客運均有增加。故此增加之數實有其需要。

四　據上分析之結果，已知二十二年份客運進款之減少，殆純係旅客人數減少所致，故第四步當研究所減少之旅客係屬於何等級者。

等級	項別	二十二年	二十一年	增減實數	增減百分數
頭等	人數	五、三六三	五、四四〇	減 七七	減 一・四二
	延人公里數	一、五六六、六〇八	一、六二六、九六六	減 六〇、三五八	減 三・七一
	每人平均行程	二九二	二九九	減 七	減 二・三四
二等	人數	三二、五三一	三五、四八五	減 二、九五四	減 八・三一
	延人公里數	五、四一五、三八〇	五、八九七、〇八八	減 四八一、七〇八	減 八・一七
	每人平均行程	一六六	一六六	…………	…………
三等	人數	二、七一〇、〇一一	二、九六九、五二五	減 二五九、五一四	減 八・七四
	延人公里數	二二九、八二五、六七〇	二三八、四七三、八四〇	減 一〇八、六四八、一七〇	減 三二・一〇
	每人平均行程	八五	八〇	增 五	增 六・二五

等級	項目			增減	百分比
四等	人數	二二、四八〇	二四、三二七	減 一、八四七	減 七·五九
	延人公里數	八、三〇九、〇七八	八、〇四六、一一三	增 二六二、九六五	增 三·二七
	每人平均行程	三七〇	三三一	增 三九	增 一一·七八

自上表可看出頭，二，三，四各等旅客人數均有減少，頭等僅減七人，爲數殊微，四等僅約二千人，二等亦僅約三千人，最巨者爲三等，計減二十五萬餘人，佔全減少數百分之九十六。由上表中，更可窺見旅客行程且有增加之象，足徵是年客運進款之減少，殆純屬三等短程旅客減少之所致。據該路之意見，以爲此項減少，係一由於東北事變後百業蕭條，客商來往較稀。而往東北之國人，因多阻碍往返甚少；二由於沿綫各地長途汽車日益普遍，鐵路之短程旅客多爲之奪去。此言尙確。至於社會人士，利用鐵路則較前爲多，此觀於睡車票，遊覽票特別費等特項進款之有增加可知也。

二　貨運進款

貨運進款分類較簡，故分析貨運進款須賴貨運統計。於分析之初，首應觀察進款之增減，係由於普通貨物之變動，抑由於外路材料或本路材料運輸之有變動，然後再分別就貨物之等級與種類，材料之類別，加以分析。玆試取民國二一—二二年份某路之貨運進款爲例·逐步分析之如左。

一 先比較二十二年份與二十一年份之貨運進款：

項別	二十二年	二十一年	增減實數	增減百分數
貨運進款總數(元)	九、九三〇、五九六・三八	九、六五六、二五〇・八九	增二七四、三四五・四〇	增一〇〇・〇〇
普通貨物(進-三-一)(元)	九、二六三、六四六・二〇	九、三一四、九〇七・八八	減 五一、二六一・六八	減 一八・六九
他路材料(進-三-二)(元)	………	………	………	………
本路材料(進-三-三)(元)	二三四、八五七・九五	一七五、四五九・六〇	增 五九、三九八・三五	增 二一・六六
調車費(進-四-一)(元)	二一四、二三五・八三	一六九、七三四・〇〇	增 四四、五〇一・八三	增 一六・二二
裝卸費(進-四-二)(元)	二一五、九三三・二一	九八六・三〇	增二一四、九四六・九一	增 七八・三五
延期費(進-四-三)(元)	一、九二三・一九	五、一六三・二二	減 三、二四〇・〇三	減 一・二八

據上引統計，該路二十二年普通貨運進款減少五萬元，但其貨運進款總數反增加百分之二・八四，爲數二十七萬餘元，考其原因，實係該年本路材料之運輸增多及調車費與裝卸費之增加所致，其中尤以裝卸費所增爲鉅，計佔全數百分之七八・三五，較上年增百分之二一七・九三。據該路之意見，此係實行負責運輸後，貨物裝卸由路自辦，將此費歸於貨運進款項下所致。

二 上表示本路材料運輸進款之增加，佔進款增加數百分之二一，六六，今試分析其增加之原因何在。

項別	二十二年	二十一年	增減實數	增減百分數
建築用材料(元)	六〇、二四〇·三五	一九、一〇三·三五	增四一、一二七·〇〇	增二一五·三三
營業用材料(元)	一一六、三六九·八〇	八九、三〇〇·九〇	增二七、〇六八·九〇	增三〇·三一
機車處用煤(元)	五八、二四七·八〇	五七、〇五五·三五	增一、一九二·四五	增二·〇九

據上引統計，建築用材料之運輸增加甚劇，營業用材料次之，機車處用煤僅增加百分之二，〇九。爲數微末。按民二十二年該路曾利用庚款，更換橋樑及軌枕，共費一百三十九萬餘元，同年復舉辦負責運輸，設備頗有添加，故本路材料運輸因而增多。

三　普通貨物運進款在二十二年有五萬餘元之減少，其原因如何，亦應研究。通常表示貨運進款增減之單位爲每延噸公里之平均進款，其變動之原因甚爲複雜，大體言之，不外爲運價之增減，業務性質之改變，貨物品類之變更及一般經濟情形之變遷。

貨運運價，常有變動，其影響貨物之運輸量及進款者甚大，故運價乃鐵路運輸學中專題之一。分析貨運進款者，首應注意運價有無變更之處。貨運業務之性質亦常予進款以重大之影響。如在遞遠遞減運價政策之下，若某期之長距離運輸增多，則每延噸公里之平均進款必見減少。又如鐵路於某種貨物採用固定運價，如膠濟路之於出口煤炭，則是項貨物如多在距離較遠之站間運輸，則每延噸公里之平均進款亦必見減少。又如整車運價較零擔者為低，故若某期之整車運輸增多，則每延噸公里之平均進款價必減少也。

我國鐵路分貨物為礦產品，農產品，林產品；禽畜品及製造品五種，分運價為六等，而將五種貨品依其所屬分別列於此六等項下。如某期中等級較高之貨物運輸量成數較大，則每延噸公里之平均進款自亦增加。

在一般經濟情形良好時，鐵路貨運較繁，進款亦呈增勢；如一般經濟緊縮或呈現恐慌，鐵路貨運卽行減少，進款自亦隨之而減少；故社會上之一般經濟狀況與貨運進款之增減亦至有關係也。

通常分析貨運進款之工具為每延噸公里之平均進款及每貨物列車公里之平均進款二單位。影響前者之原因，已見前論。影響後者之原因則一為每單位貨運業務之代價（卽每延噸公里之平均進款）之變動。一為貨物列車載量（卽每貨物列車公里之延噸公里數）之變動。茲試應用此項工具，取某路二十二年份貨運進款為例而分析之。

項別	二十二年	二十一年	增減實數	增減百分數
1.普通貨物進款(元)(進三一一)	九、二二五、〇五八·〇六	九、二七八、〇七八·〇一	減 五三、〇一九·九五	減 〇·五七
2.貨物噸數	二、二七五、五一〇	二、一五三、五六八	增 一二一、九四二	增 五·六六

3.延噸公里	五七五、三〇五、四一九	五五七、六三八、九九七	增一七、六六六、四二二	增三・一七
4.每噸平均進款1÷2(元)	四・〇五	四・二一	減 〇・一六	減 六・〇三
5.每噸平均行程(3÷2)	二五二・八二	二五八・九四	減 六・一二	減 二・三六
6.每延噸公里之平均進款(1÷3)(元)	〇・〇一六〇	〇・〇一六六	減 〇・〇〇六	減 三・六一
7.貨物列車公里	一、九五二、四二一	一、七八四、三九〇	增 一六八、〇三一	增 九・四二
8.每列車公里之平均進款(1÷7)(元)	四・七二	五・二〇	減 〇・四八	減 九・二三
9.每列車公里之延噸公里(3÷7)	二九四・六六	三二二・五一	減 一七・八五	減 五・七一

根據上表，二十二年每延噸公里之平均進款減少百分之三・六一，此指數表示在是年該路有運價減低之情事，或所運低等貨物之噸數增加之情形或二者均有。參以貨物噸數增加百分之五・六六，可知低等貨物之運輸頗有增加。更參以每噸平均行程減少百分之二・三六，而每噸平均進款竟減少百分之六・〇三，而該路所運貨物多屬低等，可知減低運價之情事亦有。

二十二年該路每貨物列車公里之平均進款較二十一年減少百分之九・二三，此固由於進款總數之減少，亦實由於列車公里增加百分之九・四二。進而言之，則由於列車裝載量減少百分之五・七一及每單位貨運業務之代價減少百分之三・六一。前者之減與行車有關，後者則已見前述。

此外，由每噸平均行程之減少百分之三·三六觀之，可見平均行程之減少亦係貨運進款減少之原因之一。

有一簡便公式，足供分析之用，以求各統計單位間之關係，茲述之於下。

甲　$R=T+A+(T\times A)$

設R代表貨運進款之增減百分數，

T代表延噸公里之增減百分數，

A代表每延噸公里之平均進款之增減百分數，

試以前表所引之統計爲例計算如下：

$$R=3.17\%+(-3.61\%)+\{(3.17\%)\times(-3.61\%)\}$$

$$=-0.44\%-(-0.114437\%)$$

$$=-0.554437\%$$

乙　$R'=T'+A'+(T'\times A')$

設R'代表每貨物列車公里之平均進款之增減百分數

T'代表每貨物列車公里之平均延噸公里之增減百分數

A'代表每延噸公里之平均進款之增減百分數

試以前表之統計爲例計算如下：

$$R'=(-5.71\%)+(-3.61\%)+\{(-5.71\%)\times(-3.61\%)\}$$
$$=(-9.32\%)+0.020613\%$$
$$=-9.2993861\%$$

丙 $R''=T''+A''+(T''\times A'')$

設R''代表每噸平均進款之增減百分數

T''代表每噸平均行程之增減百分數

A''代表每延噸公里之平均進款之增減百分數

試以前表之統計爲例，計算如下：

$$R''=(-2.36\%)+(-3.61\%)+\{(-2.36\%)\times(-3.61\%)\}$$
$$=(-5.97\%)+0.088\%$$
$$=-5.885\%$$

此三公式之用，一在表示各統計單位間之關係，二在核對統計之計算。用此項公式計算所得之結果雖與前表之統計稍有參差，然此非公式之誤，乃其中所用之數字不能求其十分準確也。

據上文分析之結果，本年該路貨運進款之減少，係由於所運低等貨物之噸數增加，運費之減低及平均行程之減少，惟究係何種何等貨物噸數之增加，何種貨物運費之減低及減低之程度如何，則均待進一步之分析，關於運費之減低可參閱車務處之減價通飭，至於何種貨物噸數之增加及行程之減少，則可根據貨物運輸統計分析之。惟於何等貨物，則因現今各路尙乏之統計可據，惟如能求出貨物之種類，其等級自明。

總稽核室制度與審計辦事處制度之比較

貢乙青

一國政務，非財莫舉，財政實爲施行一切政務之基礎，故凡屬立憲國家之財政均設有三重監督之機關。國會爲財政立法監督，其職權在制定財政法規議決歲入歲出預算審議決算，財政部爲財務行政監督，其職權在整理財務行政及核實收支，審計院爲財政司法監督，其職權在依據現行法令及預算，審定國家收支及其結果，以爲最後之報告。組織權限，極爲分明。要之以立法監督爲始基，以行政監督爲中堅，最後則以司法監督爲之結束。

今吾國試行五權憲法，所謂立法權行政權監督權同屬於治權內之一部分各自獨立，實行其職權，而互相輔助，以完治權之作用俾成一極有能力之政府。故規定審計部隸屬於監察院，係根據五權憲法精神而組織之機關，與三權憲法之審計機關其性質完全不同。三權憲法之國會，屬於人民方面之代議機關，其監督政度之權限，不僅限於預算，並得審議其決算。審計院每年編成之審計報告，尙須經由內閣送交國會爲最後之決議，是以審計機關之對于立法機關實無對等地位。惟五權憲法之立法院，其監督財政僅有制定財政法規及議決預算兩事，而關於決算之監督，惟監察院內之審計部，有最後審議之決定權，逕向主管監察院報告，無須再向立法機關請求決議。比較論之，五權憲法內之審計職權，實較三權憲法內之審計職權，具有獨立性。茲爲比較明顯起見，試列表以觀之：

甲 三權憲法下財務監督系統

財務監督
- 立法的…國會所轄 財務法規委員會及預算委員會
- 行政的…國務院所轄各部會
- 司法的…審計院

乙 五權憲法下財務監督系統

財務監督
- 立法的…立法院所轄 財務法規委員會及預算委員會
- 行政的…行政院所轄部各會
- 監察的…監督院所轄審計部

如以系統分晰而論，三權憲法下審計院工作仍須向國會報告五權憲法下審計部，不必再向立法院報告。

基於分權系統，以觀察駐路總稽核室及駐路審計辦事處，兩者截然不同。駐路總稽核室隸屬於鐵道部，所具體用均爲行政的，駐路審計辦事處隸屬於審計部，所具體用均爲監察的。行政財務監督對其所屬機關財務行爲，均有指揮監督之權，對于所屬機關預算決算，均有初審議駁之權，此鐵道部對各路財務監督行使之職掌及範圍也。監察財務監督，對於被審機關財務行爲，均可依據法案議駁，但被審機關預算法案之編審、財務法規之參訂，款項之調撥，收支之管理，不得過問，此審計部對于被審各路財務監督行使之職掌及範圍也。駐路總稽核室，爲受命鐵道部對路行使財務監督，駐路審計辦事處，爲受命審計部對路行使財務監督，其職掌範圍亦因彼此體系之不同，功用遂亦歧異。

茲請將審計部津浦審計辦事處審核津浦鐵路收支辦法條文作爲實例，分晰研究，並與鐵道部所訂駐路總稽核職掌規程，以及其他法令凡關於總稽核職掌之行使者，分別比較之。

一、關於預算之審議。查預算法案，爲一切財務行爲之最後目標，其最後決定權，自應屬於立法機關，但行政機關，對于所轄下級機關預算，在編製之時，得加以初審意見，甚至得按照所定行政計劃，增減其數額，目前國有營業預算法規，尚未頒佈，其已公佈之預算法，雖於二十一年公佈，但尚未實行，故現在辦理鐵路預算法令根據，即爲二十年頒佈之預算章程，及二十三年鐵道部所訂之國有鐵路編製概算及執行預算暫行規程。預算章程第二十三條載「各主管機關審核第一級概算應分別加具審核意見彙編各分類歲入歲出概算書……」此主管機關對于下級機關預算有初審權之明文規定也。又鐵道部編製概算及執行預算暫行規程第十八條載「各路總稽核收到各處預算時應加審核如有增減事項並應於會計處彙編以前與各處商洽辦理」此總稽核受命鐵道部審議鐵路概算權限之明文規定也。但駐路審計辦事處，絕不能有此權限。

二、關於款項之調撥　查款項調撥，在預算範圍以內主管行政機關，得指揮監督，視各路財政狀況，因時制宜，作適當之調撥或因時間之關係，作淡旺月之佈置。或因地點關係，作安穩之保存。譬如（一）簽發支票在鐵道部方面認爲愼重起見須由總稽核會簽始生效用（二）出納課庫存，至多不得過三千元，（三）支付大宗款項，應開發記名支票或劃線支票，（四）在中央銀行未經設立之處，存款處所或銀行，得由鐵道部核定（五）爲償還債款，鐵道部得命各路確立該項基金，另案存儲等等。凡此種種，咸屬于行政監督以內，總稽核得憑部令監督之，審計部對於被審機關，無從過問，故審計辦事處，對于各路，理亦不能有此權能。

三、關於管理方面內部牽制制度之效用　內部牽制制度（Internal Check System）在管理學組織學上，爲促進一企業經營效率之最主要原則。事業範圍越廣，內部牽制需要越須緊密，所謂法治精神，不外乎此。鐵路事業在公營事業之中，最爲繁複，組織上對內部牽制制度亦最爲需要。駐路總稽核室對各路管理局，可以發揮內部牽制效能之處，已經法令明文規定者，約有下端：

（一）員工薪費付出之牽制。如三十級以上之薪給及津貼公費房租等有一項在十元以上未經部令者，總稽核不得簽發。（鐵道部總字第一三七六號訓令）職員加薪進級不報部者，不得簽發。（鐵道部總字第三一六三號訓令）支領交際費應酬費或類似此項名目，未經部令者不得簽發。（鐵道部總字第五四四九號訓令）嗣後各路非路線擴展，或現有人員出缺，一概不得增派編列年度預算，以現有員工爲估計標準，不得預留空額，（鐵道部計字第一一五一二號訓令）員工薪工統計月報表須由總稽核室先行審核會署呈報（鐵道部總字第一〇三六號訓令）等等。此所以薪費支給，縱在年度預算以內據部令規定，總稽核仍得拒簽。

(二)對于訂立契約文件之牽制，駐路總稽核職掌規程第七條載「路局對外訂立契約，應由總稽核審核會同局長或委員長簽署方生効力……」云云。

(三)購定材料之牽制。路局購買材料訂立合同，均須得總稽核會署，方生效力。故購置材料。縱在年度預算以內，但鐵路財政狀況如較預定計劃已有變更時，總稽核仍得視路務之前進狀況，轉商路局改變其購料合同。凡此諸端，不過略舉一斑，表示駐路總稽核制度在內部牽制制度之下促進管理之效率，駐路審計辦事處，殊未之能也。

駐路總稽核室及駐路審計辦事處，在體系方面及功用方面不同之點，已如前述。但兩者之間，類似之點亦甚多、故常易誤被認識卽爲一體。在原則方面此兩機關共同目的，均以監督財務行爲爲唯一任務。惟駐路總稽核室係屬於行政之組織，駐路審計辦事處，係屬於監察之組織。行政之監督，除執行本身（行政範圍）之權能外，對于立法及監察範圍內之監督，因其職責之關係，尚兼有初審之任務。如核定預算立法之監督也。判定決算監察之監督也。但行政機關對所屬下級各機關預算決算，仍有初審彙編之責任。駐路審計辦事處，對鐵路財政有監察監督之權能，駐路總稽核室對鐵路財政在審計方面，有初審之權能，此兩者類似之處亦卽誤被認識爲兩者卽一體之故，在功用方面駐路審計辦事處之任務，除具有決定性最後性而外，駐路總稽核室幾無不能爲之，惟無決定權已耳。前者有決審之權，後者衹有初審之權，在審計方面，兩者功用之不同，卽在此點，現在國內已設立之駐路審計辦事處，衹有津浦一路，茲請就審計部津浦鐵路審計辦事處審計津浦鐵路收支辦法各條文一一觀察。

審計辦事處審核津浦收支辦法計共二十八條，全盤條文，除第二十七條第廿八條兩項係說明本條文立場無庸分晰外，其餘二十六條，（第一條至二十六條）均係說明駐路審計辦事處對鐵路財務監督之具體辦法。此二十六條辦法，除第二十六條一項，係審計之決定權能。非駐路總稽核室僅具有初審權能所可辦理外，其餘二十五條辦法（第一條至第二十五條）幾無一不爲現行駐路稽核室職掌規定視爲職責份內應行之事務。譬如：第一條係說明審核准預算項下之收支或核轉概算項下之收支手續，第二，三，五，條係說明審核追加預算項下之動支手續，第十一，十二，條係說明審核流用預算項下之動支手續，第十三，十四，十五，十六，十七各條係說明審核材料之訂購監標驗收收發調撥以及用料報銷點查存料等手續，第十八條係說明審核薪工之手續。第十九條說明審核轉帳之手續。第四條係說明審核預付暫付代收保管款項之手續。第六，七，二十，條係說明核簽查詢指駁之手續，及時間之限制。第二十二條係說明確定現金預算之支配。第二十一條係說明查閱表册之手續。第二十三，二十四，二十五，各條係說明計算書決算書之編送。凡此種種駐路總稽核室無一不辦理之，此其類似之處，功用相同之所在也。

駐路審計辦事處與駐路總稽核室，彼此相同之點與相異之點，大致已如前述。兩者之功用，在鐵路財務監督上，自各有其短長。概要言之，駐路審計辦事處功用之長處，爲其具有決定性獨立性。駐路總稽核室之長處，爲其具有牽制性聯綜性。因此之故。前者之運用不若後者運用之靈活，而後者之運用又不若前者運用之毅決。鐵路財政，非若普通行政機關，其收支之大部，視業務之演進，頗含有伸縮性。監督任務，如執行時一若對普通行政機關之固定，勢必窒碍滋生。然爲避免窒碍之計，又復事前含混承認，則事後審查轉受其拘束。所謂例外過多，種種約束難免成爲具文。故鐵路財政，適用駐路審計辦事處之監督，抑駐路總稽核室之監督，非本文所敢論，要在當局者審愼抉擇焉。

附錄

審計部津浦鐵路審計辦事處審核津浦鐵路收支辦法

第一條　審計辦事處審核鐵路收支，應以鐵路年度預算核定數內，預算科目為根據，如年度開始，而本年度預算尚未成立時，得暫以鐵道部核轉主計處之年度概算為根據，其不列入年度預算或概算內之收支，依照第二三四五條規定辦理。

第二條　凡因鐵路業務之激增，而連帶增加之業務等費支出，不在原列年度預算數項以內。但經鐵道部核准者，審計辦事處得先行核簽，再由鐵路局補辦追加預算手續。

第三條　鐵道部因籌劃整個鐵道財政及調劑各路款項盈絀，而命令鐵路負担提撥之特別支款，如統籌償還鐵路債款，攤墊全國鐵路建設經費，以及其他一切協款墊款等等之含有同樣性質者，審計部辦事處得先行核簽，再由鐵道部查酌款項性質，補辦追加預算或併入其他預算案內辦理。

第四條　審計辦事處對於鐵路收付款項中之預付暫付代收保管等款，有法令根據或經鐵道部核准者，應予簽發。

第五條　凡因鐵道遭受天災事變或因緊急設施，而發生之特別緊急支出，未列有預算者得由鐵路局急電呈請鐵道部核准後，送審計辦事處核簽，再行補辦追加預算手續。

第六條　審計辦事處核簽收支原始單據時，應依照現行鐵路章制會計制度，及參酌具有法令同等效力之成例辦理。

第七條　審計辦事處審核收支單據時，如有疑問得查詢之，認爲與法令成例不合，得指駁或請更正之。

第八條　審計辦事處，對于鐵路進款單據，除審核點驗單外，其他進款單據，得隨時抽查之。

第九條　凡未經審計辦事處核准簽發之支付款項，會計處不得付款。

第十條　審計辦事處對于不應支付之款項而核准簽發者，應依法負責。

第十一條　資本支出預算內各項目之分配，在不超出資本支出預算總額以外，經鐵道部核准者各項目間，得自相流用。

第十二條　營業支出預算內各項目之分配，如因營業事實之變更，而必須流用時，得由鐵路局呈請鐵道部核准。互相流用之鐵路局，應將呈准流用之事實，詳細通知審計辦事處，以爲核簽付款之根據。

第十三條　鐵路局購買材料添置機械及工程修建等，應將呈請購料單，購料單圖樣，說明書，合同，契約等，各項憑單，抄送審計辦事處核准存查。

第十四條　鐵路局購買材料，添置機械及工程修建等之各種開標驗收事項，審計辦事處應派員監視。

第十五條　鐵路材料廠或庫存於發放各處領用之材料，及接收退回之材料時，應將發料單及退回材料報告單，抄送審計辦事處，隨時檢查各領料處間，材料之調撥亦同。

第十六條　各處領用材料後，應將材料之使用退回等情事，於每月終抄單報告審計辦事處審核。

第十七條　審計辦事處，對于材料廠或庫所存儲之材料，及各領料處用料之實況，得隨時會同鐵路局材料點查員，稽察材料查核帳目。

第十八條　審計辦事處，對于工資工款之審核，如有疑問時，得派員實地稽察之。

第十九條　轉帳所用之原始單據及文件，應由鐵路局會計處列定科目，送審計辦事處審核，但帳目間互相整理之單純轉帳，審計辦事處，可無須核簽。

第二十條　審計辦事處、審計鐵路局，送處審核之單據，均應從速決定准駁，除必須查詢者外，自收到之日起，不得逾二日，其重要緊急者，不得逾三小時，

第二十一條　審計辦事處，得派員隨時赴各主管處所，查閱各項表單帳冊。

第二十二條　鐵路局應於每月二十五日以前，編造次月份現金收支預算書類，送審計辦事處

備查。

第二十三條　鐵路局於每月經過後三個月以內。編成月份營業進款計算書，營業用款計算書，總原簿懸記帳，詳細報告收支帳，資本支出報告，資本收支計算書等，連同收支憑證單據，及其他表册等送審計辦事處審查，其收支憑證單據，核畢後送回鐵路局保存之。

第二十四條　審計辦事處，審查鐵路收支計算，如有疑義得行文查詢限期答覆，或派員調查。

第二十五條　鐵路局應於年度經過後四個月以內。編成決算報告書類，送審計辦事處查核。

第二十六條　審計辦事處，審查鐵路局收入支出計算書，及證明單據，認爲正當者，應發給核准狀。

第二十七條　本辦法如有未盡事宜，由鐵道審計兩部會商修改之。

第二十八條　本辦法自鐵道審計兩部，分別呈請行政監察兩院，核准備案之日施行。

鐵道部特派駐路總稽核職掌規則

第一條　鐵道部爲稽核國有鐵路款之收支，及其他有關財務事項，以厲行預算制度，防止浮濫用款起見，特派駐路總稽核，直隸本部，常川駐紮各路辦事，於路局設總稽核室，爲總稽核辦公之用。

第二條　總稽核室，得酌設稽核員二人至四人，事務員及書記若干人，其名額由總稽核呈部核定，稽核員事務員由部派充，書記由總稽核派充，呈部核准備案，總稽核室經費，由總稽核造具預算呈部核准後，由部飭局按月撥發。

第三條　所有會計處收支款項，由會計處長負責核簽後，應再送總稽核親自簽署。

第四條　總稽核對于全路一切款項之支出，均以奉部核准之預算，爲稽核之標準，所有預算以外之開支，未經本部核准者，總稽核應拒絕簽署。

第五條　一切支款及銀行支票，未經總稽核會同局長或委員長簽署者，作爲無效，總稽核應將簽字式樣，送各來往銀行存查。

第六條　會計處一切用款之支付，送總稽核審核時，應將單據連同帳單等，檢齊附送。

第七條　路局對外訂立契約，應由總稽核審核，會同局長或委員長簽署，方生效力，其應呈部核定者，應先呈部請示。

第八條　各處一切帳册簿、單據表、契約、文件、總稽核得隨時調閱，遇有疑義，得隨時查詢主管人員，應詳細答覆。

第九條　總稽核對于其他各處，及各段站廠所帳目，應隨時親自前往，或派員查核。

第十條　總稽核遇事務上必要時，得臨時借調各處員司，協助辦理。

第十一條　總稽核應出席局務會議。

第十二條　總稽核與局長或委員長往來文件，以函行之。

第十三條　總稽核應將稽核工作情形，按旬報部，其重要事項，應隨時報部。

第十四條　凡於本規程頒佈前，所有各路已設立總稽核，其組織及權限，均依本規程之規定修改之。

第十五條　各路總稽核室，得分科辦事，其規則另行擬訂，呈部核准。

第十六條　本規程自公佈日施行。

中華國有鐵路現行行車時刻表 (四)

膠 濟 綫

民國二十三年七月一日起實行

2次各等	74次二三等	22次各等	72次二三等	52次各等	上行(東行)列車	站名	下行(西行)列車	51次各等	21次各等	71次二三等	73次二三等	1次各等
22.00	14.40	11.40		7.00	開	濟南	到	18.00	22.12		13.35	7.30
22.06	14.47	11.47		7.09	開	北關	開	17.55	22.07		13.29	7.25
22.13	14.55	11.54		7.16	開	黃臺	開	17.47	21.55		13.20	7.17
不停	15.10	12.08		7.30	開	王舍人莊	開	17.34	21.41		13.05	7.01
不停	15.23	12.20		7.40	開	郭店	開	17.23	31.30		12.52	6.50
22.48	15.39	12.36		7.57	開	龍山	開	17.08	21.15		12.35	6.34
23.03	15.55	12.52		8.13	開	棗園莊	開	16.54	21.00		12.18	6.19
不停	16.07	13.03		8.24	開	明水	開	16.44	20.49		12.05	6.09
23.28	16.30	13.20		8.41	開	普集	開	16.29	20.34		11.48	5.53
不停	16.42	13.31		8.52	開	王村	開	16.19	20.24		11.36	不停
不停	16.54	不停		9.03	開	大臨池	開	16.07	不停		11.22	5.13
0.01	17.13	13.56		9.20	到	周村	開	15.43	19.48		10.47	5.10
0.04	17.16	13.59		9.23	開		到	15.40	19.51		10.45	不停
不停	17.35	不停		9.40	開	馬尚	開	15.21	不停		10.20	4.31
0.26	17.43	14.21		9.48	到	張店	開	15.12	19.23		10.10	4.46
0.41	17.58	14.36		10.03	開		到	14.57	19.08		9.55	不停
不停	18.11	14.49		10.15	開	湖田	到	14.48	18.59		9.44	不停
不停	18.21	14.58		10.24	開	金嶺鎮	開	14.35	18.50		9.33	不停
1.10	18.37	15.12		10.38	開	辛店	開	14.21	18.36		9.17	4.05
不停	18.51	15.25		10.51	開	淄河店	開	14.08	18.19		9 02	不停
不停	19.03	不停		11.01	開	普通	開	13.58	不停		8.50	不停
1·39	19.16	15.44		11.13	到	青州	開	13.46	18.00		8.36	3.36
1.42	19.19	15.47		11.16	開		到	13.43	17.56		8.33	3.34
不停	19.35	16.02		11.31	開	楊家莊	開	13.28	17.41		8.14	不停
不停	19.46	16.13		11.42	開	譚家坊	開	13.17	17.30		8.00	不停
不停	19.59	16.25		11.54	開	堯溝	開	13.05	17.18		7.46	不停
2.22	20.12	15.37		12.06	開	昌樂	開	12.53	17.06		7.33	2.53
2.39	20.26	16.51		12.19	開	朱劉店	開	12.40	16.52		7.17	2.40
不停	20.37	17.01		12.30	開	大圩河	開	12.29	不停		7.04	不停
2.58	20.50	17.13		12.42	到	濰縣	開	12.15	16.30		6.49	2.18
3.01	20.54	17.16	7.00	12.45	開		開	12.12	16.28	20.35	6.44	2.16
3.10	21.04	17.25	7.10	12.54	開	二十里堡	開	12.04	16.20	20.26	6.34	2.08
3.22	21.17	17.37	7.23	13.06	到	坊子	開	11.52	16.08	20.13	6.20	1.56
3.37		17.51	7.38	13.21	開		到	11.37	15.54	20.02		1.41
3.52		18.06	7.54	13.36	開	蝦蟆屯	開	11.24	15.41	19.48		1.28
不停		不停	8.09	13.50	開	南流	開	11.09	不停	19.31		不停
不停		18.24	8.17	13.57	開	黃旗堡	開	11.01	15.21	19.23		不停
4.18		18.35	8.29	14.08	開	岞山	開	10.52	15.12	19 13		1.02
不停		18.54	8.48	14.26	開	丈嶺	開	10.33	14.53	18 53		不停
不停		19.03	8.58	14.42	開	塔耳堡	開	10.23	14.43	18.39		不停
不停		19.12	9.08	14.51	開	蔡家莊	開	10.13	14.32	18.28		不停
不停		不停	9 20	15.02	開	康家莊	開	10.02	不停	18.16		不停
5.04		19.31	9.32	15.13	到	高密	開	9.50	14.12	18.03		0.12
5.12		19.42	9.43	15.24	開		到	9.39	14.01	17.52		0.01
不停		不停	9.56	15.36	開	姚哥莊	開	9.28	不停	17.41		不停
不停		20.00	10.05	15.45	開	芝蘭莊	開	9.19	13.44	17.32		不停
5.47		10.17	10.23	16.02	到	膠州	開	9.02	13.27	17.14		23.30
5.49		10.19	10.26	16.04	開		到	9.00	13.25	17.11		23.28
不停		不停	10·39	16.16	開	膠東	開	8.48	不停	16.58		不停
不停		不停	10.51	16.27	開	李哥莊	開	8.36	不停	16.45		不停
6.15		20.46	11.01	16.37	開	藍村	開	8.27	12.58	16.36		23.01
不停		20.59	11.15	16.50	開	南泉	開	8.13	12.43	16.18		不停
6.41		21.15	11.34	17.08	開	城陽	開	7.57	12.27	16.01		22.34
不停		21.24	11.44	17.17	開	女姑口	開	7.48	12.18	15.51		不停
6.29		21.36	12.07	17.29	開	滄口	開	7.36	12.06	15.38		22.16
7.19		21.59	12.25	17.45	開	四方	開	7.20	11.50	15.20		22.00
7.30		22.10	12.35	17.55	開	大港	開	7·11	11.41	15.11		21.51
7.35		22.15	12.40	18.00	到	青島	開	7.00	11.30	15.00		21.40

零擔貨物處理方法與聯運直達沿途零擔車制度

沈奏廷

零擔貨物之數量零星，到達地點往往不同，應如何湊集而整理之，方能收簡捷經濟之效，洵爲鐵路運輸上之一大問題。按鐵路運輸零貨之法不外四種：(一)爲整車零擔，(二)爲合裝零擔，(三)爲沿途零擔，(四)爲中轉零擔，而後者於中轉之後仍須化爲整車零擔，合裝零擔或沿途零擔，一視情形而異。茲請先就此四種方法分別簡述之如次：

(一)**整車零擔** 凡由同一起運站(或中轉站)發出之各地零擔貨物，運往同一到達站，其數量足以湊成一車者，可合裝於一車內，由出發站加封起運，直駛到達站起卸，沿途不得啓封，是爲整車零擔車，因其由起站以至訖站之運送，交付及授受，實與整車貨物無殊，惟一車裝有兩批以上之貨物并有兩家以上之收貨人而已。凡始發站有多量之貨物運往同一地點者，自以用整車零擔法裝運爲最簡捷經濟，惟貨物之數量應加以規定，以免車輛之虛糜，按國有鐵路零擔車處理辦法之規定，凡整車零擔車所裝貨物之總重量不得少於車輛載重量四分之三，但如各路之中上下行貨運狀況有不平衡者，得就回空車輛之一方，將所應裝載之重量另定之 以資變通。由是以觀，整車零擔一法雖最爲經濟簡捷，然非有相當之貨物數量不可。否則此法卽不能適用也。

(二)合裝零擔　凡由一站發往兩到達站之零擔貨物或由兩站發往同一到達站之零擔貨物合裝於一車者謂之合裝零擔車，此法介於整車零擔與沿途零擔之間，有兩個到達站或兩個起運站，實一兩站拼裝之整車零擔車也。合裝零擔車非特須有貨物數量之規定，且須有兩站距離之限制，蓋不如是，則車輛將反多虛糜，殊非合裝零擔之本旨矣。按吾國鐵路零擔車處理辦法之規定，合裝零擔車應遵下列之限制：

(甲)貨物數量　全部貨物之總重量不得少於車輛載重量四分之三，但各路因利用回空車輛得更變通之，惟運往每一到達站或由每一起運站運出之貨物數量仍不得少於全部貨物重量十分之四。

(乙)兩站距離　兩起運站或兩到達站之距離不得超過五十公里，但各路仍得酌量變通之。

由此可見合裝零擔一法既有數量之規定，又有距離之限制，事實上較整車零擔尤難凑合，故適用之範圍尤狹也。

(三)沿途零擔　凡裝運各站至各站之零擔貨物，沿途須從事裝卸者謂之沿途零擔車。沿途零擔車既無貨物起碼數量之規定，復無各站間距離之限制，凡不合於整車零擔或合裝零擔之條件者，概須用沿途零擔車裝運之。在西國鐵路，沿途零擔車之行駛均限於路線之一段，各段均有各段之沿途零擔車，按日往來運送，故沿途零擔貨物大致可分兩種：一爲本段沿途零擔，一爲他段沿途零擔，爲便於說明起見，請設圖例以示之：

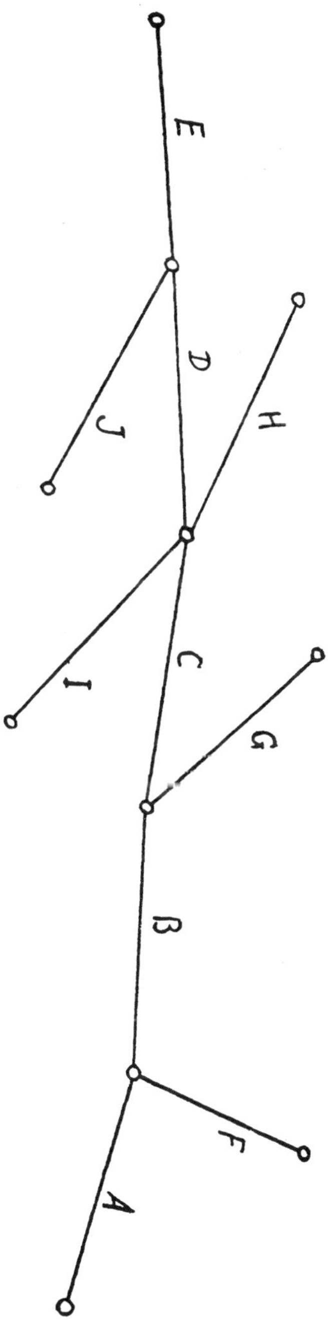

凡A段內各站起運之沿途零擔貨物運往A段內各站起卸者，可由A段內行駛之沿途零擔車輸送，是謂本段沿途零擔。若A段內某站有零貨多批運往D段內之各站，其數量足以湊集一車者，則往往由A段內之起運站按各站遠近次序裝成一車，直駛D段，迨入D段，再由D段之沿途零担列車分別輸送起卸，故自A至D段間，該車可由直達貨物列車運送，其運行情形一如整車零擔車，抵D段後，乃改挂沿途零担列車，從事起卸，如D段內有貨須裝，亦可裝貨，是爲他段沿途零担。

(四)中轉零担　整車零担與合裝零担既非有到達站相同之多量貨物不可，而本段沿途零擔又祗限於本段內各站至各站之貨物，他段沿途零擔亦以由一站至他段內各站，而路徑相順，總數量較多者爲限，故以上各法均各有其限制，未必能適用於一切沿途零擔貨物也。例如遇有下列各種貨物時，卽非另用他法裝運不可，請畢述之：

(甲)由本段某站運往其他各段之貨物　例如A段某站有零擔貨物數批，其到達地點有在G段者，有在C段者，有在H段者，有在I段者，而每段之數量又不甚多，整車與合裝零擔兩法，固不適用，卽他段沿途零擔一法亦非所宜，因到達各段之總數量祗敷一車裝載，若每段各挂沿途零擔車一輛，則共須四輛，且均不能滿載，殊非經濟之道也。爲適應此種情形計，A段某站祗得將上項貨物併裝一車，直挂C段之某中轉站，（該中轉站常位於C段與B段交界處之調車場內）由該中轉站卸車分析，連同他處送來之中轉零擔貨物，轉裝他車，或化成整車，或合裝零擔，或化成各段沿途零擔，或一部份仍作中轉零擔，挂往D段中轉站（在D段與C段之交界處），再事分析拼裝，直至化成整車，合裝或沿途零擔爲止；推一次以上之中轉僅於貨物數量不足時爲止，因其跡近耗費，力應避免者也。

(乙)由本段各站至他段各站之貨物　例如A段內沿途各小站常有零貨起運，其到達地點亦散佈於各段，數量極爲零星，其唯一集散之方法，往往由A段內行駛之沿途零擔列車沿途裝運，運往指定之某站（該站常爲該列車之終點），由該站封車待運，迨本段沿途整車列車 Pick up & Drop Train 經過該站時，乃爲之拖送至最近中轉站，從事中轉焉。

(丙)由本路至他路之貨物　在美國鐵路，凡由本路運往他路之零擔貨物，除整車零擔外，大都不問其到達地點之爲何，均併裝一車或數車，直挂他路之最近中轉站或兩路聯軌站，由接運路從事中轉。例如甲路某站（起運站或中轉站）有零貨多批，運往乙路，其到達站點甚多，而每一到達站點之貨物又不足以裝一整車零擔車，故該站卽將上項貨物併裝一車，直挂甲乙兩路之聯軌站或乙路最近之中轉站，由乙路從事卸車分析，中轉起運。除有特殊規定外，甲路例不代乙路裝成順序起卸之沿途零擔車 Station Order Car，因乙路或有他貨可以併裝，由中轉零擔化爲整車或合裝零擔，其經濟簡捷將遠勝於沿途零擔也。

(丙)由沿途小站起運之笨重貨物　沿途小站之普通零擔貨物，概由沿途零擔列車裝運，既如前述。然如遇有特殊笨重之貨，則往往另撥車輛，停留該站裝載，以免延誤零擔列車與裝載不便之患。是項車輛通常不能滿載，若直駛貨物到達地點，必不經濟。故往往由沿途整車列車挂往就近中轉站，由中轉站併裝他種貨物，再行挂運，亦中轉零擔貨物之一種也。

由是可見中轉零擔一法，實爲一種補救之方法，乃手段而非目的也。零貨中轉耗費雖多，然在其他方法不能適用時，仍以中轉爲較經濟，否則車輛之虛糜將不可勝計矣。

吾國鐵路路線較爲簡單，本路零擔貨物大致均用整車，合裝與沿途零擔三法裝運，中轉零擔尚不多見。惟聯運貨物則利用中轉一法者甚多，按部頒聯運零擔貨物處理辦法，聯運零貨之中轉路線，規定如左：

(1)由上海至漢口或至鄭州以南或以北之零擔貨物均在鄭州中轉；
(2)由上海至天津以東各站之零擔貨物均在天津總站中轉；
(3)由上海至平綏沿線各站之零擔貨物均在豐台中轉；
(4)由上海至平漢北站之零擔貨物，亦可在豐台中轉；
(5)由上海至徐州以東各站之零擔貨物，均在徐州中轉；
(6)由天津東站至石家莊以南及至正太路沿線各站之零擔貨物，均在石家莊中轉；
(7)由平綏包頭及沿線各站至平漢路豐台以南之零擔貨物，均在豐台中轉；
(8)由平綏包頭及沿線各站至天津以東各站之零擔貨物，均在天津東站中轉；
(9)由膠濟路沿綫各站至各聯運路各站之零擔貨物，均在濟南中轉；
(10)由各路及平漢路各站至湘鄂路沿綫各站之零擔貨物，在江岸站中轉；
(11)由湘鄂路至平漢路及其他各路之零擔貨物，在徐家棚站中轉；
(12)由各路及京滬滬杭甬路至浙贛路沿綫各站之零擔貨物，均在閘口站中轉；

(13)以上各路線除平漢路與湘鄂路業有往返中轉站規定外，其他各路綫，回程均適用同一中轉站。

處理中轉零擔貨物，尙有兩大原則必須遵守：卽(一)中轉零擔貨物應儘量集合，載至最速之中轉站從事起卸分發，以免一次以上之中轉；(二)凡由中轉站後方各站起運至其他中轉站前方各站之貨物，應似前方中轉站彙成一車或數車，直駛後方中轉站起卸分發。以免車輛之虛糜是也。

× × × × ×

吾國鐵路處理零擔貨物，除用整車零擔，合裝零擔，沿途零擔，(本路)與中轉零擔諸法外，對於聯運零貨，尙有聯運直達沿途零擔車制度之試行，此制爲西國之所無，頗稱新頴，殊有研究之價値。按所謂聯運直達沿途零擔車者，卽將甲路運往乙路之聯運零擔貨物，沿途裝入指定之零擔車內，迨至乙路，不必倒載中轉，卽行沿途起卸，并由車輛主有路派員押運，在聯軌站不必交付也。考此制之特點，可爲之歸納舉述者有如下列：

(一)直達沿途零擔車在起運路時，祇裝聯運零擔貨物，不得裝卸本路貨物，故與本路沿途零擔車有別；

(二)行抵到達路後，如有空位，亦得裝載本路貨物，故又與該路之本路沿途零擔車相似；

(三)自始至始，直達沿途零擔車概由車輛主有路派員押運，在聯軌站無交付貨整之手續，故與整車或中轉零擔均各有異；

(四)直達沿途零擔車係原過軌，無中轉之必要，故適與中轉零擔相反；

吾國現時規定行駛直達沿途零担車之路綫有如下列：

(一)由上海直通西安

(二)由上海直通北平

(現分滬徐及滬平兩綫前者裝徐州以南之貨，後者裝徐州以北之貨)

(三)由天津東站直通包頭

(四)由天津東站直通石家莊

以上直通路線回程亦適用之

至於直達沿途零担車之實施辦法，則各綫均大同小異，茲將滬西聯運直達沿途零擔車辦事細則錄列如左以見一班：

第一條　聯運直達沿途零擔車之運用，與附挂車次如後附表(表從略)

第二條　聯運直達沿途零擔車暫定每列車各挂四十噸篷車二輛，按照列後附表共計需車三十二輛，以經行里程計算，由京滬出車八輛，津浦出車八輛，隴海出車十六輛，該項車輛彼此均不計算車租，並不入過軌帳內，惟須按日另行登記，以便查考。

第三條 押運司事，每列車各派一名，某路車輛卽歸某路押運司事押運。其休息日期由各路自行規定。

第四條 押運司事應受所在路段長站長等之指揮。

第五條 聯運直達沿途零擔車，祇裝滬西間各站聯運零擔貨物，但其他零擔貨物，視車內有空餘時亦可裝運。

第六條 押運司事報告，應塡寫四份，一份存根，三份交上海或西安站，（自上海至西安零擔車交西安站長，自西安至上海零擔車交上海站長）分寄京滬、津浦、隴海三路車務處。報告內之年月日車次等欄，只塡上海或西安列車出發之日期及列車數次。

第七條 上海、浦口、徐州、鄭州、潼關、西安六處應預備押運司事住宿處所，上海歸京滬預備，浦口徐州兩處歸津浦預備，鄭州潼關西安三處歸隴海預備。

第八條 如因列車遲延，以致翌日無車回程時，上海或西安兩站，應另籌適當車輛及指派人員補充之。

第九條 沿途零擔車如遇中途損壞時應由所在路撥車換裝。其辦法如下：

(甲)京滬隴海車輛在津浦損壞時，應由津浦派車代替倒裝，並將損壞車修竣，於該項代替車輛囘到損壞車之原有路以前，送還原有路，原有路收到該修竣空車後，應將上項代替車輛於到達西安或上海後，卽行送還津浦。

(乙)津浦車輛在京滬或隴海損壞時，由各該所在路撥車代替，俟損壞車修竣及代替車囘至損壞車之所在路(西安或上海)後，再行換囘。

(丙)隴海車輛在京滬損壞或京滬車輛在隴海損壞時，應按乙項辦理。

第十條　其他各項事宜概按部頒零擔車處理辦法處理之。

由以上之叙述，吾人已可明瞭聯運直達沿途零擔車之性質及其實施之方法，茲請再進一步，以闡明其利弊之所在，而獲相當之評價焉。

按聯運直達沿途零擔車之利益，不外下列三端：

(一)免除中轉之時間，人力及手續之耗費，增進貨運之迅速。

(二)自始至終，由同一押運司事照料，責任分明，遇有損失，無推諉之弊。

(三)在聯軌站無交付實在貨物之必要，節省輾轉授受之手續。

然凡事有優點者亦必有缺點，聯運直達沿途零擔車制度亦然，其缺點何在，請舉述之：

(一)聯運直達沿途零擔車裝運前往到達路各站之貨物，對於到達路之路線並不劃分段落，一律沿途裝卸，如到達各站之貨物數量不多，自無問題，否則必不經濟。何以言之，例如由上海至西安之直達沿途零擔車，對於徐州西安間之路綫並不劃分數段，若京滬路有零貨多批運往鄭州至西安間各站，足資裝載　車，則此車終可由南京直挂鄭州，沿途不必啓封，與整車零擔車無異，迨抵鄭州後再行換挂沿途零擔列車，從事裝卸工作，豈非較爲迅速經濟？故若有此種情形發生，聯運直接沿途零擔車辦法如現時之所進行者應不適用。

（二）如聯運貨物在到達路尚有本路貨可以併裝，化成整車或合裝零擔時，則尚不如作爲中轉零擔裝運爲宜，例如由京滬路往隴海路之貨物原不足以併成直達整車零擔，然抵徐州站後，或尚有津浦及隴海之貨物，足資拼裝，是京滬之貨物到徐州後亦可一部化成整車或合裝零擔，僅餘一小部分仍作沿途零擔裝運，是爲車輛利用經濟起見，尚不如將京滬貨物裝成中轉零擔直駛徐州之爲愈，至時間之耗於中轉者，因整車零擔運行之較速，或反可取償之而有餘也。

（三）聯運直達沿途零擔車既由車輛主有路所派之押運司事押運。而同一列車之本路沿途零擔車又由各路自派押車司事照料，互相重複，亦殊不經濟。

綜上所述足見聯運直達沿途零擔車制度，在吾國現時貨運情形尚簡，數量尚少之際，自尚有相當之優點與存在之價值，他日貨運來源愈多，數量愈增，則此制必不經濟，爾時聯運零貨之處理，仍非常採用下列方法不可：

(甲)用中轉零擔法運至最遠之聯軌站。使與他貨併裝，大部份化爲整車零擔或合裝零擔，直駛到達地點。

(乙)對於到達路線劃分相當段落，倣照西國通行之他段沿途零擔車辦法，分裝各段沿途零擔車，直駛各該段，沿途不啓車封，迨抵各該段後，再行換挂沿途零站列車，從事分發。

或謂採用(乙)法，則起運路與到達路間不能互相授受實在貨物，設有損失，勢必互相推諉，責任無由分明，對於吾國國情殊非所宜。曰是無庸過於顧慮也。按現時整車零站貨物，兩路間亦祇授受車輛而不授受實在貨物，雖有互相推諉責任之事，然吾人並不以此而舍整車零担於不用。況鐵路對於貨物司事與押車司事均有處罰解雇之權，設屢次發生損失，形跡可疑，不難加以相當之處分，以儆效尤，而肅紀律，果能訓練員工，使能忠於其事，則情弊自不絕而自絕矣。

大學教育中之管理學程

嚴礪平

一 管理與管理學

自工業革命以後，工商業規模日漸擴大，生產組織亦愈趨複雜，復因同業間競爭之烈，管理問題遂爲世人所注意。實業之失敗或成功，其原因固爲多方的。如政治，社會，經濟，競爭諸項，均有關係，然管理之良窳，實爲最重要之因素。

對於管理之定義，學者主張，亦稍有出入，茲舉二則以資參攷。雷斯白教授（註一）謂管理乃實業組織中之各部分相互的運用，使和衷共濟，以冀能達預定之目標。金波爾教授（註二）則謂，管理乃運用經濟原理，以支配實業組織中「人」「物」二項之一種藝術。

實業組織，每依其生產目的而定；實施管理方法，亦視實業範圍之大小，與事務之繁簡而異。然管理亦有似其他科學，有原則可循。吾人之各種活動事業，初起時，恆憑臆測與個人經驗，以定處理組織中各種事務之方法。必俟經驗的紀載，充實詳盡，方可依之作爲根據，歸納成各種結論與重要之原則。此種科學方法之運用，在管理一方，殊有成効。我人認爲管理已成爲一科學。（註三）人事與物質的處理，各有種種法則與原則爲根據。故大學中，研究與講授管理科學實爲至要。管理科學，與其他科學，如理化數學等在大學教育上佔有同等之地位。

二　美國大學之管理教育

大學之管理學科講授，最早者首推德國。德國杜皮根大學在一八一七年，已聘立斯特教授講授政治經濟及公務管理學。然管理教育之發達，最爲普遍者，則爲美國。我國大學之管理教育，與美國相類者甚多。故研究美國各大學之管理學科概況，實大有稗益于吾人也，

美國大學之管理教育，現分爲三大類：其一爲商業管理科與鐵路管理科其二爲工業管理科其三爲公務管理科。除公務管理科之性質已詳見林叠教授所論列外。玆將前二種學科之成立起源，課程大概，略爲論列之。（註四）

甲　美國大學中，首授管理學程中任何課目者，應推本雪文尼亞大學之（University of Pennsylvania）華頓氏理財學院。。是院創始於一八八一年，由約瑟華頓（Joseph Wharton）之建議而設立。華頓本斐城一商人，見解頗新穎。對於教育素以正確明顯爲主。該院自始，卽講授會計，理財、商業地理等課程。

此類商業管理科，各大學中逐漸添設。在一九〇〇年已有七校。在一九二八年則有三十八校。而該年畢業生達，四千三百六十八之多。（以上數字根據美國商業管理協會會員錄其未入會者尚不列入）各大學中設有管理及會計等學系者則在一九二五年約有一八二系。

商業管理科之肄業年限。頗有出入。最短者爲二年。最長者爲五年。尙有少數大學，如哈佛等校，則以商業管理科，列入大學院。據博沙及杜赫斯二氏(Bossard and Dewhurst)之調查，二年者有十二校，三年者有二校，四年者最多；有二十三校，五年者亦祇有三校。大抵年限爲二年者，則入院生須先修大學文學院普通科二年。三年者，則管理課程分三年授畢。四年者，則與大學中其他學科相同，入學者中學畢業已可。五年者，則在校年期，仍爲四年：餘一年爲實際練習，俟實習完畢，方得學位。

各校之課程，因年限關係，頗有出入。卽年限相同，亦因各校歷史及當局見解之不同而異，惟下列諸基本課目，各校均有：卽經濟原理商業文學，商業地理，政治學，實驗心理學，社會學，數學及簡單之自然科學。據博沙及杜赫斯二氏之研究，管理學科，可分爲主要及次要二類，主要者爲六項：卽商法，統計，市場學，會計，貨幣與銀行，及公司理財，次要爲商業文學，勞工問題。商業組織與管理，經濟原理，銷售。及人事管理等項。各校所用課目名稱，雖多不一致，大概可以上項分類區別之。多數學院有八門至十門之專習科；如鐵道運輸，國外貿易，保險，銀行，公用事業，商法，會計，商業師範等科目。

乙　工程師。尤其機械工程師、因其身在工廠，故在管理機械之外，逐漸注意及于廠務組織，工作方法，及人事管理。諸項管理問題，遂成今日管理運動之先鋒。首先創是運動者，爲泰婁氏 F. W. Taylor 泰婁氏爲一機械工程師。雖與上述之華頓同屬斐城人，又爲好友，惟其思想則爲獨立的，殊非受華頓氏之影響。泰婁爲人富于研究心，凡事均用科學方法處理，其成績之燦爛，（註五）幾使聞者見疑。風會所及，本薛文尼亞省立大學 (Pennsylvania State College) 首先成立工業管理工程科。以泰婁之介紹，聘請提摩教授 (H. Diemer) 爲主任，此爲一九〇八年之事也。工程學院之兼授管理課程者，在一九〇四年已有康乃耳大學之金波爾教授，然康乃耳在一九一四年，方成立工業管理工程一科也。

此類工業管理工程科，大抵均屬於各大學之工學院。在一九一四年，全國祇有四科。在一九三一年，已有三十五科矣。是年畢業生約有六百名。

此科性質，各校不一。有二十一校。設專科，授管理工程學位。有十四校，學生雖習管理學科，並無管理學位，仍以工程學位畢業者。管理學科之講授，年限亦無一定。大抵授管理學位者，管理課程，恆分配於第二三四三年中授畢。授其他學位者，則恆將管理課程，分配於一年或二年之中，亦有數校，將管理科目，縮成爲一課程，在一年中授畢者。

課程方面，在授管理工程學位之各校，大抵將工程科目與管理科目，酌量分配，工程科目，管理科目各佔其半。工程科目大概如下：數學，理化，現代實驗，材料力學，圖畫，應用力學，水力學。(有十二校無此課)熱力工程，熱力工程試驗，電力工程。電力工程試驗，測量(有數校無此課)工廠實習，工程材料，工程問題討論等。管理科目則爲工業史，工業經濟。製造概況，人事管理，生產管理，會計，統計，市場學，理財方法，運輸，及工業組織等科目。

以上二種大學中之管理教育，在美國均甚發達，而以商業管理科爲尤甚。每年畢業生均甚多。在實業界各能得服務之機會。大概商業管理科畢業者，因于銀行及商法方面，多受訓練。故易得升遷。管理工程科畢業者，能深入工廠，故于廠務組織方面，較爲專長。至於購買，會計，及人事三項，則雙方畢業生，可云均能勝任。實則二種學科，目的均在應實業界之需要，培植明瞭管理原則之基本管理人才耳。

三 我國大學管理教育

我國大學中之設有管理教育者，計有三種：其一爲各大學之商學院，及獨立商學院，其二爲大學工程學院機械系之工業管理門，其三爲大學中之管理學院。

甲、商學院 我國除設有獨立之商學院外，各大學亦大都設有商學院。均係講授商業及商業管理方面之課程。各院亦每設有三五專門學系：如工商管理，會計，國際貿易，鐵路，銀行等。此類學院，性質頗似上節所述美國大學中之商業管理學院。課程方面，亦大致相同。惟教材則以適合國情爲主。畢業生概授商學士學位。

乙、工業管理工程科　此科均設在大學工學院之機械系或機械科，如現在北平之淸華大學工學院機械系，及民十三年時代之南洋大學機械科。課程方面以工程爲主。管理科目，殊不完全。故畢業生仍均予機械工程學士學位。

丙、管理學院　本國大學之設立管理學院者，目前祇有交通大學。交通大學之講授管理課程歷史已久。前在工業專門學校時代，已有鐵路管理科之設。民國十九年孫哲生校長掌大學校務後，擴充爲管理學院。分設公務。財務，鐵道，實業四科。分別訂定課程，以適合各該科之宗旨。學生畢業。則授予各該科之管理學士學位。

交大之管理學院，實爲集合並整理各國所現有之原則相同而應用不同之各種管理學科於一爐。另成一管理敎育之特殊統系。四科內容均較美國各大學爲充實，如鐵道管理與財務管理二科，頗似美國大學商業管理學院中之二系。惟課程則較爲詳盡。如鐵道管理科中之機車管理，鐵道工程，航空運輸，經濟統制制度，港埠管理。中國外交史等課程；與財務管理科中之鹽務行政，海關業務，中國外交史等課程，大都爲美國商業管理學院中此等學系所不備。

交大管理學院中之實業管理科，頗似美國大學中之工業管理工程科。課程則較爲充實。除講授相等之工程與管理科目外，尙有中國富源，心理學。社會學，國內外匯兌，勞工問題，預算學，估値學，廣告學及審計學等課程。亦爲美國之工業管理工程科所缺。

四　大學管理教育應注意之二要點

甲、管理教育須重基本原則之訓練　實業界範圍之廣大，及部分之繁多，欲在學校中，全盤顧及、各部分均作極精細之實用研究，在事實上爲不可能之事。故學校教育。須注重基本原則之訓練，殊不必專作狹義的專門智識的灌輸。卽實業界領袖，亦深明此理。故每於雇用畢業生時，先予以若干之練習時間，以窺其運用基本原則以處理事務之才能。米西根大學霍奇思（Hotchkiss）院長曾爲商業管理教育言曰「商業教育，非可本身獨立，實乃高等教育中之一部分。學校須以職業爲對象，使學生能得商業管理基本原則的智力訓練，與廣義的認識。」旨哉言乎。此義亦誠適用于他種之大學教育也。

乙、學校與實業界須互相合作　大學與實業界合作之最初步的，爲學生課外時作實地的參觀，與實業界人士之能到校作各種專門之演講。此均爲充實課程，爲學校所不可少者。最好學校與實業界能成立一合作辦法，使學生於假期中，可往實習。若能使實習部分，與學校課程銜接，則管理教育之効率必愈形增高。學生方面，在求學時已有實際事務的認識，畢業後，其服務能力自能加大。

吾人甚盼此種合作能實現。蓋學校與實業均蒙其利也。學校方面，教育効率提高，畢業生出路易于解決。實業方面，或有困難問題可供學校之研究。卽欲延聘人才，亦易得優良之選。實則學校與實業，均爲一共同目標而努力，卽改良與振興實業，以促進民生耳。

註一 R. H. Lansburgh "Industrial Management" 第四頁

註二 D. S. Kimball "Industrial Organization" 第一三三頁

註三 參觀「管理」第一期第五頁

註四 Lytle "Collegiate Courses in Management" Journal of S.P.E.E. 1932

註五 F. W. Taylor 'Principles of Seieniifc Management'

註六 參觀「管理」第一期第十七頁

教育之重要

一年之計，莫如樹穀。十年之計，莫如樹木。終身之計，莫如樹人。一樹一穫者，穀也。一樹十穫者，木也。一樹百穫者，人也。

管子權修篇

從價稅與從量稅之檢討

胡紀常

一 引言

關稅管理之主要工具、厥爲稅則；而稅則內含之要項，當推稅率，自稅率之編訂技術而言，稅率方式之採定，實爲一極重要之問題。稅率之方式，通常有從價與從量二種。但因此二種方式，利弊互見，故亦有設法予以改變，以求集合兩式之優點者。於是此種分化而出之稅率方式，復有混合稅 (Compound duties)，擇用稅 (Alternative duties)，滑準稅 (Sliding Scale duties)，及官定準價稅 (Official Valuation Scale duties) 四種。因此等稅率方式，皆係根據從價稅或從量稅演繹而出，故從價及從量二稅，可稱爲稅率之基本方式 (Basic forms of duty rate)，而而各種演繹而出之方式，可稱爲稅率之演繹方式 (deduced forms of duty rate)。稅率之演繹方式，其性質及運用，頗爲複雜，當另文探討。本文所及，僅以從價及從量二種基本方式爲範圍。

從價稅爲依據貨物之價格而課稅之方式，其稅率以從價值百抽若干表示之。例如我國二十三年進口稅稅則，對於汽車之輸入，從價征稅百分之三十是。從量稅爲依據貨物之數量而課稅之方式，其視爲課稅標準之數量，或爲重量，或爲體積，或爲長度，或爲個數，………

…要以貨物形體之不同而異。易言之。卽凡可將貨物數量提舉之單位，擇其便於課稅手續者，皆可用作從量課稅之標準。例如我國二十三年進口稅稅則，棉花以百公斤爲單位，酒精以公升爲單位、柚木以立方公尺爲單位，煤以噸爲單位，箱裝煤油以每十美加侖爲單位是。惟從價與從量，方式雖異，而關係綦密；蓋物價之陳示，不能不以數量單位爲根據，而從量稅率之釐訂，亦不能不以從價値百抽若干爲預定基準。是故從價與從量二種稅率，可以互相表示；例如某貨每百公斤價洋十元，則値百抽十之從價稅，可以每百公斤課稅一元之從量稅表示之，而每百公斤一元之從量稅，亦卽等於値百抽十之從價稅也。

試觀各國稅則中所用之稅率方式，大多爲從價稅與從量稅，可知此二種稅率方式，實爲各國關稅稅率方式之主體。惟此二種稅率，在各國稅則中之地位，頗有軒輊。就各國某時期之稅則而觀，從價與從量，互有消長；但就長時期之趨勢以觀，則從量稅之應用，日益普遍，而從價稅之應用，日益減少。考歐美主要商業各國之稅則，於十九世紀中葉，猶大多偏重於從價稅率，例如法國一八六〇年與各國訂立商約而形成之協定稅則，其稅率幾悉爲從價。又如美國一八三二年之稅則，因國會稅則委員會對於從價稅及從量稅利弊之研究報告，認從價稅率較爲優勝，故其所定稅率，從價爲主。迨十九世紀末葉，保護貿易主義盛倡，歐陸各國之稅則，大多盡量採用從量稅率。例如德國因欲與各國訂立有利的商約起見，曾將其稅則貨目，力求精析，從量稅目，因以增多。法國之採用從量稅制—始於一八八一年之稅則。其後一八九二年之稅則，幾悉爲從量，從價稅率，僅佔十目而已。美國一八九〇年之麥金萊稅則，對於從價稅率，雖益見信用，但此並非將從量稅稅率、悉予擯棄，多數貨物，均採用從價與從量之混合稅制。自二十世紀之初，以迄戰前，各國爲便於實施其關稅差別待遇政策起見，從量稅率之應用，益見普遍。戰後，因物價漲落無定，各國稅則中之從價稅目，曾略見增加，但以視從量稅目，爲數仍屬寥寥也。（註一）

從量稅率於應用上所以能取代從價稅率之原因，分析言之，雖可自貨物性質，物價，匯兌，商業政策及國際關係諸方面，作各別之觀察、但綜合言之，要不外乎從價稅與從量稅對於一國之經濟環境及所採商業政策能否適應之研究。簡言之，卽從價稅與從量稅應用上利弊之探討。本文目的，卽擬將從價與從量二種稅率方式之利弊，各就理論與實用，詳爲分析討論。然後根據探求所得，對於我國稅則所用之稅率方式，予以檢討，並試爲改進之建議，以供國人之參攷。

二　從價稅之利弊

自理論上觀之，從價稅之優點，不一而足，臚陳於次。

（一）從價稅對於關稅之保護目的，可以直接達到而不感周折。關稅之保護目的，原欲以人爲之方法，使外貨之價格增高若干，俾其至少與國產貨物有利之售價相等。今設若外貨與國貨生產成本之差額，能確知其爲外貨尙未納稅時價格之百分之幾而卽以此項百分數爲外貨輸入之從價稅率，則保護目的之達到，可謂直捷而簡當。

(二)公平而簡單，亦爲從價稅之優點。何謂公平？因從價稅隨貨價之漲落而自爲增減；價高者稅多，價低者稅少，極爲公平之原則。何謂簡單？因從價稅可將性質互異而稅率相同之貨物，列入一目，故其稅則貨目簡少，不若從量稅稅則貨目之繁複。從量稅對於含有多種品級之貨物，必須詳分子目，目予一率，庶幾與各級品質之貨價，有適當之比例；但從價稅自能依貨物各級品質之不同價格而爲適當之差別，其較爲簡單也明甚。

(三)從價稅所予國產貨物之保護程度，頗爲穩定。輸入貨物之從價稅額，雖依物價而增減，但其所予國產貨物之保護程度，則始終等於其對於外貨課稅，價格之百分比，或卽從價稅率，而不變；並不若從量稅之遇貨價一有變更時而卽已失却其保護國產貨物之原有的程度。

(四)從價稅對於貨物納稅後價格增高之數量，易於預測，常人對於某貨繳納百分之二十之從價稅後，可以預知此貨價格之增高，當在二成之譜。

(五)對於舊貨，古董，珍玩以及不能以形體表示價值之貨，如樂器，圖畫，彫刻等藝術作品，僅有從價稅率，可以適用。例如價值相去百倍之彫刻品，其材料之品質及數量，儘可相等，其形體亦可相若，但若課以從量稅，則直無從爲稅率輕重之區別。此種貨物，自非課以從價稅不可。

惟是上述種種之優點，多有祇合乎理論而不見諸實用者；因之從價稅乃不免於下列之缺點：

(一)從價稅能自動的隨物價之高下爲輕重，說者謂其非特能直捷的達到關稅之目的，且能予國產貨物以穩定的保護。殊不知此種適應能力，除非國產貨物與外貨生產成本之差額對於外貨之課稅價格，常保其固定的比例，而後始能實現。但實際上此項固定的比例，決不能常存，因此從價稅施行之結果，輒與關稅之保護目的，背道而馳。茲設例以明之。設若某貨之從價稅，其據以訂定稅率之標準價格，爲是貨當時在外國輸出市場之價格。在此種情形之下，若此後是貨在外國市場之價格見跌，則是此貨對於國產同類貨物之競爭力，較前增高；此時爲予國產貨物以適當之保護起見，此項外貨之進口稅，理應增高，以阻抑其輸入；但因從價之故，所課稅額，較前反輕。反之，爲該貨在外國市場之價格上漲，則是其對於國產貨物之競爭力減小；此時爲免予國產貨物以過度之保護計，理當減輕外貨之進口稅；但因從價之故。所課稅額，較前反重。此項設例，係假定以是貨在國外市場之價格，爲訂定從價稅率之標準價格。但當此項標準價格，改用是貨在國內輸入市場之價格時，從價稅之不能適應關稅之保護目的，正復相同。蓋設若國內生產增加，貨價下跌；此時外貨之輸入，須藉高稅予以阻抑，但因從價之故所征稅額，較前反低。反之，如國內貨價因生產同盟或他種原因而增高；此時應將關稅輕減，以利外貨之輸入；但因從價之故，所課稅額較前見增。

(二)從價稅之不能適應關稅之保護目的，尙有他說，可資明證。製造品之生產成本，通常包括原料及人工。若干重要原料，其市場爲無界的，各國價格，無甚差異。某貨國內外生產成本之所以不同者，祇由於工資成本之互異，亦卽保護關稅之所由設。今設若某貨國內外工資成本之差數，並無變更，則原料之價格，縱有變動，但因國內外漲落相等之故，國產貨物與外貨生產成本之差額，一如往昔。國內外生產成本差額，旣無變更，則進口稅額，亦應不變；但因從價之故，較前或增或減，一視外貨輸入課稅價格之高下爲依歸。準是以觀，則從價稅所予國產貨物之保護，固並不確當也。

(三)但從價稅之最大缺點，當爲其管理上之困難。蓋從價稅貨，於課稅之前，必經估價，而估價手續，最爲繁瑣。夫輸入貨物，種類品質各別，貿易情形異殊，欲求估價之準確，必須多聘專家，分類處理。因之行政費用，必感浩繁。且專家所估之價，時或不能得商人之聽從，於是商人與稅關之間，常起爭議，而爭議之解决手續，至爲周折，商務進行，因以稽遲。不特此也。課稅價格，旣難於確定，於是商人爲少納關稅計，輒以多報少，貪圖小利，或僞造貨單，蓄意混朦，作奸犯科之舉，層出不窮。稅關爲防範起見，於是不得不採取各種檢查方法，例如責令商人呈驗領事簽證貨單，賣買合同，以及一切有關貨物價格或生產成本之文件賬册等等；其苛細繁瑣，不僅重增關務行政之費用，抑且予商貨流通以巨大之阻滯。

(四)最後，從價課稅，必有作爲課稅根據標準貨價，而此項標準貨價之抉擇，尤感困難。故各國從價稅所用標準貨價之制度，大別之有三：一爲國產同類貨物在國內市場之價格，減去輸入貨物應納之進口稅額，是爲減去法(Subtractive Method)：一爲外貨在輸出市場之價格而加以運抵，輸入口岸前所需之運輸，保險，包裝諸費，是爲加入法(Additonal Method)；三爲本國稅關所訂定之一種正常貨價，是爲官定價格。一國從價稅之課稅價格，於此三種制度，究將何去何從，實一煞費考慮之問題。觀於各國所採制度之不同及其時有更改之情形，可以瞭然於此項問題之疑難滋多也。

綜合上述，從價稅之優點爲其(一)對於關稅之保護目的，可以直達；(二)所予國產貨物之保護極爲穩定；(三)性質簡單稅則不致複雜；(四)能順應貨價之漲落，故稅率負担較爲公平；(五)便於物價之預測；(六)可以應用於全部貨物。但自其缺點觀之，則從價稅(一)管理困難，行政費用增重；(二)對於關稅之保護目的，時或不能適應；(三)稅則訂立時，標準貨價之選擇，至爲困難。準是以觀，從價稅於理論上雖覺其頗爲公平而合宜，但於實用上則阻難殊多。(註二)

三 從量稅之利弊

從量稅之優點，不外乎下列二端：

(一)從量稅之利益，首在其便於稅則貨目精析化(Specialization)之實現。所謂稅則貨目精析化者，卽將稅則貨物，各就其種類，品質，等級或花色等等，細爲析別。吾人知稅則貨目之精析化，於關稅之效率及商業政策之運用上，至關重要，直可謂爲現代關稅問題之唯一要旨(the key-note of the modern tariff problem)(註三)嘗攷稅則貨目所以必須精析之原因，可分下列二點言之：

(1)近世生產技術日進，工業製品，極盡奇巧。因國際土地分工定理之支配，各國對於某貨之製造，輒有專事於其某種品質或某種花式之生產者。爲予本國專產之品質或花式以特殊之保護計，稅則貨目，不得不求其精析，以便釐訂富有差別性之稅率。此爲增進關稅保護效能起見不得不求稅則貨目之精析化也。

（2）一國對於外商業關係，輒訂商約以資維持，而近世商約內又輒含有最惠國條款。最惠國條款之作用，在將本國讓與締約國之利益，遍及於其他締約之國。但一國對外協定關稅交換減稅利益時，苟其稅則貨目，分析極詳，則一方面本國所予對方之利益，可僅以某類內某貨之某一品質或花色爲範圍，而不致以某類或某貨之全部優惠待遇，悉數讓與；另一方面，其讓與對方之減稅利益，可以專指由該國輸入之貨物而言，其他有約國因輸入貨物花色或品質之不同，卽不能援例均霑。此爲便利對外磋訂商約及減少最惠國條款之作用計，不得不求稅則貨目之精析化也。（註四）

一國稅則貨目，既須精析，而從量稅之要件，亦爲課稅貨物品級及花色之必須詳細析列，是則從量稅之採用，對於稅則貨目精析化之實現當可收相輔相成之效也。

（二）從量稅之又一優點，爲從量稅目有精析之可能，而從價稅目則否。從量稅目可視商貨物質組織上至微細之差異以爲別。例如布疋可以每 英寸內所含紗線之多寡爲析列之準則；金屬絲可就其斷面直徑之長度而析列。此種精析之稅目，管理上雖不無瑣細之感，然技術上並無若何之困難。反之，從價稅貨如欲就價格上至微之差別以析列多目，則必致引起估價不確及報價過低等弊端，而莫可處理。

（三）從量稅目精析之可能，實卽基於從量稅管理之簡易。夫從價稅之唯一要件爲估價，估價之事，不論其方式如何，其困難程度，必非貨物數量之查核，所可幾及。蓋貨物數量之查核，其以重量計者，權之，以長度計者，度之，以容積計者，量之，……卽至精細者，亦可藉科學儀器之助爲之。故自技術觀點而言，從量稅之管理，實較從價稅爲便利多多。因管理手續之簡易，故行政費用較省，而弊端亦可減少。

從量稅之利，略如上述，玆進而言其弊。

(一)從量稅之最大缺點，爲其不能適應物價之漲落。當釐訂稅率之時，倘某貨每單位之價格爲十元，而其所需之保護爲貨價百分之五十，則課以每單位五元之從量稅率，可以適合其所需。但貨價時有漲落，如此後是貨之價格，上漲至十五元，則原定稅率，於折合從價後，將降爲百分之三十三又三分之一，於保護上，必感不足。反之，如是貨價格，跌至五元，則此項從量稅率，於折合從價後，將增至百分之百。於保護上，必感太過。太過與不足，皆非所宜。故爲適應物價之漲落起見，從量稅率，須依時修訂，方能盡其效用。

(三)從量稅率，欲求其能有實效，非特須依時修訂，尤恃乎貨目之精析。貨目不加精析之從量稅，謂之簡單的或無差別性的從量稅 (Simple or undifferential specific dutics)。此種簡單的從量稅率所予貨物之負担，輒依貨物品質之高下而發生累增，或遞減之弊。所謂累增者(Progressivenss)，卽從量稅貨之品級愈低，則其稅率之負担愈重，所謂遞減者 (Regre ssiäeness)，卽從量稅貨之品級愈高，則其稅率之負担愈輕。茲設例以明之。設若某種棉布其品級有四，因之各級之價格，亦有高下。此種棉布，如不予析列而籠統的課以每疋洋二元之簡單的從量稅，則對於每疋價值：

4元之品級，其稅率負担爲從價50%

6元之品級，其稅率負担爲從價$33\frac{1}{3}$%

8元之品級，其稅率負担爲從價 25%

10元之品級，其稅率負担爲從價20%

觀於上表，可知簡單的從量稅，對於品質愈低之貨，稅率累增，對於品級愈高之貨，稅率遞減；此與課稅應以貨物之負担能力爲標準之原則，顯係違反，倘爲公平起見，欲使上列各級品質之棉布，俱納比較平等之稅率，或爲合理起見，欲使國產各級品質之棉布，各得適合於其個別需要之保護，則應將此種棉布，就其品質之高下，析列多目，而目予一率，庶乎有濟。

(三)復次，商人對於從量稅貨物納稅後價格增高之數量，不易預知。此因從價稅貨目，精析異常，且其視爲差別準則之質量單位，時或深奧難明。例如各國對於布疋之從量稅，輒以其精製程度與每一面積單位之重量及所含紗線數目而細爲區別；對於流質貨物，輒以其比重爲別；對於化學產品，則以其內含物質之成分爲別。商人對於此類精析之稅目，難爲準確之辨別。故從量稅所予商貨價格上之影響，除少數專家外，非常人所能共曉而預測。

（四）最後，則從量稅對於若干貨物之價值原素，有不能表示者，換言之，卽當同類貨物各種不同之價值，不能以貨物形體，或數量上之特性分別表示時，從量稅卽完全不適於用。此點上已舉例說明，無待贅言。

綜合本節所述，從量稅性質繁複，稅目有精析之可能；便於稅則貨目精析化之實現；其管理手續，較爲簡易；因之行政費用減省，而弊竇亦可較少；此其利。同時從量稅不能順應物價之漲落，必須隨時修訂；其簡單者，則稅率之負担，輒易發生累增或遞減之弊；其對於貨物納稅後價格增高之數量，不易測知；且有若干貨物。無應用從量稅之可能；此其弊。（註五）

權衡從價稅及從量稅之利弊，可得如下之結論，卽：自理論上觀之，從量稅不如從價稅之便利，但於實用上，則視後者爲簡便而有效。夫課稅方式之應用，實效是尚。從量稅制，苟能做到精析稅目及隨時修正二項要件，則其應用上之實效，自較從價稅爲勝。觀於各國稅則之多半以從量稅爲主要的稅率方式，可以信然。

四　中國進口稅稅率方式述評

我國進口稅稅則，自前清道光二十三年，中英議定進口稅則起，下迄民國二十三年之進口稅則，前後凡九次。此九次進口稅稅則之從價及從量二稅稅目之比較統計，及其對於稅目總數之百分比數，有如下表：（註六）

道光二十三年至民國二十三年九次進口稅稅則內從價稅從量稅及免稅目數之比較統計及百分比較表

年份	稅目總數	從價稅目數	%	從量稅目數	%	免稅目數	%
道23年(1843)	99	9	9.0	88	89.0	2	2.0
咸8年(1858)	177	3	1.7	174	98.3	0	0
光28年(1902)	774	133	17.2	638	82.4	3	0.4
民7年(1918)	685	179	26.1	502	73.3	4	0.6
民11年(1922)	696	188	27.0	504	72.4	4	0.6
民17年(1928)	902	394	42.8	504	56.8	4	0.4
民19年)1930)	914	455	49.8	451	49.3	8	0.9
民22年(1933)	917	411	44.8	497	54.2	9	1.0
民23年(1934)	922	411	44.6	505	54.7	6	0.7

上表有可注意之點二：一爲稅目總數之漸增，二爲從價稅目百分比數之增加與從量稅目百分比數之減少。茲分別申言之。

（一）稅目總數之多寡，足以表示一國稅則貨目之精析程度。稅則貨目愈精析，則其保護本國產業及便利對外訂立商約之效能益增强。但稅則貨目之所以能臻於精析化者，尤在從量稅目之有適當的析列。我國稅目總數，雖逐漸增加，然以視歐陸各國之稅目總數，猶大相懸殊。下列數字，表示中外各國稅則貨目總數之比較。（註七）

國別	稅則年份	稅目總數	稅則年份	稅目總數	稅則年份	稅目總數
德國	一八七一	二三三八	一九〇二	一八〇〇	一九二五	二三〇〇
法國	一八九二	一五〇〇	一九二七	四三七一	一九三一	四四〇〇以上
意國	一八九五	八三七	一九一〇	一〇八三	一九二七	三五七四
中國	一八五八	一七七	一九一八	六八五	一九三四	九二二

觀於上表，中國稅則貨目之精析程度，遠不如歐陸諸國。此中原因，自以從量稅目之未有詳細合理之分別最爲重要。試以法國相當於我國所謂本色粗細斜紋布之棉疋之從量稅目，與我國是項棉疋之從量稅目，相比較，卽知我國從量稅目之析列，實屬過於簡陋。按法國現行稅則，是項棉疋，有三級之精析。第一級以加工程度爲分析之準則，別爲本色，漂白，及染色三種。但棉布有經磨光手續者(Mercerised)，故此級中之每種棉布，又可旁分爲磨光的與

未磨光的二項。第二級之分析準則，爲棉布每一面積單位之重量；因棉布價值之高下，亦視其品質之粗細而有別，細者值昂而輕，粗者值小而重。故第一級內之各種棉布，又續以其每百方公尺之重量，而續分多目。惟是棉布之輕，未必全係質細，亦有因織法稀鬆而然者。織法鬆弛者，值低；緊密者，值高。故第二級各項棉布，又須以每五方公厘內所含紗線之數而再續分爲若干子目。若以第一級中之本色一種爲例，則其各級項目之精析，有如下列：（註八）

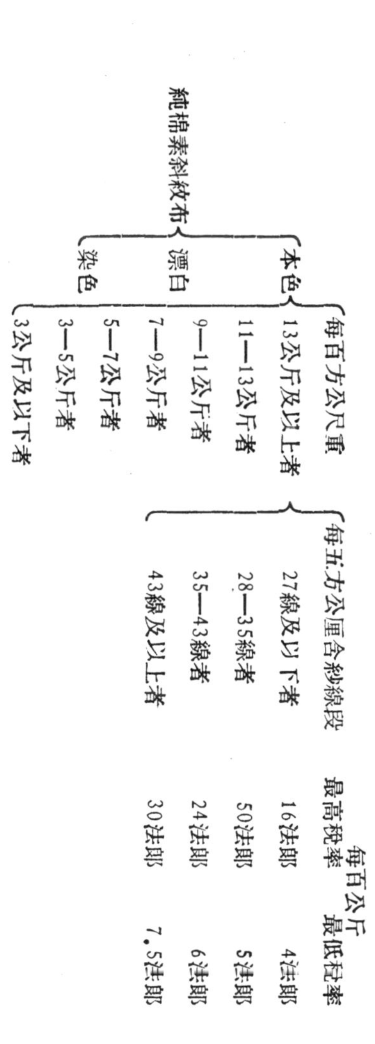

觀於上列示例，可以推知法國稅則貨目之分析，實屬異常精細。故即以此純棉，素斜紋布一種棉疋而論，其最後分列之子目，計有一百六十一目之多；以視我國現行稅則中同類棉疋所佔之稅目（計僅號列二，十六，卅六之三目）其詳簡精粗，實不可同日而語。此種情形，可以證明我國稅則雖有從量稅而未能善用之也。

（二）自一八四三至一九三四年九十餘年間，中國進口稅稅則從價稅目及從量稅目對稅目總數之百分比，自其大體上觀之，雖呈前者增加而後者減少之象；但自從量與從價二稅在稅則內所佔地位之重要而觀，則此九次稅則，顯可劃分爲二個時期。（一）一九二八年國定稅則以前之五次稅則，爲從量稅目佔重要地位之時期；（二）自一九二八年國定稅則起以迄於今之四次稅則，爲從價與從量二種稅目幾於秋平色分之時期。

在第一時期內，歷屆稅則，悉由外力片面訂定；條約之有效時期，復規定極長。此時期內，自外人之利益觀之，自以固定的從量稅率，爲最足予我以束縛；蓋從量稅之實效，恃乎依時修訂，今在極長時間內，固定不變，而此時期之大部分，又適值物價上漲之期；在此種情形之下，從量稅率，非特不能適應國家經濟之發展，即自財政收入上觀之，亦且蒙受巨大之損失。故此時期內之從量稅目，雖不失爲歷屆稅則之主體，然自我國之利害而言，反不如從價稅之可以稍裕國用也。

第二時期內，從價稅目在稅則中之地位，幾可與從量稅目相埒，一九三〇年稅則之從價稅目，且較從量稅目爲多。此種現象，顯然表示我國近年來之關稅目的，幾全爲財政收入主義所籠罩；證以一九三〇年進口稅改用金單位征收，及同年新進口稅則內從價稅目之增加，益覺瞭然。

我國關稅稅則近年來趨重於從價稅制之響影，當爲關稅管理上困難之增加，及關稅目的之難以適應，何以言之？從價稅之效用，恃乎估價之準確。我國近年來進口貨估價管理章程，雖嚴密有加，同時並實施領事簽證貨單制度以爲之輔，（註九）但當國勢陵弱，關稅行政權尚未完全恢復之時，關稅對於進口貨物之估價，未必能收切實之效，對於外商，尤難從嚴處理。至領事簽證貨單所示貨價之準確，視乎駐外領事能否實行調查管轄區域內生產及物價變動之機能，我國駐外領館，設置未遍，組織未備，駐轄區域內經濟情況之調查；大多未能施行，卽有行之者，亦未必能切實。在此種情形之下，如欲求從價稅之有實效，則其管理上所增之困難，可以想見。同時我國關稅之目的；無論其爲收入的或保護的主義，亦必不易達到；因收入主義之實現，須估價之能免於低報，而保護士義之要件，在乎從量稅之能依國產貨物各別的需要，而爲精析之釐訂也。

五　結語——我國關稅稅率方式之改進

就吾國目前關稅制定之實際情形而言，此種偏重財政收入之政策，亦係不得不然之趨勢。何則？蓋我國關稅自主權，雖已號稱恢復，實際上歷次稅則之訂立，其能不受外力之壓迫者幾希。在如此情勢之下，而欲實施與外人利益衝突之保護關稅，似屬形格而勢禁。惟是立國之道，首重國家經濟之發展。以吾國今日經濟之落伍，亟宜積極的努力於保護關稅之實施，藉以扶育各種幼稚產業，而謀國家經濟之進步。實施保護關稅之要件，不一而足，但稅率方式之改進，極關重要。根據前述，欲爲切實合理之關稅保護，自非盡量採用從量稅率不可。從量稅制之推行，並非盲目的高提稅率，卽可濟事。施行之道，首須從事於國內外生產事業實況之調查，藉以諗知本國各種產業所不可或缺之保護程度，然後按照各業之個別的需要，而詳細釐訂適當之稅率。此種合理的稅則，非特可予國產貨物以應有之保護，且可進而爲對外磋訂商約之良好工具。試觀十九世紀以來，歐美各國之關稅史，其保護關稅實施問題之焦點，何一而非集中於關稅稅則之切實與合理？而關稅稅則之切實與合理，又何一而不自稅則貨目與從量稅率之精析釐訂入手？

從量稅之效用，除精析稅目，釐訂稅率而外，尤恃乎能依物價之變動而隨時予以修正。故從量稅制之實施，復須有詳確之貨價調查。爲我國計，可將財政部國定稅則委員會以及其他機關之貨價調查事業，予以聯絡及擴充，由財政實業外交三部聯合辦理。其調查之貨價，應以修訂從量稅準爲目的，編製各項進口貨市價對於原有稅率訂定時所用標準價格之指數。同時應由政府規定此項指數對於基率之差距，達到若何程度時，卽須將從量稅訂正，俾可維持其原有之保護程度。

保護關稅實施之可能，誠視國勢爲轉移；但因噎廢食，智者不取；且籌備工作，極需時日，急起直追，不容再緩。誠能循此以進，則切實合理的保護關稅，終久必能實現。彼時保護目的既達，財政收入，亦可隨以增加，蓋『百姓足，君孰與不足』，民生充裕，國家財政，自能充裕，非特關稅收入之增加，可操左券，財政上其他各種收入，亦有增益之可能也。

（註一）Allix, Ed.—Les droits de douane, Tome Ier, pp. 227—3; Ashley, P.—Modern Tariff History, pp. 4—5, 212—2, 262, 312.

（註二）Gregory, T. E, G,—Tarilfs, a Study in Method, pp. 116—120; Allix, Ed.—Les droits de douane, Tome Ier, pp. 228—235.

（註三）Gregory, T. E. G.—Taaiffs, a Sfudy in Method, p, 143

（註四）Gregory, Les droits de douane, Tone Ier, pp. 212—213.

（註五）Gregory, T. E. G.— Tariffs, a Stsdy in Method, pp. 116—120; Allix, Ed—Les drojts de douane, Tome Ier, ppr236—240

（註六）中國銀行總管理處經濟研究室編最近中國對外貿易統計圖解坿刊道光二十三年至民國十九年間之歷屆稅則，可以參攷。惟該書對於稅則表說明內所稱之目數，實係號列之誤。本文所謂目數係指稅則內之子目而言。稅則貨目精析程度之觀察，應以子目總數爲比較，號列之多寡，無關重要也。民國二十二年進口稅稅則及二十三年進口稅稅則，分見實業部商品檢驗局，及國際貿易局合編之國際貿易導報五卷六號及六卷六號。

（註七）Trendelrnburg— Nomenclature et Classification donanières, p. 25.

（註八）Le tableau des droits.

（註九）海關法規彙編增訂版頁七八至七九

歐戰時美國鐵路軍運組織與實施概況

周世正

方今世界風雲緊急之秋，舉國上下，均亟亟以準備應付未來大戰爲務，戰時鐵道之輸送，於整個戰略，有絕大之關係，同時亦有其與平時不同之特質，本文多取材於 Walker D. Hines 原著 War History of AmericanRailroads 及 Haines. S. 所著 Efficient Railroad Operation 二籍。對歐戰時美國鐵路軍運情形，有一概括之敘述，似可爲我邦參考，尤望海內先進，對戰時交通問題，特加深切之研究，其有俾國家，定非淺鮮也。

——筆者附誌——

一　美國加入歐戰時之鐵路情形

當北美合衆國於一九一七年四月六日對德宣戰，加入第一次世界大戰之時，該國鐵路，經九十年之歷史，已有幹線二十六萬英里，若連枝線副軌及岔道等計算在內，則達四十萬英里有奇。一切鐵路，均屬民有民營，在數百鐵路公司之上，百分之七十七之鐵路，事實上併爲三十二個系統，各系統間，極劇烈之競爭存焉。蓋美國先後于一八八七年及一八八九年，訂定禁止合併及獨佔企業之法令，亟謀鐵路間自由競爭之存在，俾於最大可能之下，供給大衆以最優最廉之業務。但因此種劇烈之競爭，各路運價日趨跌落；每延噸英里之收入，自一八九九年始，卽降至不可收拾之田地(七厘半)直至參戰之年，仍無起色。且以前鐵路，雖每運輸單位收入日減，尙因工業之迅速發展，得因運輸單位之增加，而維持其生命。至一九一七年，工資物價，大爲昂貴，而工業發達。幾達限度，故運輸單位之增加，不足抵補成本之高漲，而政府之課稅與監督，變本加厲。故一般鐵路，均感到嚴重之威脅。在政府監督方面，於一九〇六年，議會卽賦州際商務委員會 (Interstate Commerce Commision) 以訂定最高運價之權，一九一〇年各州亦設監督機關，限制州內之運價，重以各路間之競爭，使運價慘跌，收入銳減。同時政府對鐵路事務上之干涉，亦使之增加不少開支，如限制列車之過長，規定列車應增設之員工，及迫令減小灣度等，均爲明顯之例證。且美國鐵路之建築，實在工業發達以前，初時草昧始開，工業不免簡陋，其後工業飛越躍進，鐵路運輸日增，建築與設備均感不足應付。故每年各路均須增募資本，以資擴充。此於利率甚高，收入減而成本大之時。極難負担。更以鐵路工人，迫于生活程度提高。要求加薪之運動，在强固組織下，進行極烈；其時歐戰巳作，各國對美貨需要頗大，各業加緊生產，勞工需要大。工資水準高，鐵路爲保有其勞動力，亦不得不徇其請，而致增加開支。故美於卽將加入歐戰之時。鐵路因競爭之影響與成本之增高，均無法增進設備，應付日增之運輸，更以歐戰發動，美貨出口多，鐵路運輸量更增，益感無法應付，且各路全係私營，彼此車輛不能互濟，尤使較繁之路感輪轉材料之缺乏，於是擁塞延誤之象，層見迭出，當美國宣戰之日，舉國上下，咸知參戰之後，運輸必更爲頻繁，則困難更將增進，於是戰時鐵路輸送。如何可以減除滯礙，適應需要，遂為彼邦一大問題矣。

二　民路自辦軍運之組織與實施概況

美國甫參戰前鐵路之窘態，已於前述。參戰以後，情形尤爲嚴重，蓋貨運方面，須輸送本國及協商國之軍需品及礦産械彈造船材料等物。客運方面。須輸送大批軍隊與工人，故均大爲增多，且各路自相爲謀，忙碌之路，如東部之Pennsylvania Rd. 及 Baltimore & Ohio Rd. 等，更感車輛及設備之缺乏，而不能得西部若干清淡鐵路之調劑。以致擁擠及延誤，輒難避免，從全國觀點說，卽是無整齊之步調與充分地使用設備，故各路合作辦理軍運。事實上成爲必要。參戰後之第五日，卽四月十一日。乃由國防諮詢委員會之交通組主席(Chairman of the Committee on Transportation & Communication of the Advisory Commission of theCouncil of National Defense) 亦卽 Baltimore & Ohio Rd. 之局長維納氏 Daniel Willard)在華盛頓城召集全國鐵路負責人，會商合作辦理軍運事宜。僉以國家在非常時期，各路爲盡力服務起見。應化除競爭，有一共同組織。以決定軍運政策與實施方法，領導各路遵行。而達最高之效果，至於組織，卽將原有之美國鐵路協會之國防委員會 (Committee on NationalDefense of the American Railway Association) 擴大爲二十五委員。均由各路負責人分任之，再由此委員會推執行委員會委員五人，連州際商務委員會派一代表，及國防諮詢委員會之交通組主席，合組戰時軍運委員會 (Raiiway's War Board) 此卽民路自辦軍運之組織，凡各路軍運上一切車輛之使用，輸送之作業。全受其控制與指揮，惟各路主權組織與普通業務之行使，仍與平日無異，政府僅立于監督地位。與各路協商合作，在財政上，亦無担保利益之規定，此委員會設下列七處，分掌各務：

(一)車輛處 (Commision on Car sservise)

(二)機務處 (Military Equipment Standards)

(三)會計處 (Military Transportation auonnting)

(四)客運處 (Miliary Passenger Tariff)

(五)貨運處 (Military freight Tariff)

(六)材料處 (Materials & Supplies)

(七)捷運處 (Express Transportation)

各處長官，均由各路職員担任，在較有系統之合作下，於戰時運輸緊張之時，自較各路自相爲謀爲佳。試觀一九一七年美國鐵路之運輸量，爲有鐵路以來最多者，延噸英里，較一九一六年多百分之九，延人公里，多百分之十二，在此運輸頻繁之情形下。各路設備，旣以物價成本昂貴，無從大量添置，一部份機車，又須送至歐陸使用，而勞工數量，亦因戰時前方及軍需工業需人，較前減少，故各路處境，較一九一六年實尤困難，惟幸在協商合作之下，得以維持耳。茲將其成效之著者述列於下：

(一)減省重複業務，如客運方面，省去二千八百萬延人英里是。

(二)改進行車規章，實行車輛通用。

(三)注意裝車，充分利用車位。

(四)減少煤斤之運價等級，使戰時急需之煤斤輸送利便。

(五)與港口調整，使鐵路輸送與出口銜接，減少港口壅塞。

關于車輛通用方面，如某路急需車輛，他路卽將空車送去。此在極端自由競爭主義下之美路。不可謂非創例，惟事實上仍感不足應付，至一九一七年秋，輪機材料之短絀，客車之延誤，港口及終點大站之擁塞，日趨於烈，其癥結所在，得於下述：

(一)鐵路最感困難之點，卽不統一而紛至頻來之政府優先運輸令 (Priosity Order) 根據一九一六年八月二十九日公佈之法令 (Navy Appropriation Act) 大總統及政府機關，於必要時，得令交通機關儘先運其物件，戰時軍運委員會，復與各軍事機關，訂立合同，凡持有特種護照 (tago) 便可享受優先運輸，於是軍事機關，各領護照，分別請求先運，甚至不問物件是否急需，鐵路能否輸送，到達站能否卸清。總求先運爲快，於是鐵路平添無數工作與用費，以應付此種不統一而數量極多之優先令。更因終點大站，往往堆積無數由先運令開到之重車，無從清卸，於運輸頻繁而車輛短絀之時。尤爲極不經濟之處。

(二)美國傳統經濟政策及一班人之觀念，厥爲自由競爭之維持，故曾先後頒佈禁止合併及取締獨佔之法令。現民有鐵路，實行車輛通用及他種協作，於法律上似有抵觸。故一九一七年十一月軍運委員會宣佈匹剌堡(Pittsburgh)以東統一軍運管理時，卽正式被司法部傳詢指摘，雖能以權宜之策爲辭，行動上總不免常受法律及輿論之牽掣，効率自減。

(三)美國鐵路，自始卽爲私人經營，未嘗停止競爭，今欲其一朝改革，澈底合作，當屬不可能。例如因實施軍運而犧牲客貨運輸，或放棄一部份競爭，卽爲全路股東之損失，本路機車車輛供他路行駛，亦非本路之利。此種損失與用費，又無政府補償，故雖惕于國家需要，合營軍運，事實上仍十分勉强，此在軍運委員會之報告上(一九一七年十一月提出，)曾痛切指出，例如軍運委員會請某路放棄某一客貨運輸，及借用機車之時，總須費相當時間於疏通上。故雖稱合作，距有系統之全國軍運組織尚遠。白未能最有効地使用全國鐵路與其設備也。

綜上三因。益以工資物價昂貴，使鐵路成本大增（按州際商務委員會統計一九一七年一至九月，雖收入較前年增一萬二千三百萬，純利則減五千七百萬）民路自動辦理軍運，漸不能亦不堪維持；就軍運成績觀，亦有更張之必要。國家經營及利益担保之議，遂先後由州際商務委員會與軍運委員會提出，一九一七年冬之國營令，亦應運而生矣。

三　國營鐵路軍運之組織與實施概況

民路自辦軍運之缺點，已于上述，蓋民路受無數政府機關之指揮與徵用。固屬疲于奔命，而整個運輸，亦非能成爲有系統的，且民路之間，未能自動地澈底合作，營軍運所蒙損失，亦非政府予以維持不可，故國家直接辦理軍運，成爲必要。事實上之開始，係在一九一七年十二月二十六日，由總統宣佈國營令，徵用全國鐵路，並附有解釋文，其主要點于下：

（一）法律根據—一九一六年八月二十九日頒佈之軍事徵發令 (Army Approprion Act) 規定總統得於必要時徵用全國交通工具，議會亦先後於一九一七年四月六日及十二月七日，議決賦總統以徵用鐵路之權，以應付對德奧之戰爭。

（二）徵發範圍—包括全國鐵路及內河沿海輪船，以及終點設備臥車棧房電話電報與一切附屬於交通之工具。市街電車與長途電車 (Interunban railway) 暫免徵用。但政府得隨時以命令徵發之。

（三）收入担保之規定—政府爲賠償徵用鐵路之損失，並確保其利益起見，規定一担保之收入額，係以至一九一七年六月三十日爲止之三年平均收入爲標準。由政府分別與徵用各路，訂定担保數額，對股東及債權人權益。絕不損害，非有特別命令，一切股息及債務之本息，均應照常支付。

（四）產業之維持——政府對鐵路一切產業俱應妥爲維持，俾於交還時與徵用日無異。

此令於一九一七年十二月十八日生効，但爲會計上之便利，係於十二月三十一日起始由政府徵用全國鐵路，劃分七區，直接辦理軍運，並以財政部長威廉氏(William G. McAdoo)兼爲領袖，設鐵路管理處(United States Railroad Administration)其組織於下：

處長 (Director General)
- 副處長 (Assistant Director General)
  - 文書科(Actuary)
  - 法律科(Division of Law)
  - 財務及購料科(Division of finance & purchasing)
  - 運輸科(Division of Operation)
  - 營業科(Division of Traffic)
  - 勞工科(Division of Labor)
  - 會計科(Division of accounting)
  - 置產科(Division of Capital expenditure)
  - 內河運輸科(Division of inland waterway)

各科職員，以及七分區之職員，均于鐵路員司中選任。但於一九一八年四月一日，規定一切管理處職員，俱應與本路脫離隸屬關係，純爲公務人員。復以各路原有局長，雖承命辦理軍運，仍不免計及本路利益，不能專謀軍運之効能。故于五月二十一日，每路另委軍運局長(Federal Manager) 一人，管理全路軍運，於是全國鐵路軍運、悉由此管理處統一辦理，各路不過保持其公司組織之獨立而已。但美國鐵路，素爲民有民營，今改爲民有國營，規章文獻，均感不足，乃於一九一八年三月二十一日，由議會通過並頒佈國營法 (Federal Control Act) ，其主要規定，除重申政府担保利率及維持資產外，更有五項：

(一)政府卽與各路訂立契約，確定担保收入額，若國營時收入超過担保，卽歸之政府，但此担保額係根據一九一七年六月底爲止之三年數目計算，若某路在此三年中全部或大部陷於衰落停頓，或過度澎漲，以致收入異常減少，則斟酌實情特予訂定。

(二)訂定契約或實施之時，發生爭執，政府鐵路兩造，均可訴之州際商務委員會所設仲裁委員會。(Board of Refrees)該委員會可籍地方法院之助，傳齊兩造及證明文件，决定公平擔保額或解决其他問題。

(三)國營期內，各路無政府允准，所付股息，不得超過一九一七年六月底爲止之三年平均數額，但於物價確已高漲，或鐵路經政府批准，大量擴充設備時，得與政府磋商增加担保收入額及股息。

(四)由國庫撥出五萬萬元，作爲國營鐵路經費。以支付各種用費，補償各路不足担保額之收入，並可用於內河沿海運輸，及設備之添置。各路爲擴充設備，或支付債務，得發行證券，政府卽以此款購置之。

(五)國營時總統得視公衆及鐵路之需要，改定分等運價及其他運輸規章，但如施行結果不滿，仍須徵詢州際商務委員會之意見，以便修改。

國營法既經頒佈，政府卽與各路分別訂約，鐵道軍運，遂於國營下順利進行，其成績較民路自辦時優良遠甚，蓋一切民路自辦時捉襟見肘之處均能消除，茲將其顯然進步之點，縷述於後。

(一)民營時最難應付，卽不統一之優先運輸令，各機關皆以政府地位，紛令鐵路儘先運送，今鐵路本身爲一政府機關，各機關請求運送，俱須由管理處決定可運與否及先後次序，結果運輸有整個系統，鐵路亦不感疲于奔命。

(二)各民路未能自動澈底合作，今由國家統一管理，車輛機車及其他設備之公用，無阻滯可言，故無此盈彼虛之弊，而獲得最大之利用程度。

(三)政府担保各路收入，使以前民路所感損失痛苦消除，不可避免之成本高昂，卽可由政府亦卽全國人民負担之。

(四)民營時機車須送回本路修理，耗時甚多。今則全國修理廠不分彼此，就近修理行駛各該路上之機車，自可增加機車之利用程度。

（五）各路由政府統一經營，軍事機關託運及籌畫運輸均易，購料可享大宗之便宜，燃料之輸送亦方便。

若更以數字觀，則一九一七年十一月十五日，全國機車剩餘可用者僅五二八隻，至年底竟完全無有，國營後之一九一八年，運輸更繁，而十一月十五日，反存一〇二一隻，年底存一三八四隻，又觀客運方面，一九一八年較前一年延人英里增百分之八，而列車英里數反減百分之八。貨運方面，一九一七年十一月車輛短少數逾十五萬，至翌年同月，減至一萬五千，足見輪轉材料之利用程度，大見增加；美國軍運，遂在國營之下，去除困難，順利進行矣。

四 結語

本文不過將美國歐戰時軍運情形，作一簡略之敘述。其中可注意之點有五，謹書而出之，即作本文之結語可已。

第一：美路雖屬民有民營，平日唯利是圖，一至非常時期，即能以國家需要爲前提，努力軍運，此種精神在我國誠屬必要。

第二：戰爭時期物價工資騰貴，使鐵路成本高昂，維持擴充，俱較平日困難，而運輸則百倍忙碌，此種艱難情形及應付方法，頗值我人研究。

第三：軍事當局，不問鐵路能力，不統一地請求優先運輸，最使鐵路難于應付。

第四：鐵路軍運，必須在整個組織下，有系統地進行，而設備公用尤屬必要。

第五：戰爭時期，人民企業爲政府徵發服務。固屬義不容辭，政府亦應顧及其利益，予以合理補償。

組織之力量

組織之力量，全視其所組織之分子而定。故凡一國，或一個軍隊，或一個企業，其强弱恆與各個份子之志趣如何，習慣如何，性格如何等，有密切之關係。…………………………組織者，所以運用人力者也，但其成功，仍繫乎此運用之結果，是否自然與順利？

(Organization Engineering, By Dennison)

THE QUESTION OF THE 10% SURCHARGE FOR CARRIAGE AT RAILWAY RISK

By

T. T. Shen (沈奏廷)

In the autumn of 1932, the Ministry of Railways began to offer to the public a better freight transportation service by the promulgation of a set of regulations under which all the national railways were required to carry goods by goods trains at the carriers' risk. At first, carriage at the carriers' risk was limited to local shipments, but later was gradually extended to through freight movements until today it becomes a universal practice.

In order to compensate the carriers for the risk they assume, a surcharge amounting to 10% of the ordinary freight rates was authorized to be collected on all shipments that move at the risk of the carriers. At present, this surcharge is being assessed almost on all shipments, except those which are specifically excluded, such as live stock, explosives and certain dangerous articles, coffins with corpses, treasure, etc. . These specifically mentioned articles are still to be carried at owners' risk.

A question has arisen as to whether this 10% surcharge is fitting and proper. It is definitely certain that the railways must have more revenue to meet their increased burden in the form of payment of loss and damage claims and provision of new shipping facilities. There is no denying the fact that in one way or another this increased revenue must be procured from increased rates. But such is no answer to the question whether a 10% surcharge should be collected. Is this arbitrary increase in the carriers' charges too low or too high? Or is there any other means to attain the same end, i.e., to yield enough revenue to compensate for the risks assumed?

It is my belief that a flat percentage increase in freight rates can never be fair and reasonable. It should be plain even to the layman that risks in transportation differ with different commodities. Some are very liable to damage, others less so, and still others are practically undamageable. The degree cf risk will also vary with the various methods of packing in which goods are tendered for transportation. If it is fair to collect a 10% surcharge on a shipment which is often subject to damage, it would be unfair to exact the same amount of contribution from shipments which are far less damageable. For instance, to impose an identical burden on cement or pig iron as on glassware or pottery would do great injustice to tne former article, which is a far more desirable commodity from the risk point of view. Similarly, to make a shipment of oil packed in metal cans in wooden boxes to pay the same rate of surcharge as one packed in carthenware would not only be unfair but have the effect of discouraging improved methods of packing.

Coming to the question of loss, we face the same difficulty. Although any article may be lost in whole or in part during transportation, the possibility for loss will differ with the different ways the shipments are carried. A less than carload shipment is far more liable to lose or pilferage than a carload shipment. A shipment well protected by packing will have less chance of being lost or pilfered than one which is improperly packed. Goods shipped loose often register more losses than when offered in containers. A flat percentage charge on all goods alike is, therefore, inequitable even for their risk of loss.

Besides, a flat percentage increase in ordinary freight rates, after all, does not produce an identical burden on all goods alike. As goods are classified into six classes on our national railways at present, their rates are graded with the classes in which they are grouped. A first class rate may be three or four times a sixth class rate, two or two and half times a fifth class rate, and so on throughout the ecale. A 10% surcharge on a fifth class rate may mean, say, only $2.00 per ton from A to B, the same rate of surcharge on a shipment of fist class goods may turn out to be as much as $4.00. On the other hand, the risk for loss or damage may be greater in the case of the fifth-class shipment than in that of the first-class, and yet a heavier surcharge has been imposed on the latter. In fact, the surcharge has been made to vary with the ability of traffic to pay instead of its risk of loss or damage.

In the United Sates, all freight is carried at railways' risk, with only minor exceptions, but no surcharge is collected by the carriers. The carriers' compensation for the risks they assume is, so to speak, already incorporated in the ordinary freight rates. For, in the process of freight classification, the American railroads or rather their classification committees take the factor of risk for loss and damage into consideration as well as other factors such as value of commodity, bulk or displacement, etc. . If there are two commodities one of which is more risky to carry than the other, they will be given different class ratings, other factors being equal. Or if an article may be tendered for transportation in several kinds of packing containers, it will be accorded several class ratings to conform with their different degrees of risk. Thus, different commodities are classified or graded on basis of the risk factor as well as other factors and made to bear different rates which include varying amounts of contribution toward compensating the carriers for the varying risks they assume. Similarly, commodity or exceptional rates are made with due consideration of the risk factor.

It is obvious, then, that our 10% surcharge for carriage at railway risk is not fair and reasonable, not because it is too low or too high in itself, but because it imposes unfair burden on different commodities which differ widely from the risk point of view. The best solution of this problem is to reclassify freight on the basis of the risk factor as well as other factors so as to put various commodities in proper classes in keeping with their varying degrees of risk to be assumed in transportation. First of all, as a preliminary step, needful statistics should be compiled from the claim files to bring into light the loss or damage possibilities of various commodities for which claims have been paid. A thorough investigation into the nature of commodities for which claim statistics are not available should also be made, so that they may also be duly treated in classification. Such a process is bound to be slow. For the present, a flat charge per ton per kilometer for carload and per 25-kilograms per kilometer for less than carload is preferable to the existing 10% surcharge, in that a flat charge instead of a flat percentage will obviate the unjustified inequality of burden on the different classes of freight.

中華國有鐵路現行行車時刻表（十一）

京滬滬杭甬綫

民國二十四年十二月廿一日起實行

上行車

站名＼車次	92 嘉滬二三等混合區間車	32 閘滬快車 餐	2 閘京聯運特別快車 餐	62 閘滬三四等慢車	34 閘滬快車 餐	94 閘嘉二三等混合區間車	12 閘滬特別快車 餐	222 新龍上南區間車
閘口開		6.30	8.30	9.00	13.25	16.30	17.30	
杭州到		7.01	8.47	9.25	13.46	16.46	17.42	
杭州開		7.10	8.55	9.35	13.55	16.55	17.50	
長安到		8.09	9.40	10.45	14.54	17.58	18.43	
長安開		8.14	9.45	10.55	14.59	18.03	18.48	
硤石到		8.46	10.11	11.53	15.31	18.41	19.14	
硤石開		8.48	10.13	11.56	15.33	18.43	19.16	
嘉興到		9.23	10.42	12.35	16.08	19.20	19.45	
嘉興開	6.50	9.30	10.47	12.46	16.14		19.50	
松江到	8.09	10.30	11.45	14.12	17.24		20.52	
松江開	8.14	10.36	11.50	14.22	17.29		20.57	
上海南站到	9.45	11.50	—	15.50	18.38		21.55	7.55
上海北站開	9.55	12.00	13.45	16.05	18.45		22.00	
上海北站到			12.20					

站名＼車次	46 錫滬三四等區間車	74 錫京二三等混合區間車	42 滬京三四等車	4 滬京特別快車 餐	22 滬京快車 餐	2 閘京聯運特別通車 餐	302 滬平聯運特快通車 餐	24 滬常區間特別快車 餐	72 滬錫二三等混合區間車	6 滬京夜特快車 餐臥	44 滬鎮三四等區間車
上海北站到						12.45					
上海北站開	0.50		5.15	8.00	9.50	13.20	16.00	16.50	17.55	23.00	24.00
蘇州到	2.41		8.18	9.27	11.56	14.47	17.51	18.43	20.40	0.57	1.51
蘇州開	2.50		8.25	9.34	12.05	14.53	17.59	18.50	20.47	1.05	1.58
無錫到	3.45		9.41	10.17	13.02	15.3[illegible]	18.46	19.37	22.00	1.57	2.49
無錫開		6.00	9.48	10.21	13.05	15.40	18.51	19.41		2.03	2.54
常州到		7.09	11.40	11.01	13.57	16.21	19.39	20.35		2.53	4.15
常州開		7.19	11.48	11.06	14.03	16.26	19.47			3.04	4.25
丹陽到		8.36	13.03	11.51	15.02	17.11	20.38			4.13	5.46
丹陽開		8.41	13.11	11.44	15.06	17.13	20.40			4.17	5.50
鎮江西站到		9.38	14.12	12.30	15.47	17.45	21.18			5.00	6.50
鎮江西站開		9.45	14.21	12.35	15.25	17.50	21.26			5.10	
南京到		12.00	16.30	13.55	17.30	19.15	22.50			7.00	

下行車

站名＼車次	93 嘉閘二三等混合區間車	31 滬閘快車 餐	11 滬閘特別快車 餐	61 滬閘三四等慢車	1 京閘聯運特快通車 餐	91 滬嘉二三等混合區間車	33 滬閘快車 餐	221 上南新[illegible]區間車
上海北站到					14.15			
上海北站開		7.00	8.55	9.05	15.00	16.30	18.10	
上海南站開		7.05	8.40	9.15	—	16.40	18.10	14.59
松江到		8.11	9.39	10.40	15.56	18.04	19.18	
松江開		8.16	9.41	11.00	16.01	18.11	19.23	
嘉興到		9.27	10.44	12.44	16.58	19.30	20.37	
嘉興開	6.55	9.34	10.49	12.52	17.03		20.44	
硤石到	7.32	10.08	11.18	13.31	17.32		21.18	
硤石開	7.34	10.15	11.20	13.34	17.34		21.20	
長安到	8.12	10.47	11.49	14.16	18.00		21.50	
長安開	8.22	10.52	11.51	14.26	18.05		21.55	
杭州到	9.32	11.51	12.[illegible]	15.42	18.50		22.47	
杭州開	9.40	12.00	12.45	15.52	19.00		22.55	
閘口到	9.55	12.20	13.05	16.15	19.15		23.10	

站名＼車次	17 錫滬二三等混合區間車	23 常滬區間快車 餐	1 京閘聯運特快通車 餐	45 錫滬三四等區間車	43 鎮滬三四等區間車	41 京滬三四等車	21 京滬快車 餐	3 京滬特別快車 餐	73 京錫二三等混合區間車	5 京滬夜特快車 餐臥	301 平滬聯運夜特快通車 餐臥
南京開			8.50			19.00	12.35	17.05	17.45	23.00	24.00
鎮江西站到			9.36			11.15	14.19	18.20	19.59	0.49	1.40
鎮江西站開			9.41		10.00	11.21	14.24	18.25	20.10	0.57	1.48
丹陽到			10.15		10.56	12.19	15.04	18.59	21.0[illegible]	1.45	2.33
丹陽開			10.20		10.59	12.24	15.08	19.01	21.10	1.48	2.35
常州到			11.03		12.16	13.49	16.12	19.44	22.13	2.50	3.32
常州開		8.00	11.08		12.24	14.05	16.23	19.49	22.20	2.58	3.40
無錫到		8.55	11.49		13.35	15.38	17.20	20.30	2[illegible].20	3.52	4.32
無錫開	5.55	9.02	11.53	12.25	13.40	15.18	17.30	20.34		3.58	4.38
蘇州到	6.55	10.06	12.36	13.41	14.51	16.49	18.35	21.17		[illegible].55	5.34
蘇州開	7.02	10.15	12.42	13.50	15.00	16.55	18.45	21.22		5.00	5.41
上海北站到	9.45	12.30	14.15	16.30	17.20	19.55	20.50	22.00		7.00	7.40
上海北站開			15.00								

CO-ORDINATION AND CO-OPERATION BETWEEN STORES AND OTHER DEPARTMENTS

Will. T. Chung (鍾偉成)

"No man liveth to himself," and this applies in the operation of the stores department of a railroad. No department of a railroad can stand alone, and no departmental organization can be truly successful without the whole-hearted support of each individual member and the willing co-operation of each department with which it comes in contact. The purchasing and supply is a service organization; it comes in contact with and serves in some way every department on the railroad, and, in serving, its aim is to serve well. The relation of the purchasing and supply to other departments is the same as that of the retailer to the consumer; while it is interested in selling as much material as possible to its consumers, it is also vitally interested in helping to conserve and in this way to cut down the ultimate cost of material to the railroad.

The lack of correct information as to the quantities required is likely to lead to overinvestment in inventories on one extreme or to delays on the other. On the other hand, failure to be fully informed as to quality or proper specifications leads to the procuring of unsuitable materials which must be either exchanged or cause the dissatisfaction of the using department.

The purchasing officer particularly must work in close harmony with all departments, and become aquainted with operations and requirements if the utmost efficiency is sought in furnishing the right material at the right time without increasing costs. He is without doubt one of the most valuable officers of the railroad organization, since his position places him in contact with all departments. He has the opportunity to consult with thestorekeepers and the heads of using departments regarding their needs and to advise them in advance as to the opportune time to request the materials and supplies they require.

It is recommanded by Section VI of the American Railway Association that the departments of purchases and stores should be co-ordinated so as to operate as a unit. This can be accomplished by having a supervising officer who is responsible for both departments. As a matter of fact, this kind of organization is common to nearly all of the large railroads in China. As the organization is centralized it can concentrate responsibility in administration and procedure. It can control efficiently the investment in materials and supplies. Furthermore, a better co-operation can easily be secured.

In order to achieve the necessary results, a railroad purchasing officer must be alert and conversant with the quick moving changes and the requirements of the modern transportation world. By the functioning of a well-balanced and active store division on which he is dependent to a great extent, he is familiar in advance with requirements of the Mechanical, Maintenance, and Construction Departments, thus, enabling him to anticipate their needs and prevent expensive delay.

The close co-operation between the purchasing officer and the storekeeper is necessary, as the latter is the buffer between the purchasing officer and the using departments. and it is the effective work of storekeeping officer which aids in the reduction and quick turnover of a roilway's material stock.

By having the full hearted co-operation of the storekeeper, a requisition reaching the purchase officer is complete, as it gives the description, catalogue reference, and other important data so that little delay is necessary in the purchasing division prior to submitting the requisition for competitive bids, and it is by prompt placement and a through follow-up system that a purchasing officer can accomplish inestimable good in the lowering of material stocks. This, of course, is one of the essentials which an railway purchase officer is striving to accomplish to secure the greatest turnover of material with the lowest investment of his railway's funds, taking into consideration all important features of equipment, etc.

There is an indirect way by which the purchasing and storekeeping divisions may be benefited by working co-operately. In buying articles of which a large quantity is needed over a considerable period of time, the railroad usually purchases in heavy volume whenver possible, to take advantage of a favorable market. But in doing so they arrange, if at all practical to place their orders with the privilege of drawing against them as needed, where the nature and uses of material are such that this can be done. By this means, it helps the stores department to avoid the accumulation of high inventories, and aid in keeping at a minimum the working capital necessary to carry the stocks of material awaiting consumption.

Co-ordination between the Purchasing Office and other Departments.

a. Relation With Engineering Department. - The engineer can co-operate with the purchasing officer in several ways. The engineering department should, subject to management control, have the final authority on what to buy. This being determined, the purchasing officer should endeavor to the best advantage to consider quality, price, delivery and related items. In co-operating with the purchasing officer the engineer will greatly aid in keeping his own departmental costs somewhere near what his budgets call for: He should constantly endeavor to keep his specifications up to date and his drawing for parts must be correct in showing any changes or revisions. Much useless material has been scrapped owing to delays in revising plants.

When some device or material new to the railroad is being considered a talk with the purchasing officer or the storekeeper will aid. They must be adviced where to make price inquiries and the question of where the material is to be stored must be settled. It is better to do this before purchase than to handle the article several times after its receipt.

b. Relation with Accounting Department. - Nowhere in railway organization is there need for closer co-operation than between the purchasing and accounting departments. The purchasing office is responsible for securing a large amount of financial obligations where it is the function of the accounting department to be prepared to discharge. Failure to cooperate upon the part of either is almost certain to be fraught with serious consequences. If the funds required for paying vouchers are not forthcoming, the railway's credit standing with the vendor is seriously injured and purchasing officer is deprieved of one of its most important elements of bargaining strength. The savings to be effected by prompt payment of liabilities are lost and in extreme eases serious financial embarrassment results. Our railway administration has been confronted with such difficult situation. This is due to lack of working capital or because the sources are not inmediatly available for meeting current obligations. This is often merely another way of saying that the management has failed to force see its needs for funds and has land no plans for their provision. If a purchasing program is planned is accordance with financial situation, this difficult situation could be avoided.

Another accounting department's relation to purchasing arises in connection with its exercise of the record keeping function. The accounting department has an interest in every purchasiag transaction, commencing when an entry is made in the records and ending only when the invoice has been paid and proper entries have been made. Ordinarily purchases are not formally recorded in the books until the vendor has presented his invoice. This evidence of the vendor's claim is usually sent by him to the purchasing division. The latter checks the invoice against the purchase order and sends it to the accounting department, which approves it if in accordance with the report of the receiving officer, prepares a voucher, and enters the transac ion in the books.

Close cooperation between the two departments is important. For it is upon their mutual efforts that prompt of obligations depends. The Account Payable Ledger Section of the accounting department is held responsible for payment, but it cannot function unless the purchasing office assumes responsibility for seeing that bills are presented promptly. The matter is of vital importance to the latter, for neglect to make prompt payments seriously reflects upon the credit of the railway and handicaps the purchasing office in its relations with vendors.

Co-ordination between Storekeeper and other Departments

a. Relation with using departments.- The storekeeping division of the Stores Department is without doubt more dependent on co-operation from the other departments than is any branch of the service, relying as itmust on advanced information from the users as to what their requirements will be. It is true that the storekeeping division has its stock ledger which is the gauge for maintenance of stocks, however this book cannot tell the storekeeper when a repair program of some nature is to be instituted which will necessitate larger stocks of certain commodities. To anticipate and prepare for such contingencies the storekeeper looks to such cooperation as he gets from the users of this material in giving him the advance information necessary, so that the material will be on hand when wanted.

Our railroads has often suffered serious losses in obsolete material due to lack of proper co-ordination. More modern locomotives, cars and tools are being constantly designed in foreign countries. The maintenance and locomotive departments are constantly recommending these improved designs and scrapping old materials without taking into consideration the investment. These losses can be avoided by an exchange of information between the operating, maintenance and construction departments with the stores department.

b. Relation with the Engineering Department. - The engineer can help the stores division in another way. He can aid in questions of design of buildings, selection of yards, interview arrangements and design of economical means for receiving, handling and storing.

From the foregoing it is evident that co-operation between Stores Department and other departments is essential for two reasons:

1. Because the operations and interests of all departments are always interdependent.

2. Because the stores department must be kept informed as to the needs of all departments for which it renders the service of obtaining them.

The first reason is not characteristic of the stores department alone. It is true that operations begun in one department are continually extending over into the sphere of others, and it is not possible to leave the depart ments to their own devices. In order to accomplish co-ordination between stores department and other departments of a railroad, some devices ore necessary:

1. The budget as a co-operating device. - Budgetary controi provides important means of co-ordinating inter–departmental relations. The essential features of this plan of control are simple. Each department is rsqui-

red to make periodical estimates what it proposes to accomplish. There are brought together, compared and co-ordinated, and approved by the high authority. When the estimates have been so approved, they comprise the budget for the ensuing period. A working guide is thus supplied for each department. The Store Department may formulate its plans for it knows what the material requirements are likelv to be. The accounting department is given advance notice as to the probable need for funds.

2. Need for some central authority. - There is a need for some central authority which is capable of assuming the point of view of the raliroad as a whole and co-ordinating its departmental activities. The best example for such device is the co-ordination Committee set up by the London Midland and Scottish Railways. This committee, though established only a few years, has done wonderful work for that railway and has been able to secure economy and efficiency for the Stores Department.

書評

『成績制度下的政府』

原名——Government by Merit

著者——Lucins Wilmerding, Jr.

出版處——Mc Graw-Hill Book Company

版期——一九三五年

定價——美金三元

任家誠

行政學得到政治學家的注意不過近三十年的事；組織，人事，財務，物料四者之中，對於人事行政尤爲前人所疏忽。以前誰都以爲人的管理是活動的，是無規跡可資遵循的，那裏談得上統治和管馭，但是久而久之，覺得行政效率的發揮，行政經濟的表現，決非行政組織之完善，財務管理之得當，物力運用之樽節所能克竟全功。組織財務和物料是死的東西，還待人去管理，人去運用，於是人事行政亦被注意了，最先是工廠方面對於勞工統馭之注意，終而及於政府機關的公務人員。

但是關于人事行政完整的書藉還是少見，有之，也是支離破碎，零落得很。美人事行政專家鮑樂克脫(A. W. Proctor)的『公共人事管理原理』(Principles of Public Personnel Administration)問世後，世人若獲至寶，誰都在他的書上下工夫，使學者們對於人事行政發生了興趣，其後華特(L. D. White)衛羅比(W. F. Willoughby)諸先進在他們行政學原理中都提起這重要的問題，使牠成爲一種光明燦爛的管理科學。可是以後就沒有良好的人事行政書藉出版；直到現在，因爲美國於一九三三年十二月成立人事行政諮詢委員會(Commission of Inquiry on Public Service Personnel)出版了七種有價值的書藉，上次介紹的『良好公務人員』和現在要說的都是其中之一。

這本書的定名—成績制度下的政府，似乎很新奇，不易捉摸牠的內容，但是一經說明，便可恍然，成績制度乃是人事行政的目標，牠便是繼鮑氏所著『公共人事管理原理』後最完備的一本。

過去人事行政的書藉雖亦有所見，但是總不能脫掉鮑氏和華衞兩氏的束縛，我們並不反對因循先進的編法，但是更贊成有新方式的開展，和新思想的介紹，這本書對於此點可以相當使我們滿意。

牠除掉職位的分類，人員的任用，升遷，退休，和俸給之釐訂以外，更注意到分工合作公民權利，和衷調劑，人事統制諸事，和中央與地方關係及其他比較次要的問題。這不能不算是該書的特點值得我們研究的。

對於良好制度的量度，作者說：『確定于(一)合宜公務員的產生，(二)適合美國傳統的合理俸給，(三)合乎經濟的原

則。』我很同意于他的主張，因爲行政學的目標是效能的發揮，工作的興奮，和行政的經濟，他說的三點，第一，二兩點正對着第一，二目標而發，而第三點更與第三目標緊相聯繫，我們不能不佩服作者的卓見。

作者認爲立法和行政的分工，不是絕對而是相對的，立法機關誠然是確定法律的中心；但是牠所定的是一般的法律，一切行政實施的計劃和政策及一切瑣屑的法規，仍應當由行政長官確定，確定的根據，當然基於立法機關所定的法律原則。所以法律和政策的擬訂，不是絕對的委託於立法機關，就行政實施上的便利而轉移分工的程度，他認爲立法和行政的絕對劃分是簡單的哲學。

對於行政人員的分工，在陳說立法和行政關係之後，也有透澈的解釋，他以爲行政人員應分兩級，就是管理級和執行級。管理級是行政長官的集團，確定立法機關所未定的行政政策和行政法律，不負一切執行上的責任，而專誠研討對於政事推進有益的計劃。執行級內的人員爲比較的中級和低級公務員，根據立法機關所訂的法律，管理級所下的政策，作實地的推行，他們的工作完全根據上級長官的指派。專司應盡的職務，而

行政推行的適當與否他們僅負在工作範圍內的責任；成功歸功於管理級，失敗也推咎於管理級。執行級下更劃分成執行級本身，辦事級，日常工作級，和速記級。這種分法的特優就是合乎分工而合作的原則。事實上所謂行政，無非是兩大部份，行政政策的決定和行政事務的推進，這二級可以相當的代表兩大部份，

但是分工合作的制度，亦有其缺點，因為立法機關，管理級，執行級的劃分太明顯而後，容易發生隔膜的裂縫，這也就是一般人所謂民主人事制度(Bureaucracy)的缺點。立法機關的人員祇負起他們份內的責任，誰也不問在行政推行時有何困難和補救方法；執行級祇是按着命令做去，更不問以後的成就是如何；至於管理級呢，相當的負起行政的責任，舉足重輕，一言可以興邦，一言可以僨事，因為立法機關的隨便，和執行級的苟且，必然是，造成了分工而不合作的現象，誠然，這一點是不容不為我們所注意的。關於此點他在後面公民權利一章中提及。

罷工，這問題在公務員管理的討論中，誰都以為不會發生的，所以認為是一個勞動問題，不被行政學家所注意，結果波士敦竟發生了警務人員罷工的事件，引起社會的驚異。作者對於這一點也提出討論，促進行政學研究者的視聽。他的觀點認為公務員的罷工是絕對可能的事，而且有設法預防及善後整理的必要，牠先引證司必魯(S. D. Spero)的意見然後加以討論，司氏說：

『麵粉廠工人的罷工足以引起全社會的恐慌，比財政部的職員罷工利害得多。……電燈廠工人罷工，停止給電，足以造成社會紛擾，人民有失其財物的危險，更比全市警察的罷工為危險。』

但是作者認為此說不確，因為公務員所幹的是全國人民福利之所繫，一罷工發生，雖然不致有立即騷然的現象，間接的影響定比直接的利害得多，所以他認為有注意的必要。

又有人說，勞工的罷工，由於勞資糾紛的不能解決，今公務員大家為公服務，無尊無卑：不致形成惡化的現象，而且在民主制度之下，國家的行動基于公共的意見，而公務員亦為公民之一，更沒有賓主之分，罷工的發生更不可能。但是事實上公務員對於工作的不滿，在在皆是，調劑無方，便促成消極的結果，不容不為我人所注意。

作者同情于胡佛總統的主張，認爲罷工不應發生，胡氏說：

『如果公務員罷工，他們的舉動非但對政府，而且對整個民族，簡直沒有法理之可言。而且國家公務人員有特別的權利，如生命的保障，職位的保障，退休養老金和恩俸等，所以實在處美國雇品中最優越的地位，公務員應該放棄罷工的權利。……』

不論罷工之會不會發生，公務不應有罷工的權利，是他的斷語，的確，公務員的地位比較勞工爲特殊，公務員的福利比勞工爲優越，他們應該努力從事，容忍可以容忍的刺激，來謀整個國家的幸福，而不應取勞工挾制資本家的消極步驟。

因爲罷工的問題，連帶的引起了本書對於工作調劑的注意。罷工誠然不應發生，但是如何避免之呢，工作的調劑，國家利益（亦即雇主的利益）和公務員利益的融合，是必要而不易的方法。國家不應極求經濟而予公務員以困難，而公務員更不應以私慾之無限而造成對政府的挾持。這點，本書裏很明細詳切地反覆申論着，值得我們的研究。

對於公務員的管理，作者主張集中統制，理由有二：『第一，文官制度集中能力利用的需要；第二，維持各個公務員良好的平均成績。』的確分工誠然是必要的事務，然而在管理上不能不有相當集中的機關處理之，不特公務員的升遷，任免，成績，可以因集中而有精密的比較和研究，使公務員的能力可以發揮，有相當的成績，而且更可以進一步改良前述的缺點，就是分工而不合作的現象，在這裏，他把全書做一個連鎖。

最後，他討論到地方的人事問題。美國是一個聯邦國家，各州並不放棄牠們完全的主權，而邦與邦間可謂是一種比較的繫聯，一切行政的集中和分化，在牠們可說是最易發生問題的。但是拿我國來講，雖然名義上中央集權，然而因爲地域龐大，四顧不易，一切行政問題，各自爲政，也確有各地不能一致的缺憾。所以人事行政同樣在美國和我國都發生各地互異的現象。

這書裏所說的是美國的情形，各地還可分爲州和州以內各地。州政府的行政較之中央政府自然簡單，因爲沒有外交，管理集中財政和州際商業的政務；所以人事方面也較中央政府爲簡單，其工作大部是屬於管理方面的。至於州以內各地，聽州指揮，牠們的事務純屬於執行，所以較之州政府更爲簡單。討論地方政府的人事問題本身，沒有什麼困難發生，但是把整個美國做單位，就不是這樣簡單，不是嗎，各州各自爲政，中央已失其統制的能力。所謂集中的統制，在美國實在發生極大的問題。使我聯帶的想到我國，蹈了美國相似的覆轍，我國現正在謀補救之道，有如各省附設銓叙委員會等。美國呢，我讀完這本書後，不能不提出一個問題：

美國因爲政體的關係，集中人事行政是否可能？

我對這本書所提出介紹和討論的，是牠特長的地方，至於職位的分類，公務員的任用升遷，俸級之釐訂等，因爲沒有與他書特別不同之處，所以不加討論。

結束前，我想說的就是這書不能脫乎一般的弊病，作者是美人　太過注意美國的情形。誠然因爲作者是人事諮詢委員會的一份子，該會旨在調查美國人事行政實況和建議改進現行制度的方針，作者爲材料搜集的便利和使命的關係，不得如此寫。我認爲何不兼採些世界各國材料作一個比較的研究，對其國家作一愈加有益的貢獻，更在世界學術界上放一異彩。當然我們不能認爲美國現在的制度是完全成功，美仍應參照他國的特長，尋求今後改進更遠的途徑。質之維爾滿庭先生以爲如何。

在此，又使我聯想到我國人研究學術的缺點，最著的是沒有比較客觀的態度，留美學生拼命表揚美國的制度，而忘却更多得些他國資料，留德法學生亦復如此。結果造成學術界的不相爲謀，各行其是，不能求得眞正於國家有益的方法，始終成爲我國科學發達的故障。在介紹這本書後，我更不能不附陳一個勸告，決不可因爲鮑樂克脫鉅著和本書的影響而認爲美國的人事行政是無瑕可擊，決不可把眼光窒塞於一個國家，好比井底觀天也似。

内政研究月報

兒童保護與教育專號

零售每册四角可用郵票（限用五分頭）函購預定全年者不加價

定全年十二册兩元

古今領袖人物言行札記

張居正的硬幹及其治術

望

明自英宗以後，內憂外患，相繼而起。至武宗的荒淫，和宦官的弄權，國勢更一天不如一天，自世宗經穆宗以至於神宗即位，離開太祖開國約二百餘年，已到日薄崦嵫之境。離明亡還有七十年光景，此後的政治，每下愈況。終於經不起新興勢力——滿清的一擊，而至於亡國。這時期的士大夫階級不是空說性理，便是標榜詩文。大家祇會議論不會做事。而且是非不分，功罪混淆，賞罰不行。祇講交情勢利，不管國家社會，一切的一切，都是因循頹唐，委靡不振。張居正在這種環境之下，做起神宗的宰相來。那時神宗不過十餘歲，一國大權，都操在居正手裏。內而整飭吏治，外而調兵遣將，應付邊患，都被他弄得服服帖帖。他的功勳確是顯赫一時。但明史本傳說：「居正自奪情後（居正父死不丁憂，仍留朝視事）益偏恣，其所黜陟，多由愛憎，左右用事之人，多通賄賂。」當時彈劾他的人是很多。都說他大權獨攬，擅作威福。至於他父死不丁憂，彈劾的人更多連他自己的學生都彈劾他。按之實際。前者是由於嫉妒，後者是由於俗儒的拘泥，居正在這種環境之下，眞是有說不出的痛苦。那時的士大夫官僚，都舒鬆疏懶，因循，舞弊驕縱慣了。你要把他們約束起來，走上軌道，是多麼困難的事。你要整頓，要改革，當然不能不用熱辣的手段，擺出無情的面孔，用人不論親疏，賞罰一憑功罪，毫無假借。可是在那麼慣了的社會，結果一定是得罪了許多人，激起很大的反動，自己弄得焦頭爛額。如果沒有極大的勇氣，不顧自己的死活利害，決不肯這樣的硬幹。就是幹了一下，覺得事不可爲，知難而退，明哲保身，發發牢騷，有什麼用處呢？我們來看看張居正是怎麼樣的硬幹。

「爲考成法，以責吏治。初部院覆奏行撫按勘者，嘗稽不報，居正令以大小緩急為限，誤者抵罪，自是一切不敢飾非，政體為肅……居正以御史在外，往往凌撫臣，痛欲折之，一事小不合，詬責隨下，又勅其長加考察。給事中余懋學請行寬大之政，居正以為風己，削其責。御史傅應楨繼言之尤切，下詔獄杖戍。給事中徐貞明等，羣擁入獄視具橐饘，亦逮謫外。御史劉臺，按遼東，誤奏捷，居正方引故事繩督之。臺抗章論居正專恣不法。居正怒甚，帝為下臺詔獄，命杖百遠戍。居正陽具疏救之，僅奪其職，已卒戍臺。由是諸給事御史，益畏居正，而心不平。當是時，太后以帝冲年，尊禮居正甚至。同列呂調陽莫敢異同，及吏部左侍郎張四維入，恂恂若屬吏，不敢以僚自處。居正喜建豎，能以智數馭下，人多樂為之盡。俺答款塞久，不為害，獨小王子部衆十餘萬，東北直遼左，以不獲通互市，數入寇。居正用李成梁鎮遼，戚繼光鎮薊門。成梁力戰卻敵功多，至封伯，而繼光守備甚設，居正皆右之。邊境晏然。兩廣督撫殷正茂凌雲翼等，亦數破賊有功。浙江兵民再作亂，用張佳允往撫，即定。故世稱居正知人。然持法嚴，覈驛遞，省冗官，清庠序，多所澄汰，公卿羣吏

，不得乘傳，與商旅無別。郎署以缺少需次者輒不得補。大邑士子額隘，艱於進取，亦多怨之者。時承平久，羣盜蝟起，至入城市，劫府庫，有司恒諱之。居正嚴其禁，匿勿舉者，雖循吏必黜。得盜卽斬決。有司莫敢飾情。盜邊海錢米盈數，例皆斬，然往往長繫，或瘐死。居正獨亟斬之，而追捕其家屬。盜賊為衰止。而奉行不便者，相率為怨言，居正不恤也。「居正以江南貴豪怙勢，及諸姦猾吏民，善逋賦，選大吏，精悍者，嚴行督責。賦以時輸，國藏日益充，而豪猾率怨居正。」——明史傳。

這就是當時所謂大權獨攬，擅作威福的實情。居正在寫給他朋友的書中說：「僕以一豎儒，擁十餘齡幼主，立天下臣民之上，國威未振，人有侮心。况自隆慶以來，議論滋多，國是靡定，綱紀倒置，名實混淆，自僕當事，始布大公，章大信，修明祖宗法度，一以尊主庇民，振舉頹廢為務，天下始知有君也。彼讒人者，欲剸刃于僕之身，又無所汚衊，獨曰專擅專擅云云，欲以悚動幼主，間僕于主上耳。僕受恩深重，當以死報國，違道干譽，直僕之所薄而不為。」可是終於不勝仇恨者的攻訐，到他死後，有人在神宗前說他寶藏踰天府，於是居正的

家，就被抄沒。他的大兒子自縊而死。居正所引用的人，一概放逐，而被居正所黜的人，統統還朝。明朝的政治從此不可救藥了。

居正死後，他的學生沈鯉和呂坤替他的文集做序，有幾句話，都是說得很動聽的。沈鯉說：「惟是人情憚檢束而樂因循，積玩既久，一旦以法繩之，若見以爲苛，而公持之益堅，爭之益力，以是遂與世齟齬。而又一二非常之事，有衆人未易測識者，其跡不無似愎，似少容，似專權，似純任霸術，似與金革變禮，終未盡合。上一時雖優容，實已不能無疑。比公謝世，言者益譸張其詞，上眷寵始移，而公家之禍，于是不可解矣。至今觀場者，猶多煩言，顧其先法後情　先國事，後身家，任勞任怨，以襄成萬歷十年太平之理，我明相業，指固未易多屈也。藉令後人循其已定之規模，而但稍濟以寬緩，亦自可以收拾人心，保囘元氣，顧乃不深惟其終，而但畏多口，遂盡反其所爲，以取悅一時。卒使紀綱陵遲，浸淫以至今日，幾無法矣。」呂坤說得更透澈：「設先生避艱險，計身家，藉一人殊眷，結四海懽心，國家威福，儘足以供之，其誰不悅？即不然，而優遊暇逸，循轍轍，守陋規，上下習而安之，其誰生怨？而先生不爲也。」

張居正的是非功罪，我們不必再加深究。我最近讀了他的全集，其中儘有不少眞知灼見，可以供行政當局省覽的。玆分類摘錄一二如左：

（一）行政　天下之事，慮之貴詳，行之貴力，謀在於衆，斷在於獨。漢臣申公云。「爲治不在多言，顧力行何如耳。」近年以來，朝廷之間，議論太多，……是非淆於脣吻，用舍決於愛憎。政多紛更，事無統紀。又每見督撫等官，初到地方，即例有條陳一疏，或漫言數事，或更置數官，文藻競工，覽者每爲所眩，不曰此人有才，即曰此人任事，其實蒞任之始，地方利病，豈盡周知？屬官賢否，豈能洞察？不過採聽於衆口耳。讀其詞藻，雖若爛然，究其指歸，茫未有效，比其久也，或并其自言者而忘之矣……臣竊以爲事無全利，亦無全害，人有所長，亦有所短，要在權利害之多寡，酌長短之所宜，委任責成庶克有濟。今始則計慮未詳，既以人言而遽行，終則執守靡定，又以人言而遽止；加之愛惡交攻，意見橫出，讒言微中，飛語流傳，尋之莫究其端，聽者不勝其眩。是以人懷疑貳，動見譸張，虛曠歲時，成功難睹。

近年以來，紀綱不肅，法度不行，上下務爲姑息，百事息從委徇。以模棱兩可，謂之調停。以委曲遷就，謂之善處，法之所加，唯在於微賤而强硬者雖壞法干紀而莫之誰何；禮之所制，反在於朝廷，而爲下者，或越理犯分，而恬不知畏，陵替之風漸成，指臂之勢難使，賈誼所謂蹠盭者深可慮也。然人情習玩已久，驟一振之，必將曰，此拂人之情者也，又將曰，此務爲操切者也。臣請有以解之，夫徇情之與順情，名雖同而實則異；振作之與操切，事若近而用則殊。蓋順情者因人情之所同欲者而施之，大學所謂民之所好好之，民之所惡惡之者也。若徇情，則不顧理之是非，事之可否而惟人情之是便而已。振作者謂整齊嚴肅，懸法以示民，而使之不敢犯，孔子所謂道之以德，齊之以禮者也。若操切，則爲嚴刑峻法，虐使其民而已。故情可順而不可徇，法宜嚴而不宜猛。

臣竊見近年以來，朝廷詔旨，多廢格不行，敘到各部，概從停閣。或已題奉欽依，一切視爲故紙。禁之不止，令之不從。至於應勘應報，奉旨行下者，各地方官，尤屬遲慢。有查勘一事，而十數年不完者，文卷委積，多致沉埋。干證之人，半在鬼錄。年月既遠，事多失眞。遂使漏網終逃，國有不伸之法，覆盆自苦，人懷不白之冤。是非何由而明，賞罰何由而當？伏望勅下部院等衙門，凡大小事務，既奉明旨，須數日之內，卽行題覆，若事理了然，明白易見者，卽宜據理剖斷，毋但諉之撫按議處，以致耽延。其有合行議勘問奏者，亦要酌量事情緩急。道里遠近，嚴立限期，責令上緊奏報。該部置立號簿，發記註銷。如有違限不行奏報者，從實查參，坐以違制之罪，吏部卽以此考其勤惰，以爲賢否。然後人思盡職而事無壅滯也。（以上全集奏疏一陳六事疏）

天下之事，不難於立法，而難於法之必行，不難於聽言，而難於言之必效。若詢事而不考其終，興事而不加屢省，上無綜覈之明，人懷苟且之念，雖使堯舜爲君，禹臯爲佐，恐亦難以底績而有成也。臣等竊見近年以來，章奏繁多，各衙門題覆，殆無虛日，然敷奏雖勤而實效蓋鮮，言官議建一法，朝廷曰可，置郵而傳之四方，則言官之責已矣，不必其法之果便否也。部臣議覆一弊，朝廷曰可，置郵而傳之四方，則部臣之責已矣，不必其弊之果釐否也。某罪當提問矣，或礙於請託之私，概從延緩，某事當議處矣，或牽於可否之說，難於報聞。徵發期會，動經歲月。催督稽驗，取具空文。雖屢奉明旨，不曰著實舉行，必曰該科記著；顧上之督之者雖諄諄，而下之聽之者恆藐藐。鄙諺曰，姑口頑而婦耳頑，今之從政者，殆類於此。欲望底績而有成，豈不難哉？（奏疏三請稽查章奏隨事考成以修實政疏）

人情玩愒已久，雖有良法美意，不肯著實奉行，一切皆成故紙，殊可恨也。當此幹蠱之時，不少行綜覈之政，惡能振之哉？（全集書牘一答總督譚二華論任事籌邊）

辱示城守保甲事宜，皆地方切務，但患有司，不能著實奉行耳，須屢省詳覈之，庶不徒爲具文。（書牘一，答憲長楊晴川）

膠河已有成議，雖費亦不敢惜。其中疏濬事宜，及調用有司等項，俱聽便宜處劃，一毫不從中制。乃近聞爲羣議所苦，頗悔昔者建言之爲易。審爾，則此事難以望其有成矣。僕聞疑事無功，疑行無名。明主方勵精圖治，詢事考成，豈宜以未定之議，嘗試朝廷哉？神禹大智，猶必親乘四載，遍歷九土，至於手足胼胝，而後能成功。方其鑿龍門之時，民皆拾瓦礫以擊之。蓋衆庶之情，莫不欲苟安於無事，而保身自便者，孰肯淹留辛苦於泥塗橫潦之中，此衆議之所以紛紛也。願公主之以剛斷，持之以必行。心乎爲國，畢智竭忠，以成不朽之功。凡粘滯顧忌，調停人情之說，一切勿懷之於中。又親歷工所，揆慮相度，分任責成。若憚勞不親細事，徒寄耳目於人，則紛紛之議，將日聞於耳，雖勉強圖之，亦具文而已，決不能濟也。（書牘七，答河道徐鳳竹）

臺工之議，始終以爲可行。確然而不搖者，惟區區一人而已。辱示云云，近來會士大夫未嘗不一一爲譬曉。但今人任事者少，議事者尤少，任事者眞見其事理之當爲，而置是非毀譽于不顧。不識事者　未覩利害之所在，而喜爲款言臆說以炫名，兩者相與，宜其說之嘵嘵而不可止也。世事如此，可嘆可慮！（書牘二答薊鎭督撫計邊鎭臺工）

（二）吏治　守令者，親民之吏也。守令之賢否，監司廉之。監司之取舍，銓衡參之。國朝之制，不可謂不周悉矣。邇來考課不嚴，名實不覈。守令之於監司，奔走承順而已。以簿書期會爲急務，承望風旨爲精敏。監司以是課其賢否，上之銓衡，銓衡又不深察，惟監司之爲據。至或舉劾參差，毀譽不定。賄多者階崇，巧官者秩進。語曰，何以禮義爲？才多而光榮。何以謹愼爲？勇猛而臨官。以此成風，正直之道塞，勢利之

俗成。民之利病，俗之汚隆，孰有留意者乎？（奏疏十二論時政疏）

乞勅下吏部，愼選良吏，牧養小民，其守令賢否殿最惟以守己端潔，實心愛民，乃與上考稱職，不次擢用。若但善事上官，幹理簿書，而無實政及於百姓者，雖才能幹局，止與中考。其貪汚顯著，嚴限追贓，押發各邊，自行輸納。完日發遣發落。不但懲貪，亦可以爲實邊之一助。（奏疏一陳六事疏）

各處有司當易者多。但甲科今已除盡，須俟新科。然僕以爲良吏不專在甲科，甲科未必皆良吏。若廉其已試有效者，就近更調可，他途亦可也。容卽與太宰公議之。大抵論廣中諸吏，官以操守爲先，廉且能上也。卽不能兼，且先取廉者。蓋數年以來，廣盜之起，始皆貪吏利其賄以致滋蔓，故唐人有送南海尉詩云，此鄉多寶玉，愼勿厭淸貧，蓋自古以爲難也。（書牘二答兩廣李蟠峯）

（二）用人　欲用一人，須審之於始，務求相應。旣得其人，則信而任之，如魏文侯之用樂羊，雖謗書盈篋，而終不爲之動。（奏疏一，陳六事疏）

臣聞人主之所以馭其臣者，賞罰用舍而已。欲用舍賞罰之

當，在於綜覈名實而已。臣每見朝廷欲用一人，當事者輒有乏才之歎。竊以爲古今人才，不甚相遠，人主操用舍予奪之權，以奔走天下之士，何求而不得：而曰世無才焉，臣不信也。惟名實之不覈，揀擇之不精，所用非其所急，所取非其所求，則上之爵賞不重，而人懷僥倖之心。牛驥以並駕而俱疲，工拙以混吹而莫辨，才惡得而不乏？事惡得而有濟哉？臣請略言其概。夫器必試而後知其利鈍，馬必駕而後知其駑良。今用人則不然，稱人之才，不必試之以事，任之以事，不必更考其成。及至僨事之時，又未必明正其罪。椎魯少文者，以無用見譏。而大言無當者，以虛聲竊譽。倜儻伉直者，以忤時難合。而脂韋逢迎者，以巧宦易容。其才雖可用也，或以卑微而輕忽之。其才本無取也，或以名高而尊禮之。或因一事之善，而終身借之以爲資，或以一動之差，而衆口訾之以爲病。加以官不久任，事不責成，更調太繁，遷轉太驟，資格太拘，毀譽失實。且近來又有一種風尚，士大夫務爲聲稱，舍其職業，而出位是思。建白條陳，連編累牘。至覈其本等職業，反屬茫昧。主錢穀者，不對出納之數，司刑名者，未諳律例之文，吏守旣失，事何由舉？凡此皆所謂名與實爽者也。若此則眞才實能之士，何由

進？而百官有司之職，何由得於哉？故臣妄以爲世不患無才，患無用之之道。各得其道，則舉天下之士，唯上之所欲爲，無不應者。臣願皇上，愼重名器，愛惜爵賞，用人必考其終，授任必求其當。有功於國家，卽千金之賞，通侯之印，亦不宜吝。無功於國家，雖嚬笑之微，敝袴之賤，亦勿輕予。（仝上）

臣聞才者材也。養之貴素，使之貴器。養之素則不乏，使之器則得宜。古者一官，必有數人堪此任者。是以代匱承乏，不曠天工。今國家于人才，素未嘗留意以蓄養之，而使之又不當其器，一言議及，輒見逐去，及至缺乏，又不得已，輪資逐格而叙進之。所進或頗不逮所去。今朝廷濟濟，雖不可謂無人，然亦豈無抱異才而隱伏者乎？亦豈無擢微玷而永廢者乎？臣愚以爲諸非貪婪至無行者，盡可隨才任使，效一節之用。況又有卓卓可錄者，而皆使之槁項黃馘，以終其身，甚可惜也。（奏疏十二論時政疏）

人是感情的動物，不是完全用機械式的方法，可以約束的。張居正的用人，除了運用他的賞罰用舍之權以外，常常以私人的資格，策勉他的僚屬，這也是補賞罰之不足的一法吧。茲舉他策勉戚繼光的書函錄一二則如左。

戚帥不知近日舉動何如？折節以下士夫，省文以期實效，坦懷以合暌貳，正己以振威棱，乃渠今日最切務也。相見幸一勉之。（書牘一，與薊遼督撫）

向有人告僕云，戚帥求望太過，志意太侈，雖公亦甚苦之。故僕以爲問。今奉來教，知昔之所怏怏者，徒以削其總理舊銜耳。今既力爲光復，更將何求？近屢得渠稟帖，極爲感奮，頗務收拾人心，漸圖實事。仍望公時時敎督之。雖然，僕何私於戚哉？獨以此輩，國之爪牙，不少優假，無以得其死力。今西北諸將，如趙馬輩，僕亦曲意厚撫之，凡皆以爲國家耳。（仝上）

戚之聲名，雖著於南土，然觀其才智，似亦非泥於一局，而不知變者。且既已被鎭守之命，有封疆之責，豈宜別有注劃乎？今人方以此窺戚之釁，恐不知者，又將以爲口實也，公如愛戚，惟調適衆情，消弭浮議，使之得少展布，卽有裨於國家多矣。（書牘一，答凌參政）

孤之此行，甚非獲已，君恩深重，寧敢亢違？到家事完，卽星言赴闕矣。薊事已悉託之鳴泉公，渠乃孤之門生，最厚，諒不相負，自被總督新命，聽其議論，觀其意向，便視薊如家。士大夫有短足下者卽力爲辯釋，可以知其用意之厚矣。願足下自處務從謙抑。凡事關利害，宜披情愫，虛心商榷而行，勿定執已見，勿心口異同，與人爭體面，講閒氣。南北軍情，務須調適，法行一概，勿得偏重。凡浮蠹冗食之人，悉宜除汰，蓄之無用，徒招物議。其處置屬夷一節，不可視爲細事，務宜恩威互用，使之知畏且懷，爲我外藩可也。邊疆事重，孤雖去，不敢須臾少忘。頃奉上諭，凡機密重務，許以不時奏聞。閫外之事，部署已定。幸足下倍加審愼，勿以孤之暫去而遂易慮也。（書牘十答薊鎭總兵戚南塘計邊事）

本刊投稿簡章

一、投稿以有關於管理者為限。

二、投稿不拘文言白話，須繕寫清楚，並加標點，如係外國文稿件，並請打印之，均不得於一紙兩面寫字。

三、論著稿中，如有譯名或引文，須分別註明原文及出處。

四、譯稿須將原文題目，原著者姓名，出版日期及地點，詳細載明，如能附寄原文尤佳。

五、稿末請簽名蓋章，並註明住址。

六、來稿文字，本院有酌量修改之權，如投稿人不願有何增删，則應於投稿時聲明。

七、來稿登載與否，概不寄還，惟附寄郵票預先聲請寄還者，亦可照辦。

八、來稿一經登載，當酌贈以每千字一元至三元之薄酬。

九、來稿請寄上海徐家匯交通大學管理學院。

中華民國二十五年七月出版

第一卷　第二期

每本大洋四角
全年五期大洋一元六角

主編者　鍾偉成

發行者　交通大學管理學院
上海浙江路五三六號

印刷者　華豐印刷鑄字所

二月刊

第一卷 第三期 二十五年九月

本期要目

交通大學管理學院編輯

管理二月刊

第一卷 第一期
民國二十五年四月

管理二月刊

第一卷 第二期
民國二十五年七月

管理二月刊

第一卷 第三期
民國二十五年九月

論著

演講

譯述

論著

評吾國最近改訂之鐵路列車及車輛統計辦法

許靖
沈奏廷

一 修訂列車及車輛統計之經過

乃者鐵部除舊布新，不遺餘力，僅就最近公布施行者言之，則有貨物運輸辦事細則，列車及車輛調度通則，與列車及車輛統計規則。此種勵精圖治精神，洵爲前所未見，不可謂非良好之現象。論上述三種規則之性質，均爲管理鐵路事務之根本大法，缺而不備，固屬非是，然若立法不臧，亦足轉貽無窮流弊；因而政府固應儘量籌維策劃於前，國人亦宜探討於后，庶幾得失易辨，改善不難。茲就管見所及，對于統計規則略抒感懷，餘則擬於另文再行論列之。

按最近修訂之列車及車輛統計規則，卽爲以前十八年頒布之鐵路行車統計車務人員應守規章，其內容同爲辦理「貨物列車統計」，「旅客列車統計」及「貨車停站時間統計」，不過新舊名稱微有不同耳。查原定種種辦法，缺陷極多，早爲識者詬病；而此次修改經過，亦有頗堪玩味者。用陳梗概、以明原委。其中大概情形，據交通雜誌第四卷第七期所載，有如下段之記述：

「鐵道部以前頒布之鐵路行車統計車務人員應守規則，施行以來，雖頗有成效，惟內容格式，尙須加以補充改善，業經令飭各路研究陳述意見，嗣據各路先後呈復到部；復經由主管廳司參酌各路意見及歐美各國關於行車統計內容，將前項統計重加改訂，改爲列車及車輛統計規則。其所有格式，業經重行審訂，加以詳細說明，先行擬定草案，再電飭各路派遣主管行車統計人員來部討論，俾明瞭此項統計之用法及作用，以期推行盡利。現在此項規則及格式說明，均已修訂就緒，一俟核定公布，卽擬於本年七月一日起實行。」

由上段之叙述，不惟可於改訂之前因後果得一簡明概念，更應有下列之認識：(一)爲事前曾經徵詢各路意見，(二)爲各路曾派主管行車統計人員到部共同討論。足見鐵部此次修改統計辦法，極爲愼重，決非草率從事者可比，姑不問其結果如何，而其認眞精神殊値吾人特殊重視。惟作者對于前段所載「舊法頗有成效」及「新法曾經參照歐美各國行車統計內容」之說，似覺未敢苟同；蓋新擬各種統計單位及方法，仍多與歐美鐵路所有者大有出入，且多相左之處；卽就統計最完善之北美鐵路而言，經作者親歷而目睹者，約計不下數百餘種，與吾國較，亦頗有不能相符者。至謂舊法行之頗有成效，尤令人不能無疑；而新法之能否推行盡利，則正爲本文行將詳爲剖析之問題，請依三種統計分別陳之。

二 對於貨物列車統計之意見

考新訂貨物列車統計，計分五種格式如左：

名稱	用途
1. 貨物列車報單	車長用
2. 貨物列車統計日報	車務處用
3. 貨物列車統計月報	車務處用
4. 貨物列車統計	鐵道部用
5. 貨車統計	鐵道部用

按新則規定：第一種貨物列車報單應由車長填造，分別交由各關係段到達站送呈車務處，再由車務處據以填造貨物列車統計日報及貨物列車統計月報，最後由鐵道部祕書廳研究室根據各路送呈之貨物列車統計月報按月編造各路貨物列車統計及各路貨車統計。所有五種表格之相互關係大致如此，而一般基本數字大抵均以第一種貨物列車報單爲根據；是故比較新舊辦法之優劣，首當衡量基本報單之內容。新訂貨物列車報單卽爲代替原有貨物列車日程單之基本表格，共分17欄，較之原有欄數不多不少，內容亦大致無甚出入。玆以新舊兩表錄列於后，以便比較：

甲 原有貨物列車日程單——車守填報由車務段填造

貨					車						備載	統計 車守不得在此欄內填寫				
何路車輛	種類	車號	噸量	車輛淨重	裝載情形	車站			掛上	摘下		貨車里程	貨車里程噸數		列車載重里程	
						由	至	貨票號數					重	空	重	空
(1)	(2)	(3)	(4)	(5)	(6)	(7)	(8)	(9)	(10)	(11)	(12)	(13)	(14)	(15)	(16)	(17)

乙 修訂貨物列車報單——車長填報由車務處填造

貨		車		貨		物		車站		附註	統計 (車長不得在此欄內填寫)					
路別	噸量種類	車號	皮重	名稱	起運站	到達站	噸數	掛上	摘下		貨車公里		貨車公噸里		列車載重噸公里	貨物噸公里
											重	空	重	空		
(1)	(2)	(3)	(4)	(5)	(6)	(7)	(8)	(9)	(10)	(11)	(12)	(13)	(14)	(15)	(16)	(17)

茲依上列兩表內容，并參照新訂填造說明辦法，論列數點於后：

(一)第5欄「貨物名稱」——若就本欄名稱表面觀之，似為新添項目，然一按其實質，實即原表第6欄「裝載情形」之變相說法，所異者不過意義上較為明顯肯定而已。觀乎對于本欄所定填寫辦法，其中無一而非表示裝載情形，即可知矣。茲錄其填寫本欄說明如次：

1.「貨物」欄之「名稱」即每輛貨車所裝貨物，在貨票上載明之貨物名稱。

2.如為合裝整車，則填數量較多之貨物名稱。

3.如爲沿途零担車；則填「沿零」二字。

4.如爲整車零担車，則填「整零」二字。

5.如爲行李包裹車，則填「行李」或「包裹」二字。

6.如裝軍隊或旅客，則填「軍隊」或「旅客」二字，不必填寫貨物名稱。

綜觀以上各項，不可謂不詳矣，然而於此有一首當認淸之問題，卽列車統計中是否有記載貨物名稱之必要是也。管見所及，以爲絕無需要。蓋鐵路如欲明瞭所運各種貨物情狀，則原有另由貨票編製之貨物統計；而列車統計所應有者，端在貨物之重量，至若名稱如何，殊與計算列車載重渺不相干。卽令每車均載一種貨物，塡寫毫不費事，亦屬無謂。何況各車內部裝載，在事實上並不如是單純，是又何取乎此徒勞無益之舉乎。明乎此，則其所定塡寫「數量較多之貨物」，與夫「沿零」「整零」等等辦法之是否合理有用，自可不言而喻矣。

(二)第6欄「貨物起運站」及第7欄「貨物到達站」——核與舊表第7 8兩欄適爲同物，謂爲虛設也可，謂爲與第9欄「掛上車站」及第10欄「摘下車站」陷於重複，亦無不可。請言其故：

第一：如爲整車貨物，車輛之掛摘車站，有時卽爲貨物之起訖地點，以整車旣係同由一站掛出，而又一至訖站，卽須將車輛整個甩下，原列車當卽離站繼續前行，絕無令同一列車在站等候該車卸完，再裝他貨，仍由原來列車掛運之理。若列車須重行編配，貨物之起訖站未必卽係列車之起訖站，然既有掛車站與摘車站之塡列，則貨物起訖站之塡註，對於編製統計，亦無必要，其結果仍不過多此一舉而已。

第二：按沿途零担車言，尤不能將每批沿途裝卸貨物一一記其起訖站點，結果仍非按照車輛掛摘地點塡寫不可。舍此而外，決無更善之法。證之第十七條所定「如爲沿途零担車，卽塡該車之起運站名」之說明，又第十八條「如爲沿途零担車，卽塡該車之到達站名」之說明，尤爲確鑿無疑。蓋所謂「該車之起運站名」者究與車輛掛上車站有何區別，而「該車之到達站名」又與車輛摘下車站有何差異。謂爲徒增煩擾，等於虛設，是又誰曰不宜。

(三)第8欄「貨物噸數」——此爲原有辦法忽略之點，今添補之，不可謂非進步。惟查所定計算各種重量方法，不無尙有研究之餘地。按第十九條說明規定，計分下列種種計算重量辦法：

1. 整車則按貨票上載明之貨物實在噸數塡寫。
2. 行李包裹車及沿途零担車則概按車輛載重量四分之一計算噸數，例如四十噸車則其噸數作爲十噸，餘類推。
3. 整車零担車則概按車輛載重量二分之一算其噸數，如四十噸車卽爲二十噸是也。
4. 合裝整車則仍按貨物實重計算噸數。

5.如以貨車裝載軍隊或旅客，則應按車輛載重量每十噸作爲一噸計算；易言之，卽爲車輛載重量十分之一也。

以上除第1 4兩項均按貨物實重計算，當無問題外，餘如種種按照載重容量折算辦法，似覺未盡妥當。其一：以沿途零担車言，因其實在貨重不便塡寫，故在北美各路，均採一種標準噸數，而所謂標準噸數者，旣非臆斷，亦非假定，乃係根據平常實際平均車輛裝載統計結果而定，如甲路每一沿途零担車平時平均裝載約爲六噸，則以六噸定爲甲路之標準數；又如乙路每一沿途零担車平時平均裝載約爲八噸，則以八噸定爲乙路之標準數；是同爲沿途零担車，各路標準噸數並不一致，以各路實際裝載情形不同也。他如直達整車零担車，亦用同樣統計方法以定其標準噸數。故在表面上似爲假定之數，實則均係經過統計手續而定，仍與計算實重無甚差別。其法之合理，卽在於此。旣能化繁爲簡，而又切於實際，較之不問實際如何，一律按車輛容量幾分之幾折算，不僅計算手續簡捷，抑且不悖於理，至若逕按容量折算比率之高低是否合理，則又另一問題也。其二：同爲沿途零担車，各路運輸情狀以及裝載情形，絕難彼此盡同，假令京滬路實際約能裝至載重量四分之一，其他平漢，粵漢，津浦各路則又未必一律裝至載重量四分之一。足見四分之一之標準噸數，縱能合理，亦不能一律施行於各路也。其三：鐵路開行沿途零担車，原爲便於疏通沿線小站零星貨運，故實際裝載數量未必隨車輛載重容積而轉移，卽車輛載重量大者，實際裝運貨物未必卽能多於載重量較小之車輛；若按一定比率計算噸數，則車輛愈大，噸數愈多，揆諸實際，亦未必盡合於事理。其四：如以貨車裝運軍隊或旅客，則該車卽與客車同其性質，按西國通例，凡屬運客車輛，類皆不算載重，以其爲數甚微也。以前法比等國，曾有以頭等客車按二噸，二等客車按二噸半，及三等客車按三噸計算載重之成例，然卒以不合實際而又無必要，亦曾早經廢止。其五：若以貨車裝載行李包裹，則論其性質，亦成爲客車之一種，縱令偶有附掛於貨物列車之場合，似亦仍應視爲客車，不必按載量算其噸數，尤不宜與沿途零担貨車同用四分之一之折算標準也。惟此項貨車既暫作客車使用，在統計上旣按客車看待，則計算車日 Car days（卽貨車輛數乘每月日數之積）之際，卽應將此項貨車輛數乘以其暫代客車使用之日數，由總數中除去，以免有所軒輊，始稱允當。此種應除去之車輛日數可由調度所主管車輛登記與稽核之人員設法供給之，要非難能之事也。

以上所述，僅以貨物列車報單內應塡之項目爲限，其次各項統計單位亦有足供商討之處，爰列述之如次，以供硏究：

（一）空貨車噸公里佔共計貨車噸公里百分數　一路空車里程之多寡及其增減情形，應以車里爲單位，不應以車輛容積噸里爲單位，而作種種之比較。因空駛小車一輛，與空駛大車一輛，同爲一種應力求避免之事，初不以車輛之大小而異其嚴重性也。或謂大車回空，損失較大，不加區別，輕重難分。曰是固誠然，惟此爲車輛空駛之結果，而不足以表示車輛空駛現象之嚴重與否者也。吾人從管理上着眼，若某路或某段無故空駛貨車一輛，無論其容積之大小，同爲應加糾正之事，並無所謂輕重之分。否則甲路對於小車調度不善或不設法利用回空，而大車則以貨運性質不同，空駛甚少；乙路對於大車調度不善或不設法利用回空，而小車則以貨運性質不同，空駛甚少；若以貨車噸公里爲單位而比較之，則乙路之空貨車噸公里佔共計貨車噸公里百分數必大於甲路，因是乙路之貨車空駛問題，似較甲路爲嚴重，而不知在車輛管理上觀之，兩路或爲一邱之貉耳。今若用空車公里佔空重貨車公里百分數以爲比較，即可免除此種不合理之觀察。乃新頒統計辦法竟舍此而不用，而用貨車噸公里以代之，不可謂非失誤。況在處用貨物列車統計月報內，原有空重貨車公里之現成數字，足資應用，無如一至部用貨車統計格式（運統2丁）內，竟不列入此數，而徒將貨車公里分成「貨物」「混合」「路務」三類，成爲一種無用之區分，以致空車公里佔空重貨車公里百分數一物無從計算，反以貨車噸公里爲單位而代之，殊未免有弄巧成拙之嫌。推其原意無非因有空重噸公里之數，即可不必再有空重貨車公里之分，而不知計算空重車輛里程，藉以比較車輛運用狀況，正須應用車里而不應用車噸里，轉增觀察之不確；且在部用格式內既不用空重貨車公里之數字，則處用月報內之編算此數，又有何種目的可言耶。總之空重貨車噸公里之比較儘可廢除，而空重貨車公里之比較則應加入，此項加入之單位卽可名之曰空貨車公里佔空重貨車公里百分數，亦分上下行以編算之，而後始稱合理。在歐美鐵路莫不有此單位，吾國鐵路又何能獨異乎。

(二)每列車公里之貨車噸公里　此數僅足表示每一列車平均拖運之車輛容積噸數，毫無實際用處可言。在歐美鐵路，原有每列車里平均貨車里之統計，用以表示每列車平均所載車數，在未編有載重噸公里之路，此數曾視爲唯一表示列車載重程度之統計，蓋此數在編算上遠較載重噸公里爲簡易也。今既有載重噸公里之統計，此數之重要性已非復昔比；至於每列車公里之貨車噸公里尤屬無用之物，在西國亦未之見，而吾乃採用之，尤無學理之根據，亦無實際之需要，似應從早廢除，以免爲整個統計之玷。

(三)每貨車每日之貨車噸公里　此數亦無意義，更無必要。蓋每貨車每日之貨車公里，固足以表示貨車之流通程度，在歐美鐵路原有 Car (or wagon) miles per car (or wagon) day 之統計，吾國倣效而採用之，固屬允當；今乃於此數之外，復加每貨車每日之貨車噸公里，未免有畫蛇添足之嫌。況比較各路時，車輛容積較大之路所有每貨車每日之貨車噸公里，自應較大，初非由於該路車輛流通程度之較高，甯非轉增誤會，弄巧而反成拙耶。故每貨車

每日之貨車噸公里一數似絕對無編算之必要，且應避免之，使無爲人誤用之可能，蓋不必要之統計往往有不如無也。

(四)貨車分類統計　在北美鐵路計算貨車里程時，莫不將守車里程 Cabin or caboose car miles 與普通貨車里程劃分，蓋守車不能載貨，自不能與一般貨車等量齊觀，若混合不分，則所有其他平均單位均將不甚正確。且守車之行程莫不與列車之行程同其終始，而貨車則往往有中途摘掛者，故守車之流通程度常較一般貨車爲高，混合計算，尤多不妥。吾國計算貨車公里，未將守車劃出，亦一缺陷，似應加以補充。此外如能將各類車輛，如蓬車，煤車，平車，牲口車，冷藏車等，分別計算其里程，則效用尤顯矣。

(五)損壞貨車輛數與現有貨車輛數之比率　此數卽美國鐵路所有之 Percent of unserviceable to total cars on line 統計也。用以表示損壞車輛之多寡與增減情形，極爲有用。吾國各路貨車維持狀況遠不及美國鐵路，尤有加入此項單位以便觀察監督之必要。而新頒統計規則於此未見提及，亦難認爲美滿。編算之法，似應由調度所主管車輛登記人員逐月計算待修在修貨車輛數與其待修及在修日數，而以所得之積與現有貨車輛數乘全月日數(按卽 Car days) 比較，而得一種比率，名曰損壞貨車輛數與現有貨車輛數之比率，此項比率應由部路兩方加以監督，以求減低。或謂部方現已有類似之辦法，按月分別各路車輛之用途與修理情形，此舉似可不必。不知車輛統計應以完備爲要着，不應有者應去之，應有者則不應漏列之，與其另訂辦法，從事補救，不如加入統計規則以求完備之爲愈也。

三　對於旅客列車統計之意見

查改訂之旅客列車統計表式，亦分五種，其名稱及填用處所如左：

1. 旅客列車報單……………………車長用
2. 旅客列車統計日報………………車務處用
3. 旅客列車統計月報………………車務處用
4. 旅客列車統計……………………鐵道部用
5. 客車統計…………………………鐵道部用

以上第一種旅客列車報單，共分15欄，較舊有日程單減少五欄，以前計算旅客列車載重辦法，在新表中予以取消，是爲最大改進之處，惟仍不無應行商榷者，請略述之。

(一)客車分類統計——按現行辦法，客車公里僅屬一種籠統之數，對於客車種類，並不區分，故行駛一列車後，其中究有若干頭等客車里程、若干二等客車里程，若干三等客車里程，若干四等客車里程，若干行李車里程，若干郵車里程，若干膳車及臥車等里程，均將無從分辨，似爲一大缺陷。誠以客車爲一籠統名詞，有用以載客者，有用以作他種用途者，在美國鐵路，客車之總稱曰 Passenger train cars，而載客用之客車則曰 Passenger cars，劃分極爲清楚，且各種車輛里程，均係按類分別計算；蓋若不分別，則其他平均單位必將受其影響，例如每客車公里之延人公里一數，卽應僅計載客用之客車公里，而不應將行李車、郵車、膳車等等里程一併牽入，轉致失其準確，其理殆甚明顯。況在吾國鐵路，載客車輛復分三等或四等，尤須按類按等分別計算其里程，而後每客車每日之客車公里亦可分類分等計算，以見各種客車運用程度之高低，較諸僅有籠統數字者其爲用不可以同日語也。

(二)每列車鐘點之列車公里　在貨物列車統計中，每列車鐘點之列車公里固有編算之必要，旨在表示貨物列車之平均速度，因貨物列車未必一律按固定時刻行駛，非特中途難免延擱或趕速情事，且常因載重之不同而異其速度焉。至於旅客列車則無須是項統計，在西國亦未之見。良以旅客列車之行駛時刻均屬固定，以不脫班爲原則，何種列車每列車鐘點之列車公里幾何，均係預知之事實，無待於逐日逐月之計算者也。若有延誤，則應於旅客列車延誤統計中求之。若謂既有貨物列車平均速度之統計，卽不得不有旅客列車平均速度之編算，則實爲昧於客貨列車性質之錯誤見解，而有迂腐固執之嫌矣。故每列車鐘點之列車公里一數，在旅客列車統計中，實根本無編算之必要也。

(三)每列車鐘點之延人公里　此數亦由貨物列車統計方面抄襲而來，與前者同犯一病。

蓋每貨物列車鐘點之貨物延噸公里一數固有重大之意義在，因貨物列車載重多則行駛緩，載重少則行駛速，管理者應於兩者之間求一適宜折衷之數，而後每列車鐘點之延噸公里乃能達於最高之點，此其所以有統計之必要也。旅客列車則不然，其編組內容與行駛速度均屬固定，管理者不能隨時左右之，祇須有每列車公里之延人公里與每客車（或客座）公里之延人公里，已足表示載客之盈虛，以爲下次改訂列車編組之參考；至於載客之多寡，則與列車速度與列車鐘點渺不相關，安能加以繫聯，造成一種不合理之統計單位，徒增觀察之不確。况旅客列車鐘點數，平時出入甚少，故每列車鐘點之延人公里若有增減，大都係由於延人公里增減之故，因分子變而分母無甚變動也。若欲於編組旅客列車時，將原由一列車運送之旅客，分成兩列車載運，以求列車載重之減少，行駛之加速，與夫每列車鐘點延人公里之增多，則非特事實上時刻有時難期便利，且往往得不償失，因所掛客車輛數減少一半，列車速度類多不能增多一倍，尤以原有列車速度已高者爲甚，不若貨物列車之速度較低，伸縮較大也。此西國鐵路之所以往往不編此數，而我乃採用之，似無學理根據可循也。

（四）延人公里分級統計　延人公里之數既由會計處方面得來，則原可分頭二三四等等級者，乃祇列一總數，不分等級，殊不可謂非一種可惜之事。至於政府、優待、遊覽等延人公里則可責成售票站編算分級統計，按月列報，似非難能。誠以吾國各路頭等客車載客最少（

據作者研究頭等客座利用程度平均約爲百分之五），二等次之（約爲百分之二十），三等最多（約爲百分之四十），四等則非各路皆有，其載客尤多於三等，今若混合計算，不分等級，則僅得一每客座公里平均延人公里之籠統數字，對於各等客車之利用程度仍不明瞭，實際上有何裨益。蓋必須知每種客車之利用程度，而後何者應添置，何者應減少，以及何者應求利用之增加，按圖索驥，始有把握。且混合計算，在比較各路時亦易發生錯觀觀念；例如今有兩路，甲路各等客車之利用程度較爲均勻，而乙路則二等車異常空間，三等車異常擁擠，然其每客座公里平均延人公里數（不分等級），兩路固無多出入，驟視之，以爲甲乙兩路客車之利用狀況大致相埒，而孰知其爲大謬不然耶。故此項統計不編則已，編則非分等級不可。

（五）每客車每日之客座公里　此數與每貨車每日之貨車噸公里相對，同爲無意義之贅物，故亦主張删去，其理由已詳於前，可不復贅。

四　對於貨車停站統計之意見

查改訂之貨車停站統計表式計分三種如左：

1. 貨車出入日報單……………………車站用
2. 貨車停站統計月報…………………車務處用
3. 貨車停站統計………………………鐵道部用

以上第一種「貨車出入日報單」，卽爲代替舊有「貨車掛出日報單」之改訂格式，在比較及分析其內容以前，先將新舊兩種報單格式並列於左：

舊有貨車掛出日報單

車輛			到站			出站			時間停留		說明			停站時間之原因（延噸時）					備考
何路車輛	貨車號數	載重噸數	日期	列車次數	時刻	日期	列車次數	時刻	鐘點	延噸時	調車及其他站務	裝貨或卸貨	延車時間	徵收機關等檢驗	軍運延車	修理	候車掛出	其他原因	
(1)	(2)	(3)	(4)	(5)	(6)	(7)	(8)	(9)	(10)	(11)	(12)	(13)	(14)	(15)	(16)	(17)	(18)	(19)	(20)

修訂貨車出入日報單

路別		噸量	車	到站					出站					停站時間						停站時間之原因（鐘點）									附註
														在站		中轉		調軌											
原屬	現屬	位	籍號	日期	車次	時刻	出發站	重或空	日期	車次	時刻	到達站	重或空	鐘點	延噸時	鐘點	延噸時	鐘點	延噸時	調車	裝貨	卸貨	空車待配	候車掛出	檢驗	修理	軍隊扣留	其他原因	
(1)	(2)	(3)	(4)	(5)	(6)	(7)	(8)	(9)	(10)	(11)	(12)	(13)	(14)	(15)	(16)	(17)	(18)	(19)	(20)	(21)	(22)	(23)	(24)	(25)	(26)	(27)	(28)	(29)	(30)

綜觀新表項目計達30欄之多，較舊有格式擴充十欄，以最初步之車站日報單，分項竟至如此繁多，其難切實用已可概見。查原有方法之缺點，不在項目之不多，乃在整個方針之謬誤，改良之道，本應首究病根所在，再爲對症下藥。今乃不此之圖，而仍斤斤於補充之是務，無怪全部重訂辦法，類皆不着邊際，始終不能跳出舊有圈套之外，故其補充結果，更使原

有辦法愈爲不合於理。茲請揭舉理由如次：

（一）規定任何統計報單格式，必須首先顧及對象之實在情況，否則小之無從塡寫，大之完全失其作用。竊以無論任何貨車，自入站以至出站，其間必須經過種種手續，手續一變，處理之場所亦必隨而更易，以一種報單必須多方處所及各方員工始能完全其記載，縱令行之可通，亦不能認爲妥當。我國貨車停站統計之最大缺點，卽在於此。請就最普通之運輸情狀分析以證明之。設有裝貨重車一輛，由北寧路前門站運至天津東站，列車一抵東站，照例應將該車甩入車場，此時該車可謂已入天津東站矣。其到站日期時刻似以由該列車車長塡寫最爲準確，但車長在事實上又不負塡報「貨車出入日報單」之責任，欲塡亦有不能。卽令退一步言之，可由站內車場員工記錄，亦必另有一種輔助記載方法，以爲車長通知車場該車到場時刻之便利，此按格式所定應記之第一種時刻與手續也。假設該車係裝零担貨物，則照例應由車場甩至零担貨棧，以便卸貨，故自進場等候甩送以至最後送到貨棧，其間皆爲調車時間，按照規定，不惟當記開始在場等候時刻，尤須登記送達貨棧時刻，必如是乃能計算費於調車方面之準確鐘點；此種甩到貨棧時刻，似非由親身執行甩掛車輛之調車員工經手記載不可，卽車場內部辦事人員亦無能爲此，然此亦非另有輔助記載方法而莫辦，此按格式所定應記之第二種時刻與手續也。此後該車卽在貨棧範圍內開始其等候卸貨時刻，及至卸完爲止，此種卸貨時刻，似又應由貨棧卸車人員塡寫，此按規定應記之第三種時刻與手續也。假令該車一經卸完，旋卽用以裝載貨物，則自開始裝車以至裝完時刻，其間經過時間又爲費於裝車方面之鐘點，又非改由貨棧裝車人員另行塡寫不可，此按規定應記之第四種時刻與手續也。及至該車裝完，當由車場派遣機車將該車拖至車場編入列車，是又入於出站前之調車範圍矣。自在貨棧裝畢開始等候時起以至編入列車時止，其間皆爲調車鐘點，但起始時刻發生於貨棧，必由貨棧人員塡記，而終止時刻又在車場，必由調車員工記載，勢非集合兩處所記時刻，無從計算確實之鐘點，此按規定應記之第五種時刻與手續也。至此則又開始其侯車掛出時刻以至實在掛出之時爲止，是卽所謂「候車掛出鐘點」，亦非車場人員另行記載不可，此按規定應記之第六種時刻與手續也。

以上乃就極單純之情形分析，尙未計及「檢驗」「修理」「軍隊扣留」以及其他等等原因，已須經過六七種手續及記載六七種時刻之多，加以各種時刻有費於車場以內者，有費於由車場至貨棧行駛間者，有完全費於貨棧者，有費於由貨棧折回車場行駛間者；又有費於第一日者，有費於第二三日不等者；論地點，論人員，論時間，彼此各不相謀，如貨棧之與車場決不同在一處，是爲最顯著之例（參閱附圖）。夫以一輛貨車之停站時間，必須牽動車場貨棧各處無數員工，又以同一報單同一車輛之種種時刻必須分由無數人員塡記，試問前後彼此

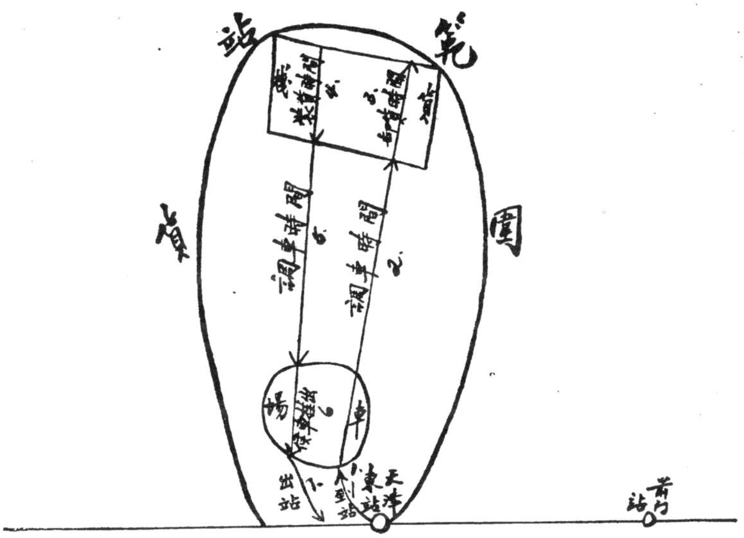

一輛貨車進出貨站之經過手續圖

何能銜接。無怪以前各路各站於此深感困難，未能切實塡報，往往先在前面「停站時間」欄內隨便塡一總共時間，然後任意劃分于以後各欄。其尤妙者，曾聞某路有一極爲巧妙簡捷塡寫辦法，其法維何，卽於各項原因時間事先規定一種固定比例劃分辦法，每日按其比例酌量分配，例如以百分之三十作爲「調車鐘點」，又以百分之二十作爲「卸貨或裝貨鐘點」，而以其餘分於「檢驗」「軍運延車」「候車掛出」等欄。此種辦法，雖屬滑稽可笑，而該日報單確爲不易塡造準確，是又何可諱言。但以迫於部令關係，不得不於無可如何之中想出此種取巧妙計。往事如此，新訂辦法亦於上述種種輔助記載方法未經明白指示，且修訂格式尤爲複雜，其不能塡得各種實在時間，是又可以預料也。總之如此考察貨車停站時間，根本上與事實發生絕大膈膜，縱令作法之人親臨各站主持其事，亦恐於事無濟。舊法本已不合，而新法復蹈其覆轍，殊足令人惋惜也。

(二)退一步言，卽令規定種種補助方法，能使各方得爲連貫之準確記載，亦不知須費幾許人工時間手續，方能完成一個車輛全部時間之塡寫，結果所費不貲，仍爲得不償失，而其所定「應於次日分別寄出」之時限，亦恐絕無實現之可能。此點在表面上似乎不關重要，然與時效問題影響甚大，要宜予以深切注意，於此可以想見凡屬以日爲單位之報單，其塡造方式必須力求簡便，否則時效易失，統計之作用勢必大受其影響也。

(三)考察貨車停站時間，既已計算鐘點，而又以每車之載重容量乘其鐘點，以求其所謂「延噸時」者，此亦吾國獨有之名詞與辦法。論者或謂各車噸量不齊，僅計時數，則大小車輛停留時間雖同，而所損耗之噸量極爲懸殊，爲求準確嚴密起見，應以連同噸量一併計算爲妥。殊不知正因各車噸量不一，故不能卽用「延噸時」以比較各站或各路之貨車停留久暫，蓋噸量乃爲不可以人力伸縮之死物，而停留時間則爲可以人力設法減少者，如連噸量一併計算，則五十噸車停站一小時爲五十延噸時，二十五噸車停站一小時爲二十五延噸時，是停站時間相同而延噸時則相差一倍之多，其不足以據爲觀察各站或各路處理車輛之快慢，蓋已彰彰明甚。此則與比較空重貨車行駛里程時應以車里爲單位而不應以車噸里爲單位，其理正復相同也。且逐車記其各種時刻，已嫌繁重不堪，而又加上各種噸時之計算，既費無謂手續，復有種種流弊，東西各國，均無一類此之統計辦法，而吾乃獨創此格，亦云異矣。

（四）抑有進焉者，查貨車之出入車站，均有事務上之必要，促進車輛運用效能，本當於其正當必需時間以外之延誤時刻求其減少，若在範圍以內之時間，自可不必枉費人工為之計算。例如車場編組列車，即可定出一種標準時間，設為一小時或兩小時，則在一小時或兩小時內編完之列車，自無所謂延誤，更無計算在場改編時間之必要，此法盛行北美各路車場，極為簡便有效。他如裝車卸車，雖不能同樣定出一種標準時間，然亦另有簡便考察辦法。乃吾國對於每一車輛進出，不問有無事務，自始至終，一一按照車號記其時刻，以本可不計算者亦計算之，殊非經濟之道也。

總之，增進貨車運用效能，減少貨車無謂停留，其道多矣，而籠統計算一切停站時間，實為至拙之辦法。考吾國現有貨車停站統計之最大錯誤，乃在不諳貨站之內容及各方與貨車運用關係之異同，而欲以同一統計方法施行於貨站範圍以內之車場，貨棧，貨場，機廠，車房以及所有岔道各方面，以致鑄成大錯而未之覺，如欲再為改進，勢非確認下列兩大原則以為前提，終恐於事無濟，而亦不能得其要領也。

第一：完全打破參照現行貨車停站統計辦法及原則之心理。

第二：另行分別規劃與貨車運用有關係之各種個別統計。

關於第二點之辦法，以限於篇幅，容當另行爲文論之。

參觀津浦膠濟兩路後之感想及意見

沈奏廷

引言

民國二十五年夏，奏乘暑期之暇，分赴津浦膠濟兩路參觀，備承兩路車務處當局懇切招待，幷荷各主管人員殷勤指導，良用感紉。此次參觀之目的物以貨運及行車兩項爲主，對於其他車務事項，亦於便中加以注意；雖爲時甚暫，所得有限，然見聞所及，亦頗有足資商討之處，爰不揣冒昧，略貢芻蕘，一得之愚，或亦足供參考也。

吾國鐵路運輸年來頗多改進，惟舊習相沿，缺陷仍多，有由於設備之不善者，有由於制度之不良者，應興應革，經緯萬端，決非一人所能盡見，尤非短時期內所能察覺，是以吾之所見僅如滄海中之一粟，其爲吾所不能見不及見者恐必數倍或數十倍於此也。

今吾所欲言者以應興應革之事爲限，對於每一事項均先之以批評，繼之以建議，無不以原則爲根據，以事實爲基礎，而絲毫無對人之意。此則當爲讀者所共見，而無須作者之多言者也。況現今吾國鐵路當局類多有識之士，對於吾之批評建議，當不至視爲河漢而能予以同情也。

吾嘗謂鐵路管理方法，無間中外，均應大同而小異，故先進國鐵路之方法經多年之實驗而來者，吾國鐵路應儘量加以變通而採用之，倣效之，而後事半功倍，收效乃宏；否則故步自封，對於一切先進國之良法善策，均斥爲不合國情，不願加以研究試驗，則非特進步綦難，抑且不免於暗中摸索自求痛苦而已。此吾之所以常取他國鐵路之制度原則作引證也。且吾所建議各點，類多平易近人，絕非鶩遠之論，如實際上仍有困難，深望當局者能設法有以解除之，或減少之，勿因噎而廢食，削足以就屨，則路事始有可爲也。茲謹就所見，逐一討論之如次：

一 整車貨場之設計問題

查吾國鐵路整車貨場之設計不合原則之處甚多，此次參觀所得，亦不能外是。舉其著者則有下列數點：(一)整車裝卸岔道之排列多爲撇蘭式，而非如歐美鐵路所採用之平行式，故各岔道之有效長度，有僅當其全長之六七成者，甚有不及半數者，非特增加地位之糜費，抑且增長調車之距離，影響調車之效率；且因岔道排列不齊，故各岔長短不一，而各岔道間所耗之無用地位，因此增加不少，要皆當初設計之不善有以致之也。(二)在美國鐵路，整車裝卸岔道旁之馬路均鋪以路面，整潔齊平，既利客商車馬之出入，復便雨天之裝卸。而在吾國對此往往不加注意，以致岔道兩旁之道路有泥濘難行如入黃泉者，尤以津浦路濟南站之貨場爲最。一遇天雨，則貨物往往須受損失，而客商出入亦深感痛苦，殊非所宜。(三)貨棧或貨場有設在正線之東而調車場設在正線之西者，如青島站卽其著例，以致調動車輛，勢必經過正線，與原則亦有未合，考其原因亦由於設計之不善，非受地位之限制也。(四)貨場之位置有設在離市窵遠之處者，如津浦路濟南站是也。此則於無形之中增加客商之車送費用，與種種之不便，亦殊不妥。考該站原有離市較近之地足資利用，今則反爲私岔及其他建築物所佔，其設計之無計畫殆可想見。(五)裝卸軌道有時失之過長，往往在同一線上裝貨卸貨，車輛不易調出，若能將此項長線分成兩條短線，則佔地相同，而運用之靈活倍之，此亦設計上之要點，而爲吾國鐵路之所未加注意者也。(六)貨場內設置調車線(如大港站之貨場是)亦與原則不合，蓋調動車輛爲調車場之任務，而貨場之岔道應僅以裝卸貨物爲職責。今既在貨場內敷設調車線，則該線卽不能用以裝卸貨物，而專供移動車輛，殊屬無謂之耗費，究其癥結，則岔道過長實有以致之耳。(七)地磅之位置均不設於調車必經之地，往往爲過磅關係，須將車輛往返搗送，既費時間，復耗機力。以上七點均爲吾國鐵路貨場設計上之缺陷而爲管見之所及者，今後改善舊有貨場或建築新貨場時，對於下列各端似應加以注意：

(一)貨場岔道之排列應採用平行式，不應再用撇蘭式，以節地位，而便調車。

(二)貨場之裝卸馬路應加修葺，并舖以堅實之路面，以利貨物之出入及裝卸。

(三)貨場裝卸線應與車場調車線聯絡一起，務以不碍正線之使用爲主。

(四)貨場之地點應擇街市交通近便之所，以便客商送貨提貨，減少其車送之費用。

(五)貨場岔道之長度應有合理之限制，以求車輛調動之便利。

(六)貨場內不宜設置調車線，致失其應有之功用，藉使貨場車場各盡其能事與職責。

(七)地磅應設於貨場與調車場之間，俾一面調車，一面卽可過磅，無須往返搗送，徒多耗費。

二　零担貨棧之設計問題

吾國鐵路之零担貨棧向亦未有完善之設計，與西國鐵路相較，其不合原則之處亦甚多。各路雖有少異之處，但弊害大抵相同。此次參觀浦口濟南(津浦)青島及大港之零担貨棧，所得觀感，可由下列各點概括之：(一)零担貨棧之前面應爲馬路，備貨商送貨出入之所，後面則爲裝貨之股道，備停放車輛之用，不若整車貨場之軌道應成對排列，而中間則爲裝卸馬路也。乃浦口站之零担貨棧(第一號棧房)，兩旁均係股道，貨棧位於中央，非特客商送貨必須繞道而入，且前後兩面均有軌道，送貨裝車勢必互相妨礙，幸該站現有零貨不多，僅用一面之軌道已無不敷，然不能以此而謂此項佈置方法之合理也。(二)零貨車輛有與整車車輛在同二軌道裝卸者，如青島站及大港站是也。此項辦法之採用，亦由於股道少而長之故，然終不合管理之原則；良以零貨車之裝畢及調出時間未必與整車相同，遇有先後，則搗車必感不便，若建調車線以變通之，則股道反多虛糜，其缺陷已詳於前矣。(三)裝卸零貨之設備，不應僅以建一棧房爲限，其棧房對面築有搬貨月台者均應覆以雨棚，并與棧房取得聯絡，使搬貨入車或由車卸貨，均可不受雨雪之侵凌；此次所見津浦路濟南站之零貨裝卸軌道共有兩股，除靠近棧房之一股足蔽風雨外，其對面之一股(俗稱小岔子)雖有月台，但無雨棚，與棧房更無聯絡，現供聯運零貨(由膠濟運往津浦者)裝卸之用，且此項聯運零貨由膠濟鐵路送來後，尙須卸於股道旁之月台，而後裝車，更非有雨棚之設備，不足以策安全也。(四)除建築聯絡雨棚外，裝卸軌道之在兩股以上者，其盡頭處卽應建築聯絡月台，以便各月台間之交通，并可免配對車門之必要，吾國鐵路之零担貨棧，旣無聯絡月台，亦不配對車門，遇有貨物須搬往對面月台裝車時，或須移動車輛，或用跳板跨越軌道以達之，均非正當合理之辦法。(五)零担貨物應以隨到隨卽裝車爲原則，故起運貨棧之地位不宜過寬，藉以減少搬送之距離，此爲西國鐵路共同遵守之定例，乃吾國鐵路之零担貨棧，與整車貨棧無或少異，且起運貨棧與到達貨棧之構造亦無二致(到達零担貨棧應較起運者爲寬)，其設計之無定則蓋可想見。雖在吾國各路，零貨裝車係先堆集棧內，所需地位較多，然此法之是否合理尙屬疑問，蓋零貨之起運，應以過磅裝車同時進行爲原則也。(六)零貨棧房之地面應向軌道之一方略形傾斜，以便搬貨，對於人力時間均多節省，吾國各路貨棧之構造均未注意及此。由以上之六點觀之，足見吾國鐵路之零担貨棧在設計上至少應加以改良如次：

(一)貨棧之佈置，應一律以前面馬路(或河流)後面軌道爲定則，不宜兩旁均設軌道，致礙搬貨與裝車之工作。

(二)零貨裝卸軌道應絕對與整車裝卸軌道劃分(沿途小站除外)，以免互相牽制。

(三)零担貨棧之有軌道二股以上者，各月台上面均應建築雨棚，并與棧房聯通，以蔽風雨而利裝卸。

(四)裝卸股道在兩股以上者，應築聯絡月台，藉以便利各股道間之交通，而免配對車門或移動車輛之必要。

(五)起運零担貨棧之寬度應與到達零担貨棧或整車貨棧不同，以節搬送之距離。

(六)起運零担貨棧之地面應向軌道一方傾斜，以利貨物入車之搬送。

三 貨運調車場與正線之聯絡問題

凡由大站出發之貨物列車應於編組完畢後，直接由貨運調車場駛入正線出發，而到達大站之貨物列車則應由正線直接駛入貨運調車場，以便卽行分配或重編，其不應經過旅客月台，殆爲極明顯之事理。乃在吾國，竟有不然者。貨物列車到達時，須先直進旅客月台，然後再由調車機車搗入貨運調車場，從事分配；貨物列車出發時，亦須由調車場搗入旅客車站，然後再由正線駛出，其辦法幾與旅客列車無甚差異，殊屬奇異。此次參觀所及之浦口站及濟南站（津浦）均用此法，雖青島站之貨物列車未必定須佔用旅客月台，而可直入貨物調車線，然其機車仍須駛入站內，交付路牌，而後駛回機房。按此種辦法所以見諸實行者，其因有四：（一）進站號誌僅有一臂，列車進站，祇許駛入規定之股道，若欲直駛調車場，則號誌不能表示平安；（二）授受路簽或路牌均在旅客月台上爲之（因路簽機設置站長室內），若列車不入旅客月台，則路簽或路牌不便授受；（三）貨站員司及站警均在旅客月台上授受貨車，辦理簽收等手續；（四）貨運調車場之軌道與機車房之軌道有未取得聯絡者（如浦口站是），若到達貨物列車直駛調車場，則列車機車無由駛回機車房，出發者則反是。以上數端，均爲造成貨物列車出入旅客站台之主因，其爲不合理，不經濟，要無待言。歷年機力時間之耗於此者實不知凡幾，似有及早加以改善之必要。且此種現象非僅津浦膠濟有之，其他各路亦有不能免者，尤宜由鐵道最高當局妥定方針，作普遍之改革也。至於改善之法，不外數點，請簡述之：

（一）改善進站號誌之構造，由單臂改爲多臂式，俾列車得由正線直接出入調車場；

(二)改造調車場之軌道，使與機車房直接聯絡，以便列車機車之出入；

(三)建造號誌樓於進站號誌相近之地，除管理號誌外，兼司電氣路簽或路牌事宜，俾貨物列車得在號誌樓前授受路簽或路牌，無駛入旅客月台之必要。

(四)貨車及貨票等之授受應在調車場內爲之，不應在旅客站台上辦理。

以上各點，對於路方所費有限，而有助於工作效率之增進者則甚多，且亦惟有加以上項之改革，而後乃能與原則相符也。

四 整車貨物之處理方法問題

按現時吾國鐵路之規定，整車貨物託運時必須先行送站，堆入貨位，而後撥給相當之車輛，與歐美鐵路之直接裝車制度頗異其趣，其不便利與不經濟之處，作者已一再爲文論之，此處可不復贅。惟既須實行此種辦法，則必廣建貨棧，使貨物於裝車之前，咸有託庇之所，乃此次參觀所及，除浦口站外，諸如濟南、青島、大港等站均僅有露天貨位，非特不蔽風雨，卽路面亦不加修葺(吾知他路亦有同樣情形)，下則賴枕木以資襯墊，上則藉篷布以爲屏障，一遇天雨，貨物之安全卽成問題。(雖北方之雨不如南方之多，然全年雨天亦不少。)以如此之設備，而必欲貨物堆存貨位，不許直接裝車，揆情度理，亦有未合。況整車貨物之託運，在原則上本應先行請求車輛，然後將貨送站，直接由託運人送貨之車裝入指定之鐵路貨車，一則人力時間均可節省，二則保管棧房無須建造，實爲一舉兩得之法。今吾國鐵路所採之方法既異乎是，而保管設備則又付缺如，事之矛盾孰逾於此。今後改善之道，吾以爲與其徒耗巨資，建造整車貨棧，不如改革託運辦法，實行先撥車輛，隨後送貨，幷直接裝車之制度、較爲一勞而永逸。至於洊請車輛之弊，應由嚴密的稽查方法防止之，不必因噎而廢食也。其無固定場所或遠道而來之客商，得於請求車輛時請其先繳定銀若干，俟貨物託運完畢，卽可用以抵付運費（如運費到付則退還之），否則用以抵償車輛留置費，而以餘額退還之可耳。

五　零担貨物之處理方法問題

在美國鐵路，零貨到站後，均係一面檢點過磅，一面卽交搬貨夫送入貨車，例不在棧內存積，所有待裝之空車均於事前安排妥貼，不必臨時配撥，故貨物源源入站概無堆積遲延之弊，迨貨已收完，則車已裝畢，迅速簡捷，可以概見。且收貨時間藉此可以延長，不必因裝車關係，而提早結束，對於客商，頗多便利。否則非特棧房地位將不敷應用，而收貨裝車既不同時進行，收貨完畢尚須裝車，無形中增多時間之耗費，而貨物之稽延隨之矣。吾國鐵路辦理零貨之起運，均係將貨檢點過磅後，分別堆積棧內，然後集合一起，從事裝車，以故收貨裝車不在同一時刻進行，遇貨物擁擠時，則棧房地位不敷支配，而平時則裝車不能迅速，致今日收進之貨或須次日始可裝車，均非促進工作效率之道。如津浦路濟南站且將零貨棧房分成兩部，一爲堆存昨日過磅今日裝車之貨物，一爲堆存今日過磅明日裝車之貨物，而貨車掛出之時間則有須待至裝車後之次日者，是時間之耗於託運及起運者須在二日以上矣。嘗考吾國鐵路之處理零貨所以必須先行堆積棧內而後集合裝車者，其主要原因不外兩端：(一)運往各到達站之貨物數量無定，究竟各批貨物應用整車零担車或用沿途零担車裝運，非俟貨物齊集，不能預知；(二)沿途零担貨物須按到達站之先後順序裝車(即最遠站之貨物裝在車之最裏面)，若集合一起，則便於依次堆裝。惟上列兩點均不無應付之法，其法維何，請分陳之：

(一)凡由大站運出之零担貨物不外三種：即(1)數量常多，每日足裝整車零担車(或中轉零担車)一輛或數輛者；(2)數量常少，須由沿途零担車裝運者；(3)數量無定，多時可作整車零担，少時須作沿途零担掛運者。對於(1)(2)兩種之貨物，可憑過去之經驗，每日指定車輛，以供裝載。第(3)項之貨物增減無定，似最感困難，惟每日由終點站出發之零貨列車通常均掛有空車，供沿途各站裝貨之用，此項貨物似可於檢點過磅後卽行裝入此種備用之空車，如數量多，卽以此車作爲整車另担掛運，否則亦可掛出，以一部分車位供沿途各站裝貨之用可也。果能如此辦理，則(1)(2)(3)三項貨物均可於過磅後直接入車堆裝，不必積存棧內，徒耗時間與手續也。

至於聯運零担貨物，或裝入聯運直達沿途零担車，或裝入整車零担車或中轉零担車（現統稱整裝零担車），更可指定車輛，隨時裝入，亦無堆積棧內集合裝載之必要也。

(二)吾國現時裝載沿途零担車，大都塞成滿坑滿谷之狀態，致貨物不易起卸或翻動，表面上似係充分利用車輛，實則妨礙工作之便利，有得不償失之患。在西國鐵路，沿途零担車之中間大都均留一空道，兩旁則堆裝貨物，均無層層擠塞不易翻動之患，故貨物得隨到隨裝，無須積壓；遇有遠站之貨後到者，稍加翻動，仍可安排，不至有礙遠近之次序。吾國鐵路對此，似應倣效他國，加以改良，則裝車自可隨時進行，時間自可因以節省，而每日貨棧收貨亦可藉此以延長鐘點矣。吾人須知沿途零担車僅爲鐵路運貨所用車輛中之一極小部分，車位縱稍有空虛，影響實至爲微末，而其有助於工作效率之增進者則甚大，權衡輕重，自應舍彼而就此。況堆裝合法，則沿途之起卸亦易，停留時間亦少，固不僅在便利始發站之工作已也。

六　零担貨物之中轉問題

吾國鐵路裝運本路零担貨物，除整車與合裝零担外，尚有專用沿途零担一法者，對於中轉零担法之應用似尚未加以普遍之注意。（津浦路對於本路零担已採用中轉辦法，指定蚌埠、徐州、臨城、兗州、濟南五站爲中轉站）在歐美各國鐵路，凡運往遠站之貨，往往不分站別，集成整車，直駛最遠中轉站從事中轉翻裝，並不一律作爲沿途零担挂運，其沿途零担列車均係分段行駛，無全線直通者。按中轉一法，一則可使運行迅速，二則可增車輛利用，雖中轉亦須耗費時間，然若運行時間之節省較多，則仍屬合算也。今見膠濟鐵路運輸本路零担貨物，除整車零担外，係一概用沿途零担法挂運，因特提出此點，以供討論。查該路每日行駛上下行沿途零貨列車各一次，由青往濟者稱一〇一次，十二時十二分由青島開，翌日二十一時三十七分到濟，費時三十三小時二十五分；由濟往青者稱一〇二次，十五時另五分由濟南開，翌日十五時到青，費時二十三小時五十五分（此係規定時刻，實際上當有出入），其上行列車之所以較速者，蓋以上行所須停留裝卸時間較少也。該路全長三九三·二四公里，下行零貨須費三十三小時以上，似嫌太慢，且青島開行時刻係在十二時十二分，故今日下午送站之貨非俟明日午時不能挂出，加以到達站卸貨交付等手續所需之時間，致由青往濟之零貨，快則二日，遲則非三日不可，時間上之損失似覺太大。改善之法雖不止一端，而下列三點似頗有加以研究採用之價值，請列述之：

（一）將沿途零貨列車分段行駛，不必全線直通；

（二）凡發往他段（指沿途零貨列車行駛之區段而言）之零担貨物，一律不分站別，集成整車，直挂主管該段之中轉站從事中轉；

（三）酌開速行貨物列車（卽沿途停靠甚少之列車），除挂整車及整車零担貨物外，兼挂此項中轉零担車，以求運行時間之節省。

除第（三）項辦法將於次節詳加討論外，試以膠濟路爲例，可將全線分成三段，卽青島坊子間爲第一段，坊子張店間爲第二段，張店濟南間爲第三段，每段應各有沿途零担貨物列車分別行駛，不必直通全線，俾時刻上彼此不受牽制；凡由青島運往坊子以西張店以東之零貨概由青島站集合裝車，湊成中轉零担，由速行列車直挂坊子，由坊子站中轉，其到坊子後能湊成整車零担者，復由坊子站交速行列車挂出，所餘沿途零担，乃交坊子張店間之沿途零貨列車運送，此其大較也。至由青島運往張店以西之貨，則湊成中轉零担車直挂張店，由張店中轉，處理一如前述。果能辦理得宜，則時間上之經濟當有可觀，且亦惟有循此途徑以謀改良，而後乃能收效。茲設一種假定時刻，以資比較如次：

（甲）中轉後化成整車零担者

（1） 由起運站至中轉站 *

起運站名	列車種類	開行時刻	中轉站名	到達時刻	中轉時間 時　分	共須時間 時　分

青島	速行	20:00	張店	5:30	4	0	13	30

(2) 由中轉站至到達站 *

中轉站名	列車種類	開行時刻	到達站名	到達時刻	共須時間 時	共須時間 分	自起運至到達共須時間 時	自起運至到達共須時間 分
張店	速行	9:30	濟南	13:00	3	30	17	0

* 速行列車速度假定平均每小時三十公里計算

(乙)中轉後作沿途零担挂運者

(1) 由起運站至中轉站

起運站名	列車種類	開行時刻	中轉站名	到達時刻	中轉時間 時	中轉時間 分	共須時間 時	共須時間 分
青島	速行	20:0)	張店	5:30	4	0	13	30

(2) 由中轉站至到達站 *

中轉站名	列車種類	開行時刻	到達站名	到達時刻	共須時間 時	共須時間 分	自起運至到達共須時間 時	自起運至到達共須時間 分
張店	沿途零貨	10:30	濟南	15:30	5	0	19	30

* 沿途零貨列車行駛時間按該路現需時間計算

上項辦法果能實行，則時間之節省幾及一半，惟上列時刻純屬假定，實際上自尙須加以斟酌。至於速行列車之是否可行，當於次節討論之。

七　貨物列車之編組問題

吾國鐵路之貨物列車大都均係沿途停靠，摘挂車輛者Pick-up & drop trains，欲求自始發站至到達站直通行駛，沿途停留甚少，如西國鐵路之所有者Through train from terminal to terminal，尙鮮其例。故列車之行駛時間甚長，貨物運輸之不能趕速，此實爲一種重大原因。間嘗考查其故。則一般意見均以爲吾國鐵路之貨運尙未發達，由同一終點站起運之貨數量不足，爲求增加機車運用效率計，不得不使各列車沿途停靠，取挂各站待運之車輛，以期滿軸。此種理由是否充分，似頗有加以研究之價值。此次參觀膠濟鐵路，見該路之貨物列車亦係逢站皆停，行駛時間甚長；試以該路之下行貨物列車爲例，每日由青島定點開行者計有七次，而以坊子及張店爲編組站，其車次及行駛時間表列如次：

（甲）青坊間列車（一七〇公里）

車次	開行時刻	到達時刻	行駛鐘點	每小時平均速度(公里)
121	〇•三〇	九•四五	九•一五	一八•三
123	三•〇〇	一二•四四	九•四四	一七•四
125	六•一四	一六•〇一	九•四七	一七•三
127	八•四四	一八•四四	一〇•〇〇	一七•〇
129	二一•五六	七•一八	九•二二	一七•九

（乙）坊張間列車（一一四公里）

車次	開行時刻	到達時刻	行駛鐘點	每小時平均速度(公里)
131	一一·〇六	一六·五四	五·四八	一九·八
133	一四·三一	一九·四七	五·一六	二一·七
135	一七·四六	二三·一一	五·二五	二一·〇
137	二〇·五二	二·一七	五·二五	二一·〇
139	二三·〇九	四·四四	五·四五	一九·九

(丙)張濟間列車(一〇九公里)

車次	開行時刻	到達時刻	行駛鐘點	每小時平均速度(公里)
151	二·二〇	七·二〇	五·〇〇	二一·八
153	六·三五	一二·〇〇	五·二五	二〇·二
155	一二·一九	一七·五五	五·三六	一九·四
157	二一·三七	二·五七	五·二〇	二〇·四

(丁)青張間列車(二八四公里)

車次	開行時刻	到達時刻	行駛鐘點	每小時平均速度(公里)
111	一五·〇〇	七·一二	一六·一二	一七·五
113	一八·四〇	一一·〇二	一六·二二	一七·三

觀上表，可見由青至濟，僅就列車行駛時間計算，已幾達二十一小時，外加編組站編配

之時間，至快當在一日一夜以上，此中似大有趕速之餘地與必要。趕速之法，不在增加列車之運行速率 Running speed，而在設法改善列車之編組，俾有行駛速行列車之可能。易言之；卽應將青島、大港，及大港碼頭起運之整車，整車零担，及中轉零担貨物，每日集成一整列車，直駛坊子或張店，沿途以不停靠爲原則，是謂速行貨物列車，專挂遠站之貨，沿途不司摘挂車輛之責；所有沿途各站待運之車，概由其他車次挂運。或謂由青島大港等處起運之貨是否足敷開行此項列車，殊屬疑問，若數量不足，徒糜機力，寧非欲益反損，得不償失。曰此可就該路之貨運統計加以研究者也。查該路主要下行貨物，大多數均由青島、大港、及大港碼頭三處起運，而其到達地點則又以濟南爲主，餘則亦多往坊子以西暨張店以西各站（見附表），可見此項大宗貨物均爲運往遠方站者。若每日集合之，使成一整列車，直駛坊子或張店，勿使分由數列車挂運，并擇每日路線較爲清閒之時間行駛，以免候車錯讓，殆爲極可能之事。此則與零貨之集成中轉零担，直挂中轉站，以免沿途停留之原則相同也。或又謂每日貨運數量增減無定，今日足敷一列車，明日或又不敷，是否此項速行列車將隨貨運數量而時作時輟耶。對於此點，請述管見如次：

（甲）吾國鐵路對於貨物列車尙一以裝載滿軸，不糜機力爲目的，而在西國鐵路則有故意減少列車載重以求行駛迅速者。良以列車行駛速，載重少，有時反較載重多，行駛緩爲有利

附膠濟鐵路下行主要貨物統計表

（二十一年份）

貨名	主要起運站	起運噸數	主要到達站	到達噸數	貨名	主要起運站	起運噸數	主要到達站	到達噸數
棉紗	青島	35,702	濟南	20,051	木料	青島	10,865	南濟	13,712
	大港	4,186	坊子以西	10,291		大港	15,902	坊子以西	14,788
			張店以西（除濟南外）	8,206		大港碼頭	2,681	張店以西（除濟南外）	5,342
		39,888		38,548			29,448		33,852
布疋	青島	9,731	濟南	10,596	高粮	大港	5,081	濟南	31,647
	濰縣	2,987	周村	1,360		大港碼頭	37,530	博山	3,212
		12,718		11,956			42,611		34,859
煤油	大港	27,093	濟南	13,835	鐵	青島	16,781	濟南	9,692
	大港碼頭	4,950	坊子以西	3,834		大港碼頭	5,359	濰縣	5,139
			張店以西（除濟南外）	9,996				博山周村	4,972
		32,043		27,665			22,140		19,803
火柴及其材料	青島	4,092	濟南	14,466	總計	青島大港及大港碼頭等	219,736	濟南	134,175
	大港	8,034						其他	75,310
	大港碼頭	2,419							
		14,545		14,466			219,736		209,485
糖	青島	24,296	濟南	20,176					
	大港碼頭	2,047	坊子以西	3,913					
			張店以西	4,247					
		26,343		28,336					

來源——膠濟鐵路沿綫大宗貨物集散概況（膠濟鐵路車務處印行）

，故欲增加機車之運用與列車之效率，不在專圖載重之大而不顧及速率之低，應在尋求一種適宜之載重與適宜之速度，使每列車鐘點之噸公重Grcss and net ton kilometers per train hour達到最高之點，而後乃收眞正之效果。鐵路對於速行列車卽應本此原則辦理，若遇某日貨運數量較少，而仍不至十分減少列車之工作效率時，仍應維持開行，勿使間斷；否則若一以滿軸爲目標，則速行列車殆永無實現之可能矣。

(乙)如遇貨運數量有相當之減少時，則可令此項速行列車停靠較大之站摘挂車輛，以免眞有機力之虛糜，但仍不必逢站皆停也。

(丙)若貨運數量繼續減少過甚時，則速行列車自應停駛。

速行貨物列車實行後，則所有整車零担車及中轉零担車均可由此列車挂運，非特整車貨物可以趕速，卽遠站零担貨物亦可減少遲延，提早到達；不然，徒將遠站零担集成整裝，以備中轉，而所挂運之列車仍爲沿途停留，行駛甚緩者，則較諸沿途零担，相差能有幾何。此速行貨物列車與中轉零担車制度之所以應同時推行也。

八　沿綫各站之死岔問題

吾國各路沿綫各小站之貨物裝卸線類多修成死岔，此次參觀所及之津浦膠濟兩路亦不能外是，且除大站外，沿路各站幾屬千遍一律，一若成爲一種標準式樣者然。按死岔祇有一端通達正線，其他一端通常止於旅客月台之盡頭處，與正線不能聯通；且各站死岔之方向不同，如爲南北線，則有南向者，有北向者，如爲東西線，則有東向者，有西向者。考其弊害，厥有三端：(1)列車編配須視岔道之方向而定，不能完全按摘車先後之次序，(例如東行列車內之車輛，凡到達站死岔通東面者應挂在前部，通西面者應挂在後部，西行車則反是。)諸多不便，(2)凡挂在列車後部之車輛甩入死岔之際，機車必須往後調送，再行駛回，增加時間與機力之耗費；(3)在站車輛須挂列車時，如方向不順，亦有同樣之耗費。足見死岔一物實足以增加行車之糜費，減低行車之效率，而吾國鐵路多數竟蹈此弊，殊堪惋惜。此後建築新路或改良舊路時對此似應加以特別之注意，幸勿貪圖區區地位之節省或建築之簡易，而貽將來無窮之患也。至於改革死岔之法應如何可稱完善，則吾人對於下列四點仍不可不加以注意：(甲)貨物裝卸線及貨棧仍應設於近街道之一邊(通常卽爲旅客車站所在之一邊)，以便客商送貨提貨；(乙)貨物裝卸線之兩端應與正線及會車線聯通，使由死岔變爲通路，以便車輛之調挂；(丙)路線及轍尖之佈置應不妨礙列車出入之安全；(丁)調車應以避免佔用車站界限以外之正線爲原則，以免動用路簽或路牌。根據上述各點，謹將應有之路線形式圖示如次，以供研究：

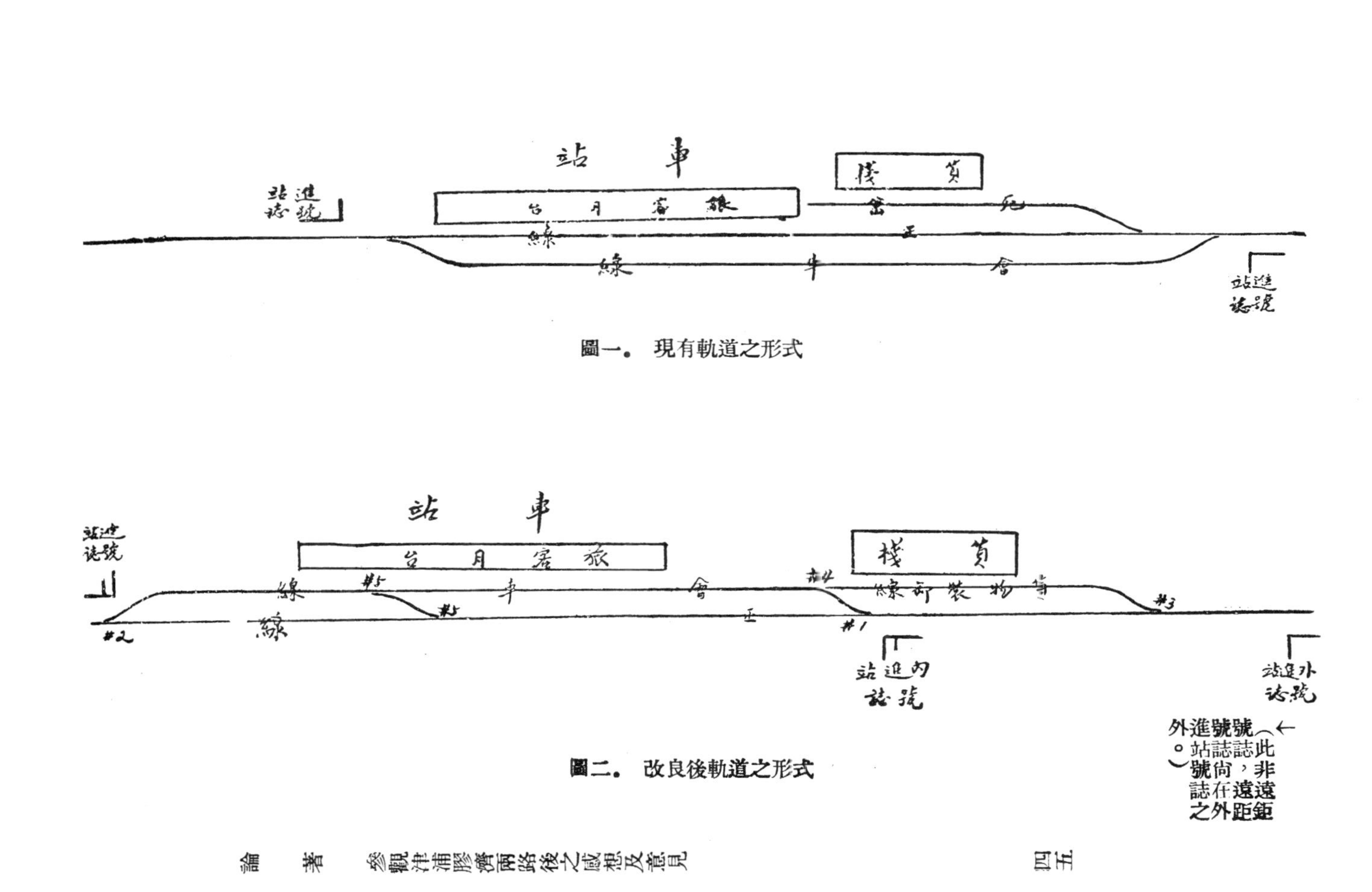

圖一。 現有軌道之形式

圖二。 改良後軌道之形式

按第二圖所示，轍尖第三號(#3)第四號(#4)及第五號(#5)專爲調動貨車而設，平時均應加鎖，使不妨礙列車之出入，故列車入站出站，仍僅使用正線及會車線，安全上決無問題。此項平時加鎖之轍尖僅於調車時使用之。此則在今日吾國鐵路尙無電氣聯鎖號誌以前所有之唯一安全辦法也。且按圖中之佈置，調車出入貨物裝卸線時，可均不必佔用車站界限以外之正線，卽不必動用路簽或路牌，徒多手續也。至於貨棧之仍居原位與死岔之變爲通路，則圖中明白指示，無待解釋也。

九　號誌設備問題

查津浦膠濟兩路之進站號誌均係單臂式，列車入站之股道均屬固定，卽上行車必須入上行股道，下行車必須入下行股道，否則進站號誌不能下落，不如多臂式之不拘任何路線也。考其優點，則在上下行列車入站時皆可避免迎面轍尖，似較安全，然其缺點亦有兩端：(一)若同時有同方向之甲乙兩列車進站，而後至之乙列車須越過甲列車先行，則須經騰道手續，殊屬費時費事；(二)大站亦僅備單臂號誌，致貨物列車不能逕入調車場，勢必先進旅客月台，而後搗入，出發時則反其道而行之，時間機力兩不經濟。關於小站騰道之辦法，可舉津浦路行車附則之規定以說明之，其例如次：

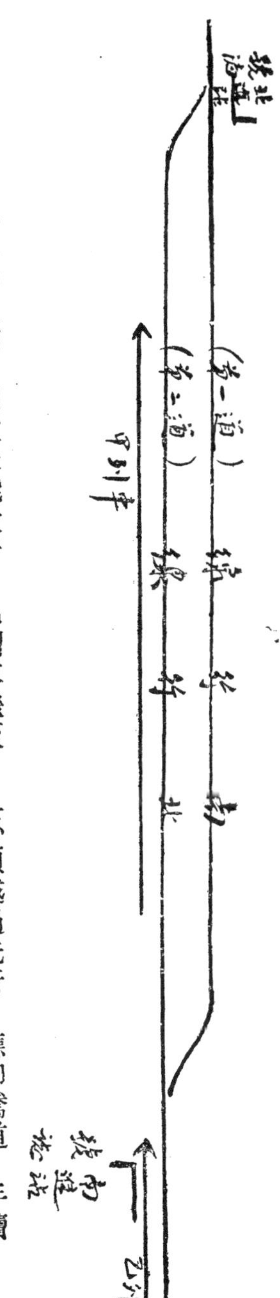

假定甲列車已先進站，因故未能放行，乙列車繼至，且必須越過先行，應即騰道，手續如次：

(1)站長塡妥讓車通知簿，向北端隣站要出讓車路簽，交與甲列車司機及車長簽字，令其開出北進站號誌，再退回入二股道；

(2)乙列車於駛抵南進站號誌外時，應先令其停止，俟甲列車騰道工作完竣，再將南進站號誌下落，准乙列車進站，如乙列車於將駛抵南進站號誌時，甲列車騰道工作業已完竣，則勿庸令乙列車停住，應將南進站號誌下落，令其入站；

(3)甲列車退回停妥後，即將路簽交還站長入機，取消讓車信號後，再將路簽要出，交乙列車向北進發。

由上列之例，可見騰道辦法非特費時費事，易致行車延誤，抑且有危險性質（例如騰道未竣，號誌因誤下落是），殊非善策；若改良號誌及其聯鎖，使由單臂改爲兩臂或多臂（隨岔道之數目而定），則列車入站不必拘泥於一線，隨時可變通之，如上例內之甲列車可直接令其入第一道，迨乙列車繼至，則令其入第二道，越過先行，蓋甲列車入第一道時，進站號誌之下臂將表示平安，上臂表示險阻，使司機者知列車須入彎道，應減低速率也。近年西國鐵路對於站外之雙軌正線，且已有裝置雙面自動號誌Either-direction Signalling，使不分彼此，上下行均可通用者，乃吾國鐵路，以設備不良，對於站內之軌道路線尚不得不劃分畛域，此疆彼界，徒使行車感受不便，其落伍殆可想見，加以改良，似不容或緩也。至於大站之有貨物調車場者，尤宜裝置多臂號誌，以便貨物列車之出入，而免機力時間之耗費焉。（按浦口站至今尚無進站號誌之設備，亦殊足異，以如此衝要之終點站而仍用手作號誌指揮行車，誠不知當初設計者之用意何在，他日添設號誌時，甚望其能採用多臂式也。）

十　到達貨物之保管問題

在歐美各國鐵路，到達貨物之應否由鐵路保管，往往視貨物之爲零担抑爲整車而定。如爲零担貨物，例由鐵路卸車入棧，代爲保管，以備領取（其辦有接送業務者除外）；如爲整車貨物，則除鮮果及候船出口之貨物外，大都均在車上直接卸交貨主，無入棧存儲之必要。故通常整車貨物祇有延車費，零担貨物乃有存棧費，而棧房（卽倉庫）之設備亦均爲零担而設，普通整車貨物概無庸建築保管之倉庫也。吾國鐵路之辦法則異乎是，到達之貨物無論零担或整車概須先行卸下，堆存待領，因是整車貨物到達後亦須加以保管，且因整車貨物數量遠較零担爲大，保管之設備及地位問題遂亦因是而發生焉。

按吾國鐵路旣實行整車貨物代卸代管之辦法，則自應廣建倉庫，以應需要。乃實際上倉庫之設備有付缺如者，有不敷用者，大多數之貨物仍須堆存露天，一與裝車前之起運貨物相同，其是否安全妥貼，自不待煩言而喩。其有倉庫之站，則以地位有限，使用上往往加以限制。例如膠濟路在青島、大港、滄口、濟南四站，均設有所謂「火險」倉庫，除供一般零貨之承運及保管外，係儘先用以保管發行提貨單之運到貨物，其發行普通貨票之運到貨物亦得請求保管（不請求者自一律堆存露天貨位），但須視有無空閒地位而定。觀此可知吾國鐵路倉庫地位之竭蹶與使用限制之嚴厲矣。茲所欲討論者卽今後吾國各路應出巨資以廣建倉庫，供運到整車貨物保管之用乎。抑應倣效西國鐵路之辦法，實行車上交貨，以免建築保管設備之糜費乎。在一般人之心目中，以爲採用後法，足以造成車輛之稽延，減少車輛之運用，雖鐵路得徵收延車費以資取償，然究不如及早卸空之有利也。蓋天下事有利必有弊，吾人應如何取其利而袪其弊，殆爲最重要之先決問題，茲就管見所及，解答如次，以供研究：

(一)鐵路交付到達整車貨物，應以在車上直接卸交收貨人爲原則；

(二)到達站應儘速通知收貨人來站提貨，期以在六工作小時內卸交爲目標；

(三)超過六工作小時尙未提取者，照章徵收延車費；

(四)如逾十二工作小時尙未提取者，鐵路乃得不待貨主之來提，逕行卸車，存儲待領，所有延車費及存棧費均應於提取時照章收足；

(五)凡按市場之習慣，貨物運到後須加以保管，以便看樣、扦樣、或辦理其他買賣手續者，得視爲例外，於運到後卽代卸車，存儲待領，祇收存棧費，不收延車費。

如按上列各條辦理，則鐵路須代囤存保管之整車貨物將僅限於下列兩種：(一)逾限不提之貨物，(二)習慣上必須保管之貨物；第一類之貨物事實上必不甚多，因延車費之負担太重(吾國延車費率遠高於美國)，人皆不願出此也；第二類之貨物並非各站皆有，僅於必要之處變通辦理之可耳。夫如是，則車輛稽延之患不至成爲嚴重，而路方所需建築之保管設備可以大事削減，折衷之法殆莫善於此矣。不然，他日貨運日益發達，整車貨物之數量將愈見增多，非特現有之倉庫不敷應用，且亦恐無如此廣大之場所，足供添築倉庫之用，其不能視爲長治久安之策，彰彰明甚。卽在今日各路設備不週之情形下，亦宜及早加以上述之改革，以免露天堆貨之必要，藉以維護客商之利益。且與其耗費巨資，以建不必要之設備，不如用以添購車輛以利運轉之爲愈也。

十一　濟南站私有岔道裝卸聯運貨物問題

查濟南一地爲津浦膠濟兩路聯軌站之所在地，故兩路貨物聯運之交付概在濟南辦理；兩路在濟設有交通站，備授受聯運整車貨物之用，零担貨物則集裝一車或數車，送達對方之貨站從事交付，與交通站無涉。津浦路濟南站現有私岔凡九處，均接津浦路軌，而與膠濟路軌不相聯絡，凡由膠濟路運至濟南之貨，現一律不得調入此項私岔起卸，而由私岔運往膠濟路之貨亦不得在私岔內裝車，一切託運裝車以及卸車交付等手續，概須在膠濟路濟南站辦理，以故客商雖有私岔，對於來去膠濟鐵路之貨物仍須往返車送，無形中增加負担與不便。查此案懸而未決者已非一日，客商迭有煩言，部方亦曾令飭兩路會商辦法，但迄今仍未解決。復查二十四年春膠濟路曾開商運改進討論會一次，其紀錄提案內有濟南市糧業公會及華慶寶豐兩公司之意見書，均與此事有關，茲爲照錄如次，以見客商方面願望之一斑：

（甲）濟南市糧業公會提：　「查敝業協泰福等二家向有津浦路岔道直達院內，膠濟路德人管理時代，二路不分界域，均能倒送貨車，後自我國收回國有，膠濟所來之貨車竟至今不能倒送車輛，不惟商等蒙重大損失，卽路局亦少得倒車費，以後請准予倒入本廠裝卸。」

(乙)華慶、寶豐公司提：「本公司設有津浦鐵路道岔，直達廠內，原爲便利裝卸起見。而津膠兩路實行聯運以來，膠濟路上車輛，依然不能調入廠內裝卸，故出入貨物每以陰雨阻礙，小車搬運既感脚力負担過重，又感運輸不便困難。竊以兩路既屬聯運，事實上同屬一線，在津路所予之特有權，自應連及膠路全線，於理似無不合，特此提出意見，懇請膠路准予過軌，調入廠內裝卸，以便商運爲感。」

上項提案，至今未見實行，考其原因約有兩端：卽(一)津浦路雖可收調車費，但須出車租及延期費，不能合算；(二)實行私岔裝卸後，原由津浦路運送之貨或將取道膠濟及沿海航路(水陸聯運)，對於津浦諸多不利。由此可見此案之癥結在津浦而不在膠濟，亦足見吾國鐵路此疆彼界之深矣。

竊以爲鐵路設置私岔，原爲便利客商起見，今以路方內部之爭，而置客商之便利於不顧，殊不能視爲事理之平。況私岔在甲路而貨物須行經乙路者，在先進國之鐵路屢見不鮮，均莫不准其在私岔裝卸，互相調送車輛，是謂 terminal switching， 吾國鐵路同屬國有國營，尤應有此種互助合作之辦法，以達便利客商之目的也。至於上述兩項之困難，自亦應加以注意，僅陳管見，申述於後：

(一)車。租。問。題。 查美國鐵路對於貨物之由甲路運送，而在乙路裝卸者，所有調車工作例由乙路辦理，而乙路應得之調車費或向客商收取，或由甲路負担，視各地情形而異。至於車租 Per diem 之計算。則另有明文規定，名曰 Switching Reclaim Rules ；茲就其規定之要點，簡述如左：

(1)每年(或其他期間)應就出入各調車路(Switching Carriers)之貨車分別計算其平均停留日數，卽作爲某年或某時期之標準停留日數，但每車平均不得超過五日；

(2)裝運牲畜之車輛，應另計之，其標準停留日數以一日爲限；

(3)凡停留八日以上之車輛應剔除不計；

(4)調車路對於車輛主有路仍照章計算車租，按月清算繳付；

(5)凡調車路應付之車租不超過標準停留日數者，得向運貨路(Line haul Carrier)收囘之。

上列各條可用下例解釋之：例如甲爲調車路，乙爲運貨路，某時期出入甲路之貨車，由過軌記錄計算，平均每車停留時間爲三日，卽以此作爲標準停留時間；某月甲路調入及調出之貨車共五百輛，每輛平均實際停留時間爲四日，應付各主有路車租二千元（美國鐵路車租每車每日一元），但得向乙路(或其他運貨路)收囘一千五百元，因在標準日數以內之車租應由運貨路負担也。

上項辦法，在原則上頗稱平允，蓋在相當必需時間以內，車租應由運貨路負担，其超過規定時間以外者則仍由調車路負担，一面顧及調車路之利益，一面仍可減免車輛之滯留，實有利而無弊之法也。吾意津浦膠濟兩路在濟南一地之聯運貨物在津浦私岔裝卸者，亦頗可適用此法，由兩路規定一種調車裝卸必需之相當時間，作爲標準停留日數，凡不超過此項標準日數之車租概由膠濟路負担，其超過者則由津浦路負担，庶幾津浦路之調車費收入不至因車租而損失過甚也。至於膠濟路負担標準日數以內之車租一點亦屬頗合情理，因此項私岔若位於膠濟路上，則該路亦必有同様之車租負担，今私岔在津浦而不在膠濟者，乃以客商廠址之故，與膠濟路應負之義務無涉也。

(二)貨運競爭問題　因私岔裝卸便利，乃恐原由津浦路運輸之貨物改道膠濟及水路運送，而予津浦路以不利，非特爲狹小之私見，抑亦爲無病之呻吟，吾知賢明之當局必不作如是想，惟既有此說，不得不將其不合理處申述之：(1)政府既在提倡水陸聯運，以利商旅，自不得用不合理之限制，故意阻止其發展；(2)客商原有選擇路徑之權利，如水陸聯運業務較優，運價較廉，則自不得用人爲方法，限制客商利用水陸聯運之機會；(3)客商之有私岔者固可因裝卸上之限制而取道津浦，然無私岔之普通客商取道自由，將何從而限制之，如不能限制，則又何厚於此而薄於彼耶；（4）若私岔客商一有裝卸上之便利，卽將改道膠濟，則現有之普通客商（無私岔者），何仍多取道津浦而南下者，可見此種顧慮，事實上亦未必嚴重若此也。蓋水陸聯運之費用，因現有轉口稅之關係，尙不如鐵路聯運（經由津浦輪渡京滬）之廉，請觀附表，卽可瞭然。是以無論從大處落目或從小處着眼，此點實不足以成爲一種理由，而用以剝奪客商應有之利益。蓋津浦路貨運競爭之難題尙在將來轉口稅取消以後也。

附濟滬間整車貨物運價表

（每公噸）

（甲）由濟南至上海

貨名	經由膠濟水陸聯運			經由津浦首都輪渡及京滬				(3)—(7)	(7)—(3)
	運費 (1)	轉口稅 (2)	合計 (3)	津浦運費 (4)	輪渡費 (5)	京滬運費 (6)	合計 (7)	(8)	(9)
棉花（普通）	$ 14.21	13.69	27.90	14.00	1.05	2.33	17.38	10.52	
花生（無殼）	13.29	5.61	18.90	8.95	1.05	2.33	12.33	6.57	
豆子	14.19	2.31	16.50	12.13	.90	2.21	15.24	1.26	
生油（新罐）	15.23	9.90	25.13	21.48	1.20	3.08	25.76		.63
羊毛	27.75	6.93	34.68	21.48	1.20	3.08	25.76	8.92	

（乙）由上海至濟南

火油	$ 33.18	——	33.18	28.01	1.35	4.54	33.90	
磁器(普通)	22.98	34.65	57.63	21.48	1.20	3.08	25.76	31.87
糖(普通)	15.35	7.59	22.94	14.00	1.05	2.33	17.38	5.56

附註：(1) 經由津浦京滬者所有聯運遞遠遞減百分率均計算在內；

(2) 負責費及各路加價均計算在內

(3) 水陸聯運接續費計算在內

(4) 裝卸費一概未計入

(5) 生油若係舊罐裝鐵桶裝或簍裝者水陸聯運費用仍高於鐵路聯運(經津浦京滬兩路)之費用

十二　浦口站京滬貨車供給問題

按由甲路運往乙路之聯運貨物，如在甲路之里程甚短者，則甲路實不啻爲一調車路，而乙路則爲運貨路，因甲路所得之收入將與調車費無多出入也。裝運此種貨物之車輛在原則上自應由乙路供給，而甲路車租之負担亦應設法以變通之，而後始昭公允。查浦口站時有聯運貨物運往京滬路，因浦口站已爲津浦路之終點，而與京滬路之南京江邊站僅有一江之隔，故津浦路對於浦口站起運前往京滬路之貨物，照現行規章，祇得核收十公里之起碼運價，爲數甚微，與調車費相較，實無多上下，故事實上津浦路實不啻居於調車路之地位，而運費收入幾全部爲京滬路所有，可見裝運此種貨物之車輛理應由京滬路供給，殆無疑義。惟因貨物由津浦起運，而車輛須由京滬路供給，遂發生客商要車之困難；蓋津浦路遇有此種聯運貨物託運時，輒思利用南下回空之京滬貨車，一面既不知回空車輛何時可到，并可到幾輛，噸位種類若何，一面又不向京滬路接洽，請求供給，遂致客商有貨待裝者，發生種種之困難，此作者參觀該路浦口站時所目擊之情形也。在客商之意，以爲津浦京滬同屬國有鐵路，何必此疆彼界，不肯通融，而在鐵路方面，則以十公里之運費爲數有限，斷不能用津浦貨車裝運，亦不能隨時向京滬路要車，用恐有回空車輛足資利用也。職是之故，客商與鐵路之利益遂處於相反之地位，殊非所宜，應如何調和而變通之，實爲鐵路管理人員應有之職責也。

按管見所及，浦口站起運前往京滬路之貨物，其所需貨車之應由京滬路供給，并應儘量利用南下回空之車輛，在原則上決無問題；惟實行上項原則之辦法，似應加以改善，勿因兩路內部之事，而使客商蒙其損失。其改善之法如何，請申言之：

(一)浦口站遇有客商託運前往京滬路(或越過京滬路)之整車貨物時，應將所需車輛種類噸量及輛數等項通知浦口調度所，請其查明沿綫有無相當京滬貨車將於二三日內回空南下，足資利用：

(二)調度所應就移動車牌并向車輛所在站立卽查明上項事實，隨卽答復浦口貨站；

(三)如在最近三日以內查無相當京滬貨車回空南下時，浦口站得向京滬路南京江邊站請撥相當車輛，以便裝貨；

(四)如由南京江邊站供給車輛時，其在浦口站停留之時間應加以規定，作爲一種標準，倘不超過標準時間，應免計車租；

(五)首都輪渡運送上項京滬路供給津浦路之空車，應概予免費。

經此規定，則津浦京滬雙方既無若何損失，而客商亦可於一定時間以內取得車輛，從事裝貨，不若現時之遲早無定不可捉摸也。客商之利益卽鐵路之利益，設法以調和之，促進之，應爲鐵路義不容辭之責，茲節所及，不過其一端而已。

結語

以上所述者凡十二點，均爲管見所及，認爲有商討之餘地與改進之必要者，其他較小之問題尙多，以限於時間，不及備述。惟作者此次參觀，爲日無多，見聞容有未週，舛誤之處，在所不免；倘蒙海內賢達進而教之，則幸甚感甚矣。

鐵路貨票制度及其塡寫方法之研究

許 靖

一 美國鐵路貨票制度之優點

鐵路辦理貨運，有種種必要之手續，除關於到達貨物者不論外，僅就起站之承運貨物而言，計有下列犖犖諸端：一曰接收貨物、二曰發給貨運收據、三曰收取運費、四曰發給運費收據、五曰計算運費，六曰稽核運費、七曰預備行車單據、手續既繁，關係亦多，故爲辦事便利及責任分明起見，不得不有各種貨運單據以資應用，而爲各方手續得收分途辦理之便利，必須對於資爲辦理各項手續之各種單據妥爲規劃，務使各能分開運用，不相牽連，妨礙各方事務之進行，庶幾客商稱便，鐵路亦收辦事迅速之效。蓋貨運手續雖繁鐵路若能於單據制力求完善，要亦不無化繁爲簡之可能也。

然則單據制度之是否完善，當依何項標準而觀察之乎？扼要言之，厥有數端：其一、單據種類之多寡，務求適合實際之需要，少則不敷應用，多則不但無益，而且增加無謂繁瑣，與夫糜費財力。其二、單據之種類既完備矣，則當進而研究同一種類之單據，究應定爲若干聯數，方能恰合各方之需要。蓋單據之爲用也，有僅須一聯者，有須二聯者，亦有多至三聯，四聯，或五聯，六聯不等者，聯數之多寡，一視事務之性質而定，用途愈廣，聯數愈多，而分聯最大之作用，乃在使同一單據可以分作多方運用，是故少則影響各方同時辦事之便利，其理至淺，無待贅言。其三、種類聯數均相當矣，尤當注意劃分各項單據之界限。用於對內者，不宜與用於對外者混於一起，易言之，卽凡屬必須直接發給托運人或收貨人收執之一切憑證，應與鐵路自身辦理內部手續之單據完全分開，俾對外之手續，不致爲內部之手續所牽制，必如是而後客商托運貨物之時，始可減少在站往返守候之苦，而鐵路始能收辦事迅速之效，凡稍諳貨運手續者，當不以此爲謬也。

嘗考美國用於起運貨物之單據，計分主要三種：卽(一)托運單(Shipping Order)，(二)貨票(Waybill)，及(三)預付運費收據(Prepaid Freight Bill)是也。托運單共爲三聯，由托運人預先一起填妥，連同貨物送站，交由鐵路外部收貨司事核對無訛。卽在三聯一併簽字，當卽以第一三兩聯交還托運人，除第三聯由托運人收執，作爲鐵路收到貨物之憑證外，并以第一聯轉寄于收貨人，俾便預爲提貨之準備。第二聯由收貨司事收下，隨後送交內部貨票塡寫處，從事計算運費及改換貨票。貨票亦爲三聯，第一聯於製妥後發交列車長持作行車之用，第二聯寄總局會計處，以便稽核各站貨運進款，第三聯則送本站會計處，計算由本站起運貨物之運費。預付運費收據共爲二聯，第一聯爲 Prepaid Freight Bill，第二聯爲收費存根——Cashier's Memorandum——，二者名稱雖異而實質均同。其格式之大小亦係按照正式貨票規劃，長短寬窄，完全一致，故於遇有預付運費之貨物，可以之夾入正式貨票各聯之內，用複寫紙一次塡就，異常省事，塡妥之後，由貨票分開，一併送交本站專管收款事務之收費處(Cashier Department)，用作催收運費根據。俟運費收到卽在兩聯蓋「印運費收訖」戳記，然後以第一聯退還托運人，作爲繳清運費之收據，第二聯則由收費處用作登記現金賬目，同時亦爲鐵路收清運費之存根。

由以上三種主要貨運單據用途之分析，可見托運單之在美國鐵路，純爲便於對外收貨及發給收貨憑證之一種單據，易言之，亦卽便於客商托運貨物及由鐵路領取貨物收據之一種單據。貨票雖係由托運單改塡而來，然各聯均係用於辦理鐵路本身之行車，會計，統計等等內部事宜，與托運人不生關係。故貨票之塡寫純屬內部事務，托運人無守候塡寫貨票之必要。加之托運單共有三聯之多，因之簽收貨物，發給收據及塡寫貨票三項得以分開辦理。托運人一經取得簽字之托運單，卽爲已向鐵路領得收貨憑證，雙方授受貨物之手續已清，卽可離站回家，在鐵路儘可根據留下之第二聯托運單從容改換貨票，較之僅有托運單一聯，非待臨時改換貨票不能取得運貨收據之辦法，孰爲便利省事，不待智者而後知也。以言收費手續叉有可以分開之兩聯預付運費收據，另由站內收費處用於貨物已經托運之後，從容辦理收費事宜，或則派員往收或則由托運人接到第一聯 Prepaid Freight Bill 之後，寄送支票支付。是故雖在預付運費之特殊條件之下，托運人亦不過於填寫托運單時，在其特備之欄內填明「預備先付運費」(To Be Prepaid) 之字樣足矣，無須先到收費處繳付運費，亦無在站守候計算運費及填發貨票之必要，所以托運貨物，極爲迅速，計在數分鐘以內，卽可了事。其所以能收如是迅速之功者，實得力於貨票與托運單之分離制度，卽以托運單辦理對外手續，而以貨票辦理對內手續，其間又有第二聯托運單專爲內部改填貨票之媒介。故內外手續得以完全劃分，而無牽連混亂之弊。用意之深，立法之善，殊有可取者也。

反觀我國起運貨物單據，亦有托運單及貨票等等名稱，但托運單規定僅爲一聯，而貨運收據又復夾於貨票各聯之中。換言之，卽以貨票一聯用作對外發給收據。故客商寄貨，雖可於事先填妥托運單，然卒以僅有一聯之故，用於發還托運人作爲貨物收據，卽無以計算運費及改填貨票；用於算費及改填貨票，托運人卽須在站守候必待貨票填就之後，方能取得收據，總計每運一次貨物，至少須費數小時之久，荒時廢事莫此爲甚，一般客商，類皆不堪其苦，嘖有煩言，又何足怪！在鐵路方面，亦因填發收據，計算運費，填寫貨票，核收運費種種手續同時集於一人，辦理異常緩慢，以致貨票之填發，往往有在託運一日至二日者，至少亦非數小時不可，舉凡行車，會計，統計等項，莫不因等候貨票而受其影響。是乃單據制度不善，誤以內部填寫貨票事務與對外發給收據兩事混成一起，互相牽制之過也。改良之道，當以貨票中之貨運收據一聯抽出，使與托運單連成一起，使托運單變爲二聯，然後可以一聯於簽收貨物後，立卽交還機運人，作爲收據，而以其他一聯送於內部改塡貨票，如是托運單得與貨票分離，而後收貨，給據，塡票等等均可並行不背，客商可免往返守候之苦矣。

二 美國鐵路塡寫貨票之程序及分工方法

貨票之性質，與夫中美兩國貨票制度之異同，大致具如前述。而貨票之塡寫，實爲主要貨運站務之一，舉凡站賬之登記，運費之計核，列車之運轉，貨物統計之編製，皆非先有貨票而莫辦，是塡票之緩慢，足以影響各方之事務至爲顯明。且製票必須輕過繁重之手續，若於人事支配不當，管理不得其法，則在一日內收進之托運單，動輒以數千張計非但不能當日一律改換貨票。卽能强爲趕辦齊全，亦必因步驟紊亂，難免發生種種錯誤，增加以後之痲煩，此種間接損失。較諸直接者尤爲重大也。故貨票制度之好壞，固宜詳加考究，然事實上究應運用何種科學方法，以管理塡寫貨票之事務，是又鐵路人事方面極堪研究之重要問題，用就管見所及，縷陳梗概如次，以供熱心研討改良吾國站務管理者之參考焉。

第一步：托運單按區分類——托運單在改換貨票以前，尚須經過種種手續，因其係由客商塡寫，故運費當爲若干，商人無從預爲計算。惟有將運價一欄留待鐵路收到貨物之後，根據貨物等級再行補塡。惟是運價等級至爲複雜，如以 人管理運往全路各站之運價事務難免辦理過於緩慢之弊。故將查填運價一事，分由多數「運價司事」(Rate Clerks) 平均担任，每人分管一個運價區域 (Rate Divisions)。凡寄往同一區內之貨物，其運價當爲若干，應由指定之人員責查明，填入托運單，以期迅速而免遲延。(見后附分區辦法表) 因有分區查填運價之分工制度，故在分送於運價司事以前，一切托運單必須先行經過一番按區分類手續，以便分別送交各個主管運價司事。此即托運單按區分類之意義及作用，而爲改填貨票以前必須經過之第一步整理手續。主管此項分類職務之職員名曰「托運單分類員」(Ticket Sorter)、由各托運單內之到達站，并視貨物之整車或零担，即知某單應行彙交何人，其法簡而易行，費時有限，較之責令運價司事自行整理，殊爲便利多矣。

第二步：分區查填運價并核定路線——托運單一面按區分類，一面隨時轉交各運價司事。一則由其審核託運人指定之路線有無錯誤，如有則爲更正之，若有未經註明路線者，由其補填之。二則由其查明相當運價，即每百磅之基本運率，填入托運單內。以貨運數量甚大，查填運價費時，故採分工合作辦法，藉以養成熟悉運價專門人材，期收辦事迅速之效，其分工劃區之原則，可於下表觀之：

趙君——專司查填由本站運往甲區之整車及零担貨物運價。
張君——專司查填運往甲區之聯運零担及整車貨物運價。

運價司事分區查塡運價辦法表

- 李君——專司查塡運往乙區之聯運零担及整車貨物運價。
- 楊君——專司查塡運往西區之一切聯運及由本站運往某站之零担貨物運價。
- 王君——專司查塡由本站運往乙區之零担及整車貨物運價。
- 陳君——專司查塡由本站運往丁區之一切貨物運價。
- 其他——類推。

第三步：計算運費——托運單一經各運價司事塡入運價，隨卽轉交「計算司事」（Comptometer Operator），進行第三步計算運費之總數。蓋前項運價司事所塡者，不過簡單之運價等級，或基本運率，例如每百磅運率(Rate)定爲五角或六角，則僅以五角或六角塡入單內，斯時運價司事手續卽爲終了。至於每批托運貨物共需運費若干，則由計算司事按照貨物總共重量一算而知，假定今有貨物一千磅，而每百磅之基本運率定爲五角，則以十倍之，卽得總共運費計爲五元，其他依此類推。

以上(二)(三)兩種步驟，因爲關於核算運費，自表面觀之，似乎應歸一種員司同時辦理，較爲簡捷。此實似是而非之見也。殊不知此等分工辦法。正所以表現西人處處運用科學方法之特長也，何以言之？原夫運價種類極繁，雖有印成表册可資查考，究不如不查卽知之更爲省事省時，然欲經管運價員司得盡如此能事，又非富有經驗而不辦。是故服務運價方面之員司，在美國鐵路上類皆經過長期之特殊訓練，前面所述之分區查塡運價制度。亦卽訓練方法之一種，關於一般普通貨物運價情況，因平時經歷日久之故，大抵均有成竹在胸，無待臨時翻查表冊，卽令偶遇特種物品間有翻查之必要亦可垂手而得，易如探囊取物，蓋所謂熟能生巧也。故托運單一到目前，運率隨可塡入，而於轉瞬之間，卽可送交計算司事，絕少停留延誤之事。倘在平時既無訓練，而於支配人事時又以「查塡」與「計算」運價兩事責成一種員司辦理，則是不但未能善於利用專門運價事務人材，抑且無從培養此等專材，蓋牢記各種基本運價等級，已非易事，而其計算複雜運費，亦須具有相當知識以及長於運用加算機器之經驗。熟悉運價者不必同時長於計算，長於計算者又不必兼知運價，將欲二者並顧，均能辦理敏捷，除實行分工制度外，別無更善之策。乃在我國貨運車站，所有收款，塡票，算費等等手續，往往僅由一人兼理，無怪遇事遲鈍，絕無辦事效率可言，改良之道，似當斟酌各站事務繁簡情形。而於前述之支配人事科學方法，深致意焉。

第四步：托運單按裝車號碼再分類——托運單既經計算運費之後，卽由計算司事轉交另一「托運單分類員」，按照單內之裝車號碼(Spot Number)分別類齊，然後分送各「貨票司事」(Waybill Clerks) 塡寫貨票。塡寫貨票員司之分工辦法，係以每人分担若干車之貨票爲標準，假令某站日常運出之貨，計有三百輛車，塡票司事計爲十二人，則每人各應塡寫五十輛車之貨票。且各車均有規定之裝車號碼以代車號，車號雖因車輛變動隨時發生變化，而裝車號碼並不受其影響，每日仍可照用、因有永久不變之裝車號碼，故各貨票司事所分担之車輛，皆可利用裝車號碼一一分別指定，如以一號至五十號之車輛劃歸於甲，及以五十一號至一百號者派歸於乙之類是也。故分類司事僅憑托運單內之簡單裝車號碼，即知某件歸何人改填貨票，對於逐日變動之車號儘可置之不理，極爲簡便。此外並特備方格木架一座，於各格之上標明貨票司事姓名，以便彙集同歸一人之托運單，而免彼此混亂，致滋錯誤，其形勢則爲上圖所示。

A君格	B君格	C君格	D君格	E君格
F君格	G君格	I君格	J君格	K君格
L君格	M君格	N君格	O君格	P君格

托運單分類架

第五步：——由托運單改填貨票——托運經過以上種種手續，始行轉至貨票司事改製貨票，由此可見貨票司事之職務，純爲依托運單而改製貨票，不負核算運費之責。製票時均用複寫紙每聯 次填完，除托運單上各項外，除其由收貨司事決定之裝車號碼，應一併填入貨票，蓋裝車號碼，除有直接便利裝車事務之作用而外，尚可用以追查短少等項情事發生之原因究係由於貨票司事誤填車號，或由收貨司事在托運上誤寫裝車號碼，抑或由於裝車錯誤。如於兩種單據行將分離以前，不以裝車號碼轉入貨票，將來如有事故發生，即不易由貨票上之車號查出與有連繫之裝車號碼，既不明其裝車號碼，即不能查出應負責任之員司，此又裝車號碼對於管理人事上之功用也。再填寫貨票之司事，一如工廠之製造工人，每日應得薪資，按其改換托運單之件數計算，每百張給薪約爲壹元七角，等於工廠所用之按件計薪制度，惟如一張托運單內之貨物項目超過八項以上及不過十六項者，則一張當作兩張計算。故爲便於計算每人薪給起見，貨票司事應在貨票上「車號」一欄之旁註明其姓名。此外並可藉以編製填寫錯誤次數之統計，考核各個貨票司事之成績，如有過於粗心屢犯錯誤者，則可根據統計之比較，隨時予以撤換，其管理員司方法之嚴密，誠無微而弗至矣。

第六步：**審校貨票及托運單**——此時貨票雖已由托運單改製蕆事，然恐其中各項難免不有遺漏或錯誤之處，所以另有「審核司事」(Revising Clerk) 之設置，此項審核司事常爲對於運價事務資歷較深之人，地位待遇均比其他員司較優，所有填就之貨票及托運單，一律由其不斷向各貨票司事提取。每半小時一次，加以嚴密審核。遇有不符之處，卽行退交運價司事或貨票司事分別更正，以免事後發現過遲，致滋種種不便。

審核司事一面核對單之項目有無錯誤，一面依據前述給薪原則隨手計算各貨業司事經填托運單之件數，登入一單，故每日終了，僅因填票一事所費之人工薪資共爲若干，以及某人應得若干，得有極敏捷之統計方法。至審核司事之分工原則，則按共有之貨票司事名額，平均分配，例如貨票司事共有八人，審核司事爲二人，則每人分担四個貨管司事之審核工作，又如貨票司事爲十六，則每人分別審查八人經辦之托運單及貨票。其他可以準此類推，是亦按照事務數量平均支配人員實行分工合作之良法也。

第七步：貨票及托運單之編號——經過審核更正之後，一併轉交「貨票分類司事」(Way-bill Sorter) 按照會計處之編號辦法，分成各類，爲二六〇〇〇號，一八〇〇〇號，二四〇〇〇號等系(Series)，是其例也。類系分妥之後，「即交編號司事」(Nnmbering Clekrs)二人，在本路及聯運貨票與托運單上分別蓋印編號之戳記，如是托運單與貨票均有同樣號碼，彼此發生密切之連繫，將來縱有短少或運價不符等等事故發生，需要調閱最初之托運單，不難按貨票上之連鎖號碼一查而知。由此可見美國之托運單及貨票之編號，均在塡妥以後辦理，且其號碼相同，方之我國事先印就固定碼號碼之辦法適得其反，兩相比較，原以美國之塡後編號辦法殊爲妥當便利。良以無論貨票或托運單，包含事項至繁，塡用時偶爾發生錯誤，蓋爲勢所難免，如在使用以前已有固定號碼之限制，則改換時前後號碼不能銜接，即須將所缺之號碼呈請會計處註銷，既可呈請取銷不用之貨票，則是原欲藉固定之編數辦法防止路員營私舞弊之作用，根本即不可靠。既於事實無補，而又徒增呈請註銷之一番無謂周折，影響應用之便利，利尚未見，害已隨之而生，法之愚笨，未有甚於此者。美國各路所以不先印定貨票號數。必待已經塡好之後再行編號者，又豈無故而然哉！

第八步：貨票與托運單分離及分類——此時一切相互之關係手續均已辦齊，貨票即可與託運單分開，除託運單當按到達站之字母次序編列保存以便將來查考外，所有貨票各聯間之複寫紙一律抽去，交由另外三個「貨票分類員」按照車號先將正張一聯分歸一起，然後使用爲附圖所示之貨票分類架，以求迅速。蓋該架分成若干方格，每格之上註有裝車號碼，故一見同屬一個裝車號碼之貨票，立即可以分入同一格內，於時司車之貨票得以彙歸一處。俟分類蔵事，即從各格取出，裝入信封，再按車次彙裝一袋，或則隨車而行。或則逕行寄至到達站，一視其爲零担或整站貨物而定。此爲處置正張一聯之大概情形也。貨票之第二聯，則彙呈總局會計處之貨運進款稽核課(Office Auditor of Freight Receipts)，用作稽核各站運費進款；第三聯則按編定號碼之次序分列一起，送交本站會計處進行會計事宜。他如關於先付途費之兩聯 Prepaid Freight Bills，則一併送于本站收費處，作爲辦理收款根據，所有全部填寫貨票程序於此始告結束矣。

No. 11	No. 21	No. 31
No. 12	No. 22	No. 32
No. 13	No. 23	No. 33
No. 14	No. 24	No. 34
其　他	其　他	其　他

貨票按裝車號碼分類架

由上觀之，自由商人收進托運單，以至貨票填寫，編號，分類，以及分送于各方面，其間經過手續計凡八九次之多，而在辦理每一手續，又各有其特殊用意與方法。且爲便利各項

由托運單改填貨票程序及辦公室內佈置圖

手續同時向前順次推進，即辦公室內之公桌亦採合於科學方法之佈置（見附圖），因而由甲至乙，由乙至丙，順次前進，毫無顛倒錯亂之現象或行動，既能整齊觀瞻，復又利於辦事。足見科學方法不僅盛行於歐美之一般工商各業，即鐵路上亦常視各項事務性質力求分工制度之施行；及辦事程度之科學化，而填寫貨票一事並非簡單問題，蓋又無可置疑者也。試更就美國鐵路管理填發貨票事務之制度，再為歸納陳述數項重要原則如次，用作將來吾國改良關於本項站務之人事及組織之參考。

（一）在美國鐵路上，辦理填寫貨票事務之員司，除主管正副主任各一人均支月薪外，其餘概係按日及按工作件數給薪，屬於後者為貨票司事之類，他如運價司事，計算司事，審核司事，編號司事，分類司事等等均支日薪。其理由不外貨運站務之數量，與運輸盛衰有密切之關係，運輸愈發達，託運批數必多；託運批數既多，則其代表託運批數之托運單及貨票，亦必隨之俱增；貨票及托運單之數目既然增加，則其連帶之查填運價，計算費，分類編號等等事務亦自隨而加重：事務既繁，用人當可隨時增加。反而推之，運輸如若逐漸衰落員司當亦隨之減少。故本項站務之用人，當採按日及按件計薪制度，幷以隨時增減員司爲原則，而後始有人事管理經濟之可言。我國鐵路員工，無分總局外站，亦不問事務之性質如何，大抵均用月薪制度，而用人與裁員，概隨主管之意思而爲之，絕無一定之合理標準，殊與鐵路商業及人事管理科學化之原則大相剌謬。此其一。

(二)辦理大站貨票事務，非採晝夜廿四小時循環不斷之辦公時間制度，不能收隨到隨辦之效，以貨票之性質關係方面太多，辦理稽延，即於行車，會計，站賬，統計各方均有妨礙。美國鐵路對於本項事務辦公時間，在貨運繁忙之站大都酌用少數夜班員司者，其意即在斯也。我國貨站票務人員，概係限於日間工作，是否應予改變，洵屬極堪研究之問題。此其二。

(三)前文所述之種種分類辦法，皆爲因事制宜之簡要科學方法，其着眼純在節省人工，及增進辦事效率，其功用又復隱而不顯，不僅在原則上至足可取，而分工之程序尤有效法之價值。此其三。

(四)其他足資比較借鑑之處，多已分別提及，勿庸再爲贅列，此其四。

(五)由託運單辦理核算運費，及填寫貨票等事，純爲內部之事務，在美國貨運衝要車站，專爲填票事務單獨設立一處，在鐵路組織上稱爲 In-FreightDepartment。亦曰 Rate and Billing Department 。因其主管職務乃在計算運費及改填貨票，似可稱爲起運貨物處，或貨票填寫處。與外部接收托運貨物之貨棧貨場立於平等地位，同受貨站站長之直接管轄，其日常服務之員司，在大站中共計不下五十餘人。茲就其組系統及主要員司職稱表示如下：

貨站站長
│
貨票填寫處
│
主任 Chief Clerk
│
副主任 Ass't. Chief Clerk

- 託運單分類司事——Shipping Ticket Sorter
- 運價司事——Rate Clerks
- 貨票司事——Waybill Clerks
- 計算司事——Comptometer Oderators
- 貨票及託運單審核司事——Revising Clerks
- 貨票分類司事——Waybill Sorters
- 貨票編號司事——Numbering Clerks
- 簡寫貨票及硬紙貨票填發司事——Slip Waybill & Card Bill Clerks
- 空白貨票預備司事——Carbon Clerks
- 總務司事——General Clerks
- 急運貨物標誌司事——Manifest Clerk
- 其他員司

註：此外尚有夜班主任一人，名曰Night Chief Cler未經列入前表。

管理淺説

管理不僅爲個人謀利益，且爲社會人羣謀幸福。管理是一種技術也是一種科學，牠的範圍，是在如何指揮有組織的人力去實施於物質的極度利用，以造成人類之最大幸福。故用分析眼光去看管理，則

（一）管理之對象有二：一曰「人」，二曰「物」。物分四種：一曰金錢，二曰原料，三曰機器，四曰土地與建築物。

（二）管理之目的亦有二：一曰「社會效用」，二曰「個人利益」。

(Manangement of An Enterprice—By Balderstin)

新路建設之經濟觀（續前期）

二 土地

土地爲建築鐵路重要問題之一，乃一般工程師及管理家所公認，蓋鐵路路線均屬固定，建造之後，卽無法遷移，况工程費用，動輒鉅萬，苟擇地未得其宜，非但資本人工材料等項，蒙受損失，卽社會經濟，亦有莫大影響，是故鐵道建設之初，路線之土質，與地勢，固須由地質學家及工程師詳爲勘測，而土地之經濟要素，更須有鐵道經濟學家，縝密考核，務須鐵路建設之後地方經濟有發展之可能，同時有運輸及營業上之便利，本節僅就建設新路其擇地及購地應行考慮之要點，詳述如次：

一、擇地建築鐵路，土方爲先，土質之良窳，關係建築費用之多寡至鉅，因人所盡知，惟尙有其他要素，爲鐵路工程及管理上所應注意者，玆分析之如下：

甲 工程上應考慮者

一、土質之輭硬及其黏性之强弱。

二、雨量多寡。

三、溫度。

四、沿綫山川形勢以及必要之坡度及灣度，

乙　管理上應考慮者

一、建築所須之材料與勞工供給之數量與距離。

二、沿綫實業情形農工商礦業之出品之產運銷情形。

三、沿綫交通狀況及運輸機關之組織。

四、各站與城鎮之距離及聯絡方法。

五、附近人口數及省市縣鎮保衞及治安情形。

凡此種種，均爲擇勘路線，對於地勢及位置應行考核之點，其功用非僅求建築費用之節省，卽估計營業收入，決定運輸方策，亦賴以參考，此種工作，須由工程管理及地質三者之專門人材，共同勘查，規定擇地之標準，以抵抗最少爲原則，同時對於地方人民之需要，營業發展之希望，運輸工作之效率，以及國防及軍事上之重要，尤應加以注意，此建設新路選擇土地所宜留意者也。

二、購地　建築鐵路，購地一項，在民有鐵路之國家，建築經濟，極關重要，倘鐵道爲國有，則所用土地，大都可由國家以法令徵收，故手續似較便易。惟細察已往我國鐵路收用民地之經驗，殊不盡然，蓋路綫所經之地，往往多爲人民私有之財產，如田畝房屋之類估價徵收難求公平。而墓地遷徙，人民惑于風水，時起抗爭，以故購地一項，在新路建設之初，極有研究之價值。茲就鐵路徵用土地應具之要素，詳述如下。

甲　規定用地種類　鐵路徵收土地其用不途同性質各異。故擇地之際必先按其用途分別種類然後定面積標價格有所準繩。茲就鐵路所需土地分別爲下列各種。

一、路線用地。

二、車站及行車設備用地。

三、局所及員工住宅用地。

四、工廠及材料存貯廠所用地。

五、取土取石運料及遷葬墳墓用地。

六、附屬業務必須用地

乙　估計用地面積　用地種類已如上規定，第二步當進而考核每種應有面積，就歷來經驗觀之所有鐵路用地之面積，最好較建築時所須要者爲廣，其理由

一、鐵路於營業發達時，路綫站房岔道貨棧車場等項須擴充，若土地廣闊隨時可以發展，不致因土地問題，阻礙其進行。

二、鐵路通車之後，沿線土地效用增大，地價因而高漲，收買徵用，困難滋多，

若能於建築時期，預留空地，則應用時當較便利矣。

三、鐵路建築之初，工程設計限于經費，以故軌道設置站棧地位，每有不能適合營業及運輸需要者通車營業之後自應逐步改進，以便應用，故必須有相當地畝，以便佈置。

根據以上理由，鐵路各種用地應有面積，約可估定如下：

一、路綫用地　幹綫兩旁地畝，至少足供敷設雙軌，或增設串道之用。

二、車站用地　車站用地最少應較初次建築時，地畝爲大，而車場貨棧附近，更須有較廣之地畝，以供改建房屋及軌綫之用。

三、各廠所用地畝宜較現用之地爲寬，以備擴充改良之用。

四、取土石及運料等用地，均屬臨時性質無須過大。

五、附屬業務用地，須視其需要臨時規定。

丙　擬訂付價辦法　鐵路用地付價辦法與土地隸屬問題，有密切關係，普通辦法計可分三種。

一、國有土地　國有土地乃包括國內各省市所有之官地而言，如驛路公溝公行路大道公路國有湖河荒地荒山等土地是也。此種土地而須徵用，可由鐵道部咨請地方政府撥用，概不給價。

二、民有土地　民有土地由鐵路徵用須按規定標準分段估定公平價值付給地價計規定此項標準所應參考者有下列各點。

甲　視土地性質種類生產量出品價值以及收益價值如租金等項規定其等級。

乙　按附近各等土地之買賣價格而規定徵用民地應付之地價。

丙　視地面附屬品房產墳墓遷移費用之大小及其剩餘價值之多寡而定應否加給津貼或增減地價。

此項地價標準規定之後，咨請地方政府指定公共評價人，詳爲評定先期公布，然後卽分段按照此項標準價目辦理。

三、公有土地　公有土地由鐵路徵用應按左列辦法處理之。

甲　屬於地方自治團體之公地，概由鐵道部咨請省政府轉飭撥用。

乙　營防屯衞軍學旗田寺院祠堂善堂義塚應由鐵道工程局與土地所有團體商酌，或給價收買或給地另還。

以上爲購地所應考慮之要素，其目的在以公平合理辦法，徵用土地。以免重斂擾民至起糾紛。但所購土地必須合乎前節所定之擇地原則，否則地價雖廉不適于用亦非經濟之道也。

（未完待續）

中華國有鐵路現行行車時刻表（六）

廣九綫

民國二十四年五月一日起實行

由九龍至各站公里	各站距離公里	No20 華段客車 下午	No18 飛星快車 下午	No12 混合列車 下午	No10 中午快車 中午	No8 直通慢車 上午	No6 飛箭快車 上午	No4 華段客車 上午	上行列車 站名 下行列車	No1 混合列車 上午	No3 華段客車 上午	No5 飛鷹快車 上午	No9 直通慢車 上午	No11 中午快車 中午	No13 飛龍快車 下午	No23 華段客車 下午	各站距離公里	由大沙頭至各站公里
	35.49		4.50	2.00	12.35	8.45	8.30		開 九龍 到	12.14		11.12	5.25	4.20	7.32			17829.
35.49	1.34	1.40	5.26 5.27	3.00 3.43	1.13 1.14	9.50 11.10	9.06 9.07		到開 深圳 開到	11.23 11.07	10.18	10.36 10.35	4.24 3.25	3.42 3.41	6.56 5055		33.49	142.77
36.83	6.34	1.51		3.50		11.20			開 深圳墟 開	11.04	10.15		3.22				1.34	141.43
43.26	3.28	·2.10		4.03		11.39			開 布吉 開	11.50	9.55		3.07				6.43	135.00
48.54	6.63	2.23				11.52			開 李朗 開		9.40		2.52				5.28	129.72
55.17	5.39	2.37 2.48		4.20 4.25	1.36 1.38	12.06 12.11			到開 平湖 開到	10.29 10.06	9.27 9.20		2.40 2.34	3.16 3.17			6.63	123.09
60.56	3.30	3.11		4.38		12.26			開 天堂圍 開	6.57	9.10		2.25				5.39	117.70
63.86	4.31	.3.19				12.34			開 石鼓 開		8.53		2.10				3.30	114.40
68.17	4.22	3.27 3.3[illegible]		4.48 4.52	1.53 1.54	12.42 12.49			到開 塘頭廈 開到	9.40 9.30	8.34 8.34		2.00 1.50	3.02 3.01			4.31	110.09
72.39	7.51	3.44				12.57			開 林村 開		8.24		1.37				4.22	105.87
79.90	7.94	3.58 4.03	6.10 6.12	5.05 5.09	2.06 2.08	1.11 1.18	9.50 9.52		到開 樟木頭 開到	9.13 9.05	8.09 7.59	9.53 9.51	1.21 1.09	2.49 2.47	6.13 6.11		7.51	98.36
87.84	4.66	4018				1.33			開 土塘 開		7.45		12.54				7.94	90.42
93.50	5.74	4.32		5.26		1.48			開 常平 開	8.50	7.31		12.40				4.66	85.76
98.24	6.43	4.43 4,50		5.35 5.38	2.27 2.29	1.59 2.06			到開 橫瀝 開到	8.38 8.3	7.15 7.05		12.24 12.14	2.28 2.26			5.74	80.02
104.67	2.80	5.02		5.49		2.47			開 南社 開	8.22	6.53		12.02				6.43	73.59
10[illegible].47	8.19	5.10				2.53			開 茶山 開		6.44		11.53				2.80	70.76
113.66	6.13	5.22	6.44 6.47	6.03 6.14	2.46 2.50	3.04 3.15	10.24 10.27	9.00	到開 石龍 開到	8.07 7.57	6.30	9.19 9.16	11.40 11.26	2.09 2.05	5.59 5.36	7.15	6.19	64.60
119.79	2.53					3.27		8.13	開 石瀝滘 開				11.14			7.63	6.12	58.47
122.32	4.05					3.36		8·24	開 石灘 開	7.47			11.08			6.57	2.53	55.94
126.37	5.23					3.46		8.36	開 石廈 開				10.56			6.47	4.05	51.89
131.90	6.13					4.01		8.59	開 仙村 開				10.46			6.38	5.23	46.66
137.73	2.54					4.15		9.11	開 沙浦 開				10.27			6o26	6813	04.53
140.27	3.12					4.24		9.18	開 塘美 開				10.17			6.19	2.54	37.99
143.39	4.30					4.35		9,26	開 新塘 開				10.07			6.11	3.12	34.87
147.69	3.07					4.44		9.34	開 沙村 開				9.56			6.03	4.30	30.57
150.79	7.26					5.03		9.44	開 南崗 開				9.48			5.55	3.07	27.50
158.02	4.55					5.14		.9.57	開 烏涌 開				9.30			5.43	7.26	20.24
162.57	2.98					5.22		10.06	開 吉山 開				9.18			5.34	4.55	52.69
165.55	12.71					5.29		10.13	開 車陂 開				9.12			5.82	2.98	
178.26			7.47	7.28	3.55	5.50	11.27	10.35	到 大沙頭 開			8.15	8.45	1.00	4.35	5.00	12.71	12.71

中國航業管理問題

司徒新

此文所論之中國航業管理問題，非組織，財務，人事等，管理問題；乃中國經營航業，或航業管理者，所弗能忽略之幾宗事理。我國航業內部之組織，是否妥善？財務管理，是否適當？用人方面，是否合乎科學？固爲航業管理重要問題。內部之組織，工作，財務，人事等，如有不妥適，可隨時斟酌實情，依據事勢，改進之，革新之、惟有幾項事理，關繫我國政策，地理形勢，國際上之財政地位，輪船業暨造船業之特質，非短期間可能變革。此諸種情事，影響國家航業之盛衰重大。我國航務經營暨管理者，弗能弗注意焉。

我國航業管理者應注意之幾宗事理，究爲何？爲易於闡明計，可別爲二類：(一)外洋航運所引生之問題。(二)沿海航運所發生之問題。二者所引發之問題，弗同；而其影響國家航務之興敗，固異。航業管理者，因須察注焉。茲分論之：

(一)外洋航運所引生之問題

外洋航運卽指本國船隻，載運客貨，航行本國與外國港埠間。如美國船隻，裝運貨客，駛行美國與中國，或別國港埠間。世界各國，每以其殖民地之港埠，爲其本國內河港埠。故一國之船隻，航駛該國港埠，及所屬地或殖民地港埠，皆認爲沿海，或內河航運，例若美國船，航行美國洛彩基與檀島間，卽視爲內河航行也。我國航務衰敗。沿江沿海之航業，尙無法維持現況。何能談發展遠洋航務？邇來輒經南洋華僑請求，「我國交通當局，已具闢設中國南洋羣島諸線之決志。惟以政局未靖，經費無着。迄未舉辦。殊爲憾事。但我國不談建設則已。不求充實國力，提高國際地位，則已。倘將來政治靖平，百業待舉。我國在現代世紀，欲與今日之先進國家，爭一席位。外洋航運，不獨中國與南洋諸島航線；卽中國與歐美諸大商埠航路，至須展辦。今言中國外洋航運所引生之問題，似嫌過早。然具廣遠眼光之中國航業管理家，對此雖未，而將設辦之遠洋航運所引生之事況，自須加考察。我國遠洋航業所引生之事理，爲我國航務管理家，應注視者；有如下數端：

(甲)外洋航務經認爲政治便利；非健全經濟問題。 一國之外洋航業，本爲一經濟活動。如該國國情，適合展建外洋航務則該國之外洋船業，自然興盛發達。無容國家輔助，津貼。航務亦自成該國一種經濟資產。惟今各國多貼助航務。遠洋航業，已成政治便利問題；非爲一種經濟活動。在政治便利上言：發展一國遠洋航務，認爲有二功用：(1)充實國防。(2)助展國外貿易。苟從健全經濟方面觀察。一國之遠洋航業，無能自興；當因該國國情，不宜設辦航務，或航業在該國爲不生利業務。如該國賴津貼，及不自然方法，補助外洋航運之建展。誠將有用資財，投於乏利營業，國家之經濟損失，匪小。惟從政治便利方面分析。

發展國家外洋航務，在建辦他種公共事業，須費若許補助金。然其對國家之效用，非可以金錢作計量也。際此國家主義極盛之時，外洋航務之視爲政治問題，更覺顯明。各國皆競加增船業津貼金。爭設法擴展固有之外洋航務。我國航業管理者，對此，不能不有深切認識。

(乙)外洋航業遭受嚴厲之國際競爭。 外洋業與他種業藝弗同。如一國之紡織業，得被保護，免受國外競爭。海洋本乃國際公路，各國船舶，皆得航駛其間。離一國海岸線三里外，卽屬公共洋海，任何國家；皆無防阻外船航行之權。因此外洋航業之競爭甚烈。一國之欲限制外船與本國船業之競爭，唯一方法，爲征收差別稅。抵制外船裝載貨物入本國港埠。如果所載貨物進口被制限。則外國船業，自蒙打擊。此種限制外來競爭方法，或奏驗效。惟此易引外國之報復。故征收差別稅，爲防制外船與本國船競爭之方法，少被採行。

外洋航業運價，大概視乎國際競爭之嚴烈，或供與求之關係而規定。當今各國皆認推展外洋航運，爲政治便利。故不顧該本國情況。是否宜於建辦此種業務；咸趨用政府津貼方法，擴建外洋航業。結果世界外洋航務之供給，遠超其需求，外洋航運之價格，因此已壓至業務成本之下。此種情況，爲我國航業管理者，所弗能忽略者。

(丙)造船業之特性 造船業是一種實業。其被經營爲大規模生產之可能性，極少。有種業藝，如製造業，能被，實常被，經營作大規模生產。苟一國因工價高，與利息厚，不利經營製造業。蓋以該業能作大量生產，亦可經營之因經營大規模製造業，一工錢與利率高之國家；所售之製造品價格，或竟較工錢及利率低之國家，所售者，爲廉。美國之汽車製造業，其例也。美國之工價暨利率，皆比別國爲昂而汽車製造成本，在美國反較在他國爲省。汽車製造業，現成美國最有利之企業。大製造業；常被認爲成本遞減，或入息遞增之事業。蓋此種藝業之出產量愈多，其每件成本則愈低。其入息亦隨產量而遞加矣。誠如英國馬蘇教授言：『某項貨品，若遵隨入息遞增律；需求高，則其產量必致增加。……同時其價格，亦因而跌落。』一種實業，爲成本遞減者；其產品之需求，則須有伸縮性。此理亦明矣。倘產品之需求情形固定。不隨價格之變動而轉移。則其產量，斷無增加之理。該業即無作大量生產之可能。故成本遞減之經濟遂不可得。

造船業不幸乃爲一種業藝，其能被經營作大量生產之可能性，極小。船舶之需要，本乏伸縮力。在一處，造船業務增多；在他處，必須有同樣減少。萬噸之貨船一艘，可供五十萬人貨運之用。二萬噸之客船一隊五十艘，可足應全球客運及郵運之需。

所以一國，如因工價及原料價昂；造船卽爲不利業務。該國自不能冀經營大規模造船業，以減低成本。化無利爲有利。我國工價素賤，原料價格亦較外國爲廉。極度工業化之先進國家，如美、法、意、德等國，工價與原料價皆高。因造船業之特性，該等國家實難經營造船而爲有利業務。故我國如向造船業方面發展，前途成有可觀。

（丁）中國國情是否宜於發展外洋航運？ 我國航業管理者，對於我國國情是否合乎建展外洋航業，不能不作精密考慮。夫一國之國情，影響外洋航務之發展之最重要，而有最近切之關繫者，則爲該國之地理特質，國外貿易數量、自足程度，天然物富，資財與勞働，暨國際財政地位。故論中國國情，於建立外洋航運，有何障助？可亦按此各種重要因素，逐一分析：

瀕海及海岸線極長之國家，其國民從事外洋航務之志趣，自較遠隔洋海，無直達海洋通道，國家之國民，爲熱烈。且一國海岸線長；其發達外洋船務，爲輔助該國海軍，以作充實國防之需要，亦較遠離洋海之國家爲迫切，我國海岸線一萬五千餘里。沿海諸省，人民對航運，志趣甚濃。而我國將來注重國防，則以擁有延長之海岸線；其發達外洋船務，以助海軍國防之需，自亦急要。故總言之，我國地理特質，於建展外洋航運，予以大助利。

一國國外貿易數量之多寡，自與發展國家外洋航業，有大關繫。如國家之進出口貨運極多，則其國之外洋航業，不難得大量運載營業。故該國外洋航務，亦較易維持。我國國外貿易總數量，比歐美先進國家雖少。此即爲現時本國發展外洋航運之障礙。然他日政治靖明，工商業發達。國外貿易數量，定有飛躍突進可能。此又足速增我國外洋航務之建展矣。

國家之外洋航業政策，常受該國自足程度所影響。一國自足程度愈低，其需要擴展外洋航務愈切。如英國須賴外國供給食料。一旦別國發生戰事，外船則被撤退，充作運事之用。故英國對興建國家外洋航務，異常重視。俾保障其國民不斷之食料。我國自足程度，雖不若英國之低。發展外洋航業，自亦無英國之急。然今之須賴外國供給之物品，亦復不少。將來工商業發展，其須靠外國之互相供銷，更多。故當今我國之自足程度，似不一定爲發展我國外洋航務之阻礙。

天然物富，有效之勞役，豐足之資財；均影響一國外洋航業之發展。統有廣博物產，特爲煤，鐵，石油，於擴建國家外洋航務，當有助益。價廉及有效之勞働，可減省行船及造船費用。如有豐富之資財，外洋航業，如上述，因難保免外來競爭。雖爲一薄利事業；國民之願投資航業者，亦自多。我國工役廉，物產亦博。資財雖不甚豐厚。但總言之；我國國情，關於勞役，資財，物富方面，於發展外洋航運，較歐美多數國家爲優也。

最末之因素，影響一國外洋航業之發展，即爲一國之國際財政地位。其他情況相同，債權國，發展外洋航務，常較債務國爲艱。蓋債權國；如欲收取外債，或外債息金，必須接納債務國，所輸進之金，貨或役務。如船務，即役務之一。世界之存金有限。而各國現有之存金，所須爲準備金之用。實難運出，充作債償。又當今各國之關稅壁壘極高，債務國欲大量輸進債權國貨品，亦非易事。故債務國，償還債務，祇得供與債權國，各種役務，或船務耳。由是以觀。債權國如建樹廣大航業，卽擋塞，或減少債務國，藉供給債權國船務，以淸償債款之機會。反之債務國建立航務，雖航業在該國爲互利事益，亦爲助該國償理債款，及維持國際酬報平衡所必須。中國乃債務國之一。故對於外洋航業之發展實有裨助。

(二) 內河航運所引生之問題

我國遠洋航運，未見大規模舉辦。前者，有小數中國輪船公司，創設中國南洋羣島諸線。然多入英荷國籍。求托庇於外人。嗣後亦有與外國合辦之輪船公司，如中比，中德等輪船公司之設立。惟皆未聞有若何成績。故今談中國航業管理問題，自以內河航運之管理問題爲主。除內部之組織，財務等問題外，中國航業管理者，對於內河航運，應注意之事理，有下列數端：

(甲)內河航權問題。　凡航行內河，或沿岸之船舶，均以本國，或揭有本國國旗者。爲限。外國船舶，皆在排斥之列。此制爲美、法、日，意，奥、西，比諸國所採納。我國內河航權之喪失，原於淸咸豐八年。我國與英訂立通商條約。該條文內三十二款，載有各口分設浮樁號船塔表望臺，由領事官，與地方官會同酌視建造，之語，此因當時航業人才缺乏，故不能不借重外人，藉資諮詢。非授以權也。嗣後同年訂立之中法通商章程，中美條約，同治二年中丹條約，同治五年中義條約，光緒二十八年，再訂之中英通商條約，內除浮椿等設置之條文，一如咸豐八年三十二款所載外，祇准予有約各國船隻通商，及噸稅特別優待，暨指通商口岸，判定口界，派人指泊船隻耳。不期外人乃由諮詢，而管攝，而攘奪。致中國今日華人自辦之內河航運，不僅遭遇外國輪船公司，如英之太古，怡和，日之日本郵船，日清等烈强之競爭；且因引水、港務管理，船舶檢查，指定泊所等權限操之外人，每受無理之壓迫。內河航政權，一日未收回，華人內河航業，自難有發展希望。

(乙)鐵路公路競爭問題。　沿海沿江航運，常遇公路與鐵路運輸之激烈競爭。此爲世界各國內河航運，之普遍現象。該類競爭，可分必須，與荒廢二種。必須競爭云者，卽如從一地到某地之客貨運輸量極大，非單一運輸工具，如水路運輸，可能勝任，作經濟之運載。有此情形，自宜添建鐵路或公路，輔助航運之不足。此不特增加該地區間運輸之效能；且既有鐵路或公路輔同水路運輸，則該地區間之運載業務，可得免受水路獨占經營。又因水路與鐵路或與公路互相競爭，而社會遂得受運輸業務改良之裨益。設若該區間成立之水鐵兩路之運輸業務已足運載貨客之用。苟再添築公路，直接與既成之水路鐵路分爭該區間之載運營業，致運輸業務之供給，遠超其需求。則水路、鐵路、公路三運輸工具，爲維持各自身之成本及業務計，不能不競減運價爭載客貨。爲虧本運載，亦所弗惜。此種情況，卽爲耗廢競爭演成之結果。不僅使各運輸工具自相摧毀，卽社會大衆亦蒙其騷害。故荒廢競爭之須力謀避免，爲我國國內運輸設計之要圖。經營暨管理我國航政者，復應注意焉。

(丙)內河航務管轄問題。　內河航運，關繫社會福利殊深，如某內河航路忽告停頓，該路沿線各港埠之客貨運載，不無受打擊。國民生計自遭影響矣。故世界各國內河航政，多歸該國政府劃一統管。俾保障國民，得不斷，有效，及平穩之內河船運業務。其立旨之深，可以想見。內河航業，亦有公營，及私營兩種。在我國亦分國營及民營內河船業。倘國家自營內河航務，則其於統制方面，自較簡易。旣有民營內河輪船公司，與國營船業公司，相並營業，則內河航務管治問題，自較繁難。故須有精密之航業法規，周善之管轄方法，方不致航業公司，民營與公營，或民營與民營間，互相制毀。或竟與鐵路公路等運輸事業，成荒廢競爭情況。於國家之經濟損失，殊大。考我國航政，在交部未接管以前，乃隸屬海關之理船廳。內河航政管治法規，類皆海關草率擬定。旣不合國情，弊病特多。今交部已接管航政，我國航律，自應重行愼密編制。以期適合國情，助利內河航務。此非獨航業界之福；亦國家全民之幸也。

(丁)政府應否津助內河航業？多數國家如美、法、日、意等國，旣採排除外輪，在本國沿岸貿易。內河航權，祇受予揭本國旗號之船隻。僅本國輪船，有航行沿岸之專權。本國船舶，航行內河故得免遭外輪競爭。各國對內河航務以可保免外來競爭多取不補助政策。內河輪船體積極小，速率有限。於國防效用上亦無大獻益。此或亦爲多數國家不補助發展內河航務之眞因。我國內河航權喪失。英日輪船公司，在我國沿海經營航務，直接與我所屬船隻競逐。以彼之資本雄厚，政府協助；且具因不平等條約，而獲得之諸種特別便利。我國自辦之內河航務，焉能與之爭？無怪乎常呈頹敗景狀。際茲航權未收回之候，津助發展我國內河船務，於國防上雖無重大價值。但我國外洋船業。既未能大規模興辦。此將危僅有之我國內河航業，誠須竭力保維。實爲至要。邇來交部頒佈我國造船，及行船獎助金辦法。或亦爲津助內河航業之先聲乎？

中國航業之內部組織，人事，財務等管理問題，如有欠當，自可隨事勢而改進。上文所論諸事理之爲我國航業管理者所應注意，乃以其關繫我國航業之展望切深也。綜析以上事理，我國情況，實非逆於發展國家航務。苟內河航權收回，政府對擴辦航運，有周全政策，妥詳計劃，我國內河航業，自蒸蒸日進。遠洋航業亦弗難推展。惟如何堪稱周全之政策？奚若足道妥詳之計劃？則非本文圍範所能釋論也。

會計與企業管理

（一）

錢素君

有組織管理（註一）之企業，一切活動，皆有一定準則，爲經營之標的或工作之規範，名曰標準（Standards）。將一切活動，納諸標準規範以內，俾其產生之結果，可與預定之成績相吻合，則曰統制（Control）。標準者，企業經營活動所應產生之目的，或達到一定目的應取之方法也。標準有三種：（一）手續上之標準（Standards of Procedures）（二）經營標準（Operating Standards）及（三）財務標準（Financial Standards）。手續上之標準，爲處理企業活動各種事務之規則或程序。與本文無關。至於經營標準與財務標準，則爲經營活動成敗之

（註一）企業管理之方式，就其演進之歷史觀之，可分四種：（一）無組織管理（Unsystematized Management），（二）有記錄管理（Record-keeping Management），（三）有組織管理（Systematized Management）及（四）科學管理（Scientific Management）第一種除極少數之小規模組織外，實際上已不復採用，第二種在國內仍佔極大多數，即自命爲採取科學管理方法之若干組織，其管理方法，仍不脫離此種窠臼。有記錄管理，僅能供給企業過去歷史，充其量，最佳亦不過可以判斷新資金投放之是否安全。有組織管理在世界各國企業界中，仍佔極大多數，在適用上無限制，而使「立法」及「行政」兩權力，嚴爲劃分，是其長處。而企業之過去歷史，詳細蒐集，一如有記錄管理，且於將來經營　亦有計劃，可以統制，實兼採科學管理之長，故即在科學管理創製之美國，此種管理方式，在整個企業界中之百分率，仍高出科學管理數十倍，良以科學管理之適用，不能普遍故也。在我國，則科學管理之不易採用，實有種種不易解決之困難，如費用之過鉅、人才之缺乏，企業家之頑固企業規模之狹小，與工業制度之障礙，其尤著者也。

所繫，而爲管理及經營者預定之努力的收獲，此種標準，類多以數字表現，如以相關之數字，彙集成表，則曰預算(Budget)。企業之預算，最要者凡五：

(一)銷貨預算 (The Sales Budget)

(二)製造預算 (Production Bddget)

(三)費用預算 (The Expense Budget)

(四)工場預算 (The Plant Requirement Budget)

(五)財務預算 (The Financial Budget)

預算爲經營活動之範疇，亦企業家所希冀之成績。經營者之活動，自須藉之爲依據，然以企業界內在外在情形之複雜，經營活動，偶一不愼，則結果卽不能如理想之圓滿；於是必須謀一切活動，遵循預定途徑，並須時以活動之結果，與標準相比較，以窺結果與標準之是否適合；如有變異，必搜求所以差異之原因，俾立謀矯正，而免兩者有差之毫釐，失以千里之憾也。

標準與統制，爲企業管理成功之要訣，然標準之訂立，統制之制定，皆以會計記錄爲主要之工具。企業欲訂立適當標準，必須先就過去情形作成藍本，始可免過於理想，不易實行。標準既立，欲謀統制，則必須知實現標準各項過程之成績，方可隨時統制活動上之異向，並瞭解事實上之成績，與標準所以差異之因果。標準與記錄，爲不可須臾分離之二大概念，猶方面之南北，地球之經緯，與簿記之借貸也。有標準而無記錄，猶如善投籃球之籃球員，投籃百次，而無法知有投出之球，若干次中入籃中；無標準而僅有記錄，猶如球員每次擲球之結果，一一記載，而無球籃之裝置。前者之球籃(標準)，形同虛設；後者之記錄，無異浪費。我人大半必具記載日用帳之經驗；一切付款，即微至一分，亦常爲記載，然並無預算，亦無確定之儲蓄計劃，以至一二年後，仍無一文之貯，是時勢必不能置信，乃就日用帳考核，得左手所得之金錢，如何自右手耗費之慘史，此種記帳，不過浪擲時間。一無用處，此我人體驗得來之經驗，足證有記錄無標準之爲浪費也。

有標準而無記錄，則統制未能就範。設或我人以個人之收支，編立預算，並有確定之儲蓄計劃，而無日用帳之記載，則即移生活上必要之費用，以補奢侈之或缺，亦難查悉，於是奢侈費用，應如何撙節，始可保持收支之平衡，並使儲蓄計劃，賡續不斷。以及謀取亡羊補牢之辦法，當不可得。企業之經營，與上舉之例，亦正相同。企業管理，雖以標準與統制爲不可少之工具，而標準與統制之施行，又以記錄爲其必要之工具，故記錄於企業管理上之貢獻，及關係之深切，又豈可小覷哉？

（二）

往昔小規模企業，事無鉅細，業主可親躬聞問；今日企業組織之規模。日漸龐大，事務之複雜，使業主親自聞問之方式，難以傚行，又兼所有權與管理權之分離 (Absentee Ownership)，及分職制度 (Functional Organization) 之擴張，管理上之權限與責任，漸歸分委，負管理最高責任之人，並不親自經營，而僅以督察考績爲職務。現代分職組織之大規模企業，職務之分掌。劃分甚細，卽在規模不甚龐大者。亦必分職掌理，以收經濟上分工之惠益。於是業主制定主要方針。而以一切權限，委諸經理，再由經理分別職務，轉委於其助理人員。經理應隨時監督助理人員之工作，是否盡責，一切付託 是否完成；而同時經理須對於業主負責，受其督察。此種督察之效力，及責任之能否卸除，皆須藉會計記錄或報告之指示，以爲徵信。

會計報告之功用，於是可簡述之如下：(一)對於業主及其代表（如公司之董事會）、或經理，供給判斷其助理人員完成之工作；是否滿意，並可以暴示整個企業之政策。應如何與其助理人員所掌管者聯繫，以謀該項政策之實施，更爲便捷合理。(二)對於掌分委權限之助理人員，供給判斷其統治下之工作者。是否能厥盡責任，並可指示工作者最簡捷最圓滿之完成責任的方法。

凡供管理上使用，以爲統制或考績之報告，當須根據完密設計之記錄、彙集而成。此種報告之編製，必須表示四種重要資料：

(一)標準——即預計的結果，此種材料，祇須就各種預算摘錄。

(二)成績——即事實上的結果，由記錄所供給。

(三)差異（Variations）——即事實上的結果與預計的結果之不同。

(四)差異的分析（Analysis of Variations）——即考求差異所以發生之因果。例如銷貨員預計銷貨數量與實際銷貨數量之差異，應分別由於價格上之差異（Variations due to Price）及由於單位之差異（Variations dus to units）。此種差異分析，可供負責推銷業務者之一種重要參考，標準之是否適當，各個推銷員之努力情形，亦藉此而得正確表現。

普通工商企業管理上需要之報告，有財務及經營之分，此種報告所載之事實，不僅應以數字表現，更須以其他相對變異之方法（如比率 Ratios）百分率（Percentages）及週轉率（Turnovers）闡明數字中所含之重要觀念，此種報告當以前述五種預算及其經營結果最爲重要。

財務報告，以資產負債之結構，及其運用情形，增減消長，以及其獲利之能力，與現金之收付及預計應付款項等各項情形，最爲重要。財務報告，亦須注意企業償債能力（Solvency）之變動，及資本使用之效能。

經營報告，包括銷貨。製造，費用，工場與工作效能各類，其種類之多，不勝枚舉，然加以細分，則尤要者凡下列各種：(一)存貨之增減（分別種類，售價。數量，進銷，手存，各部並表現銷貨百分率。）(二)銷貨（分別總額，各部，賒售，現售，貨別，各銷貨員，各地域，並求出各項之百分率）。(三)損益（分別各部，各貨，各銷貨員，各地域，並求出各項之百分率）。(四)經營成本（分別總額，各部，各項費用，並求出各項百分率）。(五)帳款（分別總額，對於銷貨百分率，及各地域。）。(六)退貨（分別總額，各貨，各地域，並求出對於各該銷貨之百分率）。(七)僱工之效能(分別利益及各部)。(八)廣告（分別總數，各部，刋物及結果。）(九)生產（分別完工數量，在製數量；耗費時間；生產總成本；單位成本；直接間接人工成本；原料成本及製造費用。(十)工資及工作時期。

財務及經營報告之良劣，則依下列標準判斷：

(一)凡讀報告之管理者所需明瞭之情形，不可或缺。

(二)報告必須具體，而極易瞭解。

(三)報告必須指示經營活動之成績，在進步抑在退步。

(四)報告必須不僅表現現在之利益，並須指示整個企業各種狀態之良健。

至於會計員在編製經營上所需要之報告之時，必須注意下列各點，以免會計報告之功用，因體裁之不當，或要點之欠缺，或意義之不確，而枉費時間：

（一）報告是否必要？

（二）報告是否能適應某種目的之需要？

（三）編製報告之目的，是否健全，而對於管理上之貢獻或關係。是否值得編製？

（四）報告是否爲管理者所取用，以供其管理上之參考？（管理者之取用，與報告本身之是否有用，並不相同。如報告確有價值，而未爲管理者採用，則其價值未爲管理者所鑑賞。）

（五）報告有否不必要之累贅？

（六）報告之編製是否已竭力免除不需要之工作？

（七）報告之格式，是否最好？

（八）報告之體裁，是否最爲適宜？

（九）編製之報告，是否能與其他報告合併，而對於兩者之功用，仍可不致喪失？

上所云云，爲會計與企業管理之重要概念，會計上之記錄或報告，總難完全免除會計上之必要技術，管理者欲完全瞭解，故須作相當準備，始克鑑賞其偉大之價值，望今之管理企業者，注意及之。

行政之主要工作綱領

第一、嚴格考驗　其方法分(甲)委任專員，將其工作，以爲考成之標準，(乙)定期考驗，驗其進退，定其功過，督促糾正，勵行賞罰，(丙)隨時考成，(丁)實地按驗，不僅憑書面報告。

第二、綜覈名實　其主要節目分(甲)明系統(乙)公銓選(丙)專責成(丁)行久任(戊)嚴考核(巳)一賞罰(庚)稽查報告(辛)面獎廉能

第三、密切連繫　各部分互相連繫以避免重複衝突與散漫分歧。

第四、政治教育打成一片　一要留意人才二要轉移風氣

第五、節約與踏實　於貧困之中完成各項建設。

第六、管理與統制　欲刷新政治除教養衛三者以外尤須特注重於「管理」管理分人事管理，生產管理，土地管理，交通管理，尤要於糧食與勞力之管理，以人盡其才，地盡其才，物盡其用，貨暢其流，爲其目的。統制者，預計其一定之功用與相互關係從而斟酌損失，善爲調劑，妥爲支配，統自籌劃以發揮管理之最高效用。

節錄蔣院長行政人員會議閉會訓詞

管理上的法律問題

俞希稷

從前注重道德的時代，祇要自己能讀書明道，言忠信，行篤敬，便可平安度日。設或有事故發生，祇須依照習慣，根據常識，不違反先賢古訓，不反背羣衆心理，即可解決一切，可是現在不同了，中西各國，莫不首重法治，法令條例，日多一日，一舉一動，莫不爲法律所拘束。我國前清時正式法律，僅有刑律一種，現在有民法，民事訴訟法，刑法，刑事訴訟法，違警罰法，戒嚴法，組織法，註册法等，關於農工商礦，尙有各業之單行法規，及共同遵守的稅法，獎勵法，公司法，破產法，商標法，票據法等，重重叠叠，不勝枚舉，所以當工商事業的管理人員，於辦理事業上，對內對外，在在涉及法律，苟一不愼，就要違背法律，失却保障，往往於不知不覺中，已吃大虧。待至事情弄僵，欲圖補救，已噬臍無及，徒喚奈何，眞是可憐之至。下列幾件事情，均因不諳法律，大受損失，可知法律已成事業管理上的重大問題。

有一家百貨商店，其招股章程，聲明爲股份有限公司，所有認股人，亦認其爲股份有限公司，各股東責任，均應以所認購股額爲限，不意開辦數年，經理人未曾注意依照公司法，辦理公司設立登記，而宣告破產，除股本蝕完外，每股東還要賠錢若干，內中殷實股東，除就其本身股份賠錢外，尙須代他股東淸償債務，董事監察人，並被處罰金國幣五百元，因爲依照公司法，未經註册之公司，仍以合夥營業論，不能爲法人，各股東須負連帶無限責任，董事監察人，違反公司法關於呈報期限或聲請登記期限之規定者，應受罰金處分，既失意外金錢，復毀原有信譽。

又有一家藥房，專賣丸藥與化粧品，每年支出廣告費國幣十餘萬元，化粧品中有一種搽面孔之白玉霜，用小方玻璃瓶裝入，外粘商標及商品名稱，每月廣告費占國幣三千元以上，在市面上已有出售二年左右，因宣傳努力漸漸著名，銷路廣大，利益優厚，但是管理人員，因專心推廣銷路，未曾將商標辦理註册。同時有一家化學工業社，亦以製造出售化粧品爲營業，見白玉霜銷路，暢旺異常，難免心動，乃仿製白玉霜出品，裝璜式樣，顏色大小，均大同小異，甚至名稱的字音亦相同。暗中侵奪銷路，並將商標向商標局註册，爲先發制人計，反控告這家藥房。冒用其商標，請求處以妨害農工商罪，且附帶私訴。請求判令賠償損失國幣二萬元，結果，藥房方面，毫無法律保障，祇好表示讓步，情願停止使用已經出名之白玉霜商標，所有存貨，均行銷毀，多數廣告費則盡付之東流，還被辦了二個月的徒刑，緩刑二年，卽二年內暫不執行，如不更犯罪，則刑之宣告，失其效力，藥房經理，總算未坐監牢。

又有一家汽車公司，規模逐漸放大，營業逐漸發達，有汽車二百輛，汽車夫四百人，均選擇誠實强壯者充任之，約定每人須繳保證金國幣三百五十元，無須其他保證，以爲汽車夫如有欺騙偸竊等事情發生，有此保證金，足以抵補。因管理嚴密，平日幸無重大事故，有一次，一汽車夫正從馬路上急駛上橋之際，適有一七歲之小學生，由對面從橋上走下來，雙方不及避讓，小學生被汽車撞倒，輾斷左足，當時流血如注，不省人事，旋由警察車送醫院，並將汽車夫帶局，轉送法院法辦結果，偵查提起公訴，因過失傷害，判處徒刑六月，此小學生爲一律師之獨養兒子，送醫院後，因重傷不治，旋卽殞命，律師悲憤之餘，對汽車公司提起民事訴訟，請求判令給付慰藉金國幣三萬元，經審問後汽車公司被判給付慰藉金國幣五千元，因爲依照民法。「受雇人因執行職務，不法侵害他人之權利者，由雇用人與行爲人連帶負損害賠償責任。」若汽車公司注意法律，事先預防，必令各汽車夫交一殷實舖保。則此慰藉金國幣五千元之損失，應由汽車夫的保人負担了。

又有一家紗布交易所的經紀人，專代客買賣棉紗棉布藉收佣金。內有一股東，與一外國銀行買辦，交情素厚，往來頗密。彼此常有銀錢進出，買辦平日奢侈豪華，已外强中乾，加之經營失敗，以致周轉不靈，有一天，買辦以其友人所出之十天期支票國幣一萬三千五百元，向經紀人貼現，取去現款一萬三千四百五十元，經紀人卽將支票轉貼現於其向往來之銀行，由銀行收現，殆至十天到期，此支票忽被付款之銀行拒絕兌現，並給一退票理由單，書明

「與出票人接洽」等字樣，是時買辦已經逃避，轉貼現之銀行，祇好訴追出票人，卽買辦之友，但是法院於審問時，發現支票上漏塡付款地點，法官謂依照票據法，支票未塡付款地點者，僅得爲借款之證據，不能認爲票據，原告卽不得享受執票人之權利，因此敗訴。

又有一家信托公司，設置地產部，專做地產押款，凡地基房屋，均可抵押，每次交易，均用自備之抵押據，令抵押人照塡，所有條件，均已印就，祇須塡入姓名，住址，數目，日期而已，內有一條件，爲如到期本金利息不能付淸時，卽由保證人負責理楚，或將抵押品沒收，以備抵償云云，自以爲穩妥周到，有一戶，押款十五萬元，利息一萬五千元，抵押人屆期不還，催討多次，亦置之不理，擬將抵押品沒收，自由出售，藉資淸償，乃抵押人忽出面反對沒收，主張將地產公開拍賣，就其賣得價金，淸償本息，於是雙方涉訟，結果信託公司竟敗訴，因爲民法規定，「約定於債權已屆淸償期而未爲淸償時，將抵押物之所有權移屬於抵押權人者，其約定爲無效。」所以無法取勝，信託公司猶不願執行拍賣之判決，復控告保證人，要求依約代負淸償責任，乃保證人於開庭時，提出抗辨，謂依照民法「有保證人於債權人（卽受抵人）未就主債務人（抵押人）之財產强制執行而無效果前，對於債權人得拒絕淸償」之規定，信託公司又敗訴，所以現在多數銀行之抵押據上面。對於保證人部分，須令其書明拋棄主張先訴主債務人或提出抗辨之權利，而使保證人負連帶淸償責任，以策安全。

又有一工程師，創辦一打樣公司，代人繪製房屋圖樣，並監督建築工程，收取公費。有一專營地產事業之業主，籌建住房二百五十幢，委托打樣公司繪圖監工，訂定報酬，依照造價抽百分之三，合國幣二萬四千元，俟落成出租時付訖，乃自一二八後，百業蕭條，地產市價大跌，且空屋太多，不易租出，此地產業主，亦受影響，入不敷出，前項打樣監工費用，無力付給，遷延二年餘，猶無具體解決辦法，打樣公司迫不得已，提起給付公費之訴，以爲無論如何，對方必托人出面和解，至少可收到一部分款項，乃此業主委任律師出庭抗辨，主張依法判決，凡技師之報酬請求權因二年間不行使，卽失時效而消滅。打樣公司職務，屬於技師行爲，已無法請求付給公費，此工程師不但不能收取分文，反受訴訟費用律師公費等之損失，悔恨萬分。

以上事實，耳聞目見幾無日無之，均因其管理人員，平日疎忽法律，以致吃虧匪淺，金錢名譽信用，損失不貲，甚至失業喪身，害人害己，寃枉之至，當其進行之際，非不小心謹愼，考慮周詳，凡百措施，莫不順人情，合事理，講道德，重習俗，自以爲萬無一失，不知法律，有特殊性質，不變條文，以國家政策，人民安甯，公共幸福，羣衆便利，爲主旨，而草擬創制，往往與普通情形，各個事實，不相符合，更非尋常理智所可推測，失之毫末，差之千里，故必賴有專門人才爲之指導。俾得有所遵循，一方面法律政令具同等效力，而爲國家最高權威，人人必須服從，關係人人之切身利害，用以保護權利，確定義務，發展生產，改良生活，引導羣衆合作，解決人民爭端，遂成管理上之重大問題。

凡事業之成敗利鈍，在乎管理得人，而管理之好壞，則須視法律上有無保障，譬如一大工廠，資本充足，房屋堅固，技術精明，工作勤奮，機器完備，出品優良，營業發達，開支節省，可謂盡善盡美之企業令人羨慕不已。然而法律方面，未曾注意，則難免有漏洞有缺點而爲人所乘，以致功敗垂成，所以經營一事業，而不注意法律之限制規定者，無異航行不問水路，飛行不察天時，其何能平安到達目的地，雖有上等機師，新式機器，仍無濟於事。所以近世講求管理制度，管理方法者，或科學化，或合理化，均不能不先注重法律。各種企業，無論國營民營，公有私有，其規模大者，均已添置法律部，聘請法律專家，主持其事，業務之發動，契約之簽訂，須先經法律部之審核，以定去留，以決進止，其範圍較少者，或係個人行爲，亦須請法律顧問，隨時指導，以期防患於未然。誠以世界日趨文明，社會情形日趨複雜，法律政令層出不窮，條文煩瑣，字義深奧，非畢生專門研究，不易明瞭，無從解釋，管理人員，既爲事務所羈，萬無暇晷涉獵法律，故欲解決此種管理上的法律問題，而爲事業謀安全，求保障，必須就正于法律專家而後可。

演講

賦稅法及整理江蘇財政之經過

趙棣華先生講
力善桂筆記

1. 地方賦稅法之意義
2. 國家稅收與地方稅收如何劃分
3. 地方租稅制度
4. 中國國家稅收與地方稅收劃分
5. 江蘇省與各縣稅收如何劃分
6. 中國田賦之沿革
7. 中國田賦之種類
8. 中國田賦之稅則
9. 中國地方賦稅之整理

1. 政府因處理人民一切事務而發生之經費，卽國家之公經濟，公經濟之來源，由人民公同攤出，卽征稅是也。征稅多寡按人民所受利益及其能力而定，賦稅法卽定賦稅之權限及征收之手續者。人民對政府之義務，及財政當局之地位，皆由以確定。

2. 劃分之理論（1）能力適應稅：謂租稅能使納稅人應其納稅力（負担力）之大小而完納者，應歸入國家稅：例如所得稅是，反是若租稅之用途，能發生特種利益使納稅人特別享受者，則宜作爲地方稅，各都市之家屋稅鄉村土地稅是，（2）賦稅範圍稅謂賦稅範圍廣而稅收數額鉅者；應歸入國稅，如關稅消費稅等是，凡範圍狹，而數額微者，宜歸入地方稅，如房屋捐車捐等是（3）征收便利稅：謂賦稅之必須一致，且須鉅額經費完善組織方能征收者，應歸入國稅，如關稅，所得稅，消費稅等是，至須按照各地狀況，且必由熟悉本地情形者征收，方可以節費用而免偸漏者，則宜歸入地方稅，如田賦房捐，營業稅等是，三者熟宜，須視各國歷史上地理上各種環境而定。

3. 地方租稅制度有四 1. 獨立稅制 2. 埘加稅制 3. 收入共分制 4. 補助金制，獨立稅者，地方稅獨立於國家稅之外，地方團體得選擇稅源，酌定方法與稅率自行征收，各田賦歸各地自征是，中央征稅而由各地加征若干者，是爲附加稅如鹽稅之附加是，又省稅有由縣征附加者亦是。某種租稅。單獨由中央或地方負征收之責但其稅收收入則由中央與地方按成分配者，稱收入公分制。補助金制，乃由中央對地方給予若干補助金，或由地方對中央每年協款若干，此制尤以分權之國家多採用之，現今一般國家，採用獨立稅或附加稅制者較多，因現在人口增加，事業日繁，公經濟愈複雜，決非後二法所能應付。

今再比較獨立稅與附加稅之利弊：

附加稅之利益——手續簡單，易於推行，且征收經費較爲節省。

附加稅之弊病——（1）不公平附加稅視何稅易征，卽征何稅，絕不顧到何者爲必須或何者爲奢侈而分別其輕重，最屬不平。（2）附加稅之征收舞弊機會極多（3）在現在環境下，地方有若干建設事業，決非附加稅可能決，必賴獨立稅（4）附加稅不易改良此又一弊也。

附加稅之利，卽獨立稅之弊，附加稅之弊，卽獨立稅之利。

大概國家範圍大者用獨立稅制者多，國家範圍小者，則採附加稅者多。

4.中國國家稅與地方稅劃分之議始於光緒三十四年，宣統繼之，卒未有成，民元討論更甚，民二祇成一草案，未實行。民國十二年以田賦契稅歸地方，亦未實行。民國十六年全國財政會議方實行劃分計國家稅爲鹽，關，常關，烟酒特稅，煤油，捲烟特稅，厘金，鑛稅，印花稅等，地方稅爲田賦，契稅，當稅，牙稅，房捐等十項。十八年取消厘金，內地漁業捐歸地方，海濱漁業捐歸中央，田賦契稅由中央劃歸地方，此爲稅制之一大改革。迄今仍舊，惟中央現又加一統稅，地方加一營業稅，二十三年第二次全國財政會議，以印花稅之三成補助地方政府，以爲廢餘苛捐雜稅之抵補，另以一成交省府爲稽查印花費用，全國印花稅局裁撤，歸郵政局兼辦，此又爲一改革。最近公佈之收支系統法規定，中央稅爲關稅，貨物出產稅，貨物出廠稅，貨物取締稅，特種營業收益稅，特種營業行爲稅，所得稅，遺產稅，省稅爲營業稅，田賦(40%歸省餘歸縣)由中央分得之所得稅，由中央分得之遺產稅，由縣市分得之土地稅，由縣市分得房屋稅。

縣稅，爲土地稅，房屋稅，營業牌照稅一行爲取締稅等等：

總之收支系統法之特點，是收入共分制，及獨立稅制之相互採用。但實行很麻煩，且窮瘠之區吃虧，富庶之區便宜，省方不能以富區所得補助貧區，是一困難。

5.江蘇省大宗收入爲田賦，契稅，營業稅其餘房捐，車捐，田賦附加，娛樂捐皆屬縣。

6.田賦卽地稅，至農耕時代始有之。我國古代行井田制，魯宣公十五年，初稅畝，餘公田外，對私田亦賦之，秦孝公時廢井田私，田皆有稅，漢高祖時對田畝征十五之一，人頭稅亦始此時。唐時行租庸調法，自此以後，賦稅議務不限於有田者，卽無田者亦有賦役之義務矣。農田可自由買賣，此後卽有兩稅法，發生第一期不能遲於六月，第二期不能遲於十二月，唐宋相沿如此。明時改兩，限爲八月及下年二月，又規定得以錢代穀，又行一條鞭法，請以人頭稅及田地合併稱地丁，完全由富人負担，雍正時，據康熙五十二年人口調查規定人口二千數百萬，再增之人口不另征稅，將人頭稅都攤到田賦上去。

7.中國田賦之種類，計有地丁，漕粮，租課，雜賦，及附加稅等。

8.中國田賦分三等九則，此以收穫好壞而定，又有以性質分爲山田旱田，草田，屯田，蘆田，官田，等者。

9.中國地方賦稅之整理

我國田賦積弊最深，中央奠都南京後，選頒整理明令，民國二十三年規定廢除苛雜，減輕附加，凡屬(1)妨害公共利益，(2)妨害中央收入之來源(3)複稅(4)妨害交通(5)變相之厘金等稅捐皆屬苛雜，一律在廢除之列，江蘇苛雜捐稅已完全取消。至取消附加頗感困難，附加稅皆屬縣款，若一概取消，影響縣之事業甚大，且賦稅高低須視每畝負担能否與人民力量適合而定，有些縣附加大於正稅十餘倍(如海門)而每畝總額不過三四角，不能謂之負担重，而欲取消之也。

減輕附加，江都吳縣宜興均曾行過，但田賦積弊甚深，從事減賦頗非易事，欲除積弊必須舉辦土地陳報，淸丈及登記，有了征粮底册，方可剔除中飽，然後再行減賦，方有成效。

至於改良征收制度，須先改革串票，並將征收機關與收款機關分立，現在江蘇有二十縣已由銀行代收稅款，積弊已廓淸不少。

整理江蘇財政之經過，時促不及細講，總之整理財政必經四步卽預算，金庫，會計，稽核是也。

事權之分離及其聯整（B 1.）

王烈望

此文著者爲 L. Urwick，原題 Executive Decentralization Wi h Functional Coodinaton 刊載美國管理協會(American Management Asscciation) 所出版之管理月刊 (The Management Revieiw) 第二十四卷第十二期。一九三五年十二月出版，此文對於企業組織方面，有深切之研究。茲譯述其大意，以介紹於留心工商管理問題者。

譯者誌

一 組織之幾種意義

(1)何謂組織？ 組織者卽爲劃分並類別對於無論何種目的所必需之行爲，以之分派於各種人員之意。其目的卽在利用工作之專門化及其調整，以達到行動一致之目的。

(2)組織原理之重要 從來對於組織問題之探討，大都皆從傳統的人事的或政治的立場着眼。舉凡行爲之區分與別類，皆從慣例，及參照現有人材之能力或依照衆所信以爲最合時宜者而定之。要知人類爲任何目的之組織，必有種種原則爲之規範、此猶建造一橋必有種種工程原則爲之準繩，正復相似。對於此種原則之考慮，應較一切傳統的人事的或政治的適應爲切要。苟於此種原則不加觀察，則衆相合作之結果，必較其應得者爲差。是爲用力之虛耗。

(3)行爲區分之兩種意義　在每一企業方式之中，無論其所關人數之多寡，行爲之區分，常有兩種意義：一爲從縱的方面分成各種行爲之種類，一爲從橫的方面分成各種行爲之等級。

(4)職位之含義　在每一組織中之任何職位，必具此兩種意義。若僅爲列舉每一職位之行爲或祇分析其與他種職位之關係，皆不足以明其意義。正確而有效之定義，必須將每一職位之責任與其他職位之種種關係，包舉並列。

(5)責任之含義　責任者卽爲個人對於其參與之企業所認定之義務，以實現其指定的行爲是也。如個人之責任，不但專爲行施特定之任務，而且爲其他任務之領導者，則所授予之權力，必須與其責任相當。

(6)統馭之限度　凡可以由一人直接指揮之屬員，其職務爲互相關聯者，無論其人如何幹練，終屬有限，大抵至多不能超過五人或六人。凡屬員之資格愈高而其責任愈大者，則其爲數必愈少。此種原則卽所謂統馭之限度(Span of Control)者是也。

在直接討論職務聯鳌(Functional Coordination)以前，有二種進一步的區別，必須加以注意。

二　組織之結構與運用

第一種卽爲組織之靜態或結構方面與織織之動態或運用方面之區別。分析對於某一目的所必需之行爲，依照正確之原則，以邏輯方法、分其類別，並將由此所設之職位，明定其間之相互關係，卽爲計劃一種組織之所有事。但計劃本身並非卽爲組織，譬如建造一橋，先之以設計繪圖，繼之以鳩工庀材。此爲橋樑工程一定之步驟。企業之組織，亦猶是也。組織計劃中所設之職位，必須延攬人材以充任之。顧人性總有所偏，或偏於疏忽，或偏於邪念，或因固執太甚而有延誤與失調之弊。因此除一定的調整以外，凡欲使組織爲有效率之運用，則設計，學習，訓練及領導等行爲，皆所必需，此種行爲應規定於組織結構之中；然欲使表現於日常行事之間，尤爲艱難之任務，故欲使一種企業爲有效率之工作，質的方面之優越較設計方面更爲需要。

三　祇重經驗忽略理論之誤謬

凡在長期間負有重要管理責任之政治家或實業家，日與其共事之人相週旋、人事之紊繁，足以掩蔽其他方面之重要。故實際上負有重大職務之人，祇在人事方面，作繼續之思考，此不但爲其已成之習慣，抑且爲其應有之責任，因之彼等實不耐於在組織結構方面，作分析之硏究，但視此爲空論而已，卽使彼等對於原則方面，有所考慮，亦將以爲人事之重要，超過其他一切而將組織結構與其本身之實際經驗，混淆不分。甚且幷結構原則之存在，亦否認之。此種態度，顯屬誤謬。否認組織結構之重要或不能辨別結構與運用之不同，實爲管理失敗之最大原因。

此點可以醫道喻之，苟欲爲一偉大之醫生，其所需之智識，自非僅知解剖學爲已足。實際臨診對於機體性格各不相同之病人相週旋，雖以冷靜之頭腦觀察各個人之心理爲臨診所必須之技術，然非有解剖學之智識爲基礎，卽不能發現癥結之所在。故僅有完善之結構，固未必能得企業之成功，但許多失敗之企業，無不有其結構上之缺陷。

四 正式的主權與技術的主權

前述二大區別第一爲組織之結構與運用方面之區別，第二則爲各種主權之區別。主權(Authority)者卽爲要求他人行爲之權力，就此意義而論，主權乃係組織本身身所賦予，其行也，從行爲之各部門而達於各等級。在某一等級之員司，接受某種責任以後，彼卽應有指揮下級人員之權力，蓋非此不能完成其責任也。此爲基於組織結構之正式主權 (Formal Authorty)。

但要求他人行爲之權，除正式的主權以外，尙有其他原則者，其效力或且在正式主權之上，如曰張君爲某一問題之權威者，竟卽張君之意見有使他人聽受或注意之權力，以其對於此一問題有專門之智識或技能故也。公司之總經理，可以任命一公司之醫生；但當醫生忠告經理有航海旅行之必要時，彼之所言，卽帶有權力者。此種權力乃從其專門智識與經驗而來。此爲基於智識或技能之專門主權（TechnicalAuthority）。

此外又有其他原因可以造成主權者，例如具有高尚人格或道德之人，其言亦有權威。顧在本文祇能討論正式的與專門的主權之區別。倘欲使行動之一致，與專門技能之充分發展，互相聯繫，則調和此二種主權實爲必要。

五 事權分離之需要

在無論何種企業必須將其行爲分成等級，正式主權之代表，必須經過許多責任之層次。決定責任層次之因素甚多，茲分述如次：

(1)空間 凡一人所能控制之權力，常受空間之限制，譬如一工頭監督二工人，苟此二人各居一室，則其監督工作必較二人同居一室者爲困難，此其例也。

(2)時間 時間的影響亦與空間因素相似。惟其影響，較不一定，因有若干判斷受時間之影響較小故也。大體言之，組織中之某一單位其所在之地不能立刻與上級主權接洽者則在該單位之工作人員必須授以一般行爲之責任及相當之正式主權。此有兩種理由可資證明。

(a)遇緊急事故時，必須有人爲當機立斷之措置，否則如無人負責，因循坐誤，結果必將大壞。

(b)如在一組織單位中之工作人員，其工作係互相依連者則必須有人主持其間以防其間發生失調之事．聯整實爲一種繼續不斷之工作，茍司調整之責者時有隔離，則聯整工作，必不能得滿意之結果。

以上所述爲造成事權分散之物質因素。此外又有心理因素者較物質因素尤爲重要。以下所述卽爲心理因素。

(3)統馭之限度 (The Span of Control) 此一原則，不論其理論上是否確當，已在經驗上證明其爲人類組織中之基本要素。高級長官之屬員。其最適宜之數，約爲四人。在組織中最低層之人員，僅爲特定之工作，而不負監督他人之責者，每部門之人數，最好爲八人或十二人。無論何種組織劃分等級，必須照此原則，分配屬員。

(4)責任與權力之相稱　凡須指定一種責任以監督他人而不授以充分之權力俾資應付其環境者，則負此責任之人，必感解除責任之困難，而餒其氣。此種屬員因其所受權力之不確定，將不能自定其身分，而其個性之足以發展其事業者，亦由此而毀損。創造爲最可寶貴之性質。足以毀損創造力者莫過於上級權力之爲無理的干涉，或其所受之權、不足以應付其所受之事。

因此種種理由，事權之分散，實爲必要。劃分行爲之等級如其爲數過少，其弊將較級數過多爲尤甚。

六　執行行爲與管理行爲

執行行爲與管理行爲（Executive and Administrative Activities）之區別，卽前者爲實施業務，而後者則爲決定應行之業務，換言之，後者爲計劃，決定並傳達政策，而前者則爲使政策發生效果。

容許屬員對於執行政策所採用之方法，有最大之創造力與行動之自由，實爲最切要之事。且在政策之發展過程中，亦應使彼等有發表與批評之自由。反之，倘不能計劃一定之政策或不能使有關係之人對於所定之政策有充分之認識，則組織之基礎必將動搖，除非人人對於共同之目標，有深切之了解，必不能收合作之效。

原則觀念在組織之中佔極重要之地位。決定政策爲管理之事，惟管理者所定之政策應使有關人員心心相印。此較決定政策尤爲重要，蓋人人對於共通原則了然於心，則其相互間之聯整必能自內而發。譬如運動比賽，隊員之間，有暗自聯絡之妙。苟欲達此目的，管理行爲應有密切之集中。

七　專門化之重要

事權之分化，要由於行爲之劃分等級，此爲組織方面之原則。惟因空間與時間的關係，必須有附屬的聯整之點，亦卽爲正式權力之分支中心點。又因統馭限制與束縛權力之不良影響，對於分支中心點所授之權限，愈廣愈佳，以與管理上之聯整相符合。

但自五十年來關於組織方面之社會生活的方式，有一種明顯之趨勢是卽爲行爲之爲橫的分化。換言之，此一趨勢乃向專門化而推進。因此事權之分化乃日形其需要。

從前之組織方式，常爲單位式的或列項式的。一人而對許多人，或某某區域，或一列事務負責。在其領屬之內握有整個權力，彼乃對於任何事物負完全責任，而每一屬員亦對彼個人負完全責任。

然自前世紀以科學方法應用於經濟生活以後，已增加許多可用以資處理各種企業之專門智識。如欲使企業爲有效能之處理，此種智識，非用不可。從另一方面言之，欲望以一人之力，週知對於其工作所需用之專門科目，實爲不可能之事。

八　效能原則之應用及其聯整之困難

科學管理之發明者泰婁氏 (F. W. Taylor) 深知專門化之重要與夫舊式籠統管理之種種阻碍，乃將以前每一工頭所有之責任，分任於八個「效能工頭」(Functional foreman)：不依區域或列項而依效能，種類或方式而定行爲之分類，實爲科學管理不易之原則。彼常謂每一管理人員之工作應限定於一個單獨效能之行施。此一原則，不但適用於工頭卽推而至於整個企業，亦無不適用。由於專門化之需要，此一原則已爲現代工業普遍採用。營業主任，總工程師，會計主任，成本會計員，廣告主任以及採辦主任等等，皆各分任一部份之事務，以總司其一部內之種種行爲，而其人則皆爲專家。此卽爲現代工業效能化最明顯之趨向。

此種趨向，自屬健全。蓋管理之效能化卽爲專門科學智識之應用，而爲無論何種企業所必需。然其結果則必增加聯整之困難，其所以致聯整之困難者有二：

(1)正式權力與技術權力之衝突　如果一企業中高級主管人員依照效能而定其職司，則依照效能原則，其所屬之下級人員，亦必按照效能而定其工作，如此則在每一下屬階級，將無一聯整之點。此種組織結構，在各部人員集中一處之企業，無論對上司對同儕日日晤面，各方有關之事，易於商洽，尙屬可行。如果一個企業分成許多重要單位，其地域上之隔離甚遠，則各部主管人員間之聯整，必將大感困難。故欲圖聯整之不缺，惟有在下層組織設置總彙之點，如鐵路之有分段段長，工廠之有分廠廠長，是其例也。

段長與分廠廠長皆應有充分之正式主權，其理由已如上述。惟在上級機關，專家智識之充分利用，亦有同等重要。

從另一方面言之，除非有正式權力爲後盾，欲得專門技能之認識與利用，至爲困難之事。上級機關所授予之忠告與指導，在下級機關之主管人員，或以爲無意義之干涉，當面商洽既不常可能，而以書函方法調整疑難，又多隔胲。故效能化之結果，總不免引起兩種權力方式之衝突。

（2）統馭限度之難於觀察　事事趨向於專門化，常使主管人員尤其是高級主管人員，有縮小其統馭限度之勢。在每一企業中至少當有三種或四種主要效能，在大規模企業，則其主要效能，可有十數。每種效能皆須有高級專門人材爲之主持，雖企業之總經理不能直接統馭許多之專門屬員，彼如欲分任其煩重責任於他人，則必須有二個或三個屬員。直接對彼負責，以處理某某區域或某某單位之事，苟於此種屬員以外，再加二三效能專員，則屬員又有過多之勢。且增加二三效能專員仍不能解決使專門智識有權力之保障。或謂凡相似之效能，可以歸併於一個主要效能主管人員之下，然此仍無俾於解除主持人聯整之困難。

譬如成本會計專家，與人事管理專家各負一部份之責任。彼等之屬員在分公司或分廠者，同時亦必受分公司經理或廠長之節制。經理或廠長因限於智識或經驗，不能應用彼等之政策或方法，於某種場合則必將上其事於主管者，一方面由經理負分公司或分廠之責一方面則由財務部主任或人事部主人負責。此兩方面之主管人員可以而且常能解決其屬下之異見。然彼一則代表負一般之責任者，一則代表負專門責任者，何以能解決其屬下之異見，並無特殊之理由可言。倘雙方不能解決，則最後之決定，仍在總經理。總經理有時爲解決此種困難起見，另設一種職務，以便雙方之銜接。例如有許多企業爲應付製造部與營業部之異見計，常將此二部份間所發生之問題，歸推銷部或商品部解決之。此實爲解決製造部與營業部困難之一大進步。然此於總經理縮小統馭限度之企圖，仍有妨碍，因多一直接統馭之職務，卽多一分心之處也。

此卽爲現代一切企業所感受之問題。執行責任，必須分離；其負組織分支部份之責任者必須授以充分之正式權力。在另一方面近五十年來科學智識之伸張及其對於社會生活各方面之應用，使任何企業之管理，大增其專門化之程度。此種專門智識之適當應用爲獲得效能所必需之工具。然此種專門權力之引入，適與執行責任分離之趨勢相抵觸。此爲組織中最新而且最大之問題。

九　問題之解決

有一管理學專家曾列述許多方法。以圖解決現代企業組織中之聯整問題。其法卽爲組織表(Organization charts) 組織紀錄 (Organization records) 手續須知 (Standard procedure instructions) 命令與報告 (Orders and returns)，施行紀錄 (Records of performance) 管理報告(Administrative reports)，與委員會 (Committees) 此種種計劃，雖各有其價值，然於

無論何種情形，並不能爲完全之解決。前七種皆係用於規定，測度並控制責任及其完成之紀錄方法。對於各方之聯整，確爲極有價值之工具。然工具雖佳，總屬死物，運用之者，仍在乎人。若謂有此種種工具便可以獲得聯整，是何異保證打字機之能自成書函也。實際上聯整乃係屬於組織之動的方面而非任何制度所能求得之者，必須同時有適當之人爲之運用而後始能得之。

委員會之在組織之中，確有極大之功用，以其能供給互相接觸與交換意見之機會。此于聯整工作固大有帮助也。然其功用仍有許多限制。委員會並不能負聯整之責，蓋如上文所云，聯整乃係繼續不斷之工作，而委員會則不過定期舉行而已。

現在最可注意者，卽爲一種新的職員方式之產生，此種職員卽爲總經理之助理員，祕書或其他類似之名稱。此種職員之責任與關係隨各種不同之企業而異。彼等權力與其地位大抵視其與主管者之關係而定。此項在商業組織中之趨向，頗與現代世界各國之軍隊組織辦法相接近。在軍隊中必須設立參謀部以扶助其長官辦理軍機。此在今日之商業組織中亦有然者。主管人員之設置祕書，蓋係一種行施權力方法之改變。如果聯整工作過於繁複時，則主管人員勢非放棄其若干領袖功能或委任若干聯整工作於他人不可。因此必須產生一種新的權力。此種權力既非區段的權力，亦非專門的權力。而爲參謀部所特有的權力。

參謀部之責任如英國軍事條例之規定卽爲襄助司令官責務之行施並襄助司令官戰略之決定。不僅此也。參謀部之組織其主要目的乃在獲得全軍各部份力量之調整及其靈動之聯絡。參謀人員有其特殊之權力方式。彼等有代替司令簽字之權，凡經過參謀部發出之命令與訓示，皆以司令之權力爲後盾，並由司令負其責任。

在大規模之組織中，各分支區域，皆有參謀人員爲每一級長官之輔佐。換言之，在每一下層聯整之點，皆有若干人員負有特殊方式之付託權力（Delegated Authority），其主要功能卽在獲得聯絡，凡專家與區段當局所措置之事，必求其互相脗合，因此參謀部在組織中係處於第三者之地位，從縱橫斜三方面聯整區段當局與專家。彼等所運用之權力雖爲長官所授予，但並不能直接指揮任何人。除若干書記以外，彼等並無其他屬員。完全責任仍由主管人員負担。故凡規模宏大組織複雜之機關，如感聯整問題之困難，當可于參謀部或祕書處之功能，求得其解決。

中華國有鐵路現行行車時刻表

平綏綫

民國二十四年八月一日實行

303次 平包通車	1次 平包快車	71次 豐張區間車	73次 張同區間車	75次 同綏區間車	77次 綏包區間車	站名	304次 平包通車	2次 平包快車	72次 豐張區間車	74次 張同區間車	76次 同綏區間車	78次 綏包區間車
17.00	7.00					正陽門	7.57	19.45				
						豐台			16.44			
17.52	8.02	10.40				西直門	7.20	18.53	16.06			
19.15	9.24	11.42				南口	5.56	17.22	14.18			
20.25	10.42	13.19				青龍橋	4.47	16.17	12.50			
21.03	12.04	14.41				康莊	4.04	15.33	12.06			
23.30	14.38	15.27				宣化縣	1.27	12.46	8.41			
0.37	15.52	18.37				張家口	0.33	11.45	7.30	22.11		
5.51	21.45	13.45	6.00	7.50		大同縣	19.18	5.45		14.50	19.54	
7.10	23.08		13.12	9.51		豐鎮	17·57	4.08			18.22	
9.15	1.43			13.14		平地泉	16.05	1.36			14.35	
14.20	7.17			19.20	9.40	綏遠城	10.56	20.04			8-00	16.23
17.51	11.31				15.18	包頭	7.15	15.35				10.35

豐台門頭溝間

83次 豐門區間車	81次 豐門區間車	站名	82次 豐門區間車	84次 豐門區間車
4.30	7.00	豐台	13.27	20.50
5.30	8.10	西直門	12.50	20.15
17.04	9.50	門頭溝	10.30	18.00

大同口泉間

93次 同泉區間車	91次 同泉區間車	站名	92次 同泉區間車	94次 同泉區間車
15.20	7.45	大同縣	11.05	18.40
16.35	9.00	口泉	10.00	17.35

各種運輸事業之聯系

白魯姆博士原著
曹麗順譯

——原文見Transport: Railway Systems, TheirO rganization & Management

交通事業，異常重要，故各國必須確定一整個的計劃，以促進其發展；並有不少關於國際性質之工作，亦須共同進行。

交通事業之所以重要，實基於其效率（精良，便宜，安全）之足以影響於人民之經濟及文化生活，甚至於全民之幸福；同時其所需要資本甚巨，僱工亦多，實爲各種實業中最重要之主顧。

在何交通工具，皆有運輸功用。惟吾人所須研究者，乃爲何種性質之運輸，由各方面觀察，以使用何種工具爲最有利之一問題耳。故在運輸政策之中，必須謀各種工具之協調；其取捨標準，不僅以私人之利益，且須以社會全體之利益爲斷。

由表面上觀之，各種交通事業，如能一概發展至於概度，豈非最佳。但此種情形，雖在最富庶之國家。亦不能實現；蓋發展過度，必有一部份流入於靡費與奢侈，故實際僅能隨國家之經濟與社會之生活情形以俱進。

交通事業大別之可分爲二類，一卽其本身有獨占之性質者，如電報，電話，無線電報，以及有定期之外洋航輪等是；一卽可以互相競爭者，如鐵路水道，汽車等，近年則更可加一航空！

次之，國家對於交通事業，必須採用一種緩和折衷之政策。蓋卽在最富庶之國家，亦必不能同時有「完善」之鐵道制度，「完善」之水道制度，以及「完善」之公路或航空制度等。故一國必須根據其特有之情形。使資本有利的投資於某特種交通事業，其費用最少而在最短時期內，卽能達到完善之效果。至於其他各種交通工具，可視爲輔助之事業。雖此舉足以引起一般私人經營其他交通事業者之爭執，但事實旣甚明顯，固不能因此而有所變更也。

在進化之國家一致認鐵路爲最重要最優良的內地交通之工具。蓋其本身之性質上，實具有若干特點，例如低廉，安全，迅速，準確。車次之多而有定時等等。均爲其他交通工具所不及。僅在數種不甚重要之處，稍次於他種工具：如電報電話於傳遞消息上，自較鐵路學尤速，但其價値過昂，爲其缺點；運貨汽車在短矩離內亦頗優良，惟運價稍貴；河道湖泊之大者對於大量貨物之長途運輸，頗爲便宜；至於空運，最適合於少數貴闊之人及豪重物品，但因其成本較大，故常需公家之補助。

鐵路—包括狹軌鐵道及電車等等—所以成爲普偏的內地交通之工具者，其理由如左：

一、鐵路業務之性質最爲繁複。蓋任何物件，如人，物，新聞，鐵路均可載運，在一方面可以便宜的裝載大量貨物，在另一方面，又因其業務之優良（如安全，迅速，準時等）。不僅可以載運旅客及郵件，且可以裝載貴重捷運之貨物。至於內河航運，普通祇能載運大量貨物；如係天然良好之河道，其費用並不較鉄路爲高，若爲人造運河或小河則高於鉄道甚多。故爲誘致顧客起見，水運須較鉄路之費用，至少便宜百分之十五，蓋顧客深知鉄路尙有其他優點也。若航空及汽車之運費，則殊太昂貴。

二、以言時間，則鉄路乃被公認爲優越者，蓋其業務無時不準備可用。鉄路在事實上，幾乎安全不爲氣候所限。甚至極大的災家，亦僅能暫時的損害其一部份，故交通可以迅速恢復。至於其他各種交通工具，均不能脫離氣候的控制，如氣候惡劣，則有時必須停止工作。內河航運遇有霧或霜以及水漲水淺往往被迫而停止—卽在進化之國家，亦常亘數月之久。此種缺點之結果，不言其他，必促使鉄路兼負水道輸運之責任。故在建築鉄路時，其運量須與全無水運相同。由此觀之，普通所謂，鉄路需要水道之救濟一語，並非準確；實則鉄路並不需要其他何種之救濟，因其運量能隨時增加，以負担無限制的澎漲。由此點而言，鉄路决不至有「業務過量慌恐」之發生。

三、鉄路在空間上之優點，亦爲一般所公認。因鉄路能達到大陸上之任何一點。在運量稀少之地點，可以建造輕便或狹軌的單線鉄道，以連接每一村莊，每一工廠，或每一礦山。

且因鉄路性質。其本身可以組成一鉄路網，對於長途重載，或窮鄉僻壤之微量運輸，均無不可。故在鉄路上並無轉裝之發生，貨物可自起運站直接運至到達站，不需要其他方式之協助，——除非街車之自店門接送耳。

此項優點，汽車與飛機在理論上，亦所同具。但因成本關係，前者之行途不能太長，後者則須視飛機場之多少而定。至於水運則其本身既不能組成一種綱系，支流亦屬自限。普通僅有一二條路綫，不能不需要許多鉄路，及他種聯絡。因此發生轉裝手續，而需要額外之費用，並常致損失。鉄路因能四向發展支綫，實勝於水道，而以文明國家需要散佈其人口爲尤甚。

鉄路又有一公認之點：卽其運貨量之可多可少。反之運貨汽車與飛機，僅能裝載少量貨物，水運又祇於裝載大量貨物；因在進步之國家內，卽指有鉄路之區域，如水道欲謀收入足以維持，至少須用四百噸之船隻，最好六百噸或甚至一千噸。鉄路所以有載多載少之特性者，卽因大單位之列車，係由各小單位之貨車，加以組織而成者也。

以上各節，已將鉄路較其他交通方式優良各點，特爲說明。所以然者，實因近時有不少通俗之人，與膚淺學者，或有私人利益關係者，以籠統貶抑鉄路之價值爲時髦，而對於他種交通方式，則以無論如何改進，而爲其性質所不能有之優點歸之。不幸此種宣傳之法，甚甚爲巧妙，非特特各國無思想無智識之羣衆，卽一般領袖及機關（國會與政府）亦皆爲其所惑。惟此事與經濟文化兩方面，有莫大之關係。故專門家不可不發爲糾正之言論。

然則何種交通方式最爲優良，此固爲一般人所急欲知者；但此一問題，殊不能加以籠統之解答，惟一辦法，祇有決定原則數項，其餘則須視各個情形而定，此法於開闢新運河，建築公路及開行汽車及航空路綫時，更爲適用切要。

在上列之探討，尤在研究整個問題之中，下列數點，應特別加以注意：

一、多數之文明國家，現皆有充足之交通工具。此種現有之工具，不僅能充分供給目前之運量，卽使有實質的增加，亦能應付裕如。同時現在各國，承歐戰之後，情形困難，故如何使用新的資本，必須加以極度之審愼。無論如何，世界許多國家，尤其是歐洲各國，在其他方面，最要者如建築住宅及開闢土地，所費甚巨，故如現有交通工具，足資應付，當無力創設新的工具也。但如有建議廢棄現有之工具，例如拆去電車道而代以他種成本重而效能低之工具，則其不合理，蓋莫過於此。

二、各種交通事業所必備之條件，必須足敷成本。如此點不爲假設所蔽或故意遺忘，則許多無識之議論，不致發生，而交通事業聯系之問題，亦大可簡單化矣。自經濟學理言之，任何一種交通事業。其自身之收入必須足敷成本—此處之所謂「成本」，不僅指營業成本，且兼指債款之利息及償還，與各種設備之更新。換言之，無論何種交通事業決不能常在成本中減去一部份，而以民衆所納租抵補之。至於國家補助，僅可用於幼稚時代之新興交通事業，如現在之航空運輸是。

三、某種交通事業，必須與其他已有之運輸系統相聯絡，而僅從事於特種之運輸，則社會上所得之利益爲最大。尤如汽車一項，在都市之內，可以與市政府所經營之運輸事業（如電車）相聯系。在鄉間之交通，則載客及運貨汽車（循適當之途徑），均可與郵政及鉄路相輔而行。

平時之軍運組織適於戰時需要

王同文譯

平時準備之意義，包括維持大量軍備，或於平時全國人民有總動員之準備，一般人之目光，均注意於人事方面之準備，而對於準備方面更重要之健全完整組織，平時未曾顧及。關於軍事運輸，雖得歐戰之教訓，但對於組織，仍有忽略。是以作者注意過去之錯誤，以免將來緊急時期，破壞我兵力以致失敗，而有討論尋常時期之軍運組織，如何可適於戰時之需要，使於軍隊中，成一有力之機關，隨時隨地與作戰軍聯絡。如是之組織，各部分各有專責，組織上之人選與職務，頗多考慮之處；或有人有不同之主張，或認爲如是之組織系統，於平時並不需要，職務與人選之分配難能適合。古諺有云，無冒險無進取，其意卽無人首先提倡組織，以供討論，則組織決無改進之可能。設我等仍取不管主義，須知戰事之災難，終有一日降臨。作者所擬適於戰時需要之平時軍運組織，爲　種建議，而非不可改善爲最後的組織系統，此僅爲貢獻於讀者，共同討論，以求得最健全完善之組織。

首先注意者，爲此組織之領袖人物，須有經驗與適合資格，等於管理美國鉄路之最優一類之行政長官；然此等優良之行政長官。無疑的不易徵得。因其在路界所得之待遇，遠勝於軍界之供給。另一方面，須注意此種爲人民謀幸福之特殊的高位，確爲榮譽，高位及其榮譽，可吸引一種富有愛國思想，而不計較待遇厚薄之行政長官充任之。如在新組織内各處處長之人選，亦受同樣考慮。各處長選擇之方法，須於現有之運輸機關中，將有才幹與經驗者任之，使確能運用其才幹與實際經驗，以求得期望之成效。

茲將附表之組織，略述各處之職務於后：

(一)事務處——該處之職務，爲辦理軍隊與軍需輸送於民有交通綫上，編制統計，處置合同與請求事項，購買材料，檢查帳目，以及其他雜務。

(二)調查處——該處之工作，關於全世界各國平時與戰時之運輸，將其材料調查收集至最近時期。如各地於平時或戰時，對於港埠、鉄路、水道、公路、空道之位置，地理上之特殊情形，設備管理與經營方法，以及其運輸物之種類數量來源與分配，並是否有能力於戰時增加其運輸量？諸如此類，須由調查處切實徵集資料。此種資料，於歐戰時全無準備，深爲遺感。將所得之資料，會同最近與過去出版之著作上有關係之材料，亦續漸收集之。如是非特能藉此增進我國運輸於平時與戰時之效用，並可相助我軍將來有國防上抵禦能力，或侵略外國之威力。

(三)工程處——該處之職務，包括設計與建築二課。設計課專於處理鉄路、港埠、終點場、水與燃料之供給、內地河道、公路、以及其他機關等之設計，建築課爲處理實地之工作，有動員人員及專門技術人員等，用最新最好之工具，以最敏捷方法，相助公衆與運輸公司，當於運輸機關之運輸，爲火災、水災、風災、地震所停頓，或其他大量破壞時，由其迅速恢復原有之運輸狀態。有動員人員之集中組織，可將一部分人員，分散全國各處，以便緊急時之需要。

（四）機務處——該處注重於設備，及其他有關於機械電機之應用與裝置，予以特殊之技術訓練。

（五）軍事處——該處專於處理人事問題，軍事上組織與訓練，及喚起民衆，受以相當訓練，適於軍事上之需要與目的。由軍事處長，從事於全國民衆有幹部組織，將有經驗之後備人員，與各處（以上四處）事務人員，於平時有伸縮組織（歐戰時無之），能於短時期之佈告，將以上有經驗之後備人員，隨時召集，或按需要能增加之。

以上所述，屬於組織表內關於行政與工程方面各處之職務與工作，以下敘述，關於直接管理運輸方面各處之事務：

（一）水道運輸與港務處——以管理現有與將來國有國營之航船，包括非特現在（指歐戰時）已在運輸軍隊與軍需之船舶，並包括業經軍政部管轄之紐約巴拿馬航綫，及密西西比河至華力羅一綫之內河航業公司，或最好能將航運局之職務，轉由水道運輸處管轄之。

(二)鉄路運輸處——除經營管理內政部所管轄之國有鉄路，如在巴拿馬運河地帶及阿剌斯加鉄路外，並指揮其他國家有權可顧問之私有鐵路，如於戰時或非常時期，全國之鐵路爲國家之利益着想，能由此處代管，較優於平時原有之行政管轄機關。

(三)公路與輕便鐵路處——現由農業部管轄受國家津貼之公路，得歸該處管理之；並該處負戰時臨時增設輕便鐵路與管理之責。

(四)汽車運輸處——由該處處長，於平時管理運貨汽車與公共汽車，以供公衆之需要，同時有準備可供戰時之急要。

(五)航空運輸處——統由該處處長管轄國家之航空運輸，於平時亦有準備可適於戰時之應用。

如是之平時軍運組織，雖能使鐵路與軍人，時有聯絡，明晰軍運戰時之需要；但尚不能稱爲完整之組織。完整與健全之組織，須產生二大全國代表會，一個全國代表會，是代表陸水空等之運輸公司，承包公司，與技術會社，另一個爲代表全國各種實業界：如鋼鐵，鐵路與輪船之設備，汽車，機器，電機與機械用具，自來水，以及其他房屋建築材料，飛機等，每一代表會，有一運輸副總監主持之，於副總監之下，各區有區代表，以協助副總監工作之進行，區代表之工作，尙須根據其本區內各地代表之報告。以上各代表，須由適合之選擇，確能負運輸事業之一部分者；又各地代表，須與有組織之動員後備人員聯絡，以便將來急要時，得臨時召集之，在動員時期內，從事於各運輸機關，各實業工廠工作，以應付戰時之非常需要。

如附圖所示虛綫下之組織，於平時爲虛設，無工作人員及工作，須至戰時方始增添有組織與平時受有訓練之後備人員塡補之。由平時之組織，變成戰時組織，其應用須切實妥愼處置之。有訓練之後備人員，處於重要地位，對於戰地軍運之各種工作，有極大相助，並須與軍隊中其他部分，有和衷共濟之精神，以完成此種組織，確有良好效用。同時此種組織，管理上有得最大效果，其關鍵全在領袖人之手，領袖人須有領導本能，管理之才力，使下屬人員信仰，及欣佩其處事努力，與愛國熱忱，並下屬人員深能服從，及與其有合作之精神。是以有適當之領袖人，處理軍運，可避免或減少運輸機關與軍事當局間意見之不調和，或其他種種誤會與弊端，可使數種運輸機關，集中其軍運力量，統由一戰時軍運機關管轄之。

作者主張，無論將來有否戰爭發現，此種軍運組織，實爲和平時期軍事組織中，不可缺少之一重要部分，作者並非見戰爭爲恐懼，但現代之人類，余認爲不能保障各國之軍事衝突，爲一過去之事實，如果云將來國家可無戰爭，卽等於說將來人類可無疾病。在此情形之下，如我國始終尙無準備，可與因距火災危險之時期尙遠，而避免保火險，同樣看待，如是因

建議中之軍運組織表

軍政部
長部
運輸總監
全國運輸代表會
運輸副總監
戰區總司令
運輸副總監（管理運輸方面各處）
運輸副總監（行政與工程方面各處）
水道運輸與港務處
鉄路運輸處
公路與輕便鉄路處
汽車運輸處
航空運輸處
工程處
機務處
調查處
事務處
軍事處
戰區軍隊與軍需之輸送
由總司令處理全美國之人事與物事
戰區運輸司令
高級副官
運輸副司令
運輸副司令（管理運輸方面各處）
運輸副司令（行政與工程方面各處）
運輸副司令分駐於每軍隊總部
水道運輸與港務處
鉄路運輸處
公路與輕便鉄路處
汽車運輸處
航空運輸處
工程處
機務處
調查處
事務處
軍事處
運輸副司令聯絡其他有關係機關

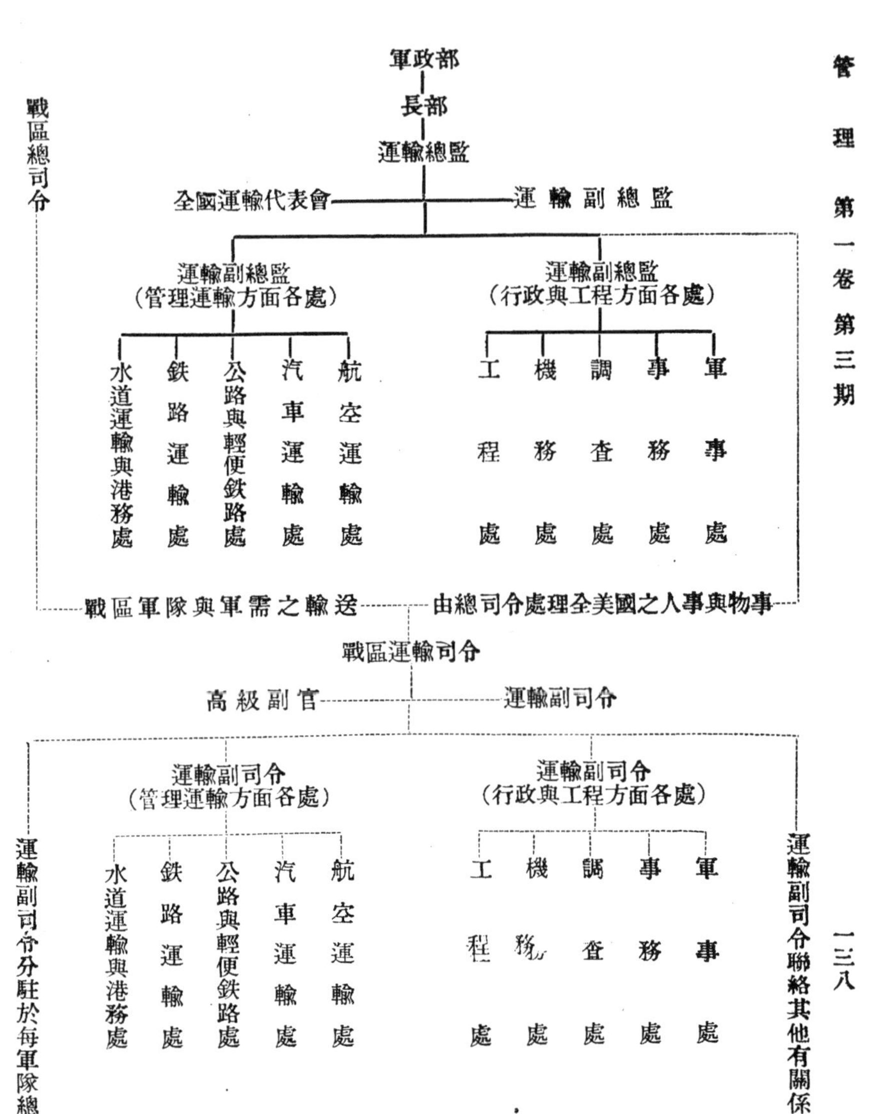

不保火險所付微細之保險費，竟致爲小而失大，若吾國如無事前準備，將來必受生命與財產之損失，有後悔莫及之歎耶。

本文譯自惠爾葛斯著之美國遠征軍在西歐之運輸一九一七——一九一九年一書中之附錄二，作者因鑒於平時軍運組織之重要，與美國於歐戰時無此組織準備，特建議一適於戰時需要之平時軍運組織，以供美國人士討論，並求改進。我國今日已處於非常時期之尖端，對於適應戰時之軍運組織，亦宜早日準備。望軍事當局與運輸機關，共同討論一適於中國戰時需要之組織系統，以便發揮其最大之運輸效用。

譯者附誌

赫脫 Col. Haupt 在美國南北戰爭的第三年曾說，鐵路在那時候只發揮得幾分的效能，他再舉出三個理由，解釋鉄路這様的沒有效能。他以爲司令官和部屬，有三個錯誤的觀念：「一、以爲鉄路和鉄路人員，是他們個人的便利和指揮之下的附屬品；二、以爲他們的命令必須卽刻施行，不管同時他方面有沒有命令，或事實上有沒有困難；三、倘若命令沒有實行，便可任意的嚴厲恐嚇，有時竟有更苛刻的處罰」。這許多事情，都是中國今日所流行的現象。

摘譯於 "Railways, Highways and National Defense", by Baker, J. E. 中國評論週報五卷五十一期民二十一年十二月

管理學院叢書之一

東北鐵路問題之研究

上下二册 王同文著

▲內容▼ 本書上册共有十章，先述中東路之史的發展，經濟價值，組織概要，營業與運輸概況。後敘日本侵略下之鐵路問題，如滿鐵會社之組織，財務，營業等概況，日本對東北之鐵路侵略政策，又分析研究南滿路之營業狀況與營業統計，及運輸狀況與運輸統計，最後論述吉會鐵路問題。共一百四十餘頁。下册計有八章，另加續編四章。內容爲：滿鐵租用地問題，南滿鐵路之倉庫管理，東北鐵路聯運及競運問題，葫蘆島築港與東北鐵路網，東北鐵路與國際關係，東北現有鐵路與總理計劃，今後東北鐵路之整理計劃。續編中有：中日鐵道交涉問題，九一八後之東北鐵路，李頓報告書中之東北鐵道問題述評，中東路出售問題。敘述甚詳，立論尤新，共二百頁，誠爲研究東北鐵路問題與中日關係之唯一有價值書籍。

定價 一元二角(直接購買對折優待)

代售處 本外埠各大書局

古今領袖人物言行札記

福特的成功

亦生

亨利福特是鼎鼎大名的美國汽車大王，他的車子遍佈在大地上每個角落里，他的財產快到十萬萬金元，他的確是世界上最偉大的製造家，並且也可算是最富有的企業家了——或許可能的地除了煤油大王洛克法爾而外。雖則最初經過重重叠叠的挫折，受着一般唯利是圖的商人的奚落，還碰到同行中人可怕的爭競與嫉妬，可是終于他是一個近代的成功者，這是誰也不能否認的；孫中山先生在民生主義的第一講里，對他的經營也是稱揚備至，卽在一向目空一切的蘇俄政府的眼睛里看來，也贊許這位美國汽車大王的制度，在他的聰明的生產組織中，很可爲社會主義的蘇俄師法，而列寧更恐懼地這樣說過，「當美國還有福特的時候，共產主義不會有在那里成功的希望」。總之，全世界上的每一宗企業，每一個地方，幾乎可說每一個人，我敢說，沒有不給亨利福特的事業與制度影響着震驚着了。

一個連小學也沒有畢業的農夫的兒子，怎樣會發明着當今最便利而時髦的交通工具「無馬的車子」，以及怎樣會在汽車界里獲得這般至高無上的地位與權威，眞是值得我們的注意與贊嘆。像這樣偉大的發明家而兼企業家，在中國一逕是貧乏了的，他的成功的事蹟，我想，也許是我們——尤其研究企業管理學的我們——所樂聞的吧。

一 汽車的發明

福特從小就喜歡研究一切的機件，他上課的時候往往忘了聽講，出神地獨自拆弄他自己所有的一個表子，等他的父親晚上睡覺以後，又時常偷偷地出去代替鄰人免費的修理鐘表。及到他有一次在路上看見了滾路機走過，就立刻發生「不用馬的車子」的觀念；從此以後，他作過許多理想的模型，拆卸又拆卸，改良又改良，可是總沒有成功。後來，他又在一本法國的雜志里，看見有人想用機器的力量開車，便更增加他繼續研究的自信心。他先在機器工場里當了四年學徒，又在別的幾個電氣之類的公司里當了技師，對于「新的馬達」，在公餘之暇時時刻刻的研究着。興致來的時候，他慣常犧牲了睡眠，妻子往往催促他去睡覺，但他總是說：「不要忙，還差一點了！」於是他又埋首在機器里，鎚子接着便響起來了。許多人都說他發了狂，而他却料定自己必有成功的一天，只顧自樂其樂地傻幹下去。他這樣百折不撓的精神，實在是他幼時受了他母親所常說的「一經想定要做的事，便非做到成功不可！」的那句話的感化，而他的妻子也能幫助他研究，使他在失敗以後還有了安慰，就更可深深地鼓勵他前進的勇氣。從他開始研究製造汽車起，晝夜不息地幾乎辛苦了十年光景，事實證明着，那奇奇怪怪的「不用馬的車子」居然成功了，「狂人」的發明品居然映入許多人驚奇的眼簾了！謝上帝，他的努力不是白費啊！

二 「天生的企業家」

福特的好朋友愛迪生曾經說過：「福特是天生的企業家，和他是天生的機器家一樣」。的確，福特不但能夠發明汽車，懂得每一部機器內部的搆造，他最大的本領，要算他能夠將自己所辦的企業，在世界連年不景氣的現象下，繼續不斷地擴展到現在的地步。雖則既經發明了汽車，沒有充裕的資本還是辦不了事業的；他最初只雇了兩個工人，自己幫同做工，可是漸漸地，漸漸地，在經他努力的奮鬥與鼓吹之下，大腹便便的商人竟也肯掏出腰包來。爲了營利的計劃與目的不同之故，他和其他的股東就分了手；而處境却更艱苦萬狀了。他再和其他的人合股着，但不久又破了產；到年節那一天，他向工人痛哭流涕地說明破產的情況，並切切實實地表示自己的計劃和希望，工人們便大爲感動，竟願全體不拿工資，繼續維持下去。恰巧歐戰爆發了，汽車的需要大增，他的營業便興旺起來；他並且以五千臺農業機器拖車送到英國去，賺了很多的錢。但是歐戰以後蔓延于全世界的大恐慌潛伏着了，並且慢慢地掀動着了！看到市面一定有極壞的反動來，他竟自動地毫無忌憚地將車價大大的跌減，同時將庫存的原料全部使用，所有的製品完全賣罄——他的意思是：「寧願閉鎖工場，不願再去折本的濫造」，而結果呢，只有福特公司還有幾百萬的現金能夠流動着哩！他在這危難時期第二點的「整理策」便是「節約浪費」：他不單節省材料的浪費，並且還節省人力的浪費。他一面有計劃地利用一切殘廢的材料，一面將統計課之類不生產的處所一律撤消，而移其人員到工場去做生產的工作——這樣一來，公司中的生產能力便立刻大大的增加了。所以別的公司在這時候一天天地倒閉着，而福特公司依然還有很多的盈餘；自從這次的難關一過、繁榮的花朵便逐漸怒放着。這不能不說福特是具有應變的幹才，也不能不說他是「一個天生的企業家。」

三 他的企業信條

福特所以能成爲「一個天生的企業家」，原來對他所經營的企業懷抱相當的信條的。他的信條有四個，他總是根據着這些信條做去而絕不違反的。牠們是：

(一)不要怕着將來，不要悔着過去。怕將來的，怕失敗的，是限制自己的行動的。失敗是指示將來不要再錯的最好機會。誠實的失敗並不算是不名譽，怕失敗的才眞是不名譽。只有指示將來發展方法的過去才是最有益處的。

(二)不要怕競爭。做最好事業的人，應當是自己能夠做到的。搶奪他人的事業便是犯罪——爲自已的利益去陷害他人，不用智力而想用强力去支配他人，那自然是犯罪了。

(三)要把服務放在利益之前。沒有利益，事業自然不能發展。利益本來不是壞東西，有良好管理的事業是必能產生利益的，至對于服務的報酬而生的利益當然應該有的。牠並不能看做事業的基本，祇能說是服務的結果。（註：福特事業的眞精髓便是「爲公衆而服務」。他的服務主義的最大標幟乃是「造出有用的物品，以最廉的價錢供給公衆，便利公衆」；他不像普通的企業家一般，祇知道貪圖一時的利益，而忘却永遠的繁榮的。他說：「以服務爲主的事業必繁盛，以利益爲主的事業必滅亡」。）

(四)製造工業不是要賤買貴賣的，而是用相當的價錢買進原料，僅僅加以少許的費用，把原料變成消費物，以分配于消費者的。投機和欺騙的買賣是妨害自己的發展的。

四 他的企業制度

福特的企業信條與其他企業家的主張是迥然不同的，而他的企業制度，正像一個巨響的霹靂，更足以震驚全世界上每個人的耳鼓的。他以爲窮苦是人間罪惡的根源。他說一個人失去了物質的安寧終日爲着吃飯問題苦惱着，自然會使他的精神漸漸地萎頓不堪而減低工作的效率的。他不顧世上有所謂窮苦，更不願在他企業里的員工還有窮苦的現象。他希望他手下的工人能夠支持一家最低限度的生活費，他使他們可以得到正當的休息與娛樂，也就是說，他不像普通資本家般地去剝削他們的血汗，他總要力求他們的幸福。大概爲了自己也是由于工匠出身便特別熟悉工人生活的苦痛吧，他贊成工人每天最低的工資爲美金五元；他贊成工人每天的工作時間減爲八小時；他贊成每星期只做五整天的工作；他贊成將福特公司每年的盈餘劃出一大部份作爲工人的紅利。這宗特別優待勞動制度的實施大家以爲福特公司不久便要關了門，但福特竟毅然決然地執行着，效果是這樣：在舊制之下，一萬六千個工人在一九一三年製造出一萬六千輛車子，而在新制之下，同數的工人在一九 四年却製造出二萬六千輛車子！他不但沒有吃虧，反而能夠獲得他們忠實的努力的服務而受到無窮的利益——他的制度萌芽着他的企業的繁榮了。

五　他的企業政策

福特的企業政策一逕採取下列的兩宗：

（一）他的是大量生産主義，或者說薄利多賣主義。利益薄了，出賣自然會多了，這是營業上一定不易的原則。他以爲以薄利賣出多額總比較以厚利賣出少額爲合算。他說大量生産一則可以使計劃的生産可能，一則可以避免商業上清淡的季節，決不至使工場中有時太忙，有時太閑，換言之，即在需要減少的季節，機器照樣的使用着，工人照樣源源不絕的做着工。他說緊縮工場——除了歐戰後的恐慌使他不得已的緊縮外，他平常總不願意這般的——是一宗浪費，製品的漲價也是一宗浪費。他說汽車不是奢侈品而是實用品，他能夠盡力貢獻于社會的，就是減低價格和增加出産。瞧着吧，福特汽車價格的低廉和銷路之廣泛實在凌駕乎其他公司的汽車之上了。

（二）假使福特單單注意于價格的低廉而不求品質的堅固，我敢說，他的企業決不會老是這般繁榮的。「要供給價廉而質美的製品，」這是他常說的一句話。的確，他既以服務主義爲標榜的，如其違反了價廉物美的原則，那便好似祇有模型而沒有靈魂的佛像一般，終究是不靈的。然而汽車是不同別的製品，材料固然要結實，而車身却是愈輕愈好的。他用種種研究與搜求的方法，才明白二十餘種鋼鐵的種類，各有特殊的用途，而一宗含有「釩」的原質的法國鋼鐵，堅固而强韌，輕巧而靈便，要算是製造汽車最適合的材料了，他寧願出了重價去購來。

在福特汽車里，任何一樣配件，他總是選擇堅固而確有耐久力的材料。他說好材料可以爲購者圖經濟，爲福特汽車圖永久的繁榮的。他的話給事實證明着了。

福特的事蹟不是這短短的篇幅里寫得完的。他振興了工商業，且還扶助着農業。他優待了工人，且還設法拯捄着農夫。他設了醫院，辦過學校。他鼓勵勞動，厭棄懶惰。他愛好和平，反對戰爭。他沒有普通資本家猙惡的面具。他擁有很多的錢，但很多的錢都用在「爲公衆而服務」的目的上去。他屏除了「自私」的野心，而懷抱着「交利」的善念。他的成功不是偶然的，而是被堅强的毅力，應變的幹才，超然的觀念，慈祥的胸懷和切實的計劃造成了的。他的一切——身家，像貌，學識，經驗等等——都是平凡的，但他却居然能夠幹出超人的偉大的事業來。「偉大往往從平凡中創造着的」，而且，只有從平凡中創造着的偉大才是眞正的偉大，才是值得我們最最欽仰的偉大！

報告

參觀自動統計機後

黃恭儀編

（一）「敘述」

統計學教授汪師仲良，此次率管理學院三年級全體同學三十四人，前往南京衛生署，參觀東亞僅有之最新式電動統計計算機，儀當隨往，司襄助之責。五月二十三日晨八時半，在京市寓所，驅車前往，當由該署指派萬國商業機器公司工程師，美人石棟君，及其秘書袁君厚載，分別招待。參觀程序，係將同學分爲兩組，先後引導，詳細解釋各機功用，並表演全部手續。按該機係紐約萬國商業機器公司（International Business Machines Corporation）製造，現存衛生署。蓋美國人口統計專家哈羅內博士（Dr. Herman Hollerith）爲計算及分析其調查所得之大宗資料，並求迅速準確起見，於是于一八八〇年，發明電動計算機。查此機運用方法，係將一切統計資料，打孔于特製之長方形表例卡片上，使機器因接觸卡片上所打之孔，而發生作用，猶如盲者誦讀書籍，必須藉凸版文字也。至打孔之地位，則須根據調查所得之資料，資料不同，所打之孔之地位，卽隨之互異。

```
00000000000000000000000000000000000000000000000000000000000000000000000000000000
11111111111111111111111111111111111111111111111111111111111111111111111111111111
22222222222222222222222222222222222222222222222222222222222222222222222222222222
33333333333333333333333333333333333333333333333333333333333333333333333333333333
44444444444444444444444444444444444444444444444444444444444444444444444444444444
55555555555555555555555555555555555555555555555555555555555555555555555555555555
66666666666666666666666666666666666666666666666666666666666666666666666666666666
77777777777777777777777777777777777777777777777777777777777777777777777777777777
88888888888888888888888888888888888888888888888888888888888888888888888888888888
99999999999999999999999999999999999999999999999999999999999999999999999999999999
1 2 3 4 5 6 7 8 9 10 11 12 13 14 15 16 17 18 19 20 21 22 23 24 25 26 27 28 29 30 31 32 33 34 35 36 37 38 39 40 41 42 43 44 45 46 47 48 49 50 51 52 53 54 55 56 57 58 59 60 61 62 63 64 65 66 67 68 69 70 71 72 73 74 75 76 77 78 79 80
```

I. B. M. 5080

上圖乃表例卡片原樣，有八十橫行每行有打孔之位置十二，其中十位以數目字○至九印出，第十一十二兩位，位於卡片頂部，未用數目字印出。運用卡片之第一步。即將行數分成若干組，每組登記資料一類，下圖爲一已分組之表例卡片：

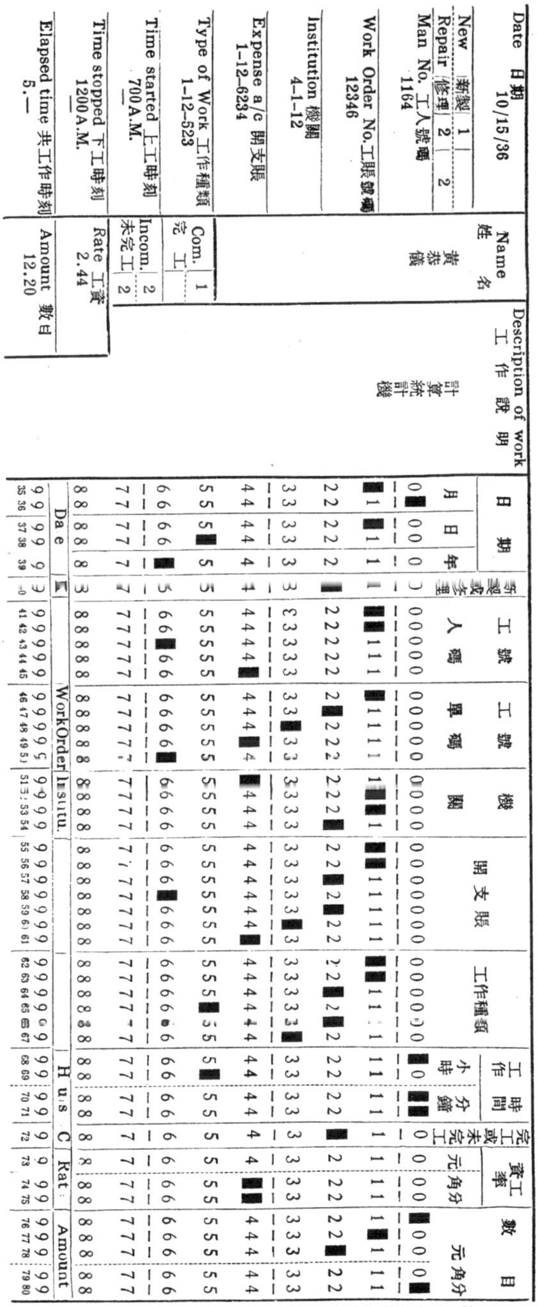

工資及工人支配Payroll and Labor Distributin

Date 日期	10/15/36
New 新製 1 / Repair 修理 2	2
Man No. 工人號碼	1164
Work Order No. 工單號碼	12346
Institution 機關	4-1-12
Expense a/c 開支賬	1-12-6234
Type of Work 工作種類	1-12-523
Time started 上工時刻	700A.M.
Time stopped 下工時刻	1200A.M.
Elapsed time 共工作時刻	5.—
Name 姓名	黃恭儀
Com. 完工 1 / Incom. 未完工 2	
Rate 工資	2.44
Amount 數目	12.20
Description of work 工作說明	計算統計機

日期（月 日 年）	新製或修理	工人號碼	工單號碼	機關	開支賬	工作種類	工作時間（小時 分鐘）	完工或未完工	工資率（元 角分）	數目（元 角分）
Date 35–39	40	41–45	WorkOrder 46–50	Institu. 51–54	55–61	62–67	Hours 68–71	C 72	Rate 73–75	Amount 76–80

例如一年有十二月，兩行已足登記任何月份，又每月至多三十一日，故對於日期亦祇需二行。上圖所記者，係一九三六年十月十五日，故卡片上所打之孔，月組內打一〇，日組內打一五，年組內打六，即行，蓋示簡捷也。工人黃恭儀，其號碼爲一一六四，工單號碼爲一二三四六，機關爲交通大學，（假定號碼爲四，蓋示鐵道部屬下之第四機關，）管理學院，（假定號碼爲一，蓋示交通大學屬下之第一機關，）統計室，（假定號碼爲十二，蓋示管理學院屬下之十二機關。）開支賬號碼爲一——一二——六二三四，蓋示管理學院統計室統計機修理費賬。工作種類一——一二——五二三蓋示管理學院統計室第

五百二十三號統計計算機。工作時間五小時另分。尙未完工，以(二)爲記。工資率每小時法幣二元四角四分，總計十二元二角。以上各種資料，一律編爲數字，因此無論用文字叙述，或數字表達者，均可用打孔法登入卡片。法極簡易，茲再例證如下：査凡用文字叙述之人名地名物名，其登記之法有二：(一)可先將一切資料編成號碼，再打於卡片上。編製號碼之方法，例如中國以(一)表之，江蘇省以(二)表之，南京以(三)表之，餘類推。人事亦能以同樣之方法表出，例如男爲(一)，女爲(二)，完工爲(一)，尙未完工爲(二)。財政事務或以一至一〇〇爲開支賬號碼。工資賬爲一〇。辦公堂開支賬爲二〇。印刷賬爲三〇。修理賬爲四〇。生財賬爲五〇等。無論何種資料，皆能依法編成一簡單之數字。(二)用英文複用打孔機，將資料打成英文字母，或數目字則無須編成號碼矣。凡統計及計算工作，通常須分三步，卽登記·分類·製表，現應用電機計算機，亦有此三種步驟，除登記資料用打孔機外，尙有分類機及電機印數機，爲分類及製表之用，分類機能將已打孔之卡片，如意分類，電力印數機，能自動計算，並能以迅速及準確之機能，印出內容及答數，成爲表格，茲將其全部機械八種，分述於下：

(一)電動打孔機，(The Electric Key Punch) 此機備將來調查所得之統計資料，打孔于卡片上，製造精巧，使用靈便，通以電流，每分鐘可打孔二百至三百個。

(二)校對機(The Mechanical Key Punch)此機係用以校對已經打孔機打就之卡片，是否準確，其使用法，係將已打孔之卡片，置於此機上，復打一次。如原打卡片有錯誤時，此機卽不前進，故校對甚簡便。

(三)英文複用打孔機，(Alphabetic Duplicating and Printing Punch) 此機式樣如打字機，能將英文字母及數字打于卡片上，並有複印功用，每分鐘可複印多份。

(四)自動倍數機，(Automatic Multiplying Punch)，此機能自動做加法，減法及乘法，應用極爲簡便，能在卡片指定之地位，將和數差數及積數，自動打出，如以八位數乘八位數，祇需時五秒，每小時能計算七百餘張，若以三位數乘三位數，每小時能計算一千五百餘張。

(五)卡片計數及分類機，(Electric Cardoperated Counting Sorter) 此機對於計算及分析卡片，能同時進行，具有迅速之效能，每分鐘可分卡片四百張，每小時達二萬四千張，同時並將每類卡片張數，及全部卡片之總數記明。

（六）卡片選擇器，（Multiple Column Selection Device）此機附裝於卡片計數及分類機上，其功效能于一疊卡片中，選出某類特需號數，而不紊亂卡片原來之順序。

（七）計算印數機，（The Electric Tabulating and Accounting Machine） 此機係一複式加減分類及印數機器，能根據已打孔之卡片，自動印成一完全之報告，併能印出類別細目分項數與總數。其印數速率，每分鐘約自七十張至八十張，卡片若僅印和數或差數，每分鐘能計算一百五十張，而無錯誤。

（八）英文計算印數機，（Alphabetic Direct Subtraction Accounting Machine） 此機能加減分類及印數，又能在報告上印出英文字母，並能將地名數字混合印出。此項機械每分鐘能同時計算及印出卡片八十張，若僅印和數或差數，則每分鐘可達一百五十張。

以上各機均有電流運動，計算者只須按鈕，如法運用，便可一一印算。觀其登記及核對之簡便，分類之迅速，印製之繁瑣，表格之整齊無誤。實屬極有價值。據石工程師云：在東方僅此一具，江海關及協和醫院所有，均係雷明敦公司所出之舊式機，較此機效能，不啻天淵。該公司祇製機出租，而不出售，蓋以不特賣價甚鉅，且結構繁複。萬一損壞，非一般人所能修理，故決以租用方式，貢獻大衆云。

（一）「例證」

一九二八年秋，美國蜜欣根大學，舉行入學試驗，有千人參加。其體格檢查表中，列載體重、高度、肩膀、胸圍、腰身、臀部、腿周等項，當由中常材能之統計技術員，做打孔及統計工作，雖卡片有千張之多，而僅費三小時弱。其二七五號之考生喬治勃浪資歷如下，打孔結果附後：

體重	一二五磅
高度	六四吋
肩膀	一六・八吋
胸圍	三四・二吋
腰身	二六吋
臀部	三四・三吋
腿周	二〇・二吋

註冊號數爲工程三十二號

GEORGE S BROWN　ENG 32　0275　125　640　168　342　260　343　202

I.B.M. 5080　LICFNSED FOR USE UNDER PATENT 1,772,492

茲利用英文複用打孔機，將考生喬治勃浪之資歷打孔，並加印其簡單摘要，（此機尙可複印數份。）上章曾談及卡片有八十橫行，每行有打孔之位置十二，其中十位以數目字〇至九印出，其第十一十二兩位，位於卡片頂部，未用數目字印出，但在打英文字母時，卽利用此兩位，以資識別，英文字母之編目如下：

第一組	A 1	B 2	C 3	D 4	E 5	F 6	G 7	H 8	I 9
第二組	J 1	K 2	L 3	M 4	N 5	O 6	P 7	Q 8	R 9
第三組		S 2	T 3	U 4	V 5.	W 6	X 7	Y 8	Z 9

凡關於第一組之英文字母，在卡片上先將其號碼打孔，然後在該號碼頂部之第十一位內打孔；如關於第二組之英文字母，亦如法先將其號碼打孔，然後在該號碼頂部之第十二位內打孔；至於第三組之頂部，已無空位，故借用零位以供第二組英文字母號碼之組號。故喬治勃浪之考試證，（其註冊號數爲工程第三十二號。）打空情形，可見前圖，而體重身長等 係用數字表識，當然更無問題。打孔工作，既已完畢，如該校需研究各考生長度重量相關，(Correlation between height and Weight)，則可將卡片，置入自動倍數機，以一二五磅爲乘數，六四吋爲被乘數，則乘積在此機之一角發現，如此逐張置入，則乘積總和亦一併發現，如欲將各項乘積在各該卡片上打孔，亦無不可。此項工作，費時五十分鐘，一千張卡片之總和

$$\sum^{1000} xy = 9477433.6$$

如欲求 x^2 則被乘數同爲 x，結果即得 x^2 之值，求 y^2 方法，仍然。

$$\therefore \sum x^2 = 4615312.2$$

$$\therefore \sum z^2 = 1969245.2$$

至於 x^3 之求也，則用 x^2 爲乘數，X爲被乘數，其結果如樣求到，x^4 x^6 y^3 y^4 等類推。

如欲將各考生依號碼分類，則可置入卡片計數及分類機中，其結果，今摘錄其首部及尾部如下：

	重量	高度	肩膀	胸圍	腰身	臀部	腿周
1	134	00.1	10.0	00.0	00.0	00.0	10.0
2	121	67.4	16.4	34.2	26.5	38.7	19.0
3	158	67.7	17.7	36.5	30.6	38.2	22.8
4	134	69.2	16.6	35.0	26.6	34.5	19.6
5	138	69.8	16.5	35.5	28.7	34.6	19.5
6	143	71.2	16.2	35.6	27.2	36.0	20.0
7	166	68.3	17.1	39.7	32.5	38.3	22.2
8	135	68.2	16.7	36.5	28.0	34.4	19.6
9	145	69.1	17.6	37.2	30.0	36.1	20.2
10	115	64.5	15.7	32.8	24.8	33.0	18.0
991	125	65.8	15.8	36.0	25.3	34.2	19.2
992	149	68.4	16.0	34.0	28.4	36.4	21.1
993	138	66.4	16.2	35.2	28.1	35.4	19.0
994	149	69.8	16.8	35.5	28.5	37.0	21.2
995	128	63.0	17.6	36.5	28.0	34.5	20.5
996	133	69.5	16.7	32.7	26.7	35.3	19.1
997	130	66.7	16.8	33.0	27.8	34.5	20.0
998	142	71.8	16.6	34.3	27.5	37.0	20.1
999	141	68.0	17.4	37.0	30.0	36.0	21.2
1000	135	68.6	17.4	34.5	28.0	36.5	20.6
	139.288	67.8896	16.5337	35.3241	28.1510	35.5165	20.1096

在統計學求平均數，（算學平均，幾何平均，倒數平均，中數，衆數等五種，）離差，（均差，標準差，四分差，等三種，）及偏度者，莫不先編次數列項。編製次數列項，須先根據資料，當然資料愈多，其準確度愈高，或然律不致深入，可是一方面是利，一方面就是弊，因爲資料愈多，人力應付愈難，錯誤百出，（譬如編者對本文忽然生興，多寫幾頁，此中錯誤，一定很多。）現在不然，因有分析機，（Sorting Machine）可以分類辨別。如下表，係錄其一部分，根據重量爲次序者，（根據長度胸圍等爲次序者，均須做成。）

Card	Weight
232	89
146	100
691	101
358	102
555	102
941	102
209	103
801	103
14	104
513	105
720	105
563	106
672	106
153	107
75	108
235	108
322	108
505	108
31	109
393	109
30	110
160	110
185	110
631	110
802	110
15	111
151	111
273	111
447	111
20	112
426	112
507	112
716	112
831	112
308	113
383	113
449	113
541	113
591	113
826	113
898	118
933	113
947	113
967	113
148	114
177	114
257	114
368	114
462	114
464	114
545	114
741	114
951	114
987	114
10	115
139	115
159	115
336	115
743	115
949	115
970	115
988	115
52	116
186	116
226	116
268	116
347	116
510	116
523	116
926	116

根據上面次數列項，（frequency distribution）統計上之分析工作，因以成立，誠如前節所述之各種單位，都可依法泡製，當然長度次數列項，胸圍次數列項等，已先做成而後開始分析工作，茲將做成之十分差，淸錄如下：

重量十分差 (Weight Deciles)

差別	重量	長度	肩膀	胸圍	腰身	臀部	腿周
第一	112.98	65.133	15.576	32.607	25.748	32.968	18.133
第二	122.41	66.659	15.980	33.663	26.777	33.927	18.926
第三	127.85	67.087	16.161	34.421	26.978	34.387	19.206
第四	131.98	67.381	16.334	34.816	27.622	34.858	19.554
第五	135.62	67.937	16.406	34.860	27.954	35.081	19.893
第六	139.54	68.189	16.651	35.608	28.065	35.511	20.112
第七	143.87	68.576	16.789	35.766	28.513	36.006	20.438
第八	149.43	68.895	16.807	36.116	28.780	36.420	20.712
第九	156.01	69.185	17.022	36.788	29.537	37.181	21.444
第十	173.19	69.854	17.611	38.596	31.536	38.826	22.678

長度十分差 (Height Deciles)

差別	長度	重量	肩膀	胸圍	腰身	臀部	腿周
第一	63.339	123.95	16.036	34.201	27.371	34.217	19.592
第二	65.295	130.97	16.261	34.856	27.984	34.944	19.929
第三	66.367	133.75	16.282	34.787	27.731	35.152	19.926
第四	67.021	136.28	16.570	35.429	28.329	35.302	80.084
第五	67.623	139.81	16.587	35.379	28.206	35.499	208223
第六	68.189	140.60	16.532	35.510	28.109	35.560	20.008
第七	68.806	142.65	16.659	35.550	28.380	35.821	20.315
第八	69.498	143.44	16.638	35.328	28.065	35.858	20.205
第九	70.410	140.71	[illegible]	[illegible]	[illegible]	[illegible]	[illegible]
第十	72.346	155.72	16.996	36.423	29.024	36.852	20.746

上面舉例，已可一一顯示，充分利用機械功能，可見一蜚，統計工作之分析，發揮異常透澈，惜無多量時間，再畢以時間列項，作一例證，則或許可使讀者聊可滿意歟？

報告　參觀自動統計機後

(三)「研究」

近來全世界各國政府、各種工商機關，學術團體，對於統計工作，莫不異常注重，良以行政效率之高低，事業進展之盛衰，非統計無以探其趨勢，窺其全豹。蓋人事繁複，關係綜雜，統計藉數字之聯繫，察變求常，以往備來。例如各國政府之人口統計，財務機關之財政統計，金融銀行家之金融銀行統計，實業機關之勞工統計，產業統計，鐵路公司之鐵路統計，公路局之公路統計等，其記載之詳盡，分類之核要，可謂極盡確切，難能可貴，但調查雖甚詳悉，而計算豈可造次，蓋統計資料，千頭萬緒，非常人之腦力，得以記憶，此則電動計算機尚矣。此項機器，不論資料之如何複雜，能處置泰然，有條不紊，萬無錯誤，至若運行之迅速，工力之經濟，猶其餘事。其效率既已如此宏遠，自當廣為利用。而凡為鐵道管理者，財務管理者，公務管理者，實業管理者，更當確切認識，方可使其管理之事業，得以科學化。

我人研究鐵道管理者，財務管理者，公務管理者，實業管理者，固已知統計之重要。而我國之鐵道統計，財務統計等，亦且略已具備，但尙未至深刻分析時期，固不能諱言，甚望將來努力編製，則我國各種事業之統計，均可蔚成大觀。屆時，電動計算機，當早已具備，分析工作，決無困難。而各種統計科目之分類，則成爲亟務，玆乘便草錄數種，其編號異常隨意，個中鉅細，或有不當，乞讀者有以指正。

（甲）鐵道統計

此項統計，共分七大類，每大類以萬號爲記，萬號之下，有千號百號十號個號，個號之下，倘再有精確分類，則可加添小數。

一〇〇〇〇 業務統計
一〇〇〇 客運
一〇〇 人數
一〇 到達人數
二〇 通過人數
三〇 起運人數
四〇 普通旅客 （一）頭等（二）二等（三）三等（四）四等
五〇 特種旅客 （一）回數票（二）路員優待票（三）政府票（四）月季票（五）遊覽票（六）來回票（七）軍用票（八）團體票
二〇〇 進款
一〇 票款
二〇 特別快車加價
三〇 附加款
四〇 月台票
五〇 定座票
六〇 床位票
七〇 捐款
三〇〇 延人公里
一〇 起運延人公里
二〇 通過延人公里
三〇 到達延人公里
四〇〇 旅客列車公里
一〇 平均行程
二〇 平均進款
三〇 客運密度
四〇 每機車鐘點之旅客列車公里

五〇〇 坐位列車公里
一〇 平均行程
二〇 平均進款
三〇 密度
四〇 每機車鐘點之坐位列車公里
二〇〇〇 貨運
一〇〇 貨物貨品等級
一〇 鑛產品
二〇 農產品
三〇 林產品
四〇 獸產品
五〇 工藝品
六〇 政府用品
七〇 本路材料
八〇 他路材料
二〇〇 進款
一〇 整車運費
二〇 不整車運費

三〇 特別加捐
四〇 免費
三〇〇 延噸公里
一〇 起運延噸公里
二〇 通過延噸公里
三〇 到達延噸公里
四〇〇 貨物列車公里
一〇 平均行程
二〇 平均進款
三〇 密度
四〇 每機車鐘點之貨物列車公里
五〇 每列車里程之貨車噸公里
六〇 貨車在站停留輛數 (一)甲站(二)乙站(三)丙站
(四)丁站
七〇 貨車在站停留時間 (一)甲站(二)乙站
八〇 貨物運輸量 (一)重量(二)容量(三)速度
三〇〇〇 軍運
一〇〇 人數

一〇 到達人數
二〇 通過人數
三〇 起運人數
二〇〇 進款
一〇 收款
二〇 記賬
三〇〇 軍用品
一〇 軍需品
二〇 軍火
三〇 牲畜
四〇〇〇 郵運
一〇〇 郵件量
一〇 到達郵件
二〇 通過郵件
三〇 起運郵件
二〇〇 進款
一〇 收款
二〇 記賬

五〇〇〇 行李及包裹
一〇〇 行李
一〇 到達行李
二〇 通過行李
三〇 起運行李
二〇〇 包裹
一〇 到達包裹
二〇 通過包裹
三〇 起運包裹
三〇〇 進款
六〇〇〇 損失及賠償
一〇〇 損失
一〇 車務
二〇 機務
三〇 工務
四〇 其他
二〇〇 賠償
一〇 車務

二〇 機務
三〇 工務
四〇 其他
二〇〇〇〇 運務統計
一〇〇〇 列車
一〇〇 旅客列車
二〇〇 貨運列車
二〇〇〇 車輛
一〇〇 客車
一〇 頭等
二〇 二等
三〇 三等
四〇 四等
五〇 合造車
二〇〇 貨車
一〇 蓬車
二〇 邊車
三〇 平車
四〇 牲口軍
五〇 冰鮮車
六〇 油櫃車
七〇 漏斗車
三〇〇 臥車
一〇 萬國臥車
二〇 頭等臥車 （一）頭等坐臥車（二）頭等連廚房車
三〇 二等臥車
四〇〇 其他
一〇 公事車
二〇 花車
三〇 自備車
三〇〇〇 車場
四〇〇〇 貨棧
五〇〇〇 車站
六〇〇〇 行車事變
三〇〇〇〇 財務統計
一〇〇〇 資產

一〇〇　地畝
二〇〇　路線
三〇〇　設備品
四〇〇　有形資產
五〇〇　無形資產
六〇〇　營業資產
二〇〇〇　負債
一〇〇　借款
一〇　種類
二〇　性質內容　(一)性質(二)內容(三)期限
三〇　數類　(一)規定數(二)發出數(三)收回數
四〇　價格　(一)發行價格(二)實收價格(三)折扣(四)息金
五〇　償還
二〇〇　股款
一〇　種類　(一)優先股(二)普通股(三)官股(四)商股
二〇　性質內容　(一)性質(二)內容(三)轉讓(四)股東
三〇　數額　(一)規定數(二)發行數(三)收回數

四〇　價格　(一)發行價格(二)實收價格(三)紅利
三〇〇　營業負債
四〇〇　其他未來負債　(一)墊款(二)準備金(三)折舊(四)救濟金
五〇〇　累積盈餘
三〇〇〇　收入
一〇〇　客運收入
二〇〇　貨運收入
三〇〇　雜收　(一)利息(二)機廠贏利(三)租金(四)附屬營業(五)互用車輛
四〇〇〇　支出
一〇〇　總務費
二〇〇　車務費
三〇〇　運務費
四〇〇　設備品維持費
五〇〇　工務維持費
六析〇　雜支　(一)利息(二)租金(三)互用車輛
五〇〇〇　財務狀況

四〇〇〇〇 工務統計
一〇〇〇 普通修養工程
一〇〇 隧道
二〇〇 橋工
三〇〇 軌道
四〇〇 信號及軌閘
五〇〇 車站房屋
六〇〇 船塢港埠
二〇〇〇 特別增建工程
五〇〇〇〇 機務統計
一〇〇〇 機車種類
一〇〇 運客機車
二〇〇 運貨機車
三〇〇 倒車（Shunting）
四〇〇 蒸汽車
二〇〇〇 燃料
三〇〇〇 機車修理
六〇〇〇〇 材料統計
一〇〇〇 材料種類
二〇〇〇 材料產處
三〇〇〇 用料
四〇〇〇 購料
五〇〇〇 收發
六〇〇〇 購料
七〇〇〇〇 人事統計
一〇〇〇 職別和姓氏
一〇〇 總局
一〇 局長室
二〇 副局長室
三〇 秘書室
四〇 議事會
二〇〇 總務處
三〇〇 車務處
四〇〇 會計處
五〇〇 機務處
六〇〇 工務處

七〇〇　警務處
八〇〇　醫務處
二〇〇〇　工資
三〇〇〇　任免告假
一〇〇　任用
二〇〇　免職
三〇〇　事假
四〇〇　病假
四〇〇〇　其他

鐵道統計，編目工作，大概如前。由此卽可應用電動打孔機，將所得之統計資料，打孔于卡片上。卡片旣已打孔，於是置入校對機，驗其是否準確。其使用方法，係將已打孔之卡片，置然機上，復打一次，至此統計之登記工作卽告完畢，完成第一步手續。

鐵道統計資料，根據各路報告，所以此間所用之卡片，可利用各種顏色：

北寧　紅色卡片
津浦　橙色卡片
京滬　黃色卡片
滬杭甬　綠色卡片
平綏　青色卡片
正太　藍色卡片
平漢　紫色卡片
粵漢　白色卡片
隴海　粉紅卡片
膠濟　淡綠卡片
廣九　褐色卡片
南潯　灰色卡片
浙贛　淡青卡片
江南　茶綠卡片

各色卡片，旣已具備，則分類機得以利用，或以分別各路，則以顏色分類。或須混合各路，以求業務統計，運務統計等總數，則以號碼分類。故卡片計數及分類機，能同時貢獻其計算及分析工作，由此統計工作之第二步手續，得以完成。

如欲將所得資料，求一結束，則應用自動倍數機，用極簡便之手續，能在卡片指定之地位，將和數差數積數自動打出，如欲臨時選擇某片，則可利用卡片選擇器，將某類特需號數檢出，絕不紊亂原有順序。如欲製表，以完成報告，則利用計算印數機。此機能根據已打空之卡片，自動印成一完全之報告，并能印出類別細目分項數與總數，至此統計工作之第三步手續，得以完成。

（乙）財務統計

一切統計，凡涉及財務者，均得謂之財務統計。此項統計，種類繁多，本篇僅編銀行統計一種。以資借鏡，考銀行統計約可分為三大類，即資產科目，負債科目，損益科目，故本篇編號即以「一」「二」「三」三個數目代表之。

一、資產科目

一——一未收資本
一——二定期放款
一——三定期抵押放款
一——四活期抵押放款
一——五通知放款
一——六往來透支
一——七往來抵押透支
一——八貼現
一——九押匯
一——一〇存放本埠同業
一——一一本埠同業透支
一——一二存放外埠同業
一——一三外埠同業透支
一——一四存放國外同業
一——一五國外同業透支
一——一六買入匯款
一——一七買入國外匯款
一——一八期收匯款
一——一九代放款項
一——二〇暫記欠款
一——二一託收款項
一——二二催收款項
一——二三期收款項
一——二四買入期貨幣
一——二五買入期證券

一——二六有價證劵
一——二七生金銀
一——二八外國貨幣
一——二九各種貨幣
一——三〇營業用房地產
一——三一營業用器具
一——三二催收押品保管費
一——三三沒收押品
一——三四銀行公會基金
一——三五公共準備金
一——三六開辦費
一——三七存出保證金
一——三八應收未收利息
一——三九發行兌換劵準備金
一——四〇領用兌換劵準備金
一——四一債劵準備金
一——四二兌換劵製造費
一——四三運送中現金
一——四四現金

二、負債科目

二——一資本總額
二——二法定公積金
二——三特別公積金
二——四釐利準備金
二——五呆賬準備金
二——六房地產提存金
二——七器具提存金
二——八盈餘滾存
二——九股利
二——一〇未付股利
二——一一定期存款
二——一二往來存款
二——一三特別往來存款
二——一四通知存款
二——一五暫時存款
二——一六本票

二—一七儲蓄存款
二—一八信託存款
二—一九本埠同業存款
二—二〇透支本埠同業
二—二一外埠同業存款
二—二二透支外埠同業
二—二三國外同業存款
二—二四透支國外同業
二—二五保付支票
二—二六活支匯款
二—二七匯出匯款
二—二八應解匯款
二—二九期付匯款
二—三〇期付款項
二—三一賣出期貨幣
二—三二賣出期證券
二—三三代收款項
二—三四借入款

二—三五轉貼現
二—三六轉放款項
二—三七存入保證金
二—三八應付未付利息
二—三九行員儲蓄金
二—四〇行員酬勞金
二—四一行員卹養金
二—四二行員保險金
二—四三行員保險準備金
二—四四發行兌換券
二—四五領用兌換券
二—四六領用券自備準備金
二—四七領用券保證準備金
二—四八債券

三、損益科目

三—一利息
三—二貼現息
三—三匯水

三一四手續費
三一五保管費
三一六有價證劵損益
三一七兌換損益
三一八生金銀損益
三一九外國貨幣損益
三一一〇各種貨幣損益
三一一一貨棧損益
三一一二雜損益
三一一三攤提營業用房地產
三一一四攤提營業用器具
三一一五攤提開辦費
三一一六攤提兌換劵製造費
三一一七呆賬
三一一八營業開支
三一一九日用開支
三一二〇特別開支

銀行科目，大要如此，至於所編號目，似太粗陋，不過如有精細分析，仍可在各項下，再行劃分，亦非難事。其應用打孔方法，仍如前節所述。此類銀行統計，並非用於銀行本身，而係管理全國銀行者，統制全國銀行者所用。蓋管理家，統制家，在某種非常時期中，亟欲知全國存款有多少？匯款有多少？發行鈔票有多少？準備金有多少？資本有多少？如一經推敲，即可瞭如指掌。故此類統計，在國家立場上，占重要地位，所以編製此類統計，可用各色卡片。分別各種銀行，藉此可明責任，同時便利應用分類機，分析一切。報告等仍可利用計數印算機配製也。

（丙）公務統計

服役公務，首重效率，苟效率低劣，則百事不舉，弊竇叢生，內則自受其殃，外則貽人口實，故管理公務者，對於公務效能，必須有嚴密之統計。鄙意下列各種統計，在目前公務上，占最重要之地位（主計處出版之中華民國統計大概已如此）

（一）人口統計（附查各人職業及專長）
（二）糧食產銷統計（包括五穀及其他可供食物者）
（三）煤鐵煤油消費統計
（四）地形地產地質統計（附查各市鄉河道丘阜）

(五)衛生機關及醫藥產消統計

(六)犯人統計

(七)牲畜統計

(八)交通器具統計

(一)汽車(二)馬車(三)驢車(四)人力車(五)小車(六)雜色車輛(七)小火輪(八)汽油船(九)帆船(十)駱駝

凡屬上級公務機關，自應在自己所屬範圍內，羣策羣力，努力完成上述各類統計，則豈特四萬萬國民有厚望，中華前途，實深幸焉。

(丁)實業統計

實業包括範圍頗廣，在中國較顯明之實業，有紗廠、絲廠、麵粉廠、火柴廠、水泥廠、造船廠、煤礦、鐵礦、金礦、機車廠、煉鋼廠、冶鐵廠、漁市場等、此項實業機關，都由新式人物舉辦，故有系統之記錄，自必具備，對於下列各點，當然甚為注意：

(一)產量(包括品質類別)

(二)銷路

(三)成本

(四)人事(包括技術)

惟最可慮者，為我國之舊有事業如內地之絲茶米磁桐油等業，因一向沿用中國舊習，其於產銷成本人事素無精密統計，以資考核，以致因循敷衍，每況愈下，時至今日，事事落後，國際貿易之由順趨逆，其誰之過歟？蓋此項事業，中國富有資格和外人競爭，而自甘放棄，宜其受人苛責也。今日中國紗廠等之不振，由於天時，處茲全世界普遍化之不景氣時代，加諸其他不言而知之因素，其情狀窘迫，國人可以原諒也，

以上報告中，敘述一節，係參觀所得。例證由翻譯而來至於最後研究一段，乃編者拉雜而成，藉以表示統計學在各種管理之重要。而編製統計之工作，非常嚴密，非常繁重，尤非有迅速而準確之電動計算機不為功。是則治管理學者固不可不知統計學，而治統計學及辦理統計者。尤不可僅究學理，而忽視統計計算機之應用。

轉載

中央及地方預算法規之研究（交大季刊第二十期）

楊汝梅予戒

(一)中國新預算制度成立之根據

預算法規之制定，以預算制度爲根據。預算制度之內容，大別爲編製議決公布執行四項。其中編製議決兩項，尤關重要，往往隨政治之進化潮流，而有所變更。吾國現行預算制度，以編製預算之職責，屬諸國民政府主計處。將核定概算之權，提歸中央政治委員會，主計處依據中央核定之歲計概數，編成總預算案，呈請國民政府，交行政院，提出立法院核議。立法院議決後，呈請國民政府公布，由各主管機關分別執行。就此制度之內容，加以分析，與舊制度不同之要點有二：

(1)編製預算機關，以超然地位之國民政府主計處擔任。由財政部內，劃出此一部份職掌，俾財政上之其他一切重要職務，均得由財政部專責處理。

(2)中央政治委員會核定概算，與他國責任內閣之決定概算，性質相近，而地位略異。因中央政治委員會爲黨與政府之連鎖機關，其職權僅在發動政治根本方案，而執行政治方策之責，仍在國民政府也。立法院之議決預算，衡以從前國會之性質，亦微有不同。因五權憲法之立法院，仍爲治權機關，而非政權機關也。

上述新預算制度之成立，吾人權衡學理，揆度事實，認爲有下列之三種根據。甲、世界政治之潮流。乙、財政分權之趨向，丙、吾國政治之背景。

茲分述其理由於左：

甲、世界政治之潮流

預算爲政府表示歲入歲出之一種平衡計劃，而搆成一國歲入歲出之現象，又多以近代之政治潮流爲背景。故預算制度；恆隨一個時代之政治信條，而有所變更，古時由封建社會，變爲中央集權之國家時，因兵農分化，而國家歲出，以維持國家威力之常備軍費爲最巨。充此經費之一切歲入，均爲特權收入。此時代之財政，對於人民之全部經濟活動，均有干涉之權。財政不公開，一國之歲入歲出，由執掌政權者，自由支配：故在此時代，無所謂預算制度也。

預算制度，實由自由主義之政治學說所促成。自十八世紀後半以來，都市工商業逐漸發達，人民對於政治，發生覺悟。咸認爲國民之經濟活動，應絕對自由，不受政治上之干涉。而政府之財政，應絕對公開。當時有不出代議士則不納租稅之要求，政治革新以後，而議決預算，遂爲國會最重要職權之一。此一時代之政治信條，爲自由主義。彼盧梭之民約論，亞丹斯密之自由競爭說，皆可爲當時之代表學說。政府之財政政策，以不干涉人民經濟活動爲原則。國家之財政設施，與人民之經濟活動，截然劃分。一般人之政治思想，均認爲國家歲出，完全歸於消費，不生產任何財物。政府之政治設施，應限於極小範圍，以保護人民之生命財產安全，爲其主要職責。於是政府歲出，大受限制。政府歲入，以無害國民經濟爲原則。國家自身，不可經營產業。所有從前之官產官業，逐漸售讓於人民，而政府歲入，遂以租稅爲中心。此時代之政治範圍狹隘，財政事務簡單，故將籌集財源與分配用途之兩種職權，歸同一機關辦理，因而編製預算之職務，在各國內歸財政部掌理。

自由主義積極發展以後，社會一般之生產消費，均在無政府狀態之下，盲目進行。社會之財富，集中於少數資本家。多數人民之生計及政府財政，悉受少數資本家之操縱支配，而貧富不均，階級爭鬬，成爲社會莫大之隱憂。於是社會政策之財政學說，乃應時勢之需要，而自然產生。此種政策，頗有緩和社會革命之功效。然此派學說，偏重分配，忽略生產。主張以財政手段。調劑社會財物之分配。對於歲入，重取直接稅，輕取間接稅。於所得稅則舍比例稅而採累進稅。對於歲出，則主張削減其他政費，而擴充社會改良費，社會救濟費、由是社會事業費，在歲出預算內，驟占巨額，而其他政費，仍爲經費膨脹之趨勢所支配，無法緊縮。軍費及因列强競爭，而逐年增加，收入反因財源枯竭，而逐年短少。其結果，財政愈陷困窮，而產業衰弱，國民之生產力降低，社會之失業問題，益加嚴重。是偏重分配問題之財政政策，亦告失敗。於是統制經濟之財政理論，乃應時勢之需要，而自然產生。所謂統制經濟之財政，乃並重生產分配之政策，其表現於國家歲出預算者，除內政外交國防教育交通衛生救貧等支出外，屬於統制企業之投資經費，增加甚巨。其表現於歲入預算者，除普通租稅收入外，而各種公有事業之收入，漸占多數。國家財政，對於社會經濟有統制指導之責任。財政機關之職責，在政治上並占重要地位。不僅整理租稅，整理國債，及統制金融貨幣之關係，益較以前爲複雜。而對於各種生產事業之財政統制，亦有賴於財政部之擘畫。從整個政治觀察，財政地位，已立於其他政治之上。苟非將舊有大政治機構，酌予改造，則政治上職權之分配，無法平衡。於是財政分權之理論，因之產生。而原歸財政部掌理之預算職務，乃首先特設機關辦理。藉以平衡政治上之職權。法國於一九二五年創設預算部。義大利曾於財政部外，創設國庫部。美國自一九二一年六月以後，以編審預算之權，提歸大總統，由預算局專任其事務。吾國特設主計處，直隸於國民政府。凡此皆爲迎合世界之政治潮流，而產生之新財政制度。

乙、財政分權之趨向

前此吾國財政制度，有一共同之錯誤，即財政部兼有籌集財源，及分配用途之兩重責任是也。夫籌集財源，本爲財政部之專責，如整理租稅，整理公債，統一貨幣，統一金庫出納，調劑金融匯兌等職務，均應歸財政部專掌，不宜另設駢枝機關，分割財政部權限，致令辦事掣肘。籌集財源之權限統一，則容易獲得巨額收入，用以滿足人民公共之需要。至於分配財政用途，以達到政治上之目的爲標準。具有分配權者，含有左右政治之威力。須屬之政治上之最高機關，始能統籌全局，公平分配。在此私有財產權時代，財之力量，足以支配一切。一國之資本家，對於其他階級之經濟生活，隱具操縱支配之力。富有資力之銀行，恆能支配社會之產業，並進而操縱政府之財政。財政部掌理國庫出納，其職權在無形中已重於其他機關。若再兼分配用途之權，則一切政治 有爲此一機關操縱把持之危險。且一機關之能力有限，使擔任過多之事務，則不免顧此失彼，放棄其應負之職責。試觀我國過去之政治事實，財政當局，常因支配款項，引起各方面之責難，致財政當局，以全副精神，消耗於敷衍周旋之中，不暇爲整理財源之根本計劃。此非主管人員之咎，實制度不良之咎也。故近代財政之新趨向，多主張將籌集財源，及分配用途之兩種財政職權，分屬於兩種機關，各別執行，以盡政治上分工合作之妙用。現代各國政府之會計收支，均劃分爲命令系統。及出納系統之兩種程序，早已認爲一定不易之原則。準此推論，可知財政上分配用途與籌集財源之兩種主要職權：更不應併於一機關之內，混合辦理也。或謂英國預算制度之產生最早，英國預算，至今尙由財政部編製，似不必另設編製機關。然英國監視國庫金之權責，不屬於財政部，而屬於審計長官。（亦稱管庫審計長，代表國會，監督國庫金。）財政部欲支出國庫金，須先編概算，送經審計長官核定，通知英蘭銀行或愛蘭銀行後，始能支出國庫金。就此點觀察，英國財政部之職權，實不如他國財政部職權之完全。且英國財政部爲委員制，其第一委員係國務總理兼任，故其地位職權，與他國之財政部，差異甚多。英國財政部之職權，注重於財務監督，不注重於執行普通財務行政。財政部對於各部之會計事務，具有監督之權限，然各部長官皆爲政務官，以處理政務爲其專責，各部之會計事務，由各部之會計長負責辦理。而財政部對於各部之會計長有直接指揮監督之權。質言之，英國財政部之性質，實可稱爲主計部，與他國財政部之性質不同。吾人認爲財政分權，乃世界政治之新趨向，不能因英國之特殊情形，致疑於財政分權之不必要也。

(附註一)因英國之國庫金，在審計長官監視之下，財政部不能直接支出國庫金，故財政部不妨有編製預算之全權。

(附註二)日本帝國大學教授土方博士，對其本國之預算制度，亦有批評曰，「我國財政部(日本稱爲大藏省)爲各部中之一部，一面司租稅徵收及其他行政事務，同時立於各部之上，有查定各部預算之權。在統制經濟必要之今日，此種制度，是否適當，大是疑問。」

丙、吾國政治之背景

吾國現行五權政治，所有政治機關之組織，與三權政治之精神，根本差異。三權憲法，產生於自由主義之政治思想，其主旨在防止政府之專制，故偏重立法權。國會對於行政方面，有立法權，有彈劾權，其地位立於政府之上。五權憲法之主旨，在充實政府之權力，故將立法權，及監察權，均列入治權之內。在訓政時期，更應斟酌吾國實際政治情形，使治權內之五權，互相監視補助，以造成運用靈敏，集中國力之制度。吾國現行之新預算制度，實以五權政治之事實爲背景，而產生者也。預算爲政府公開財政之手段，同時爲國民監督財政之工具，預算議決公布後，須有强迫施行之力。此强迫力量，出自被動，政府不得隨意伸縮。彼政府自編自決，且可自由伸縮變更者，已失預算制度之本旨。國府以前，曾設財政監理委員會。嗣改爲預算委員會，又改爲財政委員會，此等委員會，雖均稱爲議決預算之機關，然皆無憲政之根據，其自身議決之數目，仍可以自身之決議，增減變更之，不合於預算之强迫性質。故十七十八十九各年度之預算，均未能成立。國民政府爲中國國民黨之政府，在訓政時期，以黨代表人民，是現在議決政府概算之權，應屬於黨，惟黨之力量，常隱藏於政府之背後，故特設中央政治委員會，使爲黨與政府之連鎖機關。黨與政府建國大計及其對內對外政策，有所發動，須經此連鎖，而建於政府。質言之，政治委員會，在發動政治根本方案，對黨負責。國民政府，在執行政治方案，對中央政治委員會負責。中央政治委員會之地位，立於國民政府之上，有似於各國之國會，而實非國會。故中政會議決之概算，仍交主計處再編預算案。送立法院議決，以完法治手續。就中政會議決概算之權限而論，有似於他國之責任內閣，而執行之權，仍在國民政府。故中央政治委員會議決之概算，須送由國民政府發交主計處，依法編製。國民政府主計處，於二十年三月，依據第三屆四中全會之決議案，因促成二十年度預算，而正式成立。主計處掌理關於預算之一切事務，直接對於國民政府委員會負責，間接對於中央政治委員會負責。國民政府總攬治權，爲行政立法司法考試監察五院之集合權，五院各自獨立行使治權之一、而不相統屬。主計處直隸於國民政府，以超然地位，依法編成預算案，再呈國府交行政院，提出立法院核議此種新制，於各方面職權，均無抵觸，實最合五權政治之精神，在訓政時期，似無其他制度，較此更爲適宜也。

或因修正國民政府組織法，規定國民政府主席，不負實際政治責任，遂致疑於主計處所編預算，亦爲不負責任之預算，此種議論，實未就現行政治組織之內容，細加研究也。蓋世界各國，不負責任之元首，其府內皆別無其他有責任之組織，如我國北京政府之大總統，法國之大總統，英日兩國之皇帝，皆爲不負責任之元首，其府內宮內，皆別無其他負責任之組織。若我國現在之國民政府，固明明於五院之上，設有國民政府委員會，以總攬治權也。（中央政治委員會，只有發動政治根本方案之權，其執行權，仍在國民政府。）五院各自獨立行使治權之一部分，必須有一國民政府委員會，立於其上，始完總攬治權之作用也。或謂所製預算，爲行政權最要之一部份，惟有身當行政之衝，完全了解各方面情形者，方勝此任。各國編製預算之權，多屬責任內閣，如英德日本等國是。或屬責任總統，如美國是，吾國之國民政府主席，爲不負責任之元首，編製預算機關，不宜直屬於主席之下。然此說不能認爲圓滿，試就下列之各政治組織，比較而分析之，卽可證明此說之錯誤矣。

甲、三權政治組織。在三權政治之國家，如爲責任內閣，其上僅有不負責任之元首，則內閣卽爲總攬政治，全權之機關，故以編製預算之權，屬之責任內閣，由財政部專任其事務，如英日兩國之例。如爲責任總統，則總統卽爲總攬政治全權之機關，故以編製預算之權，屬諸總統，而特設預算局，專任其事務，如美國之例。

乙、五權政治組織。吾國現行五權憲法，五院各自獨立行使其治權之一，而不相統屬。五院均立於平等地位，以編製預算之權，屬之任何一院，均不相宜，財政部係屬行政院內之一部份，非組織國民政府之一權。若仍如三權政治之例，由財政部編製總預算，則顯與五權政治之精神抵觸。今依國民政府組織法第九條，設一超然地位之主計處，俾任編製預算之事務。此機關直接秉承國府之命令，間接遵照中政會之決議，從辦理程序上觀察，亦極便利，實爲施行五權憲法之當然結果也。

現行國民政府組織，五院之上，明明有一總攬治權之機關。故負有國防重大責任之機關，如軍事委員會，參謀本部，訓練總監部，軍事參議院等機關，均依此理由，直屬於國民政府，而軍事委員會，在現時政治上所負責任，與行政院相等。夫以如此重大責任之機關，尙可直屬於國民政府。今將編製預算機關之主計處，直屬於國府，似更無懷疑之餘地也。

以上三點，爲新預算制度成立之根據，亦卽各種預算法規之根據也。

（二）辦理預算必須依據之各種法令

政府財政之處理，始終不能脫離預算範圍，在會計年度開始以前。須先制定預算公佈，以爲歲入歲出之基礎。然成立預算，須經過法定手續，左列之法規，皆爲應此需要，而制定者必須大加改造，始符新法之精神。攷會計法之內容，對於簿記事務之設計處理，規定異常精密完備，在吾國會計法規內，可謂特創一新紀元。惟實係狹義之會計法，至關於廣義會計之預算決算及財務收支程序，均須另定專法，同時頒佈，始易貫徹施行。現在關於執行預算之補充法規，有暫行決算章程，及主計處對於決算附表塡法之補充說明，中央各機關經營收支款項由國庫統一處理辦法，二十二年度以前未能依限辦結之收支處理辦法，結束二十二年度收支辦法，二十三年度國庫收支結束辦法，銓釋動支第二預備費限制及追加預算限制令（以上各法令均載在歲計法令彙編內）等法令，預備制定之法律，有庫藏法，決算法，及財物經理法等，預算法自較預算章程爲完備惟現因政治上之窒礙，尚須再行酌予修訂，始易實行。

關於預算之監督，須有完善之審計法令，而超然主計制度之實行，亦於監督預算執行，大有補助。

現時關於此類法令之已行者，有審計法，審計法施行細則，支出單據證明規則，修正國內出差旅費規則，修正監督地方財政暫行辦法，公務員交代條例及關於推行主計制度之各種法令。（以上各法令均載在歲計法令彙編內）

也。

甲、現行法規

1.預算章程

2.辦理預算收支分類標準

3.預算科目細則預算書表格式及說明

4.營業機關預算科目及編製概算書實例

乙、預備施行之法規

1.預算法

2.財政收支系統法

由預算章程，改爲預算法，其差異之點頗多，主計處歲計局編有「預算章程與預算法所定辦理國家地方預概算各要點之表解」極便查對，載在歲計年鑑第二輯第六章、及二十四年度國家總預算內。

關於預算之執行，除依據預算法規外，尚須依據各種會計法規。在新會計法未成立以前，民三會計法，亦暫准援用，而財政部會計則例，及主計處所定「中央各機關及所屬編製收支報告暫行辦法」，均可爲過渡時期收支程序之準繩。自會計法公佈以後，而前此頒行之「中央各機關及所屬統一會計制度」

預備制定者；爲審計法一種。

關於公有營業預算之編製及執行，對於上列各種法令，大多不合實用。現在中央政治委員會，已另定公有營業預算暫行標準立法院亦正另定，關於營業預算之法規。

(三)辦理預算之程序

辦理預算程序，分編製，議決，公布，執行四層。茲先摘述吾國現行之程序如左：

甲、中央預算之辦理程序

中央各機關所編本機關(包括附屬機關)歲入歲出概算，爲第一級概算，(即單位機關之概算)限十一月三十日前。(即年度開始七個月以前)送達各該主管機關。各主管機關彙編之分類概算，稱爲第二級概算，限一月十五日以前送達國民政府主計處。主計處彙編總概算書，稱爲第三級概算，限三月十五日以前呈經國民政府核轉中央政治委員會。現因每年歲出概算總額均超過歲入概算總額，故主計處每年均附陳補救意見書，條列收支適合之辦法，以待中政會決定施行。中政會核定總概算於四月十五日以前，送由國民政府發交主計處，主計處編成總

預算案，於五月十五日以前，呈國府交由行政院提出立法院核議。立法院於六月十五日以前，將總預算議決呈請國民政府公布。

以上係預算能如期成立之辦法，如年度開始而預算尚未成立，則另定有救濟辦法兩項。

1.得主管機關擬定概數，送由主計處簽註意見，呈國府轉送中政會核定施行。

2.如有特殊應急之經費，得由五院之主管院長提請中政會議決先行動支，再行補辦概算手續。

預算成立以後，亦有幾種例外辦法。1.本於法令或契約所必不可免之經費，致預算發生不足時，得提出追加預算。但須自籌財源或商請財政部籌定財源，始能提出。2.因特殊事故致收入短少，不能適應原定歲出預算時，由國府提出補救方法，送中政會核定施行。3.因特殊應急之設施或處置，由五院主管院長之提請，經中政會議決，得先爲預算外之支出，事後再請立法院追認。4.因政策變更，得縮減一部份歲出。

國府建都南京以來，政治組織，時有變動，由十六年至十九年，均未能成立正式預算。二十年四月主計處成立後，始有

二十年度國家總預算，二十二年度十三類假預算，及二十三年度二十四年度國家總預算，公布施行。營業概算，亦經主計處編送中政會，惟始終未奉核准，嗣後尚須另定營業預算標準，以資依據。

乙、地方預算之辦理程序

依照新定財政收支系統法之規定，地方預算之範圍，可至縣爲止。但依現行法令，尚只有省市預算之規定。省市各單位機關，編造各該機關之概算書，爲第一級概算。限十一月三十日以前送達各該省財政廳或市財政局。各省財政廳或市財政局，彙編各該省市歲入歲出概算案，限一月十五日以前，送達各該省市政府。各省市政府，依據全年行政計劃，及收支適合原則，議定各該省市概算案，限一月三十一日以前，發還財政廳或財政局。歲出概算總額，如超過歲入概算總額，應由省市政府議定補救辦法，呈請中央核准。各省財政廳或市財政局，編成各該省市總概算書，即第二級概算，限二月十五日以前，連同行政計劃，繕具五份，以一份送行政院，一份送財政部，以三份連同一級概算書，送國民政府主計處。行政院審查各該省市行政計劃，及第二級概算，作成意見書，於三月十五日以前，轉送主計處，主計處審核各省市總概算書，簽註意見，限三月三十一日以前，連同行政院審查意見書，呈國府轉送中政會。中央政治委員會，核定總概算書，於四月三十日以前，送由國府發交主計處。主計處編成各該省市總預算案，限五月十五日以前，呈國府交由行政院，提出立法院核議。立法院議決後，於六月十五日以前，請國民政府公布。主計處應彙編全國地方總預算書，呈報國民政府。地方預算不能如期成立時，由各該省市政府，參照最近年度預算及本年度財力，議定暫行救濟辦法呈報中央備案施行。

預算成立以後，亦有幾種例外辦法。1.本於法令契約必不可免之經費得爲追加預算。2.因特殊應急之設施，得以省市政府命令，爲預算外之支出。3.因特殊事故或政策變更，得縮減一部份歲出。如不能縮減歲出，而另定加稅募債等彌補辦法，須呈經中央核定施行。

近年以來，各省市政府財政，已逐漸整理，依中央規定之法令範圍，擬定收支適合計劃，而成立正式預算者，已居多數。惟目前呈送中央正式核定之預算，只及於省及行政院直轄各市。將來逐漸推行總預算，及普通市預算，始可將整個之地方財政收支實況，完全表現。

丙、執行預算之程序

政府歲入歲出，根據預算執行，須有法令以規定其收支程序；俾繁複之收支事務，得依一定程序進行，始能互相輔助，以增加行政效率，互相監視，以減少舞弊機會。在金庫統一之國家，能將命令系統與出納系統，截然劃分，故出納人員舞弊之機會較少。吾國現因金庫尚未統一，承轉收支較多，故收支程序，極為繁雜。茲列圖解如左：

第一圖

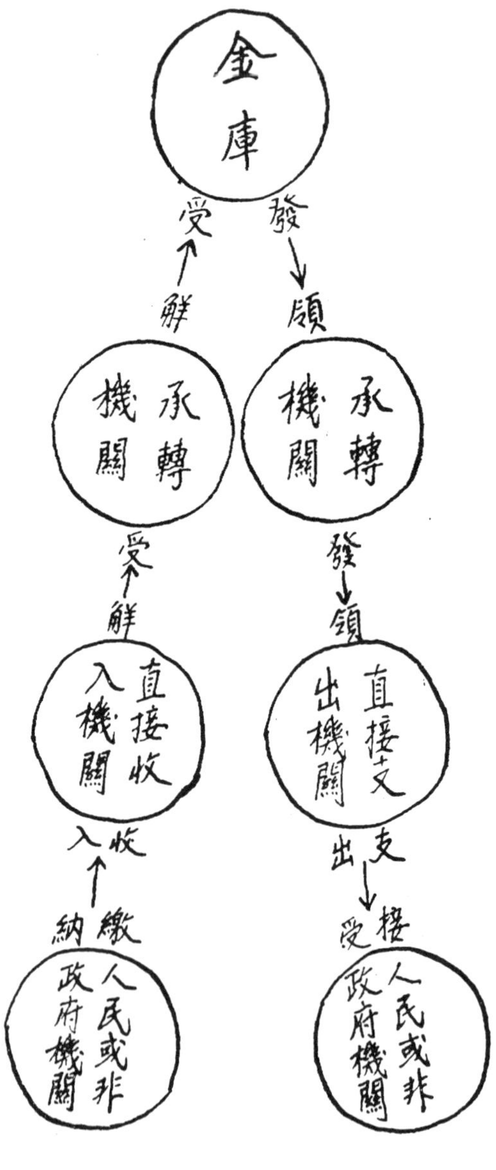

金庫
發領　受解
承轉機關　承轉機關
發領　受解
直接支出機關　直接收入機關
支出　收入
接受　繳納
人民或非政府機關　人民或非政府機關

觀察此圖，可知收入機關，自人民或非政府機關，直接收到現款，須與收入預算對照。支出機關，直接支出款項，使政府所有金錢，離開政府機關，（變為人民或非政府機關所有）須與支出預算對照。此兩類計算，均屬預算會計之範圍。

由收入機關：將所收款項，解到承轉機關，而承轉機關，又以所受款項，解送金庫。所有金庫之受款發款，承轉機關之領款發款，以及支出機關之領款等程序，均不過政府內部各機關之金錢移轉而已。其受入也，並未增加政府之財產，不得稱爲財源增加，其付出也，並未減輕政府預算上之負擔。此類計算，悉屬現金會計之範圍。故政府會計之要素，可大別爲金錢會計及預算會計兩類，官廳收支計算之唯一對象，爲金錢出納，而統制金錢出納之關鍵，即爲預算。國家普通預算之目的，以財政的統制爲主，故其預算上之收支，止於貨幣數目的表示，換言之，即金錢數目的表示也。

金庫統一之國家，其金錢移轉之責任，集中於金庫，至於承轉機關，移轉巨額款項，乃金庫尚未統一之特殊現象，政府全部之銀錢出納，以集中於金庫爲原則，但吾國各機關所收現款，不必定解金庫，多依撥付坐支等方式，在中途付出。各機關領受之款項，不必盡付於人民，或非政府機關，亦有在中途輾轉解還金庫者。

吾國政府會計之收支程序，規定較爲詳明者，有「中央各機關經管收支款項由國庫統一辦法」及「財政部會計則例」兩種法規。提要言之，其入款的方式有三，即直接收入及受款領款。其出款的方式亦有三，即直接支出及解款發款是也。同一解款，有現金解納及抵解之分。同一發款，有直放及坐支撥付之分。吾國現行法令，類皆詳定承轉收支程序，於直接收支之應如何使之互相牽制，杜絕弊端，大多不甚注意。惟海關之收支程序，較爲完善，惜乎只按多年之習慣辦法處理，並未以正式法令，將其辦理程序，規定公布也。

再列兩圖，表示金庫統一後之收支程序如左：

在金庫統一之國家，凡收稅先由徵收命令官，彙發三聯式納稅告知書於完稅人，由完稅人持赴金庫完納。金庫將此書第一聯截下記帳，將第二聯作爲收據，填給完稅人，第三聯作爲報告，送交徵收命令官記賬。凡支出先由支付命令官，查照預算，填發二聯式支付命令，留一聯存根，以一聯通知金庫，以一聯交領款人。金庫據此支付命令，發款並記賬。金庫有支庫分庫總庫。支庫每日報告分庫，分庫每日報告總庫，總庫每日報告國庫。故國庫不必直接收支現金，而全國現金出納之數，悉可於國庫帳簿上表現之。徵收命令官及支付命令官，爲命令系統之會計機關，金庫爲出納系統之會計機關，而統制整個政

第二圖　表示每日之收支程序

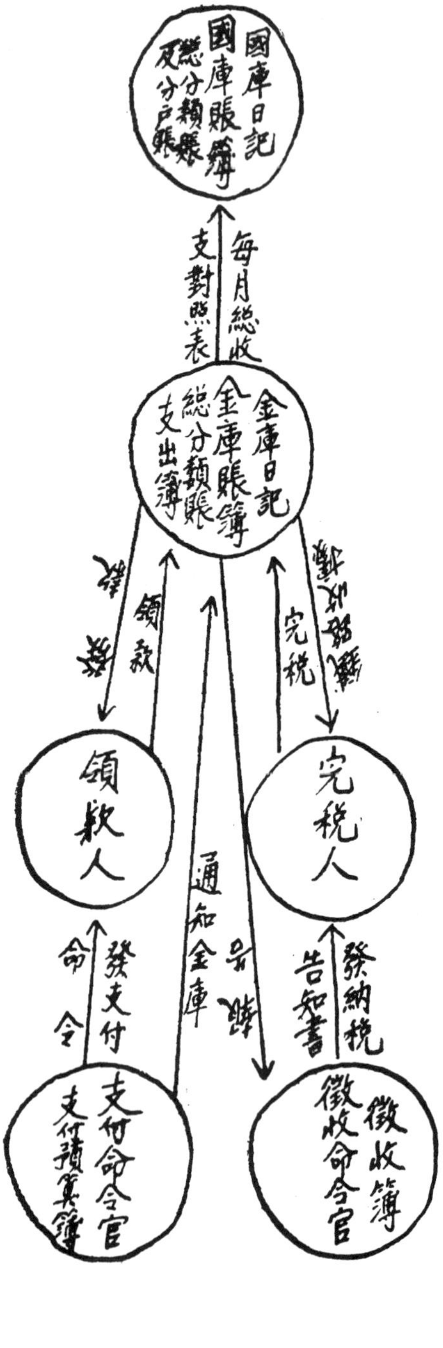

國庫日記
國庫賬簿
總分類賬
及分戶賬

每月總收支對照表

金庫日記
金庫賬簿
總分類賬
支出簿

領款

完稅

領款人

完稅人

通知金庫

發支付命令

發納稅告知書

支付命令官
支付預算簿

徵收命令官
徵收簿

府之現金會計者，厥爲國庫。

照上述程序辦理，全國各機關之現金收支實況，可依國庫賬簿，隨時編製報告公布之。

就上圖觀察，徵收命令官之徵收簿，照歲入預算科目，分戶登記。每月終了後，結算其徵收帳，編成徵收報告書，送呈其上級之主管機關。各主管機關，查照預算科目，登入歲入帳，再行彙編總報告書，送交綜理歲計事務之機關，歲計機關，查照歲入預算，分項登入歲入決算帳。支付命令官之支付預算帳，照歲出預算科目，分戶登記。每月終了後，根據帳簿，編成支出報告書，送呈其上級之歲出主管機關。主管機關登入歲出帳，再行彙編支出總報告，送交歲計機關。歲計機關，查照歲出預算分項登入歲出決算帳。（附註在五權憲法之政治，綜理政府之歲計事務者，係屬財政部之會計司。在五權憲法之政治，應爲國府主計處之歲計局。）歲計機關，於年度終結後，

第三圖　表示每月之收支程序

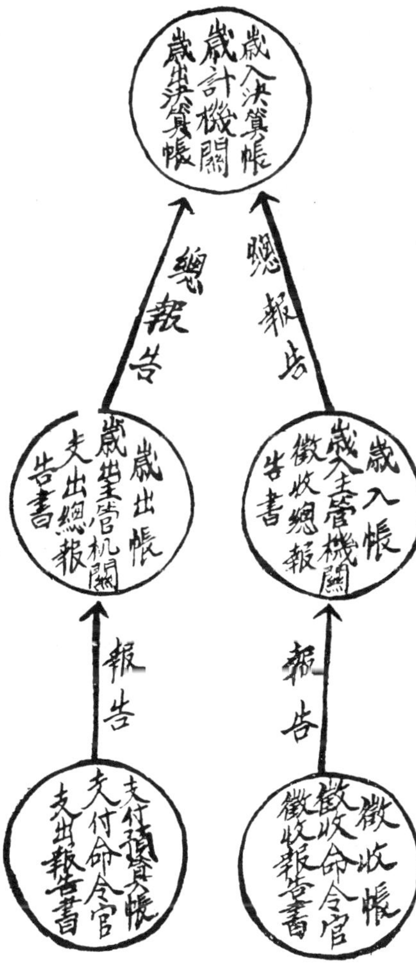

歲入決算帳
歲計機關
歲出決算帳

總報告　總報告

歲入帳
歲入主管機關
徵收總報告書

歲出帳
歲出主管機關
支出總報告書

報告　報告

徵收帳
徵收命令官
徵收報告書

支付預算帳
支付命令官
支出報告書

根據決算帳，編製歲入歲出決算報告書及歲計總平衡表。

照上述程序辦理，政府之歲計報告，（卽歲入歲出總決算），可於會計年度終了後，經過整理手續，從帳簿自然產生。現在主計處歲計局，已設有歲入歲出決算帳及其他補助帳簿，卽係爲編製歲計總報告而設也。會計局另設有政府總會計之全套帳簿其主要目的，係爲編製總平準表（會計法改稱平衡表）而設，與歲計報告有互相輔助之功用。惟歲計報告，（卽歲入歲出總決算）按照決算章程，由主計處呈請國府發交審計部審定後，尙須再由主計處呈請國民政府公布。其主旨在表示執行預算之結果，是爲政府對於國民全體之報告。故法定手續，較爲鄭重。會計總報告，由主計處會計局之帳簿產生。而會計局帳簿，以各機關每旬造送之甲種收支報告及乙種收支報告爲根據。此兩種報告之收支數目，均係各機關每旬內實收實支之現金數目，故會計報告之內容，與歲計報告迥不相同。會計報告，係屬政府內部之總報告，只須撮要公告，無須再送審計部審定，亦無須完全公布也。

中華國有鐵路現行行車時刻表

北甯綫

中華民國二十五年一月一日重訂

41次 普通客車 中膳各等	71次 平津客貨 二等慢車	3次 特別快車 膳車各等	23次 快車 膳車各等	301次 平滬特快 膳臥各等	5次 平津特快 膳車各等	305次 平浦特快 膳臥各等	401次 平津客貨 平滬通貨	1次 平瀋特快 膳臥各等	73次 三等慢車 唐津客貨	75次 三等慢車 唐榆貨客	43次 快車 唐榆各等	下行列車	站別	上行列車	2次 瀋平特快 膳臥各等	302次 滬平特快 膳臥各等	6次 津平客貨 膳車各等	72次 津平特快 三等慢車	42次 普通客車 中膳各等	4次 特別快車 膳車各等	24次 快車 膳車各等	402次 津平客貨 滬平通貨	306次 浦平特快 膳臥各等	74次 三等慢車 唐津客貨	76次 三等慢車 榆唐客貨	44次 快車 榆唐各等
5.45	7.10	9.30	13.00	15.35	17.10	20.00	20.10	21.15				開	北平前門	到	9.25	10.00	11.38	16.35	17.40	18.25	22.30	23.40	23.15			
6.04	7.56		13.16				20.54					開	永定門	開				16.03	17.23		22.15	23.13				
6.20	9.01	10.00	13.30	16.00		2.26	22.10	21.40				開	豐台	開	9.02	9.36		15.15	17.05	18.03	22.02	22.17	22.50			
6.44	10.24		13.48					21.58				開	黃村	開	8.43			13.53	16.37							
7.39	12.59		14.37			21.20	0.50	22.38				開	郎坊	開	8.05			11.42	15.41		22.54	19.15	21.51			
8.03	13.48		14.53				1.26	22.55				開	落垡	開	7.43			10.28	15.20			18.31				
8.36	15.35		15.20				2.24	23.16				開	楊村	開	7.21			9.01	14.50		20.19	17.30				
9.14	17.28	11.44	15.47	17.51	19.10	22.24	3.43	23.42				開	天津總站	開	6.56	7.45	9.40	7.08	14.14	16.10	19.55	16.22	20.54			
9.23	17.45	11.52	15.55	18.00	19.18	22.32	4.00	23.50				到	天津東站	開	6.45	7.35	9.30	6.20	14.00	16.00	19.45	15.20	20.45	停		
9.35	停	12.05	16.05	18.20	停	23.00		24.00	6.35			開		到	6.30	7.05			13.46	15.48	19.32		20.15	11.45		
10.[illegible]		13.04	17.06	開往上海		開往浦口		1.01	8.44			開	塘沽	開	5.30	由上海開來			12.46	14.55	18.35		由浦口開來	10.10		
11.46		14.00	18.13					2.07	12.10			開	蘆台	開	4.26				11.41	14.00	17.26			7.39		
12.34			19.00					2.58	14.17			開	胥各莊	開	3.30				10.45		16.34			5.51		
12.57		14.55	19.13					3.12	14.40			到	唐山	開	3.15				10.30	13.05	16.20			4.50	停	
12.52		15.00	19.18					3.15	停	6.00	8.00	開		到	3.10				10.23	13.01	16.17				21.30	20.31
13.06		15.11	19.29					3.30		6.40	8.14	開	開平	開	2.55				10.10	12.51	16.07				21.08	20.20
13.39		15.35	19.54					4.03		7.55	8.44	開	古冶	開	2.30				9.44	12.34	15.50				20.08	19.55
14.29		16.07	20.28					4.53		10.06	9.37	開	灤縣	開	1.32				8.45	11.55	15.07				17.26	19.03
15.32		16.49	21.18					5.59		12.30	10.40	開	昌黎	開	0.31				7.40	11.14	14.22				14.33	18.00
15.56			21.37					6.24		13.18	11.03	開	留守營	開	0.01				7.12		13.59				13.20	17.33
16.16		77.22	21.55					6.47		14.24	11.24	開	北戴河	開	23.42				6.54	10.43	13.45				12.00	17.17
16.43		17.42	22.17					7.16		15.30	11.53	開	秦皇島	開	23.09				6.25	10.20	13.20				11.20	[illegible]
17.05		18.00	22.35					7.40		16.07	12.15	開	山海關	開	22.40				6.25	10.00	13.00				10.45	16.20
								8.20		停		到		到	22.00				6.00							
								16.40				開	遼甯總站	到	14.00											

通縣支路

81次	83次	85次	86次	下行	站名	上行	82次	84次	86次	88次
6.30	10.10	13.30	19.00	開	北平前門	到	8.30	12.50	16.28	21.50
6.37	10.18	13.38	19.08	到	東便門	開	8.24	12.42	16.12	21.42
6.40	10.20	13.40	19.10	開		到	8.21	12.40	16.10	21.40
6.57	10.39	13.59	19.29	到	雙橋	開	8.03	12.21	15.51	21.[illegible]1
6.59	10.41	14.01	19.31	開		到	8.01	12.19	15.49	21.19
7.12	11.55	14.1[illegible]	19.45	到	通縣南	開	7.48	12.05	15.35	21.05
7.14	11.03	14.23	19.53	開		到	7.46	11.57	15.27	20.57
7.2[illegible]	11.10	14.30	20.00	到	通縣東	開	7.40	11.50	15.20	20.50

北戴河海濱支路

89次	91次	93次	95次	下行	站名	上行	90次	92次	94次	96次
7.00	10.50	13.50	17.30	開	北戴河	開	6.40	10.30	13.30	17.10
7.20	11.10	14.10	17.50	到	北戴河海濱	到	6.20	10.10	13.10	16.50

通訊

膠濟路副站長工作概況及其職責

靜勇

……前承惠寄管理二月刊一冊。內容充實，洵爲國內研究管理學術之唯一刊物。茲託烈望兄轉奉訂閱費，請按期照寄。又卒業同學通訊一欄，立意甚佳，謹將生服務情形縷陳於后：

I.引言——年來膠濟路對於運輸業務方面，大有竿頭日上之概，而以貨運業務，進展尤速，論功行賞，其歸功於該路當局之蓄心改革者，固居泰半，第於站務方面之日見推進似亦不可沒也，吾儕提及站務一項，即聯想及於副站長之重要，何則蓋副站長乃係實際督察，指示，及操作一切站務事宜之主要人物故其地位稍較正站長爲次，但其性質之重要容較正站長爲尤甚，此作者將副站長命名本題者一也，再者再依過去情形而論，凡交大同學之派入外站充當副站長者不論該路，或係其他各路，爲數綦夥，但學校方面，所側重者，似以學理居多，故一且廁身路界，或感相當隔膜，爲明晰路方情形計，自非將路方情形，廣爲介紹不辦，此作者將副站長命名本題者又一也，關於副站長之工作概況，及其重要職責，作者雖云側重該路方面但於其他各路，仍有相似之點足供參攷，值此畢業同學於廁身路界之前，其於明晰路界情形，期待必殷，茲篇愧無多大供献尙祈識者隨加指正，以匡不逮焉。

II.工作概況及重要職責——該路副站長之工作概況，及其重要職責，簡言之，有如下述。

A.工作概況

(A)以服務性質而論，則大站副站長，數人分任總務，貨運及行車等各項業務，小站副站長則一人兼任上述三項業務，且須與正站長輪流值班，蓋前者組織規模既告複雜而各項業務，又極繁冗，故以數人分任各項業務，藉收分工合作之效，至若後者不論組織或係業務，均較前者爲遜故以一人兼任各項業務，藉資撙節人位，且增辦事效率。

（B）以服務時間而論，每因分任業務不同，與夫各站等級有別，故略感參差不齊，例如

（a）大站方面，（1）其隸屬總務方面者，除每日早晨七時起，至十二時止，下午二時起，至五時止，例須值班外，至若各次旅客及混合列車到開時，亦須親自到站監視及照料一切，（2）其隸屬貨運方面者依照該路規定，上午自八時起至十二時止，下午自二時起至五時止。（但實際上，每因彙齊當日貨運款項，以便轉繳正站長關係，故非俟至六七時不辦。）（3）其隸屬行車方面者，類都依照該路規定二十四小時工作二十四小時休息制，每人每日輪流值行各項行車事宜，（惟青島站因謀劑員工精神，及增進辦事效率，故改以十二小時工作十二小時休息制爲標準，同時以二人爲一班，該站共有二班，總計四人，值班時二人務須同時到站服務，）上列（1）（2）二項，並非值班性質，而須每人每日按時值班

（3）項則係值班性質。

（d）小站方面，副站長務須一律依照二十四小時工作，二十四小時休息制，會同正站長輪流值行總務，貨運，及行車等事宜。

（C）以服務人數而論，各站亦不完全一致，其屬諸一等站，而業務較忙者，例如青島、大港、坊子、張店、及濟南等站，則副站長人數約在六七人左右，其屬諸一等站，而業務較遜者，幹線如膠州、高密、濰縣、青州、周村、及黃台等站，支線如博山，及黌山等站，則係二人左右，此外小站之副站長人數，祇有一人而已。

（D）以服務地點而論，簡言之，大站副站長之服務或辦公地點，除總務方面，類都與正站長仝處一室外，他如貨運及行車方面，乃係分處辦公，但小站副站長，則又一律與正站長同室辦公。

（E）以服務職權而論，不論大站或係小站，副站長除受該管車務分段長及正站長之節制外，其他在站服務有關員工，則靡不有指導督察，及糾正之權，例如總務以及行車（按卽值班站長或調車主任）方面之副站長，（此因不

克細分，故特一併申述之，）有權節制客票司事，行李司事，車號司事，站務司事，（以上係指員司而言），工頭，調車工頭，調車夫，轉轍夫，鈎夫，及站夫等，（以上係指工役而言），貨運方面之副站長，（按卽貨物主任，或貨物副站長）， 則有權節制內外部領班，計算司事，寫票司事，收款司事，收票司事統計司事，庶務，過磅（大磅及小磅）司事，裝車司事，卸車司事，倉庫交付司事，押貨司事，（以上係指員司而言）裝車夫，封車夫，過磅工役，倉庫交付工役，縫工，及貨房值班工役（以上係指工役而言）等是也。

上列各項，其值得注意者，卽目前青島站副站長中，乃有一人借調該路消費合作社辦事，但與站務方面，並無絲毫關係，故茲篇並不論列之。

B.重要職責，關於該路副站長之重要職責，大致可分爲總務，貨運及行車等，上列各項職責，尤以大站方面劃分較見詳明，小站方面， 則每因一人兼任關係故不克詳爲分明，再者小站副站長之職責， 初與正站長完全相同， 茲爲閱讀便利計，特將該路副站長之各項重要職責由大站立場上，分別臚述如次：

A）關於總務方面者，不外。

（a）注意站內清潔及督察服務情形

（a）注意站內清潔：副站長對於站內清潔與否，平時負有注意之責，如發現站內任何一部，不甚清潔時，則立卽命令站夫抹擦，洗刷，或掃除之，其詳細辦法，有如下述：

（1）車站方面，又分下述三端：

（一）辦公室候車室月台（或站台）及廁所等，其間各項清潔辦法，亦不完全一致，例如辦公室及候車室方面，則該路規定：（一）辦公室應於每日清晨及正午，命令站夫掃除二次，候車室則於每次旅客或混合列車開往後，卽應督促站夫掃除一次，嗣後如發現不潔部份時，則隨時督促站夫掃除之。（二）他如屋內地板門窗玻璃及裝飾品等，務須命令站夫每星期洗刷一次，並隨時注意塵垢，是否完全拂拭或光亮整潔等，（三）房屋內外牆壁，應禁止任何人用粉筆及鉛筆塗寫，或用木柴瓦片亂塗，籍保整潔，(四)桌椅及其他應用物品，務須注意是否潔淨，(五)凡辦公室內各項規章，通告，電報，及單據等，一律設法裝訂成冊，並不得拉雜凌亂，此外關於月台，(或站台)方面，則其清潔辦法，乃與上述，(一)款內候車室所列者，完全相同，特從略，最後關於廁所方面，則與上述，(一)，(二)二款之清潔辦法，大致相似，惟尚須命令站夫在每次清掃沖刷後，洒用避瘟藥水，以重公共衛生。

(二) 站內軌道其重要清潔辦法凡二，(一)凡站內軌道，如有亂紙瓜皮及其他穢物等，除由副站長指派站夫二人(此係低限度)，同時會同該路工務處指派工人，(按該路規定每日由工務處指派一人，幫同清潔事宜，但如不敷裕時，則得由副站長隨時呈請增派之)，隨時加以檢拾及掃除一空，(二)此外則嚴令站夫(或工人)將所有穢物，掃集一處以便傾入垃圾箱內，但不得掃至站台以下，以致污及軌道，有礙行車駛行。

(三)貨場關於注意貨場工役之清潔事宜，乃係貨物副站長之附帶職責，初與本節無關，茲不復贅。

(2)列車方面：該路規定列車停留站內，或尚未駛行前，則其清潔事項，乃由副站長負責注意之，如列車一經開行後，則由查票員督飭看車夫抹擦清潔之，簡言之該路列車之清潔辦法，其由副站長加以注意者，不外。

(一)洗刷例如注意車輛內外牆，三等車地板及窗門玻璃等，是否洗刷潔淨，並命令每星期舉行一次。

(二)掃除：(一)同時注意棄置地上之果皮，餅渣，煙頭，痰唾，以及頭二等車之地板地毯等，是否掃除潔淨，(二)並於每日每次旅客或混合列車出發前，由出發站副站長督飭站夫辦理云。

(b)督察服務情形，其重要者，計有下列各項。

(1)關於站內有關員工、(詳見上述)副站長隨時隨地負有督察及考勤之責。

(2)如員工在服務期內，發生任何疑竇，則副站長隨時予以相當解釋，以資開導。

(3)員工制服之是否穿着整齊初與觀瞻有關，副站長對此，似亦不容漠視。

(4)凡離差員工，不論時間之久暫，副站長爲增進服務效能計務須物色相當幹練人才，暫行庖代之。

(a)輔助正站長各項工作，正站長因平時公務極形繁冗故對於站內一切雜務，自不克一一顧及，此則副站長在可能範圍內，惟有量力輔助，以資分勞。例如

(b)處理站內公物，副站長對於站內公物，如傢俱，制服，帽章，書冊（又分規章帳目），公函，傳知(或通飭，)單據及報章等，以及其他一切應用物件等，率皆負有保管之責，並在可能範圍內，設法減少請領數量，藉以撙節公物。

(c)校閱站內文件及收發電報，凡站內次要文件，及收發電報，副站長得代爲校閱，但重要文件及收發電報，例由正站長自行校閱其因特殊原因，而由副站長代爲校閱者，則事後詳細情形，仍當稟明正站長知悉也。

(b)此外如關於接聽局用或商用電話，以及接洽其他一切事項等，亦得由副站長酌量情形辦理之。

(D)視察列車出發及到達事宜

(a)副站長在每次旅客或混合列車到開時，除親自到站照料一切外，其於旅客之上下，行李包件之裝卸，尤應特別注意。

(d)此外凡遇未明路章之旅客，副站長負有指導及解釋之責。

(c)在旅客或混合列車到開時凡站內發生任何事項，副站長當設法妥爲處理或解決之。

上列各項職責乃指副站長每日遇見及性質重要者而言，此外當有性質雖極重要，但非每日而係每月遇見一次者，即係下述一項。

(a)發放薪金查該路各站員工薪金，規定由副站長於每月十八日分發之。茲將其發薪辦法，以及應予注意

各點錄如下述。

（a）發薪辦法（1）先將會計處發下薪金之總數，詳加點驗再將每人應得薪金數目，重行分別點驗，然後將該薪金數目分別置入製就之「車務處發放薪工袋」內，以備分發全站員工。（2）員工領取薪金時咸以圖章爲憑，副站長將此圖章單之各員工名下，親自蓋章，以資存查。（3）凡員工如須預支藏金者，則事先由各該員工將其數目預爲呈請，以便於發放薪金時，再由副站長一併發給之，（4）關於車上員工之隨車飯費，則由車長領班協助副站長分發之，（5）如員工因公出差，或請假不克領取薪金者，則副站長俟其本人到差後，再行如數發還之。

（b）注意各點，副站長在薪金未發前，遇有不符短升，或僞造情事，副站長應立卽向會計處追索或更換，否則嗣後發生任何糾紛，其責任由副站長自行擔負之。（2）在發放站金時，每因人數過多，無法發放，，故副站長惟有按照到站先後依次，秉公發薪，又因人數過多，副站長對於各人面目，不克一一熟識，

此可察看其員工服務證，是否相符，以資對核，再者員工領取薪金時，副站長須命其點驗總數，是否相符，及有無損壞或僞造情事，否則一經出站或相隔多時則概不補發，或任意更換，此外爲愼重計，副站長對於員工代領薪金應極力設法避免，則嗣後一切轇轕事宜，自亦無形減除。

此外副站長平時極鮮遇見者尙有下述一項。

（f）處理旅客遺失物件，凡任何站上或車上員工，檢拾旅客遺落行李，包裹或任何物件後，副站長一方加以負責保管，再一方請示正站長，以便應用正站長名義，出示招領失主，一俟失主覓得相當妥保，到站領取該物時，再由副站長原璧歸還。

（e）附帶職責。

（a）副站長有正站長離差，但車務分收長尙未派遣替班站長庖代前則副站長負有暫行替代之責。

（b）外界有所問詢時，副站長須妥爲應付，不得任意開罪外界。

（c）平時對於一切路章，副站長應詳加研究，

以備員工之諮詢。

(B)關於貨運方面者，不外

(a)綜理及督察貨車出發及到達事宜

(a)出發計分

(1)託運，貨商在託運時，先由貨物副站長將託運司事呈交貨位憑單，加蓋印章，同時在商人領得貨位憑單，而將貨物搬入貨場前，卽行指定相當貨位，給予貨物入場許可證，迨貨物堆置預定貨位後，再行督察過磅司事過磅或過尺等事宜。

(2)裝運，貨物副站長在裝運貨物前後，除親加視察一過外，如發覺裝運貨物，並不遵章辦理時，則立卽命令裝車司事及夫役等，重加裝運，以重路運。

(b)到達再分

(1)到達，貨物副站長一俟貨車到達後，卽將貨車車長及押貨司事呈交負責貨運通知書，到達站存根，及其他有關單據等，負責保管，並依據負責貨運通知書所載件數，與到達貨車，互相對照如該

車車身各部完好無缺者，卽在貨車簽收簿上，加以簽收，否則呈報有關處所及出發站等，重加查核，日令貨車車長，在該簿上蓋章或簽字以資負責。

(2)卸車，貨物副站長除本人將車身各部，加以查核外，同時督促卸車司事，長工，或脚夫等，將貨物隨到隨卸，及小心裝卸等。

他如收票，計算及收款等，貨物副站長，僅負糾正（如有錯誤時）及解釋（如有疑竇時）之責，其關係似較前者爲次，故不詳加探討焉。

總之上述(a)(c)二項，貨物副站長應負綜理及督察之責。

(b)請求貨車

(a)在貨車未請得前，貨物副站長例須自本日十六點鐘起，至次日十六點鐘止，根據託運單所載各項，塡寫車輛請求單，交於調車房，以便轉向行車股請求車輛，再者如昨日請求車輛，雖已奉到撥給命令，但截至本日十六點鐘，尚未正式收到者，可一併請求之。

(b)如貨車已請得後，貨物副站長不外按照貨物先後，或緩急程度，與夫本諸公平原則，向客商均分車輛。

(c)保管及解繳款項

(a)先由收款司事，將貨房每日收到運費及雜費等，在每日六時前，解繳貨物副站長。

(b)再由貨物副站長逐一點驗，在款項未經解繳前，貨物副站長有妥加保管之責。

(c)迨六時左右，由貨物副站長，將此款項，繳解站長室，以便會同當日客運及其他進款，應用解款單，解繳會計處出納課，從事保管。

(a)處理各項貨運單據帳目及文件

(a)關於各項貨運單據或帳目等，事先由貨物司事，分別填寫後，再由貨物副站長重加糾正，如無錯誤而應呈交有關處課段站者，則以迅予辦理爲妥，如係存站，而非呈交性質者，尤須愼加保管。

(b)尚有其他各種公文文件，傳知，(或通飭)及規章等則係十九屬諸存站備查故貨物副站長在校閱後

亦應妥予保管。

(e)督飭處理，或保管貨車附屬品，可謂貨車附屬品云者，乃指蓬布繩索，意耳鑰平車支柱，馬栓棒，馬踏板，及車門柵等而言，該路對於此項貨車附屬品，除由貨物副站長兼行督飭處理或保管外，如係貨運業務忙繁，不克兼顧時，則每由外部領班庖代之。

(f)拍發及校閱各種貨運電報，查該路貨物副站長對於各種貨運電報，僅係側重校閱方面，至若拍發方面，則先由貨物副站長親自擬稿，或填寫，然後一併轉交調車房之調車主任，(或副站長)以便彙齊後，交由電報房拍發有關各方，再者該路各種貨運電報，其與貨物副站長拍發及校閱有關者，不外公務電報配車電報(此分臨時支配車輛通知電報，臨時請求車輛電報，車輛報告，及支配車輛電報等四種)以及商運電報等，(又分貨車載重逾量電報，請求覆磅貨車電報及遺失貨物或封誌移動及損壞電報等三種)，其中以公務及配車電報，遇見較夥，商運電報次之，惟前者因與行車方面亦有相當關係，故在嗣後申述之。至

若後者乃完全屬諸貨物副站長之職責，惟因該路遇見尚少，故不詳爲申述焉。

以上所列各項，均屬貨物副站長之重要職責，且十九係告每日發生，此外貨物副站長時常遇見，但非定期發生者，尚有下述三項。

(g)研究及調查各項貨運問題

(a)貨物副站長對於本站範圍以內或與本站有關之各項貨運問題，負有研究及調查之責，例如農場之收穫，礦產之產額，金融之變遷，物價之漲落，工商業之盛衰，水陸運輸之狀況，以及全站貨物之來源或銷路等，在在應根據過去經驗。參以固有學識，從事研究及調查工作，藉作改進貨運業務之張本。最近該路貨物副站長先後完成此項工作者凡二，一卽該路各站交通路線之調查，一卽貨物分等表之調查是也。

(b)凡其他主管段站，如須研究或調查時，亦得由貨物副站長儘量供給材料或詳加答覆。

(h)應付外界貨物副站長對於外界一切事項，自當妥善應付，例如託運規章之解釋也，客商控告或轇轕之處理也，賠償問題之解决也，以及其他各項貨運問題之處理也貨物副站長在在以妥善應付爲上策，以免開罪外界，再者尚有職責極感重要，但每月僅有一次發生者，卽係下述一項。

(i)分配貨房員工職務

(a)在分配員工職務前，務須注意各員工之工作能力，及其個人興趣，以期員工對於各項工作方面，均能勝任愉快。

(b)在分配員工職務時，務須平均分配，以免發生勞逸不均之弊徒增員工怨尤（關於該路貨物員工職務因已詳見上述，故不復贅）。

(c)在分配員工職務後，務須將其工作效能，隨時加以考核，並呈報有關各段站知照。

此外職責雖見重要，但貨物副站長平時絕鮮遇見者，則有下述一項。

(j)督飭處理貨場失火事宜

(a)貨物副站長如遇貨場失火時，除立卽督率所屬員工，會同路局或當地消防隊，迅予設法撲滅外。

(b)同時指揮調車夫將鄰近岔道內停放空重車輛，悉數移至安全地帶，以免發生意外。

(c)如火患完全撲滅後，即將起火原因，時刻，地點，路產有無波及，以及施救情形等，詳電有關之處段站知照。

(k)附帶職責：最後關於貨物副站長之施行人事管理也，(例如注意員工勤惰，避免舞弊情事，增進工作效能，聯絡員工情感，及維持清潔事項等)，稽核貨車延誤也，以及輔助員工工作也，要皆屬諸附帶職責，故本節亦不詳加探討焉。

(C)關於行車方面者，不外

(a)從事列車出發及到達工作

(a)出發工作：(1)副站長在列車出發前，應備口笛一只，紅綠號旗(晝間)或紅綠號燈(夜間)各一，時間表一只，(此於站上時鐘或大鐘失靈時應用之，)此外在迷霧、雨、雪、風、沙時、當須攜帶響墩數枚，以資應用(2)副站長在列車出發前，尙應注意站上有關員工，例如客票司事，行李司事，站務司事，(

專事剪票者) 轉轍夫，站夫，以及其他有關員工等，是否準時到站服務，他如車上人員，亦應詳詢車長，或查票員後，以便分別督促及懲處(3)列車出發前，副站長尙須親自向鄰站索取路牌，藉保行車安全，(關於索牌之詳細手續，詳見該路行車規章內，茲不復贅，)(4)副站長在旅客或混合列車出發前，再應將客車及守車號數出發日期，及車內附屬品或件數等，填入甲種車輛保管簽字簿內，(此簿與乙種車輛保管簽字均係分交各出發站，或編配列車站查收至若丙種車輛保管簽字簿則係交由警務處，轉發各編配列車站駐警查收) 以便會同該車鎖匙，及業已蓋章或簽字之保管單厚紙及簿紙一頁，移交車長保管及收執，此後該車即歸車長負責，而與副站長無涉矣。(5)無論何項車輛，其尾端非備有側尾燈牌，不得出發，但如有特殊情形發生，而側尾燈牌無法懸掛時，則副站長在該車尙未出發前得電知沿途有關各站，嚴加注意，(6)在旅客或混合列車出發前，每有旅客手持業已過期客票，赴站要求副站長簽字證明，如該票尙未超過七日時，則副站長立即准其所請，在該票面上，加以簽字證明，藉資繼續應用、(7)副站長在列車出發前務須檢視出發號誌一週。

以上所述種切，係指副站長在列車出發前之重要工作，及其應予注意各點而言，迨至列車規定出發時刻，副站長尙須從事下述各項工作。

(8)先命站夫將出發號誌顯示平安部位，(晝間號誌臂下落至少四十五度，夜間顯示綠色燈光)，(9)然後高張綠旗或綠燈，(此須穩舉頭上)同時口吹口笛一長聲，(此須與車長相互對證)，命令列車漸漸出發，(10)列車出發後，在尙未駛出最外轍夫前，副站長務須注意下述各端：(一)副站長本人所舉示之綠旗或綠燈除臨時發生意外情事，必須更換外，否則務須繼續表示，不得撤回，(二)副站長所舉示之號誌，應令車長司機及火夫等，時時迴顧，(三)此外除有相當防護外，副站長應嚴禁調車夫，在妨礙正道之岔道施行一切調車工作，(11)一俟列車駛出最外轍尖後，始克將手付號誌取消，同時一俟列車之最後車輛，超過出發號誌時，則副站長方克命令站夫將出發號誌恢復險阻部位(晝間號誌臂顯示平行部位，夜間號誌燈顯示紅色燈光，)(12)然後返至值班站長室內，按動路牌上之右方押鈕，向鄰站發放電鈴一響，表示該列車業已開入區間，(此須聽鄰站之答覆亦係一響)，再用電話通知該列車車次，此外行車股報告一切，最後副站長再在「站長行車時刻報告單上」，填寫一切。(詳見後述)

(d)到達工作：(1)副站長在列車到達前必也事前注意進站號誌，是否運用靈活或無損壞情事，否則即須派遣勝任之人，攜帶手作號誌，駐於該號誌外相當地點，執行副站長命令，及將遠距號誌，置於注意部位，直至進站號誌修復，或運用適宜時爲止，(2)如遇旅客或混合列車到達前，副站長爲審愼計得事前詢明鄰站，該列車是否準時到達，而無延誤情事，否則即於列車晚點報告及告白板上隨時記錄，以免引起旅客或員工等誤會，(3)在列車行將駛近進站號誌時，副站長即在站台向列車穩舉綠旗，(晝間)或綠燈，

(夜間)至適當停車地點，(位在準概以內)，再行穩舉紅旗(晝間)或紅燈(夜間)，以示車長及司機卽行停止列車，如該站規定不必停車者，則副站長俟該列車到站時，僅在站台，向列車穩舉綠旗或綠燈可也(4)列車到達站台後，副站長最先工作以及其應予注意各點，不外(一)從事接牌方面各項工作，此在未接牌前，注意該項列車是否完全，車尾標誌是否齊整，否則立卽通知該列之車車長，該法修整之，在接牌時卽應親至機車前，由司機手中，接收路牌，但不得假手他人，在接牌後，將接得路牌，詳加查驗，如列車未告完整，而由車長設法修整時，則副站長得將該路牌暫加保管，但不准遽行納入路牌棧內，(二)從事納牌方面各項手續(關於納牌之詳細手續，亦詳見該路行車規章內，故不復贅，(三)從事報告車長，列車正點或相差時刻，(按卽列車到達時刻及規定時刻之差)以便車長錄入車長行車時刻報單內，(5)列車到達後，副站長卽將列車到達時刻，(或延誤情形)，報告行車股，以備核查，此外(6)如旅客或混合列車到達後，先由

到達站副站長會同該車車長，詳加查驗，如查驗相符者，卽由車長交由副站長簽收厚紙一頁，以便彙呈車務處運輸課查核同時該車鎖匙，亦應一併歸站存查，嗣後副站長對於該車，卽須負責加以保管，但該車如暫不使用，而須存站，過夜或晝間停留十小時以上者，可由副站長應用乙種車輛保管簽字簿，(見後)暫時交付值班長警簽收，從事保管，但副站長仍須隨時負有察看之責。

(d)指揮調移車輛及編配列車

(a)調移車輛，再分

(1)普通調移：(一)在調移普通車輛時先由副站長事前通知有關工役，例如調車夫，鈎夫，及司機等，在列車入站後，其甩摘車輛，歸入何路股道，以便及時調移車輛，(二)如有列車已由鄰站向該站駛出後，則絕對不准在該列車方面之進站號誌所防護區域外，施行調車，(三)如鄰站駛來列車行將到站時，或進站號誌已落後，則不准在站內正道，及妨碍正道之岔道內，從事調車，除調車外，同時

亦不得在該處存留任何車輛(四)此外副站長有嚴行限制機車調移車輛之權例如最大速度，每小時不得超過十公里但遇迷霧、雨、雪、風、沙時，則其最大速度，每小時不得超過五公里，(五)在調車時副站長對於調車夫站立之位置，是否擅離開位，應負注意之責，以便隨時指示。

(2)飛甩車輛：(一)在施行飛甩車輛前，先由副站長嚴令司機，調車夫，鈎夫，及轉轍夫等，預爲接洽妥適，然後將全部列車之車鈎，詳加檢視，並注意其結聯程度，是否適合穩固，如認爲一切完備無疵後，方得施行飛甩車輛，(二)施行飛甩時，副站長值得注意者凡五(一)關於客車，起重機車，牲畜車，裝置爆發車，或易損貨物之車輛等，均應禁止飛甩，即上列各車輛停留線路內時，亦不宜施行飛甩，(二)飛甩車數，每組以換重六輛爲限，其有效制動軸數不及全軸數六分之一，或軸機失靈時則飛甩車輛即在禁止之列，(三)飛甩車輛以晴天最爲適合，如遇迷霧、雨、雪、風、沙時，則亦不宜施行飛甩，(四)此外該路規定各站具有四百分之一以上坡度線路(例如小港碼頭支線，大港，坊子，張店，濟南，及博山等站，俱有此項線路)短距離之盡頭岔道，敷設於建築物內之路線，及上列各站之第一第二及第三股道等，則飛甩車輛，均在禁止之列，(五)再者在飛甩車輛時其各種飛甩號誌之顯示，乃與行車安全有關，故亦不容漠視。

(b)編配列車，再分

(1)貨物列車之編配，貨物列車一經編配就緒後副站長即須會同車長巡視各項車輛之聯掛次序，是否適合，此則該路規定：(一)普通貨物列車之，編配乃以各車貨物到達站之先後，爲聯掛依據(二)如貨車中裝有棉花紙張等易燃物品，或其他危險及爆炸物品等，則設法使該項車輛，附掛於貨物列車後部，或遠離機車，以免發生意外危險，他如裝有動物車輛，個亦設法使之遠離機車，以免動物因震擅而促其獸性勃發，形成互相踐踏慘劇，(三)至若直達貨物列車之聯掛順序，除載有易燃，危險，及爆炸物品等貨車，另有規定外，（詳見上述）則可按照平車（前部）礦石車煤車（中部）及棚車（尾部）等次序編配之但不論普通或係直達貨物列車，最後均係聯掛守車一輛。

（2）旅客及混合列車之編配：此與貨物列車相似，即副站長務須注意其聯掛次序，是否適合查該路旅客及混合列車之聯掛次序，其最見完備者，不外（一）守車，（後端）（二）臨時加掛之客廳車，公務車，頭等寢食車，或專用車等，（如須附掛於守車後端時，則必經車務處之同意，）（三）普通規定臥車，頭等車，飯車，及二等車（氣候寒冷，暖氣不足時，可移掛列車前部，）（四）三等車，（五）守車，（前端）及（六）機車等，（如氣候較暖時，則在機車後端，尚須附掛冷藏車一輛），（二）如僅係旅客列車時，則同時注意其風軔方面是否完全貫通。

（3）外路無風管車輛之編配，（一）在編配此項車輛前，先由副站長與行車股妥爲接洽，以便電告有關車機各段及各站等，予以相當注意，（二）在編

配此項車輛時，副站長必須注意下述各端：（一）此項列車是否照章附掛於列車後部，（即守車前端）（二）掛運無風管車輛之換重，不得超過該列車原有換重三分之一，（三）由副站長指派鈎夫，值守段軔，（四）凡外路車輛設有風管，而不克貫通時，則按照無風管車輛辦理之，（五）如遇列車全部或一部份無風管時，除由出發站副站長，將司機載重電報附註欄內，註明「H.B.T.＝全部無風管或 H.B.T.＝一部分無風管等字樣外，此外將指派鈎夫人數，通知司機，以使會同車長，隨時加以查寄，（三）在編配此項車輛後，如已駛行中途，而因故摘下者，則俟該車發送時，仍由無風管之列車加以掛運。

（4）列車定數及制動軸數之編配，（一）在編配列車時，其列車編配定數，按例不得超過該路「機車牽引定數表」內規定之輛數，茲將該表附列於後。

機車牽引定數表

附表一

機車記號＼牽引車數	幹						線	
	旅客列車	混合列車			貨物列車			
		周村大臨池間下行	王村濟南間下行	其他	周村大臨池間下行	王村濟南間下行	其他	
S			12		（此數乃係倒車時之牽引定數，但有時青島至四方間拖掛混合列車時，亦屬此數）		16	
R		12	25	14	18	27	23（夏）	21（冬）
TT_1	15	21	35	23	22	37	31	28
M	9	13	18	13				
E					28	40	32（夏）	28（冬）
CC_1C_2					32	46	47	44
T_2	15	20	25	22				
P	20	25	28	28				
K							65	60

附表（二）

機車記號＼牽引車數	張店博山間		淄川黌山間	
	混合及貨物列車		混合及貨物列車	
	下行	上行	下行	上行
S			9	20
R	13	34	12	34
TT_1	18	44		
M	12	18		
E	20	46		

附表（三）

機車記號＼牽引車數	淄河礫石線
S	5
R	7
TT_1	11
M	4
CC_1C_2	14

（附註：此表機車記號之S＝六聯式（0－6－0）R＝大六聯式（0－6－2）TT_1及T_2＝十輛式（4－6－0）M＝輕快式（2－4－4）E＝八聯式（0－8－0）CC_1C_2＝凝結式（2－2－0）P＝太平洋式（4－6－2）K＝天皇式（2－8－2））

(二)再者在編配列車時，務須按照該路「列車制動軸數表』內規定之軸數，並以有效制動機（按即軔機）平均分配之，茲將該表附列於後．

列車制動軸數表

區分 制動軸數	幹線		博山支線	釁岐線
	周村明水間	其他	各項列車	
	混合及貨物列車			
	列車聯結軸數			
1	1—8	1—10	1—6	1—5
2	9—16	11—20	7—12	6—10
3	17—24	21—30	13—18	11—15
4	25—32	31—40	19—24	16—20
5	33—40	41—50	25—30	21—25
6	41—48	51—60	31—36	26—30
7	49—56	61—70	37—42	31—42
8	57—64	71—80	43—48	36—40
9	65—72	81—90	49—54	41—45
10	73—80	91—100	55—60	46—50
11	81—88		61—66	51—55
12	89—96		67—72	56—60
13	97—104		73—78	61—65
14			79—84	66—70
15			85—90	71—75
16			85—90	76—80
17			91—96	81—85
18				
19				
20				

上列(一)(二)二端，副站長亦負有注意之責。

(5)損壞機車及車輛之編配或掛運，(一)所有一切損壞機車編配或掛運時，副站長得酌量情形，將該車按照該路機務段通知辦法附掛於貨物列車，

(二)至若其他損壞車輛編配或掛運時，副站長亦得酌量情形，按照該路機務段所插之各色票附掛於貨物列車，(按該路目前所用色票，共分青票，(此再分第一號青票，表示轉送修理，第二號青票，表示

施行小部份修理，第三號青票，表示破損車輛程度，並不十分劇烈且於運轉工作，亦無任何妨碍，同時各該段無暇或短料不克修理者，得應用之）紅票（表示該車除站內調車外，應絕對禁止運轉），及白票（表示須進廠修理，或施行甲種定期檢查），等三種，其插置地點，乃在車側左方下部之鐵框內，各票均應挨次塡註號數以資識別，該票每年更換一次），上列（一）（二）二項，雖云該路副站長並未時告遇見，惟因與編配列車有關，故特一併申說之。

（c）保護列車行駛安全此分

（a）應用電氣路牌及路牌機爲明瞭該路副站長應用電氣路牌計，特先將下列（1）（2）二項，分別解釋之。

（1）採取候度：查該路乃係採取「區間閉塞制」，（Block System or Space Limit System）藉保列車行駛區間之安全，此制詳言之卽（一）每兩隣站間，各設電氣路牌一副，內貯同一式樣之路牌，端賴機械及電流之作用，故在同一路牌區間，祇能由一端之路牌機內，取出路牌一具，（同時在任何一端，不得再行取出路牌一具，）（二）然後持此取出路牌，祇准一列車駛入指定路牌區間（卽兩站間）內，一俟列車到達前站時，卽將此牌路，納入路牌機內，（三）最後方克取出另一路牌，開駛另一列車，（四）惟此制如遇行車事變發生，而亟待救援時，則副站長立卽取消此制，而另行規定相當救援辦法，直至恢復原狀後，始得重行採取之，此制簡言之卽中時列車或機車駛行時，祇准持有路牌者，始克駛入路牌區間內，此制之最大優點，不外直接避免中途列車相撞，間接保障旅客生命安全，其用意洵屬良佳也。

（2）識別標記（一）該路路牌機上，刻有三角形，（△）圓形，（○）正方形，（口）及菱形（◇）等標誌藉，以替代該機通達鄰近各站之站名，並使每上下站，及每三站間之標記，並不相同以資識別，（二）該路路牌機內，（在下部抽板上），刻有白色，（表示路線開通）紅色，（表示列車向前站進行），及綠色(表示列車向本站駛行)等標誌，藉以表示列車在區間內之行駛狀況，(如區間內路線，或列車發生障碍，而須臨時調度行車者，則此類標誌之應用，自當暫告失效)。

此外在應用電氣路牌時，其與副站長有關者。不外

(3)接遞手續(一)凡列車在站停車(一)而係接牌時則副站長在每一列車到站或接牌前，應以電話詢明鄰站，有無任何變動，以便及時接牌，如有意外變動，則立即以粉筆記於黑板上，藉以引起有關各員工之注意，或準備列車錯讓等迨列車進站到達後，副站長務須親自接受路牌，不得假手他人，凡路牌一經接受後，但尚未納入路牌機前，則屬於前站路牌，不得攜帶，(到站不停之列車除外)，又副站長不得同時攜帶兩具路牌，(二)此外關於遞牌方面，則副站長於遞牌前，得照章日間應用路牌袋，夜間應用白光燈，劃示路牌形狀，例如圓形，「○」(劃一小圓形徑約二呎)，正方形「口」(徐徐左右擺動)三角形「△」(徐徐上下擺動)及菱形「⊠」

(劃一×形)等，再者在遞牌時，可交由路牌夫或站夫轉遞司機，但副站長仍須在旁督察之。

(二)凡列車到站不停(一)而係接牌時，副站長每因一時不克分身，得臨時指派站夫執行之，(站夫接牌地位，距離副站長約十公尺左右，一俟路牌接下後先行呈交副站長查驗，如經其詳加查驗，認爲無誤後，方得將該路牌，納入路牌機內)，至若副站長本人應予注意者俟守車駛過站台時立即應用綠旗或綠光燈，按照上述方法，劃示路牌形狀。

(4、應用方法

(一)電鈴信號先由副站長按動路牌機台上之右方押鈕，藉以發送電鈴信號，同時以響數分別表示遞意義，普通一響表示路牌業已取出，或納牌手續告竣，(此項無須回復)及列車業已駛入區間傳，二響表示向鄰站索取路牌，三響表示警告注意，四響表示列車開到後，業已納入路牌機內，五響表示試驗路牌，及七響表示取消已發之信號，上列各項音響如以每日發生次數而論，則爲一響，二響，

三響，及四響，遇見較夥，五響及七響次之，再者以上乃指路牌機完好者而言，他如電話損壞時之索牌及警告音響，每因平時較鮮發生，且性質亦屬次要，故從略。

(二)尚有關於索牌及納牌方面各項手續該條雖規定極詳，惟因事涉專門，且須貴乎實地經歷，始克應用自如故，茲篇亦不詳為探討焉。

(5)注意各點

(一)關於發送電鈴信號者，不外(一)所有一切電鈴信號，除事實上不必回覆者外，其他電鈴信號，均須迅予回覆，(接收站)及靜候回覆，(發送站)藉作承認表示，否則不得認為業已明瞭，(二)凡列車由前站向本站出發後副站長即按例發送三響電鈴，警告下站注意，(三)副站長應輪流於每日早晨八時，會同接班副站長與鄰站副站長互相發送及回覆，五響電鈴，(每響相隔時間略使久常)，以資試驗路牌機是否完好。

(二)關於應用路牌機者，不外，(一)封印，副站長對於路牌機及電池箱等鎖門，務須注意是否應用特種鉛印，嚴密封印，否則立即予以更換以策安全，再者鉛印售封，雖由電務匠負責辦理，但同時必經副站長親自驗明，以出於電務工匠巡護報告內，填註並簽字證明，(二)清潔，副站長對於路牌機之內部，不得使有任何遺物遺落在內，並於路牌納入路牌機內前，驗明其中心形式號數，是否清潔，(三)其他：凡路牌一經納入路牌機內後，副站長對於下部抽板上之小窗內路牌即應注意其是否完好或有無斜立情事。

上列各項，乃指路牌或路牌機之完好者而言，他如錯誤或遺失，損壞或異狀，以及電話損壞等各項辦法，均因該路平時絕鮮遇見，及性質次要故特一併從略焉。

(b)應用或注意各種號誌及標誌：查該路目前所有各種號誌及標誌，類都與其他國有各路相似，茲由副站長之立場上，將其應用及注意各點，擇要分別臚述如次。

(1)號誌，大別之計分眼望號誌，及固定號誌兩種，其間分門別類，極感繁夥，試逐一申說之。

(一)眼望號誌，(一) 固定號誌，共分出發，進站及遠距號誌等，此因歸隸站上應用故副站長自當隨時隨地加以特別注意，尤於站夫或號誌夫將該號誌錯扳，忘扳，或顯示不正時，即應設法予以糾正，(二)臨時號誌，再分鳴汽，慢行，及停車號誌等，其中除鳴汽及慢行號誌，係屬司機職責，故歸車長督促外，他如慢行，及停車號誌等，副站長謹加注意而已，(三)手作號誌，又分號旗，號燈，及舉臂號誌等，此除屬車長，司機，調車夫，鈎夫及轉轍夫等職責外同時亦係副站長重要職責之一，尤於列車出發及到達前後，或調車時，咸須應用或注意之，再者在調車時，其實際工作，雖由調車夫負責辦理，但副站長爲職責攸關計，亦得隨時從旁監視以便有所指正。

(四)此外尙有調車及岔道號誌，該路目前尙付闕如茲不贅述。

(二)耳聽號誌，(一)號筒，此乃站上應用，即

於列車出發前五分鐘，或列車由鄰站出發後，而未到達本站前，得由站上站夫應用此項號誌，以資警告轉轍夫分路之用，副站長僅予督察或注意而已，(二)響墩，在應用響墩時，副站長必須嚴格予以保管，及試驗是否靈活，(三) 汽笛，普通係屬司機職責，其與副站長方面，並無多大關係，(四)口笛亦屬副站長重要職責之一，乃作命令旅客或混合列車出發之用。

(2)標誌，其重要分類，不外下列三端。

(一)轍尖標誌，可分爲第一標誌，及第二標誌等，而後者又有單式及複式之分，上列兩種標誌，雖屬轉轍夫之職責，但副站長仍負有注意，檢查，及督察之責。

(二)列車標誌，亦有機車頭燈，機車緩衝標誌，及列車側尾燈牌之分，此雖屬諸車長及司機等職責，然其顯示是否按章，及懸掛是否完整，副站長亦應負有察看及糾正之責。

(三)線路標誌共分成車檔標誌，公里牌，坡道

標誌，灣道標誌，及準概等，此雖泰半屬諸司機職責，但副站長得隨時矜飭及警告之，總之，副站長不論應用或注意號誌及標誌，其最大目的，不外維護行車安全而已，第欲達此目的，亦非難事，祇求本人方面，隨時以身作則，不容稍事苟且，而於所屬員工方面，尤貴明察秋毫，力避徇情隱匿，如是果能厲行不懈，則於行車安全之維護，要亦不無稍補者也。

(c)預防行車事變，關於副站長預防行車事變之方法，及其應予注意各點，不勝枚舉，此節僅就日常較易遇見者，簡爲臚列如次。

(1)關於路牌及路牌機者，(一)副站長接班後，其向鄰站索牌給牌，力避倩人庖代，而貴親自執行，以免發生意外，(二)路牌機關係行車安全者，至深且鉅，切勿任令他人妄動，亦不准派人代辦，(三)站務未了，不得輕將路牌機預交司機，(四)尚有關於應用路牌及路牌機時應予注意各點，因已詳見上述，故特從略焉。

(2)關於列車出發，或到達者，(一)凡列車出發站，編配站，或摘掛車輛，更換機車各站，於列車出發前，除外路無風管車輛，另有規定外，副站長應會同車長驗明，所掛車輛之車鈎及風管，是否聯結妥善，並試驗風軔是否貫通，同時所有列車出發前之索牌事宜，一律不得假手他人，(見上)(二)凡列車到站前，副站長務須親自到站督察或指揮一切及察看路線是否完全順妥或站內並無任何阻礙，如一切並無問題時，方得命令站夫(或號誌夫)放落進站號誌，但進站號誌一經放落後，即不准在正道或妨礙正道之道岔，施行調車或存放車輛，此外列車到達後之接牌及納牌事宜，亦不得假手他人。

(3)關於人事方面者，(一)副站長應隨時督察站內調車夫之調車工作，是否礙及行車安全(二)及察看值班轉轍夫是否於列車駛行前後，確守閘位，而無擅離或倩人私代情事，(三)此外關於其他所屬行車員工，副站長亦得隨時指示，勸誡，及糾正之。

(4)關於其他方面者，(一)副站長對於上下行之車次狀況，務須時刻加以注意，(二)同時亦應利用餘暇時間，瀏覽行車規章以便遵照規章所載，及參以固有經驗應付一切有關行車事宜。

(a)應用及督飭或協助應用行車電話

(a)應用範圍，此分，

(1)副站長本人應用者，(一)凡每次列車到達或出發後，均須由副站長將車次及到開時刻，應用行車電話，隨時報告行車股，(按該路規定報告時刻，以半分鐘爲最大限度)，如有延誤情事，或因調車關係，佔用一二股路時間，約在十分鐘，或十分鐘以上時，亦應由副站長將其延誤理由，及其大概情形，應用行車電話，擇要報告行車股，行車股根據此項報告，即可隨時察知該路全線各次列車之行駛狀況，及其差別時刻（此指與該路新頒行車時刻表之差別時刻而言），(二)關於一切聲請留軸事項，亦由副站長應用行車電話，報告行車股。

(2)督飭或協助員工應用者，又分。

(一)車號司事：(一)列車編配：凡列車編配站(按該路列車編配站，係指青島，高密，坊子，張店，金嶺鎮，淄川，黌山，博山，及濟南等站而言)，於列車編竣後，即由副站長督飭車號司事，應用行車電話，將該列車所掛之本外路車輛種類，號數，出發及到達站站名，分別空重，依照列車編配次序一一報告行車股，(按該路規定通話時間，以四五分鐘爲最大限度)以便行車股登入列車掛車單內，隨時查核車輛是否虛糜，或長度是否適合等，(二)列車車號，在應用行車電話時，車號司事對於每次列車摘掛車號，務須正確清晰，否則副站長得立予糾正，(三)列車載重，關於列車載重事項其由車號司事應用行車電話，報告行車股者亦得由副站長嚴行督飭之。

(二)他如車長及電務工匠等，其應用行車電話之機會，均較車號司事爲遜，前者僅於列車行駛中途，向鄰近站借用之，後者乃於試驗或修理行車電話時應用之，惟不論前者，或後者應用行車電話時，副站長爲職責攸關計，均應嚴行督飭或予相當協助，至其詳細辦法，則因遇見較鮮，故特從略焉。

(b)注意各點

(1)在應用前，(一)副站長必先注意該行車電話機，是否正式鳴響，如係正式鳴響時，方得開始接聽，至若平時機件內，偶有動作之聲，乃係行車股與他站呼喚之聲，初與本站無涉，自可無容接聽，(二)在通話前，副站長先行確實詢明對方或考慮此項行車事項是否屬諸本人職責範圍以內，如確屬本人職責範圍以內者則副站長立即親自接聽，並不得假手他人，上列(一)(二)二項，乃指行車股與某站通話時而言，(三)如某站與行車股通話者，則該站副站長在通話前，須將通話事項預先加以默憶，以免臨時發生遺忘或慌惶失措之弊。

(2)在應用時，(一)副站長先將聽筒貼近耳孔，並設法使話筒位置與本人口之距離相距約一寸左右，最爲適宜，(二)同時再行詢明對方，(行車股)接聽者之姓名，然後開始通話，以資負責，(三)關於本人發音方面，亦必求其簡單清晰，而免虛浮客套，如是直接既可減少時間消耗，間接亦能增進辦事效率，(四)如乙站副站長，(或小站之正站長亦可)與行車股通話時，甲站副站長(或正站長)例須靜待片刻，不得任意叫嚷妨礙他人聽聞，惟緊急事項，則不在此限，(此得預先聲明，以便行車股即時拔聽該站行車電話，(五)如通話告畢，但未將電話機放下前，副站長務須詢明對方有無其他事項經對方答覆，並無其他事項，而宣告通話完竣方得將電話機放下。

(3)在應用後，(一)副站長除將行車電話機安置妥適地點外，如不急需時，則應嚴禁任何員工，擅自接聽藉表鄭重，(二)平時尚須命令站夫將該電話機一再拂拭，以保清潔，而免應用失靈。

(c)填寫報單及簿冊

(a)列車時刻站長報告單：此單專備副站長(或小站之正站長)記載每日到開列車時刻之用，其內容除列年、月、日、外再詳列下列各項。

（1）列車號數，（如旅客列車，混合列車，貨物列車，及機車號數等）。

（2）到達，再分（一）給牌時刻（卽列車或機車到達前，某站向鄰站索牌後之實際給牌時刻），（二）規定時刻，（卽該路行車時刻表所規定之到達行車時刻），（三）現行時刻，（卽列車或機車實際到達該站之行車時刻）（四）相差時刻，（卽現行及規定時刻之差別）。

（3）出發，再分（一）索牌時刻，（卽列車或機車出發前，某站向鄰站索牌時之實際索誌時刻），（二）規定時刻，（卽該路行車時刻表所規定之出發行車時刻）（三）現行時刻（卽列車或機車由該站出發時之實際行車時刻）（四）相差時刻（見上）

上列各項，又有上行及下行之分。

（4）天氣（例如填寫晴，陰迷霧，或雨，雪，風涉等）。

（5）備考（填寫讓車，（簡寫）（），甩車（簡寫det.）及挂車（簡寫att等）此單共分三聯，（一）交車

務段，（二）寄運輸課行車股，及（三）存站備查等。

（d）車輛保管簽字簿，此簿專事記載車輛或守車之保管及簽收事宜，計分

（1）甲種車輛保管簽字簿，此簿乃在列車出發前先向編配列車站副站長會同該次車長，互相點驗明確，然後再在此簿上簽字蓋章，以資負責。

（2）乙種車輛保管簽字簿，此簿乃備機務處修整車輛後，如暫不使用而須存站或晝開停站在十小時以上者，卽由副站長填寫此簿，以備交付值班長警，暫加保管。

（3）丙種車輛保管簽字簿，此簿一經副站長通知值班長警，需用客車或守車後，（此自通知時起算，其交付時間，不得超過十分鐘，以免延誤行車，）卽由值班長警填寫此簿，故與副站長關係尚少。

此簿詳列附屬品名稱，短少件數，短少理由，（如小竊私盜或中途遺失等）附記，及點交或簽收者簽字等。

此簿每份共分三張，一係出發站存根，一爲車長簽收後，

仍交出發站查收一則由車長自行帶交到達站，再由到達站彙呈運輸課，藉作修理或添置客車及守車之依據。

(c)某站行車電話通話記錄簿，此簿專作某站副站長，(或小站之正站長)，與行車設通話時，記載或摘錄之用，其內容詳列下列各項。

(1)時期再分月、日、時、分、(即與行車股通話之時期)。

(2)命令或請求(再分來處或去處)。

(3)摘要此欄專填甩車，(遇見最多)掛車，及摘車等，倘有如行車電話損壞或運用失靈時，則將不克通話時間，及其大概情形，擇要摘錄以資參考。

(4)處理情形，(即將處理上列情形)擇要摘錄此欄)。

(5)負責人簽字，(即接班時，須與接班副站長相互簽字以資負責)。

再者此簿值得注意者凡二(一)此簿填寫後，應在每日二十四點鐘以後，隨最先到達列車，寄送行車股(二)同時將寄遞行車股之時日一併填明。

此外該路新近又設一簿。即

(d)膠濟鐵路車務處某站日記簿，此簿專將副站長每日值班時發生之一切行車事項，詳加記錄其內容除列年、月、日、外再列未結事項，經辦情形待辦事項，經辦情形，及備考等，最後再列副站長之簽字。此簿並不分聯，易言之，僅有存站一聯，以便該站副站長隨時參攷之用。

(b)拍發及校閱各種電報

(a)拍發及校閱：查該路副站長拍發及校閱之電報，計分普通，及(2)行車事變電報等兩種，前者計分公務，配車，行車，及車運電報等，後者又分事變，及道清電報等，其間除後者會當另節探討，故暫不臚列外，茲先將該路各種普通電報，其與副站長或行車方面有關者，簡為臚列如次：

(1)公務電報查該路不論行車，總務，或貨運等，均與此項電報有關，其隸屬行車方面者，不外更調行車人員，運送行車材料，摘掛或撥調列車，及處理其他一切有關行車事宜等，此則副站長負有拍發及校閱之責。

(2)配車電報，再分下列各端。

(一)臨時請求車輛電報，此項電報除貨運外，亦與行車有關。

(二)留軸電報，因與行車事項關係最切，故此項電報，完全側重行車一項。

(三)車輛報告，此項報告雖與貨運有關，但該路乃係側重行車一項。

(四)列車載重電報， 此項電報， 亦與行車有關。

上列(一)至(四)項，乃係副站長拍發有關各方者，(按即行車股及有關各站，) 此外有關各方(按即行車股)致電某站副站長而由彼加以校閱者，尚有下列二項。

(五)臨時支配車輛電報，乃與行車及貨運有關

(六)支配車輛電報，亦與行車及貨運有關。

(3)行車電報，此項電報，顧名思義。即知與

行車有關，蓋舉凡一切行車事項，例如列車誤點，車輛熱軸、及其他行車通知等，靡不詳載此項電報者也，概言之，其由副站長拍發有關各方者，計有下列各項，例如特別快車在站延誤五分鐘或五分出或五分鐘以上，普通旅客或混合列車在站延誤十分鐘至十五分鐘以上，車輛熱軸，及其他行車通知等，至若有關各方，致電副站長，而由副站長加以校閱者，尚有下列各項，例如行車緊急通知，軍運專車時刻表，通行路線之工作通知，臨時加開或取消貨物列車，及其他行車通知等，惟副站長不論拍發或校閱此項電報時，類都於行車電話失效時應用之，此外尚有車長拍發或校閱之各項電報，雖亦列入行車電報內，惟與副站長並無多大關係，特從略焉。

(4)軍運電報，又分下列二項。

(一)零星軍運請示事項電報，此項電報，乃與行車有關。

(二)掛送尋常軍運車輛電報，此項電報，亦與行車有關。

上列(一)(二)二項，乃指副站長拍發有關各方者而言，至若有關各方，致電副站長，而由副站長加以校閱者，則該路尙付闕如，故不贅述焉。

(d)注意各點

(1)拍發

(一)副站長草擬電文底稿時，不論中英文，均須力求簡明，同時關於一切簡稱名詞，尤應加以熟記，(按該路印有「站名，職名，及軍輛簡稱表」一小冊指示一切簡稱名詞極詳。)

(二)關於某某事項，其應報何處或何人，亦應加以考慮，如有連帶關係者，則一倂列入附記欄內。

(三)凡電文電稿一經草擬後，副站長務須將該電報號數，冠於電文之首，該數不容遺漏以備他日查攷。

(四)並考量事之緩急，以定列入何項等級，(按該路普通電報之等級，其分尋常電(R)，急電(XR)，加急電(XXR)，及特急電(XXXR)等四項。)

(五)最後副站長在該電報上，務須簽字，或蓋章，以資負責。

(2)校閱

(一)除熟嫻簡稱名詞，注意電報號數，及定奪電報等級等，乃與拍發方面所列者，大致相似外。此外

(二)注意電報房收發時刻，是否按時簽註。

(三)在校閱後，(一)副站長在電報回單上，必須詳加填註，及簽字或蓋章，以資負責，(二)如性質重要者，則摘錄公告牌上，以便有關員工知照。

(g)督飭校對站內時鐘或大鐘

(a)副站長對於站內時鐘或大鐘，每日負有督飭校對之責。例如

(1)時鐘方面；先由副站長指定相當員司，於每日正午十一點五十五分，前往電報房會同電報領班守候報時信號，(該信號由該路管理局電報領班依照標準鐘點，(此復依照中央無線電所廣播之時

刻爲標準，傳達各站)，一俟該報時信號傳來時先各由該站指定員司，負責予以校對由再由副站長重行，督飭校對之。

(2)大鐘方面：亦由副站長指定相當員司，於每日正午十一點五十五分，前往鐘樓守候報時信號，一俟該信號傳來後，(約於十一點五十九分傳來)，該鐘樓上之電鈴，先行鳴響三響，以資警告，再行鳴響十二響，以資代表十二小時，但在鳴響第一響時，適爲正午十二時正，該員司卽行加以校對，嗣後副站長尚須再度督飭校對之。

(d)再者副站長對於該指定員司之姓名，例須報告軍務處備案，如有更改時，則須將替添者之姓名，重行報告，車務處，以備查核。

(c)站內時鐘或大鐘一經校對後，副站長除每日將該鐘快慢或正點情形，詳細塡入，「某站掛鐘校對時刻表」外，同時每兩月將此表寄送車務課，以資存查。

綜上所列各項，類都屬諸副站長之更要職責，且係時常遇

見者；(雖其中尚有少數職責，似未時常遇見，惟因性質尚感重要，且因連帶申述關係，故特一併申述之。)此外尚有職責雖感重要，但該路平時絕鮮遇見者，卽係下述一項。

(h)處理各種行車事變

(a)以處理原則而言。

(1)凡副站長處理各種行車事變時以力求安全爲前提。

(2)在臨時處理時，貴乎膽大心細，並隨時穩妥辦理。

(3)處理事變，務求迅速，以免坐失良機，或擴大事變。

(4)除本人外，副站長應與所屬員工，及其他救護人員等，通力合作藉收事半功倍之效。

(5)隨時與行車股方面，互通聲息，以作處理事變準則。

(d)以處理人員而論

(1)關於車務方面者，則除在場之車務負責人員外，其屬諸站上或車上員工者，(副站長本人除

外），則有車長，查票員引導員，（由副站長臨時派定），司機，火夫，調車夫，鈎夫，轉轍夫外站夫）（或號誌夫）驗車匠，及其他有關員工等。

（2）關於其他方面者，員司如機務，工務及電務之在場負責人員或工務員等，工役如電務工匠，或其他工匠等是也。

（c）以處理方法而論，不外

（1）在路線未清理前

（一）致電有關各方，副站長在行車事變發生後，但尚未將路線清理或開通前，除應用普通或行車電話，（詳見上述）向有關之處，段，站，從事請援外，同時亦須拍電有關各方，以表鄭重，所謂拍電云者，乃指拍發事變及清道電報等而言，前者又分下列各項，例如兩列車或兩機車相互撞車，列車，或機車在通行路線上出軌，列車失火，路線或橋梁損壞，列車在兩站間脫鈎，車輛逸走，車場內調車相撞或出軌，（但並不阻礙通行路線）機車在中途損壞，轍夫標誌或固定號誌損壞，電氣路牌損壞，列

車或機車在中途軋斃行人，及電桿或電線損壞等，後者又分甲、乙、兩種電報，甲種乃係探詢前站清道電報，專供某站（例如甲站）詢明可否准將第某次車開往鄰站（例如乙站）之用，乙種乃答覆鄰站清道電報即係允許某站將第某次駛向該站之用，上述兩種電報，完全側重行車方面。

（二）保護障碍區間，副站長必也，（一）扣留駛向該區間之任何列車，（救險列車，或救援機車除外），（二）立即通知兩端鄰站副站長，（或正站長亦可），（三）將所有該站之進站及遠距號誌一律設法使之顯示險阻，或注意部位。

（三）採取引導制度，查該路引導制度，計有甲、乙、丙、三種之分，（一）甲種乃在正道上發生事變，阻碍列車通行時應用之，藉使該出事地點，與兩端站間之行車，繼續行駛，（二）乙種則於電汽路牌機損壞，同時電報通信，亦發生障碍，而電話尚可通達時應用之，務使列車繼續行駛於該區間內，（三）丙種乃與上列乙種大致相似，惟略感不同者，

即所有電汽路牌，以及電報電話等，全部發生障碍，以致兩端站不克互通消息時，亦得應用此制，以資補救。

再者如引導制度一經採取後，則電汽路牌或清道電報行車制，暫停應用。

(2)在路線已清理後。不外

(一)發電通知有關之處、段、站、恢復該區間之行車，(如原來路線並不阻碍時，則應將修理完好，或恢復原狀後之使用時刻通知有關之處段站知照)。

(二)如引導制度加以取消，而電汽路牌或清道電報行車制繼續使用者，則應將後者使用時刻，電告有關之處、段、、站知照，(如原來並未將後者取消時，則可毋庸通知焉。)

(i)附帶職責，此外關於注意風軓事項，保護站內閘燈，以及管理搖車及手推平車之行駛等，要皆屬諸副站長之附帶職責，其性質略感次要，故特從略焉。

(III)結論：綜觀該路副站長之各項職責，極見繁冗而所負責任，又極重大，故非有堅强之毅力，耐勞之精神，與夫審慎之態度，不克負此重任，否則影響一己名譽之事尚小，而影響整個運輸業務者實大，此則深祈新入路界同學深切注意者也，再者舉凡交大同學之初入路界服務者，以學識而言，實可問心無愧，但以經驗而論，則似稍感欠缺，故惟有利用餘暇時間，多多側重實習事項，俾學識與經驗，參融一爐，以便一旦廁身路界時，始克輕駕熟車，藉收事半功倍，之效此則深祈學校當局有以玉成者也，最後各地校友之廁身路界者爲數綦夥，其學識與經驗之豐富，固無待言，如能隨時出其學識與經驗，錄成專著刊行於世，以供在校同學之參攷，以開路校合作之先聲，其收效之宏，或將相當可觀也，此則深祈各地校友之深加襄助者也，鄙見若斯，世多明達之士，或亦笑予之愚乎　(完)

分 類 索 引

分類索引

索引類別	題目	著者	雜志名稱	發行年月	號數
A類					
A 1	關誤解管理者	鍾偉成	管理	25—4	1:1
	管理與統計	汪仲良	管理	25—7	1:1
	科學管理第一講	唐澤焱	擴播週報	25—5	88
	科學管理述要	唐澤焱	工商管理月刀	25—5	3:5
A 2	大學教育中之管理學程	嚴礪平	管理	25—7	1:2
B類					
B 2	改進工商業技術管理應設諮詢所芻議	楚聲	錢業月報	25—7	16:5
	工商事業制度改善之商榷	藹廬	銀行週報	25—5	20:19
	中國棉業現狀及其改進之方法	何文彩	交通雜志	25—6	4:4
	發展四川鹽產工業芻議	王善政	工業中心	25—5	5:5
	國產羊毛的近況及其改進的我見	朱覺方	工商管理月刊	25—5	3:3
	發展江西紙業之管見	歐陽毅	中國建設	25—5	13:5
	贛省糖業的近況及其改進的管見	朱覺方	工商管理月刊	25—5	3:5
B 3	關于工廠中使用機器及更換問題	王炳勳	商職月刊	25—5	2:1
	桐油業改進及其前途	張煒明	商業月報	25—5	16:3
	談美國工廠設備的一般情形	黃宇楨	工商管理月刊	25—4	3:4
	建設首都煤氣廠計劃書	王善政	工業中心	25—3	5:3
	一個鍊焦廠的經濟計算計算	王善政	工業中心	25—1	5:1
	工業上硬化油的製造法	王善政	工業中心	25—5	5:6
	原動機之管理法	何迪昌	工業中心	25—4	5:5
B 4	商品原料存棧最高量與最低量之核定法	張心雄	會計雜誌	25—4	7:4
	倉庫營業範圍之檢討	劉仲廉	會計雜志	25—4	16:4

	上海碼頭貨棧鳥瞰		交通雜志	25—4	7:4
B 5	推銷與廣告	何昇餘	工商管理月刊	25—3	3:3
	新式推銷術之研究	李綺迪	工商管理月刊	25—4	3:4
	商品之分配問題	劉仲廉	商業月報	25—5	16:5
	中國貿易出超原因之探索	莫　湮	時兆月報	25—5	31:5
	平漢路沿線棉花產運之研究	林　午	鐵路雜志	25—3	1:10
	日本人造絲市價前途之推測		國際貿易情報	25—3	1:3
B 6	職工代表制概論	丁馨伯	工商管理月刊	25—3	3:3
	勞役的報酬	張天澤譯	工商管理月刊	25—3	3:3
	工資問題	唐澤焱	工商管理月刊	25—4	3:3
	辦公的損失	徐百益	工商管理月刊	25—4	3:4
	勞工敎育	逸	工商管理月刊	25—4	3:4
	如何改善職員担保制度	徐啓文	銀行週報	25—3	20:10
	增進工作效能的方法	蔣中正	平漢路月刊	25—4	71:72
	職員住宅問題	屠哲隱	工商管理月刊	25—5	3:5
B 7	我國之工業化問題	魏敦夫	銀行週報	25—6	20:24
	福州之紙傘工業		國際貿易情報	25　3	1:2
	中國棉產之動態	方秋葦	東方雜誌	25—4	33:7
	日本侵略華北和中國棉花問題	向金聲	中國經濟	25—2	4:1,2
	日本之新興工業		國際貿易情報	25—3	1:3
	上海之機製煤球業		國際貿易情報	25—3	1:5
	日本製紙業概況		國際貿易情報	25—5	1:11
	塵埃之控制		工業安全	25—4	4:2
	天津之鉄紗業		津浦路日刊	25—6	1465
	一九三四年世界之鋼鉄業	知	建　設	25—6	19
	美國天然煤氣之利益	鄭禮明	建　設	25—5	18
	中國合作運動現況之分析	鄭厚博	合作月刊	25—5	8:5
	非常時期之棉紡業	馮子明	商業月報	25—6	16:6

	題目	作者	刊名	年月	卷期
	華茶對外貿易之現狀及瞻望	楊德惠	商業月報	25—5	16:5
	中國實業何以不發展	衞士生	實業部月刊	25—4	1:1
	愛翟氏論商業循環	王懿芳	實業部月刊	25—4	1:1
	減少貿易障碍的可能性	陸　慶	實業部月刊	25—5	1:2
	華北之資源與產業	楊勇超	經理月刊	25—3	2:1
	工商業實務概論	陳道曾	工商管理月刊	25—3	3:3
	盈餘的分配	屠哲隱	工商管理月刊	25—4	3:4
	商店管理講詞	唐澤焱	工商管理月刊	25—4	3:4
	什麽是工商管理學	江原祺	工商管理月刊	25—4	3:4
	軍需工業之動員	畢　立	經理月刊	25—3	2:3
	各國軍需工業與政治之連繫性	顧鈺麐	經理月刊	25—3	2:3
	華茶對外貿易之現狀及瞻望	楊德惠	商業月報	25—5	16:5
	水的經濟問題	李魯航	中國實業	25—2	2:2
	全國精鹽工業巡禮	卞傑明	中國實業	25—2	2:2
	美國農業信用貸款制度	姜炳麟	中國實業	25—2	2:2
	推進信用合作社放款方案之擬議	許昌齡	農村合作	25—3	1:8
	中國實業何以不發達	衞士生	實業部月刊	25—4	1:1
C類					
D1	建築川湘鐵路之探討	夏憲講	交通雜志	25—4	4:3
	攷察各國交通事業之觀感	李季清	交通雜志	25—3	4:3
	隴海路潼安支綫與寶漢錢之研討	蕭梅性	交通雜志	25—5	4:5
	首都鐵路之同顧與前膽	李鍾魯	鐵路雜志	25—2	1:919
	中國最低限度主幹鐵道之完成及振興實業芻議	常計高	鐵路雜志	25—3	1:10
	粵漢廣九兩路接軌之重要性	揚理之	鐵路雜志	25—3	1:10
	全國交通狀况	俞飛鵬	交通職工	25—3	4:1
	中國鐵路發展之回顧與瞻望	禹	清華週刊	25—5	44:7
	中國鐵道建設之使命及實現方法	王熙民	北寧鐵路月刊	25—1	6:1
	建築鐵路之根本問題		津浦鐵路日刊	25—2	1462

	交通統制	方顯庭	京滬滬杭甬路日刊	25—2	1498
	觀察鐵路事業消長之方法與施行經濟合理化之步驟		北寧路改進專刊	25－2	1:2
	近五年來各國鐵路因世界不景氣所受營業上之損失及所取對策之成功		北寧鐵路月刊	25—2	6:2
	粵漢鐵路湘鄂段管理局行政計劃		粵漢鐵路湘鄂線旬刊	25—1	124
	各國鐵路之特色	劉德明	津浦鐵路日刊	25—2	1507
	中國鐵路的管理問題	葉子剛	管　理	25—4	1:1
	過去我國鐵路之錯誤與今後新路建設之方針	沈奏廷	管　理	25—4	1:1
	公路管理方法之檢討	熊大惠	管　理	25—4	1:1
	新路建設之經濟觀	黃宗瑜	管　理	25—4	1:1
	我們的財政往何處去	江英志	管　理	25—4	1:1
	浙贛鐵路之經濟意義之研究	朱中良	鐵路雜志	25—4	1:11
	津浦路最近工作情形及其改進計獲	楊承訓	鐵路雜志	25—5	1:12
	鐵路管理教育與鐵路技術管理之關係	楊文璞	鐵路雜志	25—4	1:11
	鐵道部施政成績	,,	鐵路雜志	25—6	2:1
	從我國鐵道史上觀察粵漢鐵路	關賡麟	鐵路雜誌	25—6	2:1
	觀察西南各路後之感想		浙贛鐵路月刊	25—5	2:12
	最近竣工之蘇嘉鐵路	江　波	交通雜志	25—6	4:6
	由德國鐵道事業研討我國鐵道事業之改進	劉大功	交通雜志	25—5	4:5
	全國鐵路之特色	劉德明	北甯鐵路月刊	25—4	6:4
	鐵道汽車之研究	鄭禮明	建　設	25—6	19
C 2	美國鐵道整車貨場之組織及管理	許　請	管　理	25—7	1:2
	歐戰時美國鐵路軍運組織與實施概況	周世正	管　理	25—7	1:2
	論鐵路貨站外部之組織與改進	沈奏廷	京滬滬杭甬路日刊	25—2	1501
C 3	中國研究機械工程人員應注意之點		津浦鐵路日刊	25—3	1495
	南口機廠鍋爐改進工作步驟概況		平綏技術彙刊	25—3	1495

	新路軌道之提議	金　濤	平綏日刊	25—3	92-95
	軌枕長度與軌距關係		津浦鐵路日刊	25—4	1513
	鐵路號誌與保安裝置	陳鍾達	北寧路機務季刊	25—5	6:5
	德英二國鐵路幹綫軌道之構造與修養	金　濤	平綏技術彙刊	25—6	2:4
	粵漢鐵路株韶段工程完成之經過	凌鴻勛	鐵路雜誌	25—5	1:12
	在軌道外運用之工具	李恆鉞	平綏技術彙刊	25—6	2:4
	全段趕工提前接軌之經過	桂銘敬	株韶段工程月刊	25—4	4:4
	車內號誌之裝置		改進專刊	25—6	13
	流線形機車及車輛	王若佩	北寧路月刊	25—6	6:5
	流線形機車是什麽	劉德明	北寧路月刊	25—3	6:3
	我國自造長途汽車及運貨汽車底盤之商榷	張登義	工業中心	25—5	5:5
C 4	檢驗火車鐵軌之新器械	張伊耕	工業中心	25—2	1461
	轉盤之修養		平綏技術彙刊	25—3	2:3
	鋼軌之保養		平綏技術彙刊	25—3	2:3
	德國標準叉道概論	吳之翰	京滬滬杭甬路日刊	25—4	1570
	宋永明發明延年枕木		京滬滬杭甬路日刊	25—4	1570
	管理鐵路存料之幾個簡單原則	吳英豪	鐵路半月刊	25—5	1
	江南鐵路採辦本松枕木經過及研討方法	江振明	鐵路雜誌	25—5	1:11
	試驗道木		改進專刊	25—5	13
	鐵路材料常識之八非鐵屬金類	王文翔	津浦機務季刊	25—4	3:3
	鐵路材料處與用料處間之調整與合作	鍾偉成	管　理	25—7	1:2
C 5	改良我國鐵路貨票填發制度之我見	沈奏廷	交通雜誌	25—3	4:3
	中國鐵路運輸政策之我見	金士宣	交通雜誌	25—3	4:3
	改良我國鐵路貨運單據之又一建議	沈奏廷	交通雜誌	25—4	4:4
	對于我國鐵路牲畜運價之批評	沈奏廷	交通雜誌	25—5	4:5
	相互協調中鐵路與汽車運輸事業管理方法之研究	尹自强	交通雜誌	25—5	4:5
	增加鉄路營業進款方法之研討	陳鍾達	鐵路雜誌	25—2	1:9

	決定運價之三種方法	紅　葉	津浦路日刊	25—4	1521
	聯運單程及來回新票價之計算方法	紅　葉	津浦路日刊	25—2	1461
	聯運票價計算方法		京滬滬杭甬路日刊	25—1	1461
	改善我國鐵路臥車舖位預定制度芻見	沈奏廷	京滬滬杭甬路日刊	25—2	1506
	招徠小件包裹芻議	梁在平	平綏日刊	25—4	107-112
	發展平綏路貨運業務計劃書	閻述藻	平綏日刊	25—4	113-115
	廣九鐵路貨物運輸面面觀	劉建吾	鐵路雜誌	25—3	1:10
	平綏路沿線出產貨品及運狀輸況		平綏日刊	25—4	107
	英國貨車支配制度與吾國應有之改進	沈奏廷	京滬滬杭甬路日刊	25—2	1518-1519
	鐵路對于貨物火災損失之責任	趙傳雲	鐵道半月刊	25—5	1
	中國鐵路貨等運價問題	金士宣	鐵道半月刊	25—5	1
	零担貨物處理方法與聯運直達沿途担車制度	沈奏廷	管　理	25—7	1:2
	鐵路直接運輸成本之計算與運用	沈奏廷	交通雜誌	25—6	4:6
	鐵路公路聯絡建議書		鐵路雜誌	25—4	1:11
	鐵路客運業務	彭禊蘇	鐵路雜誌	25—2	1:12
	鐵路貨物特別運價制度之探討	李起濤	鐵路雜誌	25—6	2:1
	鐵路運輸成本之研究	黃漢偉	鐵路雜誌	25—6	2:1
	劃一鐵路貨物聯運運價之研究	李起濤	鐵路雜誌	25—4	1:11
	美國鐵路辦理零担貨物之概况	李希民	鐵路雜誌	25—5	1:12
	發展平綏路貨運業務計劃書	王以仁	鐵路雜誌	25—5	1:12
	發展平綏路貨運業務計劃書	梁在平	鐵路雜誌	25—6	2:1
	救濟華北白煤與核減鐵路運價	李起濤	北寧路月刊	25—6	6:3
	鐵路終點旅客車站之研究	鄭寶照	改進專刊	25—6	13
	戰時鐵路與客貨運輸	裘玄同	鐵路雜誌	25—2	1:62
	遞遠遞減率與計算方法	李起濤	鐵路雜志	25—5	1:1
	近年來鐵路損失賠賞之分析	趙傳雲	鐵路雜志	25—6	2:1
	北寧路貨運業務概況今後發展途徑	春　生	北寧路月刊	25—4	6:4
C 6	中國鐵路管理車輛登記制度實施法	蔡殿楣	鐵路雜志	25—5	1:12
	減少我國鐵路貨車停站之時間研究	劉傳書	交通雜志	25—3	4:3

	減少我國鐵路空車延頓公里之研究	劉傳書	交通雜志	25—4	4:4
	膠濟路調度制概況	何世倫	交通雜志	25—4	4:4
	增加我國鐵路貨物列車行駛速度之研究	劉傳書	交通雜志	25—5	4:5
	支配火車困難之原因及其影響	黃宗瑜	交通鐵路	25—5	4:5
	列車震動之研究	吳毓崑	京滬滬杭甬路日刊	25—4	1565-1568
	改善機車車輛調度方法		京滬滬杭甬路日刊	25—1	1492
	預防行車事變之原則		津浦路日刊	25—2	1465
	中國鐵路管理車輛登記制度實施法		北寧路月刊	25—1	6:1
	記英國倫敦東北鐵路公司互氏調車場	林　堯	京滬工杭甬路日刊	25—3	1530
	美國鐵路減除交義道事變之措施	載雲書	改進專刊	25—6	13
	鐵路統計分析與管理	葉子剛	管　　理	25—7	1:2
	總稽核室制度與審計辦事處制度之比較	賈乙青	管　　理	25—7	1:2
	整理中國鐵路統計之我見	劉傳書	鐵道半月刊	25—5	2
	統計學與鐵路統計		改進專刊	25—2	12
	鐵路人事問題之檢討	高風介	鐵路雜志	25—2	1:9
	路員合作		改進專刊	25—2	12
	鐵路人事問題之檢討		正太日刊	25 4	931
	公務人員訓練與各盡職守		京滬滬杭甬路日刊	25—2	1521
	鐵路員工福利事業之研討	馬廷燮	鐵道半月刊	25—6	2:3
	土木工程司努力之標準	曾養甫	鐵道半月刊	25—6	2
	計時分工法說明書	李維國	平漢路月刊	25—2	6970
	長辛店機廠僱用職工辦法及攷試職工技能標準規定		平漢路月刊	25—4	72
C9	招商局及航政上幾個問題	俞飛鵬	交通職工	25—3	4:2
	郵政儲金匯業局務概況	莊心在	交通職工	25—3	4:2
	南洋航空輸送事業之概況	胡一聲	交通職工	25 3	4:2
	創行運價支票制之擬議	畢慎夫	交通雜志	25—3	4:3
	日本之航空運輸	萬　琮	交通雜志	25—3	4:3
	公路運輸安全問題之檢討	曹毓才	交通雜志	25—3	4:3

各國公路運輸發達概況	王同文	交通雜志	25—3	4:34
歐戰時英國航業統制委員會之組織及管理船舶實施辦法	王　洸	交通雜志	25—4	4:4
海洋運價之基礎研究	章江波	交通雜志	25—4	4:4
公路貨運與包裝關係	楊得任	交通雜志	25—4	4:4
發展我國公路交通管見	安忠義	交通雜志	25—4	4:4
招商局及航上幾個重大問題	俞飛鵬	交通雜志	25—5	4:5
歐戰時筆用輕便鐵路之實施	王同文	交通雜志	25—5	4:5
鐵路員工對于消費合作社應有之認識	勞　勉	鐵路雜志	25—2	1:9
如何建築最經濟最適用之公路	朱定一	道路月刊	25—4	50:3
公路建設在國民經濟上之重要	任樹椿	中國建設	25—4	13:4
船員生活改造之前提	愚　人	航海雜志	25—2	2:2
民用航空之重要及其發展方法	陳　洪	社會經濟月報	25—5	3:5
遠東航空之爭霸戰	清玠夫	江蘇保安季刊	25—4	3:1
管理交通人員應有之努力	沈百先	江蘇建設	25—6	3:6
全國經濟委員會報告公路建設近況		道路月刊	25—6	50:3
四川努力公路建設		道路月刊	25—6	50:3
西北道路建設芻議	均　夫	中國建設	25—6	13:6
建設西南交通中心計劃之管見	勃　君	交通雜志	25—6	4:6
戰時公路交通之檢討	唐　志	道路月刊	25—6	50:3
公路運輸之我見	天虛我生	道路月刊	25—5	50:2
四川公路統一營業及計劃	楊得任	道路月刊	25—5	50:2
港務概論	張以禮	北寧路月刊	25—4	6:4
法國航業政策	劉莪茵	交通雜志	25—4	4:4
湖南航業現狀及其改進	謝海泉	交通雜志	25—5	4:5
招商局及航政上幾個大問題	俞飛鵬	交道雜志	25—4,5	4:4.5
一九三六年度的蘇聯水上運輸計劃	胡一聲	交通雜志	25—6	4:6
航空運輸成本概算	周鐵鳴	交通雜志	25—6	4:6

	海運的發達及其存在的意義		交通職工	25—6	4:4
	中國航業概觀	楊朝曦	交通職工	25—5	4:3
	日本的航業政策	劉銘傳	交通職工	25—6	4:4
	護證絕對安全的近代空中旅行		交通職工	25—6	4:4
	蘇聯政府統制民用航空之種種	憶　玲	航空雜志	25—5	6:5
	黄河流域鐵路造林之研究	徐　盈	中國實業	25—3	2:3
D類					
D1	讀蔣院長在十省行政會議席上之感想	林　叠	管　理	25—7	1:2
	中國行政改革論	姚崇齡	建國月刊	25—6	14:6
	民族復興之條件	邵元冲	建國月刊	25—6	14:6
	論行政權與立法權的消長	莊心在	文化建設	25—5	2:8
	論民族之發展與中國	林一新	文化建設	25—5	2:8
	中國現狀與憲政實施	楚　平	清華週刊	25—5	44:5
	民主政治在中國	殷　亮	清華週刊	25—5	44:6
	非常時期的地方行政	邵元冲	建國月刊	25—4	14:4
	行政改革的困難	李樸生	獨立評論	25—5	202
D2	中央行政組織的調整問題	張純明	政治經濟學報	25—4	4:3
	中國市政問題	董修甲	道路月刊	25—3	49:3
	近年來中央政治改革	陳之邁	獨立評論	25—4	195
	近時我國地方自治之演變與今後改進之途徑	楊幼炯	時事月報	25—6	14:6
	中國地方行政制度之起源	王文山	時事月報	25—3	14:3
	國民政府施政成績的檢討	秦　南	政治旬刊	25—2	1:14
	中國之市政	蔣愼吾	人文月刊	25—4	7:3-4
	非常時期的地方行政	邵元冲	建國月刊	25—5	14:5
	非常時期之縣政設施	博　濟	康藏前鋒	25—6	3:10
	成績制度下的政府	任家誠	管　理	25—7	1:2
	江浙各縣應有超然主計制度芻議	殷聖作	銀行週報	25—6	20:24
	解決中國市政問題的一個企望	體　揚	道路月刊	25—6	50:3

D 3	軍需人員在軍隊中之地位	雷芷京	經理月刊	25—5	2:5
D 4	軍事經理中之防銹問題	劉再雄	經理月刊	25—4	2:4
	兵器之保管	陳伯勳	經理月刊	25—4	2:4
	官廳購買論	李惕乾	經理月刊	25—4	2:4
	中國戰時的原料自給問題	鮑幼申	經理月刊	25—3	2:3
	戰時巴黎後方的糧食供給問題	田　龍	經理月刊	25—6	2:6
D 5	對於現行會計審計人員攷試制度之意見	曹寶讓	會計雜誌	25—6	7:6
	中國的犯罪問題	徐　華	時兆月報	25—5	31:5
	美國人的法律觀	谷哈特	時事類編	25—5	4:9
	由最近憲法的趨勢討論五權憲法	薩孟武	文化建設	25—5	2:8
	司法審查制與中美兩國憲法問題	陶百川	文化建設	25—5	2:8
	憲法草案上之緊急命令權問題	儲玉坤	文化建設	25—5	2:8
D 6	現代軍事經理組織與運輸	華企雲	經理月刊	25—5,6	2:5,6
E 類					
E 1	整理地方財政的重要及其應取的途徑	顧恩浩	建國月刊	25—4	14:4
	我國財政收支系統之檢討	殷孟威	浙江財政	25—3	9:1
	非常時期之中國財政		經濟評論	25—4	3:4
	從外資利用談到如何利用外資	徐　光	經濟評論	25—5	3:5
	幣制改革後的中國經濟狀況	莫　湮	錢業月報	25—3	16:3
	新公債案與財政金融的影響	陳開夫	錢業月報	25—3	16:3
	非常時期的財政政策	森　禹	錢業月報	25—5	16:5
	財務行政職權之完整與脫節	胡善恆	東方雜誌	25—6	33:11
	我國明日之戰時財政	黃　豪	經理月刊	25—2	2:2
	開源節流的國家財政	吳平章	經理月刊	25—2	2:2
	國民政府成立以來財政制度之整理	衞挺生	經理月刊	25—2	2:2
	中國之戰時財政	蕭　智	經理月刊	25—2	2:2
	整理中之四川財政	晏忠承	經理月刊	25—2	2:2
	戰爭準備中之列强財政	韜　厂	經理月刊	25—2	2:2

	國家之經濟統制與中央銀行	羅迪良	經濟評論	25—1	3:1
	公債整理與財政建設	鮑幼申	經濟評論	25—2	3:2
	整理國債與平衡國庫收支	楊汝梅	廣播週報	25—5	85
	一年來的中國財政	左治生	政治旬刊	25—1	1:9-11
	中國經濟之癥結與統制	方顯庭	政治經濟學報	25—4	3:4
	非常時期的管理經濟	馬寅初	管　　理	25—7	1:2
	非常時期國民經濟層之透視	顏悉達	經理月刊	25—5	2:5
	非常時期之冀察財政	朱光澤	經理月刊	25—5	2:5
	非常時期之中國財政問題	漆琪生	文化建設	25—5	2:8
	我國目前能否施行所得稅之商榷	董蒙正	銀行週報	25—5	20:18
	所謂非常時期之經濟	諸青來	銀行週報	25—5	20:19
	非常時期的經濟問題	馬寅初	銀行週報	25—6	20:23
	德國和平計劃中的經濟綱要	佛郎克府報	時事類編	25—6	4:12
	危難中的華北經濟	鄭曾雲	錢業月報	25—6	16:6
	一九三六年世界經濟的瞻望	朱勝愉	錢業月報	25—5,6	16:6,5
	中國鹽稅之積弊與改革方案	任樹椿	社會經濟月報	25—5	3:5
	所得稅與現代稅制	莊心在	社會經濟月報	25—5	3:5
	最近各國徵收所得稅之鳥瞰	劉絜敖	社會經濟月報	25—6	3:6
	經濟組織與景氣變動	趙懿翔	社會經濟月報	25—6	3:6
	電常時財政的基礎	殷孟威	浙江財政	25—5	9:3
	財務行政問題之綜合的研究	吳少白	浙江財政	25—5	9:3
	日本廣田內閣的財政政策	莫　湮	錢業月報	25—4	16;4
	日本馬場財政的前進	李立俠	東方雜志	25—5	33:10
	馬場財政政策與財政之非常時	家　禾	申報週刊	25—4	1:16
	關稅問題之回顧及改革方案之商榷	白方策	中國建設	25—6	13:6
	中國關稅政策商榷	李權時	經濟學季刊	25—6	7:1
	非常時的財政與財政的非常時	孫懷仁	申報週刊	25—4	1:10
E 2	蘇聯的新預算	煒　權	申報週刊	25—4	1:10

	最近各國之預算制度	唐季清	浙江財政	25—6	9:4
	我國預算編制機關問題	鍾德材	經　理	25—4	2:4
E 3	中國對外貿易指數之編製	曹立瀛	實業部月刊	25—4	1:1
	航務職工生活狀況調查統計概述	王述曾等	交通職工	25—3	4:1
	民國廿四年中國工業災害統計		工商管理月刊	25—4	3:4
	成本會計與業務管理	劉復中	銀行週報	25—3	20:19
	如何注重物品會計	郭寶珠	經　理	25—4	2:4
	就地審計與部隊經理	漆彰藩	經　理	25—4	2:4
	桂黔貿易之分折	劉古諦	統計月報	25—1	11:12
	會計人員資位之商討	袁　焯	鐵道半月刊	25—5	2
	論數字約合法—會計上最簡易之覆核法	王　璜	會計雜誌	25—6	7:6
	銀行公告資產負債表應有標準格式之建議	王　璜	會計雜誌	25—6	7:6
	工場資產價値之鑑定	施仁天	會計雜誌	25—6	7:6
	我國公司會計中之若干問題	顧　準	會計雜誌	25—6	7:6
	中式簿記貨物登銷簿之改良及應用	李夢白	會計雜誌	25—6	7:6
	查帳員職任問題舉例	錢素君	會計雜誌	26—6	7:6
	統一公路會計科目草案		道路月刊	25—4,	50-3
	估計成本制度之研究	陳新梅	工商管理月刊	25—5	3:5
	郵政與一般國營事業厲行成本會計之商榷	徐昌成	交通雜志	25—6	4:6
	公路會計之特質及其結構	楊善楨	公　路	25—5	1:4
	新會計制度之商榷	汪治桂	浙江財政	25—5	9:3
	整理財政與會計稽核制度	郭祖孝	浙江財政	25—5	9:3
	我國審計制度之特質	劉觀海	浙江財政	25—6	9:4
	合作兼營之帳務與會計	伍玉璋	合作月刊	25—5	8:5
E 4	新貨幣政策之史的背景及其將來	厲德寅	時事月報	25—6	14:6
	我國銀行制度能勝任管理通貨乎	侯樹彤	東方雜誌	25—4	33:7
	銀行票據承兌所之檢討	荆　州	新中華	25—5	4:9
	從世界通貨管理說到我國新貨幣制度	賈士毅	經　理	25—2	2:2

中國戰時財政金融之危機及其補救	鮑幼申	經　　理	25—2	2:2
四十年來中國幣制問題		中國實業	25—2	2:2
倫敦金融市場中的外匯結存問題	仲　溪	經濟彙刊	25—4	1:2
去年中國金融界的兩大事	汪疑今	中國經濟	25—2	4:1,2
都市與農村之金融組織		中國經濟	25—2	4:1,2
中美貨幣協定與幣制新開展	魏友棐	錢業月報	25—6	16:6
法幣準備品與準備銀行	宇　蒼	錢業月報	25—6	16:6
銀價的將來及其對於中國產業界的影響	井村董雄	時事類編	25—5	4:9
美國銀行統制的新階段	小島精一	時事類編	25—5	4:9
帝國主義對華貨幣權之爭霸戰	朱　炎	清華週刊	25—5	4:5
中美貨幣合作之意義	權　時	銀行週報	25—5	20:20
中央銀行與國庫之關係	漢　隱	銀行週報	25—5	20:20
評美國經濟學家貨幣宣言	權　時	銀行週報	25—6	20:21
吾國銀行與工商業	沈祖杭	銀行週報	25—6	20:21
幣制改革後之中央銀行	葉攸康	銀行週報	25—6	20:22
準備集中問題之檢討	沈祖杭	銀行週報	25—6	20:23
中央銀行應添設準備局之建議	劉嘯仙	銀行週報	25—6	20:23
論十成準備制	周順鑫	銀行週報	25—6	20:23
論當前的外匯問題	金捷琮	銀行週報	25—6	20:24
幣制改革後興利除弊之方略	俞振基	光　　華	25—6	4:10
銀行資金的構成及其動態	周耀平	光　　華	25—6	4:10
公債與財政	直　夫	商職月刊	25—5	2:3
日人目光中之我國新貨幣政策	魏敦夫	銀行週報	25—3	20:12
生產量增加貨幣數量應否隨之增加	張成達	銀行週報	25—3	20:12
新貨幣政策成功之關鍵	黃元彬	銀行週報	25—3	20:15
中國組織中央準備銀行之檢討	字林西報	銀行週報	25—5	20:17
世界黃金流動現狀	王雨桐	銀行週報	25—5	20:17
論貨幣之準備制度及我國法幣之準備問題	章午雲	社會經濟月報	25—3	3:3-5

	從貨幣改革談到銀行之命運	楊天任	交大經濟	25—2	5
	我國新貨幣政策之剖視	秦本鑑	交大經濟	25—2	5
	實施法幣政策	孔祥熙	廣播週報	25—5	88
	一年來中國之金融	徐　光	經濟評論	25—1	3:1
	中國新貨幣政策實行後的幾個問題	鮑志清	經濟評論	25—2	3:2
	現狀下我國銀行不健全原因之分析及其今後應有之動向	徐　光	經濟評論	25—3	3:3
	中國紙幣發行之現況及其前途	徐　光	經濟評論	25—3	3:3
	銀行變動與中國	閻鴻聲	經濟評論	25—3	3:3
	金融市場之眞諦	劉孔鈞	商業月報	25—3	16:3
	美國聯邦準備制度論	劉孔鈞	商業月報	25—5	16:5
	我國銀行制度問題	葉攸康	商業月報	25—5	16:6
	統制匯兌與中國	直　夫	商職月刊	25—3	2:1
	吾國最近之主要金融問題	趙蘭坪	時事月報	25—3	14:4
	最近各國貨幣制度	唐季清	浙江財政	25—4	9:2
	各省過去幣制概況	姚子山	浙江財政	25—4	9:2
	世界貨幣戰的透視	喬天佑	浙江財政	25—5	9:3
	中國近年銀行界的演變	唐季清	浙江財政	25—5	9:3
	實施法幣政策	孔祥熙	浙江財政	25—6	9:4
	整理國債與平衡國庫收支	楊汝梅	浙江財政	25—6	9:4
	中國紙幣制度之進展	喬天佑	浙江財政	25—6	9:4
E 1	討論閻錫山先生資公有制度	鍾偉成	交大經濟	25—2	5
	從價稅與從量稅之檢討	胡紀常	管　　理	25—7	1:2
	所得稅與遺產稅	鮑幼申	經　　理	25—5	2:5
	中國的關稅政策	黃　豪	經　　理	25—2	2:2
	戰時稅政	陳舉才	經　　理	25—2	2:2
	匯票之承兌背書及追索權		中國實業	25—2	2:2
	實施新鹽法的檢討	印　東	經濟彙刊	25—4	1:2
	私運問題對於財政經濟之影響	莫　湮	錢業月報	25—5	16:5

走私問題之嬗進及有效辦法	褚匯宗	錢業月報	25—6	16:6
華北走私中之中國經濟	張素民	文化建設	25—5	2:8
戰時財政與其基本條件	王克生	文化建設	25—5	2:8
我國目前能否施行所得稅之商榷	董蒙正	銀行週報	25—3	20:18
我國食鹽問題	朱體仁	廣播週報	25—5	85
所得稅之經濟影響及其在賦稅上之地位	劉千山	經濟評論	25—3	3:3
現行中央稅制整理問題	余醒民	經濟評論	25—3	3:3
中國的關稅制度		經濟評論	25—4	3:4
中國今日徵收遺產稅問題	姚同樾	社會經濟月報	25—4	3:4
中國鹽稅之積弊與改革方案	任樹椿	社會經濟月報	25—5	3:5
所得稅與現代稅制	莊心在	社會經濟月報	25—5	3:5
田賦徵收制度的檢討	王元璧	浙江財政	25—5	9:3
政現代租稅體系與所得稅	季貽謀	浙江財政	25—5	9:3
財政的社會政策	金治鄉	浙江財政	25—5	9:3
從中國歷史上觀察財政問題與盛衰之關係	吳少白	浙江財政	25—6	9:4

編後語

上期有葉子剛先生的「鐵路統計分析與管理」一篇，爲了原稿過長的原故，我們只登了一節，現在葉先生已將那篇印成了單行本子，改名「鐵路管理之分析」，每冊定價六角，由青島商務印書館，南京交通雜誌社和上海大公報館代售，凡關于鐵路營業進款之衡量，用款之衡量，設備之運用，設備之營養，人工之效率，材料之攷核等等，都有詳盡的剖析與深刻的研討，我們以爲讀者既可較早的全部讀到，在這里可無繼續刊登的必要了，這是要請讀者和葉先生共同原諒的。

沈奏廷許靖兩位先生都是本校鐵道管理學的教授。在他們的論文「評吾國最近改訂之鐵路列車及車輛統計辦法」和「參觀津浦膠濟兩路後之感想及意見」里，我們可以看出過去我國鐵道管理的淺陋，而同時知道這兩位先生于鐵道管理的各方面的確有着精心的研究。我們希冀——並且相信——鐵道當局會有鄭重的注意與攷慮。

黃宗瑜先生的「新路建設之經濟觀」在第一期里已經引起讀者不少的興趣和認識了，現在他繼續的在本刊討論着。

蘇省財政廳廳長趙棣華先生于百忙中到本校來演講，我們是很感謝的。我們希望他下次再來講講整理財政必經的四個步驟——預算，金庫，會計和稽核。

司徒新博士對于航業管理一科學有專長的，此次在他所作的「中國航業管理問題」的一篇里僅僅提出外洋和內河航運所發生的幾個重要問題作爲概括的介紹。

管理的要訣是什麽，會計與管理究竟有怎樣的一種關係，在錢素君先生的「會計與企業管理」里可以找到一個忠實的答案。凡負管理之責者——不但是會計員——都應該一讀。

俞希稷先生是律師而兼會計師。他說不諳法律會在事業管理上受到重大的損失。他舉的都是實在的例子。

王烈望先生所譯的「事權之分離及其聯整」是一篇關于組織方面的專論。牠的內容有組織的意義，組織的結構和運用，以及組織的各種理論和原則。如果有人正在着手辦理或研究改善一個事業的內部組織問題，讀了這篇文章一定會得着不少的帮助。

「如果說將來國家可無戰爭，卽等于說將來人類可無疾病」，這是王同文先生譯文里很精闢的語句。我們不是正在度着非常時期嗎，惠爾葛斯的建議中之軍運組織表是值得我們的軍事當局參攷的。

本期里還有本院卒業同學靜勇先生的一篇通訊，對于他的職務有很詳細的報告，這實是我們所非常歡迎的。我們熱誠地希望其他的校友都能夠根據着獨到的服務經驗寫給我們些切實的稿子。

本刊投稿簡章

一、投稿以有關於管理者為限。

二、投稿不拘文言白話，須繕寫清楚，並加標點，如係外國文稿件，並請打印之，均不得於一紙兩面寫字。

三、論著稿中，如有譯名或引文，須分別註明原文及出處。

四、譯稿須將原文題目，原著者姓名，出版日期及地點，詳細載明，如能附寄原文尤佳。

五、稿末請簽名蓋章，並註明住址。

六、來稿文字，本院有酌量修改之權，如投稿人不願有何增删，則應於投稿時聲明。

七、來稿登載與否，概不寄還，惟附寄郵票預先聲請寄還者　亦可照辦。

八、來稿一經登載，當酌贈以每千字一元至三元之薄酬。

九、來稿請寄上海徐家匯交通大學管理學院。

中華民國二十五年九月出版

第一卷第三期

每本大洋四角
全年五期大洋一元六角

主編者　鍾偉成

發行者　交通大學出版處

印刷者　華豐印刷鑄字所　上海浙江路五三六號

管理

二月刊

第一卷 第四期 二十五年十一月

本期要目

交通大學管理學院編輯

管理二月刊

第一卷 第四期
民國二十五年十一月

目錄

論著

譯述

書評

論著

國民大會延期之感想(D6)

林叠

國民大會，是國民黨之最高主張，是革命歷程之最後階段，爲還政於民，實行憲政之總樞紐也。考國民黨建國之程序，有軍政，訓政，憲政，三期之分，在建國之初，不惜以武力掃除一切革命障礙，反動勢力，以除民「害」。至革命已有基礎，政權在握，乃由軍政而進於訓政，在此時期中，致力於主義之宣傳，地方自治之推進，以及行使四權之訓練，以使民「知」，以敎民「行」。迨民衆已能「知」，能「行」，則由訓政而達於憲政，國民黨於此時則以整個政權，奉還於全體革命之民衆，此由全體革命民衆依法選出之代表所組成的國民大會，實若國民黨向人民辦理總交代之盛會，亦卽是結束黨治，國民執行政權，制定憲法，選舉總統，以施行民主政治，完成現代化國家之壹劃時代之關鍵。

吾人於此可以了然國民大會重要性之所在矣。顧國民黨數十年來之所努力，一以天下爲公之精神，服務社會之人生觀，爲全體民衆謀福利，不惜以最大犧牲向萬惡軍閥官僚手中奪回政權，在國民黨之立場，對於政權之取得，純係一種急公好義之手段。要以之交還於政權所從出之人民，以遂其革舊鼎新，建立民主國家之目的。惟既歷盡艱難困苦始行獲得之政權，其轉移交代，自不得不格外愼重，力求妥善嚴密，又際茲國難方殷，戰雲密佈，於事實上於情勢上，國民黨實未便苟且忽忙，舉行國民大會，亦不能遽爾卸却政權，以免有所影響於大局，是以對於國民大會不得不宣佈延期舉行。

茲就事實上言之，公民直接選舉，本爲一最繁難之事，其在吾國初次舉行，則爲難之尤難，國民黨近數年來對於地方自治之推行，實致其最大之努力，惟因種種不可避免之障礙與阻撓，未能達到所具之期望，就中如與直接選舉有密切關係之保甲制度，戶口淸查，各省尙乏顯著之成效，且教育尙未普及於民間，四權之訓練，未見有良好之表現，並益以版圖遼闊，交通諸多不便，而在此事屬創舉，初辦直接選舉之時，欲將公民登記宣誓初選複選等項，於三數月之間，辦理竣事，談何容易。試觀美國，其人民參與選舉，有百伍拾餘年之歷史，兼之教育普及，交通便利，具備選舉客觀之條件，此次改選總統，猶需用數月期間，自六月着手辦理，至十一月方能竣事揭曉，何況吾國素無選政之基礎，缺乏客觀之條件，竟欲此民選大典於短期內完成之，不亦戛戛乎難哉，雖有多處已辦理初選完竣，惟因忽忙辦理，所推出之候選人，多屬未能依法選出，而操縱舞弊之事，處處有之，且既得初選完竣，又須聽候中央將候選人圈定若干名，方可進行複選，此種選舉法，固與民主道義相違，爲全世界所未有，未免有欠妥之處，此無怪各地辦理選舉之機關，紛紛報告趕辦不及，請展緩期限，俾得蕆事也。今大會既已延期，則選舉事項，當力行改善爲宜。

再就情勢上言之，橫在吾國當前之最重要問題，盡人皆知爲中日外交之險惡，與抵禦外力之侵襲，此誠民族生死存亡之關頭，處此非常時期，自應保持政局之穩固，社會之安定，以便集中全國上下精力，爲外交之應付，與國防之佈置，苟於此時弗顧國事之嚴重，而遽要改革整個政制，變更安全局面，勢必致予國內外敵人敗類以搗亂襲擊之機會，其影響全國上下禦侮之情緒，牽動安內攘外之政策，可無疑義。且吾國自改元以來，國內之團結，力量之集中，無有逾於此時者，民意之嚴正，愛國之熱烈，亦無有盛於此時者，此正國民黨負責解決國難，復興民族之大好機會，在此情形之下，國民黨實義不容辭，責無旁貸，應該苦幹到底，把握時機，以完成國民革命，復興民族，收回失地諸偉大之事業，以慰民衆喁喁之望，則大會雖延至五年或十年之後舉行，尚未爲晚。

國民大會代表選舉，既有事實上種種困難，又值國事嚴重，時局緊張之秋，權衡利害緩急，大會自非延期召集不可。抑有進者，吾國民族意志，迄今已臻强盛激昂，對於偉大領袖之推崇信仰，已普遍於全體民衆之心裏，而反映於國防戰線上，實不讓美人之愛戴羅斯福，德人之愛戴希特拉，意人之愛戴慕索里尼，專美於前，以吾埋頭苦幹，勵精圖治之賢明領袖，領導在上，萬衆齊心戮力。共同奮鬥在下，意志統一，自力更生，國事至此，實大可爲，復興民族，排除國難，卽在目前。

二十五年十二月一日

管理二月刊

第一卷第三期　民國二十五年九月

論著

演講

譯述

報告

轉載

通訊

五十年來美國實業管理進展史（B 7）

嚴礪平

一　緒言

自美人泰婁(F.W. Taylor) 提倡科學管理迄今，已五十餘年矣。最初科學管理，僅實行於鑄鐵工場，其法則，亦祇及於研究應付工場中各項問題而已。自一九一一年後，科學管理，漸爲美國一般企業家所重示；其範圍亦逐漸推廣，由工場中推行及於工業之其他部分，寖假及於各重要工業之中。管理法則，雖依原則而定，亦漸趨複雜。欲考求自泰婁以來，美國數十年中之管理學上重要進展，頗非易事；蓋以其範圍之大，應用之繁，殊難作一有統系之叙述也。

惟美國實業管理發展，歷史最久，成効亦最宏。若能將其經過情形，跡其因果，不特可供研究斯學者參攷，抑且大有俾益於吾人。誠以我國方在復興期中，經濟建設，尚肇其端，他國之經驗，實資我以觀摩。倘能鑑其成功，而嗟其失敗，用以自勵，亦建設前途之一助也。

是篇將美國實業管理進展史，劃分爲三個時期；自一八〇〇至一九一二爲第一個時期，一九一三至一九二二爲第二個時期，一九二三至一九三二年爲第三個時期。第一期爲發軔時期，第二期爲演進時間，第三期爲發達時期。

二 第一個時期

工業歷史，實爲人類生活歷史中之一部分，故其年代，與他種歷史，同其久遠；然所謂近代工業，則爲時至暫，不過百餘年事耳。學者有主以瓦特一七六九年之發明蒸汽機，爲近代工業之起源，蓋此爲節省人力機械之最重要發明。亦有主以哈格雷夫(James Hargreaves)一七七〇年紡紗機之發明，爲近代工業歷史之始，蓋此爲近代工業機械化之起點。總之，新工業之勃興，爲時雖暫，其範圍之廣闊，生產能力之增加，以及企業組織之擴大，實使人類全部生活及思想，蒙受空前影響。吾人目前認爲若干重要問題，無論屬於經濟的，或社會的，均爲新工業所引起。以科學方法，研究處置企業組織中，各種事務，希冀增加効率，亦爲新工業所必然引起的一重要活動。

實業管理範圍，應以實業方面全部之活動爲對象：如下列五項，均爲經營任何一有規模之製造企業所不可少者：(一)企業組織之計劃，(二)廠址之選擇及廠屋之建造，(三)廠務管理，(四)採購材料及存儲，(五)推銷出品。今日研究實業管理者，以上五項均須顧及。然一般人士，恆以廠務管理，爲實業管理之全部，殊未盡然。惟廠務管理，爲實業管理進展史中最先受人注意，故早年各方之管理研究，均集中於此點。

一八八六年美國機械工程師會 (American society of Mechanical Engineers) 刊物，首先登載杜納 Towne 一文，敘述工廠管理爲一藝術，已積有若干年代之經驗矣。並主張各廠當局，須從事實上的觀察，作有系統之記載，以之分析比較，藉求出品經濟，及成本減低等語。此文當時頗引起一般注意。繼起討論之文，漸有發表。大率集於討論工廠管理中之工資一項。其中最著名者，爲一八九一年何爾山(Halsey)之獎金工資制度。因其方法，極易推行，故應用甚廣，頗爲學者所樂道。

泰婁(Taylor)自一八七八年入米達未耳鋼廠(Midvale Steel Co.)服務以後，深感工廠中人力物力之未克充分運用，卽從事于研究改進之方。泰氏於一八九○年因有他就，脫離米達未耳鋼廠，然其在該鋼廠十餘年中，已將科學管理之基楚確立。此後屢就他職，均以改良管理爲務。自一九○一年起，泰氏不復担任有酬報之工作，專事著述及演講，以宣傳科學管之原則。泰氏對於管理之研究，埋頭苦幹，孳孳不倦，前後凡數十年。積時旣久，經驗斯宏。其所經歷，非經長期間之研討，不肯輕於發表。氏於一八九五年發表計件工資新制度一文，乃在十五年不斷試行之後。此文並論及動作與計時研究，乃發前人所未發。氏於一九○三年發表工廠管理一文，對於廠務之改進，作一有統系之供獻。書中所述管理方法，多數已成過去，然其所定各種原則，與及其對於工廠管理之新態度，實爲今日實業管理發達之基本。泰氏本人對於研究管理之動機，容或受上述杜納影響，然其供獻之偉大，宣傳之努力，今日學者公認其爲實業管理學之先驅。一九一五年身殁之日，杜納稱之爲一種新科學之創造者。

自泰斐專事努力於科學管理後，扈從者甚衆：最著者有甘特（Gantt）吉耳勃士（Gilbreth）白士（Barth）及道奇（Dodge）諸氏，均以改良工廠管理爲職業，歷在各工廠推行科學管理，其臨事也，不尙臆度，全以事實爲根據，故成効頗著。一時工廠當局，鑒於泰氏及其他管理專家之成就，對於廠務之處置，已漸有變更往日態度之趨向矣。

在初期之所謂科學管理，均集中於工廠管理，內容大致如下：

一、工廠計劃部之成立，以計劃出品所應經過之詳細過程，與每一手續所必需之時間。

二、組織方面之變更，由所謂軍隊式的組織，改爲專責式（Functional Organisation）的組織，每一職員，專司一種專門的責務。

三、訓練工人，使其能依照已經研究所定之最良方法完成工作。

四、工人工資，應依照其個人出品之多寡，及品質之良窳，公平付給。

以上所述工廠管理方法，應用得當，固可減輕成本，提早交貨日期，工廠出品增多，工人工資增高等良好結果。然因應用不得當，而致失敗者，亦甚多。其失敗原因，不外下列二種：(一)工廠當局對於科學管理原則上，尚無充分認識，祇用種種刺激方法，使工人工作加忙，出品增加，而忽視管理人員本身方面之各種研究，計劃，與指導工人等項工作。(二)工廠推行新制度，過於驟速，工人方面，尚未訓練成熟，以致失其信仰，而增其疑竇，結果不特毫無成績，徒增廠方之支出耳。其時尚有一般自命効率專家者(Efficiency Man)學識與經驗二方，均甚幼稚，惟善利用時機，作種種自我宣傳，以增進工廠効率爲標題，工廠當局，每因急於求功，或炫於新奇之說，貿然聘爲顧問，以致失敗累累，而正當科學管理之發展，因之遲緩，而不易普及。

一九一一年美國州際商務委員會因鐵路增加運價問題，徵詢各方意見，白蘭的斯（Brandies)謂美國鐵路，若採用科學管理，可無須加價；同時管理學專家，殷曼生氏（Harrington Emerson）本其在聖太飛 Santa Fe 鐵路之宏富經驗，宣稱美國鐵路，若在管理方面，注重効率，則每日可省美金一百萬元之鉅。一般人士，咸震於二氏之申述，而科學管理，遂成爲當時最盛行之論題。報章雜誌，無論大小，羣爲之評論；而學校議辯，亦每以是命題。此舉實有利於科學管理之推行。據一九一二年美國機械工程師會調查，當時實業界採用科學管理原則，或其一部分者，已有五十三業。

三　第二個時期

自一九一二年後至一九二二之十年中，實業管理方面之進步，頗有足述，據夏爾福氏(Aflord)博採各專家之意見，將此十年中之成績，歸納成爲三類，第一類爲心理上之變遷，第二類爲管理方法之實施，第三類爲進展中應注意之特點。茲將其所述分類內容，附列於左。

第一類　心理上之變遷

甲　昔時關係管理學之爲科學抑爲藝術之爭執，已成過去，而管理應以科學爲根據，漸爲一般所公認。

乙　各種反對或懷疑科學管理之表現，已見絕跡。

丙　實業界負責人士，已覺悟管理問題，實有存在與討論之價值。

丁　企業家，工程師，與教育界，已漸接受管理學上之種種原則。

第二類　管理方法之實施

甲　實業界成本會計之運用科學方法，如確定成本會計制度，標準成本計算，空閒時間損失計算，銷售預測，生產數量之長期分配，與及費用預算之確立。

乙　出品單純化，工程標準化，及減除消耗運動等之利益，漸爲實業界所公認，在一九二〇年至一九二二年二年中爲尤甚。

丙　實業管理專家，均主各種判斷，須依事實爲根據，此爲運用圖表及規範，以保存及傳達管理上重要記載之主因。（如應用極廣之甘氏圖表Gantt's Chart 在一九一七方完成今日之格式）

丁　科學管理方法之採用，已普遍於實業界之各部分，自製造部分起至銷售部分爲止。

第三類　實業管理進展中之特點

甲　管理活動範圍，已自所謂泰婁氏法則，（Taylor System）擴充至於工廠中之各部分，及實業界之各業。

乙　自一九一二年起，大學中設有實業管理專科者，已有十起，

丙　人事管理問題之引起企業界之研究，最堪注意。

丁　管理專家，主張實業界，須着重服務主義，與勞工方面之各種人事爭執，應以公允的精神處理，不可專斷，或用高壓手段。

以上所述之三類，內中第二類，關於實施方法，似嫌混統。然以實業界各業之復雜情形，殊難作一普遍之叙述，以爲實施方法之根據。茲依美國全國工程學會協會消耗減除委員會，在下列四業：卽金屬業，靴鞋工業，男式成衣業，及印刷工業，五十一工廠中，調查所得

列表於左，以爲參攷：

管理法則	金屬業 計28廠 未經採用	金屬業 成績不佳	金屬業 成績良好	靴鞋業 計8廠 未經採用	靴鞋業 成績不佳	靴鞋業 成績良好	男式成衣業 計9廠 未經採用	男式成衣業 成績不佳	男式成衣業 成績良好	印刷業 計6廠 未經採用	印刷業 成績不佳	印刷業 成績良好	四業共計51廠 未經採用	四業共 成績不佳	四業共 成績良好
一、工人選擇及工作分派	10	10	18	0	6	2	0	4	5	0	5	1	0	25	26
二、獎勵工資制度	3	9	16	0	0	8	4	2	3	1	1	4	8	12	31
三、生產集中計劃	4	10	14	4	0	4	4	2	3	3	2	1	15	14	22
(甲)排列工作程序	7	8	13	4	1	3	4	2	3	5	0	1	20	11	20
(乙)預定出品期限	5	8	15	3	3	2	3	2	4	3	2	1	14	15	22
四、動作及時間研究	8	3	17	5	2	1	3	3	3	5	0	1	21	8	22
五、成本會計	6	9	13	1	3	4	2	5	2	3	2	1	12	19	20
六、閒時分析															
(甲)人力	21	0	7	7	1	0	9	3	0	5	0	1	39	4	8
(二)機械	15	1	12	7	1	0	8	1	0	3	0	3	33	3	15

七、採購管理	4	5	19	1	4	3	3	1	5	3	2	1	11	12	28
八、材料管理	3	5	20	1	1	6	3	1	5	4	1	1	11	8	32

上表詳示四業中，各廠施行之管理法則，乃以各廠採用之多寡爲次序。若依成績良好者爲次序，則應列如下：材料管理，奬勵工資制度，工人選擇及工作分派，生產計劃，動作及時間研究，成本會計，與閒時分析。

關於實施科學管理法則，有一點最有意義，卽在昔日，管理專家，最先注意生產方面之物質上的各種問題，其後漸顧及工人之訓練等事，在過去之十年中，已注意及領工與工人在管理上應有之地位。事前非徵得彼等同意，廠方似已不再任意實施，蓋非此不足引起工作上之興趣，促進合作精神，而改善勞資雙方之情感也。

此外尙有一可注意之事，卽各種管理學會之成立。管理學會之最先成立者，厥爲泰婁學會(Taylor Society)，是會實發起於一九一〇年，正式成立則在一九一二年，當時名爲科學管理促進會 (Society for the Promotion of Scientific Management)至一九一六年，因泰婁氏於上年病故，爲紀念其功績起見，將該會改稱泰婁學會。人事管理之研究組織，首先成立者，爲一九一三年之全國公司事務學校協會，(National Association of Corporation Schools)注重人事管理之研究與訓練，至一九二〇年，改稱全國公司事務訓練協會(National Associat ion of Corporation Training)自一九二二年起該會併入全國人事管理學會。(National Personnel Association)一九一七年五月，實業管理工程師學會成立，(Society of Industrial Engineers) 一九一九年五月，全國人事管理人員協會成立；(National Society of Employment Managers) 該會在一九二〇五月，改稱美國人事協會，在一九二二年亦併入全國人事管理學會。美國械機工程師學會(American Society of Mechanical Engineers)對於實業管理事務，提倡最早，一九二〇年爲便利研究起見，成立一實業管理組。以上四個管理學會，在一九二二年，會員總數達四千〇四十一人；其中機械工程學會之實業管理組，會員最多，佔一千七百餘人；實業管理工程師學會次之，佔一千〇三二人，泰婁學會又次之，佔七六九人，全國人事管理協會最少，佔五百人。(內有一二九人係團體會員)在一九二〇——一九二二年之二年中，各管理學會，曾在下列諸事，聯合進行；如管理學名詞之釐定，管理文稿之編行索引，管理圖表之統一。與考核工廠管理成績優劣之方法等事。

四 第三個時期

自一九二三迄一九三二之十年過程中，美國實業界，有極大之變化，即在中段出現空前之繁榮，而在末期，復感受極度之衰落。下表生產指數，爲聯邦準備會所發表。 (Federal Reserve Board)

一九二三　一〇一
一九二四　九五
一九二五　一〇四
一九二六　一〇八
一九二七　一〇六
一九二八　一一一
一九二九　一一九
一九三〇　八一
一九三一　六五・六

當其在全盛時期，樂觀者以爲貧困二字，不久或可在美國失其存在，孰知自一九三〇年以後，不景氣勢潮，驟然侵襲，此後二年中，實業界所感受之痛苦與及困難情形，殊難以言語形容。卽工人之失業人數，亦大見增加；按此十年中美國之失業人數，在一九二三年爲最少，約有一百五十萬餘人，在一九三二年，則爲一千一百萬人。在起首之七年中，管理人員之調動甚少，自一九三〇年起，卽管理人員，亦有顯著之變動。實業界情形，十年中雖有如是之起伏，然管理學仍有穩定的進展。且有普及於各方之趨勢。在繁榮時代，管理學上之進展，實爲促進繁榮之一要素。在不景氣時代，則管理較佳之工廠，其所經歷之過程，亦較爲良善，此爲學者所公認者也。茲將此十年中實業管理之各種進展情形，及其有關之重要條目，一併論之。

一、組織問題　自一九二一年之不景氣後，實業界對於組織方面，重加注意。組織表之結構，已不如前之依重，而員司個人的能力問題，最爲重視。爲求組織行使上增加効率起見，職務之分配，專門愈甚，而平時考核員司之成績亦愈勤。且不惜時間與人力，製成各種圖表，因數，及指數等條目，與過去情形，作隨時之比較，以求進步。

二、成本會計　此十年中，最有進步的管理法則，則爲成本會計一項。此項進步，得力於全國成本會計師協會之功爲多。下列三點，最爲顯著：(一)成本會計學地位之增高，(二)預算制度應用之提倡，(三)標準成本之推行。

預算制度應用之提倡，及其受實業界大衆採用之速，最堪注意，蓋此制度之內容，尚有相當之複雜，據一九三一年，美國工業會議委員會 (National Industrial Conference Board) 之調查，在一六二工廠之預算制度中，有十分之八，自一九二二年以後，方始採用。

標準成本，自一九一八年海立生氏(Charter Harrison) 創行之後，一切討論文字，大率發表於一九二二年以後。標準成本應用之普遍，可證工廠中預算成本之重要。

三、耗費之減少　自一九二三年以後，實業界之減少耗費工作，有三個重要之發展；即爲工廠耗費之力謀減少，出品之單純化，及工程上之標準化是也。減少耗費運動，自經一九二一年美國工程協會(American Engineering Council) 發表工業耗費報告之後，卽爲全國實業界所接受。各方均在推行，此項運動，有關一國資源之保存，實爲國家經濟上，一重要之供獻。誠如美前總統胡佛(H.C. Hoover) 所云，美國工程協會卽在五十年中，祇有此一耗費報告，該會卽有存在之價值。

至於出品之單純化，則爲各方減少出品上之非必要之尺寸，體量，式樣，及種類等項。據蓋密爾(Gemmill) 氏之調查，美國實業界，自採用耗費報告之建議後，每年可省美金約六萬萬元。若以此爲根據，則一九二三至一九三二之十年中。節省之數，必在五十萬萬元以上。

工程標準化，在一九二三年以前，已爲實業界所採用，然此後之進步尤速。參加此項運動之分子，已包括私人工廠，工廠協會，工程學術團體，及政府機關，且組有標準協會以規定各項通行之標準。已定標準之數量，在一九三一年之統計，已有一百八十一種。(在一九二三年時祇有十種) 關於標準化經濟上之節省，殊難估計，汽車工業界宣稱，每年可省美元七萬五千萬元之鉅。每年用於標準化之各種費用亦甚巨，在一九二六年，曾有調查，實業界及工程學術團體，該年約費去二百六十萬元，而聯邦政府，則該年費去約四百二十五萬元。

四、工資給付問題　奬金工資制度之應用，亦頗有進步。拉也耳 (Lytle) 根據一九二二年蓋密爾 (Gemmill) 及一九三二裘雪斯 (Jucius) 二氏在芝加哥之調查，製成下列一比較表。

	工人數		總數之百分比	
	一九二二	一九三二	一九二二	一九三二
計時制	一五、六三〇	四四、六七四	五三·五	二九·四
勵金制	一三、六〇〇	一〇七、四八九	四六·五	七〇·六

獎金制度之性質，亦由一九二四年時之十七種，增至一九三二年時之三十二種。惟各種方法，亦不過將少數之基本方式，略加更改，以適用於特殊環境而已。團體獎金制度之應用者。亦增加不少。至於職員方面之獎金制度，在一九二九以前，因市面繁榮，亦曾採用。一九三〇年起，因不景氣之故，無形取消。

五、工作分析　自一九一九至一九二七年，美國工廠中工人之生產能力，約增百分之五十，其所用之馬力，約增百分之三十。此生產能力之突然增加，得力於工作分析研究之功不小。況在高工資制度之下，欲減輕成本中之人工一項，亦非將工人生產能力增加不可，因之在一九二三年尚存在之關於工作分析中，動作及計時研究之分歧意見，已沉寂無聞。而採用計時研究之工廠，漸漸增加，且已及於紡織工業矣。

六、材料之存儲與搬運　材料管理與存貨檢點，亦有重要進展。實業界鑒於不景氣時，存貨過多之損失，恆使其材料之存儲，不超過一預定之限度。汽車工業中之進展，尤為有味。即存料已由數月之供給，減至祇數三四日之所需。外來之貨車，能直達廠中之製造部分，故搬運與存儲之費用亦可減輕。

材料搬運之經濟問題，亦已引起各方之注意。參加討論者，亦日多。不特搬運機械，時有發明，即搬運人員之組織，亦頗有進步。一九二八年中，工廠之增加搬運材料之新設備，可攷者已有三十七家，每年可省八十五萬元。搬運材料之原則，不外減少人工，及避免回後的動作，努力推行所謂直線的過程而已。搬運材料之漸趨經濟，則為此原則之多加應用耳。

七、安全問題　工廠安全問題，在一九一一年已受實業界普遍的注意。勞工損害賠償法律，亦於此時頒佈，各廠當局，均注意此問題之討論，及添置安全之設備，當時工廠意外事件，減至往日二分之一，或三分之一。自一九二三年後，因生產能力之突然增加，意外事件，亦隨之增多。惟生產率之增加較速，故實際上之比例率，尚在減低。一九二八年美國工程協會受保險業之委託，對於高速度生產時期之安全問題，作一研究，其結論如下。

一、高速度生產率之下，意外事件亦可設法減少。

二、工廠安全，則生產能力亦可增高。

三、廠務高級管理人員，應研究減少意外事件之發生。

八、人事管理與工場會議　關於人事管理之討論文件，在此期中，發表者約有八百餘篇，可見管理人員，對於此問題之興趣。蓋在十餘年前，人事管理，最初受人注意時，主其事者，均係新手。所有各種法則，如勞工選擇，心理測驗，技能考試，職務分析，勞工訓練，以及其他安，全保，險衛生等各項問題，均無往則可尋，必須本身加以考察及研究，方能應付裕如，偶有心得，即著爲文，故關於此問題之文件，發表獨多也。工廠當局，素輕視人事管理一事，及經提倡，始悟其重要性。人事管理員，今日在工廠中之地位，已與關於生產部分之其他職員相等，即在不景氣時代之調動，亦不甚多。

工場會議，在工廠人事問題中，頗佔重要。勞方與廠方之各種協議事務，在一九二三年已有七十萬工人參加，至一九二八年，參加者倍之，參加協議事務者增多，則工會之進步，即見遲緩。而不景氣之襲擊，尤足使工人地位之降低，即在繁榮時代，與廠方所訂關於勞方有利之協定，亦多所未行。

九、工資標準　十年之中，管理問題中之變化最爲奇突者，莫如工資標準問題一項。在一九二一年以前，除少數管理專家外，高度生產，須伴以提高工資標準之理論，一般人士，均所未曉。是年且有三百餘篇文字，議論工資應如何削減，及推測應減低之限度。孰知一九二二年，此類文字，已不復見，而代以提高工資標準之討論，至一九二六年，提高工資標準理論，已爲先見之實業家，及勞工領袖所公認。高度待遇，實促成一九二六——一九二九之繁榮。自一九二九以後，不景氣時代初起時，工資尚未減低。然自一九三一年起，則各廠均在削減工資矣。美國工業會議委員會根據一千七百十八工廠之調查，發表一九三二與一九二九之二年中工資比較情形如下：

職務種類	減資工廠佔全數工廠之比例	減資之限度（以一九二九年爲準）
高級職員	八〇・五	二〇・三
低級職員	八一	一五・九
勞工	七五	一三・九

上面數字。頗堪玩味；卽工資之減低，在工廠中佔數較少，而削減限度，尤少於其他職員之俸給。總之，高度工資理論之結果如何，殊難斷言，然必須與高度生產爲伴，則似無疑義也。

十、工作時間與工作環境　一九二六年起，福特汽車公司，宣稱該公司決採用每星期作工五天制度。此舉當時實業家，均引爲驚異。然此乃機械工業，以及高速度生產，所引起之必然效果。據工業會議委員會之調查，在一九二八年，已有二百七十餘工廠，實行五天星期制度，卽在一九三〇年，少數工廠，因欲維持工資，以致延長工作時間，然大部分工廠，仍趨於工作時間之減少也。

工作環境之改善，亦頗有進步．如以換氣方法，以減除塵埃及臭氣，以及調節空氣之溫度及潮度，光線之改良，採用强有力之燈光，以增進工作上之愉快，及生產效率，疲勞問題，因工作環境之改善，已不若前之嚴重；消防設備，亦與日俱新；至於避聲研究，則目前尙在初步的進行中。

十一、廠基設計與工廠設備　關於廠基設計之新趨勢有二：(一)爲選擇廠基于較小市集，或鄉村中，(二)爲工廠本身範圍之縮小。誠如美國工程協會報告所言，今日實業界，須注重製造工業之分散，方能使農工兩業，得平衡之發展，工業中除少數偉大工業，如鋼鐵等業，必須巨大規模極外，有多種類之工業，範圍較小，殊無須設於城市之中。至于工廠本身之範圍，過于宏大者，不利之點亦甚多，故此方研究，已證明美國多數大工廠，已遠超最經濟之限度矣。

工廠設備中，有二點，頗受重視：(一)各業工廠中，有無數機械設備，雖就機械本身而言，尙可供多年之使用，然爲適應新市場需要，及與新機械競爭起見，早經調換；(二)因不景氣之故，往日所添置之廠中各項財產，須重行估計，以求適合市面之新價值。

十二、推銷問題　此時期中，市場學之發達，殊爲重要。泰斐學會，實爲市場學研究之中堅。該會首先提倡以科學管理之原則，應用於銷售方面，而美國管理協會（American Ma nagemeut Association)且設有一組，專事討論市場學問題。其趨向似側重於下列諸問題之研究與發展，如銷售員職務上之分工，銷售費用之預算，銷售費用之計算，價格之規定，市場分析，推銷額之預定，與廣告之效用等項。

十三、實業計劃及統制問題　在此時間中，有一重要問題，尚爲初期的討論，卽爲整個實業的計劃與統制問題。實業界人士，及管理學者，鑑於繁榮之不能繼續，漸覺悟整個生產組織，應加以調整，使生產與消費兩方並顧，方能穩定國民經濟，而避免因商業上高度起伏所引起之不幸結果。關係調整之方案甚多，大率在下列所述之限度以內；(一)實業及商業之計劃，成爲聯邦政府之一種政務，成立一調整局，確定製造家應製造之貨品，出品之數量，及價格等事項，(二)在政府監督之下，實業界自身設法調節生產。關於實業計劃及統制問題，因係初期討論。成效如何，尙待異日事實上之證明。

十四、實業管理教育　實業管理教育，亦有顯著之發達。大學之設有專科者，自一九二二年之十校，擴至一九三二年之三十五校。畢業生亦由三百增至六百餘名。其注重學科，管理與工程雙方並重。工程科目，大概如下：數學，理化，理化實驗，材料力學，圖畫，應用力學，水力學，熱力工程，熱力工程試驗，電力工程，電力工程試驗，測量，工廠實習，工程材料，工程問題討論等；管理科目，則爲工業史，工業經濟，製造概況，人事管理，生產

管理，會計統計，市場學，理財方法，運輸學，及工業組織等科目。(參閱『管理』第二期)

十五、工業研究　在不景氣時代，實業界有許多工廠，工業研究方面之支出，反較繁榮時增加，殊足證明工業研究之價値。研究綱目，大概爲成本之減低，品質之改良，新出品之發明，新效用之發現，與副產品之研究等項。一九二七年，全國實業界，顧問工程師，及學術機關，之設有研究所者，有九百九十九個單位。一九二八年生產方面之研究費用，達二萬萬元之鉅。據全國研究委員會(National Research Council)之調查，一九三一年與一九二九年之研究經費及工作效率之比較如下；

	經費方面之百分比	效率方面之百分比
增加者	七五	八七
維持原狀者	一五	一〇
減少者	一〇	三

一九三一年研究工作之分配如下：

性質	百分比
新出品	三八
品質改良	三七
減低成本	一九

副產品研究　一一

新效用之發現　五

十六、實業界之集會組織與管理學會　近數年內，實業界對於業務，技術，及管理三方之各種智識，已願公開討論，互相交換，不復如昔日之深自秘藏。此種坦白的態度，可使全部實業界之標準提高。根據美國聯邦政府商務部之調查在一九二六年。該國有九千個實業集會，一九二八年增至一萬三千，一九三〇年復增至一萬九千餘。集會組織範圍，包括地方，州際、全國及國際各方；討論範圍，則爲各種統計、成本記算，工業研究，單純化與標準化，工廠徵信，運輸問題，及商業道德等，均在其列。

管理學業方面之會員，亦大有增加。學會之力量，亦增高不少。所出版之各種報告及論文，流行極廣。各學會亦頗能合作。交換學術之聯席會議及大會，時有舉行。管理學會組織之規模較大者。除前已論列之美國機械工程師會之實業管理組，管理工程師學會及泰裴學會外，尙有美國管理協會及全國成本會計師協會等二會。以上五會，曾屢次代表美國，出席世界管理學會議，卽對於日內瓦之國際管理學專局(International Management Institute)亦多所協助也。

五　結論

美國五十年來實業管理學之進展，在發軔時期，因各方未能卽行認識，故進步甚遲，第二期中已引起各方注意，故進步甚速，第三期中，方能普遍應用。不景氣之侵襲，尤足使實業界反躬省問，自求改進之方，故第三期之經過，最有深味。蒸汽機之發明，與工業機械化應用，固爲促進新工業之要素，學者以新工業影響於人類生活與思想之巨大，謂爲實業革命。科學管理運動之發生，使實業界減低成本增進生產，改良待遇，影響及於全球，開新工業歷史中之新紀元，時賢謂爲第二次實業革命，誠不爲過。第三期中所引起之實業計劃及統制問題，謀生產消費之調整，以免商業上高度起伏，而期國民經濟長期穩定，因目前尚在演進時期，成效猶未大著，然其影響勢將推及於國際間之實業計劃與協調，則實業革命或又將入於第三期矣。

美國數十年中之實業過程，與吾人之教訓實多，我國生產問題，尚在開始，美國之生產，則已過剩，欲採用科學管理方法，以增進生產，同時復設法避免因生產過剩，所引起之衰落，則誠今日我國政府，實業界，與管理學者，當前一大問題也。

貨運車輛載重統計之理論與實用（C7）

許　靖

一　何謂車輛載重

車輛載重者，指裝入車內之實在貨物重量而言，與車輛之規定容量截然不同。例如三十噸車之規定容量爲三十噸，但實際上所裝之貨物，或竟不及十噸之多，或又有裝至二十七八噸者，亦未可知，要之無論相差多少，其實裝貨重之不能滿足規定容量者，則常占十之八九。依經濟原理而言，實裝貨物重量與車輛之規定容量相差愈大，則車輛之運用愈不經濟，亦卽運輸上之愈不經濟，易言之，卽爲耗費愈多，損失愈大也。故爲避免或減少此項損失起見，無論任何鐵路先進國家，對于車輛裝載莫不極端重視，同時設置各種統計，考其變化，察其進展，根據統計分析之結果，而作種種之改進。此等平均車輛載重英稱 Wagon Loads 美稱 Car Loads 二者名異實同，而其用意所在，則又同爲力求平均載重之增進，以謀車輛運用經濟，與夫其他種種有形無形之利益，請析言之如次。

二　車輛載重與車輛運用之經濟關係

平均每車裝貨愈多，則極少數車輛可供最大運量之應用，而鐵路不致因添置非爲必要之車皮，增加無謂之開支，試設例以證明之。假定某路一年內運輸最旺之月，須運貨物一、〇〇〇、〇〇〇噸，按平均每四日運輸一次，及每車平均裝載三噸計算，則須四七、六一九輛貨車方敷周轉，其算法如下：

30日(一月日數)÷4日＝7次　即分7次運完之意

1,000,000噸÷7次＝142,857噸　即每次可運之噸數

142,825噸÷3噸＝47,619輛　即需要之車數

假設其他一切情狀不變，惟每車平均裝載能由三噸進至三噸有半，則僅有四〇、八一六輛，即足敷用，如 142,825 噸÷$3\frac{1}{2}$噸＝40,816 輛 是也，較之以前可以節省六千八百零三輛(47,619—40,816＝6,803) 貨車。此項節省之車輛，在財政困難之路，當初即可根本不必購置，而在運輸發達之後，亦可用以增加運輸能力，不致發生車輛供不應求之損失。以每車平均載重僅加半噸之數，其利尚且如是之大，倘能實現更進一步之裝載，則所省者當更有可觀矣。故求車輛之運用經濟，不能不於平均裝載深致意焉。

三　車輛載重與車輛修理換新費用之經濟關係

車輛因使用而遭磨損由磨損而生損壞，由損壞而修理而換新。但磨損之程度，與載重之多寡鮮有密切影響，一車每次裝運二十噸與裝運七八噸，其損壞程度並無強大之差別，故其結果每車之平均修理及換新費用 (Repair and renewal cost per wagon) 亦無若何重大變化，而可不必動用之車數愈多，則車輛修理費與更新費自可隨而減少，此增加車輛平均裝載之又一

經濟觀也。

四　車輛裝載與終點車站設備之經濟關係

世之所謂終點車站設備者，其涵義大致分三方面：一爲零担貨物之裝車線及卸車線，二爲整車貨場之裝卸軌道，三爲調車場內之編組車輛軌道。每車平均裝貨愈多，則同一數量之貨物，可以極少數車輛裝運之，車數既少，則在起訖兩站佔用之裝卸調車等等軌道設備自亦較少，如是不僅軌道可以從少修築，即地面亦可縮小範圍，推而言之，如若原有軌道設備因運輸激增而有不敷運用之現象，亦可藉裝載進步以爲暫時之救濟，而無亟於改造之必要。設甲站現有設備狀況，僅能於一日內容納三百輛車，而實際則有三百五十輛之多，如因裝車得法可以減至三百輛，甚或少於三百輛，即可騰出五十輛車之地面，不致發生擁擠之患。此種節省，爲數甚鉅。尤以處於工商繁盛地價奇昂之區域更形切要。蓋以一站之設備如能盡其利用，則合全路各站而計之，其利當更可觀。語云「涓滴不塞，可成江河」，而況車站設備費用常佔鐵路之大宗耗費，安可不力求其用之得當乎。故裝車之進步，可以減少車數，由車數之減少，轉而節省終點車站之地面與設備（Standage terminal accommodation），由是而收種種無形之利益，可謂一舉而數得也。

五　車輛載重與終點站務成本之經濟關係

站務成本，西人稱爲 Terminal costs ，其涵義大抵有二：一爲包括起訖兩站因收授，裝卸、塡票、收費、交貨、封車、檢查等等手續所費之一切人工薪資；一爲在起訖兩站或中間站之調車人工薪資；是爲歐美鐵路計算貨運車站最爲直接站務成本之通例。其增減變化，常與裝運車數發生密切關係，車數愈多，凡此種種手續愈繁；手續愈繁，需用人力愈多；人工愈多，開支愈大；開支愈大，卽爲所費之直接站務成本愈大。僅就塡裝整車貨票一端而言，每多一車，至少須多塡一張，其連帶而生之淸理貨票，會計手續，封車鎖車種種莫不隨之多費人工，因而多費開支。故同量貨物，平均裝載愈重，則車數愈少，而每噸之平均站務成本自亦低減。次如調車成本，凡稍明實況者，當知調車員工在起站之編組列車，與夫在訖站之折散車輛，皆以車輛爲單位，不關其爲空車抑爲重車，亦不關其重車內部裝貨之多少，每車經過之甩拋手續則一，淺而言之。卽一車之內，無論裝有貨物五十噸，或爲二十噸甚至完全無貨之空車，但所費之調車員工薪資，毫無二致，故按實在貨物重量計之，每噸之平均調車成本亦以裝載愈高爲愈經濟。

六　車輛載重與行車成本之經濟關係

所謂行車成本者，卽英文之Train working Costs ，指用於行車方面之一切直接費用而言，舉凡機車用煤用水，行車員工薪給，車機用油，以及其他行車用品皆屬之。此等直接行車成本常隨列車次數而伸縮，列車多，此等成本亦多，列車少，此等成本亦少；而車輛載重又與列車次數有形影相隨之關係，蓋每年之平均裝貨愈少，則同量之貨物須用多數車輛裝運，因而每列車之車數必須增加，然列車之長度，常以種種限制不能超過一定之限制，如一路之會車錯車岔道太短，則過長之列車不能容納，變度太大之地段，亦不利於行駛過長之列車，皆其例之最顯著者也。列車既受種種限制不能任意加長，故車數太多之結果，惟有改作兩列或三列行駛、由是列車次數增加，行車用煤及行車員工開支隨而膨脹，而每噸貨物之平均行車成本當亦較高，其彼此之相互循環影響可於第一表觀之。反之，如每年平均載重較多，則可減少每一列車之車數，車數既少，列車自可不致超過一定之長度，其結果同量之貨物，可以少數列車運輸之，列車少則隨行車而生之列車里程，與夫員工薪給機車煤水等等開支自可縮小，於是整個行車成本得以降落，故每噸貨物之平均成本亦低，此種相互連鎖關係可於第二表觀之。

下列兩表，揭示車輛裝載與行車成本之因果利害關係，至爲明顯，學者爲能悉心體察，不惟於裝車與行車成本經濟之理論可得深切之了解，且於行車方面基本問題亦得相當之概念，願三致意焉。

七 車輛載重與行車能力之經濟關係

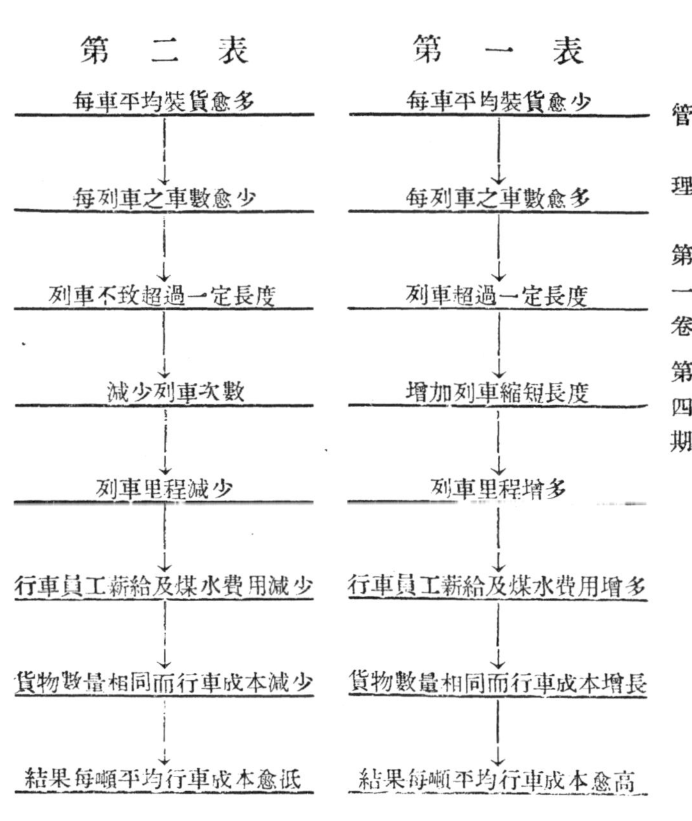

鐵路行車能力(Runing capacity)之强弱，當以軌道設備情况爲其首要條件，如單軌路線不若雙軌路線行車能力之大，是其適例。而所謂行車能力者，具體言之，乃指在一定軌道號誌設備狀况下於一定時間內可以行駛多少列車之謂也。其時間常以一日爲單位，即在廿四小時內所能開行之車數，如按某路軌道設備狀況，至多一日內可以開行一百次列車，則此一百次列車而爲鐵路之最高行車能力。所以平均裝載愈高，則運量不變而列車次數可以減少，不易超過一定之行車能力限度，而展築路軌之舉可以從緩矣。換言之，卽可利用同樣軌道設備運輸較多之貨物，直接提高運輸能力，而又不啻間接提高軌道之效用，斯卽車輛裝載愈重而固定行車能力愈可增進之明證，因其功效隱而不顯，故在實際上甚少注意及此也。

八　增進車輛載重之方法與限度

車輛之裝載，可從三方面謀其改進之道：一爲實行車輛公用制度，使各路車輛彼此可以互通有無，交相運用。而後原車不致亟於返還本路，而裝載自可增加矣。此制盛行英美各國裨益車輛運用效能至大。二爲關於人事問題者，卽裝車員工愈能按照科學方法裝車，其平均載重必愈高，歐美各國對于裝車一道，極端重視，雖此小事，無不研究入微，平時對於員工雖有嚴格訓練，復有裝車專家（Export loaders）隨時指導考察，故其效能倍增，裝工成績日有進展。迴顧我國，於此種種基本路務，往往多存卑視心理，視爲無關輕重，不特素無研究，卽欲求其能了解其重要性者，抑且寥寥不可多得，積重難返，寧不可悲！矚觀各站裝車情形，大都任憑脚行東拋西擲，雜亂橫陳，旣於安全有碍，復糜車位太甚，考其癥結，要皆歷來當事者漠不關心有以階之厲也，觀念之錯誤，莫此爲甚。次如人事而外之車輛本身容量大小，亦與裝載有密切之關係，車輛容量愈大，車重之增加比率愈低，故結果載貨之量可以提高。例如舊式小車之容量爲三十噸，車重十九•一噸，而新式大車之容量爲五十噸，車重二十一噸又半，是車之容量增加百分之六十六成尙强，而車重不過加重百分之十二，二者增加之比例差距愈大，其裝貨之能力當然更爲强大。所以歐美各國車輛構造，大都隨鐵路歷史而改進，其新製之車，容量往往較大，考其用意，無非在於增進平均車輛裝載，藉以實現前述之種種經濟耳。惟車輛容量雖能隨時擴大，倘人事方面根本缺乏裝車訓練，卽大半亦不能盡其利用，是故改進裝車方法與訓練裝車員工，尤爲切要之圖，所謂不揣能本，而齊其末，終無是處。

雖然，裝車因以愈多爲愈妙，然亦有其一定之限度，而此限度又視貨物之性質而互異，鮮有固定之標準，蓋裝車之最要原則有二：一曰求裝量之經濟，二曰謀貨物之安全，二者不可偏重，亦不可偏廢，必須同時兼顧，始爲上策。夫貨物之種類，千萬不齊，舉凡貨物本身之性質及其包裝方法，在在足以影響裝載之分量，若夫棉花麵粉一類物品，儘可盡量重疊堆裝，卽裝至與車頂齊高，亦無妨碍，然如暖氣管者則又必須豎立裝車，且須按照一定方式排列成行方爲安全，而一層之上不能再加裝，否則壓毁碰傷，勢所必至，又如蘋果、香焦、鮮菜、鷄蛋、以及甕裝流質物品，是又皆爲不能疊置堆裝之貨物。故鐵路對於如此等類物品，祇在安全首要條件之下力爲可能之裝載，不應貿然加重載量，致滋損壞，徒增鐵路賠償損失之負担。所以鐵路一面改進各站裝工之效能，尤當同時慮及此等連帶事實，庶可不致因彼而誤此也。

九　車輛載重統計之類別及其計算方式

車輛載重原有起站與全程之分，故計算之方式亦非一端。所謂起站載重者，乃指在起站運出時之每車平均噸數，其算法至爲簡單，乃以所裝車數除各車所裝噸數卽得。至全程之平均載重，則連各車在沿途各站所裝卸之貨物一併包括在內，計算之法，當先求得總共貨物噸里數，然後以重車里程除之，其商數卽爲全列各車經行全程之平均噸數。此項載重數目往往較前者爲低，以體重物品多爲短途運輸，而質輕貨物之運程又常較遠，故列車行程愈長，經過車站愈多，重貨愈少，其平均之載重愈低，不若在始發站時之高。證之下例，則知此理之不謬矣。

所裝車數	每車噸數	總共噸數	運行里數	噸里數	車里數
6	2	12	20	240	120
4	5	20	10	200	40
共計 10	—	32	—	440	160

上表中每車裝貨二噸者計爲六輛，五噸者四輛，率以行程一爲二十里一則不過十里之故，致共計十輛之起站平均載重計爲三噸又二，而全程之平均載重則約二噸又七五，相形之下，所差殊甚。其算法如下：

甲．起站車輛載重$=\dfrac{32\text{噸}}{10\text{輛}}=3.2$噸

乙．全程車輛載重$=\dfrac{440\text{噸里}}{160\text{重車里}}=27.5$噸

茲以計算兩種平均載重之中英文公式列舉於后，以便應用：

甲：中文——起站車輛平均載重$=\dfrac{\text{貨物噸數}}{\text{所裝重車數}}$

英文——Anerage wagon Load as Lorder$=\dfrac{\text{Total tons loaded}}{\text{Total wagons loaded}}$

乙：中文——全程車輛平均載重$=\dfrac{\text{貨物噸里數}}{\text{重車里程數}}$

英文——Average wagon Lcad as Carrier$=\dfrac{\text{Net Ton-miles}}{\text{Loaded wagon-miles}}$

十 比較各站平均裝載應行注意之重要事項

車輛平均裝載之重要性及其計算方法，已於前述之矣。於此更有進者，則爲實際上究應

如何運用車輛裝載統計。夫足以影響裝載之優劣者，本有關於人事及貨物性質與車輛大小種種因素，而統計之功用，又在足以考察人事之錯誤，而定補救之方針，然其所表現者不過裝車狀況而已，將欲用以比較兩站裝車員工之效能，則於各項聯繫問題勢非同時分析，不能得到正確之定評，請分陳如次。

(一)貨物之種類或性質——兩站所運之貨物種類不同，不能相比。易言之，卽平均裝載低者未必卽爲裝工不善之結果，高者未必卽裝工優良之表現，其理由可就下例說明之。假定ＡＢＣ等七站在同一月內之平均裝車成績如后：

A站……………………九・三七噸
B站……………………八・四一噸
C站……………………五・三〇噸
D站……………………三・九八噸
E站……………………三・九〇噸
F站……………………二・四一噸
G站……………………二・五九噸

論上列七站之每車平均噸數，中以Ａ站最高，而以Ｆ站爲最低。但據各站貨物統計分拆之結果，始知Ａ站之貨運其中百分之九十九爲鋼鐵土磚一類笨重物品，質輕之零担貨物不過百分之一；F站所運者，則質輕貨物幾占百分之七八成，而重貨極爲稀少；由是兩站平均裝載遂生如是懸殊之差別，並非A站之裝工技能特別優良之所致也。故當比較各站裝工成績之時，必須同時分析各站主要貨運之性質，乃能免於錯誤之判斷。

（二）貨運之數量——各站貨運數量不同，亦常影響其平均裝載。蓋運量愈大，所裝車數又多，卽爲該地工商實業發達之象徵，因而易爲較高之裝載，反之，如某站工商各業均在幼稚時期，或均係小規模之企業，資本薄弱，交易有限，運輸數量旣小，則於平均裝載之經濟當然不易實現，比較兩站尙須分析各地運輸或商業情狀之理由也。

（三）車輛之大小——車輛愈大，裝載愈易提高；反之容量愈小，裝載愈低，此乃一定不易之理。故大車多而小車少之車站，其平均噸數常比小車多而大車少者爲高，於是比較各站裝車成績，雖其貨物相同，而裝運之車輛互異，亦不能强其得到同樣之結果，斯又無形原因之一，當宜深切注意者也。

由上言之，車輛之大小不同，不能比較，貨物之種類不同，不能比較，各地商情及運輸數量不同，亦不能比較；然則車輛載重統計豈不鮮有運用之機會哉？曰是又不然，如其不有車輛裝載統計，則由前述諸般原因所生之結果，均將無從表現，能由結果而求其原因之所在，斯正統計之無上作用也。且裝車事務必須有統計者，其主要目的，原在便於分別觀察同一站地之前後變化，至於站與站比，本爲次要之作用(其他統計亦然)。何況一站之內，前後運輸情況亦復時有變遷，故不僅各站相比，當宜推求其他原因。卽就一站而論，如其前後裝工成績發覺重大變化，亦非探本溯源，不易明其眞相，而鐵路問題之錯綜複雜，彼此息息相關殊不易作一貫之研究者，是可由此一端而可概其餘也。

交通雜誌

第四卷 第十一期

管理二月刊

第一卷第一期 民國二十五年四月

管理二月刊

第一卷第二期 民國二十五年七月

中國政府購料的管理問題（D4）

張宗謙

政府購料之重要

購料事業原爲一種商業上之問題，昔日之政府完全以政治爲主要工作，其宗旨在於保障人民之生命與財產而已，今日之政府已一變而爲一大規模之科學化機關，凡事須求實際，其職務乃包括一切爲人民謀福利之工作，舉凡教育衛生公用製造等事業，無不加以管理與經營，因之材料之需要，日見增加，普通政府每年預算總數之內大致有百分之二十至三十爲購料經費，如美國中央政府每年購料經費在二萬萬五千萬元之上，全國各省市政府每年購料約七萬萬元，我國目前雖無確實總括之統計，然如鐵道部年約購料四千萬元，其他各部會各省市政府所購材料爲數當亦佔總預算百分之三十至四十，關係之重要可想而知，管理需要之迫切上可見一斑。

政府購料之重要，既如上述，然則將如何管理之，方能得到最高之效力；愚意以爲可分五大問題：曰集中，曰組織，曰人事，曰物料品質研究，曰物品檢驗研究。

（一）集中問題

集中問題，原爲科學管理要素之一，其應用並不限制於購料事業，卽生產，會計，人事等等亦宜實行之，其效果極大，昔日之政府與工商業機關，在未實行統一管理之前，因事權之分歧，往往百病叢生，弊端層出，能直接影響於事業之成敗，而習慣相沿，及缺乏科學管理之智識，雖明知其有改進之必要，而猶疑徘徊迄未見諸實行，歐美各國，直至大戰時期，始有集中購料之律令，美國於一九二一年組織國府購料委員爲(Federal purchasing Board)，加拿大於一九一五年組織戰事購料委員會(War purchasing Commission)，於一九二〇年改爲加拿大政府購料委員會(Purchasing Commission of Canada)，購料範圍乃擴充至戰事所需以外之其他物品，我國各部會及其附屬機關以及各省建設廳，近數年來始有購料委員會之設立，少數雖辦有成效，然因在幼稚時代，其集中程度尚未達到所定之標準，一部份表面上雖有正式委員會之設立，而爲一種有名無實之機關，情同虛設，除辦理購料之瑣屑手續外，既無實權，又不負責，大失集中之本意，不過變相之分購而已，此種制度有弊而無利，反不及完全分購爲爽快，蓋購料之時間或可因而減少也。

（A）集中之利益——從經濟立場言，購料集中，可以將各部份所需材料之性質及數目詳加研究，然後能合併者合併之，許多同樣材料之購料單可以合而爲一。合零爲整，結果不獨能使賣方踴躍投標，即議價方面亦可得到較優之待遇及折扣，據美人惠丁*之調查「各業實行購料集中之後，完全因折扣關係可使物料成本平均減低百分之十至十五」。

* E. Stagg Whitin: The Annuals of the American Academy of Political and Social Science May, 1924, P. 131.

購料集中之後，對於各部份所需之同樣材料，有互相交換之可能，在分購制度之下，因各部份單獨購料，雖有時某部份有餘，某部份不足，而無權力以調整之，甚至某部待用孔急，某部則視為廢物，結果大家俱感過剩，用料緩急，既不能相濟，款額之糜費自亦不能避免，實屬違反經濟之意義。

從管理立場言，購料集中能減少職員舞弊之機會，能聘用專門人才以司其事，能化簡買方與賣方之接洽，定約，會計，及其他工作，不可枚舉。

(B)集中之限制——集中購料之利益，雖如上述，然亦有其不適用之時，蓋材料種類甚多，性質既不同，需要亦相異，若一概而論之，則有時不獨不經濟，且屬不可能，故一面應規定各部份之材料，一律由購料委員會購置，以期集中，一面則授權關係部份，自行購辦不宜集中之材料，如美國各省政府均規定下列物品可以由關係部直接購辦：

(1)數值在五百元以內者。

(2)急待需用者。

(3)專門技術之物品如機械農具，醫藥大學校及專門學校書藉等。

(4)不能持久之物品如新鮮食品等。

浙江省建設廳購料委員會購料規則(二十一年十二月十日公布)第二條規定：

「各機關需用建設材料除以下三項，得由各機關自行採辦外，概須經購料委員會採辦：

(1)數量瑣屑者(每月總數值由建設廳視各該機關事業之多寡規定之)。

(2)急待應用須就地採購者。

(3)非急購材料經購料委員會認可者。

各機關自行購辦之材料，並應於每月底將所購材料細賬分別呈廳交會備查。」

(二)組織與人事問題

(A)組織　購料委員會之組織無一定之標準，須視其規模之大小及其地位而定之，但普通應設下列各組，分掌各項事務：

(1)總務組——職掌如左

關於各項文件之收發事項。

關於各項稿件之擬辦事項。

關於擋卷之保管事項。

關於營業計核事項。

關於不屬於其他各組事項。

（2）購買組——職掌如左：

關於調查物料之來源及價格事項。

關於材料說明之審查事項。

關於請購材料單之詢價及値價比較事項。

關於塡寫訂購單合同或承攬事項。

關於訂購單合同或承攬之檢討事項。

（3）審核組——職掌如左：

關於材料驗收單之審核事項。

關於商號發票收據及其他各項憑單之審核事項。

關於審核報告經主任委員判行發還後塡寫准支通知書送付款處事項。

關於一切材料請購詢價訂購驗收付款等手續之登記事項。

（4）工務組職掌如左：

關於材料之檢查及機件之試驗事項。

關於塡寫收納及拒絕通知書。

關於機料之修理及裝配事項。

(5)儲運組——職掌如左：

關於材料之儲藏保管事項。

關於材料之收發事項。

關於材料之轉運事項。

(B)人事——購料委員會乃一種專門技術之機關，故對於人事之問題，必須加以管理，方能得到最高之工作效力、普通委員會之各組主任及股長職員等，雖皆由各機關原有技術人員兼任之，而對於選擇委派之時，不可不詳加考慮，該員等之資歷能力是否可以稱職，其中尤以購買組關係爲最重大，選派之時應注意下列各點：

(1)必須有辨別材料之價値與價格之能力。

(2)必須有清高之品行。

(3)必須有公平之判斷力而不存偏見。

(4)必須明瞭各部份需要材料之詳細情形。

(5)必須有辦事之毅力與精神。

(6)必須有深遠之眼光。

上列種種乃良好購料員之必要條件，欲求購料工作達到最高之效力，此爲一大關鍵不可忽視之也。

(三)物品問題

物料品質之研究——數十年前採辦工作之效率，完全以所出價格爲標準，以爲購料工作首貴物價之低廉其他皆不必過問，從經濟方面着想，物價低廉，自屬採辦要素之一，而同時物料之優劣是否適用，較之價格問題尤稱重要，往昔購料機關，既以物價爲主體，初則選購價格最廉之物品，結果因品質過劣，不能適用，等於廢物，因貪便宜而吃虧，繼則有鑒於此，選擇價格最高者，以保障品質之優良，二者均爲耗費金錢之舉，殊爲智者所不取，顧解決此種問題，祇有以物料品質爲主體，而價格僅副之，對於某種材料，必須研究其用途，設立標準確定單，然後再比較各商行，根據確定單所提出之價格，擇其最廉者講之，此種方法既可得最低廉之價格，同時亦不致犧牲品質，可謂兼籌並顧，兩全其美矣。

物價品質之研究，除上述利益外，尚有二大功效(1)確定代價之是否公允，(2)實行統一合併各部份所需類似之材料，茲分述之於下：

(1)確定代價之是否公允——物品之代價之是否公須視其經濟效用(Economic utility)與固有價值(Intrinsic value)而確定，不能以今日之價格較往日爲低廉，卽認爲公允，亦不能以某一價格對於某種用途爲公允而卽斷爲對其他用途亦爲公允，蓋同一物品在不同之時期中，其公允之價格卽不同，在不同用途下，其公允之價格亦因之而不同，惟經濟效用與固有價值範圍太廣，不易分析，最好方法乃以物料品質(Quality)及實行(Performance)爲主體，然後分爲若干單位 (Unit) 每個單位之價值可設法與以相對的權數 (Relative weights)，或用數字的表示(Numerical expression)如六，八，十等，或用等級的表示(Grading or Rating)分派之，如A.B.C.等，結成聯合指數(Composite index)，結果應于數字或等級表示與經濟效用之間立定一種算術的相關(Mathematical Correlation)，價格之是否公允，可藉此種指數確定之。

茲以購買汽車爲例，藉以闡明確實代價之是否公允，第一先從客觀方面察其成本之是否確實，卽本節所論之取其主體分爲若干單位，然後將各個單位之價值予以愼密考查，第二再從主觀方面觀其效用之是否相對，卽本節所擬之將其用途別爲若干等級，然後將各個等級之門類予以精詳加權。

(一)客觀方面——成本說——查汽車之成本須視其內部之組織而定，其結構約可分爲二部：

(A)車身——(1)門(2)窗(3)篷頂(4)座位等。

(B)底盤——(1)車架(2)引擎(3)傳動機(4)車輪軸(5)車輪(6)鋼板彈簧等。

上述各單位，係組織汽車之主要部份，例如美國福特廠，將上述各部分材料，組合而成福特汽車，但其中所採用之各部份，或非其本廠出品，勢必從事購買，當然須注意其成本影響，又如所取質料，是否選用上品，引擎中所用汽缸之數量（於速率有關），以及車身中所占坐位之多寡（於容量有關）等等，於成本上均爲值得討論之問題，他若水箱，化氣機，眞空管抽水機。油幫浦，電箱發電機，電動機，汽油箱等，在在均須考量，惟最重要處有三：

（a）材料牌號——何廠出品。

（b）材料年代——是否最近出品。

（c）材料品質——品質優良與否。

至於歷年來材料之牌號年代質料等記載，當然有詳細統計圖表參考，並可聘專家研究某種牌號，某年出品，某種品質之材料，定爲標準品（猶如上海紗布交易所，以二十支金鷄牌爲標準紗）， 如遇品質發生優次不同時，加減其等級而詳定之，所以雖同一福特牌號汽車，因內部成本差異，價格可以隨之升降，何況不同牌號之汽車，更不可忽視矣。

（二）主觀方面——效用說——查汽車爲運輸工具，因應用不同，名稱互異，有

（A）自用汽車。

（B）出租汽車。

（C）長途汽車。

(D)運貨汽車。

(E)農用汽車。

(F)軍用汽車。

茲因上述六種汽車之應用不同，購買者對此，各有不同目光，例如學校教授，對於運貨汽車認爲不合用，出租車行對於農用或軍用汽車亦然，又如農用汽車在美國農村中普遍運用在中國猶嫌過早，因此雖然同一價格同一時代，在效用上因環境不同，在美國認爲公允，在中國認爲不然，又如廿年前中國內地公路尙未發展，內地人士對汽車價格認爲神秘，今又不然，此則在效用上價格公允與否，因時代而不同也，由上述種種例證，藉悉購買者之主觀不同，由於環境，人事，時代，變遷，因此不同之主觀，產生不同之價格估量，此項估量當然隨時隨地隨當事者臨機採納也，惟現爲得一結論起見，於汽車之行駛里程，及享用年齡，可作一具體數字研究，茲假定有甲乙丙丁四輛汽車，經專家檢驗其成本完全相同，（蓋成本完全相同者，第一步成本說之困難，當可消除，不列論究）則可將行駛里程及年齡列表如下：

按下表之效用指數，卽每加侖汽車行駛里程之約數，聯合指數係將使效用指數乘年齡，從聯合指數上看到丙車最合經濟原則，因丙車之聯合指數爲六十最高也，又假定歷年丙車每輛平均價格爲四千元，（用平均數者，目的爲減貨幣價值之漲落），間如有新出廠之丁種汽車一批，每輛價格應定若干，堪稱公允，茲可利用聯合指數以求之。

種類	每加倫汽油行駛里數	效用指數	年齡	聯合指數
甲車	三十六里	十二	四年半	五十四
乙車	三十三里	十一	四年	四十四
丙車	三十里	十	六年	六十
丁車	二十七里	九	五年	四十五

查丁種汽車之聯合指數爲四十五，丙種汽車之聯合指數爲六十。

$$\therefore 60:45 = 4000:X$$

$$\therefore \quad X = \frac{4000 \times 45}{60} = \$3000$$

從上式求得丁種汽車每輛公允售價爲三千元，假如明年汽車廠家將丁種汽車內都改良，而其成本一仍如舊，但該汽車之年齡可延長二年，於是該汽車之公允價格應爲四千二百元，計算如下：

$$60:63 = 4000:X$$

$$\therefore \quad X = \frac{4000 \times 63}{60} = \$4200$$

因該汽車之聯合指數由四十五增至六十三，（因七年乘九），所以價格由三千元增至四千二百，並不爲貴，所以明年之預定價格，比今年爲貴，並非不公允也，總之效力指數增大，或年齡增大均足以影響聯合指數之增大，如價格比例的隨聯合指數之升沉而升沉，一定公允無疑也，此例雖僅以汽車爲限，而關於購買方面原理則同，又此種方法，大概適用於大宗躉買，至於匯價變動，利率增減，亦須予以特別注意，否則勢將影響購料預算也。

(2)合併各部份所需類似之材料——購料實行集中後，其最顯明之利益，即爲合併各部份所需同樣及類似材料之可能合併完全同樣之材料，因屬簡易，毋庸瑣述，惟合併參差有限，似同而非同之材料，則必須先研究(一)該項材料品質上之種種原質爲結構，耐久，能力，大小，形狀等，(二)如實行合併購辦對於各該用料機關是否均能滿意，如以上二點皆能解決，然後應一面化簡類似材料之種類一面設立標準品質確定單，(Standardized Specifications)於是可以實行合併，換得較優之折扣及待遇，而不影響各用料部份之工作效率，故欲求眞正之經濟，必須實行合併類似之材料，而欲合併類似之材料，必須先研究物料之品質及其用途然後方不致僨事也。

(四)物品檢驗問題

從狹義言之，物品檢驗僅爲一種機械式之手續，檢驗賣方運來之貨物，是否與我方購料單上所列之物品性質與數量相符而已，但就廣義言之，則尙不止此，因檢驗工作實有協助其他部份增加工作效力之處，關係至爲重大也。

(A)檢驗組之功效：

(一)在某種物品經過標準化及簡單化之後須恃檢驗方面加以準確的調查與測驗其各種原素是否與品質確定單所載完全相符。

(二)一種品質確定單之規定，有時過於苛求，有時過於寬鬆，須恃檢驗員之經驗及研究方可切合實際，如某種物品根據確定單檢驗後，其不合格次數或數量過多時，檢驗員卽須憑其學識確定其緣因，或因承辦商之能力不足，或疏忽敷懲，或因我方確定單過於嚴厲，然後再加以改善之。

(三)對於承辦商能力，設備，及組織等情形，必須檢驗人員負責調查後，作一詳細報告，庶幾購料機關對於賣方之工作狀況有所認識。

(四)同時承辦商廠中有不妥善之處檢驗員可給與相當忠告及指示，俾雙方均可受益。

(五)新貨或代替品之產生，檢驗組應先加以查驗然後可將研究所得報告購料組。

(B)檢驗地點——政府機關所購材料普通須俟貨品送到方開始檢驗，但亦須視材料之性質而定，如所購材料爲一種極度專門性質，則不獨承辦商爲血本關係，宜愼重將事卽買方亦冀望其能夠適用，以免供給停頓，故應採用在對方廠中檢驗制度，或更進而派人常駐對方廠中在製造之時卽可監督與檢驗之職，庶幾物質設有差錯，當時卽可發覺，不必俟其達到我方再行拒絕，旣省時間又可免除來往運費，美國海陸軍部購料卽用此種檢驗制度，愚意以爲最好在購料合同上卽添入此項規定，買方可隨時派員赴對方廠中檢驗材料之製造，此舉於承辦商有利而無害當必樂從也。

(C)檢驗工作之管轄權——各購料機關雖均有檢驗組之設立，而欲完全集中檢驗所購材料，似屬困難。第一點各用料機關所在地點不同，各廳之附屬機關遍佈全省，各部會之附屬機關則滿佈全國，若在材料集中檢驗之後，再行從事交運，運費一項，豈非額外開支。第二點，購料工作雖可集中，而用料機關似宜有檢驗材料之權，若完全由購料機關包辦一切，則用料機關工作，往往發生影響故因上述困難，似應由用料機關自行檢驗，惟如有一二種材料因特別注重而規定由購料機關集中檢驗，亦無不可，我國多數購料委員會任聽用料機關自行檢驗固爲合理，不過各購料委員會對於物料品質確定單之編纂尚欠週詳，致有時，承辦商照購料單送貨後，用料機關竟遇事挑剔而拒絕接受，此種糾紛之原因，完全出於購料與用料機關事前對於物品確定單之編纂未能相互合作，彼此之誤會亦因之而產生矣。

上所云云，是我國政府購料機關目前急需研究的幾個管理問題，作者芻蕘之見，或可略供參考，因書此篇，尚希各當局注意及之。

(完)

改善吾國鐵路貨物事故處理方法之芻見（G 5）

沈奏廷

一 貨物事故之種類

鐵路承運貨物無慮千萬種，其於檢點，裝卸，起票，中轉，與運行之間，須經多數人之手，即使管理嚴密，事故仍在所不免，且貨運愈多，則事故亦必隨之而多，尤以零貨爲甚。蓋零貨數量零星，中途且常有中轉之必要，其損失之可能性自較整車貨物爲大，故零担貨物時有貨票與貨物脫離，以致發生多裝少裝之弊者，而整車貨物之票貨相離者，則往往不多見，此貨物短少之發生所以常以零貨爲多也。且整車貨物如由客商自行裝卸，則祇須車封完好，縱有短少，鐵路亦不負責，更無加以監察管理之必要，惟在吾國鐵路，整車貨物多由鐵路代裝代卸，仍難辭其責耳。茲所欲論者以零担貨物爲限，在未討論處理方法以前，請先言零担貨物事故之種類：

（一）貨物之多裝　多裝之貨物 Over freight 者，無正式貨票相隨或其件數多於票載件數之到達貨物也。若細別之，則種類不一而足，爲便於解釋計，請列述之如次：

（1）全部無票據相隨而有標誌者　例如今有某種貨物二十件由甲站運至乙站，運抵乙站時，查無貨票相隨，但其標誌之到達站則確爲乙站，並無錯誤。

(2)實在件數多於票載件數而有標誌者　例如前述貨物二十件由甲站運至乙站，運抵乙站時，貨票上僅載十五件，其餘五件卽爲多裝之貨物，但其標誌之到達站，則確爲乙站，並無錯誤。

(3)全部無票據相隨而無標誌者　與第(1)類之裝多貨物相同，惟有物並無標誌或標誌不明，無由判明其眞確之到達站者。

(4)實在件數多於票載件數而無標誌者　與第(2)類之多裝貨物相同，惟多裝之貨物並無標誌或標誌不明，無由判明其眞確之到達站者。

(5)僅有轉寄貨票相隨者　例如上述貨物二十件經過中轉站點驗裝卸時，已無貨票相隨，中轉站乃憑貨物之標誌，塡發轉寄貨票 Astray waybill ，裝入相當車輛，運至貨件上標誌之到達站，到達站收到該批貨物時，查無正式貨票，但有轉寄貨票相隨，亦應視爲多裝之貨物，從事處理，此其例一。該貨二十件經過中轉站時，查明貨票僅開十五件，其餘五件卽由中轉站按照標誌，塡發轉寄貨票，裝運一如前述，到達站收到上項五件之貨物，亦應視爲多裝貨物處理之，此其例二。

貨物多裝之原因不一，舉其著者，則如(1)託運單與貨物不符而起運站失於檢點；(2)貨票塡發錯誤；(3)貨票遺失或誤遞；(4)貨物標誌錯誤；(5)貨物未經標誌或標誌脫落，以致發生裝車之誤錯等皆是，吾人皆知鐵路貨票係根據託運單填發，若貨物實在件數爲二十件而託運單誤開爲十五件，起運站未曾於檢貨時發覺更正，則貨票自亦祇開十五件，迨抵到達站時則其中五件必將成爲多裝貨物。又如託運單上所載之到達站爲乙，而貨物標誌之到達站爲丙，前者有誤，而後者無誤，則貨票必寄至乙站，而貨物則或裝至丙站，以致乙站發生有票無貨，而丙站發生有貨無票之弊，若託運單無誤，而貨票有誤，則結果亦同。如或貨票遺失或誤遞，則全部貨物成爲多裝矣。零担貨物之標誌極爲重要，若託運單上所載之到達站爲乙，並無錯誤，而貨物標誌之到達站誤而爲丙，則其錯誤之結果或與託運單之誤填相同。倘貨物未經標誌或標誌脫落，則應裝甲車者或誤裝乙車，成爲無標誌之多裝貨物焉。

（二）貨物之少裝。　少裝之貨物Short freight與多裝之貨物適相對峙，往往甲站發現多裝，乙站卽發現少裝，惟有多裝時，未必定有少裝之發生，例如貨票填發錯誤，以多填少，卽僅有多裝而無少裝，反之以少填多，亦僅有少裝而無多裝，殆甚顯然也。貨物少裝云者，或爲有票而無貨，或爲貨物件數少於票載件數，前者爲全部短少；後者爲局部短少，其爲少裝則一也。少裝之原因有與多裝之原因相同者，有不相同者，玆爲舉述之如次：

（1）託運單之誤填　例如貨物二十件，託運單誤開三十件，未經起運站發覺，以致貨票亦開三十件，到達站核對票據，少收十件，卽成爲少裝之貨物。如託運單誤填到達站，亦足以致少裝之發生。

(2)貨票之誤塡　例如貨物二十件，託運單亦開二十件，但貨票誤塡爲三十件，其結果卽與上同。如貨票誤塡到達站名，則亦與託運單誤塡到達站名無異。

(3)標誌之錯誤　某貨之到達站爲乙，但標誌誤而爲丙，以致貨票寄至乙站而貨物或運至丙站，乙站發現全部少裝，丙站發現全部多裝，與託運單誤塡到達站名之結果相同。

(4)裝車之錯誤　託運單，貨票，及貨物標誌或均無誤，但裝車時發生錯誤，將應裝入甲車之貨裝入乙車，以致貨物應往甲站者誤往乙站，甲站卽將有票無貨，發現少裝，乙站則將有貨無票，發現誤裝（因該貨標誌之到達站並非乙站，故乙站不能視同多裝，而應視爲誤裝 Astray freight）而有卽予轉寄甲站之必要。

(5)整件之遺失　上列各種少裝均係錯誤之結果，而非貨物之眞遺遺失，但有時貨物發生少裝亦有由於眞止之遺失者，其遺失之地點不一，或在起運站，或在到達站，或在中轉站，或在中途運行之中，頗難肯定，要須視案情之如何以推斷之耳。

(三)貨物之被竊　除貨物整件被竊已在少裝之中包括外，貨物亦常有被挖竊者，卽一件貨物被人挖取一部份，以致包裝現破損之狀，是爲被竊之貨物 Stolen freight 被竊之發生可分兩種，一爲卸車前發生者，一爲卸車後發生者，前者發生於起運站，中轉站或中途運行之中，後者必發生於到達站，二者之性質不同，其追究之方法應有異。至於暗藏之短少 Concealed loss 有時亦為被竊之結果，但以其原封未動，卸車交貨時未經發覺，到達站往往無從報告查究也。

(四)貨物之誤裝　誤裝貨物 Astray freight 者，卽貨物之到達站為甲而誤運至乙，并與貨票脫離，形成有貨無票者是也。例如某批貨物標明到達站為天津東站，貨票亦未誤塡，但以裝車錯誤，誤運至北平前門站，北平前門站收到該批貨物，查無貨票，卽應視為誤裝貨物為之轉寄天津，不得視為多裝貨物，因到達站非北平也。誤裝貨物之有標誌者大都均有轉寄之可能，其無標誌而內裝貨物又無標記者，最難處理，往往成為無主之貨物，遲早不得不出於拍賣之一途，而短少之站不得不接受客商之賠償請求，由路方照値賠償，由此可見零貨標誌之重要矣。誤裝之主要原因厥為裝車之錯誤，故零貨裝車須有完密之查封制度 Ballot or Veri-check system，卽所以避免貨物之誤裝也。其次則因貨票遺失或遲誤，致中轉站發生有貨無票情事，不得不將貨物按標誌所載到達站名，為之轉寄，雖未誤裝，亦與誤裝同樣看待也。有時沿途零貨之誤卸，亦足以造成與誤裝相同之結果，惟較為少見而已。

(五)貨物之損壞　零貨混裝一車，且須中轉翻裝，其損失之機會遠較整車貨物為多，故零貨之損壞常為不可避免者，零貨之損壞有在中轉站發覺者，有在到達站卸車時發覺者，亦有在到達站交貨時發覺者，而其致損之原因則錯縱複雜，不勝枚舉，其尤著者則如（1）搬貨之不愼，（2）行車之震盪，（3）車內堆裝之不妥，（4）雨溼防護之不週，（5）車輛之不合等皆是，防止之道，自在根究其原因而後乃能籌謀補救也。

二　美國鉄路處理零担貨物事故之方法

美國鉄路零貨運輸發達，事故亦隨之而多，其處理方法之內容及用意頗有足供吾人研究之處，謹爲分別各種事故敘述之，以期明晰而便探討：

（甲）多裝之處理方法

到達站之卸車檢貨司事 Checkers 負檢點到達零貨之責，各司事監卸之車輛由領班爲之分配，故多數之到達車輛係由多數之卸車司事監卸，卸車點貨時，如發現多裝貨物（凡有貨無票者，實在件數超過票開件數者，與有轉寄貨票相隨者皆屬之），卸車司事即應就貨物之標誌或轉寄貨票之所載事項，塡具多裝貨物點驗單 Check report of over freight，送交貨站公事房備查。此項點驗單之作用有四（1）甲車卸下之多裝貨物或即乙車所缺之少裝貨物，有此單據，即可與少裝貨物點驗單核對，如核對相符，即可多補少，爲之了結，不必牽及他站或他處，徒多煩擾（2）可據以通知收貨人，囑其提出相當證據（如提單，發票或上次註有短少之運費收據或其他之證明），以便從早交付，（3）可據以向起運站追索貨票或訂正單；

(4)如逾限不能取得貨票(或訂正單)，可據以塡造貨物多裝報告書 Report of Freight Over 送達有關處所，以備進行其他步驟。有此四種功用，故點驗單實爲初步重要之單據，其應塡六項目，以(1)貨物種類件數，(2)貨物標誌，(3)起運站名，(4)車號，(5)正式貨票號數(如係實在件數多於票載件數者)，(6)轉寄貨票號數等爲最重要。蓋必須有此種項目之塡報，而後其他處理手續始能逐一進行也。

貨站公事房內有專管貨物多裝少裝之核對員 Over and short desk，貨物多裝點驗單一入核對員之手，即按收貨人之姓氏順序排列，隨即與貨物少裝點驗單(詳後)一一核對，如查有某批多裝貨物與某批少裝貨物確實相符，即將兩種點驗單互相註明號數(Cross-referenced)，仍按收貨人姓氏順序另行存放等，一面即囑棧台員司將實在貨物由多裝貨位 Over section 搬入尋常貨位，以便收貨人之具領，此多裝與少裝能即核對相符時之處理方法也。

倘多裝與少裝不能當即核對相符，則案件仍未了結，其應進行之步驟復分兩種(一)向收貨人發給通知書，請其交出提貨單 Original bill of lading 或上次註明短收之運費收據，或其他相當之證明，前來領取；(二)向起運站追索正式貨票或訂正單，以便結束站帳。如兩者均於限期內辦妥，自無問題，否則尙須進行其他手續焉。

起運站接到到達站追索貨票之請求書 Request for billing 後，即應進行查核，以便立即具復，其答復之內容當視多裝之原因而異，請分敘之：

(1)如查係貨票塡發錯誤，以致以多塡少，(如實在貨物爲十一件，而貨票僅塡一件)起運站卽應塡發訂正單，寄交到達站。

(2)如查係貨票誤塡到達站，以致貨物往甲站，貨票往乙站，起運站卽應塡發訂正單寄交乙站，註銷誤塡之貨票，並重新發一正式貨票寄交甲站。

(3)如查係貨物標誌錯誤(卽託運單與貨票均無誤)，以致貨物運往甲站，而貨票則寄乙站，起運站應卽通知甲站，將貨物轉寄乙站，以便與貨票會合，辦理結束。

(4)如查係貨票誤遞或遺失，起運站卽應塡具貨票抄件 (Copy of revenue Waylill) 寄交到達站，到達站收到貨票抄件時，應卽視同原票呈報會計處。

(5)如查係託運單以多塡少，以致貨票亦發生同樣錯誤，則起運站須請託運人改正託運單後，始得塡發訂正單，寄交到達站。

(6)如查係託運單誤塡到達站，以致貨物運往甲站而貨票則寄乙站，起運站應請託運人更正託運單後，始得塡發貨票寄交甲站，幷塡發訂正單寄交乙站，以便註銷原寄之貨票。

到達站在未接起運站之答復或收到起運站寄送之貨票或訂正單以前，應繼續將多裝點驗單與少裝點驗單逐日核對，至規定之限期(例如十日)爲止。限期已滿，仍不能核對相符而又未得起運站之回復(卽仍屬有貨無票)，到站應卽塡造貨物多裝報告 Report Freight Over 以一份送起運站(如起運站不明則寄中轉站)，一份送運輸處 Office of Superintendent of Transportation 一份存站備查。如於塡造報告後，起運站能將貨票寄來，或請到達站將貨轉寄他站時，則到達站應塡造 O.K. 報告，寄送運輸處，以便據以銷案。

至於多裝貨物之逾限不能交付收貨人者，應由到達站寄送鐵路特設之多裝貨物堆棧 Over freight Warehouse，以免佔用貨站之地位，惟在寄送堆棧以前，到達站應儘量設法查明收貨人，囑其提出證明，從事領取。

凡無標誌之多裝貨物，到達站得開箱查驗，如有查明起運站及收貨人之姓名住址者，則其處理方法與有標誌者同。否則應卽塡造貨物多裝報告寄送運輸處，一面卽將無標誌之貨物運往多裝貨物堆棧，不必待限期之屆滿也。

凡逾期而尙未了結之多裝貨物，或無標誌之貨物，旣由到達站報告運輸處，運輸處卽據以逐一登記，以便發生賠償請求時，爲之核對，以期將多補缺，避免賠償之損失焉。

(乙)少裝之處理方法

到達站卸車司事於檢貨時，如查有少裝情事，應就每批少裝貨物，塡具少裝貨物點驗單二紙，錄列貨票所載之有關事項暨車封情形，送交貨站公事房內之核對員，核對員卽將點驗單按收貨人姓名順序排列，并與多裝貨物點驗單逐一核對，如核對相符，卽互相註明號數，以資銷案，已如前述。如當日不能核對相符，仍應繼續逐日核對，如滿規定之期限仍未對出，到達站卽應塡造少裝貨物報告 Report of Short Freight 三份，以一份送呈運輸處，一份送交起運站，一份存站備查。嗣後該貨如由他處轉寄到站，應卽塡造O.K.報告，呈送運輸處，以資結束。

起運站收到少裝貨物報告時。應卽進行查對，其辦法已於多裝貨物之處理方法中詳之，可不復贅。

運輸處收到各站少裝貨物報告時，卽爲之一一登記，如遇O.K.報告送來時，亦卽記入登記簿內，以便與損失賠償案件核對。例如某批貨物在甲站短少，甲站屆期不能核對相符，乃塡造少裝貨物報告送呈運輸處，越數日，該貨由他處轉寄到站，甲站乃作O.K.報告，送呈運輸處銷案，惟在此期間客商或已提出賠償請求，經運輸處就登記簿核對，乃知該批貨物業已轉寄到站，無賠償之必要，卽可據以答復客商，免除賠償。如登記簿內並無O.K.報告之批註，則應再查轉寄貨票，因各站轉寄誤裝貨物時，皆須備具轉寄貨票，而以一份送呈運輸處備查，運輸處恐到達站忘送O.K.報告，故須再就轉寄貨票查對，以免遺漏；倘仍不能查出，乃復核對多裝貨物登記簿，其辦法已見於前，不復再述矣。

各站發現貨物少裝者，如隨後貨物由他處轉寄到站，在收貨人未提出賠償請求以前，可按尋常手續交付；倘收貨人業已提出賠償請求，則除得貨運損失賠償處 Freight Claim Agents Offiee 之准許外，不得將貨交客商，因路方或已照賠，若隨便交付，鐵路必將受損也。

中轉站翻車檢貨時，如發現少裝，卽由查貨司事在貨票上詳細註明，不必報告，一俟貨票寄抵到站後，由到達站處理之。

(丙)誤裝之處理方法

誤裝貨物之處理方法，可分中轉站與到達站兩種情形敍述之。中轉站檢點中轉貨物時，其所發現之誤裝情形復可分爲兩種：(一)爲貨物件數與貨票相符：但貨物標誌所示之到達站名與貨票所塡之到達站名不符；(二)爲有貨無票或貨物實在件數多於貨票所載之件數。對於第一種之誤裝貨物，中轉站除確能決定其貨票所載之到達站必無錯誤外，應將貨物轉寄標誌所示之到達站，Free astrayed to marked destination，一面在貨票上，註明短少，以便由到達站分別糾正；對於第二種之貨物，則應一律按照標誌，爲之轉寄。其法卽由檢貨司事於發覺誤裝貨物時，塡具多裝貨物點驗單一紙，送交中轉站公事房，據以塡製轉寄貨票 Astray Waybill，以便隨貨寄送或直接郵遞到達站，到達站收到轉寄貨票與轉寄貨物時，應視同多裝貨物處理，其法已見於前矣。轉寄貨票無論本路聯運，例不計費，故亦稱免費轉寄貨票 Free astray Waybill，與正式貨票之形式不同。轉寄貨票應分數聯，以一聯寄到達站，一聯寄裝車站，一聯寄運輸處，而以一聯存查。除存查一聯無庸敍述外，其各聯之用途可說明之如次：

（1）寄到達站聯　此聯爲貨物運輸之憑證，所以代正式貨票之用者；到達站得此，可與正式貨票核對符合，從事銷案。

（2）寄裝車站聯　誤裝貨物之發生什九由於裝車之錯誤，此聯之所以寄裝車站者，所以喚起其注意也。裝車站得此，應卽查核該站之裝車查對票 Ballots，決定有無誤裝車輛情事，如有之，應對於有關檢貨司事給以警告，以免再犯。

（3）寄運輸處聯　運輸處在核對賠償案時，如遇少裝登記簿內尙無O.K.報告之批註，應再查對各站送處之轉寄貨票，以免遺漏，其詳細情形已述於前，可不復贅。運輸處根據轉寄貨票，尙可編造各站裝車錯誤統計，設法加以糾正。以謀改進焉。

到達站收到誤裝貨物時，其轉寄之手續與中轉站無異；惟中轉站遇有有貨無票或實在件數多於票載件數時，對於多裝之貨物，應一律作爲誤裝貨物轉寄，不問其到達站之爲何站也例如某批貨物實在件數爲十八件，而貨票僅開十六件，但其到達站名，無論貨票或標誌，均載明爲甲站，絕無不符，中轉站對此二件多裝之貨物，應視同誤裝貨物，填發轉寄貨票，寄交甲站，實則此貨並未誤裝，乃貨票誤填件數之故耳。若上項情形，在到達站（卽甲班）發現，則到達站對此二件貨物，應視爲多裝貨物處理，而不應視爲誤裝貨物，因無轉寄之必要也。故就中轉站言，凡一切有貨無票或實在件數多於票載件數之貨物，均爲誤裝貨物，應按誤裝貨物，轉寄辦法處理；而就到達站言，則凡非運往該站之貨物而誤運該站者，始可稱曰誤裝貨物，而有轉寄之必要也。

中轉站及到達站遇有誤裝之貨物，均立卽按標誌所載之到達站轉寄，實爲一簡捷而有效之辦法，短少之貨物往往藉此而獲見，不至有曠日廢時，輾轉詢問之煩。蓋貨物之誤裝由於標誌之錯誤者少而由於裝車之錯誤者多也。

中轉站或到達站遇有無標誌之貨物時，得開箱查驗，如查有線索，應按照轉寄，否則惟有運交多裝貨物堆棧之一法耳。

(丁)被竊之處理方法

中轉站發現貨物有被竊之形狀時，應卽塡造貨物被竊報告 Report of Freight Stolen，一面在貨票上詳細批註。被竊報告應備四份，除以一份存查外，以一份寄裝車站，一份寄到達站，一份寄運輸處。裝車站收到被竊報告時，應立卽從事調查，將調查所得之結果連同被竊報告存站備查，聽候有關處所之查詢。到達站則僅須將被竊報告存查，運輸處有此報告，則對於應負責之各站，可與以相當之警戒，以免重犯。

到達站發現貨物被竊時，其報告方法應一如前述，惟如於卸車後在站內被竊者，並應報告段長 Division Superintendent，以便查究。其已由中轉站發覺幷填造報告者，到達站無再行報告之必要。

如遇貴重貨物被竊或案情重大者，發現站應即拍電報告，所有被竊報告則應隨後補送，以便從速查究，而免遲誤。

（丁）損壞之處理方法

中轉站發現貨物損壞時，應由檢貨司事在貨票上詳細批註，不必報告；迨貨物抵到達站，乃由到達站填造貨物損壞報告 Report of Freight Damaged，詳列貨物損壞之性質，程度，及原因，除以一份存查外，以一份寄損壞發現以前之裝車站，一份寄運輸處。裝車站收到報告時。應即查究損壞之原因。幷設法作矯正之處置，以免同樣事件之復發生。運輸處有此報告，除用以警戒有關各站外，幷可研究其致損之緣由，從事改進焉。

到達站發現貨物損壞時，其報告亦一如前述，惟如於卸車後發生者，則應自籌矯正之方，幷在報告內說明之。

三　吾國鐵路處理貨物事故辦法之規定

吾國鐵路對於貨物事故之處理方法，與美國頗有不同之處，爲便於討論起見，請將吾國鐵路現行貨運辦事細則內之有關條文，錄列如次。

(一)到達貨物與貨票不符之處理(第一〇八條) 卸車時，卸車司事務須對照貨票所載之貨名，件數等項，逐一點查淸楚，如爲沿途零担車，應會同車上貨物司事辦理。倘查有件數多出或短少情事，應卽註明於貨票附記欄內，幷報告站長電詢起運站及有關處所是否多裝，漏裝，誤裝，誤卸，貨票誤塡，抑係私運。如係多裝，應卽運回原起運站，如係漏裝，應由起運站補運，如係誤裝，應予轉寄，如係誤卸，應由誤卸站補運，如係貨票誤塡，應卽改正，如係私運，應卽按照貨物運輸通則第五七條辦理之。

(二)到達貨物包裝破壞之處理(第一〇九條) 卸車時，如發現貨物之包裝有破漏情事，須設法堵塞縫補或釘修之，並應將該項貨物置於妥當地位。以防竊取，同時電明起運站及有關處所。

(三)中轉貨物損失之處理(第九八條) 凡中轉貨物發現損壞遺失情事，除將損壞遺失情形，電知到達站及有關處所外，應將現有貨物照常中轉，其他手續，則俟由到達站辦理之。

(四)貨物損失之整理及查驗(第一四四查) 凡遇貨物全部或一部損壞或遺失時，無論係在何站發現，該站站長應卽施以整理及查驗。整理時應將餘存貨物妥爲堆置或裝載，如有殘破貨物，尤應加以修復，俾免繼續損失。查驗時，除應汼意損失情形，數量，及原因外，更應注意(一)該項損失責任應在鐵路抑在貨商，(二)該項損失如責在鐵路，應由何人負担。

(五)貨物損失之報告(第一四五條) 凡貨物發現損失，發現站於整理查驗後，應立卽電知各有關處所，并於二十四小時內塡具貨物損失報告表。起運站接到發現站之貨物損失電報時，亦應於二十四小時內，塡具貨物損失報告表，對於該項貨物在起運時之一切有關實在情形及其市價等項，均須特別詳細塡明。到達站接到發現站之損失電報時，俟該項貨物運到，經整裝查驗後，亦應於二十四小時內，塡具貨物損失報告表，對於該項貨物在到達時之一切有關實在情形，須特別詳細註明。中轉站對於該項貨物，如經辦理裝卸整理等手續者，接到發現站之貨物損失電報時，亦應於二十四小時內，塡具貨物損失報告表，對於該項貨物在改裝或整理時之一切有關實在情形，須特別詳細塡明。上述各該站於接到發現站之貨物損失電報後，在必要時，應先電復，並抄電有關處所，再行塡具貨物損失報告表。

(六)貨物損失報告表之塡造(第一四六條) 塡具貨物損失報告表時，務應確實，除非本站所經辦之事項外，務應詳明。其表內損失種類一欄，應視貨物損失之性質，按照下列名稱塡入之。

(甲)防護不週

(一)中途被竊

(二)起訖站被竊
(三)被竊地點不明
(四)焚燬
(乙)運輸過失
(五)撞車
(六)碰損(普通物品)
(七)碰損(易碎物品)
(八)汚損
(九)雨濕
(十)跌落
(十一)交付錯誤
(丙)貨物性質或包裝
(十二)包破損失
(十三)震漏(液體)
(十四)破碎(易碎物品)

（十五）腐爛

（丁）其他

貨物損失報告表每份三聯，第一聯車站存根，第二三兩聯呈主管車務段查核，第二聯由車務段轉呈車務處，第三聯由車務段存查。關於證明貨物損失責任及解決處置之重要證物，（如鉛彈、封紙、車牌、寄送貨票信封，簽字簿整裝零担車貨物點查簿單，沿途零担車貨物授受證：路警押運貨物通知單或其抄件，貨票或託運單抄件，出事地點略圖，或其他有關物件），在必要時，應隨同貨物損失報告表第二聯呈送車務處審核。

四　吾國鐵路貨物事故處理方法之缺點

由以上各種規定，可見吾國鐵路處理貨物事故之方法與美國鐵路相較，大有出入，其中足資商討之處不止一端，謹爲逐一論列之如次：

（一）關於貨物之多裝者。　貨物之發生多裝常有由於貨票遲到或貨票誤遞者，亦有於應裝甲車之貨裝入乙車（甲乙兩車均至同一到達站）者，故應先由到達站爲之核對，以期將多補少，自行銷案，不必汲汲於向起運站詢問，如不能核對相符，始有查詢之必要，既收速效，復免煩擾，吾國辦法對此未加規定，此其一。如係全部貨物發生多裝（卽有貨無票），應向起運站索取貨票，起運站應查明轉寄，因貨票或係誤送而非誤塡也。吾國辦法對此亦未提及，此其二。如係貨票誤塡到達站，以致貨物往甲，貨票往乙，則起運站應於接到到達站之詢問時，向甲站補寄貨票，向乙站發出訂正單，以註銷原有誤塡之貨票，究竟起運站補發此項貨票，應如何辦理，亦未規定，似不能以「如係貨票誤塡，應卽改正」兩語了之，此其三。無標誌之多裝貨物，到達站應如何查明起運站名，如不能查得，應如何處置，亦付缺如，此其四。到達站對於全部多裝之貨物，應請收貨人提出貨票收據聯或提貨單，從早交付，勿因內部有貨無票之故。稽延交付時日，甚或加以留難，此應切實規定之要點而未加以規定，殊欠妥善，此其五。到達站向起運站查詢而不得要領時，應限期塡造多裝貨物報告，送呈車務處，以備追究，并用以核對損失賠償案件，吾國無此規定，似宜補充，此其六。到達站卸車司事查出有貨無票情事，自應塡造多裝貨物點驗單，以備核對及查詢，并可存站備查，乃僅規定「註明貨票附記欄內」，不知無票貨物將如何能註明之，其手續之不完備顯而易見，此其七。

（二）關於貨物之誤裝者。　到達站與中轉站發現誤裝貨物，經向起運站電詢明白後，應予轉寄，吾國已有明文規定，惟吾國鐵路所用之轉寄貨票卽爲正式貨票，並無特設之格式，故不能以一聯寄裝車站，以一聯寄車務處，亦爲重大之缺陷。蓋以轉寄貨票之一聯寄裝車站（裝車站或爲中轉站，未必貨運盡屬起運站。）則裝車站可據以查究裝車錯誤之責任，以一聯寄車務處，則車務處可據以編造各站裝車錯誤之統計而從事設法糾正，均爲管理上重要之措施，似不可任其付諸缺如也。至於中轉站發現有貨無票，或貨物多出情事，自亦應由卸車司事填具多裝貨物點驗單，以便據以填發轉寄貨票，實爲必不可少之手續，而有加以補充之必要者也。

(三)關於貨物之損失者　貨物之損失僅一籠統名詞，內分少裝，遺失，被竊及損壞諸端，性質均各不同。如無被挖竊之情狀，而僅有全部或一部件數之缺少，則自尚未能斷爲遺失。其第一步手續，應由卸車司事填造少裝點驗單，先由到達站查對一過，如不能查對相符，以多補少，則第二步，手續始向起運站查詢，如不得要領或確定爲遺失後，到達站始有填造貨物損失報告表之必要，否則卽爲多事。乃查吾國辦法之規定，一面則謂如有短少應電詢起運站是否漏裝，誤裝，誤卸或貨票錯誤，一面則又謂凡貨物發現損失，發現站應於二十四小時內填具貨物損失報告表，一若二十四小時內必可斷定其爲遺失者，其不能盡與事實相符，殆甚顯然。例如發現站如在二十四小時內尚本接得起運站之電復，究竟貨物是否遺失，抑係誤裝，漏裝，誤卸，或貨票錯誤，尙難決定，則發現站是否有填具貨物損失報告表之必要，殊屬疑問；蓋如照章填造，則貨物或於次日運到，殊爲多事，如不填造，則又與規定辦法不符。又如發現站確於二十四小時內接得起運站之電復，謂貨票有誤，應予改正，則貨物原無遺失，是否仍須填具貨物損失報告表，亦無明白之規定。總之此種辦法，皆屬操之過急，一面既不先令發現站自行核對，而須立卽電詢他站，已屬增多煩擾，一面復不寬假相當之時間，藉資確定貨物是否眞遭遺失。而必欲於眞相未白之際，卽行塡具報告，更有增多無謂手續之嫌。此其不妥善之點一。

凡中轉站發現貨物之短少或損壞，按照西國鐵路之辦法，係由中轉站卸車司事在貨票上加以詳細註明，其一切手續概由到達站辦理之。其法簡捷而有效。乃吾國鐵路往往不衡輕重緩急，凡中轉站發現貨物損失時，須電知到達站及有關處所，而到達站接到此項電報時，仍須俟貨物運到以後，始能進行其他手續，然則此項電報之拍發寧非多事。何不僅在貨票上註明一切損失情形，以免發電之必要。因貨票必與貨物同時到達，並不至有貽誤之虞也。若非少裝而確係被竊，則中轉站亦應電知起運站及車務處，以便查究，更無電知到達站之必要。此其不妥善之點二。

貨物如有損壞或確有遺失時，祇須由到達站塡造貨物損失報告，以一份寄發現損失以前之裝車站，以一份寄車務處，而以一份存站備查，固不必責成起運站及中轉站一律作同樣之報告，徒多手續。若貨物並非遺失，而係誤裝，漏裝，或貨票誤塡，則責成起運站塡造損失報告更無意義。良以中轉站發現損失之情形可在貨票上註明，到達站自應參照此項批註，從實報告，決無中轉站與到達站分別塡造報告之必要。至於裝車及改裝之情形以及貨物市價等項須由起運站或中轉站報告者，亦祇須在到達站塡具之損失報告表內添列若干項目，由起運站或中轉站於收到後查明塡註，轉寄車務處備查，不必另造報告，重錄各種已有之事項（例如票據所載事項是），寗非一舉數得節省手續之法乎。此其不妥善之點三。

查美國鐵路之貨物損失報告，照例不由叚長轉呈，而係直接送呈運輸處。以免增多無謂之周折。吾國鐵路對於損失報告之塡告，既限以極急促之時間。而其寄送辦法，則反須經由叚長承轉，是急於此者而緩於彼，殊有矛盾之嫌。吾知鐵路貨運損失賠償，係由車務處集中辦理，損失報告何必由叚長轉呈，徒生曲折。主管段長得此有何用途，是否能再親往調查一過。以補站長報告之不足，殊屬疑問。卽使主管段長對於貨物損失確有負責考查與防止之責，則亦祇須由站方抄寄一份，而應寄車務處之一份仍可直接寄送豈不直捷了當，減少周折耶。此其不妥善之點四。

凡有關貨物損失之證物，在美國鐵路未嘗有隨損失報告送呈者，乃吾國竟有此規定，亦足以徒增煩擾。縱令此項證物確有吊查之必要，亦應俟車務處主管人員調查賠償案件時，斟酌情形，囑令關係站補送，斷不必由各站自作主張，隨同損失報告一併附寄。雖此項證物之寄送，有於必要時爲之規定，然何謂必要，何物必要，僅能於調查賠償案件時決定之，非站長於二十四小時內所能決定者也。此其不妥善之點五。

鐵路處理貨物損失，貴能設法糾正，以免重犯，固不僅在應付賠償案件已也。故起運站或中轉站於接得到達站之損失報告後，應卽查明損失之緣由，幷設法加以矯正，所有矯正之辦法：應在該報告內註明，而仍將該報告轉寄車務處備核，不必待車務處查究以後，始作矯正或改善之處置、吾國鐵路對此並無明文規定，而貨物損失報告表內亦無相當欄格，足資註塡此項矯正改善之辦法。實欠完備，此其不妥善之點六。

如在損失報告表塡送之後，貨物轉寄到站或貨票加以訂正，自應通知車務處銷案；方爲合理，此卽美國鐵路O.K.報告，而吾國無之，此其不妥善之點七。

五　結語

綜觀以上討論各點，具見吾國鐵路處理貨物事故辦法尚多應加補充改進之處，歸納言之，其缺點可分下列數種：

(一)對於多裝及少裝貨物，不知寬假相當時間，先由到達站設法核對，而必須立卽發電詢問，名爲趕速，實則操之過急，轉多浪費。

(二)內部手續之規定，諸欠完備，如發現多裝少裝，並無塡造點驗單之辦法、遇有有貨無票情事，勢必無從塡註，殊嫌缺乏依據。

(三)規定之欠完密者亦非一端，如全部多裝之貨物是否可憑收貨人提出之貨運收據或提貨單交付，不必待內部貨票之覓得，未見有所規定，卽其著例。又如無標誌之貨物發現多裝，不能與有標誌者同樣處理，自必另有規定，在吾國鐵路，零貨標誌未用墨戳，而用標籤，尤有脫落之虞，而通觀各條辦法對此槪未提及，安得視爲完密。

(四)損失報告表之塡造陷於極度之重複，不知利用到達站塡具之報告，分成數聯，寄送關係站，令其塡註寄回，更不知利用貨票之批註辦法，免除中轉站報告之必要。

(五)損失報告表之塡造，限時太促，難免有報告之後查明貨物並無遺失者，無形中增多不必要之手續，亦屬耗費。且查明貨物並無遺失之後，亦不令站方塡具O.K.報告，尤屬缺陷。

(六)各站轉寄誤裝貨物時，不能利用轉寄貨票，以一份寄裝車站，一份寄車務處，以爲糾正裝車錯誤之張本；而遇有貨物損失時，不知利用損失報告表，令關係站塡明矯正改善之辦法，寄回車務處備核。凡此均屬管理上之要着而不費若何額外手續者，付諸缺如，至爲可惜。

(七)處理程序之不合，亦屬處處可見，如損失報告表之須經由段長轉呈，與夫證物之不待吊取而自送；皆其著例。至於中轉站，須將損失情形電知到達站，而到達站仍須俟貨物寄到，始能辦理手續，則尤跡近兒戲，不足以稱辦事之程序矣。

有此種種缺點，則改善之道，當可思過半矣，茲不贅。

鐵路管理科學生兼習機工之我見

鍾偉成

近日之言鐵道管理者，每以運輸效率減低，其結癥所在，卽因車機兩處組織上無一貫之系統，工作上缺切實之合作，以致行動，不能一致，動多阻撓。因之效法北美合衆國鐵道之先例，將車務處之運輸課與機務處所屬之機車房合併，設立運輸處，以統制列車機車調度，車輛支配，及行車事務。另設營業處以辦理客貨業務。廠務處以管理車輛修理事務。此項制度，北寧創始于先，道濤浙贛繼起于後，然卒以車務人員不諳熟機械與工程之原理與技術，指揮殊欠靈便，以故車機二處合併未久，卽復改仍舊觀。鐵道當局鑒于車機合併辦法之失敗，其最大原因，不在制度之不良，實由于人材之缺乏，因之有本院應增與運輸行車有密切關係之機械及土木工程學科之建議。法良意美，誠屬至當。惟細思斯議，在理論上不無見地。然就教學及事實上言之，則似有考慮之必要。爰就管見略陳梗概希關心路務者有以商討之。

一、學習問題　學生之選習學科，每以其性情及志願爲轉移。性近乎管理者，因之努力于有關管理學科之研習，期造成完善之管理人材。而有志爲工程及技術人員者，其興會及志趣必偏向于工程學科之研習。因其性之相近，帥其志之所趨。以故投考管理學院之學生，其平日對於工程上基本學識，如理化數學必興趣甚少，缺乏深切之研究。若入學之後，欲授之以高深之工程學科，非特學習時，無研讀之興趣，卽聽講程度，亦虞不足。若强使硏習，非一知半解，卽囫圇呑棗積而不化矣。或謂學生程度足可于新生入學時嚴格考試其數學理化科目，則授課時學生對於機械及工程等課自不發生困難。此言似是而實非，且事實上亦有困難。蓋近年各地高級中學多採分科制度，學生之投考管理學院者，對社會經濟有研究之興趣而對於理化及數學大都程度不高。若管理學院招考新生除試驗其經濟等學科外，更試以高深之理化數學，則學力足以應考者除少數聰明傑出之士外，爲數恐極寥寥，且甄別之際亦常有顧此失彼之弊。若强欲行之，高中分科制度，必先行改革。此點是否有悖于教育原理，及社會需要，實有討論之價值。此管理學院增設工程學科所感困難者一。

二、授課問題　學生習讀及考選之困難已如上述。當進而研究授課問題。第一，爲授課之師資，蓋授機械及工程學科，其師資必兼具有工程及管理等兩種學識，且于鐵路實際工作，有豐富之經驗，而後講解之時能融會貫通，互相啓發以切實用。此種人材非本校教師中難以訪求，卽鐵道職員中亦不易多得，卽或有之，鐵道本身需材孔殷，必早爲羅致，决無暇晷充任教師。况鐵道部對于路員兼任交大課務限制綦嚴，卽有學識經驗極爲豐富之路員必格于功令，勢難兼顧。此本院添設工程及機械學科師資選擇之困難情形也。至就教材方面言之，其困難亦不易解决。蓋機械及工程之課本，大都均須引用高深之數理程式，且列舉機械圖畫及算表以資解釋，此種教材在素習工程之學生，一時尙難領悟，若取而授之素習管理之學生，則敎授非詳加解釋，學生非勤課練習，及時時實地參觀勢難澈底明瞭。然授課之時間有限，若過于加重工程科目授課時間，則須妨碍其應有之管理科學，其結果非舍本而逐末，卽草率以從事，二者均足使學生無精深之造詣可資應用。若選用淺近之課本由敎師作概括之叙述，則學生僅一知半解，反不若就管理上專用之學科，作精微之研求，庶使學有專攻，材堪致用，此本院增設工程學科敎材選擇之困難也。其他如學生解答習題，繪製圖樣等項，均與授課方面息息相關，就學生之時間技術，及學校設備上言之，皆有困難此又宜加考慮者也。

三、實用問題　由上以觀假使各中學校能預爲培養特種學生，（卽工商兼習之學生）以備投考本院鐵道管理科，同時本院能有充分經費，以供改良設備，幷能選用適當人材以充任敎師，則本院添設工程學科，培養鐵道運輸之完全人材其困難之點似可迎刃而解矣，如是則本校畢業同學出任機車調遣列車週轉事務，當可措置適當應付裕如，而鐵道運輸效率當可無形提高矣。但就實際上細爲分析之，則有未盡然者。蓋鐵路運輸效率之減低與車機二部份事務能否合併，其最大原因，不在車務人員有無機械及工程學識，而機車車輛運轉與修理遲速不能適合業務之需要，致供不應求，運輸阻滯，實爲全局之結癥。此種現狀，一方面固由于車機分處之組織使兩部份員司爲減輕責任有互相推諉之事實，而另一方面，車機而處員工，無切實合作之精神，因之而司機不聽車務人員調度，機廠修理工作，不能視車機之需要而增減其速度，其他如機件材料運轉遲緩，凡此種種，均屬鐵道管理中之人事及事務問題，非員司技術優劣有以致之也。欲袪此弊，一方面固須採用合理之組織，科學的方法，以管理列車運轉，與機車修理。而員司道德之修養，以及合作精神之鼓勵，尤爲切要。車務管理人員應否對于機械及工程學術有深切之研究，尚非急要。蓋車務人員，對於工程學術平日縱有研究，然亦只可處于設計及監督地位，而實際工作如升火，開車，檢查，加油，等項工作，仍須假手於監工及工人，苟此種工人不能合作，其效果仍等于零。況鐵道事業，日異月新，分工合作，乃鐵路管理之基本原則。車務人員致力于營業招徠，編組列車，支配車輛。而機務處則視營業上之需要，調節修理，及調度機車，以求運轉迅速。工務處盡力于路基之修養以增加運輸能力。三者苟能有眞正之合作，以互相規劃力求改良，則運輸之經濟與效能自可日臻完善，否則交大管理學院之學生縱有充分之工程學識，對於增加運輸效率實毫無補益也。

綜合上述各點，僅就管窺所及，聊抒短見，其目的在提出此項問題，以供研討，既未敢固執成見認爲必是，亦未敢忽略事實，曲爲附和，眞理俱在，事實易明，幸路界先進而教之，尤盼本院鐵路管理科畢業同學發表意見。

新路建設之經濟觀（續）（C1）

黃宗瑜

三 勞工

本刊以前各期中，作者對於新路建設之資本及土地問題，已作概括之論述矣，本節將進而研究，新路建築之勞工問題，考自社會主義流行以來，勞工問題幾爲各國社會學者，討論之中心，如工資，工時，工作場所，勞資糾紛等問題，著述宏富，美不勝收，我國鐵路工人，其情形雖與國外工人各殊，而罷工怠工事件，亦時有所聞，是則鐵路勞工問題，亦殊有研究之價值，本文限于篇幅，對鐵路勞工問題無暇詳論，僅就鐵路建築時募集勞工應行注意之點，略加研究分別陳述如左。

一、鐵路工人之分類

雇用鐵路工人，必先明乎鐵路工程之性質，考鐵路建築工程，分爲二〇類，一爲路基工作，如填土奠基砌石舖軌等工程是也，此項工作如有工程技術人員，從旁指揮監督，普通工人，類能爲之，二爲建築工作，如橋梁，涵洞，房屋，號誌等物之建築是也。其工作均有技術性質，非有技術修養之工人決難勝任，而一般普通工人，必須先受訓練，始克任之，否則工事既不妥善，材料亦多耗損，此應特別注意也。

二、工人雇用制度

鐵路建築勞工之種類，已如上述，至工人雇用制度，就各路所已經採用，及曾經計議者考之，有下列各種。

一、包工制　包工制，乃由鐵路工程局，擇其工作較爲重大者，將圖樣尺寸建造材料，製成工程規範，公開招標，由建築公司，投標承包，再由鐵路指派工程人員，從旁監督，以求工事之堅實，採用此種方法，又可分爲整包工及分包工二種，前者乃將工程全部如全線十方等交由一工程公司或工頭承包，後者亦稱小包工，乃將工程全部分爲數個單位，每一單位，由一組工人承包，如鐵路大橋，其橋基及橋架及引橋，分別由各公司承包，此項包工制速，其最大好處，卽在工事管理之簡便；工程費用之固定，以及完成日期之迅度，蓋包工均爲富有管理工人經驗之人；故雇工，給費以及監督等事均較鐵路工程人員爲諗，因之而工人之召集亦易，工資訂定亦廉，且有可爲鐵路墊付工資者近因國內公路鐵路，新工並舉。包工技術，雖亦漸養成，然大都規模甚小，工具不全，資本薄弱，嚴格繩之爲數至爲有限，加之營包工業者，以市城物料供給，工匠雇用，資本週轉，均較方便，而鐵路建築，遠在荒野，工作場所，盜匪出沒，一切工作，均帶有冒險性質，以故多不願往，是以選擇包工，必當明瞭包工爲營業性質，在工作相合，工價相當條件之下，包工應得之利益，務須顧及，包工合同，宜求公正，惟本無能力而希圖嘗試者，或開價大低而預料其難于實行者自始卽不准其承包，嚴加拒絕，以免日後之困難，又偷工減料以及虐待工人之事，則訂合同務須詳盡，監視工作必求周到，其弊自減，至於整包工與分包工，何者爲優，則應視工作情形而定，惟同一性質之工程，若採分包工制，則包價之高低，工作之遲速，工程之良窳，既可互相參照，且包工爲同業競爭顧全信譽計，亦必力求完善，此點分包工實較整包工爲優，惟小包工，其工作方法，工具數目，資本大小，工頭信用等項，均有考慮之必要。

二、雇工制　乃鐵路工程局在建築地段，自雇工人，加以訓練，以充建築之用，另派工程人員，從事指揮監督；此種辦法，在管理上極爲繁複，且鐵路工程人員，對於當地勞工情形及技能，素不深悉，因之而招募工人及分配工作等事項，均感困難且制定工資率，亦往往有過低過高之弊，惟工作之遲速工料之選擇，工人之勤惰，主管與計劃者有完全統轄之自由，而偷工減料之弊，自可減少，故較包工制爲愈也，至雇工時所應參考之要素約有下列各點。

一、當地勞工生活狀況。

二、當地普通工資指數。

三、當地工會組織及其工作。

四、當地工人居住區與工作場所之距離，此外如當地金融週轉情形，工具物料供給處所，採用雇工制度時，均應加以考慮，否則對於發放工資每多不便，而工作效率，亦無形減低矣。管理工程者，未可以其小而忽之也。

綜上兩點，爲一般工人雇用制度，在新路建築之際，如事先籌足的款，則上述二種制度，任擇其一，即可爲雇用工人之方法，惟我國現值國難時期，建造鐵路，財政竭蹶，建築材料，且須仰給外洋，而急待完成路線，爲數極多，一切建築工程費用，自宜力求減省，工資一項，乃建築費用之大宗，苟能採用其他方法，以資節省，自可分別採行，茲再就國內各種建設事業曾經試行或建議之募集工人辦法，分述如左，以冀管理工程者之參考焉。

甲、徵工制　徵工制度由來以久，古代稅制，有力役之征，即徵工之原意，後世以金錢代力役，人民納幣于官，因之免其勞力，此制遂廢，近者　蔣委員長，鑒于國民經濟建設，需要迫切，又復提倡徵工制度，實行全國國民，勞動服務，從事國民經濟建設，藉濟國家財力之不逮，而謀設事業之速成。其辦法要點爲「實行徵工制度，參加義務勞動，……以當地國民勞力，首先從事當地開發交通，修治水利，培植森林，開懇荒地，……政府方面更應同時實施兵工政策……以軍隊之勞力輔助各地徵工工務之不足……」見廿五年元旦蔣委員長演講「國民自救救國之要道」文中

由是可知，開發交通，爲實行徵工制度，目的之一，鐵道爲交通之命脈，徵工築路，地方政府，自宜首先提倡，鐵道部亦可妨擬徵工築路計劃，提交經濟建設運動委員會以爲方案，在新路建築進行之際，擇要採行，此項制度苟得地方政府盡力宣傳人民激於公義，當可見效，惟論者謂徵工時期過長，殊足妨礙農事，但每一工事苟其性質簡單如塡土舖石等工程，由沿綫各地民衆，通力合作以行之，其時期當不甚長也。

乙、兵工制　兵工政策，在清末左宗棠建設陝甘通新疆大道時，已經採行，民國十一年孫總理又復加以提倡，爰是時北洋軍閥，擁兵自衛。爲謀國家統一起見，力主必先裁兵，兵裁之後，必須授以工作俾維持其生活。因之有提倡兵工政策之議，當時格於環境，未能實現，最近晉綏兩省士兵，修築同蒲鐵路，成效卓著，實爲兵工築路最好之先例，惟國家養兵，其目的原在作戰，實行兵工政策

，對於軍隊教育原定計劃，必多妨礙，戰鬥能力，無形減低，且國防緊急之秋國家正規軍隊，一時難以抽調，以上所述一點，在我國目前情形自屬困難，惟各省駐紮省防軍保衞團或警察等項在地方承平之時，亦可事先訓練，教以築路技能，再由鐵道部測定若干路線，商請省政府，調派一部份軍隊由工程監督先行修築路基，俟有成效，再行舖軌釘道，則鐵道工程，當易進行而兵工政策亦可實現矣，查兵工築路其優點有三。

一、軍隊有組織有紀律，同時加以訓練，即可變爲良好之路工，且管理亦較普通工人爲易。

二、兵士月給餉金，若再稍給工資或奬金，工作必加勤奮，且所給之工資或奬金，可較一般工資爲低，故費用亦較雇工或包工爲省。

三、徵工有時，足以妨礙農工原有事務，間接即減少國家生產能力，而各地駐防軍隊，每日除兩操兩課之外，並無其他工作，且在募兵制度之下，士兵以當兵爲職業，殊少技術修養，一旦退伍，勢必流爲匪盜，社會安寧，影響殊鉅，苟能實行，兵工制度，一則徵工服役時期，可以縮短，二則兵士技能，亦可培養，退伍以後，當不致有失業之虞，誠一舉而兩得者也，惟實行兵工築路，須必先訂原則，管見所及，下列三點，似足以供參考。

一、兵工所築之路綫其工作以土方及道碴工程爲限，其他工事，應仍由包工或雇工辦理。

二、築路之兵，仍採軍隊組織及管理方法，由工程人員，從事指導，由軍官加以監督。

三、凡從事築路之士兵，必須先行訓練，再按其工作成績，嚴加奬懲。

以上爲實施兵工制之要點，我國現時建造新路，是否須用此項辦法，則有待於鐵道當局之擇決者也。

丙、賑工制　工賑修建路基前交通總長葉玉甫先生曾有倡議，卒以格于淸議，未能實行，當時所定辦法略爲先由各路局派員調查沿線災情，各電報報告當地歲收狀況，以爲籌賑之根據，然後擇已經計劃建築而與災區鄰近之路線首先建築路基或就災區原有路線，修築支綫；暫用雇募散工辦法，雇用災民，以工代賑，此種辦法，可旣收容災民免爲流寇，且能進行築路，於民於國，兩有裨益。近年以來，陝甘晉豫各省，災情奇重，災區廣漠，被災人民，待賑孔殷，而各該省鐵道路綫，亦亟待完成，各地所募鉅額賑款，若就地施放，雖可救急一時，終非長久之策，莫若召集災民，加以訓練，卽用其勞力以建鐵路路基，而所籌賑款，卽取其一部份，以爲發放工資之用，是賑款旣無虛縻，而災民獲有恆業，且鐵路建築資金，亦以是而減省矣。

上述甲乙丙三種募集工人辦法，在我國鐵路財政狀况之下，均可採行惟徵工制乃一般國民勞動服務，完全出于自動，其徵集及管理制度，雖國家須有法令，可資遵循然對於稽核工程成績，當不若包工制或雇工制爲便，惟按視當地民情，設法鼓勵當可稍見功效，兵工制或賑工制，雖管理較易，然各地軍隊，時有調遣，而災民築路，亦妨農事，且各地年歲，豐歉無定，故災區亦年有不同，勞工供給數量及地域，殊難固定，總之徵工兵工或賑工制度，均非建造鐵路時，募集勞之正當方法，且所集工人縱加訓練，亦只能從事建造路基工作，稍有技術性之工程卽不克勝任故新路建設之勞工，自仍以包工及雇工爲主，另採其他三種辦法，以濟其窮，如邊陲遼遠之地，爲包工或雇工所不願往者，則取徵工兵工或賑工方法，以濟之，庶幾勞工無缺乏之虞，而建設計劃亦可望速成矣。

（待續）

職位分類之比較研究（D 3）

任家誠

一

行政學之研究有二大目標，曰行政效率求其顯著，行政經費求其撙節。我人於人事行政之討論中，亦未嘗離乎此二大目標。人事行政之實施，當自職位分類（Classification of Positions）始。蓋職位旣經分類，升遷有其程序，攷績有所根據，執政人員可以盡統馭之能事，以增進公務員工作之效能。且因職位詳爲劃分，俸給之額可有合理之決定。『同職同俸』原則之實現，公務員方面，不致受不公平之待遇，政府方面於俸給之費用，亦可有所統制，而達撙節經費之目標。

我國政府近方以提倡行政效率爲已任，努力革新，對於職位之分類亦有相當確定（參照民國元年北京政府公佈之中央行政官官俸法及細則，兼採日本及清季制度分官等爲特，簡，荐，委四等，更以職列等，成暫行文官官等官俸表）。其制度是否完美有否改良之必要，爲關心行政者注目之點。請比較研究各國所用之法，以觀察我國以後應採之制度，儻亦可供政府之參攷歟。

二

英國——職位之劃分，以責任之輕重爲根據，別職爲助理 (Writing assistant)，辦事（Clerical)，執行 (Executive)，管理 (Administrative) 四級。皇家人事行政委員會 (Royal Commission on the Civil Services) 更於四級之外，建議增加速記級(Shorthand-typist Class) 與打字級 (Typist Class)（一）然現在主要之分類，仍爲四級。四級之說明如下：

『助理級——從事于機械上之工作(如打印器及計算機等)，抄寫及謄錄之工作（如書寫通知，填具表格票據及憑照等），書寫信面，計算及驗收郵件及保險單等，計劃及預備表格與書寫簡單卡片，保管卡片目錄……及其他類似之日常工作。

辦事級——此級我人任以各種一切不屬於助理級之簡單事務上之職務。更有下列之職務：

依據已定之規章，訓示及一般方法，辦理特定之案件，根據訓示，攷查及稽核直接帳目及請求案等。

依照已定方式，准備退貨，帳目及統計：

草擬簡單之稿件及要略，搜集有補判事之材料；

監視助理級之工作。

執行級——此級任以供應及會計部 (Supply & Accounting Departments) 之較高工作，

及其他人事行政執行及專門部份之較高工作。此種工作範圍極廣，更需不同程度之判斷能力，及創造力。較低各等(Junior Ranks)包含次要特定案件，其範圍未經規章及議案決定者之批判，自動的調查重要事務及直接管理範圍較小事業。較高各等決定內部組織及統制，解決種種重要之問題，負責的指導重要事務。

管理級——此級主持政策之決定，設法改良政府機構及管理各部。』(二)

四級之工作既有極大之差別，故任職資格亦大為不同。英之文官任用，必先經過攷試，故所謂任職之資格，即指應試資格而言。其資格限制可分二方面：一為教育程度，一為年齡。

各級之中，更分各等，以資歷及成績為升遷之根據。各等間升擢由各部自己決定，而級與級間之升擢則須得財政部之批准。(三)於此點上可見四級乃以職位責任之不同而分，而級與級間並不嚴加劃分，有越級升擢之可能。

德國——職位之劃分，以責任等級及俸給為依據，共分三級：(一)高級(二)中級(三)低級(四)。關於專門技術人員之分類，不在此三級之內，故置不論。高級與中級中更分不同等第若干，低級則均列一等，並不再分。低級之公務員如經攷試及格，可升入中級，故低級亦可謂中級之預備級。任職須經攷試，高級公務員須受完全之大學教育，而其餘二級則並不必要。

意國——職位之劃分亦基于責任及任務之輕重，分成五組（Groups），曰A,B,C,附屬職員(Messengers)及雇員。A組中更分十一等，B組分六等、C組分六等。(五)各組之間嚴加劃分，不能越組，換言之，升擢最高之希望，爲升至本組中最高之一等。

在一九二三年改革以前，A組有管理及顧問之職能，B組有執行及稽察之職能，C組則辦理日常事務如擬稿，記帳，及繕校等。附屬職員及雇員等爲雇用性質，而與前三組之人員有不同之處。

日本——官級可分爲四，曰親任，勅任，奏任，判任。(六)其任職概須經過攷試，高等攷試爲奏任官之攷試，而普通攷試則爲委任官之攷試。(七)任職後逐步升擢，各級間並無阻隔，各級間再按高下分成不同之等別。

日本制度之可資參攷者，厥爲官名與職名之分別。(八)故任官不一定補職，補職後方能担任職務。任官由內閣任命，任職則由主管長官就其資格才能派充。此種制度於官名視若資格，如某人已升至奏任官，而一時無職，他日再出任事時，仍可就其資格，指定職務，故職務爲暫時性質，而官名爲永久性質。雖屬世界文官制度之創見，然軍隊之編製，往往如此，非無前例也。

美國——美國之制度與前述各國迥異，爲職位分類之革命者。其最顯著之一點，爲脫離分等之羈縛，而重視於職位之性質。其根據完全以『同職同俸』爲出發點。以爲各國分職之短處在過於重視等級而輕于職務，結果俸給之定，定於等級，有違『同職同俸』之定例。其原則以職位性質絕對相同而可予以同一職名者歸入一類，任職者須有相同之資格，以相同之試驗選擇相當之公務員，而俸給之決定亦以職務之同否爲依歸。（九）制度新穎合理，已受世界行政學者及執政者之注意，而公認爲職位分類之有價值的貢獻。

攷美於一九一九年由國會組織職位重行分類聯合委員會（Joint Commission on Reclassification of Salaries），一九二三年決定職位分類之方法分爲事務（Service）與等級（Grade），事務者『相關之公務間最大之分劃也』，等級者『事務之再分劃，包括一職或數職之需相同資格及予相同俸給者，等級之差別根據工作之重要性，艱難性，責任及價值。』（十）事務之劃分可分爲五，如下：

『專門與科學之事務（The professional & Scientific Service）應包括一切職位，其任務在根據專門及科學之原理，辦理日常，諮詢，管理及研究之工作。此種工作需要專門，科學，或技術的訓練，相等於公認之專門學校及大學畢業。

次要之專門事務（The Sub-professional Service）應包括一切職位，其任務在完成附屬於專門與科學事務人員之工作及準備之工作。此種工作需要專門，科學，或技術的訓練，次于公認之專門學校及大學畢業。

日常行政及理財之事務(The Clerical, Administrative & Fiscal Service)應包括一切職位，其任務在完成日常行政或會計之工作，或其他工作之協助政府事業及理財之管理者。

看守之事務(Custodial Service)應包括一切職位，其任務在監視或完成看守，維持，或保護公共建築，房屋及器具，公務員及雇員或其財產之行旅及運輸，及公文之移轉等體力的工作。

機械之事務(Clerical-mechanical Service)應包括一切職位之不屬承認之事務，而屬於政府印刷所，印鑄局及郵件局者，其任務在完成或管理機械或人力之工作，需要特技及經驗者，或完成或管理一切人力或機械工作結果之計算，校驗，整理或攷核等。」(十一)

專門科學之事務下更分九等，次要之專門事務分八等；日常行政及理財之事務分十六等；看守之事務分十等；機械之事務分四等，故共爲五種事務，四十七等級，等級之劃分，係根據工作之重要性艱難性，責任及價值已如前述。各事務下，更以任務之類別分成各小類，如日常行政及理財事務之分爲估價，行政及監察之日常事務，會計，文書，人事庶務等。其制度可謂十分完善。六等工作載明于法案，以俸給之高低別之。分類時，事務之分別可就職務之相似或絕對相同者列入，並不困難，困難則爲分等，職務分配，俸級高下，責任輕重等，均須有嚴密之攷慮；（十二）而分等不得其法，尤易引起其公務員之反響，理論上亦將違反『同職同俸』之原則。

加拿大——重視職位之性質，而目爲分類之根據，實際上不以美國始，加拿大實先有此例。

加拿大於一九一九年以前，亦採取以責任輕重爲高下之分等法，別爲一，二，三三級，各級中更分A，B兩等。第一級A等包括助理之領袖（如我國之次長），及主要之專門及技術人員（如我國之技監）；第一級B等包括主任及較爲次要之專門及技術人員。第二級A等包括執行及技術人員，一八八五年法規規定此種人員爲主任辦事員；第二級B等包括附屬之執行人員，一八八五年法規定名爲高級二等辦事員。第三級A等包括繕校及日常工作辦事員，歸入初級二等辦事員；第三級B等包括臨時性質之職員，歸入三等辦事員。（十三）

後以分等法之不合分類原則，乃於一九一九年有『加拿大人事行政職位分類』(Classification of the Civil Service of Canada)之決定，並不一定迎合各部之組織，而以工作之種類性質及事業爲劃分之類別。各類中包含相同工作之高級人員以至低微職員。職員均須由最低級敘起，逐漸遞升，不同之類別，有不同之升擢系統，各不相混。（十四）

此種制度與美相仿，其特點在淸除一切職位及俸給上之不平，可謂新大陸之特殊貢獻，其利弊當於下節中批評之。

三

綜觀世界各國對於職位分類之方法，可分爲二，曰縱的劃分與橫的劃分是也。英，德，意，日諸國採取橫的制度，卽以分等爲原則，以責任之重輕，職位之大小爲標準，而不問所務之工作屬于何種性質。澳地利亞聯邦亦採此制，於其『聯邦公務法案』(Commonwealth Public Service Act, 1922)中，對於職位分類曾下以定義曰：

『職位分類者，將公務員與職位劃成等級，分配公務員與職位之俸給，或以工作之價值，決定俸給之限制』(十五)

其定義充分的表示分類之制度爲趨於橫的方面。縱的方面重視工作性質，以性質之不同，歸入不同之類別，然後按類研究，各類之間自定等級，以別同類工作之難易與責任之輕重。然各類之等級因均由自定，故並不一致，此與橫的劃分逈然異者。

二種制度中，橫的分類，以等級爲別，實際上我人可稱之爲職位之分等，而不應認爲分類，蓋「類」字之義顯係析工作性質之不同。分等級之高低，而名之曰類，確有不合。然爲便利說明見，均稱之曰職位的分類，而以橫直之不同別之，此點爲不可不加說明者。

橫的制度，發展較早，故其中蛻化差異亦多。就英制觀之，其別爲管理，執行，辦事，助理等級，雖有責任輕重，工作繁簡，經驗多少之別，然非絕對的爲上下級，其分等係各就其不同級而定。管理級之分等中，最低之俸或較執行級最高之俸爲低。故英制雖經歸入橫的劃分內，事實上與他國所採用者，有不同之處，請以俸給所定率證明之。

高級辦事級　三百鎊——十五鎊——四百鎊

執行級　一百鎊——十鎊——一百三十鎊——十五鎊——四百鎊

高級執行級　四百鎊——十五鎊——五百鎊

其高級辦事級最高俸可至四百鎊，而普通之執行級最高亦係四百鎊，其最低俸甚至較高級辦事級之最低俸少三分之二，即高級執行級之低俸亦與高級辦事級相近。可見各級之間，並不完全以等級之高下，爲俸給決定之標準。各級中分等之標準乃由各級自成系統定之，此其雖爲橫的劃分，與縱的劃分不無相似處。此種制度我國郵政機關亦採用之，如永遠在一級中升擢，其俸亦可較高於其上級，然如能升入上級，則俸給增加之結果，必較原級爲大。使公務員有退可以守，進可以攻之機會，誠足爲吾人取法者。其缺點與其他分等制度相同，蓋不以職位性質爲劃分，對於一切職位硬合入不同級別，不問其內容如何；事實上偏于科學及專門技術方面之俸給是否能與一般行政工作，視若一列，而强合級別，盡人知其不可。

日本，官與職劃分之法，瞀同者大有人在，蓋實施後，任用升擢之制度可以活動，而銓敘資格亦較便利。其所謂官者猶昔日我人之所謂功名，爲名譽之職，故由內閣任命，所謂職者，乃指長官所指派之工作而言。故有時身雖爲官，而並無職位，仍可保留其名譽上之資格。此種制度當然較我國之公務員一經免職根本鏟除之法爲優越。更有人主張將此種制度，加以改良，更求其發揮官與職分之優點，卽職升而官可不升，及官升而職可不升。以我國而言如職至某部之科長，例應荐任級，今則以其勞績，升擢至簡任級，以嘉其勞。然則我人知我國俸給之定，定於官等，如官等遞升，俸給增加，然所任職與俸給小於本人者相同，是否符合『同職同俸』之原則，不容不爲我人所顧及。此種理論當然亦有充分之理由，蓋以俸給之給予雖須視所任職之同否爲標準，然人類智力有敏愚，任事經驗有久暫，『同職同俸』之原則，是否宜視爲決定職位分類及俸給額唯一之條件，自成問題。此種辦法誠值得我人加以研究。言及日之官職相分，特提出此問題，願與國人一商討之。

絕對採取橫的制度者，以德國爲最明顯。此種制度如辦理之完善，成金字塔形。以德制言，低級公務員應最多，中級較少，高級更少，而其所負之責任，亦如塔形之由低而高，職愈低俸給與責任均愈少，以後比例增加，由普通之智力工作而至最高之智力工作，其優點，在權責之劃分明晰，決無推諉謙讓或攘奪之可能，使公務員對於其任務較爲專注。同時俸隨責任與經驗而增高，年復一手，攷績之有方，可以有公平之系統。其缺點，則前已言之者再，蓋在職務之類別未加劃分，一監獄之看守員，是否能與辦理日常繕校事務之書記列入同級同等，如可能，其比較之標準又復何在，諸此問題，均非主橫的制度者所能解答。全國公務員人數以萬字以上計、所謂分類者統計之工作也。統計之分析首重資料之一致性(Homogen-city)，今以各種不同之職位，不列類別，混同的別以等級，於理自有欠當。抑有進者，我人設不重理論，在事實上之觀察，技士與科員相提並論，亦無比較之可能。是我人又何必强以不合理之分等爲方法。

意國之制有橫的制度之弊而無其利，蓋其所分五級顯有高低不等之表示，然各等各相劃分，不得升擢，公務員一入某等，其終身之希望已定，永無出人頭地之日，當然使其辦事之興趣劇烈減少，轉而減損行政效率。蓋我人知公務員辦事能力之刺激最有效者爲升擢之勉勵，今升擢限於本等，希望有限，何能促其上進之心。此種理論以爲公務員之辦事能力端視其教育程度及入職資格；而不知入職之後，經驗年增，使其上升，其工作之效果，未必一定不如教育較高之公務員也。

縱的劃分在理論上言，其優異誠十百倍于橫的劃分。蓋就其方法上觀，可知非絕對着眼於縱的方面，於分類既竟後，責任不同職務高低之職位，固仍別以等級也。故其方法之眞諦，實爲先以統計學之眼光，析各不同類使之獨立，然後於相同之類別中比較其高下，此種方法自較以監獄看守員及書記列入一等，技士與科員視爲相同爲合理。故就科學化眼光觀察之，縱的劃分實較合理，且分析其制度，實已去橫的制度之缺點，而利用其責任一貫性之優點。

無論美國或加拿大之制度，於每類事務中各等級均有職位分類說明書(Classification Schedule)，內容包括(一)名稱，(二)定義，(三)職務之例，(四)資格限制，(五)升擢系統，(六)俸給差額。故此種制度不獨於分類之方法上爲合理，且以職位分類說明書之規定，無論升擢入職均有限定，不致有任用私人及少數把持之病。(十六)職務之情形有例說明，更可使初入職之人員有所遵循，對於其將來之工作亦可明晰，俾隨時可準備升擢後之工作計劃，行政之效能可以增進。

然則亦不能倖免于缺點，最著者爲過于重視職位而輕視公務員，人爲活動的，固不能若物科管理中種種日用品與設備能絕對使其標準化也。(十七)其次，制度過於複雜，以美爲例，職位之分類自五大事務中，可更析出四十七等一千六百三十三小等十萬另四千職，而每類均須加以說明，(公務人員分類局(Personnel Classification Boards)於職位之說明，佔其某書中一千三百二十七頁，誠可謂洋洋大觀)。(十八)此種繁複之制度如管理不良，不能發生良好效果，且將不可收拾。更有人且認爲此制繁重過甚，缺少伸縮性，有違乎迅速有效率及經濟之原則，（十九）此則各人見解之不同矣。

四

我國現在所採取之制近乎橫的劃分制，以特，簡，荐，委四等別責任之重輕，職位之高下，與夫俸給之大小。其有別於一般之制度者爲同時以機關類別爲縱的劃分，故亦可稱爲縱橫混合制。

縱的方面以機關別爲劃分之標準，所以說明責任之高低，有相當意義；然事實上，其所不同者僅爲地方與中央，似無劃分之必要，僅須於銓敘時別以等級。故雖爲縱橫混合制，縱的劃分並非表示工作之類別，其精神其原則，固仍爲橫的制度也。

清末民初之行政實施多有取法於日本之制度，職位之分類亦然，特任官與日之親任官相當，簡任猶勅任，荐任猶奏任，委任猶判任。然其任用及銓敘之方法，則不如日，蓋日制官與職分如上所述，而我國則無此法也。因之我國銓敘制度較日爲繁複，去職後官等不保留，以後復任他職時，更須查攷以前任職經過。作再度之銓敘，增加手續不少。我國如暫時仍維橫的劃分制度，則官與職似亦可如日之加以分開。

現行制度之缺點，可謂一如其他橫的制度，即職位之未能分類，僅注意及責任一方面。

其較他國爲優越者，則以中央與地方之權責已分輕重，故分等之方法亦加以變通，不若他國之混統。

或有反對今日之制度者曰特，簡，荐，委之名義官氣過重，不合民治之政治之潮流。關乎此點，余以爲此數字不過爲不同等級之代名詞與A，B，C，D，或高，中，低等字並無二致，其制度固仍與他國之橫的制度同，名義上之變革，換湯不換藥，並無道理。而問題則在我國應否維持現行之制度，所謂維持，並非指特，簡，荐，委名義之維持，而爲應否維持橫的劃分制度，或加以修正或加以革新。

五

於各國制度比較研究之後，我人可斷言曰，縱的制度雖不能免于繁複之弊，然以其有科學化之方法，實遠勝橫的劃分；不久之將來，各國必盡棄陳舊之分等，而注重于科學化之分類法，縱的制度必起而代橫的制度無疑。

然則我人試研究二者之關係，可以得極有趣似矛盾而實非之二大結論：即(一)縱的制度較橫的制度爲新穎，(二)縱的制度即橫的制度之改良，二者並不相悖。何以言之，在一九一九年以前，各國職位之分劃無不以等級爲前提，以責任之輕重爲移轉。後美人以分等之不合統計學原則，不同類別之職務，不能相提並論而作比較；於是有縱的制度之倡，二者以時代不同而異，縱的制度爲科學化新時代之產物極明。然自縱的制度方法上觀，其異於橫的制度者，僅爲分工作性質後，再行分等；在橫的制度採取之前，多加一步整理之工作卽爲縱的制度。故縱的制度並非新貢獻，而僅爲橫的制度之改良，又極明。

至於我國今後應採何制，爲國人矚目之點。循世界學識之所趨，應自橫的制度改爲縱的制度，殆無疑義。然爲精益求精起見，可採取混合之方法，以擷二者之長，補二者之短。所謂混合者，與現在之混合制不同，而以機關別之劃分改爲職位性質之分類。其理由如下：

一、鑒於橫的制度之不合統計學原則，我人應採用縱的劃分，以別類別，而創公平之制度，

二、鑒於橫的制度權責一貫之優點，我人不應立卽放棄其利益，故橫的劃分不可遂卽消滅。

三、美以全國事務分五大類，若干等級後，各定俸給及升擢系統，不相爲謀，過趨於極端。爲調劑計，性質之分類雖必實現，而各類之間亦不能使之漠不相關，縱的方面既各成類別，橫的方面仍應維持組別，故不應單獨採取縱的制度。

至於方式，有如下述：

(一)縱的劃分以職務性質不同而分成若干類，可多於美之五大類，而少于其所定之小類

，類別之數目，暫不一定，務須研究其是否能完全包括全國之職務。各類自成系統。有其俸額及升遷之程序。

(二)橫的劃分，仍維持分等之法，至於仍否用特，簡，荐，委等名稱或另用其他名稱表示，不必注意，蓋此爲表面之工作。各縱的劃分及其俸額決定後應聯合之，使勿漫散如美之制。

(三)二者之合併，縱的方面看可知某職之屬於何類，橫的方面看可知某職之屬於何等。至於何以須各類彙集，理甚簡單，蓋易於攷試機關管理及稽查。

請以假定之圖表，說明所擬方式：

※級別	等別	俸別	A	B	C	D	E	會計	G	H	I	J	K…
第一級	一	800											
	⋮	⋮						*主計官　會計長					
	五	⋮											
第二俸	一	⋮											
	⋮	⋮						會計科長　會計主任					
	五	⋮											
第三級	一	⋮											
	⋮	⋮						地方會計主任　會計科員					
	五	55											

* 英文字母均暫代類別之名稱，假定F爲會計。
* 級別等別係假定。
※各職位亦係假定。

．閱此表後，必有人詢曰：前既以爲不分工作性質類別，不能比較等級，今既分類之後，自應各在其自已類別內，比較已定之俸額，又何必再混入橫的制度，而與其他類相比較。混合之意義在一方面既可就自已類別，以責任重輕作比較，一方面更可參攷他類所定之俸額，以確定各類之俸給是否公平，較之他類或高或低，其結果自比獨斷決定爲可靠。且美在決定各類俸額時，余信彼亦曾對各類之俸額加以比較然後決定，所異於所擬之意見者，形式上各類合併與不合併耳。至於各類合併之利益有如前言。

在此應附帶提及者爲升擢系統問題，余以爲各類應自定系統，高等攷試或普通攷試爲入職之門，然後按年攷績擢升，不得越入他類，其理由在使分類專門化之價值增大，及增進公務員之專門辦事經驗。至於普通及高等攷試及格後應如何入職，不在本文討論之內。然欲求系統之易於實現，攷試之制度必須實行，任何公務員凡在此職位分類表內者，均須經過攷試。否則制度雖經改革，陋習仍未可泯，其結果決不能滿意。

至於劃分事務性質之方法，我人可參攷美國及加拿大過去經驗，更加以合理之籌劃及變通。最要者爲不可出以數人之獨斷，而須對現有職位不厭求詳，詳詢各機關；然後集合答解，以科學化之方法。統計學之原則，妥爲劃分，審愼各職位應屬類別。本文所討論者爲制度之研究，故僅將劃分之方法簡述如此。

六

各國制度之優點，可資申述者，爲橫的制度之責任一貫性，縱的制度之分類合理化，及日本所採官職分開之便於銓叙。後二點不同處，一在過分注意職位而不重人的要素，故亦不能免于學者之批評；一在過分否認『同職同俸』之原則，而認爲人的要素實較職的性質爲重，故俸不應僅定于職務之性質，更應定于個人工作之優劣。二者各據其理，比較之觀察，人類性情及智力之評價頗不易定，故官職劃分如與官等之遞升不相符合，是否能有公允之決定，實未可斷言。就現代科學管理之方法觀，以人類心理及性情變遷之速，頗不易尋求比較之規律，乃棄人的原素而重物質上的分析，故職位分類之方法，攷績制度之研究，均以人類之性情及智力加以分析，以觀其是否適於某職，甚或以職謀人。以攷績方法而論，世人且有譏科學化之攷績猶『用顯微鏡逐部觀察一價值連城之古畫』，其詬病蓋亦不無理由也。美之縱的劃分制度爲科學管理之產品，自決不背乎科學管理之假定，此種假定是否合理，至今未有斷論。故美，日之制孰然孰否，始終無人能以客觀之眼光確定之也。

余於第五節中，對於我國應採制度之建議，雖已盡力設法採納縱橫二制之優點，然愧未能顧及官職分離之利益，此種疏忽，當然以浸染於歐美所謂科學管理過深所致；以個人之觀察，科學管理之假定自不能謂爲天衣無縫，故極願更設法離開現代假定之立場，作比較玄理之研究，以發揚官與職分之特質。

——二十五年秋於交大管理學院

(一) Royal Commission on the Civil Service, *Report 1929-31* (His Majesty's Stationery Office, London, 1931) p. 13.

(二)摘自 *Report of the Joint Committee on Reoganisation (1920)*

(三) op. Cit., Royal Commission on the Civil Service: *Report 1929-31*, p. 74.

(四) F.M. Marx, "Civil Service in Germany." Monogrhph 5 *Civil Service Abroad* (by Commission of Inquiry on Public Service Personnel)(McGraw-Hill Book Company, New York, 1935)pp. 202—203

(五) Aldo Lusignoli, "The Italian Civil Service." *The Civil Service in the Modern State* (by L. D. White) (The University of Chicago Press, Chicago, 1930) p.303

(六) 沈覲鼎 日本官制官規之研究(南京攷試院，二十年)第一〇四頁

(七) 陳有豐 日本攷試制度調查報告書(南京攷試院，二十年)第五頁至第十頁

(八) 沈覲鼎 日本官制官規之研究第一一八頁至一二〇頁。

(九) Conference Committee on Merit System, *The Merit System in Government* (New York, 1926) pp. 34—35

(十) Joint Commission on Reclassification of Salaries, *Classification Act*, 42 Stat.1488(Mar. 4, 1923) § 2

(十一) Ibid., § 13.

(十二) L. Wilmerding, Jr., *Government by Merit*(McGraw-Hill Book Company, New York, 1935)p. 54.

(十三) V.K. Johnston, "The Civil Service of the Domain of Canada." op.cit., *The Civil Service in the Modern State* p. 77—78.

(十四) R.M. Dawson *The Civil Service of Canada*(Oxford University Press, London, 1929) p. 159

(十五) Commonwealth Public Service Act, 1922 of Aushalia; No.21 of 1922, Articl 1, part I.

(十六) op. cit, Dawson *The Civil Service of Canada* p. 162.

(十七) op. cit., Wilmerding *Government by Merit* p. 54

(十八) Ibid., p.57.

(十九) *Con. H. of C. Journals,* Appendix. §5, p. 733.

組織眞締

技術含有一種藝術，組織的技術和其他藝術一樣，有特固定的方法。然欲求此種方法的實現，則要在運用之何若。而運用之道，尤須注意各種人事的合作表現出一般原則。試觀一切政府組織，莫不有大同小異的形式，甚至教堂和古今各種實業的組織也不過是搬演故實。然而成績互殊者，卽在人事的合作一點上。

J. D. Mooney and A. C. Reiley, Onward Industry

歐戰時軍用輕便鐵路之建設與管理（C9）

王同文

一 軍用輕便鐵路之起源

當歐戰爆發初年，輕便鐵路在戰地軍運上之重要地位，尚未察覺，後於一九一七年，始悉輕便鐵路對於軍運，關係重大。於一九一七年前，後方廣軌鐵路與前線戰壕之軍運上聯絡，全憑道路運輸，當時因戰區範圍擴大，軍運繁重，道路力不勝任；又道路經數年繁重軍運，加之砲火轟炸，路面已破碎不堪，運貨汽車，亦已損舊，然仍須搬運修理道路之材料工人及工具，蓋已不能應付，對於主要之軍運，實無力顧及，至此六十公分（二三又八分之五吋）軌距之輕便鐵路以興，藉救此危急之軍運問題。此種軍用輕便鐵路，可與後方廣軌鐵路相接，前綫與重砲陣地，或有軌道路（Tramway 拖引力以大獸力或人力推進）相通，於是軍用道路與輕便鐵路之軍運範圍，得以劃分。規定道路專供運貨汽車，機器脚踏車，及客車之行駛，除修理道路外，凡輕便軍運，如高級兵士，急救傷兵，及其他臨時緊急運輸，皆屬於道路運輸。輕便鐵路專供大量與笨重之軍運；又於大雨之後，當道路之汽車軍運發生困難時，輕便鐵路能代爲解決之；並輕便鐵路與軍用道路，亦宜有相互調和與整聯之運輸。總計軍用輕便鐵路綫之里程，於歐戰停戰時約有七千哩。

二 輕便鐵路之功用

輕便鐵路對於軍運上之功用，爲專於運輸赴前綫之軍需品，糧食，道路建築材料，輕便鐵路建築材料，飼料，木板，燃料，沙袋，鐵絲網，以及其他軍用工程上之材料，如是可有大量輸送，而減省人獸力在火綫內搬運物料，致遭危險；並可有敏捷之兵士與軍馬運送，及急要之救險運輸，又可補道路運輸之不及；回程可裝載戰地之傷兵，或已精疲力極之兵卒退往後方休養，戰地之彈殼，及其他廢棄之軍用工程材料，或用舊之軍械運往後方修理；及在輕便鐵路上，應用特製之車輛、裝置八吋口徑之大砲，或以小鋼炮裝在鐵甲車上，前後左右行駛，成爲活動炮台，便於轟擊，致使敵軍不能察定我方炮火之出發地點。

三 輕便鐵路在軍運上之價值

輕便鐵路在軍運上之價值，遠勝於道路。設每一運貨汽車，平均載重量爲三噸，輕便鐵路每一列車，掛車六輛，每輛載重六噸，共爲六十噸，適等於二十輛運貨汽車所作之工作。据工程新聲週報(Engineering News-Record)第八十卷十一期，一九一八年三月十四日出版載，歐戰時英國前綫所用之輕便鐵路，每一綫一日內最多能載運二、一〇〇噸其運輸能方，可等於七〇〇輛汽車之功用，但於我方軍事節節勝利；敵軍於一日內退却十哩後之時，則我方輕便鐵路對於前進之軍運，無力相助，唯有賴於道路前進，同時趕急依照作戰地勢，延長新路綫。

輕便鐵路最適宜於戰區內短距離軍運，因其行車速率較遲，不宜於長距離軍運，又有利於防守戰爭；而不宜於進攻或退却之戰略，因防守之戰，陣地不變，輕便鐵路得源源供應前線，如進攻奪地，則難於與新進陣地聯絡，若爲退却，則根本失其效能，反助長敵人之利。

對於進攻或退却之處置，尤宜適當，若進攻奪得敵方陣地，應急于設法，將敵陣地所有之輕便鐵路，整理修築，以謀與我方聯絡；以退却論，若爲有計劃準備之退却，應將鐵路材料，路綫設備，全部拆卸，搬運後方，若爲臨時退却，應設法將鐵路設備材料等，全部炸壞，以免反資敵利用。

四　路線敷設之位置

輕便鐵路綫網敷設之位置，對於整個戰地進攻或防守之形勢，關係至重，事前需有詳細之計劃，由軍事長官與運輸長官共同設計之，先由鐵路工程隊實地測量，以附合作戰方針。其至要之原則：(一)路綫不能爲敵方偵察機覓得，收入影機，以便將來易爲敵軍用炮火或炸彈轟炸，破壞軍運。(二)最妥路綫，需築於沿樹林一帶，或於叢草之中，使敵機無從偵察，而不宜築於無草木可蔽之平地上。(三)路綫取輻射扇形，需築於第一道防綫之附近，與最前綫之戰壕及重炮陣地，各方均有連絡，後方則與廣軌鐵路，或其他主廣運輸道銜接，依軍運之繁簡，築雙綫以至於三綫四綫；但三綫不能過於接近平行，各綫須相距數十或百餘尺，並三綫之間，互有支綫相通，若左綫適爲敵軍重炮猛攻，或投彈轟炸之下，以致車輛不能前進，或竟被炸斷，失去效用，則尙可利用中右兩綫，往返運輸，仍得前後應付裕如，軍運無擁擠塞斷之虞。（四）於可能範圍內，路綫須延長至附近石礦與森林中，如是則築路必需之石子，戰壕內必需之木材與燃料，皆得有直接供應之來源。（五）路綫之敷設，最好避免工程較大之切土與塡土工作，於是不致妨礙迅速建築通車之原則。

五 輕便鐵路之運輸地帶

所謂運輸地帶，卽自前方戰壕附近一定地點，與後方一定地點之標準軌距鐵路相聯，在此區域內，一切軍運工作，全賴輕便鐵路。其運輸地帶之適當距離，應自戰壕後方五哩以上至十二哩之間，在五哩之內，輕便鐵路須受敵軍之重大破壞，標準軌距鐵路不能在十二哩內行駛，因其所受損失較大，危險尤重。據英國在戰地之多年經驗云：運輸地帶終點之距離，可由五哩改爲八哩，仍得同樣之運輸效能，而其安全，反四倍於前，是以由五哩以上至十二哩之距離，改爲由八哩以上至十八哩，後美國卽採用此制。

六 行車安全問題

輕便鐵路之使用蒸汽機車，有相當限制，蒸汽機車前進達戰綫區內之一點，不能再向前行駛，因其煤烟不能爲敵方察見，藉悉我方之行動。法國輕便鐵路限制蒸汽機車前進之一點，即距戰壕後五千碼，五千碼以內，改用汽油機車(無烟)，拖引前進，以達路綫終點，然後用運貨汽車，或獸力人力搬運軍需品等，分發於各戰壕中，較爲安全。

雖云輕便鐵路，時有出軌覆車事變發生，但因車輛較輕，速率較慢，並無重大損失，無需用笨重起重機，將傾覆於路傍之車輛吊起，人力或加以小型起重機，即能勝任之。

据美國遠征軍工程隊長 Paul Mcgechan 觀察，敵軍欲破壞我方路綫，所發射炮彈或炸彈之價值，遠過於我方路綫所受之損失及修理費；當一九一八年三月二十一日，德軍於聖昆延 Saint Quentin 北方，進攻劇烈轟炸之下。除車場內、受其損失外，於路綫上，並無重大影響。是以輕便鐵路，若不過分接近戰壕，處於火綫之內，或易爲敵方察見，則行車尚稱安全也。

七　各國造路之速率比較

各協約國興建路綫之速率，快慢不相上下。据英國稱，於一九一七年九月，興建一哩，自平路基，鋪路軌，及安置道碴，須二、一〇〇人工，据一九一八年四月出版之法國之輕便鐵路"French Manual of Light Railway稱：平均每人每日能築四分之三公尺，即等於每哩須二一四六人工。美國在法西境所建主要輕便鐵路綫之一，自後方機廠與堆場之亞巴威 Ab ainville 通達前線之索賽 Sorcy 一段，長十八哩半，平均建築之速率，爲每哩二六四〇人工，由索賽向東延長至千尼威 Canieville 一段，平均每哩爲二、三四四人工。美國之所以需多量人工，因工程較爲堅固，以便提高行車速率，增加運輸能力。

八　輕便鐵路之道碴問題

大凡戰地輕便鐵路建築工程之停頓或遲延，由於道碴問題。因道碴之來源缺乏，或竟缺少適當之道碴，用木枕之路綫，在乾晴氣候時，尚須要少量或次等道碴，如煤滓、石炭、礦泥、沙礫、亦可；但用鋼枕之路，非有優等石子之道碴不可，因煤滓石炭等，易爲鋼軌壓碎，以致路面不平。

歐戰時英國在法境前綫之輕便鐵路，因不易集得石子，採用就近比加台 Picardy 之白鉛粉爲道碴，此白鉛粉，色白質輭，若遇久雨，幾溶成糊漿，全失其功用，並白色易爲敵機偵察，藉明軍情，此其弱點。

德國所用之道碴，均爲堅固之石子，自聖密興爾 Saint Mihiel 一役協約國勝後，及和平休戰後，尚在德境可窺見有充量之石子道碴，堆存於路綫兩傍，因道碴之優良，結果運輸能力，較勝於協約國。

於美國遠征軍所用之某一輕便鐵路後方，適有一沙坑，即將坑內之沙礫，沙土，充作道碴之用，極爲方便。

据工程新聞週報戰地記者湯墨林，Robert K. Tomlin, Jr. 在法北境與比利時境內，沿輕便鐵路綫考察，得悉路基上所用之道碴，一部分係採集於戰區內被炮火所毁房屋之碎磚與石子，廢物暫時利用，得益非淺。

九　軌距問題

歐戰時在西綫 Western Front戰地。法英美所用之輕便鐵路，均一律採用六十公分（二三又八分之五吋）軌距之路綫，卽德國亦採此制。軌距旣一律，協約國方面，可互通車輛，調和軍運，設德方敗退，協約國之車輛，可利用德方之路綫、長驅直入，反之亦然。是以最初劃一軌距之規定，雙方用意，卽在此也。

後有工程專家與軍運長官批評，六十公分之軌距太狹，於軍用輕便鐵路試用初期，因機車車輛較輕，尚無問題，後採用美國鮑特文 Baldwin式機車，及十噸量之車輛，時有出軌覆車發生；有主張機車車輛，重量照舊，而軌距放闊四吋或六吋。（卽二三吋又八分之五放闊成二八或三十吋）如英國前綫之丁庫脫 Tincourt地方，時有出軌覆車事發生，當時唯一之補救辦法，卽限制行車速率，不得超過每小時八哩。

十　路軌問題

法國所採用之鋼軌，每公尺重九公斤，用一公尺長之鋼枕釘連之，英法用每碼重二十磅之鋼軌，鋼枕與木枕兼用之，（木枕優於灣度小地質軟之路面上）美國採用每碼重二十五磅之鋼軌縛於鋼枕上，鋼枕長四十三吋，闊五吋半，然大多用木枕釘連，亦有兼用標準軌距鐵路之舊路軌者。法英美諸國，在戰地先期將鋼枕配釘於五公尺長之鋼軌上，堆存於前綫車場內，若遇前綫急於修路，或伸長路線，可由人力（約六人）將裝配成段之軌道，陸續運往，如此可得敏捷之修築，並於夜間，亦易於修裝在損壞之路面上。

德國用每碼重十七磅之鋼軌，以鋼枕連之。歐戰時德國所築之輕便鐵路網，遠過於法美，彼之所以欲盡量利用輕便鐵路，其原因爲：國內缺乏橡皮汽車胎及汽油，不能如協約國之可盡量利用汽車運輸；但德曾侵奪法比邊境之煤鋼鐵區，可取煤鐵之長，以補其短，此所以對於輕便鐵路，較爲發達也。

路軌重量問題，頗有考慮，輕軌雖便於搬運鋪置，但路面須時加修理，英法爲採用二十磅軌，後英國表示二十五磅軌，較優於前者。

路軌之灣度不等，有半徑一百公尺至三十公尺者，雖二十公尺半徑之灣度，列車亦能行駛，但爲避免覆車，及行車安全計，最低限度，僅能用半徑二十公尺之灣度。至於路線斜度，不能超過百分之三，或百分之四。於建造輕便鐵路之初，路軌各種之灣度，或二又二分之一，或一又四分之一公尺長之路軌，均應俱備，以便適合應用，可免臨時缺乏之苦，以妨工程之進行，又舖以不合灣度之路軌，以礙行車之安全。是以於造路之先，須將路線地形審閱，有曲線幾處，灣度之大小如何，然後領取路軌材料。如於將轉灣處，需用二又二分之一，或一又四分之一公尺之路軌，領取全線路軌時，普通最好領取約百分之八十爲直軌，百分之二十爲曲軌，於曲軌總數內，百分之七十爲半徑三十公尺曲軌，百分之十五爲半徑五十公尺曲軌，百分之七·五爲半徑二十公尺曲軌，百分之七·五爲半徑一百公尺曲軌。

十一　機車問題

蒸汽機車之式樣，大多採美國式，爲2—6—2式，美國鮑特文機車廠出品，有五十馬力，主動輪底面 Drive-wheel base 長五呎十吋，車前引導輪與主動輪及車後之拖輪，各輪底面 Total-wheel base 總長十五呎七吋，機車全身長二十一呎七吋，闊六呎五吋，高九呎三吋，重三四、五〇〇磅。美國遠征軍所用之汽油機車，爲四汽缸，四週率，Four-cycle 三十五馬力，水冷馬達，車輪底面長三呎，機車全身長十呎九吋，闊四呎七吋半，高七呎十一吋，重八、〇〇〇磅。法國之蒸汽機車，各輪底面總長十二呎半，機車全身共長十八呎九吋，闊五呎二吋，高九呎五吋，重三一、〇〇〇磅。

某一路線上，蒸汽機車或汽油機車之需要外少，成如何比例，須於某一綫上通車前，有相當考慮。假定三輛汽油機車之拖引力，適等於一輛蒸汽機車，据惠爾葛斯氏(Wilgus; Director of Military Railways A.E.F.; Deputy Director General of Transportation, A.E.F.)之主張，全綫總運輸量之四分之三，應採用蒸汽機車，其餘四分之一再乘三（因蒸汽機車與汽油機車之拖引力比例爲三比一，）即等於汽油機車之總數，又汽油機車總數中之三分之二，爲四十馬力機車，三分之一，爲二十馬力機車。

如欲預測燃料之消耗，約計蒸汽機車，爲每一機車哩用煤四十八磅，汽油機車，爲每一機車哩用油百分之三五加侖。

十二 車輛之種類

英國輕便鐵路採用之車輛，種類甚多，其最普遍之一種爲：(一)邊車，約二十呎長，五呎闊，分平底與凹底二種，能載運軍需品十噸；但運較輕或體笨之工程材料，每車只能裝五六噸，如載軍隊，每車平均僅裝三噸。(二)次爲蓬車，如裝運新鮮易腐之糧食等貨。(三)至於拖運大炮，或於車上裝置炮位，以另備特製之車裝運之。(四)病車，於車內設上中下三層床鋪，專爲停留於戰地，救護傷兵之用，或重傷之兵，乘此車拖送後方醫院。(五)救險車，於車上裝起重機，專爲舉起已出軌之機車及事輛。(六)另有四五輛車，聯成一隊，各車長二十呎，闊五呎四吋，上裝修理機車與車輛之重要機件，名謂「車上機廠，」(Machine Shops on wheels) 其重要機件，包括鑽床，磨床，鋸機，車床，刨床等，該車上有頂，兩邊可向下掛平，無形中卽放闊車底面積，便於工作，機件之發動力，卽來自附掛於該車之石油發電機，該車停駐於戰區內，遇必要時，得前後移動，以利修理工作之進行。如機車車輛受炮火重大之損壞，非「車上機廠」之能力可修理，應卽送至後方總機廠，因總廠機件完備，零件較多，便於修理。

法國所用之車輛，亦可分下列五種：(一)蓬車，其容積有六〇〇立方呎，或二二、〇〇〇磅，車皮重一〇、九〇〇磅，車身長二四呎，闊六呎，高八呎四吋。(二)邊車，其容積有二一〇立方呎，或二二、〇〇〇磅，車皮重九、〇〇〇磅，長二四呎，闊五呎七吋，高四呎半。(三)平車，其載重爲二二、〇〇〇磅，車皮重八、〇〇〇磅，長二四呎，闊五呎七吋。(四)卸料車，Dump Car 其容積有二七立方呎，車皮重一、〇五〇磅，長五呎八吋，闊四呎八吋。(五)櫃車，專爲運飲料，依給前線戰壕內兵士，其構造與蓬車相似，惟形如櫃狀，車皮重一二、二〇〇磅。各類車輛中，法國最有用者，爲約十噸重之邊車。

美國輕便鐵路之車輛，大多採用邊車，長十七呎，闊五呎，載重量爲十噸。餘如蓬車，平車，櫃車，病車，亦備而用之。

十三 銜接站之設備

於標準軌距鐵路與輕便鐵路之銜接站，須有廣大車場，滿佈廣狹軌道，適合站台，起重機，輕便鐵路機車房等，於廣軌道傍，有汽車道，可直接卸貨於運貨汽車上，有相當之棧房與堆場，以貯藏修理鐵路之建築材料，或其他軍需品，所有狹軌輕便鐵路軌道，須插入廣軌之間，以便有敏捷之裝卸工作，對於車場設計上尤須注意。某站台爲上下兵士專用，某站台爲卸貨專用，秩序不能混亂，可免車場內調車擠塞之苦。

十四　養路工程

養路與建築工程，處於同等重要地位，其主要養路工作，卽於彈丸炸壞之路線上，加以修理，如重鋪路軌，加添道碴，疏通泄水溝渠及函洞，是以必需駐設養路工程隊，時用搖車行駛，以視察全線工程；可隨時修理。如於北歐地帶之英國軍用輕便鐵路，因氣候多濕，路基時有陷入泥糊中，因此對於泄水養路工程，應特別注意。據英國之軍用鐵路報告，每線每哩須駐有十四養路工人；並修理工作，頗爲繁重，平均每星期內，需修換被毀之路軌，約一千五百呎至二千呎，於某一段路線上，一日內曾有九十五次被炮火毀壞之修理。

十五　各國軍用輕便鐵路之組織系統

(一)英國軍運分處制組織系統表

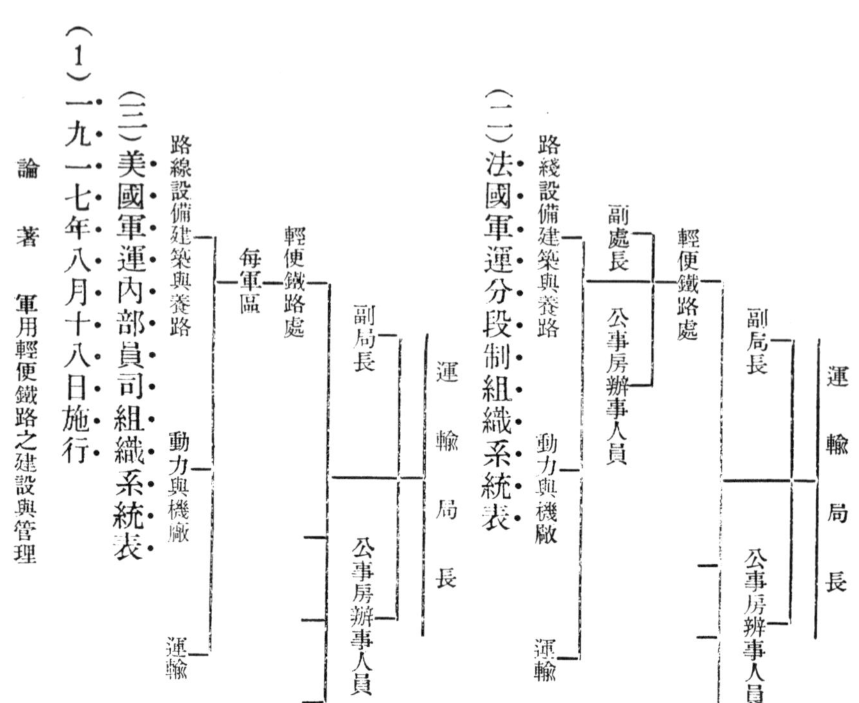

（二）法國軍運分段制組織系統表

（三）美國軍運內部員司組織系統表

（1）一九一七年八月十八日施行

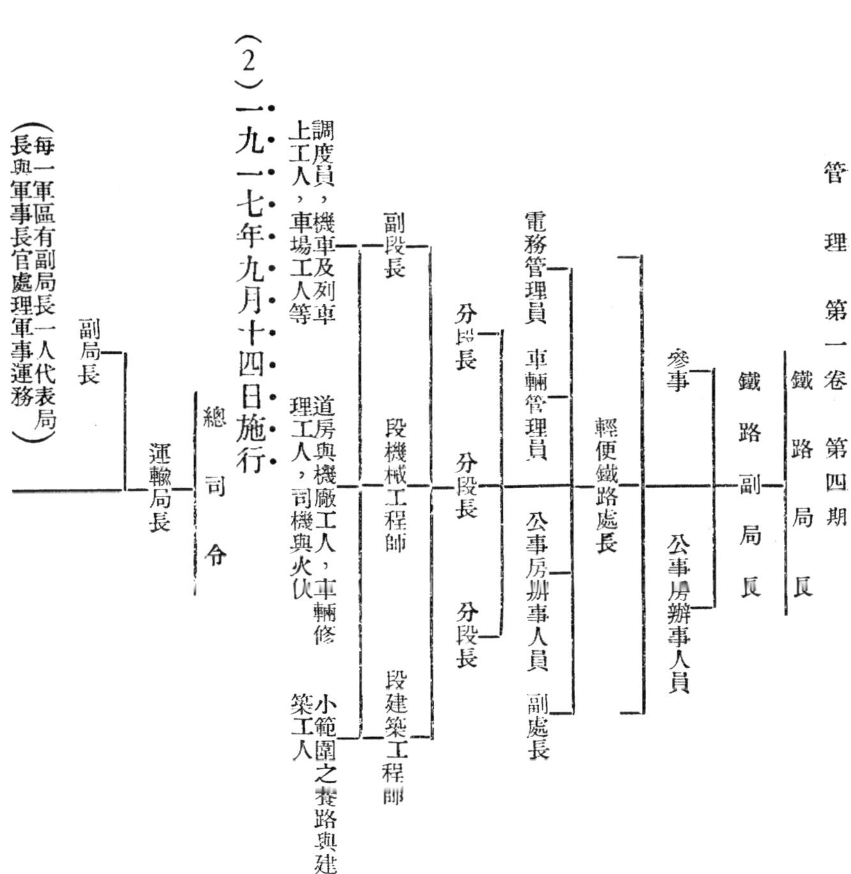
鐵路局長
鐵路副局長
參事
公事房辦事人員
輕便鐵路處長
電務管理員
車輛管理員
公事房辦事人員
副處長
分段長
分段長
分段長
副段長
段機械工程師
段建築工程師
調度員，機車及列車上工人，車場工人等
道房與機廠工人，車輛修理工人，司機與火伕
小範圍之養路與建築工人
(2)一九一七年九月十四日施行
總司令
運輸局長
副局長
（每一軍區有副局長一人代表局長與軍事長官處理軍事運務）

輕便鐵路處長
（軍便鐵路之建築運輸與養路事務）

（四）美國軍運外部組織系統表

運輸局長
- 軍事運輸長官
  - 軍事運輸段長（分區制）

上列五表，依採自 Wilgus 著之「美國遠征軍在西歐之運輸，」"Transporting the A. E.F. in Western Europe, 1917—1919"

美國之軍運管轄機關，於一九一七年七月，自參照英法成例後，至停戰日止，前後曾有八次修正，雖最高管轄幹部，叠次修正，但對於輕便鐵路內部之組織，仍照一九一七年八月所釐訂之組織系統。

於鐵路建築之初，對於造路養路及行車管理需要之員工，應早有估計。据英國之經驗談，每一路軌哩；平均需要之員工如下：行車管理十人養路十四人，建築二十人，共計四十四人。

十六 行車管理之實施

戰地輕便鐵路之行駛，與尋常廣軌鐵路之行駛，全然不同，因輕便鐵路行車之速率較慢，每小時約十哩，故無需精密之行車規章，車輛調度制，及完善之號誌設備，有一簡單之車輛調度電話，與簡易行車區截制，則可矣。其行車之主要目的，能達有敏捷可靠之軍運，與後方聯絡，則可謂行車效率，已得較優之效果矣。

英國之行車管理制，於輕便鐵路副處長下，每綫設一調度總站，於各分段另設調度分站，總站分站及各車站間，用調度電話，溝通消息，支配車輛，各站列車之開出或到站，事前須得調度總站之許可，事後須報告開出或到站列車之時間，其行車時間之制度，亦採二十四小時制，自半夜算起。於每綫調度總站壁上，掛一長木板，名謂調度牌，依照該路線地圖，以有凹形小槽之小木條，代表路軌，釘於調度牌上，無論正道岔道車站等，均應確實表現，與鐵路模型圖無異。沿綫各站，均應編號，並附註於牌上，另以有鈎之「夾子」(Clips)掛於小槽木條路軌上，以代表一列車。根據各站之行車報告，以「夾子」前後移動，表明列車之行駛，「夾子」着以紅綠顏色。紅色代表「重列車」，綠色代表「空列車」，如是一看該圖，極顯明表示重列車或空列車之行駛情形。於每一列車起運之前，先填錄一列車行運表，(見附表一)

表一　列車行運表

機車/原動車 統數……………………　等級…………

軍需站……………………　日期…………

司機……………………　上班…………

火伕……………………　上班…………

車守……………………　上班…………

車次	站名	到	開	掛上		摘下	
				號數	內容	號數	內容
57	C—1		8.00	5032	Ammo		
				154	Ammo		
				897	Ammo		
	C—3	8.30	8.35			5032	Ammo
	C—5	8.50	8.55			154	Ammo
	C—9	9.15	10.15	235	Water		
	C—103	10.25				897	Ammo
						235	Water

該表填明機車號數，起運軍需站之站名，司機，火伕，車守之姓名，到達站站名，列車次數，開與到之時間，載運貨物之內容等等；並每一輛貨車，另填單據二張：一爲「小卡片」，名謂(Chit)（見附表二或稱車輛行運單）該(Chit)表明某號貨車，於某日某時，附掛於某次車上，由某站裝某貨　重量多少，於某時至某站，如是調度總站，可知每一輛貨車之行運狀況；二爲提貨單，（見附表三）該單表明某寄貨人，於某站裝運某貨，重量多少，寄至某站某收貨人。以上三種單據，會集一起，表明一列車各車輛之情形，以調度牌上之「夾子」，夾在一處，掛於小槽木條路軌上，依照列車之行動，將「夾子」前後移動。又於調度牌上之每一站，設置一小洋

表二 Chit車輛行運單

車號 16……等級…K…日期…2--10……車次…120				
C6Line 由	裝貨時間		離站時間	
C 201			6.43	
到	到達時間	回程		
		時間	日期	
C202	7.53			
內容……………E.C.……		重量……………………		

表三 提貨單

轉便鐵路	
往……………………………	日期
起運站……………………………	噸數
貨名……………………………	
託運人……………………………	
收貨人……………………………	

鐵皮匣子，內分二格，一格代表「裝」，一格代表「空」，當一列車行至某站，將一輛貨車摘下，停該站某岔道時，即將此事報告調度總站，然後總站將該貨車之Chit自「夾子」上取下，放入某站小匣「裝」格內，當該貨車已將貨物卸空，成爲空車，然後Chit由「裝」格取出，轉放於「空」格內。照此辦法，則全綫所有車輛，是「空」或「裝」，及其所在地，總站均能一目瞭然，將來需要第二次運輸時，易將空車收集，運至請求車輛站。當一列車已行畢全程，將所有Chits均由小匣內取出，交與填錄運輸統計記錄之事務員抄填之，以備將來參考。

除此總列車調度牌外，於總站尚需有分段車輛記錄牌，於每段設一牌，以表現實情。如每一機車每一車輛之重車或空車之數目，與「工作」或「放置」之數目。每一機車與車輛，編以號目，用有空之銅牌代表之；代表車輛之銅牌，漆以紅綠二色，紅色表示「裝」，綠色表示「空」，代表機車之銅牌，有鈎可掛，分爲「工作」「備用」與「修理」三等，代表車輛之銅牌，亦有鈎可掛，分爲「存站」「裝」「立」「在路」與「延期」五等。如是於每一段內，各類車輛之實情，於車輛記錄牌上，又能一目瞭然，以後對於緊急之車輛調度，可如願以償，庶不致手足無措，難於應付，而有礙軍機也。

美國之車輛調度管理，亦採用電話制，於每隔一哩地點，駐一小木屋，妥放手提電話機，及爲管理該機者住宿。

十七　歐戰時各國路網之里程及軍運實況

歐戰時輕便鐵路網最密之國家，當首推德國，於數百哩前綫之後方，均有周密之輕便鐵路網，里程總計約在五千哩左右，法國最多不過一千哩左右，美國較少。美國輕便鐵路之最重要一綫，係起自亞巴威，該地離前綫土爾 Toul 地方，計二十二哩，在土爾之西北，設有極大之修理機廠，自亞巴威至索賽一段，計十八哩半，軍運最爲繁重，由索賽向東延長五哩至哥納威 Cornieville與法國輕便鐵路網銜接，向外輻射，聯絡其他數綫；美國在法國境所築之路網，其總里程爲一二四哩，另有一八六哩法國所築之輕便鐵路，後經美國修理，代爲管理經營，並向德國因奪復陣地後，得一〇八一哩，以上總計，至停戰日止，美國經營管轄之總里程，爲一三九〇哩，共有各類機車一六五輛，車輛一六九五輛。如是偉大之路網，美國之總運輸額，包括各類軍運，至一九一九年二月一日止，爲八六〇、六〇〇噸。

每一列車所掛車輛之多少，大有不同。如在後方平坦之路綫上，每一蒸汽機車，可拖九輛十噸重裝軍需品之車輛，或十二輛裝工程材料之車輛，若遇天雨，則載運重量，應卽減低。至於裝運兵士，據英軍運輸長官稱，一日內最多能運十六萬兵士。美國遠征軍之軍運實况，試以某一綫在一月內之運輸工作，例舉如下：軍需品四五二二噸，粮食六、二八五噸，兵士三、二八一噸，輕便鐵路道碴七、二七七噸，傷兵救護四、一四四噸，雜運六、九九二噸，總計三二、五〇〇噸。如是以某一綫某一月爲例，雖不能作眞確之標準運輸狀况，但由此可以概見輕便鐵路在軍運上之重要地位，及其價値矣。

譯　述

口試成績表之科學編製

胡亦生

本篇(The Scientific Construction of an Interview Chart)刊載於美國管理協會(American Management Association)本年八月份出版之人事特刊(Personnel)第十三卷第一期內，著者阿鄧姆君(Mr. R. Adams)及司梅而自博士(Dr. C.H. Smeltzer)，爲本薛文尼急賑管理局 (Pennsylvania Emergency Relief Administration)人事總管與顧問。篇中表格，乃經多數心理學及人事管理學專家之悉心研究，專爲該局招攷雇員而作，故項目規定，自有特性，或不適于其它企業。唯其設計之精密，編製之得當，誠可爲任何各機關口試員生之參攷。至于度量情理，斟酌損益，要在各主管者之善自抉擇耳。

譯者註

序言　一事業中人員之錄用，與職位之支配，恆根據個別接談而審定。雖今日學術試驗，已足衡量眞才，惟未能基於客觀，終難洞悉個性。蓋個性之與職位，極爲重要；在上者往往採個別接談之方法，以爲完全之鑑定。——有時此種接談固甚不可靠，然至少可作爲人事管理中一種初步的手續。

欲使個別接談之鑑定更形眞確，則應有評等表之設置。惟今之管理者，大抵重視該表之應用，而忽於該表之編製，其結果或則不適於本身之事業，或則對於應有之個性記錄，闕然不備，此誠人事管理上之一大缺憾。

考此種表格之錯誤，厥有三端。其所設忠誠堅忍等德性，實難能於立談之中，洞悉底蘊，此其一。其對於各個人之特性，並無相互高下之比較，此其二。因無相互高下之比較，口試者往往有詳細描寫之必要，比其三。

將評等表中項目，大加變更，自屬可能。本薛文尼急

口試成績表

姓名…………　性別…………　號數…………
住址…………　國別…………　區域…………
日期…………　色別…………　報告…………

	體格						人品						對工作之適合			
	身材	整潔	容貌	姿態	健康	聲調	發音	英語	舉止	[illegible]	[illegible]	自信	智識	理解力	應對	能力
項數	1	2	3	4	5	6	7	8	9	10	11	12	13	14	15	16
	○	○	○	○	○	○	○	○	○	○	○	○	○	○	○	○
	○	○	○	○	○	○	○	○	○	○	○	○	○	○	○	○
	○	○	○	○	○	○	○	○	○	○	○	○	○	○	○	○
	○	○	○	○	○	○	○	○	○	○	○	○	○	○	○	○
	○	○	○	○	○	○	○	○	○	○	○	○	○	○	○	○

總評　超等□　優等□　中等□　下等□　劣等□

說明：口試員對應試者之某項成績認為何等，卽於該項下某等之圓圈內，寫一x字，用直線連接各項內之圓圈。表中各該類項內之方塊黑影，乃顯示各該類項相互間之輕重。

口試員口試完畢後，卽於表下總評一行內，用√記號，劃定等級。

口試成績分表一

體格

說明	身材	整潔	容貌	姿態	健康	聲調
項數	1	2	3	4	5	6
超等	極得體	極講究	極美觀	極佳	似極强健	極悅耳
優等	甚相稱	甚清潔	甚動人	甚可取	似健康	甚動聽
中等	適中	尚可	尚不惡	通常	難確定	尚不惡
次等	欠合適	欠整潔	少色澤	似傴僂	頗成問題	難聽
劣等	極不稱	太隨便	極不揚	極拙劣	極孱弱	極惡劣

口試成績分表二

人品

說明	發音	英語	舉止端方否	情感	雍容自如否
項數	7	8	9	10	11
超等	極佳	文法不錯	極文雅	情理兩當	極泰然
優等	清晰	大體尚佳	端方	情理相稱	甚安閑
中等	尚可	普通	尚大方	情理尚當	通常
次等	難懂	常有錯誤	不甚好	情理欠當	欠自若
劣等	極糊塗	極惡劣	太壞	缺乏情理	極慌張

口試成績分表三

對工作之合適

說明	偏見與(或)自信	似誠摯否	懂得人事問題與關連否	能應對如流否	錄用後能勝任愉快否
項數	12	13	14	15	16
超等	極持正	極誠摯	極通達	極精贅而深遠	將無困難
優等	尚坦白	似甚明健	甚有識力	可嘉許	似少問題
中等	似有偏見或似太自信	大體不差	略知梗概	尚滿意	平時將應付裕如
次等	均欠健全	可疑	似多缺憾	無見地	或多問題
劣等	極模稜	極成問題	缺乏常識	駁雜無序	定有困難

總評　超等 □　優等 □　中等 □　次等 □　劣等 □

賑管理局以十五主試員，能在短時期中，決定雇用社會服務部職員四千五百人之多者，賴此表格之設置故也。

初，該局人事課規定資格，創議考試，應試者竟逾萬人。因社會服務部之工作，專爲救濟被難人而設，在在皆有人事上之牽連，故個別接談，在考試全程中極佔重要。上表即因此而編製，表後有三分表，乃將該表中之類別，加以詳細之分析，並定最優至最劣之等級。

此表如何編製　當此表編製之先，曾設一委員會，委員數凡十二，以熟悉人事之經歷或深知該項職位應有之才性者充之；其目的可從個別接談所得之結果，與從其它客觀方法所得試驗之成績，作一明確之比較。上表所分三類，乃在接談時可以覘得之重要才性；第一類分爲六項，第二第三類均分五項，就此十六項目中，更定最優至最劣之等級。此種表格之編製，均經會議之通過。其性質既已決定，則各類各項中相互間之輕重，自應厘訂。

相互輕重如何獲得　各類各項中相互輕重之確定，苟取決於多數人之意見，自更可靠。該管理局特請專家百人，對於社會服務部工作，均有甚深研究，將此三大類中項目應佔輕重之成分，各抒意見，確定分數，俾絕畸輕畸重之弊。

下表乃此百人意見之總平均，可用百分法書之。

百分表

類別	體格						人品					對工作之適合				
項別	1	2	3	4	5	6	7	8	9	10	11	12	13	14	15	16
項別百分數	1	3	4	1	6	3	4	5	8	10	5	9	8	13	8	12
類別百分數	18						32					50				

此種結果，可於口試成績表內各類各項中所劃黑影之大小以顯示之。類與類較，項與項別，苟視黑影，則各該類項所佔百分數之多寡，亦卽各該類項所定相互間之輕重，不難一目瞭然。

口試成績表何以必定輕重　各個人才性之輕重成分，既確定於表中，則口試員（或其他任何人）自易作合適之結論，以爲最後之評等。此種輕重之確定，既出自多數專家之意見，自較一人獨斷爲正確。

個別接談既爲雇用職員必不可少之手續，則其目的應使此手續與結果愈客觀化愈佳，且應能獲得各應試者相互比較之等級。若徒恃口頭之接談，而無可靠之筆錄，則必不能達此目的也。

在任何事業中，任何一表不能適用於各部之職位。如該表能適於許多事業者，則表中項目，必甚普遍，而某一項特殊之個性與才具，較難查考。故負人事管理之責者，應視職位之性質，以定適當之表格。惟表中等級，應劃直線以顯示（即連接x字），則口試員對於各應試者之評等，一望而可比較其高下矣。

總之，本文圖表之編製，其要點有二。應徵集熟悉個性與心理測驗者多數人之意見、於考試何種職位，則應設置何種項目，以覘應試者之是否合轍，一也。各類各項應有相互間之輕重，俾在上者可以獲得正確之評等，二也。

貨幣與復興（E 4）

王烈望

此文(Money and Recovery)刊於The Economist, Vol. CXXIV. No.4851, Ang.15,1936 Page 292—293其時金集團國已在風雨飄搖之中，此文所述，雖爲金集團崩潰以前之情形，然頗足爲當前貨幣思想之代表，不無介紹之價值也。　譯者附誌

近年來爭論最熱烈之問題鮮有過於貨幣政策對於經濟之影響者然迄無確當持平之論；故吾人所希望者能將過去七年來衰落與復興之一切重要教訓，作一精細之研究。凡注意經濟現象者對於貨幣政策，就廣義言，較之在七年以前，尤爲重視；此一印象將由國聯最近出版之「國聯評論」(The Leagne Review)而益深，該評論謂吾人對於貨幣現象之知識與理解，雖從未一致，至少已在進步中。

從該評論所得最顯著之事實卽爲世界各主要國家，未有不採貨幣膨脹政策而已克服大恐慌者。在六大資本主義國家中，英美德日四國已於一九三一至一九三五年之間，實行其膨脹政策；而法荷二國獨否，（至今年九月終，遂亦不能不步前者之後塵），此六國之工業生產指數，據該評論所載，以一九三三年二月與一九三六年二月相較，有如下列：

	%
德	+79.2
英	+25.2

美	+49.2	法	−3.9
日	+38.7	荷	−8.3

迄今猶未開始復興者惟於貨幣膨脹尚無決策之荷蘭與瑞士二國耳（今荷蘭亦已採膨脹政策矣）

在一九三一年之初與一九三二年之末雖似有復興之望，然終不過曇花一觀，可不具論，凡克服恐慌之國，其復興無不始於膨脹政策之實施，若謂不景氣之國家不採積極的膨脹政策祗須長期等待復興將自至，此種見解，雖未始不可持，然事實上，復興能自至乎？必不能也。荷蘭與瑞士期待復興已久，何復興之不見臨也？

各國所採膨脹政策，因其環境之殊異而有不同之方式。據該評論所示，其方式大致可以歸爲二類，第一類爲「銀行政策」(Banking policy)，該評論所述屬於此類之國家有英國瑞典，南非，奧國及加拿大；第二類爲「不足預算」(Deficit financing)，該評論所述，屬於此類之國家有美，德，日，荷，與智利，銀行政策之膨脹據評論之意，普通卽爲增加銀行存款與減低利率，英國取此政策以致復興可爲正例，英國自一九三一年以後黃金之流入與英蘭銀行在一九三二與一九三三年之公開購入證券（The Open market purchases）使商業銀行之現金準備擴張並使其購買政府公債藉以抑低長期利率（公債市價抬高，其利率自必低落，）英國之復興由於低利貨幣者若干，由於低廉食物者若干，固屬可資爭議之問題，但低利貨幣爲決不可省之條件，鮮有敢加否認者，由五年來之回顧與該評論所述之概況，英國復興最顯著之特點，卽在其完全採用膨脹的銀行政策而不輔以「不足預算」。

德，日，美與智利，則以「不足預算」爲主要因素，德國之創造信用(Credit Creation)大都用以重整軍備；在美國(自一九三三心理的復興開始以後，)日本，與智利，則政府支出爲增加需要最積極與堅强之因素。有許多國家，因人民心理狀態之不佳，不但有擴張貨幣數量之必要，且須監視其用途，此爲甚重要之一課，其有若干應用，似爲該評論所忽略，因該評論太偏重於貨幣數量及其流通速度方面，殊不知關係最切之因素不在貨幣數量及其流通速度(此實爲一虛擬之觀念)而在有效的需要之暢流(The stream of effective demand)，此需要之流卽爲政策所擬激勵或抑制者也。倘金平價，貨幣數量與利率之變更必須影響及於總共需要而後始可謂其有效一層能加證實，則全盤之討論，必將更爲明朗，如在英國，因戰債之變換及其他因素以鼓勵永久品之投資，引起人民之信心，此固爲英國金融政策所收之成效；但如在美國等，其政府必須採行公共工程及不足預算，以直接刺激需要則已證實其爲必要。

此不足預算之政策，如其爲增加有效的需要，必須輔以信用之創造而不能借用已有之儲蓄，此點已由該評論明白指出，該評論詰問採緊縮政策之金集團國與採膨脹政策之德美日本等國在一九三二至一九三五年之間同爲預算不足，何以前者無回漲而後者乃有顯著之回漲？其原因(姑不論心理方面之因素如何)卽在後者之不足預算由創造信用爲之彌補而前者則否故也。其情形更可從法國自一九三五年夏季以來之經驗證之，在一九三五年七八月間法國軍備費之急需，如無中央銀行之墊款，財政部早已束手無策矣，其時利率雖高，商業雖呈悲觀，而生產開始增加，物價亦逐漸上漲，由此可知有政府支出而無信用創造，固不能刺激有效的需要，反之僅有信用膨脹而無政府支出亦不能刺激有效的需要也。

在緊縮期間，金集團國之不足預算何以不由創造信用爲之彌補？良以在既定匯價之下，貨幣流通之增加必使內外成本 (Interna and external Costs) 愈益其差離，故金集團國之政府經愼重之考慮，以爲與其增加需要，不如減低成本，此如可行，容爲一成功之政策，但從此次大恐慌所得之教訓，知無一工業國家有以減低成本克服不均衡之狀態者，一部份蓋由於緊縮掙扎之沮喪的心理結果所致，該評論如能證實德意日諸國政府雖用盡約制之力，終不能由緊縮以致復興，則其價值必將尤大。因大部份貨幣成本爲無可裁減，而有效的需要必須使其增加；此則惟有採取膨脹政策，始能辦到，如其國之幣值高估卽須變更匯率或實施外匯限制。

綜言之，貨幣鬆動與利率低微，在成本不能裁減之國，已成復興不可避免之條件，但此

上海交通大学百年报刊集成·第一辑（1896—1949）·学术学科

亦不過條件已耳。實際上支出或投資之鼓勵可自心理狀態之轉佳得之，如商業信心之恢復，或對於物價有上升之一般的希望等是也。顧貨幣之流通可由政府爲更進一步之行動直接刺激之，其行動之方式甚多，如以不足預算執行公共工程等是也；究應採用何種方式，要視環境而定，其環境之最重要者卽爲一般的經濟背景；如其經濟結構已至過於失調，則僅恃貨幣或財政政策，恐亦不能奏調整之功，但若減低成本之不可能，爲吾人所認識，又若金融當局之貨幣政策不僅以變更貨幣數量，金平價或匯價爲能事而以刺激貨幣需要之暢流與夫一般就業(Level of Employment)之促進爲其主要目的，則吾人所得於此次大恐慌之教訓爲不虛矣。

陸大月刊

第二卷第十二期

目錄

本刊價目

零售：每期大洋叁角
半年：六期大洋壹元五角
全年：十二期大洋叁元

郵費

外埠：每期二分五厘 全年六角 半年一角五分
本埠：每期二分 全年二角四分 半年一角二分

編輯者 陸大月刊編輯委員會
發行者 陸大月刊社
社址：南京漢口路陸軍大學特別黨部內
電話：三一七一一三
代售處 特別黨部及各大書局

書評

『行政學之理論與實際』

任家誠

著者　張金鑑

出版者　上海商務印書館

版期　二十四年八月

定價　叁元肆角

國人對於行政學的研究，最近幾年來，如雨後春筍，很有蓬勃氣象，政府的提倡，學者的鼓吹，行政效率和行政經濟已經成爲推進中國政治的原則，這確是個好現象。行政學發展的歷史，在歐美也不過最近幾十年，我們已能深被其澤，加以注意，將來努力研究的結果，未始不能駕齊驅乎歐美，而確立眞眞良好的行政制度，這又是値得欣喜的。

但是事實不容許我們樂觀，我們對於行政學的研究，不過是略得皮毛，國中研究行政學的組織，還剛在萌芽時代；較之美國的各省有研究的機關，各校有研究的講座，英國行政學社(Institute of Public Administration) 的貢獻，德國國內政治經濟研究社(Deutsches Institute für Wirtschaftliche Arbeit) 的成績，眞有天壤之別。國中行政學研究的組織僅有行政院的行政效率研究會一處，但是全官式的機關，建議和計劃都得負相當責任，不免有所牽制。國中大學設行政學系的，也僅上海交通大學管理學院公務管理門。當然我們不能認現狀爲滿足；將來的發展，還待學者和政府的努力。

行政學專著的發表，國中也感缺乏，以前僅有兩本；民國二十二年江康黎先生的『行政學原理』在上海民智書局出版，可是祇包括總務行政行政組織和人事行政三部分，使我們有不能窺得全豹的遺憾，希望江先生再努力於續編的撰著。民國二十四年林疊博士的『行政學大綱』在南京華僑半月刊社出版（上海世界書局亦有代售）分章討論行政組織，人事行政，財務行政和物料管理四大問題，雖然是一本比較簡單的著作，但是綱舉目張，簡明扼要，完備的行政書籍，當以此著爲首創。正在感覺參攷書籍缺乏，而不得不借重西書當兒，張先生的『行政學之理論與實際』出版，一新國人耳目。我相信至少張先生的偉著，可以引起不少學者注意，刺激行政學的研究，至於他說求償拋磚引玉投桃報瑤之願，那未免太過自謙。

此書分六大部份討論：（一）普通行政，（二）行政組織，（三）政府財政，（四）物材統制，（五）公務人員，及（六）行政研究。這種分法不能不算作者聰明之處，因爲普通行政一章，可以包容行政組織以外的一切——其性質似應歸入行政組織的，爲行政工具的討論，行政長官職權的研究等。衛羅倍（W.F. Willoughby)在『行政學原理』(Principles of Public Administration) 中，把行政工具歸入行政組織內，的確不能算爲合理的辦法，懷德(L.D. White)在『行政學緒論』(Introduction to the Study of Public Administration) 中因爲覺得行政長官職權的分配一節，不應歸入行政組織，而特創行政機構一章來討論，這種補救辦法當然都有修正的必要，此書做到這一點。行政學應分爲四大部份討論是無可疑義，此書也已顧到。行

政學的將來希望何如，我人應該努力的定向如何，都值得注意，此書特設行政研究一編作專門的討論，從這幾點上研究，作者對於行政學範圍可說深深握住，絲毫沒有放鬆，值得我們欽佩。

現代學者，相當認清了科學國際化的目標，誰都不願意拘泥於一國的理論，來作他研究的根據，比較研究，已成一種普遍方法。政法方面也有這種趨向，世界行政法學鉅子古德諾（F. J. Goodnow）的著作，已經充分利用，最近英倫敦大學行政學教授房納(Herman Finer) 在他成名作『現代政府之理論和實際』(Theory and Practice of Modern Government)一書中，在討論每個問題時，必聯合採取英美法德的制度爲比較，打消過去主觀的看法，而不僅偏重於英國方面；甚至在他『英國的地方政府』(English Local Government) 中也採取不少美國的材料，作爲左證，可見比較研究的重要。此書在討論每一問題後，常加一章各國制度的現狀，使學者於明悉理論之後，還可以比較的知道各種不同制度，含有比較研究的精神。但是我以爲最好能於討論理論時，隨時提到各國的制度，使讀者能夠知道各國現行制度在理論的根據，甚至如果材料充分的話

把各國對於某一問題的理論，不厭其繁，儘量討論，做自己結論的參證。當然這種方法非身通數國文字不能辦到；但是至少也得在英美或華文譯本中尋求資料，不知張先生以爲如何。

有人說這本書太受懷德和衞羅倍學說的束縛，甚可說很多地方是譯自他們二本行政學。這一點我不反對，因爲正如李權時先生所說，中國現在的學術研究還在摹仿時代，現在雖還用他們的書做藍本，努力研究的結果，將來一定有靑勝于藍的一天，到那時候，才是中國正式踏上了完備的階段。但是此書太多地方過於偏重美國，無可諱言，譬如說在行政研究之趨勢一章中，只說到美國研究團體的發展，其實英國的行政學是聞名于世的，行政學社更是世界僅有的組織，倫敦大學於行政學也極有名，其他德法諸國，雖然說行政法的研究較行政學爲進步，事實上也有不少研究團體可資討論，此書則一些沒有提到，希望再版時能夠補充修正。

至於內容方面充實和透澈，是此書的特點，值得表揚。尤其是財務行政一編討論之不厭求詳，讀者可從此得到不少新的智識。行政組織一編對於完整制的研究，也可算相當完美，我國對於完整制雖然早已採取，但是各部的分立，內部組織的構成很多和理論相出入，有改進的必要，讀者在研究此編而後，可以明瞭改進的途徑。物材統制一編中，對於購置程序，理論和實際並重，作者以學者地位，而有如許經驗，可佩之至。公務人員一編內容是乎太過簡單，我相信假定作者有機會的時候，一定還可大加補充。

現在請提出幾點隨便討論：

此書似乎忽略了行政組織的現代化理論——決定政策職能和實行職能(Staff & Line Functions)。我們知道欲求完整制的完美表現，必須將此二大職能加以劃分，譬如說現在有幾部參事廳，秘書室，總務司同時存在，總務司的事務偏於日常工作(Institutional Service-Willonghby; Subsidiary Service-White)，而秘書室却也有處理文書等事務，參事廳應該專責理研究本部行政的推進，而秘書室更也有研究的任務，結果秘書室改不是日常事務的執行機關、又不是決定政策的研究機關，造成內部組織的畸形發展。所以我以爲要想切實實行完整制，非顧及此點不可，希望此書在再版時有以補充。

財務行政和財政學不同處，後者範圍較大，兼及財政的理論和立法。此書很多地方似乎超越了財務行政的範疇，在國家收支和國家公債三章中格外明顯，不過這也許是觀點的不同；金庫制度在現在財務行政中占着極重要的地位，現在我國正在努力於創立內部牽制的財務行政組織，金庫制度似乎更應注意，此書未曾提及，使我們不無滄海遺珠之感。

現在各國研究人事行政的改進，着眼于行政效率的發揮一點上。職位分類合理化，是俸給釐訂的根據，升擢調遷的基礎，可說是人事行政的靈魂，而此書沒有把牠詳為討論。現在世界各國於職位分類有二大趨向，一為分等制如英德，一為分類制如美和加拿大，而我國既不採分類制又沒有分等制的長處，現行制度有改革的必要；責任在研究行政學者的身上，作者也似乎不應等閒視之。其次，考績方法的施行，與公務員的工作效能生直接關係，考績得當，可以鼓勵公務員努力工作的勇氣，考績失當，可以引起種種誤會，非惟不能收其實效，甚有減退行政效能的可能，像造成公務員對上的冤恨和對同級的妒嫉等，我國現在的考績法尚不可算完備，尤其是近幾年量分制和拍樂俾司脫制度(Probst System)的成就，使我們有趨向時代，努力改革的必要。此書似乎沒有注意到這兩點，所以我說對於公務人員一編還欠完美。

最後，對於今後行政趨勢的展望，此書既已列舉美國研究團體的發達，站在國人的立場上，似乎應該有所警惕，而急求前進的企圖。所以我很希望能夠給我們一個研究計劃的具體方案，不論在研究會社的組成和研究方法的途徑上，作者一定樂於接受這一點。

最後的最後，此書不失為一完備之作，的確是國人研究行政學的良具。當我想到社會教育程度的幼稚，對於做官不必談技術和學識的無聊的諷刺，使我感覺到我們研究行政學者的責任。

我很不願吹毛求疵地指出一二句，偶然錯誤，做攻擊的資料，所以這篇書評僅把此書的大概討論一下。的確，很多地方想和作者詳為商榷，藉以匡我不逮。

分類索引

索引類列	題目	編者	雜誌名錄	發行年月	號數
A類					
A 1	事權之分離及其聯整	王烈望	管理	25—9	1:3
B類					
B 1	內都牽制組織論	李安素	會計雜誌	25—8	8:2
B 2	我國鹽業之整理問題	卞錦濤	東方雜誌	25—7	33:14
	國民經濟建設運動中之手工業改良問題	顧毓瑔	工業中心	25—8	5:8
B 3	青島貫華廠製造凍粉記實	尹喆昇	工業中心	25—7	5:7
B 4	煤灰之軟化溫度和分析	萬培源	工業中心	25—8	5:8
	存貨之統制	施仁夫	會計雜誌	25—7	8:1
B 5	中國棉花市場之組織與棉產運銷合作	履仁	農村合作	25—8	2:1
	中國棉花產銷之合作	張保豐	新中華	25—27	4:14
	華絲在國際市場之隳落	吳兆名	時事月報	25—7	15:1
	我國之鎢礦產銷狀態	吳文英	時事月報	25—8	15:2
B 6	工廠工資制度之比較	頌霖	商專季刊	25—7	11
	上海電話公司訓練職工之研究	衡	電信雜誌	25—7	4:3
B 7	日本醬油工業一瞥	蔣乃鏞	工業中心	25—7	5:7
	柴油用途之試驗	榮甫	北平研究院院務彙報	25—7	7:4
	滇邊的礦產	孟憲民	廣播週報	25—7	95
	中國的礦產	孟憲民	廣播週報	25—8	97
	德國合作中央金庫之組織及沿革	李鄉樸	合作月刊	25—8	8
	消費合作社在國民經濟建設上的價值——保證產銷	蕭涵恩	合作月刊	25—8	8
	中國合作運動今後應取的方針	董時進	農村合作	25—8	2:1
	合作社法施行上之困難	黃肇興	農村合作	25—8	2:1

	中國錦業之衰落及其救濟方法	田三立	時事月報	25—7	15:1
	我國汽油問題之檢討	周繼健	航空雜誌	25—8	6:8
	中國的棉業問題	馮奎義	浙江建設	25—7	10:1
	中國石油問題之嚴重性與解決途徑	勵伯雄	新中華	25—7	4:14
C 1	參觀津浦膠濟兩路後之感想及意見	沈奏廷	管 理	25—9	1:3
	新路建設之經濟觀	黃宗瑜	管 理	25—9	1:3
	各種運輸事業之聯整	曹麗順	管 理	25—9	1:3
	非常時期之鉄路軍運	王同文	交通雜誌	25—7	4:7
	鉄路與汽車之國際觀察	韓奎章	交通雜誌	25—7	4:7
	鉄路經濟之剖視	吳紹曾	交通雜誌	25—8	4:8
	各國鐵路適應公路競爭所採之方法	佘貽謙	交通雜誌	25—8	4:8
	國有鐵道之收入對于中央財政之關係	馮承堯	交通雜誌	25—8	4:8
	各種交通方法的比較及其關係		交通職工	25—7	4:7
	粵漢鐵路全線接道後仍應繼續努力	凌鴻勛	鐵路雜誌	25—7	2:2
	滄石路線之比較與華北經濟之關係	鄭寶照	鐵路雜誌	25—7	2:2
	鐵道部完成東南鐵道之設施	金士宣	鐵路雜誌	25—7	2:2
	德國鐵路事業最近的發展概況	韓奎章	鐵路雜誌	25—7	2:2
	蘇嘉鐵路的面面觀	胡嘯穎	鐵路雜誌	25—7	2:2
	北寧路現狀	陳宣理	中國建設	25—7	14:1
C 2	鐵路組織的現代化	馬廷燮	鐵路雜誌	25－7	2:2
C 5	變更鐵路運價利用回空車輛之我見	沈奏廷	交通雜誌	25—7	4:7
	中國鐵路貨等運價問題	金士宣	交通雜誌	25—7	4:7
	對于吾國鐵路整車貨物裝卸制度之商榷	沈奏廷	交通雜誌	25—8	4:8
	論鐵路運價率之厘定及運價大綱之編訂	畢愼夫	交通雜誌	25—8	4:8
	我國鐵路採用貨物接送業務之檢討	淙 淇	鐵路雜誌	25—7	2:2
	提貨單之面面觀	鳳 介	鐵道半月刊	25—8	7
C 6	增加鐵路貨車載重量利用程度之研究	劉傳書	交通雜誌	25—7	4:7
	機車運行之原理	安忠義	交通雜誌	25—7	4:7

	貨物列車行車效率之研究	鄭寶照	改進專利	25—7	14
	北寧鐵路號誌	鄭寶照	改進專刊	25—7	14
	比國鐵路號誌述略	戴雲書	改進專刊	25—8	15
C 7	評吾國最近改訂之鐵路列車及車輛統計辦法	許 靖 沈奏廷	管 理	25—9	1:3
	改革吾國鐵路貨物列車統計之我見	許 靖	交通雜誌	25—7	4:7
	改革我國鐵路旅客列車統計之我見	許 靖	交通雜誌	25—8	4:8
	粵漢鐵路整理計劃委員會經費收支概況		粵漢路湘鄂線旬刊	25—7	140
	我國鐵路貨運統計制度最近之改革	譚沛霖	鐵路雜誌	25—7	2:2
	改進鐵路編製暨執行預算之我見	孫寶廉	鐵道半月刊	25—7	4
	變更會計年度起訖日期與鐵道行政之關係	蔣鳳五	鐵道半月刊	25—8	6
	中國鐵路列車及車輛統計之解析	劉傳書	鐵道半月刊	25—8	7
C 8	舉辦鐵路勞工行政應有之認識與今後工作之推進	諶小岑	鐵道半月刊	25—7	4
C 9	公共運輸人之業務性質及其責任問題	湯心濟	交通雜誌	25—8	4:8
	站務處境與業務前途的關係	花 晨	道路月刊	25—7	51:1
	辦理公路事業者不容忽視幾個問題	王彥芳	道路月刊	25—7	51:1
	公路運輸之計劃與組織	洪煒冰	道路月刊	25—7	51:1
	我國航業在世界上之地位	王 洸	航業月刊	25—8	4:1
	青島航業概況	吳之璞	交通雜誌	25—7	4:7
	西北交通建設之我見	聲 然	邊疆半月刊	25—8	1:1
	籌設鐵道印刷所芻議	沈鍾鈺	鐵道半月刊	25—7	4
	恢復鐵路債信	潘光迥	鐵道半月刊	25—8	6
	交通大學設置免費及公費學額問題	袁伯揚	鐵道半月刊	25—8	6
	地下鐵道的發達構造與經營	周璣璋	鐵道半月刊	25—8	7
	中國航業管理問題	司徒新	管 理	25—9	1:3
	各種運輸事業之聯系	曹麗順	管 理	25—9	1:3
D 1	力量集中在中央	林 森	廣播週報	25—7	93
	國民對國民大會應有之認識	張道藩	廣播週報	25—8	98
	訓政的眞實基礎	王陸一	地方自治	25—7	2

	領袖態度與救亡目標	記 者	秦風週報	25—7	2:22
	中國之統一	蔭 恩	國聞週報	25—8	13:34
	行政效率的幾個問題	張茲闓	獨立評論	25—7	202
	如何增進行政效率	冥 飛	民鳴週刊	25—7	3:3
	地方行政的幾個問題	蔣廷黻	廣播周刊	25—8	97
	今後之中央政治	張佛泉	國聞周報	25—7	13:32
	論中央與地方的關係	陳之邁	獨立評論	25—8	208
	中國的地方制度與統一問題	薩孟武	文化建設	25—7	2:10
	現代市制之趨向	劉迺誠	社會科學季刊	25—8	6:4
	公務員在刑法上之責任論	李隨昌	磐石雜誌	25—7	4:7
	中國的官	陳之邁	社會科學	25—7	1:4
	從政人員的德操	張逸秋	經 理	25—8	3:2
	公務員的考績	池世英	獨立評論	25—7	210
	英國的公務員制度	郭景隆	建國月刊	25—8	15:2
D 5	原始法律	左景媛	社會學界	25—8	9
	何謂混合法律關係	張蔚然	法律評論	25—8	13:40
	行政法學之新體系	湯 怡	法律評論	25—8	13:42
	憲法草案與總統獨裁	金鳴盛	東方雜誌	25—8	33:15
	中華民國憲法草案		社會科學季刊	25—8	6:4
	中華民國憲法草案的特色	吳經熊	東方雜志	25—7	33:13
	中華民國憲法草案評	周鯁生	社會科學季刊	25—8	6:4
	評憲法草案	陳之邁	民族雜誌	25—8	4:8
	證據制度之來源	董其鳴	法學雜誌	25—7	9:3
	我國司法現況及展望	揚 鵬	法學雜誌	25—7	9:3
	國民政府司法改造之三個時期與最近司法之興革	居 正	法律評論 廣播周報	25—7 25—7	13:37 9:3
	從蘇聯新憲法談到它的政制本質	沈志遠	世界知識	25—7	4:8
	非常時期的法律知識	阮毅成	廣播週報	25—8	100
	憲法草案的精神——民主與獨裁的結合	薩孟武	時事月報	25—7	15:1

	現階級的中國司法問題	阮毅成	時事月報	25—7	15:1
	蘇聯新憲法之特質	汪馥炎	新中華	25—7	4:13
	蘇聯新憲法之精神	儲玉坤	國聞週報	25—7	13:27
D 6	國民大會組織法		新中華	25—8	4:16
	對于現代感化行政理論上與管理上之研究	江康黎	中華法學雜誌	25—8	1:1
	集體的不安全	耿淡如	東方雜誌	25—7	33:13
	從政治學理與國民心理上分析時局	茹春浦	前途雜誌	25—7	4:7
	談政治家的風度	劉眞如	明日之中國	25—7	1:4
E 1	兩廣財政問題	方秋葦	時事月報	25—7	15:1
	民國廿四年中國財政之回顧	喬天佑	浙江財政	25—7	9:5,6
	浙省半年來之財政	程遠帆	浙江財政	25—7	9:5,6
	戰時財政與平時財政	吳士俊	浙江財政	25—8	9:6
	財政與地方之研討	陶繼侃	浙江財政	25—8	9:6
	中國財政的根本問題		東方雜誌	25—8	33:16
	中國財政的特徵	魏友棐	錢業月報	25—7	16:7
	財務制度上聯綜制與總制制之採用	張柱	經濟評論	25—8	3:8
	公庫與金庫	亦有	浙江財政	25—7	9:5
	戰時財政之理論與實際	亦堅	中國經濟	25—8	4:8
E 2	廿五年度國家總預算		正風	25—8	2:12
	五年度國家總預算		中外商業金融彙報	25—7	3:7
	廿五年度國家總預算	馮子明	商業月報	25—7	16:7
	廿五年度國家總預算	劉振東	時事月報	25—8	12:2
	廿五年度國家總預算的分析	陳岱孫	獨立評論	25—7	209
	讀廿五年度總預算案	大公報	國聞周報	25—7	13:27
	中國廿五年度國家普通歲入歲出總預算		國民政府公報	25—7	2090
	銀行之開支預算制度	王琮璇			
E 3	會計與企業管理	錢素君	管理	25—9	1:3
	縣政府會計與簿記之檢討	張志鵬	浙江財政	25—7	9:5

	記帳經驗談	程養廉	會計雜誌	25—7	8:1
	清算及和解破產會計原理之研究	潘序倫	會計雜誌	25—7	8:1
	標準成本制度之研究	陸善熾	會計雜誌	25—7	8:1
	所得稅實施後若干會計問題之討論	徐永祚	會計雜誌	25—8	8:2
	改良中式簿記帳簿格式及其登記法之商榷	李夢白	會計雜誌	25—8	8:2
	會計法施行後審計上應注意各點	李夢白	會計雜誌	25—7	8:1
	會計學術進展之鳥瞰	錢素君	會計雜誌	25—8	8:2
	總計學考	超　超	週行月刊	25—7	1
E 4	穩定匯價與穩定物價	坪	金融週報	25—7	2:3
	國際金融論	李鄉樸	四川經濟月刊	25—7	6:1
	中國金融問題講話	駱耕漠	中國農村	25—8	2:8
	貨幣數量說之檢討	劉燕華	中國經濟	25—7	4:7
	紙幣本位制下之國際借貸平衡	張延年	銀行週報	25—8	20:32
	法幣政策實施後我國的金融	記　者	交易所周刊	25—8	2:20
	白銀問題之回顧與我國今後之自處	王雨桐	信託季刊	25—7	1:3
	白銀問題與中國幣制	蔣徑謝	浙江青年	25—8	2:10
	中國之銀恐慌與日英美之抗爭	蒼　生	新經濟	25—8	1
	金融改造與國民經濟建設前途	壽勉成	廣播週報	25—8	97
	美國向華購銀與中國重鑄銀幣	谷春帆	社會經濟月報	25—7	3:7
	非常時財政準備論	張一凡	社會經濟月報	25—7	3:7
	我國銅元制度與社會影響	唐季清	浙江財政	25—7	9:5
E 5	施行所得稅		銀行週報	25—7	20:28
	征收所得稅問題		銀行週報	25—7	20:27
	所得稅與儲蓄之二重課稅		銀行週報	25—7	20:28
	為所得稅問題警告國人	劉振東	銀行週報	25—7	20:28
	立法院通過所得稅暫行條例之感想	權　時	銀行週報	25—7	20:28
	所得稅暫行條例草案之批評及其修正意見	朱　偰	東方雜誌	25—7	3:13
	所得稅之研究	劉樹東	東方雜誌	25—7	33:13

中國今日徵收遺產稅問題	張景璞	東方雜志	25—7	33:14
關於我國徵收遺產稅之意見	董蒙正	東東雜志	25—7	33:13
賦稅法及整理江蘇財政之經過	趙棣華	管　理	25—9	1:3
走私的嚴重與遏制的方法	雷　震	廣播週報	25—7	93
我國幣制的觀察	陳君慧	廣播週報	25—7	95
中國所得稅問題	劉振東	廣播週報	25—7	95
對於開征所得稅的展望	陳長衡	廣播週報	25—8	97
中國經濟建設計劃之實施與蘇聯實施計劃經濟之分析比較	吳承治	廣播周報	25—8	98
中國經濟改造問題	張素民	華　年	25—7	5:29
關係經濟國防之走私問題	胡紀常	華　年	25—8	5:34
統制經濟與計劃經濟	麋中丹	商專季刊	25—7	11
走私問題的分析與對抗方法	陳叔溫	錢業月報	25—7	16:7
緝私的三種方法	鑫　伯	錢業月報	25—7	16:7
走私問題的檢視	麥　逸	錢業月報	25—7	16:7
戰時財政之調度	胡善恆	時事月報	25—7	15:1
一九三五年各國之關稅及其貿易政策	胡啓芳	社會經濟月報	25—7	3:7
城市之中特別估稅	殷孟威	浙江財政	25—8	9:6
論徵收所得稅問題	唐應晨	浙江財政	25—8	9:6
世界經濟恐慌與景气之新階段	張仲實	新中華	25—7	4:13
中國經濟的掙扎	千家駒	新中華	25—7	4:13
所得稅條例的檢討	葉　秋	新中華	25—8	4:16
論所得稅暫行條例	蔡　鼎	獨立評論	25—8	212
營業稅與所得稅之重複問題	吳　純	獨立評論	25—8	214
中國經濟改造問題	張素民	華　年	25—7	5:29
統制經濟發生的政治及經濟背景	楊桂和	中外月刊	25—7	1:8
柏拉圖的經濟思想	袁賢能	政治經濟學報	25—7	4:4
經濟學體系之新區分	劉絜敖	民族雜志	25—8	4:8

所得稅的實施	楊青田	中華月報	25—8	4:8
徵收所得稅問題		商業月報	25—7	16:7
徵收所得稅問題	子明	銀行週報	25—7	20:27
中國舉辦所得稅問題	莊心在	文化建設	25—8	2:10
國民經濟建設運動中之中國經濟	張素民	文化建設	25—8	2:11
關稅收入的激減與國民政府的財政	郭有義譯	北平研究院院務彙報	25—7	7:4

工商管理月刊

第四卷 第一期

本刊投稿簡章

一、投稿以有關於管理者為限。

二、投稿不拘文言白話，須繕寫清楚，並加標點，如係外國文稿件，並請打印之，均不得於一紙兩面寫字。

三、論著稿中，如有譯名或引文，須分別註明原文及出處。

四、譯稿須將原文題目，原著者姓名，出版日期及地點，詳細載明，如能附寄原文尤佳。

五、稿末請簽名蓋章，並註明住址。

六、來稿文字，本院有酌量修改之權，如投稿人不願有何增刪，則應於投稿時聲明。

七、來稿登載與否，概不寄還，惟附寄郵票預先聲請寄還者，亦可照辦。

八、來稿一經登載，當酌贈以每千字一元至三元之酬。

九、來稿請寄上海徐家匯交通大學管理學院。

中華民國二十五年十一月出版

第一卷第四期

每本大洋四角
全年五期大洋一元六角

主編者 鍾偉成

發行者 交通大學出版處

印刷者 華豐印刷鑄字所 上海浙江路五三六號

本刊廣告價目表

等級	地位	全頁價目	半頁價目
甲	底封面外頁	伍拾元	
乙	底面裏頁及封面裏頁	三十五元	二十元
丙	封面裏頁 底面裏頁之對面	二十五元	十五元
丁	普通	二十元	十[illegible]元

一、乙丙丁四分之一頁按照半頁價目六折計算
二、廣告概用白紙黑字如用彩印紙色價目另議
三、廣告如用銅鋅版由本刊代辦照收製版費
四、連登多期價目從廉請逕向本校出版處經理組接洽

二月刊

第一卷第五期 二十六年二月

本期要目

交通大學管理學院編輯

管理二月刊

第一卷第五期
民國二十六年二月

目錄

論著

譯述

論　著

行政組織之集權與統合（D 1.）

林　叠

一　引言

懷德(L.D. White)對於行政組織之優劣，嘗定以攷驗之標準曰：『行政效率决定于組織之是否有統一之責任及適當之權力；工作之劃分能否使專門及一般行政人員致力于各部間對外關係之調整及對內事務之管理。』(一)就此點而論，可知行政組織非可任意决定，而應下以嚴密之攷慮，蓋行政效率之發揮，以行政組織之善良爲基礎，權責之賦予，行政範圍之確立，均與行政組織有密切之關係也。整個制度之運用，其結果或完善或失當從政人員自應負相當之責任，而基礎之鞏固與鬆懈實與結果之良窳成正比例。是故各國近年來多注重予行政機構之改造，俾能充分發揮行政效率。以最近之實例觀，日本軍部力主改組現行行政制度，其最終之目的雖爲堅立政府强硬對外之能力，然有鑒乎過去日本行政之錯誤，至少爲主觀的觀察極明。

我國自國府奠都南京，對於行政組織之革新，不遺餘力，五院之成立，權責之分割趨于合理化，且能合乎國情；主計制度之創始，造成財政與計政之劃分，實現內部牽制之組織，以增加行政效率，撙節行政經費，於此可以表示政府對于行政組織改革之決心；其結果如何，雖未可預作測度，然行政制度之已上軌道，厥爲明顯之事實。

際茲政府勵精圖治，而國勢又危若纍卵之秋，求有以鞏固國基；一方面固重在非常時期計劃之籌措，對內之設施，仍未可因之而或忽，蓋國家成敗之所繫，對外有抵抗之能力雖爲唯一要事，而內顧有隱伏之憂，將不能堅立將士之決心，故對內之善爲管理及統制，亦未嘗非當務之急也。是以我人仍力主改革行政機構，使行政之效率可以發揮，政府肆應咸宜，以嚴整抗戰之陣容，行政組織之研究，實非好整以暇事也。

或曰行政組織與國情生直接關係，一國之歷史背景，傳統思想，民情風俗，執政特性，均有以左右政制之興遷，似無共通之原則，可資遵循，我人又何貴乎行政組織之理論之研究。但試稽史藉，歷觀各國行政制度之蛻化，雖因古代交通未臻便捷，音訊傳遞未見發達，各行其是，各自爲政。然在法理上推究之，仍有類似之處。分權之學說，固創于西方，東方各國亦未嘗無比先例，此蓋社會學家之所謂文化臻合（Convergence），其環境與情形雖異，而有相同之發展也。比種事實之證明，可知我人非不能在不同國家情形中求得相似之原則，以爲研究改良之助，故我人有行政組織理論之研究。

行政組織可分兩方面研究之，曰形式，曰精神。形式之研究重在表面，如中央政府之組織應爲總統制或內閣制，省政府之應爲省長制或委員制。精神之研究重在權責之劃分，如政府組織應爲集權(Centralization)或分權 (Decentralization)，統合 (Integration) 或獨立 (Independent) 等，本文所論者限于精神之研究。然分權之法，英美雖仍在繼續採用，實際上已漸有改向集權之趨勢，獨立之組織則各國多已認爲違反行政效率之發揮，而摒棄不用，故本文僅論集權與統合之組織。

二 何謂集權與統合之行政組織

世人對於集權與統合常易誤解，而認爲有相同之意義，實際上二者雖有多少相互之關係，然厥有其重大之差異，於研究二者之定義後，我人卽可明瞭其不同之所在也。

集權之組織者，不同級政府如中央與地方政府之間，有統制及附屬之關係。統合組織者，在同級政府下，不問其爲中央或地方其不同之組別成相互之關係。(二) 換言之，集權之組織者，各地方政府，不能完全獨立，而脫離與中央之關係，一方面行施其行政責任，一方面更須服從中央之法令及政策而受中央政權之約束；中央方面亦不容地方政府與之隔離，而有統制管轄之權。

統合之組織者在同一之組織下，其直轄之各組別應相互合作有合理之分配，使無衝突與

重複之現象。請以圖例說明統合組織，至集權之組織極易明瞭，故不另作圖

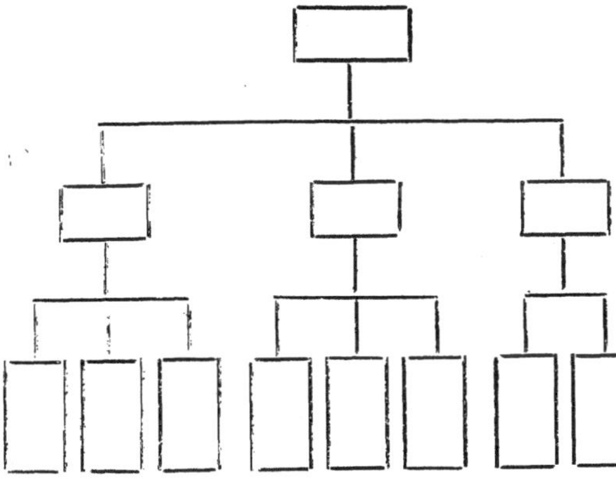

圖一 統合組織

就此圖觀之，我人可以說明統合制之意義，蓋以分工合作之辦法，分劃政整個機關之行政權，分担責任，各盡所長，以利政務之進行，而以行政長官總理全機關事務。

二者之不同，在權責之劃分上，蓋統合之組織，係在水平線上劃分不同權責於不同之組別，而集權組織則爲在直線上劃分不同權責於不同之機關級別。臘山政道言之最切，曰：

「集權組織與統合組織爲行政組織之經緯，其色澤雖各各不同，但一切行政組織，均有共通之傾向，」(三)懷得（White）亦謂二者爲縱與橫的不同。(四)此二制度原則上並不衝突，可以同時存在，不若分權與集權，及獨立與統合之爲相對之名稱。在任何環境之下，二者均自由發展，不相牽制，組織不集中時，統合之組織可以存在，而在集權之組織下，亦可能有獨立(卽統合之反面)之現象。(五)

三　集權組織之運用

在討論集權組織之運用前，我人宜先明其歷史之背景。昔時交通不便，農村制度爲社會組織之基礎，人民聚族散居各處，對於政府之觀念殊爲淡薄，故政治有分化之現象。及乎工業革命之後，科學昌明，交通發達，打破老死不相往來之習俗，衝動閉關自守之保守觀念，於是人類之關係自農村而市鎭，而國家以至國際。接觸既多，政事益繁，要之人民之有求於政府者，對內爲幸福之籌劃，對外爲國防之準備，於是政府之威力乃見發揮，爲發揮其能力計，分化之政治，不合潮流，不可復用，而有集權政治，以利政事之施行，各地人民亦不惜摒除地方之觀念，而信任政府。與集權政治而俱來者，爲集中之行政機構，蓋政府非有集中之組織，不易統馭全國，指揮自如，終而有集權之行政機構之組織也。

觀其歷史上之演變，我人易誤解集權組織之政府乃以中央政府爲執行機關，而各地行政亦受中央之直接管理。事實上地方政府散于四方，中央苟欲一一管理，既不能應付其繁複，又有鞭長莫及之感。集權組織者中央與地方之分工，而地方政府之施政受中央法令之約束及監督也，亦卽古人之所謂如身之使臂，臂之使指也。明乎此，我人可以比較的研究集權組織之運用。

英國昔日之政治制度絕對取分權制，地方政府之權力較大，甚至美國獨立後之各州分權亦源于其在殖民地時代之政策。然近年以來，工業之發達，科學之昌明，各地爲政既不能流暢商業以繁榮市面，更不能藉鉅大資力致力於建設，實不若以中央整個之力量，統籌兼顧，較易發展，於是漸覺有集權之必要。故晚近中央對於地方如縣區有統制之趨勢，其統制方式之運用大約之可分下列諸端：（一）對於地方政府需要中央財力上之臂助時，中央予以補助金（Grants-in.aid）；（二）對於地方政府法案及政策之決定必須得中央之批准，否則不得抗命執行；（三）中央發布地方政府之行政法規及命令，此卽中央授權之表示，（四）地方政府施政不當，對於訴願部份得由中央判決，甚或予以罰金；（五）指示調查事務及公共之報告。（五）就此五點觀之，中央對於地方之統制，已有相當之程度，所差者僅未直接代爲管理而已。地方政府所行者基于中央之意志，遇有不足，求于中央之補助，行政失當受中央之制裁，集權能力之發揮，昭然若揭。

世界各國最足以表示集權之組織者爲法國。其地方行政區域政事之施行，幾全操于內政部長，郡長(Prefect)及郡佐(Sub-préfect)之手。郡(Departments)(六)與區(Arrondissements)之管理均直接受制于內政長官。地方政府較有施政之權力者爲市(Commune)，然其市長(M.arie) 亦爲中央直接之代表，受部長之指揮，執行中央之法令。故地方政府最大之職權亦僅等於英之一般地方政府。

法之集權組織，可以圓形表示之，中央政府之權力可伸張至任何級地方政府。郡議會之選舉須得總統同意，郡區長官由內政部派遣，每年度之各市預算，須得郡長之審核，較大之縣猶必須經內政部長審核，市之代議機關雖亦有市議會(Conseil municipal)之組成，其權力亦極小，均受中央法令之限制，較重要之議案，更非經中央或各郡長官批准不可。(七) 圖例如上

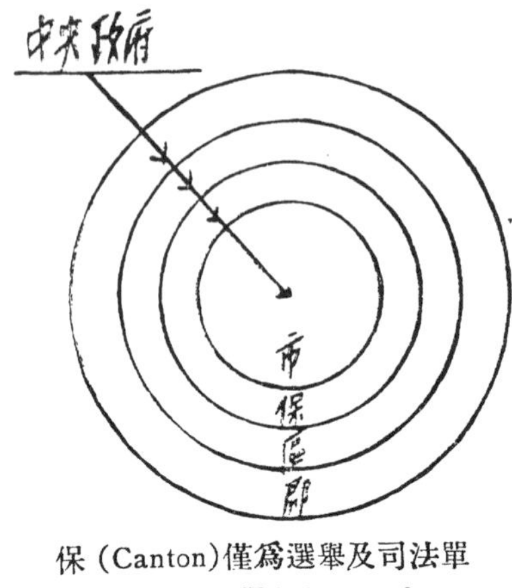

保(Canton)僅爲選舉及司法單位，普通一保包括十二市

美國爲聯邦政府，各州權力極大，有其自己之議會，選舉州長。中央政府不過爲各州代表組合而成，對於各州統制之權力有限。故一政之施，常有不能統一之現象。即各州對於各市亦僅有行政管理之權(行政管理與絕對集權微有不同，容後提及。) 晚近交通發達，商業繁盛，州與

州之關係日見密切，乃有聯邦商業委員會(Interstate Commerce Commission)之組織，爲集中政府權力之始，最近一九三二——一九三三年冬，各州勞工失業現象益見嚴重，美人咸認爲決非地方可能解決，而有集全國作共同商討之必要，集權之呼聲更瀰漫乎全美。（八）羅斯福總統(President Roosevelt)之藍鷹政策，對於全美實業之救濟，固均以整個國家爲單位也。更以商業之不景氣，地方財政，有集中管理之趨勢，以濟各州之急，而爲治本之辦法。（九）以是觀之，美之集權運動，方興未艾，他日之成就，誠非昔日倡分權組織者可能意料也。

研究過去之史實，我人可知美對於集權組織之運用方法。美可採者有如下述(十)：(一)中央及各州政府以雄厚之財力，可以聘請專家，研究地方制度之改良及發展，其結果作地方政府之參攷，或組織研究所進行研究，以收較大之效果；(二)在集權制度方在利用之始，用攷察之法，對於地方政府之施政成績，詳加攷察，善者揚之，劣者飭其自謀改革之方；(三)地方政府可自行行施其職權，然在每定期內，必須予中央政府以完備之報告以代實地之攷察；（四）凡地方政府能合乎中央或各州所定施政成績標準者，予以獎勵金，如英之補助金然，又如地方政府因須達到中央所定之標準，而經費有不足時，可請求中央予以補助，此項獎勵之法，余未敢同意，蓋各地之是否能達到標準，不一定在於施政之努力與否，或因實際上確有特殊困難而阻礙政事之推進，當不能認該級政府有不努力之表現，故此法似應改善，以適合各地實際之情形；(五)審計上監督，地方政府之一切財政收支，均須受上級機關之審核，各州有會計局之設，辦理各道(County)各市之審計事務；麻省(Massachusetts)對於各地發行公債及紙幣，均須得州政府之批准；(六)事之與中央及全國有關者，須得中央之允許，而管理之權，則仍操諸地方政府；(七)政事之施行及法案之通過，須送請中央攷覈；(八)對於地方政府有發布命令强制執行之權，此種命令雖由行政長官發布，然强制之執行，則屬於法庭；(九)於必要時，地方政府之職權可由中央收回，自己施行，如公路建設及衞生改進等事務。

我國集權組織早有先例，秦平六國廢諸侯割據，而立郡縣之制度，行政組織已有集中之方法，歷朝均因舊制；唐代藩鎮猖獗，卒移神器，後人益兢兢以分權之不利於皇室爲戒，故集權組織在我國已有悠久之歷史，固非受歐化東漸之影響也。民國而後，雖數倡地方自治，然集權之制仍復存在，其間經軍閥之割據，中央政令不出都門，北方政府時代，集權之名雖存而實亡。鼎革而後，此種現象亦不可免，今者全國統一，新憲法草案於今年五月五日公布，對於地方制度有自治之規定，具集權之精神。一般人以爲自治與集權爲相對之名詞，此則不然；蓋集權有二種一爲絕對集權，如法對郡區之管理，其長官由中央派遣對中央負責，絕對的爲中央之代表機關；二爲行政統制(Administrative Control)如英美之制，中央並不干涉，地方行政，美之州長市長均由民選對州市議會負其責任，中央僅以法令及其他方法予以統馭及牽制。我國之制度近于後者，故地方自治，正在努力推進，相輔而行，以造成一現代之國家也。

綜上所述集權之運用，可分兩方面，爲絕對的及行政的；方法則英、美、法各國所取者可作代表。至於應用集權之利，甚爲明顯，卽施政可以統一，無各自爲政之現象，如美國禁酒方行之初，因各州態度不同，結果鬧出不少笑話，其他實例不勝枚舉，又中央之從政人員其經驗及學識較爲完善，施政之計劃，亦易得合理化之決定。然集權制度亦不能說毫無微疵，卽如過分之干涉，易造成呆板不適地方情形之現象，蓋各地風俗民情各各不同，若逕律以相同之政令，必將造成南轅北轍之結果，此點之改良，貴在中央施政者能洞悉各地實況，善爲變通。其次集權組織下，中央權力至大至尊，施政人員如心存偏袒，厚其本省，則錯誤之統制難望避免，此爲悲觀者之說法，然此種弊端卽在分權制度下，省行政長官亦未嘗不可袒其縣屬，以至其鎭屬，要之，在視法令森嚴，吏治澄清與否耳。

四 統合組織之運用

統合組織爲橫的組織，在同一之政府下，劃分不同之組別，以不同之職權屬之，然其異於獨立者，在於雖以不同之職權劃入不同之組別內，其行政系統並非直接達於行政長官，而以相類似之組別歸入一類，然後與行政長官發生關係。（十二）其說已於第二節圖示中表明，現請再以實例說明之。以我國鉄道部而言，對於營業及運輸效率之增進，有營業，運輸，商務（近聞已歸入祕書廳研究室）三科及聯運處分別負責任。各科處所務之事，雖國屬於鉄道業務之推進，然一主各路營業狀況之監督推行事項，一主各路運輸方法及技術之改進事項，一主各路營業及沿線工商業農業調查事項，一主國內國際鐵道聯運及其清算事項，各有不同之責任。如在獨立之制度下，必將以之完全直隸於部長管轄之下。然因管理之便利起見，更以此三類性質均有類似之處，另設業務司主持之。既可減少部長繁重而不暇一一管理之責任，又可使此三科一處有直接之歸宿，而決定其合作程度，即我人所謂統合組織也。

就此例觀，所謂統合之制，並非新發現，似無提倡之必要，又何必加以詳盡之研究，其說誠然。然我人須研究者非其表面而爲其方法，如分組劃分之應至如何程度，分組劃分之如何方爲適當。以整個行政機關而言，世界各國對於各部之劃分，無一國完全相同，有別鉄道于交通者如我國與日本，有別農業與勞工於實業者如法國，可見統合之方法，並非易於應用。

我人欲求統合組織運用之得當，自不能忽略運用之原則；其原則有如下述：（一）組織之方法必須正確無誤而合理，對於各不相關之事務應就其性質，劃分及歸併于各部；(二)分部之時應區分行政與行政之司法 (Administrative Adjudication) 及行政之立法 (Administrative Legislation) 之事務，俾職權之行使不致十分衝突；(三)分部之法則，應以各種行使職權之目的爲標準，更應以各種事務活動之性質爲區分；(四)各部之間應相互的取得聯絡，以避免重複與衝突。(十二)

我國行政院各部之劃分尚較合理，然以分部過多，不無可議之點，深企將來憲政實行後，有以改良。至於各部內部之統合組織亦能有良好之基礎，然就一般之部而言，祕書處之組織過大，研究方面常與參事室相衝突，總務及文書方面常與總務司相衝突，就日本之制度言祕書處與總務司並不劃分，而以大臣官房總其事，於經費方面而可以撙節，事務劃分方面不致重複或衝突，我國各部實可取法之。

統合組織如能運用得當，可使國家政務趨于簡單化，避免無謂及阻礙行政效率推進之重複與衝突之現象。又可節省經費，故值得我人之研究。美昔日對於統合之組織亦不注意，一切事務，均由行政長官直轄。印第安那(Indiana)省於一九二三年以前，事務之直接隸屬於州長者達六十餘種，無分類負責之辦法，故以教育一端言，無論男生，女生，聾啞，盲目，白痴之學校均直接歸行政長官負責監督，其繁複于此可見。(十三) 自十九年世紀之始，美各省競起改組統合之制度至今已成普遍之組織。以伊立諾（Illinois）省言，卽曾將百餘小組機關及委員會歸併于九部內，節省不少經費。

五 以二種組織之聯合運用作結

第二節內曾言及統合與集權之組織並不一定同時存在，分權制度之下，亦未嘗不可採取統合之組織；另一方面講，二者成縱橫之關係，並不衝突，可並行而不背。在此二大理由下，作者正式認爲二制之合併爲行政組織最滿意之方法。

二制之合併並非難事，且爲應行之事；蓋我人知統合之方法，爲一般行政組織之方法，並不限于中央或地方。中央政府因欲避免事務之衝突，組織無限制之擴大，而採統合之組織以爲調整；地方政府亦有此種同樣之需要，故應同樣採用此種方法。使橫的行政上，得此合理之調整，而發生大量的功能。同時並應實行集權制度，以確定中央與地方縱的行政上之關係，如是上下相成，相輔並進，效率自高，而庶政畢擧矣。

總結上說，我人知行政組織之採取，以此二大方式爲最適宜，因時代背景有以促成之也。至於何者爲急需，嘗憶美哈佛大學教授華爾康(A.N. Holcombe)之言曰：『政府未曾將新政完善創導之前，權力之集中頗爲重要，而以行政統合化爲尤要。』就作者之意，二者均屬重要，最好同時採取，聯合運用。蓋華氏之言在一九一五年，美國集權之趨勢尙不及現在爲急進，故有集權不及統合爲要之說也。

(註一)L.D. White Introduction to the Study of Public Administration(The MacMillan Company,1933) p. 73.

(註二)Ibid., p. 77

(註三)臘山政道 行政學總論(昭和三年)第八章，第四節

(註四)Op. cit., White Introduction to the Study of Public Administration, p. 77

(註五)M. R. Maltbie, "English Local Government Today" Columbia University Studies in History, Economics, and Public Law, Vol. 9,(1897), p. 260

(註六)Department 一字之翻譯，各各不同，林秉中戚呂浩於其譯本現代政府原理中譯爲「部」，錢端升於法國的政府中譯爲「郡」。事實上法之Department確較我國昔之所謂「郡」爲大，而「部」之譯名較爲適合；然中央各行政組織通常我人亦名之曰「部」，爲避免衝突，本文譯亦作郡。

(註七)參攷B.C. Holt The Elementary Principles of Modern Government 第九章關於單一制地方政府一節。

(註八)J.M. Pfiffner Public Administration(The Ronald Press Company.New York, 1935),pp. 98—99.

(註九)參攷 Yale Law Journal (April, 1934), Vol. XLIII, No. 6, pp. 979—1007.

(註十)Op. cit., White Introduction to the Study of Public Administration, pp. 85—87.

(註十一)W.F. Willoughby Principles of Public Administration (The Brookings Institution, Washington, 1927),p.82.

(註十二)拙著 行政學大綱（南京華僑半月刊社，民國二十四年）第二十五頁至第二十七頁。

(註十三)Organization Chart of the Executive Branch of the Government of the State of Indiana, 1923. Compiled by Frank G. Bates, Indiana University, U. S. A.

管理旅客運輸應有之基本統計（C 7.）

許　靖

一　客貨運輸統計方式之異同

客運之對象爲人，貨運之對象爲物，兩種運輸情况根本不同，因而在統計上不能採取同樣之方式。故於計算運輸數量也，在貨運方面以重量爲標準，而於客運則以人數爲標準；又若計算平均收入也，貨運以每噸爲單位，而客運則以每人爲單位；此猶就其最淺近者而言，其他彼此互異之處不勝屈指，茲擇其最緊要而最易起人誤解或疑慮難決者提示分辨如左：

（一）**重空車輛里程之劃分**——按歐美各國雖皆對於車輛行程均有統計，然貨車則分爲重車里程及空車里程兩種，而客車則祇按車輛類別計其里程，並無重空之分別。考其理由，大抵不外因貨運較繁，空車行動較多，如若不將空車里程分開計算，則其行動是否經濟，支配是否得當，勢必無從施以考察監督，影響車輛之運用效能當非淺鮮。至若客車則不然，以車次固定者多，列車組織甚少變動，卽或偶有附掛空車之事，但亦爲數有限，故客運方面之空車行動本極微少，而無單獨統計空車里程之必要，此爲兩種統計之方式上不同者一也。

（二）**總噸里與淨噸里之計算**——在貨運方面，因欲實現管理上種種經濟之故，於是乃有統計每列車裝載重量及其行程之舉，且復分爲總噸里（Gross ton-miles）與淨噸里Net ton-miles

兩種，前者包括整個列車之全部車重貨重及其行程。後者僅爲貨物之重量與行程。但在客運則可不必强行同樣之辦法，蓋以客人之重量根本無從計算，卽令採用變通辦法强爲估計，其結果亦必不能準確。且旅客重量較之列車皮重極爲有限，影響列車之載重甚微，故在客車僅有人里 Passenger-miles之計算卽已足矣，蓋其作用正與貨車之淨噸里程相同，而又可以省卻許多無謂之煩擾與財力。此爲兩種統計之方式上不同者二也。

(三)**列車載重之計算**——依前述之同一理由，在貨運有計算列車裝載重量之辦法，復有貨物淨重及車貨總重之分，但客運則不能計算旅客噸數，因之考核旅客列車之裝載，不能同樣在重量上着眼，必須改用人數以代之而濟其窮焉。蓋人數之多寡亦可間接表現列車裝載之輕重，方之折算客人重量辦法，旣省手續，又切實用。所以關於旅客列車之載重問題，在歐美各國均用「每列車平均人數」之變通辦法，卽係以列車里程除旅客人里所得之平均人數也，其性質正與貨運列車之平均貨物噸數至相類似，在統計上具有同等之效能。此爲兩種統計之方式上不同者三也。曩者法比鐵路對於客車載重曾有估計旅客重量之折算辦法，卽頭等車每輛作爲二噸，二等車每輛作爲二噸半，三等車每輛作爲三噸，普通守車一輛作爲二噸，及帶轉向架之守車每輛作爲三噸是也。查此種辦法之精義，乃爲基於頭等客車座位較寬，數目較少，旅客亦必不若二等之多，而二等車則又必不似三等客人之擁擠，故其折合重量以頭等車爲最少，而以三等車爲最多也。此則較之我國前以「每十個座位折算重量一公噸」之種種武斷算法殊爲合理。惟此法現在法比亦已廢除而不用矣。蓋亦鑒於旅客列車本無計算客人重量之必要而然也。

(四)車輛載重之計算——貨運統計中有考察每車輛裝載貨物重量之舉，通常稱爲車輛平均載重統計，此在客運亦有之，英名Statistics of carriage goods，惟在計算方式上大有不同，亦不計及旅客重量，但以客車里程除其人里所得之平均人數作爲每車輛之平均載重，是蓋本於前項計算列車載重之同一原理，勿庸再爲申述。此兩種統計之方式上不同者四也。

上陳數端，是乃客貨運輸兩方統計上不能盡同之犖犖大者，茲更就其可以相同之處舉列數項如后：

(一)列車里程——以列車次數乘其行程里數卽得。

(二)車輛里程——以車輛數目乘其行程里數卽得。

(三)列車鐘點——以列車次數乘其行駛時數卽得。

(四)機車里程——以機車數目乘其行駛里數卽得。

(五)機車鐘點——以機車數目乘其行駛時數卽得。

(六)每列車之平均車數——以列車里程除車輛里程卽得。

(七)每機車里程之平均用煤磅數——以機車里程除機車用煤之磅數卽得。

(八)每百機車里程之平均用油品脫數——以機車里程除機車用油之品脫數(Pints)，再以一百乘之卽得。

(九)每列車里程之平均進款——以列車里程除其進款卽得。

(十)每列車里程之平均成本——以列車里程除其行車本成卽得。

(十一)每機車鐘點之平均進款——以機車鐘點除其進款卽得。

(十二)每機車鐘點之平均成本——以機車鐘點除其行車成本卽得。

(十三)其他

二 管理旅客運輸之重要統計

關於旅客運輸統計，大致可分三方面：一爲分析營業之結果，二爲考核行車之準點，三爲關於列車之本身者；惟此種界限乃相對的而非絕對的，以三者常有相互之關係，若欲嚴格劃分，實爲不可能也，請分陳如次。

甲、關於分析營業狀況者——此爲旅客運輸方面之必要初步統計，與貨運方面之貨物統計同其性質。其內容及編製步驟似應按照左列各項辦理：

第一步：計算旅客人數。

第二步：計算旅客行程里數

第三步：計算人里數。卽係以人數乘其行程里數所得之積。依吾國習慣通稱之爲延人公里，是爲代表客運數量之主要單位，人里數目愈大，斯於鐵路愈爲有利。以其對於人數及距離兩大要素兼而有之，無論因旅客增加，或因行程較遠，皆足增加鐵路之票價收入，且其變化又可隨時反映於人里數目，故客運統計中之人里實與貨運方面之噸里具有同樣之作用，是爲必不可少之重要單位。

第四步：計算平均行程。以旅客人數除人里數目，卽爲每一旅客之平均行程，其性質類似貨運方面之每噸平均行程，此項平均行程愈遠，卽爲客運愈發達之象徵。

第五步：計算客運進款。

第六步：計算每人里之平均進款。以人里除客運進款卽得。

第七步：計算行車成本。其方法與計算貨運之行車成本相同。

第八步：計算每人里之平均行車成本。以人里數除每列車之行車成本，可得各列車之每人里平均行車成本。

以上八項如能俱備，則客運統計已可蔚成大觀，卽可勝過吾國現有之旅客運輸統計，蓋就吾國現有客運統計分析，祇有「旅客人數」「進款」及「延人公里」三種基本數字，此外則爲

「平均行程」「每旅客平均進款」及「每延人公里平均進款」三種平均數字，總共不過六項，而於本篇所陳之計算行車成本等項則尚付缺如，殊難認爲十分完善。

既按上述步驟計算各項數字之後，即可反轉編製任何形式之表格，以應各項之需要，試舉一二格式於次，以例其餘：

例一

列車類別或運輸類別	人數	里數	人里數	平均行程	每人里平均進款	成本	每人里平均成本

例二

客運類別	頭等		二等		三等		四等		合計	
	人里	每人里平均進款	人里	每人里平均進款	人里	每人里平均進款	人里	每人里平均進款	人里	每人里平均進款
普通										
政府										
優待										
遊覽										
定期票										
其他										
各類共計										

以上例一之表可按每列車之類別，或按頭二各等，或按特別快車，尋常快車等等分別計算各項均可，例二則爲參照吾國旅客統計分類情形計算各種客運之人里及每人里平均進款之格式。推而演之，所有按段按路編造之日報月報或年報，皆得從心所欲酌定變通運用之，不得以此兩表視爲刻版文章也。

乙、考核行車準點之統計——行車準確統計之重要，固已早爲國內鐵路管理學者所公認，然而按諸實際，迄今尚無完善之統計方式，間嘗推求其故，大抵不出三種原因：一則國人於此專門問題素無自動研究之精神，缺乏創制之能力；二則對於西國具體辦法類皆根本隔閡，鮮有知其底蘊者；三則散見於西人之著作者又皆零星片斷之記述，遇事僅言大體，不及求詳，以致許多辦法無從探本求源，難得一貫之瞭解。因此惟有盲從書本抄襲西人一二名詞，故結果動輒失掉廬山眞正面目，莫能得其辦法之眞諦，馴至陷於謬誤而不自覺，我國一切鐵路管理問題所以至今不能得其門徑走上正軌者，正坐斯弊，固又不僅限於行車準點統計一端爲然也。因特順帶略抒所感，抑亦舉一以例其餘之意耳。

居嘗歷考歐美各國鐵路統計名著，無論關於任何統計方式，求於編製程序及運用方法能有一貫詳盡之敘述者，非惟有如鳳毛麟角不可多覯，實則比之稀世奇珍尤爲難得，着實言之，可謂一無所有，關於行車準點統計，當然亦無例外。學者如欲補救此種缺陷，勢非另覓途徑，鮮克有濟，而其唯一有效之策，則爲切實研究先進國家之實際辦法，而後西法乃能轉爲我用，抑且舍此而外，實無其他妙計可濟其窮也。作者有鑒於此，爰就個人實地所得之美國現行辦法和盤詳陳於此，惟爲便於叙述起見，特以所用兩種重要表格先行列舉於后，幷附以實在數字，以便研究全部辦法之精義及其作用：

第一表：一段長室逐日編造之旅客列車準點統計——一九三〇年九月份。

(1)	(2)	(3)	(4)			(5)	(6)	(7)
日期 (Date)	行車次數 (Trains Run)	誤點車數 (Trains Lost)	準點百分比率 (Percentage)			本段成績等級 System Rank)	全路各段客車準點百分比率 (System Performance)	誤點車次 (Trains Late)
			本月	上月	上年			
1	40	1	97.5	100	100	14	98	# 14
2	80	1	98.7	100	98.7	14	99	
3	120	1	99.1	99.1	99.1	12	98	
4	160	1	99.3	98.0	99.3	10	98	
5	200	1	99.5	98.47	99.5	9	98	
6	240	1	99.5	98.3	99.5	7	98	
7	276	2	99.3	98.5	99.6	7	99	#535
↑								
中								
略								
⋮								
⋮								
↓								
30	1184	10	99.1	99.1	99.43	8	99	# 3
31				99.18				
共計								
上月								
上年								

第二表：—總局運輸處長室逐日編造之各段及全路旅客列車準點統計—八月廿五日—九三〇

甲部：

(1) 成績等級 (Rank)	(2) 段別 (Division)		(3) 行車次數 (Trains Run)	(4) 誤點車數 (Trains Lost)	(5) 誤點分數 (Mins. Lost)	(6) 每列車平均誤點分數 (Av.-per train)	(7) 準點車次百分比率 (Percent Schedule Maintained) 本月	上月	上年
	外線段：(Line Div.)								
1	A.	本日	19	0	0	0	100	100	100
		累計	475	0	0	0	100	98	99
2	B.	本日	14	0	0	0	100	100	100
		累計	350	0	0	0	100	99	99
3	C.	本日	16	0	0	0	100	100	100
		累計	250	0	0	0	100	99	99
4	D.	本日	18	0	0	0	100	100	100
		累計	418	1	31	31	99.76	99	98
5	E.	本日	16	0	0	0	100	100	100
		累計	400	1	20	20	99.75	99	100
6	F.	本日	26	0	0	0	100	100	100
		累計	650	3	197	65	99.53	99	99
……中略……									
16	O.	本日	10	1	16	16	94	71	100
		累計	473	10	269	26	97.8	97	99
乙部：									
	終點段：(Term. Div.)								
1	A.	本日	24	0	0	0	100	100	100
		累計	600	0	0	0	100	100	99
2	B.	本日	30	0	0	0	99.6	100	100
		累計	750	3	100	33		99	98
3	C.	永日	44	1	30	30	97	100	100
		累計	1084	5	84	16	99.5	99	99
丙部：									
全路各段共計 (System)		本日	219	1	30	30	99	100	99
		累計	5178	41	1514	36	99	99	98

以上兩種統計格式，係美國意利諾中央鐵路Illinois Central Railroad之現行旅客列車準點統計。第一表爲段用格式，英文稱爲Statement of Passenger Train Performance，中爲一九三〇年九月各日實在數字；第二表由總局運輸處長室Office of General Super intendent Transportation編造，其英文名稱爲Maintenance Passenger Train Schedules By Divisions，內爲一九三〇年八月廿五日之實在數字；此二者可作美國考察客車誤點之標準統計看待，其中所含原理極爲曲折，頗費解釋，請按下列各點說明其作用。

（一）**兩表之編製程序**——按美國各路均行分段管理制度，各段皆有調度所以指揮監督行車事宜，一切列車有無誤點，在調度所隨時瞭如指掌，對於駛過段內之旅客列車，照例由調度所主任親身塡造「客車行駛狀況報告」於每日晨間電告總局運輸處長室，此爲第一步手續。運輸處長室接到各段上項日報，立卽編製如第二表之統計，一面送呈車務總管General Manager及抄致總局其他關係各處，同時發交各段一份，此爲第二步手續。各段奉到第二表時立卽由段長室負責員司轉錄於如第一表之格式，此爲第三步手續。所有由段而局及由局而段之往返造報編製情形大致具如上述，總計前後所費時間大約不過三五日之多，其編製不可謂不迅速矣。

（二）**編算表內各項之步驟**——先就第二表言之：第一步將收到之各段「旅客列車行駛狀

況報告」按段排列，計算在各段行駛之列車總共次數，如第(3)欄；第二步計算發生誤點之列車數目，如第(4)欄，但誤點時刻不及十分鐘者則不算入；此點應予特別注意；第三步計算所誤時刻之總共分數，如第(5)欄；第四步計算每一誤點列車之平均延誤分數，如第(6)欄；第五步計算未經誤點之列車佔總共行駛列車之百分數，是爲準點車次之百分比率，如第(7)欄，以總共列車次數除準點列車次數卽得，同時以上月同日及上年同日之數移於本欄之下，以資比較。表內一切數字均分「本日」及「累計」兩項，俟各段計算完竣之後，然後第六步則按準點車次百分比率以定各段成績之優劣，如第(1)欄，其百分比率最高者成績最優，以之列於第一，成績較次者第二，以下類推。若兩段此項百分比率相同，則應視行車次數多寡以定其等級之先後，車次多者應比車次少者列等爲高，至行車次數愈多，則誤點之可能性愈大，反而言之，卽車次愈繁，如能一一準點，則更爲難能可貴矣，故應列等較高。觀乎表內AB兩段之準點百分比率均爲百分之百，然A段之車數爲19，B段僅爲14，故以A段列於第一，而B段則列於第二矣。此爲編製第二表之大概程序與步驟也。

關於第一表之編製；自第(1)以至第(6)等欄，均由第二表轉錄而得，其中第(5)欄「本段成績等級」係指本段在全路各段中所佔地位之高下，如九月初一初二兩日均列於第14位，初三日列於第12位，而在初六則又進於第7位矣。第(6)欄則爲全路各段之總共準點百分比率。第(7)欄則爲用以塡明誤點列車之車次號數，如第一日內誤點者爲第14次列車，是其例也。又第(2)欄及第(3)欄之數字均係逐日累計，一至月終，則最末一日之數卽爲一月之共計。段長室有此日用統計，則於行車誤點情形隨時一目瞭然，且由第(7)欄內註明之列車車次進而考察所以發生誤點之原因，以定糾正之方策。

(三)兩種統計方式之特點與功用——綜觀兩種統計格式與其運用情形，其中優異之處足供吾人效法者不一而足，請列述之。

1.任何統計之本身原爲死物，欲其發生作用，必須使其具有能令閱者引起競勝精神之優越條件，因此非有足以表現各段成績優劣項目不可，此爲表內「成績等級」一欄最大功用，亦卽本統計全部結構中之最大特點也。

2.比較各段維持行車時刻準點之能力，不以總共誤點多少爲標準，而用準點車次數目所佔全體列車數目之百分比率，其結果實較正確，此其特點二也。

3.於百分比率相同之段又依行車多寡以定成績之優劣，於情於理，均極公允，此其特點三也。

4.於每日之本日數字另算各日累計，不僅一日內之情況各段得以比較，且可得到前後各日之累計百分比率，以爲更進一層之比較，此其特點四也。

5.有各日之累計數字，則於月終計算各段或全路總成績時無須從頭至尾另費一番加集手續，可於無形中增進編製統計之敏捷，此其特點五也。

6.在鐵路組織學上，有兩種極不相同之分段，名爲從線之段Line divisions，可稱之爲外線段，一爲限於某一大站範圍以內之終點段，英名Terminal divisions。兩種段內之運輸及行車狀況極爲懸殊，管理者必須分別考其成績，方爲合理。故在第二表內將此兩種性質各異之段分別排列、一面以外線各段相互比較，如甲部之A段至0段是也，一面另以各終點段相互比較，如乙部之A段至C段是也，思慮之周，可謂至矣盡矣，此其特點六也。

7.假設此種統計僅由總局編製而不分發各段，則各段成績好壞無由表現，自不能引起各段之注意，更不能發生爭勝之精神，此其辦法上之優點七也。

8.假設縱有第二表分發于各段，倘各段而不自辦如第一表之統計，則亦不過如吾國之辦理統計情形照例以之歸擋存卷而已，各段對於本身逐日行車準點成績必不能爲一貫之考察與監督，必難發生任何實際效用，此其辦法上之優點八也。

總之統計必賴上下均能善於運用，始能發生偉大效用，在上者當用第二表以分析各段之行車準點成績，而第一表則爲各段應有之應用統計，二者相依爲用，缺一而不可也。

上爲美國鐵路管理行車準點之詳細具體辦法，此外其他各國究用如何方式，以散見於著作者大都語焉不詳，無從窺其全豹，茲爲增加參考起見，再就英國鐵路所用格式列舉其一，雖其內容不若美國方法之嚴謹周密，然在編製上頗有類似之處，用爲比較研究之資，亦有相當價值。此項統計之英文名稱爲 Summary of the Working of Passenger Trains，其內容如下表所示：

英國鐵路旅客列車誤點統計

日期 (Date)	段別 (Section)	列車次數 (No. of Trains)		每列車到達時平均誤點分數 (Av. No. of Mins. late at destination)				誤時不過五分鐘者之百分數 (Percentage Not More than 5 Minutes late.)		超過十五分鐘者之百分數 (Percentage More than 15 Minutes late)	
		本年	上年	本年	上年	增	減	本年	上年	本年	上年
二月……	A	3,692	4,039	1.7	1.4	—	.3	92.6	95.2	.2	.1
七月……	A	4,129	4,349	1.8	2.3	.5	—	91.0	83.3	.4	1.0
二月……	B	493	673	.8	1.2	.4	—	95.1	93.6	.2	1.1
七月……	B	1,163	1,484	3.4	4.3	.9	—	79.9	77.4	4.9	7.6
二月……	列車總數 (Total Trains)	40,336	52,662	1.1	1.3	.2	—	94.3	93.6	.6	.8
七月……	列車總數 (Total Trains)	59,261	61,305	1.5	1.5	.8	—	91.6	81.6	1.3	2.9

丙、**列車統計**——所謂列車統計者，應指分析一切行車結果之統計而言，其注義實有廣義與狹義兩種，故何者究應列爲營業統計，何者究應視爲列車統計，原無一定之界限。語其大要，此種統計之性質，似應包括下列數種：

（一）**車輛載重**——鐵路開行列車，無論究爲貨運抑爲客運，其列車之組織如何或應掛車輛若干，總以適應實際需要爲原則，過少既非所宜，過多亦非經濟之道，故在客貨兩種列車均有統計每車平均裝載之必要，不過計算之方式各有不同，在客運之平均裝載爲每車輛之平均旅客人數，以客車里程除人里數目卽得。由此平均人數之增減變化，隨時可以決定增減某一列車之車輛數目，如某列車日常附掛三等客車五輛，倘三等客人人數過少，則可減少一輛，是其例也。計算旅客列車之車輛載重之作用如此，而其方式則與貨運方面不同，茲以計算方式用中英兩種文字分別列舉於后：

中文——旅客列車之車輛平均載重＝$\frac{\text{人里數}}{\text{客車里程}}$。

英文——Average carriage load＝$\frac{\text{Passenger-miles}}{\text{Carriage-miles}}$。

（二）**列車載重**——編算旅客列車平均載重，亦僅計算人數而不言其重量，其作用與車輛平均裝載統計相同，不過一爲每車輛之裝載，一爲全列車之裝載，在範圍上有廣狹之差別耳。如某列車日常客人太少，則該列車卽可取消，以與其他車次合併而省行車成本；反之如客運人數呈現蒸蒸日上之趨勢，原有列車過於擁擠，則是列車供不應求之表現，管理者自當酌量增加車次，此則旅客列車平均裝載之重要作用也。其計算方式如后：

中文——旅客列車之平均列車載重＝$\frac{人里數}{列車里程}$。

英文——Average passenger train load＝$\frac{\text{Passenger-miles}}{\text{Train-miles}}$。

(三)其他關於旅客列車尚可統計之事項甚多，試擇要列舉數項，以供參考。

1. 旅客平均行程里程——2.Passengers, average distance。
2. 旅客行程次數——Passenger journeys。
3. 每旅客行程平均進款——Receipts per passenger journey。
4. 每人里平均進款 Receipts for passenger-mile。
5. 其他。

三 旅客列車及車輛載重不若貨運方面之易於控制

夫鐵路所以計算列車及車輛平均裝載者，其作用無非欲藉統計之昭示，以謀載重之增進，而達運輸經濟之目的。特以種種原因，客運方面之平均裝載頗不易於隨時提高，其理由之主要者有九：

(一)旅客列車之車次變動甚少，每年至多三四次，且各車照例均有固定開行時刻，縱然一旦旅客銳減，亦須按時開行，而各車組織又皆大都固定不變，非若貨車可以隨時合併湊足噸量而後起運，此旅客列車往往難於實現最高裝載之特殊原因一也。

（二）辦理旅客運輸，有一舉世公認之原則不可違反，卽「每人皆有座位」—A Seat for each passenger —之政策是也。因此鐵路對於座位一層隨時應有充分之準備，寧可失之太過，不能失之不足，然事實上鮮有能盡其利用者，此爲難期客運平均裝載達於最高程度之理由二也。

（三）旅客中雖有大部分仍須由原路返回原地者，不若貨物運輸常爲一往不返之性質，然其同時未必恰爲客運清淡之日，鐵路未必卽可賴以增進其平均裝載，此其三也。

（四）客車行駛時刻之適當與否，影響旅客運輸甚鉅，然欲各種車次時刻均能博得一般旅客之滿意，則又爲事所難能，因之行車時刻愈不合於客人心理，則改乘他路之客人亦必愈多，此不利於旅客列車載重之情形四也。

（五）旅客列車之組織，在行駛時甚少變動，不裝貨車之可沿途甩掛增減車輛，加以短途客人常占十之八九，鐵路既不能於起站少掛車輛，又須預備充分座位以容納中途之旅客，故一部分之空車行動常多，影響平均載重至鉅，此其五也。

（六）如因旅客中途減少，不斷折下空閒車輛，縮小列車組織，如是固可提高平均載重，然其結果不免影響行車時刻，將有得不償失之嫌，故此策亦不可行，此其六也。

（七）卽欲彷照貨車辦法沿途變更列車組織，然中途小站居多，軌道設備極不完善，倘若勉强行之，則機車行動必感種種不便，流弊所及，損失更大，此其七也。

（八）沿途變更旅客列車組織，不僅有前述之各項困難，抑且易肇意外事變，影響旅客及行車員工之安全，此其八也。

（九）近世人類享樂慾望日高，旅客對於客車之舒適要求日奢，舉凡座位，燈光，鋪位等等設備之良窳，皆足影響客運之消長。蓋旅客之慾望無窮，鐵路之設備又難盡如人意，則因旅客之不能滿意而受營業損失者，當爲事所難免，此又不易增進客車裝載之理由九也。

總之貨運之對象爲物，客運之對象爲人，人之一切心理變化，要非他人所能左右操縱，，故鐵路之於客運，祇可遇事遷就旅客，盡量迎合客人心理，給與種種便利，切不可徒以行車經濟關係而不顧及旅客之便利，此爲客貨運輸上最大差異之處，幸管理者有以察及而明辨之，不爲一隅之見所囿，則庶乎可矣。

防範行車事變聲中吾國鐵路各站行車管理方法應有之改革（C 6.）

沈奏廷

在吾國鐵路現有單線行車制度之下，各站管理行車最重要之工具有三，一曰轍尖，二曰號誌，三曰路簽或路牌。按各路現行辦法，除少數大站外，三種工具之管理均未集中，非特轍尖與號誌尚未集中管理，卽號誌與路簽亦往往不在一起，蓋轍尖由分路夫（或稱轉轍夫）在地上搬移，號誌多由站役或脚夫主管，而路簽或路牌則歸站長主持。（事實上路簽或路牌亦有由脚夫代庖者，惟照章應由站長親自管轄。）故沿途各站所有號誌桿均設於月台之上，而路簽機或路簽路牌則置於站長室內，以致三種重要工具分散於三種不同之地點，由三種不同之員役管理，與西國鐵路之集中辦法適得其反，此管理制度上之一種重大缺陷深有加以注意改良之必要者也。

因分路誤搬而發生之行車事變，在各國鐵路已屢見不鮮，其補救辦法，作者業已另文論之。此外號誌與絡簽之不集中亦足以致事變之發生；在用電氣路簽之路，如遇站線不清或號誌失效，後站如欲索取路簽，將列車放入區間，本站應先查明站線有無障礙，或進站號誌能否對於清通路線表示平安，然後允許後站取出路簽，或拒絕之，或發出區間開通站線閉塞之信號以答復之，以便後站警告司機，入站時加以留意，此固題中應有之義也。例如某次下行貨物列車先到甲站，讓入彎道，繼有某次下行旅客列車須由乙站開來，越過貨物列車先行，但貨物列車駛入彎道後，號誌忽發生故障，致指示彎道之號誌臂不能完全回復險阻部位，轍尖遂亦不能扳向直道；爾時甲站站長覩此情形卽不應允許乙站取出路簽，將旅客列車放入區間，至少亦應發出區間開通站線閉塞之信號以答復之，同時派人在進站號誌外安置響墩，顯示手作號誌，以防列車駛入彎道而與在站貨物列車相撞。然後來列車如係速度甚高之旅客列車，尙以暫不允許取出路簽爲宜，以策安全。此固言之非艱而行之應亦不難者也。然在今日號誌與路簽分散管理之制度下，此種防範方法往往易爲一般站員所忽視。站長於允許後站取出路簽之前，大都並不外出瞭望，以觀站線有無障礙，如遇號誌不能完全回復險阻部位，除分路夫或脚夫能細心察覺報告外，站長無由知之，故儘可一面允許路簽取出，而一面站線未清，迨臨時發覺，則列車已駛近站界，補救無術矣。

誤搬分路固爲分路夫之錯誤，然苟分路誤搬之後而號誌並不倒下，則除司機不顧號誌闖入站線外，仍不至發生撞車事變。然在吾國鐵路，搬動號誌者非站長而爲站役，站役之細心者固有之，然草率者實亦不少，當分路夫誤搬轍尖之後，站役繼之以誤倒揚旗（卽號誌之俗稱）以致進站號誌竟對未清之線表示平安，一誤再誤，而列車已至，迨站長出而迎車，望見路線扳錯，雖大驚失色，亦已措手無及矣。

是以號誌不由站長親自管轄，勢必發生兩大弊害：（一）在允許後站取出路簽之前，站長例不查明進站號誌有無不能回復險阻部位之事；（二）在列車已離後站開入區間之後，站長復不及早查明轍尖與與號誌有無扳通未淸站線之誤。有此兩弊，事變之防範遂更不易。良以轍尖號誌與路簽三大工具概不集中，每人各司其一，不相爲謀，往往一誤之後，繼之以再誤三誤，欲事變之能預防自屬甚難。例如分路搬錯，而站長能及早查明，幷將號誌置於險阻部位，則一誤不至再誤，補救尙未爲晚；又如號誌失效，不能回復險阻，站長能及時察覺，拒絕後站取出路簽，則亦可防患於未然，阻止重大事變之發生。今以制度不良，將兩種重要行車工具，一律諉諸於下級站役，其危險性之大，雖局外人亦可想而見也。

在西國鐵路，站線各站之轍尖號誌等均集中於號誌樓，由一人總管之，故無指臂不相連之弊。吾國鐵路如欲將各站之轍尖集中於號誌樓內管理，恐需費較多，一時不易實現；惟號誌與路簽當可集在一起，由站長一手主管，仍由站役助之，其法卽應將各站之路簽機（用普通路簽及路牌者改革更易）由站長室移至月台，與號誌桿設於一處，外築玻璃小屋以容納之，値班站長則居此玻璃小屋內，主管路簽及號誌二物，幷應時時瞭望，以觀站線有無障礙，轍尖有無誤搬，號誌有無誤倒，以防萬一。果能如此改良，則站長不必內外奔波，而全局在望，萬事在握，其能增進安全，要不待智者知之。蓋現時站長之照料不周者非盡由其不忠於職務之故，制度之不良，設備之不妥，實司其咎也。在沿線各小站事務不繁者，站長雖移居月台上之小屋內，仍可兼管其他站務，無添用人手之必要也。

古人亦重攷績

凡南面之大務，莫急於知賢，知賢之近途，莫急於攷功，功誠攷，則治亂暴而明，善惡信，則其賢不得見障蔽，而佞巧不得竄其姦矣。夫劍不試則利鈍闇，弓不試則勁撓誣，鷹不試則巧拙惑，馬不試則良駑疑，此四者之有相紛也，由不攷試，故得然也。今羣臣之不試也，其禍非直止於誣闇疑惑而已，又必致於怠慢之節焉。設如家有五子十孫，父母不察精慄，則勤力者懈弛，而惰慢者遂非也，耗家之道也；父子兄第一門之計，猶有若此，則又況乎羣臣總猥治公事者哉。傳曰：「善惡無彰，何以沮勸，」是故大人不攷功，則子孫隋而家破窮，官長不攷功，則吏怠傲而姦宄興，帝皇不攷功，則直賢抑而詐僞勝，故書曰：「三載攷績，黜涉幽明。」蓋所以昭賢愚而勸能否也。

——節錄王節信潛夫論攷績篇——

論我國出口茶業應改爲官督商辦(B 2.)

俞希稷

我國茶葉向爲出口大宗，國計民生，關係至鉅，近年以來，一落千丈，誠非偶然，台灣爲我國最優烏龍紅茶之出產地，東北爲我國上等香片綠茶之大市場，均先後爲强鄰侵占，遂致茶葉產額銷路爲之減少，其失敗一也，蘇聯因無信用放款，而印度准許一年以上之長期賒帳，於是轉而之他，停止採辦我國紅綠茶磚茶，我於是失去一最大主顧，其失敗二也，歐戰以還，各國生產過剩，經濟恐慌，岌岌乎不可終日，乃互用保護政策，抵制進口貨物，我國茶葉適當其衝，其失敗三也，茶葉爲奢侈品，而非人生必需之飲料，際茲各國原料缺乏，食物不足之際，牛油麵包，計口授糧，茶葉已在節省之列，故各國出口進口之茶葉數量，均大爲縮小，其失敗四也，論者不察，以爲我國茶業之一蹶不振，由於商人之守舊，對於生產製造運銷方面，不知改良所致，主張政府統制，爲其唯一補救之方，殊不知此完全爲業外人不識個中底蘊者之談，無異閉門造車，蓋技術改良，固屬重要，而對症發藥，則在於積極推廣國外銷路，皖贛二省，遽信邪說，設置紅茶總運銷處，實施統制，其結果無非壓迫茶商，怨聲載道，蝕耗公帑，而茶葉之不振也如故，實業部復創立官商合辦之茶葉公司，亦係隔靴抓癢，難免與民爭利之嫌，故欲實行救濟，必須通盤籌畫，而具有世界眼光，取消統制官辦之主張，改爲官督商辦，以維特商人原有地位，同時助以營運資金，免除捐稅，減輕運費，從事國際宣傳，並設法向各國交涉，減低進口稅率，如是則我國茶葉銷路，不脛而走，不翼而飛，挽回利權，可操左券，茲將維持商辦理由，及實行官辦缺點分陳於後。

甲　商辦茶業之理由

一、以法律賦予權利言　約法第三十三條規定，爲發展國民生計，國家對於人民生產事業，應予以獎勵與保護，」又第三十七條規定，「人民得自由選擇職業與營業，但有妨害公共利益者，國家得以法律限制或禁止之，」茶業爲千萬民衆之生產事業，又不妨害公共利益，依法應有自由營業之權利，政府獎勵保護之不暇，安有收歸官辦，侵奪商人營業自由之理，政府改進茶業，其目的當然在救濟商人，若官辦則分潤其事業上利益，統制則侵犯其營業上自由，均係違法背理之舉動，是以法律賦予權利言應維持商辦。

二、以茶業本身性質言　茶業包括生產製造運輸貿易四種事業，每一種事業，均有其特殊性質，業茶者，有茶戶，茶販，茶工，茶號，茶棧，土裝製茶場，以及洋行，運輸機關，其工作又分爲種茶，採茶，焙茶，揀茶，炒茶，分篩，打堆運送，，保險，放款存棧，試茶發樣，批盤，收銀，過磅，報關，押匯等，其品質又分爲香氣，口味，顏色，形式，老嫩，濃淡，潮燥等，情形十分複雜，可想而知，非久於此業精於此道者，莫知其底蘊，一班門外漢實無從問津，故振興茶業，仍須任茶商駕輕就熟，自行改良，政府僅須居監督地位，循序漸進，因勢利導而已，是以茶業本身性質言，應維持商辦。

三、以商人地位言　商業不屬於公用事業範圍者卽無國家專利制度，旣爲商業，則在商言商，應任商人自由交易，東西各國，除特殊情形外，均不限制商人營業，更無統制可言，在昇平時期，茶業認爲普通商業之一種，對於公共利益，並不妨害，在戰爭時期，茶葉非軍事上與給養上之必需品，故無統制之必要，卽無官辦之必要，政府苟欲發展茶業，亦宜由商人自行籌劃，自行主裁，政府祇須盡督促協助之責任，例如豁除捐稅，津貼運費廣告費，調查外國市情，禁止摻假冒充等事項，固無庸省辦國營，反消滅商人之原有機能，而貽與民爭利之譏，是以商人地位言，應維持商辦。

四、以農工便利言　茶農茶工茶商，職業雖異，實係三者一體，彼此平等合作，息脈相通，已有悠久之歷史，其間接洽交易，不拘形式，至爲便利，若爲官辦，則有階級之分，一有事端，往返須經一定程序，聲請承轉，訓令批示，周折廢時，上下隔閡，況茶農茶工，多係不識字之平民，不知公文程式，呈請程序，爲何物，遇有困難，試問如何上達？且官辦人員，旣非股東，又非債權人，卽無利害關係，往往一意孤行，祇伺上司之喜怒，不問農工之痛苦，故官辦或統制茶業茶農茶工，必先惑受困難，是以農工便利言，應維持商辦。

五、以外國商情言　出口茶葉，均由各國洋行採辦販運，爲華茶對外貿易之唯一居間人，以前茶棧寄番（卽直接運茶出洋），虧累不堪，顯見洋行之不易廢除，此種洋行，均有數十年之經驗信用，勢力雄厚，可以左右市面，現因印度錫蘭爪哇日本茶葉競爭劇烈，華茶在國外市場，幾無立足地點，全恃洋行於每年上市前，分向國外顧客兜售定貨，推廣銷路，今若收囘官辦，實施統制，直接販運，剷除居間人，意非不善，但結果僅失去各洋行原有之國外主顧，而不能覓得新買客其必蹈前項寄番之覆轍，毫無疑義，洋行對於官辦，利害衝突，自然極端反對，去年夏間，與皖贛總運銷處雙方堅持，幾至不能開盤，而茶商因茶葉堆積，棧租利息旅費等，損失不貲，後由總運銷處容納洋行提出之全部條件，並由茶棧通事力事周旋，方始交易，此項條件，較之茶棧平日售茶與洋行之條件，尤爲苛酷，由是觀之，官辦統制，仍不能避去洋行之交易，與茶棧通事之贊助，卽完全官辦，已不可能，是就外國茶商情形言，應維持商辦。

六、以科學管理言　近世工商各業，均採用科學管理制度，卽分工合作，一切措施，均合理化是也，政府人民，各有確定之職務與責任，政府維持治安，發展生產，人民經營實業，圖謀生活，根據科學管理原則，各有專司，不得相混，若商業官營，政事商辦，則職務顚倒，工作錯亂，效率必見減低，各項員司職工，均不能盡其所長，以無商業專門學識經驗之公務人員，辦理情形至爲複雜之茶業，欲求成效，豈非緣木求魚，而茶商受其影響，必至兩敗俱傷，衡之科學管理原則，則背道而馳，是以科學管理言，應維持商辦。

乙 官辦茶業之缺點

一、人選上之缺點　茶業爲最複雜之商業，已一再述及，則非恃專門人才專門辦理之不可，所謂專門人才者，必須具眞才實學，積多年之經驗，能洞悉個中利弊，然後可，非徒知學術研究，或文字發表之謂，上年皖贛紅茶總運銷處，握實權者。多屬與茶業向無關係之公務人員兼任，時而蕪湖安慶，時而杭州上海，往返奔馳，席不暇暖，何能安心治事，加之情形隔閡，假題壓制，以期敷衍了事，甚至不顧茶商血本，不得茶號同意，擅與某大茶葉店訂約，將最後七千箱紅茶，躉批售出，每担扯價三十七元，美其名曰統制，後經全體茶號反對，乃改售與洋行每担售價反高六七元，總共相差二萬餘元，可見其辦事能力之一斑，所有辦事人員，均存五日京兆之心，過磅員任洋行吃磅，已到期貨款，擢收遲緩，洋行開盤，既賴茶棧各通事之流通，批盤成交，復恃各通事之周旋，否則幾無從進行，此爲官辦茶業人選上之缺點。

二、放款上之缺點　茶葉由茶號製造運銷，其營業資金大牛爲茶棧放款接濟，上年總運銷處，亦依照慣例放款，因是而發現缺點甚多、(一)放款時每縣指定二三保證人，名爲保證，但不代債務人清償欠款，僅負追繳欠款之責，凡借款茶號，依照登記章程、塡寫審查表，交驗股單，并覓得前項保證人之同意，則可領款，不問其資產信譽能力，貸以鉅款，等於所製運茶葉成本之六成，每年上海茶價，上落甚大，一經虧蝕各茶號所欠之款，雖有保證人代爲追討，但根本無財產抵償，其危險可知，幸幣制改革，金磅漲價，叶價增高，虧蝕有限，然已有小數放款無法追囘，（二）上年放款，由農工銀行經理，而由省政府担保，將茶葉提單做押匯，表面上茶號向總運銷處借款，總運銷處向銀行借款，一經虧蝕，總運銷處必扣留甲號之盈餘，抵補乙號之虧欠，以償還銀行，其糾紛不堪設想。（三）保證人規定每箱收手續費五分，此爲茶棧往年之所無。（四）因押款關係，所有棧單均由銀行執管，每次發樣提箱，先通知總運銷處，再通知銀行，再通知棧房，然後取出棧單，提貨，手續煩重周折，而茶價瞬息萬變，一日之中市價可跌落二三成，往往因時間延誤，不及發樣，不得善價而沽，（五）每月放款利息，揚言八厘，較之茶棧利率爲低，以加惠於茶號，乃每月利息，均以複利計算，卽所墊付之運貨保險費棧租營業稅上下駁力等，均以複利計算，違背民法規定，增加成本負担，（六）放款利息，既爲複利，而收進之貨款，在結帳開清單前，均以活期存款存儲農工銀行僅給週息二厘，凡銀行抵押透支，存款欠款，隨時相抵，卽存入之款，作爲還欠，以免增加欠息，今如此計算，茶號損失不貲。（七）每年茶棧將紅茶放款收囘，轉放綠茶，將第一帮茶葉放款收回，又放第二帮或第三帮，輪流週轉，各方均感便利，上年總運銷處，僅放款一次，致二三帮無力進茶，茶農損失甚鉅，此爲官辦茶業放款上之缺點。

三、運輸上之缺點　總運銷處初次營業，卽統一水陸茶箱運輸，又發現下列各缺點，（一）祁門至上海，上年每箱紅茶運費，較往年茶棧經手，增加一元三四角，（二）另加汽車運輸保險費，此爲往年所無，（三）祁門車輛缺少，每批茶葉運至上海，需三四十日，往年祗需半月，因而錯過市面機會，同樣茶葉，遲到者售價須打五六折，同時茶客旅費增加，欠息增加，棧租保險亦增加，茶號損失，苦不堪言，（四）又因車輛不足，各號箱茶用船運到祁門縣後，堆放露天沙洲，加之汽車蓬蓋不全，致多數茶箱潮濕破爛，洋行退貨數量，因之增加，此爲官辦茶業運輸上之缺點。

四、推銷上之缺點　總運銷處關於推銷方面，因管理不良，處理失當，復發現下列各缺點，（一）所附設之推銷組，看守疏忽，竟發生來路不明，未曾登記之新排面茶葉八十箱，批盤發樣，羣疑僉集剩餘樣茶，復火打堆，裝箱而成，此案已呈請查辦，（二）允許洋行一切陋規，較茶棧尤甚，（三）對洋行提供十萬元銀行保證，以備賠償洋行外國退貨之損失，此爲歷年所無之創例，（四）茶葉進口報關，新徵手續費每箱三分，此亦爲茶棧所無，（五）洋行過磅吃秤，不獨未能交涉改善，反較往昔爲甚，表面每箱約六七十磅，扣除二磅半，而實際扣除三四磅，卽總數重量，減少百分之四五，(六)過磅員辦事遲緩，人數過少，致洋行貨款，居期而無人去收總共貨款共三百萬元，平均計遲收一個月，以月息八厘計算，則損失二萬四千元，其他間接損失尚不在內，(七)茶叶可每帮結帳，而總運銷處非完全了結及各項無問題時，不結帳，且手續繁複遲鈍，茶號各項開支及欠息，均因此增加，此爲官辦茶業推銷上之缺點。

綜上論列，商辦茶業之理由如此，官辦茶業之缺點如彼，是非利害，不辨自明，查政府之統制茶業，經營運銷無非爲振興茶業，救濟茶農茶工茶商之生計，今因方法不良，管理失當，忽略國外市情，擾亂國內市面，人民不獨未受利益，反遭損失，所謂雖曰愛之，其實害之，是已，今宜迅予改弦更張，取銷官辦統制，易以官督商辦，則茶業前途，庶有希望，願我政府當局諸公，其熟思之。

再論吾國鐵路列車及車輛統計辦法（C 7.

沈奏廷
許靖

引言

自吾人合撰之「評吾國最近改訂之鐵路列車及車輛統計辦法」一文發表後，頗能引起各方之注意，良用欣慰。最近鐵道部劉傳書先生亦同時發表一文，題曰關於列車及車輛統計問題，(載交通雜誌四卷十一期）對於吾人之意見反覆指正，尤足令人欣感。蓋凡事必須討論研究，而後始有進步，在東西各國，學術上之辯論遠較吾國爲多，惟多以學理事實爲前提，不作無謂之爭執，吾人本此精神，除對於劉先生之指正表示誠意的感謝外，終覺前文有所未盡，不得不將吾人之觀點，再作進一步之闡述，仍希海內賢達予以教正，則幸甚焉。

一 貨物列車報單塡列貨名及貨物起訖站問題

貨物列車報單內塡列貨物名稱，根本與列車及車輛統計毫無關係，吾人已言之詳矣。況如爲混合整車或零担貨物，根本卽無從塡，塡亦不確，故與其徒多手續而無用，不如删去之爲愈。所謂「參考」「佐證」云者不知係何所指？至於貨物起訖站名亦與列車及車輛統計渺不相關；若謂貨物起訖站有時與列車起訖站不同，故有塡列之必要，似亦殊乏理由。例如某貨車由上海挂往長安，在京滬路由京滬直達列車挂運，則在京滬路之貨物列車報單內祇須塡挂上站爲上北，摘下站爲南京，斷無另塡長安站之必要，蓋京滬路計算該車之里程時僅以上北至南京間之里程爲限也。迨至津浦，由浦徐列車挂運，則在該列車報單內祇須塡浦口掛上，銅山摘下，既無塡長安站之必要，亦無塡上海北站之必要，蓋津浦路計算該車之里程僅以浦口至銅山之里程爲限也。在西國鐵路，貨物起訖站與列車起訖站不同者遠較吾國爲多，然未見有在車長報單 Wheel report 內塡列貨物起訖站者，誠亦以其無絲毫之用途可言耳。總之上述兩種項目，就列車及車輛統計之用途上觀之，均爲無用之物，謂爲當初失於檢點則可，謂爲合理而有用，則竊以爲不可。

二 貨物噸數之折算問題

(一)沿途零担車折合重量辦法，若果能有合理之統計根據，固屬甚好，惟一考所謂貨車裝運狀況日報，則知所謂根據者根本殊不可靠，請舉其主要缺點如次：

(1)此項零担貨物實裝噸數佔車輛載重噸數百分比統計，當係包括整車零担，合裝零担，中轉零担以及沿途零担在內，安得以之作爲沿途零担車重量之標準？

(2)各路之數字相差極爲懸殊，自百分之十至百分之八九十不等，誠所謂「適於此未必適於彼，」安得徒求簡便，以全國各路平均之數適用於各路乎？

(3)此項統計數字各路未必採用同樣標準編造，故根本未必悉數可靠，觀於零担貨車之平均載重有幾達容積噸數百分之百者可以知矣。

吾人主張各路沿途零担車重量應各定標準者，蓋有鑒於各路裝載情形懸殊，非如此不足以言統計，非謂須隨時隨地一一恰合實裝重量，強用會計之方法於統計也。統計之數有時不能完全採取實數，幾爲稍諳統計學者所共悉，惟所用假定之數，必須有合理之依據，而後方不之武斷與背謬。吾人所主張者，卽各路應就某時期內，計算一種沿途零担車之平均重量，作爲標準，卽以此種標準適用於該路。以後運輸狀況如有重要變遷，仍應擇時編算，以觀其有無劇變，藉資改正，非謂一種標準可永久適用也。然在平時固不必逐月變換，以符所謂實際，蓋如所採之編算時期選擇適當，足資代表(Representative or adequate sample)則按統計學中之平均原則，所得之數必與實數出入有限，且盈絀可以互消，此又統計學中之常識耳。

美國鐵路之車輛並非多數爲四十噸者，其種類甚多，大小不一，裝載零貨之蓬車頗多爲六〇、〇〇〇磅載重量者，亦頗多爲八〇、〇〇〇磅者，(詳後)其於沿途零担車不按車輛容積噸數幾分之幾折算者，非所用者多屬四十噸車之故，實因沿途零担車與整車不同，車輛大者載貨重量未必比例較大，小者未必比例較小，儘有用四十噸車之路，平均每車祇裝十噸者，用二十五噸車之路平均每車亦能裝十噸者，故須用統計方法，求得一種標準噸數以資代表，則結果較爲可恃。吾國各路間固有車輛大小之別，然在同一路綫，每日用於載運沿途零貨之車輛，常無多大出入，故以標準噸數計算，非特不至不合，且亦反較按容積噸數計算爲準也。

況在吾國鐵路，車輛噸量大者，容積(卽立方公尺數)未必比例較大，噸量小者容積未必比例較小，例如膠濟路之十五噸蓬車與四十噸蓬車噸量相差懸殊，而容積相差有限，卽其著例。零貨之中，輕浮貨物當佔多數，以噸量較大之車裝之，有時未必能得較多之重量，於此可見按車輛載重噸數折算一法尤難一律適用於吾國各路也。

(二)軍隊或旅客以貨車裝載者旣須計算其延人公里，則此項貨車性質上非客車而何？若所用車輛仍作貨車看待，而所載內容則作旅客統計，則猶張冠李戴，安能符合統計原則？至於計算列車載重與機車載重能力之比率一端，則凡附有客車之列車，其載重均難準確計算，例如混合列車有客貨車輛兩種，所有客車之載重卽不能加以計算。今用貨車裝載軍隊或旅客，如列車內不掛裝貨車輛卽應視同旅客列車，如附掛裝貨車輛，卽應視同混合列車，接混合列車辦法處理，初不以所用車輛之爲客爲貨而有異也，又扣除貨車代客車用之「車日」一節，事實上亦不甚難，祇須調度所備一相當紀錄卽可。

貨車裝載行李包裹亦應視作客車，其理正復相同；況在吾國鐵路，直達聯運包裹有用貨車裝載而附掛於旅客列車者，此種貨車更應作爲客車看待，旣作客車看待，卽不必計算載重。今沿途零担車按載重量四分之一折算一法，既已無合理之根據，而謂包裹行李車亦可同樣適用，尤嫌武斷。況根本客車統計之中已無計算載重之必要乎？

三　空貨車噸公里佔共計貨車噸公里百分數問題

空貨車公里佔共計貨車公里百分數一物已承採用加入，良用欣慰。吾人以為此數為必不可少之單位，舍此而用噸里代之，殊有夾雜混淆之弊。且吾人所謂空駛狀況嚴重與否云者，原指管理上之效率而言，非指鐵路因空車里程所受之損失程度而言。良以吾國鐵路貨車回空，一部分固由於自然經濟情形所致（卽在他國亦然），然因卸車遲延以致他路車輛不及裝貨而回空者有之，重車未能及時卸空利用而須另撥空車以應付者有之，不圖設法招攬貨運或變通普通運價以利用回空者有之，管理上之問題不一而足，今車輛統計既在蠡測運用之效率，則此項觀點自宜首居重要地位，至於觀察鐵路因空車行駛而受之損失程度，則反應由空貨車噸公里總數中求之，不得由空貨車噸公里佔共計貨車噸公里之百分數中求之，蓋總數為絕對數，足以顯示車輛虛糜之程度，而百分數則僅為比較數，不足以示損失之大小。例如空貨車噸公里增加，而共計貨車噸公里亦比例增加時，則百分數雖不變，而損失固已加多，用百分數以表示之，反不足以顯示損失之大小矣。

美國鐵路之貨車並非多數為四十噸者，論其載重限度，則蓬車及平車多數為六〇、〇〇

○磅（約合二十七公噸）及八○、○○○磅（約合三十六公噸）兩種，五○、○○○磅以下者亦有之。牲口車及冷藏車則較小，多數爲六○、○○○磅，煤車則較大，以一○○、○○○磅爲最多，八○、○○○磅次之。近年車輛容積逐漸加大，二○○、○○○磅以上者亦已不在少數。蓋車輛載重量之大小須以貨物性質爲衡，牲畜蔬果等物，每車載重較少，無須載重能力甚大之車，煤則質地甚重，並能滿載，故以噸量較大之車爲宜，是以一國鐵路之車輛決不能集中於一種噸位，不問貨物之性質與其需要之如何也。況美國鐵路歷年逐漸採用較大之車，以求車輛皮重對貨物實重比例之減少，其逐年車輛噸量之變遷尤甚於他國，爲先後各年比較起見，似尤有計及噸里之必要，其所以未見計及者，亦以運用之效率與車輛之大小無關耳。

四　每列車公里之貨車噸公里問題

每列車公里之貨車噸公里一數，謂係平均每列車所能裝載之貨物噸數，亦殊不確。蓋每列車所能拖運之重量均爲機車牽引力所限制，不能以所載貨車之容積爲衡：故實際上每列車平均所有貨車容積噸數決不足以表示列車載貨之能力，請言其故：某列車掛有重車三十輛，空車十輛，已滿足機車所能拖運之調整噸數，若每車平均容積爲三十噸，各車均不中途摘掛，則該列車所有貨車容積噸數（卽每列車里之貨車噸公里）應爲一，二○○噸（40×30=1,200）

試思此一、二〇〇噸是否代表該列車所能拖運之貨物噸數，則吾敢答之曰否。蓋該列車掛有空車十輛，若用以裝貨，則必不能將此十輛盡行掛走，因裝貨之後，重量增高，機車牽引力將不敷也。結果或僅能掛走五輛，計共掛重車三十五輛，所有貨車容積噸數須由一、二〇〇噸減爲一、〇五〇噸（35×30＝1050）其不能以一、二〇〇噸作爲載貨容積之標準，殆已彰彰明甚。足見每列車公里之貨車噸公里一數實無實際意義可言，亦無實際作用可見，西國鐵路之所以不編此數，蓋非無故矣。

五　每貨車每日之貨車噸公里問題

欲以每貨車每日之貨車噸公里一數，表示「每貨車每日有載運若干貨物噸公里之可能，」尤屬似是而非。蓋同一車輛，週轉速則載貨之可能數量自大，週轉緩則自小：譬如有貨車一輛全月停留不用，則其每車每日之貨物噸公里必等於零，然不可謂該車之載貨可能數量亦等於零，由此可見貨車之載貨能力，實與週轉速度息息相關，不能以實際運行所得之數爲衡。若謂每貨車每日之貨車噸公里逐月逐年必有增減，即足以表示貨車載貨能力之進步或退步，則亦屬架床叠屋之法。蓋表示貨車之流動程度，已有每貨車每日之貨車公里，表示貨車之生利成績，已有每貨車每日之貨物噸公里，兩者皆以實際運用之結果爲根據，又何用每貨車每日之貨車噸公里爲哉？若欲用以與每貨車每日之貨物噸公里比較，以覘裝貨可能數量與裝貨實在數量之關係，則何不直接比較，貨車噸公里與貨物噸公里兩數，又何庸以每車每日表示之耶？故無論從何方面觀察，此項單位非特成爲贅物，抑且易啓誤會（如以此數作爲每車每日之裝貨可能數量是，）終不如廢除之之爲愈也。

六 貨車分類統計問題

吾國鐵路之守車固有以車位之一部分載貨者，亦有以貨車代守車用者，然不能以此而謂專用守車里程亦無劃分之必要。吾人以爲原屬守車而常用以兼裝貨物者應視爲貨車，或原屬貨車而有時掛作守車之用者亦仍應視爲貨車，惟貨車之經指定作守車用而不裝貨者則應視爲守車。且各路之中儘有專用之守車，尤應加以劃分，不得以上項特殊情形而謂專用守車亦無劃分之必要也。

各種貨車分類統計，在吾國鐵路尤見需要，蓋在吾國，特種貨車雖不如外國之多，然所有普通貨車種類龐雜，大小不一，常有某種貨車以噸位及容積關係，需求較少，運用較低；某種貨車需求較大，運用較高；例如各路車輛常有噸位小而容積（立方公尺）大者，託運輕浮貨物之客商咸爭求之。有噸位大而容積並不比例加大者，託運輕浮貨物之客商咸不樂用之，亦有噸位相同而容積互異者，客商恆欲用容積大而棄容積小者：此外當有多種車輛，聯運不能過軌以致減少其運用之機會者，亦有某種車輛常有燒軸或損壞情事，以致減低其運用成績者，諸如此類，不勝枚舉，若能加以相當類別，以統計其里程，則何種車輛特別呆滯；何種車輛特別流動，以及各種車輛運用成績之高低，皆可瞭然，對於添購新車，改造舊車，與夫變通車輛之互用，增進車輛之效率，均有莫大之助益，安得謂爲「殊無必要」哉。至於編算手續亦不如理想之煩，祇須規定車輛種類，每種定一記號，將此記號塡入列車報單，卽可用算盤或計算機分別加算其里程，每一報單，可於二三分鐘內畢其事，殊無若何困難之可言也。

七　破壞貨車輛數與現有貨車輛數之比率問題

按原定統計辦法，計算「車日」時，係將損壞車輛包括在內，厥後又加修改，將損壞貨車除去不計，其意以爲損壞車輛不能運用，觀察運用效率應以完好車輛爲限，不知車輛無論完好或損壞，均爲路產，吾人須加以觀察者卽某路有如許之車輛，每月共能產生貨物噸公里幾何，與貨車公里幾何，每車每日平均幾何，以覘其生利成績與流動程度，初不以完好與損壞而有異也。不然，損壞車輛增多或修理時間延長時，其每車每日之貨物噸公里與貨車公里可仍不見減少，反之亦仍不見加多，勢必失去全部車輛運用成績之眞相矣。或謂吾國鐵路組織大都爲分處制，修車者爲機務處，用車者爲車務處，後者不能統制車輛之修理，若修理遲延或損壞車輛增多，則必減低車務處之運用成績，豈得謂平？曰此損壞貨車輛數與現有貨車輛數比率之所以應編算加入也。有此比率，則可與上項統計互相參證，一面不失全部貨車運用成績之眞相，一面仍可察覺損壞車輛對於運用成績之影響，實屬一舉而兩得者，此吾人之所以有此主張也。且爲車輛統計之完備計，亦有加入此項單位之必要，似不能謂爲無需要而又無意義也。

八 客車分類統計問題

客車分類里程統計，具有兩大作用：(一)可用以觀察每種客車流動運用之程度，尤以備用客車較多之路爲甚；(二)可用以觀察逐年客運設備與業務之演變。例如各等臥車里程逐年增加，卽可見臥車業務之發展。膳車里程之逐年增加，卽可知餐務設施之推廣，客廳車觀望車等里程之逐年增加，卽可見客運業務之改良，行李車，郵政車，包裹車等里程之逐年增加，卽可知此項客運附屬業務之推進。凡此皆不能於營業統計中求之；例如臥車旅客延人公里增加，或由於現有臥車所載人數之增多，而非由於臥車里程之增多，，膳車用膳人數與收入之增加，或由於現有膳車營業之增進，而非由於膳車里程之增加，其他各項莫不皆然，故欲觀一路各種客運設施之演變，非有客車里程分類統計不可。

計算各種客車里程，尤較計算各種貨車里程爲簡易；於此應首先認識者，卽混合車輛（如頭二等車，行李車長等）應視爲客車之一種，不必割裂計算，例如行李車長車一輛不必以半輛作行李車，以半輛作車長車計算，儘可作爲客車之一種，而獨立計算其里程，蓋吾人之目的在觀察每種車輛之運用成績與每每種車輛里程之逐年增加，按期作一貫之比較，殊無割裂之必要也。每種客車定一記號，將此記號塡入列車報單編算時每一列車可備一紙，將列車次數及其經行里程塡入該紙上端，然後羅列各種之記號。凡客車與列車行程同其終始者，卽在其記號下隨手記其輛數，不必計其里程，例如該列車有頭等臥車三輛。卽頭等臥車之記號下註一「3」字，餘類推，遇有客車中途摘掛者始有隨時註以里程之必要。迨至月終，將可將各種客車之輛數相加，而以加得之總數乘該列車之經行里程（中途摘掛之車除外，幷將其註明之里程加入，）卽得各種車輛之里程，將各列車合計之，卽得全路各種客車之里程，此法極爲簡易，在美國鐵路用之，頗不費事；以如此簡單之手續，而獲條分縷晰之統計，爲得爲失，固不必煩言矣：

九　每旅客列車鐘點之列車公里問題

每旅客列車鐘點之列車公里，卽爲旅客列車之平均速度，原可自各路行車時刻表中求之，非特每一列車之平均速度極易求得，卽各種快慢列車之平均速度，亦可平均計算，簡易之極。固不必列入列車統計，而逐月爲之計算也。且旅客列車之速度常爲旅客之需要及路線設備之狀況所限，管理者不能隨時左右之，故逐月計算其速度，對於增進行車效率，鮮有補益。至於旅客列車之延誤，原應另編列車延誤統計，分別各種延誤原因，顯示每種原因延誤之時間，與列車準點之百分數等，較諸僅有實際平均速度，功用不可以同日語。蓋僅知實際平均速度之昇降，而不知其原因，更不知何種原因較爲重要，則於改進行車效率，仍有知其然而不知其所然之患。此西國鐵路之所以不算旅客列車鐘點，更算每旅客列車鐘點之列車公里，良有以耳。

十　每旅客列車鐘點之延人公里問題

延人公里與列車鐘點爲渺不相關之物，吾人已言之詳矣。每列車鐘點之延人公里既不能表示行車之效率，復不能表示車輛運用之成績，先進國之鐵路均無此項統計單位，不知吾國果有何種本國實際情形，而需要此項統計？所謂「表示成績之好壞」者，不知係何所指？將謂客運用之成績乎？則原有延人公里佔客座公里百分數之統計，足資觀察，而此數之不能表示客車之運用又不待智者而知；將謂行車之成績乎？則列車速度均屬固定，設有延誤，應有延誤統計以顯示之，固不必迂迴曲折，求諸每列車鐘點之延人公里，徒增觀察之謬誤；且延人公里設有減少，而列車行駛均屬準點，則每列車鐘點之延人公里亦必減少，是豈行車成績退步之表現乎？即就籠統之意義言之，每列車鐘點之延人公里大者未必爲較好之現象，小者未必爲較壞之現象，例如某路爲改進客運業務計，減少旅客列車所掛車數，提高行駛速率，增加列車次數，則行駛雖較速，而每列車鐘點之延人公里往往反須較少，因列車內客座數之減少往往須甚於列車速度之增加(Th erevenue length of the train has to be reduced more than proportionately with an increase in its speed) 此則證諸任何旅客列車皆屬歷歷不爽者，可見此項統計數字之升降非特不足以辨好壞，抑且易啓相反之印象，誠宜力避之，以免錯誤觀念之發生。西國鐵路之所以不編此數者，誠又非無因矣。

至於編組旅客列車，尤無須參考是項統計，所須參考者應爲每列車旅客人數，與每客座(或每客車)公里延人公里數，藉以決定應掛各種車數之多寡；而列車速度則原應就可能範圍內力求其高，停站時間力求其少，固均不必以每列車公里延人公里爲參考之資也。

十一 延人公里分級統計問題

延人公里分級統計業已見諸實行，誠屬一種改進，故已不成問題，不必再加討論矣。

十二 每客車每日之客座公里問題

每客車每日之客座公里謂與每貨車每日之貨車噸公里相同，是固誠然。每貨車每日之貨車噸公里不能用以表示每車每日之載貨能力既已詳述於前，則每客車每日之客座公里能否代表載客可能數量要亦不辯而自明。卽使退一步言，此數果能代表每車每日之載客容量矣，然知之亦有何用？論客車流動之程度，則已有每客車每日之客車公里，論客車之生利成績，則已有每客車每日之延人公里，此外更有何種用處？若以之作各路之比較，則各路車輛種類構造與容積不同，根本無意義可言；若以之作一路各時期之比較，則反不如用每客車每日之客車公里，殊無牽及客座數之必要。若欲以之比較每客車每日之延人公里，則原已有延人公里佔客座公里百分數，甯非陷於重複，然則此數之作用，亦殊難言矣。

十三　貨車停站時間統計問題

貨車停站統計之大病，一在編造之不便，易啓敷衍蒙混之弊，致結果多不可靠；二在不論有無延誤，每一車輛自始至終一律加以計算，費力多而收效少。故吾人主張根本改造，而不主張採用輔助記載方法，徒作治標之計。蓋縱令記載方法完備，虛僞之弊盡除，亦有得不償失之患。上次文內未提改造之具體方法，因該文仍以評論爲主，故未列入，今旣提及此點，乃不得不將芻見簡述之。

在討論辦法以前，吾人須先認識者約有三點：（一）觀察貨站或車場處理貨車之快慢及其效率應作通盤之鳥瞰，不必就每一車輛記其時刻，徒增煩擾；（二）場所不同，則稽核車輛之方法亦應不同，不得以同一之刻板方法適用於貨棧，貨場，車場，等，徒使填報困難，不合實際；（三）統計數字應力求簡便而有根據，幷在可能範圍內，利用運輸上原應備具之數字，憑以填造：以節手續而增準確。循此原則，謹請參照西國鐵路之方法與吾國鐵路之狀況，作極簡要之建議如次：

（一）**整車貨場處理車輛效率統計**　整車貨場或專用岔道處理車輛之快慢大半須以裝卸之快慢爲衡，其最簡便而有效力之考察方法，不在計算每一車輛之裝卸時間，而在觀察全部車輛裝出或卸空之速度 Speed in the release of equipment 請觀下列報告，即可明瞭：

……站整車貨場貨車統計日報表

自　月　日十八點至　月　日十八點

(1) 昨日十八點鐘留站空車（包括未裝完全重車）	(2) 昨日十八點鐘未卸重車	(3) 本日收到空車	(4) 總計 (1)+(2)+(3)	(5) 本日調出空重車輛 ×一合計	(6) 本日卸空留站車亡	(7) 本日裝出及卸空車輛 (5)+(6)	(8) (7)÷4)	(9) (7)項超過(4)項車輛數	(10) 本日收到重車	(11) (9)÷(10)	(12) 本日十八點鐘留站空車（包括(6)項及未裝完重車）	(13) 本日十八點鐘未卸重車
20	110	85	215	210 45 255	10	265	132.6%	50	248	24.2%	10	198

（"×"—重車"—"—空車）

上表第（8）項用以表示本日裝出及卸空車輛，當昨日留站空車，昨日待卸重及本日收到空車之百分比，此數若在百分之百以下，即足顯示裝卸之遲緩，意即本日應裝出或卸空之車輛猶未能悉數裝出或卸空也。若在百分之百以上，即足表示裝卸之迅速，其超過百分之百以上之部分即本日到站重車能於當日卸空或卸後復行裝出者。爲進一步觀察計，乃得第（11）項，用以表示本日到達之重車即於當日卸空或卸後復裝之輛數，當全日到達重車輛數之比率，此項比率愈高，即足表現裝卸之愈速，殊易判斷也。人凡第（8）項之數字總宜不在百分之下，否則即有昨日遺下重車至今日猶未卸空，或今日收到之空車（連同昨日遺下空車及未裝重車）猶未裝出之弊。其能超過百分之百之數愈高則愈佳。第（11）項之百分數亦以愈大愈好，蓋愈大則今日到達之重車能於今日卸空或重行裝出者必愈多也。第(5)項「本日調出空車輛」應指已由貨站通知調車場調出者而言，不必問其實際上已否在十八點鐘調出也。第(6)項，「本日卸空留站車輛，」應以留站備用之車爲限（連本日卸空本日裝貨未畢之車在內，）其不必留備明日裝貨者，應通知調車場調出，列入第(5)項下，又本日收到空車或昨日留下空車至本日十八點鐘尙未裝貨或尙未裝畢亦不應列入第（5）項下，但應在第(12)項下包括之。

表內各項數字均爲貨場原應備具者，非專爲統計而編造，塡報毫不費事，而結果則與計算每輛貨車之停留時間同其功用，故繁簡之別不可以同日語。或謂如子之法，則每輛貨車平均裝貨卸貨之時間不能以數字表現，卽每車停留貨場之平均時間無從明悉，豈得謂爲完備？曰吾人觀察貨場處理貨車之快慢，原不必由每輛貨車之平均停場時間中求之，徒使陷於困難繁複，而結果轉不可恃。若欲測知每車之平均停留時間或裝貨卸貨時間，原可選擇相當時間作一次之編算，以求得一種代表之數，藉知每車平均耗於裝卸之時間若干，耗於運行之時間若干等，此則在西國鐵路亦常偶一爲之，固無待逐年逐月之編算也。

再由上表內之數字，對於待卸重車之當日卸空而又當日裝貨調出者，亦可加以相當統計，如此項車輛當待卸重車之百分率增進，卽足見裝卸速度之增高，計算極易而有助於貨場處理車輛效率之考察者甚巨，茲列算式如次，以臻明瞭：

$$\frac{\underset{(5)\times}{\text{今日調出重車輛數}}-\left(\underset{(1)}{\text{昨日十八點留站空車}}+\underset{(3)}{\text{本日收到空車}}-\underset{(12)}{\text{本日十八點留站空車}}+\underset{(10)}{\text{本日卸空留站車輛}}\right)}{\underset{(2)}{\text{昨日十八點未卸重車}}+\underset{(10)}{\text{本日收到重車}}}=\frac{210-(20+85-10+10)}{10+248}=\frac{210-105}{358}=\frac{105}{358}=29.3\%$$

上列百分數29.3%卽當日卸空當日復行裝出之車輛當全日全場待卸重車之比率，易言之，卽每百輛卸重車之中有二九．三輛當日卸空而又當日裝貨調出者，此數會高，則亦裝卸愈速之表現，計算時不必另用他數，祇須就表內已有之數字加以核計，亦一事半功倍之法也。

（二）**調車場處理車輛效率統計** 調車場與貨場之性質絕不相同，前者在司車輛之調入及調出，後者在司車輛之裝貨及卸貨，故兩者所用之統計基本數字亦應互異。觀察調車場處理車輛之快慢，亦不在計算每輛貨車之停場時間，而在表現其全部車輛流動之速度，其法亦極簡易，請觀次頁之調車場貨車統計日報表卽可知之。

每一調車場每日二十四點鐘時應編造上項報告送呈車務處，車務處卽可據以編算下列之百分數：

$$\frac{\text{本日出場車輛總數[卽(14)項]}+\text{本日備用車輛數[卽(15)(乙)項]}}{\text{昨日存場及本日入場車輛總數[卽(7)項]}}=\frac{867+17}{1032}=85.7\%$$

上項百分數卽足以表現調車場處理車輛之快慢，其數愈高，卽滯留車場之車輛愈少，例如此數若達百分之百時，卽爲全日全部應處理之車輛均已處理完畢之表現，可謂效率之最高峯，惟事實上常難達此最高紀錄耳。表內各項數字亦爲調車場原應備具者，非專爲統計而編

調車場貨車統計日報表

（自 月 日二十四點至 月 日二十四點）

昨日存場時及本日入場車輛

(1) 昨日二十四點鐘存放車輛 (甲) 待掛車輛 ×	(甲) —	(乙) 備用車輛 —	(丙) 損壞車輛 ×	(丙) —	(丁) 合計 ×	(丁) —	(2) 由到達列車掛來 ×	(2) —	(3) 由貨場或私岔調出 ×	(3) —	(4) 他路過軌本路 ×	(4) —	(5) 由零担貨棧調出 ×	(5) —	(6) 由修車房調出 ×	(6) —	(7) 總數 (1)項至(6)項 ×	(7) —	(7) 合計
120	35	20	—	10	120	65	339	88	212	95	25	37	22	26	1	5	716	316	1032

本日出場及本日存場車輛

(9) 由出發列車掛出 ×	(9) —	(10) 調入貨場及私岔 ×	(10) —	(11) 本路過軌外路 ×	(11) —	(12) 調入零担貨棧 ×	(12) —	(13) 調入修車房 ×	(13) —	(14) 出場車輛總數 (9)項至(13)項 ×	(14) —	(14) 合計	(15) 本日二十四點鐘存場車輛 (甲) 待掛車輛 ×	(甲) —	(乙) 備用車輛 —	(丙) 損壞車輛 ×	(丙) —	(丁) 合計 ×	(丁) —	(16) 總數 ×	(16) —	(16) 合計
85	92	231	75	56	65	24	25	2	12	598	269	867	115	28	17	3	2	118	47	716	316	1032

（"×"係重車記號"—"係空車記號）

造故手續上亦極爲簡便，較諸計算每輛貨車之時間，其繁簡不可以道里計。玆復將各數應有之來源列述如次，以臻明瞭：

甲 昨日存場及本日入場車輛

（1）昨日二十四鐘存場車輛——即由昨日日報表内「本日二十四鐘存場車輛」（（15）項）轉錄。

（2）由到達車列掛來車輛——每一列車應由車長備具到達列車車號單Inbound Train Consist List 一紙，於到達時交由調車場備查，此數卽由該單得之。現時吾國所用之車號記錄簿須由車號司事於列車到達後抄錄填造，實不如責成車長於中途運行時填造車號單之節省時間，車號司事祇須按單點查一過，在北美鐵路盛行此法。似足採取。

（3）由貨場或私岔調出車輛——貨場遇有空重車輛須由公用岔道或專用岔道調入車場編配或存放時，應備調車通知單Drjlling order交由車場據以調出，此單在美國鐵路均用之，吾國尚付缺如，似應加入，由此單據，則此項空重車輛數目可以一索得之。惟本日貨場業已通知車場調出之車輛，卽應一律作爲本日調出之車輛計算，不問實際上調出之爲何時也。蓋必如是，而後車場貨場之責任可以劃分，否則貨場或於本日十八時通知調出，而車場始於次日一二時往調，若以實際調出之時刻爲準，則統計將失其準確矣。

（4）由他路過軌本路車輛——可由聯運車輛交付通知書中得之。

（5）由零担貨棧調出車空——零担貨棧有車調出時亦應備具調車通知單，與整車貨場無異。

（6）由修車調出車輛——修車廠房或修車軌道由機務人員管理，如有修好之車交由調車場調出，原應有交付單據，足爲此項車輛數之來源。

乙　本日出場及本日存場車輛

（1）由出發列車掛出車輛——列車待發之前應由調車場備具出發列車輛號單Outbound Train Consist List 交由車長帶去，而以一份存查，此項車數卽可由存查之一份中得之。

(2)調入貨場及私岔車輛——調車場有調入貨場及私岔時，原應備具調車單 Switching List 交由調車夫執行，此單卽爲本項車輛數目之根據。

(3)本路過軌外路車輛——可由聯運車輛交付通知書中得之。

(4)調入零担貨棧車輛——與第(2)項同。

(5)調入修車房車輛——與由修車房調出者同。

(6)本日二十四鐘存場車輛——調車場對於存場車輛，孰爲待掛，孰爲備用或存儲孰爲損壞，原應備有紀錄，以便次日分別處理，故此數之來源亦無須另行設法尋覓也。

由以上各點觀之，可見利用現成數字，而獲有用之處理車輛效率統計，其法之合算，卽在於此。至於欲知每車平均耗於各種處理手續之時間，則列車編配時間暨自入場至出場時間，原亦應有紀錄，卽(1)到達時刻，(2)開始編配時刻，(3)編配完畢時刻，(4)出發時刻等，在西國各大車場莫不加以紀錄，幷明定標準以資遵守，然固不必就每一車輛加以計算也。他如調入或調出貨場，私岔貨棧，修車房等時間以及聯運過軌時間，雖不能每日就各批車輛一一加以計算，然亦大可擇一相當時期加以統計，以資代表，決無逐日逐輛計算之必要也。

在美國鐵路，調車場且有每日清查在場車輛之舉，凡清查時查有車輛停留逾限者（例如超過二十四小時是，惟備用或存儲車輛當然除外，）即摘錄之，列報調車場場長，以便趕速處理，亦一防止車輛滯留之有效方法也。

零担貨棧處理車輛效率可不必加以統計，因零貨車輛大都可以當日進出貨棧，不若整車之複雜，惟車場處理零貨車之成績，則已於上調車場貨車統計日報表中有之矣。

（3）沿途各站處理車輛效率統計　以上兩項均指終點大站而言，沿途各站類多無貨場與車場之分，故情形較爲簡單。其僅有零貨上下之站自無所謂處理車輛問題，所須加以統計者，可以較大之站有整車貨物或整裝零担貨用進出者爲限。若將上述整車貨場車統計日報表，稍加變通，卽可適用於此種沿途各站，惟統計之編算不妨以每旬爲單位，因車輛數目較少，且常有今日有車進出，明日無車進出者，似無按日計算之必要也。列式如次，以便解釋：

…………站貨車統計旬報表

（自　月　日十八點鐘至　月　日十八點鐘）

日期	(1) 昨日十八點鐘留站空車（包括未裝畢重車）	(2) 昨日十八點鐘未卸重車	(3) 昨日十八點鐘待掛車輛	(4) 本日收到空車	(5) 總數(1)+(2)+(3)+(4)	(6) 本日掛出空重車輛	(7) 本日十八點鐘待掛車輛	(8) 本日卸空留站空車	(9) 本日裝出及卸空車輛(6)+(7)+(8)	(10) (9)÷(5)	(11) (9)項超過(5)項車輛數	(12) 本日收到重車	(13) (11)+(12)	(14) 本日十八點鐘留站空車	(15) 本日十八點鐘未卸重車
1	2	3	1	1	7	3	2	1	6		—	2		2	2
2	2	2	2	3	9	6	2	1	9		—	2		1	2
3	1	2	2	2	7	6	1	—	7		—	1		—	1
4	—	1	1	4	6	4	1	—	5		—	3		1	3

5	1	3	1	2	7	2	1	2	5		—	3		3	5
6	3	5	1	—	9	10	2	1	13		4	5		1	1
7	1	1	2	3	7	6	3	1	10		3	4		1	1
8	1	1	3	1	6	4	1	1	6		—	—		1	—
9	1	—	1	4	6	6	3	1	10		4	6		1	2
10	1	2	3	3	9	5	1	2	8		—	3		3	3
	13	20	17	23	73	52	17	10	79	108.2%	11	30	36.6%	14	20

(註) [(5)÷(12)]−[(6)+(7)]=(14)+(15)

上表與大站整車貨場所用者計有異點二：(一)大站整車貨場待掛之車輛應於日終通知調車場調出，故可一併列入「本日調出車輛」項下，不必另立項目；沿途站之無車場者日終待掛車輛須俟列車經過，始能掛走，故應與掛出車輛劃分，另列一項填報。(二)大站整車貨場之處理車輛狀況應按日列報，按日計算，沿途站則可按日填入旬報表至旬末結總呈報，所有百分數祇須按旬計算可也。至於當日卸空復裝車輛之統計，在車輛進出較少之站，似不妨從略耳。

總之，無論貨場，車場，及沿途各站，如欲考察其處理車輛之效率，儘可利用運輸上原應備具之數字，作通盤之觀察，不必就每一車輛計算其時刻。至於每車平均時間耗於裝貨卸貨者幾何，編配調掛者幾何，過軌，檢驗修理者幾何，儘可選擇相當試算時期 Test Period 加以試算，以供研究參考之用，若每車每日一一統計之，殊有事倍功半之患也。

結論

吾人主張各點，固多以西國鐵路之良法爲依據，然決非不顧本國鐵路之現狀而盲從一切者可比。凡有合理根據與實際效用之辦法而又便於實行者吾人無不贊同，否則吾人無不反對，決不敢强詞而奪理也。此則當爲讀者所共見，應無多事聲述之必要耳。

此外猶有言者，卽一切統計單位應以有意義有效用爲要旨，不得因有現成數字，强用兩種無關之數，加以不合理之繫聯，而竟以爲有益無損。其足引起錯誤觀念者，尤宜力避之，以免發生有損無益之結果。蓋兩種無關數字之可作不合理之繫聯者，在鐵路統計數字中，實屬指不勝屈，若一一作如是觀，則統計之學根本尙有講求之必要耶？

子曰：「君子易事而難說也，說之不以道，不說也，及其使人也，器之。小人難事而易說也，說之雖不以道，說也，及其使人也，求備焉。」

子曰：「可與言而不與之言，失人；不可與言而與之言，失言。知者不失人，亦不失言。」

子曰：「君子不以言擧人，不以人廢言。」

——論語——

管理二月刊

第一卷 第三期
民國二十五年九月

論著

演講

譯述

古今領袖人物言行札記

報告

轉載

通訊

管理二月刊

第一卷 第四期
民國二十五年十一月

論著

譯述

書評

運價與物價（C 5.）

熊大惠

運價，爲構成商品生產費之一部分，就原則而論，此固無庸置疑，顧市場價格，並非以生產費爲惟一之決定因素，是以有謂農民運其產品於市，其所得之價乃包括運價在內，易言之，農產品在消費市場之價格，減去運價以後，始爲農民所得之價格，反之，農民購買工業品，其所付之價亦包括運價在內，是其所付之價除出廠價格以外，尚須加上運價，果如此說，則運價之負担者胥爲農民，蓋工業品之運價由消費者負担，農產品之運價，由生產者負担，故運價之負担者皆爲農民矣。此種說法，常爲運輸機關所炫弄，當農民或其他生產者要求減低運價時，運輸商常引運價由消費者負担一語以自辯，反之當消費者要求減低運價時運輸商常引運價由生產者或商人負担一語以自辯，並謂卽使運價影響於消費市場之價格，亦屬極微。

由此以觀，運價對於物價之關係，其情形至爲複雜，本篇目的卽在根據經濟原理，詳加分析，以明運價對於物價之關係。

就原則論，運價爲生產費中之一部分，生產費一詞，廣義言之，無論何種商品，在到達消費者之手以前一切費用，均應包括在內，運費爲在此過程中費用之一部份，故運費亦屬生產費，運費既爲生產費之一部分，則運費，在長期間內，亦如其他生產費一樣，終必由消費者負担之，在短期內，物價之變動，與生產未必一致，但在長期間內，物價祇少須能報償生產費，否則，其物必將停止生產。

在長時期中，運價雖將由消費者負担，但運價增加，未必常能轉嫁於消費者此因物價提高以後，將使消費減縮故也，消費減少、物價回跌，生產亦不能不重行調整，使供求趨於另一新平衡之點。

運價之轉嫁，實與租稅轉嫁之法則無異，在自由競爭之下，運價提高所能轉嫁之程度，要視供求性而定其原理，可以普通經濟學上之供求曲線解釋之，假定運價之提高，不致於使運貨者舍本路而就他路，或生產地點因以改變，以逃避本路高昂運價之負担，則下面之分析，甚有助於吾人對運價與物價關係之暸解。

某一商品之需要，伸縮性愈小者，其價格之變動影響於其消費者愈少，而其運價之提高轉嫁於消費者則愈多，反之，如其需要之伸縮性愈大則運價之提高所能轉嫁於消費者亦愈少，下圖甲DD表示伸縮性較少之需要曲線，SS表示供給方面之生產費運費亦包括在內，其價格爲OP，今如將運價提高，使生產數由SS增爲，S'S'，價格由OP增至OP'，消費者之購買量所減不過，Q'Q，由此可知所增加之運費大部分由消費者負担，若在圖乙，DD表示縮性較大之需要曲線，其原來之供給曲線為ＳＳ，今如將運價提高至與甲圖一樣，消費者之購買量由ＯＱ減為ＯＱ，所減遠較甲圖為大，最要者卽為乙圖所增之價ＰＰ'遠不及甲圖所增之價ＰＰ'之大，此卽表示在乙圖中所增加之運費，轉嫁於消費者遠不若甲圖之多。

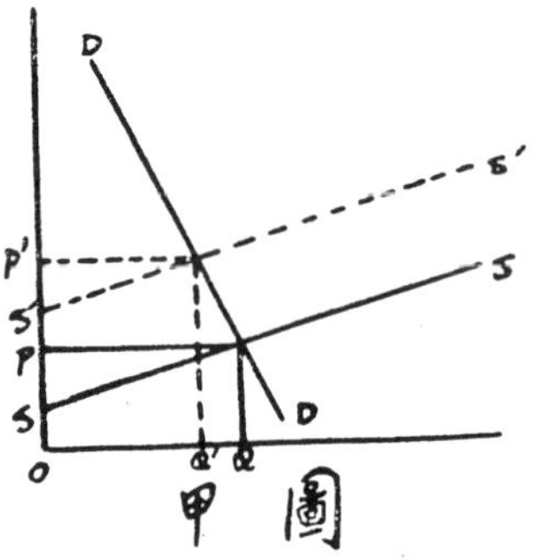

甲圖

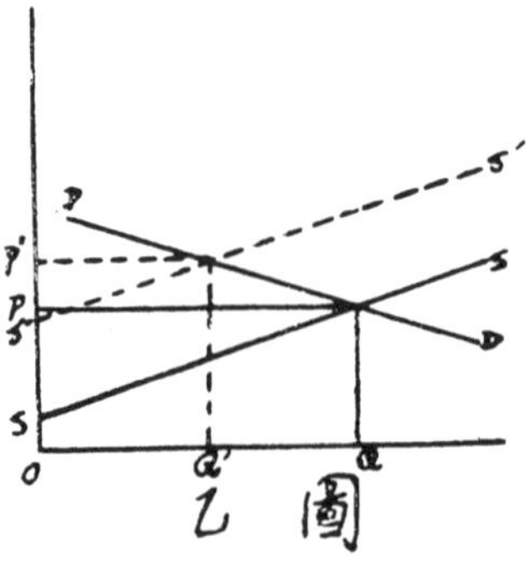

乙圖

再就供給方面之伸縮性言之，凡生產費常隨價格之變動而增減者，是為富於伸縮性之供給，反是則否，某種商品之供給，富於伸縮性者，則其運價之提高常能轉嫁於消費者反是則否，下圖丙ＳＳ表示富於伸縮性之供給曲線，運價提高以後ＳＳ變為Ｓ'Ｓ'價格由ＯＰ增至ＯＰ'圖丁ＳＳ表示甚少伸縮性之供給曲線，運價提高以後ＳＳ變為Ｓ'Ｓ'，價格由ＯＰ增至ＯＰ'，但丁圖之ＰＰ'遠不及丙圖ＰＰ'之大，由此可知供給富於伸縮性之商品運價提高以後，甚

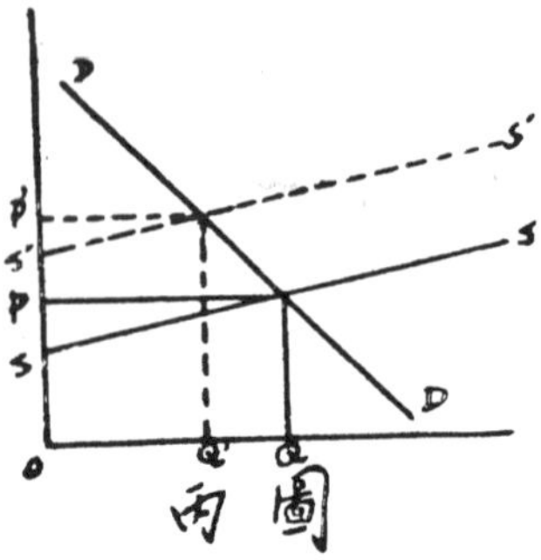

丙圖

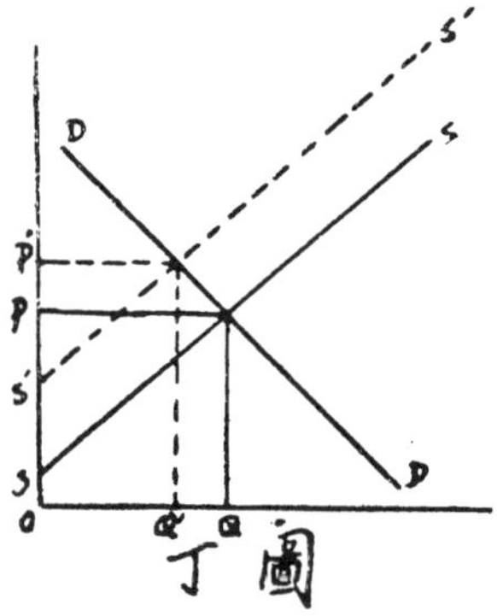

丁圖

易轉嫁於消費者，反是則否，倘供給曲線與OQ平行，則運價提高若干價格亦必提高若干，易言之，運價之提高可以使消費者完全負担之，惟其產量將視需要之伸縮而定。

上述二原則，乃係從需要與供給單方面之觀察，實際上運價之提高所能轉嫁於消費者，要視供求雙方相對的伸縮性而定，如需要之縮縮性大於供給之伸縮性，則運價之提高，大部份將歸着於生產者，如需要伸縮性小於供給之伸縮性，則運價之提高大部份將歸着於消費者。

尤可注意者，倘需要與供給同為富於伸縮性，則運價之提高，將使貨運數量大為減少，如供給與需要同為缺乏伸縮性者，則運價之提高，對於貨運影響甚少，下列二圖可以表示之：

圖戊SS與DD俱富於伸縮性，運價提高以後SS變為S'S'交易數量由OQ驟減至OQ'，圖己SS與DD伸縮性俱小，運價提高以後交易數量減少甚微。

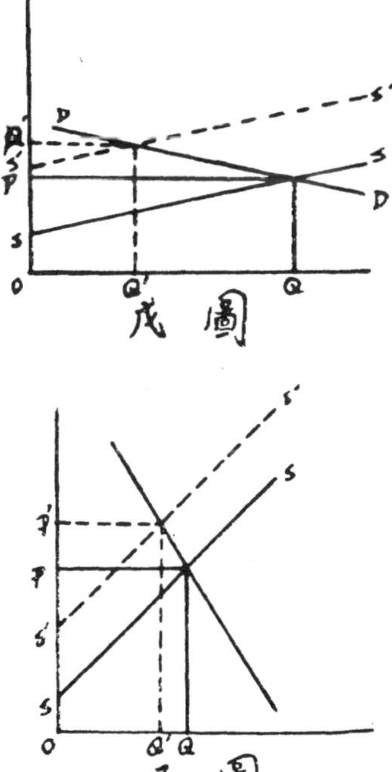

以上所舉之例，供給方面皆係屬於成本遞增者，但固定費用較大之生產組織，其成本類皆屬於遞減，在供給屬於遞減成本情形之下，運價之增加足以提高商品價格超過於運價增加之程度，此可以下圖表示之。

從上圖可以見運價之增加部分爲S'S，由此可知運價之增加反不及價格增加之多，此因運價增加以後，價格必須提高，但價格提高銷售量必減如由OQ減爲OQ'，銷售量減，生產量亦不得不減，在遞減成本之生產，生產量愈少，則每單位之生產費愈高，運價之提高，同時使每單位之生產費亦高，故PP'乃大於SS'

固定費用甚大之工業，大都有獨佔之趨勢，將有控制價格之權力，在獨佔的生產情形之下，如其出品之運價提高將會發生何種結果？亦殊値得探討，驟視之，獨佔商品之運價提高，

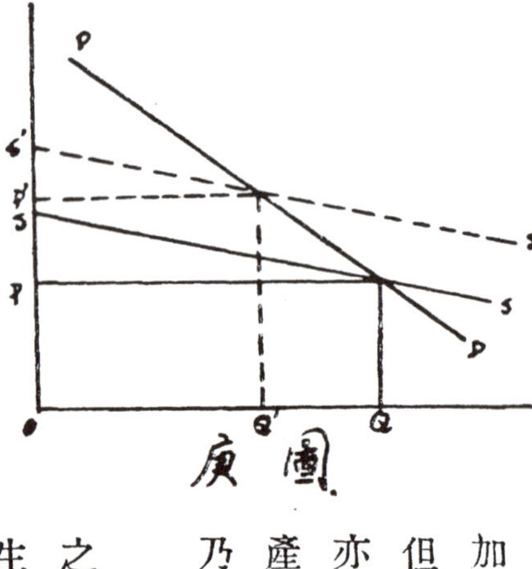

庚圖

必以爲將由消費者完全負担之，蓋獨佔者可以控制其價格也。實則未然，獨佔者之決定其價格以能獲取最大之總共盈餘爲標準，如其可以多中取利，彼寧抑其價而冀得大量之銷售也。故獨佔者之決定其售價，必須顧到需要方面之伸縮性如何，本身之生產情形如何，故獨佔商品之運價提高，是否能轉嫁於消費者亦殊不一定，供求之伸縮性，仍爲最重要之條件。

或謂提高運價如屬爲數甚微，將由生產者或中間人自行負担，而不致提高物價，此說常爲鉄路當局所持之辯護，此在短期間內，容或可信，但久而久之，物價必將隨生產費以俱增

，運價之提高，終必爲消費者之負担也。

在消費者方面，常有謂運價之提高，對於物價有積累之影響，意卽運價提高之程度行將不及物價提高之大，運價提高百分之一，物價之提高將在百分之十以上，此因中間人牟利之習慣常以其買價百分之若干爲其取利之標準，故中間人愈多。運價積累之結果亦愈大，譬如有某種物品，批發商由產地購入，包括運費在內，每件計價一元，假定取利百分之十，則其售價當爲一元一角，零售商以一元一角之價向批發商買進，取利百分之十則其售價當爲一元二角一分，今如由產地至批發商之手，每件運價增加五角，則批發商之買價爲一元五角，加上應得之利10%，其售價當爲一元六角五分，零售商以一元六角五分之價買進，其售價當爲一元八角一分五厘，是運價不過增加五角而零售物價却增加六角零五厘。（1.815－1.21＝.605），如果中間人愈多，則物價增加與運價增加之積累數必愈大，此在短時期間，容或可信，但以中間人有一固定成數之盈餘，其總共盈餘反隨運價之提高而增加（如上例批發商每件物品原來祇購一角，而運費增加五角以後，每件反可以多購五分總數爲一角五分），勢必引起競爭者之加入，結果則中間人斷難維持其原來之盈餘率，盈餘率減低，則物價自不至於隨運價之提高而爲積累之增加也。

顧吾人亦不能太重視運價提高後之長期影響，蓋供求之重行調整，必須經過相當時間，運價提高後之短期影響，自與長期不同，在短時期內，運價之提高，容或為生產者，或中間人所吸收，容或使零售物價為積累之增加要視供求之狀況而定，反之運價之減低，其利屬於買者或賣者亦須視供求之狀況而定，倘供過於求，則供者願意削價出售，運價減低之利乃為買者所得，倘求過於供則供者仍可維持原來之價格，運價減低之利乃為售者得矣。

吾人常見有許多製造品之售價，在較小之區域內不論其離原產地之遠近，皆屬一律，驟觀之，其售價似與運價無關，蓋各地之運價不同而其出品之售價則一，運價物價宜若無關，其實不然，運價仍不失為構成物價之一因素，製造家之所以取此策略，蓋有推廣其出品之作用，彼在遠地以一律之價格售出，運價之一大部份，必由另一主體為之負担，蓋其在近地亦以同一之價格出售，則運價之大部分或全部份，甚至在遠地推銷之運價，亦由近地之消費者為之負担，總之在長期間內生產者之收入至少須能報償其生產費，否則其生產必不能繼續也。

綜上所論，運價在正常情形之下，為構成商品價格之一因素，其商品價格中究竟佔若何之地位亦為吾人所應分析者，據美國農業調查聯合委員會（The Joint Commission of Agricultural Inquiry）之報告，在一九二〇—二一年，曾得許多水果及蔬菜由產地運至波斯頓，支加哥，紐約，費城及其他大城市之運費在其批發價格中所佔之百分比作一統計，發現運費所佔之成分甚高，又據美國商業聯邦委員會，一九三二年貨運進款與其所運商品到地價格之百分比統計，最高爲鮮葡萄，其運輸進款佔其在到達地點批發價百分之六十五，最低爲皮革，其運輸進款祇佔其在到達地批發價百分之一·一六，從該統計所示，可知凡貨物之價格與其重量及體積比較，係屬相對的高昂者則運費在其價格所佔之百分比必甚低，工業品大都屬於此數，反之，體質笨重，而價格低廉者則運費在其價格所佔之百分比必甚高，其次倘運價非爲遞遠遞減則運輸之距離愈長運費在商品價格所佔之百分比亦愈高。

最後吾人所欲論者卽爲運價與各個生產者之關係，由前所論，運價爲生產費之一部份，結果必將由消費者負担，此乃一般之論，若從生產者個人之立場言之，又當別論，市場價格實由社會(許多買者與許多售者)定之，市價一經定出以後，各個生產者能否在該市場推銷其出品，常受運價之牽掣，如其所得之價於給付運費以後，尙能報償其生產費，則其出品能在該市場銷售，否則卽屬不能，譬如上海小麥市場，國麥非洋麥之敵，其中有一部份原因卽爲洋麥之運費較國麥爲輕。

歸納上述之分析，吾人可以得到如下之二種結論，運費爲生產費之一部份，而加入於商品價格之內，但商品價格一經成立以後，各個生產者之銷售能力及其所得之價，要視其所付運費而異，根據此二種結論，運價提高之影響爲如何，亦可檢討而得。

第一，倘運價之增加普及於一切商品，則其結果必易轉嫁於消費者，以其不能利用代替品以避免負担之加重也，倘運價之提高僅限於一二種商品，則消費者可以利用代替品，結果，此一二種商品之銷路，必將大爲減少，甚不利於其生產者。

第二，倘某一種或某一組商品每單位之運費增加一固定之數目，不論其運輸距離之長短，則其對於所有生產者之影響均屬相同，其增加之運費所能轉嫁於消費者，要視供求之伸縮性而定，倘生產此一商品者之成本，原有高低，則成本較高之生產者或因運價之提高而不能立足矣。

第三，倘運價之增加爲比例的增加，則其結果，乂屬不同，此比例的增加，利於原來給付較低運價之客商而不利於原來給付較高運價之客商，物價雖將由此增加，但不能斷言，究將增加若干，距離市場較遠之生產者甚爲不利，距離較近之生產者則因遠距離之生產者不能在本市場立定，反因此而蒙其利也。

第四，倘運價之提高，有地方歧視性質，譬如對於來自某一生產區域之商品，提高其運價，對於別區則否，其結果至爲複雜，倘本市場之供給大部份來自該生產區域或其供給之增加甚不易由別區而得，則市價必將提高以至於與運價提高之程度相當，如此則該生產者之所得當不因運價之提高而變，但在運價不提高之生產者（卽別區中之生產者）因市價之抬高，蒙利固不淺也，且因此而增加後者之競爭力量，使前者處於不利地位，倘運價提高之生產區其供給在本市場內原屬佔據一小部份者，則運價提高之結果，彼祇好忍受所得之減少，而讓其利於別區之生產者。

子張問政，子曰：「居之無倦，行之以忠。」

仲弓爲季氏宰，問政，子曰：「先有司，赦小過，舉賢才。」曰：「焉知賢才而舉之？」曰：「舉爾所知；爾所不知，人其舍諸。」

子夏爲莒父宰，問政，子曰：「無欲速，無見小利；欲速則不達，見小利則大事不成。」

——論語——

經濟建設與國防之關係（E 5.）

鄭惠益

經濟建設爲國防上必要的準備。所謂國防工具，是指一國之陸軍，海軍，空軍，以及在要塞上的炮台，軍港，軍械，彈藥而言。國防的經濟建設，是包括交通，農田，資本，市場，工廠，財政，及一切生產設備而言。一國有國防工具而後能戰；有交通的便利與材料之接濟而戰事才能維持。所以抗敵之能否長期，全視一國之有無充分經濟建設而定。軍隊有死戰之決心，則必不致不戰而放棄領土。政府若早有經濟設建以爲國防之後盾，則國土亦不致慘遭淩夷。夫經濟建設之於國防，猶如資本土地之於生產，有此二種要素之加入，則生產可以發達。一國若有充量的經濟建設，國防上的維持力可更加雄厚。

經濟建設爲我國首宜實行之政策。我國對日本軍事之失敗，無可諱言。東三省數十萬方英里之土地與其無限的富源，事實上已經放棄，亦無須辯解；此後吾政府是否祇求維持現狀，抑將努力於國防與經濟建設？其權力與責任全在當局者之手，蓋國民熱心有餘，而其力則不足也。今我欲言者，政府今後急要之圖，當首先努力於經濟建設，其性質之緊要比任何職務更爲重大，政府遝可以經濟建設爲預算之必要支出，以節減的軍政費移作建設之用，第一年建設預算暫定二萬萬元，第二年四萬萬元，第三年又四萬萬元，其經費中之一部份，政府可舉公債，以應付之，惟舉債之前必先籌劃精密的具體計劃，而後依需要決定債額之多少，外國政府或實業團體願以資本或機械貸予吾國者，政府當盡量利用之，此而不行，則所謂十年生聚十年教養者，十年後必無成績可見，則長期抵抗更談不到。

建設之實行必待國內各派之妥協，國權統一及政治安定，爲一切建設之根本。今觀國情，統一僅有其名而無其實，國內和平無保障，建設難期實行，吾人主張開各實力派之聯席會議，覓妥協之途徑，立和平公約，以期建設之實現。妥協原非得意，但與歷年軍閥的私戰比較，妥協而能達和平之目的，較勝於空虛之統一多矣。若以各派妥協爲非，其尚有具體的和平辦法，而能於最短之時期內實現乎。

建設之種類與其性質：所謂經濟建設與國防有重要關係者如何？一曰交通；二曰生產工具；三曰農田；四曰流動資本；五曰繁榮國內市場；六曰基本工業；七曰財政；八曰農工軍隊化與軍隊農工化；九曰軍事聯盟；十曰精神建設是也。

第一先設交通網。平時可以使貨物暢流，戰時可以輸送軍隊，此誠在國防上與全國經濟發達上有無限之價值也。戰時戰鬥力之分配與防線之鞏固全恃軍隊輸送之敏捷，惟有交通設備之周全，可達此目的。交通設備包括陸路，水路，電訊與航空四種。其中以陸路的交通爲基本，以水電空三路爲輔助。陸路交通又分爲泥路汽車路，與鐵路三類。泥路祇便於人行與輕細物件之轉運：故其價値低，鋪面的道路可行汽車及輕重貨物之轉運，故其價値高；鐵路載量無限，輸運迅速，故其價値最大。水路次之。歐洲德法二國，交通設備最爲完備，設有道路交通網，全國道路四通八達，汽車到處可行。水路除天然河道外，政府又濬多條運河與天然河聯絡，以成水路交通網。鐵路非特貫通全國，聯絡都市，貫接農工業區，更由一國之中心直達邊境要塞，一日戰事發生，軍隊可迅速分配，或守或攻皆可隨意指揮。我國爲國防計，爲經濟發達計，有急起實行敷設各路交通網之必要，實因一切經濟上的活動與軍事上的行送有賴於交通之便利也。我國於交通上之建設，不應偏重建築泥路，極宜同時建築鐵路，蓋已言之於前，此二種交通線有不同之功用，與不同之價値也。

第二是建設生產工具，例如車輛，各種農工商人用的機器，船舶，商用飛機，房屋，以及其他動物之類，例如牛馬等是也。蓋生產工具愈多，一國之生產能力愈大，於國防上與物品供給上愈有利益。所謂戰時之總動員者，非特指農工商士之被徵入伍，亦指農工業生產工具之被徵發爲生產軍事必要品之謂也。世界無缺少生產工具之國而可以經濟發達者，亦無生產不發達之國而可以長期抵抗者，故生產工具之充實爲國防上一種必要條件。

然如何可使生產工具增加？則保護國民產業一也，政府助長農工商業之發達二也，調劑金融三也。由此觀之，生產工具應當多爲屬於國民，政府之職務是在保護提倡國民之產業而已。

第三是開闢農田，以增加農產品之收入，使每年國產糧食之供給足敷全國人民二年之用。一旦戰事暴發，國際間貿易發生障礙，全國人民可無絕食之患。英國在大戰時曾獎勵農礦業及開闢新農地有三四百萬英畝之多。但我國之欲闢新農田較英國爲難，因我國交通不便，或因灌溉艱難，故一時難闢荒漠爲新田。其建設之道，在立卽發展農村的長期計劃，逐漸以達到其目的。

第四是積聚資金，以爲內地農工商民流動資本之用。資金之由來，在人民之生產與積蓄；但資金之供給，以爲農工商界流動之用者，在錢莊與銀行，蓋金融機關之於農工商人猶如輪軸之於車輛，爲生產界之必要輔業，片刻不可或缺。但資金之供內地生產之用者必配置於內地，不可集中於上海一隅，庶內地不致發生金融恐慌，而上海有遊金過剩之現象；且一旦國際戰爭爆發，敵人可在上海一隅刼奪中國資金之全數，其結果將危及戰事之持久性，故一國之流動資本當平均的分配於各地，庶全國人民可蒙其利也。若欲達此目的，政府不可祇取放任政策，聽金融之自由分配。政府與社會當採積極政策，譬如設立農工銀行，或使上海商業銀行界組織農工銀行部，在內地投資，以爲內地農工商業之助。總之，全國資金之分用於內地，以爲開發國內產業之用，爲現今經濟建設上急要之圖。

第五種是繁榮國內市場，使各業之產品在國內市場流動，且當促進其交易速度，其結果可使各業興旺而增加生產，因貿易之道，在求繁榮，而不在節約，蓋有消費而產品方有出路，農工商業才可維持，但我國消費界有一種劣績：就是歡迎洋貨而輕國貨，所以國人之消費是促進外國人之產業，而於國內產業界少有利益也。是故在一方面，我人當認繁榮國內市場爲必要建設之一，再於他方面，當改變消費者之心理，以樂用國貨爲前提，蓋全國消費之力量購買國貨，是乃消費者自助其產業之發達也。

第六是建設基本工業，將來各種生產工具及物品之供給可仰持國內之自製品，使無須再購洋貨；一旦戰事發生，敵人必封鎖中國海岸，當時卽欲購買軍械與材料亦可不得。譬如我國於空中建設至少需要飛機一千五六百架，若每架以十萬元算，共計一萬萬六千萬元，中國若以此數之半卽以千萬元以建設飛機製造廠，則將來我國之飛機可以自給，卽將來國民之經濟亦可賴之以發達，故中國在經濟建設上必須計劃自製，自造，庶建設上有一種眞正的永久辦法，否則以數萬萬之金元祇供購買一種消費物，消耗後再至外國購買，於中國經濟之不利莫此爲甚，故望政府與全國國民俱遠大之目光，努力於基本工業之建設，無論遭遇若何困難，當以堅毅之力量勝過之。以達自有的基本工業爲止，此於國防上方可認爲有眞實之辦法也。

第七是財政的建設，一國之財政爲一切經濟建設與維持戰爭之關鍵，英，法，德等國在歐戰時每國共費戰爭費自一百萬萬金元至三百萬萬金元，各國合計共費一千八百萬萬金元，（我國內國公債共計約八萬萬銀元，若與外國比較則相去遠矣，）此可以證明財政之重要性。至於財政建設的原則不外增加國富及培養國民納稅能力一也，平衡預算二也，維持國家借款信用三也，若政府於平時財政上有適當的辦法，大概至國難時期亦有辦法，但欲久持戰時期間的財政，卽支出超過租稅收入的財政，則除靠國民財富以發行公債或紙幣外無他法。故財政上的根本原則是發達國民經濟與增加國富，其臨時辦法，則爲發行公債與不兌現紙幣，其後增加稅收，以淸償國家之債務也。現今政府收入之半數，是由關稅收入，若將來戰事發生，關稅收入必定無着。財政上必定發生恐慌，故今當未雨綢繆以發達內國工業爲稅收之稅源，及整理稅務行政爲着手也。

第八是農工軍隊化與軍隊農工化。歐戰時初期，法國動員三百八十萬人，英國動員二百三十七萬人，德國動員四百十萬人；自一九一四年至一九一八年，法國總共招募之軍隊爲八百萬人，英國總共九百五十萬人，德國總共一千三百萬人，由此觀之，各國人民參加戰爭之多出乎吾人意料，我國若遇正式戰爭，全國軍隊一百萬人不敷分配，故主張農工軍隊化也。夫軍隊之所以要農工化者，因爲平時軍費太大，戰時軍費反而無着，我國每年之稅收約在五萬萬元左右，而軍費支出要在三萬萬元，此種畸形的軍費支出，反於國防有害無益，因爲國防的建設費，全被軍隊消耗盡矣，故國防建設經費與普通軍費當加以區別，主張軍隊農工化，所以解決現有軍隊之消耗問題也。

第九是外交的聯絡和軍事之聯盟爲我國在戰爭上必要的補助。中國在作戰力上，缺乏技術人材，軍械，藥彈，財力爲公認的事情，我國除根本計劃建設以求自給外，更須仰求他國之補助以達戰爭之勝利。若法國者，於歐戰開始後曾製造與購置步槍三百萬桿，機關槍十一萬桿，輕炮一萬五千具，重炮七千具，又在美國發行公債數十萬萬元，以法國之預備，尚需臨時製造與購買許多之槍炮，我國將來之必要自外補助無論矣。到此時期我國可儘量利用外國技士，器械與資本，以求直達最後之目的。最好現在以最有利的條件與友國聯絡，作國防上必要的準備。一國外交之成功，本無定例，當視國內政治家之政策，計劃手段與辦事能力而定。總之，國防建設不能脫離外交政策也。

第十是國防的經濟建設，絕對不可脫離精神建設，所謂精神建設者，即提倡國家思想，培養個人生產效能，及實行責任主義是也。精神爲物質之母，由母而生子，由精神而至物質的表示也。我國多數人民，祇重個人之權利，而不注意個人權利是由國家實力的保障而來，如國家有實力以行施主權之後，則法律可以行，外患可以禦，所以爲個人權利計，則個人非維護國家之主權與領土不爲功。此所以個人必以國家之意志爲意志，國家之需要爲需要，國家之榮辱爲榮辱也，有國家思想之人，必不惜犧牲個人之生命與財產爲國家之用，亦不以個人之義務推委與他人；若四萬萬人中個個俱有國家思想，則建設之成功與國力之强盛可抵抗外來之侵略而有餘。

精神建設之關於培養個人生產能力者，當推教育與職業訓練爲最要，此種建設可啓發四萬萬人之能力，對外可以抵抗，對內可以生產，建設程序中之要素也。

責任思想爲國力發展上之必要條件，而我國於政治上，於公共事業上，負責之人最感缺乏之一種精神而急宜提倡者也。因爲責任思想之不發達，所以政治之無成績，國權之不統一，公共事業之不發達也。負責者若早俱責任思想，則陸海軍早有偉大之成績，國民之治安，必早有確實之保障。今日國權之受敵蹂躪，人民之生命自由與財産之危危乎不保，皆因我國負責者祇顧一己之利權，而對其職務多無責任思想也；故欲公僕精神之改良，國民當提倡「負責」「服務」「不貪不偸」之責任思想，此而俱備，則一切公共事業之成績必將斐然可觀，掌國權者必以民意爲歸宿，而不專獨斷獨行其是矣。

總之，上述十則，爲中國現在必要之條件，中國將來之興衰强弱，有賴於政府能否表現眞正革命精神，以最後之決心，立卽創經濟建設也。

SCIENTIFIC MANAGEMENT AND INDUSTRIAL MARKETING

By Ted. C. Chang (張宗謙)

I. THE TRAGEDY OF WASTE IN INDUSTRIAL MARKETING

China, not many years ago, has started on the drive toward scientific management in the factory. Like their fellow Americans, nowever, the Chinese experts and business men have neglected to treat the subject in its entirety. What they have done thus far is merely the application of scientific management principles to production control alone and the declaration of war on the waste of production, disregarding the fact that these wastes are of secondary importance as compared with the wastes in marketing. Although the scientific menagement of men and machinery can succeed in reducing the cost of production and in increasing the volume of manufacture savings made in this way are more than neutralized as a result of the external factors of distributive confusion and destructive competition and the internal factor of mismanagement. It is useless to turn out hugh quantities of merchandise at unbelievably low costs if it must besort to high-hand and unethical merchandising methods to force their sale to the public.

The wastes of marketing are many and varied. For instance, there is the general cry of "too many middlemen" and the distributive confusion caused thereby. This is especially true in case of marketing industrial product. The market for industrial products can be more clearly defined than the market for consumer products. Industrial products are sold to relatively few number of actual or potential users who purchase in large quantities. Industrial manufacturers, therefore, usually should make direct contact with the large buyers, even whene middlemen are used. Yet this type of waste is more or less incidental and practically indispensable in the evolution of an efficient distributive system. They are largely temporary and transient.

Then there are wastes due to destructive competition. Under the present economic system, people have been brought up to believe that free competition is essential to the welfare of the society. The tendency, therefore, has been for the manufacturers to enter into an aggressive program of supersalesmanship and super-advertising, disregarding the fact that such a scheme may not turn out to be a profitable one. But in any event, the public is made to pay the bill.

II. THE LACK OF SCIENTIFIC MANAGEMENT

The wastes hitherto mentioned are due to external conditions which are beyond the power of any one concern to reform. For the present, however, the crying need of the industrial concerns is the reformation of that internal factor named mismanagement. As has been pointed out previously, scientific management is not intended for production control alone, but should also be applied to the marketing aspect. The simple reason is that marketing is primary while production is only secondary. The wastes in marketing are much greater than the wastes due to production. The lack of scientific management in marketing industrial products may be proven by the following conditions, which are typical of the manufacturing companies of the present time.

Firstly, business managment has had no adequate facts relating to markets upon which to base their judgments and decisions. Business cycles and seasonal fluctuations have fallen upon most business concerns almost as though it were "an act of God". The determination of the relationship between supply and demand, the standardization and simplification of products have been held impossible simply because there has been no information to serve for guidance.

Secondly, due partly to the ignorance of marketing principles and partly to the prevalent erroneous conception that production is the primary consideration and marketing is merely secondary, the manufacturers have simply produced what is seemingly to the best of their interest. There was no coördination between production and demand. There has been no planning function to draw together all the various marketing activities and fuse them into a single concerted program. When marketing resistence has been encountered, either due to over production or even due to misporduction, there has been no search for the cause, but merely an added pressure in the form of super-salesmanship and super-advertising to drag the public into purchasing.

Thirdly, as a result of the over-concentration on productivc efforts, the present industrial concern has failed to functionalize marketing. Division of labor has been applied to marketing on the basis of chance and guess. They have deliberately delegated their marketing tasks to outsiders, which result in greater wastes for the producer as well as the consuming public.

III. SCIENTIFIC MANAGEMENT PRINCIPLES APPLIED TO MARKETING

What, then, are the principles according to which scientific marketing should be conducted, and how is marketing to be reduced to a scientific basis as production has been. The writer believes that Mr. Percival White, noted author and business man, in his work on Scientific Marketing Management, has probably given the most satisfactory answer in the folling study:-

(1) Objectivity of demand

(2) Division of labor

(3) Research and analysis

(4) Planning

(5) Training

(6) Control and supervision

(7) Coördination and cooperation.

Objectivity of demand. Marketing centers in all cases around the needs of the consumer. This is an absolute shift from the old practice of making the producer the focus of all business relations. It provides a definite goal based on the logic of cold facts rather than on the subjective wishes of the industrial autocrat. The high marketing costs which give rise to so much complaint are largely the result of failure to follow the principle of objectivity cf demand. Too many manufacturers have followed the tradition of making what pleased them, never dreaming they would not find a market ready and waiting. They have left out of account the fact that they have, to a considerable extent, been producing goods which did not fit the consumer's requirements.

The system of scientific marketing assumes that production exists in order to further production. Scientific marketing is based on the theory of finding out what the consumer wants and then giving it to him. Man does not consume in order to produce; he produces in order that he may consume. Business men know this, but they do not apply the law. Consumption is primary, production secondary; yet it is rare to find a business which boldly faces this fact and which produces goods always with a view to the requirements of consumption. In the future these requirements will have to be met, by the business concerns. "What does the consumer need:". This will be the standing question.

Division of labor. The second principle of scientific marketing is that all the markeing functions must be provided for in the organization, each function to be directed by an expert. This does not mean that in the small company there should be as many separate marketing departments as in the large company. But it does mean that in both large and small companies there should be a conscious separation of the various marketing functions. Even if one department should do both the analysis and the planning, these must be recognized and carried out as two distinct functions. The properly organized compay should entrust all its marketing problems to a department for the purpose. The basic purpose of this functional division of marketing is to make one individual, who is a specialist, responsible for a single line of effort, instead of intrusting him with a confusion of executive, legislative and judicial functions.

Research and analysis. Few business concenns are well acquainted with their specific marketing problems. It is a common occurence for the management to be ignorant not only of its market, but also of its sales force. Scientific marketing requires the setting up of a research organization and its analysis of the marketing problem is made the basis of all plans. Analysis is not a matter of statistics alone. It is essentially a breaking down of a problem into its constituent parts. The ordinary method in vogue to-day is to attack what appears on the surface, while the analytic methods enable an organization to go to the bottom of a problem and to give each of the factors of which it is composed a rating relative to its importance.

Planning. Plans to-day are made, as a rule, by individuals, each following his own ideas. Plans, according to scientific methods, are formulated by a specially organized division. It consists of setting pu policies and objectives, establishing standards, providing suitable methods of procedure and arranging for the actual steps involved in carrying out the work in hand.

It should be a fundamatal rule of the organization that plans will originate only from the Planning Department or at least that they shall be routed through this department, even if originated elsewhere. Any schemes for improvement which are suggested elsewhere will be submitted to the Planning Department for investigation, and for approval or reaction. Formerly, it has been customary to regard the making of major plans as a purely executive function, in which case the excellence of the plans would depend entirely on the reasoning ability of the executive in question. Under a system of scientific marketing, the function of the executives would be to pass upon plans after they had been originated logically through a process of research. They would use their judgment and experience in estimating the value of these to the concern.

Training. Scienfific marketing takes it for granted that training in principles and methods increases efficiency and there be lowers the costs of distribution. If no training is given then the salesman must learn by himself. He must acquire experience in the so-called school of experience. Here he learns how to sell through his failures, which are not only failures for him, but for his company as well.

Control and supervision. A careful system of supervision, discipline and remuneration must be worked out if scientific management is to prove successful. The organization cannot function by itself without a parallel system of control. Control when applied to production can often be reduced to an almost automatic process. With the marketing mechanism, however, on such absolute control is possible, since it is largely made up of human factors. The supervision of these human constituents is much harder than in the case of machines, since no many othor factors enter the euqation. A system of supervision is necessary to make sure that policies and methods are carried out. This may be done in some cases by personal supervision; in others by records and reports; in still others by a combination of both methods.

Coordination and cooperation. Although the principles of the division of labor is carried out on a functional basis, provision must be made for coordination of these separate functions. This coordination must be conducted in a cooperative fashion. There must be help and support all along the line. The help comes from the top and extends downward. The marketing manager supports his department managers; and they in turn back up their men. The company's representatives help the dealers. Everything is keyed to bring help to every link in the chain, and above all to that last link, the consumer.

It is important to realize at the outset that each higher grade in the organization exists for the sole purpose of sustaining what is below. Under the usual arrangement the reverse of this is to be seen. In a scientific system of a firm foundation, thus avoiding the unstable inverted pyramid, which many current organizations resemble.

IV. CONCLUSTION

By applying the above-mentioned principles to marketing, the unnecessary wastes may be eliminated. The manufacturer needs no longer torture his imagination or resort to his overguessing ability. He can determine by methods of some precision what will sell, and can thus eliminate risk and worry.

In considering the application of scientific management to marketing it cannot be too often repeated that hitherto scientific management has been a misnomer. The scientific methods have been applied to production with considerable degree of success, but it has never been extended to include marketing. In the United States, this has been the prevailing condition for almost forty years, and the Americans regret very much that Taylor's followers are his followers and nothing more; because they are doing what Taylor was doing in his time, but not what Taylor would do in the light of the present economic conditions. China is just beginning to realize the significance of scientific management in the factory, and rapid strides have been made toward that direction, but the writer sincerely hopes that our so-called experts and business men should pay just as much attention to the industrial marketing aspect as they do to production control, if not more; because after all marketing is primary while production is really secondary.

With conditions as they promise to be for some years to come, it is not to be expected that marketing will prove reducible to the almost machine-like system which characterizes manufacturing, although we believe that in the future machinery can do just as much for marketing that it has done for manufacturing. The great handicap is that marketing has always been dependent to a great extent on emotion, and emotions cannot be dealt with by using any standard system. The task of marketing, therefore, calls for higher mental caliber than that of production.

Modern Industrial Tendencies

"The new industrial methods have greatly accelerated certain tendencies that had already manifested themselves in the old, domestic factories and some of these deserve more than passing notice as they are affecting not only productive processes but our social organigation as well. Perhaps the most important of these influences are these that tend toward:

1. *Increase in size* of industrial enterprisis
2. *Specialization* or the limiting of the field of activity, not only of enterprises but also of men.
3. *Standardization* or the reduction of all lines of product to a limited number of types and sizs & cheracteristics.
4. *Extreme dinision of labor*, following aggregation, specialization, & standardization, & requiring special considration.
5. *More scientific methods in organization and management.*"

—D.S. Kimball, *Principles of Industrial Organization.*—

管理 第一卷 第五期

陸大月刊

第三卷 第三期
民國二十六年三月一日出版

九六

目錄

本刊價目

零售：每期大洋叁角
半年：六期大洋壹元五角
全年：十二期大洋叁元

郵費

外埠：每期三分五厘 半年一角五分 全年二角
本埠：每期二分 半年一角二分 全年二角四分

編輯者 陸大月刊編輯委員會
發行者 陸大月刊社
社址：南京漢口路陸軍大學特別黨部內
電話：三一七一三
代售處 特別黨部及各大書局

譯　述

介紹英國公務員制度（D 3.）

W.A.Robson著
任家誠譯述

此文載于 The Political Quarterly, April-June,1936，原名公務員制度（The Public Service），其所討論者爲英國之制，今以之介紹於本刊，故于題首冠以「介紹英國」四字，藉以表明。

［I］

今日之公務員制度幾全爲最近八十年來努力之結晶，而其主要特質之完成，更不過五十年事。以吏治(Civil Service)而言，一八五三年之屈里凡楊諾司谷報告（The Trevelyan-Northcote Report），一八五九年之恩俸法案（The Superannuation Act），一八七〇及一九二〇年之國會法令（The Order in Council）等有以造成之。然公務員制度雖無確切之內容，實吏治制度之範圍爲廣。蓋就廣義言之，除吏治制度外，凡市員制度(Municipal Service)，社會化事業服務員制度，各委員會制度，等可以歸入公務管理之範圍者均屬之。

今日中央及地方公務員爲一種新人物，猶工程師之爲新人物然。十九世紀前之官吏如驗屍員，警官，公路測量員，救貧監督員及法官，縣吏等與之有相似之處。然此種「有隸屬性質之員吏」"Subordinate Magistrates"（勃蘭克司東 Blackstone 名之）僅以個人名義受委，其任期或有定，或視其政績而定；其任務大都由法律指定，且由法庭監督，與現在僅奉負責長官或地方機關命令而執行政務之公務員絕對不同。現代之公務員實爲維多利亞(Victorian)資本主義化民主政治之產物，無此種公務員制度，民主政治將無法實現。

欲明瞭公務員制度，其關鍵在研究公務員任用之條件，及治理之法規，此二者確定公務員職業化之生命，其特質及固定性，猶兵士，教徒及醫生等。

公務員任用條件之主要者包括任用之公開競爭，或經考試，或經面談，或二法並用；就職與退職之年齡限制，職位等級之劃分；合理而固定俸給表之厘訂，規定正常的增加，對於工作成績優良公務任職之保障；贍養金制度之採行，並兼及疾病之補助，內部升擢之規定，至少以年資爲根據；確定及有增加性假期之制定。此種條件在吏治制度中已儘量利用、全國公務人員管理聯會（N.A.L.G.O.）* 及其他聯會亦已加努力，使各地採用，故此等條件之成立，僅時間問題而已，雖然苟我人離開中央或地方政府，而注意於與公務管理關係略淺之不固定組織，此種條件之運用，尚極幼稚。

治理之法規不及任用條件爲明顯，然對於公務員制度之影響則甚烈。瀆職法案（The Co

rrupt Practice Act）及公務秘密法案（The Official Secret Act）對於詐取及洩漏機密等弊，規定嚴重之處罰以防止之。立法條例限定政客不得就國家公務員有俸之職，被選議員不得就地方政府之聘；國會之選舉，亦經規定禁止公務員爲候選人，須辭職或退職後，方有候選資格。各市選舉，公務員之參與，亦受限制。財政部訓令禁止公務員參與政治或政黨之爭辯，對於政治問題，須守緘默態度，不得出頭露角，偏袒左右。公務員之兼營工商事業者亦有限制，規定在上午十時至下午六時內，不得外顧，甚至在餘暇時間兼理次要事務，亦受部令限制。因阿翁蒙格案（Ironmonger Case）發生之故諮詢委員會報告（Report of the Broad of Enquiry）制定公務員不准『辦理有投機性質之業務，』因此種事業於公務員『不獨無益且有害』也。一九二七年商業紛爭及商業集團法案（The Trade Disputes & Trade Union Act）對公務員之自由，益加限制，規定任何公務員不得加入任何商業集團或專門職業團體，然苟其團員資格乃屬於皇家人員，及其組織不與他種集團相聯合者，則爲例外。公務員集團之組成，須無政治目的，並不得與其他政治組織發生直接或間接關係，此法在使組織如郵務工會（Union of Post Office Workers）等能與同業公會（Trade Union Congress）相隔離。

再者，尙有其他未確定之義務，卽男女關係。就余所知，此點並無一般之法則，然中央及地方之公務員務望能注意禮貌，避免浪漫事跡之播傳於報章。在不久以前，郵務部對於男女職員發生曖昧事件，尚有立即予以雙方撤職之處分。以法院之程序言，避免報章宣傳問題頗易解決，然爲避免女公務員(已規定結婚後應即辭職)之任意與異性同居起見，實應有正式之限制。此問題與前問題實不可同日而語也，

* N. A. L. G. O. 似是 National Administratio League of Government Official 尚待證實，暫譯爲「全國公務人員管理聯會」

〔II〕

上述任用之條件及治理之法規，爲我國公務員制度造成之要素。盡人皆知誠信而有效的公務員制度之發展，爲我國成功之卓著者，更爲國內外所重視，我國無政治上之威脅如法之人事制度然，更無腐敗之現象，如美之中央及各市管理然。我人應欣幸在管理級內(Administrative Class)以有訓練有才幹之永久公務員担任政務之推行，美制之弱點，在未能實現此種辦法，美僅知以智囊團(Brain Trust)塡補華盛頓人才之缺乏，而不知大學教授及專家之倉卒集合，實不足以代替良好之人事制度。

雖然，吾人既已讚許我國公務員之優越及其對於工作之盡心。再一反想，當知此時，不宜徒加讚許，當再考察其情形。

〔III〕

我人可先攷慮我國制度之基礎之假定。最顯著者卽職務之分成類別，反映社會之結構及經濟之階級。外交及外務之人員因須出於委派，不能倖免于貴族及高等社會之關係，或不能不受此種社會之特惠。以管理級言，控制全國大半政務，其人員幾全爲倖能入牛津與劍橋者，二校入學試驗，亦爲錄用管理級人員之目的而設計。地方政府之主要人員，普通須爲醫生，律師，工程師等，於是所謂任用，往往限於有錢攻讀專門術科之公子；其他較爲下級之職位，則保留與年在十八七歲有錢攷讀中學之公子，蓋一般人均於十四至十六歲左右卽離學校也。

此種制度宜于昔日，蓋此制度養成行政樞紐最高級之人員，其教育程度及社會背景與其所隸屬之部長及顧問相若。外務大臣，與國務副大臣，可以平等交際共同生活，市長與市秘書可以同屬一俱樂部，故由共同觀念，而生融洽之感情，於彼此合作上可收極大效果。

就現在社會之趨向言，此種制度之收效，已成過去之事實，若非澈底攷革，於前途大有妨礙。第一倫敦及各地大學學生(大半爲社會較低階級)深蒙阻隔，不能列入政務之最高級，此等大學正在訓練社會科學方面之重要人才，而竟蒙阻隔，誠屬不可思議，第二，今日政治機會公開，務使勞働界中男女，皆有在中央及地方政府任最高職位之可能，而現制行政領袖，須由高級社會之極狹範圍中拔出，矛盾現象，最爲顯著。故就行政效率立場言，大學生之任用確爲必要，惟是大學入學之挑選，必公開於凡有智力之青年，不當如現制之有階級性，方與民主政治之目標相吻合。如我人再不注意于調整之必要，則政治領袖學專門人員間之合作關係，信任及心諒解程度將見衰落，蓋階級之分歧，教育觀念之不同，將永不能融洽也。一九二四年及一九二九年勞工政府 (Labonr government) 均遭受行政長官之優越訓練之威脅卽其明例，而威脅之結果，卽可形成喞恨。

關乎此點，確使我人感覺十分困難。我人應假定公務員制度有其完全之中立性，不受政治之影響，且不論何黨主政，均懷忠誠服從之主張。今後應重行攷查我人之假定，此故並非因懷疑公務員對於行政長官是否盡忠服役，但有時在某種情形下，或有不能盡忠服役之處，其原因在公務員自己亦不能明瞭。

過去我國大半公務管理包含調整之事務，卽凜遵法令之規定，各部實行管理各公務員個人之行爲及集團之行爲，其最切之例，爲工廠法案 (Factory Act)。然今日之公務管理，最要部份包含事務之機能，卽施行事務之機能，如運輸，建築，教育等等。在此種機能內，職官不重在施行法律上之管理，而重在自行設計，以促進遠大之政策．問題卽在是否一與社會目的漠不相關而絕對服從之職官能勝任愉快，最近毛倫脫(Sir Robert Morant)可稱爲一大行政家，因彼注重教育及公共衞生。一僅知服從部長或地方首領之職官能否振起該部或該地之事務？如一外交官被委爲駐華盛頓或莫斯科大使，而不深認其政策爲有利於人類，能否得美或俄政府之同情及合作！此疑問我人於外交部，交通部，財政部，郵務部，及衞生部，均可找得或正或反之事實根據。

然則將何以處之？我人並非建議每政治統制變化時，卽應更易各行政長官，蓋全部之更易不爲文明國家所採取也，以德意二國言，公務員幾全爲國社黨或法西斯黨黨員，此種政客把持之辦法我人當避免之。

雖我人一方面力求公務員與政黨之隔絕，然他方面仍望能獲得有創造力之人才，遠大政策之推行，庶不至爲一般消極觀之公務員所阻礙。以國家設計及建築，外交事務，失業救濟，公用事業，教育及婦孺福利事業等重要之行政工作而言，如無具創造力之公務員運轉之，其政事之推行，將蒙受重大之阻礙。富於傳統的服從觀念者，對於某部當緩工或某部當停工等命令，必能立卽遵辦。惟對於須有創造思想之政策之推進，如美國人所謂「取攻勢」之事業，則非徒有服從性之人員，所能奏效也。

[IV]

然則將何以吸引有思想，有創造力之公務員？答案甚爲簡單，現行之競爭攷試制或面試制可用以選擇有相當教育及相當智力之人才，亦可用以揭發各人之個性及性情，余信余確能計劃一種測驗方法，將有猶豫消極等個性之人類，與今日所需要之有果斷，建設，積極等個性之人類，分別淸楚。

或以爲有上述個性之人類大抵趨於經營私人投機事業，未必肯爲公務員，蓋私人投機事業範圍較闊機會較多也。其實不然，現代公共事業以宏大規模爲重要工作，其給與之機會，無可比擬，卽此一端，其吸引力已遠勝私人企業，且各人抱服務社會之宗旨，此宗旨已暫成爲有效之動力，而爲自己謀金錢之主義在我國今日已暫形消沒矣。近數十年來我國有一極有望之現象，蓋青年之野心已不若昔日之僅在謀收入富裕，更願在合理的生活標準可以維持之狀態下，努力爲國家服務。

雖然，現在之公務員制度已與社會隔離相遠，每公務員均有職業保障非如一般市民之常蒙危險，威而思 (H. G. Wells) 嘗謂各部人員已成一種高貴而不可侵犯之系統，如神父等然，『彼已將投機二字置諸度外……人民對於公務員最要之訴言，與對於神父階級及守舊派之訴言無異，蓋謂公務員已自高其地位，固守繩墨，而不敢冒險。』皮佛來其(Sir William Beveridge) 久居要津之人也，亦認爲今日各機關之公務員已有形成特殊階級之趨向。法人事行政專家寫潑 (Mr. Sharp) 亦覺高級公務員在法國恆受各種榮銜，使彼等形成一種特殊階級。』三說雖出自三人之口，而意則一致。如此說認爲合理，我人知公務員制度對內確有使之伸縮，對外使之流動之必要。

對內之伸縮全賴組織一致性。以目今而言，我國之公務員制度厥有多種：曰國內吏治制度，殖民地吏治制度，外交人員制度，地方吏治制度，社會化事業人事制度，如英國無線電播音局(B.B.C.)*，倫敦客運局（London Passenger Transport Board），中央電氣局 Central Electricity Board）等。上述各端均有獨立之制度，其俸給系統各各不同，各制間更不能互相調轉。如我人擬增加公務員之經驗，遷調之法必須採用，惟此法須在統一之公務員制度下，方可運用。雖然，我人並非謂各種情形必須全體一致，亦非謂一切公務員之任用均須經過文官服務委員會（之選錄Civil Service Commission），吾人所認為有統一之必要者，在應弭除各種公務員待遇之不同，如道議會秘書年入七千五百鎊而中央各部秘書長年僅可得三千鎊，倫敦客運局與中央電氣局之長官年入較執人事行政重任之財政部長超出三四倍之多。

其次，我人雖不能侵及各種事務自主之地位，然各種事務之人員應有遷調之可能，此法當先使各種行政之公務機關，有同一之資格標準，及任用方法。最次俸給酬報應趨於一致性，普遍性及易於調轉。

如衛生部之人員能調至各鄉村或城市服務，而以地方人員內調供職，此種中央公務員制度階級性之現象可以避免。郵務部近年已利用一極優良之法規，即青年之入為管理級公務員者，須先在各地服務，然後調至總部，如財政部人員能先在社會化之公用及建設事業機關服務，明悉大規模之投資，則財部對於經費吝撥之弊可免，而經費之劃撥，可有定向。又如各殖民地之公務員能常內調，或中央之公務員能常外調，則殖民地對於中央官員隔閡之現象，可以消弭。

以言對外之流動，司登潑(Sir Josiah Stamp)，白蘭却脫(Sir Basil Blachett)，沙而脫(Sir Arthur Salter) 內牛耶 (Sir Otto Niemeyer) 諸人均有超人之才，而均離去政府，另營他業，惟此種事實尙屬僅見，至若延攬工商界知名之士而授與公務員席位，尤屬罕覯。總言之，內外事業之流動實爲必要。公務員雖應有終身之保障，然工作不力之人員亦宜使之去職，而錄用外界之人才，此首藉俸給及其他恩俸政策之得宜。就現制言，公務員如離去本職，或遭黜除：將犧牲其養老金之權利，遂使公務員戀棧尸位，不願脫離，設養老金能推算至退職之年而給付之，不相宜之人員可隨時請其辭去，既可利其本人，又可利國家。又如能決定較高之俸給，而不另給養老金，或予以一次之獎金，則外界幹練敏達之士，年在三十至四十五者，亦必惠然肯來，因之我之公務員制度可以呈活躍之現象。

社會事業之分成公私二種已不合時代，雖社會上此種現象仍不可免，然公私界限已不甚分明，如有人間農產運銷局 (Agricultural Marketing Board)，牛乳運銷局(Milk Marketing

Board)，跑馬賭賽統制局（Racecourse Betting Control Board)，麥業委員會(Wheat Commission)等組織，何者爲公務，何者爲私務！必答曰此爲混合性質。混合之現象爲現代經濟建設過程之特點。政府對於經濟活動統制之普遍，無論爲社會主義化或國家資本主義化，上述混合組織必日見增多，其管理權則將操之於企業有專長者之手。此種事業之擴展，將有立法之根據，然財政獨立，不受度支大臣控制，其收入亦必來自他種來源，而非租稅，任用之人員亦將與刻板式之公務員有別。然我人於討論公務員制度時，不能不承認此種混合組織所任用之人員，爲政治能力最優勝之一種。

道路運輸法案（The Road Traffic Act,1930）所創之車務委員會(Area Traffic Commissioners)爲另一趨勢之明例，然與前述者定向相同。此種委員會統制全國公共汽車，領照制度極爲繁複，在在須加以小心酌裁。

各地之車務委員會主席係由交通部長委派，有一定之任期。除倫敦外，各地更另委二人，由道議會及鄉鎭機關提名，凡有瀆職及怠職行爲，可卽撤去，且法律規定『須遵部長之一般指導。』其後前交長阿虛萊（Colonel Ashley)在衆議院提出取消一般二字之議案，彼以爲部長應全權控制各委員會，否則居心叵測之委員，將有意拒絕部長之命令。現任部長摩立遜(Herbert Moirison)則反對之，彼以爲此議案實有誤解，渠不願完全控制委員會之活動。或以爲摩氏對於委員之個別行爲向國會負責，其實不然，事實上彼願注意及一般之指導，而不願問某事件處置之當否。

我人現在似乎又在注意『委員會制之政府，』此種委員之負責人員與勃蘭克司東(Blackstone)時之公務人員相似而與現在之中央公務員有不同之處。其成敗端視既脫離部長管理督促之後，我人是否能喚起從政人員之忠心，團體精神及善良品行如受部長管理督促一般。我人應知合理而有效之公務員制度不特世界少見，在英亦爲新奇之物。現在政府新立之經濟機關性質繁複，受部管理徒多掣肘，然我人如因欲使公務員制度之有伸縮性及流動性，而致政治窳敗，如十八世紀時然，則代價未免太大。然余並不悲觀，因公共利益之促進之觀念，已與我人日常生活相交織，十九世紀之保障方法，已無必要，此種保障之廢除，已有明例。今後當注意其效果。

總之，我人於某方面若冒險改進，當顧及其他方面務使公務員之魄力能見增加，能以勇敢果斷之精神，把住良機，能熔合教育與訓練於一爐，以適應現代之需要，能與整個社會共生存，能具眞實之特長，此實爲二十世紀第二四分之一時期之民主政治之目標。

*B.B.C. 似是 British Broadcast Corporation 尚待證實，暫譯爲「英國無線電播音局」

演講

鐵道部建設計畫中培養專才之定策（C 8.）

黎照寰

本年一月廿五日； 黎校長曾於 鐵道部 總理紀念週出席演講，原定題爲「交通大學之使命，」談次，臨時改爲「鉄道部建設計畫中培養專才之定策。」茲經向筆記者覓得講詞原稿，並請 黎校長核後，特附此刊。

編者謹誌

照寰去部已歷六年，茲承 部長之命出席本部 總理紀念周，藉獻蕪詞，兼敍舊誼，至爲欣幸。

本部成立於民國十七年十月，迄今尚未足九年。爲時雖短，然在建國方面則有特殊使命與重要地位。 總理有言：「交通爲實業之母，鐵路又爲交通之母。」故政府特設本部以專責成，本部之所以設立，不僅在計畫建設，除管理整頓現有各路外，當然以推動新路之建設，實現 總理鐵路計劃爲極大任務。欲於最短期間以最經濟辦法，循最有效之途徑，能建設經營管理之。不僅限於本身事業，而且及於所附帶的經濟建設，故本部在建設三民主義的國家工作中負極大任務。在民生主義方面，鐵路重要固不待言。至於教育文化之推動與發展，政治之統一與進步，國防之確立與鞏固，何一不與鐵路有密切關係？所以民族民權兩主義之實行，其物質建設之條件亦以鐵路建設爲非常重要。張部長亦嘗言之，在此時期，吾人之責任實非常重大，而職務亦非常緊要。

本部之工作當根據所定之計畫。而所定之計畫自當以 總理實業計畫中之鐵路計畫爲依歸，本部初立時即致力於此。當時 孫前部長所定計畫其中有照寰尚能記憶者可述如次：

一、整理舊債，並借款建築新路，整理舊路；

二、整理路務，發展附屬事業；

三、審定路線並定期展築；

四、整理人事，培養專才。

以上四項可謂四大方策。當時黨政軍之統一形勢尚不如近年，故進行較難。至於計畫推進之後，事業增加在在需才，是我人所深信者也。故從根本上立論，其關鍵更在能否培養專才。所謂專才者即

一、具有高深學問之人員。此項可分為四：

甲、工程師

乙、科學家

丙、經濟家及管理家

丁、其他

以上可稱為技術人員，負指導管理建設之責任。吾人期望有所創造及發明，固亦視此項人員之學問程度如何。

二、具有日常應用學問之人員。此項可分為二：

甲、職員

乙、職工

以上可稱為服役人員。吾人對於鐵路所期望的業務之安全

，全賴其職務所需之公德心知識與經驗。

一切人員固應奉公守法，任勞耐苦，然因本部計畫推進之所需，更當特為訓練使有最適宜的服務之志願，能力，精神和習慣，其不能上進者，則逐漸淘汰之。吾人在整理交通教育時，曾詳細討論及此。有以為先教育而後訓練，造就人才屬於第二項者需時六月至三年，或三年至五年；屬於第一項者需時五年至七年，或六年至十年之久。照實就記憶所及，祇計第一項之大部分人才，以期逐年增加，當時吾人以為至十年後（即民國廿九年）可得十倍，然已覺此培養專才問題不易解決。吾人深知吾國所有專才在路服務者為數不多。假定其數為百人，然事實與經驗所昭示吾人者，在鐵路建設方面，其實際需要奚止一千？現在即就鐵路計畫之中央東南東北西南西北五個系統而言，其中各種工程師，在橋梁、在養路、在衞生、以至關於公路各方面，需要若干？在機械方面，屬於鐵道及製造者需要若干？在電機方面，屬於電信及電力者需要若干？此外經濟家及管理家以分配於營業、運輸、會計、總務、機工、及乎組織設計上，又需要若干？以百數計當然不足。即以千數計，亦不為多。故當時之育才計畫，在質則求其精，在量則求其年有增加

，期使路務進展，新路建築，無虞人才之缺乏。

吾人當時更計及交大於實際上。在十年內所能教養者，約計管理家（經濟家在內）及土木工程師各可至一千，機械工程師五百，電機工程師三百，然合乎標準者兩人未必得一，蓋因環境關係，不能確定也。至育才之難，實已感及。

關於育才問題，當時談論者仍有兩說：

一、不必自辦，其理由有二：（甲）教育係國家整個的事業；（乙）可以節省經費。

二、非自辦不可。其理由有四：

一、求人不如求己，數十年自辦之經驗與結果，已足證明之；

二、節省經費有兩種可能：消極的爲節流，積極的爲開源；

三、時間空間及質的量的需要均有特殊情形，故須自辦使與其整個建設計劃適合；

四、如海陸空軍均各自造就專才，故鐵道亦宜自辦學校以應特殊之需要。

當時既決定自辦學校，故卽着手整理交通大學。因校名有

歷史之關係未曾更改。至於編制一層，則以援照教育部法規爲原則，但仍當兼顧特殊需要，不能削足適履，因教育部所定編制爲一般大學而設，非爲特殊大學而設也，當時　孫前部長曾莅校演講謂對於交大所定之進行步驟，有五年計畫及十年計畫，其中大綱可分述如下：

一、改善組織

二、增加經費

三、重建校舍

四、提高程度

五、充實內容

六、增進教學效能

七、改善教職員待遇

八、部路校聯成一貫

九、訂行有關實業計畫之研究試驗及調查工作

十、改訂畢業生實習及留學辦法

此種計畫至今祇有一部份實現，其原因有關於學校本身者、關於部路者、關於社會者、或關於政治者，頗爲複雜。

整理人事與培養專才，關係密切。而培養專才之重要，總理在實業計畫中亦有申論，現在限於時間，照寰所講述者僅爲問題之一部分耳。國人希望路務發展，尤望　總理鐵路計畫及早完成，吾人共事於鐵道部之下，負責重大，深知人才之難得，培養專才之急要。照寰以爲所負責任更有特殊關係，甚願共同努力。至於今早臨時所講述或有不當之處，尙祈　指正，不勝感幸。

管理學院叢書之一

東北鐵路問題之研究

上下二册　王同文著

▲內容▼

本書上册共有十章，先述中東路之史的發展，經濟價值，組織概要，營業與運輸概况。後敍日本侵略下之鐵路問題，如滿鐵會社之組織，財務，營業等概况，日本對東北之鐵路侵略政策，又分析研究南滿路之營業狀况與營業統計，及運輸狀况與運輸統計，最後論述吉會鐵路問題。共一百四十餘頁。下册計有八章，另加續編四章。內容爲：滿鐵租用地問題，南滿鐵路之倉庫管理，東北鐵路聯運及競運問題，葫蘆島築港與東北鐵路網，東北鐵路與國際關係，東北現有鐵路與總理計劃，今後東北鐵路之整理計劃。續編中有：中日鐵道交涉問題，九一八後之東北鐵路，李頓報告書中之東北鐵道問題述評，中東路出售問題。敍述甚詳，立論尤新，共二百頁，誠爲研究東北鐵路問題與中日關係之唯一有價值書籍。

定價　一元二角（直接購買對折優待）

代售處　本外埠各大書局

中央及地方決算(E 3.)

聞亦有

第一章 政府決算之意義

按政府決算爲政府預算之對待名詞，政府預算中所規定者，皆爲事前估計之事實及數字，期於將來完全依照執行。而政府決算則爲執行之結果，乃既成之事實及數字。故論政府會計係以預算爲起點，決算爲終點。

就一機關而言，其執行預算之結果有無錯誤或違反預算原定之意志是爲財務經過情形；又執行預算終了後，資產負債之實況如何，是爲財務現狀；均可由所編決算考覈之。再就各政府機關間而言，如收入機關支出機關及國庫等政府機關，各方面所列收支帳目，及機關間之往來帳項是否相符，可將各方面所編決算綜合考覈之。

至論担任上項考核工作者，通常由賦有超然地位之審計機關辦理之。在三權政制國家決算經審計機關考核以後應報告立法機關。由立法機關爲最後之決定。立法機關最後決定決算有兩層重大意義：

第一明瞭在前由立法機關所決定之預算行政機關依照執行其結果如何。(消極效用)

第二根據以往年度決算明瞭決定以後年度預算應如何進行。(積極效用)

吾國現時施行五權政制國家，因監察權獨立，故決算可以無須立法機關決定。

決算經立法或監察機關決定後解除各行政檢關之責任。決算公布後使人民明瞭行政機關執行預算之結果如何，解除整個行政機關之責任，人民可藉此信任政府。

基於上述政府決算意義，再分析決算名詞之涵算如下：

一、決算之定算——政府決算者，會計年度間因執行預算上所規定事實而得之確定計數也。

二、決算之根據——決算應依預算編製。如預算有普通會計預算及營業會計預算之分，則決算亦應分爲普通會計決算及營業會計決算兩種，又如預算每會計年度編製一次，決算亦按預算年度編製等。

三、決算之編製——各機關之決算應在會計年度終了後若干日編成。有直接送達審計機關查核者，有經由主管機關彙編總決算然後轉送審計機關者。如主管機關有完備之總會計制度平時即登記所屬機關之預算數字及執行預算所生之收支數字則不難就主管機關帳冊之記載編成總決算逕送審計機關查核。如此即可無須所屬機關編決算矣。

四、決算之審核——在三權政制國家決算如由各機關編送主管機關彙編總決算者，則其審核工作，應有四層：

1本機關自身之審核—本機關編成決算應爲初步之審核。

2主管機關之審核—簽註意見，供審計機關參考。

3審計機關之審核—居于超然地位披瀝其意見編成審計報告。

4立法機關之審核—將審計機關所提出之審計報告與原機關所提出之答辯對照而決定其是非。

但吾國爲五權政制國家監察院之彈劾審計兩項職權超然獨立不受立法院之拘束故暫行決算章程規定決算由審計部審定後不必再送立法院審議。

五、決算之決定公布——在三權政制國家決算經立法機關審定後應即公布以示大信但在吾國規定由審計部審定後呈監察院轉呈國民政府公布之。

六、決算之效用。

消極效用：預算所估計之事實及數字是否恰當及收入支出之執行是否與預算相適應等事項，均應依決算以審定之。

積極效用：鑑於事後之結果以定將來之計劃而期國家之財政事務能得完全之運用。

七、決算書表——決算書表宜由會計制度產生。易言之，即由會計制度產生之會計報告皆爲決算書表。會計報告應分靜態報告與動態報告兩種，吾國現行之收支決算書恰占完備會計報告中動態報告之一部。

八、決算上所採用之會計基礎——決算上計算收支應屬年度有兩種基礎1權責發生基礎2收付實現基礎前者計算準確而後者則因祇計算本期現金收付數目故計算欠準確矣。

第二章 政府決算與預算計算收支報告總平準表財產目錄及固定負債

目錄之聯鎖關係

本章所論決算係指吾國現行收支決算書，非指由會計制度產生之完備會計報告而言。

一、決算與預算之聯鎖關係

決算應依預算編製，其理由已見前述。此處再加詳細討論如下：

1 決算應依預算所分基金個別編製　如吾國預算章程規定，年度預算分為國家地方兩部分再各分普通會計營業會計兩種。故於年度決算之編製亦須依照年度預算分為國家地方兩部分再各分普通會計營業會計兩種。

2 決算應依預算所定會計年度編製　如吾國現行預算章程規定會計年度以每年七月一日起至次年六月三十日止故於年度決算之編製，亦須以預算年度為根據每會計年度編製決算一次。

3 決算應依預算所分部門及所定收支分類標準及科目編製　如吾國現行預算章程規定普通會計及營業會計預算各分為歲入歲出並按其性質各分為經常臨時兩門分別編製。故於年度決算之編製亦須依照同年度預算各分部門編製。

再如吾國現行預算章程規定年度預算應按照辦理預算收支分類標準分別編製。又規定各級歲入歲出概算書內所列科目應按照預算科目細則辦理。故於決算之編製亦須依照同年度預算所規定收支分類標準及所定科目辦理之。

4 決算應依編製總預算之系統編製　如吾國現行預算章程規定國家第一級概算由各機關編製。第二級概算由國家分類預算各主管機關分別彙編。第三級概算即國家總概算由國民政府主計處彙編。故於決算之編製除各機關在年度中有裁撤，合併，改隸等情事外國家第一級決算仍以原編第一級概算之各機關編製。第二級決算仍以原編第二級概算之各主管機關編製。第三級決算即國家總決算仍由國民政府主計處彙輯。

5 決算所根據之預算，不僅以公布之本年度預算為限。舉凡追加預算，追減預算，預算外之支出，動用預備費，轉入上年度歲計餘絀，預算內款項依法流用及其他，俱應加入計算。決算所根據之預算事實及數字，並非最初公布之本年度預算而爲本年度預算現額。故須將上述七項情形加入本年度預算，而計算本年度預算現額，以資比較。

決算所根據之本年度預算現額
- 1 本年度預算
- 2 本年度預算公布後之增減額
  - 1 追加預算
  - 2 追減預算
  - 3 預算外之支出
  - 4 動用預備費
  - 5 轉入上年度歲計餘絀
  - 9 預算內款項依法流用
  - 7 其他

二、計算與計算之聯鎖關係

計算者係根據於月份收支預算分配表(卽月份行政預算)所編之核實計數表也。蓋預算爲一會計年度之估計，一年內各月之間如何分配，得由主管機關長官就法定預算範圍之內，將各科目金額爲十二個月之分配數命令所屬機關每月依照各該月份核定分配數執行收支。此種核定月份分配數工作，無須經過立法程序，僅爲行政主管機關長官對其所屬機關所施之行政監督

而已。易言之卽主管機關長官以有月份收支預算分配表之根據可用爲考覈所屬機關每月行政效率之標準。故機關每月所編月份收支計算書卽一月過去以後視執行收支結果如何，列其既成事實及數字同時與原核定月份分配數相互排列，比較其增加或減少數額送呈主管機關考覈。通常月份收支計算書並附有收支憑證單據由主管機關轉送審計機關核銷，以解除原送機關對經理收支款項所負之責任。

就表面觀之每年十二個月計算書之合計表或計算書之採用累計表式(Gumulative Form)者其最後月份之計算書均可等於全年度之決算，但再進一步觀察則計算與決算並不盡同。爰詳其述異點如下：

決算與計算之異點
- 1 就性質方面區分
  - 1 根據不同—收支計算以月份收支預算分配表爲根據收支決算以本年度預算現額爲根據。
  - 2 對象不同—收支計算以報告行政主管機關爲對象收支決算以報告立法機關或監察機關並須明令公布昭示全國人民爲對象。
  - 3 所含之期間不同—經常費 計算乃以月份爲

單位之決算而決算者乃一年中每月計算之總和。

臨時費　計算與決算相同無甚差別。

繼續經費　計算與決算各依其事業進行每段落成全部完成時編製之。

2就所含內容方面區分

4所列之數字不同——計算書方面所列數目爲毛數。(Gross Amount) 而決算書方面所列數目爲淨數 (Net Amount) 及已經審定之數字。其詳細情形如下：收入計算書所列收入數在以後月份或有退還收入款及歲入減免額等情形，在編決算時應將上項退還收入款及歲入減免額從收入數中剔去而求得淨數列入決算書。支出計算書所列支出數在以後月份或有經審計機關剔除者，在編決算時應將上項剔除經費從支出數中剔去而求得淨數列入決算書。如編決算之最後期限已屆收支計算書尚本審查完竣爲求迅速起見得以未審定金額列入（但須與已審定金額劃分）併說明之。審計機關於審查決算時再行審定。再如審計機關提出審計

報告之最後期限已屆，仍有尚未審定金額，則將未審定金額列入審計報告(但須與已審定金額劃分)以後再行核定。

三，決算與收支報告之聯鎖關係

收支報告(年度收支報告)係表示編製機關現金出納及保管情形之報告與表示編製機關執行預算情形之決算情形不同。其異點如下．

1收支報告所列收支數目可以不與預算比較排列。而決算書則必須將收入支出各數分別與預算相互排列，比較其增減金額。

2收支報告大致採用收付實現之會計基礎(Cash basis)而決算書上所列本年收入支出各數欲求精確起見應採用權責發生之會計基礎 Accrued basis) 。如此則計算書上所列收入爲本年度之應收歲入款。所列支出爲本年度之應付歲出額。收支報告中，所列收歲入款付歲出款爲本年度實收實付之款，如就兩方面報表比較觀察。用本年度最後一份收支報告所列收本年度歲入款及付本年度歲出款之累計數與決算上所列應收本年度歲入款及應付本年度歲出款比較可以求得迄至年度終了時止之應

收未收歲入款及應付未付歲出款各若干。再者就下年度收支報告所列補收上年度歲入款及補付上年度歲出款之數目與迄至上年度終了時止之應收未收歲入款及應付未付歲出款餘額比較，可以求得迄至報告日止仍未收納之上年度應收未收歲入款及仍未支付之上年度應付未付歲出款各若干。以上所論爲其最主要之異點亦其最主要之聯鎖關係也。但亦有爲計算便利起見決算書上所列本年度收入支出各數係實收實付數者，如此則兩方面報表所列數目，可以符合。再如下年度補收上年度歲入款及補付上年度歲出款有時補記上年度帳冊重編整理決算及收支報告(Revised Report)者但過整理期間以後，卽縱有補收補付情形，則記入現年度帳冊不必整理所屬年度之決算及收支報告矣，如此則兩方面報告表數目，亦可符合。

3 收支報告附列歲入外各項收款，如代收款保管款短期借款暫收款及補收上年度款，冲收上年度付款之屬。又須附列歲出外各項付款，如墊付款暫付款及補付上年度冲款付上年度收款之屬。但以上各款在決算書內不可混入。

4 如在採用統一公庫制度國家，其國庫收支報告上所列歲入歲出各數係指由國庫代中央各機關本年度內收納或支付數目，可與各機關所編收付實現基礎之決算，比較觀察是否符合，但因各機關收款或未有達國庫帳者，及各機關簽付支票未經國庫支付者，故各機關決算數，往往與國庫收支報告數，發生差額，此時應編差額解釋表 (Reconciliation Statement) 以說明之。但如各機關所編決算係採用權責發生基礎者，則決算書上所列歲入歲出數目與國庫本年度收支報告上所列經收該機關歲入款與經付歲出款可以相互比較求得應收未收歲入款及應付未付歲出款各若干。

5 如公庫不統一祇有總基金歸國庫收付。則此時國庫收支報告上所列數目分爲兩部分：(1)國庫所收收入機關解款及國庫所付支出機關經費款(2)國庫直接收入款（如銀行交易所稅等）及國庫直接支付款（如債務費補助費撫邮費等）以上第(1)類收付祇是各政府機關現款之移轉，與決算不生影響。以上第(2)類收付屬於歲入歲出範圍，亦應另編決算與原列預算相比較。

四、決算在總平準表之聯鎖關係

政府機關之總平準表 (Fund Balance Sheet, Statement of Fund Resources and Obligations)係爲表示某項基金或某

機關某日時之資力（Resources）及負担（Obligations）等情形而設。某項基金或某機關根據預算執行收支其經過情形如何於年度終了日止或於年度終了後之整理完結日止應編成決算以資比較。而於年度終了日或於年度終了後之整理完結日實存資力若干，實欠負担若干，及歲計餘絀實數若干，須另撰總平準表以資表明。故決算為某項基金或某機關一會計年度之動態報告，屬於縱剖面（Verticle）之表示。而總平準表乃該項基金或該機關年度終了日止或整理結束日止之靜態報告，屬於橫斷面（HoriIzontal）之表示。此為決算與總平準表之聯鎖關係。

五、決算與財產目錄及固定負債目錄之聯鎖關係

政府會計普通基金所編總平準表祇列可供該項基金自由使用之資力，及由該項基金本身所歸還之負担，並求其比較餘絀數而已故凡固定資產不足供該項基金自由使用部份及固定負債不由該項基金自身歸還部分可不必列入。但上項情形不可不有表示，故在總平準表外，另應編財產目錄及固定負債目錄兩表以足成之。至論財產目錄與固定負債目錄（固定負債為負財產可與財產同編一張目錄之內）與決算之關係如下所示。

1上年度財產目錄列數＋本年度決算書上所列購置費及營造費數目－本年度財產減損數＝本年度財產目錄列數

2上年度負債目錄列數本＋年度歲入決算書上所列債款收入－本年度歲出決算書上所列債務費支出(本金部份)＋本年度債欠未付利息＝本年度負債目錄列數。

第三章　各國現行決算制度

關于各國現行決算制度茲舉英日兩國為例，詳示如下：

一、英國之現行決算制度（英國會計年度係四月一日至三月卅一日）英國之決算報告分有兩種：

財政部之國庫收支報告 Financial Accounts of United Kingdom)

各收支機關之支出決算書（Appropriation Account)

1財政部之國庫收支報告　英國國庫從會計年度開始迄至上星期六日之收支累計數，例于下星期二日編成收支報告，發表倫敦官報（London Gazette）。上項收支報告除照收入來源支出性質分類外，並依各機關分類。

每季末之決算，較為詳細，除以上收支報告外，並列資產負債目錄。

每年度末之決算更爲詳細，其中分爲五部。

1國庫收支報告。

2歲入。

3歲出。

4國債。

5其他。

以上年度末之決算全體報告，大都于結帳年之六月，印成藍皮書發表，至國庫收支報告，則于三月卅一日下午四點鐘，即行編成，播音報告全國。又收支報告上收支差額即結存數，則全數指撥爲償債之用。

查國庫收支報告中所列收入支出各類，皆爲從會計年度開始迄至會計年度終了時之現金出納數。

2歲入方面：則爲實收數之達到國庫者，其依法應當征收尚未達到國庫者、未經計入。又各機關收入經議會特准留充該機關事業補助費之用者，亦未經計入。

ii歲出方面：則以由國庫發放與支付署之撥付數爲限，其他各機關支出由其收入項下經議會特准留用者即未經計入。

是以國庫收支報告所列收入支出各數，既非本年度實收實

付數目，又非歲入歲出之應收應付數目。但英人對于國庫收支報告十分注意，認爲有決算之同等效力者，蓋有以下各種原因。

i有收支限期清理之功效　英人認爲國家應收應支之數，在權責發生時，須即時收付，不得拖延，以增進行政效率。

ii有便于財政管理之功效　在年度末時，即加清理，縱有弊竇，亦容易發現。原經手人員仍在職位，可隨時追索，以免事過境遷容易推諉。

iii有計算準確之功效　以交通便利，各地收入機關之收入數于二三日內可以完全達到國庫，此其一國庫收支報告所列收入支出各數目雖非歲入歲出確數，然因各年度間，上拉下扯，平均下來，如無非常情形發生，則每年國庫收支報告所列數目，與歲入歲出確數，亦相差不遠。

iV有結束敏捷之功效　年度末日隨時編報告公布，足使人民信任政府而解除政府之責任。且可以供下年度編製預算之參考，恰爲最近最新之資料。

2各機關之支出決算書　查英國在會計年度末之前一星期各機關在預算定額內應支各數，必趕速支付，無使拖延，然尚

有依預算可以支出而未及支出者，此項支出，分爲兩部：由財政部於會計年度終了日以前與各機關商定之。

i 停發部分　各機關未發生債務關係者，爲不必支出之經費，是爲預算上之純餘額，此後不再由財政部撥付。

ii 應發部分　年度末雖未及期償付，但仍須於下年度支付，經財政部審查後，於決算日前，全數將此項經費撥付支付署，由支付署保存。支付署保存各機關仍須支付之經費數，日後仍照常發給，但以此後三個月爲限。在三個月期內支付者，支付署記入該機關上年度原預算帳內。三個月整理期完畢後，即結束上年度預算帳。如過期而債權人始來領款者，支付署記入該機關下年度預算帳內。在此種支付署保存金額中，亦有終不支付者，其數額存於支付署可以減少下年度財政部之撥付。

各支出機關會計人員，在每年六月底（整理期間結束日期）清理一年零三個月之支出，編成支出決算書，幷彙集各項發票收據，經由財政部轉送審計機關查核。

此項支出決算書之內容，完全依照預算所列之科目排列。其格式如下：

支出決算書

科目及摘要	預算數	支出數	比較減增數	
			減	增

各項說明……………………………………

各機關支出決算書，每編一帙，每帙有一終說明。復於每節說明與預算相差之原因。

財政部彙集各機關支出決算書，成爲支出總決算書，分爲四冊。

1 政事費

2 征收費

3 陸軍費

4 海軍費

財政部於九月底將上冊送審計機關審查。海軍費之支出決算書常延至十月底送出。審計機關查訖後，編成審計報告，送還財政部，於第二年一月或二月內由財政部印就提送議會決定。

二、日本之現行決算制度（會計年度四月一日至三月卅一日止與英國同）

1 決算之編製　日本會計規則規定歲入歲出總決算，應照預算之區分，由大藏大臣編製之。按日本政府所編預算，有總預算與特別會計預算之分，故決算亦應分爲總決算及特別會計兩種。

2 編製決算之根據　大藏大臣根據以下四種材料，編製決算：

i 歲入主計簿。

ii 歲出主計簿。

iii 歲入增減計算書。

iV 各省經費決算報告書。

3 決算之審核程序　日本憲法規定國家歲出歲入之決算，于審計院審查後，由政府連同審計報告一併提出議會。

4 決算之格式：

總決算應分以下各部門：

歲入部：	歲出部：
歲入預算額	歲出預算額
查定歲入額	預算決定後增加歲出額
已收訖歲入額	已支出歲出額
歲入減免額	轉入次年度額
未收訖歲入額	剩餘額

實用格式如下：

歲入決算書

科目	預算額	查定額	收訖額	減免額	未收訖額

歲出決算書

科目	預算額	預算決定後增加額		已支出額	轉入次年度額	剩餘額
		上年度轉入額	預備費支出額			

決算書之附件，計有以下三種：

i. 歲入決算明細書

款／項目	預算額	查定額	收訖額	減免額	未收訖額	收訖額與預算額比較增減數

ii. 各省所管經費決算報告書

款／項目	預算額	預算決定後增加額		流用增減額	預算現額	已支出額	轉入次年度額	剩餘額	備考
		上年度轉入額	預備費支出額						

iii. 國債計算書應爲以下三種分表

年度末國債現額表

種類	現額

本年度國債本息償付表

種類	本金償還額	利息支付額	備考

五個年度間各年度末國債額增減比較表

種類	本年度末現額	六年度現額	五年度現額	四年度現額	三年度現額	比較表			
						比六年度末	比五年度末	比四年度末	比三年度末

5 決算之審查確定　審計院關於決算之審查手續如下：

對照所編以上各種決算報表與歲入預算，歲出預算，預算決定後增加歲出額，各項會計已決定之計算書，及日本銀行之計算額等。一一對照有無錯誤，然後作成審計報告。審計報告應載明下列各事項：

a 總決算及各省所管經費決算報告書之金額，與日本銀行提出計算書之金額，是否相符。

b 歲入之征收，歲出之支用，官有物之取得、變賣，讓渡及使用，是否違背各該預算之規程或法律勅令。

c 預算超過或預算外之支出中，有無未得議會承認者。

6 審計報告之格式

i. 歲入歲出總決算審計報告

決算額		未確定金額	
歲入	歲出	歲入	歲出

ii. 各特別會計歲入歲出決算審計報告

特別會計種類	決算額		未確定金額	
	歲入	歲出	歲入	出歲

iii. 決算額與日本銀行計算額之差額解釋表

摘要	普通會計	特別會計				
		××	××	××	××	××
歲入決算額						
日本銀行證明額						
差額						
原因						
1.…………						
2.…………						
2.…………						

7 決算之審查未確定　其主要者爲證明未了，對于審查之答辯未了及關於犯罪事件，尙須審查者。

以上審查未確定部分，應作爲決算未確定金額，載明於審計報告之末尾。以後更於審查終了之年度審計報告中，載明旣往年度決算未確定金額中審查確定數。

8 決算由議會決定　決算由政府提出議會後貴衆兩院之審議決算，恰與審議預算相同，交付決算委員會，委員會更分科辦事，最後由委員會彙齊報告本屆議會而決定之。

關於審計院在審計報告上揭載事項，政府得提出答辯，故議會通例關於各事項均先將審計報告與答辯對照，再加審議，其結果認爲政府之答辯有理由時，即議決承認。而對於答辯理由不允分者，則決定爲違法或不當，以促進政府將來之注意。

（未完）

財務管理意義之片段

國家財務管理之最大目的，在求行政計劃與行政實施之最大經濟與最高效率。行政上種種錯誤失當，以及腐敗混亂等情形，可於財務管理上一一表現無遺。此種錯誤失當，不盡由於官吏之營私舞弊。而各級機關之失却調協性與整聯性，循使各項行政，緩急失序，輕重失衡，實爲其一大原因。欲求管理上之實效，端在將計劃與實施之逐步手續，訂一集中統制之辦法。其第一步即爲編製預算。

——節譯費樂白氏著英國財務管理一書中第一章中文意——

陸大月刊 第三卷第二期

目錄

本刊價目 零售：每期大洋叁角 半年六期大洋壹元五角 全年十二期大洋三元

郵費 外埠：每期二分五厘 半年一角五分 全年三角
本埠：每期二分 半年一角二分 全年二角四分

編輯者：陸大月刊編輯委員會

發行者：陸大月刊社

社址：南京漢口路陸軍大學特別黨部內

電話：三一七一三

代售處：特別黨部及各大書局

中國統計學社湖北分社 社刊 第一集要目

定價每冊四角（郵費本埠四分外埠七分半）

寄售處 湖北省政府統計室

通訊

浙贛鐵路局南昌營業所營業概況

吳家鈞

同學吳君家鈞供職浙贛路局有年，著有勞績，近在該路南昌營業所服務。頃據吳君來函，報告該所業務至爲明晰，茲刊之以饗讀者　編者

（上略）謹將本所業務狀況分述於次：

甲、問訊業務　南昌南北二站既距市中心甚遠，客商訊均莫不趨之本所，有詢問本路沿線所經各地及往杭州上海等處票價所需時間及行李包裹貨物之運送者，有詢問貨物運價及上海交運貨物有時延滯不到幷託爲催運者，此類事件本所莫不具和藹之態度，正確之解答，使問者獲得圓滿結果，稱謝而去，尤以貨物延滯，客商託爲催詢，本所不憚煩瑣，視其經過時間之長短或發電報催問，或用電話催詢，此種業務其便利於客商，解除客商與本路之隔閡，功效甚大。

乙、接送業務　本所初備卡車一輛專爲代客接送行李包裹

貨物之用，照業務情形而論，一輛卡車實不敷用（然卡車之消費浩繁，若無相當收入，安足維持其開支，）經過月餘，爲應業務之需要，繼而增添一輛，以資循環裝運，但事實則仍感不敷，因其中延誤裝運時間情形甚多，如車站提貨之困難，稅捐查驗之繁複，裝卸搬運之阻撓遲緩等等，在在均使接送業務不能迅捷（若再增添一輛卡車，又恐業務稍淡時，收入不足維持，惟有設法盡人事力量以補救之），嗣因至九月間貨運更形擁擠，原有卡車二輛實不敷週轉，經再三考慮，決又增添卡車一輛，但該第三輛卡車僅能載重二噸，勉强堪以使用，將來業務發展，頗有增加第四輛卡車之必要。

丙、接送業務之困難與解決經過 關於本所接送業務之困難，層見迭出，解決方法極費週折，茲分述於後：

A.車站提貨之困難 南昌南站無貨倉設備，所有到達貨物，均盡量堆置於第二月台雨棚下，以防雨淋，早晨提貨時，車輛來往經過，搬運工作無法着手，須待至十時半十四次車開行後，方能搬運，並以車站貨物出口處甚少，僅有二處，倘遇停留三輛以上汽車，即感擁擠之患，妨害貨物裝車殊甚，爲解決是項困難計，乃派員駐站，於清晨五時，即督促扛搬夫，將貨物搬至第一月台，提早報捐查驗，使彼此工作不起衝突，但有時或遇天雨，則無法辦理矣。

B.捐稅局查驗貨物之困難 南昌南北兩站，均設有產銷捐徵收處各一所，運進貨物，必須報請該處查驗，納稅放行，其查驗手續，應將一批貨物全數堆置一處，一一拆包點驗清楚後，將查驗結果，攜回徵收處計算稅款，填發稅票，但其計算及填票工作之人員人數甚少，一件貨物須填稅票一張，其費時間之久，可想而知，本所惟有商請查驗人員通融辦理，將貨特隨搬隨驗，不必等候全部搬齊，以省時間。

C.稅捐覆驗處覆驗貨物之困難 產銷捐局遂於本路運進貨物，日漸增多，爲周密計，又於距徵收處一二里之遙，增設覆驗處一所，貨物裝載經過時，須拆包同樣覆驗一次，其每一車貨覆驗時間，視貨物之繁簡，多則一二少時，少則數十分鐘，因此裝卸貨物又增一層延誤，解決方法，惟有延長晚間工作時間，藉以補救，八月間該處規定。下午六時停止覆驗，影響業務更鉅，由本所向稅局請求變通，嗣該處乃自動改至下午七時半停止覆驗，但本所於貨物較多時，仍須隨時商請該處通融辦理，以利業務。

D.扛搬夫之困難 南站扛搬大，性極懶惰，動作又欠靈敏，每遇扛搬一批貨物，即須東拉西扯，將全組扛搬夫集合，方肯開始搬運，偶或欠缺一二，餘則袖手不動，迨人數到齊，工作不久，又復藉吃飯喝水等事故而散去，呼喚極費時力。至其工作情形，一組分爲裝車及扛搬二班，不知互相幫助，只知彼此觀望，且不聽指揮，延誤工作殊甚。碼頭工人亦然，卸車者不管搬送，搬送者不管卸車不致延誤車輛，但該工人等，則堅持固守死法，非卸一件搬送一件不可，遲緩達於極點，本所爲求搬運迅速，只有命自僱扛搬夫幫同裝卸，以資敏捷。

E.軍事影響 七八月間兩廣事變，本路軍運繁忙，貨運曾停頓十數日，客商因而改由水道運輸，該兩月中，南昌南北兩站，到達貨物均係零担貨物，大批整車貨物極少，而棉紗洋雜貨又值淡月，運量尤少，本所業務受此影響甚大，爲竭力維持開支計，不得不做到極步辦法，俟晚間昌南昌北兩站貨車到達，卽由本所員司，將其到達貨物名稱重量收貨人商號全數抄錄，當晚馳往各到貨商號，通知提取，以期各商直接明瞭本路辦事認眞，間接又知本所代客接送貨物便利，故本所二月以來，業務雖受軍事及淡月影響，經此一翻努力招攬，該七八月接送業務收入，仍超出一千元以上，足以維持本所開支，

丁、招徠　南昌運出貨物極少僅有鎢礦砂粗紙米穀夏布瓷器牛皮桐油等類貨物，以前運輸途徑全係取道長江，鎢礦砂爲鎢業管理處所專營，前因本路運價過高，故仍就其水道，本所籌備之初，卽注意於此，迭經與南昌辦事處鄒主任，鎢業管理處黃主任，洪技士磋商，該鎢礦砂改由本路運輸辦法，惟其水路運價比較本路與滬杭路運價僅佔百分之五十爲弱，本路及滬杭路如欲招徠鎢砂運輸，勢非減低運價莫辦，嗣由鈞與曾課長陳丰任會同鎢業管理處黃主任向滬杭路商訂減價辦法，按運價七折計算，不適用遞遠遞減，俟運價商妥後，該鎢砂於三月二

十日開始交由本路承運，於承運該第一批鎢砂時，鎢業管理處並派員邀鈞同往視察本路中轉裝卸及滬杭路裝卸情形，結果甚爲圓滿，嗣後大量鎢砂均交本路承運接送及照料，裝運事務則交由本所辦理，惟其鎢砂每交運一批，其限期到達日期甚促，致本路承運該項鎢砂煞費苦心，因本路車輛甚少，每次請求車輛均不能不能預計日期，或數日無車裝運，或一次裝運一列專車，同時本所本身業務甚忙，又不能因鎢砂而影響其他營業，更不能因顧全本所營業而躭誤行車，補救方法，惟有提早於清晨五時起工作，晚間特別延長工作時間，將鎢砂先期送至南站堆存，中午乘間裝運車站到貨，如此既不躭誤行車，復不妨碍本所營業，惟鎢業管理處堆棧工作時間因被本所牽制延長，此點堆棧工作人員頗不願意，嗣經再三情商，方勉强允爲通融辦理。南昌運出粗紙甚多，以史子記經營爲最，該紙向係銷售濟南青島等處，經由長江水運至浦口，轉津浦路聯運膠濟路，本路通車之始，因無貨倉設備，迄未改道運輸，本所有鑒於此，乃從事調查其水道運價比較經由本路確爲低廉，但中途所需時間則以本路爲迅捷，經迭次與該號經理君接洽方始改由路運，所有需用車輛。照料裝車等事，均由本所辦理，試行以來，尚

稱便利，惟運至靜江站中轉時，時有被雨打濕紙張沾霉情事，有時與別家紙混雜，俟到達後發見，牌名不符，此外貨物到達日期亦復迂緩，較水運幷不見迅速，以致該紙時由本路，時由水道，據謂倘能將以上三點解決，大批粗紙將改由路運。南昌素以米穀出口爲大宗，其由水路運往上海之運價，較經由本路之廉相距甚遠，在本所成立之初，正米穀禁止出口之時，及至最近始有大批米粮輸出，日前鈞曾數次作精細之調查，並將所調查之水運運價呈報運輸課，作訂特價之參考，現本路特價已經公布，以鈞所見，此中尙有二點，必須先行解決：(一)輪船公司備有巨大貨倉囤存米粮，且免費囤存時間甚長，鐵路方面是否有此設備，能否如此辦理，(二)靜江中轉時，米粮極易偷漏，或受濕，此層本路是否可以設法避免，以上二點倘能解決，米穀交由本路承運，當然不成問題，否則雖有特價，恐難全部招致。他如夏布、瓷器，牛皮，桐油等貨，經數度接洽招徠後，均已改由本路承運，南昌每年冬季向有大批鮮蛋運往上海，蛋商要求本所於鮮蛋運抵上海後，須代送至收貨店舖，並須代收貨價，除代送事務已函商上海南站代爲辦理外，至代收貨價一層，因鮮蛋係容易損壞物品，照章不辦代收貨價，刻已通知蛋商，聯名呈局請求，倘可代收貨價，則大批鮮蛋將全部改由路運。南昌運進貨物可謂應有盡有，惜本路設備未週，加之時間並不迅速，甚或較長江水運爲遲，故未能盡量招致，其運進大宗貨物爲棉紗，棉織疋頭，洋雜貨，南北貨，糖及紙捲菸等，本所成立之初，對於該項大宗貨物之招徠，極爲注意，首先進行者爲棉紗及棉織疋頭，該兩項貨物經鈞一再與南南昌棉紗巨商王信裕號經理王肇基中棉南記謝經理及棉織疋頭同業公會主席周子實商洽，請其改由本路運輸，彼等對於此事頗稱熱心，周君首先召集疋頭同業開會討論貨物改由本路運輸辦法，結果同業極表贊同，當場推派代表七人赴滬交涉改運手續及視察本路與滬杭路貨房設備，並邀職一同赴滬協助辦理，王信裕號王君則先期赴滬辦理棉紗改運手續，中棉南記則備函交鈞帶往上海總號，面洽一切，抵滬後，王信裕號業已委妥專人駐滬辦理棉紗託運手續，中棉南記經鈞親自前往接洽，結果極爲圓滿，允即全部改由路運，惟棉織疋頭改運事則發生相當困難，因該貨向係由南昌各號委託滬上莊客代辦，而莊客多係報關行股東莊客代辦貨物，可向輪船公司索取二成回佣，報關行辦理轉運亦可向輪船公司索取二成回佣，因此多數莊客可以從中取得雙二成回佣自故此次該棉織疋頭同業代表到滬向各莊客接洽改運辦法，渠等則竭力反對，嗣經周子實君迭次召集會議，終因同業多數主張改由路運，莊客反對無效，乃由該同業在滬另組公記運輸處，直接向路託運，並由鈞代向滬杭路辦理登記手續，四月間大批棉紗棉織疋頭均即改由本路運輸。南北貨及糖，每年運銷南昌亦頗可觀，經鈞向各商號調查招攬南北貨水運價目，確較路運為廉，糖因有濬浦捐關係，其運價亦較路運為低，鈞曾將調查該貨水運價目報課備供參考，每年暑期南昌例有大批汽水啤酒運進，經與經售商號福安公司接洽，改由路運，承允先行試運一批，其時適值本路軍運甚忙，該汽水啤酒一百餘箱擱置靜江月餘未運，在此期中，大批啤酒汽水則仍由長江水運，以致本年汽水啤酒未能盡量改由路運。紹酒每年運輸南昌達數千罎，經鈞赴各商號接洽，各商號曾試運數次，嗣因該酒曾於途中打破數罎，本路未予賠償，商人不堪損失，於是仍由水運，日前經鈞向其解釋，並告其以後如有損壞，可託本所代辦請求賠償手續，並將損壞未賠商人不由路運情形呈課，現已由課通令改善承運紹酒辦法，最近該項紹酒業已重行改由本路運到一批。至於洋紙，西藥，書籍等，經向各商接洽後，均陸續改由本路運輸，惟紙捲於除南洋公司業已改由路運外，福安公司因本路設備未週，香烟不能受濕，未敢冒險改運，現仍由長江水運，英美烟公司則因水運回佣甚大，不肯改由本路運輸。（下略）

管理二月刊

第一卷 第一期
民國二十五年四月

管理二月刊

第一卷 第二期
民國二十五年七月

書評

『行政學』

任家誠

原名——Public Administration

著者——John M. Pfiffner

出版處——The Ronald Press Company, New York

版期——一九三五年

定價——美金四元

近十年來美國對於行政學確有極大貢獻，足供我人的參證，衞羅倍的行政學原理(W.F. Willoughby *Principles of Public Administration*)和懷德的行政學緒論(L.D. White *Introduction to the study of Public Administration*)二書已成為世界行政學著作的權威，更是寰宇共通的參攷根據。但是這二書的出版，已經經過相當年份，這幾年正因為二書的提倡而造成行政學研究孟晉的結果，所以新的理論，新的學識尤值得我人注意，最近南加州大學(Uuinervsity of Southern California)行政學院(School of Government)法分諸教授(Prof. Pfiffner)薈集新論，而成此書，可為代表。

法氏執教有年，在南加州大學担任行政學教席已有七年之久（法氏於一九二九年膺南加州大學聘，此書出版時在校亦已五年，）專門研究心得的流露，著書立說當然有裨學子。尤其因為書成于執教的時候，整理教材而成，比較的可以適合基本研究的需要。明晰而詳盡是最明顯的優點。

最先請討論此書的編制。此書共分五編。(一)行政組織，(二)人事行政(三)財務行政，(四)行政法，(五)公共關係。物料管理在此書中並沒有略去而把牠歸納入財務行政中附帶討論。所以前三編可謂與衞羅倍所討論的範圍相似，而後二編則為新創。

行政法是否應在行政學中研究，這一點最值得我們注意。

行政學脫胎於行政法學，是寰宇學者所共認的事實。但是最近幾十年來由於學者的努力，科學管理方法的酌量採取，行政學與行政法學已成爲二大科學，並駕前驅，雖二者不免有節節相關而不能分離的狀態，然而混爲一談已非其時。而此書却另闢行政法一編，佔了不少篇幅，分散讀者對於行政學研究的專注力。不過行政學和行政法學到底還是同出一流，沒有互相背馳的地方，把這編插入，不能說是極大的錯誤。聽說南加川大學行政學院中的確把行政法當作行政學教材之一，這或者是新行政學研究的趨向；在我看來，總覺不盡確當。

物料的購置，保管和領用，現在已成爲行政學中一個重要的問題。雖然政府的物料不是施政的重要條件，和一般企業不同，然而也未嘗不居全國支出的大部份，有嚴加統制的必要。工商管理學中材料管理是最重要的一部份，在行政學中亦未嘗不然，所以物料管理不應在財務行政中輕描淡寫略爲提及。我國政府近來也已經確認物料管理的重要，紛紛主張改革過去的辦法，成立購料委員會，以爲統制。英美各國對於集中物料管理，購料的方法和經濟，保管的合理化，都已有相當成績，所以物料管理在今日已經不是一樁次要的事務，爲迎合此需要，物料管理的研究，更爲切要，作者似乎輕視了這一點。

『行政效率，』近幾年來在我國已成普遍的呼聲，國府勵精圖治，漸亦走向這光明的大道。以行政修明著聲世界的美國近年來也未嘗不以此自勉自勵。但是行政的良窳如何決定，施政的優劣如何測度，此書特闢公共關係一編來討論。行政的良窳和優劣最先感覺到的不是主觀的統治階級而是客觀的被統治階級，所以行政和人民最先發生關係。行政效率之提倡並非完成執政者的權能，而是圖民衆的利益，譬如說一件公事擱去幾個月，對於公務員並無害處，而痛癢相關的則是人民。所以此書提起政府行政對於公衆關係調節的方法以爲救濟，牠所討論的方法有下列三種，(一)處理人民訴願，(二)組織委員會，請平民諮商政事，(三)公開發行刊物，報告工作進行經過。吾國政府尚不能注意到這一點，此編大可供作參攷。

政府施政的良窳優劣如果必須等人民的反應或推崇而表現，未免過遲，因爲已經到了木已成舟的時候，沒有改進或變革的可能；而且客觀的批評未必公平，更不能絕對的作爲定論。因之，政府執政者應有主觀的估值，以爲改進變革的根據。此書於公衆關係中提到施政成績的標準和測度，即所以迎合此需要。牠建議標準測度的方法很多，如（一）模範法規（Model Laws）、(二)單位成本（Unit Cost）、(三)流動變數(Current variable)、(四)個人政績(Individual Performance)(五)量分制(Rating scale)等，此外更提到孟洛教授(Prof. W. B.Munro)的意見——不贊成用標尺式的標準，作呆板的測度，而主張用問題作解答。

現在各國對於行政建設最注目的就是組織的調整，這當然因爲行政組織是一切行政的基礎，成敗所繫，最關切要。美國自羅福斯繼任總統後第一炮就是改革行政機構，日本正也在討論各省的調整和總務廳的設置。在這種趨向下，行政組織的研究是不容或忽的。此書對於行政組織，討論最爲詳盡，尤對於美國的組織演變有有系統的商榷。在討論人事行政和財務行政時，也最先提起組織，的確如果人事統馭和財政統制方法十分優良，而沒有一個完備的機關來運用，還不能有良好的結果，這種討論有其重要性，此書充分地抓住這一著。所以組織一編很能迎合時代的需要。

上一期介紹張著『行政學之理論與實際』時，曾經說起張先生忽略了現代化的行政組織理論——職能之劃分。此書對於此點十分重視，在統合組織(或稱完整組織)一章中反覆申論，不厭求詳，並且還作圖說明，以便學子的研究。參贊職能和實行職能的劃分，確可以說是近年來行政組織研究的新發現，衛羅倍在他的著作中雖曾敘到，但未曾詳爲申論，懷德更一字不談，現在作者把牠提出討論，確值得我們注意。

此書人事行政一編，並沒有什麼特殊之處可資商榷，但是作者確已很忠實地逐一討論各問題。我覺得對於職位分類，俸給釐訂和退休制度的叙述似乎過簡，不能儘量歸納現代各家的學說，更少有合乎實情的例證。這或者由于主觀眼光的不同，當然不能盡歸咎于作者的忽略。

此書把財務行政的四大問題(一)計劃，(二)決定，(三)行政，(四)監督，儘量歸納于二章中：(一)預算之計劃及通過，(二)預算之執行及審計。此外更討論金庫制度，債務行政和稅務行政，以爲補充。作者很能夠把握住『行政』的本質，少有越出範圍的地方。但是會計制度在現在的財務行政中，確佔有十分重要的地位，內部牽制組織的實現，經費支出的統制，都賴會計制度來扶助，而此書對會計方面的商討却未曾加以注意，確是一個極大的缺憾。

此書把物料管理歸入財務行政中討論，其不當，前面已經說過，這不過在編制上的商榷。而作者對於物料管理問題本身也未能詳爲探討，他所提到的祇是購料一方面，對於保留和領用手續都未提起；對於集中購料也未曾有明切的建議。作者對於物料管理也許沒有深切的興趣，所以有此章編入，不過是聊備一格，以完成行政學的範疇而已。

當我讀了此書之後，有一個很深切的感想，就是行政學確乎不易研究。牠所討論的範圍兼及組織，人事，財務，物料四大問題，牽涉到政治，法律，經濟和工商管理四大學科，而人生精力有限，何能四面顧到。祇要把行政學的著作一看，我們很容易得到例證，無論那一本行政學書都不能把四問題並行研究，各具特長。以此書言，組織之討論爲最精闢，人事次之，財務又次之，物料更次之，就是一個極大的證明。同時更可以說沒有一本行政學書能分別適合政治，法律，經濟和工商管理四大學科，不是偏重前二者，便是偏重後二者。研究行政學的，大半對政治和法律發生較大興趣，所以發爲文章也較能與政治學和法律相符合；法氏之所以對組織和人事有較完美的貢獻，就是這緣故，因爲財務行政和物料管理的研究，非對於經濟和工商管理有透澈的認識必不能勝任愉快。

雜誌論文索引

索引類刊	題目	著者	雜志名稱	發行年月	號數
A類					
A 1:	非常時期之科學管理	程守中	工商管理月刊	25—11	3:6
	科學管理實施方法之檢討	顧鼎吉	人事管理	25—10	2:1
B類					
B 1:	行政上的集中購辦組織問題	李廷樑	建國月刊	25—9	5:4
	組織工業會之商榷	胡西園	工商管理月刊	25—11	3:6
	工商業組織的基本原理		科學畫報	25—10	4:6
	組織企業指導部之商榷	許體鋼	國民經濟建設月刊	25—9	1:1
B 2:	工廠管理	王國瑞	改進	25—12	19
	整理生產事業的途徑	吳景超	行政研究	25—11	1:2
	如何計劃第二年營業	程守中	工商管理月刊	25—11	3:6
	急宜整頓之我國倉儲事業	繆進三	農報	25—9	3:27
	改進江西粮食調節及農倉管理意見		經濟旬刊	25—10	7:12
	土耳其的工業化計劃	楊卓膺	中外月刊	25—12	2:1
	改進國貨工業之新途徑	大公報	國聞周報	25—9	13:38
B 3:	最近世界工業生產之發展	胡紀常	華年	25—10	5:40—41
B 5:	湘米運粤的一個問題	鄭林莊	獨立評論	25—10	221
	粮食之產銷統制問題	沈松林	申報周刊	25—11	1:45
	粮食漲價與出口問題	李芸生	國際貿易導報	25—11	8:11
	小麥出口問題	成讓	經濟旬刊	25—9	7:7
B 6:	科學管理下的康元廠職工	通原	交通職工	25—9	4:8
	職位分類之方法與效用	丁馨伯	工商管理月刊	25—11	3:6
	人事管理綱要	顧炳元	人事管理	25—10	2:1

	銀行人員舞弊之機會及方法研究	章雲保	人事管理	25—10	2:1
	舞弊與待遇	屠哲隱	人事管理	25—10	2:1
	店員與售貨效率	張一夢	人事管理	25—10	2:1
	參觀各機關人事管理部大綱	屠哲隱	人事管理	25—12	2:2
	人事管理規則彙編	顧炳元	人事管理	25—12	2:2
B 7:	研討中國茶業	黃守楨	工商管理月刊	25—11	3:6
	米麥豐收與糧食問題	孫懷仁	新中華	25—9	4:18
	戰時粮食問題	蓬 洲	黃埔月刊	25—9	6:3
	戰時粮食的準備	黃均夫	建國月刊	25—10	15:4
	中國食糧問題	西 禹	國聞周報	25—10	13:42
	工業分類之研究	唐啓賢	實業部月刊	25—9	1:6
	國貨工業散佈在農村	大公報	國聞周報	25—9	13:37
	我國之新興工業	胡 梯	商業月報	25—9	16:9
	中國工業的現狀	張素民	華年	25—10	5:38
	石油問題	朱俊臣	建國月刊	25—9	15:3
	我國棉業現勢	邁進蘭	漢口商業月刊	25—10	1:5
	我國米業現勢	吉 惠	交易新周刊	25—9	2:23
	我國火柴工業	楊德惠	商業月報	25—9	16:9
	我國之堆棧業	徐 光	經濟評論	25—9	3:9
	中國粮食問題之剖視及其解決	藍名詁	建國月刊	25—11	15:5
	浙江粮食行政述要	沈松林	浙江工商	25—10	1:1,2
	我國桐油業現狀及前途	金宜莊	中國建設	25—11	14:5
	我國羊毛業現狀及前途	陳 琴	商業月報	25—10	16:10
	我國國茶業危機及前途	王萊雨	錢業月報	25—12	16:12

C 類

C 1:	整頓路政之芻議	津浦路	鐵路雜誌	25—10	2:5
	中國鐵路建設之使命及其實現方法	王熙民	北寧鐵道月刊	25—9	6:9
	鐵路之新需要與新責任	張嘉璈	鐵道半月刊	25—11	1:12

	鐵路處理貨運之手續與辦法	朱翰譜	鐵道半月刊	25—10	1:11
	非常時期中國鐵路運價問題	劉傳書	鐵道半月刊	25—11	1:12
	改良中國鐵路起運零貨處置方法之建議	沈奏廷	鐵道半月刊	25—11	1:13
	革新鐵路業勢之要旨	蔣中正	鐵道半月刊	25—12	1:15
	貨物分等的基礎研究	熊養誠	鐵道半月刊	25—12	1:15
	英國鐵路貨運運費之研究	鄧廣熙	交通雜誌	25—9	4:9
	論鐵路運價率之釐定及運價大綱之編訂	畢愼夫	交通雜誌	25—9	4:9
	解決車機糾紛之幾個調度車輛問題	安忠義	交通雜誌	25—10	4:10
	吾國鐵路代遞貨票辦法之我評	沈奏廷	交通雜誌	25—11	4:11
	鐵路貨運商業化之動向	徐鄂雲	交通雜誌	25—12	4:12
	鐵路運價中之雜費問題	畢愼夫	交通雜誌	25—12	4:12
C 6:	如何減少行車事變	退思廬	改進專刊	25—12	19
	滬杭甬綫列車車輛調度概况	吳祿增	交大季刊	25—9	21
	平綏路車輛調度概況	呂慶溫	交大平院季刊	25—12	2:2
	如何製訂行車時刻表	范　銳	交大平院季刊	25—12	2:2
	我國鐵路貨車車輛支配問題	朱翰譜	交大平院季刊	25—12	2:2
	旅客列車行車之研究	鄭寶照	鐵路雜誌	25—10	2:5
	車務技術	退思廬	北寧鐵路月刊	25—9，10	6:9，10
	德國國有鐵路之新式貨車	秦元邦	鐵道半月刊	25—9	1:8
	車輛週轉之研究	王洪志	交通雜志	25—9	4:9
C 7:	考察貨車裝載效能之基本統計	許　靖	交通雜志	25—9	4:9
	再論吾國鐵路列車車輛統計辦法	沈奏廷	交通雜志	25—12	4:12
	貨運噸里統計之理論與實用	許　靖	交通雜志	25—10	4:10
	關於列車及車輛統計問題	劉傳書	交通雜志	25—11	4:11
	評吾國最近改訂之鐵路列車及車輛統計辦法	許　靖 沈奏廷	交通雜志	25—11	4:11
	貨運車輛載重統計之理論與實用	許　靖	管理	25—11	1:4
	統計學與鐵路統計	張漢炎	改進專刊	25—9，10，11	17，18，19
	論編製及運用鐵路統計之基本原則	許　靖	交大季刊	25—9	21

	評鐵部各路機車用煤統計及其改善之我見	許 靖	交大平院季刊	25—9	2:1
	中國鐵路列車及車輛統計之解析	劉傳書	鐵道半月刊	25—9	1:8,9
	鐵路預算之重要性	張紹元	鐵道半月刊	25—9	1:9
	貨運車輛里程統計之理論與實用	許 靖	鐵道半月刊	25—12	1:14
	我國現行列車車輛統計與原有行車統計之比較	宗之琥	鐵道半月刊	25—12	1:15
C 8:	交通服務人員效率之增進	何清儒	交通職工	25—10	4:9
	鐵路員工應如何努力以盡國防之責任	張公權	鐵道半月刊	25—11	1:13
	各國鐵路人員考績制度概況	薛光前	鐵道半月刊	25—11	1:13
	鐵路員工應有之認識	潘光迥	鐵道半月刊	25—12	1:15
	論鐵路管理人才之訓練與交大管理學院之使命	湯心濟	交通雜志	25—9	4:9
C 9:	鐵道單軌人工區截法之保安制度	宗之琥	交通雜志	25—10	4:10
	重整軍備中的德國汽車路	尊	交通雜志	25—10	4:10
	德國商業航空的發展	胡 侗	交通雜志	25—10	4:10
	最近告成之粵漢鐵路	薛正斗	交通雜志	25—10	4:10
	經濟復興政策下之美國交通事業	王 洸	交通雜志	25—11	4:11
	我國郵政局所發展之趨勢及今後應取之方針	王希祥	交通雜志	25—12	4:12
	航空運費之檢討	田惜庵	交通雜志	25—12	4:12
	最近我國中部貨運動向觀	劉堦平	交通雜志	25—12	4:12
	軍用輕便鐵路之建設與管理	王同文	管理	25—11	1:4

D類

D 1:	今後政治之展望	張佛泉	獨立評論	25—9	219
	平治之道	宋哲元	正風半月刊	25—9	3:3
	兩種民主政治	蔣昌聲	蘇俄評論	25—11	10:11
	我的行政經驗與感想	蔣廷黻	行政研究	25—10	1:1
	新政的透視與展望	張 銳	行政研究	25—10	1:1
	日本行政機構改革的展望	框子青	獨立評論	25—11	228
	行政效率與民衆利益	呂學海	獨立評論	25—10	224
	美國新政成績之總檢討	馬星野	新中華	25—9	4:17

	行政效率與民衆利益	呂學海	獨立評論	25—10	224
	行政效率之測量標準與方法	張金鑑	政治經濟學報	25—10	5:1
	論提高行政效率	賀嶽增	國聞週報	25—11	13:46
	政權運用與行政效率	甘乃光	行政研究	25—12	1:3
D 2:	中央地方關係之調整	大公報	國聞週報	25—9	13:37
	縣行政改進之要點	趙　澍	獨立評論	25—9	218
	縣政改進之心理的基礎	一　鷗	福建縣政半月刊	25—9	1:1
	縣政改革之新動向	愼　庵	福建縣政半月刊	25—10	1:3
	今日縣政之重要性	靜　觀	福建縣政半月刊	25—10	1:3
	論今日之縣吏治	程清舫	國聞週報	25—11	13:44
	地方自治的理論與實施	汪德裕	黃埔月刊	25—11	6:5
	城市計劃之要素	馮秉坤	市政評論	25—12	4:12
	中國之縣地方財政	孫曉村	社會經濟月報	25—12	3:10
	論中央地方事權之劃分	高青山	獨立評論	25—10	223
D 3:	現代政治中吏治的地位	鄭宏述	東方雜誌	25—10	33:19
	論政治犯的大赦	賀　知	自由評論	25—9	40
	人才問題	楊　勃	民鳴週刊	25—9	3:7
	行政效率與公務員任用法	成　言	國聞週報	25—9	13:38
	怎樣培養縣政人才	翁初白	國聞週報	25—10	13:42
	攷試人員儘先任用問題	陳曼若	國聞週報	25—10	13:42
	英國的公務員制度	郭景隆	建國月刊	25—10	4:10
	論魏晉九品用人之制	許同莘	河南政治月刊	25—10	6:10
	攷績的理論與實際	謝廷式	行政研究	25—12	1:3
	縣政人員對于人生應有的認識	一　鷗	福建縣政半月刊	25—10	1:3
	縣政府人事管理	吳文枏	人事管理	25—12	2:2
	職位分類之比較研究	任家誠	管理	25—11	1:4
	口試成績表之科學編製	胡亦生	管理	25—11	1:4
D 4:	中國政府購料的管理問題	張宗謙	管理	25—11	1:4

E類

	中國戰時財政問題	陳永年	河南政治月刊	25—10	6:10
	中國戰時財政問題	賀憶嚴	前途雜誌	25—12	4:12
	改良我國財政制度商榷	李超英	東方雜誌	25---12	33:24
	最近中國財政之分析	懷　仁	交易所周刊	25—11	2:27
E 2:	預算編製機關之研究	吳國雋	中行月報	25—10	5:10
	美國中間預算之內容	吳國雋	中行月報	25—11	13:5
	預算法之提要研究	唐休武	會計季刊	25—10	2:2
	新憲法施行後之預算編製問題	鄒兆京	會計季刊	25—10	2:2
E 3:	合作倉庫會計制度	謝元莊	合作月刊	25—12	8:1,2
	幣值變動時會計方法之研究	盧其昌	會計雜志	25—9	8:3
	論財產目錄之本質	陸善熾	會計雜志	25—9	8:3
	我國銀行主要帳簿制度之研究	顧　準	會計雜志	25—9	8:3
	商業成本會計之研究	李夢白	會計雜志	25—11	8:5
	中國統一會計制度與會計法	王文鈞	會計雜志	25—11	8:5
	主要原始憑證之單據與管理	周成勛	會計雜志	25—11	8:5
	改革會計年度問題	權　時	銀行週報	25—11	20:43
	所得稅與會計改革	顧鍾琦	華年	25—11	5:46
	開徵所得稅一般商人對於會計上應有之認識	徐永祚	銀行週報	25—10	20:41
	英國所得稅額計算述例	徐祖齡	會計季刊	25—10	2:2
	中國地方審計制度概論	王立貴	會計季刊	25—10	2:2
	會計學原理	陳恕鈞	計政學報	25—9	2:2
	怎樣研究會計學	潘序倫	綢繆月刊	25—9	3:1
	出納整理與會計整理	楊澤章	計政學報	25—9	2:2
	成本會計中之費用攤配問題	刁民仁	計政學報	25—9	2:2
	英國審計制度論	章長卿	計政學報	25—9	2:2
E 4:	金融統制論	王先璟	四川經濟月刊	25—9	6:3
	論金融季節		金融週報	25—9	2:4
	中國金融資本之研究	王宜昌	中國經濟	25—10	4:10

	國際匯兌率之釐定	鄔志陶	華年	25—12	5:12
E 5:	對于所得稅率之管見	羊冀成	社會經濟月報	25—9	3:9
	英美法三國遺產稅制度	王丕烈	社會經濟月報	25—10	3:10
	吾國地方財務行政之檢討	何　廉	行政研究	25—11	1:2
	我國走私問題之檢討	蔡致通	青島工商季刊	25—9	4:3
	長期投資之計算	沈曾定	交大學生	25—9	5:1
	我國現行所得稅之計算	力　行	交大學生	25—12	5:3
	遺產稅制之研究	張稺琴	新中華	25—9	4:17
	所得稅與資本之性質	徐永祚	銀行週報	25—10	20:41
	對于所得稅研究之結果	銀行學會	銀行週報	25—12	20:50
	中國推行所得稅的得失	丁　夷	華年	25—12	5:49
	英國所得稅制度之研究	姜佐宣	中央銀行月報	25—9	5:9
	華北走私與所得稅	于　眉	錢業月報	25—10	16:10
	所得稅之理論與實施	陳圭懋	中央時事週報	25—10	5:38
	所得稅暫行條例之檢討	劉樹東	中國經濟	25—9	4:9
	所得稅暫行條例之檢討	陳德容	銀行週報	25—9	20:36
	所得稅問題之面面觀	李啓鋒	中外月刊	25—10	1:9
	關于開徵所得稅的幾點商榷	蔡　鼎	國聞週報	25—9	13:35
	我國所得稅開徵的搜討	文　平	交易所週刊	25—9	2:23
	德國所得稅的發達及其特點	絢　文	留東學報	25—10	2:5
	中國現在實行的所得稅	謝　霖	光華半月刊	25—12	5:3,4
	評所得稅暫行條例	祈之晉	錢業月報	25—12	16:12
	現行所得稅制度之研究	張一凡	經濟評論	25—10	3:10
	所得稅之研討	秦貢武	木鐸半月刊	25—10	1:3
	鹽務改造之商榷	蔣方正	鹽政雜誌	25—10	65
	整理鹽務基本問題之檢討	秦中行	鹽政雜誌	25—10	65
	公債之最後歸着	蔡　鼎	之江學報	25—9	5
	資本主義列强之國債政策	秉	交易所週刊	25—11	2:27

編後記

流光不居，倏又經年，本刊與讀者相見已五度矣。一年以來，承校內外專家不棄，廣賜珠璣，使本刊能欣然向榮，更使編者不致因力之不勝，而有隕越，至感至幸。五期之中，刊論著、譯述、演講、轉載、名人傳記、通訊、書評、書報索引等八欄，約凡百篇，對於管理科學之理論及實施，多有論列，雖不可謂啓國內研究斯學之嚆矢，抑或可作國人研討參證之資。今後我人更當抱定邁進之精神，去蕪陳青，擷採各家之說，嚮我國人，藉以爲學術之提倡。雖然編者既以學識淺陋，不敢膺此重寄，更以螳臂之力，難以當車，所深望者，學者專家能廣輸卓見，發爲宏文；讀者能善加愛護，廣爲宣揚，則編者雖以蟬翼而負千鈞，將瘁其心力，竭其駑鈍不之辭。

本期內容之分配，較前四期爲平均，言鐵道管理有許靖先生之「管理旅客運輸應有之基本統計，」沈奏廷先生之「防範行車事變聲中，吾國鐵路各站行車管理方法應有之改革，」沈奏廷許靖二先生合撰之「再論吾國鐵路列車及車輛統計辦法」及熊大惠先生之「運價與物價」等三篇。我國對於鐵道之建設，日見孟晉，然行車事變常有所聞；使人民發生不良之印象，於鐵道之發展殊有阻礙，沈奏廷先生有鑒乎斯，爲文建議防止事變之改革方法，可供執政及學者一讀。我國晚近鐵道事業對於運輸及業務兩方面，已有相當成績，然積極之調整工作尚待注意，統計之彙集以爲改進之參攷其尤要者也，沈許二先生深明此點，發爲文章，以示提倡者前已數見，而「管理旅客運輸應有之基本統計」一文，尤爲許先生最近精心之作，本刊得之，彌足珍貴。沈許二先生合擬之文，乃發揮其前作「評吾國最近改訂鐵路列車及車輛統計辦法」之未盡處，故所提各點尤爲透切。運價爲造成生產費之一部份，與物價發生密切之關係，我國當局近方努力於物價之調整，對於運價問題不可不作連帶之注意，則熊先生「運價與物價」一文，可供當軸之參攷。

言公務管理，有林蝨先生之「行政組織之集權與統合，」及任家誠先生譯述之「介紹英國公務員制度。」林先生爲本刊柱石，其文已數見本刊，無待介紹，此篇以行政學學理觀察行政組織之精神，更以比較研究之方法，忠實的敘述行政組織應循之路徑，以供國人之研究。英國實施人事行政最早，故其成就亦最明顯，任先生之譯文，所以介紹其成就於我人也。

言財務管理，有聞亦有先生在本院演講之「中央及地方決算」，聞先生為主計處會計局副局長，對於國中政府會計制度之設置，多有貢獻。此文乃以實際之經驗，宣道我人，其內容之精確，不問可知。

言工商管理，則有俞希稷先生之「論我國出口茶業應改為官督商辦，」及張宗謙先生之「科學管理與市場。」實業部近方籌劃創設公私合辦之茶業公司，良有鑒乎國產茶葉品質優良，應即大量生產，以競爭于國際市場，故茶業之改進已漸為國人所注意，俞希稷之文可謂確得其時，且別具卓見，理直識當，確為提倡茶業聲中，一應加注意之文字。張先生之文乃以科學管理之理論為立場，討論產品之推銷，亦為僅見之作。

黎校長之「鐵道部建設計劃中培養專才之定集，」為在鐵道部紀念週中演講辭，與本校前途，有直接關係，更對國家之育士植才，有充量之發揮，故特刊之。其餘如鄭思益先生之「經濟建設與國防，」吳家鈞先生之「浙贛鐵路南昌營業所營業概況」等均有一讀之價值。

編者尸位一年，承專家及讀者不棄，厚加扶助，本刊得能按期出版，倖免挫折，銘感良深。然編校之餘，常覺心有所感，不能不一獻芻見，就商於愛護本刊者：

一、管理之蔚為學術，聳人視聽，在歐美亦不過近數十年事，然已成為世界公私事業公認之工具，無不藉以為業務推進之原動力。我國積弱已久，觀夫歐美之前驅，不免興望塵之嘆，追跡之道何自始，行政效率之表現，事業經濟之推進，科學管理之提倡，確為目前當務之急。本刊問世，正所以應此需要。然本刊之力量有限，深覺不能促國人之注意，故於此刊普遍流傳之後，更應進而組管理學會，集專家，合羣智，以圖宣揚與推進之道，以為切實之研討。故本刊之發行，雖為異日成敗之試金石，不過啓提倡管理學之端，深盼在最近期內，移此責任於全國之學者。

二、本刊既以管理名，第一卷，第一期發刊例言中，更確定研究之範圍爲鐵道、工商、公務、財務四者，所刊之論文，應平均的以玆四者爲對象。然過去五期之中，編者雖盡力循此範圍，以來稿之關係，仍不免有輕重之別。其中以鐵道管理之討論爲最多，公務次之，工商及財務更次之。以後深望工商管理及財政學者，多賜宏文，以維持平衡之發展，以符本刊發行之宗旨。尤於管理學原理之商討，管理學方法之研究，更企有所論列，以爲鼓吹提倡之助。

三、過去惠稿者，多係本院同仁及同學，外界學者少有見賜，因之稿件來源極受限制，不免影響今後之發展，深望國中同志，以發揚管理科學爲懷，時賜金玉，俾本刊得以增光，而年在髫齡之管理學亦能漸趨于精壯之候，間接的挽救我國政治經濟在在落後之現象。

四、本院同學卒業後，服務於國家社會者，不可勝數。如能常以服務之所得，研究之結果，賜登本刊，或常惠最近工作情形，因切磋而增進學問，藉交換而貢獻心得，因之更可有互通聲氣之機會，於公於私，兩得其益。本刊設通訊一欄，可以適應此需要，然過去承通音問者極少，深願今後常有所獲。

上述四點，爲其犖犖大者。至如編制之方法，內容之搜羅，均覺不能自滿，而亟欲改革。對於應行改善，應加努力之處，尚望海內明達不棄淺陋，時賜敎言，則本刊感甚，管理學之前途幸甚。

本院教員著作一覽表

行政學大綱 林奋著

中國政府（英文） 林奋著

法律大綱（英文） 林奋著

研究科學之方法（英文） 林奋著

鐵路經濟論文集 沈奏廷著

鐵路貨運業務 沈奏廷著

鐵路運價之理論與實際 沈奏廷著

中央銀行論 崔曉岑著

錢幣與銀行 崔曉岑著

鐵道經濟論叢 鍾偉成編

鐵道材料管理 鍾偉成著

公路運輸 王炳南 熊大惠合著

運輸學水道編 熊大惠著

東北鐵路問題之研究 王同文著

本刊投稿簡章

一、投稿以有關於管理者為限。

二、投稿不拘文言白話，須繕寫清楚，並加標點，如係外國文稿件，並請打印之，均不得於一紙兩面寫字。

三、論著稿中，如有譯名或引文，須分別註明原文及出處。

四、譯稿須將原文題目，原著者姓名，出版日期及地點，詳細載明，如能附寄原文尤佳。

五、稿末請簽名蓋章，並註明住址。

六、來稿文字，本院有酌量修改之權，如投稿人不願有何增刪，則應於投稿時聲明。

七、來稿登載與否，概不寄還，惟附寄郵票預先聲請寄還者 亦可照辦。

八、來稿一經登載，當酌贈以每千字一元至三元之薄酬。

九、來稿請寄上海徐家匯交通大學管理學院。

中華民國二十六年二月出版

第一卷第五期

每本大洋四角
全年五期大洋一元六角

主編者 鍾偉成

發行者 交通大學出版處

印刷者 華豐印刷鑄字所 上海浙江路五三六號

本刊廣告價目表

等級	地位	全頁價目	半頁價目
甲	底封面外頁	伍拾元	
乙	底面裏頁及封面裏頁	三十五元	二十元
丙	封面裏頁之對面 底面裏頁之對面	二十五元	十五元
丁	普通	二十元	十二元

一、乙丙丁四分之一頁按照半頁價目六折計算

二、廣告概用白紙黑字如用彩印紙色價目另議

三、廣告如用銅鋅版由本刊代辦照收製版費

四、連登多期價目從廉請逕函本校出版處經理組接洽

管理

二月刊

第二卷 第一期 二十六年四月

本期要目

交通大學管理學院編輯

管理二月刊

第二卷 第一期
民國二十六年四月

論著

譯述

論著

人事行政組織之研究（D 3.）

林疊

一 組織之分類

在人事行政改革聲中，人事行政之組織漸因改革之需要而日趨于完備，然因各國改革過程之不同，其組織上之發展，因之亦各異其趣。要之觀現存之狀態，可析爲兩種，曰集中之組織及分部之組織。集中之組織者將全國之人事行政歸入一集中之機關辦理，分部之組織者人事管理由各部或各組織單位分別担任。可以爲前者之例者爲英美之制度，可以爲後者之例者爲德法之制度。

英國因攷選印度公務員而組成人事行政委員會 (Civil Service Commission) 迄今已有攸久之歷史，爲世界集中公開制度之嚆矢，美亦因分贓制之奔潰，于一八八三年成立人事行政委員會，追踪英制之成就。故集中之制度可謂英吉利首創之，而美利堅發揚之，迄今各國起而仿效者極多，已成爲世界各國人事行政普遍之模型。我國將人事行政歸由攷試院辦理，亦有集中之精神，其與英美異者僅在形式上而已。

法國對於人事行政之革新較遲，故其成就亦較差。至於今，法政府仍以爲政府事務繁複，職位各各不同，不應有統一而集中之組織，此種觀念完全由於傳統思想之造成。法對於人事行政之管理，往往由各部設局辦理，各部之組織較大，部務較繁，甚有由數單位分別担任者，如教育部 (Ministry of Public Instruction) 設六局管理，財政部設十局管理，(一)此種形式實爲世界之創見。德國因昔日各邦分立，政治上之集中尚無攸久之歷史，故人事行政方面集中化之發展亦較遲緩。然人事行政委員會 (Beamtenausschuss) 之組織則普羅士 (Prussia) 於一九一九年時已有規定，其性質與英美之制度不同，蓋此種委員會之存在，並非以整個中央或地方甚或全國爲單位，而以各行政組織爲單位，一九一九年『普羅士政府人事行政委員會組織及責任規章』(Regulations of the Prussian Government Regarding the Formation & Duties of Civil Service Committee, Mar. 24, 1919) 第一條中規定『凡各機關至少有常任公務員二十人以上者應組織人事行政委員會』(二) 此種組織如能逐漸擴充，則其發展之途徑不難與英美之制度相吻合。

人事行政在集中而後，既可利於流轉，更可便於比較，政府之統制既可得力，成績之表現又復昭然，故現代言人事行政者，應以集中之方法爲標準，我人於此際討論，自亦不宜放棄此目標，故以後各節所述者，爲分別討論集中之制度，而分部之法不與焉。

所謂集中，因政治制度之不同，亦有程度上之差別，以美而言，各省及市政府之權力，尙有一部份獨立之形態存在，故人事行政之組織中央與地方亦不能統一，各地及中央均分別設立人事行政委員會，不相關聯，其人選或出於選舉，或出於長官指派，均以各級機關爲單位——中央或地方——，不能絕對表現統一之精神，故美制可謂集中之程度較淺者。

過去一般行政學者認爲人事之駕馭，乃爲行政之一部份，故其組織及權限均由行政長官賦予之，隸屬於行政權，故事實上行政機關仍有管理人員進退之機會。是以人事行政雖有獨立之形態——如人事行政委員會之組成——，而無獨立之精神，行政長官之操縱統制，舉薦助引，仍不能完全免除。且國家之辦理政事，舍行政而外，更有司法立法等端，其人員之銓選亦需合理的管理，則行政權下之人事行政機關是否可以越俎代庖，尙成問題，故我人未能認爲過去觀點完全無誤，因之有析攷試而獨立之說。我國攷試院卽爲過去觀點欠缺之糾正，其成立之原因大部分卽基於此。雖然歷史上之背景使我人不願隨便放棄昔日之成就，亦爲主要之原因。

目前更有一般前進之行政學者，於詳細分析之結果，以爲人事行政工作之大部分實爲財務統制之一，故應歸入財務組織。此種主張認爲職位之分類，俸給之釐訂，退休制度之創立，無不與財務行政發生極密切之關係，且國家支出中，公務員俸給之費用實居大部份，爲使財務行政易於駕馭起見，人事行政之統制宜歸入財政機關辦理。首創此制而實行之者爲英國，其理論及實施之方法頗爲時下學者所稱頌，故他日人事行政組織之發展，舍我國之根本獨立而外，殆將逐漸走入英制。

綜上所述，舍分部制已不適宜外，我人可歸納人事行政組織於英美及我國之制度中，蓋此三者可以代表獨立制度中不同之形態也。雖然，如從大體上着想，則三者之形態雖異而原則則一，蓋均欲使人事行政漸趨於相對的獨立，使能運用自如，而發揮其人才主義之原則也。

茲請於下列各節中分別討論英、美及我國三種不同之制度。

二　英國之人事行政組織

英國將人事行政之責任分別付之兩大組織中，一爲財政部之人事制度司（Establishment Division），一爲人事行政委員會。二者互相合作，故制度可謂十分嚴密。然其與一般國家異者，則人事管理之大權幾多半操於財政部之手，而人事行政委員會則僅有舉行攷試及頒發候補人員之資格證。(三)因之，我人名英之制度爲財政統制之人事行政。

英國之財政部爲委員會組織，以首相，財政大臣及其他閣員組成之，一九一九年時於其下設人事制度司，專職辦理人事行政事項，故其負責長官往往由對人事行政素有專長之人員任之。其職權至爲龐大，舍攷試由人事行政委員會担任外，其他事務幾均由該司辦理，故其工作可包括(一)實習之監督，(二)升擢，(三)遷調，(四)退休，(五)不重要事務之停止，(六)公務員儲蓄制度之採取，(七)維持人員進退記錄等事務。

該司爲促進各部人事行政之合作及便於比較各部施政之成績起見，更召集主管人事長官組成常務委員會 (Standing Committee) 由該司之司長 (Controller) 任主席。委員會重要之工作爲以商討之結果，建議於財政部，俾便酌量採取，如此則各部對於財部所發表之人事管理辦法如認爲應加修改時，可以有參加意見之機會，而各部與財政部之關係可以日趨於密切，相互之諒解，促成行政效率之推進。

人事行政委員會雖名義上爲獨立之委員會，事實上處處受財部之牽制，故雖攷試一項，尙有種種限制，以下各種程序之履行均須得財部之批准：(一) 決定招攷辦法 (如決定攷試爲公開攷試，或有限制之公開攷試，或及格攷試等)，(二)決定給予獲雋人員證書之辦法，(三)決定舉行攷試之情形及時期，(四)分配錄取男女之職位，(五)確定免試辦法。(四)此四點明白表示人事行政委員會於攷試之種種條件均無決定之權力，而其任務可謂僅至於奉命執行之程度而已。

人事行政委員會由委員三人組織之，委派之權屬之英皇，然往往由財部推薦，故實際上可謂仍在財務管轄之下。三委員之任務不同，一爲主席(First Commissioner)，其餘二人，一任攷試長(Deiector of Examinations)，一任祕書，分別辦理應辦之事務。三人之任期均無定，隨時可以更換。然如任期較長，則政事易於實行，政治之地位可以中立，因之委員之人選不常更動。

我人應加注意者爲人事行政委員會雖處處受財部之干預，然在行政系統上仍不失其獨立之地位，而非隸屬於財部者。

舍茲二者外，更有皇家人事行政委員會(Royal Commission on the Civil Service)之組成，無行政方面之責任，而專事調查全國人事行政施行狀況，集中資料，加以研究，將其所得之結果建議於政府，故實具有諮詢之意。近年以還，常有報告書之刊印，此種報告之編成，乃爲彙集全英實況而成，彌足珍貴。此委員會之人選由英皇任命，自國內人事行政專家中選任之，其任期亦無定。

茲列圖說明英制如下

內閣
皇家人事行政委員會
各部
人事行政單位
財政部
人事制度司
常務委員會
人事行政委員會

圖一。英國人事行政組織系統圖

三　美國之人事行政組織

美國人事行政組織係採取人事行政委員會制，然因各省及各城市有比較獨立之行政組織，其人事行政組織亦各各不同，故於討論美之制度時，對於地方之人事行政組織應作比較的研究，俾可盡羅各種不同之制度。請先述其中央之組織。

中央政府之人事行政委員會由委員三人組成之，各代表不同之政黨，使不致發生一黨把持之陋習。此亦美人所以主張組織委員會之理由。委員由大總統派充，惟須得上議院之同意，因其工作須涉及法律，商業、政治、經濟、以至工程等端，故人選之決定甚非易易，然人類之能力有限，於一切學術及經驗，決不能廣收並蓄，故在選擇時，最好能分別挑選三不同之人才，極力使之能包涵於一切任務之需要內。委員之任期無定，由總統觀察各個人之成績及能力而定。其任務可分爲三方面，曰立法的，行政的，司法的，而尤以行政的如攷選任用等端爲要。

至其內部組織，初創時設攷試行政處（The Office of Chief Examiner），祕書處（The Office of the Secretary）及總務處（The Office of the Executive Assistant to the Commissioner）分別掌理全會事務。自一九三二年起，漸加改革，分處設科，以便管理而節省行政經費，故截止現在，其組織與前相較已迴然異，無論在辦事系統或組織形式上，均較前爲簡

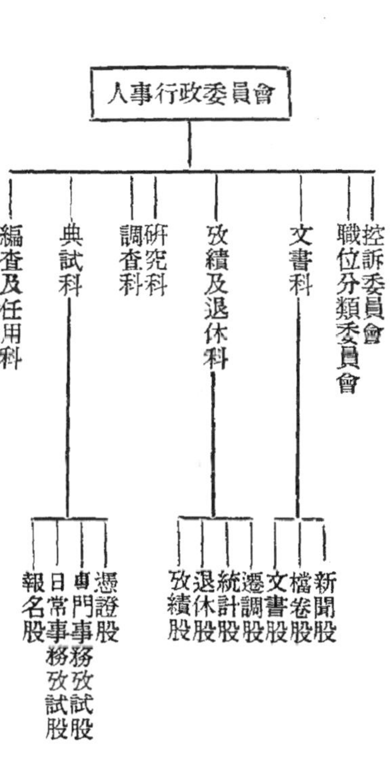

圖二 美國中央政府人事行政委員會現行組織圖（五）

便，可分為六科二委員會，見圖二。

美國地方人事行政組織從管理上之觀點言，可分兩種，曰省府管理制 (State Administration Plan)及地方管理制 (Local Administration Plan)。如對於各市鎮成績制之施行集中於省府之人事行政組織者，為省府管理制，如對於各市鎮成績制之施行由各市鎮自組人事行政委員會者，為地方管理制。(六)

省府管理制僅麻省 (Massachusetts) 及紐袭賽(New Jersy) 二省採用。前者對於各市鎮之人事行政有委任統治之性質，各地均由省府管理，後者則可任意由市鎮政府公民投票決定，較為自由，故可謂絕對採取省府管理制者僅麻省一處。省府管理制之利極為顯著，蓋有數市鎮經濟能力薄弱無力自組人事行政機關，然成績制之施行又為全體公民所企求，如能由省管理，經濟方面可免支出，而目的以達。

地方管理制亦有二種方式，有數市人事行政機關雖有其獨立之組織，須受省府之監督，如紐約及渥海渥 (Ohio) 之各市。其他省份之市鎮則較有完全獨立之精神。然相對言之，二者均有其弊，其弊即前述省府管理制之利也。

美地方人事行政機關之內部組織，經二十餘年來逐漸之改革，已較中央之人事行政委員會為合理化，故實較為前進。

初，本特爾登法案方告通過，中央設立三委員合組之委員會組織，其中須有二人以上代表不同之黨別，各地痛分贓制之積弊，乃羣起倣傚，組人事行政委員會。然委員之人選仍不能與黨派相分離，雖云異黨混合之組織可以調和黨爭，避免分贓制之死灰復燃，惟委員既選自黨員行政方面遂不能與政治相劃分；違反行政之原則，行之既久，積弊又生，分贓制之名雖去而實在，各地有志之士羣主改革，法官奧台（Judge S. H. Ordway）其最著者也。卒因先後倡議，相繼改革，而漸臻完美之境。

現在美各地所採之組織方式，歸納之，可分爲四種，（一）委員制，（二）行政長官下設一人事行政指導員，更設半司法（Quasi-judicial）或半立法（Quasi-legisletive）之委員會輔之，（三）獨任制，無輔助之委員會，（七）及四有財政監督意義之獨任制。

在委員制之組織下設三委員，一爲專任之委員，担任行政工作，二爲輔助委員僅担任偏於立法及司法之工作。此種制度往往由省政府採用，創之最早者爲加利福尼亞省（California）一九一三年。加省於一九二九年時更於財政部下另設人事科，人事行政委員會雖仍維持，已削去其行政權，最近人事科長往往由指導員担任，故可謂已轉入第二種方式內。（八）

派任人事指導員，更設委員會輔助之法，倡於新新納底（Cincinnati），該城於一九二六年由新新納底大學董事會及新新納底學校區教育局（Board of Education of the Cincinnati

School District) 及市長各委一人組成委員會，另由市經理就專門人事行政人才中選派一人爲祕書，担任指導員職務，且予一任免部屬之權。（九）委員會與指導員雖爲合一之組織，然實有不同之工作，蓋委員會可担任之工作爲偏於司法及立法方面的，而指導員之工作爲行政的，其利取其分工合作也。

新新納底之組織較爲特殊，故特引以爲例。就一般採取委員會及指導員混合組織者言之，委員之人選往往由省議會或市議會决定，而指導員則由行政長官派遣。

獨任制之採用，在美國地方人事行政機關之組織中，亦已取得極重要之地位。其組織爲廢除委員會制，而將管理權付之人事行政指導員一人統合的執行一切政務，人員由行政長官委派，在行政系統上亦隸屬之。採取此制者有干薩斯(Kansas)及密蘇里(Missouri)等市

美之行政學者近頗同情於英之財政統制之法，以是人事行政機關直接受財政之監督者亦有所見。聖保爾(St. Paul)城以市審計員(City Comptroller)兼任人事行政指導員，即爲首創之例。

四制之中，以何者爲佳，殊不易下以斷語，各有利弊，當就情勢及辦理人員之能力而斷。均衡輕重，當以第二式較爲可取，蓋其將司法及立法之應加商討事務歸委員會諮商，而行政事務歸獨任之指導員辦理，與行政學之原則極相符合也。

四 我國之攷試院

我國爲遵守總理遺旨，及發揚歷代攷政獨立之優越性起見，將人事行政之執行及計劃歸入攷試院辦理，故我國之人事行政機關，爲攷試院。然爲避免公務人員之枉法瀆職之現象，更將彈劾及督察之責歸之監察院，及公務員懲戒之責歸之司法院之公務員懲戒委員會，故我國之人事行政雖云獨立，尚無澈底之系統。

懲戒責任之旁貸，是否合理，論者各異其說。或謂人事行政之要旨爲澄清吏治，故監察及懲戒之責任殊屬重大，攷試院於處理攷政及銓敘攷績之餘，實無兼顧之暇，否則徒然造成顧此失彼之錯誤，故應另由監察院及公務員懲戒委員會專責辦理，俾可以組織上之嚴密，防止公務員之違法。或謂事務官之懲戒，本爲澄清吏治之一部份，攷試院既負人事行政之全責，自應聯同辦理，俾系統上可以合理，而管理上可以統一。以美國之人事行政委員會而言，此類責任均由會負，成績昭著，我國既以攷試院之獨立爲提倡，責任之專一化統一化自屬必要故不應將監察及懲戒之權，歸入監察院及司法院辦理（十）。揆之情理，二說之中，自以後者爲合理，蓋如懲戒之權可以另行歸隸，則其他人事行政之權能亦未嘗不能因政治之關係而逐一脫離攷試院，則將來之攷試院將等虛設。我國目今雖有攷試院之成立，而人事行政仍不能完全獨立，甚至攷試本身亦不免有各行其是之現象，故爲切合總理遺敎及人事行政原則起見，權限之調整及歸屬有其必要，懲戒權之調整其一也。

我國自國府奠定，卽有籌設攷試院之議，至民國十七年而正式成立，前以新型初試，工作方面不免因陋就簡，然經茲數年之積極努力，成績已斐然可觀，攷試之舉行，公務員資格之調查，公務員工作之攷勤，其尤著者也。茲討論其組織如後。

攷試院之組織法於民國十七年公布，院下設攷選委員會及銓敘部二機關，一主全國攷選事務，一主人事行政之一切重要事務如公務員之登記，攷績，升降及轉調，任免與資格審查，及俸給與奬卹審查等。院內設祕書處，參事處及統計室，一主文書及機要事務，一主法令之徵核事務，一主人事行政資料之搜集及整理事務。（十一）

攷選委員會以委員長一人，副委員長一人，委員五人至七人組織之，對於較爲專門攷試之襄理，由院聘請專家担任。一切事務均先經委員會會議公決，然後由委員長執行。爲便於施政計，其下設祕書處及專門委員室，分別處理會內一切事務。祕書處下分設六科，担任總務、文書、高等攷試，普通攷試，特種攷試與候選人員攷試，及統計等事。專門委員室下分設八組曰（一）法學商學組，（二）文學教育組，（三）理學工學組，（四）農學組，（五）軍事學組，（六）醫學組，（七）編審組，（八）設計組。

銓敘部設部長一人，次長二人，主持全部之部務，其下分設（一）祕書處，（二）登記司，

(三)甄核司，(四)育才司，(五)銓敍審查委員會。祕書處掌理機要事務，文書及庶務等。登記司掌理各機關公務員及攷試及格人員之登記事宜，甄核司掌理各機關公務員之攷績，升遷等審查之事務。育才司掌理各機關公務員之俸給，獎卹及補習教育等審查之事務。銓敍審查委員會掌理各司所審查結果之覆核事務，其組織以次長，各司長，甄核司各科長，育才司一二兩科科長爲委員(必要時登記司科長得出席會議)，以政務次長爲主席。

攷試院於攷試時，因工作忙碌，人員不易分配，得臨時設立典試委員會及襄試處，襄理一切攷試事務。典試委員會以委員長一人，委員若干人組成之；襄試處設正副主任各一人主持之。委員及主任爲簡派，於高等攷試時由中央任之，普通攷試則由省市政府委派。

我國幅圓廣大，中央對於各地之統制，頗非易事，人事行政亦然，故攷試院於舉行銓敍會議時，多主於各地設立分處，受中央之節制，以明管理上之系統，至民二十五年六月銓敍處組織條例公布，地方之人事行政組織乃有基礎，今後如能循此途徑，人事行政之普及化可必而國家澄清吏治之目的可以達到。

各地之分處爲銓敍處，由銓敍部於各省中組織之，辦理各該省委任職公務員之銓敍事宜，並兼辦隣近省市委任職公務員之銓敍事宜。其下設二課，曰總務，曰審查，其所有之職掌與中央之銓敍部相似，惟具體而微而已。（十二）

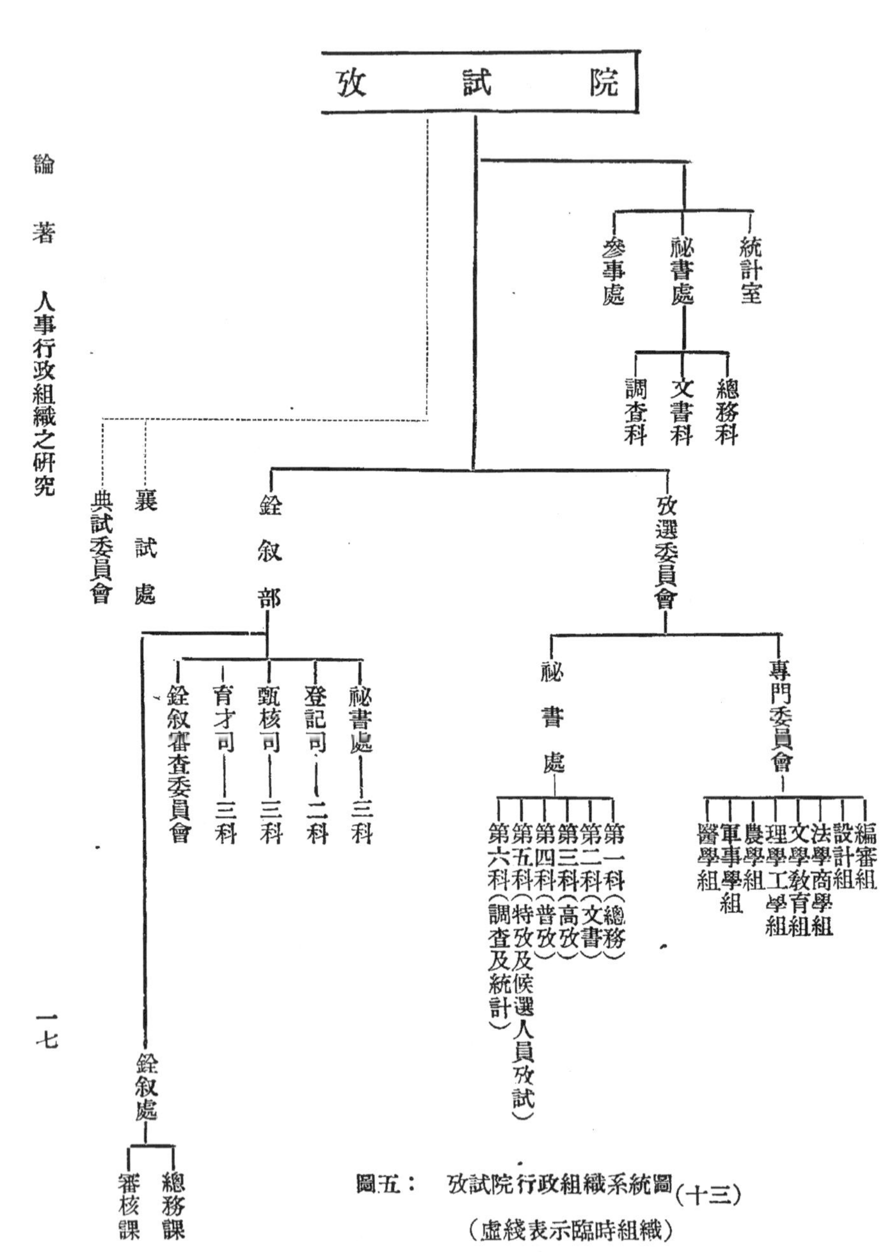

圖五：　攷試院行政組織系統圖(十三)
(虛綫表示臨時組織)

(一)一九二九年時法財政部在下列各不同單位下，設各自獨立之人事行政組織：(一)中央行政，(二)直接稅，(三)間接稅，(四)海關，(五)印花稅，(六)國家製造廠稅，(七)貨幣及金屬獎章，(八)試驗所，(九)國立印刷局。

參攷 W.R. Sharp, "Public Personnel Management in France," Civil Service Abroad, edited by L. D. White, C. H. Bland, W. R. Sharp, F. M. Mart (McGraw-Hill Company, New York, 1935), pp. 92—93.

(二)C. H. Friedrich, "The German & the Prussian Civil Service" The Civil Service in Modern State, edited by L. D. White (The University of Chicago Press, Chicago, 1930), p. 427.

(三)Sir S. Leathers "The Qualification, Recruitment, & Training of Public Servant" Journal of Public Administration Vol. 1, No. 4 (Institute of Public Administration, London, 1923), pp. 343, 348—351.

(四)L. D. White, "The British Civil Service," op. cit., Civil Service Abroad, p. 10.

(五)職位分類委員會初爲獨立之組織，與人事行政委員會相分立，秉承大總統之命令，專司職位分類事宜。以過去辦理之成績不佳，政府人員多主歸併人事行政委員會以節經費，至一九三三年乃告實現。故現在已成爲隸屬於人事行政委員會之機關。

(六)W. C. Beyer, "Municipal Civie Service in the United Stale's" Problems of American Public Service, edited by C. J. Friedrich, W. C. Beyer, S. D. Spero, J. F. Miller, G. A. Graham (McGraw Hill Book Company, New York, 1935), pp. 90—92.

(七)J.M. Pfiffner Public Administration (The Ronald Press Company, New York, 1935), p. 157.

(八)W. C. Beyer, "Municipal Civil Service in the United States," op, cit., Problems of American Public Service, p. 97.

(九)Ibid., p. 98.

原文見Charter of the City of Cincinnati (City Council, Cincinnati, 1933), p. 12.

(十)薛伯康中美人事行政比較(商務印書館，上海，民國二十三年)第二十二頁

(十一)『攷試院統計室組織規程』於民國二十五年三月二十日經國民政府指令核准，係根據『國民政府主計處組織法』，『國民政府主計處辦理各機關歲計統計人員暫行規程』，暨『中央各機關統計室組織及辦理通則』制定。原文見攷試院公報第七期(攷試院祕書處，南京，民國二十五年七月)第三頁

(十二)攷試院公報，第六期(見前，民國二十五年六月)第二頁至第四頁

(十三)關於攷試院之組織，詳細內容及職掌等可參攷試院法規彙刊(攷試院祕書處文書科，南京，民國二十三年)。前述各段均參證此書，特附註

注：原刊影印件缺20页。

美國鐵路管理到達貨運事務之組織與方法（C 5.

許 靖

處理到達貨運事務，內而涉及會計及收費等處，外則與零担貨棧，整車貨場，調車車場，種種方面皆有連帶關係，其中手續繁複，錯綜萬狀，不獨創立制度之初，關於組織人事不易擘劃支配得當，即能實地考察西人成規，亦有千頭萬緒之感，若非悉心體察，多方揣摩，終難得其辦法之妙處，至欲徒從文字而得西人管理方法之秘訣，自屬更爲困難。作者深知本篇所擬陳述各節，至爲複雜曲折，加以我國站務組織尚不健全，又無類似情形足資參證，因就重要者扼要言之，以期删繁就簡，易於瞭解。

處理到達貨運事務，本爲站務方面極端重要問題，因其性質繁難，故在美國各路貨運大站，類皆以之劃歸一處管轄，單設一部組織，名曰Inbound Freight Department，舉凡關於到達貨物一切票據之審核，到達通知之塡發，運雜各費之計算，車輛之處置等等，概由此處負責辦理，按其性質，可以稱之曰到達貨運處理處，或簡稱爲到達貨運處。在全部貨站組織中，此爲內部機構方面最關緊要之一部分，有正副主管首領各一人，名曰 Chief Inbound Clerkand Assistant Chief Inbound Clerk，吾人可稱之曰正副主任。其下則有不少辦事員司，若以大站爲標準，約計不下五十餘人。正副主任之地位，適與外部零担貨棧及整車貨場之總副監工相等，同對貨運站長直接負責。茲將全部事務從頭至尾順序列述，一則以明分工合作處理之程序，一則以示人事支配之方法，而又同時順帶列舉各種員司之職務名稱，以見西國鐵路用人定職，無往而不專門與具體化也。

一 貨票之收集查對及分類

到達貨票乃辦理到達貨運之基本單據，在美國各路，貨票有由客車郵寄者，亦有隨列車而行者，除郵寄者應由旅客車站提取外，其隨貨車而行者類皆於列車行抵到達站之車場時，卽由車長交於車場接收，車場與本處通常相距甚遠，而貨票之運用又在本處而非車場，處此情形之下，若無一定辦法，則貨票難免滯留場內，影響本處之應用，因有下列之規定，以謀雙方授受貨票之便利。第一，在車場方面應將收到之貨票隨時開列一單，單內祇塡車號路屬，凡屬同一列車之貨票，一律列入一單，是謂車號單 List of Car Numbers，共塡二份，以一份連同關係貨票裝入專用封袋，其餘一份則由車場存查。第二，由本處指定差役 Messenger 按時前往車場提取，每日往返五次，平均兩小時一次。如是車場不斷收到貨票，又可隨時轉交本處備用，不致發生延誤，而地域上之障礙乃得消滅於無形矣。

貨票旣按上法分由各調車場收集提取，而提回之時，卽交副主任根據車號單逐張查對，如有短少失落，立可發現。且查對之際，同時卽將貨票按照貨物性質分別彙集，如以煤運，糧運，零担，整車鮮貨者各爲一類，是其例也。因貨運種類繁多，必須分由多數員司同時辦理，而后能收分工合作之效，故此時順便分類，既可節省時間，一俟查對無訛，卽可分發各關係員司分途進行其他處置手續。此外并於查核貨票之時順手摘錄關係事項，以編下列兩種報單，其性質及作用亦有足資注意者：

（一）爲**整車鮮果靑菜車數日報** Daily Report of Carlots of Fruits and Vegetables其單如左：

整車鮮果靑菜車數日報　　＿＿站＿＿年＿＿月＿＿日

貨　　名	截至昨日上午七時存站車數	截至本日上午七時新到車數	起運州名	已卸車數	改運他處車數	尙存車數
(1)	(2)	(3)	(4)	(5)	(6)	(7)

此單共分七欄，僅塡水果菜蔬一類農產物品，例如蘋果，香蕉，白菜，芹菜，白薯，等類是也。共塡三份：以正張寄呈政府設立之農業經濟局 Bureau of Agricultural Economics，第二張呈送總局鮮貨運輸經理 Manager of Perishable Freight Service，在前者根據各路同樣報告，可以按照供求關係統制農產鮮貨市價，以防商人操縱市面，影響日常民食。在後

者則可藉以明瞭鮮貨運輸狀況，而作管理之參考。

（二）爲每日新到貨場之鮮貨車輛報單 Daily Report of Perishable Cars Received at Team Tracks 內分車號，貨名，收貨人，起運站，重量，及託運人指定之加冰或通風辦法 Instructions regarding icing or ventilation 等項，與前面第一種報告之性質迥不相同（參閱附式），共塡二份，一份存查，一份送交整車貨場，俾得有所遵循，按照開示各項執行保護業務。以鮮貨運輸，託運人對於冷藏業務性質照例先有一定之指示，有要沿途加冰者，有應僅

每日之到貨場之鮮貨車輛報單　＿＿站＿＿年＿＿月＿＿日

車號及路屬	貨物名稱	收貨人	起運站	貨物重量	託運人規定之加冰或通風辦法
(1)	(2)	(3)	(4)	(5)	(6)

加一次而不再加者，亦有需要標準通風 Standard Ventilation 辦法不用冷藏業務者，更有於用冰之外另加若干成分食鹽者，雖然同爲鮮貨運輸，但辦法極不一致，故各站外部人員究應如何執行加冰業務，非待得有貨票上之根據，殆將無從着手。此時車輛停在外面貨場，貨票

又須留在本處用以辦理各種手續，既不應以貨票送於貨場，而貨場因無貨票亦不能執行加冰加鹽種種事務，欲求雙方兼顧，應於此時先從貨票摘編此項報單，以應貨場之需要，蓋貨場得有此項報單，即可依照第六欄之指示辦法辦理各車加冰事務，同時內部又可不斷辦理種種重要手續，不致影響貨票之運用，故本報之編造，純為便利內外同時分途管理事務而作，欲知西人管理鐵路秘訣，當於此等微妙關鍵之處着力求之。

二　分配貨票及辦理車輛處置手續

貨票一經查對無訛而又同時經過摘取報告材料之後，即行發交關係員司，分別辦理其他事務：

(一)關於煤運車輛者交煤運司事 Coal Clerk。

(二)關於糧食車輛者交糧運司事 Grain Clerk。

(三)關於零担車輛者交貨棧司事 Freight House Car Clerk。

(四)關於中途改運之鮮貨車輛者交鮮貨改運司事 Perishable Reconsigning Clerk。

(五)關於郵寄貨票之硬紙路單 Card or Slip Bills，則交郵寄貨票司事 Mail Waybill Clerk。

(六)其他。

貨票既按類別分交上述各項司事之後，應卽進行車輛處置事宜 Car disposition，因在美國各路，除零担貨物外，所有整車貨運，如糧食煤運一類車輛，往往多於中途改變貨主或運輸地點，故貨物雖已按照原來貨票運至原定之到達站，然而到後又常發生種種變動情形，不能遽作最後之處置，必俟臨時得到貨主命令，方能決定交車交貨。車輛處置之涵義大致如此，然因貨物種類不同，而其處置情形亦不一致，試就煤運一端述其概要，以資例證。

煤車交車通知登記簿

______站

路局	車號	車到日期	起運站	交車通知書號數 Order No.	收到交車通知日期	連續號碼 P-O No.	收貨人	送往何路 To What Road Ordered	填發車牌日期 Date Carded
(1)	(2)	(3)	(4)	(5)	(6)	(7)	(8)	(9)	(10)

煤運司事處理煤運車輛，一以商人之通知爲依歸，煤商決定如何交車以後，照例可以隨時通知鐵路，煤運司事日常不斷收到商人交車通知 Disposition Orders，隨手登入簿內，是謂交車通知登記簿 Coal Order Book，其式如上。及至收到貨票，則卽檢查各通知書，以視已否收到通知，如某車處置命令或通知早已收到，卽可將關係貨票抽出，編上連續號碼，并

按通知開示交車地點填發車牌 Carding，同時在登記簿內第七十兩欄分別填入連續號碼及填發車牌日期，再以同樣連續號碼填入以前收進之散張交車通知，斯時貨票對於處置車輛之作用畢矣，可以轉交運價司事 Rate Clerks 繼續辦理計算運費等事，而其散張交車通知亦可從此編存，於是全案結束矣。

如貨票已到，商人尚無交車通知送達，又或運費必須先付而後始能交車，則應通知商人速示處置方法，同時對於稽延時日過久之車輛。則按貨主或商號名稱分別開列車數填具日報，以一份呈總局營業處煤運經理 Coal Traffic Manager，一份呈車務處運輸處長，一份呈叚因而甲乙丙丁各商每日尚有未經起卸之煤車若干，在上級關係方面亦可明瞭，以便多方設法催促貨主趕速繳費卸車，較之僅由車站單獨交涉，當易發生效力。似此分途呈報辦法，亦爲管理方法之表現，吾人亦當明其作用。其次如在列車未到之前業已接到商人改運通知 Reconsigning Order，則煤運司事卽可依照通知先將車牌填妥，交由差役送至車場，以便車到場內，卽可遵照改運，而免臨時辦理，轉多延誤。

以上是爲車站內部處理煉運貨票及車輛之大概方法，他如糧食鮮貨車票處置情形，繁簡不盡相同，若欲一一叙述，未免過於煩瑣，故從略耳。

三　核算運費與貨票之編號登記

斯時貨票對於車場方面處置車輛之關係終了，此後則爲辦理與會計，卸車，交貨，各種事務有關之手續，惟本節所敘述者祇限於核算運費，貨票編號，及登記三種手續，其處理程序應分三步：

第一步——貨票一經前述各司事用畢之後，即由各人分別轉交運價司事 Rate Clerks，以便一面審核原算運費有無錯誤，一面加算運雜各費，因貨物運到本站以後，尙有繼續改運種種情形，故有重單補算或改變運費之必要。

第二步——運雜各費確定之後，則又轉交連續號碼及路線司事Pro Number and Routing Clerk 辦理下列兩事：

(一)於各貨票上加蓋連續號碼，其作用在將零散貨票編成有系統之號碼，他日如須查究多裝少裝損壞種種事故原因，即可便於檢閱關係貨票，且於會計方面計算到達運費，登記賬目，均有莫大便利。蓋到達貨票係由各站填發，號碼各異，若不以連續數字另行編號，則各張不相連貫，在運用上卽感種種不便。

(二)此人一面編號、一面對於改運貨物之路線 Routing 附帶加以審核，有錯誤者更正之，缺而不備者則補填之。

第三步——此時以貨票轉交連號登記司事 Pro Boy，由其一一登入簿內，此簿名曰 Pro

Book，每月換用一本，以車號末尾二字代表各頁之號數，如欲查明某車貨票何時經過本處辦理經過，因此有案可稽，一索卽得。

四　由貨票塡製六聯收費單據之作用及其塡製方法

既經編號登記以後，隨卽轉交審核司事 Revising Clerk 分發各製票司事分途塡製六聯收費單據，以備各方同時運用。此項用於處理到達貨物之收費單據，足以表現美國貨運票據制度之最大優點，請折言之如后：

（一）收費單據之各聯名稱及其作用——美國鐵路鑒於到達貨運事務牽涉內外各處，非於貨票之外另行採用一式多聯之單據制度，不足以收內外各處同時辦理各事之效，因有收費單據之發明，共分六聯，總稱之曰 Expense Bill，各聯實質相同而名稱用途各異：

（1）第一聯爲運費收據 Freight Bill，於貨主接到通知來站繳付運費後，蓋上「運費收訖」戳記，交其收執，作爲付淸運費之收據。

（2）第二聯爲收費存根 Cashier's Memorandum，由鐵路存留，作爲運費收訖之收據。

（3）第三聯爲交貨收據 Delivery Receipt，由交貨司事 Delivery Clerk 用於交付貨物後，留作鐵路交貨憑證。

（4）第四聯爲運費記錄 Record of Freight Received，連同由起站收到之貨票一併轉文站內會計處，用作稽核及計算到達貨物運費之根據。

（5）第五聯爲卸車點單 Tally Bill，交于卸車司事用作卸車點貨之根據。

（6）第六聯爲到達通知 Arrival Notice，作爲通知貨主提貨之用。

由上觀之，可見六聯足以代表六項用途，亦卽表現處理到達貨物必須經過之六種手續，若此六種手續均非依賴一份貨票而莫辦，則在同一時間祇能辦理一種手續，以視六事同時並舉，相差何啻霄壤。單據制度之好壞，影響站務管理竟有如此之甚，然則吾國專恃一聯貨票輾轉爲用之辦法，豈可認爲妥善而無亟待改良之必要耶。

（二）**貨票分配法及收費單據塡製法**——審核司事分配貨票，當視貨物性質而異其先後，零担貨票應最先分配，鮮貨整車貨票次之，中轉貨物之票據 Transfer Bills 又次之，其餘不緊要者則視由登記司事轉到之先後陸續順次分發。其次分配貨票之時，尤應注意數量上之均勻，蓋製票司事 Expense Bill Makers 不止一人，每人一次應分多少貨票，不可無一定之標準，考其辦法，則爲零担者每人一次分發貨票一百張，整車者則按每人平均十輛車數分配，不以貨票張數爲標準。

各製票司事各按分得之貨票改塡六聯收費單據，各聯夾以複寫紙，一舉而六聯可以同時製成，至爲簡便迅速。此等製票司事之待遇，一如起票處之貨票司事，均按所塡票數計薪，每百張貨票約給一元六角之譜，如某張貨票有超過七種項目以上者，則一張按兩張計算。塡製關於零担貨物之六聯收費單據，尙須另外每車加塡卸車點貨總單二份，卽凡屬同一車輛之零担貨票各種情節，均應總共開入一單，以便貨棧卸車之用。此單共分七欄。名爲 Tally Sheet，其式如左：

卸車點貨總單　　＿＿站

貨票號數及日期	起運站	到達站	收貨人	貨物件數	貨物重量	運輸路線 (Route)
(1)	(2)	(3)	(4)	(5)	(6)	(7)

（三）貨票及收費單據之審核——六聯單據塡就之後，尙須經過一番審核手續，以昭鄭重，故製票司事每經塡完一批單據，應卽檢同貨票送交審核司事，并用便條塡報所塡貨票張數，各自署名一併送交。如是審核司事一面審核收費單據，如有錯誤，立卽退還更正改塡，同時又可根據便條計算各製票人員經手改塡之貨票數目，以便將來用作支付薪資之憑證。

（四）六聯收費單據及貨票之分開應用概況——此時貨票所載事項，業經移轉於收費單據，卽可分開發交各處應用，其大概如左：

（1）所有第四聯運費記錄，一律由審核司事順便撕下，以與貨票釘於一起，轉送運費更正單司事 Correction Clerk，俟將運費更正單填發以後，再行轉送站內會計處進行計算運費事宜。

（2）關於整車鮮貨之第六聯到達通知，亦由審核司事順手先行抽出，轉送通知司事 Notice Clerk，俾便提前辦理整車鮮貨到達通知事宜。

（3）關於貨棧方面之零担貨物單據，則將餘下五聯連同前述之卸車點貨總單一齊裝入封袋，按車別分開幷應在封袋外面填明車號路屬及卸車地點，交由差役送至到達貨棧，俾得進行卸車，交貨，收費各種事宜。

（4）整車貨物之第一聯運費收據，則交派駐貨場之收費司事Cashier's Teller on team track，而交貨收據則又交於貨場監工 Team Track Foreman

（5）關於交付外路之聯運車運費收據，則一律交於站內收費處 Cashier's Department，俾得與外路清算聯運運費事宜。

五　運費更正單之塡發

斯時第四聯運費記錄與到達貨票業由審核司事送交運費更正單司事，接到之後，卽將運費有改正變動之貨票，一律彙出，發交另一按件計薪之司事 Piece-Worker 填寫運費更正單 Correction Sheets。此項更正式分本路聯運兩種格單，填就之後，仍與貨票一律交還運費更正單司事，由其分別寄送本路或外路之起票車站 Billing Stations，俾得依照更正錯誤。另以一聯更正單附於到達貨票，即可轉送站內會計處進行計算運費事宜，蓋以關於貨票一切手續此時已經本處辦理完畢，再無留用之必要也。

六　到達通知之送達方法

到達通知送達方法，可按整車與零担兩種分別述之：

（一）**整車者多採分區遞送辦法**，其法即為將全市商業中心地帶劃為若干區域，凡在同一區內貨主之通知，指定由某一差役負責遞送，例如某站運輸發達，通知事務繁忙，非用專遞差役五人不可，即可將全市分為ABCDE五區，而令甲乙丙丁戊五人各管一區，如圖一所示，規定每日上下午各送一次。通知司事 Notice Clerk 接到各散張到達通知，即行按區開列一單，是謂到達通知總單 Skeleton Notices，共分七欄（參閱上列格式），然後檢同散張通知一併交於送差役 Notice Boys，分途

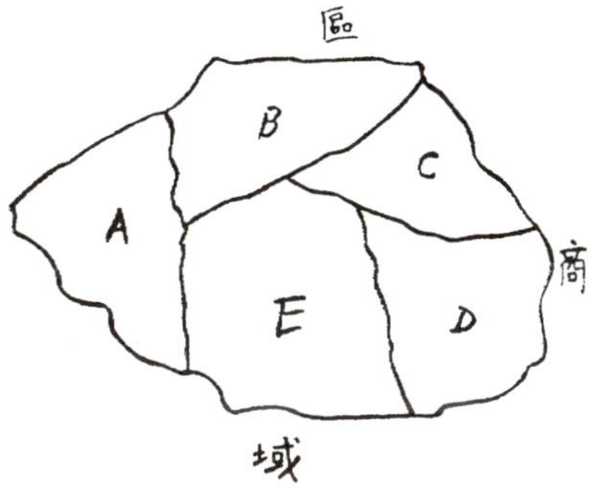

圖一

到達通知總單

第＿頁 ＿＿站 ＿年＿月＿日 遞送差役簽字＿＿

運費收據號數	車號	路屬	收貨人	收貨人簽名	收到通知之	
					日期	時刻
(1)	(2)	(3)	(4)	(5)	(6)	(7)

按區遞送。送到時一面交付散張通知，一面請貨主在此單內第５６７三欄簽名及填寫收到日期時刻，完畢卽以原單繳囘通知司事保存。

（二）**零担貨物通知多用郵寄辦法**，因零貨通知太多，不便派人遞送，故用郵遞方法。其法則爲先由貨棧用以卸車，隨卽送囘本處通知司事，其最後一次不得遲過下午三時以後。通知司事對於零担通知另行先開一單，作爲紀錄，然後裝入貼妥郵票之信封，於每日下午六時前送至郵局，如是次日上午如貨主卽可接到來站取貨，其在偏僻地帶之整車貨主，亦以相隔太遠，不便派人走送，則亦改用郵寄辦法。由此可見到達通知雖有零担整車之別，然送達事務則係集中一處辦理，不但用人經濟，辦事敏捷，抑且事權統一，可免紛歧遲延錯誤種種流弊，較之分由貨場貨棧各自寄送，實爲便利經濟。

總上所述，自貨票收進以至六聯收費單據塡發分送運用，其間經過手續，錯綜複雜，卽就貨票一端而言，前後不知經過若干分合變化，而其一分一合。則又在在足以表現管理人事之方法。例如點收貨票一事，如不限由一人辦理，則編製報告與分配貨票卽不能同時完成，又如處置交車事項，如不將貨票按其性質由多數煤運，糧運，各司事分途辦理，則又必不能收同時並舉之功效。茲爲便於瞭解本處處理事務程序及人事支配起見，更就上述各節撮要表列於后。

到達貨運處處理事務程序表

- 第一步
  - 1. 收進貨票
  - 2. 查對貨票
  - 3. 摘錄報告事項
  - 4. 貨票分類
- 第二步
  - 1. 分配貨票
  - 2. 處置車輛
- 第三步
  - 1. 審核貨票
  - 2. 審核運費
- 第四步
  - 1. 貨票編號
  - 2. 貨票登記
- 第五步
  - 1. 由貨票塡製六聯收費單據
  - 2. 審查收費單據
  - 計算製票司事改塡貨票張數
- 第六步
  - 1. 塡造運費更正單
  - 2. 寄送運費更正單
- 第七步 據分送各處貨票及收費單
  - 1. 站內會計處
  - 2. 站內收費處
  - 3. 整車貨場
  - 4. 零担貨棧
  - 5. 收貨人

七 其他

本處之主要事務大致如上所述，茲更擇其次要者略陳數端，以補前文之所未盡。

（一）特別託運單之彙報與保管——吾之所謂特別託運單者，即爲英文之 Order-Notify Bill of Lading，在吾國稱之爲提貨單。其實美國所用之 Straight Bill of Lading 與 Order Bill of Lading，同爲託運貨物單據，不過用前項單據託運者，提貨時可以不必交回鐵路，而用後項單據託運者，則非交出原來單據，即不能提取貨物，是故前者可稱爲普通託運單，而後者則可稱爲特別託運單。特別託運單既然如此重要，故其處理亦極愼重，所有已經交貨收回之特別託運單，由一雜務司事 General Clerk 兼負保管繳銷之責，每日造具報告一份，共塡三聯，以兩聯連同各託運單送呈總局會計處貨運進款稽核室 Office of Auditor of Freight Receipts 稽核室收到時應在一聯之右角蓋一收到戳記，退還站內，作爲收據，如日久不見退回，則應注意催查，以免遺忘失落，俟接退回一聯，則即以之連同原來存站之聯一併存查。

（二）郵遞貨票之管理——由客車郵寄之貨票，類皆在貨車到達以前寄到，到後即交郵遞貨票司事 Mail Waybill Clerk，先行登入簿內 Waybill Book，分本路聯運兩類。以後隨車到站之硬紙路單 Card or Slip Bills 由車場轉交本處時，即交此人持與登記簿核對，倘路單已到而貨票尚未寄到，應即按路單上之車號登入簿內，并須不斷電達起票站催促趕速補票，以至收到貨票之時爲止。同時對於已經收到之貨票，一經登記完畢，當即轉交運價司事審核運費有無錯誤，以免延誤他項手續。

（三）每日全處員工薪資統計——Daily Expense Report其作用與貨棧方面每日造報之成本統計相同，節制站務成本，此乃必要辦法，且本處事務多可採用按件給薪制度，例如製票司事之開支，即爲顯著之例。故其性質不僅止於計算員工薪資而已，將欲比照事務變化裁員減薪，亦非有此統計不可。

（四）夜班工作辦法——本處夜間須留少數人員繼續辦公，如夜班審核司事，製票司事，及運價司事等等，皆爲不可缺乏之人，蓋本處事務處理之快慢，影響卸車交貨種種事宜，至爲重大，票據不齊，即不能進行卸車交貨，故非採用日夜工作制度，不足以謀各事進行之順利。

（五）本處組織系統及員司職務名稱——本處爲貨運車站內部組織之一部，直隸貨運站長，所有主要員司職務已於前文分別述及，茲再表列於后；俾臻明瞭。我國貨站組織結構，人事管理，尙皆缺乏合理規劃，內外各處在工作上尤無嚴密之聯繫，其情形實如一盤散沙，彼此各不相謀，鬆懈遲鈍，貽誤實多，將欲改弦更張，則斯篇所陳，或多足供借鑑效法之處。至若我國現行制度之缺陷，當於另篇詳爲討論。

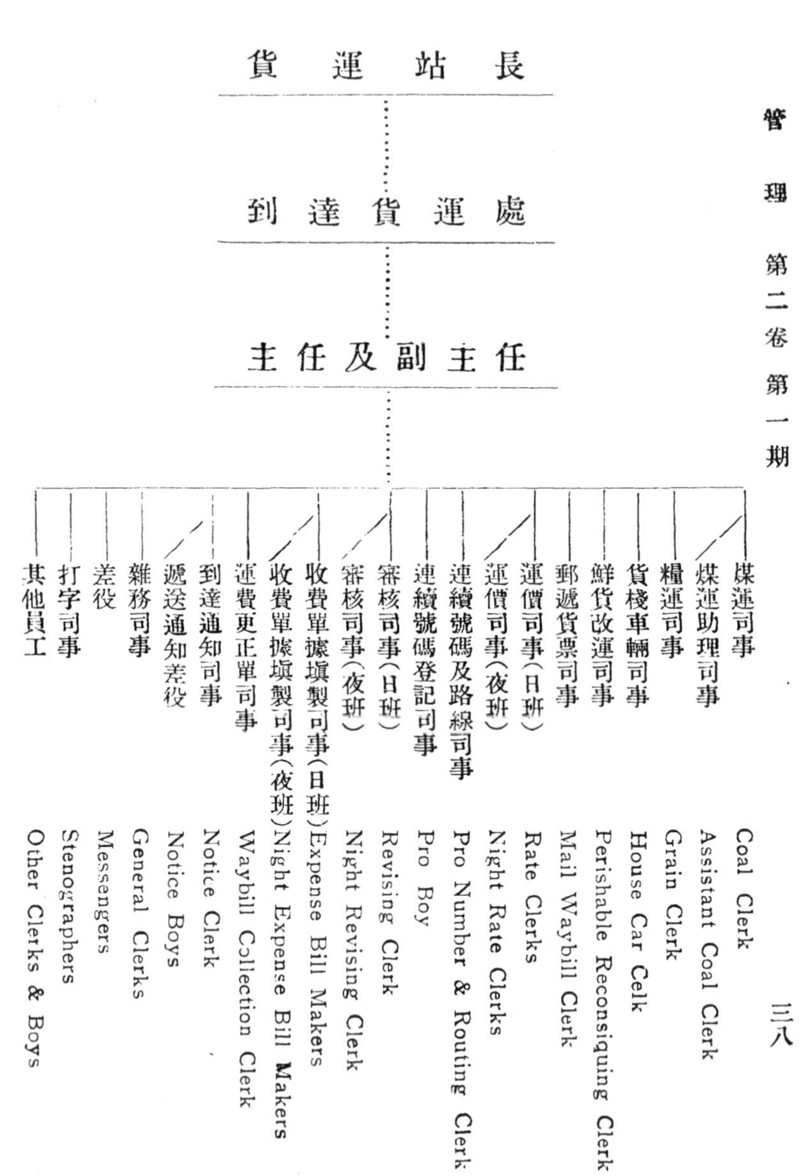

貨運站長
到達貨運處
主任及副主任
煤運司事 Coal Clerk
煤運助理司事 Assistant Coal Clerk
糧運司事 Grain Clerk
貨棧車輛司事 House Car Celk
鮮貨改運司事 Perishable Reconsiquing Clerk
郵遞貨票司事 Mail Waybill Clerk
運價司事（日班） Rate Clerks
運價司事（夜班） Night Rate Clerks
連續號碼及路線司事 Pro Number & Routing Clerk
連續號碼登記司事 Pro Boy
審核司事（日班） Revising Clerk
審核司事（夜班） Night Revising Clerk
收費單據填製司事（日班） Expense Bill Makers
收費單據填製司事（夜班） Night Expense Bill Makers
運費更正單司事 Waybill Collection Clerk
到達通知司事 Notice Clerk
遞送通知差役 Notice Boys
雜務司事 General Clerks
差役 Messengers
打字司事 Stenographers
其他員工 Other Clerks & Boys

經營比率（E. 3）

錢素君

一 導言

經營效能之强弱，管理方法之良窳，投資及債權之安全，皆可以經營比率（Operating ratio）爲測驗判斷之根據。經營比率，最初爲測驗鐵道經營效能之一種方法，自一九〇〇年經美人依頓（J.S.Eaton）(1) 倡導後，首先用諸實務者，爲費斯克（Albert Fisk）(2) 其後以理財學者之提倡，美國政府之强制採行，爲用更廣。凡今日測驗公用事業及工商企業之經營狀況者，亦罔不用之。

經營比率，爲生產成本營業費用與營業收益間之一種相互關係，以校驗經營上相對的經濟者也。此乃一般的或通俗的定義，固不足剖析在不同情形下所計算之經營比率之確切意義。本文之作，卽在補充此種通行定義之缺漏，並介紹不同情形下適用之要旨，故卽謂全文爲新的定義而作，亦無不可。

二 計算項目之釋義

就上述一般定義而論，計算經營比率，必須先得生產成本營業費用與營業收益二項之數目。此兩大項目，皆可自事業之損益計算書中取得。然以鐵道，公用事業及工商業活動之各異，損益計算書之編格式，與項目包含之內容，頗多區別，茲以實例列示如下：

工商業		鐵　道(3)		電氣事業(4)	
銷貨淨額	$1,000,000	營業進款	$5,000,000	電費收入	$4,000,000
製銷(或銷貨)成本	700,000	營業用款	3,500,000	電雜項收入	20,000
銷貨毛利	$ 300,000	進款淨數	$1,500,000	收入共計(5)	$4,020,000
營業費用(銷售，總務及管理)	200,000			發電，供電，營業及管理費用	3,020,000
營業淨利	$ 100,000			營業淨收入(5)	$1,000,000

上示例舉，除工商業外，皆以標準制度為根據；而公用事業僅列電氣事業一種，良以其他公用事業，除公共汽車(成本，費用與收益之性質，與鐵道極為相似，惟無貨運耳)外，在國內舉辦者尚少，而讀者舉一反三，固不難想見也。至於細目方面，名目繁多，且無關宏旨，亦不贅。

三　經營比率之計算縱的方面

計算經營比率之方法，隨運用之範圍，與事業之組織而各異。在縱的方面，則經營比率之計算，可依組織之不同而分別為三：

(一)工商業

(二)鐵道及其他交通事業

(三)公用事業

在橫的方面，則依運用之範圍，解析之目的，而可分為下列五項：

(甲)經營及管理效能

(乙)債權上利息(或本息)之保障

(丙)投資報酬之豐嗇

(丁)股票投機

(戊)資本結構之規劃

茲請先述縱的方面之計算方法。

(一)工商業　計算工商業之經營比率，乃在求出生產及或銷售上之成本及費用，與銷貨所得之相互關係，算式如下：

$$\text{經營比率} = \frac{\text{製銷(或銷貨)成本} + \text{營業費用}}{\text{銷貨淨額}}$$

如以上例代入算式，得經營比率百分之九十，或〇・九〇：

$$\frac{\$700,000 + \$200,000}{\$1,000,000} = 90$$

以此項比率，自百分之百中減去，則可得營業純利與銷貨之關係，即所謂營業純利與銷貨比率是也。如以營業純利與銷貨比率逐年計算，歷年比較，則昇降消長之趨勢。亦易於觀察矣。此種比率，能助判斷產銷管理之成敗，故通常應用，每分別部分，產品及商品之門類或其他單位，逐一計算之。

(一)鐵道及其他交通事業　此類企業之經營比率，則依下式計算：

$$經營比率=\frac{營業用款}{營業進款}=\frac{\$3,500\ 000}{\$5,000,000}=70$$

經營比率，在鐵道及他種交通事業，雖較其他測驗經營效能之比率（如修繕比率，運輸比率等）更爲通用。然其所能指示者，僅獲利能力與收益間之一定比例而已。在財政解析方面，則利息數額之成比，每一股份所獲之利益，咸較獲利能力爲重要也。然而，此種比率對於公平費則之釐訂，容或有不可掩沒之重要；有變動性之費用之撙節浪費，亦藉以評斷經營者之責職也。

(二)公用事業　計算公用事業經營比率之方法，與鐵道同；其式如下：

$$經營比率=\frac{營業費用}{營業收入(包括主要收入及雜項營業收入)}$$

如以上例電氣事業爲例，得經營比率百分之七十五強：

$$\frac{3,020,000}{4,020,000}=75$$

此比率之意義。乃在指示營業收入每元之成本若干？易言之，取得一元之營業收入，須支付之代價爲若干？

四　變動與固定費之分野

當我人晉而闡述經營比率橫的方面計算方法之前，費用之變動與固定之劃分。實爲一極重要之問題。會計學上，對於兩者之區分，除計算成本時稍加討論外，並不以爲一重大問題。經濟學原理雖有變動與固定費用之分別，然不甚適合計算經營比率之需要，因以經濟成本與會計成本之畛域，不相融洽故也。是以經濟學上之討論，頗不適於會計學上決定成本之用也。

就事業營理上之統制可能性，費用可分爲二大類：（一）變動費用，（二）固定費用。前者爲事業管理者所能統制之費用，後者爲不能統制之費用。茲以習見項目，列示如左：

變動費用	固定費用
薪給工資	租金
旅費	捐稅
廣告	折舊
運費包裝	利息
水電薪炭	
法律及會計費用	
郵電	

文具印刷
保險
呆賬

據上以論，變動及固定費用之分別，亦原以費用之伸縮性爲標準。申言之，凡費用隨營業之大小而高下者，爲變動費用；不問營業之大小，費用之數額絕無伸縮增減者，爲固定費用。

然上列綱要中變動費用方面之保險，與固定費用下之租金捐稅及折舊，都有解釋之必要。

保險可分爲三種：曰貨物保險。曰房屋及設備保險，曰職工人壽及傷害保險。此三類之中，貨物保險，顯屬隨營業數量而變動，故爲變動費用，實無疑義。至於其他兩種保險，爲變動費用，抑固定費用，則須視情形而定，尤以人壽及傷害保險，更有確切分別之必要。房屋及設備保險，爲維持事業生產力常態之必要支出；就今日通行實務觀察，實爲良健管理上不可或吝之負担，而保險費數額之大小，雖不若借款利息數額之一成不變，然其增減亦極微小，且爲構成經營成本間接費用之一種，故可謂固定費用；良以此種費用，爲管理者不能統制而使其伸縮者也。至若職工人壽及傷害保險，則須以有無強制規定，爲區別變動與固定之標準。依一般而言，任意投保之人壽及傷害保險，既由管理上自由意志決定，故爲變動費用，強制投保之人壽及傷害保險，乃由契約或協約之約定而發生，故爲固定費用。然即屬有契約或協約之強制規定，保險之荷負，固隨營業之大小而異其輕重，營業大，職工之僱用多，保險之負担，自須添重，故與工資津貼等費用之性質，並無區別，其爲變動費用也，自無庸疑。但高級職員之保險，則與營業顯無聯繫，故爲固定費用。

租金及捐稅兩項，雖列入固定費用方面，且實際上亦每作如此處置，然其中亦不無變動費用之性質者。如貨物徵賦出廠稅統稅者，則此種稅納之大小，與出貨之數量成一正比，不若房捐地稅等，不隨產銷數量而直接增減者。他若倉庫之租賃，亦隨銷量而異其需要，故此種費用，當屬變動。

折舊爲常人最易誤解之一種費用。凡百有形物體，無不受自然界毀損定律之支配。鋼筋水泥之巍峨大廈，終將隨時日之消逝而毀杞；機器設備，亦將變爲廢鐵而非修理所能恢復。此種物質的消蝕。或效用的減少，謂之折舊。常人以折舊與利益混爲一談，要知折舊非爲一部分利益之運用，而係產生利益所不可不負之一種費用，故此種費用，自非隨營業之增減而有所變動，即使事業一旦間斷經營，折舊固依然繼續發生也。是爲固定費用，無待贅言。

五　經營比率之計算——橫的方面

事業之關係者，對於事業之收益，每因其地位之各殊，其觀察之根據亦隨之而不同。事業之關係者凡五：(一)經營事業者，卽負責執行業務之人，如執行董事，經理及直接負責一部分經營之職員；(二)管理事業者，如公司之董事會；(三)長期債權人，如抵押借款債權人，及公司債持券人；(四)優先股股東；及(五)普通股股東。此外以公司股票作投機牟利者，則此輩對於事業收益之變化，關切更較上述諸輩爲甚。

就工商業損益計算書之通行格式，分析上述各種不同觀點，可得下列比較表：(6)

營業損益(固定費用除外)	經營事業者之觀點
加：其他損益(包括利息以外之固定費用)	
總損益	管理者及事業本身之觀點
減：流動負債利息	
餘　額	長期債權人之觀點
減：固定負債利息	
淨損益	優先股股東之觀點
減：優先股股利	
餘額	普通股股東之觀點

此種觀點，甚爲重要，因其能限制經營比率之計算。而就不同目的所計算之經營比率，

欲界需要者以正確的營業結果之概念，則必須確切瞭解其需要，否則其價值必不能爲人所共賞也。

（一）經營效能之測驗　經營效能之測驗，要在明經營者之成敗，故凡以此種目的而計算之經營比率，應以經營者不能統制或不應負責之各種費用，全部剔出。易言之，算式分子之中不得包含折舊及租金以外之其他固定營業費用。故與初倡時所用之算式同，茲列示如下：

$$經營比率 = \frac{製銷成本+（變動營業費用+折舊+租金）}{銷貨淨額}$$

式內變動營業費用，係採上節變動費用之解釋。折舊一項，雖爲固定費用，且其數額決定之權限，係操諸管理者之掌中，然因其爲經營上不可不負担之主要成本項目，故經營者雖無統制之權，仍須由其負責。他若租金之支付，亦非經營者所能左右，惟生產要素之租賃，爲事業經營上不可或缺之生產力策源，如事業自行置備此種要素，則使用之費用，當以折舊之形式，歸經營者負責。倘此種生產要素，事業係租賃而使用者，則使用之代價，基於同一原則，當歸經營者負責，實爲公允之舉。

此種比率。乃供內部之用，故計算資料，蒐集甚易；若外界關係者，欲就公開之損益計算書中，確定算式內分子方面三大項目之數額，容非易事；良以事業所公布之決算表，大抵以各種細目，彙列一款；此種手段，尤以損益爲甚，作者曾據民國二十四年上海工商業五十二家之公布損益計算書作一統計各種營業費用以一款表示者，凡四十五家，佔全部百分之八十七。由此可見國內商人對於損益科目之態度，大都保持緘默之一班矣。

（二）管理效能之測驗　測驗管理效能之經營比率，依下式計算而得：

$$經營比率=\frac{製銷成本+(變動營業費用+折舊+租金利息)}{銷貨淨額}$$

上式與測驗經營效能之經營比率，所不同者，爲分子方面多利息一項。蓋經營與管理之分別，卽在於斯。經營爲直接活動之管理，而管理者，除經營以外，尙負調濟財政及釐訂理財政策之責任。利息爲理財政策所產生之後果，其責任之歸屬，自須由管理者負担也。

（三）債權上利息（或本息）之保障　此處所謂債權，係指事業對外之負債，其種類大別之，有二：曰短期債權，曰長期債權，短期債權人測驗其利息給付之保障，可用測驗經營效能之經營比率，蓋此項比率與百分之百之差額，卽表示短期債權利息所佔營業總損益（卽銷貨淨額與利息以外之變動及固定費用之差額）之比例，易言之，每一元利息所佔總損益之成比。例如某公司之經營比率（測驗經營效能之經營比率）爲百分之八十，銷貨淨額爲二百萬元，短期債務須給付利息者十五萬元，債務到期應付之利息總額爲八千元，則短期債務利息之保障爲五十與一之比，卽每一元之短期債務利息，有五十元營業總利益爲之保障，算法如下：

經營比率　＝80%

利息與總利益之比例＝100%－80%　＝20%

可供支付利息之總利益金額　20＝$200,000×20%＝$400,000

$$利息保障之比率＝\frac{400,000}{8,000}＝50$$

至若測驗長期債權利息（或本息）保障之經營比率，應依下式計算：

$$經營比率＝\frac{製銷成本＋（變動營業費用＋折舊＋租金＋短期債務利息）}{銷貨淨額}$$

其個計算方法，與短期債權利息同，茲不贅。

（四）投資報酬之豐吝　公司之投資者，有優先股股東，與普通股股東之分。測驗投資報酬豐吝所計算之經營比率，故亦須分別，其算式如下：

$$測驗優先股報酬之經營比率＝\frac{可供支付股利之純利}{銷貨淨額}$$

$$測驗普通股報酬之經營比率＝\frac{可供支付股利之純利－優先股股利}{銷貨淨額}$$

所謂可供支付股利之純利（Net Profit Available for Dividents），係採會計學上之解釋。有人容或以此種比率，既以經營以外之其他損益及純利分配項目一併計算，即不足再膺經營比率之名；或以此種比率實無顯著之意義相非難者，則下文解釋，可爲答辯也。

企業利潤之泉源，以銷貨或供給勞務而取得之報酬，最爲主要；投資之報酬，亦不外取給于斯。依今日企業組織之規範而言，投資報酬之限度，居於銷貨或供給勞務上收入，提減各種成本，費用與其他提存後之餘額，而此種餘額之產生，以銷貨或勞務上之收入，爲最初之來源；故餘額與其來源兩者間之關係，自予享受此種報酬者重大之意義，——卽其應享之報酬，與報酬來源之關係或比例何若？夫構成此種關係之一項要素，既爲主要經營活動，則以經營比率名此關係，就名詞論，浮泛則有之，不足以膺固未也。

(五)股票投機　以公司股票作投機者，除『非參加累積優先股』外，經營比率與其毛利之關係，至爲密切。證券市場上對於股票價格之決定，咸取決於市場利率與股利率之差異，及獲利能力之强弱。前者與本文無涉；後者之測驗，則經營比率實甚重要。以股票投機所計算之經營比率，其方法與測驗投資報酬者同。惟依國外經驗而言，投機之股票，大抵以普通股占多數。投機者所以深切注意經營比率之昇降，無非欲於決定股票價格之一大要素有確切之認識，以佐其牟利之決斷耳。經營比率愈高，普通股股利之享受愈少希望；經營比率低，則股利分發之希望大。股利分發之希望愈大，股票之價格當漸趨上漲，投機者如屬空頭可早日補進，俾免損失更鉅。如係多頭，則可不爲脫手，俟價格漲至利益極大之時，始行抛去。此種利用科學方法之投機，其牟利之希望，較僅憑臆測或幸運者，自屬不同也。

(六)資本結構之規定　在決定資本結構之時，經營比率之應用，幾爲每一科學訓練之理財家所必採。資本結構在理財上之先決問題，爲舉債營業(Trading on the equity)之可否。

此一問題之解答，有恃收益平穩性之强弱，收益之豐吝，及使用借入資本之代價等三端。就原則而論，收益豐厚而且平穩者，舉債營業常爲一種得計。然舉債營業最大之弊害，莫如本利到期不能償還，債權人即可管理或淸算事業。故當舉債營業之先，對於債期之長短，每期還本付息之數額，須有愼密之考慮，務使每年之固定負擔，不超逾最歉年度之最低收益，此爲理財者之金科玉律，嚴遵不渝者也。

爲決定歉吝年度最低收益而計算之經營比率，其算法與測驗經營效能者同。玆列示根據經營比率，計算最高還本付息負荷之方法如下：

設M爲尋常年度之銷貨淨額(或營業收益)，d爲最歉年度銷貨淨額之減少數，r爲經營比率(7)，X爲歉年還本付息之最高負荷系數，則尋常年度與最歉年度之銷貨淨額(或營業收益)及營業成本與費用(包括折舊及租金)，之數額，可以符號代表，表列如下：

	尋常年度	最歉年度
銷貨淨額(營業收入)	M	M-d
營業成本與費用(包括折舊及租金)	Mr	(M-d)r
營業純利(營業淨收入)	M-Mr	(M-d)-(M-d)r
還本付息之最高負荷系數	X(M-Mr)	

以上僅 X(M-Mr) 爲未知數，此未知數係固定性質，故不論其數目太小，而各年度均不

變動，且其數與尋常年度之純利相乘之積斷不容超逾最歉之年之營業純利，但可能與最歉之年之營業純利數額相等。職是之故 X(M-Mr) 可等於(M-d)-(m-d)r。解析X之因數，則得下式：

$$X=\frac{(M-r)(I-r)}{M(I-r)}=\frac{(m-d)}{m}$$

例如某公司尋常年度之銷貨淨額爲二百萬元，最歉年度爲一百五十萬元；經營比率爲百分之八十，則該公司還本付息之最高負荷數爲三十萬元，適等於尋常年度純利之百分之七十五。算式如下：

M＝$2,000,000

d.＝$2,000,000－$1,500,000＝$500,000

r＝80%

x＝?

$$x=\frac{(2,000,000-500,000)(1-80\times)}{2,000,000(1-80\%)}=75\%$$

尋常年度之純利＝(M-mr)＝$2,000,000-($2,000,000×80%)＝$400,000

歉吝年度之純利＝$400,000×75%＝$300,000(即最高還本付息負荷數)

六 經營比率應用上之注意及其限制

經營比率，爲測驗事業活動結果之便捷方法。事業之經營者及管理者，對於事業之經營管理，每預定一種經營比率，作爲事業之尋常標準。就原則言，經營比率以愈低愈佳。較低而傾向下降之經營比率，表現經營管理之撙節與進步；較高而趨向上昇之經營比率，可表現經營管理之奢糜與浪費。

事業之健康否，與人體相同，亦以有無疾病爲判斷標準。事業疾病之最流行者，爲利益之菲薄，此種病態，猶我人之貧血症。貧血未必爲險惡之徵象，有時亦非主要病患，事業利益之菲薄亦然。經營比率，爲測驗事業有無貧血症之方法，恰似我人患貧血症時驗血確定病狀，驗血雖爲確定病症之主要試驗，然不能指示疾患之來，由於造血機能之窒礙，抑由於他種疾病之消耗。以經營比率測驗事業利益之菲薄，亦不能確定疾患侵襲之原因，究因浪費所致，抑由於事業自身之貧瘠羸弱？約言之，以經營比率測驗事業之利益菲薄病，僅能確定病態之是否存在，而不及於診斷也。

但在另一方面，我人如憂慮貧血症之襲來者，常以血液試驗，確定徵象之有無，以事預防，則驗血對於健康者之欲防是疾者，其功不可沒已。事業如在若干連續之年度內，表現經營比率之瀕昇趨向，洵屬大難將臨之預兆，主持者固可藉以立謀療治，以免因病勢之日趨險惡，終致奪事業之生命。

經營比率之適用，與其他比率同，必須互相比較，而後意義昭彰。比較之法，或以同業，或採各年。如以同業比較，則於構成計算項目之內容，必求相同。通常經營比率之解析，必須輔以純利所占利息之倍數，及每一股份所能享受之利益，方可得正確概念，而營業利益與固定資產及營業利益與現値之關係，更須參證，以資正確判斷之根據。

經營比率之解析，尤須參照經濟情形。在物價上漲之時，貨物售價高漲，而若干費用，因有固定性質，或其昇張之比例，低於售價之上漲，致經營比率，乃呈下降傾向。惟在公用事業，因收費標準缺乏伸縮性，故費用之增減，恆大於收入。職是之故，當物價逐漸降落之時，工商業之經營比率，必呈向上趨勢，而公用事業則下降。倘物價既呈下降，而業務又現減色，則公用事業收入之減少，必超逾費用之節省，於是其經營比率，反而上昇矣。

各業於經營比率之高下，及其影響投資報酬之多寡，每因其生產策動力投資之大小而異。依原則而言，個人勞務爲生產策動力泉源之事業，即使經營比率極高，其投資之報酬仍甚可觀。貿易業之投資如需獲適當之報酬，其經營比率必須較低，製造業更低；若公用事業交通事業及地產業，則必須較製造業爲尤低，否則投資之報酬，必太菲薄矣。

經營比率，可以以生產步驟有聯繫之若干事業合併(Vertical integration)而抑低，若同業合併(Horizontal integration)則無影響也。經營比率，於股權公司則不能適用，蓋以此種公司，全恃投資利息及股利爲主要收益來源，故事實上無所謂經營也。

（1）見氏著"Railroad Operations," 1900

（2）Louisville and Nashville Annual Report of 1873—1904

（3）見部頒則例營業帳

（4）詳見全國電氣事業指導委員會電氣事業標準會計科目草案

（5）非草案規定名稱

（6）以現行之公司組織爲依據

（7）就經驗論，尋常年度與歉吝年度之經營比率，每極相仿，蓋以收益雖減，開支亦可節省。實際上容或兩者增減之比例不一致，而致經營比率稍示昇降者：固不乏實例，惟據大量觀察，卽有出入，所差亦極有限。但公用事業則適成反比例。要以其收費爲政府所箝制故也。

交通大學出版刊物

一 期刊

1. 交大季刊	每册三角	全年一元
2. 交大三日刊	半年五角	全年一元
3. 科學通訊(全年八期)	每册二角	全年一元四角
4. 管理二月刊(全年五期)	每册四角	全年一元六角

二 本校一覽

1. 中文本	每册四角
1. 英文本	每册六角

三 本校研究所編輯刊物

1. 油漆試驗報告,第一號	每册二角
2. 油漆試驗報告,第二號	每册六角
3. 油漆試驗報告,第三號	每册八角
4. 地下流水問題之解法(英文本)	每册三角
5. 美國鐵道會計實務,第一編(英文本)	每册六角
6. 解決中國運輸問題之途徑 (英文本)	每册四角
7. 解決中國運輸問題之途徑 (譯本)	每册三角
8. 鐵路零担貨運安全辦法	每册四角
9. 中國國民經濟在條約上所受之束縛	每册六角
10. 皖中稻米產銷之調查	每册六角
11. 小麥及麵粉	每册五角
12. 平漢沿綫農村經濟調查	每册一元六角
13. X 射綫檢驗材料法	每册一元二角

經售處 上海徐家匯本校出版處

改善吾國鉄路大站行車房之我見（C 6.）

沈奏廷

吾國鐵路大站行李房之零亂無序，雖不如貨棧或貨場之甚，然其紛雜之情形亦足令旅客望而生畏。旅客託運行李，大都均由脚伕照料，所謂行李員者伏案寫票且不遑，何暇接待旅客，甚有將行李員納入一室，不與旅客見面者；而一切行李，無論大小輕重，概由櫃上出入，以致爾擠我擁，備極紛擾之能事，加以包裹之托運亦多與行李混在一處，大有治絲而棼之概，欲其井然有序，自更不易言矣。有此情形，故一般旅客均以行李掛牌爲畏途，羣願自帶上車，以節手續而免煩擾，吾國旅客列車上旅客自帶笨重行李之多，雖原因不止一端，而一部分實由於此，其流弊所及，因不僅在旅客之不便已也。

查吾國行李房混亂之由來，不外四大原因：(一)以笨重行李不與輕便行李劃分；(二)以行李票之形式不良，塡寫費事；(三)以包裹行李混在一起；(四)以到達行李缺乏合理保管制度。明其原因乃可進而言改良之途徑，茲請分別討論之如次：

一、**笨重行李與輕便行李之劃分**　按在美國鐵路，笨重行李之收受大都均與輕便行李劃分，收受笨重行李之處所名曰行李室Baggage room，收受輕便行李之處所名曰掛牌處Checking Courter，前者位於站屋之旁，前面卽爲街道，笨重行李車送到站，卽可直接送入此室，從事過磅，無須送入站門，穿過待車室等處，更無搬至掛牌處之必要，故笨重行李通常不爲站內一般旅客所見，根本無由造成站內之擁擠。此項笨重行李，在美國都由捷運商或旅館等代客車送到站，捷運商或旅館對於每件行李，發給臨時收據 Claim Check 一張，臨時收據分兩聯，一聯交由旅客收執；旅客持此收據。可卽於到站上車之前，向掛牌處換取正式行李票 Baggage Checks，手續極簡。掛牌處業於事前由行李室取得磅條，載明臨時收據號數及重量，故旅客前來換票時，卽可爲之對照，查明重量，以定免費或收費，法至便也。由此可見笨重行李之收受，過磅，裝車等均由行李室辦理，絕對不經掛牌處之手。掛牌處類多位於售票處之旁，僅司輕便行李之收受起票與笨重行李之換票工作，所有行李員 Checkmen 均鵠立櫃前，接助旅客，故旅客有賓至如歸之樂，而無四顧無人茫無頭緒之苦，與吾國較洵有霄壤之別也。

（二）行李票之形式　吾國鐵路之行李票向採薄紙票式，無論免費或逾重，均須逐項填寫，頗費手續。查旅客所挂行李終以免費者居多，免費行李既無收費之必要，其行李票之形式及製發手續大可使之簡易化，美國行李均用卡片式，免費者二聯，逾重者三聯，免費行李票之到達站名等項均於事前加蓋戳記，分別懸掛於行李員之前，遇有行李起票，卽可隨手取下，以一聯交旅客收執，一聯輊繫於行李上，手續極簡；且明明可以免費之行李，卽不爲之過磅，行李票上亦無塡寫重量之必要，與吾國之繁重手續較，相差甚巨。蓋吾國鐵路承運行李，即使明明不至逾重，亦須過磅，并將實在重量與規定免費重量塡入行李票，一若非如此不足以資考核者，實則此項重量之可持與否仍須視員司之忠實而定，若行李員將一百公斤塡爲五十公斤，亦屬難於查察，然則不至逾重之行李又何必爲之過磅徒費手續耶。然在吾國笨重行李與輕便行李尚未劃分，笨重行李仍須入掛牌處過磅，究竟有無逾量，自難臆斷，勢非一一過磅不可，故欲使掛牌處之工作簡易，僅就改良行李票形式入手尚嫌不足，必也將笨重行李與輕便行李劃分，過磅事宜概由笨重行李室爲之，則改良票式始有助於工作效率之增進焉。輕重行李劃分與票式改良之後所有掛牌處之行李員，均可一一鵠立櫃前，招待旅客，不必假手於行李夫，而旅客自無痛苦矣。

最近京滬路之上海北站對於免費行李，已倣效美國鐵路辦法（按此爲吾友周賢言君之建議）採用三聯式之卡片行李票，誠爲一大進步，在國中已不可多得，惜輕重行李尚未劃分，工作亦難充分簡易，尙有待於他日之改良耳。

(三)**包裹與行李之劃分** 我國鐵路之包裹，除聯運直達包裹外，類多與行李同裝一車，故其起運及交付亦與行李混在一起。按包裹均爲貨物，較諸笨重行李尤爲龐雜，在西國鐵路，笨重行李且與輕便行李劃分，何况貨物。吾國鐵路行李房之繁雜零亂，手續遲緩，包裹之與行李混雜，亦爲一重大原因。在美國鐵路，捷運包件，在火站均另有承運之所，是爲捷運終點設備 Express terminal，規模甚巨，吾國之包裹業務固不能與之比擬，然亦可倣照笨重行李辦法，另闢門道從事收取，勿令送入車站行李掛牌處等場所，或與笨重行李同在一處收進亦無不可。果能如此處理，則掛牌處之工作又可簡易化矣。

(四)**到達行李之保管制度**　查吾國鐵路對於到達行李多無規定之管理制度，往往隨便堆放，檢認費時，交付手續爲之增繁，而遲延錯誤隨以發生，其堆放地位不敷應用者，更有上下堆疊層層擁塞之患，交付時更覺不易應付，皆非促進工作效率之道。按美國鐵路到達行李之保管方法，類皆井然有序，笨重行李亦與輕便行李劃分，前者堆存地上，四周墻上編有號碼，自0至9，行李卽按票號之某一字歸類堆放，檢尋極易；輕便行李置於架上，架上亦編號碼，自0至9，歸類亦如之。故旅客前來提取時，對照票號，一索卽得，手續簡易之至。其次保管行李之地位必須寬暢敷用，切忌層層堆叠之弊，庶幾搬動不難，先到之行李不至擁塞在內也。

今欲改良我國鐵路之行李房，根據上述各點，作者以爲非實行下列諸端，決難收效，請列舉之：

(一)實行笨重行李與輕便行李劃分辦法，前者應另闢沿街之門道收進，過磅掛牌後，直接搬送上車，絕對不經掛牌處，如旅客携有輕便行李與笨重行李兩種者，其輕便行李亦得與笨重行李同交該門收受，每件各給臨時收據一紙，收據上祇須一簡單之號碼，製發極簡；旅客即攜臨時收據，至掛牌處換票。

(二)輕重行李劃分之後，掛牌處之免費行李票應一律採用卡片式，預先蓋戳製就備用，所有行李員均不必伏案寫票，而須一一鵠立櫃前，招待旅客。

(三)包裹與笨重行李同一門道收進，或另闢門道收受之，絕對勿許搬入掛牌處；收受包裹之行李員隨即製發包裹票，不必如笨重行李之經過換票手續。

(四)到達行李應有合理之保管制度，自0至9，編列號碼，行李即按票號之最末第二字歸類排列之，幷將重件與輕件劃分，前者可置地上，後者須置架上，以免夾雜混淆。

上述四端皆非難能之事，爰特加以討論，以供吾路界之參考。

本院教員中文著作一覽表

林　叠	行政學大綱（南京華僑半月刊社，民國二十四年）定價一元
沈奏廷	鐵路問題討論集（上海商務印書館，民國二十五年）定價一元五角
沈奏廷	鐵路運價之理論與實際（大學叢書）（上海商務印書館，民國二十四年）定價二元九角
沈奏廷	鐵路貨運業務（大學叢書）（上海商務印書館）民國二十四年定價二元五角
沈奏廷	鐵路經濟論文集（上海中國鐵道運輸學會，民國二十三年）定價八角
俞希稷	匯兌論（上海商務印書館，民國十四年）定價九角
夏晉麟	上海租界問題（上海太平洋國交討論會，民國二十年）定價二角
鍾偉成編	鐵道經濟論叢（上海交通大學管理學院，民國二十二年）定價二角
鍾偉成	鐵道材料管理（在印刷中）
熊大惠	運輸學水道編（上海交通大學管理學院代售，民國二十三年）定價平裝二元五角，精裝三元
王炳南 熊大惠 合著	公路運輸（在印刷中）
王同文	東北鐵路問題之研究，上下二册（管理學院叢書）（上海交通大學管理學院，民國二十二年）實價一元二角
崔曉岑	中央銀行論（大學叢書）（上海商務印書館，民國二十四年）定價平裝二元二角，精裝三元二角
崔曉岑	幣制與銀行（上海生活書店代售，民國二十五年）定價平裝一元五角，精裝二元五角

現代企業組織問題之檢討（B 1.）

王烈望

不佞於本刊第三期發表譯述『事權之分離及其聯整』一文，已指出現代企業組織問題之焦點所在，茲復就美國管理協會所發表之意見，參以己意，草成本文，以就教於讀者。

一 組織問題在管理中之地位

組織問題爲管理問題中之一種，現代之管理問題約如下列：

(1)政策問題(Problem of policy) 此爲關于擬定目標及實施計劃方面之問題。

(2)組織問題(Problems of organization) 此爲關於責權之如何劃分，各部份機構之如何調整，使政策能從各部份機構之合作而得最有效率之實施問題。

(3)人事問題(Problems of personnel) 此爲關於人材之如何獲得，員司之如何發展與利用，使組織計劃中所定之責權，得充分之表現問題。

(4)設備問題(Problems of facilities) 此爲關於行施政策所必須之各種物質財產之如何取得及如何維持問題。

(5)方法問題(Problems of method) 此爲關於在政策中規定之目標所必須之行施實務及手續之如何建立與運用問題。

上述五項雖不足以盡管理者所遇之一切問題，且問題之來往往有互相關聯錯綜而不能如上述之劃分者，然大致則不外乎此。

實業家對於設備及方法問題，已甚注意，蓋在十九世紀末葉以前，管理者但求商品之生產，足以應市場之擴大；故彼等專致力於可以增加生產之物質設備之獲取以及可以增加物質設備效能之實務與方法，對於其他問題，不及此二者之重視也。

自前世紀末葉以來，實業家對於政策問題始漸增其注意，但於組織問題與人事問題，仍未重視。彼等之所以忽略組織問題者，大概由於下列各點：

(1)組織問題之性質，較難捉摸，故其對于管理者之重要性，亦不若其他問題之顯著，譬如適應定貨單之需要，不能不添置新機器，此類問題爲管理者最所關心，以其不能不迅予解決也。組織機構之調整，容亦爲管理者所注意，但其需要之迫切，遠不若改進設備之明顯，蓋前者之效果著於無形而後者之效果則成於有形，無形者不易計其價值而有形者之價值，歷歷可數也。

(2)對於決定政策，設備以及方法之錯誤，顯而易見，一有錯誤，管理者自不能不亟予糾正。至於組織與人事方面之決策，其錯誤隱而難明，故組織問題之考慮乃不若其他有形問題之急要。

（3）組織問題之解決，須有深沉之思想，此種思想似不易爲繁忙之實業家所能發展，蓋組織方面之思想，至爲抽象曲折，慣於處理有形事物之實際家，往往無暇運用組織方面之思想，此組織問題之所以不爲世所重視者之又一因也。

由於上述三點之故，組織方面之改進，遂遠不若其他管理方面進步之速，然現代各種事業之組織既日益其膨脹，而其內部之分工亦愈見其精密。組織問題之日趨繁複，實爲必然之勢。

二 組織問題之所以複雜

組織問題之日趨繁雜，既爲必然之勢，請申言其所以日趨繁雜之原因：

（1）由於專門化程度提高

（2）由於生產過程與經濟狀況變動之迅疾

（3）由於政府干涉或參與經濟活動權力之擴大

茲就上列三點分別言之：

（1）專門化程度之提高，何以能提成組織問題之複雜？

自家庭工業衰而工廠制度興，一物之成往往經數十百人之手，一人所作之工僅爲全體中之極小部份，此就一廠之內而言，已含有如何分配工作，如何劃定職務之問題，此種問題即爲組織問題之原形。生產技術愈進步，分工亦愈精細，參與同一生產部門之人數亦愈多，而嗣後分工之原則不僅適用於製造工作部門卽事務上之工作亦皆依分工之原則而進行，分工愈細卽專門化之程度愈高，專門化之程度提高，一方面固爲增進工作之量與質所必由之途徑，然同時必益增組織問題之複雜，請更分析言之：

(a)分工愈細所分之部門愈多，各部門之間，其關係有如連鎖，此環與彼環，必須呼應靈活，而後乃能協調進行，否則一環步伐失調，全部工作，必將爲之遮斷，故分工愈細，部門愈多，愈需要有高度之聯繫。如何獲得高度之聯繫？實爲今日企業管理中最難解決之問題其問題之中心卽爲不易選取領袖人才而居之於聯繫之責。

(b)因專門化之結果，工作員司之思想目光隨其環境而日趨狹隘，因之領袖人才之造成，亦日見其困難。

上述二點卽謂專門化之結果益增管理之困難，同時因專門化而更不易造成管理人才，此二種問題之發展，實大可促研究管理問題者之注意也。

(2)生產過程與經濟狀況之變動，何以能促組織問題之複雜？人類最富惰性，生活於其種社會習慣或社會制度之下，終不願見其所素習之制度有所紛更。故卽使生產方法，經濟關係已發生根本之變動，制度之改革，終不能與之相應。此在新舊勢力交替之時，最爲顯而易見，就中國之現狀言，有許多現代企業如紗廠，麵粉廠，及其他輕工業，已需要有科學化之管理，蓋企業之目的原爲圖利，欲求利潤之增加，必須提高管理之效能。欲求管理效能之提高，必須按照生產過程與經濟狀況之需要，調整工作之機構，然後就工作機構中之各種職務，配置合宜之之工作人員，務使人盡其才，物盡其用，而後方可以言管理之效能，今之經營現代工業者，亦未嘗不知此，然往往牽於舊習，礙於人情，遂以組織去適應人事，而不能就組織以配置人才。私企業固多如此，公營企業尤有甚者，政務機關，更無論矣。此種社會環境之牽制，足使組織問題之解決，甚感棘手，蓋一方因生產過程經濟狀況已起變更，非調整工作機構，不足應付新的事實之發展，一方則因社會環境之牽制，亦不能不與之周旋。欲調和於此二者之間，豈易言哉！豈易言哉！

（3）政府干涉經濟活動或參與經濟活動權力之擴大何以能促成組織問題之複雜？在資本主義的經濟制度發展之初，政府因事實上之要求而採取放任政策，學者亦認爲政府對於私經濟之干涉，愈少愈好。然採取放任政策與自由經濟之國家，亦僅十九世紀之英國耳，其他後起之資本主義國家，如德，美，日，意等國政府殆皆參與經濟活動，洎乎歐戰爆發，政府乃一躍而兼爲經濟之統制者，戰後經濟秩序，漸次恢復，然政府之經濟活動範圍，則已日見伸張，自一九二九年以來資本主義國家因救濟經濟恐慌，政府之經濟活動，愈形擴大。彼社會主義與法西斯主義的國家，固已合政治與經濟爲一體，卽資本主義國家，亦以統制經濟爲政府之職責。處於次殖民地之中國，更須於集體力量，推動經濟建設之進行。故大勢所趨集體行動必將超越一切個人行動。今日個別經營之一切企業及其他社會組織，必將逐漸失去其單獨行動之性能而成爲集體機構中之一小器官，個人者直將視同集體內之細胞耳。此趨向之發展將使組織問題愈形複雜而亦愈見其重要也。

三 解決組織問題之途徑

總上所論：組織問題有日趨複雜，日形重要之勢，此一問題之如何應付，自爲注意管理學術者與實業家所欲探討，茲就管見所及，概舉如下：

(1)調協個人行動與集體行動之齟齬。

(2)劃分企業行爲之類別。

(3)取得各部門單位之聯繫。

(4)注重領袖人材之選用與訓練。

(5)激發個人對於事業之興趣。

茲就此五點分別討論之：

(1)個人行動與集體行動之調協　人類自原始時期，已知合作之有利於己，有利於羣，因之乃有種種政治，社會與夫經濟之集團組織，社會愈進步，各種合作之方式亦愈多，就政治言，則有政黨之組織，就社會言，則有宗教團體，學術團體以及其他各種社交團體之組織。至於經濟方面之組織，乃隨生產方法而推移，初則爲個人企業，合夥企業，嗣以生產之規模，漸次擴大，非個人或少數人之財力所能濟，於是乃有公司之組織，再進則合併許多企業單位而有託辣斯，卡推爾之獨佔組織，集體範圍愈大，力量亦愈雄厚，顧集體之構成分子，爲個人，集體之是否健全，要視其構成分子之是否協調。惟各人之天賦不同，禀性亦異，而利己之心往往急於利公，是以個人與個人及個人與團體之間，遂不免有衝突生焉。個人主義者以團體爲個人之堆積，團體之利益即爲個人利益之總和，利於個人者亦必利於團體，故個人之行爲應任其自由發展，不應加以束縛，集體主義者則視個人如機械，其一舉一動，皆受集體之指示，個人完全處於被動之地位，此二種見解，各有所偏，皆非確當之論也。余則以爲個人之於集體，猶細胞之於全身，如細胞之新陳代謝作用，靈動活潑，則身體之生長發育自能臻於健全之境…健全之身體，各部份必須爲平均之發展，如有所偏亟須加以治療。依個人主義者之說社會雖有畸形之發展，可不必加以糾正；依集體主義者之說，直以個人無創造之餘地，二者之所見皆失其當。質言之，今日之個人，僅爲組織中之一小單位，其所爲之工作僅全體工作中之一微細部份，顧人類好勝之心，始終未泯，如能予以自由動作之機會，個人必喜展其所長，以自炫其能，社會之進步，實基乎此。然同時必須加以適當之控制，以防其行動之失去正軌，礙及各部門之聯整。惟如何始能不妨礙個人創造力之發展而獲得各部門之聯整？則有賴乎管理人材之用得其當。而此卽爲一最難解決之問題。第一，管理人材必須識見卓越，手腕靈活，學識豐富，而能面面俱到，始爲上選，此種人材，百不得一，卽有其人，而不知所以用之，亦屬徒然，故生才難，生才而得其用亦難。第二，專門化程度愈高，欲求具有多方面智識之管理人材亦愈難．此一問題是否能由敎育或訓練方法而獲得滿意之解決，尙未易遽下斷語也。

（2）企業行爲之劃分　建立組織之第一要點，卽爲責任之規定。而責任之規定必須依據企業行爲之類別。故劃分企業行爲之類別，實爲規定責任之初步工作。卽使企業行爲，甚爲簡單，一二人行之，已可蕆事，但行爲之劃分仍爲必要，蓋非此將無以定各人所負之責任故也。如企業之行爲愈複雜，則事權之分離必愈甚，而行爲之劃分，亦愈感其重要。

企業之行爲隨其性質目的範圍而不同，然大體言之，無論何種企業，必有二種行爲爲管理者應負之責，一爲計劃的行爲，一爲實施的行爲。計劃的行爲屬於問題之研究，何者應爲，何者不應爲胥取决於是，實施的行爲屬於業務進行之指揮與監督。管理者旣有其所負之責任，亦必有其行使責任之權力。其權力可別爲二種方式，一爲職能的權力，一爲領域的權力，前者所以決定行爲之方法與手續，後者所以管轄行爲之實施。管理者或僅有一種權力或二者兼而有之，要視情形而定矣。

企業行爲應依照何種標準，劃分其類別？非本文所能詳，或有依功用而分者，或有依商品而分者，或有依地域而分者，或有依顧客而分者，或有依生產過程而分者，或有依二種以上標準而分者，要視實際上之需要而定。

(3)聯整之取得　企業行爲因區劃而分成許多個體，所以明權限而專責成，然僅爲組織之一方面。其另一方面卽爲如何取得個體間之聯整，每一個體之領袖，因其權責所在勢必以其本體之利益爲前提，爲其本體之利益作主張。各個體間之利益，如何使其均衡發展，如何使其不起衝突，則爲總領袖之責任。聯整之法，原無一定公式可循，惟下列各點，足爲注意聯整問題者之參考。

(甲)確定企業之政策，使各個體明瞭全體所赴之目的。

(乙)全體之政策必須明白表示，以祓各個體懷疑猜度。

(丙)各種委員會有助於合作思想之發展，應酌視情形設立之，每一委員會，設主席一人，以總其成。惟委員會祇能作爲討論或研究問題之機關，不宜干涉各部份之責權。

(丁)激發團體精神，此惟有領袖人員，以身作則，始能得之。

（4）領袖人材之訓練　吾人在上文已謂專門化之程度愈高，領袖人材之選拔將愈感困難；然領袖人材之需求，反因聯整問題之重要，而愈感迫切。此一問題雖未必能由訓練教育而得滿意之解决，然訓練教育，仍不失爲造就領袖人材之良法。至於如何訓練？非本文所能詳，容另文論之。

（5）個人對於事業之興趣　領袖人材之造成，除由學校之訓練與教育外，各業領袖亦應負一部份之責任，凡屬員之有能力有思想者，應善導之而奬掖之，以增進其向上之心，則彼對於本業之興趣亦必日感濃厚，此亦造成領袖人材之一途也。

四　結語

組織問題千端萬緒，本文所論，僅舉其概。就現代經濟組織之變動趨勢而論，因專門化之程度日高，人類互相依賴之關係愈密，個人活動之範圍日益縮小，集體行動之範圍，日益擴大，故昔日認爲無足重輕之組織問題，至今日而漸感迫切。本文目的卽在指出此一問題之趨向，並建議應付之途徑，是否有當於理，願世之明達，有以敎之。

ACCOUNTING SYSTEM FOR COTTON MILLS

Robert Cheng-Sien Chen（陳振銑）

NATURE OF BUSINESS.— As the cotton costs are computed on the basis of the weight of cotton entering and emerging from eace manufacturing process, a knowledge of the mechanics of the industry is a necessity to accountants. Almost all cotton comes to the mill in the form of bales compressed to about 22 pounds per cubic foot. After the iron hoops and jute bagging are removed, the bales, consisting of about 500 pounds of cotton, are fed by hand into the feed apron of a machine, called the "bale breaker," which loosens the compressed cotton and forms it into tufts, about a handful in size, on a belt conveyer. The belt conveyer delivers these tufts into machines called "openers" which are similar to the "bale breakers," the function of which is to reduce the large tufts into smaller ones and remove a certain amount of foreign matter.

The small tuffs are delivered by an air chute to the picker room, in which there are three kinds of machines, known as "pickers." The first, or "breaker-picker", beats out the coarse impurities by pounding the tufts over grid bars, by means of rollers armed with short, flail-like projections. and then compresses them into a continuous sheet, or "lap". This sheet, or lap is wound on a large spool and delivered to the second, or "intermediate" picker. This macnine practically repeats the operation of the first machine, and then combines the four laps from the first picker into one lap, which it delivers to the last, or "finished picker." The latter again takes four intermediate laps and forms them into one sheet, or lap. The pickers are all set to make a standard 48-yard lap.

The laps from the finished picker are fed to machines called "cards", which disentangle and arrange the fibers in parallel rows. This machine removes most of the remaining dirt, by placing the cotton on a revolving cylinder bearing wire teeth, which draws it over a set of knives and passes it on to a large cylinder armed with millions of fine wire teeth. The latter carries the cotton past a slowly revolving chain of flats and on to a smaller rapidly revolving roller, called the "doffer," from which it is taken by the "doffing comb," passed through a funnel, and condensed into a single untwisted rope, called a "sliver" The sliver, which is less than an inch in diameter, is automatically coiled into a can, not unlike an umbrella stand, as it emerges from the machine. Up to the sliver stage, all operations are practically identical, regardless of the kind of yarn to be spun. From here on the processes may vary, ordinary coarse and medium yarns being simply drawn and reduced, and the fine yarns requiring additional combing.

The drawing of ordinary coarse and medium yarn (the object of which is to draw out the fibers and to cause them to be porallel to each other), is done by feeding sjx "card slivers" simultaneously between two pairs of rollers, the second of which revolves faster than the first. This operation is usually performed three times, in each case combining six slivers into one, the final sliver having the same diameter as the original card slivers, but containihg more parallel fibers. The sliver delivered by the third "drawing machine" is reduced in size and twisted in "roving frames." The first roving frame, or "slubber," passes the "drawn sliver" through rollers without combining, and twists it as it winds it on bobbins. The slightly twisted sliver, called a "roving," is about the size of a clothes line. The three other roving machines, the "intermediate," "fine frame," and "jack frame," are much the same as to mechanism, each combining two rovings into one of smaller size and more twist, but in each successive frame the spindles are smaller and revolve faster, thus reducing the thread until it is small enough to spin.

When fine yarn is desired, 20 card slivers are combined in a machine similar to the draw frame, called a "sliver lapper," where they are drawn into a narrow ribbon, or laps, and spooled. Four of these laps are combined by a machine, called a "ribbon lapper," into a single band less than a foot wide. Eight rolls from the ribbon lapper are placed end to end, fed through rollers between the teeth of a very fine and rapidly oscillating steel comb, and then condensed into a single "combed sliver," which is coiled into a sylindrical can as it emerges from the machine. The combed slivers are usually passed through two drawing frames, each combining six slivers into one, and then they are put through the roving frames.

The combining of two or more laps, slivers, or rovings is known as "doubling", the process serving to counterbalance inequalities in the cotton. The roving as it leaves the jack frame has been doubled 27,648 times if the cotton has not been combed and 2,959,120 times if the cotton has been combed. Instead of being spun on "mules" as would be done in Europe, the rovings are run through a "ring frame," very similar in principle to the roving machines, and wound on bobbins.

There are two kinds of yarn, "filling", or yarn which goes crosswise of the cloth, and "warp", or yarn which goes lengthwise of the cloth. The separation is made at the intermediate roving machine, filling yarn being drawn and twisted less than warp. Filling is ready for the loom as soon as spun, while warp is sometimes "twisted" (two or more threads being united) and "sized" (run through a bath of beeswax, starch, etc., and dried quickly on the steam filled drum of the "slasher"

ORGANIZATION.— The president of a cotton mill is not usually the chief directive force— he acts as the chairman of the board of directors. The treasurer performs the two all-important functions of buying the raw cotton and selling the product. The treasurer may have an office either at the mill, or in the office of a selling house of which he is a member. In the latter case, the same treasurer usually acts in that capacity for more than one mill, each mill being managed by a superintedent, known as an "agent". The organization chart (Fig. 1) presents in diagrammatic form a typical organization of a cotton mill.

LEGAL STATUS.— Cotton mills have no legal peculiarities other than their contractual relationships. The trading device, called the "hedge", is an insurance against fluctuations in cotton prices by the purchase or sale of future contracts for cotton against sale or purchase made for actual delivery. As the cotton mill sells the finished product for future delivery based on the current price of cotton, it can buy futures now, and any loss or gain made on the actual purchase of the cotton will be offset by the gain or loss made when it sells the future contracts. Assume for instance, that a cotton mill sells yarn at a price based on the current cotton price of 25 cents in July for October delivery. The mill would then buy October futures on the Exchange. If the price of cotton rises 5 cents, the mill will lose on its cloth contract but will gain an equal amount when it sells it October futures.

ACCOUNTING BOOK AND RECORDS.— The outstanding features of the accounting books and records of a cotton mill are the unusual importance given to invoiced cotton (because cotton is paid for within three days from date of receipt) and the usual failure to book interdepartmental transfers of partly finished product. While labor and overhead are usually divided into departmental accounts, the departmental accounts are all closed into the yarn account, and the cost of the various kinds of yarn then computed on

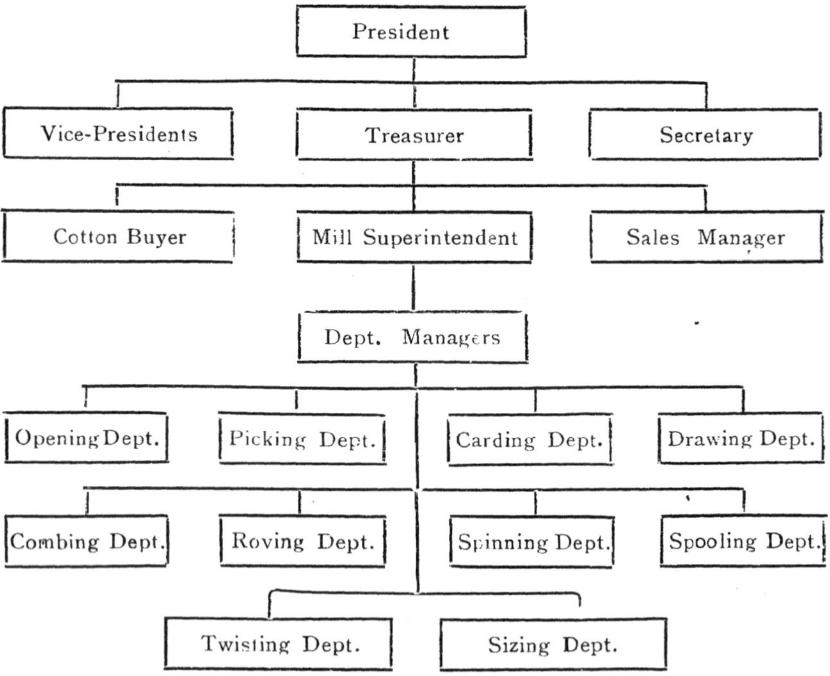

Fig. 1.- Organization Chart.

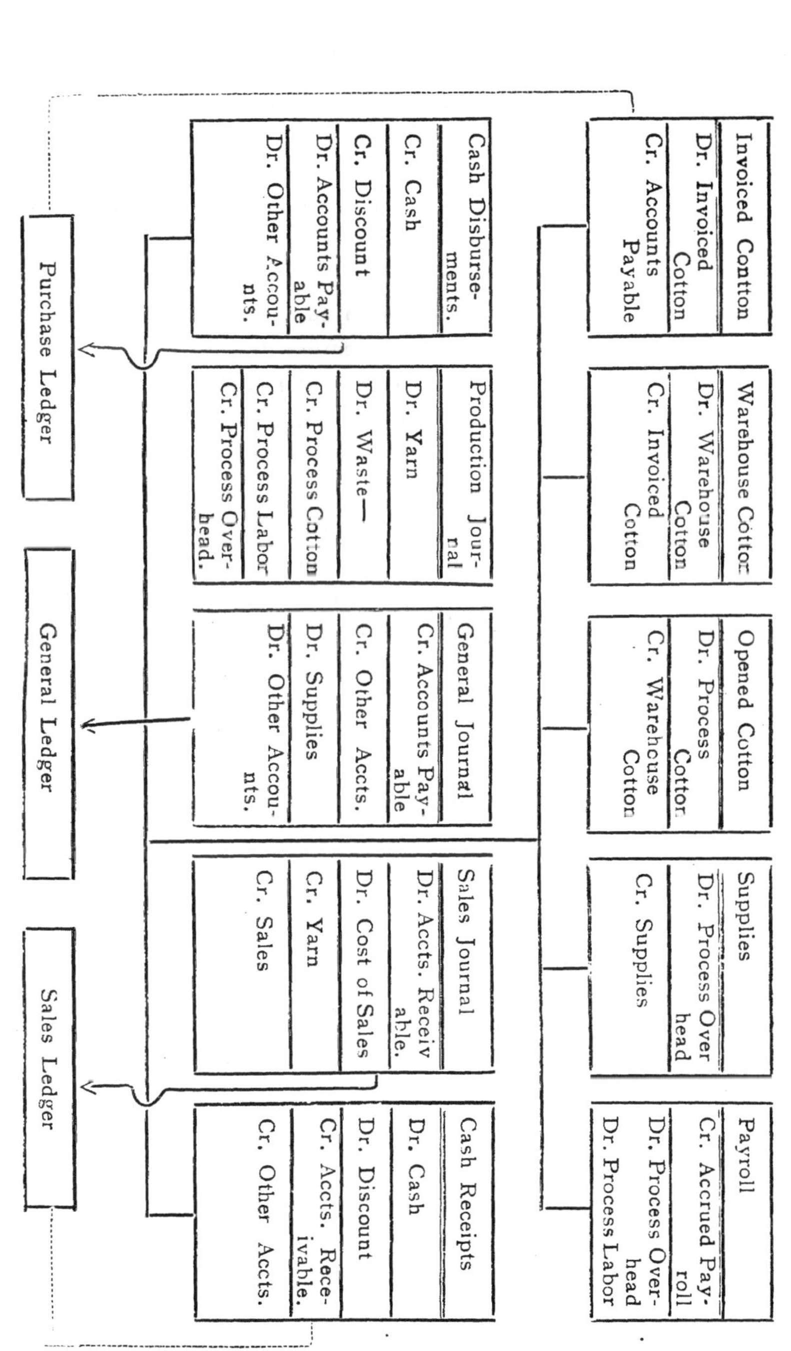

Fig. 2.— Chart of accounting books and records

one of the following bases: (1) the "average number" of the yarns produced, (2) the "theoretical ration of production", of the yarns produced, and (3) the "number of spindles employed." Each of these bases will be discussed later. Some cotton mills follow the product from one process to another, but this is not the usual practice.

Figure 2 presents in diagrammatic form the accounting books and records used in a cotton mill. These are arranged and connected so as to show the functions of each, the course of the entries from one to another, and the general relation each bears to the other and to the system as a whole.

MATERIAL COSTS.— Material costing requires careful attention to consumption and production weights. As the length delivered by each process is based on delivery roll circumference, speed, and running time, the weights con be computed by means of occasional tests to determine the weight per yard. Loss or gain on hedging contracts, a practice discussed above under the caption "Legal Status", is a cost of cotton.

There are two kinds of cotton waste: (1) visible, or cotton unfit for the making of yarn, yet having a sales value, and (2) invisible, or the intangible loss due to the evaporation of water content and the elimination of impurities. The cost of the cotton consumed is the cost of the opened cotton less credits for the sales of the waste. The adjustment for waste as made by most cotton mills and by all agents constitutes the final step in mill-cost production. Visible waste reduces both the poundage and value, while invisible waste reduces only the poundage of the product manufactured. The mathematics invovled in invisible and visible waste is shown by the following statement:

	Pounds	Value	Value per Pound of Yarn Made
Goods in Process, Initial Inventory	20,000	$ 2,000	$0.005
Cotton Put in Process	450,000	80,000	0.200
Total	470,000	$82,000	$0.205
Visible Waste Sold	40,000	2,400	0.006
Invisible Waste	5,000		
Goods in Process Final Inventory	25,000	5,600	0.041
Total	70,000	$8,000	$0.020

Yarn Made—Cotton	400,000	$74,000	$0.185
Yarn Made—Labor		16,000	0.040
Yarn Made—Overhead		6,000	0.015
Total cost of Yarn Made	400,000	$96,000	$0.240

If the product is passed from one process to another, an estimated value should be credited to the process and debited to a waste account; and then, if the actual sales of waste do not conform to the waste account, after adjustments for inventories, an adjustment should be made to the profit and Loss account. The effect of waste on costs, if the product is followed from one process to another, is shown by the following illustration:

	Weight Pounds	Cotton		Labor		Burden	
		Total	Cents per lb.	Total	Cents per lb.	Total	Cents per lb.
Opening, picking, carding	10 000.0	$2 000.00	20.000	$28.50	0.300	$19.00	0.200
Waste	500.0Cr.	60.00	.421				
Drawing	9 500.0	$1940.00	20.421	28.5	0.300	19.00	0.200
				6.65	0.070	.95	0.010
Roving	9 500.0	1 940.00	20.421	35.15	0.370	19.95	0.210
				292.19	3.268	29.68	0.332
Waste	558.7Cr	23.00	0.381		0.023		0.013
Spinning	8 941.3	1 917.00	21.439	327.34	3.661	49.63	0.555
				262.88	3.000	30.67	0.350
Waste	178.8Cr.	5.00	0.381		0.075		0.011
Total	8 762.5	1 912.00	21.820	590.22	6.736	80.30	0.916

SUMMARY OF WASTE

	Cents per Pound			
	Cotton	Labor	Burden	Total
Opening	0.421			0.421
Drawing				
Roving	1.018	0.023	0.013	1.054
Spinning	0.381	0.075	0.012	0.467
Total	1.820	0.098	0.024	1.924

The average per cent of waste in the various processes is given below:

	Percent		Per Cent
Breaker lapper	5	Ribbon lapper	Negligible
Intermediate lapper	2	Comber	20
Finisher lapper	2	Draw frame	Negligible
Card	5	Roving frame	2
Silver lapper	Negligible	Spinning frame	4

INVENTORIES.— As many cotton mills calculate costs on the assumption that the conversion cost of each pound of cotton in process is one-half of the conversion cost of each pound of yarn, this method of valuing inventories is worthy of consideration. As an illustration, calculate the value of the final inventories from the following information:

Raw Cotton Purchased (480,000 pounds)	$ 81,600
Sales of Yarn (480,000 pounds)	175,000
Sales of Waste (45,000 pounds)	1,000
Productive Labor	30,000
Factory Overhead	8,020
Losses on Hedging Contracts	2,400
Initial Inventories:	
Raw Cotton (120,000 pounds)	30,000
Goods in Process (100,000 pounds)	
Cotton	25,000
Conversion Costs	5,000
Yarn (40,000 pounds)	10,000
Waste (1,000 pounds)	20
Final Inventories:	
Raw Cotton (100,000 pounds)	?
Goods in Process (60,000 pounds)	?
Yarn (50,000 pounds)	?
Waste (2,000 pounds at market value)	40

COTTON ACCOUNT (Schedule A)

	Pounds	Value	Per Pound
Raw Cotton, Initial Inventory	120,000	$30,000	$0.25
Cotton Purchased	480,000	81,600	0.17
Loss on Futures		2,400	
	600,000	114,000	0.19
Raw Cotton, Final Inventory	100,000	19,000	0.19
Cotton Fed during Perion	500,000	$ 95,000	0.19
Cotton in Process, Initial Inventory	100,000	25,000	0.25
Cotton to be accounted for	600,000	120,000	0.20
Cotton in yarn Produced	490,000	98,000	0.20
	110,000	$ 22,000	0.20
Cotton in Process, Final Inventory	60,000	12,000	0.20
Waaste, Visible and Invisible	50,000	10,000	0.20

PRODUCTION STATEMENT (Schedule B)

Yarn:	Pounds
Sales	480,000
Final Inventory	50,000
	530,000
Less Initial Inventory	40,000
	490,000
Goods in Process:	
One-half Final Inventory	30,000
Total	520,000

CONVERSION COSTS (Schedule C)

Productive Labor			$30,000
Factory Overhead			8,020
Conversion Costs in Initial Inventory.			
Goods in Process			5,000
Waste:			
Initial Inventory	$ 20		
Current Period (Schedule A)	10,000	$10,020	
Less Inventory (Final)		40	
		$ 9,980	
Less Sales of Waste		1,000	8,980
Total			$52,000

$52,000÷520,000=$0.10, Conversion Cost per Pound

YARN INVENTORY (Schedule D)

	Per Pound
Cotton Cost (Schedule A)	$0.20
Conversion Cost (Schedule C)	0.10
Total	$0.30

50,000×$0.30=$15,000, Final Inventory

GOODS IN PROCESS INVENTORY (Schedule E)

	Per Pound
Cotton Cost (Schedule A)	$0.20
One-half Conversion Cost (Schedule C)	0.05
Total	$0.25

60,000×$0.25=$15,000, Final Inventory

The division of the inventories of goods in process into two sections, cotton cost and conversion cost, while theoretically correct, is frequently ignored in practice, as the division is rendered unimportant by the fact that the conversion costs per pound and the poundage of goodsin process inventories do not vary materially between accounting periods. If the division is not made, the entire cost of both inventories would be entered in Schedule A, and the conversion costs in the initial inventory of goods in process would not be entered in Schedule C.

Some cotton mills, using the plan of estimating that the conversion costs of goods in process is a fractional part of the conversion costs of the comleted goods, use the fraction one-fourth, instead of one-half.

LABOR AND OVERHEAD COSTS.— After being charged to the various manufacturing processes, the labor and overhead costs are combined and prorated to the various kinds of yarn on one of the following bases: (1) the "average number" of the yarns produced, (2) the "theoretical ratio of production" of the yarns produced, and (3) the "number of spindles emloyed."

Average-number Method. The numbering system for cotton yarn is based on the number of hanks of 840 yards to a pound, viz., 1 hank of No. 1 yarn weighs 1 pound; 20 hanks of No. 20 yarn weighs 1 pound; 30 hanks of No. 30 yarn weighs 1 pound, etc. Assume that 12,500 pounds of No. 20 yarn, 10,000 pounds of No. 25 yarn, and 17,500 pounds of No. 40 yarn were put through a process at the total labor and overhead cost of $144. The conversion costs would be prorated, according to the average-number method, as follows:

Yarn No.	Pounds	Equivalent of No. 1 Yarn
20	12,500	250,000
25	10,000	250,000
40	17,500	700,000
	40,000	1,200,000

1,200,000÷40,000=30, average number

$144÷40,000=0.36 cents per pound of average number.

36 cents÷30=0.012 cents per pound of No. 1 yarn

Yarn No.	Multiplier	Cost per Pound, Cents
20	0.012	0.24
25	0.012	0.30
40	0.012	0.48

Care must be taken, if costs of multiple-ply yarns are oomputed with single ply yarn, to reduce all yarn to its single-ply equivalent, i. e., a 2/20 yarn (two strands of No. 20 twisted together) would be taken as a single ply No. 10.

Theoretical Ratio of Production Method.— The above problem in prorating conversion costs would be calculated on either of the following methds by the "theoretical ratio of production" basis.

Method No. 1.

(1) Yarn	(2) Pounds Produced	(3) Theoretical Production	(4) Quotient (Col.2÷Col.3)	(5)[1] Multiplier	(6) Conversion Cost	(7) Cost Per lb. Cents
20	12,500	100	125	$0.24	$30	$0.24
25	10,000	80	125		30	0.30
40	17,500	50	350		84	0.48
			600			

1. Sum of Col. 6 divided by sum of Col. 4 i. e., $144÷600=$0.24

Method No. 2.

(1) Yarn No.	(2) Theoretical Production	(3)[1] Cost Ratio	(4) Actual Production	(5) Equivalent of 20's (Col.3X Col.4)	(6)[2] Multiplier	Cost per Pound Cents (Col. 3 X Col. 6)
20	100	1.00	12,500	10,500	$0.0024	0.24
25	80	1.25	10,000	12,500		0.30
40	50	2.00	17,500	35,000		0.48
				60,000		

1. Let cost ratio of the yarn with smallest number equal unity; calculate other cost ratios by dividing the respective theoretical productions into the theoretical production of the yarn having the smallest number, i.e. 100 divided by 80 equal 1.25.

2. Cost of conversion divided by sum of equivalents, i.e. $144 divided by 60,000 equal $0.0024

Spindlage Method.— The same problem calculated by the "number of spindles employed" method would be as follows:

(1) Yarn No.	(2) Spindles Operated	(3)[1] Spindle Cost	(4) Conversion Cost (Col. 2X Col.3)	(5) Pounds Converted	(6) Cost Per Pound Cents (Col.4 Col.5)
20	20	$1.50	$30	12,500	0.24
25	20		30	10,000	0.30
40	56		64	17,500	0.48
	96		$144		

1. Conversion cost divided by total number of spindles employed. i.e. $144 divided by 96 equal $1.50.

BALANCE SHEET.— The balance sheet accounts of a cotton mill vary in name only from those of ordinary factories, the nature of the accounts being the same as the corresponding accounts in other industries. The most unusual account is the asset account entitled "Hedging Contracts", which is set up at cost at date of purchase of the cotton futures and adjusted to market value on the balance sheet by a Reserve for Hedging Contracts account, which is established by debiting or crediting the Cotton account with the difference between the cost and market values of the cotton futures. When the cotton futures are sold, the Hedging Contracts and Reserve for Hedging Contracts accounts are closed into the Cash and Cotton accounts.

BRDFIT AND LOSS STATEMENT.— The profit and loss statement of a cotton mill is very similar to that of other departmentalized industries which do not follow the product through the manufactuuring processes. While the names of the accounts are different, the manufacturing section of of the profit and loss statement consists merely of the usual divisions: (1) Raw Materials (of course, headed Cotton), (2) Productive Labor (departmentalized), and (3) Manufacturing Expense (departmentalized).

SPECIAL AUDITING FEATURES.— Cotton inventories must be carefully verified by the auditor, special care being taken to account properly for consigned and hypothecated cotton. The process inventories are sometimes divided into major classifications, viz., "fixed", or goods in the machines, and "loose", of the process cotton in laps and cans and on bobbins ready to feed. Some mills and a constant amount for the "fixed" process cotton to the value of the machinery, a practice which misclassifies the assets and, in case of a material change in the price of cotton, misstates the net income of the period. Process cotton should be valued according to the varying stages of production but many mills assume that the inventory is exctyl one-half completed. Contracts for undelivered cotton purchases and unshipped yarn sale must be carefully examined and any contingent liabilities resulting therefrom booked. The calssification of the payroll and the factory overhead must be examined, and the proration of the conversion costs to the various kinds of yarn must be verified. The handling of waste and waste sales must be carefully examined, especialiy if the cotton mill carries the costs from one manufacturing process to another. This is especially important when it is desired to verify the production figures of the mill agent. The official's authority to buy cotton futures must also be verified. All losses or gains from "hedging" should be clearly ascertained and entered in the Cotton account.

交大季刊 第二十三期要目

經售處——上海徐家匯交通大學出版處

每册三角　預定全年一元

科學通訊（交通大學科學學院編輯）第三卷 第一期 目錄

定價　每册二角

經售處　上海徐家匯交通大學出版處

SCIENTIFIC ORGANIZATION IN INDUSTRIAL MARKETING

By Ted C. Chang (張宗謙)

In the last issue, the writer made an effort to link scientific management to industrial marketing, which is a task that any modern marketer should do at the outset, in order that it may be applied thereafter to the problems of organization, research, planning, and control. The present discussion, therefore, is made in the light of such an understanding.

The Necessity for a Scientific Marketing Organization

In was not very long ago when marketing management consisted merely of sending out salesmen, allowing each to get orders as his personal methods dictated, and paying his salary. Salesmen were employed without much thought and discharged quite as readily. To-day these easy-going ways have been discarded because the selling costs have risen to alarming proportions, so high in fact that selling cost threatens to absorb all the profit margins of the business.

In the past, instead of systematically undertaking to overcome the deficiencies of marketing management as then practiced, the common method most business men choose was to cover them up. Our way of covering up the high costs of selling was through the lowering of factory costs by the application of scientific management principles to production, which may imply a number of things, such as: the installation of better equipment, together with time and motion study; scientific purchasing of materials and supplies; personnel administration, etc. At one time, such a method did bring the desired result, because there were wide differences in the cost of manufacturing similar products, and any manufacturer could lower his cost by adopting better methods and new equipments of the labor-saving sort. To-day most concerns have already gone far enough, if not too far as is the case in the United States, in this respect to hope for any further advantage. Even in China where scientific management in production is just beginning, still this is not the best way of covering up high selling cost, because isn't it a fact that most authorities are unanimous in the belief that marketing wastes are many times as great as the wastes in production?

Anther source, in former times, was that of rising prices. Once it was possible to raise prices almost at will. Today, however, few products come on the markets which are not quickly duplicated by competitors. Many former specialties have now become little more than staples. Advances in prices cannot be easily made, because each advance reduces the possible market. Competition is a far more active element in fixing prices than ever before.

A third resource was that of increasing at will the volume of sales. This also is a doubtful advanture. Only during a period of business prosperity can we expect it to materialize. The conditions of 1923—1929 when the world seemed able to absorb endless quantities of goods will possibly never by repeated again. The natural increase in demand due to expanding population will continue, but this increase will be on fairly normal level.

Functional Basis of Organisation Most Scientific

By organization is meant the bringing of men into working relations with each other. The purpose of organizaing in business is to achieve harmony of effort, remove friction and insure the best results at the least cost. For in business the ultimate purpose of organizing a concern or a department within that concern is to earn profits.

Before we undertake to draft an organization chart for the Marketing Department, we must first determine the task which the Department is expected to do. These tasks are then broken down, analyzed and classified, and the Department organized to fit the requirements. Naturally, the larger the concern, the more are the tasks it will have to perform, but since common problems run through all organizations, we may safely and logically say that the work of the Marketing Division of a representative manufacturing concern should consist of the following headings:—

(1) Building or shaping up the sales organization, and determining its relations to other departments.

(2) Sales research and planning as a basis both for sales policies and for sales operation; forecasting sales and quota making.

(3) Formation of policies for selling the product, such as quantities, quality, simplification, unit of sales, brands, trademarks, etc.

(4) Policies in distribution; relation to the channels of distribution to be utilized.

(5) Policies as to price—including the policies relating to price level, discounts, price maintenance, etc.

(6) Sales methods—including personal selling and advertising, combining all forms of personal selling and advertising to fit the peculiar needs of the enterprice.

(7) Management of the sales force—selection, training, compensation, supervision, control, etc.

(8) Financing—terms of sale, credits and collections, instalments and deferred terms, etc.

(9) Problems in connection with filling orders and delivery-cancellations, claims and adjustments, filing systems for orders, warehousing, stock control, etc.

(10) Problems in the control of sales-accounts, statistics, records, and reports.

With these tasks in mind, the management should then work out an ideal scientific organization on a functional basis. Functional organization means laying out the work of the Department on the basis of tasks to be done. This involves the adoption of the principles of scientific management as was made clear by F. W. Taylor. Taylor, in 1930, revealed the great waste of awkward and ill-directed work. He heaped derision on executives who are constantly searching for more competent men, because they want to find these men ready-made, trained by some previous employer. Taylor declared that "progress begin when we realize that our duties as well as our responsibilities lie in devising ways and means for training and developing competant men. In the past, the man has been first. In the future, method must be first. The object of this method must be to develop first-class man, and if the method is right the best men will rise to the top more rapidly than ever before."

Such scientific management differs from the old management chiefly in that it assumes the responsibility for the planning. It must lay out tasks or functions. The plan must cover four kinds of work:

(1) The gathering, recording, and tabulating, by the management, of the great mess of traditional knowledge of the job which in the past has been in the heads of employees, and developing a plan for each step of man's work, to replace the old rule-of-thumb. A man will be hired to do a job as defined, instead of trying to find a man who knows all about the job.

(2) The scientific selection, training, and development of the men.

(3) Hearty cooperation with the men to insure their use of the scientific principles which have been developed and to make them work according to the plan.

(4) Almost equal division of the work and responsibility between management and workmen. The management takes over all work for which it is better fitted than the men, while in the past almost all the work and the greater parts of the responsibility were thrown upon the men.

Under functional organization, therefore, the department is laid out with reference to tasks to be done. One part of the organization will specialize in management of the field force, another in filling of orders, another in helps for dealers, and so on through all the tasks to be done. Within the department at the home office, there will be also a so-called "staff" organization for such tasks, as research, quota making, checking of performance, records and statistics, business forecasting, formulation of policies, study of competiton, market planning, and so on.

Centralized vs. Decentralized Authority

The size of an industrial concern brings with it a significant question which must be decided at the outset, namely: Should the marketing organization be based upon centralized or decentralized authority?

In the small organization all employees report directly to the marketing manager and all responsibility is centralized at his desk. Here, the marketing manager is a one-man executive. He must himself perform all the planning and directing, the few salesmen making their reports directly to him. The stenographers and clerks are directly under his supervision.

In large organization, however, there is today a general tendency to place reponsibility on those lower down, holding them responsible for results without prescribing minutely how results are to be obtained. It then because the task of these subordinates to plan and harmonize the work of others. Such a plan is known as "decentralized" because final responsibility is broken up. Such a plan gives the subordinate a chance to exercise initiative and demonstrate his ability, but at the same time, it involves risk to the company when the subordinates make mistakes.

The management must therefore, decide whether the marketing manager should retain all authority in himself by requiring all major decisions to come to his desk or whether he should assign extensive authority to subordinates and require them to consult him only for far-reaching policies and plans which involve other departments. Centralization brings unity of action, but it quickly burdens the excentive to the breaking point; for that reason, in very large concerns it is impossible. Decentralization develops strong men, although it the threatens rivalries and underhand check-mating of each other. Further, it frees the executive's brain and his time for the biggest tasks.

Relation of the Marketing Division to Other Departments

The Marketing Department should always be considered as a part of the company. It exists only as one means to the purpose of being in business: to earn profits. Unless all departments corperate to that end, costs will rise and the enterprise ceased to succeed. As a rule, the marketing production, shipping and finance departments must cooperate. Cooperation does not imply that the Marketing Department gives in to another or another department to it, no matter what the disagreement may be. It does implydefinately bearing in mind the real object of being in business, namely, to earn profits by serving the consumer and the market.

正風雜誌半月刊

第四卷 第六期要目

余天休主編

▲每期十餘萬言 零售每冊一角

▲另印有副刊商業經濟評論零售每冊五分訂閱本刊全年者函索即贈

每月一日十六日出版，全年廿四期，材料豐富，思想健全，銷路最廣，廣告效力宏大，定價全年二元四角。郵費本市二角四本國四角八外國四元八，

▲發行所 北平北長街五十五號

陸大月刊

第三卷 第五期

目錄

零售：每期大洋叁角 半年六期大洋壹元五角 全年十二期大洋三元

郵費 外埠：每期二分五厘 半年一角五分 全年三角
本埠：每期二分 半年一角二分 全年二角四分

編輯者：陸大月刊編輯委員會
發行者：陸大月刊社
社址：南京漢口路陸軍大學特別黨部內
電話：三一七一三
代售處：特別黨部及各大書局

譯述

行政專門化（D 1.）

L.D. White著
任家誠譯

此文載于 The Annals of the American Academy of Political & Social Science: Improved Personnel in Governmentat Service, Jan. 1937 題名爲"Administration as a Profession"

百年前政府事業之管理，舍教育而外，鮮有需要專門職業者。可包涵于專門職業者僅如司法部(Department of Justice)及各省檢察機關之法律人員，建築河道及測量公路人員，醫生及少數科學人員。至如法律執行人員，收稅員，簿記員，辦事員，破產人之財產管理員，臨時救火員及普通之勞工等僅須有日常智識，良好之判斷力，工作之志願及對於辦理特務之程序有相當知識，而不需專門或技術的訓練。

專門職業團體之增加

美國最早之專門職業團體爲美國教導社(American Institute of Instruction)成立於一八三〇年。自南北戰爭以後，專門及技術團體逐漸浸入公務員制度內，以一九〇〇年以後爲尤多。例如一八七二年之美國公共衛生會(American Public Health Association)，一八八四年之官方農業化學技師協會(Association of Official Agricultural Chemists)，一八八九年之省圖書館全國協會(National Associations of State Lifraries)，一八九七年之美國牛乳製品及藥劑師協會(Association of American Dairy & Drug Officials)等。其他專門職業團體同時亦漸有浸入者，今日政府之管理幾多操于專門人才之手。一八三○年普通公民執政說漸成爲傑克遜哲學(Jacksonian philosophy)之中心，而一九三○年時，政府之管理，已遠越乎一般人民或少數專門團體能力之外。

以一九三三年所發表之研究結果觀，專門及科學團體之管理公務有極速之發展，其所佔比例已大爲增加。(一)一八六九年在聯邦公務中，專門及技術之職位僅三千六百個，佔全國職位百分之二，一九○七年時近九千七百，約佔百分之三·四許；至一九三○年時，竟增至三萬五千之譜，佔百分之六弱。

試研究各省之數學，我人知合衆國之專門公務員在各省中亦有相當之增加，以密歇根省(State of Michigan)之台屈落埃(Detroit)而言，公務員制度性質大有變更。一九○○年時僅有專門及科學職位四十一個；一九一八年爲三一九；至一九三一年時達一九一四；其中近

(一)L.D. White, Trends in Public Administration, Ch. 19.

千餘爲看護，多自一九一八年起入職。

此數字之例舉，可使人知公共服務對專門及科學階級人才之需要日趨嚴重。昔日之專門職業如法律及工程，現已析爲各種不同之類別，同時新創之專門職業亦逐漸插入，佔據全國公務員重要之地位。

例如昔日政府雇用之工程人員僅限于公共建設及建築而今日則可分爲下列各種：航空工程汽車工程，地產工程，測量工程，航海工程，建築工程，無線電工程，運輸工程，航空傘工程，及航空測量等。其他各農事學，水類生物學，微生物分析，菌學，細胞生物學等，均需專家研究。

同時專門或半專門之類別如經濟學家，社會學家，森林種植學家，獸醫，藥劑師，會計員，統計員及計算員等，亦年見重要而漸增加。

公務員制度性質之變更

上述各點形成公務員制度性質之變更，專門及科學人員之雇用予公務員之性質及工作狀況以極大之影響。現在我人雖無暇作此種影響勢力之詳細估價，然請研究其較爲顯著之特質。

專門及科學人員之雇用，促成恩惠制度（Patronage）之改革，無論何人甚至任用私人者之本身均承認專門及科學化之事務不能由不合資格之人員主持，否則政治上之反響必造成極大危險。此種專門職業引進不少男女大學生，蓋專門及科學工作之準備，必須從高等教育機關中得到也。因之公務員之水準亦自中學生之標準而提高至大學生。

受有專門訓練之公務員之增加，改良公務員制度之威信及地位，結果造成一種環境，能優容無政治色彩而有專門技術之管理員。就其發展之歷史觀，公務員制度雖已與專門人員以相當之地位，然對行政方面，專門化之趨勢，尚不十分普遍。

『行政』之意義

何謂『行政』，此辭雖有合理而切實之定義：然常被隨便使用。最近人事行政諮詢委員會(The Commission of Inquiry of Public Personnel)之報告書良好公務人員(Better Government personnel)一書中，解釋行政之意義如下：

『無論私營或公共事業，凡屬複雜之組織，均需要相互之關聯，計劃及集中指導，與工作之委派，總括之曰行政。行政本身之智識及經驗有確定之範圍，其本身技術日漸發展，需要特種才能，適當訓練，獨具經驗及本能之廣爲應用。』

法實業家兼管理學家翻欲耳(Henri Fayol)之定義中，言行政應包括計劃，組織，命令，聯繫及統制。此五者確爲英之管理級(Administrative Class)，德之高級公務員，及世界殖民地佔有國殖民地管理人員所應完成之職能。一方面行政不是解決政策決定問題，與立法機關有別，他方面行政亦不是執行固定政策之日常事務。然其界限之劃分，不能如數學中數字之準確。

英國高級公務員協會(Association of First Division Civil Servants)於一九三〇年致皇家行政委員會(The British Royal Commission on Civil Service)之呈文中，描寫行政之特性，至爲完美：

『政府之任務，如欲執行妥善，須運用遠大的眼光，以應付種種複雜問題。在一切事務上須有準確方針，彼此不相矛盾，順從公意；在環境許可時，須有繼續執行之可能；否則亦須設法調整。任何行政決議於政府既行之後，常可發生種種結果，故吏治行政職能及管理級公務員之責任在乎於日常工作中，以遠大之攷慮，支配目前急切待辦之事務。使今日之議會不致爲明日議會之阻礙……躊躇懷疑及前後矛盾爲窳政顯明之徵象。

故各部有效的行政工作之完成，需要良好的智力訓練，至遇特殊情形時，特殊之能力亦見重要，有時最要者爲判斷力練達之能力，識別力及公正心。遇複雜難解之問題如租稅及其他經濟問題等時，更需智力之準備；舍此外，有時亦需創造及理想之能力。』

(二)

上文所述之英國行政工作，適與美國行政工作相同。我人試詳爲攷察中央政府，省政府，及市政府之組織，極易發現一切職位之責任與翻欲耳所言者相似。行政人員對此五點固早在從事，然對於其職能尚未充分認識，在整個管理機構中，其個人所任之職份如何可貴，大都尙未明瞭。

專門職業之定義

翻欲耳主義所定之行政是否爲一種專門職業，實成問題。其答案之關鍵在明白『專門職業』之定義。專門職業可作爲一種行業解，從事者自以爲有該項技能而可以永久執此業，如職業拳術家，經紀人，新聞記者，舞蹈家或其他。或謂專門職業應以更確定之職業解釋之，爲一種職業，係應用某種科學智識，爲他人作事，或實施其根據於此種智識之技能。

任何人承認行醫爲專門職業之一種，任何人更承認汽車上擦油工作不可稱爲專門職業。然在此顯著之兩極端間，有頗難分斷者，實例極多，如行政之技術卽其中之一也。

爲合乎本文之目的，我人應下以更準確之定義，專門職業包括各要素如下：

一、須有一種有組織，有結合，廓而益大，研而益精之智識，及基於此種智識之技術。

二、須有訓練此種智識之便利與步驟。

(11)摘自 White, Bland, Sharp & Marx, Civil Service Abroad, pp. 19—20.

三、須有公認之執業資格，此種資格有時可由法律規定，如給予執照等，然領有執照之職業，並不一定專門。

四、須有有執業資格之多數人員之集合團體，能發生維持該項職業之地位之效力。

五、須有倫理法典，普遍的規定該業人員與公衆之關係，及與同業者之關係，並宜認定爲公服務乃一種責任，不僅爲經濟之目的而已。

行政人員之專門地位

在地方行政中顯具專門職業之特點者，至少有二實例，卽學校校長及市經理。此二種人均屬于專門行政人員，蓋彼等有計劃，組織，命令，聯繫及統制之責任也。二者各有一種組織完善之智識，及特別管理之技能。此種智識與技能，範圍日益加大，內容日益加豐，實基于執業經驗，及賴有業務刊物之記載也。該兩項職業皆可於高等教育機關中，受正式訓練，學校校長已有公認之任職資格，惟市經理則尙不然；又該兩項職業均有根深蒂固之組織，然一部份市經理尙有在此種組織勢力之外者，彼等祇以地方行政員自視，其與學校校長之不同，卽在此點。

各省高級行政人員尙未深受專門職業之影響，蓋各省省長及憲法規定之各公務員皆出于選舉，其興趣集中於政治上，而不在行政。各部之長官，所任無論何項專職，皆可歸納爲往日之數門，如檢查長屬律師，公共視學員屬教師，衛生部長屬醫師，而無與市理事長相當之職。法庭及公安機關之長官往往無專門學識之準備，乘省府政變之事機，捷足登場。省府雖亦有不少受過專門訓練之人才如工程師，衛生技師，統計員，經濟學家，典獄員，菌學家等，然欲求一專門管理人員，其程度與其他專門人員相當者，不可得也。

再研究中央行政人員，則我人可下以結論曰，中央行政尚未成爲專門職業，彼等自己亦否認爲專門人員，而他人更不以此目之。實際上吾人已發覺多數執行普通管理職權之官吏，其上場時，均有政治背景，而時局一變，全無留戀繼續之可能。其他如聯邦各部管理員雖受科學訓練者，則或自以爲屬於醫學，法律，化學，森林種植或工程等等之專家，而非屬於管理之專門家。各部必有不少職位純粹屬於管理性質者，但全無組織，而中央政府對此種職位亦不承認其有一種有組織之智識與技能。雖各大學近已介紹各種行政智識與方法，然受正式訓練者，幾等於零。專門行政人員資格未經認定，更無特別論理法典。觀此種情形可見祇久於行政，不足以實現行政之專門化也。

專門職業與職位分類法案

『專門職業』一辭之法律上意義在一九二三年職位分類法案（The Classification Act of 1923）已有解釋，此法案規定專門及科學之職務包括『其任務乃基于專門及科學之原則，需要專門，科學及技術的訓練，其程度與公認之專門學校及大學畢業相當者，』並規定此種職位最低之年俸爲二千元。

職位分類法案更規定次要之專門事務，其職務爲『輔助專門科學及技術的工作，』亦爲專門的，然爲輔助而已。故二者之不同不在工作之性質，而在工作之難易及工作之責任上。最實際之劃分爲年俸二千元。

試就某職務言，其爲專門或次要之專門，論者各異其說。又就某事業言，其爲專門或非專門，論者亦各異其說，而大都有歸屬專門之趨勢，人事管理，其實例也。

人事管理中之日常工作如記錄員司進退，調遷，復任等僅屬於日常事務之執行性質，固不得謂爲專門，然已有不少工作須應用專門技術，如攷試方法，適當人員之任用力求適合其個性及能力，以及發生問題時之調整等。

至森林事務與其他部份中，人事管理之職位其工作屬於上述性質者，已委專門人才充當，然在大部份之事務上，錄事工作與人事管理之專門工作尚未劃分清楚。於管理之專門方面，若不加以相當注意，使與錄事工作相劃分，則終不能認識管理人員係屬專門之人員也。

如何造成專門職業

中央職務分類之決定，並非指定何種職業屬於廣義的專門職業。凡與一九二三年職位分類法案所定『專門職業』之界說不符者，則須視其事實上之情形如何，是否已得社會上一般人之公認。人事行政委員會(Civil Service Commission)內分類科(Classification Division)之責任，並非以命令做成專門職業，必須依據法律條文。欲將一般人所公認之專門人員安置於各專門科學之職位，有時因礙於法律，不能實行。

公務員制度專門化之趨勢爲社會趨勢之一部份，任何專門職業各有其威望與地位，更有經濟之價值，尤以工會爲最，然亦僅限于有組織者。

一團體決不能自命爲屬於專門職業，蓋一切專門職業之特質乃出於數千百年逐漸累積的發展，並非成于旦夕者也。專門職業之特點，在執業者對社會能盡有價值之義務，該業之組織能以其團體勢力，對執業個人施行管理。

就一般言，行政團體雖時欲提高其專門化之程度，以冀得法律承認，然其策勵專門化行爲之方法尙屬幼稚，如何策勵之法，雖有人提出，終以組織脆弱，基礎欠固，對犯法者不能施以斷然之處置。

當然專門職業並非徒有組織而已，專門職業之精神繫于個人之智力及其對己對人之態度，組織者僅便于發展態度，及廣擴知識而已。

專門化之可渴慕

專門職業之廣場中，尙有容納外人加入之餘地，故團體之演進，達於專門地位者，繼續增高，公務員有趨向專門之態度，此種態度值得鼓勵。行政之性質已因專門化而改造，團體精神漸見提高，行政威望日加降重人員品質，益見優良，施政成績，益收美效，而違法越規之舉動則見減少。由內心之自責，以達專門職業之最高目的，不必藉外力之指導，方爲公務員之儀表及行爲。

水平線之提高，基礎之鞏固，行見組織日趨優良，而行政人員與社會對於『專門職業』之含義，亦有漸更深刻之認識。

中國主計制度之特點（一）

望

「超然」卽各機關辦理預算決算會計統計之人員對於所在機關雖受長官之指揮而有超然之地位。

「聯綜」卽各機關之主計人員以聯綜組織隸屬於各機關；卽一方面爲所在機關之職員辦理其預算決算會計或統計事務，對其機關長官負責；而另一方面又爲主計處派出之職員，不但直接受主計處之監督指揮而並直接受其任免遷調訓練考績。

中國主計制度之特點（二）

望

「連環性」卽歲計會計統計，合併組織成爲一個有連環性而不可破判之機關——主計處，所謂連環性者卽統計產生歲計，歲計產生會計，會計又產生統計，執統計可以覘歲計會計之虛實，執歲計會計亦可以證統計之當否，三者相爲因果，相爲體用，正如連環之不可破判。

「隸屬」卽中央主計機關隸屬於擔負全國全部政治責任之機關，而地方主計機關亦直隸於各該級政府之最高長官。

何謂管理能力（B 2.）

G. U. Cleeton與C. W. Mason著
胡亦生譯述

本篇(What Is Executive Ability?)闡明管理家之能力，異乎它人；其應有之才能，與不應有之性格，篇中逐條稱述，足資借鏡。原文刊于美國管理協會(American Management Association)去年五月份出版之人事特刊(Personnel)第二卷第四期內。

譯者志

「管理」二字，可引用于各種不同之人，爲今日極普遍之名詞，應定解釋，以供研討。吾人以爲管理家應負責于它人之工作，决定政策及實際上之問題，並施全權以觀察决議之是否實行。此解釋與監督有異，與理事董事亦不同；蓋監督祇負責于它人之工作，而無取决之權力，理事董事有决議之權力，而無監督它人行動之必要：此種人祇有管理家局部之職權，皆未能稱之爲完全之管理家。

有時領袖與管理家二者，混而爲一。最好之管理家，自富有領袖之才具。但今世最成功之管理家，往往缺乏領袖之才能，而極多偉大之領袖，亦不必具有管理家之能力。領袖有時可不必有智慧之判斷，而須有感化它人之魔力，蓋賴情感以獲得效果，自勝于徒恃威力以致之也。故領袖之才具，實可爲管理家共有之資產，而領袖未必即管理家；管理家如無領袖之才具，即不能得下屬之信任，自不免視爲失敗之領袖，但彼能自知其短，善用具有領袖才能之下屬，則雖無感人之魔力，仍不難爲一成功之管理家。

在資本主義社會中，企業機關本爲多數人設計，生產，銷售與經理之集會，其成功實有賴于財政上之管理。管理能力與財政措置，易于混淆。財政措置固需要管理才能，而財政家往往未必眞能有此。將設計，生產，銷售與財務等問題，作一適當之聯繫，斯卽所謂管理家之才能。

管理家爲人事組織之焦點，總管理又爲全部組織之中心。各部主管員乃隸屬于總管理之下，爲該組織內各部之中心。任何企業機關均可以圖表顯示此種組織，惟眞有能力之主管員，可以處理得當，不受此圖表之限制。其綜合之職權，可以隨時創造，其學識與引力，其識別與決斷，其想像與遠見，其對物質與人事之感覺，能使其管轄範圍爲一有生氣之機構。在錯綜紛歧之局面中，如能善自措置，以獲得經濟上之聯絡，則譽之爲有創造力之天才，誰曰不宜？

以管理能力作一抽象之分析，實至不易。唯此乃超乎一般普遍之能力，自可斷言。所謂才能者有時可以衡量，有時則須用等級表及其它方法以窺測。爰擬后列資格，以爲設置「管理能力等級表」之參考：

一、決斷能力。

二、合法的負責能力。
三、明察它人之特徵與反動。
四、足使它人深信之個人習慣，像貌與態度。
五、高深專門學識，普通經驗與教育。
六、公正與誠摯。
七、努力與堅忍。
八、吸引，教導與發展它人之能力。
九、辨別高下之分析權力。
十、坦白。
十一、機敏，自治與滑稽。
十二、超人體格。
管理家之分等，可有數種，惟何者爲最適當，殊難確定。玆錄一種，依次列后：
一、爲獨裁以達目的者。
二、雖爲獨裁，但亦願順從輿情。
三、如爲評判或證人，專事協調紛爭之目的與行爲。

由是以觀，則知眞有創造力之管理家，卽爲第三種之協調者。惟無論其用獨裁與協調，總冀少費周折與時間。若固執某種，未免太愚，其必因時制宜也審矣。

另有一種分等，與上述不無相似，其法如下：

一、賴原有之權力，資財，聲望或技能者。

二、賴恫嚇及處罰它人（此種人視管理爲兒戲）之能力者。

三、賴勸導他人之能力者。

此三等亦顯有歧異，其能視環境之需要，以定何種之管理，斯可謂得管理之眞諦。管理家應有之資格，旣縷陳于上，如徒知其才能，而忽視其弱點，則眞正之管理能力，仍無從完全鑑別。下述才性，足以限制管理之效果．

一、對雇員有疑慮及恐懼。

二、欲獨裁以貪得權力。

三、不能得下屬之信仰，使態度與意見無從暴露。

四、以爲雇員無權建議，或以爲建議之無値。

五、不願負社交之責。

六、祇顧近因缺乏遠見。

七、過爲錢財所引誘，祇謂改進在乎獲得生產與利益。
八、雇員意見之不當或太偏，忽于觀察。
九、專賴賞罰爲進陞之階梯；及用壓迫與賄賂之辦法。
十、不能與它人合作，以謀公共之利益。

管理家實應有社會之觀念，存乎其中，上陳十項，已多指示，此固無庸置辯。將來之管理家，必更爲具有社會觀念之一人，殆可斷言。

管理 第二卷 第一期

陸大月刊

第三卷 第四期

民國二十六年四月一日出版

目錄

本刊價目

零售：每期大洋叁角
半年：六期大洋壹元五角
全年：十二期大洋叁元

郵費

外埠：每期二分五厘 半年一角五分 全年三角
本埠：每期二分 半年一角二分 全年二角四分

編輯者 陸大月刊編輯委員會
發行者 陸大月刊社
社址：南京漢口路陸軍大學特別黨部內
電話：三一七一一三
代售處 特別黨部及各大書局

演講

中央及地方決算（續）

聞亦有

第四章　吾國歷年辦理決算情形

一、民國十七年度以前之制度

我國舉辦決算之動機，發生於前清光緒季年憲政編查館奏准在九年立憲期內自第三年起試辦決算。然終清之世，未經定有決算制度。民國肇興，財政部曾定辦理臨時決算例言如下：

一、各部及在京各機關，應編歲入決算分冊咨部彙總。

二、在京各機關，應編歲出決算分冊咨送主管部彙編。

三、此次所編臨時決算。以前清宣統三年舊歷正月一日起，至十二月底止爲斷。

四、交通部所管郵、電、航、路四政，作爲特別決算。

五、決算冊格式，照預算格式辦理。

當時五項辦法，僅係籌辦在京各機關之決算。迨二年春，財政部始通電各省辦理元年決算表冊。三年一月，又訂元二兩年度決算辦法七條。

一、京內外歲入歲出各款，截至民國二年六月底止，開單銷結。

二、民國二年度歲入歲出各款，依據修正預算，造具決算表冊，送財政部全份，並將歲出之款，分送各主管部核編，轉送財政部彙編總決算，送審計院審定。

三、歲入按實收數開列，並將有無尾欠及欠收確數，逐款詳晰聲叙。

四、京內外業經呈咨准銷之款，仍編入決算，註明奉准案由。

五、超過修正預算及臨時支出款，經主管部核准有案者，應聲叙案由，其未經報部核准者，應聲叙確實理由。

六、編造決算表冊至項爲止，先列決算數，次列修正預算數，次爲比較增減數。

七、元年度歲入歲出清單，限三年十月底送部。二年度決算表冊，限十二月底送部。

以上辦法由財政部電達各省照辦。

民國三年頒布會計法所規定者，略舉如下：

第廿四條 總決算先經審計院審定後。由大總統提交國會，其分門之次序，與總額預算同，並須開具下列各項之計算。

歲入部

歲入預算額 查定歲入額

已收訖歲入額 歲入斷短額

未收訖歲入額

歲出部

歲出預算額 預算決定後增加歲出額

支付飭書已發之歲出額 轉入次年度之歲出額

歲出剩餘額

第廿五條 總決算提出國會時，由大總統提出報告書，並附送下列各書類：

各官署所管歲入決算報告書

各官署主管歲出決算報告書

各官署主管特別會計決算報告書

國債計算書

會計法關於決算事項，僅規定編訂程式及附送書類，既如上述。而編送程序及期限，則散見於審計法施行細則如下：

第六條 中央各官署，應於年度經過後三個月以內，編成歲入歲出決算報告書，送主管部查核，京外各官署同。

第七條 各省各特別區域及蒙藏等處各官署，應於年度經過後三個月以內，編成歲入歲出決算報告書，送財政廳或財政分廳彙核，於年度經過後六個月以內編成全省或全區域歲入歲出決算報告書，送財政部全份，並分送主管部查核，未設財政廳或財政分廳之處，由行政長官查核編送。

第八條 各部應於年度經過八個月以內，編成所管歲入決算報告書，主管歲出決算報告書及特別會計決算報告書，送財政部查核；但關於雲、貴、甘、新、川、桂六省之決算，得展限一個月，蒙藏等處之決算，得依特定之期限，另案編送。

第九條　財政部應於年度經過後十個月以內，彙核各部及本部決算報告書，並國債計算書，編成總決算，連同附屬書類，送審計院審查：但關於蒙藏等處之決算，得另案編送。

以上編訂決算之程序及期限，經審計法施行細則規定者，爲上述四條。蓋在北京政府時期，關於決算制度，祇東鱗西爪，時見一端，卒未有具體之方案故亦未能編成總決算。

二、民國十七年度至十九年度之試行制度

民國十七年度決算之編製，於十八年五月經審計院依據審計法施行細則關於決算事項各規定，呈請國府令飭財政部將決算報告書格式，以及編製方法，詳密規劃。呈候核定施行。經財政部於是年七月參照法理，兼顧事實，擬訂編製十七年度決算章程二十三條。大體如下：

（一）總則。京內外各級機關編製中央地方及特別會計年度決算，均照本章程辦理。中央地方特別會計決算之區別，悉依同年度預算辦理。各級機關歲入歲出之決算分爲經常臨時兩門，亦依同年度預算區別之。

（二）編製程序及時期。屬於中央收支之機關應編中央歲入歲出決算報告書四份，限十八年八月底以前送主管機關。由各主管機關審核後，編製各該管轄事務歲入歲出決算報告書三份，連同所屬機關原報告書各三份，限十八年十月底以前送各該彙編分類決算之機關。由各該彙編分類決算之機關審核後，編製中央各分類歲入歲出決算報告書，連同原附報告書各二份，限十八年十二月底以前送財政部由財政部彙核後，編製中央歲入歲出總決算一份，連原附各報告書一份，限十九年二月底以前送審計院審核。

屬於地方收支之各機關應編地方歲入歲出決算報告書四份，限十八年八月底以前送各該省或各該特別市主管機關。由各該省市主管機關審核後，編製各該省市分類歲入歲出決算報告書三份，連同原附報告書各三份，限十八年十月底以前送財政廳或財政局。由各該廳局彙核後，編製各該省市歲入歲出決算報告書，經各該省市審核後，連同原附報告書各一份，限十八年十二月底以前分送各該監督機關查核。財政部彙集各省市總決算各特別會計決算編製地方歲入歲出中央及地方特別會計歲入歲出總參考書，限十九年二月底以前送審計院備查。除附訂各級決算報告書式五種，表式四種，各附說明外，關於中央地方決算之分類，復附訂中央地方分類決算辦法。中央計分黨務、國務、行政、立法、司法、考試、監察、軍務、內務、外交、財務、教育文化、農鑛、工商、交通、衞生、建設、官營業、內外債。特務等廿類。地方計分黨務、行政、立法、司法、公安、財務、教育、農鑛、交通、衞生、建設、官營業、債款、特務等十五類。其用意係將中央地方收支劃分編製，不相混淆，較爲明晰，呈奉國府核定後於十八年九月公布施行。但十七年總決算未能編成。

迨編製十八年決算時經財政部呈由行政院轉呈國府核准十八年度決算辦法仍照十七年度決算章程賡續辦理。惟將原規定各年份各予遞展一年不再另訂規章以省手續。但十八年度總決算亦未能編成。

至編造十九年度決算時主計處已經成立編造總決算依主計處之職掌應劃歸主計處歲計局辦理。惟經財政部與主計處商定十九年度預算既由財政部辦理故該年度決算仍以由財政部辦理爲宜。財政部遂復參酌當時事實另訂十九年度決算章程凡十六條於二十年九月呈經國府公布施行大體如下：

(一)中央及地方收支機關應編之國家及地方歲入歲出決算報告書限二十年九月底以前按照同年度預算辦法送達中央各主管機關及各該省財政廳或市財政局。

(二)中央各主管機關審核後按照同年度預算辦法編製國家各分類歲入歲出決算報告書，各省財政廳各市財政局審核後按照同年度預算辦法編製各該省市歲入歲出決算報告書經各該省市政府審核後，均連同各原附報告書限二十年十二月底以前送達財政部。

(三)財政部彙核國家各分類決算編製國家歲入歲出決算連同各該原報告限二十一年二月底以前送達審計部審查。財政部彙集省市總決算營業會計決算加具按語限二十一年二月底以前送達審計部備查。

十九年度總決算亦未能編成。

三　民國二十年度以後之制度

民國二十年度之決算制度卽爲現行決算制度詳見下章敍述茲不復贅。但自民國二十年度起至目前爲止，國家總決算均未能編成。

四　歷年總決算未能編成之原因

歷來總決算何以未能編成，可分析爲兩種主要原因．

1.政治上原因——北京政府時代所定總決算係將全國中央及地方各機關之收支一律包括入內如一地方政府之決算不能如期送達財政部，則總決算卽無由編造矣。民三以後中央權力不能統馭全國，故歷年總決算俱未能編成，有目共見。國民政府成立以來所訂決算章程，均採國地分別編造原則，自表面觀之，似較以前簡便。實則各院部會之直屬機關仍然分佈於全國，苟一方面因特殊原因不造送第一級決算，亦必同受影響。

2.技術上原因——共十四點詳見下章。

第五章 吾國現行決算制度

一、編造決算之主管機關

國民政府主計處組織法第六條規定歲計局辦理事項其中第八款規定「關於各機關歲入歲出決算書之核算及總決算書之編造事項」足覘編造決算之主管機關爲國民政府主計處。

二、現行法規摘要

國家、省市——現行法爲暫行決算章程（民國二十一年十月十二日中央政治會議第三二七次會議通過）

縣市——由各省自行規定茲舉江蘇省爲例，詳述於後。

暫行決算章程

1.通則及編製方法

I 年度決算種類

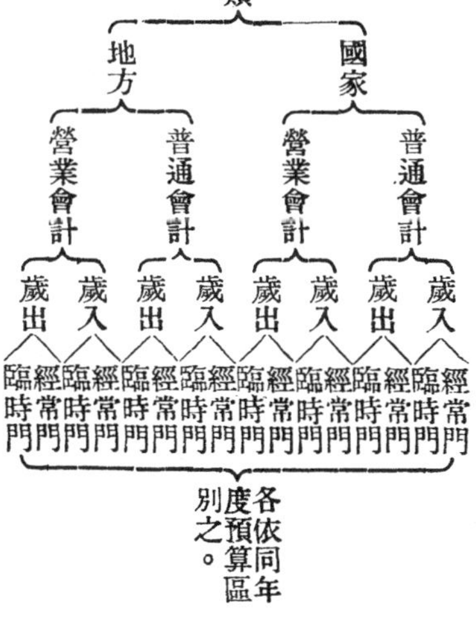

- 國家
  - 普通會計
    - 歲入：經常門、臨時門
    - 歲出：經常門、臨時門
  - 營業會計
    - 歲入：經常門、臨時門
    - 歲出：經常門、臨時門
- 地方
  - 普通會計
    - 歲入：經常門、臨時門
    - 歲出：經常門、臨時門
  - 營業會計
    - 歲入：經常門、臨時門
    - 歲出：經常門、臨時門

各依同年度預算區別之。

II 年度決算之級別——三級決算制——與編造概算之三級制相同。

III 年度決算之科目——按照同年度預算科目塡列如有新增收入未列預算及新增支出因情形緊急當時不及辦理追加預算程序事後補請追認有案者均得列入決算。

IV 編造年度決算之機關

第一級決算——原編第一級概算機關但有以下五項例外：

1. 機關之裁撤者應由主管機關代爲編製。

2. 機關之改組者應由改組後之機關合併編製。

3. 機關之名義變更者應由變更後之機關按名義變更之前後分別編製。

4. 數機關合併爲一機關者在未合併以前各該分設機關之決算應由併存機關代編。

5. 數機關之預算先合併而後分立者在合併期內由原機關合併編製分立以後由分立機關各自編製。

第二級決算——國家第二級分類決算主編機關如因第一級機關有改隸情事歸改隸之主要管機關彙編第二級分類決算。

（民國廿五年二月一日國府第一五七號訓令）

Y總決算應有之計算（暫行決算章程第五條規定）

歲入部：
歲入預算額　歲入追加預算額
已收訖歲入額　歲入減免額
未收訖歲入額　上年度剩餘額

歲出部：
歲出預算額　歲出追加預算額
歲出預算實支額　歲出剩餘額

?國家決算之編審之秩序及時期

級別	編製機關	期限	份數	送達機關
第一級決算	國家第一級概算機關	十月卅一日以前	第一級歲入歲出決算書各三份（並各項附表）	各該主管機關
第二級決算	國家第二級分類概算主管機關	十二月卅一日以前	第二級國家各分類歲入歲出決算書三份連同第一級決算書各二份	國民政府主計處
第三級決算	國民政府主計處	二月二十八日以前	國家歲入歲出總決算書連同第二級決算各一份第一級決算各一份	呈國民政府令交監察院發交審計部審核
審定國家歲入歲出總決算書附入審查報告	審計部	四月卅日以前	審定國家歲入歲出總決算書附入審查報告	呈監察院轉呈國民政府交主計處
審定之國家總決算並開具暫行決算章程第五條規定各事項之計算	國民政府主計處	五月卅一日以前	審定之國家總決算並開具暫行決算章程第五條規定各事項之計算	呈請國民政府公布並繕具一份呈轉中央政治委員會備查

3. 地方決算之編審之程序及時期

級別	編製機關	期限	份數	送達機關
第一級決算	地方第一級概算機關	十月三十一日以前	第一級歲入歲出決算書各三份（並各項附表	各該省財政廳或市財政局
第二級決算	各省財政廳或市財政局	十二月卅一日以前	第二級省市歲入歲出總決算書連同第一級決算各二份	各該省市政府
審核完竣之第二級決算	各省市政府	二月二十八日以前	審核完竣之第二級決算	發還財政廳或財政局
第三級決算	各省財政廳或市財政局	四月三十日以前	審核完竣之第二級決算三份連同第一級決算各一份	呈由省市政府送達國民政府主計處各省市審計處成立後各省市政府應將各該省市歲入歲出決算送審計處審定後再行送達國民政府主計處轉呈公布
各該省市歲入歲出總決算書附具暫行決算章程第五條規定各事項之計算	國民政府主計處	五月卅一日以前	各該省市歲入歲出總決書附具暫行決算章程第五條規定各事項之計算	呈請國民政府公布並各檢具一份呈轉中央政治委員會並逕送審計部備查
全國地方總決算	國民政府主計處	未規定期限	全國地方總決算三分	呈報國民政府並呈轉中央政治委員會暨逕送審計部備查

4. 決算書表格式

決算書

i. 格式

決 算 書

第________號

編製機關____ 中華民國___年度___處___門 第___頁

___年___月___日起至___年___月___日止

科目	本年度決算數	本年度預算數	比較增減數		說明
			增	減	

編製日期 中華民國__年__月__日 編製機關長官____

會計主任____

ii. 說明

第……號—第一級歲入/出決算書為第1/2號第二級歲入/出決算書為第3/4號第三級歲入/出決算書為第5/6號。

科目——第一級決算書科目欄內之科目祇塡款項目三級第二級及第三級決算書科目欄內之科目均塡款項目節四級。

第一級決算書決算數欄內各數卽將同年度計算書所列各計算數分別款項目併計塡列。

預算數欄內各數均照同年度預算書所列之數塡列其曾經追加及追減者須一併計算塡列。

預算書內所計之期間不足十二個月及預算實行期間不足預算書內所計之月份者均應照預算總額塡列但須於說顯欄內詳細說明之。

其他各欄及各標題下之塡法與數目之分色畫線等均依同年度施行之預算科目細則內預算書塡法說明辦理。

收支對照表

i. 格式

收支對照表

編製機關________　　中華民國______年度

收入	科目	支出
	總計	

機關長官________　　會計主任________

ii. 說明

本表所用科目如下：

上年度結存數——在會計年度終結後應將所存餘款悉數繳庫以期劃分清楚。但事實上或有上年度終結未經將餘款繳庫者應以之列入本表收入欄。

本年度收入各項——凡正雜款項在本年度內收入者分別列入本表收入欄。

本年度支出各項——凡坐支撥抵解繳款項在本年度內支出者分別列入本表支出欄。

本年度結存數——在本表收入兩抵後所餘存之數列入本表支出欄。

總計——本表各項塡完之後於科目欄塡總計於收支各欄各

列總數。

貸借對照表

i.格式

編製機關＿＿＿＿ **貸借對照表**

資產(借方) 中華民國＿年＿月＿日 負債(貸方)

減	增	本屆數 年月日	上屆數 年月日	科目 資產	 負債	上屆數 年月日	本屆數 年月日	增	減
				總	計				

機關長官＿＿＿＿ 會計主任＿＿＿＿

ii.說明

資產欄——應列土地房屋器具機械圖書儀器車輛雜件裝置積存消耗品現金存款證券應收款項等科目。

負債欄——應列欠薪欠銀行欠商號暫存款項欠出納員保證金欠房租等科目。

資產負債之金額應登記結算日期分類簿經整理後之結算金額。

資產內土地房屋係舊有官產未有定價者得酌量估價記入其他一切資產悉記購買時之原價。

本屆數欄內年月日塡註本屆結算日期。

上屆數欄內年月日塡註上屆結算日期。

本屆數大於上屆數者列其增加數於「增」欄內其小於上屆數者列其減少數「減」欄內。

資產數大於負債數者應用紅筆記「純餘額」科目於負債欄，其小於負債數者應用紅筆記「純短額」科目於資產欄。使資產之總計與負債之總計相等。

所有本年度以內應支未支之款應列入本表之負債欄其未經列入之款，即不得再在翌年度內動支。

財產目錄

i.格式

編製機級＿＿＿＿ **財產目錄**

中華民國 年度

種類名稱	編號 字	 號	數量	單價	價值	購置 年	 月	備考

總計									

機關長官＿＿　　會計主任＿＿　　庶務主任＿＿

ii. 說明

種類名稱欄——凡土地場圃池塘房屋一切建築物之新建或購買或撥入以屬於支出計算書購置各項物品除消耗品及每具價值不滿一角之物品外均列入本欄。

編號欄——除地產房屋及零星小件不能編號外其餘均應逐項編列號數就一欄之起訖號數分別列入本欄。

數量欄——地產之畝數房屋之間數其他物品傢具之件數均列入本欄。

單價欄——各項財產之單價列入本欄。

價值欄——每一類財產之總價列入本欄。

購置年月欄——各項財產購置之年月列入本欄。

備考欄——各項財產之購入按外幣定價折合數額分列單價及價值兩欄外仍將原幣數額列入本欄並註明折合率。

江蘇省各縣編造縣地方決算暫行辦法（二十三年十二月四日江蘇省政府委員會第七〇八次會議通過）

1. 年度決算之種類｛歲入（收入類）〈經常門、臨時門；歲出（經費類）〈經常門、臨時門｝悉依同年度預算區別之。

2. 年度決算之科目——按照同年度預算科目填列。如有新增收入及新增支出均應列入決算。

3. 編造年度決算之機關——由原編預算機關編製。但年度內各機關各有裁撤或改組情事者亦規定五項例外辦法。（完全與暫行決算章程所規定者相同。）

4. 編造年度決算之程序計有以下三項：

i. 各縣地方機關於年度經過後兩個月編造決算書二份一份送縣政府備查一份送交會計主任轉呈財政廳審核。

ii. 縣政府應於年度經過後三個月彙核縣地方各機關決算報告編成縣地方總決算送會計主任轉呈財政廳審核。

iii. 凡縣補助款及總預備費項下動支之款其決算由公款公產管

理處編造。

5.決算書表

決算書

格式及說明與暫行決算章程規定者相同

（惟缺少「第……號」之記載）

收支對照表

i.格式與暫行決算章程規定者相同　　ii.說明

收支對照表分為兩種：

收支對照表第一號記收入類收支各款說明如下：

一、上年度結存數列入本表收入欄。

二、本年度收入各項應依預算（至目為止）列入本表收入欄。

三、本年度解庫各項列入本表支出欄。

四、本年度結存數係收支相抵之餘數列入本表支出欄。

五、總計　本表各項填完之後於科目欄填總計於收支兩欄各列總數。

收支對照表第二號記經費類收支各款，說明如下：

上年度結存數　列入本表收入欄。

二、本年度收入各項　凡本機關實領經臨各費分別列入本表收入欄。

三、本年度支出各項　凡本機關各費支出分別列入本表支出欄其科目至目為止。

四、本年節餘經費　本機關節餘經費除填列支出決算書外列入本表支出欄。

五、總計　本表各項填完之後於科目欄填總計於收支兩欄各填總數。

貸借對照表

格式及說明與暫行決算章程規定者相同

財產目錄

格式及說明與暫行決算章程規定者相同

三、對於吾國現行決算制度之批評

對於吾國現行決算制度，足資討論之點，試列舉於後：

1.編造決算依理言應由會計制度產生不必另立系統。但依國民政府主計處組織法規定：

歲計局辦理事項中第八款規定：「關於各機關歲入歲出決算書之核算及總決算之編造事項。」

會計局辦理事項中第四款規定：「關於各機關會計報告之綜核記載及總報告之彙編事項。」

基於上述組織法規定，歲計局主管編造總決算會計局主管彙編會計總報告。因之總決算與會計總報告之內容，似乎完全不同。此種觀念，實出誤解。現時一般人觀念以為

總決算＜1.為與預算對照之書表。2.另由編決算之三級決算系統產生總決算。

會計總報告＜1.祇為收支總報告可以不與預算對照。2.由會計局之總會計制度產生。

其實依理論而言，決算書表應自帳冊產生，即在工商業機關其決算書表，莫有不從會計制度內產生者。故現時因會計制度不完全而另立三級決算系統產生總決算之辦法，實為畸性狀態，而徒增彙編之繁重手續。此其一，且由完善會計制度產生之完備會計報告。當然不止收支總報告一種。凡表示動態及靜態之會計報告當然應有盡有。故為補救目前不能編造總決算起見，首在設計各級機關會計制度。將來由會計制度否生完備會計報告，使會計報告包括決算書表，而不再另立編造決算系統，以資敏捷。

2.營業會計決算書表應另行規定

暫行決算章程規定之收支決算書，收支對照表，貸借對照表及財產目錄等四種不適宜於公有營業機關。在公有營業機關所編決算應與工商業機關所編造決算書相仿為下列六種：

1.營業報告書　2.資產負債表　3.財產目錄　4.損益計算書　5.盈虧撥補表　6.其他（二十四年九月國民政府主計處公函通行謂「各附表之說明祇有適用於此種會計而不適用於彼種會計者應補充說明以便各會計人員容易填記」）

3.繼續經費決算書表應另行規定

繼續經費以完成該項事業為段落，應不受年度之拘束。故在普通基金內應依撥付繼續經費數目列入決算。而由繼續經費自編基金決算。不與普通總基金決算相混。以示界限。

4.收入支出決算對於收支計算基礎不一致

暫行決算章程規定第一級決算十月卅一日送出故有四個月之整理期限，按現時決算上收支計算基礎如下：

i.收入決算書所列收入數目係本年征獲數——權責發生基礎。

ii.支出決算書所列支出數目係本年應支並已實支數——權責發生與收付實現聯合之基礎。

基於上述，收入決算書因已採用權責發生基礎，故各級機關。於年度終了時，可隨時核計應收數目，結束帳冊，不必期待收入款，何時實際納入。惟由分支機關報告送達第一級決算主管機關，必須定一會計整理期間，便於彙編而已。故收入第一級決算在年度終了時四個月後送出當無困難。

惟支出決算書現定辦法係於應支數支付完畢，實支數等於應支數時，始行結束。然後將已等於應支數之實支數列入決算，故各級機關年度終了時不能編決算必待應支數完全支付完畢始克編造，再加以第一級主管機關彙編分支機關決算之期間，四個月之整理期限卽恐不敷應用。故支出決算書之基礎有改爲應支數之必要。如此不但時間敏捷且收支兩種決算之計算基礎相埒。

5.缺少劃分收支應屬年度之規定　現行預算章程及決算章程對於收支應屬年度之劃分未有規定故決算上計算應收應支數目，何者應屬本年度，何者應屬次年度，不易決定。如各機關所定標準不同，則編造總決算卽失去一致性。將來關於劃分收支應屬年度辦法，應在決算法內規定，或在預算法或會計法內規定爲尤宜。

6.缺少出納整理期間之規定　現時決算章程規定有四個月之整理期間。依理言收支採取權責發生基礎，凡年度末應收未收歲入款及應付未付歲出款，卽可一律轉入次年度，此爲最理想之辦法。有四個月整理期限，專爲整理會計事務，已儘足用，但如英國之制度各機關之支出，在年度過去後三個月內，仍能支用，補記上年度帳冊。如此情形卽有出納整理期限矣。吾國現時支出決算書上之計算支出基礎。係待應支數支付完畢時始行列入。如一時不能改爲純粹應支數基礎。亦可仿傚英國訂出納整理期間，以期決算容易編就。此項規定，應列入決算法內，或在預算法或公庫法內規定爲尤宜。

7.缺少上年度應收及應支各數轉入次年度辦法之規定

上年度末或上年度出納整理期末日應收未收及應付未付各數轉入次年度應編追加預算或自動轉入，此點應列入決算法內，或在預算法內規定爲尤宜。

8.缺少消滅時效之規定

凡應繳納及應給付之款項，經過本年度後若干年內，不經政府通知令其繳納之收款，應列入減免額內。又不經債權人請領之付款，政府得免予發給。以上兩點，在決算法內應有規定

，或規定在會計法或公庫法爲尤宜，

9.決算章程所規定之決算書格式與第五條應計算事項不能適應。

按決算章程第五條內規定總決算歲入方面應開歲入預算額，歲入追加預算額，已收訖歲入額，歲入減免額，未收訖歲入額，年度剩餘額等六事項之計算。又歲出方面應開歲出預算額，歲出追加預算額，歲出預算實支額，及歲出剩餘額等四事項之計算。但所規定決算書格式，祇有預算數，決算數，及比較增減數三欄，是不能相互適應，尤易明瞭。

10決算章程規定之收支對照表不適用

決算章程規定之收支對照表將收入類經費類合併一齊，殊不適用，此點江蘇省規定縣市決算辦法內，已加更正（二十四年九月國民政府主計處公函通行謂「收支對照表之收支及結存均係現金數其塡法說明包含收入類會計及經費類會計之兩種塡法在內其1.2.3.4.係說明經費類收支對照表之塡法1.2.3.5.係說明收支類收支對照表之塡法。」）

11決算章程規定之貸借對照表不適用

各機關固定資產與固定負債，不屬普通基金範圍之資力與負擔，已見前述。且兩方面不形成相互間之關係，所計算之純餘及純虧額，毫無意義。故規定强爲合編一表全無是處。（現主計處已准各機關免予造送。）

12缺少總平準表

總平準表爲表示某基金運用完畢時之資力及負擔數額，爲主要靜態會計報告，故應加入決算書表之內。

13缺少固定負債目錄

貸借對照表既不適用。關於固定資產方面現已訂有財產目錄。故爲表示固定負債起見，可視事實需要，另編固定負債目錄一份。

14審計程序應加更改

，現時規定編成國家總決算後，送審計部審核，但現有審計辦事處之設置，故以後設有審計辦事處之機關，其決算應先送該管審計人員審查。

（未完）

『人事行政學』

任家誠

原　名——Public Personnel Administration

著　者——William E. Mosher & J. Donald Kingsley

出版處——Harper & Brothers Publishers, New York

版　期——一九三六年

定　價——美金五元

在行政學的研究中，人事行政佔着最重要的地位，在行政的實施中，管理人員是一件最困難的任務。因爲這兩種緣故，人事行政學的研究最爲世人所注意，努力的結果，引發了不少光明燦爛的發展。

我人試把全部行政學分析研究，在最近的幾部偉著中，人事行政的討論，最可以表示研究的進步。就是科學管理的移植，也以人事行政爲最明顯。考試，升遷，考績的敘述已漸從理論而趨于實際，已經脫離了理想而逐一有科學方法的根據，理論和實施的熔合是研究進步的鐵證。

人事行政學的專著在十餘年前僅有拍樂克脫（A.W. Procter）的『人事行政原理』一書，此書雖然是一本創作，然已因時代的進展，而漸失其固有的地位。最近幾年來因爲美國人事行政諮詢委員會(Commission of Inquiry on Public Service Personnel)之成立，很有幾本值得參考的書籍刊行，然因爲該會負有特殊的使命，其論列或是偏于美國，或是立場固定，作爲正式的課本讀是不相宜的。最近我們才得到了這本『人事行政學』，一本完善而新穎的課本。

在序文中，我們很容易察出這書的觀點，牠是一方面根據行政學的原則，發揮人事行政應加討論的範疇，同時注意到科學管理的紹介，想把工商業管理的成就移植到行政學上來，所以牠說很多基本上的哲學是採自墨脫卡夫和推特（H.C. Metcalf & Ordway Tead)的『人事管理』(Personnel Management)這二點的兼收並蓄，就是這書的優越處，更適合我們目前的需要。

行政科學化和商業化的呼聲，在十餘年前已經有人高唱，但是事實上並沒有切實做到，尤其是人事的統馭，無論中外仍舊脫不掉衙門的氣味，我相信這書的問世，可以矯正時弊，

把此書和拍樂克脫的創作相較，我們很可以看出不少不同之處，這種差異也就是進步的象徵。拍氏書中對於公務員工作的激勵（Incentive）祇談到升擢和考績，而此書提到俸給釐訂的公平，退休制度的籌劃，公務員福利事業的推進等等，其他如任用方面的討論，考試方法的研究，多較拍氏之作爲完備。

此書第一編敘述人事行政的進展和特質，雖多偏于美國方面，很有些資料可供我人參考。牠把人事行政的組織反覆申述至爲詳盡，最後並且提到人事行政機關的任務，把一切任務分成二十六類，並別其性質，逐一加以簡短的解說，在暗暗中說明了今後各章所討論的範圍，不啻爲全書的總綱。

過去研究人事行政的，大都着重方法的商討和原則的推敲，然而對於管理機關的組織却很少注意，其實制度的優劣，方法的能行與否，完全看執行機關的能力和方策，組織的討論是必要的，此書補救了過去各書的疏忽。

第二編研究任用的原則，牠對於考試方法很加注意，更注意到面試問題。的確，人品之良莠很不容易在試卷中察出，所以當面口試的方法是必要的，但是因爲人類偏袒心理的難于免除，面試的結果，往往不能十分公平，此書利用科學方法，分析人類的性格，編成面試記錄（Record of interview）其中分爲七欄，更在每欄中分成若干項，面試員於試驗時可以逐一填入記號，然後由另一人歸納總成績，所分的七欄爲(一)工作的準備，(二)容貌與態度，(三)體格，(四)對人的態度，(五)自信力與勤惰，(六)品性，(七)對面試員之態度。牠的優點就是避免隨便定分，而造成種種弊誤。

對於正式考試的討論，此書亦較他書爲詳盡，牠把考試的方式分成兩方面討論(一)筆試和口試——方法的研究，(二)態度試驗，特種能力試驗，人品試驗，成績試驗，體格檢查——形式的研究，用意可謂周密之至。

第三編是訓練和任用條件。在事前訓練的商討中，牠指出了英美所用方法的不同——一般智力的訓練(英)和專門的訓練(美)，這種清晰的劃分，於行政學的研究上，很有貢獻，因爲從這一點上我人可以明瞭英美研究行政學的異同。

事後訓練的討論比任何書籍都詳盡，牠把整個訓練方法析爲幾種研究，曰：(一)入職訓練，(二)增進行政效率的訓練，(三)升擢的訓練，(四)其他訓練。各節之中，更舉出實例，便于參攷，自不必言。我國對於人員的任用，事前既無完善的訓練方針，事後更沒有注意到入職應受的種種訓練，結果辦事的人多，而眞能辦事的人却很少，行政效率之減退，政績之不彰，訓練不得其當之罪，實不可逭。所以這一章我人應詳加研究，以便擷人之長而補己之短。

作者因爲有意把工商企業行有成效的人事管理移植于人事行政，在在視重科學化問題。所以在調轉升遷的研究中顧到公務員的流轉 (Turnover)，在任用條件中顧到請假和辦公時間等問題。的確過去很多學子認爲公務員有他尊嚴的地位，所以對於公務員的工作方面不應有過分的干預，但是這種思想已經不合時代，此書能夠明白認識，進而討論改革，在此我們不能不欽佩作者提倡的勇氣。

第四編所討論的是對於公務員工作的激勵，內容包括三點：(一)俸給問題，(二)攷績問題(三)退休問題。

俸給的釐訂，以前也有種種不同的論辯，行政法學者認爲公務員的俸給是終身努力效勞公共團體的贍養金，所以應該較工商業基于契約的工資爲優裕；經濟學者認爲從國民經濟方面觀察，俸給與工資並無多大的差異，俸給不過爲工資之中之較爲特殊。二種觀念的不能相謀，造成種種錯誤的結果。現在無論中外，工商業高級人員的薪金常較行政人員爲高，結果使學有專長的幹才，一個個走向工商界上，這種公私競爭的態度，於整個國家來說自然是不利的，所以我們需要調整，需要合理而公平的調整。此書很注意這一點，所以在俸給的討論中，先說到生活費與俸給的關係，並搜集了不少資料，以便參證。其次說到釐訂俸給的一般原則，牠把俸給釐訂的原素，分析成三方面，(一)經濟上的攷慮，(二)社會及論理上的攷慮，(三)其他有關之各方面，同時提到公私薪給的調協，設法弭除人才羅用的競爭而促進公私事業之合作。我國現行俸給及分等制度，並不完善，人所共見，尤爲行政學者所不滿，提議改革者大有其人，我相信，此書可以供給不少有利於改革的資料。

關於攷績，現在已成爲升遷中最重要的原素，方法的公平與否，更切切與公務員工作效能相關聯。但是攷績方法的優劣是相對的，各有利弊，我人決不能斷何者爲善，何者不善，就是最新的量分法和拍樂比司脫法 (Probst system)也不能說十分完善，無瑕可擊。在這種情形之下，往往使施政者感到十分猶豫，但是如果我們能夠決定幾個原則，然後利用不同的方法來迎合需要，其結果一定較爲有效，此書在比較各種方式之後，就着眼于這一點，牠所提出的十幾點有加以研究的價值。

最後一編，牠提到公務員的合作問題，特別注意英國的懷德萊會議 (Whitley Council) 組織，當然牠唯一的目的就是想促成政府當局和公務人員諒解和合作的可能性。但是舍此之外，牠也提到公務員聯合會組織問題，討論到公務員聯合組織與外界工會組織的聯合問題，和罷工權問題，牠的觀點在在沒有放棄合作的原則。

從上面各段觀，我覺得確有把這書介紹給對行政學有興趣的學者的價值，但是牠的編制，也未嘗無可以商榷的地方。

第一，立場問題——此書的立場是創造化的，前進的，但是工商管理中對於人事統馭的方法是否能完全搬演於人事行政上尚是問題。傳統觀念和習俗的造成，公務員所處的地位，至少在公務員自己看來已佔着社會上比較崇高的一層，他們是否願受種種科學化的統馭。特別是我國，官是了不得的，這種改革一旦實行，是否會造成種種反響，轉而謀利不成反爲害，確值得我人注意。我覺得生長在這種烏烟瘴氣的社會中的我，雖然受到科學管理的陶鑄，還不能完全避免社會思想的左右，我的過慮，或者作者二位先生會感到大可不必。

第二，編制問題——牠的編制的確已避免了過去幾本行政學編制的呆板，而趨于生動醒目，尤其是分編得當，值得我們欽佩，這一半是作者卓裁的妥當，此外取材的新穎亦爲原因之一。但是其中亦有數章可資商討。譬如像工作時間和請假諸問題應和安全問題聯合討論，列成專編，以爲合理的歸納，訓練的討論應該有其獨立的地位等。

總之在人事行政專書的缺乏中，這本書確可以救濟我們的渴望，而值得注意。

雜誌論文索引暫行分類方法

管　　理

A. 管理總論

A1. 管理理論　　A2. 管理教育　　A3. 其他

B. 工商管理

B1. 工商組織　　B2. 計劃與行政　　B3. 生產管理

B4. 物料管理　　B5. 推銷與市場　　B6. 人事管理

B7. 其他

C. 鐵道管理(附公用事業管理)

C1. 概論　　C2. 鐵道組織　　C3. 工程與機械

C4. 鐵道材料管理　　C5. 鐵路業務　　C6. 行車管理

C7. 鐵路會計與統計　　C8. 鐵路人事問題　　C9. 其他

D. 公務管理

D1. 概論　　D2. 中央及地方政府　　D3. 人事管理

D4. 物料管理　　D5. 法制　　D6. 其他

E. 財務管理

E1. 概論　　E2. 豫算　　E3. 會計與統計

E4. 金融管理　　E5. 其他

分 類 索 引

索引類別	題目	著者	雜誌名稱	發行年月	號數
A類					
A 3:	成本制度與科學管理	顧鐘奇	華年	26—1	6:2
B類					
B 1:	論我國出口茶葉應改為官督商辦	俞希稷	管理	26—2	1:5
	商業組織常識及鐵路沿線商情調查	譚沛霖	鐵道半月刊	,,	2:4
	施工制度	范揚	行政研究	26—1	2:1
B 2:	改良桐油芻議	許寶駿	浙江建設	,,	10:7
	棉業統制與紡織之我見	王德明	染織紡週刊	,,	2:23
	經濟建設之當前工作	吳鼎昌	廣播週報	,,	118
B 3:	最近世界工業生產之發展	胡紀常	華年	,,	6:3
	英日紗廠生產費之分析比較	欣奇	紡織時報	,,	1353—1354
	福建糧食的生產及其消費	杜俊東	福建縣政半月刊	,,	141
B 5:	廿五年中國對外貿易與工商業	孫懷仁	商專月刊	,,	1:1
	如何發展出口貿易	葉抱賓	商業月報	,,	17:1
	湘米運粵情形及重要性	余丹忱	申報週刊	26—2	2:6
	我國及歐美各國抵制傾銷述略	董家鏐	商學理刊	,,	1:1
	科學管理與市場	張宗謙	管理	,,	1:5
B 6:	商業輔導員應如何養成	韓玉書	教育與職業	,,	182
	管理紗廠女工之簡例	欣寄	紡織時報	26—1	2:26
	練習生的問題	何清儒	工商管理月刊	26—1	4:1
	雇用前的測驗	屠哲隱	工商管理月刊	,,	,,
B 7:	一年中實業建設之回顧	吳鼎昌	商業月報	26—2	2:2
	我國的紡織工業	楊德惠	錢業月報	,,	17:2
	浙江各縣桐油調查	陳强	浙江建設	26—1	10:7
	嘉興米業調查	方悴農	浙江建設	,,	,,

	中國工業化問題檢討	吳景超	行政研究	26—1	2:1
	我國鄉村工業檢討	林凡野	國聞週報	26—1	14:5
	日本工業進步之原因	馬寅初	銀行週報	26—1	21:2
	實業部湘米檢驗所與中國米穀檢驗事業之前瞻	周抬祿	農報	26—1	4:2
	中國豐收問題	編　者	中外經濟拔萃月刊	26—1	1:1
	商業的要素	陶朱公	正風半月刊	26—2	4:1
	促進商業的便利方法	陶朱公	正風半月刊	26—2	3:12
	宣傳技術	余天休	正風半月刊	26—2	4:1
C類					
C 1:	中國鐵路建設的展望	馮享嘉	錢業月報	26—1	17:1
	蘇聯遠東交通建設之計劃與實現	王國樑	交通雜誌	26—1	5:1
	水陸空運輸網的主要性	黃伯樵	鐵道半月刊	26—1	2:1
	津浦路一年來之施政經過及今後計劃	楊承訓	鐵道半月刊	26—1	2:1
	隴海路一年來之施政經過及今後計畫	錢宗澤	鐵道半月刊	26—1	2:1
	膠濟路一年來之施政經過及今後計劃	葛光廷	鐵道半月刊	26—1	2:1
	廣九鐵道最近之措施及概況	李祿超	廣九季刊	26—1	4
	粵漢鐵路通車後之情況及整理步驟	凌鴻勛	粵漢月刊	26—2	1:1,2
	最近美國鐵路情況的蠡測	韋　愿	鐵路雜誌	26—1	2:8
	平漢路一年來施政經過及今後計劃	陳延炯	鐵道半月刊	26—1	2:1
	中國鐵道事業之檢討	羅　魯	鐵道半月刊	26—2	2:2
	正太路一年來施政經過及今後計劃	顏德慶	鐵道半月刊	26—1	2:1
	汽車業務社之組織及其實施計劃	丹　心	道路	26—1	52:3
	中國公路交通當前之幾大問題	趙祖康	道路	26—1	52:3
	鐵路政策之研究	園	改進季刊	26—1	20
C 2:	鐵路營業組織改進芻議	陳家騏	交通雜誌	26—2	5:2
	我國鐵路組織之檢討	陳家騏	鐵路雜誌	26—1	2:8
C 3:	京贛鐵路贛境工程籌備經過及將來工程進行計劃	容祖誥	鐵道半月刊	26—2	2:3
	平漢鐵路改善軌道橋梁之概況	陳　琯	工程	26—1	12:1

	鐵路車輛鈎承減除磨耗之設計	封雲廷	工程	26—1	12:1
C 5:	淮南鐵路沿線生產交通情形及其業務發展之計劃	張善瑋	鐵路雜誌	26—1	2:8
	鐵路貨物運輸論	倘省三	改進季刊	26—1	20
	鐵路與公路之聯絡	夢　候	希進季刊	26—2	21
	鐵路沿線水陸競爭之調查	吳文蔚	鐵道半月刊	26—2	2:4
	鐵路沿線投資機會調查	許傳音	鐵道半月刊	26—2	2:4
	鐵路沿線之農業調查	李恭亮	鐵道半月刊	26—2	2:4
	鐵路沿線之工業調查	王炳南	鐵道半月刊	26—2	2:3
	鐵路沿線特產及礦產調查	譚沛霖	鐵道半月刊	26—2	2:4
	鐵路電化及運輸問題	譚沛霖	鐵道半月刊	26—2	2:3
	改善吾國鐵路貨物事故處理方法之商榷	沈奏廷	交通雜誌	26—1	5:1
	粵漢路廿五年度貨客運改進計劃		粵漢月刊	26—2	1:1,2
	整理粵漢鐵路運輸事宜紀要	陳清文	交通雜誌	26—2	5:2
	運價與物價	熊大惠	管理	26—2	1:5
	我國鐵路沿線國煤產運銷之研究	譚沛霖	鐵道半月刊	26—2	2:3
	一九三五年度俄國鐵路運輸的實績		鐵路雜誌	26—1	2:8
C 6:	高速度茅塞爾列車的制動問題	黃昌言	交通雜誌	26—2	5:2
	鐵路行車管理之連鎖問題	周世正	交通雜誌	26—2	5:2
	防範行車事變聲中吾國鐵路各站行車管理方法應有之改革	沈奏廷	管理	26—2	1:5
	吾國鐵路整車貨場應採用之車輛管理方法	沈奏廷	鐵道半月刊	26—1	2:2
C 7:	評鐵道部編各路機車用煤統計及其改善之我見	許　清	改進季刊	26—1	20
	改進鐵路預算之意見	葉崇勛	會計季刊	26—1	2:3
	修訂鐵路步計帳盈虧帳及盈撥補帳三則之商榷	林兆棠	鐵道半月刊	26—2	2:3
	管理旅客運輸應有之基本統計	許　清	管理	26—2	1:5
	再論吾國鐵路列車及車輛統計辦法	沈奏廷	管理	26—2	1:5
	關于營業進款類數日報	吳文蔚	鐵道半月刊	26—2	2:3
C 8:	鐵道部建設計劃中培養專才之定策	黎照寰	管理	26—2	1:5

C 9:	公路路基排水法	楊士文	道路	26—1	52:3
	一年來之公路建設	建 白	道路	26—1	52:3
	改善汽車車身之設計	高國恕	道路	26—1	52:3
	英德法美俄鐵道公路運輸業之鳥瞰	何乃民	鐵道半月刊	26—2	2:3
	日本國有鐵路之防災計劃	高鳳介	鐵路雜誌	26—1	2:8
	經濟調查的重要與經濟調查員的使命	黃 卓	鐵道半月刊	26—2	2:4
	經濟調查之原理及方法	王炳南	鐵道半月刊	26－2	2:4
	調查結果之整理	吳文蔚	鐵道半月刊	26—2	2:4
	航業合作與統制	洪賓雁	航業月刊	26—1	4:6
	廿五年份之交通建設		中行月刊	26—1,2	14:1,2

D類

D 1:	日本政治之動向	周伊武	外交評論	26—1	8:1
	蘇聯政治之理論與實際	繆培基	外交評論	26—1	8:1
	獨裁政治的興起	陳之邁	社會科學	26—1	2:2
	一九三六年國際政治總檢討	丁作韶等	外交月刊	26—1,2	10:1,2
	現時國際政治概況	周鯁生	廣播週報	26—1	118
	實現三民主義之方法	黃旭初	廣播週報	26—1	122
	行政組織之集權與統合	林 疊	管理	26—2	1:5
	增進行政效率之幾個問題	高秉坊	行政研究	26—1	2:1
	對于蔣委員長政治思想方法之管窺	茹春蒲	前途雜誌	26—1	5:1
	獨裁政治的興起	陳之邁	社會科學	26—1	2:2
	論政治領袖的要素	楊振先	民族雜誌	26—1	5:1
	我國政治的展望	丘 鋒	綢繆月刊	26—1	3:5
	如何加强三民主義的革命陣線	陳長蘅	東方雜誌	26—1	34:2
	日本政治之實際及變遷	楊定成	日本評論	26—1	9:5
	日本行政機構改革問題之檢討	鄭宏述	東方雜誌	26—1	34:1
	國際政治之新趨勢	耿淡如	東方雜誌	26—1	34:2
	論民主政治	丁 平	清華週報	26—1	45:12

	現代獨裁政治述要	杜秀瓊	新北辰	26—1	3:1
	日本今後的政局	文　彪	申報週刊	26—2	2:6
	日本政治之動向	周伊武	外交評論	26—1	8:1
	日本政治的前途	秋　郎	中外問題	26—2	18:2
D 2:	鄒平實驗縣政的剖視	馬博丁	行政研究	26—1	2:1
	劃分地方政府行政費與事業費之檢討	董修甲	行政研究	26—2	2:2
D 3:	事務官的保障問題	沈乘龍	行政研究	26—1	2:1
	怎樣增進公務員的工作興趣	張金鑑	行政研究	26—1	2:1
	青年心理研究	朱自蘋	青年月刊	26—1	3:4
D 4:	省市購辦制度之檢視	孫澄方	行政研究	26—2	2:2
D 5:	美國使舘人員之致選制度	朱馭歐	行政研究	26—2	2:2
	介紹英國公務員制度	任家誠	管理	26—2	1:5
	中國司法制度	阮毅成	廣播週報	26—1	122
	日本憲法論	隴本英雄	時事類編	26—2	5:4
	廿五年之所得稅法則	陳岱孫	社會科學	26 | 1	2:2
	中國憲法草案特色	吳經熊	中蘇文化	26—1	2:1
D 6:	論行政處分之拘束力	徐道隣	行政研究	26—2	2:1
	議官等官俸	錢端升	行政研究	26—2	2:1
	日本政治支配形態與軍事法西化	小岩井淨	時事類編	26—1	5:1
	戰時政府的行政組織	孫慕迦	行政研究	26—2	2:2
	戰時政府的特徵	莫寒竹	政問週刊	26—1	55
	五權憲法中之行政權	金鳴盛	東方雜誌	26—2	34

E 類

E 1:	財政劃分類	董問樵	民族雜誌	26—2	5:2
	讀廿三年度財政報告	褚匯宗	錢業月報	26—2	17:2
	非常時期之經濟統制	童世芳	青年月刊	26—1	3:4
	實施財政收支系統法的研究	林鐘秀	商業月報	26　1	1:1
	一年來之中國經濟	范苑聲	中國經濟	26—1	5:1

分類索引

	中國非常時期財政之出路	劉世仁	中國建設	26—2	15:2
	中國非常時期財政之出路	劉念中	中國要設	26—2	15:2
	中國非常時報財政之出路	劉星晨	中國建設	26—2	15:2
	非常時財政與國民經濟建設	胡亦山	中國建設	26—2	15:2
	非常時我國財政之肆應	梁登高	中國建設	26—2	15:2
	中國財政的回顧與展望	鄭森禹	錢業月報	26—1	17:1
	浙江一年來財政設施概況		浙江建設	26—1	10:7
	現代財政新原則及最近日本稅制改革之鳥瞰	壽景偉	東方雜誌	26—1	34:1
	中國財政的新階段	崔敬伯	月報	26—1	1:1
	中國財政之劃時代的展開	崔敬伯	國聞週報	26—1	14:1
	如何打破中國財政難關	唐宗蔭	民族雜誌	26—1	5:1
	中國戰時財政的一個切實方案	朱　偰	東方雜誌	26—1	34:1
	中國平時和戰時財政問題	千家駒	東方雜誌	26—1	34:1
	廿五年度財政收支狀況		正風半月刊	26—1	3:11
	廿六年度財政的展望	要家珂	綢繆月刊	26—1	3:5
	國民政府之財政	蕭堯松	清華週刊	26—1	45:12
E 2:	日本新預算案之分析	昂　千	外交評論	26—1	8:1
	改善地方預算制度意見	董蒙正	銀行週報	26—2	21:7
	日本新預算的特徵		月報	26—1	1:1
	吾國現行預算制度之檢討及其應有之改進	唐休武	會計季刊	26—1	2:3
	日本新預算的解剖	趙俊生	中央時事週報	26—1	6:3
E 3:	家庭記帳之設計	朱愛廬	商專月刊	26—2	1:2
	編製物價指數選擇物品數研究	林鍾秀	商專月刊	26—1	1:1
	中國每日物價指數	吳大鈞	廣播週報	26—2	125
	統計方法論	朱君毅	青年月刊	26—1,2	3:4,5
	錢莊的內部管理與會計制度	魏友棐	錢業月報	26—2	17:2
	會計制度之設計問題	姚仰山	浙江財政	26—1	10:1
	縣之就地審計與集中審計	沙　莫	浙江財政	26—1	10:1

	會計年度改用曆年制之研討	林鍾秀	浙江財政	26—1	10:1
	全國各港輪船統計	編　者	航業月刊	26—1	4:6
	世界各國商船統計	編　者	航業月刊	26—1	4:6
	論江蘇省推行縣總會計制度之動機	黃啓超	會計季刊	26—1	2:3
	安徽地方總會計制度述要	汪友明	會計季刊	26—1	2:3
	改進吾國現行財產會計制度擬議	沈欽祥	會計季刊	26—1	2:3
	所得稅征課會計制度論	朱符遠	會計季刊	26—1	2:3
	所得稅第一類營業事業所得之會計原理研究	王逢章	會計季刊	26—1	2:3
	近兩年推進主計制度概況	聞亦有	會計季刊	26—1	2:3
	我國都市政府應採用成本會計制度	董修甲	道路週報	26—1	52:3
	所得稅實行後各業應編司業會計規程之建議	盛　寅	銀行週報	26—2	21:7
E 4:	讀廿四年度郵政儲金匯業事務年報感言	權　時	銀行週報	26—2	21:5
	中國債務行政之檢討	楊壽標	行政研究	26—2	2:2
	管理通貨與中國金融機構之改造	趙蘭坪	時事月報	26—2	6:2
	新貨幣政策實施一週年	林經英	社會科學	26—1	2:2
	金融季節之研究	王家棟	信託季刊	26—1	2:1
	近年美國之金融風潮及一九三五年銀行法述要	姚慶三	信託季刊	26—1	2:1
	美國各洲存款保證制度之研究	劉仲廉	信託季刊	26—1	2:1
	最近世界黃金之供給	馮秉坤	浙江財政	26—1	10:1
	最近各國之匯兌管理政策	唐季清	浙江財政	26—1	10:1
	一九三六年國際金融之回顧	程紹德	外交評論	26—1	8:2
	中國金融事業之展望	魏友棐	錢業月報	26—1	17:1
	經濟運動與金融業	朱宇蒼	錢業月報	26—2	17:2
	管理通貨之理論與實際	徐自昌	錢業月報	26—2	17:2
	廿五年份銀行業之回顧		中行月刊	26—1,2	14:1,2
	廿五年份上海金融市場之回顧		中行月刊	26—1,2	14:1,2
	戰時財政金融概論	鍾光祖	中國建設	26—2	15:2
	戰時金融的特殊性	劉耀榮	中國建設	26—2	15:2

	農業金融論	邱 燻	華年	26—1	6:2
	一年來新幣制政策對于全國經濟之影響	唐廣永	中國經濟	26—1	1:4
	廿五年銀行對農業投資狀況	慕 傑	商專月刊	26—1	1:1
	廿五年上海儲蓄銀行之進展	丁瑞芬	商專月刊	26—1	1:1
	新幣制下金融之進展	受 百	商業月報	26—1	17:1
	救亡時期的金融政策	李蔭南	中華月報	26—1	5:1
	金集團組織崩潰之檢討	陶中安	中國經濟	26—1	5:1
	金集團的崩潰對中國的影響	袁 釗	銀行周報	26—1	21:3
	日本滙兌管理的强化	希 超	國聞周報	26—1	14:5
	日本强化管理匯兌的前途	魏友棐	國聞周報	26—1	14:5
	日本强化管理匯兌的展望	文 彪	申報周刊	26—1	2:4
	一年來的國際金融	徐自昌	中央時事周報	26—1	6:1
	一九三六年世界金融概觀	侯樹彤等	外交月報	26—1	10:1
	一年來金融紀要	潘恆敏	金融周報	26—1	3:1,2
	一年來之拆息與票據交換	陳天表	金融周報	26—1	3:1,2
	上海金融之季節變務	吳大業著	政治經濟學報	26—1	5:2
	江蘇金融資本之新形態及其應有之動向	姚曉廉	銀行周報	26—2	21:4
	通貨管理與貿易統制	傅堅白	金融周報	26—1	3:4
	管理通貨與吾國金融機構之改進	趙蘭坪	時事月報	26—2	16:2
	中國債務行政之檢討	楊壽標	行政研究	26—2	2:2
	中國國債總數		中外經濟拔萃月刊	26—1	1:1
	市債問題檢討	陳主懋	市政評論	26 2	5:2
E 5:	我國徵收遺產稅之管見	馬雄軍	商專月刊	26—2	1:2
	國民對于所得稅之認識	孫嵩齡	青年月刊	26—1	3:4
	非常資產稅	周學謙	中國建設	26—2	15:2
	今日世界經濟與中國經濟	莫 湮	錢業月報	26—1	17:1
	中國經濟的回顧	陳叔溫	錢業月報	26—1	17:1
	整理舊稅與開征新稅	楚 聲	錢業月報	26—2	17:2

所得稅與地方財政	董修甲	信託季刊	26—1	2:1
所得稅暫行條例之分析與批評	朱通九	信託季刊	26—1	2:1
中國遺產稅制度之商榷	朱 楔	時事月報	26—2	6:2
所得稅實行後應編新複利年金表之建議	李鴻壽	銀行周報	26—2	21:5
粵請求洋米免稅問題	權 時	銀行周報	26—2	21:4
上海市商會所得稅問題研究會議決案之總檢討		銀行周報	26—2	21:5
民國廿五年全國關稅收支狀況		浙江經濟情報	26—1	2:2
一年來之關稅收支狀況		國際貿易情報	26—1	2:1
華北走私之嚴重	大 槃	申報周刊	26—2	2:7
所得稅概說	王蘊玉	商學期刊	26—2	1:1
所得稅問題		中外經濟拔萃月刊	26—1	1:1
各地商會對于修改所得稅問題研究會議決案之總檢討		銀行周報	26—2	21:6
遺產稅研究	侯仲桓	商學期刊	26—2	1:1
遺產稅與不動產估價問題	金國寶	社會經濟月報	26—1	4:1

管理

二月刊

第二卷 第二期 二十六年七月

本期要目

交通大學管理學院編輯

管理二月刊

第二卷 第二期
民國二十六年七月

目錄

論著

譯述

演講

論　著

送別本屆畢業同學 (B 6.)

鍾偉成

諸君經四年之努力，終於得到今天的收穫，這是値得我們向諸君慶賀的。自今日起，諸君求學的梯階暫時可算告一結束；此後諸君努力的方向當然在於擇業與做事。說得再莊重點，諸君此後最大的問題，卽是建立畢身的事業。

交通大學因她所負特殊的使命，所設特殊的學科，所以諸君大部份都已擇定鐵路爲終身事業。學而能致用，是人生一大快事；而况政府當局正在建設新路廣羅人才，諸君事業前途，可以說是十分光明。

求學的成功途徑在于深思勤學，卽孔子所謂「學而不思則罔，思而不學則殆」，學與思必須相輔而行。做事的成功秘訣，在于深思力行；行與思也是不可偏廢的。諸君初入鐵路服務，第一固然要下決心努力工作，但是求學時代所練習的深思習慣，仍然要繼續培養。孟子說過：「行之而不著焉，習矣而不察焉，終身由之而不知其道者衆矣」，這種人在社會上是隨時隨地可以碰到的。在鐵路上，好些員工祇知緊守長官命令絲毫不加思索不知所云地埋頭苦幹；這種人誠然是勞苦，但於鐵路却并不算功高，有時甚而至于賣力不討好，對於鐵路，對於社會反而有害。這種人刻苦耐勞絕對服從的精神，固可值得我們敬佩，然而我們不可不知道這種人工作效能之高下，是要完全靠着長官之能力而決定。果指揮的長官是十二分細心，所指示的方法又是十二分地精密，此輩之工作效能，或可十分滿意。如果指揮者稍有疏漏，外立的環境稍有變更，便隨時可以敗事，小則僅僅影響鐵路本身，大則有害於社會。所以諸君初入鐵路，雖然第一要下決心力行；但是要想眞有貢獻於鐵路，除了力行之外，還得時時磨練你的思想。一個大學畢業生的學問，眼光，理解力，分析力自然要比一班沒有受過高等教育的人高強一些，因此想像的能力已必然地比人家高一些。我并不是說沒有受過大學教育的人不能思想；也不敢說受過高等教育的人都有思想；可是一個受過高等教育的人，假使更富於直覺習於深思，他的思想比較未受過高等教育的人來得獨到；這種思想可以說是比較上多具建設性；這一層我想誰都不能否認的。因此我希望鐵路當局能充份利用這一班大學畢業生，拿做事的機會來鼓勵他們向上。如果以大學生可做的事讓中學生去担任，開支上一時雖或可稍有節省，但總結果是決不會經濟的。

鐵路事業至為繁複，諸君在學校所受書本上基本知識決然不能夠用，因此諸君要想在鐵路上有所建樹，必須要時時刻刻追求新知。經驗愈多，知識愈豐富，知識愈豐富，思想愈周到工作成績自然會卓越過人。深思力行仍然要先從求知做起，中庸所謂：「博學，審問，愼思，明辨，篤行，」大學所謂：「欲誠其意者先致其知，致知在格物，物格然後知至」，所以博學致知，無疑地是深思力行之根本。

求知之不二方法，即是事事須從下層工作做起，然後一步一步地向上。每做過一種事，即增加一種經驗，這樣逐漸累積起來，你的鐵路知識，自然融會貫通，應用起來，自然會左右逢源。等到你有機會做一部份首領或全部份首領的時候，你的屬下知道你曾經事事經歷過，他們自然不敢朦弊，自然會樂爲爾用。青年人大抵好勝心極盛，總不免希望一入世途，馬上通顯；什麼事都想一帆風順，悉如己意。這種心理，不知耽誤了多少青年，埋葬了多少功業。嫉世，悲觀，自放等種種罪惡，都是名場頓挫必然的現象。我們要明白平步青雲的青年不是沒有，然而千萬人中能有幾人，這種例外的倖運，值不得我們羨慕，更值不得追求。倖運是可遇而不可求；但是機會是可求而又可遇的，自求向上之機會條件有三：(一)要你能自別于人；(二)要你能時時刻刻有準備；(三)要你能有耐心去等。工作成績，學識，品格，體魄都是自別于人主要因素。小而至於儀容，談吐，運動，音樂及戲劇藝能等等均足以引起他人對爾良好之印象。總而言之，能自別于人方能引起他人之注意。有美國青年某初入某大公司辦事，日與其同事數百人稠坐一大辦公室中工作。適巧此君之寫字檯位於走道之旁，爲總經理每日所必經由之路，此君次日上班衣深紅背心據案工作。總理過其旁，見此鮮明觸目之紅色背心，隨即加以傳喚，詢以何故服裝奇異。此君笑對曰，「爲欲使汝確知本公司中尙有某在耳」，此君後來竟然因此而受知于總理，得發揮其才能而致于通達。可見一衣之微，亦足以引人注意。此人之手段，雖卑不足取法，然亦可謂苦求機會。機會之來，遲早不可預定，吾人應絕對自信我之機會必有降臨之一日。因而時時自作準備。美國潘雪凡尼鐵路公司前有總理富而登君（S.E. Felton）初年任該路一分工務段長，碌碌無所見長，一夕，段中有一雙軌大橋忽遇火焚。次晨六時富君即集工就山伐木，迨至午後工務處長來勘，知新橋之設計與施工準備，早已完全妥帖。又某年美國擘此堡城Pittsburgh 羣衆對鐵路示威，終之以暴動，有多人擁入車場，見物即燬，車務段長某君，預知或將有變，先時將滿裝貴重物品之列車多列拉入山洞。更組織員工四周保護，因而得免于難。兩君若非平日有備無患，決不致於成功。上述兩事，足見鐵路機會所在皆是，所要在平時準備與耐心等候耳。

做事最困難的一點，即是對人。往往在學校內成績優異者到社會上做事竟爾成績平常；反之，有些在學校時成績平凡，一到社會做事倒反成績優異。其中重要關鍵，可以說是在于善于對人與不善于對人。諸君入鉄路服務，上有長官，下有工友，內有同事，外有顧客，日日所接觸的人，何止千百。對像既如此之廣，應付當然不是一件容易事。然而假使我們處處能克己服禮，處處先爲對方一着想——人家的立場，人家的見解以及人家的困難。能如此，你對于長官或同事間之誤會，自然不致發生。兩方面的信仰，自然能以樹立。我以爲應付人事最要條件卽是知人，能知人然後可望見知于人。見知于人的方法在上文已經說過，要求爲可知要自別于人。換言之，卽是要培養自己的人格——學問、才力不算數，還要能處處接物處世合乎人情。不但使人敬佩你的才學而且歡喜你的爲人，冷酷與違反人情之長官決難得下屬之忠心亦決不能馭衆，同樣的，青年人初出問世單憑學問竟爾時時存一種「固」「我」觀念亦決難遇長官之歡心，同僚之同情，因而也不能獲得升遷之機會。

我以爲在鐵路服務之青年至少須具有下列條件：(一)誠實不欺，(二)工作正確，(三)辦事勤肯，(四)學識充裕，(五)精神愉快。近年來國內各鐵路用人行政雖漸上常軌，然舞弊之事不免仍時有所聞。尤以買材料收回扣引誘性爲最大，事前既不露痕跡。事後更難于追究。諸君遇此務須特別注意。其次鐵路工程與營業有絕對準確之必要，毫厘之差會闖大禍。因此鐵路員工——尤其是担任下層工作者，必須具事事準確之習慣，馬虎的人絕難在鐵路立足的。辦事正確與工作勤肯又是互爲因果，眞勤于所事者不肯馬虎的。更次，諸君到路工作當然以學校所習爲基本學識，此書本知識必得時時以經驗對證方能充分領悟。再則鐵路學科範圍至廣，諸君所知當屬有限，虛心求知是必要的。如其以問人可恥，以所足已足，甚而至於强以不知爲知。是可謂自暴自棄。最後青年人初到社會無論對人對事，務須以愉快之態度出之。孔子曰：「君子坦蕩蕩，小人常戚戚。」俗語所謂「哭喪面孔卽是失敗之照會」。

除上述五者外，諸君將來欲圖非常之成功，仍必以深思爲根本。每遇一問題思所以解決之，每思一事思所以改進之。富於思想者終有一日成領袖；拙於思想者雖上述五德俱備，亦不足言非常之功，辦理例行事務，雖綽乎有餘，付以大事則決難勝任。惟深思力行方足以任重致遠。

俸給釐訂之原則 (D 3.)

林叠

在人事行政之實施中，目今最重要之點爲公務員工作之激勵(Incentive)。激勵之法不一端，較爲主要者厥有三種，一、俸給釐訂之公平，二、考績獎懲之嚴正，三、退休制度之確定。三者之處置與人員之管理關係最切，蓋行之得當，可以鼓勵公務員上進之意向，間接的推進行政效率；行之失當，常可以引起公務員間嫉視不滿之心理，結果非特無以促激勵之效，益將因而發生種種紛擾，求其功效之彰不可得，轉而適以造成陋政之端，是激勵方策之採取，不可不審愼其得失及利害也。

三者之中，尤以俸給釐訂之公平爲尤要，蓋人員之供職政府，雖所以發揮其能力以效勞國家，而最大之目的，無非藉工作而維持其生活，故公務員與勞工之地位雖不同，其爲生活而奮鬥則一。今者勞資間之關係常因工資之不能調協而發生種種糾紛，成爲社會人士着眼之中心。而公務員因俸給之不足而釀成風潮之舉，則尚不多覯，因之一般執政人員誤認爲俸給之分配已極公平，然不知公務員有其智識之修養，地位之牽制，其不滿之表示，常潛伏于各個人之心，或怠於所務，放棄其忠矢之誠意，或故意作祟，以洩其鬱鬱之忿，其發也漸，而其禍之烈雖工潮之橫生，不可及也。

俸給與工資之差別

俸給與工資性質之漸見符合，爲最近厘訂俸給原則之根據。故我人在科學管理之原則下，研究俸給之厘訂，不可不注意工資決定之原則。先請討論二者差異關係之演進。

俸給與工資之差別，在昔極爲明顯，蓋「官」與「民」絕對劃分，所享之權利不同，所處之地位不同，諸有以形成公務員優越性之現象，因之俸給之授受並非表示服役勞務之酬報，而爲一種維持其地位之贍養金，以與視勞力爲商品之工資學說相劃分。

至十九世紀之初，俸給之形態更有一新奇之發展，蓋此時方當資本主義之發軔，功利主義(Utilitarian)之盛倡，邊沁(Jeremy Benthan)之義務勞動說風行一時，政府官職均尚榮譽而無俸給之供應，因之担任種種政府工作者均爲地方碩望，富有資產之階級，無產平民之執政幾成絕響，觀其發展誠非無因，蓋可以符合物競天擇，優勝劣敗之資本主義原則也。當時英國各級重要公務員每多援用此例，凡著者爲倫敦市長，蓋至今仍爲無給職也。主張此種制度者所持之理由，以爲政府左右全國事務，握人民生殺之權，如此重要之事務，應以社會地位崇高之人士担任，以免發生營私舞弊之習尙。當時之名流固皆爲資本家也，無形之中造成資本階級專政之現象。然則義務勞動之說固未必盡然也，蓋金錢無絕對的邊際效用，貧者誠汲汲乎求之，以增進其生活上之享受，與以就任公務員之機會，誠將變本加厲，以隨其貪得之目的；富者亦未嘗棄金錢若敝屣也，亦未必能淸廉自守。蓋貧者求富，富者求益富，以至於無限，如制度之不良，內部牽制之不密，其欲藉機而貪得，以償其私慾者，貧富固無殊也。且因富者之專政，人才之選拔致極有限制，顯已反乎人才主義之原則，故自十九世紀之後，民主政治之替興，社會主義之勃發，中下階級之抬頭，此種義務務動之說遂並時代而逝去。

至於最近，社會主義學說之紹介，俸給與工資意義之解說益趨于接近，蓋政府人員不過爲社會之一份子而已，其所處之地位與工廠之職工無殊，其俸給亦不過代表其服務所應得之報酬而已，故經濟學家衞拿納(Adolf Wagner)等均認爲工資與俸給有相同意之點二者實非對立，而俸給可謂工資之一較爲特殊者。

然則在今日之觀點下，工資與俸給亦有其相異之處乎，曰有之，俸給舍酬報其勞務外，並須維持其相當之地位，以鼓勵發揮其廉潔之精神。雖然使就世界各國俸給之現狀觀之，此說僅不過爲一種理論而已，蓋無論英美以及加拿大等國(一)，公務員之俸給常較實業人員之薪給爲低，我國雖工商業不發達，此種現象亦有所見，求其二者之平衡尚不可得，更無論俸給之優越矣。

俸給與工資之高低，常可造成公私事業對于任用人才之爭執，然則公私事業均與國計民生切切相關，求其合作奮進之不遑，更何可重而造成不相調協之結果。最近有知之士，不特已深覺二者有合理的分工之必要，抑更進而主張互相流轉，俾可交換人才，增進生產及施政效能，今設二者之報酬相別天壤，則已處優越地位之幹練企業家，更何願棄其成功而他向，如是則流動之法將不能進行，求其利不能反而爲發展之彰礙，此我人研究人事行政者所不能不加以切實注意者也。

決定俸給之要素

天下無絕對公平之俸給，厘訂之公平與否僅可就程度上之深淺別之。蓋即以生活費一項而言，往往隨時間空間而變易，欲求其平衡穩定不可得也。要之，我人如能比較的尋求厘訂應行注意之點，使適合此假定，即可謂爲滿意。俸給與其他社會關係不能分離，故其厘訂常與社會政策與習慣，勞工之生產能力及供求等等發生連繫，茲數者實爲厘訂俸給時所不能不加攷慮者，易言之，我人可名之爲厘訂俸給之要素。試再歸納言之，可別爲二大要素，曰經濟的與社會的。

在私營企業中勞工之勞務往往可以生產之數量及利潤獲得之數額表示之，蓋生產事業爲物質的有形的，計算其成績，並無困難也，然在公營之事業中，公務員對於國家社會以及國民之貢獻多少，不能有確切之估計，如私營企業之生產數量及利潤然，因之俸給之給付更不能以進益之多寡而作合理的分配。且也政府事業往往有獨占性的，無競爭之現象，不能藉比較而斷其優劣，不若在工商業之廣場中，競爭劇烈，優勝劣敗，顯而易見，因之俸給之定，亦不若私業企業對於勞工之適合邊際生產說(Marginal productivity theory)。俸給之決定可與整個政府經濟關係發生關聯之處僅在國家歲入之多寡上。從此點觀之，俸給之釐訂似與經濟原素無深切關係。然則不然。我人於前一、則中已提及現在及過去私營企業之工資常較俸給爲高，造成才能卓越公務員離職他去之現象，致使公私事業對於人才之爭執，試反而言之，如俸給高出工資極多，則人將競騖於功名，而使私營企業發生人才之恐慌，其對於整個社會之影響，正與公務員之離職相同。故爲調節計俸給之決定不可不以工資之率爲參考。換言之，工資因市場懋遷及供求之多寡而有伸縮，則公務員之俸給亦應隨而調整，庶可造成二者之貫通，以流轉二者之關係。然此種辦法亦有事實上之困難，最顯著者工資之率頗不易決定，而尤以特種性質之事務爲甚。蓋各地情形不同，工資亦有高低，各人能力不同，工資亦有多少，勉强用平均之方法裁斷之爲工資普遍之比率，於理似有欠通，自不能更以之介紹于俸給之決定之也。抑又有進者，私營企業之事務並不與政府之事業相同，工作之不同，性質之各異，加以比較，實違乎統計之原則，徒作不合理之推敲，不如放棄之爲愈，以是觀之，經濟之要素雖爲釐訂俸給應加注意之點，然因事實上之困難，仍使我人有無以着手之感。

從社會的要素上觀，我人於公務員俸給之釐訂時須顧及其自存養家之能力，豐裕其收入，以安其服務之心。故此種俸給厘訂之標準爲適合其生活標準(Standard of living)，我人在科學管理中稱之爲最低生活工資(Minimum living wage)，其基點完全出于社會之論理，而與經濟要素之適合邊際生產說(Marginal productivity theory)者不同。

俸給厘訂之基于生活標準在公務員方面觀之，可謂顧慮週到，理直氣當，無瑕可擊，然從整個政府之管理上觀之，尚有不安之處，請討論之如下：

一、各地商業繁榮之程度不同，農業與工業之地帶，更有絕大之差異，因之生活標準各各不同，苟我人放棄此實際上之差異不同，而貿然訂一全國一致之俸給率，則生活標準較低之地方將無形中獲得提高俸給之利益，或反之，於理既有欠當，政府預算之分配更將有不合理之結果。且也因生活標準不同而俸給相問，狡黠之流更將乘機避重就輕，設法服務于生活標準較爲低落之地帶，如是則全國人才之分配將失其公平之論據。美國近數年來有心國政之人目擊私營企業工資給付之不公，嘗屢議決定最低俸給之率，然而久久不行者，其所見蓋與我人之所慮者相同。

二、政府對俸給之支配，當與其歲入相應，故如俸給過於重視公務員之生活標準而失預算平衡之旨，當非我人所企求，同時最低生活俸給之厘訂完全基于公務員之生活福利，對於其工作之優劣無兼顧之暇，亦非淬勵服務之道。

爲補救此種缺憾計，我人於俸給之釐訂，誠宜注意其經濟化及社會化，而於工作能力，工作情形更不可不作相當之攷慮。公務員之地位更宜與俸給之收入相當，蓋地位有高低，其生活之所需因是亦不能避免差異，所謂生活標準誠不能一概言之也。

生活費用與俸給

前述之最低生活工資之法雖其定義未見確切，施行時難免困難，然以整個社會之福利觀之，當不失爲一良好之釐訂方法。我人對此種俸給之釐訂乃根據生活標準（如前述），而所謂換言之，即其所入應與最近之生活所需相適應，故我人於俸給釐訂之時當注意及生活費用之比率（表示生活費用之比率者爲生活費指數）。

大戰而後，二十年來社會上有劇烈之變化，尤以交通之便捷，商業上之盛衰常可頃刻間影響全國甚或全世界，因之物價上落無定，生活之費用亦受直接及間接之影響，此種變端輒與公務員之俸給以極大之影響，蓋如物價高漲，生活費用隨而上升，而俸給不增，則公務員之金錢收益（Money income）雖仍舊觀，而實在之收益（Real income）將日見減低也。職是之故，爲維持公務員之生活計，不得不逐漸增加其金錢之收益，以求實在收益之穩定。美國近年來對于此點常下以極大之努力，故生活費指數與俸給之率能約略相應，使實在收益不致發生慘烈之暴跌，而影響公務員之生活。然就事實上觀之，俸給之調整仍不若工資爲積極，舍一九三〇年後商業不景氣，工資之率一蹶不振。自一九一四起至一九三〇年之工資率常高于俸給率，近數年之低落爲一種循環變化（Cyclical Change），不能據爲定論，就大體觀之工資之率仍高于俸給也。茲附表如下：(二)

公務員及職工平均收入之變動與生活費指數表

年份	平均收入指數 1914＝100				生活費指數
	聯邦行政人員	郵政人員	一切製造業工人	低級男工	1914＝100
1914	100	100	100	100	100
1920	145	159	231	246	206
1922	143	159	192	189	165
1924	154	167	209	209	169
1926	160	184	216	217	174
1928	171	187	220	223	171
1929	181	190	225	228	171
1930	185	190	204	205	166
1931	189	189	179	179	152
1932	175	178	135	136	137
1933	160	166	139	139	131

我國對於公務員之俸給向未下以具體的研究，故歷年俸給率之增減未見有翔實確切之計算。以觀察所得加以估計，則數年之俸給實未有若何增進，反觀生活費指數則十餘年已有增加，尤以最近爲著，去年新貨幣政策實行，物價高漲，商業雖有起色，月受薪俸之人員則未受得任何金錢上之增加，近年以來實在進益之減低可無疑義（附上海歷年生活費指數表以供參攷）。在此種情形下，我國俸給應否調整，不問可知。

上海歷年生活費指數變動表（以一九二六年爲基年）(三)

年份	生活費指數
1926	100
1927	016.7
1928	102.5
1929	107.9
1930	121.8
1931	125·9
1932	119.1
1933	107.2
1934	106.2
1935	106.6
1936	113.3
1937（三個月之平均）	119.0

調整俸給之補救方法

社會之生活標準既因時代之流轉而有變化，而變化又若是其速，欲求俸給能無時無刻不與生活標準相吻合，乃爲不可能之事。且俸給之釐訂决非草率之間可以决定而應經過適法之手續，如欲隨時因生活標準之轉移而修致，則一修正之方案方告通過，社會之情形已經大變，求其適合已失其時。時間上之不能湊合，手續上之麻煩，確爲『最低生活工資』釐訂之事實上困難。

爲解决此種困難，我一人可採用英國所盛行之滑準制(Sliding Scale)其法爲利用津貼之給予，譬如某期之俸給率與生活費用指數相當，一年後生活費指數增加百分之十，則俸給亦應有相等之增加，爲避免立法上之週折，名其所增加之部份爲生活費津貼，每年於三月一日及九月一日計算，其增减之數，根據俸給之多寡。其理論爲收入較優者原則上每月應有餘裕，不致因生活費之增加而受影響，故不必予以補償。法國亦有相似之津貼。然其增加之數額並不根據俸給，而予各公務員以相同之整數，名爲生活費補償金 (Indemnités de résidence)(四)。

法國舍生活費補償金外，更有一種所謂家庭負担補償金 (Indemnités pour chargés de famille)，此種補償金之給予係因公務員子女兄弟之逐漸增加而生，故其所給之率並不以俸給之多寡爲比例，而隨家庭份子之增加，累進的給予。此種政策之採取有兩重意義，一爲鼓勵公務員服務之忠心，一爲刺激國家生殖率。其實行及調查之制度至爲嚴密，故已成爲世界人事行政中一可述之點(五)。

我國對於此種補救，不特不爲政府所採取，抑且不爲行政學者所注意，故可謂十分新穎。然如他日行政方法日見改良，人事行政漸見進步，深信此種方法必可得熱烈之同情。

釐訂俸給與職位分類

上述釐訂俸給之要素乃爲理論上之觀察，最終之歸結我人仍着眼于俸給與工作相當一點上。同職同俸，爲人事行政中堅定不易之律，蓋職既相同，責任相若，能力相若，其所處之地位亦必所差不多，予以同俸，必較妥適也。爲當應此原則我人不得不先事愼爲劃分職位以合理之分職，以爲決定俸給之助。

我國職位分類原則上尙不能稱爲合理，而此不合理之分類竟亦不能普遍應用于全國一切政府事業，因之俸給之分配可謂絕不公平，而尤著者爲關、郵、鐵諸政人事系統之獨立。

所謂原則上之不合理者蓋指分等之方法而言，我國之分等既不基于責任之輕重、更不基于職務之難易，稱之爲歐陸之制(歐陸以責任之不同分等)不可，稱之爲美國之制（美國以職務之不同分職）更不可。此種傍徨歧途之分等辦法，何能企求合理之俸給釐訂。故我國對於俸給釐訂之不當，雖不能完全歸咎于分等之不科學化，苟我人能設法改善職位分類之方法，則俸給之釐訂亦可隨而有好轉之結果。(職位分類之研究可參攷本刊第一卷第四期)

(一)W. E. Mosher & J. D. Kingsley Public Personnel Administration (Harper & Brothers Publishers, New York, 1936), p. 395.

W. A. Robson, "The Public Service", The Political Quarterly, Aprie-June, 1936, (MacMillan Co., London) p. 190

R. M. Dawson The Civil Service of Canada (Oxford University Press, London, 1929), p. 176

(二) Report of the Commission of Inquiry on Public Service Personnel Better Government Personnel (Mc Graw-Hill Book Co., New York, 1935) pp. 161, 162.

(三)國定稅則委員會編製，刊於中央銀行月報第六卷第四號(中央銀行經濟研究處，上海)第七六九頁

(四)W. R. Sharp, "Public Personnel Management in France", Civil Service Abroad, edited by L. D. White, C. H. Bland, W. S. Sharp. F. M. Marx (McGraw-Hill Cor., New York, 1935), p. 123.

(五)Ibid., p. 123.

本院教員中文著作一覽表

林 蔭 行政學大綱（南京華僑半月刊社，民國二十四年）定價一元

沈奏廷 鐵路問題討論集（上海商務印書館，民國二十五年）定價一元五角

沈奏廷 鐵路運價之理論與實際（大學叢書）（上海商務印書館，民國二十四年）定價二元五角

沈奏廷 鐵路貨運業務（大學叢書）（上海商務印書館）民國二十四年定價一元五角

沈奏廷 鐵路經濟論文集（上海中國鐵道運輸學會，民國二十三年）定價八角

俞希稷 匯兌論（上海商務印書館，民國十四年）定價九角

夏晉麟 上海租界問題（上海太平洋國交討論會，民國二十年）定價二角

鍾偉成編 鐵道經濟論叢（上海交通大學管理學院，民國二十二年）定價二角

鍾偉成 鐵道材料管理（在印刷中）

熊大惠 運輸學水道編（上海交通大學管理學院代售，民國二十三年）定價平裝二元五角，精裝三元

王炳南 熊大惠 合著 公路運輸（在印刷中）

王同文 東北鐵路問題之研究，上下二冊（管理學院叢書）（上海交通大學管理學院，民國二十二年）實價一元二角

崔曉岑 中央銀行論（大學叢書）（上海商務印書館，民國二十四年）定價平裝二元二角，精裝三元二角

崔曉岑 幣制與銀行（上海生活書店代售，民國二十五年）定價平裝一元五角，精裝二元五角

吾國鐵路實行貨物夜間裝卸制度之商討（C. S.）

沈奏廷

鐵路運輸工作原應日夜川流不息，無時或輟，如行車、調車、以及旅客站務皆係二十四小時連續進行，鮮有中斷者，惟貨站裝卸及收交貨物之工作，大都均以日間爲限，蓋貨車以日間裝卸夜間行駛爲原則，而客商之送貨提貨，又宜於日間爲之，故貨站之開夜工者殊鮮其例，有之亦惟限於一部分必要之事務，如美國鐵路對於到達之零貨，有於夜間製填收費單據 Expense pills 以便清晨卸車交貨者，但裝卸工作仍於日間爲之。吾國鐵路現爲增加車輛利用提速貨物運輸起見，乃有實行夜間裝卸之議，有已進行實施者，有尚在擬議中者，其爲得爲失，尚無人加以討論，爰特提出此點，申述管見，以就正於讀者。

按夜間裝卸之辦法，在西國鐵路尚未之見，有之則爲鮮果蔬菜等物有於夜間卸入棧台以便翌日清晨進行拍賣手續者，其他貨物，無論零担整車，要皆於日間裝卸之。以言零担，貨棧莫不隨到隨收，隨收隨磅，隨磅隨裝，夫收貨既限於日間（夜間重車出發在途行駛），而收貨裝車既在同一時刻進行，是裝車工作決不至延至夜間爲之，其理甚明，此就起運之零担貨物而言也。至若到達之零貨，亦均於清晨或夜間到達終點大站（終點大站非路線之盡頭處，乃列車之終點站），例於上午卸事，更無夜間工作之必要。以言整車，則貨物多由客商自裝自卸，除私有岔道之貨物得由貨主隨時處理外，所有公共岔道 Public team tracks 貨物之裝卸均在日間行之，因運往終點大站之貨車多數於夜間或侵晨到達，而由終點大站出發之貨車又多數於夜間或傍晚挂出，故裝卸工作儘可於日間進行，無須夜以繼日，徒增路方之耗費；且日間裝卸於鐵路固屬經濟，於客商亦屬便利，否則夜間裝卸，日間運送，一反其道而行之，則必發生下列諸弊：卽(一)日間行駛貨物列車太多，妨礙客車之運行，造成路線之擁擠；(二)貨站日夜工作，增加員工薪給之耗費；(三)客商於夜間送貨提貨，諸感未便；(四)夜間光線較差，輒易發生檢點錯誤，堆裝不妥等弊，使貨物之損失增多。有此數害，故貨物之裝卸類多以日間進行爲常例，不然，夜間裝卸制度必已盛行於西國鐵路矣。

吾國鐵路處理貨運之方法與西國鐵路逈然不同，故有以爲夜間裝卸不能適用於他國者可適用於吾國，茲將其主要之觀點列述於後，以便討論：

(一)吾國鐵路之起運零貨類多不採隨收隨裝之制，往往收到過磅以後，堆積貨位，集合一起裝車，且按現行辦法，須候貨票塡發後，對照貨票點裝，故若能於日間收貨，夜間裝車，則可不必待至翌日，以免妨礙翌日之收貨，并藉以趕速貨物之裝出。

(二)吾國鐵路之起運整車貨物，亦不如西國鐵路，隨送隨卽裝車，往往先由託運人將貨送站，堆存貨位，而後酌撥車輛裝載，各路以車輛缺乏，常多不能隨時撥車裝運，故存站待運之貨物爲數頗多，設有貨車於日間或傍晚卸空，儘可利用夜間光陰，將存站待運之貨裝入，以免空車停留過夜，徒多延擱，寧不於路於商皆有裨益。

(三)到達之貨，無論零担整車，在吾國鐵路均未必能於淸晨以前運抵大站，以備日間起卸，往往以列車時刻關係，於下午或傍晚運到，若不夜間卸車，又必使重車停留過夜，徒多延誤。

(四)吾國鐵路整車貨物之裝卸由路方工人辦理，不若西國鐵路之由客商自裝自卸，故客商儘可於日間送貨。日間提貨，而由鐵路於夜間裝車，夜間卸車，對於公衆，應無不便。

上列各種理由均係根據吾國鐵路之現實狀況，頗有一加討論之價値，謹就管見所及，一一爲申論於後：

(一)起運零貨之應隨收隨磅隨磅隨裝實爲鐵路處理貨運之不易原則，作者已屢作如是之主張，其詳細辦法已見拙著其他文內。(參閱拙著「改善吾國鐵路起運零貨處理方法之建議」，又拙著「參觀津浦膠濟兩路後之感想及意見」)吾國現有之裝車辦法須將貨物分別堆積貨位，并須候貨票塡發以後，集合裝車者，根本有改革之必要，卽根本不能作爲夜間裝車之理由。故零貨若於夜間裝車，不可謂非一種錯誤之措施，易言之，即以一種錯誤補救乃一種之錯誤而已。其爲得爲失，不待煩言而喻也。

（二）貨物列車刻之編排，應以大多數之貨車能於淸晨以前到達列車終點大站爲準繩，俾大多數之重車得於日間起卸，幷儘量當日卸後復裝，而於傍晚或夜間復行挂出行駛。若列車時刻編排失當，而欲以夜間裝卸之法從事補救，則倒果爲因，必無益而有害，蓋日間造成路線之擁擠，而夜間增加貨站之開支，有得不償失者在也。吾國鐵路之於此點，頗有加以檢點調整之必要，雖不能使全部貨車均於淸晨到達大站，全部貨物列車均於夜間行駛完畢，然應以大多數之貨車及貨物列車遵照此項原則運送爲目標，要無疑義也。

（三）貨物列車之時刻雖照上項原則規定，然其中必有一部分之貨車不能於侵晨以前到達大站者，亦有因貨物列車延誤時刻不能準時到達者，此種情形，在吾國鐵路決難避免，然則鐵路對於此種貨車，是否有實行夜間裝卸之必要，誠爲一大問題，管見對於此點擬貢述如下之意見：

（甲）實行夜間裝卸，非特須有裝卸二人，且檢貨起票等員工亦應加工雇用，若大多數貨車通常能於晨前到達，則爲局部少數貨車而開夜工，頗不値得；

（乙）若因列車延誤以致多數貨車不能準時到達，則非每日皆然，不能視爲常例，即不能每日加開夜工，以應付或有之延誤！且是否應在夜間卸裝，亦須視貨車裝卸後是否能卽行掛出，若仍須候翌日夜行列車掛運，則又何必汲汲若是，徒增貨站之開支。

（丙）我國鐵路貨車在站之延誤往往以候車掛出之時間爲最巨，其原因常在機車缺乏，或列車時刻不合，故趕速裝卸所省之時間，常爲候車掛出之延誤所消耗。今若實行夜間裝卸，則此弊尤必變本加厲。因大多數之貨物列車不宜於日間開出，尤以客運較繁之路爲甚，然則名爲減少車輛之滯延，實則多增貨站之開支而已。

由是以觀，夜間裝卸一法絕對不應適用於零貨，至於整車貨物，亦應從調整列車時刻以減少車輛之停留入手，不能以夜間裝卸之法代之，更不能以有夜間裝卸之故，反使列車時刻編排失當，以誤致誤。惟若遇非常情形，貨車急於卸載待用，且卸裝以後確能利用挂出時，則偶用夜間之法，臨時召集員工應付，亦屬權宜之策，有益之舉；若以夜間裝卸立爲一種經常之制度，與日間裝卸並重，則竊以爲未可也。

管理二月刊

第二卷第　期
民國二十六年四月

論著

譯述

演講

書評

美國貨運大站處理貨物事故之組織與方法（C 5.）

許靖

一 處理貨物事故之組織

在貨運上發生之多裝、少裝、遺失、損壞、以及被竊一類情事，皆爲貨物事故。運輸愈繁，事故發生之機會愈多，良以貨運情況複雜萬狀，自起運以至交貨，其間須經無數員工與無數手續，若在驗票、對貨、塡票、裝車、卸車、轉車、交貨種種方面稍一失愼，即有招致事故之可能。故貨物事故既不可絕對防止避免，亦不可聽其自然不加管理，吾人研究處理事故方法，其目的不僅止於明瞭如何依例辦理事故案件而已，尤在如何籌劃改進方策，積極養成各方員司認眞作事之精神，勿令同樣錯誤一再發生。所謂處理方法果能發揮如是偉大效用，方得謂有管理學上之價値，學者必須首先認淸此點，然後乃能了解處理貨物事故問題在管理學上所佔地位之重要性矣。

考美國鐵路處理貨物事故之組織，原有總局與外站之分，在總局者除有賠償處 Freight Claim Agent's Office專辦賠償損失案件外，尚有貨站及中轉站務管理處 Office of Superintendent Stations & Transfers，其職責則在綜合全路各站處理貨物事故狀況與夫指導各站改進防止事故發生之方法。至在局外最大車站，則亦有賠償處之組織，名曰 Local Claim Department，若夫答復商人問訊，追查失踪貨物，處理無人認領貨物，以及辦理車站範圍以內一切事故案件，乃其主要職務也。本文限於陳述站內組織及其管理方法，至總局貨站及中轉站務管理處之組織管理，則擬另文論之。

在最大貨運車站之賠償處，通常設正副主任各一人，名曰 Chief Claim Clerk 及 Assistant Chief Claim Clerk, 以下共有員司約五十餘人，分為若干小組，分別辦理各事。各組事務性質既殊，人數多寡亦不一致，大抵同一事務需要三人以上共同分担者，則可劃為一組，并設組長 Sub-head Clerk 一人，以便提綱挈領而專責成。核其全處職務，極為繁瑣，本文所陳，不過其中寥寥數端，餘則概俟另文補述。

二 到達零担貨物短少及多出事故之處理方法

零担貨物運抵到達站後，當在貨棧卸車，故其事故發現之地點，亦捨棧貨而莫屬也。惟貨棧之職責只在檢查貨物，及發現意外事故，至事故之應如何處理，則又責在車站內部之賠償處。茲就處理程序依次列述於后：

(一)卸車點單之審核及登記——零担貨物在貨棧卸車時，由卸車司事 Check Clerk 主持驗票對貨之事，凡貨物中遇有短少多出或損壞種種情節者，一概由其負責填入卸車總單 Tally Slips 及卸車點單 Tally Bills，前者每車一張，後者每批貨物一張。每車卸完以後，此等點單卽由卸車司事繳還貨棧辦公室，依照車號登記後，隨卽彙送站內賠償處。當由貨棧送到之際，先由組長Head OS&D Clerk簽收，并卽逐單審核，遇有事故各單，則用藍色鉛筆在各單上特加標記，以資注意而防止辦理之時發生遺漏。各單審核完畢，旋卽由其登入簿內，名曰貨棧卸車點單簿 House Tally Book，依單上車號最末一字記其車號，卸車日期及點單編號File Number。有此登記，則單簿分離以後，檢查仍極簡便，或由登記以查點單，或由點單而查登記及原裝車號，貨物種類件數等項，要皆不難一索而得。

（二）事故之查對及報告——卸車點單之性質，實爲車站處理貨物事故之初步基本單據，，一經如是登記完畢，卽行發交事故核對員 OS&D Clerks。核對員卽按收貨人姓名字母順次排列，再又記入多裝少裝簿 Over and Short Book內，然後以點單分彙置於查對架內Post Office Matching Boxes　如是則在同一站內發現之多出短少貨物，卽可在相當時日以內自行查出。蓋在甲車檢出之少短貨物，或卽乙車檢出之多出貨物，又或今日收到無票相隨之多裝貨物，明日或由起站接到補來之貨票，故爲避免枉費手續起見，不必遽爾填發正式事故報告，換言之，卽在正式向外發生報告以前，必須首先自行經過一番查對手續，如在相當時以內不能自行查出銷案，則再填造正式報告，繼續進行其他手續。請依短少事故之例述其大概辦法如后：

(1)由到達站填造短少貨物報告Short Report四份，以第一份寄總局貨站及中轉站務管理處，第二份寄主管段長，第三份寄起運站，第四份存站自用。

(2)總局站務管理處接到短少報告，亦可根據所報各項情節進行調對，蓋該處爲各站事故報告總匯之所，甲站之短少，或即乙站之多出，如有甲乙兩站所報告各種情節適相吻合，即可證明係屬同一事件，可以轉令兩站查照結案，此總局接到報告之大概作用也。

(3)起運站接到短少報告，如其不能查明錯誤原因，應即按照報告開列各項填妥，轉寄第一次轉車站 First-break-bulk point，再由該處依次轉送第二次轉車站，凡屬誤車經過轉換手續之車站，均應依次查明車站記錄填入，由最後之站寄回填發站。經過如是從頭至尾澈查辦法，則錯誤發生之地點不難綜合各方報告而得之矣。

(4)其存站一聯，則視貨物之最終到達站 Final destination 分爲兩類，以終于本站者爲一類，以仍須由本站繼續運出者另爲一類，前者按收貨人姓名字母次序排列，置於查對架內，後者則照到達站名字母次序分彙置於查對架內。對於多出報告亦在查對架內各置一份，於是凡屬一事之報告，經過如此集合核對考察辦法，常有不待向外調查即可自行了結之便利。

三 到達零担貨物損壞事故之處理方法

貨棧卸車司事發現貨物有損壞時，亦在卸車點單註明，賠償處接到此項點單後，應立即塡發損壞貨物報告Bad Order Report四份，以正張寄總局貨站及中轉站務管理處，第二份寄主管段長，第三份寄至發現損壞之前一裝車站或中轉站 Lastloading or transfer station that made no exception notation on waybill，其詳參閱後段，第四份存作本站辦案之用。

貨物損壞事故之性質，與貨物件數不符之事故大不相同，故其處理情形頗不一致。鐵路對於損壞貨物，重在確定損壞程度及查明發生原因，不似短少事故之須追究貨物，故卸車司事應對損壞之性質程度詳加批註，以爲將來決定賠償之參考，一面應於發現損壞後廿四小時內塡發正式報告，調查損壞發生之地點。惟貨物常有在中途經過多次中轉手續之情事，發現損壞之站，不必卽爲發生損壞之地，故損壞如非在本站卸車以後而發生者，則應向他站發出報告，查究損壞原因。至第三份報告交應寄至何站，則可頗堪研究之問題，此則必須設例如下分別說明之。

(一)假定某貨係由A站裝車起運，中間經過DG等地中轉手續，至抵K站，方始發現損壞，則前述第三份報告卽應寄至G站，蓋貨物如在D站轉車之後卽已發生損壞，則G站必可早已發覺，必已早在貨票之上加以批註。如在G站轉車之時尙無損壞發現，足證係在G站轉車之後方始發生，故應向G站發出報告，請其查究致損緣由。

(二)如損壞之發現在G站，則其致損之時間必在D站轉車以後，卽應向D站發出報告查究原因。

(三)如該車係由A站直達K站，其間並未經過DG兩地轉中。則該報告卽應寄至最初起運之裝車站A (Originating station) 以憑查究原因。

以上三種情形各異，寄法各有不同，茲再爲圖示於后，俾易了解。要之無論寄至何處，其接到報告之站，大抵卽爲應負損壞責任之站，應卽查究致壞原因，設法糾正錯誤。至總局接到損壞貨物報告，亦可據以研究致損緣由，熟籌改進方法，令行各站注意改正。如係由於行車震盪或調車不愼所致。則應令行關係各段設法查究矯正，以免同樣事故，再發生。

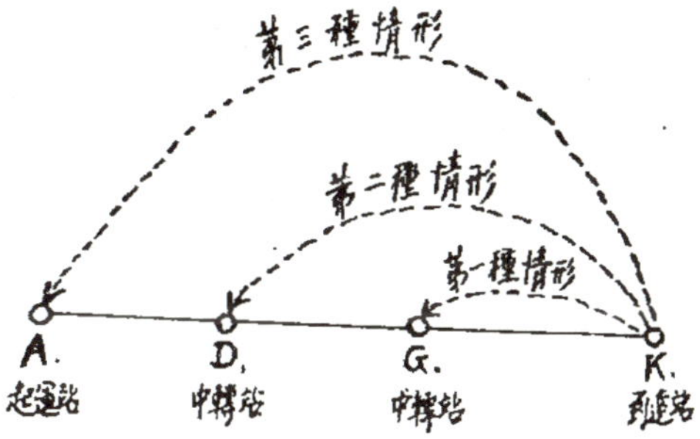

第三種情形
第二種情形
第一種情形
A. 起運站
D. 中轉站
G. 中轉站
K. 到達站

西　到達整車貨物事故之處理方法

整車貨物之裝卸事務，雖在西國例由商人自理，然在鐵路公用貨場 Team Tracks or Yard 卸車之時，仍有鐵路交貨司事到場交車監視卸貨，藉淸手續而明責任。遇有意外事故，例由交貨司事在交貨收據 Delivery Receipts or Sheets 之上詳加註明，并令提貨人簽收署名。此項交貨收據卽爲鐵路調查短小損壞事故原因之根據，亦爲將來決定損失賠償之重要證件，於每日交車卸貨之後，由貨場辦公室彙繳賠償處。

賠償處收到時，逐單詳加審核，對於發生事故之件，亦均特加標記，并按車號最末數字妥爲登記，然後發交核對員分途進行查對及塡發報告各種手續。其處理情形則與零担貨物事故大同小異，故不詳贅。

總上各種事故，統歸一組處理，約由七人分別担任，其組名爲Inbound L.C.L. and C.L. OS&D Division，凡屬到達貨物事故，無論關於零担整車，概由本組負責辦理。

五　查究貨物事故發生原因之方法與作用

貨運上無論發生任何事故，要皆不合運輸安全原則，於路於商，均爲不利。管理者一面固應設法補救，如當賠者之應從速決定賠償，短少者之應從速追查，同時仍須查究各種錯誤原因，以期一切同樣事故得以防於未然，全體事故得以逐漸減少，方爲管理之能事盡矣。

因欲實現上述管理功效，要以美國各路所行方法最爲周密，茲僅扼要舉述兩項如次，以資參考而供研究：

（一）上述總局之貨站及中轉站務管理處收到各站報告，除一面詳究事實確定責任而外，每日按照站別編製事故報告，名曰 Exception Reports Charged against……Station，內分（一）多出 Overs，（二）短少 Shorts，（三）損壞 Bad orders，（四）誤裝 Astrays 及（五）總計

Grand total等項，以一份存查，以一份發交各站。於是各站在同一期內發生事故若干次數，隨時得有比較，則在監督完善之車站，此項事故自可減少，在管理不善者此項事故必多，可以於無形中啓發各站力求進步之精神，誠爲以上馭下之最爲有效方策。因其性質既在揭示各站成績之優劣，而在編製上係採取統計形式，故如以之視爲一種管理貨運站務統計，亦無不可。

(二)各站應負錯誤責任之事故件數，既由總局站務管理處運用前述方式製成統計公佈，同時各站亦復自行辦理查究工作，如有應由本站負責者，第一步首先查明錯誤發生原因，第二步進而查明應負責任之員司，追根究底，窮源溯委，均有一定步驟方法，其大概可於左列各例覘之：

(1)例爲指定各件零担貨物應裝之車輛，本爲收貨司事Receiving Clerks之責任，是故調查事故結果，如有因誤裝車輛而致短少者，則應由該站之收貨司事負責，此則一查當日在託運單上簽註之裝車號碼Spot Number，卽可知其有無錯誤及其應負責任之司事姓名。

(2)又如零担貨物因裝車方法不合規則而致損壞者，則應由貨棧實際監理裝車事務之各副監工Assistant Foremen負其責任，此則又可檢閱當日裝車表Loading Chart卽知某人監理某車裝工，蓋每一副監工分管若干車輛，每日各有一定分派，可按裝車表一查而知也。

（3）他如因貨票與託運單不符而致發生短少事故者，則應由起票處 Billing Department 主任及經手填寫貨票之司事 Way bill Clerks 共同負責，此則既可由一聯存站貨票查出關係託運單，亦可由託運單查出關係貨票，查出貨票之後，即可知其當初填票之司事究為何人。蓋由託運單改填貨票之時，各貨票司事照例應將本人姓名順手填入貨票頂端左角，而貨票又與託運單早經編有同一號碼，有此重重連鎖記載，故能化繁為簡，得收查究便利之奇效。

各站一面接受上級事故統計，一面按照上述諸法查明錯誤原因及負責員司，每日自行另編站用事故統計報告，分發關係處所，以起注意而資警惕。關於填寫貨票錯誤之報告，則送致起票處主任查核，關於裝車錯誤者送致貨機監工 General Foremar，由其分別轉告各關係員工。同時各送站長室一份，俾隨時明瞭全站員工服務狀況，統籌改善管理方法，茲以美國伊中鐵路芝城貨運車站賠償處用以報告填寫貨票錯誤事件 Daily R-

起禁處誤填貨事故報告

賠賠處填報員姓名　　　　起報處主任姓名

日期	貨票號數	連續號碼	到達站	收貨人	原填者 (Read)	應改正者 (Shoned Read)	貨票司事 (B.C.)

償處主任姓名

eport of Errors in Billing 之格式列示於左，以資參考。

似此上下層層節制考察辦法，可收極大效果，一則各站成績好壞得有比較，優良者有表現能力之機會，惡劣者無從隱避，由是全路各站競勝精神可以自然養成。二則各站員司雖多，然而功過均極分明，既不能掩飾錯誤，更不能推諉責任，由是全站各方員工自非加緊認眞辦事情緒不可，莫敢稍存苟且敷衍心理。推而演之，則是不但全路各地貨運管理方法得有不斷改進，貨物事故得以盡量減至最低限度，而其無形中所收之直接間接利益，尤爲不可思議。學者如能透澈切實了解大站辦理貨運之緊急復雜繁瑣情態，然後方知此種內外上下因果並顧之處理貨物事故方法在管理學上殊有極端重大之意義與價值矣。

公務員退休與贍養金制度（D 3.）

任家誠

意義

在一優良而穩定之行政組織中，對於其公務員之年邁力衰者應設法使其退休，給予豐裕之贍養金，足以維持其晚年之生活，此種辦法我人稱之爲退休制度。世界各國類多先後施行，以維持行政氣象之蓬勃，且著有成效。我國人事行政方在改良，對於退休之制尚未創立，僅於去年通過公務員儲蓄條例，由中央信託局集中辦理，考其內容與世界各國頗有出入之處，故退休制度之採取在我國尚屬必要，草此文以爲提倡。

退休制度之採取有二重意義。從政府方面看，人事系統最宜維持其流轉之靈活，使低級職員有上升之機會，而提高其工作之興趣，設年邁力衰之人員高踞不去，則下級人員之遞升將遭阻塞，故應有退休之辦法，以便于流轉。且在一良好之人事行政系統下，升擢基於辦事能力及資歷，故重要之事務往往由經驗宏富之人員担任，此輩人員至年事十分衰老後，其工作之效能及種種智力上之應付，必較壯年時爲減退，故應使之退職，以讓較爲幹練，智力健全之人員担任，俾行政之設施有維持其良好精神之可能。故政府爲增進行政效率及流通人事系統起見，應採退休制度。

從公務員方面看，既已亟其一生勞瘁，爲國服務，於其年邁能力不勝之時，自應予以優容之辦法，使之退休，以維持其生活，以娛其餘年，更所以堅其壯年時爲國服務之決心。此處所謂優容之辦法，即我人所欲討論之贍養金。

贍養金學說今昔頗有差異。昔日之贍養金爲一種恩賜性質，蓋憫其年老力衰不能工作之苦，而予以相當之補助。現在則認爲一種延遲給付（Deferred payment）之俸給，而爲俸給之一部份。其理由有二：一、公務員既犧牲其他事業發展之機會，爲國服務，國家自應負贍養之責任。且公務員既以年邁而被擯於政府之外，精疲力竭，自不能直接再營他業，以贏利而終其天年，如是則個人甚或國家之生計將生困難，此種困難，實因國家剝削其其他贏利之機會所致，故國家應負贍養之責任。二、我人試研究贍養金之性質，無論此種資金由公務員自儲或由國家出資，實均爲每年或每月中俸給減少一部份積聚而成，故亦爲俸給之一部份，僅以其給付期限之延遲而有較爲特殊之形式而已。

從上述之意義中，我人可以窺出其利益。公務員因年邁後可無衣食之慮，而將黽勉從事，力圖振作；政府方面可因衰老人員之退休而促進工作之質量，增加行政上之效率。現代人事行政學者往往將退休制度視爲一種激勵公務員工作效能之工具，其方法可謂十分確當。

贍養金之來源

贍養金之積聚有三種方式：(一)由公務員自己出資積聚，(二)由政府出資積聚，(三)雙方聯合出資積聚。主政府出資者，認爲公務員之贍養金爲廣義俸給之一種，所以補償公務爲公服務犧牲其他贏利機會也。主公務員自己出資者，認爲贍養金乃爲公務員之儲蓄，應由公務員自己担任，而政府僅須負代爲保管之責，且政府誠根據廣義俸給之原理而出資積聚，結果政府必減少俸給以爲挹注，「羊毛出在羊身上，」於公務員並無實益、不如自資之爲愈。昔者英之公務員曾因此種關係而請求改政府出資爲自己出資之舉，卽有感於此而發者。(一)故衡之二者之論辯均不免過趨極端，爲補救計，第三法實較爲合理，且可與延遲給付及協謀雙方利益之理論相符合。司丟鄧司史監(Paul Studensky)所舉聯合出資之利益至詳且切，摘錄之如下(二)

『(一)此法較他法爲經濟而切實用，蓋減少政府或公務員間單獨負担之重責，可以造成良好之贍養金制度。

(二)此法使政府與公務員間之費用趨于公平及需要之調節。

(三)此法如合理採用，限制對公務員鉅額之需索，蓋政府亦出資，隨俸給而增加，結果可以造成健全之制度

(四)此法可使公務員參與管理贍養金之事務，造成政府與公務員合作與調協之利益。

(五)根據哲理之觀察，此法頗爲合理，如前所述，蓋退休之法於公務員及政府雙方各有利益，雙方自應各負出資之責任也。

(六)公務員之勞力因工作而耗費，而他方面自己身受因公服務之便利，故雙方均應負担出資之責任。

(七)人事行政首重政府與公務員間之公平，決不應使一方面負其責任。

(八)聯合出資可以引導公務員與政府間之相互合作及諒解』

聯合出資之法較爲新穎，故尚未十分普遍。然歐美諸國已漸有採取此法之傾向，絕對維持政府出資者現僅有英，比，德三國。

我國政府贍養金制度尚未經採用，有之，亦僅爲一般西人所手創之機關，尤著者如鐵道，海關，郵務及鹽務等。我國各鐵道現已有統一之退休制度，其所積聚係採取政府出資辦法，給付之方法，係根據入職年限及年齡，比照最後每月俸給，而定應得之百分數（例舉於後節中。）(三)此外如京滬滬杭甬路局等更有聯合出資積聚之贍養金，於退職時一併取出，此則爲一種儲蓄性質。

贍養金之管理

關於贍養金之管理有二法焉，曰現金分配法(Cash disbursement) 及計算準標法(Acturial

reserve）

現金分配法者以年入抵年出也。換言之，今之爲甲所積之贍養金（無論何方出資）即以之付與乙（退休者），而甲將來按月或按年所應得之贍養金，則至臨時再以丙所積聚者付予乙，如是川流不息，至於無限。此法頗爲學者所不滿因其所計及之眼光過短，將來必可造成種種困難，且未能預計每年退職之人數，假定因公致命及由於其他理由中途退職之情形在某年突然增加，豈非將發生所入不敷所出之問題。然此法亦有其利，蓋管理方面較爲簡便，而贍養金之籌措亦較爲安全，不若計算準法之需複雜之程序及機密之保存。

計算準備法合乎科學化計算之原則，而爲矯正現金分配法之缺點，于按月存款交入時，按照複利計算每人可儲之總額，於退職時分期給予，以贍養其晚年。此法與現金積聚法之不同，爲此種方法之贍養金乃由儲入金及利息二項積聚而成，而現金分配法僅靠現金，故較合經濟及投資之原則。其缺點爲手續煩冗，不易管理，且可因一髮而牽動全身。故爲管理之得當，利益顯然。否則徒然造成種種困難問題，其中尤著者爲所積鉅款之投資問題。

贍養金與儲蓄之不同

世人往往將贍養金與儲蓄二事混爲一談，不相分別，其實二者頗有不同處。儲蓄者於每年積聚若干數額計算複利，至公務員退休之時，一筆返還。我國於去年經立法院通過公務儲蓄條例，按月由公務員儲出若干俸給，由中央信託局管理，此種計劃卽屬於儲蓄性質。贍養金者，於公務既經退休後，並不付予一筆整數而爲按月給付，至死而後已，其計算更與公務員生命之長短有關，故實較儲蓄方法更進一步。

至儲蓄之制度，計算之唯一根據爲複利表，猶如銀行之零存整付然。而贍養金制度則因與公務員生命之長短發生關係之故，舍複利表外，更應注意及生命統計表(Mortality table)，其性質蓋與人壽保險相若。

由上觀之我人知贍養金與儲蓄之不同有二點，一爲給付形式之不同，一爲積聚計算之不同。

贍養金積聚之方式

贍養金之積聚無論爲公務員出資，政府出資或聯合出資，恆由俸給中抽出一相當之百分數，作爲留存之資。此種情形以公務員出資或聯合出資之法爲明顯，蓋公務員所積之一部份顯由俸給中提出也。政府出資之法則因往往先事於無形中減少俸額，故較爲隱藏，然其原則則一。

百分數之決定並不一致，各國均各不同，其原因有四（一）各國人民生命長短之不同，(二)各國經濟狀況及投資情形之不同，(三)計算方法之出入。及(四)退職年限規定之不同。

然其數不宜超過全俸百分之十，因所扣過多，於公務員將來之幸福誠屬有利，不免影響其目前之收入。故過少雖不能免于不敷，亦不能過事苛求。

於百分數之決定時，更須注意一事，卽對各人所扣之百分數應否一致；如有高低，應以何者爲標準。此點各國辦法不同，以法國而言，根據一九二四年法案之規定，由公務員自出俸給百分之六爲養老金，並無高出或低於百分之六之規定。(四)以美國新新納底(Cincinnati)之制度而言，在二十歲時入職之公務員月納俸百分之四·七六，四十以上入職者則年須納百分之五·四一，而五十九歲以上入職者須納百分之六·八四(五)。此種高低之規定有其合理之根據，蓋二十歲入職者離職之期自較四十歲者爲遠，故年付之養老金儲備額之所積亦較多，爲公平計，自應較在後入職者酌爲減低。主張一定之百分率者，則無非將入職時期作一統計上之平均，俾求計算上之便利。不可謂爲完全不妥也。

關於納費多少而有不公平之結果，現在已有補救辦法，卽退休之條件舍年齡之規定外，更有入職久暫之攷慮，容於後述及。

贍養金數額之計算

公員於退職時按月或按年所領取之額，應爲幾何，亦爲研究退休制度者所應注意之點。其確定之根據有三，(一)根據退職前最近之俸額，(二)自入職時至退職時各年俸額之平均，

(三)規定一離退職時相當年限之平均。

根據退職前最近之俸額之法不便于預測，蓋退休之年齡誠可預爲決定，然公務員之發展之經過，固不能預期，故退職時俸給爲若干，不易預先猜度，在計算及預爲估計上極有困難，此種困難足以破壞整個退休制度。從公務員方面講亦未免不公，蓋各人有各人之機會及才能，設某甲與某乙同時入職，在退休前數年中某甲較某乙之俸給爲高，其贍養金儲備之繳納常較某乙爲多，在退休前不久，某乙忽因某項特著成績或夤緣高陞，俸給竟與某甲相等，甚或過之，退休後某甲之贍養金乃與某乙相同，甚或不如，豈可稱爲公平。此種不公常可引起公務員間之誤會，甚而發生傾軋之現象，我人亟應避免。

入職後各年俸給平均之法，在資金之積聚上自可稱爲公平，然因每年俸給之多寡與其終身有利害之關係，致使公務員隨時有求職位之提高以提高其俸給之心，將使公務員競騖於功名，而無暇顧及工作。且公務員之職位及供職地點常有變更，數年中俸額之升降，變化多端，欲集整個材料，而作全盤之平均，決非易事。故此法僅可謂合理，在執行方面尚不免有困難。

相當年限之平均之法，不若前法之平均爲冗長，故無論在俸給增減之調查方面，或計算方面均較前法爲妥當，故可謂補救前法方法上之缺憾者。所謂相當年限，往往爲五年，最多爲十年，美各省每多採取。

退休期限之規定

公務員究竟應於何時退休，諸人之主張往往不同，然多認爲年齡之限制爲最主要者。各國地土風俗各異，人民之智力之卓發與衰退並不一致，大概體力較健之民族，智力減退之時期較遲。故退休之年齡規定務須根據國民能力，作準確而合理之統計，以觀察其智力衰退之情形。以吾國人而言，年屆六十者，無論在體力上或智力上，已不能如壯年人之奮發有爲，故我國如創立退休制度，可定六十歲爲退休年齡。

於上述贍養金之積聚討論中，我人曾言及退休之年齡誠有規定，然入職之期限必有先後，如於退職時予以相同之待遇，則所積有多少，未免不公，我人更提及以積聚之百分數多寡之法以補調節。然此爲消極之辦法，百分數高低之決定常有種種計算上之困難。爲補救計，我人舍年齡應有規定外，更須確定入職年數以定贍養金之數額，如入職已有二十五年，年齡達六十歲可按照退職時之月俸按月給予半俸，而年齡達六十，入職僅二十年者應減少至退職時月俸之相當百分數，又如入職已滿二十五年而年齡僅五十五者亦可予以退休之機會，法亦在減入贍養金之數額，餘以此類推。

此種聯合規定之法可使入職年數及年齡二項互相顧應，自較單獨之決定爲妥善。我國鐵

道部之退休養老金卽採取此種聯合規定之法，茲例舉如下（六）

『第一條 國營鐵道員工服務滿二十五年，年齡滿六十歲，自請退休或由局令其退休者，均得給與退休養老金，每月應給養老金額照最後之月薪資，給與百分之五十，發給至身故日爲止。

第二條 員工服務滿十五年，年齡滿六十歲，自請退休者，得給予退休養老金；每月應給養老金額，按其服務年數計算，發給至身故日爲止。

服務滿十五年者，照最後之月薪資給與百分之三十；

服務滿十六年者，照最後之月薪資給與百分之三十二；

服務滿十七年者，照最後之月薪資給與百分之三十四；

服務滿十八年者，照最後之月薪資給與百分之三十六；

服務滿十九年者，照最後之月薪資給與百分之三十八；

服務滿二十年者，照最後之月薪資給與百分之四十；

服務滿二十一年者，照最後之月薪資給與百分之四十二；

服務滿二十二年者，照最後之月薪資給與百分之四十四；

服務滿二十三年者，照最後之月薪資給與百分之四十六；

服務滿二十四年者，照最後之月薪資給與百分之四十八；
服務滿二十五年者，照最後之月薪資給與百分之五十。

第三條　員工服務滿二十五年，年齡滿五十五歲以上，自請退休者，得給予退休養老金，其每月應給養老金額按其年齡計算，發給至身故日爲止。
年齡滿五十五歲者，照最後之月薪資給與百分之四十；
年齡滿五十六歲者，照最後之月薪資給與百分之四十二；
年齡滿五十七歲者，照最後之月薪資給與百分之四十四；
年齡滿五十八歲者，照最後之月薪資給與百分之四十六；
年齡滿五十九歲者，照最後之月薪資給與百分之四十八；
年齡滿六十歲者，照最後之月薪資給與百分之五十。

第四條　員工服務滿十五年以上，年齡滿五十五歲，因身體衰弱，經派醫師檢驗，證明確係不勝職務，經呈部核准退休，給與退休養老金，每月應給養老金額，按其服務年數，依第二條所定金額三分之二計算，發給至身故日止。」

其他

前述各節爲退休制度應加注意之基本各點，舍此外我人爲完備計，更應提出較爲次要之各問題。

一、退休贍養金與卹金之不同　贍養金爲公務員退休後，供其養老之用，故其給予之期限僅至身故日爲止。卹金爲撫卹公務員遺族生活及教育之用，故於公務員身故後發給，往往爲整數之給付而非按月或按年的。通常公務員須因公病故，其遺族方可領取卹金，其卹金應包括兩部份，一爲公務在職時按年所積聚之贍養金之儲備金，加以複利，一爲正式之撫卹之部份，此部份發給之理由，因公務員既因爲公服務而遭喪身，在倫理上政府自當負絕對之責任，同時卹金之給予可以促進後起者奮力之志願，故實撫卹而有獎勵之意。

卹金中既包括一部份贍養金在內，故二者雖各不同，而實有聯帶之關係在焉。我國鐵道部更規定凡受領退休贍養老金未滿十年而亡故，其遺族得更領取一次卹金，此種卹金數額隨退職後亡故之年代之近遠而增減其百分比，故更有補充贍養金不足之意。(七)

二、中途離職之處置　凡公務員中途離職，自已放棄其養老金之權利。然爲公平起見，彼歷年所自存之數應予發還並加給利息。在完全由政府出資之情形下，政府雖已無形中於俸給內扣除；然此數額不易作準確之計算，公務員無需索之權利，此乃爲不得已之故，自不能完全歸咎於政府措置之不公。

三、因病休致之處置　如公務員未滿退休期限，因病不能繼續供職，當視其致病之原因而斷贍養金之給付。如因公致病，政府應負責任，自應按月給予贍養金；如自己致病，政府應退還其自存之一部份，並給予利息。

四、管理問題　爲易於取得公務員之信任起見，贍養金之管理應由政府代表及公務員代表聯合爲之，（尤以採取公務員出資之制度者爲甚）。雙方之代表可組織理事會會同商討論種種問題，另由政府指定區分單位担任行政上之責任，而其主任之人選則應徵得委員之同意。

所有金額如完全擱置庫中，未免太不經濟，而應設法妥爲投資或設法存儲，使其生利。然以全國之大，公務員之多，所積款必不在少，如投資不妥，可以影響全國公務員之利益，故資金之處置實爲管理上最大之問題。在政府信用卓著之國家，將此款借于政府，舉辦種種事業，自屬可靠，然如政府之信用不振，國帑奇拙，則種種困難棘手之問題必可發生，我國遲遲之不能舉辦贍養金制度，此點亦未嘗非較大之原因。

（一）H.D. Brown Civil Service Retirement in Great Britain Sen. Doc. No. 290, 61st Cong. sd sess., p. 183

（二）.P. Studensky, "Pension in Public Employment", National Municipal Review Vol. 11. (National Municipal League, N. Y. C. 1922) p. 105.

（三『國營鐵路員工退休養老金規則』，二十四年四月十三日參字第一四二號部令公佈，見鐵道部人事法令彙編（鐵道部秘書廳，南京，民國二十五年九月）

（四）W.R. Sharp "Public Personnel Management in France" Civil Service Abroad, edited by L.D. White & others (McGraw-Hill Book Co., N.Y.C., 1935) pp. 125—129.

（五）W.E. Mosher & J. D. Kingsley Public Personnel Administration (Harper & Brothers Publishers, N. Y. C 1936) p. 458

（六）『國營鐵路員工退休養老金規則』，見前。

（七）同上

管理 第一卷 第五期

管理二月刊

第一卷 第四期
民國二十五年十一月

論著

譯述

書評

管理二月刊

第一卷 第五期
民國二十六年二月

論著

譯述

演講

通訊

書評

A STUDY OF FILING SYSTEMS FOR OFFICE MANAGEMENT

H. C. Cheng (鄭惠益)

When we come to the subject of filing in office administration, however, we find definite systems and rules of procedure. The growth of large business organizations in the 20th century, in which definite records must be substituted for some one's memory of the location of important papers, has gradually and systematically developed complete system of filing, and their introdution into business houses through special courses in business schools and colleges, and through, the sale of standard equipment and systems by office-furniture and supply houses. Much has been borrowed and adopted to business needs of the excellent library practice of filing and index.

As a result of this inattention many offies are familiar with the confusion that arises on frequent occasions when executives ask for important papers that can be found in the files. The work of the office stops, papers are pulled from desks or file drawers until the missing papers are found, or until all hope is abandoned.

A succession of these occurrences usually leads to the decision on the part of the manager that something must be done about tne files. The real remedy lies in a study cf filing systems and equipment, the installation of the right system or combination of systems according to the needs, and the employment of a trained file clerk in taking charge of it. The proper solution of the filing question will contribute as much to the general welfare of any office as will any other one improvement, because all individuals and departments are effected by it in one way or another.

The functions of a filing system are as follows:—

1. To relieve executives and employees of the necessity of keeping in or on their desks letters and papers to which they may refer at some future time.

2. To keep these papers systematically and safely in which a way that they can be produced definitely and quickly.

The first step is to get all papers out of desks and private drawers. The evils of having papers kept individuals are many.

Other clerks or executives may need such papers, and be unable to discover who is holding them; a letter coming into the office referring to previous correspondence cannot be associated with it; letters unattended to can be filed away with closed matters without the fact being discovered by the manager; each individual files his papers unsystematically, wasting time in both filing and finding them, clogging his desk, and distracting his attention from the day's work. Finally if he should leave the organization or if he finds too many papers accumulating he will destroy those that he judges non-essential. Later his indgement mav be found to have been very poor.

Following the conclusion that material is not to be kept in desks and small private filing systems, comes the question as to whether all material should be kept in a central file. Many up to-date offices, as I know, have a central filing room, others have departmental files, still others have central files for some kinds of material, departmental for others.

Whenever a central file does not defeat other purposes it is desirable; it is de·irable; it probides standard equipment, and methods, one location only for material, and definite responsibility on the part of all individuals in the office for sending materials to the central files, and on the part of the file clerks for filing and finding it.

When the system is being selected that will produce the papers most surely when they are needed, the matter of expense have some influence, especially where there is a great mass of material to be filed, in which case a more expensive system might have to be set aside for one not so infallible, but sufficiently satisfactory, and cheaper to operate.

There are six main systems of filing, such as:—

I. Alphabetic Files:—

The alphabetical system is the simplest and most commonly used. It varies in degrees of complication from a system that has 26 guides, one for each letter of the alphabet, to a system that has 400 guides for the alphabet. (A) The advantages of the alphabetical system are: (1) there is only one place for each paper filed, (2) filing can be done very quickly, (3) no index of any kind besides the file is required, (4) the alphabetical method of filing is the best known and most natural to every one, because it is used in libraries, telephone books, directories, and so forth. (B) The disadvantages of this system are: (1) that it is not always clear whether a letter should be filed under the name of an individual or his company, (2) that no matter how many guides are in the system, it is inevitable that some places in the file will be undesirably crowded, (3) if a paper is misfiled there is no cross-reference to it.

II. Numeric Files:—

Under this system each correspondent is assigned a number arbitrarily. If a letter from Chester Cheng is received for the first time he will have no previous number and the next number in order will be assigned to him.

This number will be placed on his correspondence and all future correspondence sent to or received from him will bear this number. An index card, preferably 3 by 5 inches in size, usually numbered in advance, is filled in with the name and address of Mr. Cheng. The chard is then filed alphabetically to an index box or drawer. The paper is put in a folder which bears Mr Cheng's number, and the folder is filed in numerical order, which throws out all other order.

III. Combined alphabetical and numeric system:—

Is is easy to file numerically but easy to find alphabetically. To combine the two features in a filing system has long been the aim of filing experts. An alphabetic series is divided into a given number of parts to which numbers are assigned in consecutive order, these numbers respresenting the main division of the file.

IV. Geographical Filing:—

A geographical system of filing has a separate section in the files for each province or section of the country accordingly. Within each section matter is filed alphabetically by the name of the town in which the correspondent lives. If there are several correspondents in one town, their correspondence is filed in alphabutical order with respect to that town.

(A) The advantages of this system are important. It throws the material into small divisions, which make it easy to find, the unit of filing being the town in which there are not usually more than a few correspondents or customers. But in large cities, where there are many correspondents, a set of alphabetical guides can be inserted behind the city guide.

(B) The chief disadvantage of this system is that it is the most difficult way of filing, because the material to be filed must be sorted first by province, then by town, and then by customer's name.

V. Chronological Filing:—

Under the chronological system of filing, material is filed according the date. This system is used only in cases where the date is the mast important feature of the paper and name and address are unimportant. Paid cash vouchers which are supported by entries in a cash book will probably be called for by date.

There is however, a chronological element in numerical or alphabetical filing in that, in each division of the file, papers are arranged chronologically, those of the latest date on top.

(A) Central Tickler-There is one small filing systen with a chronological arrangement that will be found extremely useful in any office. That is a tickler system that is located centrally and operates as follows:

Certain executives or employes should have some method of remembering that certain things must be done on a definit future date. The president of the company may want certain statistics on the last day of the month in order to make his report to the directors meeting on the first day of the following month, or the manager of the advertising department may decide in June he will sent out certain circular-matter in July. A thousand matters may come up in the meantime to prevent them from remembering these things. Under the central tickler system an executive may mark on the paper "Ct July lst." and send the paper to the filing department. On July lst., as though be magic, it will appear on his desk for his attention without any further thought on his part in the meantime.

This is accomplished in a very simple way. A section of the file is set apart for all such papers, which section was a guide for each day on the month and each month of the year. The guides for the days of the month are arranged behind the guide for the current month, the other monthly guides behind them.

At the beginning of ecah month the papers which have been placed behind the monthly guide are placed behind the daily guides. Each morning the file clerk takes out and distributes all papers requireing attention on that day.

(B) Card File:— In the way of handling orders the mail order house, instead of keeping its thousands of orders of all shapes and sizes, prepared a card for each customer on which was entered a record of sales. A ledger system also usually consists of a card or page in a loose-leaf-book for each customer giving all charges and credits made on his account.

This shows at a glance the present status of his credit transactions with the house. In this case, however, copies of the bills are filed to support the ledger entries in case of any dispute.

The advantages of transferring information to cards to replace or supplement the filling of the original documents are:

1. Cards take much less space.

2. Cards cover transactions over a long period, the accumulation of which at one place is very valuable for reference.

3. Cards are uniform in size, beavies in weight, and file more easily.

The disadvantages, on the other hand, are the time taken for transferring the information, and the possibility that the transfer may be inaccurate or cannot be complete enough to do away with the originol papers. Nevertheless, in every office there will be cases where it is advisable to install some card records, a part of the filing system that should not be overlooked.

VI. Subject or Data Files:—

The old way of running a business by common sense and intuition is passing more and more insistence is placed on scientific and organized methods. Careful study of all phases of industry is made, data of all kinds are gathered, and standard methods and procedures are being worked out. The larger the concern, the more widespread its operations, and the less the dependence on one man who is proprietor, memory, judge on all questions, the more important it becomes to have some way of preserving the written record of studies and achievements of both the business libraries and special subject files, work where their library technique becomes extremely valuable.

Works in English by Members of the Faculty in the School of Administration

K. D. Lum, *The Political Influence of the Orientals in Hawaii* (Columbia University Press, New York, 1923) G. 1.00

K. D. Lum, *The Evolution of Government in Hawaii* (New York University Press, New York, 1926) G. 2.00

K. D. Lum, *The Government of the City & County of Honolulu* (Co-authorship with Robert Littler & K. C. Leebrick, Honolulu Star Bulletin Press, Honolulu) G. 1.00

K. D. Lum, *Methods of Research & Thesis Writing* (The Mercury Press, Shanghai, 1932) $ 3.00

K. D. Lum, *Outline of Law* (The Mercury Press, Shanghai, 1932) $ 9.00

K. D. Lum, *Chinese Government* (The Mercury Press, Shanghai, 1934) $ 3.00

C. L. Hsia, *Studies in Chinese Diplomatic History* (Commercial Press, Shanghai, 1924) $ 3.00

C. L. Hsia, *The Status of Shanghai* (Kelly & Walsh Book Co. Shanghai, 1928) $ 4.50

C. L. Hsia, *English Translation of the Chinese Civil Code* (Kelly & Walsh Book Co., Shanghai, 1931) $ 15.00

C. L. Hsia, *English Translation of the Chinese Criminal Code* (Kelly & Walsh Book Co., Shanghai, 1936) $ 6.00

譯述

人事行政上一新的著要點（D 3.）

原名 A New Emphasis in Personnel Administration, 爲美國 Gordon R. Clapp 所著，見 P. 111—118, The Annals of The American Academy of Political and Social Science, January, 1937

G.R. Clapp 著
韋愿 譯

在大多數行政範圍上公務人員的增加和政府工作的擴充，已使人事行政上有了新的和較重的責任。因爲近代國家的各種問題須用新的方法來解決，人事行政人員便受了一番嚴重的試驗。人事行政上特殊的工作，不獨是要物色那些合格的，能盡心竭力於公務的男女僱員，但亦要幫助創造工作的環境，俾公務人員能充分施展他們的才智。

這項工作合理的成功就是試驗良好行政的最高標準。人事行政機關有一主要的責任，就是把下列各種特點在一個組織裏樹立起來：有卓立的工作精神，有創作的思想，自由提出可行的計畫，忠實地努力，效忠於公務上最高的理想等。

積極地解決這項問題的主要途徑有二：一是僱員在內工作的組織的機構；一是僱員的工會組織和獨立的社團。經這兩組織的途徑，辦事的、行政的、和全體的工作人員，對於職務上和他們的集體幸福上，都有貢獻。

本文目的在主張人事行政上須研究和解決各種組織問題，又須憑着獨立的僱員組織來發展監督人員和僱員雙方的合作關係，俾有一特殊的機會來改善公務人員。

人事行政與組織機構

行政上最困難的問題有一項就是怎樣使各種職務、職責、責任、和關係成爲組織化，而這些，合攏起來，便是人事行政機關全部工作的表現。人事行政人員顯然要注意他自己的職員內部的組織和那些完成人事行政工作的各種單位的組織。這就是行政人員在公務責任上固有的一部份責任。但是，人事行政人員在他自己的公務範圍上所遇到的各種組織問題，亦爲任何在公務上與人事行政機關有聯絡的其他行政單位的長官所遇到的。因爲專門性質上，技術上和工作主體上都日益複雜與變化，而政府工作的範圍亦有正常的和迅速的擴充，公務行政本身已變爲一專門的工作範圍了。因爲了這些發展，人事行政機關遂不能不担任着研究和解決各種組織問題的特殊職務。人事行政機關又須擴充了它處置各種職位分級問題的責任，才最有效地來執行這項職務。

人事行政須有什麼的基礎來担負這工作範圍內的責任呢？除非小心地和不斷地把注意集中在各種組織問題上，行政的方法或許變爲呆板而又有虛飾；這些虛飾倘依照那些要被執行的工作來評價，或依照工作計畫的變遷、擴充、或收縮來評價（這些變遷擴充，或收縮等等都是近代公務行政機關的特質），却值得很少的辯護——甚或連一點辯護也不值得；這層可無庸贅說。所謂組織的機構，根本是對於各種關係、職責、權力、

責任、和工作計畫所有的一種活的規定。在工作的實踐上，組織的機構是一種明晰的指導，對各僱員一一曉以他所負的責任的限度和程度，且又使他認識各種在他的上下左右可受他自由支配的途徑和人才。（這些途徑和人才俱屬能夠——而且應該——被用來執行工作的。）

僱員對於本人在內工作的組織的機構所有的普通認識和特殊認識，倘未達到相當清楚的程度，那末就會惑於權限的衝突、工作分配和上司命令的矛盾、工作的重複、權力的獵等、和一般的紛亂而失却了主宰。那些具有創作力而又能夠有聰明思想的僱員，也許數在不少，但他們若對於『怎樣才能夠順利進行』這一點還沒有適當清楚的認識，那末他們的努力常是枉費的，或則在他們的背景以外便不能產生任何實際效力的。甚或更壞些，對於組織上缺乏了清楚的認識，就會使下列這種人佔了便宜．（一）個人很野心的僱員，或（二）國內的政客，他存心計畫各種不合理的方法來弄權而辦事絕不計及圓滿妥善的結果，像組織完善的機關所產生出來的。

這些就是行政人員必須遇到的問題。工程師，律師，公共衛生員司——簡單一句話說，一切職業專家，——倘担負行政責

任，而又要使他所負責的專門事項辦理得有些成績，那末他必須具有那些與公務行政的原則和技術有關係的知識。他所遇到的各種行政問題，和怎樣使他的下屬的工作成爲系統化的問題，都與他的特殊職業的範圍有些關係，但不是屬於該範圍內。因此，於解決各種組織問題時，職員的輔助，就是一種職務，而這種職務必須作爲一個偌大的政府機關管理部職務上的一部份；這是明顯的。

有缺點的組織的影響

各種組織問題的應付方法，對於人事行政機關順利執行它徵募、選舉、和安插工作人員等因襲的職務，有了一種非常重要的關係。倘安插着這些僱員的組織在機構上有了缺點，自必不能「人盡其才」，因此人事行政機關的努力亦會失效。人事行政機關，於執行它的尋常職務時，須認識各種人的能力：唯其如此，它才能夠自己準備起來，對於幫助研究及解決各種組織問題這一層，有了一番有效的貢獻。人事行政上健全的工作計畫，須負主要的責任來處斷這些問題。

人事行政機關自然而然的就會被牽入了這些問題的漩渦。人事行政機關重視着職務上各種建設的方面，亦注意下列各項問題：（一）工作精神的問題，（二）不善處置僱員的問題，（三）僱員擢陞機會的問題，和（四）僱員和他的監督人員雙方的關係上所發生的各種難題。人事行政人員於應付這種專門的問題時，不久將覺着：倘若他依照因襲的方法去進行，又以爲其他行政單位內部組織的缺點，在公務上對於他本人是沒有關係的，那末他僅能應付問題的結果而不能應付問題的原因了。

萎靡的工作精神，不善的處置，各種因不公平待遇而起的怨懟及其他類同的情形，乃是種種象徵：都可表明僱員的工作制度發生了一種有機的缺點。當然，這些困難的發生，常因爲僱員不能適應職業環境。但不應該使那些在才能上和品質上經過了精細選擇的僱員們，把他們自己來適應着那些不合理的和不適宜的職業環境；這些環境也許深深地根伏在組織的機構上的。人事行政人員，常遇到了這些象徵發現的時候，要不是常在事後來應付各種人事問題，那末就要用專門的方法積極地來解決那些屢次發現的困難的基本原因。

我們並不主張：設立特殊的組織來收容那些具有特殊才能的各個特種人物；我們也不主張，使組織的機構完全合理而不必顧及各個在內工作的人員。這項歷久無法解決的問題的答案，必在乎兩種極端之間。欲尋出其中中央的地段，必求之於積極的人事行政的方法。這項問題的答案，亦須建設在一些基本的因素上面，這些因素就是：普通的和合格的僱員的志願、才能、和動機了。

職位的說明與分級

對於各種組織問題，人事行政機關怎樣才最能貢獻意見呢？在人事行政的普通工作範圍的各種特殊技術職能之中，職位的分級和職位上各種專門性質的說明，可以作為工具，幫助職員來研究和解決各種組織問題。

在職位分級的過程中，調查分級的人員，必須常常把一種重大的職務或工作計畫，分作許多組織的部份。一種由一個行政單位指導的重大工作計畫，必須成為系統化，俾每一個工作人員都曉得他個人責任和職責。最重要的，工作人員應該認識他本人與同一機關的同事所有的關係，此外又須認識他本人與其他有關係機關的工作人員所有的關係。因此，想要分析一工作位置，就常常非要分析許多其他的工作位置不可。

這樣一來，許多事實都可看到了。各有職司的工作人員的種種混亂情形可以發現了；權力上明確的衝突和責任上的重複可以顯明了；又有時，監督人員將得調查分級的人員幫助而發現了某一下屬違背了該監督人員所委任的責任和職守。行政方法向有不能運行的情形，此種情形的真因，以前祇可忖測，現在可以具體表現出來。又在一較廣泛的衡量上，權力的猶豫與空虛以及種種因為組織的機構有缺點而造成的工作關係，現在可以初次作為事實上的說明了。

這些有缺點的組織所有的標記，若非影響着職位說明書上所開列作為分析和分配職位的根據用的事實，對於分配特殊的工作位置不會有什麼關係的。但尋求更有效的方法來研究組織的機構，便發覺着調查分級的人員能夠在他的因襲的責任以外努力來增加他的工作效力。未把那有缺點的組織內部的工作位置分配之前，調查分級的人員或他的工作監督人員，就有優良的機會來共同修正或更改該組織的計畫。人事行政機關能夠有這一種合理的責任，而分級的職員又可協力來執行它；這是可以相信的。照這樣做去，人事行政機關便成為一主要的助力，可以改善一個組織的機構使它能鼓勵和發展一切公務人員的才能，而不是牽制他們的才能了。

人事行政和僱員組織

僱員們的正當職位和工作所在的組織，並不是他們發表思想和能力的唯一途徑。政府機關的僱員們，覺得應該要把自己組織起來成為各個獨立的會社，俾對於解決公務問題上有集體負責的貢獻，可見他們深明團體責任的意義，實堪嘉許。

鮮有人事行政的問題，比較起僱主僱員間關係的問題與僱員組織和代表的附帶問題，更使人頭腦昏亂和發生感情衝動的。美國的勞工運動和政府機關僱員雙方發生了密切關係，對於公務上僱主僱員間的關係，已注入了一種新的因素，這種因素對於某些人會係可恨的與使人迷惑的。

學員和練習生不能不承認在人事問題的行政上有這種力量存在。因為已有了全國的政策，無疑的將來還繼續有這全國的政策，全國僱員當然享有組織權和結合權，而不發生問題。這問題早給一九一二年福利德法案(The Lloyd-La Follette Act of 1912)在法律上解決了。人事行政人員所遇到的問題就是他是否以為僱員的組織必然妨礙和威脅着管理部的權力，抑或他肯定地和積極地承認僱員的組織作為有用的工具，在公務上可幫助得收「人盡其才」的功效。

美國田納西河流域行政處的政策

剛才所說的第二點就是美國田納西河流域行政處（The Tennessee Valley Authority 以下簡稱該行政處）所確立的處斷僱主僱員間關係問題的政策的特點。在該行政處管轄下的工作人員，約有僱員一萬七千人，包括在內的有真實的工會集團的會員，而這些工會集團又與美國勞工聯合會(The American Federation of Labor)有聯絡的，至於那些自由職業、書記部和行政部的僱員，亦係政府機關僱員獨立聯合工會的活動份子。該行政處對於普通問題的研究和解決，甚願經由僱員們和僱員工會所選的真實獨立代表採取集體方式來應付僱員們。簡略地檢閱該行政處在這項工作範圍內所有的經驗，可知人事行政上可尋求方法來清除一切障礙，俾僱員和管理部雙方有更密切的合作。

該行政處的態度和宗旨，可於它正式公布的政策見之。（原註："Employee Relationship Policy"，見第十三頁，

Knaxuille, Tenn.: Tennessee Valley Authority, Aug. 1935)該行政處的理事會，經過了一年半以上的時間集會討論後，已於一九三五年八月通過該政策；而參加集會討論者有職員和僱員的代表，其中又多為真實的僱員工會的負責人員。

總括來說，該行政處的政策承認僱員有權隨意組織與結合，指派代表而不受干涉或威脅，且又可與該行政處的管理部進行集體磋商。該政策又制定一種方法來處置各種因不公平待遇而起的怨懟、又使管理方面與獨立勞工僱員組織方面的能發展合作關係。它規定了關於僱傭標準，工作時間，工作報酬，職業訓練，職業安插等各種原則；規定了僱傭的最低年齡限度，排除了任用私人的惡習；設置各種保護僱員的安全和衛生設備；又把發言權授與真實的僱員組織來成立各種關於僱傭和工作情形的政策，規則、和條例。有了這些基本的認識，在解決人事問題上自然可以應付它的原因而不是應付它的結果，照這樣做去，就可得到一種有意識的辦法來對付下列兩種因素：一是常常妨碍着僱員們和監督人員完成滿意工作的因素，一是消滅了他們的職務興味的因素（這種興味是造成興奮的工作精神所不可缺少的。）

不公平待遇的起訴程序

舉例說來，適當地應用着處置怨懟的規程，就使監督人員切實負責對僱員有公開平允的應付。這樣一來，關於降級、遷調、離職、或撤職等項給予僱員們的理由，當然要與事實符合。這就是說：僱員應該知曉這些事實的，而那些作為人事行政的根據的成文紀錄，必須係一種從監督人員說出來正直坦白的陳述。根本上，政策上規定的程序；不獨要僱員或僱員代表必須經由那些業已設立的監督機關來解決他的因不公平待遇而起的怨懟，并且要該管的監督人員須採有條理正直迅速的方法來應付這種怨懟。這種程序亦承認：解除誤會最適當的場合就是這些誤會所由發生的地方，而不是在於那些遠離了工作場所的辦公室內。

至於那些起訴不公平待遇的僱員，亦有一種明確的責任。他必須把一切他能夠自由提出的事實向該管的監督人員申訴。倘若把適切的消息隱瞞着，到了他的案件上訴至美國田納西河流域行政處人事科(The Personnel Division of the Authority)請求處斷時才露佈出來，便是對不起了監督人員。

人事科因此須執行一種司法的職權來判決那些於上訴時交它處斷的怨懟和誤會事件。人事科必須謹愼維持着不偏不阿的地位，其唯一目的在確定那些在糾紛中的僱員和監督人員曾否竭誠去探訪適切的事實，又確定那種根據這些事實的解決是否合理並是否由誠意來造成的。僱員或監督人員見解錯誤時，若非有明證，亦不得認爲無誠意。

但是，不公平待遇的起訴程序不僅爲改善工作條件和給予僱員們公平待遇的一種企圖。該政策的程序大綱，倘能由一切有關係的人們誠意來實行，那末結果將會產生較好的監督人員與更負責的、更有效的、和更努力的僱員了。

怨懟事件的調整問題

因爲應用了處置怨懟事件的程序的規程，該管理處於手續統一方面有了明顯的進步。有些由僱員或僱員代表提出而經已按照規定的程序來調整的更普通的訴願，包含着下列的問題：某種工作報酬之不適當；關於解除職務，擢陞，遷調，分配工作等方面的差別待遇和徇私；關於解除職務，降級，分級紀績，和懲戒辦法等理由之不充分或不合理；監察人員之不勝任或不適當；工作條件之不生效或不穩安，不肯攷慮遷調請求，或不肯承認遷調資格；關於離職與再任職的手續上沒有適當地攷慮資格問題；停止不滿意的職役之前監督人員對於該項工作未能加以批評；分配那些違反公認的行政範圍內的裁定的工作；以及過度的工作，在規定時間以外的工作時間，不一定的工作時間，太長的工作時間等等。

由一九三五年八月二十八日起至一九三六年六月三十日止，上訴至人事科請求最後判定的不公平待遇訴願案件有十二宗，其中所爭執的有下列的各項問題：僱員職務之解除，僱員之遷調，合法代表之選舉，工作時間之延長與加工工資率之支付，以及不利於有工會組織的僱員之差別待遇。人事科經過了小心調查後——有好幾次還要正式開庭審訊——宣告各種判決如下：判決雙方讓步者計一宗，判決監察人員得直者計八宗，又判決僱員得直者計三宗。試檢閱處置應付各種怨懟和原因的最近經驗，可知這政策係一重要因素造成一種更有意識的方法來樹立良好的工作精神，適當美滿的工作條件，和監督人員與僱員雙方更和諧的關係。

當『僱員關係政策』(The Employee Relationship Policy)

被採用的前一年，正式由人事科註冊和處斷的訴願案件有九十四宗。後來這些案件的數目減少的原因有下列三種：

（一）採用了一種明確的勞工政策後，對於一切計畫的工作條件，俱已達到了更高的標準化程度；

（二）監督人員現有一種明確的責任，要依照該勞工政策來審理及處斷各種怨懟的訴願；

（三）因為迅速消滅了一種新的和發展迅速的組織本有的一切問題，已減却了許多發生怨懟的原因。

就該政策的術語說來，對於僱員和管理部雙方有系統的合作方面，『僱員們負責的組織和社團是很有用的』，至於僱員們為着這種目的而組織起來的限度，則完全由僱員們自定。為着保證僱員組織獨立性起見，該政策亦明白地承認僱員有權組織會社和選擇他們自己的代表而不受限制，干涉，或因為是否係任何僱員組織或僱員會社的會員而有差別的待遇。

僱員參加編制規例的問題

該政策又規定：規則條例必須提出與僱員和僱員代表商議，方能採用、更改、或修正，用這種方法來鼓勵僱員去參加規定他們的工作條件，却有深切的意義，可使人事行政機關的工作易於執行而那些被通過的條例亦易於實施。

有了這種規定，那末僱員們和管理部雙方當然要費相當的時間和努力來討論和制定規則和條例。這些規則和條例，倘是需要的，大抵都是可行的。這種規程實際上承認着，條例僅是工具，使習慣更加統一，公平的工作條件更加普遍，而這樣的工作條件又為合理的效率標準所必不可缺少的。它又承認着，沒有那些有關係的人員的合作而欲遵守着這些規則和條例的精神和字句，那是不可能的。採用民主化的程序來編制工作的規例，結果不獨得到更好的更可實行的規例，但亦更能認識各種有關係的問題，此外又獲得一種比較，平常所企料着更大的服從程度。關於規程的起草和通過，恪遵着這些規定，就使僱員們負責維持一種更高的服從程度，因為那些規例係他們自己或代表所參加制定的啊。

自採用了該政策以來，就可以觀察許多在該政策上的規程的實行性。現今依照該政策來實行的已有幾種主要的工作，如制定給假的條例與工資和薪俸計畫，以及處置和消除各種因不公平待遇而起的怨懟。

該政策所包含的各種主要責任

在整個的政策上主要的規定有二：一是爲着管理部規定的，一是爲着僱員們規定的。管理部有一種責任，須不斷努力着改善監督工作的性質，承認着監督人員，就他的人事管理地位來說，不獨要負責完成堤壩、道路、或研究計畫等工作，還須負責保儲和使用那些受他們支配的人才。此外管理部又有一種職責要訓練監督人員，使有積極的領袖的技能和公平的處斷方法，其目的在使該計畫能有效地進行並可表示公務員應有的尊嚴和謙恭。

至於僱員們所有的責任，則須具有較優的能力和創造力來奉行職守，對於他們的工作效率必須自加批評，提出各種可行的改良方法，承認着他們若不盡自己的責任，那末指揮工作的監督人員亦不能盡他的責任，此外又須注意在個人在集團和在同事中發展「自治」(Self-discipline) 使監督人能有餘力，在生產和管理各種問題上更求改善。

僱員方面，無論是否爲監督人員，都有一種責任，須對於職務有一種智識上的貢獻。能行的計畫都是難能可貴的；凡切實可行的計畫的起源往往出乎意料之外。一個組織若能夠認識和運用良好的計畫，便是開發人才的資源，而人才的資源的價值，斷不是可以用金錢來估量的。

各種僱主僱員間關係的原則的採用，最近已有進展。這表示複雜問題的積極解決，已使該行政處的人事行政計畫更得到了充實的內容。把許多造成怨恨、不安、和其他不良的因素的原因消滅後，已建立了一種基礎，使僱員負起責任共同發展興奮的工作精神和促成「人盡其才」的目的。

——完——

中央及地方決算（續）

聞亦有

第六章　吾國現行普通會計之收支報告

總決算既不易編成，退而求其次，則現時吾國普通會計之收支報告尙矣。茲分別述之於後：

中央＜財政部所編中央收支對照表
　　　主計處會計局所編中央會計總報告。

地方——以江蘇省收支對照表爲例詳述於後。

財政部所編中央收支對照表

中央收支報告表係自民國十七年度起由財政部會計司逐年編製。其性質屬於現金收支報告。其編製方法係將國庫現金及抵解收支數目及總稅務司與鹽務稽核總所等大宗收入機關所報告之收支數目合併而成。是以此項報告，既不能包括中央各機關及所屬全體之收支數目，又不能包括財政部所屬機關全體之收支，內容極爲狹溢。此其一。又收支應屬年度以列入本年度國庫總稅務司鹽務稽核總所收支報告爲限幷未加以整理。收支應屬年度既未整理故不能表示本年度各該收支眞實數目此其二。又上所列國庫現金及抵解收支數目：收入方面之分類方法祇就各收入機關解款及抵解款時所附解款書各聯上塡寫收入來源分類。是否各該機關之眞正收入來源，不得而知。支出方面之分類方法祇就項款機關之性質分類亦不準確。此其三。基於上述三點中央收支報告表似不能代表國家總決算書。祇是財政部爲執行財務行政於年度終了時卽就財政部直接或間接經收經撥款項，所編之現金收支總報告而已。

茲舉民國二十二年度中央收支報告表於後，以窺全豹。

二十二年度中央收支報告表

（收入之部）

I 稅項收入			
1.關稅		$352,398,5[illegible].32	
2.鹽稅		177,375,2[illegible].57	
3.統稅			
a.捲煙統稅	$70,910.039.50		
b.棉紗統稅	17,986,916.23		
c.麥粉統稅	5,784,548.82		
d.火柴統稅	4,884,564.69		
e.水泥統稅	1,853,823.23		
f.薰菸統稅	3,558,072.27		
合計		104,977,96[illegible].74	
4.菸酒稅		13,073,58[illegible].79	
5.印花稅		8,378,91[illegible].82	
6.鑛稅		1,619,95[illegible].93	
7.交易所稅		25,20[illegible].00	
8.銀行稅		1,526,94[illegible].79	
9.國有財產收入		2,541,29[illegible].80	
10 國有事業收入			
a.國有鐵路收入	16,781,162.17		
b.其他	957,273.33		
合計		17,738,435.50	
11 國家行政收入		3,186,972.25	
12 營業純益收入			
a.中央銀行	2,000,000.00		
b.其他	452,446.79		
合計		2,452,446.79	
13 協款收入		252,888.87	
14 其他收入		3,939,907.98	
稅項收入總計		689,488,337.15	
減：坐撥征收費及退稅			
a.坐撥征收費	67,048,909.51★		
b.退稅	780,470.50		
合計	67,829,380.01		
稅項收入淨計			$621,658,957.14
II 債务借款收入			
1.公債及庫券		80,220,444.62	

2. 銀行借墊款

借墊總額	395,099,185.51		
減：歸還額	303,660 297.97		
未還額		91,438,887.54	
3. 美棉麥借款		88,300,000.00	
借券借款收入總計			179,959,332.16
收入總計			801,618,289.30
上年度結存			
國庫		1,505,689.95	
海關總稅務司		21,997,659.40	
鹽務稽核所		3,590,049.51	
合計			27,093,398.86
收入總計及上年度結存			$828,711,688.16

★坐撥徵收費內計關務類$32,161,285.51，鹽務費$19,994,863.09，及其他各項$14,892,760.91。

（支出之部）

I 黨務費	$5,589,584.93
II 政務費	

1. 國務費

a. 國民政府	$3,290,270.68	
b. 行政院及其直屬機關	2,094,990.45	
c. 立法院	1,589,500.00	
d. 司法院及其直屬機關	936,760.00	
e. 考試院及其直屬機關	1,145,371.27	
f. 監察院及其直屬機關	1,571,500.00	
g. 其他各機關	4,844,720.28	
合計		$15,473,112.68
2. 內務費		4,190,780.09
3. 外交費		9,920,548.82
4. 財務費		4,917,385.73
5. 教育文化費		13,338,008.28
6. 實業費		1,578,072.12
7. 交通費		4,909,033.96
8. 蒙藏費		1,576,823.90
9. 建設費		6,812,363.67
10 補助費		

a,補助各省市	26,038,121.94		
b,其　　他	5,963,210.87		
合　　計		32,001,33[illegible].81	
11 撫卹費		1,191,18[illegible].10	
12 救濟費		3,923,86[illegible].54	
政務費總計		99,832,51[illegible].70	
減：繳回經費餘款		930,01[illegible].11	
政務費淨計			9[illegible],893,495.59
III 軍務費			37[illegible],895,202.52*
IV 稽核所撥當地長官款			2[illegible],003,728.78
V 稽核所撥各項基金款			942,222.58
IV 債務費淨額			20[illegible],601,983.65
VII 賠款淨額			4[illegible],676,254.99
VIII 暫記各款淨額			2[illegible],519,882.43
支出總計			76[illegible],122,355.47
本年度結存			
國庫		19,307,15[illegible].80	
海關總稅務司		33,880,54[illegible].44	
鹽務稽核所		6,401,633.45	
合　　計			59,589,322.69
支出總計及結存			$828,711,688.16

*軍務費內有$46,376,864.80係以前年度款項在本年度內轉帳者

主計處會計局所編中央會計總報告

中央會計總報告係自民國二十年度起由主計處會計局逐年編製。內分普通會計及營業會計兩部營業會計部份容於下章敘述。茲先就普通會計分言之。

中央會計總報告普通會計部分計分以下十一表

1.收支總表
2.收入附表一（按科目分類）
3.收入附表二（每種收入占百分比數）
4.收入附表三（與預算數比較）
5.收入附表四（以二十年度數為標準按百分比）
6.支出附表一（按經費支出機關分類）
7.支出附表二（每種支出占百分比數）
8.支出附表三（與預算數比較）

9.支出附表四(以二十年度數爲標準按百分比)

10支出附表五(各種債務費預算與償還數比較)

11支出附表六(每種徵收費佔稅收款百分比較)

按上述收入附表支出附表中有與預算數比較者就表面觀之似與國家總決算相類似。但有以下三點不可不注意第一、編製上述各表之根據爲主計處會計局之帳册。而斯項帳册之根據爲各機關造送主計處會計局之甲乙種收支報告及國庫收支報告等。如此項收支報告有一二機關漏送情事卽不完全。不能認爲全體機關之決算，第二多數軍務外交機關甲種收支報告不能造送，故爲支出數目比較完全起見，不得不用發放經費作爲支出分類之標準，故與嚴格方面用各機關支出應付數或實付數作爲決算之標準者，迥不相侔。第三現時關於收支報表所列收支年度之劃分爲比較完全起見，於次年度收支報告內補收補付上年度款一律補記上年度帳册，惟有一期限，過此期限以後，卽縱有次年度收支報告列補收補付上年度款亦不再補入，是以年度劃分未爲明晰。基於上述三點中央會計總報告亦不能代替決算。但因稍有期待，比較年度劃分清楚一點，所根據收支報告範圍亦較擴大一點，故比財政部所編中央收支報告比較有準確性。

又因期待整理，所需時日甚多，故每年編成日期落後，比較財政部所編中央收支報告表失去敏捷性。

茲舉民國二十二年度中央收支總表於後以窺全豹。

二十二年度中央會計總報告

收支總表

▲收入

I稅款		
1.關稅	337,647,767.21	
2.鹽稅	174,414,230.55	
3.菸酒稅	12,332,394.25	
4.印花稅	8,182,864.58	
5.統稅	98,870.926.22	
6.礦稅	2,465,814.05	
7.交易所稅	3,063.45	
8.銀行稅	1,526,690.79	
合　計		635,444,001.10
II稅外款		

1.國家行政收入	8,029,570.23	
2.國有事業收入	516,489.36	
3.國有財政收入	1,264,533.52	
4.協款收入	659,551.12	
5.國營機關撥款收入	54,475,827.86	
6.國有營業利益收入	2,275,506.12	
7.其他收入	15,695,361.22	
合計		82,916,842.43
III 債款		
1.債券款	64,364,606.03	
2.借入款	79,437,876.11	
合計		143,502,482.14
IV 保管款		4,545,988.32
V 暫收款		5,138,621.72
收入共計		371,547,935.71
上年度結存		26,491,260.54
總計		398,039,196.25

▲支出

I 黨政費		
1.黨務費	5,628,800.00	
2.國務費	16,527,108.06	
3.內務費	4,389,904.09	
4.外交費	8,091,655.00	
5.財務費	71,550,125.22	
6.教育文化費	13,912,480.19	
7.司法行政費	2,028,663.43	
8.實業費	4,046,230.09	
9.交通費	5,732,677.38	
10 蒙藏費	1,617,064.21	
11 建設費	1,300,725.86	
合計		134,825,433.53
II 軍務費		361,920,225.68
III 國有營業資本支出		2,645,233.56
IV 補助費		
1.地方補助費	33,533,151.05	
2.教育補助費	8,719,508.19	

3.事業補助費	363,204.00	
4.其他補助費	4,044,451.39	
合計		46,660,314.63
V 撫卹費		1,636,237.92
IV 債務費		
1.內債本息金	107,093,004.53	
2.外債本息金	56,800,319.14	
3.庚子賠款	38,850,256.32	
4.其他	18,219,105.55	
合計		220,962,685.54
VII 墊付款		18,390,584.98
VII 暫付款		18,256,339.94
VI 以前各年度付款		6,235,115.50
X 整理內外債基金		5,000,000.00
支出共計		816,522,171.28
結存		81,507,024.97
總計		898,039,196.25

江蘇省收支對照表

江蘇省收支對照表亦係現金收支報告。惟在決算未編成以前代替決算觀察歲入歲之實況則可。若即作爲決算觀察，又恐不能確當矣。

茲舉江蘇省收支對照表於後，以窺全豹：

收支對照表 江蘇省二十二年度

1.田賦省稅	$12,104,585.10
2.契稅	1,055,815.86
3.營業稅	3,739,157.49
4.財產收入	291,975.89
5.事業收入	350,780.90
1.黨務費	$146,200.00
2.行政費	2,065,120.00
3.司法費	1,145,517.03
4.公安費	2,682,794.61
5.財務費	1,062,719.30

6.行政收入	387,474.3
7.司法收入	11,604.9
8.補助款收入	1,203,603.0
9.其他收入	1,584,039.7
10 繳還款	1,052,295.6
11 暫收款	1,059,636.6
12 借入款	5,086,532.6
上年度庫存	156,165.6
總計	28,083,669.6

6.教育文化費	3,469,544.05
7.建設費	1,943,453.99
8.衛生費	51,997.00
9.協助費	590,156.14
10 其他支出	515,396.70
11 償還借入款	7,388,393.64
12 補付上年度款	6,244 296.14
本年度庫存	240,698.22
總計	28,083,669.63

第七章　吾國現行營業會計之決算書表

中央會計總報告包括普通會計及營業會計兩部，已見前述。民國二十二年度中央會計總報告包括營業會計決算書表，內容如下：

路政

二十二年度各鉄路資產負債總表暨分戶表

二十二年度各鐵路資本帳總表暨分戶表

二十二年度各鐵路營業帳總表暨分戶表

二十二年度各鉄路損益帳總表暨分戶表

二十二年度各鐵路盈虧撥補帳總表暨分戶表

電政

二十二年度全國電政機關資產負債總表

二十二年度電政司有線電無線電京內電話長途電話其他機關資產負債總表暨附表四種

有線電資產負債各區附表

無線電資產負債各區附表

全國電話局資產負債各區附表

觀於上述各表國營機關決算報表送達主計處會計局者尚未完全此其　。因營業會計預算從未正式公布故所編各表未與預算比較。此其二。學者主張營業機關因營業盛衰其支出得按收入比照增減故預算之拘束力不大所編決算可以不與預算表比較排列，即採用工商業機關決算報告，已備足用，此其三。但又是學者主張公營事業既編預算則所編決算應與預算數比較排列。不過審核決算時管理費用（Fixed Expenses）如局長等之俸給有一定數目即不得超過原定預算數。其他隨營業增減之費用(Variable Expenses) 則就實際情形並比照原定預算內支出與收入之比率而審定之此其四。以上四點爲觀察營業決算之要點。

第八章 進行中之編造總決算底册

主計處歲計局因各機關編送決算不完全，即編送亦愆期日久，於彙編國家總決算，困難之至。爰仿倣日本大藏省所設歲入主計簿及歲出主計簿之辦法，擬定歲出決算帳及歲入決算帳登記實例兩套，以後預備根據此兩套帳册，編造總決算。如各機關日後第一級第二級決算送到，又可以根據此兩套帳册，加以核對。故一舉可以兩得其便矣。舉例如下：

1. 歲出決算帳登記實例

第一級歲出決算帳——根據各機關月份支出計算書登記

機關建設委員會（第一級概算機關）

科目俸給費（以第一級歲出概算科目『項』爲單位）

第一級歲出決算帳

月份	摘要	預算數	決算數	比較增減數	
				增	減
7					
8					
9					
……					

餘類推

第一級歲出決算書——根據第一級歲出決算帳各項十二個月合計金額填入。

機關：建設委員會　　處出決算書

科目	本年度決算數	本年度預算數	比較增減數		備考
			增	減	
俸給費合計					
辦公費合計					
購置費合計					
營造費合計					
特別費合計					
合計					

第二級歲出決算書——根據第一級決算書填入

編製機關：建設委員會　建設費分類歲出決算書

科目	本年度決算數	本年度預算數	比較增減數		備考
			增	減	
第一款設備費 第一項建設委員會 第一目俸給費 第二目辦公費 第三目購置費 第四目營造費 第五目特別費 第二項模範灌溉管理局 第一目俸給費 餘類推					

附註：其他科目可以類推

2.歲入決算帳登記實例

第一級歲入決算帳——根據各機關月份收入計算書登記

機關江蘇印花菸酒稅局（第一級概算機關）

科目菸酒稅（以第一級歲入概算科目「項」為單位）

第一級歲入決算帳

月份	摘要	預算數	決數數	比較增減數	
				增	減

7					
8					
9					
……					

第一級歲入決算書——根據第一級歲入決算帳各項十二個月合計金額填入

格式與第一級歲出決算書相同

第二級歲入決算帳——以主管機關及稅別分戶登記

編製機關財政部

科目菸酒稅　　第二級歲入決算帳

機關及摘要	預算數	決算數	比較增減數	
			增	減
江蘇印花菸酒稅局 浙江印花菸酒稅局				
合計				

第三級歲入決算書——根據第二級歲入決算帳填入

財政部主管歲入決算書

科目	預算數	決算數	比較增減數	
			增	減
關稅合計 鹽稅合計 菸酒稅合計 …………				

第三級歲入決算書——根據第二級歲入決算書彙編

編製機關國民政府主計處

科目菸酒稅

主管機關	預算數	決算數	比較增減數	
			增	減
財政部主管				
合計				

附註 其他科目可以類推

上述編造決算底冊係根據計算書登記。如一機關不送決算，可斷定其計算亦不能如期送出。此其一。計算所列數目爲毛數而非淨數如某月份收入在以後月份退還或從寬減免部分及某月份支出在以後月份被審計部剔除部分俱未列入故決算底冊之登記必須設法搜集上項資料始能準確。此其二。現定決算底冊祇列預算數決算數及比較增減數三欄但依決算章程規定總決算應開左列事項之計算1.歲入部：歲入預算額歲入追加預算額已收訖歲入額歲入減免額未收訖歲入額上年度剩餘額等六項2.歲出部：歲出預算額歲出追加預算額歲出預算實支額歲出剩餘額等四項。但依現定決算底冊於以上各事項之計算將無法著手此其三。現定決算底冊祇是過渡辦法所能編造決算祇有決算書一種，其他應有各項主要會計報告皆未列入。故日後應仍就會計制度產生完備會計報告，以代替決算書表方屬正辦此其四。

第九章 論將來決算法應規定事項

完備財務行政法規中既有預算法，會計法，公庫法及審計法等是否再有製定決算法必要恰爲應討論問題。

第一派主張不應另定決算法者所持理由——決算法中所規定者不外下列十點但均應分別規定于預算法會計法公庫法及審計法內，故不必另定決算法。

一、決算之根據—— 依會計法所設置之會計制度卽爲編造決算之根據。而會計制度之設計應以預算法之所定辦法爲根據。故由會計制度所產生會計報告自然與預算法相適應。

二、決算書表之種類——即會計報告應在會計法規定。

三、決算之報告程序——會計報告程序應在會計法規定。

四、收支計算基礎——應在會計法規定。

五、收支應屬年度之劃分——應在預算法或會計法內規定。

六、出納整理期間——應在會計法或公庫法內規定。

七、會計整理期間——應在會計法內規定。

八、上年度應收及應支各數轉入次年度辦法——應在預算法規定。

九、消滅時效——應在會計法或公庫法內規定。

十、決算書表審核公布之程序及期限——應在審計法規定。

第二派主張應另定決算法者所持理由——鑒於決算書表編造審核程序之重要除預算法會計法公庫法及審計法已有規定者外應將決算方面有關事項另加詳細及一貫規定，以昭鄭重。

依現在趨勢而論持上述第二派主張者占多數。故日後將由立法院製定決算法。但所規定者，亦不外下列十點而已。茲將其應有內容，申述于後：

一、決算之根據——依預算法及會計法之所定辦理。

1. 決算每會計年度辦理一次。
2. 會計年度開始終了名稱依預算法之所定。
3. 各級政府每一會計年度之一切所入及一切費用均應編入決算。
4. 決算所用之機關單位及基金，依預算法之所定。
5. 決算所列金額之單位(即本位幣)，依會計法之所定。
6. 決算所用歲入歲出科目，應依照其年度之預算科目如有合法收入預算未列科目者及新增費用僅于追加預算有科目者均應列入決算。
7. 各級政府之決算依法定收支系統之劃分，各自獨立，同級地方政府之決算亦同。
8. 各級政府之決算其內容應依照預算，分為下列三種：
   - (i) 總決算，
   - (ii) 機關別之單位決算及分決算。
   - (iii) 基金別之單位決算及分決算，(各特種基金之決算另有合法之決算辦法者依其辦法。)

二、決算書表之種類——凡依會計法辦理結帳之年度會計報告均爲決算報告。

三、決算之報告程序——會計法開始會計報告程序即爲決算報告程序。惟須將會計法未規定事項在決算法補行規定。

四、收支計算基礎——依會計法之所規定採取純粹權責發生基礎。如現行支出決算書所採用權責發生及收付實現聯合之基礎應予改正。

五、收支應屬年度之劃分——收支應屬年度劃分既因權責發生制度之採用，易於區別。但爲周詳起見，不妨詳爲規定。

六、出納整理期間——既採權責發生制度，可以不必採用出納整理期間。

七、會計整理期間——決定分會計機關呈送該管單位會計或附屬單位會計整理報告之期限。

八、上年度應收及應支各數轉入次年度辦法——詳細規定如下：

1.歲入方面

將應收轉入次年度，毋庸經追加預算程序。

6.歲出方面

i.歲定經費——將應支數（包括預計保留數及應支數兩種）轉入次年度毋庸經追加預算程序。

ii.繼續經費——如實支數未達其年度應支之預定額者，得以其年度之餘額，全數轉入次年度預算，毋庸經追加預算程序。

九、消滅時效——分歲入及歲出兩方面詳定之。

十、決算書表審核公布之程序及期限——詳細規定如下：

1.各分會計擬開之決算報告由主辦會計人員編就後經機關行政長官簽名蓋章後送交該管審計人員審核加具審計報告。

2.各彙編單位決義之機關接到所主管彙編之決算報告應即查核彙編之。如發現不當或錯誤時除通知原編機關外應附加修正之報告，並依其修正彙編之。

3.主計機關彙編總決算亦準用前第二條之規定。

4.主計機關編成總決算書後，以送該政府最高審計機關爲最終之審定。

5.中央審計機關爲最終之審定後附加最終之審計報告送呈監察院

省市之總決算報告經該管審計機關審查完竣出具審計報告呈中央審計機關核轉監察院。

6.各級審計機關所附審計報告應通知原編機關提出答辯。

7.監察院接到總決算審計報及答辯後應爲最後之決定。

8.已決定之決算提請政府公布之。認爲應賠償之項目移交公庫主管機關執行賠償。認爲應懲處案件應移付懲戒。

学術界之巨擘 —— 交通界之權威

交通雜誌

第五卷 第五期

定價

月出一冊
每冊三角
兩期合刊
定價六角
預定半年
連郵一元
六角全年
連郵三元

總發行所

南京新街
口燕慶坊
一號交通
雜誌社

通訊

車站帳目之審核(C 7.)

高國棟

票據爲進款之根據，站帳爲進款帳之基礎，款求進款之翔實，不能不求站帳之完善，是站帳之完備與否，關係路收至重且鉅，故對於站帳之審核，實爲切要。各路均派有查帳員，隨時出巡其本路各站，查核站帳。茲將在京滬滬杭甬鉄路實習所得之審核方法，約略報告，就正於母校師長及同學。

甲、客運單據帳簿之審核

(一)售票員銀櫃之審核

售票員銀櫃之審核，必須於車站每次列車開出後爲之，其法將售票員銀櫃中之款項數目，分類點清，並按其類別，列一細表，其式概可如左：

類別	張數或個數	銀額
法幣		
拾元	—	$ —
五元	—	—
一元	—	—
紙輔幣	—	—
硬輔幣	—	—
小洋	—	—
銅元	—	—
		$ —

上列細表，係供參攷，如銀洋檢點無訛，則應責成售票員或站長蓋章簽字，以防發現款項不符時，有所狡賴。

上述售票房之銀洋，係指當日售出客票進款，惟內有備用金係存站備找換之用，其數視其營業情況而定。售票房當日之銀行，除備用金外，須與當日售票應得數相符，售票盈餘或虧短，照章均所不許也。故如發現不符時，各相差無幾者，則應嚴詢其由，或即責令賠償，並當面告誡之；如情節重大者，則須呈報會計處長，轉車務處處長查辦之。

檢點現金時，應予注意者爲下列數點：

一、有無僞鈔之攙入

二、檢查時有無款項等攙入或攜出售票房

三、應使售票員不與外界多所接觸

上述三者，係防止售票員之舞弊。如在檢查時，遇有僞鈔，應令售票員賠償；如檢查時，有款項等之攙入或攜出，即有舞弊之可能，故檢查時，注意其有無款項之攙入或攜出，即所以防止售票員之舞弊也；又在檢查時，所以不應使售票員與外界多所接觸者，蓋唯如此，則舞弊之機會，方得以減少。

售票房之現金，雖如上法檢點，然猶不能知其數之確否，故即須檢查本日出售票數，其法：可檢視售票房自至該時止之各種各級客票訖數，以之與該日名片式客票日報單上所列之各起號相減，即可知當天之出售票數，惟同時須查有無孩童劵及退票，並視當日有無填寫客票（空白票）出售，如有開立填寫客票者，應查視其報會計處聯，然後依其票數及票價，核算其票款，是否與上述現金相符。

檢查各大站售票房現金時，除根據上述客票日報審核外，亦可根據售票員登記簿核查之。茲將此登記簿之性質及審核方法略述如次。

售票員登記簿（站帳六一（二））係大站所用，其設立之目的，係記載每次列車客票之起訖號數，以便登記每次列車之進款數。此簿由各售票櫃分別將當日每次客車各級客票之起號登記於起號欄，待該列車開行後，則將各訖號，出售票數及共計國幣等，分別列入各相當欄中，並即結總一次，如有售出月台票，則將其起訖號註明於此簿下端，而將其款額過入該次列車進款中，然後將此簿上每次列車之進款數，分別車次，登記於客貨營業現款登記簿（站帳六一（一））。

客貨營業現款登記簿：係記載每次列車之進款數，如分櫃出售者，則此簿分數本，如滬杭甬路之杭州站，則分兩本；每次進款登記畢，由經手者簽字，將款項交與站長，由銀行派員前來取去，給與臨時收據。至其收據上之總數，則應與此簿（站帳六一（一））上所記之數相符。

至於審核現金之方法，除先依前法檢點現金外，即將售票員登記簿該列車之訖號，與售票房所存之客票訖號相比對，是否無誤；再按票價，計算其該次列車進款共計數之是否無誤；再次，將該簿各該次列車進款共計數，與客貨營業現款登記簿所列各該次列車進款數比對。

依上述方法核對現金，雖屬無訛，然猶不能確知其解銀行額數，故猶須與銀行所出臨時收據所列之數比對。其法：即將各客貨營業現款登記簿所載該日各次列車進款數相加，其所得總數，應與收據上所列之數相符。

上述現金，係指當日之進款，如有昨日之款，尚未解會計處者，應將解款袋解開檢點，以防今日之款，補昨日之款之用。

售票員銀櫃之審核手續，不論滬杭甬路蘇嘉路或京滬路，均如上法行之。至於審核時間，在原則上言，可於每次列車開行後爲之，惟京滬路(除小站外)數大站，如吳縣站，以日間列車來往甚密，出售客票幾無停時，各欲斯時檢點現金，極感困難，且非所宜，故恆在深夜爲之，此與滬杭甬及蘇嘉路情形稍異之處也。

(二)名片式及簿紙客票日報單之審核

1. 本路及聯運名片式客票日報單

車站出售各級名片式客票，按日記載於名片式客票日報單(站帳五(一)及(二))。此單除聯運方面不分段外，本路方面，則按客票之種類及等級，分段如下：

第一段　頭二等尋常客票及特別快車客票

第二段　三四等尋常客票

第三段　三等特別快車客票

第四段　其他各種名片式客票

第五段　本路記帳客票

上列每段之下，各列共計，第三段之下，於本段共計之外，另列三段之共計，第四段之下，於本段共計之外，另列四段之總計，此即本報單之現款總計。

審核是項日報單時，首將本月各級客票之起號，與上月末日之各該級客票訖號一一比對，以核定本月之各起號，有無錯誤；次用昨日(查帳日前一日)之客票訖號，減去本月一日之各該起號，如是，可核算該站出售票數，以之與該末日日報單本月累計欄之實發張數相對，次再計核其進款數，其法：即將本月累計之出售張數，與各該票價相乘，其積乘數，則與本月累計欄之進款相對。

此項日報單之審核，不論本路或聯運，均依上法行之。惟審核時，尚須注意者，卽應查其有無廢票及孩童劵，前者每張作一張，後者二張作一張計算(孩童票每張作半張)；又成人客票價，其尾數若爲單數，如一元五角五分，則其半價，爲七角七分五厘，惟依規章，尾數不滿一分者，亦作一分計算，故一孩童劵價應爲七角八分，有二張孩童劵時，應較成人票價增加一分，卽一元五角六分是；再此項廢票及孩童劵，均應記入作廢客票及孩童劵日報單(站帳七)，審核時，除與名片式客票日報單除去欄所列共計張數相核外，又須逐一視其有無記入廢票及孩童劵日報單中。

本路及聯運名片式客票日報單，經上法核對後，應將其結果與客運業務進款撮總簿(會檢一二三)各該項之數比對，核其是否相符。

2.本路及聯運薄紙客票日報單

薄紙客票日報單，係塡本路及聯運(站帳八(一)及(二))之各種薄紙客票。審核此項日報單，須先查核塡寫客票。玆將查核塡寫客票所應注意之處，略述如下：

查核塡寫客票時，最應注意者，爲塡寫票(空白票)之種類

有幾。按車站之塡寫客票，普通概分下列三種：

(1)尋常——普通，用以代替硬票，供無硬票站用

(2)利益票或優待票——供鐵路員工及其家屬用

(3)軍用票

(一)甲種——現付半價

(二)乙種——記帳半價

此外有團體票。照最近站帳，每種均分尋常與特別，而各立一簿，每種中各有頭、二、三等三級，有時且有四等；本路與聯運，則又分立，本路者，每張客票，分旅客聯報會計處聯及存根三聯，聯運客票，則除上述三聯外，多報清算股一聯。

又審核塡寫客票時，對其所塡銀行數與日期，局編號數之有無遺漏，及當天之款是否當日繳解，均應予注意外，尤恐注意報會計處聯有否誤給旅客，以防一張客票二用，惟報會計處聯已解局，當不能見，如有發現，應向主管人員詢問其由，以防遺漏，並查有存根在否。又當每本塡寫客票查畢時，應在該簿背面，將滾存數註明，以備下次查核時，參考之用。

上述各種各級塡寫客票之審核，須按順序爲之，不可顚亂，蓋塡寫客票簿種類如多，若不按順序審查，則難免不有遺漏

之患。

審核塡寫客票應注意之點，已如上述。至簿紙客票日報單之審查，則祇須在審核塡寫客票時，同時與該日報單逐張核對。其法：本路對本路，聯運對聯運。此外則查其每日累計數有無錯誤，並如審核名片式客票日報單然，將其結果，分別與客運業務進款撮總簿各該項之滾存數比對，是否相符。

(三)行李包裹及雜項客運進款之審核

行李包裹收入現金之檢點，法與檢點售票員銀櫃現金同。至審核此兩種收據時，所應注意之點，與審核塡寫客票同，即核其日期，號數及銀數，並逐張與運出行李包裹及雜項客運日報單(站帳十(一)及(二))比對，是否符合是。惟審核時，當須注意者，即行李有免費及收費兩種，前者，祇須注意其車票號數與等級(以便與客票日報單運對)；及有無逾限重量；後者，除注意上述各點外，又須注意其逾限重量，及逾限運費；如有溢收，則應過入客運進款撮總簿盈餘一欄中。至包裹方面，除核其重量及運費外，如有由鐵路代裝，則又須注意其裝力，如裝卸力由站直接劃給裝卸承辦人，則不對亦可。

除上述行李包裹進款外，尚有雜項客運進款，如囤存費，延期費，電報費，裝卸費，退票手續費，及其他雜項客運收入等是。審核方法：可將其收據，如車站雜項客運進款收據（站長七三），與運出行李包裹及雜項客運日報單（站帳十(一)及(二)）逐張核對；對於其磅單，是否認眞塡列，亦須隨時抽查，以杜弊端而裕收入。

運出行李包裹及雜項客運日報單所記上述各項進款，其結果，應與客運業務進款撮總簿各該項之數相符。

以上所言，係指本路及聯運行李包裹及雜項客運之運出方面。至於本路及聯運運進方面，則應注意到付包件及代收貨價，逐項與運進行李包裹及雜項客運日報單(站帳十一(一)及(二))核對，到付包件，又應與站帳六一(四)相核對。

上述運進行李包裹及雜項客運日報單所記各項進款數其結果，亦應與客運業務進款撮總簿各該項之數相符。

(四)其他各項客運報單

各項客運報單之審核，概述如前。茲再略述所缺如後。

日報單之分類　日報單如站帳五、六、七、十及、十一等，均依下列旅客運輸之分類，而分類開列。

(一　本路

(二)聯運

(1)本兩路

(2)蘇嘉路

(3)國內聯運

(4)水陸聯運

(5)其他

客運進款撮總日報單(站帳十五)：此單係本日客運方面各項進款及解款之撮總表。除站帳十四(渡船客票日報單)外，所有其他各種客運日報單內本日共計之數，均應轉入之。至本報單之內容，則分四段如下：

第一段 現款

第二段 解款

第三段 進款撮總表

第四段 會計處用之結欠表

凡發出先付，及運進到付之客運進款，以及到達站所收之代客收款，均列入第一段；解款單內，客運各項實解及補解扣回之數，列入第二段；發出先付，到付，及記帳之客運進款，則列入第三段；第四段係記該站客運結欠，由會計處填入。審核是項報單，祇須將第一段之本月應解現款累計數，與客運進款撮總簿每日進款總數欄之共計數比對；解款部份，則與解款單及各種單據相核。

「客貨運費雜費訂正單(站帳六四)」 此單因票據內運費雜費計算之錯誤，或變更到達站等項，應補收或退還之時，由收款或退款之車站填造之，及或由站根據清算股之更正清單，及檢查課之錯誤通知書填造之，計分本路與聯運兩種，客運與貨運分別填造。此項訂正單，應隨客運進款撮總日報單解交會計處。

「無」字報單(站帳六十)凡某項客運，某日無進款，應於每月末日，填造「無」字報單，以代替其他各種報單，如寄繳與寄繳收到本路及聯運業務各種報單點驗單(站帳一六(一)—(四))，渡船客票日報單，以及各種報單點驗單內所列之各種報單，除每月末日，不須填造，均應填用此「無」字報單代之。惟無聯運客運之小站，聯運客運報單，如站帳五(二)，六(二)等，均毋須填造，故不須填用「無」寫報單。

各種票據點驗單 各種客運票據，應隨寄繳及寄繳收到本路及聯運客運業務各種票據點驗單(站帳十六(一)—(四))寄交會計處。各種客運寄送報單票據及信件，則應隨「客運寄送報單票據及信件清單」（站帳一〇〇(二)）分別寄送會計處客帳股及聯運股。

(五)客運業務進款撮總簿之核對

客運業務進款撮總簿（會檢一二(三)），係按日記載一站之一切客運進款，其式如下：

客運業務進款撮總簿　　一站　　年　月份

日期	旅客總數	普通旅客 本路	普通旅客 聯運 本路	普通旅客 聯運 他路	官員票	優待票 本路	優待票 聯運 本路	優待票 聯運 他路	遊覽票 本路	遊覽票 聯運 本路	遊覽票 聯運 他路	[illegible]價票	臥車床位 本路	臥車床位 聯運 本路	臥車床位 聯運 他路	特別快車加價 本路	特別快車加價 聯運 本路	特別快車加價 聯運 他路	行李 本路 公務	行李 本路 營業	行李 本路 附帶	行李 聯運 本路	行李 聯運 他路	行李 聯運 公務	包裹 本路 公務	包裹 本路 營業	包裹 聯運 公務	包裹 聯運 本路	包裹 聯運 他路	雜項運輸 本路 公務	雜項運輸 本路 營業	雜項運輸 聯運 本路	雜項運輸 聯運 他路	裝卸費	其他營業進款 月台票	其他營業進款 退票費	其他營業進款 電報費	會計處通知補收進款	每日進款總數

此簿之審核：先將上列每行相加，再與各該日報單之累計數，逐項相核，有無錯誤。茲將所列各行之核對法，略述於下：

普通旅客欄之本路及聯運進款本日止之共計數，分別與名片式及簿紙客票日報單（站帳五及六）普通旅客一類，兩累計數之和相對，惟簿紙客原日報單中應減去利益票進款數，蓋此欄所記，專指尋常客票之進款也。

優待票欄本日止之共計數。則與簿紙客票日報單利益票一項之累計數相對。

補票費欄之共計數，應與站帳十八之補票費一項共計數相對，或與車站雜項客運進款收據逐張核對。

行李包裹兩欄諸數，則與行李房報單逐張核對。

雜項運輸及裝卸費，則與雜項收據，如站帳七三逐張核對。

其他營業進款欄之月台票，電報，及退票費共計數，分別與站帳十八各該項共計數相對。

每日進款總數欄之數，則按日與解款單核對，其至本日止之總計數，則與客運進款撮總日報單第一段之本月應解現款累計數比對，是否符合。

（六）解款單之審核

解款單（站帳六一）正面所載之數，係指該日繳解之客貨運及雜項進款數，其背面則將客貨運及雜項分別記載，故如先查客運進款時，則可將解款單背面之客運業務計數，與客運業務進款撮總簿之每日進款總數欄所列該日之數相對，無訛後，再將此數加上貨運業務及其雜項進款，其總數應與該單正面之總計數相符。

各站所解款項，會計處尚未將解款單收據寄還者，則查時，應在已解未退還之解款單存根聯上，加以註明，以便下次查時，再查之，蓋解款單之審核，不依存根，而以經會計處出納課蓋章後發回之解款單收據聯為根據也。

（七）客運營業進款平準表之審核

客運營業進款平準表（會檢一八七（客）），係補各站結算一月間客運業務進款之收支帳目而設。凡一切客運收入，列於此表借方；繳解之現金，墊付款項，特別貸項等，則列入貸方。

借方所列各款，係由各該站，自客運業務進款撮總簿內轉錄而來；貸方各款，則依解款單及核准由站墊付之各種單據，或會計處特准貸餘各數而得。

此表之審核，可分借貸兩方言之：

借方之審核：上月結存，則與上月份平準表之本月結餘相查對，並應視其上月結餘各項之解款日期；惟此項結存，係包括上月各種進款，故在共計欄內，應獨立，不能包括於本路客運進款小計中，必須各種進款各作小計後，而後始可加入共計一欄之共計數中，此點車站司帳者，每易疏忽，故審核時，尤應注意。至本月份之各項收入，則可與客運業務進款撮總簿，或各項日報單，逐項核對。例如本路，本兩路聯運，及國內聯運之名片式客票收入，則可分別與名片式客票日報單本月之尋常及特別費兩累計數之和相對；簿紙客票，則分別與簿紙客票日報單本月之尋常與特別費兩累計數之和比對；各種行李包裹及雜項客運則分行李包裹及雜項客運報單，各該項之本月累計數相核；雜項進款與站帳十八本月累計之共計一數相對；運進到付包裹，則與站帳六一（四）相核等是；核畢，將上月結存，與上述各項相加，而核其借方總計然否。

貸方之審核：現金總數一項，可與客運業務進款撮總簿每日進款總數欄之總計數比對。至特別貸項，如本路公務包裹，政府及他路記帳，退票收等等，審核時，須視其支付憑證，記帳憑證及其他各種單據。核畢，則將上述各項相加，而與借方總計相比，如有本月結餘，則應在此表背面，將結餘細帳開立，如有久未繳解者，應註明其原因。又本月如有未清之到付包件，及代收款項，則應檢視其包件等，是否實際在站。

乙、貨運單據帳簿之審核

（一）現金之審核

審核貨運方面之現金，可先檢點其現金手存數；再將（一）當日之先付票據，（二）運進到付及代收貨價貨票，及（三）其他雜項貨運收入單據，逐張核對，再將以上三種進款總數相加，而與客貨司事現款登記簿相對，如未備上項登記簿者，則與貨站所備之貨運進款草簿之記載核對，然後與現金手存數相核，是否相符。

（二）貨票之核對

貨票之種類甚多，以付款時間言，可分：

（1）運出先付

（2）運出到付

（3）運進到付

（4）運進先付

（5）記帳

上列五種，以運輸範圍言，又各分本路，本兩路及國內聯運等數種。茲就付款時間之分類，而略述其核對之方法如次。

運出先付貨票　各種運出先付貨票，須與貨物進款登記簿（會檢一一四）逐張核對，按貨物進款登記簿係記載有現款收入之先付到付貨票及其他雜項收入，其式如下：

貨物進款登記簿

貨票		站名		收款	收項											附註
號數	日期	由	至	日期	運出貨票		裝卸		調車費		保管延期等費	代收貨價	代收貨價手續費	其他	總計	
					前月	本月	裝費	卸費	起運站	到達站						

核對本路及本兩路聯運貨票時，應注意其局編號數，日期，訖站，及銀數。國內聯運貨票方面，則除上述各點外，又應核其裝力。至代收貨價貨票，則不論本路，本兩路及國內聯運，均須核其手續費，並與車站雜項進款收據（站帳七三）逐張核對。此項手續費起碼為二角五分，每五分為單位。

運出到付貨票　此項貨票，除國內聯運貨票，須核其裝力，及代收貨價貨票，應核其手續外，餘則祇須注意其局編號數是否連續及運出日期。

運進到付貨票　此項貨票，除須與貨物進款登記簿核對外，並須與運進到付及代收貨價登記簿（站帳三二（四））逐張核對，前者，須記載已付之運進到付貨票，後者係記載一切運進到付貨票各費之總數及代收貨價，其式如下：

運進到付貨物包裹及代收貨價代客收款登記簿
（附運進先付代收貨價代客收款）

一站

收到		票據				應收各款				附記
日期	車次	先付或到付	號數	起運 路名	起運 站名	到付票內各貨總數	代收貨價代客收款	費用	運貨出門證或包裹件寄收數運貨號數	

運進到付貨票，與上述兩簿核對，除核其銀數外，應注意其起運，到達，及提貨日期，起運與到達日期之檢視，係查其貨之提取，是否已逾該貨到達後　星期，如然，則應收延期費；又對此種運輸，應視其為整車抑零担，以便明瞭運輸情形。

運進先付貨票　此項貨票之核對，亦應注意其提貨及到達日期，以便視其有無延期費；如屬代收貨價者，則又應與運進到付及代收貨價登記簿及貨物進款登記簿相核對；又貨票如為國內聯運者，則又須核其卸費。

記帳貨票　此項貨票，祇須視其局編號數，是否連續，及其日期，暨記帳憑證可也。

（三）各項單據之核對

聯運到站卸費收據（站帳二八（三））　此項收據上所載之卸費，逐張與貨物進款登記簿相核。其法：依收據號數，按日逐張核其銀數符否，再與車站雜項進款日報單卸費欄之數相核。

貨物保管費收據（站帳四七）　審核是項收據，法將收據上所列銀數，與貨物進款登記簿上所列銀數，按收據號數，逐張核對，並依其收據上所載貨票號數，在該簿附註欄註明貨物保管費收據號數，以便核對貨票時，即可查知保管費已收；（反之，如先查貨票，後查此項收據時，若發現應收保管費時，亦應在附註欄內註明，以便查閱保管費收據，並與之核對）。又運進先付之貨票，在貨物進款登記簿上無記載，如收有保管費，則查時，應在此簿加以註明。再此項收據又應與車站雜項進款日報單保管費欄之數相對。

代收貨價收據（站帳七三—無進款收據） 此項收據，除注意其號數是否連續外，收據上所列代收貨價，可按收據上所列貨票號數，與貨物進款登記簿該號所列之代收銀數相對。

接送費收據（站帳七三） 本兩路貨運中，有接送費一項，此係代客接送貨物，其收入係直接撥付裝卸承辦人，然承辦人出具收據，繳解會計處，是故，是項接送費，非本兩路之收入，所以入賬者，以其接送費收據係由鐵路所出也。在解款單上，則將收據號數及銀數列入，由會計處認其款已解，而冲銷之。其所出之收據。則可與車站雜項進款日報單（貨運）（站帳三五）逐張核對。

調車費及延期費收據（站帳二八） 關於調查費之審核，應先考核各該管商用岔道出入車輛號碼，照後到站查核站帳二八，曾否照章核收，車輛出入號碼，次數，時間，是否相符。至延期費之審核，應根據車輛登記簿，查視發交商號裝卸之車輛，有無逾越鐘點，曾否照章核收延期費。此外再與站帳三五相核，以期涓滴歸公，而杜侵蝕之弊。

訂正單 貨運方面之客貨運費雜費訂正單（站帳六四） 所列之訂正數，可按訂正單號數，與貨物進款登記簿查對，惟此係指少收而言，如多收須退還者，在貨物進款登記簿上無記載，故查時，若遇此項訂正單，則應在登記簿附註欄內註明其訂正單號數。

（四）各項貨運報單之審核

運出運進貨物日報單 此兩種日報單，各分本路與聯運。運出貨物日報單（站帳三一），則與本路及聯運出口貨票，按運出先付，運出到付，及運出記帳分別核對。運進貨物日報單（站帳三二），則按運進到付，運進先付，及運進記帳，分別與本路及聯運進口貨票相對。

脚伕裝卸貨物日報單（站帳三四（二）） 此單內之出口貨物裝費，可與上述運出貨物日報單裝費欄諸數比對；進口貨物卸費則可與運進貨物日報單卸費欄諸數核對。

車站雜項進款日報（單帳三五）以單係記載各項貨運雜項收

入，如調車費，延期費，接送費，代收貨價手續費，罰款，取保領物手續費，變更費，及國內聯運之卸費等。其審核方法；係與站帳七三車站雜項進款收據貨運，站帳[illegible]八調車裝卸及延期費收據，站帳四七保管費收據，站帳八一變更單，及站帳二八(二)聯運到站卸費收據，分別核對。

上月運進未提貨物月報單(站帳三八) 此單由到達站按月填造。凡每月末日，車站應將該日晚間所存未提之運進貨票通知書聯查閱一次，如查有填發日期，係在上月，而本月末日，仍未提取者，應逐號列入此單。例如三月末日晚間查閱各種票據之通知書聯，如其填發日期係在二月廿八日以前，而二月末日仍未提取者，則應於三月末日，列於三月份月報單。如其填發日期，係在三月一日以後，則不須填入。至此單之核對法，可將其總數，與上月份貨運營業進款平準表本月結餘數相對照，並與未清貨帳報單核對。

未清貨帳報單(站帳四一) 此單亦由到達站按月填造，內包括本月份及上月份之未清貨帳。核對時，將所有本月份及上月份未清貨帳，先根據運進到付及代收貨價登記簿所載之號數，至貨棧檢查，是否各該貨均在棧中，並在運進到付及代收貨記價登記簿上，加以記號；各貨已提去，則運費等已收，應解會計處，故再依未清貨帳報單所列之貨票號數，按號與貨物進款登記簿各該票號相對，核其銀數然否。未清貨帳報單之本月未清總數欄之總計數，則應與本月份貨運營業進款平準表貨方之本月結餘數相符。又此單之本月未清總欄之數，如在下月解清則應與次月收入欄之現款或滙單欄所列之數相符，若在次月，全部償清者，則本月未清總數與現款或滙單兩欄之兩總計數，亦必相符。

貨運進款撮總日報單(站帳三九) 此單係本日貨運方面各項進款及解款之撮總表，所有各種貨運日報單內本日共計之數，均須轉入，故其性質與客運進款撮總日報單相同。內亦分四段：

第一段 表明應收現金，凡運出先付，及運進到付之貨運進款及加價，以及到達站所收之代收貨價，均列入之。

第二段 表明解款概況，凡解款單內貨運各項實解之數及補解扣回之數，均列入之。

第三段 表明營業概況，包括運出先付，到付，及記帳之貨運進款及加價，並非專指現金之數而已。

第四段　表明車站貨運結欠數，由會計處填入。

核對時，將第一段本日止之本月應解現款累計數，與貨物進款登記簿總計欄同日止之共計數相核；第二段所列之數，則與解款單及各種單據相對。

各種票據點驗單　各種貨票之點驗單應隨「寄繳及寄繳收到本路及聯運貨運業務各種報單點驗單」(站帳四二(一)—(四))寄交會計處。貨運寄送報單票據及信件，則應隨貨運寄送報單票據及信件清單(站帳一〇〇(二))分別寄送會計處貨帳股及聯運股。

「無」字報單　此單之用法，與客運同，故不多贅。

代收及扣付各款日報單(站帳五九)　此單登記車站代收及扣付各種款項，此均爲借方，其貸項均在貨運進款撮總日報單之站帳五九一行內對銷之。

(五)解款單之核對

解款單之核對，與客運方面相同，即將此單背面所到貨運及其雜項進款數，按日與貨物進款登記簿總計欄所列之數相核對。茲有一點尚須注意，故略述如下：

會計處收到各站解款，所出收據，四五日內概可寄到原解款站，如該站久未將收據粘貼於解單簿，除查詢外，可查閱解款通知書此書係大站解款于銀行時所用，計分兩聯，一聯交于銀行，一聯存根，在存根上，由銀行收支員蓋章，並另出臨時收據，由站隨解款單寄會計處，憑此可查知款項是否已解。惟此猶不足憑，不能與客運營業進款撮總簿之每日營業進款數，及貨物進款登記簿之每日進款總計數相對，若欲核對，必須以會計處出納課所出收據爲根據。

(六)貨運營業進款平準表之核對

貨運營業進款平準表亦爲車站結算一月間貨運收支帳目而設。借方係記載一切貨運收入，貸方則記各項解款數。

此表之審核，亦可分借貸兩方言之：

借方之審核：首將上月結存與上月份貨運營業進款平準表之本月結存相對，並檢視其解款日期。至於本月之各項收入，則與各該項日報單之本月累計數核對。例如本路及聯運之運出先付各項，則分別與站帳三一(一)及(二)各該項之本月累計數比對；其中雜項進款一項，則另與站帳三五之本月累計相核，本路及聯運之運進到付各項(包括本月運進未清)，與站帳六一

（四）逐項核對，訂正一項，則與結帳六六比對。核畢，將上述各項，與上月結存相加，核其借方總計然否。

貸方之審核：所列已解現金數，則可與貨物進款登記簿之總計數相對；特別貸項之各項，則與支付憑單，記帳憑證，及其他各種支付單據相核，然後將上述二項相加，而與借方總數相比，如有本月結餘，則應在此表背面，將結餘細帳開立。

書評

汽車運輸學原理

王同文

原　名——Principles of Motor Transportation

著　者——Ford K. Edwards

出版處——McDraw-Hill Book Co.

定　價——美金四元

當今吾國各省積極興築公路網，以利內地陸運，對於汽車運輸，尤需注意。本書內容，計分十六章，其大綱如下：(1)載客汽車運輸之發達史，及晚近業務上之進展，運輸之範圍，及其經濟概。(2)裝貨汽車運輸之發達史，及晚近貨運業務上之進展，並詳述美國開發農村運輸之實況。(3)汽車營業公司之組織，與各處之工作。(4)營事處內部之組織，員司之責任，尤以發展貨運之方法，及營業之分析，研究敘述為詳。(5)運輸處之組織與工作，客貨運業務實施之方法、範圍、種類、及手續等等，對於接送業務各項，著者加以注意。(6)養路處對於汽車及應用材料各項之檢查，與保養事宜。(7)會計處之組織、事務之範圍，賬目之分類，損益方面之種種審查，聯運賬目之清算，成本會計之應用，各項用費之分析。(8)管理與訓練開車夫一章，關於人事管理之方法及制度，大可參用於吾國各地之公路局，或私營汽車公司，並提及災禍之避免等種種問題。(9)運價與運價表一章，說明釐訂運價之要素與原則，客貨運價要素之應用，貨運分等，客貨運價表之編訂，各種運價之舉例，讀者凡欲研究公路汽車運價，此章不可不讀。(10)討論汽車營業公司之估值，目的與方法，對於應用折舊方法一點尤詳。(11)敘述汽車營業公司之監督機關，及其組織與實施。(12)至於汽車營業公司之稅捐，著者曾列舉各種稅捐制度，並參以美國各地之實施情形。

著者曾與汽車運輸業各公司，相處多年，此時已有著書之意，乃由各處廣取材料，是以書中所列統計，及所舉實例，均由汽車營業公司方面，直接得來，誠較為真實；其文體清簡，最適宜於為大學讀汽車運輸學之教本。惜本書寫述，全依汽車公司本身為立場，偏重於論述各處之職務，關於公路方面之建設與管理，及公路與汽車公司之種種關係，均未提出，實為最大缺點。又關於行車管理，不及 George W. Grupp 著之「汽車運輸之經濟」Economies of Motor Transportation 為充實。

專載

參觀崇德及吳興兩縣羊種及羊毛展覽報告書

A. F. Barker 著
夏循元 譯

民國二十五年十一月二十七日，余應浙江省第一第二兩區所主辦的羊種，羊毛，及製品展覽會的邀請，前往崇德參觀，並就檢查所得，作一研究的報告如下：

體格的類別

體格的類別很多，惟當地所產的羊，大部屬於長脚的一類。體格的形狀，與所產毛的重量，很有關係。圖一是一隻崇德羊，其體格的形狀，可算是本地羊種中的最優者，其身體厚壯，是一種健全的表現。其頭大而其鼻類似維馬式(Roman type)，這是世上牧羊人所喜求的。圖二爲吳興羊種之一，牠的體質與圖一的崇德羊大同小異，惟其頭部及尾部的形狀，尚未到第一等標準。圖三是崇德羊的另外一種，其頭部形狀尚佳，惟其體格不如圖一之壯厚。圖四的羊體格的構造更爲輕小。圖六爲本地所畜的美利奴(Merino)羊種，但是這個羊種，已非純粹。美利奴的鼻形是尖的，不像維馬式的，這也是體質比較孱弱的一種表示。

以上所述的羊種，除美利奴種外，其餘的皆屬於所謂『闊尾類』者。這類羊是否爲中國羊種主要的家種，是一問題，在本報告中的後部，再論及此一點。大概言之，迄今中國的闊尾羊，能渡過有定的食料缺乏時期，和無定的食料缺乏時期，而得傳延其種，是這類羊特有的長處。關於配種方面，體格問題是很重要的，本報告中的後部，特別論及這點。

毛皮的類別

由羊毛方面而論，毛皮的類別是很重要的。圖二甲是表明普通吳興毛皮之一，毛皮係精細纖維的組成，在檢驗每一叢纖維時，（如圖二乙與二丙），發現一種普通的外層粗纖維，但比較其他多數羊種爲少。圖中還可以看到的一點，就是纖維有捲曲的趨勢，這也是品質優良的一種表現，這類毛發展的結果，就成爲圖四甲與四乙的毛樣。毛中的粗纖維可見的極少，而大半都是捲曲精細的纖維。這類毛是本地羊種中所產的最優者。圖三甲與三乙，是表明纖維構成的點劣，其中長而粗的外層毛有明顯的發展，致使這種毛不易紡製，因而製成的紗與布等，品質粗陋。這種羊看來好像有『髭』蘢罩着的，由檢查所得，證明這種「髭」的現像，是由於粗纖維比細纖維更長(卽圖三)，而細纖維祇占全毛較小的部份。圖五甲與五乙，是值得注意的一種羔羊毛纖維的組合，其中纖維沒有分爲內層與外層的現像，而有一種粗細整齊的分配。還可以看到的是纖維的末端是尖形，這是表明羔羊第一年所生長的毛皮。毛皮的內外層，無淸楚界綫，祇由外層而漸變爲內層。由這種現像，可見在中國的羊種中，毛皮生長的變化，比世界上無論任何處爲多。(按毛皮生長的變化愈多，則所產毛的品質愈劣)關於這點以下再討論。

美利奴的毛皮是具有個性的，並且在這裏有兩種毛皮——卽「單純的毛皮」與「不單純的毛皮」。所謂「單純的毛皮」，卽毛皮中的纖維，是具有同一性質的。這種纖維的粗細，從肩部到股部雖有不同，大概言之，全體纖維，同屬一類。所謂「不單純的毛皮」，卽有顯然的外層與內層的分別，因而纖維的構造，在顯微鏡下有不同的顯現。

普通美利奴羊毛，具有優美的波紋每一寸纖維上，常有十至二十波紋數，波紋數與纖維直徑（卽纖維細度）的關係，可用下列公式表明：

$$\frac{D}{60}=\text{每寸波紋數}$$（D代表纖維直徑英寸分數的反數）

上面已經說過，中國土產羊毛以有波紋或捲曲的爲最優。惟中國羊毛的波紋，因爲纖維如V字形，所以往往不如美利奴羊毛的波紋占據纖維的全部份。由製造一方面而論，纖維的波紋愈多愈佳。

以上一節報告可以結論如下：在所檢驗的本地毛皮之中，崇德的捲曲毛皮爲最佳（圖四），其次是普通的吳興毛皮（圖三）。雖然這幾類毛皮，都沒有均勻的生長。但是現在認爲在可能範圍之內必須有最均勻的生長，縱使要犧牲一部份的內層細毛，亦在所不計。爲製造起見，將來或須能有方法能將細毛與粗毛分開。但是現時對於毛皮的品質，須有整個的鑒定。假使能有方法將細毛與粗毛分開，則毛皮的品質，可就其內層細毛鑒定——而最細的內層毛可在最粗的外層毛底下得到。

雖然是雜種的美利奴羊的毛皮，也比無論任何種類的中國本地毛皮爲均勻。所以用美利奴羊與本地羊配種，或可得到「單純的毛皮」。然而這種工作，尚須有積極的研究及試驗方可。假使能設法將內層細毛與外層粗毛分開，則牧羊的事業，當另有新的發展。

纖維直徑的分析

羊毛的纖維直徑是檢定羊毛品質最主要的一點。下列的表中，是上述的幾種毛，每一種測量到一百次的結果。

直徑次數分配表

直徑單位	吳興毛（圖一）	崇德粗毛（圖三）	崇德捲毛（圖四）	崇德羔毛（圖五）	美利奴毛（圖六）
1＝1/7800″	—	—	—	—	
2＝1/3900	—	—	—	—	—
3＝1/2600	—		2	1	—
4＝1/1950	3	2	17	15	16
5＝1/1560	12	12	20	10	19
6＝1/1300	27	24	18	5	19
7＝1/1110	21	16	18	8	11
8＝1/975	15	7	9	8	10
9＝1/867	2	4	4	7	6
10＝1/780	1	11	1	8	5
11＝1/710	1	3	—	5	3
12＝1/650	1	3	1	5	3
13＝1/600	1	1	—	3	2
14＝1/560	1	1	1	4	2
15＝1/520	1	—	—	3	1
16＝1/485	1	—	—	2	2
17＝1/455	1	—	1	3	—
18＝1/430	1	—	1	2	—
19＝1/410	1	—	1	4	—
20＝1/390	—	1	1	1	1
21＝1/372	—	1	1	—	—
22＝1/355	1	2	1	—	—
23＝1/339	1	1	—	—	—
24＝1/325	2	2	—	—	—
25＝1/312	1	1	—	—	—
26＝1/300	1	1	—	—	—
27＝1/289	—	2	1	—	—
28＝1/278	—	2	1	—	—
29＝1/269	—	—	1	—	—
30＝1/260	—	1	—	—	—
31＝1/252″	—	—	—	—	—
32＝1/244	1	1	—	—	—
33＝1/236	—	—	—	—	—
34＝1/229	1	1	—	—	—
平均直徑＝1/	890″	755″	1080″	890″	1075″

從上表可以得到下列的幾個論點：——

（一）圖二，圖三，圖四的毛顯示內層細纖維的集中，其直徑從 $\frac{1}{3900}$ 到 $\frac{1}{1950}$ 英寸。但是其中少數的 $\frac{1}{500}$ 英寸以上的粗纖維，是不可忽略的，這種粗纖維有時占全部毛皮百分之五十的重量，因而足以減少原羊毛紡紗的能力百分之五十以上。圖四的崇德捲毛平均細度爲 1/1080 英寸。而圖六之美利奴毛平均細度爲 1/1075 英寸。惟中國毛中含有在 $\frac{1}{400}$ 英寸以上的粗纖維，或能使其紡紗的能力比美利奴毛減少一倍。假使能將中國毛中含有少數的粗纖維分出，則中國原有的羊毛，可以有完全新異的用途。由分析圖五之羔羊毛，可知與美利奴羊配種，或可產生粗細均勻，品質良好的羊毛。

(二)配種的目的，不但要能使毛的粗細均勻，約在 $\frac{1}{1000}$ 英寸，並且還要使每單位纖維全部的粗細均勻。圖一的外層毛中纖維粗細的變異由 $\frac{1}{1000}$ 至 $\frac{1}{600}$ 英寸，而內層毛的變異，由 $\frac{1}{1300}$ 至 $\frac{1}{400}$ 英寸之間。圖五的羔毛每單位纖維的粗細變異較少，這大概是因爲羔羊受氣候的影響，比長大的羊爲少。

在這裏可以得到一點有科學意味的討論。美利奴羊常認爲能脫去其外層毛而保留其內層毛。英國的黑面羊(Blackface sheep)也有兩層毛，每年春季，脫去其內層毛而保留其外層毛。惟美利奴羊向不脫去其毛，並且若是牠的來源是屬於英國羊一類的羊種，那末牠也應在每年的春季脫去其毛。再看圖二丙的羊毛，其中粗纖維的末端是尖的，而細纖維的末端反是平的，這表示細纖維已經剪過，而粗纖維的生長，每年更新。倘是如此，則在中國可得與美利奴相彷彿的羊種，即是每年脫換其外層毛而繼續生長其內層毛。這一點假若能證實，則或許能使中國羊進化至如同美利奴羊一般。然而粗毛或黑毛的生長，據說是一種强壯體格的表示。這或許是農人所喜求的。但從製造方面而論，這兩種毛都應完全消滅的。

顯微鏡下的檢驗

在顯微鏡下檢驗所表明的幾點，是很值得理論上及實際上的注意：——

(一)所有檢驗的纖維可以分爲下列幾種：——

(甲)有髓的(圖七甲)

(乙)無髓的(圖七乙)

(丙)有斷續髓的(圖七丙)

有髓的及有斷續髓的纖維，均認為不能得有優良的紡製，故現在所需的是要能檢定這種纖維在每一束毛中占有的百分數。檢定的方法，可將纖維浸入輪質(Benzene)之中，則有髓的纖維立可檢出。這種髓，普通在顯微鏡下也可看出，若將纖維加以坎拿大香油(Canadian Balsam)少許，置於小玻片上，則有髓之處，在顯微鏡下更為明顯。

(二)纖維上鱗狀的結構，可分為下列數類——

(甲)鋸嵌鱗狀的結構。即普通所謂『死纖維』者。既粗且脆而毫無彈力性（1/400英寸直徑）；（圖八甲）。

(乙)髮形的結構。此項纖維上有鱗形，成不整列的條紋（1/500英寸直徑）；（圖八乙）。

(丙)碎塊鱗形的結構。在外層的粗纖維，及內層的細纖維均有（1/600英寸直徑；（圖八丙）。

(丁)圍抱鱗形的結構。此項結構，一律為細纖維所含有。並且事實上似乎全靠纖維的細度，始能有這種鱗形。（1/800英寸直徑）；（圖八丁）。

(三)中國羊毛纖維上鱗片的形狀不一，而最普遍的要算圍抱鱗形或近乎圍抱鱗形的結構。其他如圓形或尖形以及伸長形的鱗狀，也常有可見（如圖九甲與九乙）。中國羊毛何以無如美利奴毛的波紋，且粗纖維上鱗形的結構何以有偌大變化，其原因尚在進行研究中。

現在可大概說明羊毛品質之優良者，須具有下列的幾點性質：——

(甲)無髓的纖維。

(乙)具有圍抱鱗形或細碎鱗形的結構。

(丙)每單位纖維，由根至尖，無極端粗細的變異。

(丁)毛皮上最粗與最細之纖維的差異，不超過百分之二十五以上。

（戊）每寸波紋數與公式 $\frac{D}{60}$ 適合。D等於纖維直徑英寸分數之反數。（譯者按：例如纖維之直徑爲 $\frac{1}{1000}$ 英寸，則D＝1000）。

（己）纖維長度之用於紡毛紗者（Woollen yarn），須有一英寸半至二英寸長。如用於梳毛紗者（Worsted yarn）須有三至五英寸長。這裏跟着發生兩個問題，即是每年當剪毛一次或兩次。及春季拔毛是否應視秋季落毛與否而定。

結論

（一）本地的羊大都是長脚的，並應具有厚壯的體格，與强壯的頭，及羅馬式的鼻。

（二）是否應要毛產量多的羊用以替代闊尾類。這問題是應當考慮的。想得到這效果，可用 Romney Marsh 羊（英國種）配種。

（三）在上節所說的變更時，須特別注意飼料均勻的供給。不然羊毛的生長，亦必不均勻，而致使其價值減少。

（四）研究擇配本地羊種的方法，使消除其外層粗毛而發展其內層細毛。同時要求其產量的增加。

（五）與美利奴羊配種；假若需要較有伸縮力的毛，則與英國的Down 類羊（如 Ryeland 種）配種。並應有持久及悉心的研究，務使消除其外層毛，而專使其內層細毛生長。在這裏，單純的毛皮是最理想的。

（六）選擇本地羊中有產量最多可能性的羊種，而發展其毛。同時要發展其腹部及腿部的毛。

（七）毛皮的生長不但是要求其一律，而且每單位纖維的直徑，也須求其一律。有規則的飼餧，是主要的方法。

（八）纖維平均直徑，須在 $\frac{1}{1000}$ 英寸左右，而最重要的是不得有「死纖維」或粗毛的存在。

（九）除第一年的羔羊毛外，每一束纖維應有平頭的末端。

（十）有髓的或有斷續髓的纖維，應用選擇的方法消除之。

(十一)有關抱鱗形結構，及有整齊波紋的纖維（每寸波紋須有十至二十之多）是在所必求的。

(十二)纖維的長度如何，及每年剪毛一次或兩次，須視紡毛與梳毛製造的需要而定。

關於在冬季以桑葉飼羊的附註： 從羊毛這一方面而論，這裏有兩重要點應當考慮的。第一點纖維的生長不宜有任何突變，所以應注意及（甲）由飼草變至飼桑葉之時是否突然而變的，（乙）由飼桑葉復變為飼草之時是否突然而變的。在這兩個時間，羊毛纖維均生長有變遷的趨勢。故如有變更飼料之時，最宜使其逐漸變更。飼料的變更有時能影響及纖維的長度。譬如英國的Wenslcydale羊種，當從飼草變為飼萊菔之時，及懷孕之時，纖維的長度減短，而於纖的粗細，則不甚影響。另一方面，氣候的變遷也能影響及纖維的生長。如以桑葉為飼料，是於羊毛的生長有特別利益，則在支配情形之下，應作小規模的實驗。南京金陵大學或許能實行這種實驗工作。

第二點應考慮的就是飼桑葉與飼草時所產的毛品質優劣的比較。飼料的不同是否於製造方面有實際的影響，也應考慮的。並應檢驗飼草與飼桑葉的毛，以作製造上準確的試驗。

（附插圖於後）

圖一：崇德羊中最優的體格

Figure 1: Chungteh Sheep showing the best body characteristics.

圖一甲：羊之四種

Figure 1A: Illustrating four types of sheep.

圖二: 吳興羊
Figure 2: Wushing Sheep

圖二甲: 吳興羊毛皮
Figure 2A: Wushing Fleece

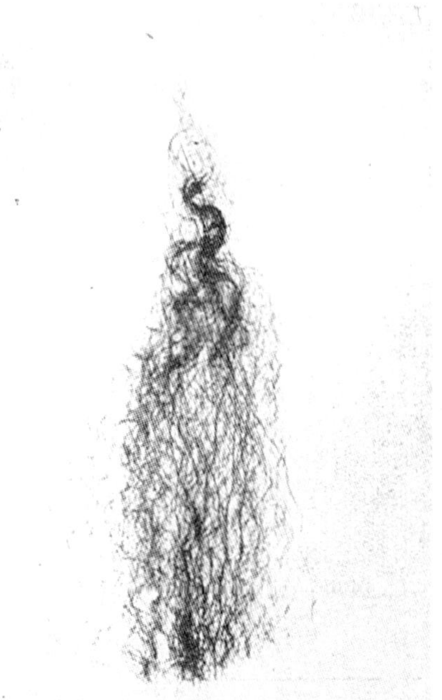

圖二乙: 吳興毛之一束
(注意其中之粗纖維)
Figure 2B: Wushing Staple
(Note the strong fibres)

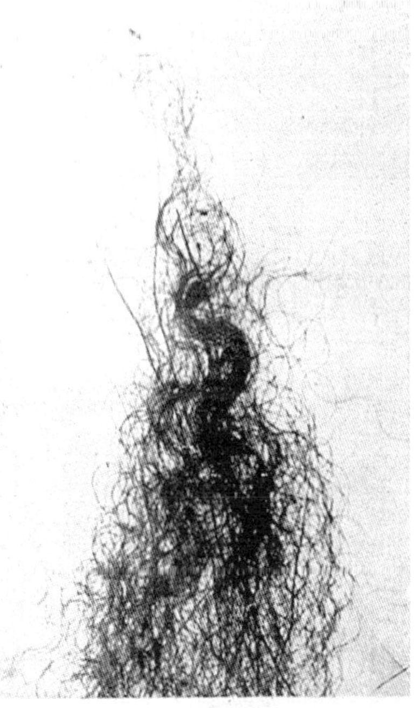

圖二丙: 吳興毛之一束
(注意其中粗毛之尖頭)
Figure 2C: Wushing Fibres
(Note the pointed fibres)

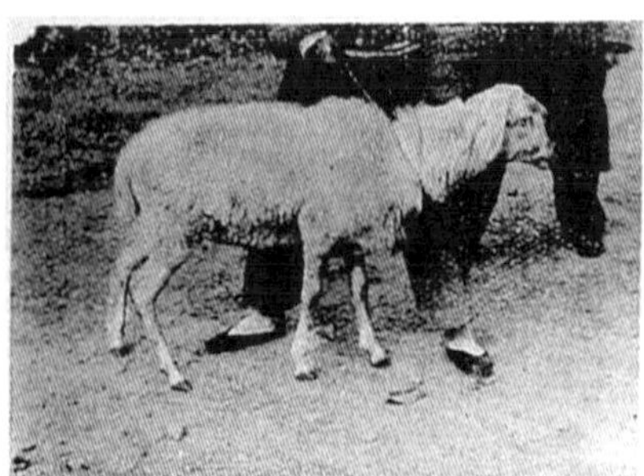

圖三：崇德羊
Figure 3: Chungteh Sheep

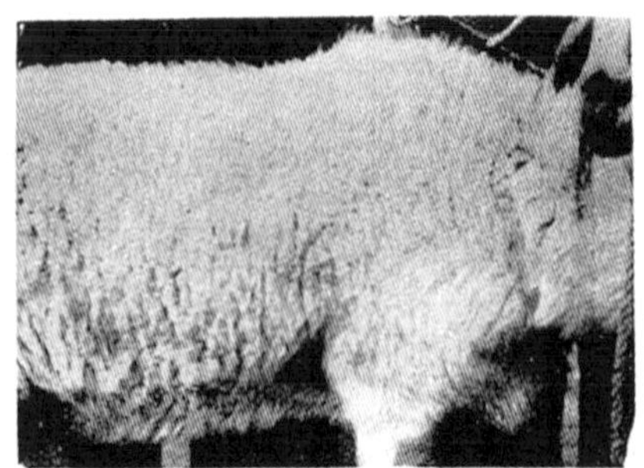

圖三甲：崇德毛皮
Figure 3A: Chungteh Fleece

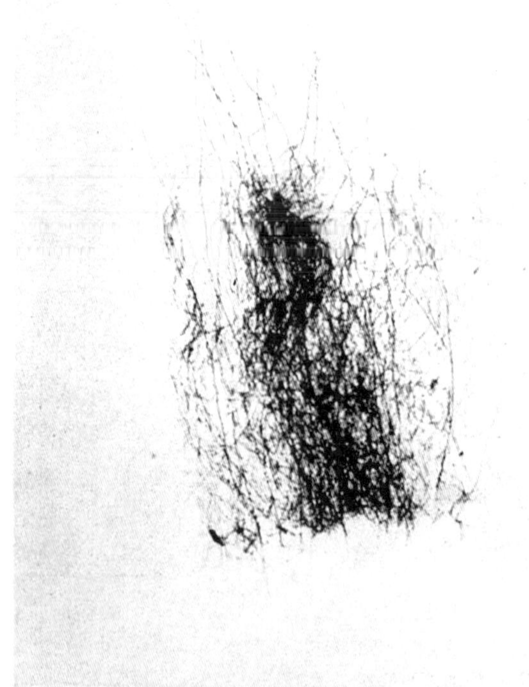

圖三乙：表明「粗毛」之一束
Figure 3B: Showing "Hohlo" staple.

圖四： 輕小之體格
Figure 4: Light Body

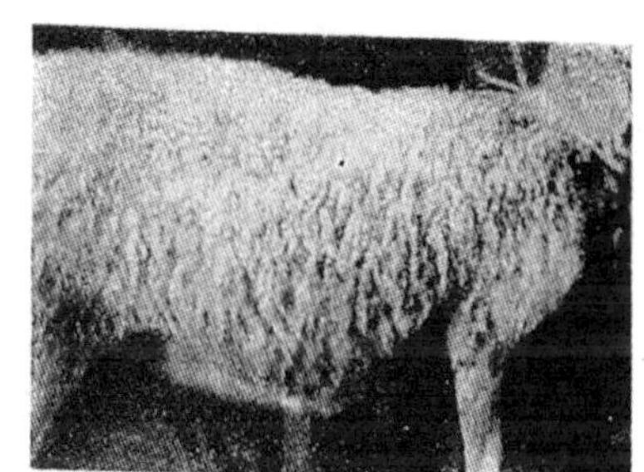

圖四甲； 捲毛皮
Figure 4A: Curly Fleece

圖四乙； 捲毛之一束
Figure 4B: Curly Staple

圖四丙： 捲 毛
Figure 4C: Curly Fibres

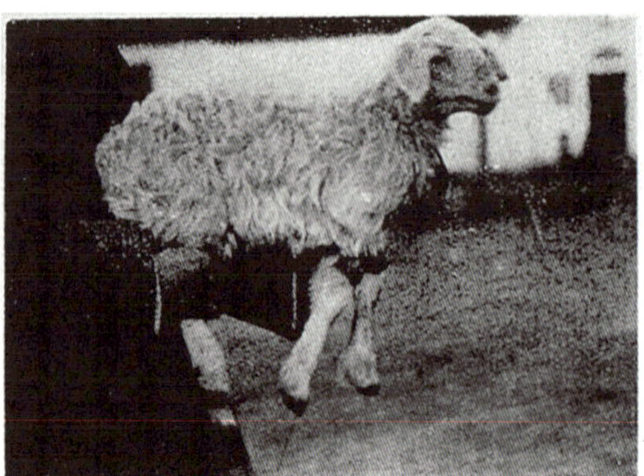

圖五： 崇 德 羔 羊

Figure 5: Chungteh Lamb

圖五甲： 羔毛之一束

Figure 5A: Lamb's Staple

圖五乙： 羔羊毛（尖頭）

Figure 5B: Lamb's Fibre (Pointed)

圖六：美利奴羊
Figure 6: Merino Sheep

圖六甲：美利奴羊毛皮
Figure 6A: Merino Fleece

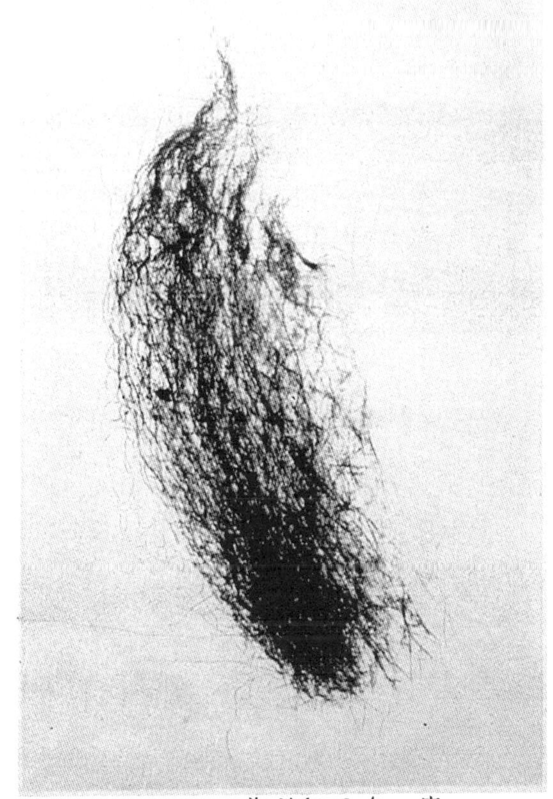

圖六乙：美利奴毛之一束
Figure 6B: Merino Staple

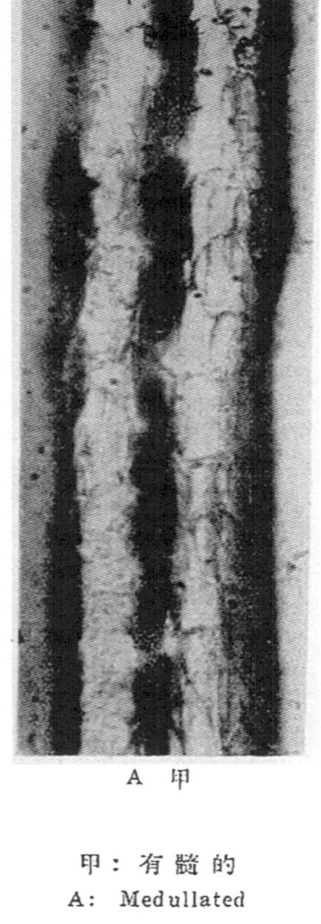
A 甲

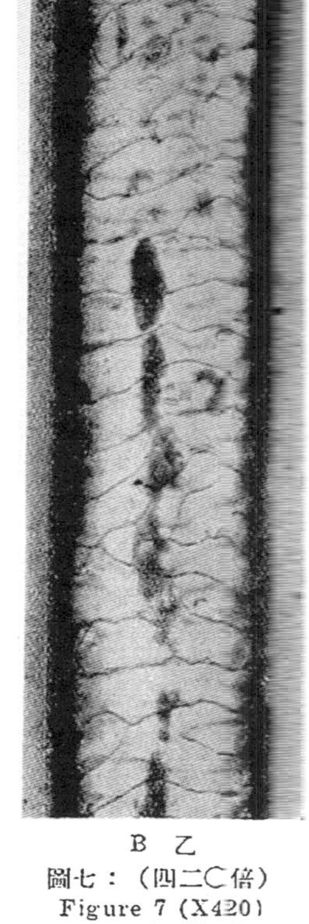
B 乙

C 丙

圖七：（四二〇倍）
Figure 7 (X420)

甲：有髓的
A: Medullated

乙：無髓的
B: Non-medullated

丙：有斷續不連之髓的
C: Broken Medullated

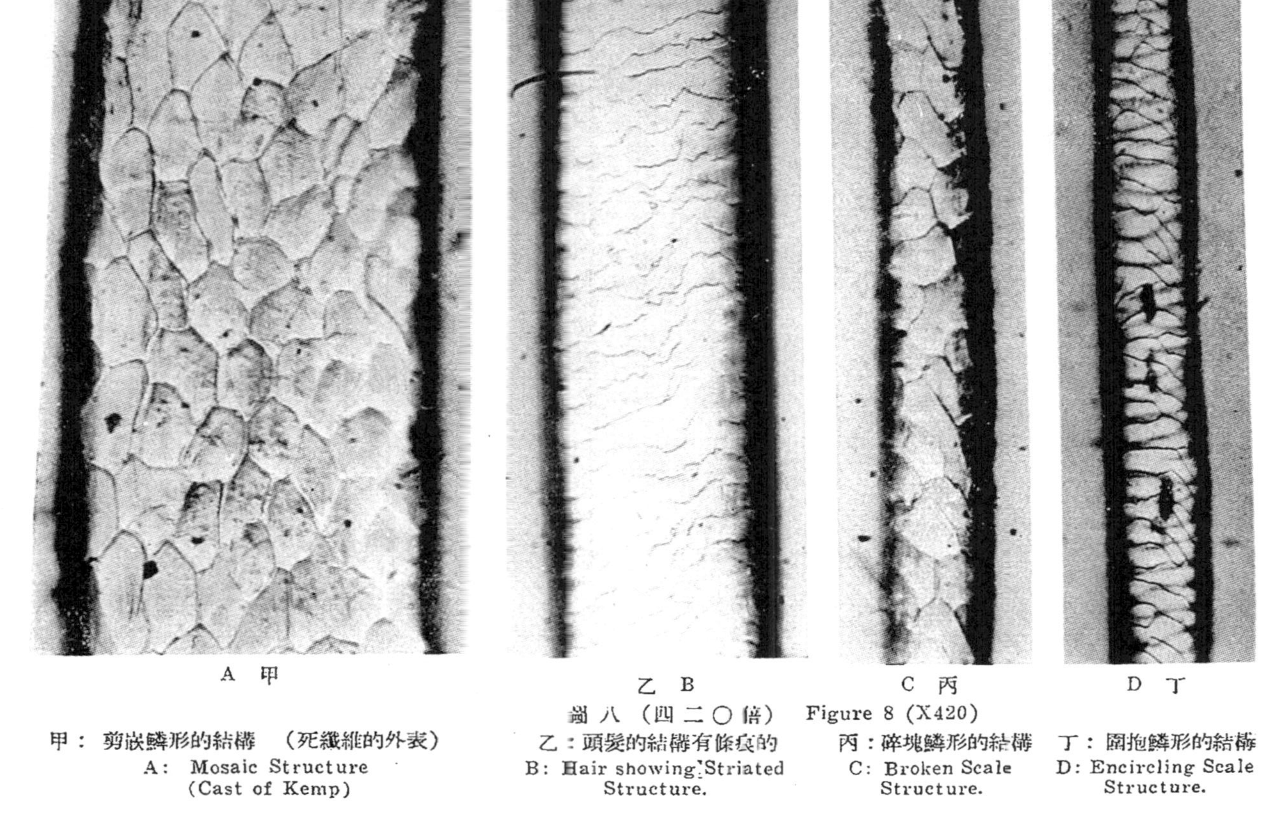

A 甲　　乙 B　　C 丙　　D 丁

圖八（四二〇倍） Figure 8 (X420)

甲：剪嵌鱗形的結構　（死纖維的外表）
A: Mosaic Structure
(Cast of Kemp)

乙：頭髮的結構有條痕的
B: Hair showing Striated Structure.

丙：碎塊鱗形的結構
C: Broken Scale Structure.

丁：圍抱鱗形的結構
D: Encircling Scale Structure.

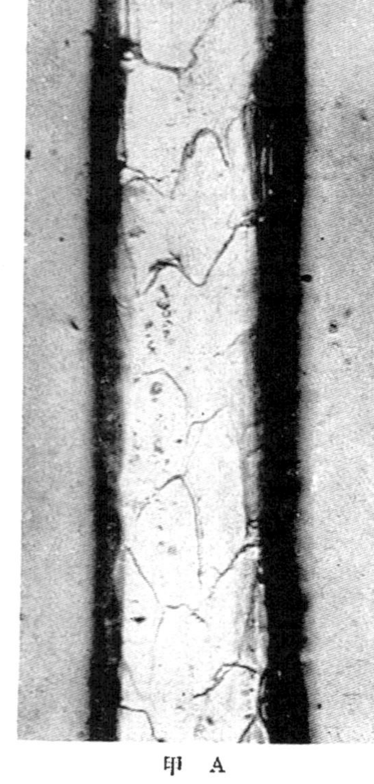

甲 A

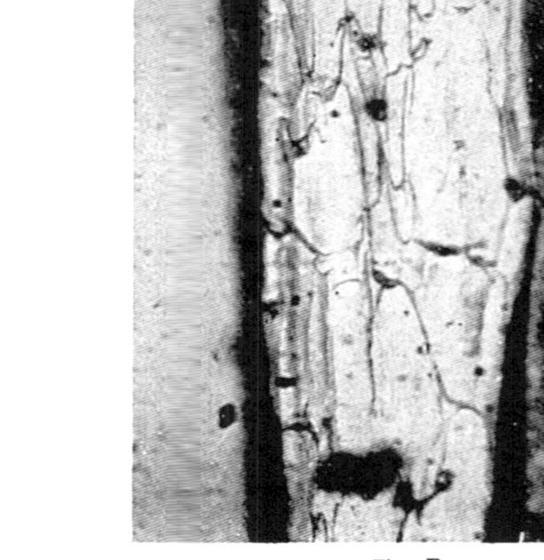

乙 B

圖九 (四二〇倍)
施以膠質的兩種奇形鱗狀的外表
Fig 9 (X420)
Gelatine Casts of Curiously Shaped Wool Scales

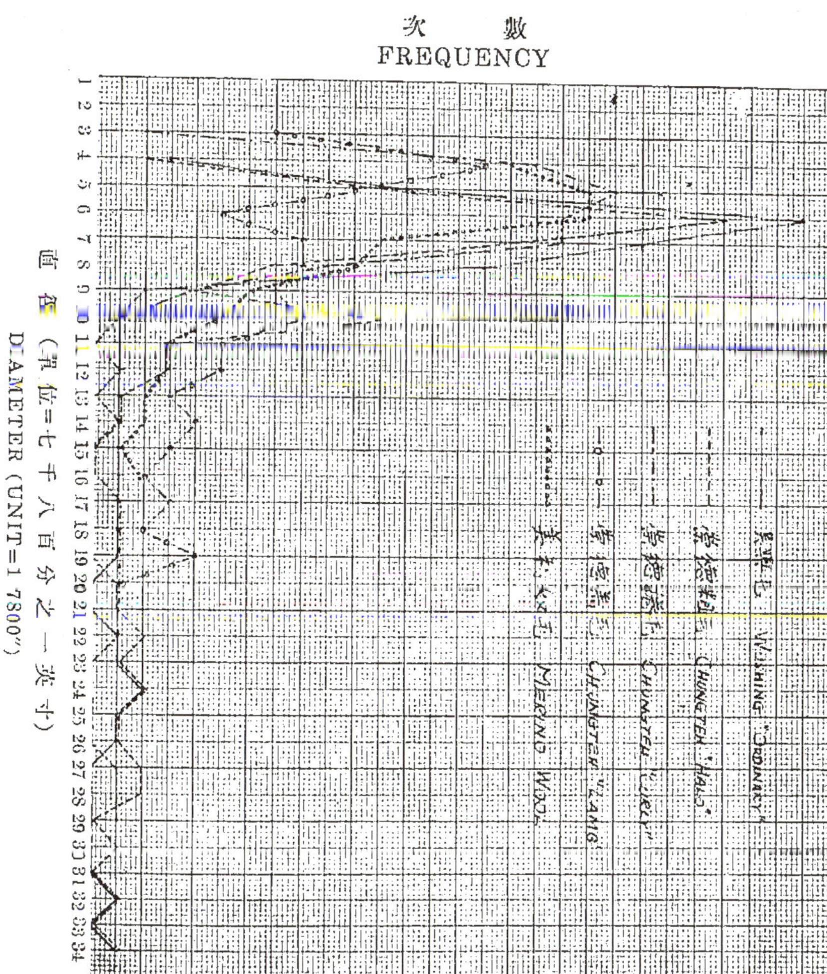
次 數
FREQUENCY
直 徑 (單位=七千八百分之一英寸)
DIAMETER (UNIT=1/7800")

分 類 索 引

索引類別	題目	著者	雜志名稱	發行年月	號類
A 類					
A 3:	何謂管理能力	胡亦生	管理	26—4	2:1
B 類					
B 1:	現代企業組織問題之檢討	王烈望	管理	,,	,,
	福建林木市場組織		社會統計	26—3	121
	組織機構之建造剖視	丁馨伯	工商管理月刊	,,	4:2
	日本公司組織發展史略	余文輝	留東學報	,,	3:3
B 2:	論雙邊貿易平衡政策	何炳賢	民族雜志	,,	5:3
	振興我國毛織工業之切實方案	章復辞	中大校風	26—4	509
	糧食統制之面面觀	卞錦濤	實業部月刊	,,	2:4
	糧食自給的途徑	草　方	時論	,,	50
	救濟粵米缺乏之辦法	凌道揚	廣州評論	26—3	3
	非常時期的勞工政策	陳振鷺	社會科學月報	,,	1:1
B 3:	最近世界工業生產之發展	胡紀常	華年	,,	6:11
	福建糧食生產與消費		統計月報	,,	29
	蘇俄的茶葉生產	賀更蘇	正風風志	26—4	4:4
B 5:	工業製品推銷法	周寶軒	海王	,,	9:21--22
	介紹巴黎國際市集	馮執中	社學月報	,,	1:2
	世界資本市場之轉變	孔士諤	東方雜志	,,	34:8
	我國桐油的產銷及其將來	張覺人	實業部月刊	,,	2:4
	日本資本主義與中國的市場	伍徵之	時事月報	26—3	16:3
	南洋棉布市場之探討		國際貿易情報	,,	2:8
B 6:	雇用前的測驗	屠哲隱	工商管理月刊	,,	4:2
B 7:	武漢之工商業		漢口商業月報	,,	1:10

食糧儲備問題	胡鳴龍	中國新論	,,	3:3
越米輸華之將來	胡紀常	東方雜志	,,	34:6
粵米問題	趙劍豪	地理教育	,,	2:3
粵米荒問題及對策	吳鉄峯	國聞周報	,,	14:11
粵米問題的兩點建設	揚青田	中華月報	,,	5:3
所得税與工商管理之關係	潘序倫	立信月報	,,	8
世界鋼鉄問題與日本的地位	胡小米	時論	26—4	50
世界鋼鐵問題與日本所佔的地位	陸　棟	國論月刊	26—3	2:7
中國煤礦業問題之嚴重性與應有之策略	王潔卿	國本半月刊	26—4	1:10
綏遠之工業		中央銀行	26—3	6:3
中國之自力更生與工業化		化學工程	,,	4:1
成都之製革業	世　尊	建設周訊	,,	1:2
日本棉業之現勢	張劍萍	國際貿易	,,	9:3
我國食粮盈虧的估計方法	張培剛	中山文化	26－4	4:2
急得解决之中國粮食	董汝舟	正風雜志	,,	4:4,5
天津麪粉業概況	翔	津浦日刊	,,	1815:7
杭州油業概況	來醒華	浙江經濟	26—3	2:9

C 類

C 1:	鐵道管理觀之進步	朱瀚譜	鐵路雜志	,,	2:10
	法國的鐵路概況		,,	,,	,,
	德國航業近况	韓奎章	交通雜志	,,	5:3
	日本航業政策	周雪城	交通雜志	,,	,,
	我國戰時交通管理芻議	關星三	國本半月刊	,,	1:8
C 2:	美國鐵路管理到達貨運事務之組織與方法	許　靖	管理	26—4	2:1
C 3:	錢塘江鐵橋工程誌略		鐵路雜志	26—3	2:10
	路簽自動交換機	華浦圭	工程	26—4	12:2
	美國新奥林橋工程誌略		平綏技術實刊	26—3	3:3
	各式激水機功力比較		平綏技術彙刊	,,	,,

	錢塘江大橋一瞥	楚　寶	京滬杭甬日刊	26—4	1855
	低值柏油路之築造	洪文瀚	道路	,,	53:2
	冷舖瀝青路面之建築法	郭增望	道路	,,	,,
	成渝鐵路興工與四川建設	袁　著	地理教育	26—4	2:4
	茅塞爾機車與其經濟性	劉德明	鐵道半月刊	26—3	2:5
	技監室修訂鋼橋規範之經過	錢昌淦	鐵道半月刊	,,	,,
C 4:	鐵路材料常識之九——一非鐵屬合金	王文翔	機務季刊	,,	4:1
	銲接長軌之實驗		平綏技術彙刊	,,	3:3
	電風信號聯鎖之理論與實用	濮思本	平綏技術彙刊	,,	,,
	用水率與混凝土關係	胡伯文	平綏技術彙刊	,,	,,
	德美鐵路蒸木事業之概況	吳慶源	鐵道半月刊	,,	2:6
	我國鐵路國煤產運銷之研究（中下）	譚沛霖	鐵道半月刊	,,	,,
	修正鐵路材料帳目則例之檢討	張廼修	鐵道半月刊	26—4	2:8
	發行購料期票之原因及經過	朱文熊	鐵道半月刊	,,	,,
	視察各路材料狀況報告	莊其士等	鐵道半月刊	,,	,,
	鐵路大宗材料圖說管理問題	李法端	鐵道半月刊	,,	,,
	[illegible]鐵路材料[illegible]希望	曾[illegible]甫	鐵道半月刊	,,	,,
	整理鐵路材料之基本工作	莫　衡	鐵道半月刊	,,	,,
	籌設中央枕木廠之建議	朱文熊	鐵道半月刊	,,	,,
	中央枕木廠採辦國產枕木之我見	康　瀚	鐵道半月刊	,,	,,
	中央蒸木廠籌設之旨趣及其經過	朱文熊	鐵道半月刊	,,	,,
C 5:	鐵路客運業務	朱光中	鐵路雜志	26—3	2:10
	鐵路電化及運輸問題	俞次恆	鐵道半月刊	,,	2:5,6
	鐵路副業之研究	畢愼夫	鐵道半月刊	,,	,,
	廿六年二月份各路營業進款	吳文蔚	鐵道半月刊	,,	2:6
C 6:	製定行車時刻表之研究	思　維	改進專刊	,,	22:15
	列車製動距離與時間計算法之比較	思　律	改進專刊	,,	22:1
	平漢鉄路調度制之實施	何世倫	鐵路雜誌	,,	2:10

	改善我國鐵路大站行車房之我見	沈奏廷	管理	26—4	2:1
	列車制動距離與時間計算法的比較	思律	北寧專刊	26—3	22
	編製鐵路行車時刻表之研究	劉傳書	鐵道半月刊	26—4	2:7
	製定行車時刻表之研究	思統	北寧專刊	26—3	22
C 7:	中國鐵路統計之商榷	王乃棟	鐵路雜誌	,,	2:10
	貨運行車成本統計之理論與方式	許靖	鐵道半月刊	,,	2:5
C 9:	如何收回我國航行權	章勃	交通雜誌	,,	5:3
	水路運價之檢討	畢愼夫	交通雜誌	,,	,,
	發展航業與改進我國輪船經理之研究	曾白光	交通雜誌	,,	,,
	改進招商局業務之我見	熊大惠	交通雜誌	,,	,,
	美國航政機關之組織與職權	王洸	交通雜誌	,,	,,
	船用柴油機之運用		航海雜誌	26—4	145
D類	中外交通史之簡述	葉高	政治學報	26—3	7
D 1:	行政專門化	任家誠	管理	26—4	2:1
	如何增進行政效率	鄧漢祥	四川合江	26—3	1
	從日本政局的癥節說到中日前途	鄭宏涂	共信周刊	,,	1:1
	評國民大會之組織與發展	費鞏	國聞周報	,,	14:9
	日本的新政府		世界知識	,,	5:12
	我國地方行政機構的檢討	葉高	政治學報	,,	7
	論縣政視察	翁初白	國聞周報	,,	14:10
	重要縣政問題改進意見	胡次威	行政研究	,,	2:3
	衡山實驗縣政推進概況	彭一湖	民間	26—4	3:24
	劃分地方政府行政費與事業費之檢討	董修甲	市評月刊	,,	5:4
D 2:	人事行政組織之研究	林壘	管理	,,	2:1
	縣長當爲地方培養元氣	伯承	四川合江	26—3	1
	病態的公務員考績制度	朱惟祺	是非公論	26—4	35—36
	攷績之理論與實際	謝廷尤	行政研究	26—3	2:3
	主計人員任用條例之施行	周保民	會計季刊	26—4	2:4

D 5:	論我國行政與立法的關係	陳之邁	行政研究	,,	,,
	憲法草案中的政治制度	江發正	行政研究	26—3	2:3
	理行保甲制度之檢討	張純明	行政研究	,,	,,
	中國的銓敍制度	沈世英	民族雜誌	,,	5:3
	論英國政府對地方自治機關帳目稽查制度	何會源	民族雜誌	,,	,,
	英美文官考試制度之比較	謝遠崙	中國新論	,,	3:3
	美國文官制度	張逢珺	政治學報	,,	7
D 6:	僑務行政幾個重要問題	李樸生	行政研究	26—4	2:4
	行政處分拘束力之討論	陳汝德	行政研究	,,	,,
	論違法與失職	湯吉禾	行政研究	26—3	2:3
	從行政學上論合署辦公	汪德裕	汗血月刊	26—4	9:1
	各省合署辦公之實施與成效	張景瑞	汗血月刊	,,	,,
E 類	我國財政內容之解剖	陳揚鑣	中國公論	,,	1:8
E 1:	中國財政經濟問題	高　植	時事類編	26—3	5:5
	法國政府挽救財政危機	松　山	外交評論	26—4	8:3
	近五年德國之財政		中央銀行	26—3	6:3
[illegible]	[illegible]預算之剖視	楊丙炎	軍事雜誌	26—4	100
	立院通過預算修正案		正風雜誌	,,	4:5
	一九三七年蘇聯國家預算	甘　棠	蘇俄評論	26—3	11:3
E 3:	我國會計年度起訖時期之我見	林　少	禮拜六	26—4	684
	記帳管理與選擇僱員	陶朱公	正風雜誌	,,	4:4
	浙江縣會計制度批評	張心徵	會計季刊	,,	2:4
	中國主計制度之研究	張國藩	會計季刊	,,	,,
	論國有營業機關審計制度之重要性及其改進	胡世學	會計季刊	,,	,,
	論稽察在官廳會計中之地位	陳以剛	會計季刊	,,	,,
	會計行政效率之研究	汪友明	會計季刊	,,	,,
	商譽的研究	何作岩	會計季刊	,,	,,
	江蘇省事後審計概況	郭劍初	會計季刊	,,	,,

E 4:	非常時期金融上的準備	朱宇蒼	錢業月報	26—3	17:3
	上海的拆票借票與票據習慣	魏友棐	錢業月報	,,	,,
	日本低金利政策及對滿投資	吳容爐	錢業月報	,,	,,
	美國之貼現市場	潘世傑	銀行周報	,,	21:9
	國際匯兌之益趨穩定		銀行周報	,,	21:11
	銀行實務研究	銀行學會	銀行周報	,,	21:8-12
	內部牽制與外部牽制	吳仲蝦	銀行周報	,,	21:11
	特種現金保證辦法各論	王展千等	銀行周報	,,	21:8-12
	上海各銀行存款之現金準備	程紹德	金融周報	,,	3:13
	日本銀行業務方針演變之研究	鑑　深	金融周報	,,	3:10
	美國抵銷現金輸入影響之政策	傅堅白	金融周報	,,	3:9
	蘇聯的金融	高　植	時事類編	,,	5:6
	從貨幣貶值說到國際貨幣戰	郭　恆	中國經濟	,,	5:3
	各國幣制前途	丹　楓	國聞周報	,,	14:11
	日本管理外匯及其經濟的動向	梁子青	中央時事周報	,,	6:8-9
	中國之國際收支對照		中經援萃	26—4	1:4
	英國之國際收支平衡		中經援萃	,,	,,
	國際貿易之前瞻		中經援萃	,,	,,
	中國經濟之復興與減低利息之必要	馬寅初	中山文化	,,	4:2
	籌設中央儲備銀行之意義	沈麟玉	金融周報	,,	3:14
	中央銀行改組之檢討	狄超白	中山文化	,,	4:2
	中央銀行之改組	朱鶴賓	中外月刊	,,	2:4
E 5:	中國平民借貸制度研究	劉自强	文化建設	,,	3:7
	中國財政史上的一頁重要教訓	千家駒	中山文化	,,	2:4
	結城財政的剖析	魏友棐	東方雜誌	,,	34:8
	結城財政之全貌	鈴木茂三郎	文摘	,,	1:4
	從馬場財政到結城財政	周伯棣	新中華	26—3	5:5
	外僑抗稅問題	許持平	外交評論	26—4	8:3

陜西的田賦問題	嚴仁賡	行政研究	,,	2:4
評所得稅暫行條例	吳平章	正風雜誌	,,	4:5
冀察平津施行所得稅問題	嘉　定	現代評壇	,,	2:15
關于所得稅的研究	江問漁	人文月刊	,,	8:3
走私的再度猖獗及其現狀	喬　抵	文欄	,,	1:4
各國遺產稅制度概要	陳朝俊	立信月報	,,	9
遺產稅概說	鮑昌勛	立信月報	,,	,,
國家經濟論	姚鐵心	銀行周報	26—3	21:8
國民經濟建設運動的重要性	潘家驥	留東學報	,,	2:3
非大量生產之中國經濟及其救濟辦法	馬寅初	銀行周報	,,	21:10
陰曆年關結帳聲中之中國經濟	張素民等	文化建設月刊	,,	3:6
各國景氣的分析	馮亨嘉	錢業月報	,,	17:3
日本經濟的特殊發展與日圓的暗礁	魏友棐	東方雜誌	,,	34:5
德國經濟的窮途	賓　符	世界知識	,,	6:1
德國經濟的難關	蔭　恩	國聞周報	,,	14:10
最近日本在華之經濟動態	[illegible]	錢業月報	,,	17:10
日本經濟侵略的烟幕彈	學　鵬	共信周刊	,,	1:1
日本侵華經濟實力的透視	周泰京	東方雜誌	,,	4:6
所謂中日經濟提攜	張樂然	西北論衡	,,	5:3
我國地方財政之改造	許華楨	中國新論	,,	3:3
租稅理論的進展與動向	朱炳南	社會科學雜誌	,,	8:1
培養稅源問題	蔣元新	東方雜誌	,,	,,
華北走私之面面觀	佘漢三	時事類編	,,	5:5
怎樣徵收所得稅	朱鶴賓	中外月刊	,,	2:3
地方營業稅與中央所得稅	權　時	銀行周報	,,	21:9
改革吾國地方政府財務管理制度之建設	開亦有	會計季刊	26—4	2:4

鐵路雜誌

第二卷 第十一期

要目

編後記

編者

依照本刊出版期的規定，本期應在七月中出版，因為畢業典禮的關係，特地提早了幾天，使可以和參與盛會的來賓見面就正，我們認為這是一樁有相當意義的辦法，何況過去已有成例。

本院造就的人才，負起管理一切事業的責任，尤其是鐵路管理一方面，每年畢業同學大部份供各路的驅策，把過去的成績加以檢討，雖不能說有什麼貢獻，至少也盡了些應負的責任。今年部方因為建築新路的計劃，逐漸推行，需才孔亟，本院畢業同學大有供不應求的情形，在這種情形之下，我們感覺到國家對於人才的重視，應該十分欣慰，全時更使我們顧慮到畢業同學責任的重大。因之，在同學未離母校的一剎那，我以為有予以最後勉勗之必要，所以草擬了一篇送別的文字！

管理的有效與否，不祇靠管理者的能力和系統的嚴密，同時工作人員本身的自覺也是一個重要的條件，我國近年來工商鉅子政府要員也未嘗不注意于管理方法和行政效率的促進，然而因為從事者的沒有自覺，才造成種種隔隔不入的現象，所以本期所刊的『送別畢業同學』，並不是祇對本屆畢業生而發的。

沈奏廷先生在準備出發各路考察的百忙中，為本刊寫一篇極新穎而極重要的文章，我們應該十分感謝。貨運佔鐵道業務中最重要的地位，甚而較客運為尤要，而我國對於貨運的技術方面尚有精益求精的必要。沈先生建議暫行貨物夜間裝卸，當然是看到各路的需要而寫的。

鐵道管理的進步，向來美國佔着權威的地位，我國各路的現制，更有很多所法的地方，許靖先生近來致力於美國鐵道管理方法不遺餘力，『美國貨運大站處理貨物事故之組織與方法』，就是他最近的代表作。

人事管理的核心是對於工作人員的勉勵（Incentive），勉勵的最好方面就是酬報決定之公平。林森先生和任家誠先生二文分別討論在職時的俸給的厘訂，和退職後贍養金的規定：可說是有相當連繫的文章。林先生之文着重在俸給之厘訂應與生活費相吻合，切實地把握住國民經濟的立場。任先生之文在沒有放掉公務員和政府雙方的利益，他的解說可謂十分公平。我國實行退休制度的政府機關除掉海關和路郵之外，尚少有所聞，在目前，確有提倡之必要。

韋愿先生所譯的『人事行政上一新的著要點』，原文內容很有意義，而且至為新穎，牠所提到的人事行政機關組織，僱員組織，不公平待遇的起訴，怨懟事件的調整等等，都是最近人事行政中重要的問題，很可一讀的。

高國樑先生是本校的畢業同學，離校後即在兩路會計處實習，勤奮的精神，素為上司所稱許，最近他把站帳審核實習的結果，作一簡要的報告，翔實的內容，可供鐵道管理學者和會計學者的參考。

總之，本期的文字，很有幾篇是值得一看的。同時本期仍沒有放棄質量平衡的分配。

歡迎投稿

歡迎批評

本刊投稿簡章

一、投稿以有關於管理者為限。

二、投稿不拘文言白話，須繕寫清楚，並加標點，如係外國文稿件，並請打印之，均不得於一紙兩面寫字。

三、論著稿中，如有譯名或引文，須分別註明原文及出處。

四、譯稿須將原文題目，原著者姓名、出版日期及地點，詳細載明，如能附寄原文尤佳。

五、稿末請簽名蓋章，並註明住址。

六、來稿文字，本院有酌量修改之權，如投稿人不願有何增删，則應於投稿時聲明。

七、來稿登載與否，概不寄還，惟附寄郵票預先聲請寄還者　亦可照辦。

八、來稿一經登載，當酌贈以每千字一元至三元之薄酬。

九、來稿請寄上海徐家匯交通大學管理學院。

中華民國二十六年七月出版

第二卷第二期

每本大洋四角
全年五期大洋一元六角

主編者　鍾偉成

發行者　交通大學出版處

印刷者　華豐印刷鑄字所　上海浙江路五三六號

本刊廣告價目表

等級	地位	全頁價目	半頁價目
甲	底封面外頁	伍拾元	
乙	底面裏頁及封面裏頁	三十五元	二十元
丙	封面底面裏頁之對面	二十五元	十五元
丁	普通	二十元	十二元

一、乙丙丁四分之一頁按照半頁價目六折計算

二、廣告概用白紙黑字如用彩印紙色價目另議

三、廣告如用銅鋅版由本刊代辦照收製版費

四、刊登多期價目從廉請逕向本校出版處經理組接洽

中華民國卅六年四月復刊

季刊第一期

本期要目

交通大學管理學院主編

現代管理發展方向與管理者之責任

鍾偉成

一 管理問題之劃分

管理乃應用科學之一，其本身之性質及研究方法，與工程、教育、醫藥大致相同，即利用其他有關科學之成果，從事於自身所遭問題之解決。按法國管理家費堯(Fayol)之分析，管理問題計有五種：(一)「設計」問題亦可名為「政策」問題，(二)「組織」問題，(三)「奉行」問題(Command)(四)「聯繫」問題(Co-ordination)(五)「檢討」問題或作「控制」問題(Control)(註一)筆者以為管理之最大對象，曰人與物。故主張加「人事」問題與「設備」問題兩種。「奉行」問題應可併入人事問題之內，聯繫問題則可併組織問題之內。故現代之管理問題可分作下列：

1 設計問題 (Planning) 此為預計目標，擬定方針，及實施計劃方面之問題。

2 組織問題(Organization) 此為關於責權之如何劃分，職位如何分等，各部份機構如何聯繫，使設計之方針，能從各部門之合作，而實施而開展。

3 人事問題 (Personal) 此為關於人材之如何徵選，如何訓練，如何利用，工資、勞工政策、工作時間之規定、考績之實施、使組織之所定責權能充分表現。

4 設備問題(Facilities) 此為生產所必須之各種機器，原動力機、工具、材料之如何取得，與如何利用及維持問題。

5 檢討問題(Control) 此為關於在設計方針中規定之目標所必須實行之事務及其手續之建立，與原定方針之比照。

二 前此被人忽視之人事問題

美國交通及工業建設，開始於一八四〇年左右。自彼時至第一次世界大戰結束，為美國私人資本極度澎漲時期，成品供不應求，市場逐年擴大。管理者但求商品之生產與成本之減低，故彼等專致力於可以增加生產之機器，工具之物質設備，以及可以增加物質設備效能之實踐與方法。泰勒及其信徒之科學管理法，殆集中精力於此，如高速度鋼工具之倡用，設備之改善，排列之順序，工作方法之改良等等。對於現代人事問題未加重視。即對於組織問題，設計問題，亦不及設備問題之受重視也。彼等之所以忽視人事問題者大概由於下列各點：

1在此期內政府採放任政策，資本家之聲勢不可一世，趾高氣揚，獨行獨斷。管理者對於工人可以隨意去留進退。加以工人本身知識淺弱，組織不强，且大半自東歐貧窮國家移民而來，慾望不奢，因此資本家毫無顧忌，得以恣意實行其高壓手段。

2人事問題及組織問題較難捉摸，故其對於管理者之重要性，亦不若其他問題之顯著。譬如鐵路旅客業務劇增時，即不能不添置機車客車及車站設備。管理者因利之所在，對之自特別關心，力謀解決。但對於人事之改進，機構之調整，容亦為管理者所注意，但其需要之迫切遠不若改進設備之明顯，蓋前者之效果著於無形，而後者之效果則顯而易見。無形者不易計其價值，而有形者之價值則歷歷可數也。同理，設備之錯誤，顯而易見，一有錯誤，管理者自不能不亟予改正。至於人事方面之決策，其錯誤隱而難明，故人事問題之考慮，遂覺不若其他有形問題之急要。

3人事問題之解決，須有遠大的眼光，深沉之思想。此兩條件似不易為繁忙而又一帆風順之實業家所兼具。蓋人事方面之問題至為曲折抽象。欲求改進，須外省世界潮流，內察社會輿論，旁徵各種科學之成果，（如經濟學心理學社會學生理學倫理學等）方足以言效果。彼慣於處理有形事物之實際策，往往無暇及此，或竟以為不屑加以研究。此人事問題之所以不為世所重視者又一原因也。

由於上述三點之故，人事方面之改進，遂遠不若物質方面進步之速。然現代科學日新月異，企業組織日益膨漲，管理科學發展之趨向必隨時代而演進，庶能與複雜的社會環境互相配合，若僅抱『人惟求舊，器惟求新。』之陳腐觀念，忽於全豹而專及一隅以手工業時代之頭腦，管理廿世紀之企業，欲其不失敗也，難矣！

三　人事問題何以成為現代管理的中心問題

前章已述管理者僅注意生產方面之物質上的各種問題，其間雖稍稍注意工資與訓練等事，然管理者之出發點仍以片面的私利為前提。故所定辦法每缺乏誠意，盡狡滑欺騙之能事。大受工人之責難。因此怠工、罷工、及種種勞資鬥爭之現象幾於司空見慣，無日無之。自廿世紀至第一次大戰結束時，一日以上之罷工計四萬餘次之多。當其初，資本家尤雄心不死，作困獸之鬥，對於工人運動盡威脅利誘之能事，但終以大勢所趨，自身犧牲過大，不得不改絃易轍，由壓迫而對立，由對立而合作，蓋明知非精合作不能互存，人事管理與勞工問題遂成為管理科學之中心研究。戰前之十年中討論人事問題之論文，美國一國即有八百餘篇，此亦可以察人心之趨向矣。請再申述其理由：

1 由於勞工勢力之擴張

自第一次世界大戰以至現在，勞工者之地位與權力日益擴展。此乃全世界之大趨勢。所謂勞工陣綫，工黨執政，工會聯盟，集體談判 (Collective Bargaining) 等習見名詞皆足以表示勞工今日之地位與權力，與十九世紀之聽人支配者已不可同年而語矣。蘇聯英國姑不具論，即以私人資本最發達之美國而言，工人團結力之堅，「集體談判」力量之大，罷工對於國家社會破壞力之猛，令人驚駭，美國工人組織除縱面的各同業工會， Trade Unions) 工業工會，手藝工會等外，橫的方面有三個國際性的工聯會：（一）美國工聯會 (American Federation of Labor) 會員約四百五六十萬人。（二）工業組織工聯會 (Congress of Industrial Organization) 會員人數約與工聯會同（註二）（三）鐵路工人聯合會，會員約七十萬人。

工聯會成立於一八八一年。當時會員尚不足四萬人，第一次大戰結束時劇增百餘倍，達四百十萬人。（註一）該聯會會員可以歸入六大系統：1.手藝工會(Craft Unions) 2.多業手藝工會 (Multiple Craft Unions) 3.同業工會，4.工業工會 (Industrial Unions) 5.半工業工會 (Semi-Industrial) 6.其他。工組聯議會 (C. I. O.) 雖成立於一九三五年，但其聲望有後來居上之勢。大規模生產企業如鋼鐵、汽車、橡膠之工人皆加入此會。鐵路工人兄弟會包括三十餘個單位，主要者僅鐵路隨車工人兄弟會 (Brotherhood of Trainmen) 鐵路火伕兄弟會 (Firemen) 鐵路司機兄弟會(Engineer)，與鐵路車長(Conductors)兄弟會四大單位而已。會中之首領年薪有至十萬元以上者，即分區首領亦在四五萬元。各地有工會自辦之報紙，其財產之雄厚可知。

於上述概況中，有一點值得吾人特別注意。即從美國工聯會構成份子之中，無論其性質何如，均能不分畛域，使會與會之間，相互交流，職業與職業之間，貫通聲氣，整個組織上下縱橫，打成一片。在麥飛(Murphy)格令(Green)路易司(Lewis)强生(Johnson)惠特尼(Whitney) 五巨頭領導之下，陣容如此整齊，步伐自然一致。宜乎管理者除輸誠合作外，蓋無策足以應付也。

工會之步伐，不論其為鬥爭，為合作，在現在堅强團結之下，均胸有成竹。其鬥爭之最後武器自為罷工。在昔日一廠罷工不過一二百工人加入，今則三大工聯會之會員已將一千萬人。據美統計，以過去多年之經驗作根據，每一次因罷工所加諸資方與社會之損失，（大工業與交通事業）每一工人約攤目一萬元至三萬元。（註四）假如某次罷工有一百萬人捲入旋渦，則社會之損失已達一百億至三百億金元之鉅。不亦可畏也哉！工人合作的方式為「集體談判」。洽商工資，工作時間，與工作環境等事。代表均屬工會中之優秀。

綜上所述，足見美國今日之勞工藉堅强之組織，憑迅速有效之武器，（罷工怠工集體談判等）指揮若定，左右逢源，今後美國勞資糾紛隨時可以觸發，策防亘患於未然，免挽狂瀾之既倒。管理者之責任不在政府之下也。

2.由於政府勞工政策之開明

一國之政治設施，經濟改造，常爲經濟環境之自然產物，幷賴以改造社會環境者也。各國勞工法令，百餘年來由桎梏而至開明，由偏袒而至公正，亦猶是理也。蓋自機器生產以來，資本萬能。政府對之縱容放任，首受其直接榨取魚肉者，厥爲工人。工人爲生存與洩怨計，以團結爲對象，以罷工爲武器。由一廠工人之團結推而至於一國工人之團結。由一隅聯繫推而至於全面合作。演變至此，勞資兩大階級之對立現象，遂勢均力敵，旗鼓相當。社會安定大受威脅。美國政府有鑑於此在過去廿年中乃逐漸改變方針以圖糾正。尤以美已故前任總統羅斯福爲澈底。政府的新法令賦予工會組織以更大的自由。勞工失業、退休、救濟，更予工人以更大之保障。昔日管理者所掌握之進退大權，亦在「無理處置條文」(Unfair Labor Practice)以及「集體談判」下予以限制。工人對勞工管理政策亦可在集體談判方式中參加意見。（註五）

一九三五年之「國家勞工關係法」(National Ladcr Relation Act)制定後，資方處處須與工會協商。服務年份較久之工人恃「資歷條文」(Seniority Clause)之維護，公司不得將其撤職。職工之升遷進退，管理者不能任意作主。以上種種均須在「集體談判」中明文規定。華盛頓之國家勞工關係委員會(National Labor Relations Board)之任務，即爲防止資方一切不公平之措施而設立者也。

上述之美國政府開明態度，吾國可以斷定將繼續維持。資本家在政府此勞工雙重緊壓之下，管理者之責任遂更形加重。在昔手工工業時代，組織簡單，雇主對於每一職工兼負有道義上的責任。有此共同甘苦情感上之維繫，遂收工作精進，出品優良，營業蒸蒸日上之效。然在今日無感情化之企業關係中，工人對於雇主的心理大有死活不關。觀於近年來美國各企業勞力成本之高，電氣事業中竟有至佔成本百分之八十，平均之百分比亦在四五十之間，長此以往力所不勝。如何解決此勞力成本問題，將爲今後企業成敗之最大關鍵。然欲減低勞力成本必先管理勞工。欲求管理收效，先必恢復感情，樹立互信。美國開明人士有企業民主化之口號。完成其目的，管理者之責任必較任何人爲大也。（註六）

3.由於大規模生產促成職能專責化

不論其企業私人資本化，抑爲資本社會化，大規模生產在近代社會絕對需要。其數量多多益善。蓋苟無大規模生產，資金不能累積，建國所必需之重工業，鐵路，輪船將不能完成其使命。在大規模生產之下，一物之製成往往須經數十或數百人之手，一人所作之工僅為全體中之極小部份。就一廠之內而言，數萬員工之工作分析，釐訂薪級，職能劃分，工作分配，均屬難題。且分工愈細，部門愈多。各部門之分界線乃愈顯著。然各部門間之關係有如連鎖，此環與彼環必須呼應靈活。切忌有人事上之隔閡。但因專責化之結果，工作員工之思想、目光、能力往往隨此環境，而日趨狹隘。各部門間之隔閡又必在所難免。在此情形之下，如何一方面維持原定方針，而另一方面又須顧及培養工作興趣，刺激創造能力，啓發自由思想，鼓勵合作精神。此又一有待於管理領袖者解決之矛盾問題也。

四 解决人事問題是管理者的責任

現代企業之目的極為繁複，絕非前人想像之單純，自社會觀念言之，企業之目的在能供給貨物與勞務，使社會大衆隨時隨地得以享用，即經濟學上所謂滿足社會慾望是也。但在另一方面自參加生產過程各個人言之，經濟活動之目的，又復不同。蓋其孜孜終日辛苦勤勞之目的，不在社會慾望之滿足，而純由其個人在生產過程中所處之立場為出發點，或為獲得工資，或為獲得利息，或為獲得地租，或為獲得利潤。因此勞工與資本者之利益，因分配多少問題，利益常相對立。蓋勞工者之希望在，獲得最高工資之進益，至於其所出勞力是否值得換取此項代價則置之不顧。資本者之目的，在欲竭力抑低每一單位之勞力成本，其直接而有效之方法常為減低工資，雙方衝突大半由此發生，其實，雙方所想像之結果有時每背道而馳，蓋勞工者之工資如其增加，增加之結果使社會對於此種勞力之需要反而減低，社會上即發生勞工過剩之現象，則此種工資之增加對於勞工大衆幷非眞有所得，同理，如僱主將工人之工資增加，其結果如能使生產效率增加，因而單位勞力成本減低，則僱主前此認為增加工資之損失，亦非眞有所失。不但此也，生產成本減低之後，於爭取市場，防止競爭，增加國家富力，是於勞資兩方，國家社會均有利益。

孔子有云，「為富不仁」。筆者以為此語應有雙重解釋。以一國對另一個國言之，在世界今日局勢之下，一國欲求富强，對於別國，似有非「為富不仁」不可，蓋甲國不富而乙國富甲將受乙之欺侮；甲仁而乙不仁，則甲必受乙之壓迫。

但在一個國家以內之個體（各個企業單位）言之，在現代潮流趨向之下，孔子對個人「為富不仁」之警告，實已不復適合。蘇聯之禁止資本，民生主義之節制資本，均不許「為富不仁。」且有由求仁以致富之意，固不具論。即美國近十餘年來之作風，由前章所列舉之勞工法令，人為的「新政」，以及各種捐税政策等等，亦足以證明美國之企業，亦在逼向「為富亦仁」之路，以我國之窮，必須人人抱「為富」（註七）之決心，方能生存。但更必須認識「為富亦仁」之意義，方可完成「為富」之目的。蓋不富，則國家之物質匱乏，何以「為仁」；不仁，則工作之效率不高，何以「為富」。欲求仁富兩全，其責任一在於政府，一在於管理者。政府之責任，一方面在提高勞工之智識，與開導資方之認識形勢，一方面善用各種政策與法令以平衡勞資之利益，而求取勞資之協調。然於日常實施之際，仍有待於管理者依據政府所規定之政策法令，運用其豐富之常識與科學之成果，措理千變萬化之人事關係，庶可克奏厥功，所謂執一定以御萬變。管理者地位之重要概可想見。約其要點，計分三端：

一、為人事政策之決定 。蓋勞資雙方對於任何人事問題之意見，總難盡同，偶有誤會，每成殭局。管理者以科學的客觀的立場，擬訂綱目，徵集雙方各種見解，綜合分析為合理之研討，就大同而去小異。對於選擇、訓練、薪級、位置、工資、工作時間、升遷降調、福利、安全、及勞工代表評議組織等等各項均為訂立雙方所瞭解而承諾之契約，共同遵守。

二、為人事政策之執行。蓋政策既定之後，貴在執行。而執行之條件有三：（一）須有科學訓練之頭腦，庶不致因情感而有所變異；（二）須有管理之學識與技術，庶不致因紛繁困難而從事敷衍或停頓；（三）須有專一之責任，庶可收確切執行之效。

三、為執行效果之考核與研究。執行之後，尤須有管理者為之經常注視，經冷靜之考核，加精密之研究，契約內原訂各條有無困難或窒礙之處，工作狀況，是否美滿，有否可以改進之點。工人工作是否適合，是否可以設法再行提高其效率，以資隨時與勞資雙方討論改進方法，與另訂新標準。

準此以觀，可知現代管理之發展方向 ，實以人事問題最為重要。而人事問題，對於管理者之需要亦最為迫切而嚴重。此為研究管理者所應有之認識。然欲實行其管理之職責，則對於各種常識及一切管理之學術均需有充分之準備，方能勝任而愉快。良以人事乃最活動，最抽象，最複雜之問題，初非如管理設備之確定簡易也。

註一 Principle of Industrial Administration, Henri Fayol

二 Personnel Management, Yoder

三 Report of the Proceedings of the Annual Convention, 1941

四 Social Control, E. A. Ross

五 Personnel Management. Yoder

六 Problems in Labor Relations, Feldman

七 此處「為富」意義為工作

鐵路編配調車之方策

沈奏廷

第一節　長路車與短路車之介說

鐵路空重貨車由一地掛運者其目的地繁多，有遠至數千哩者，有近達數十哩或僅數哩者，然大別之不外二種，即一為長路車，一為短路車，二者運送之方策不同，故有加以區分之必要。惟所謂長路短路者，雖與里程之遠近有關然亦非有一定不易之關係，如運送十哩者固為短路車，運送五十哩者或亦為短路車，運送三百哩者固為長路車，運送二千哩者亦為長路車，是猶整車與零担之區別，雖與託運貨物之數量有關，然五十磅為零担，五百磅亦為零担，二十噸為整車，五百噸亦為整車，其理正復相似也。茲將長路車與短路車之界說申述如次：

一、長路車之意義　凡由某一終點站（列車編組站）掛往次一終點站或其以上前方各地之車輛 Cars destined to the next terminal & beyond，就掛出此種車輛之終點站言，均可稱曰長路車，所謂以上前方各地者包含甚廣概括言之，可分下列數種：

（一）前方第二終點站 the second terminal in advance

（二）前方第二段內各沿途站 all wayside points on the second division or district in advance.

（三）前方第三終點站 the third terminal in advance

（四）前方第三段內各沿途站 all wayside points on the third division or district in advance

（五）前方第N終點站 the Nth terminal in advance.

（六）前方第N段內各沿途站 all wayside points on the Nth division or district in advance.

（七）前方第一終點站以外之他路各站 all points on foreign roads beyond the next terminal

上述地點可為圖示之如次：

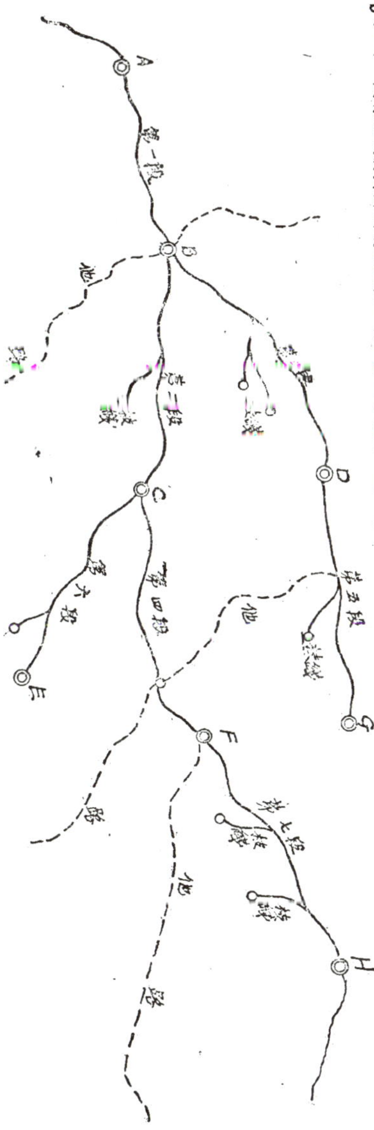

如以終點站A爲出發點，則凡須由A運往BCDEFGH各終點站之車皆爲長路車；凡須由A運往第二段以至第七段幹枝綫各沿途站之車亦爲長路車；更如由A運往圖內各他路之車，亦爲長路車。由此可見長路車之目的地實幾無遠弗屆，範圍至廣，此一路運送之車輛所以常以長路車居大宗也。

長路車所載運之貨物種類亦不止一種，舉其要者列述如次：

（一）整車　凡須運往次一終點站及其以上各地之整車均屬之

（二）整車零担車　凡須運往次一終點站及其以上各地之整車零担車均屬之。

（三）中轉零担車　凡須運往次一終點站及其以上各終點站之零担車準備在各該終點中轉者均屬之。

（四）沿途零担車　凡須運往次一終點站以外某段沿途各站之零担貨物在車內裝成先後順序，以便到達該段後始行沿途起卸者均屬之。

二、短路車之意義　既明長路車之爲何物，則短路車之意義可不言而自喩矣。蓋短路車者不外二種，卽（甲）由某一終點站（列車編組站）運往前方第一段內沿途各站之車輛。（乙）由某段沿途站掛往該段其他沿途站或次一終點之車輛是也。就上圖觀之，下列各種車輛均爲短路車：

（甲）由終點站掛出者

(1)由A掛往第一段內各沿途站者；

(2)由B掛往第二段內各沿途站者；

(3)由B掛往第三段內各沿途站者；

(4)由C掛往第四段內各沿途站者；

(5)由C掛往第六段內各沿途站者；

(6)由D掛往第五段內各沿途站者；

(7)由F掛往第七段內各沿途站者；

（乙）由沿途站掛出者

(1)由第一段沿途站至第一段其他沿途站或至B者；

(2)由第二段沿途站至第二段其他沿途站或至C者；

(3)由第三段沿途站至第三段其他沿途站或至D者；

(4)由第四段沿途站至第四段其他沿途站或至F者；

(5)由第五段沿途站至第五段其他沿途站或至G者；

(6)由第六段沿途站至第六段其他沿途站或至E者；

(7)由第七段沿途站至第七段其他沿途站或至H者

以上指東行車輛而言，其西行者亦如之，如由H掛往第七段內沿途各站之車，由F掛往第四段內沿途各站之車，由E掛往第六段內沿途各站之車皆爲短路車，餘可類推。

短路車所載運之貨物或爲整車或爲零担，其種類如下：

（一）整車　凡須由終站運往前方第一段內各沿途站之整車或

由沿途站至同段其他沿途站或次一終點之整車均屬之。

（二）整車零担車　凡須由終點站運往前方第一段內各沿途站之整車零担車，或由沿途站至同段其他沿途站或次一終點之整車零担車均屬之。

（三）沿途零担車　凡運往前方第一段內各沿途站之零貨裝成一車沿途起卸者均屬之。

以上所述乃指重車而言，此外空車亦有長路車與短路車之分，茲爲分述如下：

（一）長路空車　凡由某一終點站挂往次一終點站或其以上前方各地之空車均爲長路空車。此種空車類皆按照餘車自動集中計劃挂運，由餘車之段挂往缺車之段，以便集中配用，其目的地大都爲前方各終點站，因終點站爲空車集中最適宜之地點故也，就上圖觀之，凡由ABCDEFGH挂往各終點之空車均爲長路空車，其由B挂往CDEFGH者亦然。

（二）短路空車　凡由某一終點站挂往前方第一段內沿途各站之空車均爲短路空車，如由C挂往第四段或第六段內沿途各站之空車卽屬此類。蓋空車集中終點站後，除供該終點站本地裝貨之用外，尚有一部分須撥送前方段內各沿途站應用，撥送之際，卽產生短路空車。此外由某段沿途站挂往該段其他沿途站或次一終點站之空車亦爲短路空車。此短路空車之由來也。

抑有進者，貨車之爲長路或短路尚不如上述者之簡單，蓋一輛貨車固有始終爲長路車者，亦有始終爲短路車者，然亦有先爲長路車而後爲短路車者，有先爲短路車而後爲長路車者，更有先爲短路車後爲長路車而最後又爲短路車者，錯綜不一，其故安在，請分敍之：

（一）始終爲長路車者　凡貨車起運站爲終點站而到達站亦爲終點站者卽始終爲長路車。如由A起運至B到達之車，由A起運至D到達之車，由C起運至E到達之車，由C起運至H到達之車，均自始至終爲長路車而不變，餘可類推。

（二）始終爲短路車者　凡貨車由一段沿途站起運至該段其他沿途站到達者，或由一段沿途站起運至前方次一終點站到達者，均始終爲短路車，如由第二段某沿途站起運至第二段某沿途站到達之車或由第二段某沿途站起運至C到達之車，均屬之。

（三）先爲長路車而後爲短路車者　凡由終點站起運至前方某終點站以外之沿途站到達者均屬此類，如由A起運至第四段某沿途站到達之車，其由A至C時爲長路車，因由終點站至終點站 From Terminal to terminal也，由C至沿途站時爲短路車，因由終點站至前方第一段內之沿途站也。

（四）先爲短路車而後爲長路車者　凡由沿途站起運而至前方較遠之終點站到達者卽屬此類。如由第一段某沿途站起運至F到達之車，其由沿途站至B時爲短路車，因由沿途站至次一終點站也。由B至F時爲長路車，因由終點站至終點站也。

(五)先爲短路車次爲長路車而最後又爲短路車者　凡由某段沿途站起運至較遠之他段沿途站到達者即屬之，如由第一段某沿途站起運至第五段某沿途站到達之車，其由第一段沿途站至B時爲短路車，因由沿途站至次一終點站也。由B至D時爲長路車，因由終點站至終點站也，由D至第五段沿途站時又爲短路車，因由終點站至前方第一段內沿途站也。其餘皆可舉一反三而知之。

第二節　長路車與短路車分別行駛之方策

各種貨車既因起運與到達地點之不同而有長路車與短路車之分，然則挂運之際，是否長路車可與短路車合併成一列車，抑須分成兩種列車運送，洵有加以考慮之必要。請申論之：

一、長路車與短路車分別行駛之必要　長路車之目的地既在次一終點站或其以上各地，吾人若能編組一列車，專挂長路車輛，不挂短路車輛，則自此終點至彼終點之間，該列車即祗須運行，而無沿途摘挂車輛或裝卸貨物之工作，其行駛全段所需之時間必可減至最低限度。反之，吾人若不將長路車與短路車分開，而混合編成一列車，則列車內所有之長路車，皆將因短路車之關係而沿途作無故之停留，因短路車或須沿途摘挂，或須沿途裝卸也。故兩者若不分別行駛，長路車即有被短路車延誤之弊。若某輛長路車須行經十段之路程，每段多費六小時之時間，則其延誤將達六十小時，即二日半之久，其嚴重可以想見。考長路車分別運轉之利益甚多，舉其著者述之如次：

(一)貨車利用程度之提高　因分別行駛而貨車在途滯留之時間減少，故每車日平均貨車里 Car-mile per car-day 增加，貨車週轉之速度加快，其利用程度自必提高。例如每輛長路車若平均每四日週轉一次，每次來回平均行駛四百哩，則每車日平均貨車哩應爲 100 (400÷4=100)，若列車運行速度平均每小時爲15哩，則耗於運行之時間約爲二十七小時。今因與短路車混合行駛之故，列車運行速度每小時降爲八哩，則其耗於運行之時間將由27小時增至50小時，(400÷8=50)其每次週轉之日數將由四日增至五日 ((4×24−27+50)=119÷24≒5)，於是每車日平均貨車哩將由 100 降至 80 (400÷5=80)，若其他條件不變，則貨車利用程度即須降至百分之八十，易言之，即一千輛之貨車祇抵八百輛之用，其損失之大可想見也。

(二)機車利用程度之提高　運送長路車輛之列車沿途既少停留，故其機車之週轉亦快，每機車日平均機車哩 (Locomotive miles per Locomotive day) 亦多，與貨車之情形相似。例如每輛機車每日平均若行駛一五〇哩，以每小時十五哩之速度計，則耗於運行之時間為十小時，若因沿途摘挂短路車輛，每小時僅行八哩，則非十九小時不可，於是一五〇哩之行程即非一、二六日（24－10＋19）÷24＝33÷24＝1.36)不能完成，故每機車日平均機車哩非由150降至110不可(150÷1.36＝110)，因是機車之利用程度即須由100%減至73.3%(110÷150＝73.3%)，易言之，即一百輛之機車祇能作七十三輛之用，其損失亦殊可觀也。且專運長路車輛之列車因不必沿途摘挂車輛，其載重可與機車牽引能力相符，耗費較少，因是每機車哩平均載重噸數(Gross ton-miles per locomotive mile)可以提高，亦增加機車利用程度之一道也。

（三）行車費用之節省　運送長路車輛之列車既能迅速完畢其行程，故行車員工工作時數 Man hours 可以減少，工資可以少付，且因過時工作須給過時工資 over time wage，其率較高，故列車運行過快，過時工資即可減少，甚或全部避免，此行車費用之所以節省者一。列車在中途既少停留，則燃料費用亦省，因每次停開必須多耗燃料也，此行車費用之所以節省者二。

（四）正線容量之增加　行車正線之容量視列車密度及列車速度而變，如速度快，則每次列車佔用正線之時間少，其結果等於減少列車次數，使正線容量發生餘裕，可供行駛更多之列車運輸更多之貨物之用。是以長路車與短路車分別行駛，既足以提高列車平均速度，故亦足以增加軌道之容量，因而可以遲延雙軌或多軌之建築，而仍無運輸上之困難其功亦殊不可沒也。

（五）貨運業務之改善　長路車與短路車分別行駛，對內固足以實現種種之運轉經濟，對外亦足以改善業務品質，良以貨車在途滯留之時間既少，則貨物亦可以早到目的地，使商人之資金積壓減少，貨物損壞程度降低，其結果等於減低運價，促進地域分工之生產，對於鮮活貨物，其利尤大。

二、長路車與短路車分別行駛之可能　或謂長路車與短路車既須分別由不同之列車挂運，則數量分散，是否能編配成列，恐有問題。不知所謂長路車者包括之範圍甚廣，所有須往次一終點站以上各地之車輛，不論空重，均可編入運送長路車之列車，此種列車逐段改編，故不必集合同一目的地之車輛而後始能編成一列車也。且每一終點站之長路車來源甚多，並不以本地起運之車為限，凡來自他站他路至該終點集中改編續運者均可加入編配，與本地起運之車無異。職是之故，除貨運極稀之路線外，長路車為數往往不少，每日非特可編成一列，抑且必須編成多列，其湊集實不如意想之難也。惟在貨運較稀之路線，湊集確有困難，此則當視情形而變通辦理之。例如長路車可與一部分短路車合併行駛，在段內少數地點停留，摘挂車輛，其餘短路車則仍另挂列車運送，如是則長路車被短路車延誤之程度仍不至十分嚴重，而機力糜費可免，列車組成較易，不可謂非一種折衷之策。若併此而不能實行，則該路之貨運必極爲稀少，有如一般之枝線，若不分別行駛，亦屬無甚妨礙，蓋分別行駛之結果，將使得之於車機週轉之趕速者失之於列車載重之減少也。

三、長路車與短路車分別行駛之辦法　欲使長路車與短路車分別行駛不相牽制，則吾人必須開行兩種性質絕對不同之貨物列車，以便分工合作，各得其宜。此兩種列車爲何，卽一爲直達貨車列車 Through freight train，一爲沿途貨物列車 Local freight train，前者專挂長路車，後者專挂短路車，兩者之分工與合作情形可爲分述如次：

(一)兩種列車之分工　直達貨物列車者行經全段或兩終點站之間沿途以不摘挂車輛亦不裝卸貨物爲原則之列車也。故其所挂之車輛輒以長路車爲限，卽凡須運往次一終點以上之車輛均可由此列車挂運，除有特殊需要外，其他短路車概不附挂，因若附挂短路車，則仍須沿途停靠，從事摘挂工作，將與直達列車之本質背馳矣。反之，沿途貨物列車者在行駛之區間內沿途摘挂車輛及或裝卸貨物之列車也。故其所挂之車輛以短路車爲限，蓋若附挂長路車，則長路車將被短路車無故延誤矣。有此分工，故一切運轉方面之耗費，如車機週轉之遲緩，機車引力之虛糜，行車費用之增加，軌道佔用之延長等皆可限於少數沿途列車，而與直達列車無涉，全部運輸效率之提高，運轉經濟之促進，與夫運輸能力之加强，莫不有賴乎是。

(二)兩種列車之合作　直達列車與沿途列車之間，除分工外，又須合作，所謂合作者，其義有二：卽(甲)兩種列車有互相聯繫之處，(乙)兩種列車有互相協助之處是也。何以言之，請申論於后：

(甲)聯繫　前既言之，貨車之中有先爲短路車而後爲長路車者，有先爲長路車而後爲短路者，更有先爲短路車次爲長路車而最後又爲短路車者。此種車輛之行程一部分須由直達列車挂運，一部份須由沿途列車挂運，故直達列車挂到之車輛常須轉挂沿途列車，沿途列車挂到之車輛常須轉挂直達列車，而後乃能運抵目的地，可見兩者之間實有密切之聯繫如臂與指，不可或分也。質言之，編成直達列車之車輛頗多來自沿途列車者，編成沿途列車之車輛亦頗多來自直達列車者，此貨車之所以能由長路變爲短路或由短路變爲長路也。故吾人於此聯繫之中，必須遵守一種重要之原則，卽每輛貨車之行程既有分長路短路者，其由直達列車運送之行程應儘量求其長，由沿途列車運送之行程應儘量求其短，例如一千英里之行程，前者或佔九百英里，後者僅佔一百英里，蓋必如是，而後運轉之經濟與效率乃能達於最高峯也。

(乙)互助　有時某沿途站爲一較大之站，貨車到發較多，其出入之貨車亦得由直達列車爲之摘挂，以資變通，蓋此種摘挂既限於一二沿途大站影響於直達列車之運行者不多，而沿途列車免除此種重負，可免中途發生機力不足妨礙沿途加掛車輛之患，此即直達列車協助沿途列車之法也。反之，直達列車所卅之車輛，如因熱軸逾重等原因，中途摘下，則於整理後應由沿途列車代爲挂運至終點站，藉免後來直達列車因須加挂此種車輛而發生延誤，此卽沿途列車協助直達列車之法也。

第三節　長路車編配之方策

長路車既須編成直達列車，則其編配之方策應若何，亦爲運轉經濟方面極關重要之問題，所謂編配之方策 Train Make up Policy-者，其義有二：一爲列車之目的地點 Destination of Train，一爲列車之編組內容 Make-up of Train，茲請分論之：

一、列車之目的地點　列車之目的地點卽列車須再折散或改編之地點也。直達貨物列車之最近目的地卽爲前次一終點 Next terminal in advance，此乃無可置疑者，惟在貨運發達之路，其目的地點並不以此爲限，如車數湊集不難，儘可編成列車，至前方第二第三甚或第四第五終點站始行改編，當其經過中間終點站時僅換機換班而已，其內容可不加改組，而原列車仍繼續前進。此種列車實可視爲超級直達列車，英語名曰 Train, Relay Train, or Main-tracker，以別於一般普通直達列車。行駛此種列車之利益可得而言者如次：

（一）調車費用減少　因列車目的地放遠，中間越過一處以上之終點站而無須改組重編，故車場調車費用可以減少 Reducing Intermediate yarding Cost，尤以終點站之工作已忙，增加少數車輛卽須添用一輛機車及一班人手者，其節省尤爲可觀。反之，吾人若不辨車輛目的地遠近而混合編成列車，一律至前方次一終點站改組，則一部份遠路車輛亦須逐段拆散重編，調車之費用無形中卽須增加不少矣。

（二）貨車週轉加快　因列車中途改編之次數減少，故貨車停留之時間縮短，良以貨車每經一次改編，輒須多一日之延擱，因先到之車必須等候後到之車，而後乃能編結成列，繼續運行，非謂實際編配之時間須耗一日之久也。反之，若僅換機換班，則所費時間至多數十分鐘而已，其出入之大可以想見也。因貨車運行之時間縮短，故貨物亦可提早運到，對外業務之品質亦因此而大見改善矣。

雖然，列車目的地愈遠，則車輛湊集愈難，故非貨運發達之路，輒難編成此種超級直達列車，惟車輛湊集之難易，一方面固視貨運之繁簡而異，一方面亦視彙集時間之長短而定，如等候時間較長，則車數湊足自必較易。按通常之慣例，若將車輛遲延一日（二十四小時）挂出，而能湊成足數，將列車目的地放遠一段時，亦應視爲合算，蓋始發站雖多一日之延誤，而中途可少一次之改編，在時間上仍無損失，而在調車費用上則可節省不少，故仍有此勝於彼之利也。

由上所述，可見直達列車之目的地，在可能範圍內，自應儘量放遠以資經濟，故編配之際應將遠路直達列車之車輛與近路直達列車之車輛分開，以便分別編成列車行駛，其情形可再爲解析如次：

直達列車類別	附挂車輛別	改編地點
(1)甲種直達列車	須往前方第一終點站以上第二終點站以下各地者	前方第一終點站
(2)乙種直達列車	須往前方第二終點站以上第三終點站以下各地者	前方第二終點站
(3)丙種直達列車	須往前方第三終點站以上第四終點站以下各地者	前方第三終點站
(4)丁種直達列車	須往前方第四終點站以上第五終點站以下各地者	前方第四終點站

一、列車之編組內容　就通常情形言之，直達列車所挂之車輛應不必排成任何次序，卽不論車輛目的地之遠近，儘可隨意編配，不妨遠近倒置因列車抵達前方終點站時終須全部拆散重編，無待未雨綢繆也。例如參照上圖，今有直達列車一列，由A編成，至B改編，其所挂車輛之目的地如下：

貨車目的地	輛數	記號	貨車目的地	輛數	記號
(1)B站	5	B	(2)BC間各站	10	BC
(3)BD間各站	8	BD	(4)C站	8	C
(5)CE間各站	3	CE	(6)CF間各站	5	CF
(7)D站	7	D	(8)DG間各站	4	DG
(9)E站	3	E	(10)F站	2	F
(11)FH間各站	6	FH	(12)G站	2	G
(13)H站	2	H	合計	65	

上列六十五輛貨車目的地遠近不同，編配成列時，以其爲直達列車，儘可不必顧其遠近次序，隨意夾雜排列，如BD儘可在B之前，FH儘可在D之前，CE亦可在G之後，CF亦可在E之後，甚至同爲CF之車，亦不妨二輛在C之前，三輛在C之後，餘可類推。惟其若，則以排成遠近順序，往往既無必要，亦不可能，誠以列車至B，既須全部解散重編，在A排列成序並無用處，復以目的地類別相同之車輛爲數過少，若欲分排，則佔用車場軌線太多，亦屬不可能也。

雖然，有時因前方終點站軌線不敷，或工作太忙，不得不作相當之編排，藉以減輕前方終點車場之編配工作。其最折衷適宜之策，莫如將列車之車輛分兩組，一爲運往前方第一終點暨第一與第二終點站間各沿途站者，一爲運往其他目的地者，如按上例，則全部六十五輛貨車應分成兩組如下：

第一組 B BC BD 共23輛 (cars for the first yard advance & cars for poin between the first & the second advance yards)

第二組 其他 共42輛 (All other cars)

如此分組，則第一組車輛到B後，即可先行分開，留待稍緩處理，其編配工作可先就第二組進行，事畢乃將B車分析，以便調送，并將BC及BD之車編成順序，以便轉掛沿途列車運行，故若B站工作太忙，分組以後，即可減少其緊張程度，免除直達列車重編續運之延誤，其得失殆可想見也。

第四節 短路車編配之方策

短路車編成沿途列車時，其編配方策與用直達列車不同，因兩者沿途工作之性質有異也。茲亦就(一)列車之目的地點與(二)列車之編組內容二者申述之：

一、列車之目的地點 沿途列車之目的地點必不出一段範圍以外，因其所挂者爲短路車，自無將目的地放遠之必要也。不甯唯是，直達列車往往自此終點開往彼終點，絕無以段內中途站爲目的地或始發地者沿途列車有時則不然，以其運行時間延長，速度遲緩，爲免員工工作時間過久起見，其行程不能太長，故全段沿途列車常有分成區間行駛之必要，不若直達列車之必在終點站起訖也。由此可見沿途列車之目的地或爲終點站，或非終點站，其情形可圖示如次：

(甲區間)
(乙區間)
A (終點站)
X (沿途列車起訖站)
B (終點站)

沿途列車分成區間行駛原爲適應員工工作時間之需要，惟因此甲區間挂出之車輛須往乙區間或以上各地者須在中途站（圖中之×站）轉換列車，常須增加等候時間，不能早達目的地，此亦沿途列車之另一缺點也。

枝線沿途列車之行駛方式有二：一爲與幹線沿途列車分別開行，不相牽連，卽枝線列車以聯接站爲目的地 Junction station between main & branch，不再前進，其須往幹線之車輛等候轉挂幹線列車繼續運行。一爲與幹線沿途列車合併運轉，不另開行枝線列車。其法卽令幹線沿途列車開入枝線，去而卽返，再上幹線繼續運行，故亦稱來回行駛法 Turn-around Runs。兩者各用適用之場合，一視情形而定，大凡枝線較長或枝線貨運較多者，宜用分別開行法，反之宜用合併運轉法，藉收因地制宜之效。

二、列車之編組內容　沿途列車所挂迭車輛不外三種類別：卽(1)須運往列車目的地或其以上各地之車輛，(2)須運往列車目的地以下各地之車輛；(3)沿途裝卸零貨之車輛。此三者必須分成三組，不可夾雜編配，蓋第一組之車輛乃不必沿途摘下者，若與第二組混雜，則沿途摘車之際必將增多不少手續，殊屬無謂；第三組車輛因須裝卸零貨故宜挂在列車後部，亦卽挂如守車之前，以便車長處理裝卸，若與第二組混雜，則摘挂車輛之際卽不能同時裝卸零貨，列車之延誤必將大爲增加矣。

第一組之車輛，因須在列車行程以內沿途摘下，故又須按到達站之遠近順序編排，以免途中摘挂之不便，蓋若遠近倒置，則不必調動之車輛亦須調動，遠近夾雜，則同一目的地之車輛並不聯結一起，原則一次搗送者非變成多次搗送不可，其不經濟尤甚於遠近倒置矣。

至於第一組車輛之編配通常應無排成順序之必要，蓋至列車目的地後再行編排可也。如因目的地軌線不敷，調車機車缺乏，或其他特殊原因，則加以編排，使成順序，亦未始不可，惟到達列車目的地後，往往以有他車加入，仍須改編，全部編配調車之工作因而增加重複，輒非經濟之道。裝卸沿途零貨之車輛如有二輛以上時，概不必編排次序，因此種車輛既不在列車行程以內摘去，實與列車始終同起同訖者，故無遠近順序之可言也。

由心理學及社會學的觀點應認識之人事問題

曾世榮

人事方面的智識，是比較狹義的技術，缺少客觀性，若欲進一步了解各人的或一個團體的各種人事問題，更格外困難。但若干心理學及社會學方面，已經獲得資料與結論，對於人事問題，頗多貢獻，玆扼要說明之：

心理學上之貢獻

由心理學之研究我人應認識下列各點——

第一：我人應認識各人的性情互不相同，甚至無一個以上的絕對相似。所謂「人心之不同，如其面。」然此種結論，實太籠統。我人應具體的說明各人所以互異之原因，其中要之理由，爲：（一）各人生理上及精神上遺傳之不同。（二）自幼年以迄成人之家庭環境不同。（三）所受教育不同。此點復可分爲學校之地點，學科之種類，及在學時期之長短。（四）工作經驗之不同。（五）工作時間以後消遣方法不同。簡單言之，其個人在某一時間之性情，是受出生以至該時期各種經驗之總和，及生理精神方面遺傳之背景所影響。由於此種經歷的影響不同，因之各人的思想，性情亦各互異。

第二：我人應認識人類之性情，是極複雜而不易了解。其原因由於人之性情，既由各種背景模塑而成。傍觀者對於他人之經歷，缺少確切之智識，對於每一問題所能得到之資料不能全盤明瞭某人所有之經歷。又以感覺敏銳之人，不願被人刺探其過去之歷史，及內心之蘊藏，致瞭解更爲困難。

對於了解他人性情，有一種誤解或迷信，我人必須鏟除。往往有若干人士以爲人與人接觸，可於短時間或簡短之談話中，由面部表情，了解各人之性情。實則成人所表達於外者，不若幼年人之率直爽快，往往將眞情隱蔽，不使他人窺見。故藉此種印象所得到之結論，往往不正確而易引入岐途。

假使我人必須了解他人，則我人應認識上述各種限度。對於人事問題方面之消息情報或可能知悉之消息情報，於應用之時，必須十分審愼，應將每一事實與其他事實，互相研討，方能體會整個複雜的人的性情。

第三：我人應認識成人仍是喜歡學習，且無時不在學習。此點可由現代社會上成人生活習慣變換極快一點推想而體會得之。換言之，雖成年之人，無時不被環境驅策，繼續學習，而隨時調整其思想行爲。主管監督人員，假使對於部下在學習方面之調整方法予以特別協助或鼓勵，則對於適當工作所需之調整，可以改變，格外加速，而亦格外可以有效果。

有人以為人類一到成年，即不能再學習新技能，誠然，成人對於必須應用肌肉之學習有若干限制。其原因則由於成年人之肌肉逐漸缺乏彈性及骨格逐漸發脆。且肌肉已習得之許多習慣，對於需用肌肉之新技能，確屬不如年輕之人容易學習。然最近二十年來對於成人之能力問題，有許多著名之研究，而認為成人不能學習新技能之見解，為不可靠。在各種研究中Herbert Sorenson氏，於一九三八年在成人教育雜誌（Adult Education Bulletin）上，所發表論文之結論，可以直接應用於日常工作情形。Sorenson 氏之結論，以為年齡本身對於學習，并無特著之影響。一般的成人，假使體格健全，而有正常的能力且願意學習者，直至老死，均可容易學習，質言之，無論何種年齡，「願意」二字，為學習的主要因素。

第四：除上述各要點外，復有若干一般的成人特性，值得為我人所認識。此等特性，雖不普遍，然往往在某某問題中，可以遭遇之。

A　成人喜歡被人認識其姓名，且喜歡被認為對於某一問題或可能辦到之某一問題之特殊人物。而不願為無名之人。再成人不願被人以勢力壓服，而願意率直的直接的予以平等機會，互相商討。

B　成人願意知悉，本人果有若干進步。對於此問題，許多率領部屬之主管人員，往往祗在經濟的酬報方面着想，實則上級人員，如果得悉其部下在工作方面有若干進步，給予善意的批評與鼓勵，其意義與價值，往往超出經濟報酬之上。

C　成人需要工作及收入有保障。因一般的情形，成人均需維持家庭，最少亦需與其家庭互助的維持家庭，保障工作及保障收入是每一家庭必需之條件，許多成人在工作時所表現之態度及動作，是受此種强有力的動機影響之結果。

D　成人極易受其所敬佩之人之影響。假定上級人員處理事務或日常工作，採取積極之態度，并嚴格遵守規章，可以預期其部下之工作人員，必能互相效法，反之，假使上級人員，時時超出常規，對於規章不加重視，則其部下亦必逐漸效法。

E　成人極喜他人對於其工作以外之活動及其家庭發生熱忱的關懷，而尤以有兒童者為尤甚。人與人接觸，對於工作以外之活動及其家庭，如果缺乏誠意，其例應特別明顯。假使主管人員能熟知其部下之一個個人，則熱忱的關懷，必受歡迎。

社會學上之貢獻：

茲特提出社會學方面對於增進瞭解工作人員在工作關係中之若干貢獻。

社會學較心理學為後起之學問，其應用於事業管理方面，亦較心理學為少。但最近若干年來，曾有許多有價值之研究與實用，其中最著明者，當推西方電氣公司 Hawthorn 工廠內之研究。Hawthorn 工廠之研究，曾有許多報告，其中尤以 F. J. Roethlisberger 及 W. J. Dickson 二氏合著之 Management & the Worker 巨畧，值得介紹。

第一：我人應認識各種工作人員，自爲一個集團。每一集團，有一個非正式所確實之關係。此種集團，由若干具有密切關係之工作人員，非正式的無形的自動形成。每一集團對於某一問題，無形中公認有一人爲其領袖，如果一個集團內，有若干問題時，對於各個問題，可能有各個公認之領袖。一旦有此無形中公認之領袖，則此後一切行動，均以此領袖之行動爲依歸，而不再注意其他人對於同一問題之行動。有時且對不爲其集團所公認之行動或其種申明予以制裁。惟管理人員，往往對於此非正式之集團不加重視。事實上此種集團之控制情形，雖在正式組織圖表上無任何明文，然實際確屬存在。我人如需瞭解其所率部下集團的態度及集團的反應，必須認識此種非正式關係之存在。

某一集團態度及集團動作，均有一定之標準。其所以形成某種標準之因子，可能的能在整個工作環境中研討其各種情況及各種關係以尋求綫索。各種態度及動作之標準，復有各種水準。其水準之高度與集團風氣有關係，而風氣二字可解釋爲各人相互間對於希望之態度及信心。

第二，我人應認識者，上述非正式之集團與其領導人之關係由其集團自己決定。主管人與其所率領部屬之關係，雖在機關組織內有一定明文之規定，然事實上各人對於其所率之部屬在工作方面，不能有同樣之效果。失敗者所遭遇之困難，由於專門智識者較少，大都由於缺少人事方面的智識，及缺少能力將人事智識施之實用。假使我人欲期造就其自身成爲一個有能力之領導人，則不能僅憑藉組織規程所賦予之地位與權力，而必須對其所屬部下之個人及集團有所瞭解。主管人員在組織規程內所處之地位爲一事，而事實上其權威之由來，由於上述非正式集團之公認及尊重。主管人員之所以能爲主管人員，并在實際上可以成功者，其人必瞭解其所率部屬各個個人及其形成之集團。

第三，我人應認識單調之工作，苟能使工作人員有所瞭解，并改善其工作環境，亦能予工作人員以刺激。一般的信念，以爲祇有各種不同而內容複雜之工作，方能引起工作人員之興趣與刺激。另有若干工作僅需高度重複之作業，或在大量生產過程中所製造之零件，在製造人并不知究有何種用途。工作人員對此類工作往往感到單調與乏味，而不能引起刺激。但如能對工作人員說明工作之目的及其工作對整個作業之關係，則亦能予工作人員以有興趣之刺激。如果工作需要變動時，應使工作人員有機會澈底瞭解改變之原委。各個工作人員對於更改工作所發生之反應，應加以細密之研究。我人必須瞭解者，大部份之工作人員，在工作時間內，一方面固在工作，一方面仍在思想也。

以上所述，心理學及社會學方面之貢獻，實爲認識人事問題之主要關鍵。人事問題處理之目標在爲期使各個人或一個團體對其工作或工作關係，能得到愉快而平衡之適應。當人事問題發生，有時雖祇由於特殊之原因，然在處理之先，採集針對某一問題之整個背景，認識以上所述各點，則瞭解問題比較容易。

我國金融制度之改進與經濟建設

莊智煥

民國肇建，三十六年矣，然以政治不定，內亂頻仍，致破壞多而建設少，國民革命統一全國後，政府多方努力，謀作有計劃之建設，而日本發動侵略戰爭，使初茁之萌芽，復受摧殘，九年抗戰中，敵騎縱橫，蹂躪我大好河山，瘡痍滿目，物資缺乏，勝利之後，又以共產黨不肯以政爭而以兵爭，使全國經濟敗殘，民不聊生，現在之經濟復興，經緯萬端，然現代國家之經濟，爲一繁複之有機體，而職同經濟血液之金融，要爲關鍵，良以一國之生產，運輸、消費之進行，莫不有賴於金融機構之參與，而經濟與財政政策之順利推行，亦惟健全之金融制度爲之樞紐，抑金融制度爲經濟制度之一部，吾國經濟制度既以三民主義爲依歸，則金融設施，自應依據此項立國原則，而爲因時因地之改進，至吾國金融現狀，銀行專業之形態尚未具備，專業運用之效能，尤待加强，茲姑提供意見，以供討論：

一、工業金融體制之建立

當前吾國經濟建設之首要目標，在於全國工業化之完成，欲達成此一目的，必須具備若干基本條件，而工業金融體制之建立，尤爲基本條件中之最要者，攷工業資金之調劑業務，在歐美先進各國，大都由投資公司，投資信託公司，及產業證券市場等金融機構任之，投資公司之作用，在代替一般產業機構，發行證券，此種公司大率皆由國內外著有聲譽之金融機構，由其發行之證券，能獲得一般投資人之信任，故其推銷工作亦較一般產業公司爲易，投資信託公司爲便利一般人民投資之組織，其業務在發行其本身之證券，以取得資金，然後將此項資金，轉投於各種產業之證券，產業證券市場，乃一種繼續性市場，凡新證券之發行，有賴此一市場之連綴活動，始能發揮其高度效率，吾國目前雖有證券交易所之設立，但新證券市場尚付闕如，一般產業機構所需之長期資金，大都僅向銀行或其他方面舉借，而無法向廣大之投資大衆吸集，此實爲吾國工業發展中最大病態，欲期吾國產業金融制度之健全發展，自以上述三類機構完全具備，最爲理想，但此種產業證券市場之建立，非一朝一夕之事，而在產業落後，資本蓄積低弱之吾國，其過程當尤爲遲緩，爲[illegible]之計，自須另闢途徑，以資適應。

吾人認爲在當前經濟及金融現狀下，爲求產業資金之充裕供應，並謀證券市場之漸次形成起見，最好參照美國「復興金融公司」，及英國「工商業金融公司」之前例，創辦一「工業金融公司」，美國之「復興金融公司」創立於一九三二年，以協助工業復興爲主旨，資本五億美元，並具有發行債券之擴大權力，開業以來，對於挽救經濟恐慌中之美國產業，裨益甚多。英國「工商業金融公司」係設立於一九四五年，此一公司，由英蘭銀行各大合資銀行及保險信託公司等共同組設，資本五千萬鎊，貸款額度，可爲資本之三倍，運用以來，亦極著成效，英美以工業資金素稱豐厚之國家，猶爲復興工業而另立機構，則在工業資金微薄之吾國，自更有其迫切需要。

吾人所建議之「工業金融公司」，不僅須具有辦理工業貸款，及代理廠商發行債券之權力，且可用爲利用國外資金之中介，茲將其組織方式及業務要點，擬定如次：

（一）該公司可定名爲「中國工業金融公司」，（以下簡稱公司）由國家銀行主要商業銀行及信託與保險公司共同籌設，其資本分國幣及外幣二部份，國幣部份假定爲五百億元，外幣部份假定爲美金五億元，其主要目的，在籌集長期工業資金，並任利導外資之中介。

（二）公司之主要業務，除對國內廠商直接辦理投資及貸放外，並得代理廠商發行投資證券，代理廠商向國外接洽長期投資與放款，代理廠商訂購生產器材，代向國外作信用担保人，並代付外匯價款，

（三）爲適應國內工業界對長期資金之需要，並兼顧國內資本之貧乏和資本市場尚未建立起見，公司得按廠商實際需要，接受各廠商所發債券，或以廠基房屋作抵，貸放中長期國幣資金，此項資金之來源，除公司之國幣資本外，得以債券或其他憑證，向國家銀行及其他股東銀行質押借款，其通融數額，可達資本額若干倍。

（四）凡公司代廠商向國外廠商接洽投資放款，與金融界所作之擔保，政府可再代公司向國外政府及人民作無條件之全面担保，以增强公司在國外之信用。

（五）凡廠商向國外訂購器材，需要政府協助接洽，或代爲借款者，概歸公司統籌辦理，以一事權，並便利在國外獲得優惠條件。

（六）俟公司在國外之信譽確立後，得與外國金融機構洽商在國外資本市場，發行外幣投資證券。

上列辦法倘獲實行，不特工業金融體制之中樞，得以建立，且因其擁有代理廠商發行證券之權力，故產業證券市場，亦可漸次健全發展，在目前並可吸收國人在國外之外匯存款，及現在國內之黃金。

「中國工業金融公司」既爲實業金融之中樞，欲求其效運用，仍賴其他實業金融機構之輔助，國內之各實業銀行，無論公營商營，均應與之密切聯繫，而由政府指定爲實業銀行之交通銀行，更應以下列方針協助工業：

(1)發行實業債券；爲增闢工業資金之來源計，交通銀行除應具有收存國營及民營工業存款之特權外，並應賦予發行實業債券之權，按美國復興金融公司及日本興業銀行等機構，均有發行實業債券之權，對於吸收民間游資，頗著成效，交通銀行爲增强其營運實力，自亦應具有同樣之權力。

(2)辦理實業票據重貼現及工業品轉抵押；今後實業銀行之工作，應以通融中期及短期工業信用爲主，俾能配合上述之「中國工業金融公司」而爲相輔之運用，融通中期工業信用之重要方式，不外實業票據之重貼現，與工業品轉抵押，故實業銀行在此方面，應具有相當權力，俾利其業務之展開。

(3)倡辦投資信託事業；投資信託，爲近代歐美各國融通產業之主要手段，吾國欲期產業證券化之完成，非推行此項業務，不足爲功，實業銀行如交通銀行，既爲特許之實業銀行，應肩任提倡促進之責。

二、農業金融系統之完成

吾國素稱以農立國，但數十年來，農村日就凋敝，農產愈益萎縮，其原因雖多，而農村資金之枯竭，當爲其主因之一，自中國農民銀行成立以後，農業金融之基幹已告樹立，但其業務與運用，仍待向專業方面繼續加强，今者全國合作金庫亦告成立，兩者正可分工合作，同謀農業長短期資金之調劑，吾人如欲期農業金融機構善盡厥責，則首先須放棄其一切普通銀行業務，而將其機構與業務重點，移入廣大之農村，同時並可利用遍及全國鄉鎮之郵政儲金匯業局機構，向全國農村吸收小額資金，以供農業金融機構之運用，如此則來自農村之資金，仍用於農村，則農村資金偏枯之象，當可避免，至其業務方針，似應依據下列原則，妥愼厘訂：

(1)展開土地金融業務；土地金融業務之推展，對於民生主義經濟制度之建立，關係綦鉅，應根據國父遺敎原則，制定之土地金融綱要，以爲吾國土地問題之合理解決。

(2)發展中期信用業務；現代之農業經營方法，對於機械之使用，及生物學化學之利用，日趨擴大，故在農業上，對於中期信用之需要，亦日見殷切，如美國之設立聯邦中期信用制度，即其顯例，吾國今後果欲促進農業之現代化，則對於畜牧農具農田水利農場設備及農村副業等，均應予以最大限度之融通。

(3)提倡農業票據重貼現及農產品轉抵押；此種業務之推行，足以加强全國農業資產之流動性，對於整個農村之復興，爲益甚大，昔年日本人經營之南滿鐵路，曾舉辦實物撥付辦法，例如商人爲便利出口起裝輪船起見，可按大豆之品級數量另加運費手續費等，在長春繳款，則鐵路即可在大連將規定數量之大豆交指定之輪船運出，甘便利農產之流通，實非淺鮮。

(4)推展農業保險業務：農業保險業務之推展，不特可以直接促進農業之發展，抑且可保障農村秩序之安定。此在災禍頻仍，經營落後之吾國，尤屬迫切需要。

農業金融機構倘能集中全力於上項業務，則農村金融問題，大致可望解決，其運用資金之來源，亦應賴國庫撥款及發行長期債券，以為挹注。

三、商業銀行組織之健全

吾國銀行，初期以歷史關係，大都由官商創辦，均富衙門色彩，自上海商業儲蓄銀行崛起，始有真正之商業銀行，現在之銀行，不問其名稱為何，均屬商業銀行，但其組織及運用，則猶未臻於健全，組織則大都規模狹小，資力微薄，業務則多趨向於短期性營業，及投機性事業，此種病態，自應予以糾正，吾人認為欲求商業銀行之業務健全，必須採行下列措施：

(1)厘訂有關商業銀行組織資本公積及其與一般負債之標準；吾國新銀行法，迄未公佈，依民國二十年制定之舊銀行法，曾規定銀行組織分為有限公司，兩合公司，股分兩合公司，及無限公司等四種。無限公司因股東責任關係，不能設立分支行。就美國銀行之經驗視之，單行制度(Unit system)，弊害甚大，不足取法。故無限公司之規定，理宜取消。至於資本額之微小，亦為現代金融之大病，晚近先進各國，對於銀行最低資本額，多有限制。依擬議中之銀行法，規定銀行最小資本為一百萬元，此數在目前實嫌過小，似須參照物價水準，而作適當之提高，且銀行資本與公積，為一般負債之最後保障。現在各國立法，對資金及公積與一般負債之最低比率，均有規定，吾國亦應參照此法，規定一適當之比例。

(2)確定商業銀行之業務範圍；商業銀行之業務，應以工商業短期信用之融通為限，並應以貼現及承兌為放款之主要方式，押放之期限與條件，均可有妥善之決定，以保障商業銀行資產之流動性，至於一切長期性投資與貸放，以及投機性之證券買賣業務，均須完全禁止，此外對於商業銀行，保有第二準備(即穩妥之證券與票據)之比率，亦須切適規定，以期保證存款人之安全。

四、中央銀行效能之加強

中央銀行為銀行之銀行，其在推行國家經濟及金融政策中，所負之責職，特別重大，比年以來，中央銀行所必需具備之基本條件：如獨佔發行，經理國庫，集中準備，以及辦理重貼現及轉抵押等，吾國中央銀行亦已大致具備，但其實際效能，仍待繼續加强，吾人認為為發揮中央銀行之效能起見，今後中央銀行業務，似應採取下列方針：

(1)存款準備政策之靈活運用：存款準備之集中，為現代各國之共同趨勢，此項政策如推行盡利，當可控制市場信用，而有裨於整個金融之穩定，反之如運用不當，則難免阻礙整個經濟及金融事業之發展。依吾國現行法令，存款準備率規定為百分之二十，在目前情勢下，此一比率已嫌過高，抑且缺乏彈性，為糾正此一缺陷，存款準備率，似應規定一最高及最低限度，並賦予中央銀行以隨時伸縮之權，此種伸縮，並許其對某一銀行個別實施，以便此種信用控制，能兼具質量之效。同時為適應各地之經濟趨勢計，應顧及此項準備率，在地域上之差別性，蓋大都市與小鄉鎮之市場，組織信用狀況以及支付習慣等，恐有不同，故各地之準備率，殊不應作硬性之劃一規定，美國之所以分設中央準備，區準備，及鄉鎮準備者，其原因亦即在此，

(2)重貼現與轉抵押之推行：重貼現為中央銀行管制利率，安定市場之重要工具，而轉抵押則為中央銀行支持一般銀行及促進經濟發展之有效手段，吾國一般銀行與工商界之往來，仍多取押放方式，故資金極易凍結，為補救此一弊害，今後中央銀行對此自應積極展開，惟重貼現政策之運用，應與經濟政策密切配合，故重貼現之對象，應以產業證券及正當工商業所發出之票據為限，此外並應對各銀行請求重貼現之種類及各類票據之比額或數量，加以適當規定，俾以防止投機取巧。

(3)公開市場活動之參與：公開市場政策之運用，足以控制整個市場之信用，惟吾國中央銀行，迄未參與公開市場活動，最近上海股票市場，波動劇烈，此乃游資紛集股市之必然結果，僅賴行政力量，予以取締，絕難奏效，故中央銀行之參加證券買賣，實屬必要。

以上乃中央銀行所應致力之積極方針，在消極方面，中央銀行為造成其超然的最後貸款人地位起見，對於若干業務：如私人存款，私人匯款，及直接投資放款等業務，均須完全放棄，尤以直接投資與貸放業務之放棄，最關重要，蓋中央銀行既獨佔發行，如恃其無限制之紙幣，對各業作大量投貸，則不特其他銀行將無立足餘地，抑且將促成嚴重之信用膨脹，非惟經濟金融將趨紛亂，即整個銀行制度，亦必趨於崩潰。

以上係就改進吾國金融制度，以配合經濟建設之犖犖大者，簡作擬議，卑之無甚高論，果能切實推行，則吾國金融業務，始能漸入正規，而健全之金融制度，亦能隨以建立，對於輔助「迎頭趕上」之建設之完成，亦實為必要也。

鐵路中央控制行車制控制總機運用之方法

陳樹曦

吾國鐵路復員以後，多數鐵路倡用中央控制行車制(C. T. C.)之呼聲，喧囂塵上，惟C.T.C.制調度所控制總機(Control Machine)之運用如何，尚無人介紹，茲特將在美實習C.T.C.調度所控制總機運用之方法陳述如后。

美國製造C.T.C控制總機及各項號誌與轉轍器之公司，計有兩家，即聯合號誌及轉轍器公司(U.S.S.Co.)與鐵路號誌總公司(G.R.S.Co.)是也。兩公司出品大同小異，效能亦大致無差，茲以聯合公司出品之控制總機運用之方法及各種示意之解釋分述如下：

(甲)C.T.C.控制總機為一書桌式樣並附有自動列車運行圖，茲將其各部門運用情況分述如次

(一)在總機之上部為一軌道模型，共分兩部：

1.上部份為一直綫圖，表示此總機所控制之區域，各站正道及岔道(指受控制者而言)相互關係，及岔道內可容車輛數目，均註明於其上，其略圖如下：

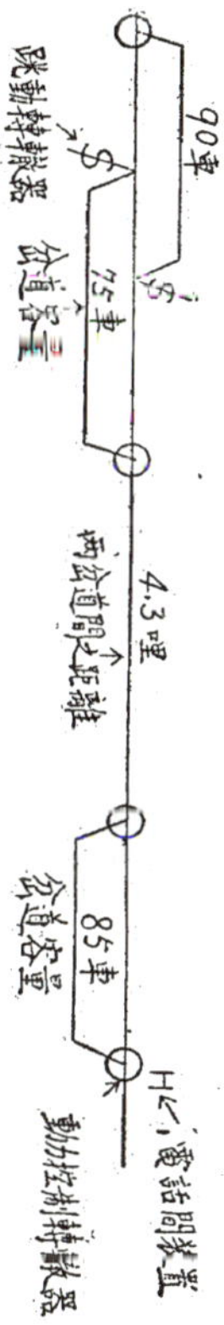

90車
75車
岔道容量
4.3哩
兩岔道間之距離
85車
岔道容量
HK，電話間裝置
動力控制轉轍器

此項簡圖，可予調度員一個概況，使知全區各站岔道容量，以解決錯誤車之問題也。

2.下部份軌道圖，包括軌道示意燈光，此項燈光電流，可使正道顯示燈光連續顯示，以指明此控制區域各次列車之地位及行駛概況，受控制之號誌及轉轍器均在此圖上註明，並註明其號數使與搬鈕上之號數相同，其略圖如下：

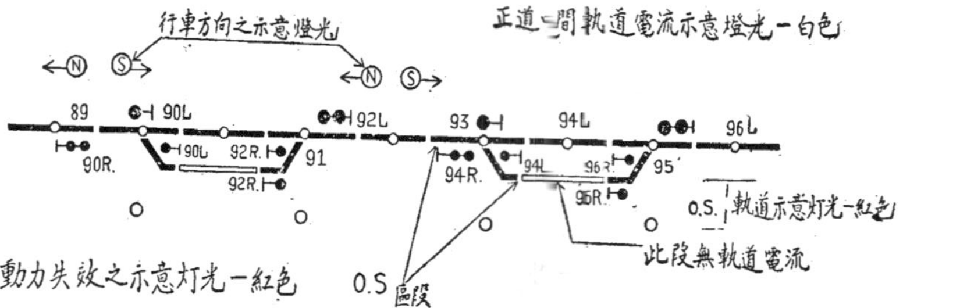

上項軌道佈置圖上，軌道燈光爲白色，用以指示列車之位置者，此項燈光指示軌道部份如下

a. 在號誌控制下，須經過一控制或跳動之轉轍器之一段軌道，此段軌道謂之"O. S. Section"，即紙上區段(On Sheet)，換言之，即在自動列車運行圖上，其O.S. 雖可接受其控制而記載列車經過該區段是也。

b. 在O.S. 區段間之正道，每一區段，均裝置一區截軌道顯示之燈光（如上圖）

上述二節之軌道燈光示意方法，無論在站內或兩站之間，所有列車在正道上行駛，均係連續示意。至"O.S."區段亦由軌道電流顯示之，無論列車佔據該區段或已離該區段進入岔道（無軌道電流）之區段（見上圖），均由圖上示意之。

所有區截示意，均受號誌控制電流之影響，如號誌電流開放時，則一佔據區截之示意燈光，即於圖上顯示，此種情況，係由於以下諸原因之結果，如一列車佔據此區間，或一軌道電流損壞或失效，電綫綫路損壞，控制之轉轍器開放或動力控制以外之轉轍器失效等原因。

當一列車進入北向或東向第一個號誌以後區段之軌道以內，即發生一單響災聲之鈴聲（音響較O.S.鈴聲爲强），可使調度員注意其位置，如列車進入南向或西向第一個號誌後之區段內，亦有一單響災聲之鈴聲，使調度員注意知悉一列車由另一端進入此控制區內。

4. 軌道圖下爲動力失效之示意燈光，每一控制區段，均有一動力失效之紅色燈光，以促使注意。

5.行車方向示意燈光，係位於每一個區截燈光之上（見上圖）此項燈光可示意控制區域業已封鎖穩當之行車方向，每一組燈光兩個各有箭頭一個以示方向並用白地黑字『北』或『西』以表示行車綫路業已封鎖妥當，應爲北向或西向列車行駛，另一燈光，則以「南」或「東」代表，以示行車綫路業已封鎖妥當應爲南向或東向之列車行駛，當路綫上封鎖情況與控制總機，封鎖情況不同或有錯誤時，則此行車方向示意燈光即黑暗不明。

6.所有以上燈光，均係用小電泡裝置於有色玻璃之後，如燈泡更換時，可自總機前面，用特製之工具更換，此項工具隨同總機供應，隨時使用。

（總機上其他部位及撥紐所用之小電泡，均用上述電泡相同）

(二)轉轍器撥紐，位於上述軌道圖內各轉轍器之下面，每一撥紐，均有一固定之號數，此號碼與軌道圖上位置相當之轉轍器之號碼相同。

1.轉轍器之撥紐，爲兩個位置之撥紐，其撥動位置或右或左，正常位置，是在左方，（即撥紐撥在左方時，轉轍器撥通正道），反常位置爲右方（即撥紐撥向右方時，轉轍器撥通岔道）。撥紐上註明"N"（正）及"R"（反）兩字，以代表其位置（但鐵路號誌總公司之式樣，正常位置，撥紐位於垂直形狀態，反常位置，撥向右方）。

欲使外站轉轍器撥通正道或岔道時，先將撥紐依照上述位置，依樣撥妥，然後再將傳遞密碼按紐（Code Starting Button）按一下，始發生作用也！惟軌道圖中白色"O.S."燈光亮時，證明有一列車佔據該"O. S."區段，此時不能傳遞轉轍器之密碼(Code)，即按「密碼按紐」亦無效。又當其號誌撥紐上之燈光全暗或當一個綠色號誌燈光顯示於總機上時，在此種情形下，即係此轉轍器業已封鎖矣。欲使已封鎖之號誌轉轍器"O. S."區段或區截重發生同一效用，僅須將傳遞密碼之按紐，再按一次，即生作用也。

2.轉器示意燈光，係按下述辦法排列，即「撥紐」撥向反常位置，則反常位置上之燈光明亮，撥向正常位置，則正常位置上之燈光明亮。

3.反常位置之示意燈光（當路綫上轉轍器業已撥妥反常位置『撥通岔道』其密碼電流傳回至總機以後此燈即明）爲紅色。

正常位置之示意燈光（當路綫上轉轍器，業已在正常位置，即搬通正道」，其接受密碼由電流傳回以後，此燈即明）爲琥珀色。

故此項示意燈光，可指示外綫上轉轍器之確實位置。

上述兩種轉轍器之示意燈光，自上述情況觀之，無論任何時間內，兩燈之中，必有一燈明亮，因轉轍器僅有兩個位置，非搬通正道（正常位置）即搬通岔道（反常位置）也。但當轉轍器搬紐搬動傳遞密碼電流時，此兩燈均暗。如兩燈均暗時，調度員應揿密碼按紐一次，以視轉轍器位置係在何方，如兩燈仍保留黑暗時，即應通知號誌保養員修理（普通校對時間甚短，但如已搬妥一方，而臨時又變易其位置，則需時約六分鐘）

4. 此項搬紐控制之轉轍器，其設備係一種雙用機械式，此項雙用機械式設置，爲一選擇搬閘及手用搬閘，其選擇搬閘可有兩位置，「動力」及「手」，並在轉轍器上註明其位置，通常此搬閘係搬在「動力」之位置，當須要用手搬動時，始可搬向「手」之位置也。

此項選擇搬閘與手用搬閘，係互相聯鎖，故選擇搬閘，能常搬向「手用」位置，俾乘務人員於站內調車時，便於用手管理，并不注意轉轍器之位置或動作，但除非手用搬閘完全搬向「正常」或「反常」位置時，此選擇搬閘不能搬回「動力」位置也。

又轉轍器非經調度員許可，不能用手搬動，俟調度員允可，而工作完畢以後，乘務人員始得將搬閘搬回「動力」位置并加鎖，然後報告調度員此轉轍器已恢復動力位置。

5. 有時，在許多錯讓車道，係用跳動轉轍器 (Spring Switch)，並不用搬紐控制，此項跳動轉轍器如欲使列車逆向行駛時，乘務人員必須得調度員之許可，始能用手搬動，但當工作完畢時，應將轉轍器搬回正常位置，並告知調度員，此跳動轉轍器業已恢復。

（鐵路號誌總公司式樣在轉轍器搬紐中裝置一燈，自正常位置搬向反常位置，此燈即明亮，俟轉轍器搬妥後，始滅去，又當乘務人員使用手閘，此燈亦明）

（三）號誌搬紐是在轉轍器搬紐之下方（鐵路總公司式樣正相反，即轉轍器搬紐在號誌搬紐之下方）每一號誌搬紐控制與其有關位置兩方向之各個號誌，號誌搬紐之號數較與其有聯鎖之轉轍器搬紐之號數多一，如第二號號誌搬紐，控制第一號轉轍器搬紐所控制之轉轍器（鐵路號誌總公司式樣，號誌搬紐號數較有關轉轍器搬紐號數少一）。

1. 每一號誌搬紐有三個位置：

a. 垂直位置——即此搬紐所控制之各號誌位於最限制之位置，搬紐之上立即顯出一紅色燈光。

b. 左方位置——控制左方號誌，在紅燈之左，顯一綠色燈光。

c. 右方位置——控制右方號誌，在紅燈之右，顯一綠色燈光。

2.所有燈光熄滅時，其意義爲號誌顯示「停止」，轉轍器已封鎖，時間傳遞器正在工作，當所有燈光熄滅後上述之(a)紅色燈光即明亮，以指示時間傳遞已過去，轉轍器未鎖，惟號誌顯示「停止」。

欲使左或右號誌顯示安全，則將該號誌搬紐搬在左方或右方之位置，并撳動密碼傳遞按紐，當搬至所欲搬之位置後，則號誌搬紐該方向位置上之綠燈即明亮，一直到列車進入"O.S."區段後，綠燈始熄滅，而號誌搬紐上正常位置上之紅燈與軌道圖"O.S."區段之示意燈光同時明亮，當列車業已接收此項號誌後（即綠燈熄滅時），應迅將號誌搬紐搬至正常位置（即垂直位置）。

欲使任何號誌顯示危險，即「停止」意義，即將號誌搬紐放至正常位置，再撳動密碼傳遞按紐一次（如列車尚未經過"O.S."區段時，時間聯鎖(Time Locking)對轉轍器有效，俟一列車經過"O.S."區段後，其時間連鎖自動解除）。

3.以上三種示意燈光之一，在所有時間內，必須明亮，除當時間傳遞器正在工作以外，無論何時，如所有燈光均熄滅時，調度員確知時間傳遞器並未在工作，其必須撳動密碼傳遞按紐一次，以視號誌之位置，如應亮之號誌燈未亮時，必須立即通知號誌保養員，以便修理。

轉轍器搬紐及號誌搬紐佈置圖如下：

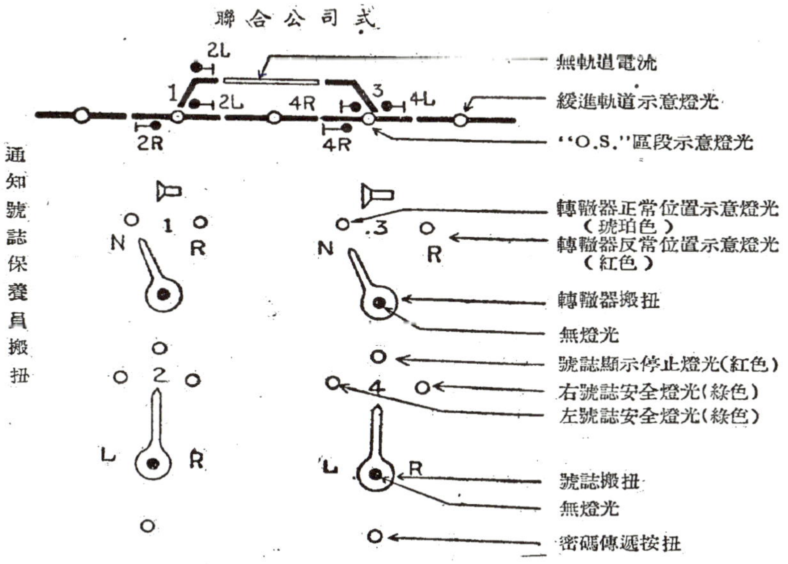

聯合公司式

鐵路公司式樣

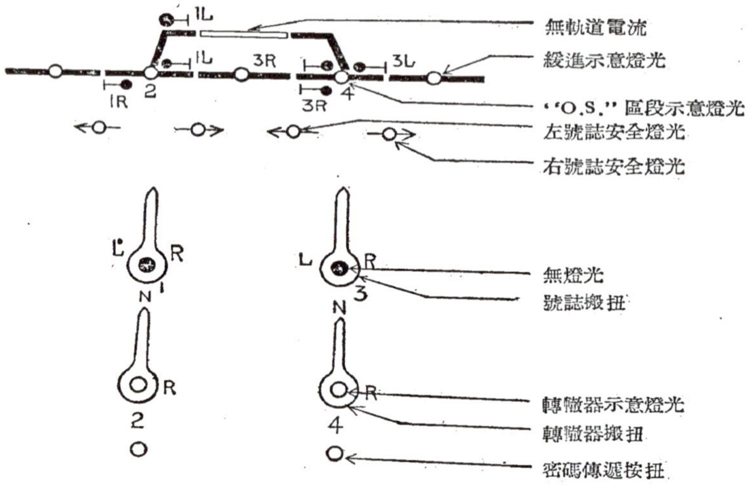

1L
1L
3R
3L
1R
2
3R
4
無軌道電流
綏進示意燈光
"O.S." 區段示意燈光
左號誌安全燈光
右號誌安全燈光
L
R
N
L
R
3
N
R
2
R
4
無燈光
號誌搬扭
轉轍器示意燈光
轉轍器搬扭
密碼傳遞按扭

(四)複合的密碼　Composite Code

總制密碼爲複合的，所有控制均在此特製之總機內，當上圖下之密碼傳遞按紐揿按時，所有複合的密碼均可同時傳遞至路綫上，此複合的密碼包括號誌，轉轍器，及通知號誌保養員之搬紐等在內，故如欲易轉轍器於另一位置及使號誌顯示另一意義時，均可於同一時間傳遞至外路綫上。

各種示意燈光之密碼，亦爲複合的，其意義起始傳遞電流於路綫上，俟完成時，可同時將密碼傳遞返回調度所之總機上，而變幻成爲各種示意燈光，以示不同之意義也。

(五)通知號誌保養員之搬紐　(Maintainer's Code Switches)

通知號誌保養員之搬紐，緊位於轉轍器搬紐之上，如號誌保養員在路綫上控制區域工作或巡視時欲通知此保養員欲與其在電話上商談，則將相當該區域之搬紐向上揿，同時將下方之密碼傳遞按紐，揿按一次，則此密碼即傳遞至路綫該有關地區繼電器房屋外之一燈上，此燈即明亮，號誌保養員看此燈明亮時，即知調度員有事通知，即可與調度員以電話商談也。繼電器房屋 (Relay Housing) 多設在轉轍器之附近，其電話間亦在轉轍器附近，但欲取銷此意義時，則將此搬紐向下揿並按動下方之密碼傳遞按紐，以取消之也！

(六)出碼傳遞按紐　(Starting Code Buttons)

密碼傳遞按紐在每一號誌搬紐下裝置一個由此可知所有控制外站各個地點情況之各種有關之搬紐及按紐在總機上，均各排列為一直行。如上述之號誌搬紐，轉轍器搬紐，密碼傳遞按紐，通知號誌保養員搬紐等等，均同一"O. S."區段內之各種有關作用之樞紐，均在總機軌道圖上之"O. S."區段下，排列成一直行。

控制號誌之電流機構，在錯讓車道兩端以內及兩錯讓車道之中間，均固定包括有一行車方向性質（Traffic Direction），換言之，如變更任何區間內之行車方向，其控制密碼係送達至此區間之進口及出口，其密碼電流之設計，可為任何方向之行車運用，傳遞之法，僅憑搬動號誌搬紐，而以搬紐之方向為轉移，故當搬動搬紐時，須注意其鄰近搬紐或其區間出口處之搬紐之方向，以避免抵觸，此意此法在注意其搬紐位置，俟檢視不抵觸時，始能撳按傳遞密碼按紐也，以此之故，此項設計，包括有 A. P. B. 原則，（即絕對允許區截原則）之使用，如上述一錯讓車道兩端之內，或兩錯車道中間之區截，如使其相鄰之號誌搬紐之方向相抵觸時，換言之，即使其行車方向相抵觸（即於兩站之區間內開向列車），如是則外路綫上所受之密碼，其先接受者發生作用，而此後一密碼，即不能承受，以資保護行車安全，此為控制總機之功效也。

（七）鎖轍搬紐 (Switch-Lock Levers)

此種搬紐為三個位置推動搬紐，係管理封鎖轉轍器之用，設置於密碼傳遞按紐之下，此項搬紐有其自備之電流，不須用撳動密碼傳遞按紐，即可傳遞於所欲控制之鎖轍作用也！

鎖轍搬紐傳遞密碼無論何時，均可傳遞至外站兩端轉轍器之內，故當傳遞密碼時，必須注意轉轍器及號誌搬紐在該有關站點之位置。

當一列車行駛離開正綫進入岔道，經過封鎖之轉轍器時，不須要搬動鎖轍搬紐。

惟當須要轉轍器開鎖時，則與該轉轍器相當之鎖轍搬紐有關，必須先根據下述原則推按轉動搬至或左或右之位置，始發生效用，例如一列車岔道進入正道，乘務人員必得調度員之許可，將鎖轍搬紐搬動，始能開鎖，其次序如后：

1. 乘務人員先以電話請求調度員開鎖。
2. 調度員先注意控制總機上之情況，如此時無列車開往該區間（即應准開鎖之區間未被佔據時），始可按動鎖轍搬紐，搬向該列車進入正道應開往之方向，此項動作，可使控制總機軌道圖上顯示該區截已被佔據，以使其他列車及調度員注意，以資防護。

3.管理鎖轍搬紐有兩種手續：

a.乘務人員於開鎖搬閘及完成任務以後應立即報告調度員，由調度員將該搬紐恢復正常狀態，如是則恢復原有控制狀態，其他列車可以跟序控制行駛也。

b.如乘務人員開鎖搬閘後，即向前行駛，並未通知調度員，在此情況之下，如調度員確已知該乘務人員業已開鎖完成工作（以二至四分鐘為估計完成時間），可立將鎖轍搬紐恢復正常狀態。

（鐵路號誌總公司之式樣，無鎖閘搬紐之設備，僅於轉轍器搬紐內置一燈光，如乘務人員用手開鎖搬閘時，則此燈明而不滅，可使調度員予以注意，但乘務人員用手轍時，必須得調度員之許可）

（八）"O. S." 鈴聲截斷按紐 ("O.S." Bell Cut-out Button)

此一按紐位於控制總機右手之下方：

1.此按紐上註明有 "O. S." 鈴聲截斷按紐字樣，有兩個位置，即「推進」與「拉出」是也。當此按紐拉出時，則為表示佔據 "O. S." 區段之鈴聲已截斷，如推進時，即 "O. S." 區段被列車佔據時即響亮。

2.最好是推進，可使調度員聞鈴聲而注意該列車之所在地是也，但調度員已付其全部精神於總機時同軌道圖時，則亦可截斷此鈴聲。

（九）取銷按紐 (Reset Button or Cancel Button)

在 "O. S." 鈴聲截斷按紐之右方為取銷按紐，當調度員欲取消其已發送之任何控制密碼，可撳此按紐即取銷也。

（十）外站失效按紐 (Field Station Disconnect Button)

位於取銷按紐之右方，為外站失效按紐，當綫路失效而懷疑係其一站失效之故，可用下述辦法，將此站臨時取銷。

1.按外站失效按紐約十五分鐘，其結果使所有車站在一不動作狀態之下，其時間自各種指示燈光得之。

2.然後有一密碼傳遞，自各站依次檢視，正如依次將各站恢復控制狀態，直至發現某站不能恢復為止。

3.將該站密碼傳遞按紐拉出，並掛一符號牌，以明其為失效，拉出按紐之意，在不再發密碼至該站。

4.再將失效外站按紐按十五分鐘，即可將此失效之站取消。

5.各站除失效之站外，再依次恢復控制。

（十一）封鎖牌 (Lever Blocking Devices)

如號誌保養員或工程列車在外站綫路工作或其他原因須封鎖搬紐時，則用封鎖牌 (Lever B'ocking) 放於控制總機有關之搬紐上，俾得注意，而免撥動，俟工作完畢或不須封鎖時，再將該牌取下。

封鎖牌式樣不一，有用圓形轉紐，插入有關撥紐之旁，以免該撥紐轉動，或用方形之牌，插入有關兩撥紐之間，使其不得左右移動，方法不同，用意則一，當撥紐鎖於正常位置之後，調度員並放一指示牌於其上，以示該撥紐封鎖。

(十二)自動列車運行圖 (Automatic Train Graph)

控制總機，均設置有自動列車運行圖，用以記載列車經過控制區域之各個規定地點：

1. 自動列車運行圖，位於控制總機正面之中央，正在調度員之前，易於劃綫及檢視。
2. 運行圖係裝訂於總機之內，運行圖直接上方，另有一小軌道佈置圖，各個規定地點均用綫代表書於運行圖上，當圖轉動時，按照一定速度在許多筆下經過圖上，每一支筆所畫之直綫係爲一指定之地點。(即"O. S."站)
3. 在運行圖極左方之筆，爲一個導筆(Pilotpen)其作用當墨水槽(Inkwell)之墨水積存過低時，此筆可予調度員以警告。
4. 列車運行圖自動紀載列車經過"O. S."區段，正如自動預備一全控制區域之列車運行表。
5. 自動列車運行表之設計如下：

a. 一卷適宜紙張，正合記載行車卅日之用，此卷紙係置於一電氣機械之上，此卷紙經過此機械係有一定之速度，每日恰轉動至廿四小時，其作用等於一個電鐘，此項機械係用電力，如商業電力失效時，其下備有儲備電池仍可繼續工作也。

b. 此捲紙上有許多橫格，每格代表兩分鐘，紙張之兩端註有時間（五橫格即有一較粗橫格代表十分鐘，六個粗橫格「六十分」即爲一小時）此卷紙行動，係由後向前捲動，經過調度員之前，(C.R.S. 式樣，係自前向後轉動)

c. 有許多筆（代表各個"O.S."區段）位在近於此卷紙之處，每一筆代表一"O.S."區段，筆正在紙上，當紙繼續轉動時，每經過筆下，即劃出許多平分綫，每綫係即代表一"O.S."區段，如一列車經過此"O.S."區段，此筆即另於平行綫上劃一小橫綫，代表此列車於該時間經過該區段。

d. 筆充滿墨水，其墨水來源，係由於一公用之墨水槽供應。

e. 紙上有一平板玻璃蓋着與桌面平。

6. 運行圖之轉動，係有兩個圓柱形之轉動器，兩端各有齒輪，運行圖紙捲在後一圓柱上，叫做「供給圓柱」(Supply

roll)，而由前面之圓柱，叫做「前轉圓柱」(Take-up roll) 向前轉動，紙之兩端有許多距離相同大小相等之小圓孔，扣住於齒輪之上藉電機之力，經前轉圓柱根據一定時間，慢慢向前轉動，每捲容 200 呎，前轉圓柱可轉動卅小時之紙張，故每過廿四小時，即應將其剪下。號誌保養員應注意紙卷上至少應留有二天至三天之紙量（指後圓柱上）如不足時應即準備更換。

7. 圖上平行綫爲紅色墨水畫成，而筆上墨水則爲綠色，可互相對照，故僅有綠墨水可用於墨水槽及筆上。

8. 列車運行圖之保養，則係號誌保養員之責任，但調度員亦應了解此自動機之構造及工作情形，因保養員有時不在調度所時，遇有更換或障礙時，調度員可以臨時處理之。

9. 如運行圖轉動時間不正確，或筆失效畫綫時，其程序如下：

a. 將控制總機右手前方之多節揑手 (Knurled knob) 拉出，旋轉幾次，以校對紙張之自由行動，如齒輪不能自由轉動時，應將前圓柱之彈簧鎔合子用力解放，如解放後，仍不能轉動時，則用一種炭製化合物清潔齒輪。

b. 如齒輪失效時，應校對其機械動力視當電力聯結時是否動做。

c. 任何時間內，應保持機器清潔。

10 運行圖紙張前後拉動之校正方法

a. 前轉圓柱 (Take-up roll) 係控制向前拉動運行圖紙張，供給圓柱，(Supply roll)，可控制向後拉動。向前拉動可以變動，係根據校正齒輪之數目，校正齒輪，係校正左手前方鑄造之螺旋。向後拉動，亦可以變動，係根據手閘壓力（在供給圓柱上），用供給圓柱向後拉動應恰可禁止紙張在筆下凸出，及平板上發生皺紋，向前拉動亦不能用力太强以免爲輪齒之齒撕破紙張兩端之孔。

b. 圓柱之轉動，可使紙張之移動有一規律之速度，其方法在使紙張兩端之孔，每孔恰與齒輪之齒吻合，漸漸向前移動也。如撕破紙孔，指明前轉圓柱前曳及供給圓柱後拖之力量不勻，超過紙張撕破之力量。如撕破紙孔之後面，證明前轉圓柱齒輪磨擦力量應予減低，撕破紙孔之前面，證明供給圓柱之轉閘壓擦力量超過。

11 畫綫不當之校正

a. 如磁石筆下所畫出之綫變薄，並將紙畫破時，其原因在：

i 筆有妨礙。

ii 墨水槽起汽泡，使墨水不能達到筆尖。

iii 筆對於紙之壓力不充分。

b. 如筆有妨礙應先查墨水槽是否清潔此時可將球形充墨水器多捏一兩次，以檢查墨水槽內墨水是否清潔。

c. 如墨水能順利充入筆內，而畫綫時仍繼續尖銳及紙破時，此或係不勻之壓力在紙上，調度員不移動紙上之筆，此時應通知號誌保養員或號誌部份人員予以修理。

12 筆磁石 (Pen Magnets)。

筆磁石係控制各筆動作之用各筆所畫之綫成為破亂不全之邊緣，其原因如下：

a. 如畫出之綫前端為破亂不全時，證明筆磁石不能控制各筆之動作使達到即刻完整運用之位置，此種殘亂之端即由於紙張前移時，筆之工作經過運用緊張而未能鬆放適當位置也。

b. 如畫出之綫後端為破亂時，證明筆由後端緊張運用突變為完全鬆放之位置，在此情形下，其殘亂之端，即由於紙張前移時，筆之工作經過一完全鬆放之位置也。

c. 磁石失效使筆不能運用或即刻鬆放至完全運用位置，或係因筆不潔，或筆在紙上之壓力過多或筆磁石不正當之校正等緣由所致。

i 筆清潔及校正筆之角度，應由號誌保養員司之，調度員不負此項任務責任。

ii 清潔墨水槽，亦亟重要應時常保持清潔，至少每六個月完全清潔一次，必要時亦可增加清潔次數。

13 集中控制行車制各單位之繼電器 (Relays) 係按時間傳遞，其控制與燈光顯示密碼同時包括在內，惟控制密碼係優先傳遞，換言之，即控制密碼 (Control code) 傳遞在前，而顯示密碼 (Indication Code) 傳遞在後，控制總機上有一路綫電表 (Line Ammeter) 指示路綫上密碼情況。

如密碼綫路失效，調度員可按下法試驗：

a. 開 (Opens)，說明表針穩定位置小於正常情況

i 決定「開」之地位，電表上顯一「開」字，應起始傳遞各個站之密碼，按照車站排列之順序，起始於最近調度所之站，「開」字可以發現於最後一站（即顯示密碼接受之站）與最初之站（即顯示密碼不接受之站）之間。

ii 通知號誌保養員告以「開」字之位置。

d. 少 (Shorts)——當「少」字在電表上發現時，表針穩定位置大於正常情況，通知保養員，該員可能決定「少」之近似位置在何處，彼可自所中測量綫路抵抗力量 (Resistance) 大小，以發現「少」之位置。無論「開」

或「少」，其位置發現後，號誌保養員應即前往修理

（乙）集中控制行車制之運用實列

以實例言之，集中控制行車別之運用，可如下述：

（一）兩列車在中途站相錯

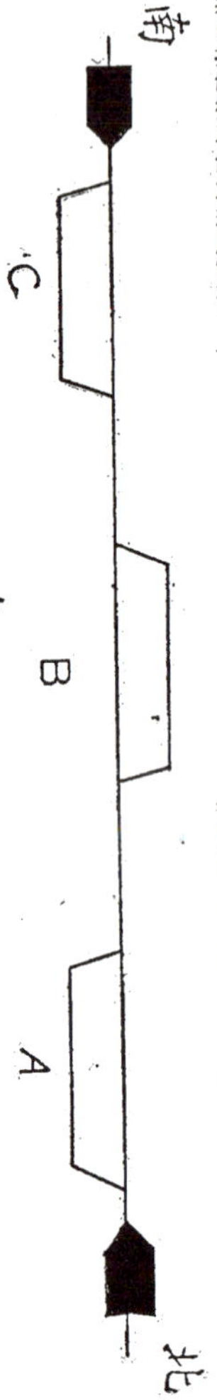

南
C
B
A
北

圖一

如一南行旅客列車已駛近A站，而北行加點車在C站之南（如圖一）自南行旅客列車行駛時刻觀之，北行加車可按時進入站之岔道以錯南行客車，而不延誤客車之時刻，調度員可按下述方法控制，使此加車由C站至B站。

1. 先將B站南端轉轍器撥鈕撥至反常位置，即撥近岔道，而C及B兩站間之號誌撥鈕應撥至右方，為北向加車之行駛，然後再撳按密碼傳遞按鈕，其結果使C及B兩站間之北向號誌均顯示「安全」，僅「B」站南端之進站號誌顯示進入岔道（上紅下黃）之指示。當控制C站北端號誌之號誌撥鈕撥向右方後，所有CB兩站間之南向號誌（即反向號誌），均顯示「危險」(Stop)意義，以樹立絕對北行之區間，此即為絕對允許原則(A.P.B.)是也，如此則完成此加點車自C站開至B站之直接控制。

2. 次建立自A站至B站客車之直接控制，其法係將AB兩站間號誌撥鈕至左方，再撳按密碼傳遞按鈕，當控制A站南端號誌之號誌撥鈕，撥向左方後，所有AB兩站間反向北行號誌均顯示「危險」(S:op)以建立絕對區間，為南行客車安全行駛。（如圖二）

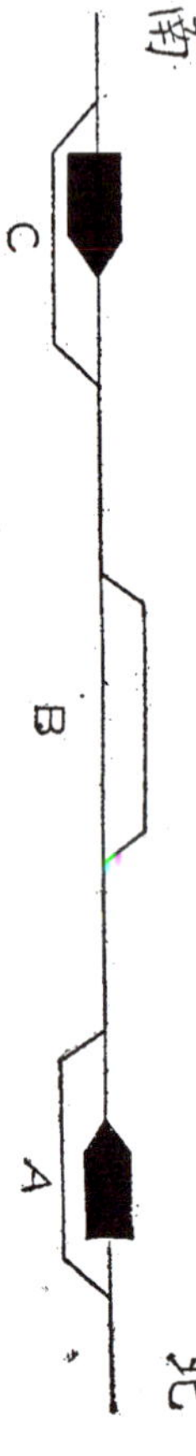

南
C
B
A
北

圖二

如上圖所示，俟AB間路綫已清之時，北向加車已駛近B站並按照號誌指示進入岔道，等錯南行客車。如圖三

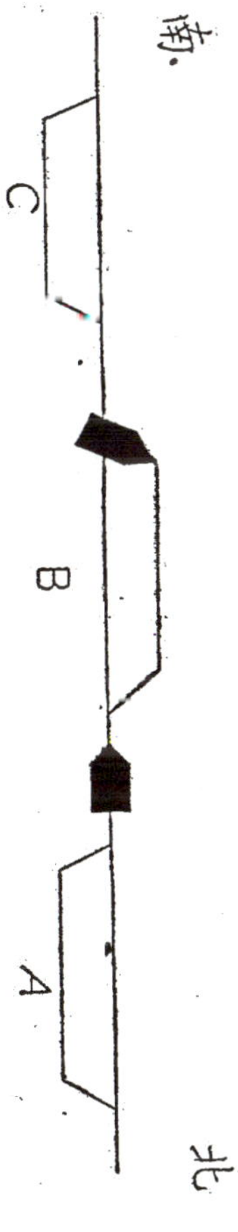

圖三

3.當此時，南行客車駛近B站，北行加車已進入B站岔道，調度員應將總機軌道圖上B站祇軌道電流岔道之白色燈光開明，以免遺忘。此時B站南端號誌之號誌撥紐上綠色燈光已滅，紅燈復明，調度員乃將此號誌撥紐撥至中間即正常位置，並將B站南端轉轍器之撥紐亦撥至正常位置，即撥通正道，並掀按密碼按紐，此時此轉轍器撥紐上紅燈熄滅，琥珀色燈光明亮，然後再將B站南端號誌撥紐撥向左方，以使B站南端出站號誌顯示安全，俾南行客車得以通過也。當B站南端號誌撥紐撥向左方，所有反向北行號誌在CB兩站之間者，均變為「危險」(Stop)指示，調度員然後將C站南北兩端號誌撥紐均撥向左方，則南行客車可直通過BC兩站控制區域。

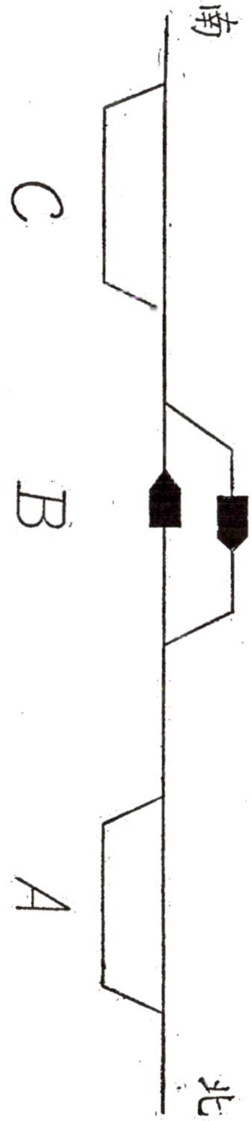

4.當南行客車駛過B站北端"O.S."區段後，調度員應即將B站北端號誌撥紐撥至正常位置，並俟將轉轍器撥紐撥至反常位置，即撥通岔道後，再將該北端號誌撥紐撥向右方，並按密碼傳遞按紐，如是則岔道右方低位號誌 (Dwarf Signal) 顯示安全 (Clear) 指示北向加車乘務人員，該加車可自B站岔道開入正道前駛也。當北端號誌撥紐撥向右方後，所有反向南行AB站間各號誌均顯示危險 (Stop) 再將A站南北端號誌均撥向右方（如無其他列車相錯讓時）再按密碼按紐一次以備加車可直通A站也。

俟列車每經過一軌道區段或"O.S."區端後，各有關號誌及轉轍器均應撥回至正常位置，俟再有其他列車駛近，再根據實際情況撥動控制也。

（二）兩列車在中途站相讓

如上例軌道佈置情形，有一南行加車自A站至B站進入B站岔道，避讓跟隨之定點列車，俟該列車經過後再繼續前駛，在此情況下，調度員應先樹立為此加車由A站至B站之控制，其辦法如下，

1.第一假定控制總機有關各站之號誌撥紐，均在正常位置，然後將有關各站之號誌撥紐，均撥向左方。在A站兩號誌撥紐均撥向左方，為南行加車經過該站之控制以後，次應將B站北端轉撥器之撥紐，撥至反常位置，即撥通岔道，再將B站北端號誌之撥紐撥向左方，其結果該號誌應顯示「上紅下黃」即進入岔道之指示，如上例所述，當A站南端號誌之撥紐撥向左方時，則所有反向北行號誌均顯示「危險」之指示，以策安全。

2.如上條所述，則此南行加車由A站駛入B站岔道之各項控制準備，業已樹立完成，當此加車經過A站及A站北端軌道電流，均可在由控制總機上軌道圖內之軌道燈光指示及號誌燈光指示中，得悉其行駛情況，當此加車繼續前駛進入B站岔道之際，南行客車亦駛近A站，所應注意者，每當有跟隨列車行駛時，因其方向相同，如勿須錯讓列車時，調度員業已為前行列車將號誌撥紐撥向其行駛之方向，跟隨列車行駛方向相同，則有關號誌撥紐，即勿須再行撥移，僅當前行列車每經過一控制號誌，其號誌轍紐上之綠燈熄滅紅燈明亮時，彼僅應再將密碼傳遞按紐掀按一次，即可紅燈變為綠燈也。其結果則有關各號誌均能自動顯示安全，以便跟隨列車跟隨前駛也。

3.當前行之加車進入B站岔道時，此時控制總機軌道圖上軌道燈光亦同時予以顯示，俟此加車駛入岔軌道電流之軌道以後（即駛過"O.S."區段），調度員應將該軌道之白色燈光開明，以免遺忘「該軌道中尚有一列車」也。（G.B.S.Co.,無軌道電流之軌道，無燈光設置，而用一種箭頭符號插入該軌道之中以表示之）再將B站北端號誌搬紐搬回正常位置，次將該北端轉轍器搬紐，搬回正常位置，即搬通正道，然後再將號誌搬紐搬向左方，再撳按密碼按紐，其結果該號誌顯示「上黃下紅」即進入正道綫行前駛之意(Entering main track to approach)通常搬法，多不將號誌恢復正常位置，僅俟前行列車進入岔道駛過"O.S."區段後，即可將該轉轍器搬至正常位置，再撳按密碼按紐，即可得同樣之結果也。B站南端號誌之搬紐，然後再搬向左方，以便後行客車自正道上通過，其結果所有C B兩站間各反向北行號誌，均顯示「危險」，然後再將C站各號誌搬紐均便向左方，以轄南行客車繼續前駛也。

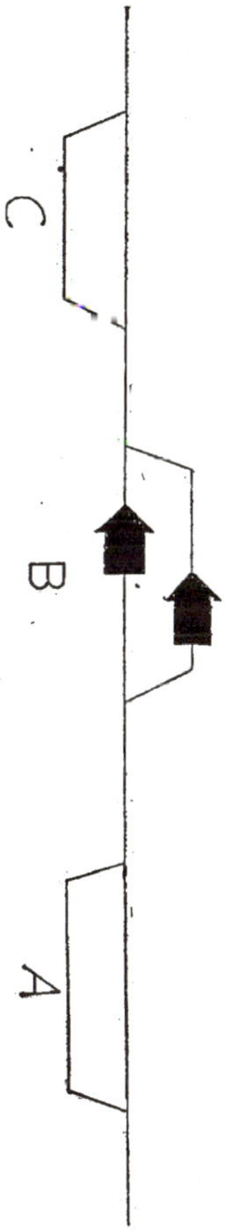

4.當南行客車業已經過B站南端"O.S."區段後，調度員應即將該號誌搬紐，搬回正常位置，再將該南端轉轍器搬紐搬至反常位置，即搬通岔道，再將號誌搬紐搬向左方（通常不用搬回號誌至正常位置，僅搬動轉轍器搬紐即可得同樣結果）撳按密碼按紐，以便允許該南行加車自岔道開入正道前駛也。當此加車駛出"O.S."區段以後，所有該南

端號誌及轉轍器各搬紐均應即恢復正常位置，俟再有南行或北行列車行駛時，再行搬動。當每一列車駛出控制區域經過每一控制"O.S."區段，其相當之號誌及轉轍器各搬紐均應即恢復正常位置，以備其他列車行駛時，再行斟酌錯讓車情形而搬動之也。

C

B

5. 控制總機搬紐之管制，可根據實際情形，調度員可隨時變易其計畫，但當正綫行駛業已樹立完妥而欲變易使從岔道進入正道，或正道進入岔道時，應先將號誌搬回正常，然後再將轉轍器搬至反常。

行政之寶

政之所興，在順民心；政之所廢，在逆民心。民惡憂勞，我佚樂之。民惡貧賤，我富貴之。民惡危墜，我存安之。民惡滅絕，我生育之。能佚樂之，則民爲之憂勞。能富貴之，（則民爲之貧賤，能存安之，）則民爲之危墜。能生育之，則民爲之滅絕。………故從其四欲，則遠者自親；行其四惡，則近者叛之。故知予之爲取者，政之寶也。

管子牧民四順篇

鐵路終點貨運車場之調車管理制度

黃宗瑜

一、緒言

調車爲行車之準備工作，亦爲行車之結束工作，蓋列車開行之前有調車，列車到達之後，亦有調車，調車與行車，實有密切之關係，調車不得其法，行車必受其影響，故各調車場，在國外鐵路爲一獨立之運轉單位，每一貨運終點，均有調車場，其主要工作爲到達車輛之接收，分析，與調送，出發車輛之調集與編組，其中接收，分析與編組工作，多行之於調車場之內，而調送及調集工作，則伸展至車場之外，但均受車場之管理與指揮，茲爲便於研究起見，特分爲車場內之調車工作與車場外之調車工作，又本文所討論之範圍，則僅以一終點調車場管轄範圍爲限，其他沿線調車則當於另文述之。

二、管理原則

查調車管理之最高原則，不外二端，一爲提高調車之效率，一爲增加行車之效率，一切調車場之管理方法，莫不以此兩端爲目標，茲請分別申論之。

(原則一)提高調車之效率。所謂調車效率即以最少數之調車機車鐘點調移定量之貨車，欲提高調車之效率，即如何縮短貨車通過及停留車場所需之時間，查貨車通過或停留車場所需之時間，計分六種，就到達車輛而言，計共三種(一)等候編析之時間(二)實行編析時間(三)待卸車輛調送時間，就出發列車而言，爲(四)車輛調集之時間(五)等候編組時間(六)準備掛出時間是也，凡此六種時間，均因儘量求其縮短，而後貨車在場停留之時間可以減少，若調車管理得宜則每一調車機車鐘點所能調移之貨車增多矣，茲就上述六種時間分別解釋如下。

(A)關於到達貨車者

(一)準備編析之時間　爲自到達列車入場以至開始編析之時間，在此時間之內，車場需辦理列車入場手續，時間固非浪費，但所費時間，不宜過長，若手續辦理遲緩，或車場管理人員事先毫無準備，迨列車到達以後，再行辦理手續，時間必須延緩，實爲車場管理之病象。

(二)實際編折之時間　自某一貨車開始分析，以至該車靜止於某一軌道與其他貨車組合一起之時間，在此時間之內，各車實行分析與集合，乃到達貨車通過車場時，工作人員之主要任務，自非有相當之時間不可，然或緩或速，其伸縮性亦大，管理是否得法，影響於此一時間之長短亦鉅。

（三）待卸重車調送時間　為到達重車調至規定地點（如貨棧貨場實業岔道碼頭等地是）此種時間之長短一方面須視調車機車工作之繁簡，一方面須視各地卸貨手續之遲速，最要者須使調送時間適宜，可與各地卸車工作配合，過早過遲均不合宜，

（B）關於出發貨車者

（四）車輛調集時間　已裝重車或卸空不用之空車必須調集車場，再行編組，此一時間，雖非完全由車場控制，但若裝畢重車或卸畢不用之空車久留棧場岔道，不予調集，既須影響列車出發時間，且久佔棧場裝卸軌道，亦足以影響棧場工作，殊不經濟，必須合理配置，以資銜接。

（五）車輛等編組時間　車輛調集以後，必須等候同行車輛編成一整列車，方能出發，調集雖經濟，若尚須等候編配，貨車在場停留，時間虛糜於此者，為數仍大，若等候之時間，為調整機力，自亦不能視為浪費，蓋失之於時間之滯留者，將得之於機車載重之提高，自屬有利，若等候時間，超過合理之需要，殊有失管理效率，必求有以改善之者也。

（六）準備出發時間　為自整個列車之貨車開始編組以迄完竣而至開始離場出發之時間，其到達本地，尚須再行前進之車輛，亦有此種準備時間，即須待相當輛數集結以後，開始掛於某一列車離場出發，亦為等候編組時間是也，在此時間以內車場管理人員自亦有相當手續待辦，若所費時間，並非無故延長，仍屬合理。

（原則二）增加行車效率　車場辦理調車工作一方面求調車效率提高，一方面仍須顧及行車之效率，否則調車管理雖嚴，行車受其妨礙則殊失整個運輸工作配合之本旨矣，車場管理事務足以促進行車之效率者其要點約有四端：

（一）避免編析錯誤　編析貨車，若編入軌線發生錯誤，則貨車即掛往錯誤的地點，迨發覺以後，再由錯誤的地點送回，往返轉運，非但行車費用增加，且時間亦因延誤，故必須有種種管理方法，為之考核，使錯誤不致發生，雖多費少許時間，亦屬合算。

（二）調整列車載重　編配列車之目的，即在以車輛配合機力，若配合不當，則編配之作用已失，若車場祇顧自身之便利，不問行車之經濟，或車輛集結未多，即已掛出，表面雖可縮短車輛在場時間，而機力虛糜殊大，實有得不償失之弊，反之不問機力，有車即掛，或天氣嚴寒，仍不減噸，雖亦可減少停留待開時間，而列車中途發生障故因而停滯，其他列車亦被延誤，影響全部行車效率，殊非所宜。

（三）規定列車內容　列車編排內容，對於行車之速度及安全

均有莫大之影響，且此二者皆足以左右行車之經濟，如編排不當，次序零亂，中途摘車費時，影響於行車之速度，又如編排不當各車位次不合，中途發生事變，影響行車之安全尤大，凡此皆應切實管理者也。

三、管理方法

調車場之工作大別之有五種階段，一為收車 Receiving Trains，二為編車 Classifying Trains，三為送車 Distributing Cars，四為集車 Assembling Cars，五為開車 Despatching Trains 五者均各有其管理之方法，茲分述之：

甲、收車管理方法　自到達列車入場以至開始編析為準備編折時間，所謂收車工作即在此時間內一種準備工作，其程序計分：

（一）預告列車組織內容　到達列車之組織內容應由後方終點站（即前一編組站），於開行時，即行電告，其中途有摘挂車輛者，應由車長在中途隨時電告（交由站方拍發），其電告之主要項目，厥為各車之目的地，與各車所裝貨物性質，最近美國各終點調車場各均裝設電報打字機 Teletype，此項列車內容報告，多用電報打字機傳送，同時調度員應向車場報告列車將到之時刻，因沿途或有晚點不能按規定時刻到達也，有此預告，則（甲）調車人工是否敷用可以預為佈置，以免延誤編配，（乙）列車內有無急運貨物俾可預定出發列車，以便挂出，（丙）查明各車目的地是否有相當軌線可供到達車輛編列，有此報告，足以減少貨車之停場時間，提高調車工作效率，同時足以趕送急運貨物（如鮮貨牲畜等）。

（二）核對列車組織內容　到達列車開入收車線後，車長應交出到達列車組織單 Inbound Train Consist，連同運輸貨票，交由車場處理，車場得此，應先將貨票與組織單核對，察其車號，是否一一相符，然後將組織單與車輛實地核對，察其有無錯誤，若貿然以貨票為準，從事編析，若車輛誤送其他目的地，將來再予送回，行車之經濟，已大受影響，又核對之方法尤須求其迅速，惟如何可使此項核對工作加快，則必須

（甲）到達列車組織單內所列車輛之次序必須完全與實在之車輛次序相符，核對時可以順序觀看，無前後查對之煩。

（乙）運輸貨票摺疊之次序，亦須與實際之車輛次序相符俾組織單與貨票核對時，亦可依次察看。

（丙）組織單與貨票應核對後，即將組織單交由車號司事在外核對車輛，貨票可留存於內部，供編填軌線（編車線）號數之用，則二種工作同時并進，免誤編配之時刻。

（三）加蓋收車時刻圖記　每一貨票背面應按經過車場加蓋圖記 Yard Stamp，內有車場名稱及到達日期與時刻，各車場應依序加蓋，該車通過車場若干處，即有若干次圖記，順序排列，何時到

達何地車場，一望可知，其中有無延誤并在何處延誤亦可查明，則該貨車在兩終點中途運行之時間，可以估計，如某車到達甲車場之日期時刻，距到乙車場之日期時刻，相差甚遠，即知甲車場之延誤，必甚嚴重，以此各車場工作時間，有無延誤，一查可知，責任分明，無從規避，無形中即足以促成貨車停場時間之縮短。

（四）檢驗車輛　調車場內例須駐有驗車夫，列車一到即開始檢驗，其目的即在標明壞車，俾可扣修，惟檢車必須迅速以免延誤編析時間，車場監工必須切實督察機務人員，在規定檢驗時間以內檢驗完畢以資限制。

（五）記錄車封　核對車輛之際，車號司事，應同時將各輛重車之車封號數，在車封登記簿 Seal Record 內，逐一記錄，記錄之目的，即在確定車封，有無破損，是在何處損壞或失落，日後查究追緝，諸多便利，如記錄時，發現不完整之狀，即應由車場重行加封，此項登記車封之手續，亦應迅速辦理，以免延誤編車。

（乙）編車管理方法　收車以後，即繼之以編車，編車工作遲速，非但影響本列車被編車輛運轉之效率，且對於後來車輛之等候編配時間，亦有深切關係，反之後來之車，若須等候編析，則先編之車亦須等候集結相當數目始能調送，陳陳相因，其影響之廣，可以想見，故管理編車方法必須加以嚴密，否則調車效率，難以提高也，茲請依次述之如次：

（一）製調車單　在小型車場調車單 Switch List 即以到達列車組織單充作調車單之用，其法即在組織單內，每一車號之旁，填註編車線號數，交由調車員工，從事編析，如有變更到達站者，則組織單及貨票內之到達站名，必須先加更改，然後規定車線，再行編析，在較大車場或坡度車場而有止車器者，調車單常須多份，以供各有關員工之應用，其填製方法，乃先在貨票內填註編車線號數，其係空車而無貨票相隨者，則按組織單內填註之，然後根據貨票及組織單編製，調車單用複寫法一起製成若干份，再如各處裝有電報打字機即分打若干份，所需份數及分配情形視各車場之工作情況而定。上述工作，採用分工辦法，即填註編車線號數者為一人，此人熟悉編車規則，能立刻決定軌線號數，至編造調車單者乃為一打字員，分別進行，工作自能迅速。

（二）標誌車輛　標誌車輛 Car Marking 之作用有二，一為便利解鈎，一為便利調送，蓋編析之際，各車必先解鈎，而後乃可編入不同之軌線，以達分組之目的，惟各車之中有二三輛或三四輛可以連結一起，而入同一軌線者，有須單獨分開而入不同之軌線者，加以標誌，則解鈎時，有所依據，不至有誤，此項標誌有以粉筆為之者，然若到達之車甚多，且須分送不同之地點起卸或交付者，則以用卡片標誌制度為宜，其法即備各種顏色不同之卡片，表示各輛貨車分送之目的地點，復在卡片上書明軌線號數及連結輛數（Number of cars per cut），如本地貨棧貨場與專用分道不止一處，則每種卡片又可加印顯明之號數，以識別之，又如聯軌路在二路以上者，亦可將路名用大字印入卡片，以利辨認，卡片標誌制度除用於編析外，并可便利調送，蓋自編析以至調送，中間須經相當時間，如用粉筆標誌，易被雨水冲去，且卡片顏色不同之車，若發現在同一編車線上，即知編配有誤，極易糾正。

（三）實行編析　上述數端，係編車工作之準備，實行編配乃為管理車場之主要工作，茲述之如下：

（1）坡度車場　近代鐵路多建坡度車場，其較為新式者均使用止車器 Car Retarders，因其設備較多，工作較繁，當另為專文以述及之，較為舊式坡度車場，編車時則用駕車夫 Car Riders，在車頂上管制手軔，以防車輛高速溜駛，發生撞擊出軌之危險，其編車之遲速，須視（a）駕車夫之人數與技巧（b）駕車夫之週轉速度而殊，此項車場，除應備相當人數，從事駕車外，尤須使駕車夫返回迅速，以免編車工作停頓，增進駕車夫週轉速度之法，即於編車線中指定一股或二股軌道專供行駛自動車 Rider Car 之用，駕車夫隨車下坡後，即乘自動車返回坡度之頂端，繼續登他車，極為迅速，并須由調車員一人記錄，每一駕車夫所駕之車數，以便觀察各人之勤惰情形，編車時，列車由推送機車 Hump Engine 在後頂送，其速度亦須加以統制，統制之法或用號角 Horn，或用號誌 Hump Signal，由調車員用以轉達命令，使頂送機車，速度適中，而利工作，各車駛入軌線後，未必一一相接，有因速度太緩，而中途停住者，後至之車，即無法編入，故又須有整理機車 Trimmer 加以推送，使各車一一相接，此項整理機車，亦由調車員管制，每當一列車全部編析之後，即以號角或號誌，召喚整理機車前來，告以應加整理之軌線，使迅速整理，若各車之中有不宜自動溜駛下坡者，（如裝有爆炸品之車或內裝牲畜之車輛等）調車員應注意調車單內所開各車之內容，另由整理機車推送之。

（2）平地車場　平地車場之編車万法係由調車機車將車輛往返調移，而由調車員工解鈎掛鈎與撥移轍尖，既不用駕車夫駕車，亦不利用坡度溜駛，故前述各種管理方法，均不適用，至平地調車管制之法，以限時完成為原則，其法即在調車單內，註明交付調車員工之日期時刻，調車夫取得調車單後，即應開始編調，全列車編調完畢，乃將編配完竣之日期時刻，填入調車單，送還車場主管人員，後者得此，即可核計編配所費之時間，以觀有無過分之延誤。

（四）車輛排列　凡經過本場不在本地卸貨且須掛出之車輛既須分成組別，尚須排列順序，此項車輛排列工作類皆以平地調車法為之，且須另備機車，將此項車場調往另組軌道辦理，以免影響其他編析工作，又凡須由沿途列車掛出之車輛於編析時業已編成一組，此後乃就此組車輛，再備調車單一份，註明各車之目的地及其

先後次序　交由調車員工，從事編調。

丙、調送管理方法　凡到達本地之車輛，須調至裝卸地點卸貨者，亦宜有規定之調送時刻，既不可一到卽調，亦不可調送過遲，前者使每次調送之車數減少，虛耗機力，增加調送次數。後者使貨車待調之時間延長，均不經濟。尤須注意者，卽與各地卸車工作時間。在美國鉄路，重車多於夜間或侵晨破曉時到達終點，并於上午七時以前調妥備卸，使貨場及岔道客商或貨棧工人，可以及早卸車交貨，客商可當天取貨，免一天延期費之損失，故此種車輛之調送時刻，頗爲急迫，若時刻一到，雖減少每次送車輛數亦應爲之，若貨物列車均能準點開行，多數重車均按時到達，則車數不至太少，機力之利用亦不至十分虛耗也，欲達上項目的，車場人員應將待調之車列入一種送車通知單 Placement List 載明車號及應送入之軌綫名稱或號數，并塡註日期時刻，交由調車員工從事調送，當調車員工進行調送時，應將每輛貨車調入裝卸地點之時刻註明，迨調送完畢，卽於此項通知單註明調畢日期及時刻，然後以此單送交貨站，以供登記貨車延期記錄，蓋延期費之計算與貨車實際調入裝卸線之日期時刻有關也。

丁、調集管理方法　零担貨棧之空重車輛，例有規定之調出時刻，車場人員可按時刻，派機調集，其他各處如每一專用岔道以及整車貨場每日規定調集一次，其調出時刻亦應加以規定，并先使客商週知，俾裝卸工作能與調車工作配合，而後車輛乃可及時調出，此種調出時刻之規定，應一面參酌裝車卸車需要之時間，一面顧及列車開行之時間，勿使調出過早而妨礙裝卸，亦勿使調出過遲而延誤挂出，庶幾貨車待調與待挂之時間乃能減至最低可能之限度，每次調集之車數亦可增加，機力亦可儘量利用，至調集車輛管理方法，則各貨場岔道或貨站人員應將待調之車列入一種調車通知單 Drilling order 載明車號及停放軌線名稱或號數，送至車場，車場將此單交給調車員工并註明日期及時刻，當調車員工進行調車時，應將每輛貨車調出裝卸軌線之時刻記入，迨車輛調集到場，調車員工應將此單交回，然後由車場註明調車日期及時刻，以資考核，則其間有無過度之延誤，若因故延誤，其延誤原因，亦應在單內註明，以便査明責任。

戊、開車管理之方法　車輛雖已調集完竣，尙非立卽開行，在開行之前，尙須經過各種必要手續與程序，此種手續與順序，與行車之經濟關係綦切，其重要性，實不亞於收，編，送，調也，玆次第言之。

（一）整理貨票　重空車調集之後，須列車編組規則重新編組或按到達站點之先後順序排列，此種車輛已分集各線重新集中，新編車輛內容不同，運輸貨票多係新製，卽車輛內容未經變動，而各車位置亦必改變，必須重加整理，整理方法，每一編車線備一木格，凡調集編入同線之車輛，其貨票應納入同一架格，仍按一定順序安放，故整理以後，非特同一列車出發之貨票可以彙集一起，且其次序仍與車輛之置在次序相符，整理工作應與調集後之編車工作同時進行，迨貨車編竣，貨票早已整理就緒，庶免延誤開車時刻，又整理之際，應注意每一貨票之編車線號數是否錯誤，有則尚可糾正也。

（二）調整噸數　出發列車所掛之車輛有係經過本地重須掛出者，有係本地起運及過軌之車輛，均各分別編入各次出發列車掛出，何種車輛應掛何種列車，例有詳細規定，惟此種車輛，所構成之噸數，是否恰當，能否配合機車牽引能力，則須視實際貨運情形而定，故開車之前，對於列車載重，必須注意調整，以免有超過與不及之患，茲將此項習見調整辦法述之於下。

（甲）按級補噸法　在美國鐵路直達貨物，列車常分三級，（一）爲急行列車 Preference or Manifest Trains，專運鮮貨牲畜及零担貨物，非特定點開行，抑且載重較小，速度較高。（二）爲定時列車 Time Freight Trains 專運一般貨物之須按定時到達者，必須按定點開行，載重應與速度配合，（三）爲慢行列車 Slow Freight Trains 專運無時間性的貨物，須視噸數湊足而後開行，雖有規定時刻，並不必絕對遵守，而載重大，速度低，車輛對於此三級列車之載重，輒採按級補噸之法，Filling-Out Tonnage 調整之，如急行列車，噸數不足，即以定時列車應掛之車輛補充之，而該列車仍按急行列車行駛，如定時列車噸數不足，即以慢行列車之車輛補充之，而該車仍按定時列車行駛，如慢行列車之噸數不足，則祗能延長時間俟湊足噸數，而後開行，此項按級補噸辦法，對於急行與定時列車不致延誤，而機車可能充分利用，若遇重車不足，則又可以空車補充之，蓋空車原有自動向指定區段輸送之制度。

（乙）延緩開行法　列車噸數不足，除補噸辦法外，在慢行列車可以遲開，但急行或定時列車因到達列車晚點或調集延誤，以致噸數不足時，亦可酌量情形而遲延其開行，嘗若晚點不多（普通以半小時爲限）則遲開較補噸更爲經濟，晚點太多仍宜以補噸法應付之爲宜。

（丙）另開加車法　如急行或定時列車載重過多，則宜另開加班列車 Sections 以應付之，如一列有餘，但不及兩列之三分之二，則應以補噸法湊足之，若係掛慢行列車之車輛，則多餘部份，自可暫留俟足噸時掛出之。

（丁）中途補噸法　有經過二段以上之長途列車，若在起運終點，車輛噸位不足，但其他鄰段，則有急於待運貨物，雖噸位不足仍可開行，迨至鄰段，再行補噸，此種辦法在本段或不經濟，但可以顧及全路之急切運輸，對於客商可以得良好之服務。

至於沿途列車，則有異於是，無論噸位若何，每日必須開行，且不能用補噸辦法，但若噸數太多，必須加開列車以免積壓。

（三）編排車輛　車輛編入各編車線後，僅係分類分組，並無一定次序，其中裝有爆炸品之車輛，是否位於中央，裝有牲口之車輛是否排在後部，性質互相侵犯之車輛，是否連結一起，均須開車之前，應參照貨票（業已按出發次序整理），査看有無應加重排之車，有之，即應令由調車機車在開車線或編車線上，採用平地調車法爲之重排，同時將貨票次序更改，以符實際，此點關於行車安全甚巨，亦不可不加以注意也，此乃就直達列車言，至於沿途列車則原應按到達站點重編，不必贅述矣。

（四）召集員工　沿途列車之員工班次固定，直達列車之車長及司軔夫均無固定之車次，何人輪值何次列車，係按先入先出 First in First out之原則指派之，即誰先到達，誰先出發，蓋直達列車之次數，逐日常有更變，固定派班，不易實行，輪流制不可因班次不固定，事前必須召集，是謂叫班 Calling Crew，由叫班員Crew Caller 專負其責，或至場內宿舍召集，或往員工家中通知，務使輪值員工均於規定開車時間以前半小時上班簽到，從事開車準備工作，否則必增加車輛等候挂出之時間，如輪值之員工因故無法召集，則依次通知已到達之員工，不到員工即無工資，如其次到達員工倘未經過應有之休息時間，則可喚備用人員 Extra men 充任，遇有加班列車時亦如之，故無論如何不至無人應點致誤開車時刻。

（五）試驗汽軔　列車開行之前必須試驗汽軔 Testing air以觀風管是否貫通，軔閘是否靈活，汽醎有否洩漏等，以策安全，惟試驗手續，須費相當時間，若因此而延誤開車，又與行車效率有關，若將機車提早出房，專備試驗汽軔之用，則又須增加機車用煤及人工，亦非經濟辦法，故在車場內開車線之旁，均設有汽壓管 air Line 各管有接頭通至地面，可將壓汽輸入各車之風管暨試驗器內，故不待列車機車之挂上，已可將汽軔試驗完畢，待機車到場，即可開行，此種試驗工作，例由駐場之驗車員 Car inspector 爲之，車場人員亦應加以監督，以免延誤。

（六）核對車輛　車場對於出發列車，應塡造出發列車組織單 Out bound Train Consist List，列各車車號內容到達站名車封號碼及噸數等項，按照實在次序排列，不得錯亂，重車可由貨票轉錄，空車可由調車單得之，其車封號碼，應由車號司事抄錄而得，噸數指車輛皮重及貨物噸數之總噸數而言，如屬重車可得於貨票，如屬空車，則其皮重均於車旁標明，一覩即得，此單以一聯存査，一聯交由車長隨帶，車長取得此單以後，應先自行査對一過，各車車號應與場方所備之組織單及貨票相符，始將貨票及組織單接收之，如是雙方分別檢點，互相校核，錯誤自不致發生矣。

以上三節爲終點貨運車場之管理原則與方法，乃美國鐵路習見者，其主要之點即在減少車輛在場停留時間，亦即將貨車之收、編、送、集、開候，六、種時間求其緊湊，以期貨車週轉加速，貨物運送加快，但同時對於機車運用之經濟，列車行駛之效率與安全，亦處處顧及，我國鐵路各站無分開之調車場，以及調車亦無完整計劃，殊屬不合，爰因觀察所及，依次述敍，以供國內之有志改革路務人士之參考。

卅六、三、十、上海交大

國際貨幣基金與我國

鄒宗伊

根據第一次大戰後國際經濟紊亂之教訓，世人深信欲消弭戰爭奠定永久和平，必先以集體的努力，消除經濟戰爭之因素。基於此一信念，英美兩國同時於一九四三年四月各自提出其穩定國際匯兌計劃。嗣經聯合國專家研究討論，越時一載，於一九四四年四月發表共同宣言。同年七月一日遂在美國紐亞什爾州（New Hampshire）布里敦森林（Bretton woods），舉行聯合國貨幣金融會議（The united nations monetarg and financial conference）會中對於設置「國際貨幣基金」（International monetary fund）和「國際復興開發銀行」（International Bank for reconstruction and Development）兩機構，通過協定。此二協定已於一九四五年十二月二十七日經佔有攤額百分之八十會員國政府簽字而生效。兩大國際金融合作機構，辛勤籌議，幾及四年，現已大體就緒，即將與世界需要各國援手。國際銀行已於一九四六年六月廿五日正式成立，貨幣基金則定於本年三月一日開始匯兌交易。我國認繳國際銀行股額及貨幣基金中之攤額，均佔相當重要地位，其對我國今後幣制匯兌以及經濟建設，關係綦切。是以此兩國際金融合作機構之內容業務與效用，深值國人注意。本文僅就國際貨幣基金一方面，申論於后：

國際貨幣基金之設立，係爲協助會員國維持穩定之匯率及避免不必要的匯兌限制。促進國際貿易之平衡發展，藉以維持國民就業及實際收入於高度水準。會員國若遇國際短期收支不能平衡時，可由中央銀行以本國貨幣向基金換購一定限額內之美元或其所需要之外幣，以平衡之，而不致引起匯率之波動，所以國際貨幣基金，可說是一種抵制國際匯兌戰爭之因素。

基金總額依布里敦森林協定應爲八十八億美元，而現有會員基金認繳總額祇有七十三億九千七百五十萬美元。美國攤額達二十七億五千萬美元，約佔總額的百分之三十七。其餘四十六億四千七百五十萬美元，由其他四十二會員國分別攤認。我國攤額爲五億五千萬美元，次於美英蘇而佔第四位。因爲各國攤額之多寡對於各該國在基金理事會之投票權數及向基金融通款項之數額息息相關，所以在布里敦森林會議時，各國爭持頗久。當時我國出席代表力爭我國攤額應爲六萬萬美元，經會議決定減爲五萬萬五千萬美元，佔第四位，法國攤額爲四萬萬五千萬美元，佔第五位。據美財長摩根索解釋，第四位與第五位之間，無論如何必須保持一萬萬美元之距離，故有此項決定。然戰後法國勵精圖治，國勢日降，經濟情況，日有進境。最近乃向基金申請提高攤額，已經核准提高至五萬萬二千五百萬美元，與我國僅差二千五百萬美元之距離。我國政府以國際地位有關，故亦向基金申請提高攤額，但基金方面認爲中國經濟情況，逐漸退步，又未便拒絕，乃給予中國以機會，自動「撤回」。執此一端，即足證中國在政治上及經濟上之國際地位，較並肩作戰時已有降落，將來國際基金可能給予我人之協助，概可想見。

各會員國認繳攤額中，一部份須以黃金美元或其他可以兌換黃金之外匯繳付，其數額或爲各該國攤額二五%，或爲各該國持有黃金美元外匯數額一〇%，二者擇其較小者爲準，於基金通知即將開始匯兌交易會員依照規定得以利用基金資源時支付。其餘額則以會員本國貨幣支付，實際上仍存於各會員國中央銀行收基金戶而已。我國認繳攤額爲五億五千萬美元，其中應以黃金美元支付之數額，如照攤額的二五%計算，應爲一億三千七百五十萬美元，但依協定，我國爲被敵人破壞佔領之國，應繳黃金美元數額可減爲四分之三，即一億零三百萬美元。

各會員國之國際收付仍照舊辦理，但爲抵補短期交易方面國際收支之不足，可以用本國貨幣向基金換購美元或其他所需之外幣，以平衡之。此項向基金換購外幣，實際等於向基金透支款項，其透支限額每年（每十二個月）不得超過各該國攤額百分之二十五，逐年透支累計總數亦有一限度，即以基金保有各該國貨幣達到各該國攤額百分之二百爲度。以我國爲例，攤額爲五億五千萬美元，每年透支限額不得超過攤額的百分之二十五，即爲一億三千七百五十萬美元。逐年累計透支限額不得超過攤額百分之二百，即爲十一億美元，惟我國攤額中百分之七十五即四億一千二百五十萬美元係以本國貨幣繳付，換言之，基金原已保有我國國幣四億一千二百五十萬美元，故我國可能向基金透支數額逐年累計之最高限度，祇有六億八千七百五十萬美元，兩者合共十一億美元，相當於我國攤額百分之二百也。

現在有一問題，即依上述計算方法，基金究竟擁有多少黃金美元資源？是否足資應付全體會員國透支限額內之需求？我們既知現有會員認繳基金總額爲七十四億美元弱，其中百分之三十七，即二十七億五千萬美元爲美國所認繳，此部份全數係黃金和美元。其他會員國認繳總額共爲四十六億美元强，其中應以黃金美元繳付者，最高爲十一億五千萬美元，扣除被敵人破壞會員國及存金量較小會員國應予減低之數外，據估計最高不過八億五千萬美元，連同美國之二十七億五千萬美元，合共基金持有黃金美元資源幾達三十六億美元。美國以外所有會員國向基金透支數額逐年累計之最高限度，以各該國認繳攤額合計之二倍減除基金持有各該國認繳攤額之國幣部份後，應爲五十五億美元弱。據此推算之結果，基金擁有之黃金美元資源，僅及美國以外所有會員國透支總限額的百分之六十五。

但有些國家並不使用其全部透支權，同時基金保有美元以外之其他國貨幣如加拿大金元，當亦可供各會員國部份之需求。且基金之資源僅用以抵補短期交易收支之不足，各會員國而有向基金透支者，一面理應自行改善其短期收支狀況而有陸續分期償還其透支者。基金如此週轉運用，自可應付裕如也。以我國情況而論，祇須繳付黃金美元最多一億零三百萬美元，即可獲得約七倍之信用透支。每年透支限額爲一億三千七百五十萬美元，且可繼續增加同額透支達五年之久。按我國一九一四至一九三〇年間平均每年短期收支逆差按戰前匯率計算，約合美金九千萬美元。故我國參加國際貨幣基金，本可獲得抵補短期收支不足之利，惟在戰後初期生產力未能恢復，出口貿易與僑匯收入大減，所需進口物資又增，預料短期收支不足額將遠超過戰前情況，是則一面有賴我國內部經濟之自行努力改善，一面引用協定中過渡辦法之規定，繼續實施合理而有效之匯兌管制。

國際貨幣基金之主要目的，既在維持國際匯兌之穩定，消除阻礙國際貿易之匯兌競爭。故基金在未開始匯兌交易以前，先要決定現有會員攤額百分之七十七會員國家貨幣之平價。此一步驟，已由基金會於上年九月廿八日通知各會員國，請其於三十天內各將本國貨幣按黃金或美元計算之平價，根據協定生效前六十日（即一九四五年十月二十七日）之匯價爲準，提出於基金會審核，如基金會認爲有不滿意時，可於十月二十八日起予以六十天之之期限，重訂適當匯率。惟中國情形特殊，在六十天期限後得再延緩。會員國提出之平價，如基金會與會員國雙方均無異議，則定爲基金協定下該會員貨幣之初期平價。以後變更平價在百分之十以內可由會員國自主，超出百分之十以外之變更，非經基金會之批准不可。各會員國接得此項通知後，紛紛於去年十月二十八日提出平價，截至十二月十八日止業經基金會正式接受之會員貨幣平價，除中國、巴西、多明尼哥、希臘、波蘭、南斯拉夫、越南及荷屬東印度等國外，計有其餘英法等三十五國。茲將主要會員國貨幣之法定平價列左：

英帝國每金鎊	四·〇三美元
南非聯邦每金鎊	四·〇三美元
法國每法郎	〇、〇〇八三九九美元
埃及每鎊	四·一三三美元
加拿大每金元	一·美元
墨西哥每比索	〇、二〇五九七美元
菲律賓每比索	〇·五美元
荷蘭每盾	〇、三七六九五美元
挪威每克降	〇、二〇一五〇美元
印度每羅比	〇、三〇二二五美元
丹麥每克降	〇、二〇八七三美元

在上列各會員貨幣平價，皆係根據現有匯率爲準，其中加拿大金元曾於上年七月將對美匯率由〇·九對一提升爲一對一，法國法郎在去年亦曾貶值。若依照協定須根據一九四五年十月二十七日之匯率爲準，則該二國所提平價，未能符合。不過基金會發出文告有謂：「基金會深知在現有匯率之下，若干國內均有物價與工資水準相差甚鉅之事實。但若干國家今方從事壓制通貨膨脹之工作，匯率之變更，具有激動通貨膨脹之危險，自不宜於目前有此冒然之舉」。言外之意，乃承認現有匯率，而將協定以「一九四五年十月二十七日匯價」爲準之原意，已經打了個折扣。基金會復再三聲明，現在接受的各會員貨幣平價，不能視爲永久固定之價值。百分之十以內之變更，固可由各會員國自主爲之，即百分之十以外之變更，亦非絕對不准，不過變更的大權操在基金會之手而已。

我國現正處於惡性通貨膨脹之困境中，國內物價急劇上漲，法幣對外購買力自難期其長期穩定，故目前不宜申報法幣之匯兌平價，以免作繭自縛。依照協定，我國雖未申報匯兌平價，仍可享受向基金透支款項之權利。惟我國匯兌平價既未能確定，財政幣制尙無整理之望，則此項透支款項亦不過飲鴆止渴而已。最近報載紐約所傳，由於中國財政歲出中過半數用於軍事方面，貨幣基金會條款，可能自動阻止中國向基金會申請貸款，以彌補收支差額。果如所傳，則不啻摒棄中國於國際貨幣基金之外。環顧國內局勢與政治上經濟上之國際地位，撫今思昔，實令人痛心疾首不置，國人其共勉諸

曾文正公函牘摘錄

（一）京官之辦事通病有二：曰退縮，曰瑣屑。外官之辦事通病有二：曰敷衍，曰顢頇。退縮者，同官互推，不肯任怨，動輒請旨，不肯任咎是也。瑣屑者，利析錙銖，不顧大體，察及秋毫，不見輿薪是也。敷衍者，裝頭蓋面，但計目前，剜肉補瘡，不問明日是也。顢頇者，外面完全，而中已潰爛，事實粉飾，而語無歸宿是也。有此四者，習俗相沿，但求苟安無過，不求振作，將來有一艱鉅，國家必有乏才之患。

（二）唯天下滔滔，禍亂未已。吏治人心，毫無更改，軍政戰事，日崇虛僞。非得二三君子，倡之以樸誠，導之以廉恥，則江河日下，不知所屆。默察天意人事，大局殆無挽回之理。鄙人近歲在軍，不問戰事之利鈍，但課一己之勤惰。蓋戰雖數次得利，數十次得利，曾無小補，不若自習勤勞，猶可稍求一心之安。

鐵路貨車停留時間之監督問題

顧家騏

鐵路投資於貨車購置爲數可觀，佔資中支出之極大部分，而鐵路運輸之表現要賴貨車。是以發生一種矛盾心理：即一方面爲節省資金計，貨車購置務求甚少；一方面爲適應貨運之需要以及工作之方便計，貨車購置以愈多爲愈佳。此爲兩人極端，皆非所宜。是故鐵路購置貨車，其數量務求適中，不宜太多，亦不宜太少，一方面儘可能之節省資金，一方面須顧到貨運之實際需要，求得一折中數字，以爲購置貨車之標準。此項標準如何求得，乃爲一困難之點，惟以屬於購置問題範圍，筆者不欲論述。至吾人對於「利用貨車之最大效率」一點，務須三致其意；蓋鐵路決定貨車購置數量，須以鐵路工作之相當效率爲根據，若數量之決定如彼，而工作效率之減退如此，則現有之貨車不能盡其最大利用，欲以適應貨運之實際需要殆矣。反之，數量之決定如彼，而貨運數量之增加如此，鐵路不即添置車輛，而欲增進工作效率，以增加貨車之利用程度，則以現有之貨車數量以適應增加之需要，或爲事實所許可。由是觀之，增加工作效率即爲增加貨車利用程度，而增加貨車利用程度適足節省貨車之購置數量，此爲鐵路工作經濟之一大樞紐，吾人務須深切研討者也。

然則何以增加貨車之利用程度？曰，有數端可述：一爲增加貨車之活動程度，貨車之活動愈劇，其所產生之車里愈多。二爲減少貨車之空車里程，蓋車里既增加矣，又須儘量減少無謂之空車里程。三爲增加貨車之平均載重，貨車載貨愈多，鐵路運輸之單位成本亦愈減少。凡此三者，均足以增加貨車利用程度，宜爲鐵路管理者所注意；減少空車里程爲車輛支配問題，增加貨車平均載重爲站上裝車方面之問題，初非屬於本文範圍之內，筆者自不欲加以論述。惟增加貨車活動程度一端，爲本文討論之中心，蓋所謂貨車停留時間之監督，原欲減少貨車之停站時間，以增加貨車之活動程度是也。

監督之範圍　筆者早已申言，貨車停留時間監督之目的，在於避免貨車無謂之停留時間，以期產生較多之車里，而盡貨車之利用也。吾人之最高理想原爲根本免除貨車之停留時間，然此種理想決不能實現，蓋貨車或有在進行裝卸工作者，或有在編組列車者，或有在修理者；凡此均含有必要之停留時間，雖可減至最小程度，但究不能全然免除。至所謂減至最小程度，亦即吾人監督之目的；惟所涉範圍初有四處：一爲整車貨場或私有岔道Team tracks a private

Sidings；二爲零担貨棧 Freight house；三爲車場；四爲修理廠。夫貨車在修理廠之時間，乃爲機務方面之問題，卽有停留監督之制度，亦本文所不及論述。惟車場之貨車停留時間直接與貨棧貨場或私有岔道之處理程序發生密切關係；蓋貨車雖已自貨棧貨場或私有岔道拖出，但仍留滯車場而不組成列車出發，則於事實總爲大害；反之，貨車雖已到達車場，而仍不拖入貨棧貨場或私有岔道，則停留之減少豈又可能。抑有進者，貨棧貨場或私有岔道方面之停留時間，除裝卸工作須由路方或客商負責外，其他均屬於車場所應負責之範圍以內。是以筆者討論貨棧貨場或私有岔道貨車停留監督之制度時，雖以貨棧貨場或私有岔道爲出發點，但仍以車場爲討論之中心也。

監督問題之兩面觀　貨車停留時間之監督問題，可分兩方面觀察，一爲一般工作趨勢之監督，一爲臨時工作狀況之監督。所謂一般工作趨勢之監督，乃爲吾人利用統計方式，考核貨車停站狀況，觀察工作效率趨勢爲上升抑爲下降，爲進步抑爲退步；若有退步現象，則可詳加分析，探求癥結所在，然後據爲事後之補救，而期日後之改進。所謂臨時工作狀況之監督，爲利用檢查制度暨追查制度等，作隨時之處置，以便及時改進。前者之觀察乃爲一般的，據此可以大體明瞭工作效率是否有進，貨車停留時間是否儘量減少，對於個別貨車停留狀況之良否尚未能作及時之改進。後者則不然，對於每一貨車之停留，皆須予以監督，若爲停留時間過分延遲，則必隨時警告有關人員加以注意，督促其立時改進。對於個別貨車停留狀況，均宜迅速發現其有否正在發展之病態，如有之，則須及時避免其再予發展。進一步言，臨時工作狀況之監督亦可視爲一般工作趨勢監督之實行階段，蓋前者僅止於不著邊際之監督而已，而後者則爲運用實際之監督工作而貫澈監督之全部效能也。由是觀之，二者雖在施行之時，性質不同，但亦爲相輔而行一事之兩面，蓋一般趨勢之監督，其功效偉大，而臨時狀況之監督，其功效切實也。

監督之原則　貨車停留時間之監督，既屬如此重要，而對於監督之實行，則又不能不遵守合理之原則。不論爲長期趨勢之監督，抑爲臨時狀況之監督，而其應循之原則則一，今請論述之：

甲　經濟　監督之工作，務求切合實際而符經濟原則，不必要之監督事務必須絕然免除，而必要之監督事務不能節省一絲半毫。視事務之繁簡而決定適當之工作方法，既不可支離破碎，亦不能大而無當，要在簡單切實，扼要不煩。如是，則在監督者，既感工作之便利，而在被監督者，亦感應付之有方。此爲監督問題之「經濟」原則也。

乙　迅速有效　監督工作亦須迅速而有效，在臨時狀況之監督，此點尤爲重要，蓋某一貨車之停留，業已超過應有之適當程度，今實行監督工作，務須立刻加以督促改進；設若監督手續複雜，工作進行緩慢，及至實行改進工作，為時已晚，時機既失，監督之意義全無，欲求改進，病入膏肓矣。至於一般趨勢之統計監督，雖其應用之時效較長，但有以一日為依據者，有以一週為依據者，又有以旬以月以年為依據者，要皆有一規定之期限，若統計之編造極煩，費時頗久，而致監督工作全失時效，毫無意義，成為明日黃花，則既有監督之麻煩，而無監督之實效，斯可謂徒自擾矣。是以吾人欲求監督之有效，務須工作迅速，切合時效，依照事務之繁簡，工作之性質，而規定適當之工作期限為標準，在不傷害工作需要之範圍內，監督之進行以愈迅速為愈佳。抑有進者，「迅速」與「有效」，原為形影相隨之二事，迅速而切合時效，庶幾有效之監督工作得以成立。若監督工作雖迅速而無用，於事亦無所補，可謂鐵路工作之累贅，在合理之監督制度下，自當不應存在。凡此，皆為監督問題「迅速而有效」之原則也。

丙　準確　監督方法，又須準確；蓋手續既簡單矣，工作既迅速矣，然若監督方法全屬謬誤，則亦不能獲得監督之利益。抑有進者，監督之根據若屬非是，則監督之結果必致荒謬無疑。譬如觀察貨車停留時間，設所填報之時間不確，停留久者填報為暫，停留暫者填報為久；或貨車已經離站而仍填報為在站，貨車在站而仍填報為離站；依照此種錯誤之紀載，而作為監督之根據，必致笑話百出，監督之尊嚴性盡失，而其意義全歸烏有矣。至若監督之根據並無錯誤，而監督之授受手續全然錯誤，則所得結果亦同，小之影響監督之效力，大之造成張冠李戴，責任不明，懲譽不明之結果。由是觀之，監督之準確性，亦為健全監督制度之先決條件，若欲強行監督制度，而內容全係荒謬不經之雜亂物，則無監督制度，亦無損也。此為監督問題「準確」之原則也。

結論　筆者對於貨車停留時間監督之意義、範圍、目的以及原則諸端，均已予簡略探討，循此理論之指引，吾人可得實際監督制度之工作方法。西國鐵路所用之統計監督以及檢察監督均屬貨車停留時間監督之標準方法。本文所述監督之理論體系，大部由其實際工作方法推演而來，讀者既已把握監督之理論，則於研究監督之實務時，自可得一方便之門矣。

貨幣數量說述評

吳羣敢

在近代（所謂『貨幣信用經濟』的）社會經濟結構里，貨幣扮演着極端重要的角色，它底運動是社會經濟的脈絡，它底循環是社會再生產的前提；甚至近代社會經濟的癥結和祕密也可以說是潛伏在貨幣形態里，貨幣政策已經成爲各國政府穩定社會經濟的重要武器了。因此，對於一個這麼重要的範疇，已經越來越引起學者專家們的興趣和爭論。

但在所有的貨幣理論里，再沒有比貨幣數量說更重要——在理論上更輝煌奪目，在影響上更深徹遐邇的了。差不多整整兩個世紀以來，貨幣理論分爲金屬說（Metalism or commodity theory）和名目說（Nominalism or claim theory）兩大壁壘，前者堅持有確定價值的金銀，排斥不能兌現的紙幣和信用貨幣；後者恰恰相反，只把貨幣當作本身沒有任何價值（只由政府法令或者商業習慣制定）的流通媒介，當作分享社會財富的憑證（tickets）。這兩大派別相互爭辯論戰，但這兩大派別大都接受了數量關係的概念；特別是在近百年來完全統治着貨幣思潮的名目說學派里，更倚貨幣數量說爲其靈魂與梗概。

對於在近代社會經濟結構里占着這麼重要地位的貨幣有着這麼深刻研究和廣泛影響的貨幣數量說，加以介紹和批評，對於有志於貨幣金融理論者，想非無益。

二

什麼是貨幣數量說（Duantity theory of Money）呢？對於這一問題的答案卽使是同爲貨幣數量說的學者專家們恐怕也未必一致。我們只能從其根本精神立論：貨幣數量說，可以說是關於商品價格的一種理論，依照這種理論的邏輯，商品價格水平決定於流通領域的貨幣數量，在商品數量不變的條件下，商品價格比例於貨幣數量的減少而降低，比例於貨幣數量的增加而提高；換句話說，就是：貨幣價值（購買力）決定於流通領域里商品與貨幣數量的比例。

這種理論由來已久，早在公元三世紀意大利學者底經濟思想里已見端倪，羅馬高等法院法官鮑爾斯（Julius paulus）早就講過：『貨幣價值依其數量而左右』（註一）；但最先倡導的還是洛克（John Locke 1632—1704）和孟德斯鳩（Montesquien 1689—1755）。洛克曾經肯定地說：『金屬底價值不是別的，而是數量』『金銀之缺乏價值，是跟數量決定金銀價值的事實有直接關係。』（註二）孟德斯鳩認為：『商品的價格受決定於全世界的商品數量與全世界金銀數量之間的關係，全世界的商品集合體乃與全世界的貨幣量相對立。』（註三）

往後范德林(J. Vanderlint)和休謨（David Hume 1711—1776)也加宣揚，范德林說：『不論在那一個民族中，商品價格當然應該隨着民間所流通的金銀數量之增加而逐漸昂貴起來；所以，某一個民族所特有的金銀數量減少了，那麼價格應當也跟貨幣之減少同比例地減少下去。』（註四）休謨更依據當時（十七世紀）美洲金銀礦山發現後大量金銀流入歐洲而引起歐洲物價非常上漲的教訓為證，提出了更完全的貨幣數量關係的理論；但休謨跟孟德斯鳩不同的是：休謨不是用全世界範圍內商品與貨幣的絕對數量，而是用流通領域內的貨幣量來說明在流通領域內商品的價格水準。

到了古典學派（Classical school）大師李加圖（David Ricardo 1772—1823)和約翰穆勒(John Stuart Mill 1806—1873)手里，貨幣數量說又獲得發揚光大，李加圖雖然曾經承認貴金屬內在獨立的價值（承認金銀也是商品，金銀底價值也被決定於其生產所必需的勞動時間）；但在其名著政治經濟學與賦稅原理里他又說：對於貨幣的需要要完全由其價值決定，而其價值又由其數量決定。』（註五）在跟波桑格(Bosanpuet)論爭時，李加圖更坦率地說：『商品價格比例於貨幣的增減而騰落，我認為這是無可爭辯的事實。』（註六）

但是，這時期貨幣數量說的發展，還祇是侷限在一個簡單的概念里，除了反覆說明貨幣數量與商品價格成反比例的關係以外，並無其他。這跟往後縝密透徹的理論體系和確切簡要的數理公式比較起來，實在只能算作貨幣數量說初期發展的萌芽階段。

三

在近代貨幣思潮史里，貨幣數量說一直占着支配的地位，馬歇爾(Alfred Marshall)費雪(Irving Fisher)加塞爾 (GustavCaocel)庇古(Pigou)凱思斯(John, Maynard Keynes) 眞不愧是名師輩出，慧光四射。首先是耶魯大學教授費雪，在第一次世界大戰前夕，提出了貨幣數量說新的詮釋。

費雪教授認為所有過去的貨幣數量說，都忽略了貨幣流通速度（時間）和銀行制度（信用）兩大因素的影響；費雪理論的特點，就是以貨幣流通速度和銀行制度來解釋（補充）貨幣與商品價格間數量關係的內容。他認為：第一、如果貨幣流通速度平均加快一倍，出現在市場上的貨幣量（即使絕對量不變）也無形增多一倍，商品價格水準也隨着上漲一倍；反之如果貨幣流通速度平均減慢一半，商品價格水準也隨着下跌一半；第二、如果銀行存款或其流通速度增多一倍，商品價格水準上漲一倍；反之，如果銀行存款或其流通速度減少一半，商品價格水準也就下跌一半。

為了展開這種理論，費雪在其名著貨幣購買力(The purchasing power of Money)里列出了著名的交易方程式(Exchange equation)他假定以M代表貨幣流通量("the volume of money in circulation")，以V代表貨幣流通速度("the velocity of money in circulation")，以M'代表銀行活期存款量("the volume of bank deposits subject to check")，以V'代表支票流通速度("the velocity of checks to circulation")，以T代表商品交易總量("the volume of trades")以P代表商品價格水準("level of price")，那麼，整個商品世界與貨幣對立的數量關係，費雪以$MV+M'V'=PT$的公式來表示，這公式的另一種寫法是：商品價格水準（即貨幣購買力）$P=\frac{MV+M'V'}{T}$

這公式說明了：商品價格水準（貨幣購買力）與貨幣數量（包括現金和存款）及其流通速度成同方向和正比例變化的關係；同時這公式又說明了：商品價格水準（貨幣購買力）在貨幣數量及其流通速度不變的條件下與商品交易總量成反方向和反比例變化的事實。這公式於是費雪教授全部理論的集中表現，也是貨幣數量說新發展的標誌。

四

費雪教授充份反映了近代社會貨幣信用經濟的發展，在貨幣數量說里穿插了貨幣流通速度和銀行信用這兩個新因素，而且用了許多精密透徹的數理公式和曲綫圖解來說明和發揮；我們可以說：費雪教授是把貨幣數量說從一個抽象的概念發展成為嚴密的理論體系的第一人。

但最先反對費雪理論的是安德生教授（Prof.B. M. Anderson），他認為貨幣數量或其流通速度的增減，不但影響商品價格水準（P）的高低，而且也會影響商品交易總量（T）的多寡；例如商品價格水準因貨幣數量或其流通速度的增加而上漲時，一方面可能發生投機性交易數量的增加，另一方面同時也可能逼使大衆消費性交易數量的減少。這種商品交易總量的變動，會加强或者抵消貨幣數量或其流通速度增減所喚起的傾向，會破壞交易方程式兩端的均衡：而費雪教授居然忽視了這個極有意義的因素，把它（T）假定作一成不變。（註七）

再進一步根本推翻費雪教授交易方程式，並且從動態經濟學的觀點來繼續發展貨幣數量說的，是所謂『劍橋學派』("Cambridge school")的霍德萊（R. G. Hawtrey）、庇古（Pigou）、和凱恩斯（J. M. Keynes）。

霍德萊認為商品價格水準（貨幣購買力）的高低，決定於社會上『餘存差額』("unspent margin")的貨幣數量的多寡；換句話說就是決定於『社會上沒有用去的購買力總額』("Unspent purchasing power in Circulation")的多寡。

霍德萊認爲：『餘存差額等於流通中的貨幣量（銀行的庫存貨幣除外）加上銀行信用的總數，銀行信用只等於銀行資產減去其資本。如果貨幣由民間流入銀行，或由銀行流出，只是表示人們所留存的某種數額的信用變爲現金或某額的現金變爲信用，餘存差額可不受影響。但如果流通中的貨幣量增加或者減少，如果銀行擴加或其減少其放款實額，餘存差額就要發生變動。』（註八）

但『餘存差額』爲什麼會有這種變動呢？霍氏在其一九一九年出版的通貨與信用 (Currency and credit) 一書里，對於影響『餘存差額』的諸種因素分析甚詳，他從個人主觀的觀點上立論，認爲第一、收入和支出的時間常常不能一致，收入和支出的數額亦其難於配合，人們必須將其一部份收入留存起來，等待應付支出的時機；第二、每個人都感到好景不常，難免將來不有意外，因此大都設法儲蓄貨幣備用；第三、個人過賸資金如非儲蓄，定欲投資。個人心理上這三要素的變幻，決定着社會貨幣量『餘存差額』的大小。

霍德萊把商品價格水準）貨幣購買力）決定於『貨幣週轉速率』("Circuit velocity of money") —— 就是『餘存差額』與消費者支出("Consumers outlay")的比率，就使得貨幣數量說的理論排斥了費雪教授機械論的因素添進了許多消費者心理，或用諸觀念的影響；這跟庇古教授所謂的『收入週轉比率』("Income velocity of money")——就是把商品價格水準決定於『餘存差額』與消費者的收入("Consumers income")的理論，有異曲同工之妙。

到了近代貨幣學權威凱恩斯教授手里，貨幣數量說更被注入了動態經濟學的新精神，一九三〇年凱恩斯在其名著貨幣論("A Treaty on Money")里，就以『提供一種新的理論，不特可以用來說明靜態的均衡狀態，而是可以用來解釋不均衡的現象。獲得貨幣制度從一種均衡狀態到另一種均衡狀態的動態支配法則』（註九）自命。

凱恩斯把商品與貨幣分析成許多機動的組合（把商品分爲消費品和投資品，把貨幣分爲開支貨幣與儲蓄貨幣），從其內部各成員相互間因果關係里來把握商品與貨幣間數量關係的複雜性和多樣性。凱恩斯全部理論的核心，就是把儲蓄和投資當作物價結構（乃至整個貨幣數量說體系）里兩個機動的因素，認爲(一)消費品的價格決定於社會貨幣總所得與消費品總產量的比例；(二)投資品的價格決定於儲蓄貨幣與投資品價值的比例。爲了要展開這個觀念，凱恩斯列出了兩個著名的公式：

依照凱恩斯在其貨幣論里原用的符號，假定——

E＝社會貨幣總收入量（包括工資、利息、地租以及正常的利潤）

I＝社會投資品的成本；∴ E－I ＝社會消費品的成本

S＝用於儲蓄的貨幣量；∴ E－S ＝用於消費的貨幣量

I'＝社會投資品的『價值』——售價

O＝社會生產品總量

R＝社會消費品與勞務數量

C＝投資品數量；$\therefore C=O-R$或$O=R+C$

$$\therefore EC=OI' \text{或} I'=\frac{EC}{O}$$

P＝消費品價格水準

P'＝投資品價格水準

X＝一般物價水準

凱恩斯的出發點是：消費品數量（R）與其物價水準（P）的乘積，應等於社會總收入中用以購置消費品的貨幣量，即$PR=E-S$

$$\because O=R+C \quad =\frac{E}{O}(R+C)-S$$

$$=\frac{E}{O}R+\frac{E}{O}C-S$$

$$=\frac{E}{O}R+I'-S$$

$$\therefore \quad P=\frac{E}{O}+\frac{I'-S}{R} \text{（第一基本公式）}$$

同理，社會生產品總量（O）與其物價水準（X）的乘積，應等於社會總收入中用以購置消費品和投資品的貨幣量的總和，即

$$OX=PR+P'C=(E-S)+I$$

$$\therefore X=\frac{E-S+I}{O}=\frac{E}{O}+\frac{I-S}{O} \text{（第二基本公式）}$$

這兩個基本公式的第一項（E/O），是社會生產品總量除社會貨幣總收入量的結果；如前所述、社會貨幣總收入量（在正常情形下）應等於社會生產品成本（工資、地租、正常的資本報酬）的總和，換句話說，E/O也就應等於每一單位出品的平均生產成本。所以，物價水準如只等於E/O，就是說每一單位出品的價格與成本相等，——在這種情形之下，企業家除了應得的報酬外，並無意外的利潤或損失（"Windfall Profits or Losses"），因此既不會增加生產，也無意縮小生產，整個經濟制度進入均衡的，隱定的狀態。

但是，E/O只是一種觀念上的常態，實際上價格與成本很難完全相等，價格與成本如一有差略，S也就與I'或I有別，意外的利潤或損失發生，基本公式的第二項就不等於零，物價水準亦或漲或落。

由第一公式可以看出，當投資品的生產成本（I'）等於儲蓄（S）時，消費品價格水準（P）就恰可均衡；但如果投資品生產成本（I'）大於儲蓄（S）時，換句話說就是不用在投資品生產上的貨幣總收入（E－I'）比較不用在儲蓄方面的貨幣總收入（E－S）小，即消費品的生產成本小於社會總收入里用於消費的開支貨幣；於是消費品價格上漲，消費品生產者獲得意外利潤，引起該部門的生產擴張與繁榮。反之，當投資品生產成本（I'）小於儲蓄時，引起消費品價格下降，使消費品生產者蒙受意外損失而致減縮生產。

同樣，由第二基本公式可以推論一般物價水準的漲落（以及意

外利潤或損失的是否發生），也是決定於投資品價值與儲蓄的比例：如果投資品價值大於儲蓄，一般物價水準上漲，生產者獲得意外利潤；如果投資品價值小於儲蓄，則一般物價水準下跌，生產者蒙受意外損失。

『凱氏公式的優點，在其能把他所認為物價結構中的變動因子（即投資與儲蓄）與穩定因子分開』。『凱氏自謂其公式的好處即在於此：由公式的第一項單位成本的變動，使物價從一個均衡水準到另一個均衡水準；而第二項儲蓄與投資數量的變動，引起經濟的失調以及再度趨向均衡的變動。』（註十）

凱恩斯的理論體系雖然如此錯綜繁雜（甚至不是這篇短文所能儘意介紹）；但其根本立場（揭穿來說）仍是一種貨幣數量說的精神，當他從貨幣總收入與物品總產量的比例（E/O）解釋物價水準的穩定時，當他從投資品價值與儲蓄貨幣的比例$\left(\frac{I-S}{R}, \frac{I-S}{O}\right)$來解釋物價水準的波動時，凱恩斯所沿用的邏輯還不是貨幣數量說所因襲的數量關係嗎？凱恩斯底貢獻，只是從商品與貨幣內部的許多組合里來解釋相互間機動複雜的數量關係；而且把數量關係的變動與市場心理相聯系而已。

將貨幣理論與心理效用聯系起來，使其合於近代價值論的主觀傾向，這就是劍橋學派『現金餘存觀念』（"Cash Balance concepts"）的特徵；這也是費雪教授機械的交易方程式（貨幣流通速度與心理習慣無關）的再揚棄。

五

我們已經從貨幣數量說發展的全過程里多方面地介紹了各派貨幣學者的理論，要批評（甚至要詮釋）這些大師底思想體系，至少要寫好幾本專書，決不是這幾千字短文所可奏功。現在所能致力的只能從其根本精神方面來批評；因為這些大師們底體系雖各有不同（甚至彼此攻訐），但其理論前提却只有一個：否認貨幣內在獨立的價值，假定貨幣價值（購買力）的高低，完全決定於流通中商品量與貨幣量的比例，用費雪教授的話來說就是：『貨幣的本質是數量而不是重量。』（註十一）

這理論前提如不細加推敲，彷彿是無瑕可擊；特別是在紙幣通貨膨脹刺激物價狂漲的今日中國，似更顯得入情近理；但若肯多加辯證，若向深處發掘，我們將會發現這理論前提的空虛和背理。

貨幣數量說理論前提的第一個基本錯誤是：在商品交換關係的兩端里，忽視了『如果沒有質的共同，就不可能有量的相等。』在化學領域里，當我們把水(H_2O)跟雙氧水(H_2O_2)比較時，我們底理論前提是水和雙氧水都可以還元為氫(H)和氧(O)。在幾何學領域里，當我們說甲三角形面積等於乙平行四邊形的面積時，我們底理論前提是三角形和平行四邊形的面積都可以還元為高與低的乘積（四邊形可以還元為高與低的乘積三角形可以還元為高與低乘積之半）；不管怎麽笨拙的初中學生，如果他不懂得這點，他就不會說甲三角形的面積等於乙平行四邊形。在商品與貨幣的交換關係里，道理也是一樣，哲學祖師亞里斯多德(Aristoteles)早就講過：『沒有等一性即不能交換；沒有公約性即不能等一。』這共同的基礎非他，即商品與貨幣內在的『價值』(註十二)是也。關於價值的如何決定，是經濟學自威廉彼得(William Petty)有史以來爭辯不休的中心問題(註十三)，在這里不必（也不能）作任何武斷的結論；我們在此地所必須把握着的只有兩點：第一、商品與貨幣自身都必須先有獨立的價值實體，然後才可能有彼此交換的數量比例，惟有『同質』然後才能『等量』，第二、這價值實體是社會客觀的存在，是完全發生和決定在生產過程里的，絕不是那些與大利心理學派從享受者主觀立場出發的限界効用說("The Marginal Utility Theory")所能解釋(註十四)。貨幣數量說理論前提錯誤的淵源，就在這里。

貨幣數量說理論前提的第二個基本錯誤是：在貨幣諸機能里，混淆了價值尺度("Measure of value")和流通手段("Medium of exchange")這兩個本質上完全不同的機能。當作價值尺度（如前所述），貨幣本身必須具有獨立的價值，才可以測定一切商品體的價值量；但當作流通手段，貨幣本身可以毫無價值，它只是流通過程里最常用（最便利）的公認的交換媒介而已。在貨幣經濟里的任何一個時期，充當價值尺度的貨幣永遠是金銀；但執行流通手段的貨幣却屢有更易，各種各色的鑄幣和紙幣都以金屬象徵的姿態充當交換的媒介，其所能代表之金量決定於其發行數量與社會所必需的金（銀）幣量的比例。以時下盛行的不兌換紙幣爲例，紙幣本身毫無獨立的價值；所以商品價值尺度的機能必須仍由金銀來執行（這直接表現在國際貿易必須由金銀來結算上）；但紙幣却可以在國內執行流通手段的機能，它所能代表的價值量決定於紙幣流通量與流通所必需的金幣量的比例（如果紙幣流通量恰等於社會流通所必需的金幣量，那一元紙幣可以十足代替一元金幣流通；如果紙幣膨脹紙幣流通量超過流通所必需的金幣量十倍，那麽，每一元紙幣只能代表一角金幣的價值，過去用一元金幣表示的商品價值，現在必須用十元紙幣表示；換句話說，物價水準上漲了十倍。）貨幣數量說的錯誤，是把僅僅具有流通手段機能的紙幣，當作價值尺度的担當者；唯其如此所有的貨幣數量說都認爲紙幣可以脫離金幣而獨立，都把紙幣數量直接跟商品數量比較，從來沒有考慮到紙幣與商品間不可踰越的媒介：『流通所必需的金幣量。』

貨幣數量說理論前提的第三個基本錯誤是：倒果爲因——在金幣流通的條件下，不是貨幣數量的增減引起商品價格水準的上下；而是跟貨幣數量說恰恰相反，商品價格水準的騰跌，喚起了貨幣數量的增減。上面曾經提起的『社會流通所必需的金幣量』，（暫且假定流通速度不變）永遠決定於商品與金幣自身內在的價值。在這里有三個可能的場合，第一是在貨幣價值不變的場合，如果商品價值因生產力增加而降低，商品的流通所必需的貨幣量也隨着減少，過賸的金被鎔化、窖藏以至輸出外國；反之如果商品價值因生產力降低而提高，商品流通所必需的金幣量也隨着提高，金便由產地、國外以至民間的藏窖里流進流通領域，總之，存在流通領域里的金幣量，永遠就是流通領域所必需的金幣量。第二是在商品價值不變的場合，如果金幣價值因豐饒金礦的發現或者採礦技術的改善而降低，商品內在價值雖然不變，但却必需更多單位的貨幣作爲商品相對價值的表示；反之，如果金幣價值提高，商品內在價值雖然不變，但只需要較少單位的金幣作爲商品相對價值的表示。第三、在商品與金幣價值同時變動的場合，這時有不同方向與不同比例的多種結合，商品價格水準的變動或因相得益彰而更加激烈，或因彼此抵銷而轉趨平和，種種錯綜複雜的場面完全不必在此細表，而且也可以由上述兩場合得到推論。在此地我們所要說明的僅有一點：價格水準的變動（如果把市面上供求關係及貨幣流通速度撇開不談，假定其等於零），起因於商品或金幣內在價值量的變動，而不是起因於商品與金幣數量的變動。休謨所曾引證的當時南美洲大量金銀流入歐洲，引起歐洲物價普遍高漲的事實，實際上不過因爲南美洲發現了大批豐饒的金銀礦山使得金銀價值下跌，才需用更多的金銀才能測定商品內在價值的緣故吧。休謨從數量方面來解釋；但眞正的原因却是在價值方面。只有像狄爾 (Karl Diehl) 之流，才會相信金銀貨幣也可以通貨膨脹，也足以刺激物價。

總結來說，貨幣數量說理論前提的根本錯誤是：否認貨幣內在的價值，歪曲紙幣流通的法則，『把沒有價格的商品和沒有價值的金銀投進流通；所以他們決不說商品的價值或者貨幣的價值，而只說兩者相互間數量的關係。』（註十五）而且『無視紙幣是金幣的代表者抹煞紙幣的購買力是取決於紙幣與爲流通所以需的金幣量之比例。他們看到某些國家使用不兌換紙幣，就被這種現象迷住，因而沒法更進一步地去把握這一現象里的本質。』（註十六）

兩百多年來膾炙人口的貨幣數量說，這麼說來，豈不像是一座建築在沙灘上的大廈嗎？

（註一） "The value of money depends on its quantity" 見牧野輝智著（李陸南譯）最新貨幣學原理第一一五頁。

（註二） 見 D. Rosenberg 著（李侠公譯）政治經濟學史卷一第一〇五頁

（註三） 見Montesquien 著法底精神導論。

（註四） 見D. Rosenberg著上書卷一第一一三頁。

（註五） 見 D. Ricardo; "The Principles of Political Economy and Taxation" P. 138

（註六） 見D. Ricardo; "The Essay" P. 189

（註七） 見B. M. Anderson; "The Value of Money" P. 123

（註八） 見梁慶椿編近代金融學說第九頁朱炳南文。

（註九） 見J. M. Keynes; "A Treaties on Money"P. V.

（註十） 見梁編近代金融學說第四十一至四十三頁，陳振漢教授文。

（註十一） 見I. Fisher; "ThePurchasing Power of Money."P. 25

（註十二） 價值一辭，有使用價值(Value-in-Use)與交換價值 (Ualue-in-exchange)兩種意義，前者爲商品本身的有用性，不在經濟學討論之列；後者是商品的可換性，是經濟學研究的中心。在交易方程式X量商品A＝Y量商品B里的兩端，在使用價值觀點看來，必須是異質，就是說A與B必須是不同的使用價值，但在交換價值的觀點看來却必須是同質，就是說X量的商品A與Y量的商品B必須有等量的交換價值。兩者涵義不同，絕不容混淆，普通經濟學中所用『價值』一辭應指後者而言。

（註十三） "Value Theory is the Heart of Economic Doc:rine"– by Prof. A. Haner. by Prof. Du.hing『價值論是決定經濟學體系的價值的試金石』

（註十四） 限界効用學說的最大錯誤就是把使用價值與交換價值混爲一談，純粹從商品有用性方面着眼，從寄生階級驕奢淫逸的慾望出發，只抓住幾個偶然的個人的事實就以爲很滿足，從來不去分析社會的普遍的現象。

（註十五） 見Karl marx;"A Critique of Political Economy."P. 545

（註十六） 見許滌新著：經濟論衡第三十五頁。

管理原則是燈塔

偉成

吾輩司管理之責者，苟不熟知管理原則，有如暗中摸索，混亂紛爭將爲必然的結果。合理的原則，更益以經驗與果斷，可使吾人辦事無往不利。原則有如港外之燈塔，航行者賴之辨別方向，避免危險，不致走入歧途。然而苟操舟者并進港正路亦不辨，則燈塔無補於事也。（譯法國工業管理家費堯語）

經濟之戰

經濟之戰，較武力之戰，尤爲重要。吾人試以都市等於營盤，關稅等於溝壘，國貨等於鎗砲，交通等於前線，工廠等於武庫，銀行等於後路糧台，行政長官等於主師，羣衆等於小卒，而經濟學說之宣揚，則爲最效之戰略。今觀吾國所謂營盤如何，溝壘如何，鎗砲戰線如何，主帥小卒又如何，思之眞不寒而慄：此實有關我國眞正存亡問題，而有待於舉國上下共同籌謀者也。

鐵路客運業務之重要

周健民

一、客運業務之功用

(1)工商事業之促進　鐵路旅客以勞工及商賈佔大部分，因各種技術工人，全國難以平均，每有一地勞工過剩，一地相形缺少，生產地需要專門技工，往往須求諸遠地。工廠主持者爲改進生產品，減低成本，增加產量，推銷製成品，亦須時赴各處參觀接洽。商賈爲探聽商情，或批購貨物，或調査其商品運輸簡捷之方法，亦應時有旅行之必要。此均賴鐵路旅客運輸之便利，而鐵路以工商業之發展，工廠與商賈即有大量之製成品或商品，須經鐵路運銷各地，是以旅客運輸尙能簡接發展鐵路貨運業務也。

(2)人口分佈之平衡　繁榮都市之區，居民麕集，雖工廠商肆林立，而失業者仍屬衆多，此係人口過剩所致。而窮鄉僻壤之地，人口顯見稀少，雖有富源厚藏，未能從事開發，此則少人力也。鐵路辦理客運業務，政府即可實行移民政策，將人民由謀生不易之地，移至急待開發之區。使人口分佈平衡，人民可各得其所需，地可各盡其利，因此無論何地工商事業，得以平均發展，人人安居樂業，社會秩序，賴以維持。

(3)難民死傷之減少　一國之內水災旱災戰爭等不幸之事在所難免，每遇此種天災人禍之發生，則災區內之人民，全賴鐵路之客運業務運往各處避難，否則惟有束手待斃。況且鐵路暢通，賑濟搶險亦易到達災區，受災難民大可減少死傷。

(4)學生集散之便利　學生求學因有鐵路旅客運輸之便利，不論遠近，均可前往投考或負笈求學。近者朝往而暮歸，遠者假期乘車返里，而使學生易於往返，讀書之機會，可以均等。加以運輸迅速，票價低廉，學生隨時集體旅行參觀，藉此增進知識，是與以前交通閉塞之時代比較，其相去曷可以道里計耶。

(5)新式都市之發展　鐵路沿綫各城鎭，初甚冷靜，因有旅客列車之經過停靠，旅客上下往來頻繁，當地人口自然增多，繼之道路開闢，高樓大廈建設，各種商店工廠林立，市內交通便利，居民相繼遷往，逐漸形成近代繁榮之都市。

(6)言語風俗之統一　凡欲謀文化之發達，必須賴文字語言印刷之傳播，惟各地語言風俗習慣等等，每不一致，必藉鐵路客運業務之媒介，不能使其逐漸同化，免除畛域觀念，以期聯絡統一。

二、客運業務之目標

(1)安全　旅客出行乘坐鐵路客車，其生命已托付於鐵路，故辦理運輸者，對於行車設備，應不惜費用，力求完善，務使行旅安全，儘力防範失火出軌撞車等等之危險。

(2)舒適　旅客購票乘車，利用途中時間，瀏覽沿綫風景，務必使其舒適，一若家庭樂園，毫無疲勞之苦，而其最低限度每客必有其座。因此車內一切設備，應求精緻華美，造成舒適清潔之環境，引起旅行之興趣，增加旅客之滿意，然後旅客運輸始能發展。

(3)便利　旅客列車開到時刻，不宜過早或過晚，務須按照旅客一般習慣與需要，而後妥定適當之時間。切不可祇顧鐵路自身之方便，並須注意銜接他路客車之時間，以免旅客在途中多費金錢與時間之不經濟。如列車行駛在用膳或深夜時間，應掛餐車或臥車，以便解決旅客在行程中之膳宿問題。至於行李係旅客出行不得已而帶之，鐵路對於行李之處理，務使旅客托運與提取之簡捷，並須防止其損失，倘路方能辦到上述種種之便利，旅客始可不視旅行爲畏途。

(4)經濟　鐵路客票票價，不能祇顧運輸成本及利潤方面着想，尚須注意供給旅客之舒適程度，及人民購買能力，而制定合理低廉之票價。使人人多願放棄其他交通工具，並羣趨鐵路而旅行，於是鐵路旅客運輸數量，大可增加。

(5)迅速　人們旅行均希望行程時間之縮短，迅速到達其目的地，故鐵路對於旅客列車應用高速度機車行駛之，並須在出發之前詳細檢驗機車及客車各部分，以免在途中各站停留修理。至於不必要之車輛，應取消附掛，致礙行駛，而求沿途運轉之迅速，滿足旅客之慾望。

(6)準確　旅客列車在中途行駛，固然需要迅速，然列車到達時刻，務須準確，以便旅客預計到達後應辦之事務，或換用其他交通工具轉往別處，故鐵路對於列車之準點，應加重視，以達盡善盡美之境。

三、旅客運輸之特質

(1)節省人力與特殊設備　客車停靠月台，旅客即可自行上下，毋須站員照料，亦無其他特種設備，人力與設備兩可節省。不如貨運需要貨棧或貨場等設備，及設置各種貨運員工處理貨物。西國旅客列車祇有車長一人，除辦理行車事務外，尚須兼辦查收客票照料旅客，此可爲吾國鐵路改進客運管理之借鏡也。

(2)旅客往返數量之平衡　旅客外出，無論時期久暫，往而必返，極少一去不回，或改用其他交通工具，因此旅客數量大都往返平均，路方對於列車所掛客車之輛數，亦可預計固定。如臨時旅客突然增多，因站上有停備客車，亦可隨時添掛應用。

（3）座位不致有虛糜之弊　旅客上下行數量，雖大致平衡，然不能預計每次確實之人數，如多掛車數有虛糜座位之慮，少掛車數，則影響其收入，故須根據平時某一次列車旅客人數，及每車平均旅客人數，或旅客站立報告，規定應掛適當之車數。惟旅客旅行有短程長程之別，車內座位之利用，勢難與列車之起訖同始終，故仍有少數座位之虛糜，但其損失究屬有限，不能認爲靡費也。

（4）旅客列車時間之固定　旅客列車開行之時刻一經規定，不論氣候之變化，或旅客之有無，均應按時開駛，以便旅客準時上車，而免在站久候之苦悶。

四、客運業務之種類

（1）普通客運業務　鐵路旅客大部份皆因有事務而旅行，若路方辦理未能適合上述之目標，則此種客運不但在服務上大受阻礙，甚至欲求往返平衡，亦難維持。此所以辦理客運之不易，而應由鐵路管理者多加注意也。現代鐵路爲應付一般人之需要，並兼顧路方辦理客運之經濟起見，故普通客運可分爲左列四種，請分述之：

A. 長途客運 Long Distance Passenger Service 旅客出外，行程較長者，尤求時間之節省，及途中之舒適，路方爲適合此種需要起見，乃有長途旅客列車之開行，速度特高，車內設備，較爲優良，沿途各小站，均不停靠，祇限於各大站，而求迅速，其行駛範圍均在一段及二段以上，或有通行全綫者。

B. 短途客運 Intermediate Passenger Service 鐵路爲便利旅客短途旅行，而免影響長途客運，故有短途旅客列車之開行，其行駛區域以兩終點站爲起訖站，而對於該終點站之間，各站旅客尤爲便利，而其需要亦爲迫切也。

C. 近郊客運 Suburban Passenger Service 西國各大都市以生活較高，居大不易，工商人士大都在附近各鄉鎮住家，而都市居民亦有利用空閒赴郊外遊覽，因此路方辦理近郊客運業務，而有近郊旅客列車往返之便利。鐵路爲適應近郊旅客之心理，此種列車早晚行駛次數特多，而速度極快。車內設備雖可稍爲簡單，但必須有充分之座位也。

D. 市內客運 Urban Passenger Service 鐵路爲便利市內居民交通之便利，減免汽車之擁擠，而有市內鐵路客運業務之設施。此種鐵路有設於高空，亦有設於街面，或設於地下。其列車行駛迅速，次數甚密，均利用電氣行車，而不用機車，日夜繼續行駛，惟深晚次數較少耳。

（2）遊覽客運業務　鐵路旅客中有少數爲遊覽名勝古蹟而旅行，以求消遣娛樂爲目的，鐵路辦理此種業務，仍應本六大目標爲原則。惟爲擴充客運起見，對於遊覽所用之車輛，應較普通客車爲優，行程須短，而所耗旅費及遊覽雜費應較少，以資引起一般遊覽旅客之興趣。此非僅爲發展客運業務，並可鼓勵社會人士作正當娛樂之良法也。

(3)行李運輸業務　旅客所帶行李，係旅行時必需之物品，鐵路爲便利旅客計，則有行李運輸業務，解決旅客之困難，並須保證行李與旅客同時到達，毫無損傷。

(4)包裹運輸業務　包裹可視爲貨物之一種，原與旅客無關。以旅客列車掛車較少，機力所餘頗多，乃在列車後附掛包裹車一輛或二輛，裝運包裹，以期迅速，而增加旅客列車之進益，亦可謂客運業務之一種。

(5)郵件運輸業務　郵件包括信扎公文報紙雜誌書籍等等，此均有時間性之關係，旅客列車行駛迅速，而時間又準確，殊屬適宜傳遞郵件之條件，亦可以稱爲客運業務之一種。因此鐵路利用旅客列車附掛郵車，而利文明之傳佈，消息之流通，影響社會者甚鉅。一面又可使路方增進客運之收入，誠一舉兩得之事也。

五、結論

鐵路運輸業務，可分爲兩種，一爲貨運業務，一爲客運業務。前者以其進款爲鐵路總收入之大部分，因此吾國管理鐵路者，對於貨運不得不注意，而爲維持鐵路之關鍵，但貨運業務之如何發展，其制度之如何改變，尚無暇顧及也。後者以其進款有限，似屬無關輕重，而爲路方有所忽略。吾人應知客運對於社會經濟政治文化，莫不有直接之關係，惟彼是賴。鐵路有了客運，纔始產生貨運，因客運的發達，而後間接促進貨運的發達，兩者相依相關，有同等之價值，故客貨兩種業務，實爲鐵路兩大生命綫，與鐵路上兩條軌道有相同的效用，豈可輕視哉。

吾國鐵路自開辦起，一直到目前，根據以往的見聞，月月窮，年年窮。究竟是想了辦法後，依然的窮，抑是未想辦法而呼窮，實在是一個疑問？復員一年後，鐵路方面，固然比較以前改良的多，但是旅客購票之困難，車中之擁擠而無座位等等問題，實使平民痛苦萬分，怨恨載道。其所以如此者，因爲鐵路當局，不能支配特殊環境，祇可按照數十年的傳統原則去苦幹，即以原有設備限制營業的發展，並以原有制度來應付近代人民需要的運輸，一般旅客焉得不以旅行爲畏途，此種原則實爲運輸業務發展的致命傷。

對學生進一言

凌鴻銘

昔子夏問政，孔子教以無欲速，無見小利。重子將介，孔子責以非求益而欲速成。大抵無論在行政上，在求學上，「欲速」是最大毛病。讀書須澈底，寧慢勿急，寧少勿多，準少多寡，不可以書頁計。試問中學六年，所讀書本幾何，得益又幾何。平心而論，「多食不化」之弊，恐不能免，虛耗物質其害小，而耗光陰其失大。余以爲課本程度，不當與作文程度相差太遠。一個原則，即是讀到如何程度之書，亦當能作如何程度之文。若不然，即是評本太深。與其略深而覺些微困難，不如略淺而瞭解愉快。祗求自己之實益，不唱高調，不尙虛飾。或云「取法乎上，僅得其中，取法乎中，僅得其下。」但就事實言，「取法乎上者，未必能「得其中。」恐「其下」亦不可得。學者之目標，應是「取法乎中，」而「得其中。」假使「取法乎中，」而「得其下，」亦暫可滿意。蓋可以由「下」而「中」由「中」而上，拾級而登山。昔孟門公孫丑，歎聖道高如登天。自願降低程度。求其師「使彼爲可幾及，而日孳孳。」學者宜有深刻之自覺，不以暫時降級爲恥。教者勿易於「變其彀率，」放棄「能者從之」之態度。更有一個毛病，即是嫌教師太多，嫌自己太少。往往以爲得一位好教師，便可減輕自己之努力。不知「學無捷徑，乃西哲名言。「先難後獲，」是古聖明訓。正常用功之法，自修時間，至少三倍於上課時間。自修不限於溫習課本，除課本外，應博覽雜誌。文字不是自然科學，隨時代而變。英文變化，比國文變化更速。我國數百年以前之文字，仍與今日無大差別。要唐虞三代之文字，才是佶屈聱牙。若英文，則二三百年前之文字，已不可讀。十八九世紀之英國文學，須有相當程度，方可閱讀，故余不取，其或有淺易者，有中文註釋者，有趣味者，未嘗不可一讀，現代文選，比前世紀文學，更爲重要。中文註釋，以葛傳槼氏所著爲最詳盡。欲多識現代文字，最宜閱報。競文與開明等書局，皆刊有「英文報讀法入門。」學者可先讀此等書，得其門徑，閱報自無難處。此外英美雜誌，亦可作自修讀物。但淺易者不易得，學者往往嫌其太深。且美國雜誌中，多有新字，或新義之字，不易瞭解，若葛傳槼先生，已從事搜集此種字彙，加以詳釋，不日出版，學者可俟機購閱之。與其讀美國雜誌，而覺費解，不如讀實用雜誌競文雜誌等，經編註者一度之選擇與配備，更適合學生口味。尙有一種書，尤宜人手一卷者。即是坊間所刊行之英文月刊。據余所知，開明書局有英文月刊。中華書局有英語半月刊，分高初兩級，學者可自行抉擇。讀書宜注重文字，不宜偏重內容。書中每逢一個句法，一個習語當熟記之，作文當從摹仿書句，應用習語入手。習語之用法，在葛著「日用英文習語，」言之綦詳舉例豐富。（競文版）英文句法，彷彿有一定公式。多事摹仿，慣用公式，寫起文來，自然有道地英文氣味，無中式英文之弊。學生更有一種毛病，即是査字典太少。一本好字典，除査某字之拚法及意義外，更可以査得文法上及該字用法上與發音上之教訓。現時坊間所有，可稱完善者，爲世界書局版之「四用字典。」惜該字典每字祇有中文意義，而無英文意義。學者於此字典之外，更宜有一本英義字典，如縮本牛津字典，及袖珍牛津字典均佳。但恐太深奧。欲求簡明者，商務版之雙解實用字典，可稱標準。更有競文版葛著「英文用法大字典，」全以中文解釋，最爲詳盡。此書不獨供臨時檢査，且可供平時閱讀也。嘗見學生作文，錯誤處多在文法與拚字母。文法上之錯誤原因不是文法知識不够，而在寫時不小心，不肯將文法應用於作文上。矯正之法，第一在乎讀書與學文法打成一片。不可視文法爲獨立科，即是不可脫離書句而談文法。讀書時當以文法爲工具，闡發書句之蘊義。讀書時有顧到文法之習慣，則作文時自然會顧到文法。第二在乎作文時不要怱遽。例如本星期一出家課，星期六繳卷。不可待至星期五晚，方草草了事。星期一即要開始起稿，但未可謄正。祇可暫置抽屜內。星期二取出來，自己修改。再置抽屜內。星期三再修改。星期四又修改。如是者數次，文法錯誤，自然少了。至於減少拚字母之錯誤，當然要有多査字典之習慣。祇要知某字之首兩個字母，便可査得全字之字母。養成査字典之習慣，自是進步之一個祕訣。至於講話方面，對外國人，不能達意，大抵有三個原因，第一無講英語習慣，往往口將言而囁嚅。第二發音不正確。第三說話不表情。第一原因，如何補救，暫置不論。第二三兩原因，皆可從萬國註音符號之研究而得糾正。關於此類之書，有中華書局之「英語發音一助，」及開明書店之「英語發音學，」皆可參考。（世界書局四用字典，有萬國註音符號，爲普通字典所無。）發音學不獨教人如何發音，且教人如何朗讀。無論讀書或講話，表情作用，全在抑揚頓挫，高低疾徐之間。學者目的。不在背誦，尤不可爲背誦而背誦，更不可爲考試而背誦。宜以自然活潑之朗讀，替代機械化之記憶。朗讀無須有連續之一段時間。又不必有一定時間。花前月下，飯後茶餘，有二三分鐘之暇，亦可捧起書來，朗讀一二頁。嘗於晨早在公園內，見學生捧書，來往朗讀，甚可效法。朗讀爲講話之第一步法門，餘對教師與同學，不論課內課外，多講英文。不要怕難爲情。多多集會，彼此講英文故事，或練習演講，亦可爲講話上之一助。於讀書寫作與講話各方面，得修養之道。進步可期。諸同學勉旃。

經濟學教材改革芻議

（譯自一九四七年六月四日經濟學人）

張明炯譯

對於我們英國的經濟學教材，人們時常表示不滿。這類批評，主要是關於給學生的教材的抽象和不現實性。有時它也認爲，在通俗課本和學校教材中，沒有充分反映近二十年經濟思想所表現的變革。

假若連大學之外的課本也包括在內，大多數的經濟學教材便都在大學水準之上。大學一年級的課本，主要不外是敍述承繼馬歇爾傳統的古典派的價值學說，分析和描述貨幣制度，以及研究近代經濟史。學校裏很少人選讀這一科，但假若選讀的話，內容總是差不多的。職業學校和專門學院裏，爲了應付校外的或職業團體的考試，所要準備的功課也幾乎一樣。但職業學校只採用『商業』課本，反對這種傳統的經濟學概論，因爲它的內容枯澀而且脫離現實。這些『商業』課本集中在商業實務與經濟制度的平凡的描述上。

關於研究經濟學的方法，當然沒有一種是絕對令人滿意的。對於初學者，敍述古典經濟學，一定會太片面而又不够嚴正確切的。因爲經濟學的許多基本假定沒有充份說明，以致不能令人注意到它的引申。同時也很少有人想去糾正經濟學的理論方法，因此學生自然迷惑起來。現在的情形却變得更糟，因爲一般課程總力求趨時，要插入現代理論的一些片段。這裏包括不完全競爭的學說和凱因斯的就業理論；一本普通的入門書，也包含一節無差別曲線（Indifference Curves）。事實上，初學者既然沒有相當基礎，這些複雜的理論當然無法作系統的介紹。學生面對着這許多明顯的矛盾的論斷，於是對經濟學失去研究的勇氣。在專門學院裏的一些銀行行員以及在大學裏爲求得學位而選讀經濟學的人們，只得到一種無用的分析工具，而且會爲了理論與他所接觸的現實脫節而感困惑。在他們的經驗中，并沒有經濟學上常講的羅賓遜和沙漠中缺水的人。他們在日常生活中探求知識，而且發現自己投入一個永無休止永無矛盾的世界中，它充滿着自私，這種自私明顯地是不能爲無知所寬恕的。大多數的討論的抽象都超出了學生的水準，經濟學對他們實在成了一種壞胃口的笑柄。甚至那些鄭重地想成爲經濟學者的，也沒有得到更好的收穫。一個有價值的起點已經變成了各種理論的混合。

『商業』課本，甚至更少把握到這一點。它常常過分注意苦燥的事實，完全引不起興趣。至少就研究機關來講：討論支票的起源和目的，公司組織與經濟規模和經濟力集中的關係，以及廣告在經濟上的意義，總比各種支票背書的方法，各種企業的形式，和窗飾的技術，來得重要些，而且也間或有興趣些。

一般學生對經濟學發生興趣，多半由於想知道經濟學的實用情形，對經濟問題以及各種論爭能有進一步的了解。他已微微地感到經濟學有某種體系存在，而且更確切地領悟到這種體系的不完全性，以及它引申出的不良的結果。但他需要知道「爲什麼」和「如何」的問題。商業課本却僅僅告訴他一些經濟現象。經濟學想獲得一種體系——譬如採取一些分析工具（例如彈性 elasticity 等），特殊觀念（例如消費者剩餘 consumers' surplus 等），或者支配經濟機構各部分的原則（譬如價格比例與邊際替代率相等），但這些偏頗的觀念很少是適當配合得起來的。

這是必要的，學生在開始學習時，非脚踏實地不可。最需要的，正是分析與描述兩種方法的結合。在十年或十五年以前，這種方法也許是很困難的。那時，理論的方法都是抽象的——定下一些在簡單情況中價格制度運用的法則。但不管這種方法如何困難和不實際，它必須經過若干修正，才會令人滿意。敍述的方法不免會遭到好多人的訾議，認定它不出平板敍述經濟制度的範圍，因而令學生對經濟制度的整個機構不能有所了解。但是在今天，由於數理經濟學的進步，用實證的與數量的方法來討論經濟問題，因此有了一個新的機會。

赫克斯教授曾經揭示這一方法開始的步驟，皮果教授也曾粗疏地說明怎樣繼續赫克斯教授的辦法。一個合適的起點，可以講述國民所得的定義、大小、及其估值。對於產生國民所得的許多生產因素，可以作實際的解釋——譬如勞工，可以用人口趨勢，工作人口的內容組合等等來參證，對於資本可用它的實際組合、大小、所有權等等來參證。國民所得的物質的與服務的內容是受價格制度作用所支配着，這種價格制度，用不着公式地來詳細解釋，就可簡單明確地表明了。國民所得可以分開來，歸屬於各種有關的生產因素，作爲分配問題的介紹。對於社會所得的支出分析，要注意到儲蓄與投資；牠們與就業波動的關係，可以用有效的統計資料來解釋它，敍述它。社會生產品用貨幣計算的困難，加强了指數的重要性和貨幣與價格的關係。由於在計算上要涉及對外關係，於是要講到國際貿易；對於國際收支衡估的作用，正如國民所得在國內經濟之中一樣重要。

這種內容雖不能算是模範的，但牠總足以說明這種經濟學教材可能得到的成果。按照這種方法所設計的教材一定會是現實的，而且決不致失去學生的興趣。既然各種討論都根據同一顯明的事實，注意力自然要集中在主要的經濟研究的一致性了。

在得到這些利益中，難得找到什麼缺點。不錯，這樣的方法，不能有精確的邊際分析，而只能對需求給與模糊的概念，像流動願望和准地租一類的名詞，學生也不會知道。但這總不難證明，對只想得到一點經濟常識的人，并不算太大的損失。如用純粹算成一種思想訓練，那麽傳統經濟學雖然有這種好處，但是假若經濟學只成思想訓練的學課，倒常常不如哲學與數學。

那些想成爲經濟學者的，公式的理論分析也不妨後一步再去研究。作爲初學者，對於傳統的經濟學課程的取消，很少會有所抱恨；因爲他們并非專家，傳統經濟學早已爲對他們所作的讓步而毁棄。從經濟數量的知識和資本、所得、投資等一類概念的了解中，他們儘可以得到很大的益處，成爲學者的萌芽；但這也正是現在入門書所最缺乏的。這種從收入開始的方法，常會引起對純粹理論的更好估價，而且更願意接受純粹理論的訓練。在我們開始想編做一本好書的時候，唯一的希望便是好好地把經濟機構分析開來，再把它造成簡單化了的雛型。一般情形，經濟學成績優異的學生，他們雖然痛苦地努力追求這種理論工具，但對牠的基本目的却知道很少。

學院經濟學的整個職務，教授法的這一變革，將會有極大的利益，使外界得以公認經濟學的現實性，而且有好多可以應用於世界的現實問題。工業家、銀行家、和政治家也不至於再像現在一樣，從大學經濟學課程的記憶中，相信經濟學教授不過是不實際的學究，他們的學說，雖然在他們的定義裏是正確的，但並沒有實際的價值，而且比那些神學教授更少道德價值。

帳目不清

當然，賬目不清，是認爲有營私舞弊侵呑公款的嫌疑，是一種重大的案件。其實賬目不是專限於金錢方面。物品也可以有賬目，人事也可以有帳目，所以賬目也就是一種記錄。

人事記錄是辦理人事，研究人事所必需的。人事記錄，種類很多，但不妨按性質的重要，來先後次第保存，人事記錄若是不完整可靠，那亦等於金錢上的賬目不清，是與整個的組織有害的。

管理淺說

管理不僅爲個人謀利益，且爲社會人羣謀幸福。管理是一種技術也是一種科學，牠的範圍，是在如何指揮有組織的人力去實施於物質的極度利用，以造成人類之最大幸福。故用分析眼光去看管理，則

（一）管理之對象有二：一曰「人」，二曰「物」。物分四種：一曰金錢，二曰原料，三曰機器，四曰土地與建築物。

（二）管理之目的亦有二：一曰「社會效用」，二曰「個人利益」。

(Management of An Enterprice—By Balderstin)

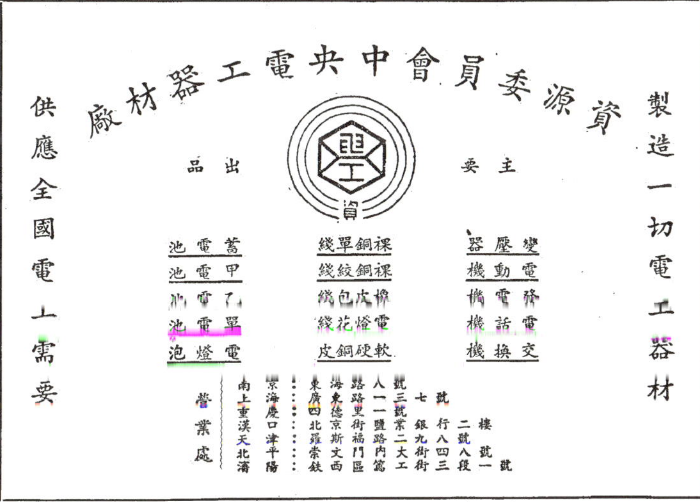
資源委員會中央電工器材廠
製造一切電工器材
供應全國電工需要
主要出品
變壓器
電動機
發電機
電話機
交換機
裸銅單綫
裸銅絞綫
橡皮包綫
電燈花綫
軟硬銅皮
蓄電池
甲電池
乙電池
單電池
電燈泡
營業處
南京：東海路八號
上海：廣東路一三七號
重慶：四德里一號
漢口：北京街鹽業銀行二樓
天津：羅斯福路二九八號
北平：崇文門內大街四八號
瀋陽：鉄西區篤工街三段一號

永興倉庫股份有限公司
遠東最大貨物倉庫—永興倉庫
自建六層大廈 全部鋼骨水泥
電梯可載卡車 裝卸迅速便捷
設備新式安全 歡迎各界賜顧
總公司：—上海中正東路160號六樓 電話：17016，16794
倉庫：楊樹浦路61號 電話：51525